Jon Heath

A HISTORY
OF THE
CHRISTIAN
CHURCH

A HISTORY
OF THE
CHRISTIAN
CHURCH

by
Williston Walker

and
Richard A. Norris

David W. Lotz

Robert T. Handy

FOURTH EDITION

CHARLES SCRIBNER'S SONS · NEW YORK

Copyright © 1918, 1959, 1970, 1985 Charles Scribner's Sons; Copyright renewed 1946 Amelia Walker Cushing and Elizabeth Walker.

Walker, Williston, 1860–1922.
    A history of the Christian church.

    Bibliography: p.
    Includes index.
    1. Church history. I. Norris, Richard Alfred.
II. Lotz, David W., 1937– . III. Handy, Robert T.
IV. Title.
BR145.W34 1985   270   84–23614
ISBN 0–684–18417–6
ISBN 0–02–423870–8 (Macmillan)

1 3 5 7 9 11 13 15 17 19   F/C   20 18 16 14 12 10 8 6 4 2

PRINTED IN THE UNITED STATES OF AMERICA.

Contents

Period III

THE IMPERIAL STATE CHURCH

Period IV

THE MIDDLE AGES TO THE CLOSE
OF THE INVESTITURE CONTROVERSY

Period V

THE LATER MIDDLE AGES

Period VI

THE REFORMATION

Period VII

Maps and Charts

Preface

THE FIRST EDITION of Williston Walker's *A History of the Christian Church,* published in 1918, quickly became a standard, highly serviceable textbook. Walker, professor of ecclesiastical history at Yale University, achieved a rare combination of directness, competence, and balance in this work, which became an unparalleled success as a basic one-volume treatment of church history from the first to the twentieth century. After forty years, its usefulness in providing a concise coverage of the sweep of Christian history was still widely recognized. Hence, when the second (1959) edition of the work was undertaken, the aim of the revisers, Cyril C. Richardson, Wilhelm Pauck, and Robert T. Handy of Union Theological Seminary in New York, was primarily to revise those parts where some errors of fact had come to light or where the interpretation had become seriously out of date, and to do a more thorough reworking of the section on modern Christianity, where much research had been done since Walker's time. The third (1970) edition was little changed except for additions to take account of important developments of the 1960s, with particular reference to the Second Vatican Council and the spread of the ecumenical movement.

Since then, continuing historical research and methodological changes have led to important new discoveries and to fresh interpretations of the earlier periods, necessitating a much more thorough revision. This fourth edition undertakes this. The basic outline of Walker's original text, previously modified only for the last period, has proved to be sound, and with some emendations has been generally followed again, but there has been extensive reconception, recasting, and rewriting of the content of many sections, incorporating the result of recent scholarly work in these areas. The work was divided as follows: Professor Norris has rewritten the sections from the beginning through the early Middle Ages (Periods I–IV). Professor Lotz has recast and extensively rewritten the sections treating the later Middle Ages and the Reformation (Periods V–VI). Professor Handy has further edited the sections covering the years from Puritanism to the present (Period VII). Cross references in the text are indicated by citing the appropriate period and chapter numbers in parentheses.

For example, "(see I:2)" refers the reader to period one, chapter two. For the reader's convenience, period and chapter numbers run along the top of right-hand pages in the book. The bibliography has been redesigned; following a listing of selected general works, attention is focused on the seven main periods of the text. It is our hope that our labors wil perpetuate and add to Walker's original achievement in his revised and considerably rewritten work.

RICHARD A. NORRIS
DAVID W. LOTZ
ROBERT T. HANDY

Union Theological Seminary, New York
September 1984

Preface to the Third Edition

A NUMBER of significant events in church history took place in the 1960's. Therefore, though it was not advisable fully to revise this useful volume again so soon after the thorough revision of 1959, it was decided to make some changes in the latter part of the book, to add an additional chapter, and to update the bibliographical suggestions. It is instructive to observe how much of the history that is recounted in this long-standard work has been reconsidered again in the epoch-making deliberations and actions of the Second Vatican Council and the Third and Fourth Assemblies of the World Council of Churches.

ROBERT T. HANDY

Union Theological Seminary
September 1969

Revisers' Preface

FOR NEARLY half a century Walker's *History of the Christian Church* has been a standard textbook. It was written by a scholar of ripe learning, who profited especially from the rich fruits of German historical scholarship in the later 19th and early 20th centuries. Its rare combination of clarity, compactness and balance has been responsible for its unparalleled success. Moreover, despite the advances made in historical scholarship, the main text of Walker has held up remarkably well. Nevertheless, sections have inevitably become out of date, and especially in the later portions has extensive rewriting been necessary. It has been the aim of the revisers to retain the main structure of the original, and only to revise those parts where there were errors of fact or where the intepretation was seriously questionable. Occasionally sections have been added to introduce a better balance or to take note of modern discoveries. In the modern period a more radical reworking of the material has been necessary in order to bring the text up to date.

The division of labor between the revisers has been as follows: Professor Richardson has been responsible for the work to the early Middle Ages (pp. 1–215), Professor Pauck through the Reformation (pp. 219–401), and Professor Handy from Puritanism to the Modern Day (pp. 402–545). Grateful thanks are due Dr. Edward R. Hardy of the Berkeley Divinity School, New Haven, for his scholarly help on the section dealing with the Greek Orthodox Church. It is our hope that by bringing the text up to date we have added to its usefulness and so prolonged the life of a worthy and popular volume.

CYRIL C. RICHARDSON
WILHELM PAUCK
ROBERT T. HANDY

Union Theological Seminary
September 1958

xii

A HISTORY
OF THE
CHRISTIAN
CHURCH

Period I

FROM THE BEGINNINGS TO THE GNOSTIC CRISIS

Chapter 1

The General Situation

*A*T THE BIRTH OF CHRIST, the lands which surrounded the Mediterranean Sea were under the political control of Rome, whose empire embraced not only the coastal territories but their hinterlands as well. Bounded by the ocean and by the Rhine and Danube rivers to the north of the Mediterranean, it encompassed North Africa and Egypt and stretched in the East to the borders of Armenia and of the Persian Empire.

In the century and a half before the appearance of Christianity, the sway of the Senate and People of Rome was extended from Italy to include not merely Gaul, Spain, and North Africa in the West, but also, in the East, the Hellenistic monarchies which had succeeded to the empire of Alexander the Great. This time of expansion coincided with an era of growing conflict and instability in the social and political life of the Roman republic. The assassination (44 B.C.) of Julius Caesar, carried out by a party which feared his subversion of traditional republican institutions, was followed by civil wars which affected all parts of the territories ruled by Rome. It was generally with relief and hope, therefore, that people greeted the final triumph of Octavian, Caesar's nephew and adopted son, whose task it became to reconstitute the Roman state and to reform the administration of its provinces. Preserving the form of republican institutions, Augustus (as Octavian was officially and reverently named in 27 B.C. by the Senate) eventually concentrated all effective power (*imperium*) in his own hands, receiving lifetime status as tribune of the people and then as consul, with the title "leading citizen" (*princeps*). Acting with this authority, he brought order to the government of the provinces and relative peace to the whole of the Mediterranean world.

The imperial system which Augustus thus established embraced peoples of many languages and cultures. In most regions of the empire, the basic political and social unit was—or came to be—the *polis,* a term commonly but inadequately translated into English as "city." This was a corporation of citizens tending the affairs of a modest territory whose heart was an urban center of greater or smaller size. Under Roman aegis, such civic corporations—which were ruled

5

oligarchically for the most part—were responsible for their own local affairs as well as for the taxes which supported the imperial establishment and its armies. Each city thus provided for the worship of the god or gods who were its patrons, for the administration of justice, and for the welfare of its citizens and other residents. Each was a focus of local pride, with its economic roots in the surrounding countryside.

Put together as it was out of a multitude of ethnic, cultural, and religious groupings, the empire was held together by a common political allegiance, by economic and commercial interdependence, and by a shared higher culture. Politically, everything depended upon Rome, its emperor, and its armies, both for the maintenance of internal order and for the protection of the outer frontiers of Mediterranean civilization, where most of the legions were stationed. Within the empire, the principal source of wealth was the land and its products, and agriculture was the chief industry. Communities distant from the Mediterranean and its tributary rivers lived for the most part on local produce, but the cities of the seacoast—and especially great cosmopolitan centers like Rome—were dependent on a lively trade in the staples of life: grain, wine, and olives. North African grain fed the population of Rome as, at a later period, Egyptian grain transported from the seaport of Alexandria sustained the inhabitants of Constantinople. Italy itself was a center of viniculture, and its wines were exported extensively. The Mediterranean cities, then, which were the core of the empire, were increasingly bound together in a nexus of commercial relationships.

The unity and cohesion of the empire, however, depended also upon the existence of a common higher culture—the "Hellenistic" culture which grew up in the wake of the conquests of Alexander the Great (356–323 B.C.), as Greek language, education, and civic institutions were diffused through the eastern Mediterranean world. Even Rome, in the century and a half before the birth of Christ, became a cultural and intellectual tributary of the Greek tradition. As Greek became the daily speech of city-dwellers in the East, it also became a normal second language for educated persons in the West, where Latin was the common tongue. Other languages—Aramaic, Coptic, Punic—by no means disappeared, but they tended more and more to become languages of the uneducated and of the rural population. In this way, Greek science, Greek religious philosophy, and Greek art and literature enriched and were enriched by other traditions and created the possibility of a shared world of cultural and religious values for the urban civilization of the Mediterranean area.

In this complex, variegated, and remarkably sophisticated world, religious concerns, beliefs, and practices were central in the lives both of individuals and of communities. At the same time, however, the religious currents of the time were diverse. To speak in general terms, one can distinguish three broad categories of religious belief and observance. First, there was the traditional religion of the family and community gods—what one might call the "civic religion" of the Roman-Hellenistic world. Second, there were the so-called "mystery cults."

These were for the most part oriental cults which had their mythic roots in local fertility rites, but which, in the cosmopolitan world of the Greek-speaking empire, underwent a transformation and became voluntary brotherhoods which offered their initiates salvation from the trammels of Fate and Fortune. Finally, there was the way of life which sought human fulfillment and blessedness through the pursuit and practice of philosophical wisdom: a wisdom founded upon criticism of the traditional gods of the Greek pantheon, but capable, as time went on, of offering a "demythologized" version of traditional religion. In practice, these different styles of religion coexisted peacefully, and some individuals were, to one degree or another, involved in all three of them. They responded, however, to different needs, and to some extent they presupposed differing perceptions of the human situation.

On one matter, however, the various types of religion were at one. People in the Roman world were acquiring—had, indeed, for the most part already acquired—a new picture of the cosmos. Gone was the flat earth and overarching heaven of ancient myth. Educated and half-educated persons alike now saw the earth as a sphere set motionless at the center of things. Around it in their orbits moved the seven planetary spheres, and around this whole system moved "the heaven," the realm of the fixed stars. To the ancients, however, this cosmos was no mere machine. They perceived it rather as an ensouled—that is, a living—thing, in which orderly change and motion were maintained by divine Mind. The world was pervaded by life, and the gods who inhabited the heaven and the planetary spheres were the manifestations or representatives of the ultimate divine Power which extended to all things, even to affairs in that sector of the cosmos—earth—which was farthest removed from the divine realm.

Traditional religion in the Roman-Hellenistic world was a public and social affair, an affair of family and community. Since human well-being depended at every moment on the good will of the gods, the cosmic powers, religion sought their help for the common concerns of life: the growing of crops, the conduct of business, the difficult enterprises of war and diplomacy. Its rites were age-old and traditional, seldom rationalized, and conducted by the normal leaders of the community: the head of the family or the elected magistrates of the city. It used divination, dream, and oracle to seek the will of the powers; it used prayer and sacrifice to gain their alliance.

It is in the setting of such traditional religion that one must understand the phenomenon of emperor worship or worship of the state that grew up in the Roman Empire. The triumphs of Roman arms and the benefits which the imperial order conferred on the Mediterranean world convinced the Romans themselves, and most of their subject peoples too, that Roman power was a manifestation of the power of the gods—that Rome had a divine mission. Augustus himself, conscious that the imperial city's destiny could only be fulfilled if she maintained her covenant with the gods, undertook a revival of traditional religion. Furthermore, just as he erected an altar to the goddess Peace in the Senate-House in Rome, so he followed earlier eastern precedent by encouraging a cult of the goddess Roma—the divine power manifested in the conquering and ordering work of the Roman state. A similar outlook lay behind the establishment and growth of the cult of the divine emperor—whose actual origins lay in the East and not in Rome itself. When first permitted in Italy, this cult took the relatively modest form of veneration of the "genius" of the emperor (that is, of the divine *alter ego* of the human ruler), or else of the "deification" of an emperor after death. Roman sensibilities did not originally permit the declaration that an ordinary human being was himself a god; only an acknowledged madman like Caligula (37–41 A.D.) could have taken such a step. In the provinces, however, and especially in the East, such restraint was less common. There, following age-old custom, worship was offered to the emperor in his own person as a living manifestation of the divine. This cult evoked no deep personal piety, widespread and carefully organized as it eventually was; it belonged to the realm of formal civic religion, and its role, as people generally recognized, was political. It did, however, represent a real conviction: that the basis of political order lay in the divine realm.

This traditional religion, however, was in many if not most cases irrelevant to personal needs and longings. Its rites, carefully maintained as they were, were impersonal, and its concern was with public order and public welfare. Hence the ordinary people of the cities turned to other religious cults to achieve personal security, prosperity, and a sense of having a place and a positive destiny in a confusing and impersonal world.

The cosmos as these folk experienced it was not a perfectly ordered and harmonious whole. The earth of their experience was far removed from the blessed realm of the gods. It was the realm of chance and necessity, and one in which demonic powers, whose territory was the lower region between Earth and Moon, worked their unpredictable will. Much popular religion, therefore, was concerned with understanding and control of the nonhuman powers which —often capriciously, it seemed—ruled human life. The practice of magic—the use of charms, spells, and amulets—was rife. There was also a great vogue of astrology, imported in Hellenistic times from Babylonia and diffused throughout the Mediterranean world. To consult the stars was to gain some insight into one's destiny. It was also to confess that one's destiny was in the hands of alien forces.

It is this situation which makes the popularity of the mystery cults comprehensible. These, as we have seen, were oriental "nature religions" which, in Hellenistic times, were diffused through the Mediterranean world as religions of salvation. The most popular of them were the cults of the Great Mother, which originated in Asia Minor; of Isis and Serapis, which derived from Egypt; and of Mithras, which spread at a later time from Persia. Rome originally viewed such religions with suspicion. They involved enthusiastic, even orgiastic, rites which seemed inconsistent with public decorum and morality. Nevertheless, it was the Roman authorities themselves who, at a time of crisis in the wars against Carthage, had introduced the worship of the Great Mother (suitably cleansed of its excesses) within the sacred enclosure of the Roman gods (204 B.C.); and by 80 B.C., the cult of Isis was established in the vicinity of Rome, though it endured long governmental opposition. In time, these cults were accepted even in the West as a normal element in the religious life of populace and rulers alike.

What did they offer? For one thing, they offered, in their rites of initiation and in worship, an experience of the Divine which touched and evoked deep emotions of awe, wonder, and gratitude. The initiates of these secret mysteries "saw" the god and entered into fellowship with a divine being who had reached out to care for them. At the same time, these cults offered the gift of a blessed immortality in fellowship with the gods. Rooted as they generally were in the myth of a dying and rising god, they provided an experience of rebirth to a new quality of life. The initiate, become a sharer in the life of the god, was raised above the earthly realm controlled by fate and chance and so was liberated for the immortality proper to those who enjoy fellowship with the Divine. The mystery cults, then, were religions of salvation which both drew and fed on a sense of the transcendent.

A third way which people could follow in their search for a fulfilled and happy life was the way of philosophical wisdom. In the Roman-Hellenistic era, "philosophy" was not the name of an academic discipline concerned with a special range of abstract questions. Rather, it denoted the quest for an understanding of the cosmos and of the place of humanity within it—an understanding which was achieved only by participation in a certain way of life and which issued in happiness or beatitude. The philosopher's vocation, then, was not for everyone. It entailed a life of intellectual and moral discipline which only the few could pursue. On the other hand, the pictures of the world and of the human situation which philosophy evolved had a way of turning into commonplaces of popular religion and morality. In the end, philosophy provided the framework of understanding which made sense of the myths and rituals of religion.

The origin of the Roman-Hellenistic philosophical schools is found in the fourth century before Christ, in the movement of inquiry and speculation stimulated by the teaching of Socrates at Athens. This movement had its first great leader in Plato (d. 347 B.C.), whose ideas were communicated in popular form in his series of dialogues. The Academy which he founded—and which was finally closed only in 529 by the Christian emperor Justinian—was the first of the great "schools" of Hellenistic philosophy. Plato's pupil Aristotle (384–322 B.C.) broke away from the Academy after Plato's death and became the founder of the Peripatetic school, but the influence of Aristotle's teaching was most strongly felt in the Christian era, after the republication of his scientific and philosophical works in the first century B.C. Subsequently, there appeared the school of Epicurus (342–270 B.C.) and that of the Stoics, so named from the Porch (*stōa*), a public hall in Athens where its founder, Zeno (d. ca. 264 B.C.), originally taught. Each of these schools became, in effect, a continuing brotherhood which expounded and developed its founder's teachings. The differences among them involved a wide range of issues: epistemology, cosmology, and theology as well as ethics. The focal problem which was debated in the Hellenistic age, however, was that of the nature of the "happy" or fulfilled human life.

The school of Epicurus taught that pleasure—in the negative sense of absence of mental disturbance (*ataraxia*)—was the highest human good. The good life is the life which maximizes pleasure by minimizing the pain attendant upon unnecessary desire and anxiety. Thus, paradoxically, the greatest pleasure is attained by a life of quiet, retirement, and restraint: a life characterized essentially by self-control. Epicurus and his followers regarded religion—fear of the gods and anxiety about an afterlife—as one of the principal sources of disturbance and pain. They believed, however, that all such religious fears were baseless. The gods exist, they taught, in an empyrean world of their own and have no responsibility for, or interest in, the affairs of human beings. Death, moreover, marks a mere end to human existence and is therefore not evil, since with death awareness of pleasure and pain disappears. This doctrine admirably fitted the Epicurean conviction that the cosmos is formed, as Democritus (d. ca. 380 B.C.) had earlier taught, by the fortuitous and ever-changing combination of eternally existing atoms within the Void. This philosophy enjoyed a brief vogue in the first century B.C. in aristocratic circles at Rome and its greatest literary product is the brilliant poem *De rerum natura* of the Roman Lucretius (d. 55 B.C.). In Christian times, Epicurus's doctrines were not influential or widespread, but they were often unfairly pilloried, by Christians and others, for polemical purposes.

Much more influential, especially in the Latin West, was the philosophy of the Stoics with their teaching that the sole human good is virtue or "the life according to nature." The doctrines of Zeno, expanded and developed by his successors Cleanthes (d. ca. 232 B.C.) and Chrysippus (d. ca. 207 B.C.), found notable western exponents in Lucius Annaeus Seneca (d. 65 A.D.), the former slave Epictetus (d. ca. 135 A.D.), and the emperor Marcus Aurelius (121–180 A.D.). Like the Epicureans, the Stoics were materialists. Roughly speaking, they conceived the cosmos to be composed out of two kinds of "stuff" or "substance": a passive matter, and the active, fiery "spirit" or "breath" (*pneuma*) which transfuses matter, forms it, and causes it to cohere. This *pneuma* functions in the cosmic body much as soul does in the human body; that is, it is the source of life and of harmony. Called "God" or "Fate" or "Reason" (*logos*), this "spirit" is the indwelling divinity whose outflowing powers are the gods of popular religion. The human soul, itself rational, is a spark or portion of the divine Reason.

The good for human persons, then, consists in their being fully what they are—that is, in living and acting according to their interior nature and identity, which is *logos.* Only such a life is the excellent (or, in other words, virtuous) human existence. What is more, only the virtuous life is free, for it alone is within people's power to achieve, and it alone lets people be truly themselves. Whatever depends, therefore, on external circumstance—health, for example, or worldly success, or sensual pleasure—is no essential part of the human good. In fact, dependence on external circumstance alienates the person from himself. It is a sickness of the soul which the Stoics called "passion" (*pathos*), because the person who is subject to it is passive in relation to influences stemming from outside and to that degree unfree and unfulfilled. This outlook led the Stoics to the view that differences of rank and status are secondary. All persons are ultimately equal, fellow citizens with one another and with the gods in a cosmic city.

In the Hellenistic era, it was Epicurean and Stoic teachings which were most widespread. The future, however, was to belong to Platonism, which underwent a revival in the first century before Christ, though in a significantly altered form. The teaching of Plato was based ultimately on his distinction between that-which-is (Being) and that-which-comes-to-be (Becoming). Searching for the true basis of order in the moral, political, and natural realms, Plato discerned it in the system of Ideas or Forms—the models or originals of empirical reality. These Forms were characterized by two essential qualities. First, they were seen simply to *be,* unchangeably, self-identically, and hence eternally. Second, they were seen to be *intelligible,* capable of being grasped by mind. In contrast to this realm of Being and Intelligibility, Plato saw the visible world of immediate experience as a realm of continual Becoming—a world about which it was impossible to have stable knowledge because it was always slipping through one's mental fingers.

These two realms of Being and Becoming, however, were not in Plato's view divorced. The empirical world images and participates in the eternal world of Being. That it does so, moreover, is owing to the activity of living, self-moving soul, which is a denizen of both spheres. As soul contemplates and internalizes intelligible Being, conforming its own life to that truth, it orders and harmonizes the world of Becoming, so that the temporal order becomes "a moving image of eternity." The cosmic order is thus the product of the contemplation and action of the Soul of the World; the vocation of human beings, themselves rational souls, is to imitate that contemplation and action: to rise to knowledge of the Forms, of that-which-is, and in that knowledge to confer moral and political order on human affairs.

Plato's immediate successors in the Academy carried on his tradition of thought and the mathematical inquiries which had arisen out of his theory that the Ideas or Forms were archetypal "numbers." With Arcesilaus (315–241 B.C.), however, and Carneades (213–128 B.C.), the Academy took a new turn.

Convinced that Socrates and Plato had never propounded a positive, "dogmatic" system but had always examined issues from all sides without reaching firm or final conclusions, these thinkers taught the doctrine of "suspension of judgment" (*epochē*). In this spirit, they mounted critical attacks on belief in the gods and on the dogmas of other philosophical schools (especially those of the Stoics), teaching that the wise man finds in probability, not certainty, the only "guide of life." This spirit of "Academic doubt" much impressed the Roman philosopher Cicero (106–43 B.C.) and through him the young Augustine of Hippo.

In the end, however, skepticism did not reign in the Platonist Academy. In the first century before Christ—and at roughly the same time as Aristotle's philosophical and scientific works were rediscovered and beginning to circulate —a movement, generally known as "Middle Platonism," appeared which sought a return to the positive teachings of Plato, especially as those were set out in the dialogue *Timaeus*. It was typical of this movement, however, which in the course of the first and second Christian centuries rose to virtual dominance, that its understanding of Plato fused his ideas with themes drawn from Stoicism and, increasingly, from Aristotle.

Thus Middle Platonism took over from Aristotle the idea of formless matter as the ultimate substratum of all visible things, as well as the conception of a transcendent God understood as Mind (*nous*). This God had the Platonic Forms as the content of his thought and so was identified with Plato's realm of Being. The visible cosmos is shaped as the eternal World-Soul, formed and enlivened by its contemplation of God, in its turn confers form and harmony on formless matter. It follows from this account of things that the philosopher who seeks self-fulfillment by conforming his way of being with ultimate reality must take the cosmos and its order as the starting point of his search, for the cosmos is the image and reflection of eternal truth. In the end, however, he must transcend the visible world. He must rise in his thought to its original, the everlasting Good. There the multiplicity of the time-and-space world is harmonized in an ultimate unity, and there the rational soul finds its proper companion and the fully worthy object of its love. For the soul, too, is eternal and immortal, and its natural affinity is not for the passing world of time and space, but for Being. Thus the end of the philosophical quest is "likeness to God": a knowledge of God which amounts to a sharing in the divine way of being.

As has already been said, this philosophic quest was not for everyone. The philosopher's way to self-fulfillment involved not only long education and study, but also a moral discipline (*askēsis*) designed to cleanse the soul of the passions which prevented it from being its true self. Yet the philosophical quest as it was understood in the era of the early empire had more than a little in common with the mood of popular religion, especially as the latter was expressed in the vogue of the mystery cults. Both sought a kind of salvation from the changes and chances of life on earth. Both envisaged this salvation as a liberation—whether from the passions which bound people to the space-and-time world or from indifferent or hostile cosmic powers. Both, finally, saw the human person as capable of a transcendent destiny in the fellowship of the Divine. It is no surprise, therefore, that a Platonist philosopher like Plutarch of Chaeronea (d. ca. 120 A.D.) should be able and willing to make philosophical sense of the myth of Isis and Osiris—to see it as an allegory of humanity's situation and destiny. No more is it surprising that when another oriental religion of salvation—Christianity—began to make its way in the social and cultural milieu of the Hellenized cities of the Roman Empire, it should find sympathetic resonances in the philosophy and the religion of that era.

Chapter 2

The Jewish Background

*I*N THE SIX CENTURIES prior to the birth of Christ, the Jewish people were subjected to the rule of the series of empires which controlled Syria and Palestine. After Israel's deportation to Babylonia by Nebuchadrezzar (586 B.C.), a portion of the people returned to Judaea under Ezra with the blessing of the new Achaemenid (Persian) monarchy, and there, under the authority of a local satrap, was left undisturbed in the practice of its own religious customs and under the rule of its own law. This tolerant policy of the Persians was continued by Judaea's Hellenistic rulers, the Ptolemies of Egypt, and then, after 200 B.C., the Seleucids with their power bases in Syria and Mesopotamia. Judaea in the Hellenistic period thus had in effect the political status of an "ethnarchy," ruled in domestic affairs by a hereditary high priest and his advisers. It was a tiny state, isolated both by geography and by culture from the increasingly Hellenized areas along the seacoast and to the north, and it had at first little share in the prosperity of its neighbors.

This same period—in particular the centuries of Ptolemaic and Seleucid rule—saw a marked expansion in the number of Jews who lived outside of Judaea in the so-called Diaspora. Since the conquest of Jerusalem by Nebuchadrezzar, there had been a substantial community of Jews in Babylonia, and even prior to that time there had been small settlements in Egypt. During the Hellenistic era, however, both the Ptolemies and the Seleucids discovered the

Jews to be useful subjects and able soldiers and gladly settled them, or allowed them to settle, outside their heavily overpopulated homeland. Thus Egypt, Asia Minor, and Syria came to have large Jewish populations. By the first Christian century, perhaps as much as a third of the population of Alexandria was Jewish, and there were settlements not only in the East but in Rome and other western cities as well. Diaspora Jews did not ordinarily become citizens of the towns where they settled, for to do so they would normally have had to participate in the worship of the civil gods. They retained their national and religious identity and formed specially privileged communities of "resident aliens" (*metoikoi*), or else, as in Alexandria, a *politeuma*—that is, a civic corporation within a larger community. Their relative isolation caused them to be objects of interest and sometimes of envy and distrust to other inhabitants of the cities where they settled.

The foci of Jewish identity were the temple at Jerusalem and the Law of Moses, which functioned not only as a religious but also as a civil code. Jews of the Diaspora paid an annual tax to the temple until its destruction (70 A.D.), and temple worship was the formal center of national life. In Judaea as well as in the Diaspora, however, the functioning bulwark of Israel's identity, its sense of being a separate people dedicated to the Lord in holiness, was the Law. To study, understand, and keep the Law was the calling and the delight of the serious Jew.

This overriding concern to understand and keep the practical wisdom of the Law found outward expression in two institutions. The synagogue, whose origins probably go back to the exile, was typically an assembly of all the Jews in a given district, presided over by a group of "elders" who often had a "ruler" (*archōn*) at their head. This assembly gathered to pray and to bless the name of God, but also to read and interpret the Law and the Prophets. The officials of the synagogue were responsible for the administration of the Law and thus for the punishment or excommunication of offenders. Further, however, the need to interpret the Law and to sanctify the community's life by bringing all aspects of it under the Law's rule produced a class of religious functionaries called "scribes," of whom Ezra himself was counted the first. These men, who in Judaea and elsewhere became the real religious leaders of the people, sought both to expand the range of the Law's application and to guard against its violation by interpreting it in the most cautious and stringent way possible ("building a fence around the Law"). Consequently, they gradually evolved an oral tradition of interpretation (to be incorporated much later in the Talmud), whose content was for practical purposes treated as part of the law itself. It was out of these scribal circles that the Hasidic and Pharisaic movements subsequently arose.

The great crisis of Jewish life in the Hellenistic age arose in the middle of the second century B.C. out of a conflict within the Judaean community itself, a conflict which had both economic and religious sources. One party in the community, drawn from the landowning aristocracy in Jerusalem, sought and gained, from the Seleucid monarch Antiochus IV Ephiphanes, permission to alter the constitutional basis of Jewish life by making Jerusalem a Greek-style city, with the new name of "Antioch." In accord with this policy, Greek educational institutions—a *gymnasion* and *ephebeion*—were established to train new citizens; but above all, the Mosaic Law, under this arrangement, lost its status as the constitution of the community, since legislative power was now lodged in the newly created (and no doubt carefully restricted) citizen body. This attempt on the part of the monied classes to bring Israel up to date enjoyed no support from the common folk of Jerusalem or of the countryside, and certainly not from the scribes and devotees of the law. It was destined to fail, with tragic consequences. When the reforming party made the mistake of replacing the high priest, the people rose. Their successful rebellion, however, compelled the intervention of Antiochus IV, who to assure the safety of his realm took the strongest possible line by way of punishment. He abolished the practice of Judaism and installed the worship of Zeus Olympios in the Jerusalem temple.

In this way, a religious struggle over Hellenization among Jews in Judaea became tied in with the larger political problems of the weakening Seleucid Empire. Antiochus's abolition of Jewish worship provoked the revolt of the Maccabees (167 B.C.), whose guerrilla tactics ultimately compelled him and his successors, distracted as they were by war and by dynastic struggles, to compromise with the Jewish leaders. The final result of all this was threefold. The worship of the Lord was restored in a cleansed and rededicated temple, and with it the traditional constitution of the Jewish ethnarchy. The Hasmoneans—that is, the family of Judah the Maccabee—who in the person of Judah's brother Jonathan assumed the high priesthood with Seleucid support (152 B.C.) —became after 140 B.C. the hereditary rulers of Judaea. At the same time, the Jewish state, which in 142 B.C. had become effectively independent, grew in military power until, under John Hyrcanus (135–105 B.C.), it came to control the whole of Palestine. In this process, however, the aims of the original rebellion were frustrated. The high priesthood itself grew into a Hellenistic monarchy, and the religious forces which had impelled and supported the revolt against Antiochus found themselves in growing opposition to the Hasmonean dynasty.

This era of the Maccabean revolt and Hasmonean rule was the matrix of the religious parties and the religious ideas that dominated Palestinian Judaism in the time of Jesus. The advent of the Romans in 63 B.C. under Pompey the Great changed the situation only by rendering the internal conflicts more acute. Rome began by intervening to settle a struggle over the succession in the Hasmonean house. It solved the problem by putting most of the Jewish kingdom under the rule of its propraetor in Syria, but Jerusalem itself was constituted a temple-state, its domestic affairs governed by the Hasmonean high priest. This system might have worked, had Rome not changed its mind and violated Jewish sensibilities by installing Herod, called "the Great," as a vassal king (37–4 B.C.) over the former territories of the Hasmoneans. An Idumaean whose people had been forcibly converted to Judaism in the days of Hasmonean power, Herod was almost universally hated, in spite of his magnificent reconstruction of the Jerusalem temple, his contributions to the material prosperity of the land, and his occasional interventions at Rome to protect Jewish interests. His very presence as king violated the Jewish people's traditional theocratic constitution. He was, moreover, not only a foreigner but a manifest if sometimes cautious Hellenizer. Above all, however, his taxation impoverished the peasantry, drove more land into the possession of the great landowners, and forced many common folk into beggary or brigandage. Rome tried to retrieve its error by making Judaea a province under a Roman procurator (6 A.D.), but the damage was done. The religious, political, and economic strife which had been triggered under Antiochus IV and continued under the Hasmoneans was only exacerbated by Roman policy. It is no wonder that the first response to the Roman census of 6 A.D. was a local rebellion led by the founder of the Zealot party, Judah the Galilean.

It is against this general background that one must understand the division which arose in Hasmonean times between an aristocratic, priestly party and a popular, devout, and religiously more exclusive party: the Sadduces and the Pharisees. The former were the group with which the Hasmoneans gradually became associated. This was an essentially worldly party, whose attitudes were determined more by an interest in political and commercial expansion than by strong religious conviction. Most of the religious principles it stood for were simply conservative. The Sadducees were loyal to the Law, for example, but would not accept the oral tradition of the scribes. They denied recently popularized doctrines of resurrection or immortality, and they rejected the notion of good and evil spirits. Though very influential politically, they were unpopular with the mass of the people, who saw them as representing economic oppression, as open to foreign influences, and as lax in their attitude toward the Law.

Over against this group stood the Pharisees—"the Separated." This party stood in the tradition of the ancient scribes and of the Hasidim, who had originally rallied to the support of the Maccabean revolt. Its primary concern was with the sanctification of life through a minute and joyous observance of the Law. It evinced no great interest in political action (though the party of Zealots, who advocated rebellion against the power of Rome, seems to have sprung out of the Pharisaic movement), yet it did take stands on issues affecting political life. The Pharisaic party not only broke with the Hasmoneans over the latter's policy of national expansion, but also questioned their title to the high priesthood, the very basis of royal power. The Pharisees were influential and widely admired, so much so that the Hasmoneans were eventually forced to give them representation on the Sanhedrin, the high priest's council of advisors. Nevertheless, they were not numerous, since most people lacked either the education or the leisure to devote themselves utterly to the Law. They stood for certain popular beliefs that had grown naturally out of Jewish religious experience since the time of the Exile. They held strongly to the existence of good and evil spirits and to a doctrine about angels and Satan which was partly the product of Persian influence. By the same token, they taught belief in resurrection of the body and in future rewards and punishments: eschatological beliefs which, together with messianic hopes, flourished in the intense and troubled era of the two centuries before the birth of Christ.

Connected with the Pharisaic party in its opposition to the Hasmonean settlement of religious (and therewith political) affairs were the Essenes. The teachings of this sect are known to us chiefly through a library of scrolls discovered at Qumran, on the northwest shore of the Dead Sea. There one community of the sect lived a quasi-monastic life in isolation from the rest of Israel. The origins of the movement are obscure. Previously it was known only from reports of Philo, Josephus, and Pliny the Elder, writing in the first century A.D. The community at Qumran, however, whose buildings possibly date back to around 135 B.C., seems to have assembled as the result of a conflict over the high priesthood. Its members looked back to a "Righteous Teacher" as their founder and set him in opposition to a "Wicked Priest"—perhaps an illegitimate high priest whose assumption of office represented, at least to a small body of the pious, a repudiation of the religious foundation of Israel's existence. Some historians have sought to identify Simon the Maccabee's recognition as hereditary high priest (140 B.C.) as the offense that generated the sect. In any case, this movement, unlike that of the Pharisees, withdrew from the mainstream of Jewish life, refusing to have anything to do with the worship of the temple and believing that it alone was the true congregation of Israel, the faithful remnant. Its members esteemed the Law and claimed, by following the Righteous Teacher, to preserve the Law's correct meaning as against current perversions. They observed periodic lustrations, an annual rite of entering and renewing the Covenant, and a sacred meal of bread and wine. They lived under a strict discipline, which is preserved for us in *The Manual of Discipline* —a work which also reflects the careful organization of the community, with its overseers, priests of Zadok, elders, and others. Above all, though, they looked forward fervently to the future redemption of Israel. They expected the appearance of a messianic figure or figures who would arise to gather the scattered hosts of Israel together, to defeat her enemies, and to inaugurate the age of God's rule.

Such hopes were not confined to the Dead Sea sect. The religious, political, and economic frustrations of popular Judaism in Palestine generated a mood of combined despair and hope—despair of the present and hope in a future, decisive intervention of God to set things right. This mood was reflected above all in the rich "apocalyptic" or "revelation" literature of the first and second centuries B.C. (and later). Such writings recorded visions in which the mysteries of the heavenly world, of the course of human history, and of God's plan for overthrowing wickedness were revealed—almost invariably to an ancient sage. The best known of these is the canonical Book of Daniel, composed in the setting of the struggle against Antiochus IV Epiphanes. Alongside it one can set such other examples of the *genre* as *The Book of Enoch, The Assumption of Moses,* and the later Christian Revelation to John. The burden of this apocalyptic literature is the assurance that God himself will "visit and redeem his people"[1] to frustrate the cosmic and earthly powers of evil and to assert his own righteous kingdom. There were of course variant accounts of how this could come about. In some sources, God himself was expected to step in; in others, he was to act through the agency of an angelic or supernatural being. In some quarters, as we have seen, there is mention of the Lord's "Messiah," a human king in the Davidic line who was expected to restore the kingdom of his father. Whatever the form of the expectation, however, it reflected a belief not only that God would act, but also that God's action alone was sufficient to overcome evil.

Equally prominent in post-exilic Jewish life was the genre of thought and literature concerned with the theme of wisdom. Wisdom traditionally meant the practical insight necessary for the successful conduct of the affairs of life, and the wise were people who saw into the structures and meanings of things.[2] In later Judaism, this meant in particular understanding of God's law, which was equated with wisdom and thus became the basis for inquiries into cosmological and anthropological as well as moral and legal questions. Such human wisdom, however, was thought to be the result of openness to the inspiration of a divine Wisdom, who was both God's plan and God's agent for creation, and who is described in *The Wisdom of Solomon* as "a pure effluence from the glory of the Almighty . . . the flawless mirror of the active power of God and the image of his goodness."[3] Wisdom (not unlike the Stoic *logos* or the Platonist World-Soul) orders creation, but she also seeks out and summons people to understanding and makes them friends of God. She, too, is thus a saving agent, though one conceived in a framework of thought different from the saving figures of apocalyptic expectation.

These literatures were known and pondered not only in Judaea and Palestine but in the Diaspora as well, where the great majority of Jews was to be found. Under the Romans, Judaism was an "authorized religion" (*religio licita*), not only in Palestine but in Greek and Roman cities, and Roman law protected the communities of Jewish farmers, craftsmen, and traders throughout the empire. This protection was necessary, since the Jews' religious exclusiveness, their legal privileges, and their unwillingness to participate in civic life

---

[1] Luke 1:68.   [2] Wisd. of Sol. 7:17–21.   [3] Wisd. of Sol. 7:25.

sometimes made them unpopular. In fact, Diaspora Jews had made many adjustments to the Hellenistic world, most notably in the matter of language. They spoke Greek almost universally, even in their synagogues; and by the time of Augustus, the Greek version of the Scriptures known as the Septuagint (LXX) was completed and everywhere employed. Further, the Diaspora Jewish communities entered into dialogue with pagan religion. As a result, they not only made converts (proselytes) but gathered about them a large penumbra of partially Judaized inquirers ("God-fearers"), which was to serve as a recruiting ground for much of early Christian missionary propaganda.

This dialogue produced its most remarkable fruit in the Jewish community at Alexandria in Egypt, where, in the work of Philo (d. ca. 42 A.D.), themes from the Jewish scriptures were combined in a remarkable syncretism with Stoic and Platonist philosophical ideas. A faithful Jew, Philo sought to show that the Law—that is, the Pentateuch—intimated a wisdom which agreed with the best in the teaching of the philosophical tradition. To do this, he used the method of allegorical interpretation well known to Hellenistic exegetes of Homer, and by this means uncovered in the pages of Moses not only an ethic but also a philosophical doctrine of God and of creation. According to Philo, the cosmos is the product of God's outflowing goodness. Incomprehensible in his transcendence, God is linked to the world by the divine powers. Of these, the highest is the Logos, which flows out of the being of God himself and is not only the agent through whom God created the world but also the source of all other powers and the ultimate model of the spiritual and visible creations. Philo's picture of the Logos thus fuses together elements from many sources: from Jewish Wisdom speculation, from Platonist ideas about an intelligible realm of Forms, and from the scriptural notion that God creates by his Word (Logos). This kind of thinking, which has less sophisticated parallels in New Testament ideas of God's Word and Wisdom, was to prove a fertile model in the development of later Christian theology.

Chapter 3

Jesus and the Disciples

*T*HE WAY WAS PREPARED for Jesus by an apocalyptic-messianic movement led by John the Baptist, who in the thought of the early Christians was the forerunner of the Messiah. Ascetic in life, John, in the region of the Jordan, preached that the day of judgment upon Israel was at hand and that the Messiah was about to come. In the spirit of the ancient prophets, he proclaimed the message: "Repent, do justice." He baptized his disciples in token of the washing away of their sins, and he taught them a special prayer. Jesus, we are told, classed him as the last, and among the greatest, of the prophets. Some of John's disciples later became followers of Jesus, but his movement continued to have an independent life.[1]

Materials are lacking for any adequate biography of Jesus. The Gospel records are primarily testimonies to the divine event of Jesus the Christ, and their details have doubtless been colored by the differing experiences, situations, and memories of early Christian communities. Scholars are thus divided concerning the accuracy of many incidents recorded in the Gospels. Nevertheless, the career and teaching of Jesus stand out on the pages of the Gospels in their essential outlines.

Jesus was brought up in Nazareth of Galilee. This land, though despised by the more purely Jewish inhabitants of Judaea because its people were of mixed racial stock, was loyal to the Jewish religion and traditions, the home of a hardy, self-respecting population, and particularly pervaded by the messianic hope. Here Jesus grew to manhood through years of unrecorded experience. From this life he was apparently drawn by the preaching of John the Baptist. He went to John and was baptized by the prophet in the Jordan River. With his baptism there came the conviction that he was appointed by God to fulfill a special role in proclaiming the kingdom soon to be inaugurated by the heavenly Son of Man. Whether Jesus actually viewed himself as Messiah is a

[1] Cf. Acts 19:1–4.

much contested question. In any case, he seems to have rejected popular conceptions of the messianic office and to have anticipated not political triumph but suffering as his own lot, even while believing that in his ministry the power of the coming kingdom was already at work.

After his baptism—or, as Matthew would have it,[2] after the arrest of the Baptist—Jesus began an itinerant ministry of preaching and healing whose message was the near approach of God's kingdom and the consequent necessity for repentance and faith. He gathered a company of associates—the Twelve, symbolizing the fullness of the tribes of Israel—and attracted a larger group of less closely attached disciples. His ministry was brief: it lasted for three years at the most, and perhaps no more than one. It aroused opposition from the religious authorities, and no doubt from others as well, because Jesus' actions and teaching made him seem blasphemously critical of the Law and its traditional interpretation. He journeyed northward toward Tyre and Sidon, and then to the region of Caesarea Philippi, where the Gospels record that his disciples acknowledged his messianic mission. He judged, however, that at whatever peril he must bear witness in Jerusalem. There, in the face of growing hostility, he went; and there he was seized and crucified, certainly in the administration of the procurator Pontius Pilate (26–36 A.D.) and probably in the year 29. His disciples scattered to their homes, but speedily gathered once more at Jerusalem, in the glad conviction that God had raised him from the dead.

The kingdom of God, in Jesus' teaching, meant the manifest assertion of God's loving and righteous rule. Hence, in those who discern its nearness it demands practical acknowledgment of God's sovereignty and fatherhood. This comes about only through a complete reorientation of values and attitudes (repentance and faith), which issues in love of God and neighbor and is crowned and empowered by divine forgiveness. To live in view of the coming kingdom is, as Jesus portrays it, a costly and demanding business. It entails willingness to relinquish all lesser goods, to transcend the normal moral demands of the Law, and to practice unlimited forgiveness toward others. The fulfillment of such a life is an unending fellowship with God and his holy ones. For those, on the other hand, who fail to discern and understand the kingdom which is dawning in Jesus' ministry, there is only destruction.

Most of Jesus' teachings have parallels in the religious thought of his age, yet their total effect was disturbing and revolutionary—the more so, apparently, by reason of the style in which he taught. "He taught them as one that had authority, and not as the scribes."[3] He could say that the least of his disciples is greater than John the Baptist, and that heaven and earth should pass away before his words. He called the heavy-laden to him and offered them rest. He promised those who confessed him before men that he would confess them

---

[2] Matt. 4:12.   [3] Mark 1:22.

before his Father. He declared that none knew the Father but a Son, and he to whom the Son should reveal the Father. He proclaimed himself Lord of the Sabbath, than which, in popular estimate, there was no more sacred part of the God-given Jewish Law. He affirmed that he had power to pronounce forgiveness of sins. On the other hand, this teacher-with-authority experienced all the limitations of the human condition. He prayed and taught his disciples to pray. He declared that he did not know the day or the hour of the ending of the present world-age, which was known to the Father alone. It was not his to determine who should sit on his right hand and his left in the kingdom. He prayed that the Father's will, not his own, be done. On the cross, he cried out: "My God, my God, why hast thou forsaken me?"[4] In reporting all these utterances, the Gospels in effect confess their sense of the mystery of his person: the person of one who is on the one hand a normal human being and on the other the bearer of God's authority and active presence.

What Jesus taught and did was, in the experience of his disciples, vindicated by his being raised after death to the life of the kingdom which he had proclaimed. The "how" of this conviction is one of the most puzzling of historical problems. The fact of it is unquestionable. It seems to have come first to Peter,[5] who, in that sense at least, was the "rock" leader on whom the church was founded. All the early disciples shared it. It was the turning point in the conversion of Paul. It gave courage to the scattered disciples, brought them together again, and made them witnesses. Henceforth, they had a risen Lord in whom the reality of God's kingdom was already fulfilled and whose present glory they could, in a preliminary way, share, even while they waited for its universal manifestation.

These convictions were deepened by the experience of the eschatological gift of the Holy Spirit, which Acts associates with the day of Pentecost. The exact nature of this pentecostal manifestation is perhaps impossible to recover. Certainly the notion of a proclamation of the Gospel in many foreign languages is inconsistent with what we know of "speaking with tongues" from elsewhere in the New Testament,[6] as it is also with the impression given onlookers that the speakers were "filled with new wine."[7] The point of significance, however, is that these phenomena appeared as manifest evidence of the gift and power of Christ. They demonstrated the inauguration of the new age which Jesus' ministry had promised. If the disciple visibly acknowledged his allegiance by faith, repentance, and baptism, the exalted Christ, it was believed, would in turn acknowledge the disciple by bestowing the Spirit; and this gift attested the disciple's part in the coming age of "the restoration of all things" promised in God's oracles through the prophets.[8]

---

[4] Mark 15:34.   [5] I Cor. 15:5.   [6] I Cor. 14:2–19.   [7] Acts 2:13.   [8] Acts 3:21.

Chapter 4

The Early Christian Community

*I*N ITS EARLIEST PHASE, the Christian movement had its center in Jerusalem, where it took shape not as a new religion but as a sect or grouping within the parent body of Judaism. Presumably there were, from the beginning, followers of Jesus in the towns and villages of Judaea and Galilee as well, but of these little is known. Indeed, our knowledge even of the Jerusalem community is limited and obscure, since the Acts of the Apostles, our only source of information, must be read by the historian with caution. It embodies early and authentic traditions; but at the same time it is written in the "creative" style normal for Hellenistic histories and handles its materials from the point of view of the second Christian generation, which already tended to see the events of four or five decades before its time as constituting a kind of golden age of the church.

What is clear is that the original communities were composed of Palestinian Jews who, on the basis of Jesus' resurrection, proclaimed his imminent return as the fulfiller of God's kingdom, and who lived in anticipation of that event. They called themselves, apparently, "the poor"[1] or "the saints,"[2] and also, from an early time, "the *ekklesia*"—i.e., "assembly" or "church." What all of these styles or names meant was much the same. The early community saw itself, in virtue of its allegiance to Jesus, as the true "assembly" of Israel, the end-time community which the Lord will recognize when he comes in glory. That they saw themselves simply as Jews, as a renewed Israel, is made clear by the fact that they were faithful both in attendance at the temple and in obedience to the Law; and this being the case, they lived at peace with the religious authorities in Jerusalem. Needless to say, this community had its own special institutions which expressed its particular identity. It practiced baptism, with which the eschatological gift of the Holy Spirit was associated. It gathered regularly for prayer, mutual exhortation, and "breaking of bread,"[3] in which

[1] Gal. 2:10.　　[2] Rom. 15:25.　　[3] Acts 2:46.

historians have no doubt rightly seen the origins of the eucharist as well as a community fellowship-meal. It expressed the faith which defined its identity in expressions like "Jesus is the Messiah"[4] or "God raised Jesus from the dead."[5]

The founding members of this community were no doubt the Eleven (restored, Acts tells us, to twelve by the election of Matthias). By the time that Acts was written, these men were being called "apostles," a title which was originally applied to traveling missionaries like Paul. Apart from the case of Peter, however, and perhaps John, nothing is in fact known about the careers or activities of the Twelve, who fade almost immediately from the history in Acts and thus become apt subjects for later legend. When Paul visited Jerusalem, leadership seems to have been in the hands of two or three "pillars," James the Lord's brother, Peter, and John.[6]

Trouble came to the community of believers in Jerusalem as a result of the incorporation into its life of Greek-speaking Diaspora Jews resident in Jerusalem. There was, we are told, a complaint brought by Greek-speaking Jewish believers against the local Aramaic-speaking Christians. According to Acts 6, the sole reason for this was that the "Hellenists" were aggrieved because "their widows were neglected in the daily distribution."[7] The brief quarrel was settled by the appointment of seven Hellenists to administer the community's common resources[8]—a fact which no doubt accounts for the tradition that these seven were the first deacons.

There was, however, more at stake in this situation than a mere administrative problem. That much is apparent from the continuing narrative of Acts. There Stephen, the apparent leader of the Hellenists, is found in acrimonious debate with members of other Greek-speaking synagogues, who accused him of speaking "blasphemous words against Moses and God."[9] As a result of this, Stephen is hauled before the Sanhedrin and eventually condemned to death by stoning. Presumably, then, Stephen and his Greek-speaking fellow-believers lacked the respect for temple and Law which the Palestinian Christians habitually evinced, and they were persecuted not on grounds of their belief in Jesus as Messiah, but because they talked as though they were prepared, Jews though they were, to jettison certain demands of the Law in the light of their new faith.

This view of the matter is confirmed by two further reports given in Acts. First, we are told that Stephen's death was the opening scene in "a great persecution . . . against the church in Jerusalem,"[10] yet it is made clear at the same time that "the apostles" were not affected by this persecution.[11] In other words, the persecution was selective and touched only those Christians—the Hellenists —who spoke "words against this holy place and the law."[12] The Aramaic-speaking community was left relatively undisturbed, as the ongoing narrative in Acts clearly presupposes. But, in the second place, the scattering of the

---

4 Cf. Mark 8:29.
5 Rom. 10:9.
6 Gal. 2:9, and cf. 1:18–19.
7 Acts 6:1.
8 Acts 6:3.
9 Acts 6:12.
10 Acts 8:1.
11 Ibid.
12 Acts 6:13.

Hellenist leaders which the persecution produced turned out to be the beginning of a new phase in the life and mission of the church. For "they went about preaching the word,"[13] carrying it to Samaria,[14] and afterward to Phoenicia, Cyprus, and Antioch, where, it appears, there arose the first Christian *ekklesia* which mixed Gentiles and Jews.[15] The Hellenists, then, first carried the message of the risen Christ into the Diaspora. What is more, their actions confirmed the impression they had given to the Jerusalem authorities about their attitude toward the Law. They admitted Gentile "God-fearers" into their fellowship in violation of orthodox practice.

The Jerusalem community, however, enjoyed relative peace, obviously maintaining its loyalty to temple and Law and having, at least for a time, no direct involvement with the new mission or with the new centers of Christian life in places like Antioch and Damascus. This peace was briefly broken under the kingship of Herod Agrippa I (41–44 A.D.), to whom the emperor Claudius had restored part of the kingdom of his grandfather, Herod the Great. Perhaps in order to build up a reputation for enthusiastic orthodoxy, Agrippa had James ("the brother of John") executed and Peter thrown into prison.[16] It may have been this brief persecution which led to Peter's departure from Jerusalem and his subsequent activity as a missionary apostle. At all events, the leadership of the Jerusalem community fell to James the brother of the Lord, who exercised it until his martyr's death in about 63, in association, Acts suggests, with a body of elders.[17]

---

[13] Acts 8:4.   [14] Acts 8:5, 25.   [15] Acts 11:19–20.   [16] Acts 12:1–3.   [17] Acts 21:18.

Chapter 5

Paul and Gentile Christianity

*T*HE PERSECUTION which resulted in Stephen's martyrdom started the movement which planted Christianity in the cities of the Jewish Diaspora. More than this, however, it created at Antioch what was in effect a second focal center of Christian life. Capital of the province of Syria and former seat of the Seleucid monarchy, Antioch was a city of first rank, with a large cosmopolitan population, including a significant Jewish community. There, the message about Jesus was preached to Gentile "God-fearers" and such persons were admitted to the

Christian assembly without first becoming Jewish proselytes. One result of this development was that people in Antioch began to perceive the followers of Jesus as a body distinct not only from paganism but also from normative Judaism, and hence it was there that the church's members first acquired a label. The populace, no doubt half-contemptuously, called them "Christians"—a term little used by the church itself until well into the second century. Another result of it was, inevitably, to raise the question whether persons who could not be members of the synagogue could be members of the *ekklesia,* the eschatological people of God. If the rule of the Law were imposed on Gentile converts to Christ, the church would continue to be a grouping within Israel; if such converts were free of the Law, the church could understand itself to have a universal mission. In this debate—one not without some precedent within Judaism itself—the decisive role was to be played by the apostle Paul.

Paul, whose Hebrew name, Saul, recalled the ancient hero of his native tribe of Benjamin, was born in the Cilician city of Tarsus. His father was apparently a citizen of Rome as well as a Jew in the Pharisaic tradition. At the time of Paul's birth, Tarsus was an intellectual and cultural center of some note and a center of Stoic teaching. There is no reason to believe, however, that Paul, brought up in a strict Jewish home, received a Greek-style education. Greek, to be sure, was his normal language from childhood, and he could not have failed as a youth to become familiar with the popular commonplaces of Hellenistic moral and religious thought. Nevertheless, it was in the rabbinical tradition that he was raised. Acts, in fact, makes Paul assert that he was "brought up" in Jerusalem "at the feet of Gamaliel,"[1] a famous teacher of the Law. This may have been the case, though it seems to presuppose that his family moved from Tarsus, and it finds no confirmation in his letters, which give the impression that Paul had very little to do with Jerusalem until after his conversion. On the other hand, the report in Acts is consistent with what we know of Paul's original convictions and commitments. He was devoted to the Pharisaic ideal of a nation made holy by strict observance of God's Law, and he insists that his own conduct, measured by that standard, was beyond reproach. It was no doubt this ideal which motivated Paul's persecution of the church. Whether or not he was present, as Acts maintains he was, at the stoning of Stephen in Jerusalem, it was Stephen the Hellenist, who spoke against the Law and the Temple, who represented the strain in early Christianity that would have given offense to Paul, "so extremely zealous"[2] was he for the traditions of Judaism. It is therefore no matter for surprise that we hear nothing of any actions of his against the Palestinian Christian community in Jerusalem, yet we find him traveling to Damascus, a Diaspora city, to bring discipline to bear against Christians there (who must, incidentally, have had some connection with the synagogue). His antagonism

---

[1] Acts 22:3.   [2] Gal. 1:14.

was directed not against believers as such, but against those whose faith went hand in hand with a tendency to bend the requirements of the Law.

Though the dates of Paul's history are somewhat uncertain, it may have been in about the year 35 that the great change in his life occurred. Journeying to Damascus on a disciplinary errand, he was seized up in an encounter with the risen Christ, who called him to a special mission. The nature of Paul's experience can only be conjectured; of its effects on his life, there can be no doubt. He joined the very folk whom he had been attempting to restore to Judaism by disciplinary means. More than that, he discovered in the risen Lord of his vision the one in and by whom his own identity was determined. He could say: "It is no longer I who live, but Christ who lives in me."[3] Most important of all, he was convinced that fellowship with the crucified and risen Jesus, not observance of the Law, was the necessary—and sufficient—condition of people's participation in the renewed creation of God's promise.

In Paul's case, conversion showed itself at once in action. He relates that he went first of all to Arabia—i.e., the territory of Nabataea south of Damascus, with its capital at Petra. There he seems to have preached his gospel to some effect, since the Nabataean authorities pursued him even in Damascus.[4] Three years after his conversion, he made a two-week visit to Jerusalem, "to visit Cephas" (Peter),[5] and there he met James the Lord's brother as well. For almost a decade—of which Acts tells us nothing—he worked in Syria and Cilicia (of which province his native Tarsus was the capital), no doubt founding churches. Eventually, however, he was brought to Antioch by Barnabas,[6] a Hellenistic Jewish Christian whose home was in Cyprus and who may have been one of those who scattered from Jerusalem after the martyrdom of Stephen.

At this point, however, the inevitable crisis arose. Christian visitors from Jerusalem came to Antioch. In accord with the tradition of the Jerusalem church, they insisted: "Unless you are circumcised according to the custom of Moses, you cannot be saved."[7] The debate thus occasioned took Paul, Barnabas, and Titus, an uncircumcised Gentile convert, to Jerusalem to confer with the leaders of the church there. Paul describes the meeting in Galatians 2:1–10, and a different account of what seems to be the same meeting is given in Acts 15. On the general result of the meeting both accounts agree. The leaders of the Jerusalem church and the leaders of the new Gentile mission reached a portentous accord. The calling of persons like Paul and Barnabas was recognized as legitimate, and it was acknowledged that the Gospel belonged to Gentiles as well as to Jews. Thus, there were to be two strands in the church's missionary enterprise; but the new Gentile congregations and their leaders were to "remember the poor"— that is, they were to symbolize their fellowship with the Jerusalem congregation by contributing to its material needs.[8] The account in Acts 15 records that the

---

[3] Gal. 2:20.   [5] Gal. 1:18.   [7] Acts 15:1.
[4] 2 Cor. 11:32.   [6] Acts 11:25.   [8] Gal. 2:9–10.

apostolic council required Gentile Christians "to abstain from the pollutions of idols and from unchastity and from what is strangled and from blood"[9]—in other words, it passed a decree governing the conditions of table fellowship among Jewish and Gentile Christians. Paul, however, indicates that the problem of table-fellowship arose only after the apostolic conference,[10] and in any case his letters show no knowledge of such a decree. Likely enough, the author of Acts is attributing to the council an arrangement which had become traditional in his own day.

It is in all probability at this point—after and not before the apostolic conference—that Paul and Barnabas, responding to the guidance of the Spirit, set out on a journey which took them to Cyprus and thence to Perga, Antioch of Pisidia, Iconium, Lystra, and Derbe. This is the so-called "first missionary journey" described in Acts 13 and 14. On their return from this trip, there arose at Antioch the debate between Peter and Paul over the matter of eating with Gentile Christians.[11] This disagreement, needless to say, did not concern the bedrock issue of whether Gentiles could belong to God's people without submitting to circumcision and the other ritual prescriptions of the Law. That matter had already been settled. Paul, however, was not prepared to compromise even on the subsidiary issue of table-fellowship, since for him what was at stake was the principle that "a man is not justified by works of the law but through faith in Jesus Christ."[12] In this debate, Barnabas, Paul's friend and companion, took the side of Peter. The result was that when once again Paul set out on his missionary travels, he "chose Silas" as his companion, while "Barnabas took Mark with him and sailed away to Cyprus."[13]

Now came the short years of Paul's great missionary effort "to win obedience from the Gentiles"[14] by planting the Gospel in every region of the civilized world, even as far as the western extremities of the Roman empire.[15] His journeyings opened with return visits to the communities he had already founded in southern Asia Minor. He was kept for a time in Galatia by illness,[16] taking occasion to found new churches there. With his companions, however, he was guided to leave Asia Minor. From Troas, he crossed into Macedonia, and pursued his way along the great Via Egnatia, which led westward toward the Adriatic Sea and Italy. Having founded communities at Philippi and Thessalonica (the seat of the Roman proconsul of Macedonia), Paul was diverted from his route when troubles in Thessalonica forced him to leave "by night" and turn slightly south into central Greece. Persecution pursued him, however, and he continued south to the seaport of Corinth by way of Athens. At Corinth, he spent eighteen months preaching and teaching in the house of one Titius Justus, a Gentile God-fearer. From there, Paul traveled with two new friends and colleagues, the Roman Jews Aquila and Priscilla, to Ephesus, but he soon left them there to

---

[9] Acts 15:20.   [11] Gal. 2:11–12.   [13] Acts 15:39–40.   [15] Rom. 15:24.
[10] Gal. 2:11–13.   [12] Gal. 2:16.   [14] Rom. 15:18.   [16] Gal. 4:13.

return to Palestine and Antioch, reappearing in Ephesus after another visit to his churches in Phrygia and Galatia. On his return to Ephesus, he began a ministry there of several years' duration (53?–56?)[17]—a ministry which produced his Corinthian correspondence and also, in all probability, his letters to the Galatians, the Philippians, and Philemon.

Paul's departure from Ephesus took him back to Corinth for a three-month stay; there he wrote his letter to the Romans, from which we learn of the two great projects which now governed his actions. One of these was to bring to the church at Jerusalem, as a healing gesture of thanks and solidarity, the offering he had collected from his new Gentile congregations. He was determined to do this himself, even though he was uncertain of his reception by Jews and Jewish Christians in Palestine. The second project was to carry out his original plan of bringing the Gospel to the western parts of the empire in order to discharge his "obligation both to Greeks and to barbarians."[18] As it turned out, it was his journey to Jerusalem, where in the end he was arrested by the Roman government, which ultimately brought him to Rome, but only after two years' imprisonment in Caesarea and only as a man under indictment. Little is known of Paul's last days. Some scholars have argued that he was released from his imprisonment and made further journeys, but the weight of the evidence is against this hypothesis. The probability is that Paul was executed at Rome some time before 64 A.D.

Paul's letters, which were circulated and no doubt gradually collected in the churches he founded, are the earliest body of Christian literature. The extent and degree of the authority they acquired is reflected in the fact that later generations cited them simply as containing the words of "the Apostle." Next to the four Gospels, they have exerted, in every age, a more profound influence on Christian thought and piety than any other set of writings. The reason for this influence does not lie in the clarity or the systematic character of Paul's thinking. In the modern sense, Paul was not a "systematic" theologian, and his writings (even the carefully planned and argued Letter to the Romans) are occasional and personal in nature. Their influence is grounded rather in the richness and suggestiveness of Paul's thought and occasionally in its unfinished and even ambiguous character.

There is no ambiguity, however, about the foundation of his teaching and preaching. It lies in what he calls simply "the gospel" or "my gospel" (for it was given him by revelation,[19] even though its content was also a matter of tradition[20]). This was the good news that in Jesus, God had acted to provide salvation for all who should believe—a salvation whose complete realization lay in the future but whose beginnings could be experienced even in the present. This salvation had its roots in Jesus' death and resurrection—two events which in Paul's thought stand forth as transactions of transcendent significance. "Christ

---

[17] Acts 19:8–10.   [18] Rom. 1:14.   [19] Gal. 1:12.   [20] 1 Cor. 15:3.

died for our sins"[21] in accordance with the prophecies of the Hebrew Scriptures; he "gave himself for our sins to deliver us from the present evil age."[22] More than this, "Christ was raised from the dead by the glory of the Father" so that, just like him, believers "might walk in newness of life."[23] Christians, therefore, united with Christ through faith and rejoicing in the gift of God's Spirit, wait for the time when the Lord will return and the work of salvation will be completed, when "we shall bear the image of the man of heaven."[24]

At the heart of Paul's understanding of this gospel is his conviction that believers are indeed joined to Christ in the Spirit. The events of the Lord's death to sin and his resurrection to new life are not simply "objective" happenings which have effects on the cosmic state of affairs. They are events which happen in and for the believer. "We were buried therefore with him by baptism into death";[25] "our old self was crucified with him so that . . . we might no longer be enslaved to sin."[26] Consequently, he tells his correspondents, "we believe that we shall also live with him."[27] "You must . . . consider yourselves dead to sin and alive to God in Christ Jesus."[28] This idea of unity or identification with Christ works, for Paul, in two directions. On the one hand, it issues in his picture of the church—"the saints"—as Christ's body, enlivened and made one by the Spirit of God which comes from the risen Lord. On the other hand, it is the source of his understanding of the ethical imperative which is laid upon Christians. They were, Paul insists, "washed . . . sanctified . . . justified in the name of the Lord Jesus Christ and in the Spirit of our God."[29] Hence they are "united to the Lord,"[30] and this is a state of affairs entirely inconsistent with immoral living. Being "the body of Christ and individually members of it," believers are to cultivate the graces showered on them by the Spirit and, above all, to make the greatest gift of all, love, their aim.[31]

This conviction, however, that Jesus the Christ is the one in whom God's salvation is to be found inevitably occasioned a problem for Paul: the problem of what to say about the Jewish Law, the basis of the "old" covenant. This issue was raised for him by a concrete circumstance—namely, the contention of some Christians that even Gentile believers must keep the Law in order to be a part of the covenant of God's grace. To Paul this was a puzzling and, in the end, intolerable demand. As he saw it in his role as one whom Christ had charged with a mission to non-Jews, the crucified and risen Christ embodied the new life for "every one who has faith,"[32] whether Jew or Greek. To demand more than union with Christ in faith was, therefore, to question the sufficiency of what God had done for humanity. It was, in fact, to fall away from reliance on God's gracious act in Christ. "You are severed from Christ, you who would be

---

21 Ibid.
22 Gal. 1:4.
23 Rom. 6:4.

24 1 Cor. 15:49.
25 Rom. 6:4.
26 Rom. 6:6.

27 Rom. 6:8.
28 Rom. 6:11.
29 1 Cor. 6:11.

30 1 Cor. 6:17.
31 1 Cor. 12:27–14:1.
32 Rom. 1:16.

justified by the law; you have fallen away from grace."[33] Hence, Paul insisted that "a man is not justified by works of the law but through faith in Jesus Christ";[34] and to prove his point he appealed to the example of Abraham, the father of God's people, who "believed God, and it was reckoned to him as righteousness."[35] From the beginning, God's intention had been to bring redemption to all through Christ as a "free gift"[36] which needed only faith's acceptance. Therefore "God has consigned all men to disobedience, that he may have mercy upon all."[37] Nothing but God's grace in Christ avails or ultimately matters.

This does not mean that for Paul the Law is evil. As far as its teaching is concerned, "the law is spiritual."[38] Paul never suggests that what the Law inculcates is wrong or inconsistent with God's will. It does mean, however, that the Law is preliminary. "The law was our custodian until Christ came."[39] It is at once God's reaction to sin and the revealer of the reality and power of sin.[40] Nevertheless, salvation is "apart from law,"[41] "for if justification were through the law, then Christ died to no purpose."[42] And so we are back to Paul's bedrock conviction: as with Abraham, faith "will be reckoned to us who believe in him that raised from the dead Jesus our Lord, who was put to death for our trespasses and raised for our justification."[43]

---

[33] Gal. 5:4.
[34] Gal. 2:16.
[35] Gal. 3:6; Rom. 4:3; and cf. Gen. 15:6.
[36] Rom. 6:23.

[37] Rom. 11:32; cf. Gal. 3:22.
[38] Rom. 7:14.
[39] Gal. 3:24.
[40] Gal. 3:19; Rom. 7:7.

[41] Rom. 3:21.
[42] Gal. 2:21.
[43] Rom. 4:24–25.

Chapter 6

The Close of the Apostolic Age

THE PROMINENCE of Paul's letters in the New Testament and the devotion of the author of Acts to Paul's missionary career leave the average reader of the New Testament with the impression that primitive Christianity and Pauline Christianity were virtually coextensive. In fact this is not the case. Paul himself knows of churches founded by other missionaries.[1] The church at Rome was

---

[1] Rom. 15:20.

established before Paul wrote his famous letter of introduction to it. The so-called First Epistle of Peter addresses (among others) Christians in Pontus, Cappadocia, and Bithynia—provinces to which Paul's mission did not extend. The Gospels of Matthew and John testify to the existence in Syria, and possibly in Asia Minor, of Christian communities and traditions whose roots were planted quite independently of Paul's work. The original churches of Jerusalem, Judaea, and Galilee owed nothing to the Pauline mission. One must thus assume that primitive Christianity was, both in its thinking and in its organization, more various than a superficial reading of the New Testament might suggest.

From the historian's point of view, therefore, it is unfortunate that, for the period after the deaths of Paul and of Peter, data for reconstruction of the church's development are sparse, and difficult to interpret with assurance. It is possible, however, to identify with reasonable certainty the Christian writings that belong to this last third of the first century, even though it is not always easy to date them or locate their place of origin with any precision. At the same time, there are references in non-Christian writings which illuminate the history of the church in this period. By piecing these various sorts of evidence together, one can arrive at some very general conclusions about the life of the Christian community in the last third of the first century.

Thus, from the Roman historian Tacitus we learn that in 64 A.D. a fire "more serious and terrible"[2] than any that had ever afflicted the city of Rome raged for more than a week and ruined ten of the city's fourteen districts. In spite of the emperor Nero's relief efforts and his expenditure of personal monies on reconstruction, many suspected him of having started the fire in order that he might have the opportunity of rebuilding Rome in a more splendid style. Nero's response to this rumor was to find scapegoats: "those whom the populace called Christians, who were detested because of their shameful deeds." Christians were arrested and tried, not so much for arson, we are told, as for "hatred of the human race"; and they were put to death by methods calculated to provide lurid entertainment for the public.[3] Apparently, then, by Nero's time Christians were recognized in Rome as a distinct group, independent of the Jewish community, and were unpopular because they did not mix with others but kept to themselves. The authorities—and the populace, for that matter—may have regarded them as an illicit secret society dangerous to public order.

This local attack on the church at Rome, while portentous of things to come, had little real effect on the Christian movement, whether at Rome or elsewhere. Of much more significance for the future of the church was the Jewish rebellion of 66–70 A.D., which, while it did not involve the Jews of the Diaspora, devastated Judaea and Galilee and resulted in the burning of the temple and the near destruction of Jerusalem. By the time this rebellion started, the Christians at Jeru-

---

[2] *Annals* 15:38.   [3] *Annals* 15:44.

salem had lost their first leader, James the brother of the Lord, who had been put to death by the Jewish authorities. The only report we have of the fate of the church in this catastrophe comes from Eusebius of Caesarea, who in his fourth-century *Ecclesiastical History* relates that an oracle led believers to migrate from Jerusalem to the Transjordanian city of Pella before the serious fighting started.[4] Whether or not one accepts this account, it seems likely from indirect evidence that Christians in Palestine took a neutral stance during the Jewish war, and that this fact exacerbated the conflict between synagogue and church and made it less and less possible for believers to live as practicing Jews and synagogue members. By the last decade of the first century, the rabbis who reorganized and reinvigorated Judaism after the destruction of the temple had inserted in the synagogue prayers an anathema which made it impossible for a "Nazarene" to participate officially in the liturgy. This great crisis in the history of Judaism, then, brought about as one of its results a separation of the church from its parent body, even for Christians of Jewish parentage and practice. It meant, therefore, that Christians who continued, as many in Palestine apparently did, to keep the Law and to celebrate the Jewish feasts became an increasingly marginal and anachronistic group, at odds both with Judaism and with the growing Gentile churches.

The last third of the first century thus represents a time of crisis not only for Judaism but for the new Christian movement as well. The great leaders of the early years—Paul, Peter, and James—were dead. Furthermore, the church was beginning to be noticed, if only occasionally and locally, by the authorities; and in spite of its continuing dependence on Jewish thought, tradition, and literature, it now stood ever more clearly apart from the synagogue. Not surprisingly, morever, this time of trouble and transition brought to light serious debates and differences within the Christian communities themselves. Questions arose about the meaning and the practical implications of their message concerning the risen Christ. It is understandable, therefore, that this era produced a significant spate of Christian literature and that this literature almost uniformly reflects the churches' need to stabilize their life and witness—to define their tradition and thus to establish their independent identity.

From the point of view of the Christian future, the most significant contributions to this literature are the four Gospels, each of which, in its distinctive way, represents an attempt to bring together in a single work both the apostolic message about Jesus' death and resurrection and the traditions about his teaching and ministry. Each of them carries this task out from the point of view both of a particular Christian community or group of communities and of its own editor or author, who puts the story together in a way that reflects at once the life of that community and his own grasp of the sense of the Gospel. There are,

---

[4] *Ecclesiastical History* 3.5.3.

nevertheless, literary and traditional relationships among the four Gospels. It is the consensus of scholars—questioned by some—that Matthew and Luke at once follow, revise, and supplement Mark, which thus seems to have been the original representative of the Gospel form, dating from the period 65–75 A.D. The Gospel of John, a distinctive work in more than one sense, almost certainly has no literary relation to the other three; there can be no doubt, however, that it handles and interprets in its own way many of the same traditions—as, at least in part, does the later, quasi-gnostic *Gospel of Thomas,* which presents a different version of the traditions concerning the sayings and teaching of Jesus. The aim of these works was to articulate and define the ground and substance of the Christian message by telling the story of Jesus as Christian preachers and teachers had traditionally conveyed it; and they do in fact appear to have incorporated whatever recollections of Jesus' teaching and ministry were extant in the last decades of the first century.

It is not in the Gospels alone, however, that one can discern the efforts of late first-century Christians to order their lives and define their message. A variety of writings—many of which claim apostolic authorship and may well represent the thinking of disciples or "schools" in the tradition of one of the church's original leaders—address themselves to the problems of the Christian movement and to the interpretation of its life and message. In this category, for example, belong the letters attributed to Peter and James, as well as such Pauline writings as the Pastoral Epistles and the Letter to the Ephesians. A special place belongs to the Acts of the Apostles, a companion piece to Luke's Gospel, which not only has its own theological perspective but also offers an interpretation of the early history of Christianity calculated to stress the basic coherence and agreement of the several traditions. All of these writings respond to needs in the life of the churches, and all alike testify to an increasing sense of the necessity for a settled, authoritative "apostolic" tradition to provide a basis for the churches' self-understanding. The Christian movement was beginning to realize that it lived by the message about Jesus as that was based in his own life and teaching and proclaimed by the witness of the leaders and founders of the earliest communities.

Chapter 7

The Interpretation of Jesus

THE QUESTION of crucial importance for the churches of the late first century was that of understanding Jesus in and through the events of his ministry, death, and resurrection. What was the significance of his person and his career? It goes almost without saying that reflection on this Christological question started with the same datum as originally inspired the preaching and faith of the primitive community: that is to say, the experience of Jesus as risen. To the first followers of "the way," this experience, accompanied as it was by the gift of the Holy Spirit,[1] meant that for Jesus and in him the "life eternal,"[2] the life of God's fulfilled rule, had already dawned. The Risen One was the "first fruits" of God's new creation[3]—of the re-formation of the cosmos. As such, he was also the bearer of God's kingdom, the one in and through whom it comes and is made accessible.

It was natural, therefore, that in the first instance the significance of Jesus should have been expressed in messianic categories. His resurrection had shown him to be the one whom God would send to fulfill all things.[4] Thus Paul, using what was no doubt a traditional formula, tells the Roman Christians that the good news concerns God's "Son, who was descended from David according to the flesh and designated Son of God in power according to the Spirit of holiness by his resurrection from the dead";[5] and in another letter the same apostle explains that the calling of Christians is "to wait for [God's] Son from heaven, whom he raised from the dead, Jesus who delivers us from the wrath to come."[6] In these basic summaries of his proclamation, Paul's attention, like that of the speeches attributed to Peter in Acts, is focused on the resurrection and the *eschaton*—the final day of the Lord; the significance of Jesus is seen in the fact that as the person for whom the resurrection to true life has already happened, he will be God's designated representative—God's "Christ" and "Son"—on the last day. As such, Jesus is the bearer of salvation.

---

[1] Acts 2:32–33; John 20:22.
[2] Cf. Acts 13:48.
[3] 1 Cor. 15:23.
[4] Acts 3:20–21, 10:42.
[5] Rom. 1:3–4.
[6] 1 Thess. 1:10.

Such a messianic Christology also lies behind the primitive use of the titles "Son of Man" and "Lord." Over the origin, history, and sense of the first of these titles, there was and is a great deal of scholarly controversy. There can be little doubt, however, that in the synoptic gospels as we now have them, "Son of Man," as a title applied to Jesus, is meant in the first instance to describe his eschatological role as the representative of "the saints of the Most High,"[7] who will come "with the clouds of heaven."[8] The title has also, of course, come in the gospels to be associated with his resurrection and, indeed, with his role as one who suffers. Similarly, the style "Lord" seems, in its original use, to have denoted Jesus as the Coming One[9] who in virtue of the resurrection[10] is even now the exalted representative of God's power.

The resurrection of Jesus, however, meant more for early Christians than could be conveyed by statements about his messianic function as the embodiment and bearer of God's coming kingdom. The future which he represented as the one whom God raised to the new life was, after all, not his alone. It was the future of all believers and, indeed, the destiny to which God had called all his human creatures. More than that, the new life actualized in the risen Christ was a gift in which believers could even now, through the gift of the Spirit, have a preliminary share. Thus, the Christ appears in early Christian thinking not only as the bearer of the kingdom, but also as the one in whom believers discover their own true identity because they share in his life and find their own lives transformed in him. In this strain, the Johannine Epistles testify to Christians' sense of abiding "in the Son,"[11] of being "in him who is true, in his Son Jesus Christ."[12] Similarly, the author of Hebrews insists that the "son of man," now "crowned with glory and honor,"[13] is nevertheless of the same "origin" as those whom he sanctifies and "is not ashamed to call them brethren."[14] This sense of oneness in the Christ and of participation in his life is, however, nowhere more clearly expressed than in the Pauline letters. There believers are said to be "in Christ"—to be baptized "into Christ Jesus," so that in sharing his death to sin they may also come to share his resurrection.[15] Paul can say that it is no longer he who lives, but Christ who lives in him,[16] and by the same token he understands that the "life" of believers "is hid with Christ in God."[17] Hence, the followers of Christ are, collectively, "one body in Christ,"[18] and can even be called simply "Christ."[19] This same theme takes shape in Paul's idea of Christ as "the last Adam,"[20] the "second man" who is "from heaven" and whose image believers are to bear.[21] In this role, the Christ is contrasted with the first Adam, who represents and sums up humanity as it is caught in the state of death which sin brings. Jesus for his part is the person through whom the power of sin is

---

[7] Dan. 7:18, 22.
[8] Cf. Mark 14:62.
[9] I Cor. 16:22; cf. Rev. 22:20.
[10] Acts 2:36.
[11] I John 2:24.

[12] Ibid.
[13] Heb. 2:6–8; cf. Ps. 8:4–6.
[14] Heb. 2:11.
[15] Rom. 6:3ff.
[16] Gal. 2:20.

[17] Col. 3:3.
[18] Rom. 12:5.
[19] I Cor. 12:12.
[20] I Cor. 15:47.
[21] I Cor. 15:49.

conquered and "grace" reigns "to eternal life." The Christ thus embodies the new humanity, and believers enter into this identity of his through the faith by which they are joined to him as his members.

Clearly, though, this portrayal of Jesus as Messiah, Son of God, and Lord on the one hand, and, on the other, as the Second Adam in whom the identity of humanity is realized, can make sense only on the hypothesis that the whole career of Jesus is the work of God, a deed and a declaration through which and in which God actualizes his purposes for humanity. Thus, we find, beginning with Paul, a tendency to interpret not merely the resurrection but also the ministry and death of Jesus as events which spring from God's initiative. Peter in Acts is made to declare that it was "by the definite plan and foreknowledge of God" that Jesus was executed.[22] This statement, however, merely echoes Paul's conviction that God "sent" his Son[23] and "put [him] forward as an expiation."[24] It is, therefore, not merely in his resurrection and his return to restore all things that Jesus is the Christ. It is also in his whole ministry and in his death that he is the bearer of God's redeeming activity. "I delivered to you," writes Paul, ". . . what I also received, that Christ died for our sins according to the Scriptures."[25]

It is not surprising, then, when we turn to the Gospels, to find that the role and significance which were initially ascribed to Jesus in the light of his resurrection are now seen to have belonged to him in his life and ministry as well. In Mark, the status of Jesus as Son of God is traced back to his baptism at the hands of John—that is, to the very beginning of his public career. Luke and Matthew, however, carry this logic one step further. Their accounts of the birth of Jesus make it clear that his very presence in human history has to be understood as God's doing. Even his conception in the womb of Mary was the work of God's Spirit, announced by an angel in accordance with a prophecy of Isaiah. In the course of his ministry, he is recognized by demons as God's Son, and he presents himself as the "Son of Man," who is called to fulfill in his death the role of the Suffering Servant of Isaiah. In the temptation which follows his baptism, he is seen in the role of the new Adam, "tempted," like the original human being, "by Satan" and living "with the wild beasts,"[26] but triumphing where his ancient counterpart had succumbed. Thus, the messianic and Adamic roles of Jesus are his from the very beginning of his story.

Throughout his career, then, Jesus is the very embodiment of God's purposes and the one in whom they are carried out. This conviction—that what God is for humanity and what humanity is for God are both realized and made concrete in Jesus—gave rise to yet another, and centrally important, strain in primitive Christology.

The origins of this strain are also to be found in Paul. In his Corinthian correspondence, the apostle finds that he has to deal with a group of believers who claim to possess a superior understanding of the mystery of God's way with

---

[22] Acts. 2:23.   [23] Gal. 4:4.   [24] Rom. 3:25.   [25] 1 Cor. 15:3.   [26] Mark 1:13.

his creation. They have, or assert that they have, a special insight into that transcendent wisdom of God which is worked out in the salvation of humankind. These converts, accordingly, find Paul's preaching of a crucified human being to be "foolishness," and they criticize him for not offering his churches a more profound teaching. In reply, Paul answers that "the power of God and the wisdom of God"[27] are to be found not in any human knowledge or accomplishment, but only in "Christ crucified."[28] Christ is the one whom God has made not only "righteousness and sanctification and redemption" for his creatures, but also "wisdom."[29] In other words, the Jesus who was crucified and raised from the dead embodies and expresses the divine Wisdom which is at once God's mind and purpose in creating and the "power" by which God carries out his purpose.[30] Paul makes these statements, of course, in a polemical setting. He identifies Jesus the crucified as God's Wisdom only in order to stop his converts from looking for that Wisdom elsewhere. Nevertheless, he takes his idea quite seriously once he has formulated it. It is in effect repeated at 1 Corinthians 8:6, where Paul speaks of "one God, the Father, from whom are all things, and one Lord Jesus Christ, through whom are all things and through whom we exist." Here, language traditionally used of the divine Wisdom is explicitly applied to the risen Lord, and it is made clear that Jesus is the focus, not for the church alone but for the whole cosmos, of the active power and purpose of God.

This theme, though, is not sounded solely by Paul. Matthew's gospel identifies Jesus in his earthly ministry as the presence of divine Wisdom.[31] The Epistle to the Hebrews opens with a passage which describes God's "Son" as the one through whom the world was created and who, like God's Wisdom, "reflects the glory of God and bears the very stamp of his nature."[32] In the Epistle to the Colossians, moreover, there is found an early Christian hymn which portrays God's Son as "the image of the invisible God," in whom "all things were created" and in whom "all things hold together."[33] The messianic Son who was raised from the dead to be the bearer of God's Kingdom is now seen as the embodiment of that Wisdom which has been the bearer of God's universal rule from the beginning of the creation.

Thus, almost inevitably, the logic of this theme leads on to the kind of Christology which is formulated in the Fourth Gospel. There too, a form of the idea of the divine Wisdom is determinative of the understanding of Jesus. Wisdom now appears as *logos,* the "Word" of God. The Logos pre-exists creation itself, being "in the beginning . . . with God."[34] As God's own self-expression, the Logos is both divine and creative: "All things were made by him and without him was not anything made that was made."[35] This same Logos, however,

---

[27] 1 Cor. 1:24. [30] See I:2. [33] Col. 1:15–17.
[28] 1 Cor. 1:23. [31] Matt. 11:19. [34] John 1:1.
[29] 1 Cor. 1:30. [32] Heb. 1:2–3. [35] John 1:3.

who is God's creative power is also the carrier of divine life and "the true light"[36] —in a word, the power of God for redemption. The saving power of Jesus, then, the fact that in him God's "grace and truth"[37] are actualized and made available to those who love him and keep his words, means that his human life and death have as their inner meaning and reality the eternal, life-giving Wisdom of God: "The Word became flesh and dwelt among us."[38] So Jesus in the Fourth Gospel can say, "Before Abraham was, I am."[39]

This Christology of the incarnation ("enfleshing") of God's pre-existent Word and Wisdom was of crucial significance both for what it said about Jesus and for the influence which it had on the formation of Christian belief. On the one hand, it served to explain a claim which had always been implicit in the designation of Jesus as Messiah, Lord, and Second Adam—the claim, namely, that his career is the fulfillment of God's eternal purpose for humankind. It articulated this claim by envisaging the human life of Jesus as the embodiment of the Word, "the only Son from the Father,"[40] who was God's personified power and purpose as exercised in creation and redemption. On the other hand, this Christology was a strong assertion of the universal meaning of Jesus' ministry, death, and resurrection. What these events brought about, it asserted, was the fulfillment of what God in his Wisdom had been up to always and everywhere. They manifested in a concrete way the meaning implicit in the very creation of the cosmos and of humanity, for their ultimate subject and agent was that divine Word in whom all things have their being.

Though in a variety of particular forms, the Christology of incarnation dominated the literature of the end of the first century and beginning of the second.[41] It appears, for example, in the letters of Ignatius, the bishop of Antioch in Syria, for whom Jesus the Christ—"the life from which we are inseparable"[42] —is to be understood as "our God." This does not mean, however, that Ignatius ignores or plays down the ordinary humanity of Jesus. On the contrary, he polemicizes against Docetism (the view that the fleshly, bodily side of Jesus is mere "appearance") and insists that Christ was truly born, truly suffered, and was truly crucified.[43] Thus, for Ignatius there are two dimensions of the person of Christ. In Jesus, spirit and flesh, divine and human, are at one. "There is only one physician—of flesh yet spiritual, born yet unbegotten, God enfleshed, genuine life in the midst of death, sprung from Mary as well as God."[44]

Christologies of this incarnational form were in evidence in other sectors of the church as well. The document called *1 Clement*, a letter from the Roman congregation to that at Corinth, speaks in a Jewish-Christian theological idiom quite different from that which shapes the thought of Ignatius. Nevertheless, it

---

[36] John 1:9.
[37] John 1:14.
[38] Ibid.

[39] John 8:58.
[40] John 1:14.
[41] On this literature, see chapter I:8.

[42] *Ephesians* 3.2.
[43] *Smyrnaeans* 1–2.
[44] *Ephesians* 7.2.

uses the language of Hebrews to portray Jesus as the reflection of God's splendor, the "mirror" of "God's . . . transcendent face,"[45] and "the scepter of God's majesty"[46]—in other words, as the Wisdom and Power of God who comes into the world to suffer but who is at the same time a descendant of Jacob "according to the flesh."[47] A somewhat later writing from Rome, *The Shepherd of Hermas,* combines the idea of "the holy pre-existent Spirit which created the whole creation"[48] with the picture of Jesus as the suffering and exalted servant.

This Christological trend or theme, however, was not universally favored. In some circles in the church, the very notion of a unity of flesh and spirit, worldly and divine, seemed both incredible and offensive; and gnostic Christologies, as we shall see, tended to deny or to qualify any doctrine of the true "enfleshing" of God's Word. At the same time, there was a persistent strain in Jewish Christianity which came to reject the Pauline and Johannine traditions and insisted upon a picture of Jesus as the one human being who had completely fulfilled God's law. Constituted Son of God and Messiah at his baptism, Jesus would return in glory as the heavenly Son of Man. Called "Ebionites" by later Christian writers (who had forgotten that *ebionim* meant "the poor": see Galatians 2:10), the groups which espoused this "adoptionist" view were no doubt the heirs of the primitive Judaean churches, whose influence, along with their numbers, dwindled after the Jewish war of 70 A.D.

There was, then, and continued to be, a variety of Christological ideas in the early church. However, the end of the first century and the beginning of the second saw the emergence of one dominant line of thought. One might, after the fashion of Ignatius and the Johannine letters, envisage the Christ as the bearer of a new and immortal life, divine in quality, which believers are called to share. Alternatively, one might view him primarily, in the style of *1 Clement,* as the teacher, model, and revealer of the divine righteousness, which believers are called to imitate and embody in their own lives. In either case, however, the human person of Jesus was understood to express and body forth the divine life of the pre-existent Son, Word, or Wisdom of God, with whom, by God's gracious sending, it was one.

---

[45] *1 Clement* 36.   [46] *1 Clement* 16.2.   [47] *1 Clement* 32.2.   [48] *Similitudes* 5.6.

Chapter 8

Gentile Christianity of the Second Century

By THE YEAR 100, Christianity was represented in Asia Minor, Syria, Macedonia, Greece, and the city of Rome. It may well have been—and by about 130 certainly was—present in Egypt, although nothing is known of its origins there. In the western portions of the empire, it had spread very little, if at all. Asia Minor was unquestionably the most extensively christianized territory in the empire. About 111–113, Pliny the Younger, governor of Bithynia, reported to the emperor Trajan that "the contagion of that superstition [i.e., Christianity] has penetrated not only the cities but also the villages and country places"; and he intimated that until he took steps to combat its spread, pagan temples had been "deserted."[1] In this there may be some rhetorical exaggeration (Pliny is obviously very troubled by the phenomenon of Christianity), but his testimony is at any rate reliable evidence of the liveliness of the Christian movement in the territories along the shore of the Black Sea.

An equally reliable testimony to its liveliness is the variety and quantity of Christian writings that can be dated to the closing years of the first century and the first half of the second. To this period there belong, of course, some of the works later included in the canon of the New Testament: the two letters attributed to Peter, for example, as well as the Johannine letters, the Revelation to John, and, in all probability, the Pastoral Epistles. In addition to these books, there is the body of literature (which a series of relatively modern discoveries has gradually expanded) traditionally referred to as the "Apostolic Fathers." This description dates back to the seventeenth century, when scholars thought that these works had been written "in apostolic times" by immediate disciples of the church's founders.

Among these works, a place of honor has always been given to *1 Clement,* a letter written in the name of the Roman church to the Christians at Corinth around the year 95. This, the earliest known piece of Christian writing which failed finally to be included in the New Testament canon, has generally been

---

[1] Pliny, *Epistle* 96.

attributed to Clement, a prominent presbyter (or perhaps the bishop) of the Roman church. It deals with problems of church order in the face of a rebellion in Corinth against the authority of that church's presbyters. Alongside *1 Clement,* there are seven letters written (ca. 113) by Ignatius, bishop of Antioch, to churches which had received him (or, as in the case of the Roman church, were about to receive him) while he traveled under strict military guard to be tried at Rome for his faith. Ignatius, too, is concerned with problems of church order, though in his case this concern is stimulated by theological issues. He urges his readers to unity in Christ, a unity to be realized in practice through obedient fellowship with the bishop, presbyters, and deacons of the local church. In the process, he argues against the Docetic and Judaizing doctrines which, as he sees it, are dividing the communities. Bound up with *1 Clement* and the Ignatian Epistles are a letter of Polycarp, bishop of Smyrna, and a document called the *Epistle of Barnabas.* The latter, perhaps written in Alexandria around 130, is in fact not a letter but a treatise which by allegorical methods explains the "true" (i.e., Christian) sense of the Jewish Law. To this treatise there has been appended a primitive Christian ethical instruction. Finally, the traditional list of the "Apostolic Fathers" included an early Christian sermon, probably of Alexandrian origin, mistakenly called the *Second Epistle of Clement (2 Clement).*

Later eras, however, added to this list of "Apostolic Fathers." Most notably, there was the apocalypse or revelation called *The Shepherd,* written around the turn of the second century by a Roman Christian prophet called Hermas, who was troubled by the moral state of his community and by the question of whether there can be a "second repentance" for serious sins committed after baptism. Also included among these works was the so-called *Letter to Diognetus,* although later scholarship has assigned this piece to the last half of the second century and identified it as a work of Christian apologetic. More recently still— as the result of a discovery made in Constantinople in 1883—there has been added to the list a work whose full title is *The Teaching of the Lord through the Twelve Apostles to the Gentiles.* Commonly called *Didachē,* this work, like the *Epistle of Barnabas,* is composite. It contains a version of the same primitive ethical instruction which is appended to the latter, and it goes on to provide a simple church order—a set of instructions regarding baptism, the eucharist, and the governance of the church. It is commonly assigned to Syria and dated around the opening of the second century.

Not even these works, however, exhaust the list of the literary productions of the Christian movement in the early second century. For one thing, it seems likely that this is the period to which one must assign the beginnings of a Christian Gnostic literature. Even approximate dating of the Gnostic materials known to us is difficult, but it is clear that the great Gnostic teachers, Basilides and Valentinus, were functioning in Alexandria prior to about 140, when Valentinus appeared in Rome. The fragments of Valentinus's letters and homilies that have been preserved for us by Clement of Alexandria may well, therefore, date to this period—as, for that matter, must the Gospel which is attributed to Basilides and his commentary on it, the *Exegetica*.[1] And quite apart from Gnostic literature, there are remains of a number of other works from this period: for example, *The Preaching of Peter;* the influential *Revelation of Peter,* which was known and used by the Roman church as late as the end of the second century; and the *Letter of the Apostles (Epistula Apostolorum)*, an anti-Docetic writing that testifies to a struggle between Gnostic and non-Gnostic groups in the church.

A survey of this literature makes at least one point quite clear. Christianity in the opening decades of the second century was a movement beset with debate and conflict. It still moved in the shadow of the thought-world of late Judaism. That thought-world itself, however, was no monolithic structure, but a loose and variegated affair, as is shown by the varieties of emphasis, interest, and doctrine which are reflected in Christian writings of this era. The fact appears to be that questions were being raised on every hand that the primitive proclamation of the church had neither contemplated nor answered: questions about the meaning and value of the church's Scriptures, which at this time were simply the traditional scriptures of Judaism; about the framework of beliefs and values within which the proclamation of "Jesus and the resurrection" was to be understood; about the order of the communities and the style of life which Christians were called upon to lead. Time, moreover, would make these problems not less but more acute.

At the same time, however, this literature makes it clear that there were forces at work which were pushing the churches toward common solutions of these problems—forces which, in effect, demanded that they make up their collective mind about what they stood for. One, and perhaps the most important, of these forces was the Christian movement's most basic conviction about itself: that its members and followers belonged to "a chosen race . . . a holy nation, God's own people."[2] However scattered and various the communities of believers, they were conscious of being a single people whose shared citizenship was not in Rome but in the heavenly Jerusalem.[3] This fact is attested to not merely by their words—as, for example, Ignatius's reference to the "catholic" (i.e., universal) church which is "wherever Jesus Christ is"[4]—but also by their habit, for which there is no ancient parallel, of writing each other letters of rebuke, advice, and exhortation. This sense of unity, of belonging to one elect people, helps to explain the seriousness with which these groups took their disagreements. It also explains their compulsion to seek shared settlements and resolutions.

This sense of unity was enhanced by the surprising unanimity with which they accepted certain norms or authorities for their common life and teaching,

---

[1] Clement of Alexandria, *Stromata* 4.12.81; Origen, *Homilies on Luke* 1.2.
[2] I Pet. 2:9.
[3] Hermas, *The Shepherd* ("Similitudes" 1.1.)
[4] *Smyrnaeans* 8:2.

and also by the persistence and development of certain common institutions. All communities appealed to the Jewish Scriptures (though these, as the future was to show, constituted a shared problem as well as a shared resource), and all appealed as well to the words of the Lord and to the testimony of the leaders of the primitive community—"the ordinances of the apostles," as Ignatius puts it.[5] There was, in short, general assent to the belief that the churches' teaching and practice had to be consistent with its origins in the work of Christ and of the first generation of his disciples. The seriousness with which this conviction was held is demonstrated by nothing better than by the tiresome regularity with which early Christian writings are attributed to one or another of the Twelve— or, like *Didachē* or *Epistula Apostolorum,* to the entire college of the church's founders.

The common life of the churches, moreover, was shaped by shared institutions which functioned as instruments of unity and continuity. The disciple was admitted to the church by the rite of baptism. This involved not only washing but also the making of a traditional confession of faith, and it presupposed instruction in the meaning of that faith and in the style of life that it demanded. The regular assemblies of the community, which took place on the Lord's Day (Sunday) in celebration of Jesus' resurrection, involved not only prayer, praise, and the reading of the Scriptures, but also preaching, prophecy, and the celebration of the Lord's Supper or eucharist. These regular common actions were occasions which both shaped and interpreted the life and identity of the community, and they provided a matrix in which a common symbolic language was preserved and developed.

Of equal importance in the life of the second-century church was the discipline of the community. The church was a "separated" body whose members were expected to conduct their lives in a certain style. There were disciplines of fasting and prayer.[6] It was understood that Christians did not enter into second marriages, put unwanted babies to death by exposure, or practice abortion. They were to have nothing to do with pagan festivals or with any occupation which could be construed as putting them in the service of the "demons" they understood the pagan gods to be. All this meant, of course, that they could have little to do with the public life of any city in which they dwelt, since pagan religion was inevitably part of the very fabric of that life. Above all, however, they were to love the brethren and to practice almsgiving and charity. "Fasting is better than prayer, but almsgiving than both."[7] Ignatius's most eloquent condemnation of heretics comes in his allegation that "For love they have no care, none for the widow, none for the orphan, none for the distressed, none for the afflicted, none for the prisoner, or for him released from prison, none for the hungry or thirsty."[8] *1 Clement* knows of believers who have sold themselves into slavery to supply the needy.[9] Christian communities not only lived by a discipline, but they

[5] *Trallians* 7.1.   [6] *Didachē* 8.   [7] *2 Clement* 16.   [8] *Smyrnaeans* 6.2.   [9] *1 Clement* 55.2.

also functioned as close associations in which systematic mutual assistance was organized and practiced. This fact, too, no doubt contributed to a sense of cohesiveness and to a low threshold of toleration for fundamental disagreement or conflict.

Chapter 9

Christian Organization

N° QUESTION in church history has been more darkened by controversy than that of the origins of the church's official ministry. Owing to the scantiness of the evidence which has survived, few questions are more difficult to answer in detail. In all probability, the course of institutional development was slightly different in different places. In other words, not all first-century Christian communities had the same structures at the same time. Yet by the middle of the second century, a substantially uniform pattern of local ministry was coming to prevail throughout the Christian world. In each city, the Christians tended to have a principal leader and pastor, called *episkopos*—"bishop" or, more literally, "overseer" or "superintendent." The *episkopos* worked on the one hand with a body of colleagues called *presbuteroi* ("elders") and on the other with a set of assistants who "served" him in his administrative and pastoral functions—the *diakonoi,* or "deacons." These officers did not, of course, get appointed or selected out of a body of more or less trained professionals, as has been the case with the Christian ministry in most places since late classical and medieval times. They were members of the body of Christians in a particular city, selected for their personal talents and qualities.

The reasons for the emergence of such a pattern of ministry and governance are, in general, clear. As we have seen, the Christian community in any given city was a closely knit body. It gathered regularly for the performance of its characteristic rites. It also served as a society for the members' mutual assistance, and it provided support for the poor, for widows, and for parentless children. In addition, not unlike the Jewish communities out of which they had originally grown, these churches seem by and large to have regulated their own affairs and the relations among their members without appeal to Roman courts of law, enforcing their own standards of behavior and settling disputes.[1] Finally, these communities found their raison d'être in the new life of the risen Christ, communicated to them by God in the Spirit and articulated in the proclamation and teachings of the original disciples and apostles. They were sure, therefore, that the preservation and transmission of this Gospel in its authentic form was essential to their life. The emergence of community officers, in these circumstances, to serve as leaders of worship, rulers of the community life, administrators of its affairs, and teachers of the truth by which it lived, can hardly be a matter of surprise.

On the other hand, this set of conditions, which encouraged or demanded a settled organization of the churches, only gradually had its effect. For one thing, the performance of these functions demanded an official ministry only as churches grew and ceased, bit by bit, to be face-to-face groups that could meet in a single dwelling. For another, problems about the life, order, and beliefs of the community had to appear before the shape of the official ministry could be settled and its authority established. Nevertheless, there is no puzzle about the "why" of the appearance of an official ministry nor about its nature and functions when it appeared.

By contrast, there is, and will no doubt continue to be, a puzzle about the "how" of the development of the official ministry. The Acts of the Apostles informs us that the church at Jerusalem was in the end governed by James the brother of the Lord in association with a body of "elders." Some scholars have argued that, since James's successor, who presided over the Jerusalem church after the Jewish war, was also a relative of Jesus ("a cousin of the Savior"[2]), the original constitution of the Jerusalem church was that of a "caliphate," in which the community was to be ruled by collateral descendants of Jesus. Others, discounting this hypothesis, have nevertheless thought that the picture in Acts of "James and the elders" provided the model which was later imitated (perhaps originally at Antioch) in the institution of the bishop with his council of presbyters.

In fact, however, the first hint of the existence of such a structure comes, as we shall see, from the first decade of the second century. In spite of the statement in Acts that Paul and Barnabas "appointed elders for them in every church,"[3] the letters of Paul make no mention of established church officers and certainly none of elders. It is true that 1 Thessalonians 5:12 refers to persons who "are over you in the Lord," and that Philippians 1:1 includes "the bishops and deacons" among the "saints in Christ Jesus who are at Philippi." On the other hand, Paul's Corinthian correspondence contains no such references, nor indeed do any of the others among his undoubted letters. There may have been, in some of the Pauline churches, the rudimentary beginnings of a structure of

---

[1] See 1 Cor. 5:3–5, 6:1–2; Matt. 18:15–18.
[2] Eusebius, *Ecclesiastical History* 3.11.
[3] Acts 14:23.

ministry and governance, but there is no indication either that Paul himself was directly responsible for its institution or that it had become established and formalized. And this is more or less the state of affairs one would expect to find.

This is not to say, of course, that Paul took no interest in the functioning of the "varieties of ministry"[4] in his churches. Moreover, his discussion of this problem in the Corinthian letters suggests that in Corinth there was already some conflict over the question of whose ministry, or what sort of ministry, was the most important. Paul's response to this situation was to emphasize that all ministries are gifts of God and the Spirit and that all are essential to the welfare of "the body," even those that seem obscure or dishonorable. What he meant by "ministry," then, is any gift which expresses itself in constructive service to the community, from healing to administering; and these different gifts of the one Spirit are given to all members of the body. Paul believed that, among these gifts, some are of first importance: those which constitute individuals as "apostles ... prophets ... teachers," in that order.[5] In other words, what the church cannot do without are those gifts and callings which concern the proclamation, interpretation, and explication of the new life "in Christ Jesus." Even in this case, however, he was referring not to offices but to forms of activity into which people are called by the Spirit, even as he himself had been "called by the will of God to be an apostle."[6] Paul himself exercised a very active ministry of superintendence and governance over the congregations he had founded, and indeed he employed assistants in the work,[7] but he never regarded himself as being in any sense an officer of the church.

Yet by about the end of the first century, officers had appeared, not only in the Pauline churches, but in the church of Rome and, apparently, in the region of Syria and Palestine as well. What is more, the structure and nomenclature of these offices seem to have been roughly the same in all these regions. Thus *1 Clement* speaks of "bishops and deacons"[8] and traces these offices back to apostolic foundation. The letter presupposes that such officers exist not only at Rome but also at Corinth. They are persons appointed "with the whole church's consent";[9] this fact and the fact that they stand in a succession which goes back to the apostles[10] makes it both impious and destructive of divine order for Christians to rebel against their authority. *1 Clement* also mentions elders as officers in the church, but everything in the letter goes to suggest that it uses "elder" and "bishop" as interchangeable words for the same office.

The same twofold structure appears in the Pastoral Epistles and *Didachē*. The latter document almost certainly reflects a transitional situation, in which the authority of local officers has to be commended in the face of the charismatic appeal of traveling "apostles" and "prophets," who occasionally showed a tendency to charlatanism. *Didachē* accordingly gives rules for distinguishing false

---

[4] 1 Cor. 12:5.   [7] E.g., Timothy in 1 Cor. 4:17, 16:10.   [10] *1 Clement* 44.1–2.
[5] 1 Cor. 12:28.   [8] *1 Clement* 42.4.
[6] 1 Cor. 1:1.   [9] *1 Clement* 44.3.

prophets from true (the false prophet asks for money and does not practice what he preaches[11]) and exhorts its readers to "elect" for themselves "bishops and deacons who are a credit to the Lord. . . . For their ministry to you is identical with that of the prophets and teachers."[12] The Pastoral Epistles, unlike *Didachē*, mention elders as well as deacons and bishops, but one passage in Titus[13] seems to suggest that here, as in *1 Clement*, "elder" and "bishop" denote the same individuals. Also in the same vein as *1 Clement*, the Pastorals intimate that these officers exercise authority with apostolic approval and at apostolic direction. In describing the work of the elder-bishop, the Pastorals place emphasis on three matters. The bishop is, first, to be a model of Christian life: "no drunkard, not violent but gentle, not quarrelsome, and no lover of money."[14] Second, he is to be an apt manager of affairs—an administrator. Above all, though, he is to be a "teacher,"[15] to "follow the pattern of sound words"[16] which embodies the doctrine of the apostle himself and to "hold firm to the sure word as taught, so that he may be able to give instruction in sound doctrine."[17] There are false teachers abroad, and the leaders of the local churches find their primary responsibility in bearing witness to the style of life and doctrine which the first generation of Christian preachers had inculcated. They are, in fact, the guardians of the apostolic "deposit" (*parathēkē*).[18]

This concern for maintenance of the authentic (i.e., original) Christian witness is reflected equally in the letters of Ignatius, who commends the members of the congregation at Ephesus for having "always been of one mind with the very apostles."[19] In fact, however, Ignatius puts his emphasis less on agreement with the apostles than on the believers' unity of life with Christ himself and, through Christ, with God. When he discusses the official ministry, he dwells on its character as an effective symbol of this unity. "The bishops," he says, ". . . reflect the mind of Christ,"[20] and believers, if they continue in unity with and submission to the bishops, by that very fact enter into the unity of Christ with God.[21] What stands out, however, in the Ignatian letters is the fact that in all the churches he addresses (except that of Rome), he presupposes not a twofold ministry of elder-bishops and deacons, but a threefold structure in which the office of bishop is clearly distinguished from that of elder. In each of these churches there is one bishop, who governs with a body of elders and has his "ministers" in the deacons. It is thus in the Ignatian letters that the historian first encounters the ministerial structure which, in the course of the second century, came to prevail in all the churches.

The question of how, by what process, this development occurred, has been the subject of much debate. One hypothesis is that it came about almost naturally, and certainly informally, as special status and responsibility in each church

---

[11] *Didachē* 11.8–12.
[12] *Didachē* 15.1.
[13] Titus 1:5–7.
[14] 1 Tim. 3:3.

[15] 1 Tim. 3:2, 5:17.
[16] 2 Tim. 1:13.
[17] Titus 1:9.
[18] 2 Tim. 1:12; cf. Acts 20:28–31.

[19] *Ephesians* 11.2.
[20] *Ephesians* 3.2.
[21] *Ephesians* 5.1–3.

came to be assigned to an elder who regularly chaired meetings of what Ignatius calls "the presbytery." This hypothesis finds some confirmation in the fact that, even after the development of the monarchical episcopate, bishops seem often to have been referred to as "elders." The third-century church order known as the *Didascalia Apostolorum* identifies the chief pastor of a local church as "bishop and head among the presbytery,"[22] and it is clear that for a long time elders were regarded not as the bishop's representatives or delegates but as his colleagues. It finds further, albeit indirect, confirmation in the facts that at least for a while the two different structures must have existed simultaneously and that no one (including Ignatius) seems to have taken offense at this fact. At the turn of the second century, the system which acknowledged elder-bishops and deacons and that which spoke of bishop, elders, and deacons may well have looked, in actual practice, very much alike, if one assumes that most local Christian groups would, at least informally, have treated one individual among their elders as their principal leader and teacher.

With the establishment of this pattern of church order, there also appear the bare beginnings of the idea of "apostolic succession" or "succession from the apostles." It is in *1 Clement* that this development is most obvious. There the authority of the bishops and deacons is made to depend, at least in part, on the fact that their offices were established by the apostles;[23] and one sentence in the letter—a sentence which, unfortunately, is quite ambiguous—may mean that the Roman church regarded its elder-bishops as "succeeding" to the apostles.[24] This idea, however, even if it represents the thinking of the Roman church, was not widespread at the beginning of the second century. The Pastoral Epistles claim the authority of Paul for the institution of episcopal and diaconal ministries but do not suggest that local officers "succeed" to apostolic authority; and Ignatius of Antioch, convinced though he is of the necessity of strengthening the authority of bishop and presbytery, makes no effort to claim apostolic foundation for these offices. The full flowering of the idea of apostolic succession had to wait for the controversies of the later second century over Gnosticism.

Even by the beginning of the century, however, a regular pattern of ministry and governance was in the process of being established. The unit of the church—as one might expect, given the social and political organization of the Roman world—was the body of Christians in a particular *polis*. Each of these churches tended to have a principal pastor, called the bishop, who not only presided at liturgical gatherings but also directed the administrative and disciplinary business of the community and, above all, was the church's official teacher, the guardian and interpreter of its ethical and doctrinal tradition. With the bishop there were associated in this work the body of elders, to which he

[22] R. H. Connolly, ed., *Didascalia Apostolorum* (Oxford, 1929), p. 28.
[23] *1 Clement* 42.1–4.
[24] *1 Clement* 44.2.

himself was seen to belong, and the "ministers" or deacons who apparently came to assist the bishop in his liturgical, administrative, and disciplinary work. Each such body, with its officers, was understood to be the *ekklesia,* whole and complete in its particular place. In spite of the obvious fact that each local church frequently exchanged ideas and admonitions with other churches, there was no organization of the church above the level of the *polis.*

Chapter 10

Christianity and the Roman Government

*I*N MATTERS OF RELIGION, Rome was normally tolerant, following in this regard the policies of the earlier Hellenistic monarchies of the East. The Roman authorities understood that each of the cities and nations under their sway had deities, rites, and religious practices which it cherished, even as the Senate and People of Rome cherished theirs. Under Roman rule, such local or ethnic cults were permitted and protected as long as due honor was given to Rome and her gods. Thus, Judaism was a *religio licita* ("authorized religion"); and while the Romans tended to dislike Jewish proselytism and tried more than once to make Judaism less visible in Rome itself, they nevertheless went to the length of dispensing Jews from participation in the imperial cult.

This toleration of pluralism, however, had certain limits, which became apparent where the interests of Rome or the welfare of Roman citizens was concerned. Some religious practices seemed to the Romans to be immoral and thus offensive to the gods on whose good will the city—and the empire—ultimately depended. Such practices were liable to be suppressed, whether in Rome itself or in the provinces. Thus, we learn that while "Augustus had been content to prohibit any Roman citizen in Gaul from taking part in the savage and terrible Druidic cult," which practiced human sacrifice, "Claudius abolished it altogether."[1] At the same time, the Romans were traditionally wary of voluntary religious societies (*collegia*) that practiced their rites in private. The members of such groups were likely to be suspected of taking blood-oaths that pledged them to crime and sedition. In short, religious cults which seemed to threaten

---

[1] Suetonius, *Life of Claudius* 25.

the Roman state and public order—whether by offending Rome's gods or by appearing to encourage conspiracy—were regarded automatically as illicit, even though little or no action might in fact be taken to suppress them.

For such status as an unauthorized and potentially dangerous association, the Christian movement was a natural candidate. It was not the traditional religion of any nation or city and could therefore scarcely claim the sort of recognition which Rome gave to the Jewish or Egyptian religions or to such a local cult as that of the Syrian Baal. What is more, Christians gathered in private, and their exclusive monotheism compelled them to refuse all participation in pagan religious observances. This meant not only that people tended to suspect them of being up to something indecent or sinister, but also that in any *polis* where they dwelt they were marked out as a small group of willful dissenters from the very basis of communal life. Paul conveys the Christian attitude by saying, "Our citizenship is in heaven";[2] to the Roman historian Tacitus, this attitude looked more like "hatred of the human race." Thus, when Pliny, during his term as governor of Bithynia, wrote to the emperor Trajan about the problem of Christians, his very language betrayed the reaction which believers evoked from their contemporaries. They "assemble before daylight," he says, "and recite by turns a form of words to Christ as god." What is more, they bind themselves "with an oath," and though they insisted that this oath committed them not to crime but to good behavior, Pliny obviously had difficulty in crediting any such disclaimer. Accordingly, he tortured two slave-girls who were Christian deaconesses in order to find out the truth, but, he reports, "I discovered nothing else than a perverse and extravagant superstition."[3] He does not for a moment doubt that the Christians are guilty of "secret crimes," but he is uncertain whether they are to be prosecuted for these crimes or for "the mere name" (i.e., simply for being Christians).[4]

The emperor Trajan's reply is just as instructive as Pliny's report. There is no question in the emperor's mind that the Christians represent an unauthorized, and in principle dangerous, association. Nevertheless, he obviously does not believe that they constitute much of a problem in practice. He directs, therefore, that when caught they are to be punished (though if they recant their faith, they can be pardoned), but that they are not to be sought out actively. The governor, then, is not to involve himself in a systematic attempt to extirpate this sect. Trajan's successor, the emperor Hadrian, seems to have taken much the same attitude. His pronouncement on this subject, embodied in a rescript to the proconsul of Asia (ca. 125), assumes that Christianity is unauthorized and therefore punishable; his primary concern, however, is to assure that proper judicial procedures are followed and that persons are not punished for Christian belief as a result of mob tumults or false or anonymous accusations.[5]

---

[2] Phil. 3:20.
[3] Pliny, *Epistle* 10.96.
[4] Ibid.
[5] J. Stevenson, *A New Eusebius* (New York, 1957), p. 17.

Even from these scanty sources, there is much to be learned about the situation of Christianity under Roman rule during the second century and later. For one thing, it seems clear that the emperors of this period were neither greatly interested in nor greatly disturbed by the phenomenon of Christianity. Nonetheless, they assumed that it was undesirable and punishable, and by this judgment they exposed Christians to the hostility of local populations and so to prosecution and punishment by imperial governors. Further, Hadrian's rescript suggests that Christians caused far more trouble to the imperial authorities by being the occasion of local disorders and tumults than by any threat they posed to the empire in their own right; and in this intimation there is a clue to the real source of the Christians' troubles—a clue which is confirmed by the evidence of early Christian martyrologies. These documents indicate that it was not imperial policy but popular hostility that instigated the early persecutions. At Lyons and Vienne in Gaul, it was the rage of "an infuriated populace against its supposed enemies and foes"[6] which started the persecution in 177 A.D.; and at Rome, Justin, the Christian apologist, was not sought by the authorities but was betrayed to them by a fellow intellectual, the Cynic philosopher Crescens. One is bound to conclude that the actual incidence of persecution depended largely on the attitudes and feelings of local citizenries toward the Christians and on the degree to which provincial governors were willing to pacify popular feeling by co-operating with it. This conclusion is supported, moreover, by the sporadic character of the early persecutions. More important than the deliberate policies of the emperors (who seem in fact to have given very little thought to "the Christian problem") were popular fear and mistrust of the Christians, who were widely believed to be atheists (since they would not worship the gods), seditionists, and habitually given to unspeakable crimes.

What was the Christian response to this situation? In the face of persecution, imprisonment, and death, believers understood that they were being called, by unwavering confession of their Lord, to share the suffering by which Christ had overcome the forces of evil abroad in the world. The death of a martyr—a "witness"—was thus the glorious culmination of a struggle that led to eternal life. When the slave-girl Blandina hung in the arena at Lyons, believers "saw in the form of their sister him who was crucified for them" and knew "that all who suffer for the glory of Christ have for ever fellowship with the living God."[7] This struggle, though, was not envisaged as a fight against Rome and its emperors. It was directed against Satan and his hosts, who held the world in thrall; and the Roman *imperium,* in spite of its blasphemous pretensions, was an instrument of God to keep evil under relative control.[8] Thus, in the very face of a "fiery ordeal" of persecution, the First Epistle of Peter can urge Christians, "Be subject for the Lord's sake to every human institution, whether to the emperor

---

[6] Eusebius, *Ecclesiastical History* V.1.8.   [7] Ibid., V.1.42. See also 1 Pet. 4:1.   [8] Rom. 13:1–7.

as supreme, or to governors as sent by him to punish those who do wrong and to praise those who do right."[9] Rome, the imperial order, was perceived not as the real source of the evil by which Christians were afflicted but rather as a power which, in God's providence, kept things from getting much worse—and this was a judgment which, no doubt in a very rough way, reflected the actual state of affairs.

[9] 1 Pet. 4:12, 2:13–14.

Chapter 11

The Apologists

THE CHARGES brought against Christians, not to mention the official policy of treating the church as an unauthorized association, impelled believers not only to bear witness in suffering but also to explain and defend their faith. There arose, therefore, in the course of the second century a new genre of Christian literature, the "apology"—so called from the Greek *apologia,* meaning "a speech for the defense." The authors of these works are known collectively as the Apologists; and though writings of this type were produced long after the close of the second century, the period from about 130 to about 180 A.D. is frequently referred to as the age of the Apologists.

The first of these writers was one Quadratus, probably an Athenian, who in about 125 wrote an apology addressed to the emperor Hadrian. The work is now preserved only in fragments. Better known is the similar appeal of Aristides, another Athenian and a philosopher of sorts, who addressed his argument to Antoninus Pius in about 140. Most famous of all is the *Apology* of Justin Martyr, a Christian philosopher who apparently ran a school in Rome and wrote in about the middle of the century. Justin's disciple Tatian (who also harmonized the four Gospels in his famous *Diatessaron*) wrote a *Discourse to the Greeks,* which is perhaps less a defense of Christianity than an outright attack on pagan culture and religion. Also to be reckoned in this group of writers are Melito of Sardis, who wrote between 169 and 180; Athenagoras, of whom nothing is known save his authorship of the *Supplication for the Christians* (ca. 177); and the bishop Theophilus of Antioch, who wrote the lengthy apology, *To Autolycus.*

There is no evidence that any of these works greatly influenced heathen opinion (though one of them, Justin's *Apology,* eventually stimulated a pagan counterattack, in the *True Word* of the philosopher Celsus) or that they were read by the emperors to whom they were technically addressed. They were, however, valued in Christian circles, because they offered the first reasoned explications of the church's tenets. Their authors were men of some literary and philosophical culture, who took pains to speak the language of the educated classes. At the same time, their work shows that they were acquainted not only with the content of traditional Christian preaching and catechesis, but also with some of the leading ideas and themes of earlier Hellenistic Jewish apologetic, on which they drew for their own purposes.

The most prominent of them, Justin Martyr, was born in the Roman colony of Flavia Neapolis near the site of ancient Shechem. The account of his life and conversion that is given in the opening chapters of his *Dialogue with Trypho the Jew* indicates that he was a student of philosophy who belonged to the Platonist tradition. The teaching of this school, he reports, "furnished my mind with wings,"[1] and he "expected forthwith to look upon God, for this is the aim of Plato's philosophy."[2] Justin goes on to report, however, that in extended conversation with "a certain old man,"[3] he was persuaded that some tenets of the Platonist position were questionable. Above all, he learned that true knowledge of God could come only by revelation and that such revelation had been given through the prophets, "who spoke by the divine Spirit."[4] These prophets "gave glory to God the Maker and Father of the universe and announced his Son, the Christ whom he sent."[5] Thus, Justin was convinced that the goal of the philosophical quest could be achieved only through God's revelation of himself in his Son and that the truth of this revelation was evidenced and guaranteed by the inspired testimony of the Hebrew prophets. It might be true that "the work of philosophy is to inquire into the Divine";[6] but anyone who wants to "come to be with God in a state of inalienability [*en apatheiai*]"[7] must know God as he is revealed in Christ. Christianity, then, for Justin, was the oldest, truest, and most divine of philosophies because it was the wisdom revealed by God himself, through the prophets first of all, but then in his own Son.

Justin's *Apology* was written after he took up residence in Rome, around 153 A.D. It opens by arguing the injustice and irrationality of punishing believers simply for the name "Christian" rather than for proven criminal acts. Further, it insists that Christians are not guilty of the charges commonly lodged against

---

[1] *Dialogue* 2.6.
[2] Ibid.
[3] *Dialogue* 3.1.
[4] Ibid., 7.1.
[5] Ibid., 7.3.
[6] Ibid., 1.3.
[7] *2 Apol.* 1.2. Justin's *Apology* is normally cited as two works, though the "second" one is actually an appendix to the first.

them. They are not atheists, though they worship the true God rather than the demons who pass themselves off as gods. They are certainly not seditionists or anarchists, for the "kingdom" they seek is God's and not a human kingdom to rival Caesar's. They are not criminals, but inculcate a strict morality in accordance with Jesus' teaching and seek to promote peace and decency. Having made these points, Justin then passes on to establish the superiority of Christian belief over pagan religion and to set out its credentials by showing how the Hebrew prophets had predicted the Christian dispensation.

At the center of Justin's apologetic is his use of the idea of the divine Logos. This word in Greek means not only "word" or "speech," but also "reason." As Justin uses it, it can of course refer to human reason—that endowment by which a human person understands reality and exercises freedom of choice. Primarily, however, the Logos for him is "the first-born of God,"[8] "the Spirit and the Power from God,"[9] whom Justin seems to identify with the creative World-Soul of Plato's dialogue *Timaeus*.[10] This Logos has been active throughout human history as the revealer of God, and all human persons partake of, or participate in, God's Logos/Son insofar as they are rational. Hence, Justin can say: "Those who have lived by the aid of *logos* are Christians even if they were adjudged atheists—such as Socrates and Heraclitus and their like among the Greeks, and, among the barbarians, Abraham . . . and Elijah."[11] What Christian faith distinctively knows and declares, however, is that this divine Logos "was born as a human being of a virgin, and given the name Jesus, and was crucified and died and rose and ascended into heaven."[12] Thus, it is not true to say that the Christ came into existence only "one hundred and fifty years ago." He has always been the companion of humanity, but he has not always been present in the way that Christians know him—as a human person named Jesus.

From one point of view, then, Justin's Logos-doctrine is nothing more than a reiteration of themes already to be found in Christian—and Hellenistic Jewish —tradition. It draws on the Wisdom Christology which we have already noted in earlier Christian writers, and no doubt, too, directly or indirectly, on the speculations of a thinker like Philo Judaeus (see I:2). Still further in its background lies the ancient Stoic use of *logos* to denote the Divinity immanent in the cosmos. Justin, however, has assimilated these ideas to a Middle Platonist world view, and he sees the Logos as a mediatorial figure, begotten "before all creatures"[13] to be the agent of the unbegotten and unnamable God in creation and in revelation. This line of thought, shared by all of the Apologists, was to occasion much controversy and difficulty in later Christian theology. On the other hand, Justin's own interest in the Logos doctrine did not center primarily around its relevance for the doctrines of God and creation. More important for his apologetic task was its capacity to give expression to the universal claims of

---

[8] *1 Apol.* 46.2.   [10] Ibid., 60.1.   [12] Ibid., 46.5.
[9] Ibid., 33.6.   [11] Ibid., 46.3.   [13] *1 Apol.* 61.1.

Christian faith. It enabled him to say that the truth which Christians knew in Jesus the Christ was a truth for all human beings, and a truth to which all historical traditions bore witness, because Jesus is the concrete human presence of the universal and creative Reason of God, the very principle of the world-order itself. Justin's theology thus lays the basis for an open dialogue between Christian faith and the tradition of Gentile religious philosophy, and in that sense marks the beginnings of a "scientific" theology.

Period II

FROM THE GNOSTIC CRISIS TO CONSTANTINE

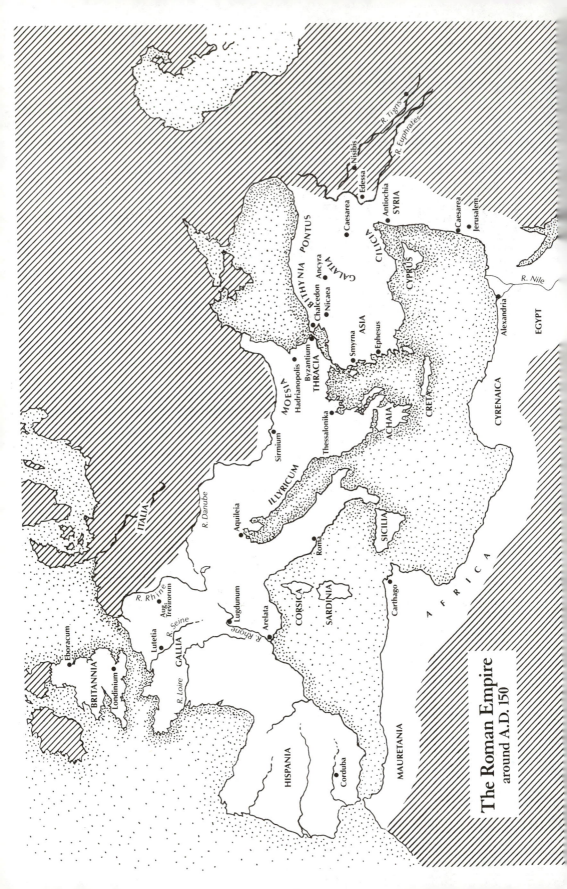

The Roman Empire
around A.D. 150

Chapter 1

Gnosticism

D URING THE LIFETIME of Justin Martyr—that is, in the period between roughly 130 and 160 A.D.—there surfaced within the Christian community a debate whose roots reached back into the first century. It was the controversy between groups which came to be called "gnostic" and defenders of what might be termed a common-sense interpretation of the churches' teaching tradition. The debate raised difficult and fundamental issues, not merely about particular questions—for example, the nature of evil, the meaning of "God," and the character of redemption—but also about the way in which the language of the church's catechesis was to be interpreted. As a result, it compelled significant developments in the range, depth, and precision of the Christian theological tradition, as well as in the institutions by which that tradition was shaped and handed on.

In spite of the historical importance of this debate, it has not proved an easy matter for scholars to bring the phenomenon of Gnosticism into clear focus or even to decide upon a uniform way of characterizing or defining it. One reason for this lack of clarity is no doubt the fact that Gnosticism represents less a specific set of teachings than a religious mood of world-rejection coupled with what might best be called a transcendentalist habit of mind. Its cultural and social setting seems to have been the urban world in which Jewish religious texts and symbols were being drawn into syncretism with popularized philosophical notions and themes drawn from Hellenistic religion. Since it was precisely this world which Christianity entered when the Gospel was carried "to the Gentiles," it is hardly a matter for surprise that much of the gnostic writing and teaching with which we are acquainted is either partly or thoroughly christianized. Nevertheless, it is necessary for the historian to distinguish, for the sake of clarity, between the general phenomenon of Gnosticism itself and the particular and definite forms which it took through an association with Christianity.

Another reason for this lack of clarity lies in the character of the sources on which historians have until recently had to draw for their knowledge of

Gnosticism. It is true that modern scholars have had access to a few complete works of gnostic authorship. The Christian Gnostic Ptolemy's *Letter to Flora* was preserved in its original Greek by the fourth-century heresiologist Epiphanius, and eighteenth-century finds in the Egyptian desert produced some important texts in the Egyptian vernacular, Coptic. Among these were the *Pistis-Sophia,* a dialogue of the risen Jesus with his disciples; two works contained in the so-called Bruce Codex, one untitled and the other called *The Mystery of the Great Logos*; and the vastly important *Secret Teaching of John,* first published in 1955. Nevertheless, the principal sources for a knowledge of Gnosticism have been the works of its Christian opponents and critics of the late second and early third centuries: writers such as Irenaeus of Lyons, Clement of Alexandria, Origen, Tertullian, and Hippolytus of Rome. From such authors, we have summaries of gnostic teaching and, not infrequently, quotations drawn from gnostic writings. (Thus, Origen provides us with extensive citations of the earliest known commentary on the Fourth Gospel, from the pen of the Gnostic Heracleon.) Even when there is good reason to think, however, that the sources these writers use are trustworthy and their reporting accurate (which is often but not always the case), their testimony is of limited value. For one thing, their theories about the origins and sources of Gnosticism (which they liked to trace back through a succession of teachers to Simon Magus, as portrayed in the narrative of Acts 8:9–24) were mostly produced to serve the needs of their polemic. For another, their understanding and handling of gnostic ideas could be biased and unsympathetic even when their reporting was faithful.

It was, therefore, an event of great importance for the scholarly world when, in 1945, a small library of thirteen codices was discovered at Nag Hammadi in Egypt, on a site not far removed from that of a fourth-century monastery at Chenoboskion. These codices contain some forty-eight short tractates in Coptic translation, of which the great majority are gnostic works. They have now, after many years of controversy and negotiation, been edited and translated, and are being studied systematically.[1] It is from this find that we have such works as *The Gospel of Truth, The Gospel of Thomas,* the so-called *Tripartite Tractate,* and the *Treatise on the Resurrection,* often referred to as the *Epistle to Rheginos* —all works which illuminate the character of a Christian Gnosticism. The library also contains, however, works of gnostic provenance which show little or no interest in or acquaintance with Christianity.

From a study of the gnostic materials, two things at any rate have become clear. The first is that Gnosticism was by no means a uniform phenomenon. Both the reports of early Christian critics and the materials in the Nag Hammadi collection itself indicate that there was no single body of teaching common to all

---

[1] For an English version, see J. M. Robinson et al., *The Nag Hammadi Library in English* (San Francisco, 1977).

the writings or all the teachers belonging to this stream in ancient religion. Beyond this, though, and equally important for an understanding of second-century Christianity, it is now clear that not all Gnosticism was Christian and that the movement or religious tendency which it represents existed independently of the church, even if it did not greatly antedate Christianity. From the point of view of second-century Christian writers and thinkers, Gnosticism may often have looked like a *hairesis*—"sect" or "heresy"—bred up within the church. But if it did, the explanation seems to lie in the fact that, no doubt from a very early date, there were persons of a gnostic habit of mind who became converts to Christianity, or were attracted by its teaching, and who interpreted the meaning of this new faith in a way consonant with their habitual beliefs.

But what were the salient characteristics of this stream or movement in ancient religion? A student approaching the sources for the first time is bound to be struck initially by the very mood and style of gnostic writings. For one thing, what they have to offer is always a *secret* teaching, revealed to the few and mysterious in its very substance. Not everyone is capable of the knowledge (*gnōsis*) which the gnostic possesses, and one (though not the only) reason for this is that it concerns things which are not apparent—truths about a primordial reality that is not only beyond ordinary thought and experience but positively alien to them. There is, therefore, a deliberately riddle-like quality about much gnostic discourse, a delight in the obscure, the complex, and the mystifying. Again, much gnostic teaching—indeed, the very core of it—is couched mythologically. That is, the *gnōsis* which comes as a revelation to those "in the know" takes the form of a story (*muthos*) about the transcendent, primordial realities. Yet gnostic myth is distinctive in kind. The actors in it are not those gods and goddesses of primitive lore whom Greek philosophy was in the business of demythologizing. Quite often they are abstract philosophical or theological notions, or general religious symbols, which are used not as symbols but as names—"remythologized," as it were, and made the subject of a tale. Finally, as we have already suggested, no one who looks at these sources can miss for long the syncretistic character of gnostic thinking. Certain elements in the Jewish Scriptures—the creation story, for example—figure largely in gnostic writings. But so do themes from pagan mythology, from popular astrology, and from magic, not to mention philosophical ideas with parallels in Middle Platonism, Neo-Pythagoreanism, and Hellenistic Judaism. There is inevitably, therefore, something of a phantasmagoric quality about gnostic literature.

This does not mean that its message is trivial, however; and in spite of the variety of gnostic myths and systems, they seem to have certain general themes and concerns in common. If one were to summarize as briefly as possible the content of the *gnōsis* which is revealed to the elect, it would turn out to be the assurance that they are "displaced persons" in the system of things. They are spirit-selves from the hidden world of Light and Knowledge, lost and cruelly imprisoned in the visible, material cosmos of darkness and ignorance, but destined inevitably to be restored to their true home. Thus, the Christian gnostic Theodotus can explain that in baptism "it is not the washing alone which liberates, but also the *gnōsis* which tells who we were, what we have become, what situation we have been cast into, in what direction we are hastening, from what we have been redeemed, what coming-to-be is, and what coming-to-be-anew is."[2] It is these questions—about the identity, fall, and redemption of the spirit-selves—which the gnostic myths seek to answer.

The basic device of these myths, then, seems to be the idea of a duality or replication of worlds. In some accounts, this division between two realms—one of light and one of darkness—is conceived to be original and primordial. In such myths, the displacement of the spirit-selves, who are potential gnostics, is pictured as the outcome of an unhappy encounter and mingling of the two orders. In other accounts—and it is this second type of myth which prevailed among second-century Christian gnostics of the dominant schools of Basilides and Valentinus—the darkness-world, the "cosmos," is not original but secondary and derivative. It was not there "in the beginning." Rather, it was produced as the result of a tragic fall or error, a disturbance within the higher realm. According to a common version of this myth, the lowest and weakest member of the light-world, the "Eon" called Sophia or Wisdom, fell into error and passion through her desire to know the unknowable Father. Her redemption and restoration to order, however, entailed the exiling of this error and passion from the higher world; and as a result of this extrusion of evil, the process began by which an inferior cosmos—a cosmos in which exiled spirit-elements are trapped—came into being.

Thus, there turn out to be two parallel worlds: the original, divine world of spirit-stuff, which is called "the Fulness" (*plērōma*), and the inferior, material world, which is sometimes called "the Void" (*kenōma*). It is characteristic of Christian gnostic thinking that the parallelism between these orders is stressed. Whatever is real and important transpires in the Fulness, but it is imitated in a transposed key on the lower level of the visible cosmos. Thus, for example, the drama of redemption as Christians understand it is a shadow or image of the true redemptive drama which transpires in the spirit-world. However, this parallelism is developed in a way that is calculated to emphasize not the union but the separation of the two orders. For one thing, the "stuff" of which they are constituted is different, and the difference amounts to irreconcilability. The light-world is made of spirit (*pneuma*), whereas the lower world is made of soul (*psuchē*) and matter (*hulē*). By the same token, the two worlds are headed by two different deities. There is a God-figure who is the "Fashioner" (Demiurge) of the material cosmos. This, in fact, is the "Lord" and "God" of whom the Jewish Scriptures speak. In spite, however, of his foolish claim to be the only God, he is not a member of the spirit-world at all but is made of mere soul-stuff

---

[2] Clement of Alexandria, *Excerpts from Theodotus* 78.2.

and is ignorant of the true source and ground of things. "The Lord God," in short, is a copy—a kind of second-rate imitation—of the Mind from which the spirit-world and its inhabitants issue.

So the situation of gnostics is clear. In their inner, true selves they are spirit, and their proper home is in the Fulness. Lost as they are, however, in an alien cosmos, they are condemned to ignorance of their true nature and destiny. It is only through the grace of a revelation by which they become self-aware that they are "formed" for restoration to their proper state. Once they receive this "formation in knowledge," though, they understand themselves to be the elect—beings of an order superior even to the Creator-God of the Jewish Scriptures and thus liberated from the trammels of the oppressive world-order which he tries to rule. Inevitably, then, their situation as recipients of *gnōsis* sets them apart from other people. The Christian gnostics of the second century in fact came to recognize three classes of human persons, which corresponded to the three kinds of cosmic "stuff." There were those—the pagans, perhaps—who were hopelessly caught up in the world of flesh or matter and so destined ultimately for destruction. Then there were those—apparently the ordinary Christian believers—who belonged properly to the God of the Jewish Scriptures because they lived, like him, at the level of soul. These "psychics" were destined not for destruction but for a kind of second-class salvation, along with the God whom they served. Finally, of course, there were the "spirituals," the gnostics themselves, with their destiny in the Fulness of the divine world. Needless to say, this sense of constituting an elite whose salvation was assured and whose status put them beyond concern with the mere externals of life in the cosmos made the gnostics troubling neighbors in the life of the churches. They frequently professed indifference to the life of "faith and works" and to the need for witness in martyrdom. They had, or seemed to have, little commitment to the communal, institutional life of the church. They were apparently, at least in the impression they conveyed to others, quite literally above it all.

To this picture of the meaning of redemption and of the divergent destinies of humankind there corresponded a teaching about the Redeemer himself. Christian gnostics were distinguished from others by the fact that they identified the bearer of saving revelation with the Christ or Jesus. Given their doctrine of two worlds and two levels of salvation, however, their natural tendency was to envisage two parallel Christs. One of these was a merely "psychic" Christ, the Messiah promised by the Creator-God of the Jewish faith. His were the work and the message which ordinary believers appropriated. The true Savior, however, came from the Fulness and descended upon his psychic counterpart at the moment of the latter's baptism. In this version of the incarnation theme, the deeds and words of the "ordinary" Christ were seen, in accord with the principle of the parallelism of worlds, as intimations of the higher revelation borne by the Word from the Fulness; and this nobler revelation only gnostics could grasp. However, saving knowledge could not touch the flesh, the material order, in any way. Consequently, gnostic thought was prone to docetism: that is, to the conviction that the Savior did not operate in the realm of the flesh at all but had only the appearance of a body.

It is perhaps too easy for modern students of early Christianity to discount the seriousness with which the gnostic message was intended, and frequently seen, to declare the authentic burden of the church's faith. Similarly, it is much too easy to underestimate the degree to which certain gnostic ideas were modified or qualified as a result of their being christianized. What we know of the great Christian Gnostic teachers of the early second century suggests that they were sincere and significant interpreters of early Christian literature and tradition. To be sure, they appealed to a special secret tradition of their own, an "apostolic tradition, which we have received by a succession."[3] They traced it back to revelations given by the risen Christ to his disciples after the resurrection, and much gnostic literature is devoted to such revelations. At the same time, however, it is clear that the followers of the gnostic thinker Valentinus (fl. 130–160) found much of their inspiration in the letters of Paul. Their distinction between "spiritual," "psychic," and "fleshly," for example, as applied both to human persons and to levels of being in the universe, owes much to Pauline language; and Valentinus's disciple Theodotus appeals to Colossians in order to justify his way of speaking about "the Fulness."[4] It was noted above that Heracleon, who was another follower of Valentinus, wrote the first known commentary on John's Gospel, and Irenaeus of Lyons supplies abundant evidence that Valentinian teachers were diligent allegorical interpreters of the synoptic Gospels. Nor did the Christian Gnostics neglect the Scriptures of the Old Covenant. Ptolemy, also a follower of Valentinus, devotes most of his *Letter to Flora* to a discerning and troubling analysis of the "sources" of the Jewish Law, which he then builds on to intimate the mystery of the three levels of being—spirit, soul ("the Midst"), and matter.

In spite, however, of this gnostic appeal to the sources of Christian belief, it seems that most leaders of the churches (including some, such as Clement of Alexandria, who liked to call themselves Gnostics) saw in Christian Gnosticism a systematic distortion of the meaning of the teaching-tradition. They were shocked and outraged at the suggestion that the ultimate God is not identical with the Creator of this cosmos. They were angered at the contention that in rejecting gnostic revelation they proved themselves to be second-class "psychics." In gnostic criticism of the Jewish Scriptures, they saw a denial of the continuity of God's self-revelation in history, and in gnostic interpretation of the Gospels and the letters of Paul they saw deliberate avoidance of the plain sense of words. They deplored the gnostic tendency to reduplicate the Christ and to deny or qualify the statement that he came "in the flesh." They doubted the claim

---

[3] Ptolemy, *Letter to Flora.*
[4] Clement of Alexandria, *Excerpts from Theodotus* 31.1.

of the Gnostics, as "spirituals," to be superior to the Creator-God and his commandments, and they often suspected that the claim did no more than conceal a taste for libertinism. Above all, they repudiated the gnostic suggestion that good and evil are substances or kinds of being: that "spirit" is automatically good and "flesh," as such, evil and irredeemable. To them, such a view had the odor of fatalism or determinism; they preferred to insist that evil is no "thing" or kind of thing, but a way of choosing. In short, they were systematically offended by the developed implications of the gnostic dogma of two worlds, and on this issue battle was joined.

Chapter 2

Marcion

IN THE MINDS of those who opposed the wedding of Gnosticism and Christian faith, the figure of the heretic Marcion represented a threat equal and very similar to that posed by the followers of Basilides and Valentinus. Marcion, however, in spite of the presence in his teaching of gnostic ideas, did not, at least to begin with, share the basic assumptions and prepossessions which shaped the gnostic world-view, and the movement he began and organized in fact took a radically different shape from Gnosticism.

Born in Sinope in Asia Minor, where he was a wealthy Christian ship-owner, Marcion, already something of a storm center in the churches of his native land, came to Rome in about 139. There he joined the Roman congregation, making it the substantial gift of two hundred thousand sesterces for its charitable work, and began teaching his own understanding of the Gospel, which was based on an interpretation of the letters of Paul. His views created enough stir, scandal, and opposition to bring about his excommunication and the return of his money in 144. Marcion's response to this repudiation was to gather his followers into a separated church, which was apparently carefully organized. For this body, he provided an official canon of sacred books: ten letters of Paul (he did not know, or decided not to include, the Pastoral Epistles) and a form of the Gospel of Luke. The community which he founded spread quickly over wide areas and existed as a rival to churches of orthodox persuasion well into the fifth century. It became especially strong in Syria.

The problem with which Marcion's teaching began was that of the relation of the Christian Gospel to Judaism and to the religious teaching of the Jewish Scriptures. From the letters of Paul, which he seems to have read with a fresher mind than many of his contemporaries, he learned that the Christian dispensation was founded on the revelation in Christ of a loving and gracious God. He also inferred from his reading of Paul that between this Gospel of a loving God and the law-religion of Judaism there was opposition and inconsistency. This conviction was, in Marcion's view, strengthened and confirmed by the contents of the Jewish Scriptures. These he read in a fashion which was new in Christian circles. Rather than taking the Law and the Prophets as symbols and foreshadowings of the Christian dispensation, he insisted upon reading them literally. His conclusion from this exercise was that the God of the Mosaic covenant and the God of Jesus and Paul were two quite different things. The latter was a God of love and mercy. The former was a God of harsh justice—arbitrary, inconsistent, even tyrannical. This contrast he set forth systematically in his only written work, of which fragments alone remain. Called the *Antitheses,* it developed Marcion's understanding of Christian faith by exhibiting what he saw to be the inconsistencies between the Jewish Scriptures and Christian belief.

It is in Marcion's development and articulation of this basic conception that certain gnostic themes surface in his thought. So insistent was he upon the absolute novelty of the Christian dispensation that he refused to see any anticipation of it in the Jewish (or in any other) history. The God and Father of Jesus Christ was unknown prior to the manifestation of Jesus. Accordingly, the God of the Jewish Scriptures must be seen as a second, inferior deity, distinct from and opposed to the true God. In this fashion—and perhaps under the influence of the gnostic teacher Cerdo in Rome—Marcion adopted a strict dualism. The visible cosmos, as the creation of the God of Israel, and a creation out of matter at that, was an evil work destined for destruction. The Christ, who came as the agent of the unknown God of Love to rescue souls ("since the body, derived from earth, cannot possibly partake of salvation"[1]), simply appeared in Galilee, having undergone no human birth and possessing no real human body. Consonant with this view of materiality and of the body, Marcionite believers were required to abstain from all sexual intercourse, even in marriage. Marcion's rigorism is also shown in the requirement that his followers refrained from eating meat.

Marcion's teaching did more than confront the churches with the threat of a rival institution. It also forced them to consider the question of the continuity of Christianity with its Jewish heritage and, as one aspect of that issue, the problem of the unity of salvation-history under God. Furthermore, Marcion's

[1] Irenaeus, *Against Heresies* 1.25.1.

establishment of a canon of authoritative Christian writings (which he carefully expurgated of all passages that seemed to lend authority to the Jewish Scriptures) undoubtedly provided a model and a stimulus which pointed the way to the church's later and gradual adoption of its own canon of twenty-seven books.

Chapter 3

Montanism

M ARCION'S TEACHING and the contemporaneous debate about the fusion of Christian faith with Gnosticism combined to create in the churches a crisis of self-understanding. This crisis was rendered, if anything, more acute by a third movement which rose and spread during the last decades of the second century. Called by its followers "the New Prophecy," this movement is known to history as "Montanism," after its founder, Montanus, a convert to Christianity who lived in the region of Asia Minor where the borders of the Roman provinces of Phrygia and Mysia met. Around the year 170, he began to proclaim to his fellow believers that he was a prophet—that, indeed, he was the mouthpiece of that Spirit which the Lord had promised to the church as the one who would "teach . . . all things" and "guide you into all truth."[1] Montanus was soon joined by two women, Priscilla and Maximilla, who shared his inspiration and, like him, delivered portentous and occasionally obscure oracles in a state of ecstasy, speaking not in their own persons but in that of the Spirit himself. They soon acquired a substantial local following for themselves and their message, and as their movement spread it evoked almost instant opposition from the leaders of the Christian communities, who rightly perceived it as a threat to their own, none-too-secure, official authority, to the orderly life of the churches, and to the established tradition of teaching, which the New Prophecy claimed in effect to supersede.

The problem was not that Montanus was a prophet, for prophecy had existed in the church since its beginnings, and there is no reason to think that it had died out in the last third of the second century. The problem was that

[1] John 14:26, 16:13.

this was a *new* prophecy. It was unfamiliar in its form (Montanus uttered the words, "Behold a man is as a lyre, and I fly over it like a plectrum,"[2] where the "I" can only refer to the Spirit). It was also new in the substance of what it conveyed. Montanus and his companions represented a revival of the apocalyptic spirit and announced the forthcoming end of the world. The Lord was about to return, and the new Jerusalem would be set up in the vicinity of the town of Pepuza in Phrygia. In a spirit consonant with this apocalyptic outlook, Montanus and his followers saw themselves in a relation of complete alienation from the world. Their calling was martyrdom, and their duty was to hope for it and never to flee from persecution. As a preparation for the end of all things, they purified themselves and cut themselves loose from their attachments to society. The Phrygians, as they were frequently called, fasted longer and more elaborately than other Christians and discouraged—if they did not, like Marcion, forbid—marriage. Priscilla and Maximilla in this spirit left their husbands.

The movement spread with great rapidity, even though the last of the original prophets, Maximilla, died in 179, remembered for the words, "After me shall be no prophetess any more, but the consummation."[3] It spread through Asia Minor, reached Syria and Antioch, and was known in Rome and the West by the end of a decade. Montanism made its most illustrious convert in the North African Christian writer Tertullian, who was attracted to it not so much by its apocalypticism as by the seriousness and moral rigor which it required of Christian believers. To him, Montanism represented the pure church, uncorrupted by compromise with the world and endowed with the living presence and authority of the Spirit. The bishops of Asia Minor held one or more synods (the first such synods of which we have any record) to deal with the "Phrygian problem" and in the end condemned the New Prophecy. In the West, its reception was more mixed. Zephyrinus, bishop of Rome (199–217) at first received it tolerantly, but later, in the words of Tertullian, "put to flight the Paraclete."[4] In North Africa, it seems to have been a movement interior to the church, which only later separated itself from other Christians, and it lived on there until the time of Augustine of Hippo.

[2] Stevenson, *A New Eusebius*, p. 113.　　[3] Ibid.　　[4] *Against Praxeas*, 1.

Chapter 4

The Catholic Church

NEITHER GNOSTICISM nor Montanism, persuasive and attractive though they were to the religious mentality of the second century, was embraced by the majority of Christians. What emerged, however, from the controversies of the middle and late second century was a church that had made choices and in the process of doing so had not only defined its moral and doctrinal teaching but also—and perhaps even more importantly—acknowledged and established certain institutions as the definitive bearers of its tradition. In no case were these institutions new; what was new was the clarity and uniformity with which their authority was accepted and, at the same time, the insistence, or recognition, that their meaning was inconsistent with the teachings of people like Marcion or the Valentinian Gnostics. In other words, the "early catholicism" which emerged as normative Christianity from this time of debate represents a fresh stage in the development of Christian tradition—an appropriation of the Christian message which was, at the same time, a closer and more elaborate definition of its sense and implications.

One sign and form of this development was the increased prominence and authority given to credal or confessional formulas. Such formulas had always figured in the life of the church. Sometimes they had taken the form of teaching or preaching summaries—for example, the traditional formula which Paul cites to remind his Corinthian converts of what he had "delivered" to them,[1] or Justin Martyr's summary reference to "Jesus Christ, who came in our times, was crucified, and died, rose again, has ascended into heaven and has reigned."[2] In other circumstances, confessional formulas had served a polemical purpose and sought to specify more narrowly the meaning of a traditional belief. An instance of this is the Johannine formula, "Jesus Christ has come in the flesh."[3] Of equal if not greater importance, however, were forms of speech which were preserved and handed on as standard parts of the liturgical tradition. Certain

[1] *1* Cor. 15:3ff.   [2] *1 Apol.* 42.4.   [3] *1* John 4:2.

hymns thus had a confessional character,[4] as did the eucharistic prayer, in which God's saving works were set out in the form of a thanksgiving.

Most central of all, however, by reason of the psychological and ceremonial solemnity of the moment of initiation, was the confession of faith which constituted the formula of baptism. In first-century communities, this confession may have been a Christological affirmation like "Jesus is Lord." By the middle of the second century, however, the baptismal confession was triadic in shape. Candidates for baptism were asked three questions as they stood in the water, to each of which they replied "I believe"; and with these three affirmations and the washings which accompanied them, the candidates were understood to be baptized "in the name of the Father and of the Son and of the Holy Spirit."[5] The baptismal confession, then, was the basis of an individual's membership in the community and, in consequence, the most fundamental expression of the community's self-understanding. We have a sample of such an "interrogatory" baptismal confession in the well-known formula of Hippolytus, which reflects the practice of the Roman church in the last decades of the second century.

> "Do you believe in God the Father Almighty?"
> "I believe."
> "Do you believe in Jesus Christ the Son of God, who was born of Holy Spirit and the Virgin Mary, who was crucified under Pontius Pilate and died, and rose the third day living from the dead, and ascended into heaven, and sat down at the right hand of the Father, and will come to judge the living and the dead?"
> "I believe."
> "Do you believe in the Holy Spirit, and the Holy Church, and the resurrection of the flesh?"
> "I believe."

It would be a mistake, though, to think that any such form of words was universally employed, or that formulas of this sort were officially composed and "enacted." These confessions—or "symbols," as they later came to be called—were essentially oral forms, and they evolved not by conference and decision but by informal traditionary processes. Each church had its own baptismal confession, whose wording might or might not coincide exactly with that of some other church. What was uniform was the structure of confession; what everyone was sure of was that each local confession embodied and expressed the one faith. It is not surprising, then, that in the second-century debates about the meaning of Christian belief, appeal was made to the terms of baptismal confession as embodying the commitments by which the church would stand or fall. This appeal took the form of insistence upon a "rule" (*kanōn*), variously called the "rule of truth," "rule of faith," "ecclesiastical rule," "tradition," and also "kerygma." What these terms referred to was not a form of words but a pattern and content of teaching. The "rule" was essentially a syllabus of the catechetical instruction in which neophytes learned the meaning of the church's

---

[4] Phil. 2:5ff.; Col. 1:15ff.   [5] Matt. 28:19.

baptismal faith. When summarized, it tended, not unexpectedly, to have the same structure as the triadic baptismal confession. In the course of the third century, this "rule" was formulated by the several churches in the brief form of "declaratory" symbols: i.e., creeds formed not as questions to be answered with an affirmation of faith, but as direct declarations on the part of the believer. Such creeds were used as a basis and outline for prebaptismal instruction and are the direct ancestors of the so-called Apostles' Creed as well as of the creed commonly referred to as the "Nicene."

Alongside the *kanōn* or rule provided by traditional confessional formulas, however, the second-century churches in their debates with Gnosticism and the Marcionites established the core of yet another rule or norm: that of the "canon" of New Testament Scriptures. The procedure, if that is the word, by which the formation of this collection came about was informal and decentralized—a drawn-out affair of increasing consensus which was completed only in the fourth century. This development involved three simultaneous processes. The first was a growing recognition of the need for a fixed, written tradition, especially where the teachings of Jesus were concerned. The second was the process by which such Christian writings as the Gospels and the apostolic letters were acknowledged to have the same essential place in the life of the churches as the Jewish Scriptures and so came to be cited and treated in the same way: i.e., as inspired by God's Spirit. The third was the complex business of deciding just which Christian writings qualified for this status. Where this last problem was concerned, there seem to have been two coordinate criteria employed. Books were established as "canonical" if they were regularly read at the liturgical assemblies of the churches and if they were thought to be "apostolic"—i.e., if they could reasonably be regarded as written by an apostle or by some other person of the founding generation whose testimony was identical with that of the apostles. These two criteria did not always agree, and there were debates (sometimes extended) about such writings as the Epistle to the Hebrews (which the Roman church quite rightly suspected of not being an authentic Pauline letter) or Hermas's *Shepherd,* which, while clearly not apostolic, was established in liturgical use. A third, more informal, criterion was also brought to bear, that of doctrine. The Fourth Gospel was for a time suspect because of the delight taken in it by Gnostics and followers of the New Prophecy; its establishment as canonical was no doubt owed both to its widespread use and to the fact that an apostolic name was associated with it.

The central core of this developing canon were the Pauline corpus and the four Gospels, together with the Acts of the Apostles. There was apparently a collection of Pauline letters in use fairly early in the second century, and they were already (at least in some quarters) being thought of as "scriptures" and as "hard to understand."[6] The case with the Gospels is somewhat different. It

[6] 2 Pet. 3:15–16.

appears, from the evidence of such a document as *1 Clement,* that even after the four Gospels had been composed, people for some time appealed to oral tradition rather than to written documents for the teachings of Jesus. By the time of Justin Martyr, however, at least the three synoptic Gospels were in liturgical use at Rome, and it seems probable that by the opening of the last third of the second century all four Gospels were in widespread use. There was a problem, however, about the fact that there were four of them and that they were not perfectly united in their testimony: a problem which Justin's disciple Tatian dealt with by creating a harmony of the four, the famous *Diatessaron,* and Irenaeus of Lyons sought to solve by arguing that they supplemented one another and thus bore a single total witness. Yet another problem was created by the fact that, while most churches acknowledged the authority of the four Gospels of Matthew, Mark, Luke, and John (though certain Jewish Christians, we are told, admitted only the authority of Matthew), in some churches, Alexandria being a notable example, other gospels were read as well. It seems to be the case, however, that by the turn of the third century this basic canon was firmly established, and in fact churches also knew and used others of the books which finally came to be included in the canon. In the end, the New Testament included works that represented most of the significant streams of tradition in primitive Christianity, though it excluded works which were explicitly gnostic.

With the articulation of the credal-confessional tradition and of the emerging New Testament canon, the churches defined what they meant by authentic and apostolic Christianity. There was, in their mind, no conflict between these two "rules of faith" because the credal tradition simply summarized the basic and obvious message of the prophetic and apostolic scriptures. In this way, moreover, it provided the church with the necessary key for the interpretation of the scriptures' more obscure parts—a key which, not just incidentally, ruled out gnosticizing exegesis. It is true that Gnostics of the Valentinian school argued that they had an apostolic tradition of their own—a secret (i.e., non-public) tradition that conveyed what the risen Christ and the apostles had taught when they were speaking "wisdom among the perfect."[7] This proposition, however, was denied categorically by Irenaeus of Lyons and those who followed the lines of his anti-gnostic polemic. Just as these thinkers were convinced that the apostles had "perfect knowledge," so too were they convinced that whatever the apostles had received from Christ had been entrusted to those whom they appointed as their public successors to govern the churches. There was, indeed, then, as the Gnostic Ptolemy had argued, an "apostolic succession," but it was constituted by the orderly succession of the church's official teachers, the bishops, and what this succession passed on as apostolic was precisely the credal-confessional tradition of the churches. Go then, they

---

[7] 1 Cor. 2:6.

argued, to the churches of apostolic foundation—those like Smyrna, Ephesus, or Rome, which can trace the line of their bishops back to an apostolic founder. It is the public tradition of these churches which represents authentic teaching, and that tradition can be confirmed by the fact that it agrees with the plain testimony of the apostolic Scriptures. Thus, the church is the one repository of Christian teaching, for "the apostles, like a rich man in a bank, lodged in her hands most copiously all things pertaining to the truth."[8] To preserve and convey this truth—the message of the Gospel—was the responsibility and privilege of the bishops.

In this way, through the struggles of the second century, the churches were strengthened as they bound themselves to their first-century roots by the threefold cord of creed, Scripture, and official teaching office. At the same time, by this institutional definition of the sources of their life and teaching, they initiated a new phase in the history of the Christian movement—differentiating themselves from their past in the very act of appropriating it.

[8] Irenaeus, *Against Heresies* 3.4.1.

Chapter 5

The Growing Importance
of the Roman Church

No one who consults the sources of early church history can fail to be impressed by the prominent role played in church life by the Christian community at Rome. The origins of this community are obscure. It may have begun with the conversion of a large body of Hellenized Jews—perhaps of an entire synagogue—in the earliest years of the mission from Jerusalem. However that may be, this congregation was, even by the end of the first century, beginning to speak with a weighty voice in the affairs of the church generally.

To explain this phenomenon, several factors can be mentioned. Peter and Paul both died at Rome, and the luster of their names was associated with the church there from an early date, even though neither was actually its founder. In addition, it had the prestige lent it by location in the capital of the empire and by the fact that at the opening of the second century it was apparently the largest single congregation of Christians anywhere. Rome's influence was, as time went on, increased by the well-known generosity of the church there. Ignatius of Antioch praised it for "having the presidency of love";[1] and a few decades later Dionysius of Corinth commended the Roman congregation for sending "contributions to the many churches in every city . . . relieving the poverty of the needy, and ministering to the Christians in the mines."[2] Given these circumstances, one can understand the sense of authority with which the church at Rome addressed the Corinthian church in *1 Clement*. The letter clearly expected to be heeded, and its tone, if brotherly, was big-brotherly.

There is more to the story than this, however. To understand the influence of the Roman church in the second and early third centuries, one must take account both of its special problems and of its response to them. Its location at the principal crossroads of the empire seems to have made the Roman church from an early date a crossroads in the life of the Christian movement. It was, until the third century, a Greek-speaking church and therefore an immigrant church, and as it grew its members came to include believers from many regions of the empire. From Irenaeus of Lyons and other sources we gather that there was in Rome a large group of North African Christians as well. Justin Martyr came there from Asia Minor, Valentinus from Alexandria, Marcion from Pontus. Not too long after its beginnings in Phrygia, the New Prophecy arrived in Rome and had supporters there. As it turned out, then, whatever went on anywhere in the church tended to be a matter of domestic concern to the church at Rome. If Rome seemed to have a finger in everyone's pie, that was because it had a piece of everyone's pie on its own table.

How did the Roman bishops deal with this situation? As far as we can tell, monepiscopacy was established more slowly and with more difficulty in Rome than in some other churches, perhaps just because of the size and variety of the community. As a central authority did develop, therefore, it was with a conscious understanding of the bishop's role and of the basis of his claim to obedience. The bishop was the voice and representative of the tradition on which the Roman church was founded—the tradition which stemmed from Peter and Paul, who by the time of Irenaeus were understood to have been the church's founders. This meant that Rome was seen, especially in the West, to be the apostolic church par excellence (Jerusalem, refounded as a Roman colony after the Jewish revolt of 135, could make no such claim), and its bishop the focal witness to apostolic tradition. It also meant that when a Roman bishop acted, within his own sphere, to resolve some problem or settle some debate, his word often affected, and also carried some weight in, other churches as well; for Rome's problems, as we have seen, frequently had their roots in other sectors of the Christian world.

The signal illustration of this situation can be seen in the lengthy quarrel over the proper date for the celebration of Easter, commonly known as the

---

[1] *Romans.*   [2] Eusebius, *Ecclesiastical History* 4.23.10.

"Quartodeciman" controversy. While there is reason to think that Easter had been kept from early on in Christian history, the first explicit record of its celebration is in an account of the visit of Polycarp, bishop of Smyrna, to Anicetus, bishop of Rome, in 154 or 155—a visit no doubt connected with the prominence of believers from Asia Minor in the Roman church. At that time, the practice in Asia Minor was to observe Easter with a vigil, culminating in the eucharist, through the night of the fourteenth of the month of Nisan: that is, the celebration coincided with the date of the beginning of the Jewish Passover, regardless of the day of the week on which it fell. The Roman custom, on the contrary, which was also observed in some parts of the East, was to keep the feast always on the Sunday following the Jewish Passover. Polycarp and Anicetus could not resolve this difference of practice, but nevertheless parted with expressions of good will.[3] Their agreement to differ, however, meant that the Roman church was divided between those who kept the Asian custom and those who followed the local use.

The local situation in Rome became so acute and divisive over the years that Victor, bishop of Rome (189–198), contrived synods in Rome itself, in Palestine, and elsewhere that decided in favor of the Roman practice. The churches of Asia Minor, however, led by Polycrates, bishop of Ephesus, refused to conform. Thereupon Victor excommunicated the recalcitrant congregations. This high-handed action met with much protest and does not seem to have been very effective in Asia Minor, but it no doubt enabled Victor to impose a uniform practice on his own church. It was also a sign that the Roman church and its bishop were acquiring authority and influence beyond their own immediate sphere—an authority and influence which no other church could equal.

[3] Eusebius, *Ecclesiastical History* 5.24.16f.

Chapter 6

Irenaeus of Lyon

*W*HATEVER THE BASIS of the growing influence of the Roman bishops, it did not rest upon their contribution as thinkers or theologians. The earliest theological leader of distinction in the debate with Marcion and the Gnostics was, in fact, the bishop of a relatively new and obscure church in Gaul, Irenaeus of Lyon, himself an immigrant to the West from Asia Minor. Born around

135 A.D., he is first known to history as a presbyter of the church at Lyon. During the great persecution which occurred there in 177, he was absent in Rome on an official mission. On his return, he was chosen bishop in succession to the martyred Pothinus. It was at Lyon that he wrote the two works which we now possess: the *Demonstration of the Apostolic Preaching,* which was first published in the early twentieth century; and the much lengthier work in five books which he called *An Indictment and Overthrow of the Falsely Named "Knowledge,"* but which tradition has more conveniently styled *Against Heresies.* This major work was probably completed around 185. Irenaeus died in about 200, according to tradition as a martyr.

Irenaeus believed and argued that the teaching-tradition of the churches as it was ordinarily expounded represented the authentic version of the Christian faith. It was he, accordingly, who first developed the appeal to tradition (the "rule of truth") and to the successions of bishops and presbyters who had transmitted it, as a weapon against his gnostic and Marcionite opponents. The great weight of his argument, however, was borne by an appeal to the prophetic and apostolic Scriptures, which, he was convinced, would themselves confute heretical teaching directly if attention were paid to their plain sense and if their obscure passages were understood in the light of those whose meaning was obvious.

In Irenaeus's view, the "first and greatest"[1] issue raised by Marcion and the Gnostics arose out of their denial that the true God and the World-Creator are one and the same. In reply, he insisted that rule of faith and Scripture alike know only one God, the Creator, who "contains all things" while being himself contained and limited by nothing.[2] The Creator called the world into being when before it did not exist ("out of nothing"), and the world which he thus created was not some distant spiritual "Fulness" but this visible cosmos. As the world's immediate Creator, moreover, God is not distant from the world but intimately present to it. By his own "two hands," Logos and Wisdom, Son and Spirit, God formed humanity lovingly, adapting this creature of body and soul to grow to fulfillment and maturity by "receiving the Spirit of the Father"[3] and thus coming to immortality in the vision of God. The one God, in other words, just because he is the sole Creator of everything, is alien to nothing that he creates.

On the basis of this understanding of God as the unique Creator, Irenaeus can take up the second issue which Marcion and the Gnostics had posed for him: that of salvation. Repudiating the gnostic segregation of spirit, soul, and flesh as inconsistent "substances" or "natures," and the corresponding belief that flesh is incapable of salvation, Irenaeus insists that salvation is not the correction but the fulfillment of creation. The original humanity which God made of earth and imbued with life is the very "Adam" who in the end is fulfilled in

---

[1] *Against Heresies* 2.1.1.   [2] Ibid., 2.1.2.   [3] Ibid., 5.6.1.

likeness to God—who indeed is the "figure of him who is to come."[4] Even the sin and disobedience of this earthly humanity did not cut it off finally from God, for in his Logos and Wisdom God has been its constant companion through history, educating and guiding it toward the supreme moment when the Second—and true—Adam should appear: the Christ, in whom humanity, flesh as well as soul, is united to the Logos of God. Using Ephesians 1:10, Irenaeus thus sees the Christ as the one in whom the whole historical relationship of God and humanity is "summed up" or "recapitulated" in all its dimensions—reiterated in order to be set right and fulfilled. The Christ therefore represents for Irenaeus the destiny and true identity of the Adam whom God originally created. Christians follow, he writes, "the only true and steadfast teacher, the Logos of God, our Lord Jesus Christ, who did through his transcendent love become what we are, that he might bring us to be even what he is himself."[5] This destiny which the Christ embodies and enables for humanity will be finally realized for believers in the last days, when all things are marvelously renewed.

Irenaeus saw himself as above all a preserver and interpreter of tradition, and so he was, weaving together in his anti-gnostic synthesis themes from Pauline and Johannine thought, from the tradition of his native Asia Minor, and from the apologetic of writers like Justin Martyr and Theophilus of Antioch. At the same time, like many "traditionalists," he was an innovative thinker. In his confrontation with the dualism of Gnostics and Marcionites, Irenaeus caught a vision: that of the unity of human nature and of the continuity of salvation history in their character as the work of the one God in his Son and Spirit.

[4] Cf. Rom. 5:14.   [5] *Against Heresies* 5; preface.

Chapter 7

Tertullian and Cyprian

ABOUT THREE YEARS AFTER Irenaeus was chosen bishop of Lyon, in July of the year 180, there occurred an event whose record provides our first knowledge of Christianity in the province of North Africa: the martyrdom in the capital city, Carthage, of twelve believers from the town of Scillium. The nature of this event is, for the historian, portentous, for the North African church, from the second century to the fifth, understood itself as above all a church of martyrs. It saw itself as a church marked by opposition to the powers which rule this world—as a Spirit-filled elect whose hope was focused on God's future vindication of people who had been faithful to him in the midst of a society which denied him. This outlook is manifest not only in the account of the witness of the Scillitan martyrs, but also in *The Martyrdom of Perpetua and Felicity,* which records the experiences of a group of Carthaginian martyrs in the persecutions set off by the emperor Septimius Severus (193–211). Above all, though, it breathes for us in the numerous tracts of Tertullian, the first Christian writer of any note to use Latin, and the man who gave to Latin theology its vocabulary and its basic agenda.

Of Tertullian's life, little is known save what can be gathered from the uncertain chronology of his writings. He was a convert to Christianity, a native of Carthage who probably never strayed far from home, and a man with a professional education in rhetoric. St. Jerome, writing two centuries later, asserts that Tertullian was a presbyter, but this is most unlikely. He burst on the Christian scene in North Africa in 197 with the appearance of his *Apology,* an angrier imitation of Justin Martyr's, and he seems to have died around 225. In the interim, he published a spate of eloquent, witty, and argumentative tracts on doctrine and morals which reveal him to have been a masterful and tendentious debater as well as a Christian of radical and uncompromising spirit.

At the heart of Tertullian's theology lies his concern for the purity and holiness of the church—the practical authenticity of its life and teaching. The church lives by the revelation of God—"We meet to read the books of God"[1]— and that revelation, focused in Jesus Christ and his Gospel, is the law which governs its life. By keeping that law in action and belief, the church and its members appropriate for themselves the promises of the Gospel and await with confidence "the judgment to come."[2] On that day, the world and its rulers, who have served and worshiped the demons that stand in opposition to God, will, to their dismay, see the truth they have spurned vindicated, and believers rewarded by the God whose words they have kept.

Keeping God's words, though, meant for Tertullian existence in separation from the world, which had the idolatrous service of demons built into the very structure of its life. Christians prayed to God for the emperor and for the peace and welfare of the empire; but they understood, too, that "when the nations are rejoicing, we [Christians] are in mourning."[3] In Tertullian's view, therefore, as in that of many Christians before him, believers had no business serving in the army, in government, in educational institutions, or in any business which directly or indirectly supported pagan religion. They were to have nothing to do with public entertainments of any sort, since the latter, quite apart from their immoral content, were celebrations in honor of the "gods" of

[1] *Apology* 39.3.   [2] *Apology* 39.4.   [3] *On Shows* 28.

the pagan world. This rigoristic spirit extended to other matters as well. Baptized Christians were people whose past sins had been forgiven by repentance and by washing with water and the Holy Spirit; but having been thus set free to do God's will, the remainder of their life after baptism was the strenuous one of "competitors for salvation in earning the favor of God."[4] Like many New Testament writers,[5] then, Tertullian had little use for believers who fell into serious sin after baptism. In his treatise *On Penitence* he argued that one—and only one—such fall might be compensated for by a "second repentance." Later, however, reflection on the failures of Christians, as well as opposition from high quarters, drove him into the sterner position of the Montanists, and in his Montanist period he denied the possibility of any repentance and restoration at all after baptism. There was no room in the church or in Christian life for a serious and deliberate failure to live by the precepts of the Gospel—just as there was no room for any attempt, under persecution, to escape the privilege of martyrdom, the only real "second repentance."

Tertullian's stance on Christian life and morals was paralleled by his stance on doctrinal issues. Well read though he was in the philosophy of his day, he insisted that Christian belief had nothing to do with the traditions of the philosophical schools stemming from Athens. Its tradition came from Jerusalem—from Christ and the apostles—and was maintained, as Irenaeus had argued, by the successions of bishops in the apostolic churches. The business of the church was simply to maintain this tradition: to adhere unquestioningly to the "rule of faith" which was the one key to the Scriptures. Tertullian accordingly turned his skill with the pen against the heretics of his day. He wrote five books entitled *Against Marcion* and another treatise, *Against the Valentinians*. He defended the doctrines of creation, of the fleshly incarnation of the Logos, and of the resurrection of the flesh. His most notable contribution to theology, however, was made in the tract *Against Praxeas,* in which he mounted an attack on a "monarchian" teacher who had denied the substantive reality of the Logos as distinct from the Father (see II:8). In this work, Tertullian evolved the earliest systematic form of the doctrine of the Trinity, arguing that there is one divine "substance" which is articulated or "administered" into three distinct but continuous "persons": Father, Logos/Son, and Spirit. At the same time, he offered a reflective account of the incarnation, explaining that the person of Christ is a union of two distinct, unconfused "substances," divine and human, in a single "person." This terminology—hard to interpret by reason of the differences between the meanings of Tertullian's Latin terms and those of their modern English derivatives—became the basis of all later Latin and western trinitarian and Christological discourse.

---

[4] *On Penitence* 6.   [5] Cf. Heb. 10:26; 1 John 5:16–17.

Tertullian, then, saw the church as the society of those who lived under God's rule in the midst of a world ruled by demons, and therefore as the society where alone God's Spirit was given and salvation attained. For him as for the writers of the New Testament, it was the end-time community, which must sustain its identity and its purity in order to be the home of the Spirit and eventually enter into "the inheritance of the saints in light."[6]

In Tertullian's time and after, Christianity spread with remarkable rapidity in North African and Numidia, but in the generation after his death it underwent a severe testing, when the emperors Decius and Valerian unleashed the first universal persecutions of the churches (see II:10). At that time, the bishop of Carthage was Cyprian, a former teacher of rhetoric and a careful student of Tertullian, whose conversion around 246 had brought him to almost immediate prominence in the church. Elected bishop on the very eve of the persecutions, Cyprian found it his lot to guide the African churches through the pain, disillusionment, and divisions engendered by the imperial effort to make Christians apostatize. In the end, in 258, he too suffered martyrdom, by beheading, but not before he had reconsidered and reinterpreted his inherited understanding of the church in the light of its response to persecution.

One basic premise Cyprian never doubted. For him as for Tertullian, "There is no salvation outside the church,"[7] for "He can no longer have God for his Father who has not the church for his Mother."[8] The church for him, too, is the sole ark of salvation. The events of the persecutions, however, raised questions about how this premise should be understood. For one thing, great numbers of Christians took steps to avoid imprisonment or death. They either sacrificed or else purchased fraudulent certificates (*libelli*) to assure the Roman authorities that they had done so. By Tertullian's standards, such persons had simply placed themselves outside the sphere of salvation. The African bishops, however, under pressure from their own pastoral consciences as well as from confessors who claimed authority to forgive and restore apostates, agreed to readmit to the church, on condition of "long protracted"[9] penance, those who had procured forged certificates. By this act, though, they implied that the identity and holiness of the church could no longer be grounded in the purity and fidelity of its individual members. Not even the holiness of the martyrs could compensate for the lapse of so many of their sisters and brothers. In what, then, was the holiness of the church grounded? Furthermore, the persecutions produced schisms (see II:10), as groups in Carthage and Rome formed separate bodies because they thought the bishops too lax or too rigorous in their treatment of the lapsed. Thus the question of the unity of the church arose in an acute form. On what was the unity of the church founded? Were schismatic—but admittedly not heretical—bodies also "church"?

[6] Col. 1:12.
[7] *Epistle* 73.21.
[8] *On the Unity of the Church* 6.
[9] Cyprian, *Epistle* 55(51).6.

Cyprian thought not. As he saw it, the church was founded ultimately upon the apostles whom Christ commissioned. It was therefore the apostles as a single college (*collegium*: a body of "colleagues"), severally exercising a single undivided authority, who were the foundation of the church and hence the basis of its identity, holiness, and unity. The apostolic office, however, had in Cyprian's view (and not his alone) devolved upon the bishops, the successors of the apostles, who severally exercised the authority of a single collective ministry. "There is one God, and Christ is one, and there is one chair [episcopate] founded upon the rock by the word of the Lord."[10] Hence, to depart from communion with the bishop in any given place was, quite simply, to depart from the church, the ark of salvation. By the same token, on the principle that "the bishop is in the church and the church in the bishop,"[11] the character of the church as the home of God's Spirit and the Mother of saints also depended, as Cyprian saw it, on the legitimacy, integrity, and holiness of the bishop. If the church's leader and president, who taught the Gospel, administered the sacrament of baptism, and offered to God the church's sacrifice in the eucharist, were himself unworthy or unholy, then the community itself ceased to be "church."

These views—which in effect made the unity and holiness of the church dependent on the person of the bishop—had both logical and historical consequences. For one thing, they led directly to the system of synodical government by bishops, a system which Cyprian encouraged and to which he submitted. Each bishop in his place succeeded to and exercised the apostolic authority. Each bishop therefore had a right to a voice in the common concerns of the whole church, which was governed properly not by any individual but by the college of bishops itself. Even the bishop of Rome—who certainly enjoyed a special dignity and a special right to leadership, as successor to St. Peter—was nevertheless, substantively, the colleague and therefore the equal of his brethren. At the same time, Cyprian's way of focusing the holiness, and in that way the identity, of the church in the person of the bishop led almost inevitably to the theological position taken by the Donatist church in the fourth and fifth centuries (see III:1).

---

[10] *Epistle* 43(39).5.   [11] *Epistle* 68(66).8.

Chapter 8

The Logos Theology and Monarchianism

ROME IN THE EPISCOPATES of Victor (189–198), Zephyrinus (198–217), and Callistus (217–222) was the principal arena for a debate over the implications of the Logos theology as it had been developed by Justin Martyr and other Apologists. The interest of this debate lies less in any useful issue to which it came (it seems to have been conducted for the most part with excessive heat and even more confusion) than in the fact that it represents a first encounter with problems which were to engage the churches in the great trinitarian controversy of the fourth century—problems in the first instance about the Christian understanding of God.

There can be no doubt that the Logos theology raised many serious questions. Rooted in the Wisdom Christologies of the first century (see I:7), it used the expressions "Son of God" and "Christ" to denote a mediatorial figure who was, in Justin's phrase, "another God"[1] alongside "the sole unbegotten,"[2] the Father. This distinction between Father and Son was, Justin insisted, one of mere "number" and not of "will";[3] the Logos was like one torch lit from another,[4] divine as its progenitor was divine. Nevertheless, in Justin's picture, as later in Tertullian's, the generation of the Logos takes place only with a view to the world's creation. The Son, therefore, is not co-eternal with God; moreover, he exists to provide a mediator between God and the cosmos in creation and revelation, as the language of John 1:3 and 1:18, not to mention 1 Corinthians 8:6, seemed to suggest. Thus, the Logos theology appeared to introduce a "second God," inconsistently with the principle of monotheism; and further, it suggested that the Logos represented a secondary grade or kind of divinity. It "subordinated" the Son to the Father.

It was against the first of these implications of the Logos doctrine—that of a duality (or trinity) of divine beings—that a small movement arose that took as its watchword the Greek term *monarchia,* which meant (roughly) "uniqueness of first principle." This "monarchianism" came to Rome, from

---

[1] *Dialogue with Trypho* 56.4.   [2] Ibid., 5.6.   [3] Ibid., 128.4.   [4] Ibid., 61.2.

Asia Minor, in two successive waves which represented significantly different points of view; both were repudiated because of the way in which their strict monotheism led them to understand the person of Jesus.

The first of these waves arrived ca. 190 in the person of one Theodotus, a tanner from Byzantium. This man, despite his excommunication by Victor, found energetic disciples in a certain Asclepiodotus and another Theodotus, called "the banker," who briefly established a schismatic church. Their circle was unpopular among ordinary Christians in Rome, because its members enjoyed the study of Aristotle and his commentator Theophrastus, not to mention Euclid the mathematician and Galen the writer on medicine, and practiced dialectical reasoning (no doubt to the frequent discomfiture of their opponents). What really troubled the church, however, was their teaching that "Christ was a mere man,"[5] born of the Virgin Mary and the Holy Spirit, on whom the divine *dunamis* ("power") descended at his baptism and who was "adopted" into the divine sphere by his resurrection. In this way, these "dynamic" or "adoptionist" monarchians were able to dispense with the Logos doctrine—though only at the cost of denying the identification or union of God and humanity in Christ.

The second, and historically more important, wave of monarchianism arrived in Rome ca. 200, when Zephyrinus was bishop, with a man from Smyrna named Noëtus. This Noëtus had been expelled from the Smyrnaean church for teaching that "Christ was the Father himself, and that the Father himself was born, and suffered, and died."[6] Unlike Theodotus, then, he did not deny the doctrine of incarnation; but in dispensing with the figure of a distinct Son or Logos, he made God himself the subject of the incarnation. This same line was evidently followed by Tertullian's opponent Praxeas (see II:7), who (in addition to his anti-Montanist activities) denied any distinction between Christ and the Father and used the term "Son" to mean the human Jesus. Thus, in his view, too, it was the Father who was born and who suffered in union with Jesus's humanity—a contention which caused later critics to label this position "Patripassianism."

A more persuasive and enduring form of the monarchian position was developed by one Sabellius—a man who, despite the fact that little was remembered about his person or career, eventually lent his name to the whole movement. "Sabellianism" attempted to take serious account of the triadic structure of the church's baptismal faith. It did so by using the terms "Father," "Son," and "Spirit" to denote, not distinct realities within the Godhead, but three roles or "modes" in which the one God successively shows himself in relation to the world and to humankind: viz., as Creator, Redeemer, and Sanctifier. Hence, modern scholars have described Sabellianism as "modalistic

---

[5] Eusebius, *Ecclesiastical History* 5.28.6; Stevenson, *A New Eusebius*, p. 157.
[6] Hippolytus, *Against Noëtus* 1; Stevenson, *A New Eusebius*, p. 159.

monarchianism," or, because the roles in question refer not to what God is in himself but simply to ways in which he "manages" his external relations, as "economic" trinitarianism (from the Greek *oikonomia,* which literally means "household management").

The principal opponent at Rome of modalistic monarchianism was Hippolytus (d. ca. 235). This presbyter—the probable author of the works to which we owe most of our knowledge of the history and liturgy of the Roman church in this period—was engaged in simultaneous controversy with the Roman bishop, Callistus, whom he accused both of being taken in by the monarchians and of relaxing the rigor of the moral standards exacted of Christians at Rome. Against Sabellius, Hippolytus reiterated eloquently the view that the Logos is a *prosōpon* (in Tertullian's language, "person") distinct from the Father, but created by God for the carrying out of his will. In the end, Hippolytus set up a schismatic community at Rome, so alienated was he by the success and the teachings of Callistus, whom he regarded as being in any case morally and intellectually unsuited for the office of bishop. It was, perhaps ironically, Callistus who eventually excluded Sabellius from the communion of the Roman church, for even though the bishop was firmly persuaded of the unity of God, he was also sure that "it was not the Father who died but the Son."[7] With this judgment, unclear and ambiguous as it was, the matter rested for the moment.

Needless to say, the same or similar issues arose at other times and in other places in the third century. A species of adoptionist monarchianism was taught in Syria by Paul of Samosata, who was condemned by a synod at Antioch in 268. Sabellianism reared its head in Libya and the Pentapolis, and it was attacked by Dionysius, bishop of Alexandria, in terms so extreme that he was rebuked in a significant correspondence by his namesake, Dionysius of Rome (259–268), who was as troubled as Callistus had been by the pluralism and subordinationism of the Logos theology. It was Tertullian—and even more, perhaps, his Roman disciple Novatian (fl. ca. 250), from whom we have an important treatise, *On the Trinity*—who came closest to indicating ways in which the Logos theology might be reconciled with the principle of monotheism. Settlement of these issues, however, had to await the debates, explorations, and decisions of the fourth-century church.

---

[7] Hippolytus, *Refutation of All Heresies* 9.11.13; Stevenson, *A New Eusebius,* p. 164.

Chapter 9

The Alexandrian School

TERTULLIAN'S CARTHAGE AND Hippolytus's Rome were cities far different in history, ethos, and culture from the Hellenistic metropolis of Alexandria in Egypt. Founded by Alexander the Great himself in 332 B.C., Alexandria was successively the capital of the Ptolemies' bureaucratic empire and the center of the Roman administration of Egypt. At the same time, it was one of the principal trading centers of the Mediterranean, from which the produce of the Nile valley flowed to other sections of the Roman world. Above all, it was an intellectual center, whose great library had made of it a focus of literary, scientific, and philosophical culture since the reign of the first Ptolemy. Every philosophical school had its representatives there; commerce in ideas was in the city's blood. One consequence of this fact was that Alexandria provided an arena in which religious ideas and movements of varied origin encountered and influenced one another and in which all were subject to philosophical criticism and interpretation.

Of the origins of Christianity in Alexandria, little is known. The movement must have appeared there, however, at a relatively early date, since at the time when we first hear of it, around the end of the second century, it appears to be firmly rooted. The available evidence, however, suggests that from early on Christianity in Alexandria had been divided between a learned and intellectual Christian Gnosticism (Basilides the Gnostic was teaching in Alexandria in the reign of Hadrian, ca. 130) and another community of traditionalist "simple" believers who vastly distrusted the compromises with pagan religion and philosophy which this sophisticated Gnosticism seemed to represent.

It is against this background that one must understand the work of the first great Christian teacher of Alexandria, Clement (?–ca. 215). Like Justin Martyr a convert to Christianity and, also like Justin, a professional intellectual, Clement came to Alexandria, after studying with a series of Christian teachers elsewhere, to hear the wisdom of a man whom he does not name, but whom Eusebius the church historian identifies as one Pantaenus, who had charge of the school of the faithful at Alexandria.[1] Clement settled in Alexandria and eventually, like Justin in Rome, had a "school" of his own. What is interesting and characteristic about him is that on the one hand he regarded himself as a defender and interpreter of ordinary Christianity, conscious of an obligation "in no way to transgress the rule of the Church,"[2] while on the other hand he represented that sympathetic attitude toward "secular" learning and culture which most ordinary Christians thoroughly distrusted. He was, then, very much a man in the middle, who took seriously the Gnosticism he repudiated and offered a defense of the teaching tradition that was calculated to suggest that Hellenistic philosophy was as much its ally as its foe.

The most important surviving works of Clement are three in number. There is first of all his *Exhortation to the Heathen,* a critique of pagan religion which issues in a call to follow God's Logos. Then there is the work titled *Instructor,* which seeks to spell out the logic of a Christian way of life (and is, incidentally, a mine of information about the mores of Clement's age). Finally, he wrote a work called *Stromata* or *Miscellanies,* a collection of his thoughts on the religious and theological issues of his time. Set out in seven books (a promised eighth book was never completed), the *Stromata* is deliberately unsystematic in form and allusive in style. It intimates rather than states a theological position, though it develops with great clarity Clement's position on certain issues: denigration of the flesh and of marriage, the relation of the Greek philosophical tradition to revelation, and the goal and character of the Christian life. For Clement as for Justin, the divine Logos had always been the teacher of humankind everywhere. "Our instructor is the holy God, Jesus, the Logos who is the guide of all humanity."[3] Hence, it is his inspiration which lies, in one way or another, behind the philosophical tradition of the Greeks. "God is the cause of all good things; but of some primarily, as of the Old and the New Testament; and of others by consequence, as of philosophy." In other words, Clement wanted to follow the commonplace Hellenistic-Jewish belief that the philosophers had originally gotten their best ideas from the writings of Moses. But he is capable of entertaining a yet more radical hypothesis: "Perchance, too, philosophy was given to the Greeks directly and primarily, till the Lord should call the Greeks. For this was a school-master to bring the Hellenic mind, as the Law the Hebrews, to Christ."[4]

Clement thus followed Justin and Irenaeus in seeing the history of God with humankind as a process of education—a case of *paideia.* More clearly than either of his predecessors, however, Clement used this same model to describe the Christian life of the individual believer, which for him was an affair of learning, training (*askēsis*), and growth in the knowledge of God. Where the North African Tertullian envisaged Christian life primarily in

[1] Eusebius, *Ecclesiastical History* 5.11.2.
[2] *Stromata* 7.15.90 (Stevenson, *A New Eusebius,* p. 200).
[3] *Instructor* 1.7.55.
[4] *Stromata* 1.5.28.

moral terms, as an affair of obedience to divine precept, and where Gnostics saw it to consist in a once-for-all enlightenment, Clement conceived it rather as a gradual process of moral and intellectual transformation which issued in likeness to God—the destiny implied in Adam's creation "after the image of God."

Such likeness to God is, for Clement, as for Irenaeus before him, coincident with knowledge of God, since to know something is to participate in its way of being. Thus, the Christian ideal is that of the "true gnostic," who to faith has added knowledge, "to knowledge, love; and to love, the inheritance."[5] "There seems to me," Clement writes, "to be a first kind of saving change from heathenism to faith, a second from faith to knowledge; and this latter, as it passes on into love, begins at once to establish a mutual friendship between knower and known," until, continuing to advance, the self "presses on . . . to that which is indeed the Lord's abode" and remains there as "a light standing and abiding forever, absolutely secure from all vicissitude."[6]

Clement left Alexandria in 202, in the face of the persecution which occurred there in the reign of Septimius Severus; nothing is known of his life thenceforth. At Alexandria, however, the sort of work he had done was continued, though in a vastly different style and spirit, by his pupil Origen, the greatest and most influential Christian thinker of his age, whose work won him the grudging respect even of such a radically anti-Christian philosopher as the Neoplatonist Porphyry.

Born into a Christian family at Alexandria between 182 and 185, Origen, after Clement's departure and the death of his father, Leonidas, in the persecution, gathered a group of inquirers and constituted a school, which may or may not have been a continuation of the catechetical school of which Eusebius speaks. In any case, Origen was able to continue his work there, with the approval of the bishop, Demetrius, until 215, when the emperor Caracalla drove all teachers of philosophy from Alexandria. Origen had already done some traveling—to Rome (ca. 211–212), where he met Hippolytus, and to Arabia (ca. 213–214), where his services were wanted to deal with a problem created by monarchian teaching. This time, however, he went to Caesarea in Palestine, where he made friends of permanent value. He resumed his teaching in Alexandria in 216 and continued there until 230 or 231, when he set out on a journey to Greece. In the course of a stay in Caesarea, he was ordained presbyter at the instance of his friends there, probably in order that he might be free to preach. However, Bishop Demetrius—who had in any case become doubtful about some of Origen's unusual ideas, was almost certainly jealous of his success, and tended to listen to hostile gossip about him—regarded this act of the Caesarean church as an invasion of his rights; accordingly, he seized the opportunity to have Origen severed from the communion of the Alexandrian church, and

[5] *Stromata* 7.10.55.   [6] *Stromata* 7.10.57.

Origen spent the remainder of his career writing, teaching, and preaching in Caesarea, with a discipline and dedication that earned him the nickname "Adamantius." He was imprisoned and tortured in the Decian persecution of 250 and died either in Caesarea or in Tyre, probably in 251 (254?), as a consequence of his sufferings.

Origen was a man of many-sided learning. He was an adept of the philosophy of his day, with an exact and thoughtful grasp of the ideas of the several schools of thought. His general outlook, moreover, was shaped by the eclectic Middle Platonism prevalent in Alexandria and the East, whose commonplaces he took, quite naturally, for granted. Nevertheless, he had a much more distant and less enthusiastic view of philosophy and culture in the Hellenic tradition than either Clement or Justin. He was not given to cordial or needless quotation of poets or philosophers, though he knew them well enough, as his learned apologetic work *Against Celsus* demonstrates; and his way of handling the commonplaces of Middle Platonism seemed, to a pagan thinker like Porphyry, to mingle "Greek ideas" with "foreign myths."[7] The explanation of this complex attitude is that by conscious conviction Origen was certain that the only way to wisdom was through prayerful and exacting study of the divine revelation in the Scriptures. It was this task to which he dedicated his life. The vast majority of his writings took the form of commentary on Scripture, and even his occasional "systematic" writings proceeded by a method which was largely exegetical. If the wisdom which he discerned in the Bible was in fact informed by the philosophical assumptions that he brought to its interpretation, the resultant understanding was nevertheless, for him, scriptural. Perhaps Origen's most significant gift to the churches was the principle, by which he himself lived, of *sola scriptura*.

Origen's study of Scripture had systematic textual work as its foundation. In an effort to assure a correct text for the Septuagint version of the Hebrew Scriptures—the version regularly used in the churches—he compiled over the years his monumental *Hexapla,* which in parallel columns gave the Hebrew, a Greek transliteration of the Hebrew, the Septuagint, and three other Greek versions. In his exegesis, he repudiated the literalism of the rabbis and of Marcion. For one thing, he was convinced that in many places the literal sense was absurd, as in the fable of Jotham, where trees are found talking;[8] or unworthy of its subject, as where God is portrayed losing his temper; or inconsistent with other passages, as in many Gospel pericopes. For another, he was certain that writings inspired by God's Spirit must superabound in meaning, so that even where the literal sense is important, much more is meant than is directly said. The task of the exegete, therefore, is to disengage not merely the literal but also the higher or deeper "spiritual" sense, in accordance with Paul's admonition and practice.[9] This way of conceiving and handling

---

[7] Eusebius, *Ecclesiastical History* 6.19.7.   [8] Judg. 9:7-15.   [9] 2 Cor. 3:6; Gal. 4:21-27.

the Scriptures owed much to earlier precedent—to Stoic allegorization of the Homeric poems and, above all, to Philo's allegorical exegesis of the Pentateuch. At the same time, Origen was indebted to early Christian typology, which interpreted the Hebrew Scriptures retrospectively, finding their key and their "deep" meaning in Christ and in the Christian dispensation. Accordingly, for Origen, the fundamental bearing of the spiritual sense of Scripture is on our understanding of the human self's relation to God in Christ, of the life of the church as the community of the new dispensation, and of the fulfillment of that life in the "restoration of all things" (for the Law, we are told, is a "shadow of things to come"[10]). In the third book of his treatise *On First Principles* (*Peri archōn*), he justifies and attempts to systematize his exegetical procedures; but since his practice was more flexible than his theory, this earliest Christian treatise on hermeneutics offers only a very imprecise idea of what Origen actually did.

Even in the midst of his exegetical labors, however, Origen could not ignore the immediate problems of the church in Alexandria. Like Clement, he was bound to address himself to the problem created by the presence of a vocal gnostic community and to do so in a way which enlisted philosophical learning on the side of orthodoxy. It is typical of him that he carried out this task not by engaging in lengthy polemic but by developing systematically a position which handled the questions and ideas in which Gnostics traded, but did so in a different sense: that is, in accord with the church's teaching tradition, which Origen understood to be not (as Tertullian had argued) a sufficient formulation of truth, but the foundation and starting point of theological inquiry. The result was a theological cosmology in which Platonist and even gnostic themes were sounded, but only as transposed into a key defined by the principles of the Alexandrian teaching tradition.

This theological cosmology, set out in the early treatise *On First Principles,* turns on three central ideas. The first of these, which was equally central for Irenaeus, is simply the monotheistic axiom that there is one God, who is the sole ground and source of all being, material and immaterial alike. The second idea, also crucial for Irenaeus, is the anti-gnostic principle that evil is not a substantive thing or kind of thing (such as matter or flesh) but a disorder introduced by the free agency of created selves. If there is evil in the world, it is not ultimately an external affliction of humanity but a product of human choice. Finally, Origen accepted an old tradition of interpretation, already exploited by Philo, which held that the two accounts of creation in the opening chapters of Genesis reflected, in fact, two stages of divine creation, the first concerned with the appearance of the immaterial, intelligible order and the second with the formation of the visible cosmos. Accordingly, it was Origen's conviction that God's original creation was a society of immaterial "spirits," finite because created, self-determining because rational. Images or reflections of

---

[10] *On First Principles,* preface.

God's own image, the Logos, these spirits lived in the harmony of perfect equality, rejoicing in that knowledge of God which was the proper fulfillment of their nature. Evil intruded when these spirits, becoming satiated with the vision of God, chose to fall away from their own happiness, God, into a self-willed state of separateness, variety, and multiplicity. Some became demons and others angels and yet others the souls of human beings, but all, to one degree or another, fell from their original focused identity into distraction and alienation. As a consequence and symbol of their altered state, God then brought into being the physical, visible cosmos, to be for these creatures a second-best world—a world in which harmony was imposed on disorder and in which the fallen spirits could be "schooled" back to their original glory.

From this account, it is apparent what redemption meant for Origen. It meant "the restoration of all things" to that original unity and harmony where, as Paul had said, "God will be all in all." The process by which this final restoration comes about is, for Origen as for Clement, essentially one of education and training, for God respects the freedom of his creatures and will not (indeed, cannot) save them in spite of themselves. The central moment in this divine tutelage is the incarnation of God's eternal Logos, in whom, as Wisdom, God's mind and being are articulated for creatures. The Logos draws near to fallen human beings through the mediation of the one rational creature that did not fall: the human self which is Jesus. It was Origen's understanding that this one unfallen spirit, by the intensity of its love for God, was so united with the Logos as to be virtually indistinguishable from him—in the same way, he says, as iron is indistinguishable from the fire which turns it red hot. In turn, the union of Jesus' soul with a body brings about the incarnation of the divine Son/Logos. This fleshly existence of God's Son enables human beings to rise through faith to a knowledge of the eternal truth which the historical life of the Christ bodies forth—a truth which is always the same, yet always adapted to the varying capacities and needs of its recipients. Origen seems in fact to conceive the Christ in a way analogous to that in which he conceives the Scriptures: what the letter of Scripture is to its deeper meaning, the flesh of Christ is to his Logos-nature—an adumbration of the truth which is life. And the destiny of the individual human being is to share the identity of the human Jesus as he participates in divine life through the Logos.

Like all great theological creations, this scheme of Origen's raised as many questions as it answered. It seemed, for example, to take the gnostic side on the issue of bodily resurrection; for plainly, in Origen's view, though flesh is not evil, neither is it, as Irenaeus had insisted, an essential or original constituent of human nature. Again, Origen's stress on the mutability and freedom of rational creatures raised, for him as for his critics and followers, the question whether redemption could ever be truly final—whether, in fact, the cycle of fall and restoration might not be everlastingly repeated. By the same token, his conviction that the final restoration must indeed include "all things" led him to the universalistic conclusion that even Satan and the demons did not fall outside the scope of God's love, a view that accorded ill with most earlier eschatology, which had as definite a place for Hell as it did for Heaven.

It was not merely in the realm of eschatology, however, that Origen's scheme made difficulties, but also in the whole area of the problem of creation and of God's relation to the world. Skeptics had often raised a needling question about what God was doing before he created the world. Origen's answer to the challenge implied in this question was simply to deny that there is any "before" and "after" in God. If God's being and doing are strictly timeless, however, and if, therefore, he is the Creator unchangeably, then it seems that the world he creates must be without beginning or end in time; and this conclusion Origen appears to have considered seriously, though he was uncertain about it. He did, however, insist that the "beginning" of which Genesis and the Fourth Gospel speak is not the world's temporal start but its eternal ground, God's Wisdom. If this be true, however, then God's Wisdom—that is, God's Son and Logos—is also eternal or timeless, coeval with God as God's first self-expression and perfect image. Did this mean, though, that Logos and world, since each in its different way is coeval with God, are therefore equally primordial with God? And is such a conclusion consistent with monotheism? Origen had good answers to these questions. The "eternal generation" of the Logos did not for him imply that the Logos is God's equal; being "generated" or "begotten" entailed being secondary—i.e., subordinate. On the other hand, this subordination of the Logos to God, as of radiance to source, did not rank the Son among creatures, since he was not, like them, generated "out of nothing" as a mutable and so a temporal being. This distinction, however, depended entirely on Origen's denial that God exists, and hence that God generates or creates, "in time"; and not enough people understood him on this point for his solution to the problems of creation and of the Logos theology to prevail. This fact became all too apparent in the Arian controversy, where one side espoused Origen's subordinationism, and the other, his idea of the eternal generation of the Logos, while neither seems to have understood what these notions meant in Origen's system.

Chapter 10

Church and Roman Society
from 180 to 260

THE OPENING and middle decades of the third century—the era of Tertullian, of Hippolytus, of Origen and Cyprian—marked a period of crisis and change both for the Roman empire itself and for the Christian communities within it. Where the empire was concerned, this crisis had many roots. The most obvious of these, and the one which increasingly dominated the consciousness of rulers and people alike, was military in nature. Beginning in the reign of Marcus Aurelius (d. 180), the barbarian tribes beyond the empire's Rhine and Danube frontiers, now organized into larger and more formidable groupings, again and again invaded and ravaged its provinces. After 235, there was added to this pressure that of the new Sassanid dynasty in Persia, which was bent on reconquest of the territories that had once belonged to the empire of Darius and Xerxes. Rome therefore found itself engaged in a struggle for survival, and there were times in the later part of the third century when its prospects for survival looked dim indeed.

These military pressures, moreover, did not stand alone in troubling the Roman world. They revealed and accentuated other weaknesses in the life of the empire. The army of necessity grew in size and in power. Its needs absorbed more and more of the wealth of the ordinary citizenry. Taxation became heavier and accelerated the flight of overburdened peasants from their land, even as it progressively impoverished the upper classes in the provincial cities. To get more money, emperors allowed the coinage to be debased, with the result that, as the third century wore on, a galloping inflation overtook the empire. These economic and social problems were accompanied by what amounted to a constitutional crisis. Marcus Aurelius had deserted the practice by which each emperor chose and "adopted" a successor capable of carrying out the imperial office. The hereditary principle to which he and his immediate successors returned ultimately failed to produce men who were able to lead the empire in its time of crisis. In consequence, emperors after 235 came and went (with startling frequency) at the will of the armies, their survival depending upon their military success and their ability to command the loyalty of their troops.

This situation of growing crisis and instability—which the empire survived in the end only by unparalleled military exertion and by its reconstitution under Diocletian and Constantine—had a religious dimension as well. Never had the good will and assistance of the gods seemed more necessary to Rome and to its individual subjects. Never had the imperial office itself stood in greater need of a religious sanction for its authority. It is symptomatic of these facts that early in the third century there was a revival of the imperial cult, and that with the later Severan emperors (218–235) there was an effort at religious unification under the aegis of the "Unconquered Sun" (*Sol Invictus*), whose rule the emperor symbolized.

In these circumstances, the Christian communities in the third century found themselves in an ambiguous and uncertain position. One factor in this situation was, of course, their own continuing expansion and consolidation. By this time, Christianity was widespread in Egypt, Asia Minor, Syria, North Africa, and Italy. It was a growing movement in Gaul and in Spain. It was predominantly urban and so eminently visible; in some places, moreover, its followers were sufficiently numerous that writers like Tertullian and Origen could question whether it could ever be extirpated. Furthermore, the Christian movement was not merely a trend of opinion or belief, a "school of thought." To join it was to become part of a separately organized, centripetal community, which not only had its own leaders and officers, its own characteristic rites in baptism and eucharist, its own calendar of observances and celebrations, its own properties and finances, but also maintained a continuing hostility toward the religious foundations of Roman society. Not all Christians shared the rigorist outlook of the Montanists or of a thinker like Hippolytus of Rome, who identified the Roman state as Antichrist. Origen, devotee though he was of the martyr's vocation, had room in his vision of things for the work of the Roman empire, and his and Clement's intellectual labors had staked a claim for Christianity in the cultural heritage of the late antique world. Nevertheless, he and his fellow Christians were clear in their minds that the reality on which their common life was based—the reality of God's gift in Christ—was inconsistent with the claim of pagan religion, which they persisted in regarding as a trafficking with demons. Even in its more "liberal" moments, therefore, the church tended to appear in the cities of the Roman world as that most knotty of problems for any political or cultural order: an alternative society.

Christianity, then, in the third century found its position altered. Whereas before it had been an affair of too little significance to be taken seriously by either political or intellectual leaders, it now attracted attention in high quarters, the more so since the third century was an era of crisis. The philosopher Celsus had already, in the time of Irenaeus, attacked the Christians in his *True*

Word, which eventually required a reply from Origen himself. In the third century, Porphyry (232–305), the Neoplatonist philosopher and interpreter Plotinus (205–270), went further and directed a learned work in fifteen books against the Christians. Among the emperors, on the other hand, some were tolerant of Christianity and some positively interested in it. Caracalla (211–217) let believers alone; although Scapula, the proconsul of Africa (211–212), proceeded against Christians during his brief administration there, this was apparently on his own initiative. Alexander Severus (222–235), under the dominant influence of his mother Julia Mamaea (who once summoned Origen to Antioch to converse with her on religious issues), practiced a conscious tolerance and even employed a Christian scholar, Julius Africanus, to supervise construction of a library near the Pantheon in Rome. It is true that Septimius Severus (192–211) had issued a decree forbidding conversions to Judaism or to Christianity and that this decree had brought about local persecutions both in Alexandria and in Carthage in 202. In general, however, the first half of the third century was a time of peace, expansion, and growing confidence for the churches.

In 247, the emperor Philip the Arab, known for his sympathy toward Christians, participated in solemn rites to celebrate the millennium of the Roman state. Christians refused to take part in these ceremonies, even though they occurred at a time of military danger and incipient civil disorder, for it was the ancient gods of Rome who were being glorified. It is perhaps not surprising, therefore, that Origen should, in 248, have observed among the general populace a growing distaste for Christians, who had thus called attention to themselves as noncooperative outsiders. In the same year, a series of Gothic invasions of the empire began. Unable to cope, Philip the Arab was overthrown by a conservative Illyrian soldier-emperor named Decius (249–251), whose aim was the restoration of Roman glory through a return to the virtues and the gods that had made Rome great in the past. In the very year of Decius's accession, there was a popular uprising against Christians in Alexandria. Then Decius himself acted, instituting what was in effect the first universal persecution of the churches.

He began in January 250 by arresting leaders of the churches. Fabian, bishop of Rome, was executed; Cyprian of Carthage and Dionysius of Alexandria went into hiding. In June, Decius decreed that all inhabitants of the empire must call upon the gods for aid by sacrificing to them and further must prove that they had done so by procuring official certificates (*libelli*) to that effect. Imprisonment and torture, such as Origen suffered, were the consequences of refusal. The persecution was brief; Decius went off on a campaign in the Danubian provinces and was killed in 251. But the effect on the church seemed little short of catastrophic. Origen and Cyprian alike record that great masses of Christians rushed to sacrifice or to purchase the requisite *libelli* from friendly officials. The bishop of Smyrna, successor to the martyred Polycarp, apostatized, as did (to Cyprian's dismay) two North African bishops. In the last years of Decius's successor Valerian (253–260), the persecution was renewed. This time the decree was explicitly aimed at the leaders of the churches—clergy in the first instance, and then prominent laypersons, the latter of whom were threatened with loss of property and privilege. It was this phase of the persecution which claimed the lives of Cyprian and of Sixtus II of Rome.

These persecutions gave the churches a shock which no doubt had a permanent effect on their life and self-understanding. We have seen how they induced in Cyprian a reinterpretation of the traditional North African understanding of the church. What they did not accomplish, however, was a significant reduction in the numbers of Christians. Both those who had sacrificed (*sacrificati*) and those who had purchased certificates (*libellatici*) seem in general to have sought readmission to the churches. It was not their beliefs but their courage which had failed. They were, moreover, encouraged in their desire by the confessors (those imprisoned for their faith), who assumed that the witness they had borne gave them authority to forgive and restore those who had lapsed, and who, at least in North Africa, proposed to make indiscriminate use of this privilege. Others, of a more rigorist disposition, thought that there could be no forgiveness for apostasy. The bishops, their authority challenged by the confessors, were inclined on the whole to readmit the lapsed, but only under conditions that would maintain the discipline of the church. Thus, the North African bishops prescribed lengthy penance for the *libellatici* and even permitted the restoration of the *sacrificati,* though only at the moment of death.

This middle-of-the-road policy, followed in its essentials at Rome as well, produced reactions on both sides. At Rome, the presbyter Novatian, author of an important treatise, *On the Trinity,* led a rigorist schism in the conviction that a church that restored apostates betrayed its own nature and calling. In Carthage, on the other hand, another presbyter, Novatus by name, created a schism in support of the authority of the confessors and their "laxist" policy. Even if the persecutions did not greatly reduce the numbers of Christians, then, they thoroughly troubled the churches and brought the problem of discipline and forgiveness, long a source of debate, to a head (see II:15). The cessation of the persecutions, moreover, while it introduced a period of peace for the Christian communities, by no means marked a settlement of their status in the Roman world. In the end, such a settlement could be produced only by significant changes in the life of church and empire alike.

Chapter 11

The Constitutional Development
of the Church

WHATEVER the uncertainties and crises of Christian existence in the third century, the fact remains that during the greater part of that period the churches enjoyed relative peace. It was, therefore, an era of expansion for the churches in most parts of the Roman world, and with expansion there came a development and consolidation of the church's organization on the foundations already laid in the second century. These developments affected the status and articulation of the official ministry, the internal organization of individual churches, and the relations of churches to one another.

The word "church" continued to denote primarily the assembly of Christians in a particular place—that is, in practice, a particular *polis* with its urban center and rural hinterland. Such "cities," however, varied greatly in size, from cosmopolitan centers like Rome, Alexandria, or Antioch, to what were by modern standards no more than small towns, and the size and complexity of Christian congregations varied accordingly. In some places, all the Christians could meet together in one location for their regular eucharistic assembly; in others, like Rome and Alexandria, subsidiary centers developed which eventually came to have something like the character of the later "parish" (*paroikia*). Whatever the size and complexity of the congregation, however, its unity or *consensio* (to use Cyprian's term) was represented in the fact that the local bishop was the leader and pastor of the entire congregation. Chosen by the congregation, the bishop was ordained with laying-on of hands by neighboring bishops—an indication of the fact that in his pastoral charge he was the representative not merely of the congregation to which he belonged but also of the universal church. Once elected and ordained, he was the ruler in the congregation. The bishop administered the community's financial affairs, was its principal teacher, chose and ordained its other ministers (presbyters, deacons, and others), enforced its discipline, and presided at its baptismal and eucharistic assemblies. In virtue of the fact that he "offered the sacrifices" (as *1 Clement*

98

put it at the end of the first century[1]) in the eucharistic liturgy, the bishop came to be called *sacerdos* or *hiereus* ("priest"), a title that could also be applied to his colleagues, the presbyters.

The bishop, however, was not alone in the exercise of administrative, pastoral, and liturgical leadership. The third century saw a growth in the number of offices (Greek *klēroi,* whence the English "clerk," "cleric," and "clergy") or orders (Latin *ordines,* whence the English "ordination") that served the churches. Increasingly distinguished from non-officeholders, who were called *laikoi* or *plebs* ("laity," "people"), the occupants of these offices and orders included not only bishop, deacons, and presbyters, but also, from time to time, lectors, widows, subdeacons, virgins, deaconesses, catechists, acolytes, exorcists, and doorkeepers. Needless to say, such development was more elaborate in large communities than in small and in any case occurred at a slow, informal, and uneven pace. Most prominent among these officeholders were undoubtedly the deacons, who, as the bishop's personal assistants, not only played an important liturgical role but also were in direct charge of carrying out the community's charitable work. Their number was often (as in Rome) limited to seven in accordance with Acts 6:3. Bishop Fabian of Rome (236–250), a martyr in the Decian persecution, appears to have divided his city, for purposes of ecclesiastical administration, into seven regions, each of which had a deacon as its supervisor. It is understandable, then, that when a bishop died it was most often one of his deacons who was elected in his place.

The order of presbyters, however, was gaining in importance during this era, particularly in churches where the number or geographical distribution of Christians made a single local gathering under the bishop's presidency difficult or impossible. Originally the bishop's associates, counselors, and colleagues, presbyters had played a role which, if dignified, was also shadowy. In their new circumstances, however, they became the bishop's representatives or delegates at local gatherings for instruction and, ultimately, for celebration of the eucharist. Thus, a presbyter might travel to, or become resident in, a suburban or rural area within the bishop's charge, or he might preside over neighborhood assemblies within a large city. In a few places, where a bishop's charge came to embrace more than one city, it was presbyters who became, at least for a while, the principal pastors for newly established congregations. The tendency was, however, to believe that every center of Christian population should have its own bishop; in the province of Africa, by the end of the third century, there were bishops in approximately two hundred cities and towns.

Alongside deacons and presbyters, members of the so-called minor orders functioned in central roles in the life of the churches. The order of deaconesses, for example, appears to have been more than minor, at least in the Syrian churches whose practice is represented by the injunctions of the third-century

---

[1] *1 Clement* 44.4.

Didascalia Apostolorum. In this text, they are referred to simply as "deacons" and are assigned a special ministry to women, on the ground that "our Lord and Savior also was ministered unto by women ministers."[2] Subdeacons, who are known from Carthage as well as Rome, were assistants to the deacons in their liturgical and administrative work. The order of widows, whose membership and regulation was a problem as early as the end of the first century, was devoted to prayer and to the visitation of the sick and needy. One of the most frequently mentioned of the orders is that of the lector, to whom the public reading of the Scriptures in the liturgy was assigned and who may well have been the custodian of the books from which he read. Another common office was that of catechist, and in the third century, with the more elaborate organization of the catechumenate (see II:13), this would have been a post of great dignity and responsibility.

Apart from the elaboration of offices and orders in the churches, the third century saw another development of special importance for the life of the Christian communities. In spite of their extralegal status, and no doubt because in many if not all places their existence was recognized de facto, the churches in the person of their bishops became the owners of property. They had, of course, from the beginning disposed of monies contributed as offerings by the faithful. They had not, however, owned buildings or other real property. Their places of assembly were private homes made available to them by individual believers. In the course of the third century, though, they began to acquire, if not to build, their own places of assembly, as excavations at Dura-Europos (in eastern Syria) and at Aquileia have revealed. The Roman church seems to have begun to acquire its own cemeteries in the time of Zephyrinus. This evidence, sparse though it is, probably represents a common and general trend, for the issue of the restoration of church properties looms large in the imperial decrees of toleration at the beginning of the fourth century. Whether such properties were normally acquired by purchase or (as seems the more likely alternative) by legacy and gift is unknown. In any case, their acquisition would have meant additional administrative burdens (as well as additional temptations) for the bishop and his deacons, as well as a potential source of regular income both for charitable works and for support of the church's activities and officers.

Finally, it is in the third century that we see the beginnings, though the very bare beginnings, of an organization of the church above the local level. Already in the second century, as a result of the Montanist crisis in Asia Minor and the debate over the date of Easter, councils of bishops had been held on a regional basis to discuss and resolve common problems. In many sections of the Christian world, this practice became a common one. The bishops, as representatives and leaders of their churches, would meet to deal with some burning

---

[2] R. H. Connolly, ed., *Didascalia Apostolorum* (Oxford, 1929), pp. 147f.

issue (as in the series of councils held in the East to consider the case of the monarchian Paul of Samosata) or simply to discuss common problems. In some areas, such councils or synods came to be held on a regular basis. In the province of Africa—in accord with Cyprian's teaching about the nature of the bishop's office and his example in resorting to conciliar action to resolve the problem of the lapsed—councils came to be held annually.

Hand in hand with the development of conciliar institutions, a system began to appear in which certain churches and their bishops were recognized as having a special eminence and authority in a particular province or area. These were ordinarily the churches of the provincial capitals and also, for just that reason, the centers from which Christianity had originally spread in their region. Thus, Carthage was the site of the "mother church" of the province of Africa, and its bishop, at least from the time of Cyprian, summoned and presided at councils of bishops in that province. Similarly, the Roman church and its bishop had a natural superintendence over the churches of most of Italy, as did Alexandria over those in Egypt. Eventually—but not until the fourth century—this nascent system of organization gave rise not to one but to two levels of higher jurisdiction. In the East, and much more gradually in the West, each province came to have its "metropolitan" church and bishop. But some churches—notably Rome, Alexandria, Antioch, and Carthage—were acknowledged to have an authority which extended over an area much larger than that of a single province. Such churches came, at a later period, to be called "patriarchal," and in the West, as also at Alexandria in the East, it was the bishops of these sees to whom the style "pope" (*papas*) came regularly, though not at first exclusively, to be applied.

Chapter 12

Public Worship and Sacred Time

FROM THE EARLIEST TIMES, Christians assembled regularly on the first day of the week,[1] whose beginning they reckoned, in traditional Jewish fashion, to the sunset of the day before. The observance of this day was central in the pattern of their lives, and they had their own names for it, even though they

---

[1] Acts 20:7; 1 Cor. 16:2.

were accustomed to its common pagan name, *dies solis* ("Sun-day"). They called it "the Lord's Day,"[2] presumably because it was by tradition the day of the Lord's resurrection. They also called it "the eighth day,"[3] because as the day on which "God inaugurated a new world"[4] it fell "beyond" the confines of the ordinary week in the same way that God's kingdom transcends the ordinary world. It was, therefore, a day of celebration, unsuited to gloom or sadness. The tradition grew up that on this day no one was allowed to fast or to kneel.

The business of these first-day assemblies was to celebrate the new life and the hope which believers shared in the risen Christ. Accordingly, one of the marks of the day was participation in a ritual meal that repeated and bore the sense of the Lord's actions at his Last Supper with the disciples. On that occasion, according to the liturgical tradition whose earliest form is found in 1 Corinthians 11:23–25, Jesus, when he came to the customary thanksgiving over the bread (at the beginning of the meal) and over "the cup of blessing" (at the meal's end), set these elements apart. They were to be symbols of himself in his triumphant dying and of the "new covenant" between God and humanity which was the fruit of that dying. The meal, therefore, as the church repeated it, was understood to be a proclamation "of the Lord's death until he comes"[5] and at the same time a way in which the church participated, here and now, in the new life of the risen Christ, the "life of the age to come." In the earliest times, this ritual meal was just that: a common meal of the community into which, at one point or another, the crucial thanksgivings over bread and cup and the sharing of them were incorporated. In time, however—perhaps because of the sorts of problems that Paul had encountered in his Corinthian congregation[6]—the thanksgiving and communion were separated from the communal meal and became an independent rite. The transition was complete by the time of Justin Martyr. In his description of Christian worship on the Lord's Day,[7] the eucharist ("thanksgiving") figures prominently, but the actions of the Last Supper no longer occur in the context of an ordinary meal. As a result, there is one thanksgiving said over bread and cup together, in which "the president of the brethren . . . sends up praise and glory to the Father of the universe through the name of the Son and of the Holy Spirit, and offers thanksgiving at some length that we have been deemed worthy to receive these things from him." Afterward the "deacons give to each of those present a portion of the 'thanksgivinged' bread and wine and water, and they take it to the absent."[8]

It was not celebration of the eucharist alone, however, which marked primitive observance of the Lord's Day. From the time of the first Christian generation, believers had regularly gathered—and not merely on the first day—

[2] Rev. 1:10. [4] *Epistle of Barnabas* 15:8. [6] 1 Cor. 11:17–22. [8] Ibid., 65.
[3] Cf. John 20:26. [5] 1 Cor. 11:26. [7] *1 Apol.* 67, and cf. 65–66.

for an exercise of praise, instruction, and prayer: a service modeled on (and no doubt in many cases simply identical with) the worship of the synagogue. By Justin's time, such an assembly, with added emphasis on the reading of Scripture, was the normal beginning of the liturgy of the "first day." "On the day called Sunday there is a meeting . . . and the memoirs of the apostles or the writings of the prophets are read as long as time permits. When the reader has finished, the president in a discourse urges and invites to the imitation of these noble things. Then we all stand up together and offer prayers."[9] Such gatherings were not, and were not intended to be, brief or brisk. The readings, as Justin suggests, were long. Other sources indicate that they were interspersed with, and perhaps also preceded by, the singing of psalms. In some places in the third century, the bishop's "discourse" followed upon similar homilies by any of the presbyters who wished to speak, and no doubt this was the primary setting for the utterances of prophets. The prayers which followed the preaching were the community's intercessions; before they began, those who had not yet been baptized were dismissed (for "you must not let anyone eat or drink of your Eucharist except those baptized in the Lord's name"[10]), and when they had been completed the celebration of the eucharistic meal followed. Thus, the cycle of the week was fulfilled, as Tertullian phrased it,[11] by administration of "the word" and offering of "the sacrifice" of bread and wine with thanksgiving.

This cycle of the week was early supplemented by a second which had the year as its basis and which centered in the Christian observance of the *Pascha*—Passover or Easter. That the early Christians—even the Gentiles among them—understood the symbolism of the Passover and attached great significance to it is evident from the way in which Paul insists upon a Christological interpretation of it ("Christ our Passover has been sacrificed"[12]), not to mention the emphasis placed by the Fourth Gospel (which in this point differs from the other Gospels) on the fact that Jesus died "on the day of Preparation of the Passover,"[13] when the lambs for the celebration were being slaughtered. Easter, then, became for Christians the celebration of the new Exodus—the dying of Christ into life, which had been prefigured in the liberation of the Israelites from Egypt. The churches of Asia Minor long preserved what was probably the original custom of celebrating the feast on the fourteenth day of the Hebrew month Nisan, the traditional date of Passover, but the Palestinian, Alexandrian, and Roman habit of adapting the Passover celebration to the pattern of the Christian week eventually prevailed, and Easter became a "first day" festival. It was marked, however, by special observances (notably by a great vigil during the hours of darkness preceding the dawn of the Sunday), and it followed a solemn fast, which by Hippolytus's time in Rome extended back through the

[9] Ibid., 67. [11] *On the Apparel of Women* 2.11.2. [13] John 19:14, 31.
[10] *Didache* 9.5. [12] 1 Cor. 5:7.

Friday. The third century in the East saw the fast extended to encompass the entirety of what was to become "Holy Week." Easter thus became the central festival of the Christian year, and by the third century it was celebrated not for one day only but, in effect, for fifty days—the whole season from Passover itself to Pentecost (the Jewish feast of Weeks), which commemorated the total "mystery" of salvation as comprised in the triumph of Christ and his gift of the Holy Spirit.

Chapter 13

Baptism

*T*HE RITE OF BAPTISM, closely associated with the Christian Passover both in its use and in its meaning, was from the most primitive times the mode of formal initiation into the eschatological community of God's people in Christ. The use of washing in water to symbolize penitence and purification had ample precedent in Jewish (not to mention pagan) tradition. Quite apart from the various lustrations prescribed in Leviticus and those ritually employed in the Qumran community, there is the probable use of washings in the making of a proselyte to Judaism. The immediate precursor of Christian baptism, however, was that practiced by John "the Baptizer"—a baptism which signified penitence and conversion and so is described in Mark 1:4 as being "for the forgiveness of sins." John's was apparently a rite which looked forward to the messianic era and to the renewal of the gift of the Spirit which that would bring.[1] It was an act which aimed to prepare a people to greet the Messiah.

The Christian use of baptism began, as far as we can tell, only after the experience of the resurrection. It differed from John's, therefore, because it symbolized entry upon the new relation to God that had been realized in the death and resurrection of the Messiah, Jesus, and so conferred the eschatological gift of the Spirit. This much is evident from our earliest witness, Paul. In spite of his assertion that his own calling was to preach and not to baptize,[2] Paul knows and assumes that all of his converts "were washed . . . sanctified . . . justified in the name of our Lord Jesus Christ and in the Spirit of our God."[3] What this means to him is that in this washing and the confession of faith

---

[1] Mark 1:7–8.   [2] I Cor. 1:17.   [3] I Cor. 6:11.

which accompanies it,[4] believers have "put on Christ."[5] They have been "buried
. . . with him by baptism into death."[6] Hence, they are no longer enslaved to
sin but in baptism have made the crucial transition to a new order of existence.
"You . . . must consider yourselves dead to sin and alive to God in Jesus
Christ."[7] This participation in the death and new life of Christ, moreover, is
effected by the gift of the Spirit. "By one Spirit we were all baptized into one
body . . . and all were made to drink of one Spirit,"[8] with the result, Paul says,
that the community of believers is "God's temple," in which God's Spirit
dwells.[9]

   In the light of this Pauline understanding of baptism, it is not surprising
that later writers also take a serious view of it. For the author of the Fourth
Gospel, baptism means being "born anew . . . of water and the Spirit," and
apart from it none can "enter the kingdom of God."[10] In the First Epistle of
Peter, the water of baptism is compared to the waters of the flood which saved
Noah and his family.[11] Hermas, in his *Shepherd,* records a prophetic vision of
the church as a "tower" which is "built upon the waters" for the reason that
"your life was saved and shall be saved by means of water."[12] For Justin
Martyr too, baptism is "rebirth" (*anagennēsis*) into a new mode of life, which
he explains to his readers by contrasting the condition of "children of necessity
and ignorance" with that of "[children] of choice and knowledge," whose sins
have been forgiven.[13] Baptism for him is a liberation which frees people from
sin and by "enlightenment" (*phōtismos*)[14] enables them to do the will of God.
In all these testimonies, from Paul to Justin Martyr, there appears the conviction
that baptism represents a decisive moment of transition between old and new
identities, between death and life. And it is in this sense that it was universally
understood in early Christianity.

   As one might expect, there is little evidence in the largely occasional literature of the first and early second centuries which bears on the components or
the form of the baptismal rite. Nevertheless, this literature supplies indications
of the central moments of the initiatory process. At its heart, of course, lay the
washing itself. According to *Didachē,* this ought if possible to take place in
"living [i.e., flowing] water," presumably by immersion. In the absence of a
stream, however, it was acceptable to use standing water and even to "pour
water on the head."[15] Clearly, moreover, this washing was always accompanied
by a confession of faith, the only "baptismal formula" known to the early
church. Paul was baptized as he "called on [the Lord's] name";[16] and the
treasurer of Queen Candace, according to an early corrective addition to the
text of Acts, was baptized with the confession, "I believe that Jesus Christ is

[4] Rom. 10:9–10.   [9] 1 Cor. 3:16.   [14] Ibid., 61.10.
[5] Gal. 3:27.   [10] John 3:3, 5.   [15] *Didachē* 7.2–3.
[6] Rom. 6:4.   [11] 1 Pet. 3:20–21.   [16] Acts 22:16.
[7] Rom. 6:11.   [12] Hermas, *The Shepherd* ("Visions" 3.3.5).
[8] 1 Cor. 12:13.   [13] *1 Apol.* 61.3, 10.

the Son of God."[17] As we have seen (see II:4), this confession of faith began early to assume a triadic form in accordance with the language of Matthew 28:19. Believers entered upon their new life by acknowledging and affirming the threefold source of that life: Jesus the Lord, the Father who sent him, and the Father's Spirit by whom they were united in Christ's body.

The initiatory process seems, however, at least in some places, to have involved more than just washing accompanied by confession of faith. The Acts of the Apostles understands this process to consist of three elements: repentance, baptism "in the name of Jesus Christ for the forgiveness of . . . sins," and reception of "the gift of the Holy Spirit."[18] Of these three, the first is obviously in some sense preliminary or preparatory. It was a necessary presupposition of Christian initiation and took shape eventually both in certain ceremonies of the baptismal rite itself and in the institution of the catechumenate. The second element is the washing-with-confession, which Acts associates specifically with forgiveness of sins (perhaps taking a narrower view of the sense of this rite than did Paul). The third element, reception of the Spirit, the author of Acts regards as the essential *differentia* of initiation into the Christian life,[19] and he associates it (though not in the case of Cornelius the Centurion[20]) with a rite of laying-on of hands, which seems normally, though not invariably, to follow immediately upon baptism proper.[21] What Acts seems to reflect, in its somewhat confusing testimony, is the bare beginning of a process by which different moments in the meaning of Christian initiation came to be associated with successive elements in the rite itself.

The first relatively full accounts of Christian initiation come to us from the beginning of the third century—principally in the *Apostolic Tradition* of Hippolytus of Rome, but also in the reports contained in Tertullian's treatise, *On Baptism*. Both of these works testify not only to the articulation of the rite but also to its solemnity and gradual elaboration, a reflection of its pivotal place in the life and consciousness of the churches. Unlike the eucharist, which took place each Lord's Day, baptism normally occurred just once (or at most twice) in each year. It belonged, in other words, to the annual rather than the weekly cycle of celebration and occurred in connection with the observance of the Christian Passover, either at Easter itself or at Pentecost. According to Hippolytus's account,[22] the preparations for the rite began on the Thursday before the feast, at which time the candidates were instructed to bathe. On Friday and Saturday, they fasted in token of repentance. The ceremony itself began "at cock-crow" on the Lord's Day, when prayer was said over the water and the candidates stripped themselves of clothing and ornaments. Naked, they solemnly renounced Satan and his servants and his works and were anointed with "the oil of exorcism." They were then taken by a deacon into the water—

[17] Acts 8:37.   [19] Acts 8:12–17.   [21] Acts 19:6.

[18] Acts 2:37.   [20] Acts 10:44–48.   [22] *Apostolic Tradition* 20–22.

infants (for whom their parents spoke) and children first, then men, then women—where a presbyter washed each candidate three times as each made the threefold confession in response to the presbyter's questions (see II:4). Coming out of the water, the candidates were anointed a second time, with "the oil of thanksgiving," then dried, clothed, and brought to the assembled church. There the bishop laid his hand on each of them with prayer, and anointed each of them on the forehead, making the sign of the cross. The rite continued with a celebration of the eucharist, in which the newly baptized participated for the first time.

In the structure of this rite (details of which varied from church to church), it is easy to discern the lineaments of the Lucan sequence of repentance, baptism, and laying-on of hands (though neither Tertullian nor Hippolytus is at any pains, as Luke apparently was, to separate the gift of the Spirit from the baptism proper). It is also easy to appreciate how dramatically the rite symbolized a transition from one order and context of life to another.

In the course of the third century, this sense that Christian initiation represented a radical "turning" from death to new life was enhanced by the systematic development and institutionalization of the catechumenate, which lengthily extended the preliminary or preparatory stage of initiation. Already in Hippolytus, the beginnings of this development are apparent. Tertullian insists that people must prepare for baptism by prayer, fasting, and confession of sin.[23] Hippolytus, however, is not content with exhortation: he prescribes an orderly discipline for those seeking baptism. When they first offer themselves, their manner of life and their occupation is to be scrutinized; if finally admitted as candidates, they are to spend up to three years in this marginal state, being instructed (*katēchoumenoi*) and tested, before they are actually brought to baptism. As this sort of procedure became common, churches organized the progress of catechumens, bringing them solemnly by stages to an understanding of the mystery of Christian faith and life—which, as Hippolytus insists,[24] was not to be revealed to unbelievers. It was in this setting of the organized catechumenate that declaratory creeds, of the type of the later Apostles' Creed, arose to serve as bases for instruction and as summaries of Christian belief which candidates for baptism might learn by heart. One result of this whole development was that many folk spent much of their lives as catechumens. Tertullian himself—even in the face of the practice, well established by this time, of baptizing infants and children—thought it prudent for people to delay baptism until they were fully and truly prepared to lead the life which it demanded. "If there are any who understand the weightiness of baptism, they will be more afraid of attaining than of delaying it,"[25] he wrote; and to this conviction of the "weightiness" of baptism, the institution of the catechumenate was, and was meant to be, an enduring witness.

---

[23] *On Baptism* 20.   [24] *Apostolic Tradition* 23.14.   [25] *On Baptism* 18.

In the early Christian communities, then, the rite of baptism was envisaged as a matter, quite literally, of life and death. Where its significance was concerned, there were differences of emphasis, but little debate. It meant and conveyed forgiveness of sins and rebirth in Christ through the gift of the Spirit. It was therefore in the strictest sense constitutive of the church. Just because of this fact, however, debate inevitably arose, not so much about the significance of the rite as about the conditions requisite for its "true happening." Everyone would doubtless have agreed with Tertullian that any baptized person might in principle administer baptism.[26] But could baptism truly take place—could forgiveness of sins and life in the Spirit be truly conferred—in a heretical or schismatic community?

Debate was joined on this issue by Cyprian of Carthage and Stephen of Rome (254–257) when both faced the same problem: what to do about persons baptized in a schismatic body if they sought restoration to the Catholic Church. Stephen's view was that one received and restored them as penitents by the laying-on of hands—a policy which, since it treated them as properly baptized persons, seemed to admit either that schismatic bodies qualified as "church" or else that baptism could occur outside the church. Cyprian, however, would admit neither of these premises. He took the view that, since the Holy Spirit is given only in the church, the temple of God's Spirit, such persons had not been baptized at all and could be restored only by being (re-)baptized. Since Stephen died in 257 and Cyprian suffered martyrdom the following year, the debate was not settled. The North African churches continued to follow Cyprian's view, which was to become an issue again in the Donatist controversy.

[26] *On Baptism* 17.

Chapter 14

The Eucharist

OF THE EARLY understanding of the eucharist, some account has already been given. The term "eucharist" became, at least from the end of the first century, the prevalent and ordinary word for the rite which had originally, perhaps, been referred to as "the breaking of bread."[1] It denoted in the first instance, and most properly, the offering of thanksgiving to God over bread

[1] Luke 24:35; Acts 2:46.

and wine at the church's ritual meal. It came to denote, by extension, the whole of the liturgy of the Lord's Day, including the ministry of the word (see II:12), and, further, the "thanksgivinged" bread and wine itself, which the faithful shared at the climax of the meal. Since, as we have seen, what this total action symbolized was the Christ in his death and triumphant new life (the same "mystery" of Easter into which baptism initiated the believer), what its performance intended was the involvement or participation of the assembled church in the eschatological and transtemporal life of the crucified and risen Lord. This participation was consummated in the sharing of the bread and wine to which Jesus had assigned the meaning of his body and blood.

There is no lack in second- and third-century sources of references to the eucharist or of clues to the way in which early Christians saw and understood it. There is, however, almost no debate or speculation on this subject of the sort which characterized medieval and reformation attempts to systematize understanding of the rite and to rationalize it. Early Christian speech and teaching about the eucharist, like early Christian speech and teaching about baptism, move in the realm not of "literal" description or explanation but of living metaphor. Indeed, they see the rite itself as acted metaphor—not a mere figure of speech, to be sure, but the grasping of (or the being grasped by) one reality in and through another.

The clue to early Christian understanding of the eucharist perhaps lies in the idea and act of thanksgiving itself. Rooted in the Jewish "benedictions" over bread and cup, which were blessings of God for his gifts in creation and redemption, the "great thanksgiving" of the eucharist gave praise to God by confessing before him, and thus making commemoration (*anamnēsis*) of, his work of salvation in the Christ. This commemoration, however, which took place in the giving of thanks, was no mere mental act of remembering. Jews who at the Passover meal "commemorated" the Exodus were constituted, in that act, the Exodus people: the commemoration brought about a participation in the event recalled. By the same token, Christians who recalled the Christ in his saving death and resurrection through their thanksgiving to God were constituted, in that act, participants in the Christ—in all that he was and did and meant. They made this commemoration, moreover, not simply in the words of their thanksgiving but in the acts which they performed as well—the acts of taking, blessing, and sharing bread and wine. For these acts themselves were a commemoration—a reenactment of the very deeds by which Jesus had signified the New Covenant in his blood. The whole liturgy of thanksgiving, therefore, was an offering of praise to God in and through which the assembled church was grasped by the new life in Christ. There is little, then, of the unexpected in Ignatius's description of the eucharist as "the medicine of immortality,"[2] since "immortality" is his word for that new life. Nor is it incom-

---

[2] *Ephesians* 20.

prehensible when a writer like Tertullian can in one place simply identify "the Lord's body" with "the eucharist"[3] and in another assert that the bread of the eucharist has the "figure" of Christ's body[4] or "makes his body manifest"[5] (*repraesentat*). For Tertullian's purposes, the two forms of language interpreted each other and asserted, in different ways, the coincidence of the Christ in whom God once for all worked salvation and the bread and wine which "mean" him.

This conviction that the church's action in the eucharist coincided, in virtue of Christ's promise and God's graciousness, with the reality it recalled and commemorated led to a further development which can be studied in the teaching of Cyprian. From very early on,[6] it had been common to refer to the action of the eucharist as an "offering" or "sacrifice." Such language gave expression to the fact that the eucharist was an offering of praise and worship and prayer to God, and also to the fact that in it the people's "gifts" were presented to God. Thus, in the model eucharist prayer which Hippolytus provides in his *Apostolic Tradition,* the bishop says at one point, "We offer you this bread and this cup."[7] This offering of the material things of the creation for God's use had already been stressed by Irenaeus in his anti-gnostic polemic.[8] With Cyprian, however, the idea of the eucharist as sacrifice is developed in a way that had at best been implicit in some earlier writers—a way that depended ultimately on the picture of Christ as the "high priest" who effected salvation "when he offered up himself."[9] It was Cyprian's idea that the church, which through its human priest "imitates what Christ did" at the Last Supper in order to commemorate and enter into his saving work, is in fact, when it offers its own sacrifice of praise, participating in the once-for-all self-offering of Christ; for, he writes, "Christ bore us all, in that he also bore our sins," and in the eucharist "the assembly of believers is associated and conjoined with him in whom it believes."[10]

It is the idea expressed in these last words which seems most fundamentally to underlie early Christian appreciations of the eucharist. Paul had asked his Corinthian converts, "The cup of blessing which we bless, is it not a participation in the body of Christ?"[11] Cyprian, following out Paul's thought and developing a traditional figure, asserts that in the eucharist "our people are shown to be made one, so that just as many grains, gathered and ground and mixed together in one mass, make one bread, even so in Christ, who is the heavenly bread, we may know that there is one body, with which our number is joined and united."[12]

---

[3] *On Modesty* 9.
[4] *Against Marcion* 3.19.4.
[5] Ibid., 1.14.3.
[6] See *1 Clement* 44.4.

[7] *Apostolic Tradition* 4.11.
[8] Cf. *Against Heresies* 5.2.2.
[9] Heb. 7:26–27.
[10] Epistle 63 (62).13–14.

[11] 1 Cor. 10:16, and cf. 17.
[12] Epistle 63 (62).13.

Chapter 15

Forgiveness of Sins

*I*T WAS GENERALLY understood in early Christianity that baptism carried with it God's forgiveness of past sins. It was also understood that one moment in, or condition of, the baptismal gift of forgiveness was the believer's conversion or repentance (*metanoia*), which was to be evidenced not merely in acknowledgment of sin and in fasting and prayer but also in change of life—including, if necessary, change of occupation. The new Christian was expected to lead a new life, confessing Christ, avoiding idolatry, living in charity with all, practicing strict sexual purity, and eschewing the accumulation of wealth and other worldly entanglements. The standards of the Christian *disciplina,* then, were both strict and high. Inevitably, believers fell short of them—sometimes in small and ordinary ways, but at other times in ways that seemed not merely dramatic but scandalous, and, in the end, inconsistent with profession of Christian faith. Hermas, in his *Shepherd,* is shocked and outraged at "deacons . . . who devoured the living of widows and orphans,"[1] "those who quarrel with one another,"[2] "those who have the Lord on their lips but not in their heart,"[3] "those who are rich and those who are involved in a great deal of business."[4] There was, then, a serious problem for the churches in the question of what to make of, and what to do about, sins committed after baptism. Did such sins exclude the sinner from the Christian community—from the elect people of God? Could they be forgiven?

Hermas reveals a great deal about attitudes in the church of Rome at the beginning of the second century when he announces the burden of the message conveyed in his vision: that to those who heed his words, repentance will be followed by forgiveness, but "if there is still sin after this day [for repentance] has been set, they shall not have salvation."[5] Hermas's idea, however—that

---

[1] Hermas, *The Shepherd* (Similitude 9.26.2).
[2] Ibid., 9.23.2.
[3] Ibid., 9.21.1.

[4] Ibid., 9.20.1.
[5] Hermas, *The Shepherd* (Vision 2.2.4–5).

God has allowed his people, the church, just one historical opportunity for repentance—does not seem to have been representative of the normal view. It is true that the Epistle to the Hebrews (which may itself have been written at Rome) insists that "if we sin deliberately after receiving the knowledge of the truth, there no longer remains a sacrifice for sins."[6] In the Johannine churches, however, it was taught that "if we confess our sins, [God] is faithful and just, and will forgive our sins"[7]—though the author of the Johannine letters qualifies this by admitting that there is a "sin which is mortal."[8] As he sees it, then, some sins or kinds of sin are in themselves death-dealing, and for them there can be no forgiveness; but for other, more ordinary sins, God's forgiveness is always available to those who repent.

By the opening of the third century, the Johannine view had prevailed, but in a significantly developed form. On the one hand, it was generally believed that there were certain sins that were unforgivable. Commenting on the statement in 1 John that "there is a sin which is mortal," Origen makes it clear that idolatry, adultery, and fornication are sins which God does not forgive, and he upbraids bishops ("priests") who pretend to pardon such sins.[9] Tertullian also distinguishes between "remissible" and "irremissible" sins,[10] and in the latter category he includes not only idolatry, adultery, and fornication but also blasphemy and apostasy.[11] On the other hand, both of these writers are agreed that the majority of ordinary sins are to be dealt with by mutual forgiveness, by prayer, and by making satisfaction through almsgiving and fasting.

For grave sin, however, which did not figure on the list of unforgivable or "irremissible" offenses, there was, by the opening of the third century, a public penitential discipline in use at least in Egypt, North Africa, and Rome. The roots of this discipline no doubt reach far back into the history of the church. Paul instructed his Corinthian converts to exclude from their fellowship a man who was "living with his father's wife,"[12] implying that the assembled church had authority to judge and excommunicate sinners; and Matthew's Gospel accorded to the Christian assembly and its leaders the authority to "bind" and "loose."[13] In the later penitential discipline, in which just this authority was exercised, what was sought by the penitent and granted by the church was an opportunity for that "second repentance" which Hermas's vision had announced as a once-for-all possibility. The process was long and formal. Called *exomologēsis* ("acknowledgment"—i.e., of sin), it involved open confession before the assembled church, a period of penitence and exclusion from the eucharist, and finally a public restoration to the full fellowship of the church, symbolized by the laying-on of the bishop's hand. The length of the

[6] Heb. 10:26.　　[8] 1 John 5:16.　　[10] *On Modesty* 2.12.　　[12] 1 Cor. 5:1–5.

[7] 1 John 1:9.　　[9] *On Prayer* 28.8–9.　　[11] Ibid., 9.9.　　[13] Matt. 18:18, 16:18–19.

period of penitence varied with the gravity of the individual's sin or sins. It required, Tertullian tells us, that penitents "exchange for severe treatment" the sins they had committed: that they dress as mourners, eat and drink the plainest fare, and "feed prayers on fastings."[14] What is more, the privilege of *exomologēsis* was available only once in the Christian lifetime of any individual.

By the time of Origen and Tertullian, however, there was a vigorous debate over the matter of "irremissible" sins. Origen, as we have seen, knew bishops who, in his mind, exceeded their authority by allowing the repentance and restoration of idolaters, adulterers, and fornicators. Tertullian rebelled against the policy of a bishop (very likely the bishop of Carthage) who allowed penance to be performed for adultery and fornication, and whom he calls, with bitter irony, "pontifex maximus" and "bishop of bishops."[15] Hippolytus reports that his own favorite adversary, the bishop Callistus (217–222) of Rome, claimed the authority to remit (no doubt after penance) sins of the flesh and apparently even mortal sins. Callistus seems to have argued that the Lord's command to let wheat and tares "grow together until the harvest"[16] meant that the church had a place in it even for sinners,[17] a view which portended a fundamental alteration in the church's picture of itself. Tertullian and Hippolytus saw the church in the same way as had Hermas a century earlier: as the society of the redeemed, where serious sin could not be tolerated. Callistus's argument suggested that it was rather a "mixed" society, whose aim was precisely to bring sinners to salvation.

In the end, as the aftermath of the Decian and Valerian persecutions showed, it was Callistus's view which triumphed. When the bishops of North Africa, with the final assent of Cyprian himself, agreed to allow the discipline of *exomologēsis* to be applied even to those who had lapsed under persecution, the ancient doctrine of unforgivable sin itself lapsed (see II:10). The discipline of confession, penance, and restoration could be applied to all sins.

---

[14] *On Repentance* 9.4.
[15] *On Modesty* 1.6.
[16] Matt. 13:30.
[17] Hippolytus, *Philosophoumena* 9.12.

Chapter 16

Patterns of Christian Life

THE DISCIPLINES associated with baptism and penance, not to mention the moral demands and ideals upheld by Christian writers from Hermas to Origen and Tertullian, make it plain that the churches of the second and third centuries continued to see themselves as a society somehow "set apart"—governed by a Spirit other than the spirits that ruled the world at large. The original source of this attitude can no doubt be sought in the world-view of the Jewish apocalyptic. Repudiating the political, moral, and religious corruption of a world trapped in the nets of evil, the apocalyptist had looked to the future for that world's overthrow—to a new age when God would punish evil, reward suffering righteousness, and so set the creation right. Since, however, those who had believed the message of Jesus' resurrection and had entered, by baptism, upon his new life knew themselves to have a share even now in the good things of the age to come, they also knew that it was their business to live as people "crucified . . . to the world."[1]

No doubt this commitment was honored as often in the breach as in the observance, but it was honored nonetheless. Of this fact, one primary evidence is the respect and devotion which early Christians accorded to martyrs and the ideal of martyrdom. The martyrs were not, for them, merely courageous persons who stood by their convictions. They were contenders in the struggle between good and evil, who shared in the triumphant suffering of Christ and—for just that reason—attained the fullness of Christ's life in the age to come. The martyr in fact was the perfected imitator of Christ, who with the Lord was indeed "crucified . . . to the world" and therefore a model for all Christians.

Not all believers could—or wanted to be—martyrs in the proper sense, but each Christian could, in his or her own way, share in Christ's death to this age and in his new life for and with God; and it was just such a life which the early churches sought not merely to encourage but even, by their discipline, to institutionalize. This life had two sides, which corresponded to two central

[1] Gal. 6:14.

114

moments of baptism: repentance—a turning away from the old life—and in-corporation into Christ through the Spirit. Thus, on the one hand, the believer was to be detached from, even hostile to, the concerns and interests of the world: the pursuit, that is, of power, riches, and pleasure. On the other hand, he or she was to participate in a new communal life whose central motif was "brotherly affection" supplemented by "love."[2] Even if they did not seek to achieve "all things in common,"[3] these communities continued to set a high value on transcendence of conventional social barriers, sharing of goods, and mutual support among members, and indeed they organized themselves to this end.

What is more, the churches received encouragement and guidance in the pursuit of these ideals from the very world they criticized. The mood of Jewish-Christian apocalyptic—its sense that the world as presently constituted was no proper place for human beings, that its way must be rejected and its life transcended—had analogues in the pagan religion and philosophy of the day, and it was not long before Christians were using the popularized wisdom of pagan moralists and philosophers to express their own ideals. Paul uses the language of Cynic and Stoic philosophy when he commends his own "self-sufficiency" (*autarkeia*)[4]—that is, indifference to or independence of externals, which was the correlate of interior freedom; and Acts does the same when it pictures Paul discoursing on "justice and self-control" (*enkrateia*) in his ex-position of the meaning of "faith in Christ Jesus."[5] In a similar way, the language of a Platonized Stoicism is used in 2 Peter to characterize the shape and goal of Christian life. In the spirit of apocalyptic, this letter calls for "lives of holiness and godliness" to hasten "the coming of the day of God,"[6] but it interprets the sense of this demand in the language of popular philosophy. Christians are to "escape from the corruption that is in the world because of passion (*pathos*), and become partakers of the divine nature."[7] In thinkers like Clement of Alexandria and Origen, such philosophical ideas and ideals became the common currency of Christian moral discourse and shaped the understanding of repentance and rebirth for centuries to come.

There were, however, serious problems occasioned for the churches by this demand for simultaneous conversion from the world and participation in the new life of God's kingdom. The nature of these can be illustrated by the second-century conflict over the place of marriage in Christian life. There was much in the New Testament, not to mention the mood of the times, to sug-gest, on the one hand, that sexual relations in marriage were a sure way of binding oneself to the world and its values, and, on the other hand, that they had no place in the life of the new Kingdom. Paul had insisted that "those who marry will have worldly troubles,"[8] and Jesus had pointed out that "in the

---

[2] 2 Pet. 1:7. [4] Phil. 4:11. [6] 2 Pet. 3:11f. [8] 1 Cor. 7:28.
[3] Acts 2:44. [5] Acts 24:25. [7] 2 Pet. 1:4.

resurrection they neither marry nor give in marriage, but are like angels in heaven."[9] Such sayings as these go far to account for the universal esteem in which virginity or continence (again, *enkrateia*) was held in early Christianity. To practice it was both to separate oneself from the world and to live the life of the age to come, and by the third century many—perhaps most—Christian communities had, and honored, their virgins, male and female. In some quarters, admiration for the life of continence was allied with outright condemnation of marriage. This was the case with Marcion and his followers, with many Gnostics, with Justin's disciple Tatian and the "encratite" movement which he led in Syria, and with writings like the *Acts of Thomas* and the *Acts of Paul*.[10] Such uncompromising radicalism, though, seemed excessive to most believers, who, like the author of 1 Timothy, defended marriage.[11] Like Clement of Alexandria later, they saw no inconsistency in affirming both that marriage was to be honored and that virginity represented an authentic—and a higher— calling for Christians.

A similar middle-of-the-road position emerged on the equally difficult issue of wealth. The Gospels made it clear that Jesus had regarded "great possessions"[12] as an obstacle to entrance upon God's kingdom, and a similar distrust of riches and rich folk is apparent, for example, in the denunciations of them in the Epistle of James,[13] as well as in 1 Timothy's appeal to the well-known aphorism which asserted that "the love of money is the root of all evil."[14] When, according to a legendary but instructive story, the apostle Thomas was given a large sum of gold to construct a palace for a king, he spent it instead to tend the poor—and so procured his royal patron an even finer palace in heaven.[15] Early Christians, then, tended to regard possession or acquisition of personal wealth as inconsistent with that detachment from the world which the Gospel required. What they praised was contentment with the necessities,[16] remaining "unstained from the world,"[17] and the sharing of goods with the needy. The early social shift of the church from the peasant society of Palestine to the cities of the Hellenistic world meant, however, not only that more persons of relative prosperity joined its ranks but also that it lost a primary identification with the rural "underclass" of Roman society. In these circumstances, it was again the message of Clement of Alexandria—this time in his little treatise, *Who Is the Rich Man Who Will Be Saved?*—that best expressed the later mind and expectations of most believers. Possession of wealth was not in itself

---

[9] Matt. 22:30.
[10] See Hennecke-Schneemelcher, ed., *New Testament Apocrypha*, vol. 2.
[11] 1 Tim. 4:3.
[12] Mark 10:22.
[13] James 2:1–7, 5:1–6.
[14] 1 Tim. 6:10.
[15] Hennecke-Schneemelcher, *New Testament Apocrypha*, 2:451ff.
[16] 1 Tim. 6:8.
[17] James 1:27.

wrong, but it could be justified only if the wealth was employed in charitable works.

This did not mean, however, that the radical ideal of the martyr—who surrendered, and indeed fought, the world for the sake of the new life in Christ—had disappeared from the churches. Just as Clement and his contemporaries would have maintained that the continent or celibate life was a higher one than the married state, so they would have argued that the straightforward surrender of wealth was nobler even than its administration for the good of others. What is more, as the third century wore on and Christianity spread among the non-Hellenized rural peasantries of the Nile Valley and the Syrian countryside, the radical and rebellious martyr-spirit was reawakened. A new asceticism reasserted the ideals of continence and poverty and eventually created the monastic movement of the fourth and fifth centuries.

Chapter 17

Rest and Growth

IN THE YEAR 260, the emperor Valerian (253–260), campaigning against the Persians, was defeated and captured by Sapor I (234–270). His son, colleague, and successor, Gallienus (253–268), thereupon revoked his father's edict of persecution, and for the next forty-four years the Christian churches enjoyed a period of respite from official persecution—a respite which, however, was occasioned not so much by a fundamental change of attitude on the part of the imperial authorities as by the fact that they had little time to address the religious issue directly. This period of growth, consolidation, and peace for the churches was the time of the empire's most acute crisis, when its very survival was in doubt.

On the Rhine, Danube, and eastern frontiers there were constant and simultaneous pressure and invasion. Moreover, the ability of the emperors and their armies to cope with these external threats was impaired by the repeated appearance of usurpers and the consequent necessity to fight distracting civil wars. The Persians three times invaded the eastern provinces, once overrunning Syria and capturing Antioch itself. The Gothic tribes forced their way across the Danube and not only ravaged the Balkans and Greece but twice pierced into Asia Minor. At one point the confederation of German tribes called the

Franks reached as far as Spain in an incursion across the Rhine, and even raided North Africa. Under these pressures, the emperors seemed for a time unable to hold the empire together. For fourteen years (259–273), there was an independent "empire" in Gaul with its capital at Augusta Trevirorum (Trier). In the East, the client kingdom of Palmyra, under its queen, Zenobia (267–273), annexed Syria, Mesopotamia, Egypt, and parts of Asia Minor and ruled them as an independent state. It was only under Claudius Gothicus (268–270) and the great Aurelian (270–275) that the tide began to turn and the empire was reunited against its enemies. And it was only with Diocletian (284–305) that the emperors were able seriously to turn their minds to the internal reform and re-creation of the shaken Roman order. Until that time, the question of the Christians and their status—that is, the question of the religious stance and allegiance of the empire—remained in abeyance.

By the end of this period, Christianity was represented in all parts of the empire and its adherents may have numbered as many as five million—a significant if not a large minority of the population. Its greatest concentrations were in Asia Minor, Egypt, Syria, North Africa, and central Italy. In Egypt and North Africa in particular, it had been successful in winning the allegiance of rural peasant populations, a fact not without significance for its future history. At the same time, its membership had come to include persons of higher social rank. By Diocletian's time, there were Christians on the imperial staff and, in provincial cities, Christians who belonged to the order of those liable to service as magistrates (whence the Council of Elvira in Spain had to legislate, at the beginning of the fourth century, that Christians who, as magistrates, had to wear the garments of pagan priesthood might be restored to communion after two years' penance, provided they had not actually sacrificed or paid for sacrifices). Furthermore, there were, by Diocletian's day, Christians in the army—perhaps as a result of conscription—who occasioned uproars from time to time by their scruples in the matter of honoring pagan gods. Thus the churches spread not only geographically but socially, and their membership approached the point where it would represent something of a cross-section of the general population.

The last half of the third century seems, however, to have produced little in the way of original theological thought. The very last years of the century saw Eusebius of Caesarea (ca. 260–ca. 340)—a pupil of the presbyter Pamphilus, who had himself been a student of Origen's—beginning work on his monumental *Ecclesiastical History,* which was finished only in 323. In his close association with the Origenist tradition, Eusebius was apparently typical of a great many Christian teachers of his time. The successive bishops of Alexandria, especially Dionysius (d. ca. 264), encouraged and represented a kind of popular Origenism; and Palestinian Caesarea, where Origen had taught during the last years of his life and where his library was kept, became a center for the diffusion of his ideals. On the other hand, there were not a few opponents of this tradition. The city of Antioch, in particular, produced two notable teachers whose ideas stood in radical contrast with those of people like Dionysius and Eusebius.

The first of these was the notorious Paul of Samosata, who became bishop of Antioch ca. 260 and flourished there under the rule of Queen Zenobia of Palmyra. Paul held views very like those of the dynamic monarchians of an earlier generation in Rome. Against the trinitarian pluralism of the Origenists, he stressed the unity of God and explained the incarnation as an instance of the divine Logos's indwelling of a human person. He was condemned and deposed in 268 by a synod of bishops who represented the Origenist tradition. Antioch was also the home of the presbyter Lucian (d. 312), a famous exegete who, like Origen, worked at the text of the Septuagint and of the Gospels, but who repudiated Origen's allegorical methods and held to a more literal interpretation of the text of the Scriptures. Concerning Lucian's theological views, almost nothing is known save what can be inferred from the fact that Arius and his protector, Eusebius of Nicomedia, were both pupils of the Antiochene teacher. Lucian died as a martyr in the last of the great persecutions. A contemporary of Lucian's, Methodius of Olympus (d. ca. 311), also took up the cudgels against Origen. A shadowy figure, of whose life little is known and most of whose works survive only in fragments, Methodius attacked Origen not merely on the subject of the resurrection of the body and the doctrine of the "pre-existence" of souls but also on the subject of his views on creation "in time." His best-known work is the so-called *Symposium* or *Banquet of the Ten Virgins*—an imitation of Plato's *Symposium* written in praise of virginity.

Chapter 18

Rival Religious Forces

*I*F THE THIRD CENTURY was a time of expansion and consolidation for the churches, it was also a time of religious change for the Roman world as a whole. Paganism itself experienced a shift of religious mood. Attention was focused less on the many intracosmic gods of classical religion and more on the transcendently holy and life-giving God whose power they, in their diminished way, represented. This development is manifest particularly in the evolution of the imperial cult. Emperors, human beings as they were, were no longer seen as gods. Rather, they were seen as persons who, in virtue of their office, were "begotten of the gods": that is, who shared in their mortal way in the holiness of the Divine and enjoyed its protection. It was in this spirit, for example, that Diocletian called himself "Jovius," a style which meant not that he was identified with Jupiter (the supreme god of the Roman pantheon) but that he represented him and belonged to his "family."

Behind this shift in the sense of the imperial cult lay the third-century development of solar monotheism—worship of the life-giving sun as a symbol of the ultimate God who is the source of all things and who was not infrequently identified with Apollo. Encouraged by the emperors of the Severan dynasty at the beginning of the third century, the popularity of this cult grew as time went on. The emperor Aurelian built a great temple to the Unconquered Sun, which he intended to be center of the empire's religious life. Christians in the fourth century could find no better way of rivaling this popular deity than by using his birthday, December 25 (the winter solstice), to celebrate the birth of Christ, the Sun of Righteousness. At a more popular level, the worship of the sun and of the transcendent life which it represented took shape in the widespread cult of Mithras, the Iranian deity of the Morning Light. More popular in the West than in the East, and especially influential in the ranks of the Roman army, the mysteries of Mithras not only offered immortality to their initiates but also inculcated a severe ethic of fidelity, good conduct, and self-control.

Not dissociated from these developments in religion was the rise of Neoplatonism, the philosophical school whose teachings became, in the third and fourth centuries, the vehicle of a pagan revival and a source of opposition among educated persons to the claims of Christianity. The source and inspiration of the Neoplatonic movement were the teachings of Plotinus (205–270), whose written essays, intended simply for his students at Rome, were assembled by his disciple Porphyry (233–304) in a collection called the *Enneads*. A careful and creative interpreter not only of Plato's writings but of the whole tradition of Greek philosophy, Plotinus discerned his Sun, the First Principle of all reality, in a transcendent Unity (he called it "the One" or "the Good"). This Principle was "beyond being" and so beyond the powers of mind to grasp or describe; yet on the other hand it was the fecund source of all being—boiling, as he once put it, with a life which overflows and disseminates itself. From this center and source, everything moves out and down in a graded series of "hypostases," which represent levels at once of being, of awareness, and of value. The highest of these is Intellect, in which being and the awareness of it are as nearly as possible one thing. The second level is that of Soul, where time appears and awareness first takes the form of serial apprehension and reasoning. The final level is that of Nature, in which being and awareness become external to each other and body appears. Each of these levels, however, images in its own way the reality of its Source, and each strives to turn back and to rise, by a process of self-concentration, to Unity. Neoplatonism, then, as Plotinus represented it, called the human person to follow an ascesis which led on an inward path toward unity of being and awareness in the One. In the hands of Plotinus's immediate successors, Porphyry and Iamblichus (ca. 250–ca. 325), Plotinus's thought was not only systematized but put to the service of popular religion, losing in the process much of its mood of transcendent optimism. Such was its power and attraction, however, that Neoplatonism, in spite of its open alliance with the cause of pagan religious practice, became a source and dialogue-partner for the thought of many fourth-century Christian teachers—most notably, perhaps, the Cappadocian Fathers and Augustine of Hippo.

The same cannot be said of another influential religious movement of the third (and fourth) centuries which entered into rivalry with Christianity. Manichaeanism, which evoked the hostility of pagans and Christians alike, entered the Roman Empire from Persia. Founded by a Persian teacher named Mani (216–277), who was called in a series of visions to be the founder and apostle of a new, universal religion, Manichaeanism was a dualistic faith with many affinities to Gnosticism. Mani's fundamental theme was the conflict between Light and Darkness, two irreconcilable but equally primordial realms of being, each of which is ruled by its own king. The creation of the present world-order, as Mani saw it, was the result of a conflict between these two kingdoms, in which Darkness attempted to swallow up Light and at least partially succeeded. The calling of the human person, then, was to recognize that its nature is a mixture of light and darkness and, with the help of the emissaries of Light—Buddha, Zoroaster, Jesus, and Mani himself—to be purged of darkness. Purgation was brought about by abstinence from everything that binds the individual to materiality. Full initiates into the Manichaean faith therefore renounced the world entirely. They did not labor or marry, they owned nothing, they rejected all "impurity." In short, they worked, by self-denial, to hasten the purification of the world—the segregation of Light from Darkness. These full initiates, "the elect," were served and followed by a second class of believers who were called "hearers." Manichaeanism spread rapidly and far in the Roman empire, especially in North Africa and Syria; its indirect influence reached as far as the Middle Ages, when a similar movement appeared as Albigensianism in the south of France.

Chapter 19

The Final Struggle

IN 284, Diocletian succeeded to the imperial throne. A Dalmatian of humble origin, he came to prominence in the army and was raised to the imperial dignity, after the custom of the times, by his soldiers. Though it continued to be necessary for the empire to wage defensive war on its frontiers, the military crisis of the third century was well enough in hand for Diocletian to be able to turn his mind to internal reconstruction—dynastic, military, and economic. The first step in his program, which was evolved gradually, was to appoint, in 285, a second emperor to share his authority and to supervise affairs in the western portion of the empire. By this step, Diocletian plainly hoped to assure not only that there would be more effective supervision of the administrative machinery in each sector of the empire, but also that one emperor would never again have to conduct military campaigns on two fronts at once. His next step, taken a few years later, was to associate with these two "Augusti"—that is, himself and his colleague, Maximian—two junior emperors, called "Caesars," who were assigned sections of the empire to rule and defend and were also designated heirs apparent to the two Augusti. As his own Caesar, Diocletian selected Galerius, yet another soldier of Dalmatian origin; and to Maximian was assigned Constantius I, father of Constantine the Great. This did not mean, of course, that there were now four separate empires. Though each Augustus and each Caesar had his own capital, his own administrative staff headed by a praetorian prefect, and his own mobile army, all laws and decrees were issued jointly: the empire was one even if its rulers were four.

Diocletian's changes did not stop there. He doubled the number of provinces by redrawing boundaries and then grouped these new provinces into larger administrative areas called "dioceses," each of which was put under a "vicar" or governor general. He began the process of reorganizing the army and separating civil authority from military command. In the interest of imperial autocracy, he withdrew from the Roman Senate the last vestiges of its ancient political authority. In an effort (unsuccessful) to cope with the economic problems of the empire, he attempted to freeze prices of goods. He was more successful in freezing certain essential occupations by binding sons legally to their fathers' responsibilities, a policy which was continued under his successors. Diocletian, in short, began the creation of that form of the Roman empire which was to survive, with its capital at Byzantium, until 1453.

Religion, however, was as much a problem for the empire as issues concerning efficient military and civil administration. Diocletian and his colleagues, like their predecessors and successors, understood that the fate of Rome depended ultimately on its alliance with the gods. For Diocletian, and for his Caesar, Galerius, "the gods" meant the ancient protectors of Rome—as witness his deliberate association of himself with the power of Jupiter. This did not mean, however, that he was bent, as a matter of principle, on the extirpation of other religions. During most of his reign, he exhibited the same toleration which had marked the policy of his predecessors, and this in spite of the fact that Galerius (not to mention others in court circles) was openly hostile to Christianity. Toward the end of his reign, however, circumstances conspired to convince him that the existence of Christianity was rupturing the covenant between Rome and her gods. Not only were Christians in the army insulting the gods by refusing to acknowledge them, but Diocletian was informed by his priests that, because of the presence in his court of "profane men" (presumably Christians), the traditional auguries, by which emperors learned the will of the gods, were void of effect: the gods were not answering. And when Diocletian sent to the oracle of Apollo at Miletus to inquire what course he should take in the face of this situation, the answer was unfavorable to the Christians. Thus, Diocletian was induced to follow the line favored by Galerius, and he began a series of actions which were calculated to rid first the court and the army, and then the empire as a whole, of Christians.

Beginning in February 303, three edicts of persecution came in rapid succession. Churches were to be destroyed, sacred books were to be confiscated, and finally, clergy were to be imprisoned and compelled to offer sacrifice. In 304, a fourth edict required all Christians to offer sacrifice. Where the persecution was intense—as in the East generally and in North Africa and Italy—the effects of these edicts were not dissimilar to those of the earlier persecutions under Decius and Valerian. Some believers were martyred, many suffered, and many lapsed. In 305, troubled by ill health, Diocletian retired from his office as Augustus and compelled the simultaneous resignation of his colleague Maximian. This unprecedented event, however, did not stop the persecution. Peace, it is true, came to the churches in the West, because the new Augustus there, Constantius I, was among those who believed a policy of persecution ill-advised. In the East, however, the senior Augustus, Galerius, and his new Caesar, Maximinus Daia, continued the persecutions unabated.

While the severity of the persecution was growing in the East, however, a new star was rising in the West. The retirement of Diocletian had removed from power the one man whose authority could have maintained the new system of succession in the imperial office. In his absence, the power of the armies to make and break emperors was reasserted. In 306, the new Augustus of the West, Constantius I, died suddenly at York in Britain. His son Constantine, who had just returned to his side after long residence at the court of Diocletian, was promptly acclaimed emperor by Constantius's troops. On the strength of this support from the army, Constantine compelled Galerius to acknowledge him as "Caesar," and was given Britain, Gaul, and Spain as his charge. He was, in theory, to be the subordinate and heir apparent of Severus, who had succeeded Constantius as Augustus in the West. Severus, however, was overwhelmed and deposed by yet another usurper, Maxentius, the son of Diocletian's original colleague Maximian, who thus made himself the master of Italy and North Africa. As the first decade of the fourth century drew to a close, then, the West was divided between Constantine and Maxentius, who maintained an increasingly uneasy truce.

Before the decisive contest for the West took place, however, the emperor Galerius in the East issued, from his deathbed, an edict of toleration for Christians. Published in 311, the edict admitted that the purposes of the persecution had not been accomplished. Christians had not returned to "the persuasion of their forefathers" or stopped "making themselves laws for their own observance." What is more, not only were they not serving the gods of Rome, but they had also been prevented by persecution from worshiping their own god. In view of these circumstances, and no doubt with some idea that his sickness might be due to the ill will of the Christians' god, Galerius decreed that "Christians may exist again" and that "it will be their duty to pray their god for our good estate."[1] This act of indulgence, however, did Galerius little good. He died almost as soon as he had proclaimed toleration.

The death of Galerius left four contestants for the empire. In the East, Licinius, who controlled the territories north of the Hellespont, faced Maximinus Daia, who held Asia Minor, Syria, Palestine, and Egypt. The latter renewed the persecution of Christians not long after Galerius's death and allied himself with Maxentius in the West in order to counter the already established entente between Constantine and Licinius. In 313, Licinius defeated Maximinus in a battle near Heraclea Pontica and took control of the eastern sector of the empire. In the West, matters had been settled almost exactly a year earlier. There Constantine, with an army which seemed much too small for its task, had crossed the Alps in a brilliant march and won several engagements against Maxentius's troops in northern Italy. Risking everything, he continued south to confront Maxentius, who, with superior numbers, had retired behind the walls of Rome itself. Disturbances in Rome, however, where he was not popular with the local population, led Maxentius to bring his troops out of the

---

[1] Lactantius, *On the Deaths of the Persecutors* 34.

city and to confront the forces of Constantine before the Mulvian Bridge across the Tiber.

It was at this point that there occurred the event which was to change the course of the history of church and empire alike. Constantine, like his father, had been a firm opponent of the persecution of Christians. Also like his father, however, he had associated himself with the vague solar monotheism popularized by the emperor Aurelian—a cult entirely consonant with pagan sensibilities. But on the eve of the battle at the Mulvian Bridge, Constantine had a dream in which he saw the initial letters of the name of Christ with the words, "By this sign you will conquer."[2] Taking this as an omen, he resolved to trust his cause to the God of the Christians and had the Chi-Rho monogram painted on the shields of his soldiers. In the ensuing struggle, Maxentius lost the battle and his life. Constantine had won the control of the West. When he entered Rome in triumph, Constantine remembered to whom he owed his victory. The customary tributes of thanks to the gods of Rome were omitted. The emperor had cast his lot with the minority cause of the Christians, and henceforth he regarded the Christian God as the protector of the empire and the sponsor of his own mission of reform and reconstruction. Rome had a continuer of the work of Diocletian, but Diocletian's task was now to go forward under the patronage of the very God whose adherents he himself had persecuted.

It need hardly be said that Constantine practiced caution in the manner in which he made his new allegiance known. He accepted the pagan title of Pontifex Maximus, and his coins still showed the emblems of the Sun-God. At a meeting at Milan in 313, he and Licinius reached an agreement about the treatment of Christians which, while it went beyond mere toleration, fell well short of any kind of establishment of the church. It proclaimed freedom of conscience, accorded to Christianity a full legal equality with other cults, and ordered the restoration of all church property confiscated in the persecution. Licinius, however, carried this agreement out somewhat grudgingly. He was no persecutor, but—still a loyal adherent of paganism—neither was he prone to give privileges to the church. As tension between him and Constantine grew in the decade following their meeting in 313, Licinius imposed severe restrictions on the public life of the churches. It was therefore as a champion of the Christian faith, and not solely as a man with a sense of political mission, that Constantine found an excuse to invade Licinius's territories in 324. Defeated in two engagements, Licinius was retired to Thessalonica and finally put to death. Constantine was the sole ruler of the empire, and the churches awoke to find that the cause of Rome and the cause of Christ had become one.

---

[2] Lactantius, *On the Deaths of the Persecutors* 44.

Period III

THE IMPERIAL
STATE CHURCH

Chapter 1

The Changed Situation

*I*N THE MIND of Constantine, there was probably, at least to begin with, little difference between the monotheism of the Christians and that of the Sun-cult which the emperor Aurelian had fostered and which he himself had consciously espoused after 310. Each proclaimed the supremacy of a single transcendent deity by whose rule the subordinate "powers" of the cosmos were ordered. Each, therefore, projected a picture of the world-order consonant with Constantine's sense of his own mission: to restore a universal monarchy which would integrate and unify human society on earth. Nevertheless, it was the Christian God who had brought Constantine victory before the walls of Rome, and after that victory it was the Christian churches on which Constantine relied to offer the one God, the "summa divinitas," the worship which alone could assure the well-being of the empire and the successful issue of his own enterprise. It was in this—classically Roman—spirit that he instructed Anulinus, the governor of the province of Africa, to exempt the clergy of the "catholic church" from civic obligations, in order that they might devote their full time to the service of God and thus "confer incalculable benefit on public affairs."[1] He had come to regard it as his duty to assure the welfare of the churches in order that they, by their worship, might assure the good estate of the peoples of the empire.

Of this commitment, Constantine's actions after 313 give clear evidence. Even by that early date, he had taken on an ecclesiastical advisor, in the person of the Spanish bishop Hosius (Ossius) of Cordova. Gifts of money were made to individual churches for charitable use. The emperor constructed basilicas at his own expense to serve as Christian places of worship. In 321, he issued a decree that allowed churches to receive legacies, thus conceding them the legal status of corporations. He legislated that the Day of the Sun, the Christian "first day," should be kept as a weekly holiday from work. In cases where both parties to a civil suit agreed voluntarily to the arrangement, he allowed them

---

[1] Eusebius, *Ecclesiastical History*, 10.1.

to take their case to the court of the local Christian bishop, whose decision would have the effect of law. When he built himself a new capital on the site of the ancient Byzantium—a city which he, to symbolize the spirit and achievements of his reign, called "New Rome," but which posterity called "Constantinople"—it was liberally furnished with Christian shrines but had no place for pagan worship.

In following this policy, Constantine was taking a serious risk. For one thing, Christians were and for some time remained a minority in the empire. The emperor's support and interest did not produce immediate conversions to the Christian cause, paganism continued not only to exist, but even to exhibit symptoms of considerable liveliness, and the wealthy and educated classes did not support the emperor's shift of religious allegiance. More than that, however, as Constantine soon discovered to his frustration, the churches themselves, after a period of intensive and sometimes cruel persecution, were troubled and, in some places, seriously divided. His commitment to their cause meant, therefore, not only that he had to support and encourage their service of God, but also that he must take a hand in the resolution of their conflicts. How difficult and thankless a task this could be Constantine learned very early, as, in the years immediately after his defeat of Maxentius, he found himself involved in a schism in the churches of Africa and Numidia.

The Donatist schism, as it came to be called, like the schisms at Rome and Carthage in the time of Cyprian, was rooted in a conflict over the ideology of martyrdom. In the tradition of Tertullian and of Cyprian himself, popular North African Christianity continued to glorify the martyr's calling and the spirit of opposition to the world which it embodied. Its adherents were also convinced of the truth of Cyprian's teaching that the Holy Spirit could not be given in a church whose bishop was, by reason of apostasy or other great sin, unworthy of his office. There was, therefore, during the persecution under Diocletian, great opposition to the bishop of Carthage, Mensurius, and his archdeacon, Caecilian, when they openly discouraged the cult of martyrs and gave the impression of being less than wholehearted in their opposition to the powers of evil. Accordingly, when Mensurius died and Caecilian was hastily elected and ordained bishop in his stead, many Christians in the province of Africa—and all the Numidian bishops, who had not been consulted as had been the custom—were alienated. This alienation became schism when it was alleged plausibly that one of the bishops who had ordained Caecilian had apostatized (by handing his church's sacred books over to the authorities), for this meant that the ordination could not have been valid and that Caecilian was in fact no bishop. Thus, by the time Constantine came on the scene, the African church was divided. Caecilian headed the body which was called "catholic" because it was in communion with the churches elsewhere in the Roman world; his rival was Donatus the Great, a charismatic figure who headed "the church of the martyrs." When Constantine in effect recognized Caecilian's group as the Christian church in Africa, the Donatists appealed to him for a formal judgment, insisting that they and they alone were the legitimate church. The emperor thus found himself involved in the internal affairs of the churches.

Constantine at this point initiated a procedure which was to become imperial policy with regard to ecclesiastical questions. He referred the question to two successive councils of bishops: first, to the bishop of Rome, Miltiades, who was to sit with three Gaulish bishops as a court; then, when the Donatists appealed from Miltiades' decision against their cause, to a larger council held at Arles (314), in Gaul itself. Again the Donatist accusation, that Caecilian's ordination was invalid because one of his ordainers was an apostate, was rejected on grounds of fact; and the Donatist principle that a morally unworthy cleric cannot perform valid ecclesial acts was denied. These efforts to overcome the schism, however, were fruitless. Constantine tried briefly to repress Donatism by force, but he soon gave the effort up. The schism endured and the "pars Donati" prospered and grew in Africa, claiming to be the only true church and indeed embodying much of the authentic traditional spirit of African Christianity.

Chapter 2

The Arian Controversy
to the Death of Constantine

W HEN IN 324, after the defeat of Licinius, Constantine assumed control of the eastern half of the empire, he found a debate raging which divided not a single province but the whole of Licinius's former dominions. This time the issue was theological. It concerned the old problem of the Logos-theology: the question of the nature or status of the Word or Son of God and his relation to God on the one hand and to the created order on the other. It was a debate which was not to be resolved officially for almost sixty years and which, in the end, required a rethinking of the way in which Christians expressed their understanding of God.

The controversy had begun in Alexandria, probably in the year 318. There the presbyter Arius, who presided over the suburban "parish" of Baucalis and was a prominent and popular figure in the Alexandrian church, had propounded the view that the Logos is a creature called into being by God "out of nonexistence." As a creature, the Logos was subject to change and capable, at least in principle, of either virtue or vice, just as human beings were. Moreover, Arius taught, there was a "time"—a "when"—in which the Son/Logos did not yet exist. The pope of Alexandria, Alexander (312?-328), heard these views presented in a debate between Arius and another teacher and gave his decision that Arius was in the wrong and must cease setting forth such opinions. Arius, however, was not without supporters among clergy and laity alike. He made it clear that he intended to continue disseminating his views. The scale of the controversy grew. In the end, about 320, Alexander had Arius and his associates deposed by a council of some one hundred Egyptian bishops; but by that time Arius had fled to Palestine, certain that outside of Egypt he would find sympathy and support for his views, as indeed he did. Among others, he won over the influential Eusebius of Nicomedia (d. ca. 342), bishop of the imperial capital in the East and, like Arius, a former pupil of the martyr Lucian of Antioch. For a time, Arius stayed with Eusebius at Nicomedia, and it was there, in all probability, that the wrote his *Thalia,* a work (now known only in fragments) in which he presented his views more or less systematically. Between them, Arius and Eusebius, through a campaign of letters, brought pressure to bear on Alexander to restore Arius; Alexander in response mounted his own correspondence campaign, insisting that Arius's denial of the divinity of the Logos/Son was blasphemous. The bishop held that the Son is generated eternally, without reference to time, comes "from God himself" rather than "from nonexistence," and is changeless and perfect. This position, however, which echoed Origen without clearly reproducing Origen's subordinationism, evoked from Arians the response that Alexander was teaching two coequal Gods—two "unbegottens."

The central issue in this debate as it opened up was, then, that of the Logos. This issue hinged in turn on interpretation of the Greek term *gennētos* as that was applied to the Son. Traditionally translated "begotten," in Greek philosophical terminology it had a broader and hence vaguer sense. It denoted anything which in any way "came to be" and hence anything "derivative" or "generated." Christian thought had early learned to express its monotheistic stance by insisting that God is the sole *agennētos* ("underived," "ungenerated"): that is, the unique and absolute first principle. By contrast with God, all else that exists—including the Logos, God's Son—was described as generated. This implied, of course, not only that the Logos was subordinate to God (as any "image," even an exact image, is secondary to the reality it represents), but also that the Logos had something in common with creatures which God did not—some quality of "generatedness." "Something in common," though, does not necessarily imply identity of status, and the tradition of Greek theology normally differentiated the way in which the Logos/Son was generated from that in which creatures—like the human soul or body—were generated. The latter came to be "out of nonexistence"; the former, on the other hand, was "born" from God and was thus in a secondary but real sense divine. What the Greek tradition envisaged, therefore, was a pluralism of divine persons within a hierarchy of being. There was an eternal and unchanging first principle, God, who gives rise to a Son and Image, the Logos, and through this Image of himself calls "out of nonexistence" a world of creatures.

Arius at once affirmed and challenged this tradition. He maintained the hierarchical idea that the Logos mediates between God and world, but at the same time he argued that between the ungenerated and the generated, God and creature, there can be no ontological middle term. The mediator must be either God or creature, and since there cannot be two Gods, it follows (as Proverbs 8:22 seemed to say clearly) that the Son is a creature. No doubt he is the most glorious of creatures, God's instrument in creation and redemption, and therefore a creature on a different level from the others. Nevertheless, a changeable creature he is, and perhaps for just that reason a more adequate pattern for a humanity which had been created "after the image of God," i.e., on the model of the Logos. By contrast, the position of someone like Alexander, who wanted to stress the deity of the Logos and his exact likeness to God, seemed to involve one of two impossible assumptions. Either there were two coequal Gods, or else there was, as the monarchians had taught, no real distinction between Father and Son. In short, both Arius and Alexander questioned in effect whether the traditional hierarchical scheme, which bridged the gap between an immutable God and a mutable creation by appeal to the Logos as a halfway house, could be sustained. In the first act of this drama, the confused and uncertain bishops of the eastern churches ended by rejecting both positions and reaffirming the tradition which Arius and his bishop had, in different ways, jeopardized.

It was not merely confusion, however, which Constantine found in the East in 324. Many church leaders had already picked sides, and there was open warfare of the most embarrassing and acrimonious sort, in which theological issues had become inextricably mixed with questions of personality and prestige. At first, the emperor seems not to have grasped this fact. His opening move was to send his advisor, Hosius of Cordova, to Alexandria with a letter that called for reconciliation and suggested that the issue being debated was "unprofitable"—a minor disagreement over a point of detail. This well-meant but bungling effort was in vain, as Hosius quickly discovered. On his way back to the emperor's side, however, he presided over an assembly of bishops who had come to Antioch to install a new bishop there. After selecting one Eustathius, a firm anti-Arian, the bishops issued a confession of faith which insisted against Arius that the Logos/Son is "begotten not from nonexistence but from the Father, not as made but as properly an offspring," and that he "exists

everlastingly" and is "immutable and unchangeable."[1] This repudiation of
Arian teaching, couched in terms familiar to the eastern tradition in theology,
no doubt encouraged the emperor to think that his, and the church's, problem
might be settled by the same method he had tried with the Donatist issue in the
West—that is, by a council of bishops. He proceeded, therefore, to summon all
the bishops of the empire to the city of Nicaea in Asia Minor for what was
to be the first universal council of the church.

This council, which assembled in May 325, has lived in Christian tradition
as the one whose confession of faith defined the very foundations of orthodoxy.
The bishops, most of whom had suffered in one way or another in the recent
persecutions, were no doubt astonished and gratified to find that they could
now travel at imperial expense. The great majority of them came from the
East: of about two or three hundred who attended, only six were westerners.
They represented three schools of thought. A small number, led by Eusebius
of Nicomedia, were thoroughgoing Arians. Another small group, including
Eustathius of Antioch and Marcellus of Ancyra, were fervent supporters of
Alexander. The majority—the most prominent of whom, perhaps, was Eusebius
of Caesarea, the church historian—were conservatives in the sense that they
represented, if not always thoughtfully or knowledgeably, the pluralism and
subordinationism of the eastern tradition. The emperor himself was present at
the assembly and dominated its proceedings.

The actions of the council, as well as the texts of its creed and canons,
are known only from unofficial, and sometimes much later, reports. Soon after
it opened, the assembly showed the direction it was going to take by rejecting
a confession of faith presented by the Arians. Later, however, Eusebius of
Caesarea, who had consistently shown sympathy for the Arian cause (though
he was not in the strict sense an Arian), read out the baptismal creed of his
native city to clear himself of suspicion; and on this occasion, the bishops, led
by the emperor himself, agreed that the confession was entirely orthodox, even
though it did not actually exclude an Arian interpretation. What emperor and
bishops alike were searching for, it seems, was a way of repudiating Arius's
teaching that did not explicitly exclude the traditional eastern stance. Accordingly, they took another baptismal creed, of much the same type as Eusebius's,
and altered its text to serve their purpose, in the process creating a new, non-
liturgical type of confession. At its end, they added a short series of anathemas
which directly condemned the basic propositions affirmed by the Arians. In
the text itself, they inserted the significant expressions "true God from true
God," "begotten not made," "from the substance [*ousia*] of the Father," and—
most important of all, as it turned out—"of one substance [*homoousios*] with
the Father." The general force of these expressions was plain. They excluded

---

[1] J. Stevenson, ed., *A New Eusebius* (New York, 1957), p. 355.

absolutely the idea that the Logos is a creature, they asserted that he is truly the eternally generated "Son" of God, and they insisted that he belongs to the same order of being as God.

From the very beginning, however, people like Eusebius of Caesarea had doubts about the creed, doubts that focused on the word *homoousios*. This was, to be sure, a vague and nontechnical term which was capable of a fairly wide range of senses. It could in principle be taken to mean exact sameness of being, but it could also be taken to suggest no more than a significant degree of similarity between Father and Son—which, of course, everyone was glad to affirm. On the other hand, the term was non-Scriptural, it had a very doubtful theological history, and it was open to what, from Eusebius's point of view, were some dangerous misinterpretations indeed. He notes, for example, that "of one substance" might, in the light of ordinary popular usage, suggest that the Logos is some sort of "extension" or "piece" of the divine "stuff," and thus suggest that God himself is corporeal, divisible, and changeable. At the same time, there was no doubting that it could be understood to deny that there is any distinction between Father and Son and thus to open the door to monarchianism, the bête noire of the eastern pluralist tradition. Eusebius was assured, however, that the term was intended only to say that "the Son bears no likeness to generated creatures, but is likened in every respect solely to the Father who begat him, and that he is not from some other reality and substance, but from the Father."[2] On the basis of this explanation, he, along with Eusebius of Nicomedia and all save two of the other bishops, signed the creed—willing, no doubt, to go along with what the emperor wanted. Yet he and many others continued to suspect its language, to put a minimizing interpretation on it, and to make as little reference to it as possible. The creed achieved the aim of excluding Arianism and providing the eastern church with a formula to which all could assent in one sense or another. Its positive implications for a Christian understanding of God, however, could only be drawn out through debate about the questions it raised.

The council dealt with other matters beside the central issue of Arianism. For one, it passed a series of canons which for the first time defined a formal church structure above the local level. This structure, which took shape in the East much sooner than in the West, was based on the provincial divisions of the empire. The council in effect limited the authority of local churches and their bishops by calling for regular provincial synods of bishops, by assigning to the bishop of the provincial metropolis a veto over the election and ordination of bishops in his area, and by insisting that no one could be made a bishop without the participation of at least three other bishops of the province. In

---

[2] H.-G. Opitz, *Urkunden zur Geschichte des arianischen Streites* (*Athanasius Werke* 3.1, Berlin, 1934), p. 46.

addition, it recognized an exceptional jurisdiction, more extensive than the territory of a province, for the bishops of Alexandria, Rome, and Antioch—a first step toward the acknowledgment of patriarchal sees.

The council was also called upon to find a way of mending a schism in in the Egyptian church which dated back to the persecution under Diocletian. At that time, Peter, bishop of Alexandria, had withdrawn into hiding. In his absence, Melitius, bishop of Lycopolis, had taken it upon himself to ordain clergy for Alexandria. Peter saw this act as a usurpation of his authority and responded by excommunicating Melitius, who then in turn organized separate churches. Guided no doubt by Constantine, the council sought to heal this schism—which had persisted, even after the martyrdom of Peter, into the episcopate of his successor, Alexander—by a compromise. Melitian clergy were to retain their functions, but under Alexander's authority. Melitian bishops, if properly elected for the purpose, might succeed their catholic counterparts upon the latters' death.

Constantine's desire for peace and reconciliation, embodied in the legislation of the Council of Nicaea, did not flag after the close of the council. His manner of pursuing it, however, only brought about an increase of conflict. In 328, the very year in which the former deacon Athanasius succeeded Alexander as bishop in Alexandria, the emperor recalled Eusebius of Nicomedia (whom he had exiled shortly after Nicaea for communicating with Arius) as bishop of the imperial capital. A brilliant and resolute politician as well as an Arian, Eusebius soon became Constantine's principal ecclesiastical adviser. With the emperor's ear and confidence, he forthwith mounted a campaign to rid the church of the enemies of the subordinationist theology of the eastern tradition. In the end, he not only accomplished his goal but did so without any hint that the real issue was Constantine's cherished Nicene formula, which, as Eusebius no doubt saw it, was a tool of the monarchian interest.

The first victim of Eusebius's campaign was Eustathius of Antioch, an open and notorious anti-Origenist, whom Eusebius of Caesarea had accused publicly of monarchianism. Informed by his advisers that Eustathius was a disturber of the church's peace, a man of doubtful moral character, and one who had voiced uncharitable judgments on the emperor's mother, Helena, Constantine acquiesced in the deposition of Eustathius by an Origenist synod at Antioch ca. 330 and enforced this action by exiling Eustathius to Thrace. Eusebius's next, and more difficult, victim was Athanasius, the new pope of Alexandria (328–373). A determined and single-minded champion of the Nicene formula, which he saw as representing the views of his predecessor, Alexander, Athanasius opened himself to attack by the high-handed methods he employed in dealing with the Melitians and consolidating his authority over the Egyptian church. In 335, Athanasius was hauled before a synod at Tyre composed entirely of his bitter theological enemies. He was accused, among other things, of contriving the murder of a Melitian bishop named Arsenius. The charge was false

(Athanasius had done no more than sequester Arsenius), but there was no hope of justice for Alexander's successor at such a council. Athanasius therefore fled Tyre secretly to appeal to the emperor in person at Constantinople. In the end, however, the appeal accomplished nothing. Eusebius of Nicomedia and his associates persuaded Constantine that Athanasius had threatened to cut off the capital city's grain supply from Egypt. This amounted to a charge of treason, and Constantine, accepting it as proved without investigation, exiled Athanasius to Trier in Germany. Eusebius's last triumph was the deposition and exile of Marcellus of Ancyra, another extreme anti-Origenist.

By the time, then, that Constantine, whom Eusebius of Nicomedia baptized on his deathbed, expired in May 337, the enemies of Nicaea and defenders of subordinationism had triumphed. Arianism in any open form had been ruled out by the council, but the vocal opponents of Arianism had been defeated in its aftermath, and the traditional theology of the East had prevailed. It was one form or another of this traditional theology, the position of the majority of eastern bishops, which was to enjoy imperial support in the East until the advent of Theodosius I.

Chapter 3

Controversy under Constantine's Sons

THE DEATH of Constantine led to a division of the empire among his three sons. The eldest, Constantine II, received Britain, Gaul, and Spain. Constantius II was assigned the East: Asia Minor, Syria, and Egypt. To the youngest, Constans, went the central sector of the empire, including North Africa. Constantine II, while striving to assert his authority over his youngest brother, fell in an ambush at Aquileia in 340. After that date, therefore, the greater part of Rome's dominions was ruled by Constans, a fact which was not without significance for the history of the controversy over Nicaea.

The first focus of that controversy—which soon embraced the whole church, Latin as well as Greek—was not the creed of Nicaea itself but the standing of those bishops, Athanasius and Marcellus of Ancyra in particular, whom the eastern leaders had deposed. The new emperors at the beginning of their joint reign permitted these exiled bishops to return, and Athanasius was back in Alexandria before the end of 337. The influence of Eusebius, however, who had moved from Nicomedia to become bishop of Constantinople (339) and who still functioned as the effective leader of the eastern bishops, made it impossible for Athanasius to remain. Driven from Alexandria in the spring of 339 and replaced by an Arian, Gregory of Cappadocia (who arrived with an escort of troops), Athanasius fled to Rome, where Marcellus of Ancyra soon joined him. There the exiles enlisted the support and sympathy of Julius, the bishop of Rome, whom the Eusebian bishops had earlier requested, in a moment of weakness, to review the case of Athanasius.

Julius, now enjoying the support of the emperor Constans, convoked a synod in 340 which declared that the depositions of Athanasius and Marcellus had been unjust. The eastern leaders, refusing to be represented at an assembly they themselves had requested, expressed outrage at this interference in their affairs. As far as they were concerned, Athanasius and Marcellus had been legitimately deposed and the question of restoration could not legally be raised. They were, moreover, motivated in this attitude by a theological concern. They suspected both Athanasius and Marcellus—the latter with good reason—of using the creed of the Council of Nicaea as camouflage for a monarchian denial that Father, Son, and Spirit are three distinct realities (hypostases). Accordingly, ninety-seven of them, when assembled at Antioch in 341 for the dedication of Constantine's "Golden Basilica," repudiated the suggestion that they were Arians, denied Rome's right to act as a court of appeal in cases involving eastern churches, and clarified their theological position by issuing three creeds. These were apparently intended to supplement and correct the Nicene formula by systematically excluding monarchianism in general and the views of Marcellus in particular. A fourth confession—plainly not Arian in intent, but equally plainly representing the eastern tradition of pluralism and subordinationism—was presented to the emperor Constans at Trier when he requested an explanation of the position of the eastern bishops.

This portentous split between the Latin and Greek churches could be remedied only by a major effort. Constans, acting at the suggestion of Pope Julius, persuaded Constantius to join him in summoning a general council of the churches at Sardica (the present-day Sofia). Gathering in the autumn of 343, the council in the end merely aggravated the problem. Confronted by a western demand that Athanasius and Marcellus sit with the council, the outnumbered easterners simply withdrew. The Latin rump of the council proceeded to pass canons that confirmed the appellate jurisdiction of Rome and to issue, against the advice of Athanasius, a theological statement whose language could only appear, to easterners, to support monarchianism. The western bishops insisted in so many words that there is but one hypostasis of Father, Son, and Holy Spirit; and while they also asserted that they did not deny the real distinction of the three, this language (no doubt intended to render in Greek the sense of the Latin "one substance" formula; see II:7) was bound to be taken as an attack on the whole Origenist tradition of the East.

In the face of this deadlock, the two emperors decided that concessions must be made on both sides to break it. On the death of his rival, the Cappadocian Gregory, in 347, Athanasius was restored to his church at Alexandria amide passionate manifestations of popular support. In the West, all efforts to rehabilitate Marcellus of Ancyra were quietly abandoned. The peace thus attained, however, was not to endure for long. In 350, Emperor Constans was murdered by the supporters of an usurper, Magnentius by name. After a struggle of three years' duration, Magnentius was defeated in his turn by Constantius II, who thus in 353 became the sole ruler of the empire. This critical change in the political situation was accompanied by a revival of the theological battle in a new and more explicit form. Restored to his see, Athanasius launched an open and aggressive defense of the Nicene creed and of the term *homoousios* (which hitherto had scarcely been mentioned in the controversy) by publishing a treatise, *On the Decrees of the Nicene Synod* (350–351). From the second-generation Arian teacher Aetius (d. ca. 370), who was resident in Alexandria during this period, Athanasius's argument evoked a reply which was to become the trademark of a renewed and radical Arianism: the assertion that the Logos/Son is "unlike" the Father. A new stage had been opened in the controversy over Nicaea.

These theological developments were overshadowed at first by the heroic efforts of Emperor Constantius to create unanimity by enforcing an essentially noncommital, middle-of-the-road imperial orthodoxy. His first step in this direction was to rid himself of Athanasius. At synods held in Arles (353) and Milan (355), he forced the western bishops to abandon Athanasius and to resume full communion with the eastern churches. Those who resisted—Liberius of Rome (352–366), the aging Hosius of Cordova, and Hilary of Poitiers (d. 367)—were promptly exiled. Athanasius was driven from Alexandria in 356 and took refuge for the next six years among the monks of the Egyptian hinterland. This much accomplished, the emperor proceeded, under the guidance of Arian advisers, to deal with the doctrinal problem. A synod held at the imperial residence, Sirmium, in 357 published a declaration which insisted that "there ought to be no mention" of terms like *substantia,* or *ousia,* or *homoousios,* which were unscriptural, or of phrases suggesting that the Son is "subordinated to the Father."[1] This formula, which repudiated Nicaea and in effect made room for Arianism, has gone down in history as "the blasphemy of Sirmium," a label given it by Bishop Phoebadius of Agennum in Gaul. Despite opposition, however, Constantius did not relent. Through a series of councils and synods in 359, he compelled the unhappy assent of eastern and western bishops alike to a formula which was finally established as representing imperial orthodoxy by a synod held in Constantinople in 360. This formula— a vacuous compromise which in effect marked the official triumph of the

---

[1] J. N. D. Kelly, *Early Christian Creeds,* 3rd ed. (New York, 1972), pp. 285f.

Arian cause—forbade the use of the terms *ousia* and "hypostasis" and contented itself with the statement that "the Son is like the Father." This "Homoean" (from the Greek *homoios,* "like") formula did repudiate the "Anomoean" doctrine of Aetius and his followers, who held that the Son is "unlike" (*anomoios*) the Father, but it did not exclude the original doctrine of Arius himself.

The political triumph of a form of Arianism, however, was accompanied by other, less obvious, developments, which portended a change in the theological climate. Led by Basil, bishop of Ancyra (336–360), many of the eastern bishops in the Origenist tradition reacted strongly not only against Aetius's Anomoeanism, but also against the new orthodoxy of Constantius's court bishops. In opposition to the minimizing formula that the Logos is "like" the Father, they insisted that he is not only "like" but "like in respect of substance" (*homoiousios*). The fear of monarchianism, which had hitherto blinded them to the implications of Arian language, was now joined to an equal fear that the Son's divinity would be negated. They were still hesitant to use the term *homoousios* (which to them seemed to imply a denial that God, Logos, and Spirit are distinct hypostases), but their position was now approaching that defined by the Nicene formula. In the meantime, Athanasius from his exile in the Egyptian desert was also resisting Constantius's theological solution by defending the language of Nicaea. To Athanasius, as he was swift to say, *homoousios* did not mean that the Son is "identical with the Father." It rather meant that the Logos is "in full possession of whatever belongs to the Father," that there is an "unalterable similarity—not to say identity—of . . . qualities" between them, even though the Logos "has from the Father whatever he possesses."[2] The point of this contention for him had already been made plain in his earlier (339?) apologetic treatise, *On the Incarnation.* With Arius, Athanasius accepted the view that there can be no halfway house between Creator and creature. Unlike Arius, however, he was convinced that creation and redemption alike imply and entail a direct presence of the Uncreated God in and for creatures—an immanence of the Transcendent. It would not do, therefore, to attribute creation and redemption to a glorified creature like the Arian Logos and thus to isolate God from God's world. No more was it possible for humanity to come to share in the divine way of being—to be "divinized"—except through the presence of one who is truly God. Thus, the Logos, in and through whom God creates and redeems, must be all that God is. This, to Athanasius, was the message of Nicaea; and his understanding was not so far removed from that of the homoiousians of Basil of Ancyra's school that a meeting of minds was out of the question. Everything depended upon the discovery of a way of combining the eastern insistence upon three hypostases with the Nicene language of "one substance" (*ousia*).

---

[2] *Orations against the Arians,* 3.36.

Chapter 4

The Later Nicene Struggle

CONSTANTIUS II DIED in 361 and was succeeded as sole ruler by his cousin Julian (332–363), called in Christian tradition "the Apostate." The son of Constantine's half-brother Julius Constantius, Julian at the age of five had seen his father and all save one of his brothers slaughtered by Constantius II's troops. Raised to be a Christian, but governed by an abiding distrust of his imperial cousin, Julian was made Caesar in 355, by which time he had become, under the influence of Neoplatonist teachers, a convinced if discreet pagan. An able and imaginative military leader and administrator in Gaul, he was marching at the head of his troops to overthrow Constantius II when the latter died. Once he had come to power, Julian pursued his ideal of a reform and revival of pagan religion, to which he had a serious, not to say romantic, commitment. In the process, he took various steps to limit the influence of Christians and to discourage Christian customs. In particular, he excluded Christians from teaching in imperially supported schools (and thus, in effect, from the rhetorical education which was the key to public advancement) and from occupying high imperial office. Further, from the beginning of his reign, he allowed the various bishops—both homoousian and homoiousian—whom Constantius had exiled to return to their churches, "to the end that, as this freedom increased their dissension, he might afterwards have no fear of a united populace."[1] In Alexandria at least, this policy failed. Athanasius returned from his hiding-place among the monks of Egypt in 362, and he was received with such enthusiasm by a united populace that Julian exiled him for the fourth time before the end of the year.

The brief reign of Julian—which ended in 363 when he lost his life on campaign against the Persians—showed the weakness of the Arianizing party which Constantius had supported. For one thing, Athanasius, at a synod convened in Alexandria in 362, held out an olive branch to the homoiousian party by admitting, on the one hand, that "three hypostases," the cry of the eastern

[1] Ammianus Marcellinus, *Rerum Gestarum Libri* 12.5.4.

conservatives, was not intended to mean "three Gods" or three "subsistences
. . . alien in substance from one another," and then insisting, on the other,
that *homoousios* meant "identity of nature" but was not intended to deny the
truth that Father, Logos, and Spirit are distinct.[2] This synod also made it clear
that (as Athanasius had argued in a correspondence with Bishop Serapion of
Thmuis) the Holy Spirit also is to be regarded as being "of the same substance"
as God. Thus, the synod, under Athanasius's leadership, decreed that for reconciliation of the parties it would be enough for all to repudiate Arianism, to
"confess the faith confessed by the holy Fathers at Nicaea," and to "anathe-
matize . . . those who say that the Holy Spirit is a creature."[3] These were
generous terms to come from so single-minded a combatant as Athanasius—
and one who had suffered much from the very group with which he was
attempting to achieve reconciliation. Like the homoiousians themselves, he was
obviously convinced by now that it was the imperial orthodoxy of Constantius
II which was the real threat to Christian faith, and in this conviction he opened
a way for the settlement which was to be brought about by the Cappadocian
Fathers after his death in 373.

Julian's death was followed by the brief reign of Jovian (363–364), a Nicene
Christian who had little opportunity or inclination to meddle in church affairs.
Jovian—whose accession brought Athanasius back from his fourth exile—was
succeeded by Valentinian I (364–375), who assigned sovereignty over the East
to his brother Valens (374–378), in order to facilitate the defense of Rome's
embattled frontiers. Valentinian as far as possible eschewed interference in
religious problems and practiced an evenhanded tolerance; but his brother,
who was strongly influenced by the Arian clergy of Constantinople, actively
followed out the policies of Constantius II. In 365, he condemned Athanasius
to yet a fifth exile, but his wrath fell indiscriminately on both homoousian and
homoiousian leaders and thus furthered the process of reconciliation which
Athanasius had begun in 362.

By the time of Athanasius's death in 373, both intellectual and political
leadership in the struggle against Arianism had passed into fresh hands: those
of the so-called "new Nicene" Party. This group, led by Basil the Great, metropolitan bishop of Cappadocian Caesarea (370–379) and Meletius, bishop of
Antioch (d. 381), was composed of eastern Origenists and former homoiousians
who had rallied to the support of the Nicene faith under the influence of
Athanasius. It was their task to work for reconciliation of the various groups
and schools that had stood against Arianism but were themselves divided by
past antagonisms or misunderstandings, and at the same time to formulate and
defend a theological framework within which the full divinity of Word and
Spirit might be confessed.

Basil himself was the heart and soul of this new party. Born of a prominent

---

[2] *Tomus ad Antiochenos* 5–6.   [3] Ibid., 3.

Cappadocian family in about 330, Basil was educated at Constantinople and Athens. At Athens, he began a lifelong friendship with Gregory of Nazianzus, whose eloquence and learning would eventually win the people of the imperial capital to the Nicene cause. After completing his education, Basil turned away from the public career as a rhetor which would ordinarily have been his. For a year, he traveled among the ascetics of Egypt and Palestine. On returning to his native land, he established a community of monks on a family estate in Pontus. Though soon called to a more active life, he continued until his death to be the untiring guide and leader of the monastic movement in his homeland. Once elected bishop of Caesarea, Basil worked to reconcile West and East, "old" and "new" Nicenes, in the struggle with Arianism. At the same time, he confronted two new theological problems. Among those former homoiousians who now confessed the full divinity of the Son, there were some who persisted in denying the divinity of the Holy Spirit. Against these so-called Pneumato-machi ("Spirit-fighters") or "Macedonians," Basil wrote his classic treatise, *On the Holy Spirit*. Of even greater importance than this debate, however, was that with the Anomoean teacher Eunomius, a disciple of Aetius, who argued that, since God is by definition ungenerated and the Son generated, the two must be unlike in nature.

In these theological battles, Basil had the assistance of two men whose teaching, together with his own, would play the same seminal role in eastern Christian thought as would that of Augustine of Hippo in western theology. The first of these was his friend Gregory of Nazianzus (329?–389?), who like Basil himself was drawn to the contemplative life but unlike Basil had little taste in, or capacity for, the conduct of affairs or the compromises and ambiguities of politics. An orator of great distinction and an imaginative and discerning theologian, Gregory was also a man of almost excessive sensitivity, with a tendency to retreat from the positions of public responsibility which others thrust upon him. His permanent monument is the body of sermons which he left behind him, sermons whose thoughtfulness and eloquence show well enough why it was that his contemporaries sought again and again to violate his retirement.

The second of Basil's associates was his younger brother Gregory of Nyssa. He, too, lacked Basil's flair for leadership and administration, but he surpassed both Basil and Gregory of Nazianzus in theological depth and penetration. His extensive writings, which mostly came from the period after his brother's death, when Gregory took up his pen to defend and develop Basil's teaching, include sermons, treatises, tracts, and commentaries. He addressed not merely the issues of the Arian controversy (especially in his works against Eunomius) but also the problems of theological anthropology and of the spiritual life. In the process he achieved a major critical revision of the Origenist and Platonist tradition in eastern theology. The time of his death is unknown, but he lived until after 394.

The key to the Cappadocian reconciliation of the "old" Nicene party with the eastern tradition represented by the homoiousians lay in a careful distinction between the senses of the words *ousia* and *hupostasis*. Beginning with the presupposition that Father, Word, and Spirit are three distinct hypostases (concrete, subsistent realities), the Cappadocians argued that each of these hypostases instantiates a single, identical being or nature (*ousia:* the Latin "substance")—that, namely, of Deity—and are for this reason properly called *homoousioi*. Thus, the divine hypostases ("persons" in the Latin idiom) are seen to be three distinct ways in which the same being exists. The Cappadocians further argued that the unity of God's being or nature implies the unity of God's activity or operation. The three "persons," in other words, are not distinct from one another because they engage in different activities. All are involved, though in distinguishable ways, in every divine action. What alone sets the hypostases apart from one another is the way they are related to one another—as Source, Offspring, and Procession, respectively, of the one Deity. In developing this doctrine, the Cappadocians not only carried through the logic of Nicaea's confession that God and his Word are "the same sort of thing," but they also completely revised the traditional Hellenic-Christian picture of God and God's relation to creatures. If Word and Spirit are fully God and not "mediating" powers, then there is, as Anthanasius had contended, a direct and non-mediated presence of God with creatures. If this is true, moreover, then the transcendence of God has to be understood in a way quite different from that in which the traditional Logos-theology had expressed it. The Cappadocians did not conceive God's nature or being as something "opposite," and hence opposed to, that of creatures. Rather—against Eunomius, who defined God's being as "ungeneratedness" over against the "generatedness" of creatures—they argued that the divine being or nature is in the strictest sense all-encompassing because it is infinite and indefinable.

The political and theological work of the Cappadocian Fathers bore its fruit only after the defeat and death of the emperor Valens at the hands of the Visigoths. This event, which occurred in 378 near Adrianople, led the surviving emperor, Gratian (367–383), who was Valens's nephew, to appoint a new Augustus for the East. For this task, he selected a forceful Spanish soldier and administrator named Theodosius (379–395), who assumed office in the year of Basil the Great's death. As a westerner, Theodosius I (likewise called "the Great") was sympathetic to the Nicene cause. Gregory of Nazianzus was called to Constantinople, where, in the oratory of the Anastasia, he delivered the famous "Theological Orations," in which he set out the classic defense of the Nicene cause. In 380, Theodosius and Gratian issued an edict decreeing that "all the peoples" of the empire should "practice . . . the religion that is followed by the pontiff Damasus [of Rome] and by Peter, bishop of Alexandria"—that orthodox Christianity, namely, which confessed "the single Deity of the Father, the Son, and the Holy Spirit."[4] This decree, which marked the triumph of the Nicene party over Arianism, also marked a new moment in history of the relation of the churches to the Roman state. Clearly, in the minds of Gratian and Theodosius, Christianity was now the official religion of the empire, and all others were forbidden, including deviant forms of Christianity itself.

In 381, Theodosius summoned a synod of eastern bishops to meet at Constantinople. This council, recognized eventually as the second ecumenical council of the church, had as its primary business the affirmation of the full Deity of the Holy Spirit against the Macedonian party. It naturally confirmed the symbol (i.e., "creed" or "confession") of the Council of Nicaea. At the same time, its members seem to have considered another formula as well: a declaratory baptismal symbol in which the key Nicene words and phrases had been inserted, and which also contained the anti-Macedonian declaration that the Holy Spirit "is worshiped and glorified together with the Father and the Son." This confession, though not officially adopted by the Council of 381, continued to be associated with its name and was later, at the Council of Chalcedon in 451, declared to be the "faith" of the one hundred and fifty bishops assembled under Theodosius. It was this symbol which, by reason of its growing use as a liturgical and baptismal formula, gradually achieved universal acceptance. It was and is called "Nicene" because it incorporated the anti-Arian phrases—and so expressed the faith—of the creed of Nicaea.

Theology, however, was only a part of the business of this council. One of the most difficult problems of the last years of the Arian controversy was that of the reunification of the church at Antioch. There the long debate over Nicaea had produced internal schisms, not only between Arians and orthodox but also between a small group of "old Nicenes" led by one Paulinus, who enjoyed the support of the bishops of Rome and Alexandria, and the majority body led by the bishop Meletius, a "new Nicene." The emperor, Theodosius, signaled his own judgment in this matter by appointing Meletius president of the council (and thus qualifying, in the light of eastern realities, his earlier judgment that orthodoxy consisted simply in agreement with the bishops of Rome and of Alexandria). Meletius, however, died in the course of the meeting. Gregory of Nazianzus, on the other hand, who had been elected at the opening of the council to replace the Arian Demophilus as bishop of Constantinople, was frustrated by the unwillingness of the bishops to conciliate Rome (and the West generally) by recognizing Paulinus. Accordingly, in a gesture of disgust, he resigned his new honor and returned home, leaving the council to elect a successor to himself as well as to Meletius. This it proceeded to do by naming two supporters of the "new Nicene" party: one Flavian as

---

[4] J. Stevenson, *Creeds, Councils, and Controversies* (New York, 1966), p. 160.

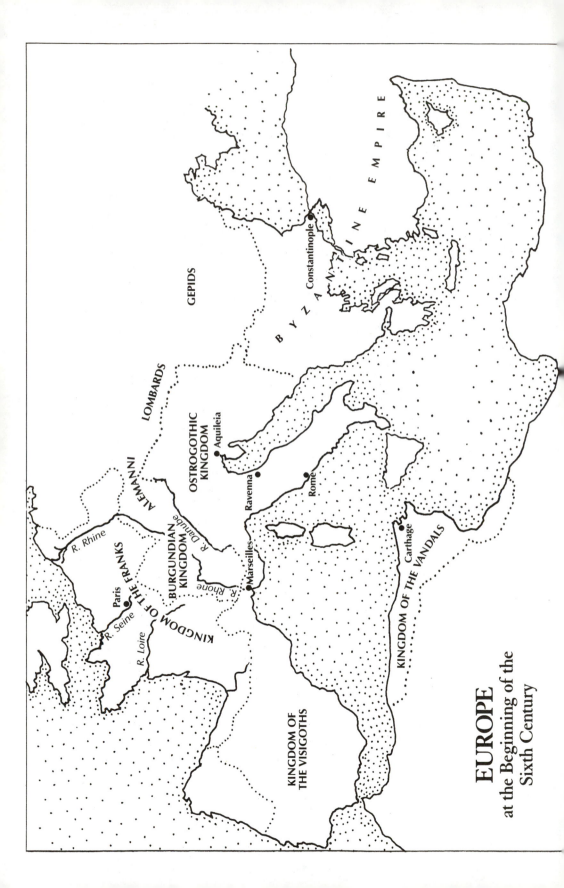

EUROPE
at the Beginning of the
Sixth Century

BYZANTINE EMPIRE

GEPIDS

LOMBARDS

ALEMANNI

OSTROGOTHIC
KINGDOM

Aquileia

Ravenna

Rome

R. Rhine

R. Danube

BURGUNDIAN
KINGDOM

R. Rhone

Marseilles

Paris

R. Seine

KINGDOM OF THE FRANKS

R. Loire

KINGDOM OF
THE VISIGOTHS

Carthage

KINGDOM OF THE VANDALS

Constantinople

bishop of Antioch and an imperial lay official, Nectarius, as bishop of Constantinople. This course of action, which entirely disregarded the views of Damasus of Rome (not to mention those of Timothy, the new bishop of Alexandria), meant that the council's work was regarded with a certain hostility in the West; and this reaction was enhanced by the synod's Third Canon, which stated that the bishop of Constantinople should have "the primacy of honor" after the bishop of Rome, on the ground that Constantinople was "the new Rome." This action violated the custom of seeing Rome and Alexandria as the "senior" churches, and it also violated the commitment of the Roman church to the view that the "honor" of a church depended not on the political status of its city but on its early relation to the apostle Peter. The upshot of the Council of Constantinople, therefore, was not only a triumph of Nicene theology, but also a new source of friction between West and East and, in the East itself, of tension between the ancient see of Alexandria and that of the new imperial capital, which the Council's Second Canon had constituted as a patriarchal see.

Chapter 5

The Germanic Invasions

*T*HE BATTLE OF ADRIANOPLE (378), in which the emperor Valens lost his life as well as his army to the Visigoths, marked the effective beginning of a new crisis in the relations of the Roman Empire with the Germanic tribes across its Rhine and Danube frontiers. This battle initiated the process—which took two full centuries for its accomplishment—by which the western half of the empire was invaded, conquered, and divided by Goths, Franks, Vandals, and Lombards. These invasions, which involved not armies merely but whole peoples, were made possible by the combination of clans and tribes into confederacies and nations under unified leadership. They were made almost inevitable by the westward movement of Hunnic peoples from the steppes of Asia, a movement which pressed the Germanic tribes closer to the borders of Rome and ultimately forced them to seek safety by crossing in force into Roman territory.

By the fourth century, the Franks occupied the right bank of the lower Rhine and indeed lived partly as a "federated" people within the borders of the empire. The confederation known as the Visigoths or "West Goths" occupied the bank of the Danube north of Thrace, and ranged behind them, under direct pressure from the Huns, were their kinsmen the Ostrogoths or "East Goths," whose center was north of the Black Sea. Between the Goths in the south and the Franks in the north were a variety of groups: Vandals, Alans, Burgundians.

By this time, there was frequent intercourse between Romans and Germans across the frontiers. Germans served in the Roman armies in increasing numbers. Roman traders brought their goods into Germanic territories. Many Germans were settled in border provinces, where they became accustomed to Roman ways.

It was inevitable, in these circumstances, that the Germanic tribes come into contact with Christianity. Prisoners of war from Cappadocia—probably taken during a Gothic raid of 264 into Asia Minor—planted the seeds of Christianity among the Visigoths before the end of the third century. It was one Ulfilas, however, who began formal evangelization. Born around 311, Ulfilas, a descendant of the Cappadocian prisoners, was himself a Goth. As a young man, probably because he was a lector in the church, he began a translation of the Christian scriptures into Gothic. After accompanying a Gothic embassy to Constantinople, he was ordained in 341 by Eusebius of Nicomedia (who by this time was bishop of Constantinople) to be bishop of the Goths. An Arian, Ulfilas eventually espoused the views of the Homoean party—the imperial orthodoxy of Constantius II. He worked for seven years among his people, until persecution forced him and his fellow Christians to seek refuge on Roman soil. The final conversion of the Visigoths took place only when their king, Fritigern, in 376, led his whole nation into the church after they had themselves taken refuge from the Huns on Roman territory. Thus, the Goths—who defeated Valens at Adrianople in 378, in a battle growing out of a dispute with the Roman authorities—were a people who had accepted Valens's own faith: Arian Christianity. It was not just the Visigoths, however, but their neighbors as well—the Ostrogoths, the Vandals in part, and the Burgundians—who had embraced Christianity in its Arian form before invading the empire. Only the groups farthest removed from the Visigoths, the Franks and Saxons of the north, were predominantly pagan at the time of their incursions. The Germanic tribes, then, did not on the whole come as enemies of Christianity. Indeed, they did not come as enemies of Rome. If they had adopted Christianity, it was because Christianity was the religion of the Romans; and what they sought was to have a share in the benefits of Roman civilization.

After the disaster of Adrianople, Theodosius I managed to restrain the Visigoths, at first by concessions and payments of money. On his death in 395, however, the empire was divided between his two sons, Arcadius (393–408) in the East and Honorius (393–423) in the West. With its counsels and interests thus divided, the empire proved unable to resist the Gothic attack. Under their new king, Alaric, the Visigoths turned on Constantinople and ravaged Greece as far as Sparta. Diverted to the West, by 401 they were pressing into northern Italy, but were successfully resisted at first by Theodosius's able Vandal general, Stilicho, to whom he had entrusted the welfare of the young Honorius. In 408, however, Honorius brought about Stilicho's assassination. This act opened the road to Rome itself, and in 410 Alaric and his warriors captured the imperial city—an event which shocked the Roman world. Wanting to secure Roman Africa, the granary of Italy, as a kingdom for himself, Alaric continued south, but he died on the verge of crossing into Sicily. His successor, Athaulf, led the Visigoths back north. In 412, he invaded southern Gaul, and by 419 the Goths had settled there. In the course of the fifth century, they came to dominate not only the south of Gaul but Spain as well, subjecting the Roman inhabitants and appropriating much of their land.

During the long trek of the Visigoths from the Danube provinces to Gaul, the German tribes across the Rhine had recognized and seized an opportunity. At the close of 406, the Arian Vandals together with the pagan Alans and Suevi crossed the Rhine, pushed across Gaul, and descended upon Spain, where they arrived before the Visigoths. At roughly the same time, the Franks had pressed into northern Gaul, while the Burgundians occupied the region around Strassburg. Britain, from which Roman troops were finally withdrawn in 410, came under increasingly frequent attack from the Saxons, Angles, and Jutes, and the Romanized Celts were driven westward into Cornwall, Wales, and Strathclyde. The Vandals in Spain, under pressure from the Visigoths, crossed into Africa in 429 in full force. Their king, Gaiseric, soon established a powerful German state there, and his ships speedily dominated the western Mediterranean. A Vandal raid sacked Rome in 455.

In a space of about fifty years, then, Roman power, if not the influence of the Roman name and the order which it symbolized, was destroyed in Britain, Gaul, Spain, and North Africa. The kings of the new barbarian nations were, it is true, technically servants of the Roman state, whose authority they were proud to bear. From time to time, they were glad to co-operate with the imperial authorities in Italy. It was at Roman behest that the Visigoths attacked the Vandals in Spain. It was a united Roman and German army which fought the invading Huns under Attila to a standstill at a battle near Châlons in 451. Although Attila went on to invade Italy, he eventually retired to the seat of his empire, in what is now Hungary, and died there before he had consolidated his conquests.

Even in Italy, however, the power of the western emperors declined, and they gradually became the puppets of their generals. On the death of Honorius, the imperial office devolved upon Valentinian III (423–455). His long reign was marked by a quarrel between Boniface, count of Africa, and Aetius, count of Italy—a quarrel which permitted the Vandal conquest of North Africa. It was Aetius, leader of the Roman forces against Attila in 451, who gained the empire's last military victory. Between the death of Valentinian and the year 476, no fewer than nine emperors were set up and deposed in the West, while Italy was effectively ruled by a series of dominant military leaders. The last emperor, called Romulus Augustulus, was set aside by the German general Odovakar, an event which is normally spoken of as the "end" of the Roman Empire in the West. In fact, it had little significance. Neither Odovakar nor his contemporaries had any notion that Roman rule was at an end, for he ruled in Italy, even as the Visigoths did in Gaul and Spain, as a deputy of the Emperor in Constantinople, though the latter had little influence on events.

Odovakar's sovereignty in Italy was ended in 493 by a new set of German invaders, the Ostrogoths led by their king, Theodoric. Under this successful conqueror, an attempt was made to fuse Roman and Germanic institutions, an attempt which ultimately failed because the social and religious barriers between Goth and Roman were strictly maintained. Theodoric ruled from Ravenna until his death in 526. It was shortly after this that the emperor Justinian (527–565) embarked upon the enterprise of reconquering the western empire from the barbarians. In 533, his general, Belisarius, invaded North Africa and reestablished imperial authority there. In 535, the reconquest of Italy was begun, to be completed, after years of warfare and devastation, two decades later. Justinian's triumph, though, was short-lived. Three years after his death, yet another Germanic people, the Lombards, invaded the Italian peninsula. By 572, they controlled most of the north of Italy. Rome, Ravenna (which was the seat of the imperial governor), and the south remained under the authority of Constantinople.

In the meantime, events of great significance for the future were under way in Gaul. The Frankish nation had long been pressing into the northern sector of the ancient Roman provinces. From about 481, when one Clovis became king of the Salian Franks, this pressure turned into conquest. Clovis soon extended his rule as far south as the river Loire. In 493, he married Clotilda, a Burgundian princess who was, unlike most of her people, a catholic and not an Arian. After a victory in 496 over the Alemanni, Clovis declared for Christianity. He was baptized, together with three thousand of his followers, on Christmas Day at Reims, and, what is more, baptized as a catholic. The Franks thus became the first of the Germanic nations to espouse the orthodox Christianity of the empire—a fact which gained them favor not merely at Constantinople but also among the people and clergy of the Roman population of Gaul. By the time of Clovis's death, the Frankish kingdom extended to the Pyrenees in the South and beyond the Rhine in the East (see IV:2). There was now, once again, a potentially powerful catholic state in the West: a fact which was to have far-reaching effects in the future, when the Roman bishops were compelled to turn to France rather than to Constantinople for support.

The conversion of the Franks also influenced the other Germanic rulers and peoples, though the example of the native populations among whom they had settled worked even more powerfully. The Burgundians abandoned Arianism in 517 and became a part of the Frankish kingdom in 532. Justinian's conquests ended the Arian kingdoms of the Vandals and the Ostrogoths. In Spain, the Visigothic king, Reccared, renounced Arianism in 587, an act which was confirmed at the third Council of Toledo in 589. In about 590, the gradual conversion of the Lombards to catholic Christianity was begun, though it was not completed until about 660. In this way, Arianism finally disappeared.

Chapter 6

The Growth of the Papacy

THE FOURTH CENTURY and the era of the barbarian invasions saw a significant development both in the effective influence of the bishops of Rome and in the claims made on their behalf. The roots of this authority lay originally as much in the location, wealth, and make-up of the Roman church as in the association of the apostles Peter and Paul with its early years. Nevertheless, as time went on, the claims of the Roman see to pre-eminence were increasingly—and in the end exclusively—based on the accepted fact that its bishops were the successors of Peter. This was neither meant nor understood, however, as a mere claim about the past. The Roman church was in fact the keeper of the tombs of the martyred apostle and of his colleague, Paul. The emperor Constantine had honored it, and them, by constructing the two shrines of St. Peter, on the Vatican hill, and St. Paul without the Walls. The spirit and presence of these apostles, therefore, brooded over the Roman church and, in a special way, defended it. It is scarcely surprising, then, that this church was seen to possess an exceptional authority, not merely among the churches of southern Italy, where it was acknowledged to have a rightful jurisdiction, but in the West generally and even, up to a point, in the East.

When Pope Damasus (366–384) began the custom of describing the Roman church simply as "the apostolic see," he was no doubt in a certain sense innovating and, at the same time, trying to make a point. He wanted, on the one hand, to insist on the pre-eminence of Rome even among patriarchal churches and, on the other, to protest the elevation of Constantinople, which had no claims to apostolic foundation, above Alexandria and Antioch, which had. His point was not without justification in precedent. The status of the Roman bishop had been recognized by Constantine when he turned to Pope Miltiades to adjudicate Donatist claims in Africa; and in the days of Julius (337–352), it had been tacitly acknowledged by the eastern bishops, who asked Roman approval of the depositions of Athanasius and Marcellus of Ancyra. Damasus's successor, Pope Siricius (384–399), though overshadowed by his great contemporary, Ambrose of Milan, exercised a disciplinary authority not only over churches in Italy but over those in Gaul and Spain as well. By the end of the fourth century, Rome did not merely claim, but possessed, a special role and authority among the churches generally. It was the senior patriarchal see. Its word was weighty even in the East. In the West, it was beginning to exercise an authority almost legislative in character.

The popes of the fifth century expanded this authority. Innocent I (402–417), although his attempt to intervene in eastern affairs in defense of John Chrysostom (see III:8) came to nothing, successfully asserted the prestige and authority of the Roman bishop in the West. He referred to the Roman bishop as "head and apex of the episcopate,"[1] and, on the basis of the canons of the Council of Sardica, which he attributed to the Council of Nicaea, he claimed a universal jurisdiction.[2] The same spirit animated Pope Leo I (440–461), called "the Great." He insisted upon the primacy of Peter among the apostles and taught that the popes, as Peter's heirs at law, inherited his role as supreme ruler and teacher, so that Peter could be said to speak in and through them. It was in this spirit that he intervened in the Eutychian controversy (see III:9) with his *Tome* addressed to Flavian, bishop of Constantinople. This document was ultimately accepted, at the Council of Chalcedon (451), as definitive of orthodox belief, with the cry, "Peter has spoken through Leo." Though partially frustrated in his attempts to assert Rome's authority in the East (Canon 28 of this same Council of Chalcedon accorded the see of Constantinople an honor and authority equal to that of Rome), Leo saw his position vindicated in the West. In North Africa, Spain, and Gaul, he established his authority as the supreme judge of appeal in questions of church order; and this authority was confirmed by the emperor Valentinian III, who decreed by "perpetual edict that it shall not be lawful for the bishops of Gaul or of the other provinces . . . to do aught without the authority of the venerable Pope of the Eternal City."[3] The popular and official view of Leo and of his office is further revealed in an ancient account of the embassy he was asked to lead to Attila the Hun when the latter was approaching Rome with his troops. "The king," it was reported, was "so pleased at the presence of the chief Christian priest, that he gave orders to desist from the war."[4] The Roman bishop was becoming not only the teacher but also the leader and guardian of the Christian people of the West.

Later, in the struggle with Monophysitism (see III:10), the bishops of Rome regularly asserted their authority against the efforts of eastern emperors to placate the Monophysites of Syria and Egypt by qualifying the Chalcedonian

---

[1] Innocent, *Epistle* 37.1.
[2] Innocent, *Epistle* 2.25.
[3] Leo, *Epistle* 11, in Stevenson, *Creeds*, p. 304.
[4] Stevenson, *Creeds*, p. 359.

doctrine that there are "two natures" in Christ. This policy led, in the pontificate of Felix III (483–492), to the excommunication by Rome of the patriarch of Constantinople, Acacius. The schism which resulted—the so-called "Acacian schism"—was resolved in 519 in favor of the papal position. This triumph, however, while it demonstrated the importance of the Roman see in the ecclesiastical affairs even of the eastern empire, evidenced at the same time a growing alienation between the western and eastern churches—an alienation which was underscored not many years later, when Pope Vigilius (537–555) was carried off to Constantinople by the emperor Justinian and held in virtual imprisonment to force his assent to what looked, to westerners, like yet another imperial attempt to compromise with the Monophysites. The East acknowledged the patriarchal status (and the political weight) of the Roman bishop, but not the universal authority claimed for him by Leo I and his successors. In the increasingly barbarian West, on the other hand, the popes remained, even when their actual power was severely restricted, the symbols of both apostolic authority and Roman tradition.

Chapter 7

Monasticism

BEGINNING IN THE LATER THIRD CENTURY and burgeoning in the course of the fourth, the movement which history has labeled "monastic" (from the Greek *monachos,* "solitary") contributed a new dimension, both institutionally and spiritually, to the life of the churches. In many ways, this movement was a continuation of tendencies already established in the Christian communities. Baptism, as we have seen, had traditionally been understood as entrance upon a life marked by renunciation of the present order of things and entire dedication to the new order manifested in the resurrection of Christ. The model of this new life, moreover, had been discerned in the witness of the martyrs, who, like Christ himself, had fought against the powers of evil and triumphed over them through death—counting the world and its values things to be spurned for the sake of the kingdom of God. From early on, therefore, the churches had known their ascetics, who, whether individually or in household groups, sought, in imitation of Christ and his martyrs, to live the Christian life in its fullness by systematic renunciation of all attachments to the world. Leaving the pursuit and possession of riches, committed to sexual continence, and devoted to prayer, fasting, and the study of the Scriptures, such persons sought to live in the present age as citizens of the age to come. In this enterprise, moreover, they found encouragement in the Hellenic ideal of the "philosophical life," a life which turned from dependence on externals and, through the practice of virtue, sought attunement with, and contemplative knowledge of, ultimate reality.

But if the monastic movement had roots in an earlier Christian asceticism, it also differed from it. For one thing, monasticism arose originally among the peasantry, a class of persons which Christianity, hitherto an essentially urban movement, had only begun to touch. Its initial growth was coextensive with the conversion of the non-Hellenized populations of the Egyptian and Syrian hinterlands. At the same time, monasticism was a movement of withdrawal and retreat. It instinctively sought the desert: that is, sought physical and social separation from city, town, and village, and so from the normal life of the churches as well. Such withdrawal (Greek *anachorēsis,* whence the English "anchorite") had no single or simple significance. In part, it reflected a quest for solitude; in part, it was a gesture which dramatized rejection of worldliness and even contempt for civilization and culture. But it was also, at least in some areas, a manifestation of the continuing flight of an overburdened peasantry from the demands of the estate steward and the tax collector. Since, at the same time, this movement of withdrawal represented an impulse at once lay and popular and embodied an irresistible upsurge of religious enthusiasm, monasticism created a problem for the churches and their leaders, the bishops. It threatened, in effect, to create a separate and parallel organization of the Christian life. This problem was resolved only as the leaders of the churches themselves became sponsors, organizers, and, in the end, products of this movement.

The spirit of early monasticism is most easily studied in one of its earliest and most influential leaders, Anthony of Egypt, whose *Life,* written by Athanasius of Alexandria, was a notable piece of propaganda for the movement, widely read in East and West alike. Anthony, a man of native Egyptian (Coptic) ancestry and language, was born around 250. At the age of about twenty, he was seized by Christ's words to the rich young man.[1] He sold his parental inheritance and took up the life of a hermit at the edge of his native village, under the tutelage of an older ascetic. As he progressed in this life, he gradually moved farther into the desert, eventually spending twenty years in the solitude of a ruined fort near the coast of the Red Sea. During all this time, he was engaged in a heroic struggle, like that of the martyrs themselves, against the demonic powers, whom he had challenged in the very desert places where they dwelt. In the name of Christ, by constant work, fasting, and vigil, and by unremitting prayer and recitation of the Scriptures, he overcame these forces of evil. When, in the opening years of the fourth century, Anthony emerged from this retreat,

---

[1] Matt. 19:21.

he seemed to others not merely a hero and a man imbued with holiness, but one who represented human nature restored to its proper glory. He healed the sick, reconciled enemies, and by example and word taught the wisdom he had learned. Others gathered around him, and a loose community of hermits appeared, in training under Anthony for the salvation of their souls. During these same years after the opening of the fourth century, other such leaders and communities appeared, first in the desert of Nitria, southwest of Alexandria and the Nile Delta, and then, as numbers increased, farther out in the desert of Scete and the area known as "the Cells." By the time Anthony died, in 356, there were probably some thousands of ascetics practicing the following of Christ in the desert.

Of this number, however, a significant proportion were practicing a new, communal form of the monastic life which appeared in Upper (southern) Egypt under the leadership and inspiration of Pachomius (ca. 290–346). A native of the village of Chenoboskion, Pachomius, after brief service as a conscript in the Roman army, presented himself for baptism and immediately took up the life of a hermit under the supervision of an older ascetic named Palamon. Around 320 or shortly thereafter, in response to a divine call, Pachomius established an organized monastic community at the village of Tabbenisi. The members of this community lived a strictly common life (*koinos bios,* whence the English "coenobite" or "cenobite"): that is, they followed a common schedule of work, prayer, and meditation (i.e., in practice, recitation from memory of passages from the Scriptures); they ate together and treated all property as common; and they practiced strict obedience to their superiors, who governed the monastery as a whole and its constituent houses in accordance with the *Rule* which Pachomius, no doubt gradually, developed. In time, the Pachomian *koinonia,* as it was called, came to include a number of such monastic centers (including communities of women) and thus constituted the first monastic "order." These communities supported themselves by their work (agriculture and weaving, for example) and were dedicated to mutual assistance and encouragement in practicing the way of salvation.

Whatever the tension between them in principle, both Anthony's eremetical monasticism and Pachomius's cenobitism persisted as the monastic movement spread. In Syria, where the ascetic ideal of Christian life had deep historical roots, the eremetical impulse seems to have appeared as spontaneously as it had in Egypt, but with a characteristic tendency toward extremes of self-denial and eccentricity in ascetic practice. Simeon the Elder (ca. 390–459), for example, the most famous example of such eccentricity, was called "Stylites" because he spent thirty years of his life living at the top of a pillar, where he prayed and preached to the pilgrims who came to visit him. Such holy men were objects of great popular reverence in Syria, and Simeon himself was appealed to by the imperial authorities for assistance in settling the controversies surrounding the councils of Ephesus and Chalcedon (see III:9). At the same time, the fourth century saw the development in Syria and in Palestine of a native form of the cenobitic life; Simeon himself, in fact, had begun his career in a monastery at Teleda, north of Antioch.

In Cappadocia and Pontus, and later in Asia Minor generally, cenobitism became the rule. Introduced around the middle of the fourth century by Eustathius of Sebaste (ca. 300–ca. 377), the monastic life in this region owed its spread and its organization to the efforts of Basil of Caesarea (see III:4) to promote and nourish "the philosophical life." Basil's conviction was that the full Christian life demanded both love of God and love of neighbor. His monks, therefore, were to imitate the life of the apostolic community in Jerusalem, where "all who believed were together and had all things in common."[2] Disapproving of the extremes of asceticism which he had witnessed among some solitaries, Basil, like Pachomius, added obedience to the lists of monastic virtues. The monk was not only to live in community, practicing charity toward neighbors, but was also to renounce self-will by submitting himself to the rule of the community, represented in the person of the abbot. In addition, Basil encouraged monasteries to situate themselves on the edges of cities, where they could be of service to the populace, offering example and instruction as well as hospitality to travelers and care for the sick and needy. These principles and others Basil enunciated as he visited groups of ascetics to deal with their problems and answer their requests for advice. His instructions were committed to writing and edited even during his lifetime, and they were eventually circulated as his *Longer Rules* and *Shorter Rules*—the bases of Greek and Russian monasticism to this day.

It was not only institutionally, however, that Basil and his school (including Gregory of Nazianzus and Gregory of Nyssa) influenced the future of monasticism. At once adepts in and critics of the tradition of Platonist theology which stemmed from Clement of Alexandria and Origen, they provided the ascetic movement with a theoretical framework—a theological and anthropological foundation which could be employed to map the soul's progress from the beginning of its life in Christ at baptism to the fruition of that life in contemplative knowledge of God. A version of this Hellenized and intellectualized asceticism was brought to Egypt by Evagrius Ponticus (346–399), who, after a career in Constantinople, where Gregory of Nazianzus had ordained him deacon, came to the desert of Nitria in 382. His teaching there won some disciples but created opposition among the Coptic monks, who no doubt distrusted his Hellenism and certainly suspected him (not without reason) of dangerous addiction to the views of Origen. The "Origenist Controversy," which began on his death and which ultimately figured in the struggle between the sees of Alexandria and Constantinople that led to John Chrysostom's exile and death (see III:8), had the effect of bringing Evagrius into permanent disrepute (he was condemned

---

[2] Acts 2:44.

for Origenism by the ecumenical council of 553); but it also scattered his disciples and disseminated his teachings, with the result that his understanding of the ascetic life, and of the contemplative knowledge of God at which it aims, significantly influenced western and eastern monasticism alike.

The monastic ideal was first communicated to the West by Athanasius himself and by his *Life of Anthony,* which was swiftly translated into Latin (ca. 360). The earliest hint of monastic institutions in the West is connected with the name of Martin of Tours (ca. 335–397), a hermit around whom a community of anchorites gathered at Liguge and who brought this mode of life with him when he became bishop of Tours. At roughly the same time, Eusebius, bishop of Vercelli (340–371), introduced a new form of monastic community by organizing the clergy of his church under an ascetical rule—a practice later followed by Augustine of Hippo. At Milan, in the 380s, there was a monastery of men just outside the city, whose community was sponsored and supervised by the bishop, Ambrose; and the ascetic life, if not monastic institutions as such, was much popularized by Jerome during his stay at Rome, 381–384. By the last decades of the fourth century, monastic communities seem to have been multiplying in Italy. In Gaul, the monastic movement was given encouragement by the gradual growth, after 410, of a community on the island of Lérins off the coast of Cannes, and then, after 415, of another founded by John Cassian (ca. 360–435), a disciple of Evagrius Ponticus, at Marseilles. Cassian's *Institutes* and *Conferences,* designed to acquaint western ascetics with the Egyptian tradition of monasticism, became foundational documents for western monasticism.

The continuing establishment of new monastic communities in Italy, Gaul, and Spain, and concern for the interior regulation of their life, led in the fifth and sixth centuries to the multiplication of formal rules for individual monasteries—a development no doubt encouraged by Jerome's translation of the *Rule* of Pachomius into Latin. Of these rules, one, the *Rule* of Benedict, was eventually to become the norm for western monasticism. It is almost certainly to be attributed to Benedict of Nursia (ca. 480–ca. 550), the outlines of whose life are known from the *Dialogues* of Pope Gregory the Great. Originally a hermit who dwelt in a cave near Subiaco, he organized the disciples who gathered around him into small communities. Eventually, he removed to Monte Cassino, between Rome and Naples, where he founded the cenobite monastery for which his *Rule* was designed. In the composition of this rule, which is striking for its simplicity and clarity, Benedict no doubt drew on his own experience. He also knew, however, a Latin form of the rules of Basil of Caesarea and Pachomius, and he used a near-contemporary document known as *The Rule of the Master*.

Benedict's conception of a monastery was that of a stable, self-supporting community of persons devoted to the following of Christ. Its members were required to renounce personal possessions, to practice continence, and to remain in their community for life. The head of the community was the abbot, who must be obeyed implicitly but was bound, in his turn, to consult all the brethren in grave matters of common concern. The principal occupations of the monks were three in number: communal praise of God in the sevenfold daily office; manual labor in the fields; and *lectio divina*—the meditative study of Scripture. Like Basil of Caesarea before him, Benedict was skeptical about the value of extremes in asceticism and even more skeptical about the individualism and uprootedness of the anchoritic tradition. His *Rule* was strict but not severe, and it insisted on the communal, even familial, character of the monastic establishment, in which mutual love was to govern. Since all monks had to read in order to carry out the divine office and to study the Scriptures, Benedict's monastery, like most others from the time of Pachomius himself, ran a school whose primary purpose was to teach the brethren reading; and this institution of the monastic school (together with the library which the practice of the *lectio divina* required) was eventually, as the Middle Ages approached, to make monasteries the primary centers of learning in Europe. Benedict's contemporary, Cassiodorus (ca. 485–ca. 580), who was for a time a minister of the Ostrogothic king Theodoric, retired to his estate in the south of Italy to found, in the monastery of Vivarium, what he hoped would be not only a center for the ascetic life but also a center of biblical and humanistic learning. His hopes were not fulfilled, but his typically Roman and aristocratic association of the "withdrawn" life with the cultivation of letters was in fact prophetic of a future function of monasticism in the West.

The Benedictine *Rule* spread very slowly, though it enjoyed the patronage of Pope Gregory the Great, who increasingly used monks as missionaries, as bishops, and as ambassadors. In early seventh-century Gaul, in the reigns of the successors of Clovis, the primary impulse to the further development of monasticism came from the monasteries founded by the Irish monk Columbanus (ca. 543–615), whose *Rule for Monks,* introduced to govern the monasteries of Annegray, Fontaine and, most important of all, Luxeuil, mirrored the life of his home monastery of Bangor (in Ulster), itself a recent foundation. The roots of Irish monasticism lay in the eastern tradition introduced by John Cassian to Provence, whence it had been carried to Britain. This tradition, however, underwent significant modification in Ireland, where, in an essentially tribal society, the monastery and its abbot (rather than the urban congregation with its bishop) became the center of all pastoral work, and the bishop was often the abbot himself or, in some cases, one of the monks. Such monasteries retained their concern with the ascetic life, but they also became centers of missionary endeavor, of care for the poor, and of sacred and secular learning, for which Irish monasticism of the seventh and eighth centuries was famous. As a result of the work of Columbanus, this tradition flourished in Gaul and Italy (where he founded the monastery of Bobbio). Gradually, however, the *Rule* of Columbanus was modified by contact with that of Benedict; and in the age of Charlemagne and the abbot Benedict of Aniane (ca. 750–821), who systematized the Benedictine Rule and made it the basis of a far-reaching reform of monastic life, Benedict's pattern became the norm for all of European monasticism (see IV:6).

Chapter 8

Ambrose and Chrysostom

T HE CONTRASTING SITUATIONS and problems of the churches in the West and the East toward the end of the fourth century are reflected in the almost contemporaneous careers of Ambrose of Milan and John Chrysostom. Both men were preachers and thinkers whose ideas continued to be influential in the church long after their deaths. Each was called, at a significant moment, to serve as bishop in an imperial capital. Both represented, in their different ways, the ideals of the growing ascetic movement. Yet the issues and circumstances which shaped their stories were significantly different.

Born in Trier, probably in the year 339, Ambrose was the son of a praetorian prefect of Gaul and was educated in the rhetorical schools of Rome for a career in the imperial service. He practiced for a time in the Roman law courts, but was eventually (ca. 370) appointed civil governor of the province of Aemilia-Liguria, with its capital at Milan. There, on the death of the Arian bishop Auxentius in 374, a bitter controversy broke out between Arian and Nicene Christians over the question of Auxentius's successor. Compelled to intervene personally in order to keep the peace, Ambrose found himself being acclaimed loudly as the candidate of the Nicene laity. With some reluctance, he acceded to this informal election. Since at the time he was only a catechumen, he was first baptized, then swiftly ordained. He marked this change in his life by giving up his property, adopting the personal discipline of an ascetic, and taking up the study of theology with his former tutor (and later his successor as bishop of Milan), Simplicianus.

Ambrose must be seen in the first instance as a man of affairs, who devoted himself not merely to the care of his flock but also to the welfare of the church at large. Persuasive, practical, and a man of commanding personal authority, he became the counselor and guide of a series of western emperors: Gratian (367–383); Gratian's younger brother, junior colleague, and successor, Valentinian II (375–392); and Gratian's choice to succeed Valens, Theodosius I (379–395). The goal which he sought is clear: the alliance of the Roman state with orthodox Christianity as against Arianism, paganism, and Judaism. It was no doubt under the influence of Ambrose that Gratian in 382 removed the altar (but not the statue) of the goddess Victory from the Roman Senate. Certainly it was his influence which prevailed when, after Gratian's death, the pagan senators under the leadership of Symmachus unsuccessfully petitioned Valentinian II to restore the altar. It was Ambrose who resisted the effort of Valentinian's mother Justina to procure church buildings in Milan for the use of the emperor's Gothic—and therefore Arian—troops. Above all, it was the views of Ambrose which were reflected in the series of edicts that Theodosius I issued after 391 forbidding pagan worship. But if Ambrose was thus a principal architect of the close alliance between Roman state and Christian church in the West, it was also he who gave that relationship the character of an alliance and not an identity. In Ambrose's view, the emperor was the church's sponsor and faithful child, but emphatically not its ruler. Where the internal affairs of the church were concerned—its teaching and discipline—imperial interference was not welcomed: "for the emperor is within the church, not above the church."[1] Thus, when Theodosius I's troops carried out a massacre of civilians at Thessalonica in retaliation for the murder of an imperial official, Ambrose demanded that the emperor imitate King David's behavior in the case of Uriah the Hittite[2] and do public penance in the streets of Milan. Church and state were separate authorities with separate spheres of competence.

It is not only as a man of affairs, however, that Ambrose is remembered. In his time and place, he was a theologian of importance, not so much for his originality of thought as for his introduction of Greek ideas and idioms into Latin Christian thinking. He drew unashamedly on the philosophical, theological, and exegetical work of the Greek past for his preaching and writing. It was this learned quality of his preaching, as well as its eloquence, which attracted the young Augustine of Hippo and started him rethinking his youthful Christian faith. Ambrose's greatest and most influential work was an ethical treatise, *On the Duties of Ministers,* in which he imitated a classic work of Cicero's in the spirit of the new Christian asceticism.

Very different was the life of that John to whom later generations gave the name "Chrysostom," "golden-mouthed." Born of noble parents (his father was an imperial "Master of Soldiers"), John was educated at Antioch under the pagan rhetor Libanius, and later, in theology, under Diodore of Tarsus. Upon his baptism (ca. 370) he, like many others of his time, took up the ascetic life and even, for a period of some years, became a hermit. His austerities, however, affected his health, and he was forced to return to Antioch, where he was ordained successively deacon (381) and presbyter (386) and entered upon the career of regular preaching which won him his reputation. A skilled orator, he was also a faithful exegete, attuned to the needs and problems of his auditors. At the same time, he was, in the spirit of an ascetic, severely critical of the social

---

[1] *Sermon Against Auxentius,* 36.　　[2] See 2 Sam. 11–12.

and economic circumstances of the times. He pilloried the rich for their blindness to the needs of the poor. He argued that private property was introduced only as a consequence of Adam's sin. He criticized vanity in dress and the "double standard" of sexual morality as between husbands and wives. His preaching was not only edifying but on frequent occasion prophetic and blunt even to the point of indiscretion.

In 398, after the death of Nectarius, a complaisant official who had become bishop of Constantinople in 381, John was more or less forcibly imported from Antioch to succeed him. In Constantinople as in Antioch, he soon won a wide popular hearing. Nevertheless, he had enemies in high places. The imperial court of the emperor Arcadius, under the domination of the eunuch Eutropius, was not in the habit of hearing criticism of its ways or of tolerating a bishop who did not behave like a court chaplain. The clergy of Constantinople, grown lax in the days of Nectarius, were soon restive under John's harsh discipline. Outside the city itself, moreover, there was fear among prominent ecclesiastics that a strong bishop of Constantinople would try to assert the patriarchal authority which had been assigned to John's see by the second Ecumenical Council. In particular was this the case with Theophilus, the bishop of Alexandria, who resented the reduction of prestige which he and his church had suffered as a result of the council's decision that Constantinople should rank second after Rome. Theophilus's resentment was shared by the churches of Asia Minor, since theirs was the area over which a bishop of Constantinople would naturally seek to extend his jurisdiction. And as a matter of fact, John did step into the affairs of these churches, deposing a series of bishops who had paid money (to the metropolitan bishop of Ephesus) for their episcopal ordinations.

Caught, then, in the jurisdictional quarrels of the eastern churches and involved with a court which did not appreciate his single-minded devotion to holiness of life, John's fate was sealed when he intervened in the controversy then raging over the teachings of Origen. This controversy had begun in Palestine with the effort of bishop Epiphanius of Salamis (ca. 315-403) to extirpate Origenism in the church of Jerusalem and the monasteries in its vicinity. It had early spread to the West as a result of the involvement, on different sides, of Jerome and Rufinus of Aquileia (see III:15), both of whom had been translators of Origen's works into Latin. Bishop Theophilus of Alexandria, who had originally favored the Origenist cause finally gave in to pressure from the monks of the Nitrian desert and outlawed the teachings of Origen, exiling his advocates from Egypt. Four of these exiles, known as "the tall brothers," fled to Constantinople and were well received by John Chrysostom. Theophilus retaliated almost immediately by going to Asia Minor and holding a synod (403) at an imperial estate near Constantinople known as "the Oak." The synod, composed as it was entirely of John's enemies, deposed him; and since the imperial court had no use for John and the empress Eudoxia was enraged at his criticism of her greed and injustice, the imperial court confirmed the verdict. Almost immediately the empress, troubled by an earthquake and the discontent of the populace, relented of this decision, and John was briefly reinstated; but adversity had not taught him discretion. He was soon inveighing once more against the ways of the court and comparing the empress not only to Jezebel but even to Herodias. In the end, he was exiled to Armenia. The intervention of Pope Innocent I (402–417) accomplished nothing save a schism between Rome and Alexandria. Chrysostom died in 407 as he was traveling to a yet more distant exile, the victim not only of a corrupt imperial court but also of the theological and jurisdictional quarrels which were agitating the eastern churches.

Chapter 9

The Christological Controversies

STIMULATED BY THE TEACHING OF ARIUS and the response of the Council of Nicaea, the trinitarian controversy was focused in the first instance on the status of the divine Logos/Son—his relation to God and his role in God's relation to the created order. Inevitably, however, this debate also raised questions about the person of Christ, for the first axiom of ancient Christology was the belief that Jesus the Christ is the divine Logos "made flesh"—existing, that is, in a human way, or united to humanity. This axiom was not questioned by any of the parties to the Arian controversy. Nevertheless, in raising the question of the nature or status of the Logos, the Arians at the same time compelled the churches to reflect more explicitly on the meaning of the formula, "Logos made flesh." Exploration of this problem gave birth in turn to debates about the divinity and humanity of Christ and the mode of their relation, and in the course of these debates two Christological schools arose—the so-called Alexandrian and Antiochene. The conflict between these schools, theological and political, required three ecumenical councils for its settlement and even so produced two enduring schisms within the Christian movement.

This christological issue surfaced first in an argument which the early Arians apparently used to support their thesis that the Logos is a creature. Appealing to the Gospels, they pointed out that there Jesus is a person who hungers, thirsts, weeps, exhibits ignorance, and suffers. From these data, they concluded that the Logos has the sort of nature which is subject to all the limitations of an ordinary human being: that, in a word, he is finite and creaturely. Athanasius eventually took them up on this argument, because he believed it touched a basic issue. He insisted, against the Arians, that the Logos must be truly and fully God, on the ground that it is only through the gracious presence of one who is himself God that human nature can be divinized—elevated to fellowship with, and likeness to, its creator. Athanasius judged, in short, that the redemption of humankind required a nonmediated presence of God with and for humanity, through which the creature might come to participate in divine life; and for him, the incarnation of the Logos was the "moment" in which just such a union of the truly human and the fully divine occurred.

In stating this principle, Athanasius sounded the central motif of the whole Alexandrian tradition in Christology. At the same time, however, in defending his principle he showed that he and his opponents shared at least two assumptions about the person of the Christ. First of all, both sides agreed that the Logos is the real, the ultimate, subject of everything which the Christ does or suffers. To be sure, Athanasius stated this conviction in a carefully qualified way. If, he insisted, it is true that the Logos thirsts or suffers, it is true only insofar as he has taken on a human way of being. It is not in his proper divine nature, but only in his human nature, that he is susceptible of such characteristics. Nevertheless, Athanasius was sure that it is the divine Son, and not some other, to whom such attributes were ascribed. But then, in the second place, both sides habitually referred to this humanity which belongs to God's Logos through the incarnation as "body." Even when Athanasius wanted to counter the charge that the Christ —that is, the Logos enfleshed—could suffer from ignorance, he never seems to have thought of attributing that ignorance to a human mind or soul in Christ, natural though such a course might appear. What was important to him, it appears, was the union of the Logos with the bodily dimension of human nature— that side of human nature which most obviously requires redemption from mortality. Athanasius certainly did not deny a human center of awareness in Christ, but neither did he display much interest in it.

What was merely implicit in the thought of Athanasius, however, became explicit in the first thinker of this era to develop a systematic Christology— Apollinaris, the bishop of Laodicea in Syria (d. ca. 390). A strong supporter of the Nicene faith, a friend of Athanasius, and the person largely responsible for converting Basil of Caesarea to the homoousian position, Apollinaris enjoyed the respect of his contemporaries both for his skill as an exegete and for his ascetic mode of life. His christological position, like that of Athanasius, sprang from a desire to affirm that in Christ, the divine Son is immediately present to transform and divinize the sinful mortality of the human creature. For him, however, this conviction of the immediate union of the Logos with humanity in Christ entailed the belief that the true "ego," the very life-principle, in Jesus was simply the Logos himself. Hence, there could be no question, for him, of the union of the divine Son with a complete, normal human being, for in that circumstance, he insisted, there would be two competing wills, two minds, two selves and hence two Sons, human and divine. The unity of the Christ would be destroyed and, with his unity, the essential truth that he is, simply and truly, "God with us."

The way to grasp and affirm this unity, Apollinaris thought, was to say that, just as an ordinary human being is made up of spirit, soul, and body[1]—or, to use what for Apollinaris was equivalent language, intellect, animal soul, and body—so the Christ is made up of the same structural elements, but with one crucial difference. "Christ, having God as his spirit—that is, his intellect— together with soul and body, is rightly called the human being from heaven."[2] In other words, the Christ as Apollinaris conceived him is a single organism— "one composite nature"[3]—in which "the earthly body is knit together with the Godhead"[4] and "the Logos contributes a special energy to the whole,"[5] because he is the sole source of life in this divine-human organism. This unity of life in turn means, as Apollinaris pointed out frequently, that "both that which is corporeal and that which is divine are predicated of the whole Christ."[6] The trouble with this teaching was that in insisting on the displacement of human spirit or intellect by the divine Logos, it presented the humanity of Christ as incomplete. To Apollinaris this may have seemed unobjectionable, since it was the "vivification" and "sanctification" of flesh which he took to be the essential thing accomplished by the Incarnation. Once human flesh, which occasions sin by its domination of the finite intellect, is in Christ controlled and enlivened by divine Intellect (the Logos), and once our flesh is in its turn sanctified by its union with the body of Christ, then the "self-moved intellect within us" can share in the destruction of sin by assimilating itself to Christ.[7]

Once explicitly stated, however, this view turned out not to be widely shared, and Apollinaris's ideas were attacked from several quarters. Gregory of Nyssa composed a treatise, *Against Apollinaris*. Gregory of Nazianzus insisted that since it is not merely the flesh which sins, but soul and mind as well, it was necessary for the divine Logos to take a complete human nature, intellect as well as ensouled body: "For that which he has not assumed he has not healed, but that which is united to his Godhead is also saved."[8] As represented by his disciple Vitalis, Apollinaris's teaching was condemned in 377 by a Roman synod under Pope Damasus, and then, two years later, by a synod at Antioch under Meletius, which assented to the Roman proposition that the Son of God was

---

[1] 1 Thess. 5:23.
[2] Fragment 25, in R. A. Norris, Jr., ed. and transl., *The Christological Controversy* (Philadelphia, 1980), p. 108.
[3] Apollinarius, Fragment 111, in Lietzmann, H., *Apollinaris von Laodicea und seine Schule* (Tübingen, 1904).
[4] *De unione* 4 in Norris, ed., *The Christological Controversy*, p. 104.
[5] *De unione* 5 (ibid., p. 104).
[6] *De unione* 17 (ibid., p. 107).
[7] Fragment 74 (ibid., p. 108).
[8] Letter 101, in E. R. Hardy & C. C. Richardson, *The Christology of the Later Fathers* (Philadelphia, 1954), p. 218.

born as a complete human being. The Council of Constantinople in 381 included Apollinarianism in its lengthy list of erroneous teachings to be condemned (Canon 1).

The principal opponents of Apollinaris, however, were the representatives of the so-called Antiochene school, elements of whose tradition can be traced back through Eustathius of Antioch (see III:2) as far as the monarchian Paul of Samosata (see II:8) in the third century. Favoring a more strictly literal interpretation of Scripture than the followers of Origen and the Alexandrian tradition, these Antiochenes stood in a tradition which had also regularly stressed the role of the Christ as "Second Adam"—as one whose human obedience had a central place in the work of salvation. Even more important is the fact that, as defenders of the Nicene dogma of the full deity of the Logos, they were troubled by any language that attributed human characteristics or limitations to the divine Son. Hence, Apollinaris's view that the whole Christ is the subject of divine and human characteristics alike struck them as blasphemous. How could one say of God's Word, if he was himself truly God, that he thirsted or suffered or died?

It was this problem above all which troubled the Antiochene presbyter Diodore, later (378–394) bishop of Tarsus. A participant at the Council of Constantinople, Diodore was the teacher of a whole generation of Antiochene thinkers, including John Chrysostom. He used the same christological language as did the Arians, Athanasius, and Apollinaris: that is, he spoke habitually of the Christ as the union of Logos with flesh and, at least to begin with, had little or nothing to say about the presence of a human soul or self in Jesus. In spite of this, however, Diodore insisted—and not merely against Apollinaris—that there must be a clear division or distinction between "flesh" on the one hand and "Logos" on the other. They could not be conceived, as Apollinaris had argued, to constitute one nature or hypostasis or *ousia*. For Diodore, that is, flesh and Logos did not compose one single "thing." It was only to the flesh, and not to the Logos, that one could refer such statements as Luke 2:52, "Jesus increased in wisdom and stature, and in favor with God . . ." Somehow it must be the case that in the Christ there are two distinct factors which, though intimately united, are nevertheless not fused or identified. Otherwise, it seemed, Logos would cease to be truly God, and flesh, to be flesh.

It was, however, in the thought of Diodore's pupil Theodore—a monk of Antioch, a notable exegete, and eventually the bishop of Mopsuestia in Cilicia (392–428)—that the logic of the Antiochene theology became explicit. Condemned in effect at the fifth ecumenical council (553) as the originator of Nestorianism, Theodore opposed the Apollinarian idea that the Christ is "one composite nature" with the view that in him there are two subjects of action and predication—two "natures" and two "hypostases"—which he understands to be the divine Logos and a complete human being, "the Man." The problem, then, was to give an acceptable account of how the Son of God is truly united with the human nature. To do this, he employed the old image of indwelling. By "good pleasure" (*eudokia;* see Psalm 147:11) or grace, he taught, the Logos indwelt the Man from the very moment of the latter's conception—and in a way so special and so intimate as to share with the Man his own status, identity, and dignity as God's Son. In this way there was constituted, of the two natures, one *prosōpon*—one "person" in the sense of one public, functional identity. This doctrine of so-called prosopic union enabled Theodore not only to assert that the humanity of Christ is complete, but also to stress the significance of his human obedience and suffering for the redemption of the rest of humanity. At the same time, the doctrine enabled Theodore to deal clearly with the issue which had troubled Diodore of Tarsus. Because Logos and humanity are two natures, subjects, or hypostases, there can be no question of attributing the characteristics of the one to the other. On the contrary, Theodore insisted, one must "divide the sayings"—i.e., in any scriptural statement by or about the Christ, one must refer to the Logos what is proper to divinity and to the Man what is proper to humanity. On this ground, Theodore questioned the propriety of calling the Virgin Mary "Mother of God" (*theotokos,*), a style which had been popular in the East since at least the beginning of the fourth century. To have a human birth, he argued, is not a proper attribute of the Logos himself, but only of the human being whom the Logos indwelt. If the title *theotokos* is used, then, it must be understood in a nonliteral sense. Thus, to the christological monism of the tradition which had stemmed from Athanasius and had found extreme and eccentric expression in the teaching of Apollinaris, Theodore opposed an equally strict Christological dualism.

With the elevation in 428 of the Antiochene monk Nestorius to be patriarch of Constantinople, the debate between these two christological traditions entered a new phase. It became the focus of another stage in the political struggle between the sees of Alexandria and Constantinople. Whether or not Nestorius was a personal pupil of Theodore of Mopsuestia, he revered and essentially reproduced Theodore's teaching. This is apparent even from the recently discovered *Book of Heracleides of Damascus,* Nestorius's most thorough treatment of the Christological issue, but one which was written long after his deposition and exile in 431. In that work, he refines the sense of the terms 'nature" and "hypostasis," which Theodore had used as virtual synonyms, but he continues stoutly to maintain the doctrine of prosopic union as Theodore had taught it. Certainly, in any case, it was the Christology of Theodore which he brought with him when, in the footsteps of John Chrysostom, he moved from Antioch to Constantinople.

On his arrival in the imperial capital, Nestorius found in progress a burning controversy over the use of the title *theotokos* as applied to the Virgin Mary. After hearing the arguments of both sides, he delivered a sermon in which he gave his judgment that the title was inappropriate because "that which is formed in the womb is not . . . God." He added that "God was within the one who was assumed" (i.e., the human nature) and that "the one who was assumed is styled God because of the One who assumed him"[9]—a repetition of Theodore's doctrine of prosopic union, and in Theodore's own language. Nestorius preferred, he said, the title *Christotokos* ("mother of the Christ"). These views gave great offense to those who maintained that the Logos and his humanity are so truly one that what is said of the humanity has the divine Son as its ultimate subject. Accordingly, Nestorius's statements were reported to Cyril, the patriarch of Alexandria and a strong supporter of the *theotokos* and of the Athanasian tradition in Christology. As it happened, Cyril was already at odds with his colleague at Constantinople over the case of some Egyptian monks who had appealed to Nestorius against a judgment of Cyril's. On consideration, however, he resolved to fight his battle with Nestorius over the doctrinal issue; for in his mind, this involved a central matter of Christian faith and, at the same time, offered grounds for a more serious onslaught on the authority of the see of Constantinople.

A nephew of the same Theophilus who had brought about the exile of John Chrysostom, Cyril had succeeded his uncle as bishop in 412 and shared not only Theophilus's jealousy of the church of Constantinople, but also the lack of scruple in the pursuit of power which had marked the patriarchs of Alexandria since Athanasius. At the same time, Cyril had a keen theological mind and a sincere devotion to the religious ideal represented by the Alexandrian tradition in Christology. In the history of that tradition he played, in fact, the same role as had Theodore of Mopsuestia in the formation of the Antiochene outlook. He gave it a finished and all but definitive form.

For Cyril, the touchstone of orthodoxy, in christological as in other matters, was the inspired "symbol of the 318 holy Fathers"—the creed of the Council of Nicaea. In the second paragraph of that creed—which in this regard, as Cyril saw it, followed John 1:14 and Philippians 2:6–11—it was laid down that the "one Lord Jesus Christ" was identical with "the only begotten Son of God" and that this divine Son "was enfleshed . . . and became a human being." The effect of this language, Cyril thought, could be summed up nicely in the expression "one incarnate nature of the divine Logos"—a phrase he found in a work attributed to Athanasius but which in fact (though he was not aware of it) had been written by Apollinaris. What Cyril meant by this expression, however, had nothing to do with the Apollinarian denial of a human soul or intellect in Christ. For Cyril, what this phrase—not to mention the creed of Nicaea—was saying was that in Christ there is one *subject*, one nature or hypostasis, that of the divine Logos; and that the humanity of Christ, body and soul, was a mode of existence which the Logos had made his own through his birth of a woman. The humanity, in other words, could in no way be separated from the Logos as "another" beside him. It was in the strictest sense *his* humanity, his way of being a human

---

9 "First Sermon Against the Theotokos," in Norris, *Christological Controversy*, p. 130.

person. This view Cyril summed up in expressions like "union in hypostasis" or "natural union." Nestorius and his partisans, perhaps understandably, took such phrases to assert or imply that humanity and divinity had somehow been fused in Christ into something which was no longer either divine or human. Cyril, however, had no such intention. "One nature" and "one hypostasis" did not, in his vocabulary, denote Apollinaris's "composite." They denoted the divine Logos himself, but the Logos as he had taken upon himself "the measures of humanity." On this view, it made perfect sense to speak of Mary as "Mother of God," just as it made sense to think of God as "Father" of Jesus' humanity.

Cyril began his attack on Nestorius by writing to the Egyptian monks in defense of the word *theotokos*. But he did not confine himself to cementing the necessary local alliances. He appealed to the emperor and empress, Theodosius II (408–450) and Eudocia (ca. 401–ca. 460), and the emperor's pious, able, and influential sister, Pulcheria (399–453). At the same time, he set about rallying the support of the Roman pope, Celestine I (422–432). Nestorius also wrote to Rome, but succeeded only in offending Celestine, who was annoyed, among other things, by the fact that Nestorius had extended hospitality to certain exiled leaders of the Pelagian party (see III:17). In the meanwhile, Cyril and Nestorius had exchanged two sets of letters, Cyril demanding that Nestorius "think and teach . . . in company with us,"[10] Nestorius insisting that Cyril had misunderstood the creed of Nicaea. At a synod in Rome in 430, Celestine took action against Nestorius. He decreed that the patriarch of Constantinople must recant or be excommunicated. This action licensed Cyril to write a third letter to Nestorius, which demanded of the latter that he assent to a series of anathemas stating the most extreme version of Cyril's position. Nestorius responded with anathemas of his own.

By this time, it was clear to the emperors—Valentinian III in the West and Theodosius II in the East—that the matter would require an imperial general council for its settlement. Accordingly, they summoned such a council to meet at Ephesus in 431. Cyril and his allies were early to arrive, as was Nestorius. However, Nestorius's supporters, the patriarch John of Antioch with the oriental bishops, were delayed beyond the date set for the opening of the council. Cyril, sure of the support of his own bishops and of those from Asia Minor (who still no doubt resented the jurisdictional claims of the see of Constantinople), insisted that the council convene. In the face of a hostile assembly, Nestorius refused to attend, though he was summoned peremptorily to appear. In a single day's session, this body, affirming the sole authority of the creed of Nicaea and standing on Cyril's interpretation of it, condemned and deposed Nestorius.

A few days later, Nestorius's supporters arrived, assembled, and in their turn set about the condemnation of Cyril and of Memnon, the bishop of Ephesus.

---

[10] *Letter 2 to Nestorius*, in Norris, *Christological Controversy*, p. 135.

Finally, the delegates of Pope Celestine arrived. Following their instructions, they joined the Cyrillian assembly, which then proceeded to add John of Antioch to the list of those deposed and—as a gesture of friendship to the westerners— to condemn Pelagianism. In so confused a situation, the emperor Theodosius was temporarily at a loss. He temporized by interning the leaders of both parties, but his own sympathies and the aggressive diplomacy of Cyril and his allies led him to restore the patriarch of Alexandria to his see. Nestorius, on the other hand, was deposed and retired to his monastery near Antioch.

It was still necessary, however, to restore communion between the sees of Alexandria and Antioch. Not without imperial pressure, an arrangement was achieved. The orientals would consent explicitly to the condemnation and deposition of Nestorius; in return, Cyril would assent to a compromise confessional formula (which was probably drawn up by the Antiochene theologian Theodoret, bishop of Cyrrhus). In 433, John of Antioch sent Cyril the text of this document (called the *Formula of Reunion*). It approved the term *theotokos* but at the same time explained not only that the Christ is "complete God and complete human being," but also that "a union of two natures has occurred, as a consequence of which we confess . . . one Son."[11] In the famous letter *Laetentur caeli,* Cyril greeted this confession and the reunion it signified with enthusiasm, though some of his followers were troubled by the notion of a "union of two natures," which seemed to contradict Cyril's earlier position. Nestorius's cause was now lost (though there is little doubt that he too could have assented to the compromise formula, which, like most such documents, was not without its ambiguities). He was finally banished to Upper Egypt, where, just before his death around 450, he completed his *Book of Heracleides of Damascus,* in which he justified his position as against Cyril's.

The reconciliation of 433 turned out to be a mere truce. By 438, his suspicions of Antiochene duplicity aroused, Cyril entered the lists again, this time with a work against Diodore of Tarsus and Theodore of Mopsuestia, whose teaching, still honored among Antiochene signers of the *Formula of Reunion,* he was determined to extirpate. In fact, each party to the compromise felt that the other had betrayed the terms of the agreement. The old debate was renewed, though now the power was all on the side of the Alexandrian party. On his death in 444, Cyril was succeeded by Dioscorus (d. 454), an arrogant and unprincipled man who had little use for the reunion of 433 and sought a complete triumph for Alexandria over its theological and political opponents. At roughly the same time, Proclus, Nestorius's successor at Constantinople (434–447) and a moderate supporter of Cyril, was succeeded by Flavian (447–449), who inclined toward the Antiochene point of view. The stage was thus set for a full renewal of the conflict.

[11] Norris, *Christological Controversy,* p. 142.

Occasion for conflict soon arose. The principal supporter in Constantinople of Dioscorus's campaign against the Antiochenes was the archimandrite Eutyches. This popular figure was head of a monastery in the city and a person of influence at the imperial court, where the emperor's chief minister, the eunuch Chrysaphius, was his godson. At a meeting of the "home synod" of Constantinople under the presidency of Flavian, Eusebius, bishop of Dorylaeum, mounted a counterattack against the Alexandrians. He accused Eutyches of teaching that the human nature of Christ was altered or absorbed by his deity. Summoned before the synod, Eutyches significantly refused to assert that Christ's humanity is *homoousios* with ours and maintained that Christ was "of two natures before the union [i.e., the Incarnation], but after the union, one nature." This cryptic statement was taken to mean that he did indeed teach an absorption of the human into the divine. The synod accordingly deposed him and declared him a heretic. Eutyches appealed at once to the imperial court. The court responded—ominously—by demanding not of Eutyches but of Flavian that he present a confession of his faith, while Dioscorus in Alexandria called for, and obtained, an imperial summons for a general council.

Another factor was introduced into the situation when Eutyches and Flavian alike appealed to Leo I, bishop of Rome (440–461)—Flavian transmitting the minutes of the meeting at which Eutyches had been condemned. After studying the matter, Leo replied in a long and carefully argued letter to Flavian, which has become known as his *Tome*. Referring to Eutyches as "an extremely foolish and altogether ignorant man,"[12] Leo appealed to the baptismal creed of the Roman church to substantiate the traditional western view, inherited from Tertullian (see II:7), that the Christ has two substances or natures and that "the characteristic properties of both natures and substances are kept intact and come together in one person."[13] Furthermore, each of these natures "carries on its proper activities in communion with the other. The Word does what belongs to it and the flesh carries out what belongs to it."[14] It is clear that by this declaration Leo intended to settle the christological debate finally, in accordance with Roman and western tradition. His strong doctrine of the two natures, however, which insisted that they were distinct principles of activity, set Rome in this case against its normal ally, Alexandria. In the end, conservative supporters of Cyril's position were to see Leo's *Tome* as teaching a doctrine which was little better than sheer Nestorianism.

Dioscorus in the meanwhile was taking steps to have Eutyches restored. At his instance, Theodosius II called a general council to meet at Ephesus in August 449. When the council gathered, Dioscorus had his way without contradiction, and not least because he had at his disposal squadrons of imperial soldiery and of monks from Constantinople. Flavian of Constantinople and Eusebius of

[12] *Tome* 1, ibid., p. 145.   [13] *Tome* 3, ibid., p. 148.   [14] *Tome* 4, ibid., p. 150.

Dorylaeum were condemned. Eutyches was vindicated. The *Tome* of Leo was denied a reading. The council took its stand on the principle stated in the seventh canon of the previous council of Ephesus (431): nothing was to be added to the Nicene Creed. Flavian died, under suspicious circumstances, on his way to exile. Dioscorus had achieved a great victory, but only at the cost of a final rupture of the ancient alliance between Alexandria and Rome. Leo I no sooner heard the results of the council than he denounced it as a "synod of thieves" (*latrocinium*). The pope besieged the emperor with demands for a new council to be held in Italy, but Theodosius II was a firm supporter of the Alexandrian cause.

The situation was altered when the accidental death of Theodosius, in July 450, placed on the throne his sister Pulcheria and the undistinguished soldier Marcian, whom she took as her husband. The new sovereigns denied Leo's request for a new council to be held in Italy, but they called one nonetheless, and it met in the city of Chalcedon, just opposite Constantinople, in the autumn of 451.

This council—the fourth to be recognized as ecumenical—acted swiftly to depose Dioscorus and to rehabilitate the Antiochene supporters of the *Formula of Reunion*—most notably two well-known critics of Cyril of Alexandria, Theodoret of Cyrrhus and Ibas of Edessa. The bishops present agreed that the creed of the Council of Nicaea and its daughter creed which they attributed to the Council of Constantinople (381) should under normal circumstances have been adequate for the definition of the faith. They admitted, though, that new heresies had arisen in their time. For this reason, they accepted—in effect, canonized—the Second Letter of Cyril of Alexandria to Nestorius and the letter *Laetentur caeli,* in which Cyril had assented to the *Formula of Reunion,* as adequate expositions of the meaning of the Nicene faith against the errors of Nestorius. In the same way, they accepted Leo I's *Tome* as a document which, agreeing with Cyril's doctrine, explained the orthodox faith as against Eutyches. With these decisions, the bishops were essentially satisfied. They did not wish to offer any substitute for, or formal addition to, the Nicene faith. The imperial court, however, insisted that they go further and provide a formula which would effectively settle the christological conflict. Under this pressure, the bishops appointed a commission which, after one false start, produced a formula composed largely of phrases and ideas drawn from previous documents—Cyril's letters, Leo's *Tome,* the *Formula of Reunion,* and the confession which the patriarch Flavian had submitted to the imperial court after his condemnation of Eutyches.

This formula, usually referred to as the "Definition" of the Council of Chalcedon,[15] insisted, in a Cyrillian vein, upon the unity of the Christ. He is "one and the same Son . . . complete in his deity and complete . . . in his hu-

---

[15] Ibid., p. 159.

manity." Christ is, then, "one *prosōpon* and one hypostasis"; but he exists "in two natures," which are at once unconfused and unaltered (against Eutyches) and, on the other hand, undivided and inseparable (against Nestorius). This language reflects most closely the position taken by Leo I in his *Tome*. It presupposes—what in fact the debate hitherto had never really conceived of, even though the notion had been adumbrated in the *Formula of Reunion* and was basic to the trinitarian settlement of 381—a distinction of meaning between the terms "nature" and "hypostasis." Cyril's central conviction, that the ultimate subject or reality in Christ is the divine Logos, was reaffirmed, but at the same time the council insisted that, in the Incarnation, this one subject had two genuinely distinct ways of being. Christ is indeed "God with us," but in him God is "with us" as a complete, and in that sense ordinary, human being.

The victory of Rome in the doctrinal conflict did not carry with it, however, a victory in the political sphere. By its Canon 28, the Council of Chalcedon gave to the see of Constantinople equal privileges with that of Rome (on the ground that Constantinople was the "New Rome"). Furthermore, the downfall of the see of Alexandria, emphasized by the continuing distaste of the Egyptian churches for the Chalcedonian Definition, meant that the Roman church had lost its most regular ally in the East and at the same time its ability to play a "balance of power" game as between the claims of Alexandria and Constantinople.

Nor in fact did Rome's (and Constantinople's) victory guarantee the unity of the churches. A second and not less important consequence of the Council of Chalcedon was the creation of a separate Nestorian church within the confines of the Persian Empire. Many oriental—west and east Syrian—bishops had, even at the time of the *Formula of Reunion,* been reluctant to condemn Nestorius, and some of these settled, after 433, across the borders of the Roman Empire in Persia, where there were already Christian communities. The real roots of the new body lay, however, in the great School of Edessa, where a learned tradition carried on exegetical and theological work in the spirit of Theodore of Mopsuestia. Ibas of Edessa had himself, prior to 435, been head of this school, and when he returned from the Council of Chalcedon, officially restored to his see as bishop, he continued to support its work and that of its new head, Narses. On Ibas's death in 457, when he was succeeded by a strict Chalcedonian, Narses moved his school and many of his pupils to Nisibis in Persia, where gradually it became the center of a renewed—and Nestorian—Christianity. This church had as its head a "catholikos," who came to be styled "Patriarch of the East" and had his seat originally at Seleucia-Ctesiphon (after 775 it was shifted to Baghdad). Nestorian missions carried Christianity to Arabia, India, and even Turkestan. The church survived and on the whole flourished under Islamic rule, but it was virtually destroyed by the Mongol invasions of the later Middle Ages.

Chapter 10

The East Divided

*T*HE CHALCEDONIAN CONFESSION was now the official doctrinal norm of the empire. To Rome and the western churches, for which Leo I had spoken in his *Tome,* it represented an unquestioned orthodoxy. In the East, however, the situation was significantly different. Not only was there a body of Nestorian Christians beginning to take shape around Edessa and in the Persian Empire, but conservative supporters of Cyril of Alexandria's teaching could make little sense of a doctrine which spoke of the Christ as one subject or hypostasis "in two natures." They might tolerate such language as that of the *Formula of Reunion,* which had said that Christ was one hypostasis "out of two natures," but in their opinion Leo's Christology was no better than Nestorianism. To them, "two natures" meant two subjects, two realities, "two Sons," and so denied the unity in Christ between God's Logos and human nature—a unity which was the very basis of redemption.

Nor was the dissension created by this body of Monophysites (i.e., supporters of the formula "one nature") a matter to be taken lightly. The vast majority of eastern bishops was devoted to the teaching of Cyril, however little they might think of Eutyches or the unpopular Dioscorus. Even those who affirmed and supported the Chalcedonian doctrine did so on the ground that "Leo agrees with Cyril"—as, indeed, they had shouted at the council itself. Yet Cyril himself, as the Monophysites insisted, had regularly spoken of one nature and one hypostasis in Christ, and hence it was no easy thing to argue that the true teaching of Cyril—his intent, if not his language—had been preserved by the Council of Chalcedon. Furthermore, the Monophysite movement had firm popular roots. It did not depend merely upon the authority of individual bishops, however numerous. Both in Egypt and in northern Syria it enjoyed the whole-hearted and even fanatical support of monastic communities and, for just that reason, the support of ordinary believers as well. In the end, then, the failure of the emperors at Constantinople to reconcile the Monophysites to the imperial church created not only ecclesiastical schism but also political dissidence among the peoples of Egypt and Syria.

The depth and seriousness of the Monophysite reaction can be seen in the fact that, at Alexandria, imperial troops were required to control a raging mob which refused to accept one Proterius as successor to Dioscorus for the simple reason that he had been ordained by four Egyptian bishops who had approved the work of Chalcedon. Juvenal, patriarch of Jerusalem, was driven from his see by his own people and forced to retire temporarily to Constantinople. On the death of the emperor Marcian (457), Proterius of Alexandria was lynched, and a new patriarch—Timothy, called by his enemies "the Cat"—was installed by Monophysite leaders. Timothy was subsequently (459) sent into exile by the new emperor, Leo (457–474), but only after the emperor had assured himself through a series of provincial councils that the eastern bishops would support Chalcedon and the disciplining of Timothy—an assurance which they loyally gave, even while making it clear that they understood Chalcedon's stance in Cyrillian terms. In Syria, the strength of the Monophysite movement was revealed when, in 469, during a temporary absence of the patriarch Martyrius of Antioch, a Monophysite named Peter the Fuller was ordained in his place. Before his removal and exile in 471, Peter inserted in the Antiochene liturgy an expression which became a rallying cry for his party. To the doxology of the *Trisagion* ("Holy God, Holy and mighty, Holy immortal One"), he added the phrase "who was crucified for us"—a clear testimony to the faith that indeed there are not two subjects in the Christ.

After the death of Emperor Leo, a palace revolution temporarily replaced his successor Zeno with the usurper Basiliscus (475–476), who promptly sided with the Monophysite party. He not only restored Timothy the Cat to the see of Alexandria, and Peter the Fuller to that of Antioch, but he also issued an encyclical letter in which he anathematized the *Tome* of Leo and the decisions of the Council of Chalcedon. This encyclical was subscribed by a majority of bishops in the East and evoked extensive popular approval. It did not, however, command the assent of Acacius, patriarch of Constantinople (471–489), who quickly discerned that it favored the claims of Alexandria and was thus a threat to the authority of his see. Acacius even called Pope Simplicius (468–483) to his aid, as well as the revered Constantinopolitan pillar-saint, Daniel Stylites. Basiliscus, humbled and overwhelmed, yielded, and in 476 the emperor Zeno (d. 491) was restored.

Basiliscus, however, had revealed by his policies the strength of the Monophysite party in the East. Zeno, with the encouragement of the patriarch Acacius, determined upon a course of religious compromise and reconciliation. In 482, he issued his famous *Henōtikon,* which took the stand, popular with the followers of Cyril of Alexandria, that the creed of Nicaea, as reiterated at Constantinople (381) and Ephesus (431), was sufficient to define the faith. The document condemned Eutyches, but on the subject of the Chalcedonian Definition it permitted, in effect, difference of opinion by depriving the council's teaching of official status. Zeno thus canonized the Christology of Cyril but left open the question of whether the "two natures" doctrine of Leo's *Tome* and the Chalcedonian Definition was consistent with it, hoping by this policy to achieve a reconciliation of the two parties.

At first, this policy achieved a remarkable success in the East, so much so that it remained the official norm of imperial orthodoxy through most of the reign of Zeno's successor, Anastasius (491–518). In the end, however, the *Henōtikon* failed in its purpose. For one thing, the see of Rome, seeing its honor and its orthodoxy attacked by this rejection of Chalcedon, excommunicated Acacius and broke off relations with the East. This "Acacian" schism continued until 519, when the emperor Justin (d. 527) restored the authority of the Chalcedonian Definition of Faith. More important, however, the debate between Monophysites and Chalcedonians continued and grew in intensity.

The fact is that this era—the close of the fifth and the opening decades of the sixth century—was one of great theological fertility in the East. It produced the works of the unknown author who wrote under the pseudonym of Dionysius the Areopagite, allegedly a disciple and so a contemporary of St. Paul. Strongly influenced by the late scholastic Neoplatonism of writers like Proclus (ca. 412–485), the pagan head of the Platonic Academy at Athens, this thinker, through his influential treatises *On the Celestial Hierarchy, On the Ecclesiastical Hierarchy, On the Divine Names,* and *Mystical Theology,* greatly strengthened the tradition of the so-called negative or apophatic theology in the East. At the same time, through much later Latin translations, he familiarized the West not only with Neoplatonist metaphysics but also with the style of mysticism which accompanied the negative theology.

Of more importance for the christological controversies of the time, however, was the monk and presbyter Severus (ca. 465–538)—to whom, as a matter of fact, some scholarship, though without much justification, has attributed the works of the pseudo-Dionysius. An adept in the writings of the Cappadocian Fathers and of Cyril, Severus gave learned and insightful theological leadership to the Monophysite cause. Though he rejected Eutychian and Apollinarian views entirely, Severus nevertheless repudiated Chalcedon as a Nestorian council which had not only taught the doctrine of two natures but had also rehabilitated the notorious Antiochene teachers Theodoret of Cyrrhus and Ibas of Edessa, both of whom had openly attacked Cyril's teaching. In his carefully argued defense of the doctrine of one nature, Severus had the co-operation of the fiery Syrian preacher, theologian, and agitator Philoxenus, bishop of Mabboug (485–519).

With such leadership, the Monophysite cause, in the last decade of the fifth century, came close once more to winning the eastern empire. Resident in Constantinople after 508, Severus gained the ear of the emperor Anastasius and became, in effect, his ecclesiastical advisor. In the end, Severus and Philoxenus between them won the emperor over to a policy that explicitly condemned the Chalcedonian Definition and Leo's *Tome.* At Antioch, the pro-Chalcedonian patriarch was replaced by Severus himself (512) and the patriarch of Constantinople, Macedonius, was sent into exile.

As it turned out, however, this triumph was local and short-lived. In Palestine, Asia Minor, and the European provinces, Chalcedonianism, legitimized by the *Henōtikon* which Anastasius's new policy had overturned, had strong supporters, who did not hesitate to appeal to Rome against the new imperial policy. When, in 518, on the death of Anastasius, Justin I, a Latin-speaking Chalcedonian, acceded to the imperial throne, not only was Severus deposed from the see of Antioch but the representatives of Pope Hormisdas (514–523) were permitted to dictate the terms for restoration of communion with the Roman see. The result was that eastern supporters of Chalcedon got rather more than they had bargained for. The *Henōtikon* itself was condemned, and with it the successive patriarchs of Constantinople who had supported it. This astonishing papal victory, however, turned out to be superficial and temporary. The East had not given up Cyril for Leo. The majority of church leaders was willing, at imperial behest, to accept the Chalcedonian Definition and its authority, but only if its teaching could be shown to be consistent with the real orthodoxy of the East, the teaching of Cyril of Alexandria. Their Chalcedonianism was represented and summed up in the famous "theopaschite" formula of John Maxentius and his fellow "Scythian monks," who appeared in Constantinople in Justin's day: "One of the Trinity suffered in the flesh." This formula no doubt qualified the uncompromising bluntness of the Monophysites' shibboleth, "Holy immortal One who was crucified for us"; but it left little doubt of the seriousness with which eastern believers generally took the doctrine that the divine Son is the ultimate subject of all that can be said about the Christ. The new emperor had merely added, to his task of reconciling Chalcedonians and Monophysites in the East, the equally difficult one of reconciling eastern with western understandings of Chalcedon.

It was in the reign of Justin's nephew and successor, Justinian I (527–565), that the attempt was made to carry this policy out—to reconcile all parties around the Council of Chalcedon itself, but Chalcedon interpreted and understood as a restatement, against Eutychianism, of the Christology of Nicaea and of Cyril of Alexandria. This attempt was entirely consonant with Justinian's general policies. His political ambition was to reunite the empire by reconquering the West—an ambition which, at excessive cost to his treasury and to the integrity of his eastern frontiers, he partially realized in the restoration of North Africa and, eventually, Italy to the empire. Justinian in effect sought a single, unified confession of faith for the five great Christian patriarchates—Rome, Constantinople, Alexandria, Antioch, and Jerusalem. He further intended—though the firm Monophysite sympathies of his wife Theodora (ca. 508–548) often blunted the edge of his resolution in this regard—that the Council of Chalcedon, together with those of Nicaea, Constantinople, and Ephesus, should be the foundation of this confession. In pursuit of this goal of a thoroughly united and thoroughly Christian empire, he passed, at the opening of his reign, severe decrees outlawing paganism and requiring the baptism of all remaining unbelievers. He closed the Platonist Academy at Athens (529), a center of pagan learning and loyalty. He violently persecuted the Samaritans and put severe limitations on the religious and civil rights of Jews. He outlawed Manichaean-ism, Arianism, and other heresies. In his attempts to unify the church, however, he met failure in the end, despite the absolute authority he asserted and enjoyed over its business and despite his capacity for conciliation and compromise when circumstances seemed to call for them.

Justinian's first effort was directed at persuading the exiled Monophysite leaders that acceptance of the Council of Chalcedon did not entail a dualistic Nestorian Christology. In this attempt, he was no doubt encouraged by Empress Theodora, but also by the fact that the exiled Severus of Antioch, living in Alexandria, had been engaged in violent controversy with the radical Monoph-ysite Julian of Halicarnassus, who taught the doctrine, seemingly Apollinarian, that the body of Christ was incorruptible ("Aphthartodocetism"). Severus's passionate defense of the normal humanity of Christ gave reason to think that Monophysites might accept an interpretation of Chalcedon that insisted, in Cyrillian idiom, that the one hypostasis of the Logos is the sole ontological sub-ject of both the human and the divine natures—the very doctrine implied in the theopaschite formula, "One of the Trinity suffered in the flesh." Justinian ac-cordingly invited some Monophysite bishops to a conference with a group of Chalcedonians at Constantinople; and though there was no indication that the Monophysites had changed their minds about the council of 451, the emperor nevertheless proceeded to publish an edict (533) setting out his own official definition of christological faith, which declared that Christ is the divine Word who assumed human nature and himself endured suffering in that (though of course not in his divine) nature. This "neo-Chalcedonian" theology found its most able theological proponent in one Leontius of Jerusalem (fl. ca. 534), who carefully distinguished the senses of "hypostasis" and "nature" and taught that the human nature of Christ has no hypostasis (i.e., principle of concrete exist-ence) of its own but exists "in" the hypostasis of God's Son, who is thus the true subject of the being of a complete human nature. Leontius's teaching, some-times referred to as the doctrine of "enhypostasia," justified theopaschite lan-guage and, with it, the central thrust of Cyril's Christology, while at the same time maintaining the doctrine of two natures.

Justinian's decree, reiterated in letters to the patriarchs of Rome and Con-stantinople, brought with it a brief moment of toleration and reconciliation, during which Severus himself was received in the imperial capital and Theodora was able to place supporters of the Severan Monophysite position in the sees of Alexandria and Constantinople. The fears and opposition created by this situa-tion, however, brought about another intervention from Rome, this time by Pope Agapetus (535–536), who, on a visit to Constantinople in the interest of the Ostrogothic rulers of Italy, deposed the new patriarch in Constantinople and ordained a Chalcedonian successor. Justinian, in an apparent volte-face, assented to the banning of Severus of Antioch and his followers and, further, ordered the writings of Severus burned. A Chalcedonian was placed in the see of Alexandria. Although Justinian continued to try to win Monophysite leaders to his orthodoxy of "the Four Councils," there was never again an effort to achieve compromise over the question of Chalcedon. It was, indeed, to please the strict Chalcedonians that, in 543, after a bitter controversy originating among the monks of Palestine, Justinian condemned the teachings of Origen.

His next step—which in his own mind may have been intended to mollify the Monophysites—was to condemn, in 544, the "Three Chapters": the writings of Theodore of Mopsuestia and certain works directed against Cyril of Alexandria by Ibas of Edessa and Theodoret of Cyrrhus. Since Ibas and Theodoret, disciples of Theodore, had been accepted as orthodox by the Council of Chalcedon, this gesture came close to questioning the authority of the council itself, but Justinian was careful, in this final attack on the Antiochene Christology, to condemn only particular writings, and not the persons, of Ibas and Theodoret. The neo-Chalcedonian orthodoxy of the "Four Councils" was to stand.

Justinian's condemnation of the Three Chapters did little to reconcile the Monophysites to Chalcedon, but it proved to be the stimulus which evoked Latin and western opposition to his neo-Chalcedonian policies. The bishops of Africa (now freed from Vandal domination), large numbers of Italian and Gaulish bishops, and the papal representatives at Constantinople refused to sign or assent to the condemnation of the Three Chapters. Justinian succeeded in bringing the weak and indecisive Pope Vigilius (537–555) to Constantinople. There, the pope was induced to issue his notorious *Judicatum* (548), which consented in all essentials to Justinian's action. The West, however, did not in this case follow its leader. A synod of African bishops excommunicated Vigilius himself, and the African author Facundus, bishop of Hermiane (d. after 571), already in Constantinople, composed the treatise *In Defense of the Three Chapters*. He argued that Justinian's action was tantamount to repudiation of the Chalcedonian Christology. Eventually, Vigilius, given temporary courage by the western reaction to his *Judicatum,* not only withdrew his assent to the imperial action, but also, in spite of imperial attempts to snatch him by violence from churches where he had taken sanctuary, excommunicated the patriarch of Constantinople as well as Justinian's principal theological adviser, Theodore Askidas, who had originated the emperor's policy. In the end, the matter was committed to a council, which met in Constantinople in 553. Vigilius, because of the composition of the council, which contained only a dozen western bishops, refused to participate. The council duly condemned the Three Chapters and reiterated the condemnation of Origenism, which had continued to flourish among the monks of Palestine. Since Justinian ultimately compelled the assent of Vigilius to the council's actions—an assent which led to a long schism between the churches of

Rome, on the one hand, and those of Milan and Aquileia, on the other—this synod is recognized as the fifth Ecumenical Council.

In the meanwhile, the process was already under way by which the Monophysite party ceased to be a mere party and became a series of separate, nationally based churches in Syria, Egypt, Armenia, and eventually Ethiopia and Persia. The process had in fact begun almost at the start of Justinian's reign, when, under persecution, Monophysites in Syria and Asia Minor who would not accept the sacramental ministrations of Chalcedonian priests were supplied with clergy of their own confession by John of Tella, with the consent of the exiled Severus of Antioch, who also licensed the ordination of bishops for Monophysite Christians on the Persian side of Rome's eastern frontier. Within the empire, however, the creation of a separately organized Monophysite hierarchy was largely the work of Jacob Baradaeus (Bar'adai), an east Syrian monk who, with the connivance of Theodora, was made metropolitan bishop of Edessa (ca. 542) and spent the rest of his life as a traveling missionary, working often in disguise, for the Monophysite cause. By the time of Justinian's death, therefore, there was already an independent Monophysite church, centered in northern Syria and Cilicia, with its own traditional head, styled the patriarch of Antioch. This "Jacobite" church (so called after Baradaeus, who died in 578) used Syriac as its liturgical and theological tongue—in distinction from the Greek of the imperial state church—and had its base in the monasteries and villages of the north Syrian countryside, where it exists to this day.

In Egypt, the resistance to Justinian's theological and religious policies was rooted not only in the firm opposition of monastics and people to the Council of Chalcedon, but also, increasingly, in their sense that the cause of the Cyrillian Christology was a native, Coptic, and Egyptian cause, to be maintained firmly in the face of imperial attempts to impose a foreign orthodoxy from Constantinople. From about 575—and in spite of serious divisions among the Monophysites themselves—there was a Coptic patriarch of Alexandria to rival his "Melkite" (i.e., "royal" or "imperial") counterpart, and it was this Coptic-speaking, Monophysite church which, because it embraced the vast majority of Egyptian Christians, survived both the Persian and Arab conquests of Egypt to become the prevalent and characteristic form of Christianity in Egypt down to the present day. Furthermore, it was this Monophysite Christianity which—thanks again in part to the empress Theodora—was transmitted by missionaries to the kingdoms of Nubia and shaped the Christianity of Ethiopia (the kingdom of Axum), for which Athanasius himself had consecrated a first bishop, Frumentius, in about 348. Syrian and Egyptian monks of the anti-Chalcedonian party were responsible for the expansion of Christianity in Ethiopia in the sixth century, and the church there has remained, to this day, formally dependent on the Coptic patriarch of Alexandria.

Alongside the Monophysite churches of Syria and Egypt, a third arose in Armenia, where Christianity had been introduced at the beginning of the fourth century by Gregory the Illuminator, a missionary from Cappadocia who (ca. 301) converted King Tiridates, and with him his nation, to Christianity. Represented at the council of Nicaea, the Armenian church, headed by its own supreme bishop, the "catholicos," belonged to the tradition of Greek Christianity, welcoming teachers and leaders from Cappadocia, until the nation came under Persian domination after 363. The resulting introduction of Syrian Christian influence exposed the Armenian church to Antiochene and Nestorian ideas. When these were challenged as a result of the condemnation of Nestorius at Ephesus, the leaders of the Armenian church sought to settle the ensuing debate by appeal to the judgment of Proclus, the patriarch of Constantinople (434–446). He in turn addressed to the Armenian church his *Tome,* a letter which set out in clear terms the christological position of Cyril of Alexandria. As a result, the Armenian Christians, who took no part in the Council of Chalcedon, eventually adopted the imperial orthodoxy of Zeno's *Henōtikon* and rejected the Council of Chalcedon as Nestorian.

Thus, the controversies over the councils of Ephesus and Chalcedon had, in the end, divided the churches throughout the Mediterranean world. Not only did they exacerbate the tensions between West and East, Rome and Constantinople. They also produced an independent Nestorian church in Persia and national churches of Monophysite confession in Ethiopia, Egypt, Syria, and Armenia. Their effects in the life of the Christian movement have continued until the present.

Chapter 11

Controversy and Catastrophe in the East

JUSTINIAN'S RESTORATION OF Roman power was to last no longer than his life. After 568, Byzantine power in Italy began to crumble before the invasion of the Lombards, who eventually occupied the northern and much of the central part of the peninsula, for a time isolating Ravenna, the seat of the imperial exarch, from Rome and from the remaining imperial territories in the south. North and west of Constantinople, the Balkan peninsula and Greece were subjected to constant raids and invasions on the part of the Avars and the Slavs, who settled large tracts of Byzantine territory. The inability of imperial troops to resist this migration was due, at least in part, to the fact that from the time of Justin II (565–578) the Romans were engaged in constant warfare with the Persian Empire to their east.

In the second year of the reign of the emperor Heraclius (610–641), who inherited an empire weakened and demoralized by the excesses of his predecessor, the Persians invaded Syria, capturing Antioch and eventually Damascus. By 618, they had conquered Palestine and Egypt, where, as in Syria, the Monophysite population, though it did not welcome the invaders and quickly learned to fear and hate them, gave little support to imperial forces. While this disaster was in progress, Slavic raids pierced to the walls of Constantinople and the last Roman forces were driven out of Spain by the Visigoths. Heraclius responded to this apparently hopeless situation by raising and training a new army, which he financed in part by appropriating gold and silver valuables from churches; and in three brilliant campaigns which he conducted in the years from 622 to 628, he carried the war into Persian territory. The resulting peace (630) restored Syria, Palestine, and Egypt to the empire.

At this moment of his greatest triumph and prestige, Heraclius attempted to heal the religious division which rent and weakened his empire. The means of doing this, moreover, seemed to be at hand. As early as 622, Sergius, patriarch of Constantinople (610–638), had suggested that a way to compromise might be found by conceding the Monophysite position on the controverted question of the Christ's *energeia* ("operation," "activity"). Apollinaris of Laodicea had spoken of "one *energeia*" in Christ to correspond with his one nature, and Severus of Antioch had in this regard followed Apollinaris against the tradition represented by Leo's *Tome*, which asserted that each nature had its own operation. Sergius's idea, of which he persuaded Heraclius, was that the formula "one *energeia*" could be reconciled with the Chalcedonian doctrine of two natures if it were understood that *energeia* properly pertains, not to a thing's nature, but to its ontological subject or hypostasis. Since Christ (according to Chalcedon) is one hypostasis, he would necessarily, on this view, have a single "energy" or operation. At the successful conclusion of the Persian campaigns, Heraclius attempted to win the Monophysite leaders to this formula, and his attempt enjoyed initial success.

In the end, however, it stumbled. In the first place, it evoked the opposition of the Chalcedonian monks of Palestine, whose aged leader, Sophronius, was elected patriarch of Jerusalem in 634. This opposition forced Heraclius and Sergius to seek the support of Rome. Pope Honorius (625–638), however, judged that the introduction of new dogmatic teachings was the business of ecumenical councils alone, pointed out that the term *energeia* was unscriptural, and intimated that "two natures" implies "two operations." In an unfortunate afterthought, however, he said that he was prepared to speak of "one will" in Christ.

This diplomatic and on the whole friendly opposition from Rome was accompanied, though, by events which seemed to make Heraclius's whole enterprise meaningless. Out of the Arabian peninsula, in the years following the death of Mohammed in 632, burst the storm of the Islamic invasions. Damascus fell to the Arabs in 635, Antioch and Jerusalem in 638. Nevertheless, in 638 Heraclius published his *Ekthesis,* which followed Pope Honorius in forbidding all talk of "one energy" or "two energies," but went on to make dogma of his suggestion that in Christ there is but one will ("Monothelitism"). Since Syria was already lost to the empire, the only effect which this decree had was to inflame the opposition between Chalcedonians and Monophysites in Egypt and thus render that province the more ready for Arab conquest of it in 641. By the time Heraclius died in 642, the portions of the empire he had recovered from the Persians had fallen again—and this time permanently—into foreign hands. The Monophysite problem was no longer his to solve. Heraclius's *Ekthesis* stood, however, as the standard of imperial orthodoxy, and the so-called Monothelite controversy continued. Maximus the Confessor (ca. 580–662), one of the formative minds behind Eastern Orthodox theology and spirituality, entered the debate in defense of the Cappadocian doctrine that will and "energy" pertain to nature and not to hypostasis. The implication of this view was that if Christ has, according to the teaching of Chalcedon, two natures, then there are in him two wills corresponding to his divine and human ways of being. This brought Maximus into alliance with Pope Martin I (649–655), who in 649 assembled a synod in Rome which proclaimed the existence of two wills, human and divine, in Christ and went on to condemn not only Heraclius's *Ekthesis* but also the *Typos,* in which the reigning emperor, Constans II (642–668), had forbidden discussion of the question of Christ's will or wills. This defiance of the emperor brought Pope Martin imprisonment in Constantinople and, later, exile to the Crimea, where he died.

Constans's successor, however, Constantine IV (668–685), was willing to come to terms with the see of Rome, which in this matter had remained adamant. Entering into negotiations with Pope Agatho (678–681), Constantine summoned what was to be known as the sixth Ecumenical Council, which met in Constantinople in 680 and 681. This assembly declared that Christ has "two natural wills or willings . . . not contrary one to the other . . . but his human will follows, not as resisting or reluctant, but rather as subject to his divine and omnipotent will."[1] It also condemned Patriarch Sergius; Heraclius's appointee as patriarch of Alexandria, Cyrus; and Pope Honorius. With this decision, the course of the great christological controversies came to an end. The tendency of Justinian's neo-Chalcedonian orthodoxy to drift in the direction of Monophysitism—the very tendency which Heraclius's Monenergism and Monothelitism had represented—was arrested. It was affirmed that the human nature of Christ is a principle of human willing and acting—willing and acting which, because they are indeed natural and not sinful, are harmonious with the divine will that informs and guides them.

---

[1] J. C. Ayer, ed., *A Source Book for Ancient Church History* (New York, 1913), p. 669.

Like Chalcedon itself, the sixth Ecumenical Council was a triumph for the West. It was followed, however, by another synod which marked the increasing alienation between Rome and Constantinople. Since neither the council of the "Three Chapters" nor the council of 681 had formulated any disciplinary canons, Justinian II (685–695, 704–711) summoned an assembly to meet at Constantinople in 692 to complete their work. Called the Trullan Council (from the *trullus* or domed room in which it met) or the Quinisext Council (because it completed the work of the fifth and sixth ecumenical councils), this assembly was entirely eastern in composition. While it renewed many ancient canons, some of its enactments directly contravened western practice. In agreement with Chalcedon, it decreed that "the see of Constantinople shall enjoy equal privilege with the see of Old Rome." It permitted marriage for deacons and presbyters and condemned the Roman prohibition of such marriages. It forbade the Roman custom of fasting on Saturdays in Lent. It prohibited the favorite western representation of Christ under the symbol of a lamb, ordering instead the depiction of a human figure to emphasize the reality of the Incarnation. The acts of this council were never recognized in the West, and they are significant of the growing estrangement in feeling and practice between East and West— an estrangement which the policy of the iconoclastic emperors of the eighth century was, as we shall see, to aggravate.

Chapter 12

The Constitutional Development of the Church

As in the second and third centuries, the normal basic unit of the church continued, after the recognition of the church by Constantine, to be the assembly of Christians in a particular *polis*—that is, a particular "city" with its rural hinterland. Such a local church, whose geographical extent varied widely from one sector of the empire to another, continued to be headed by a single chief pastor, the bishop. Under the bishop were the other officeholders of the congregation, who were called "clergy." These came to be divided into two categories. Bishops, presbyters, and deacons—known in civil and ecclesiastical law as "superior" clergy—were distinguished from "inferior" ranks by the fact that they were invariably ordained by bishops. The number of grades of "inferior" clergy—such officials as subdeacons, acolytes, lectors, and exorcists—varied from locality to locality. There was, then, no fundamental change in the structural order of the local church from the third to the fourth and fifth centuries.

Nevertheless, Constantine's recognition of the church brought about significant alterations in the function and status of the local clergy. For one thing, they were progressively exempted from certain taxes and civic responsibilities, in order that their full attention might be given to the duties of their office, especially to the work of public worship. At the same time, the role of the bishop was significantly expanded. During most of the fourth century, bishops were accorded the privilege of sitting as judges in civil suits where both parties to the suit consented to accept their decision—an extension of their long-standing function as judges within the confines of the Christian community. Furthermore, when the local church came to be recognized as a corporation which could own property, and when its work came increasingly to be supported by endowments of land as well as by the regular personal offerings of the faithful, the bishop and his deacons frequently became the administrators of extensive properties, whose income was used to support clergy, to provide for the construction and upkeep of church buildings and furnishings, and to support the church's work in relief of the poor and deprived. For all of these reasons, the prestige of clerical office was increased. More and more, the local bishop became not merely the pastor of his flock but also a principal leader and benefactor of his community. The exemptions, privilege, and prestige of the episcopal office (and of clerical office in general) is best attested by imperial legislation which, from early in the fourth century on, sought to prevent persons of property—who might otherwise serve as local secular officials and be responsible for the payment of taxes—from escaping, by way of ordination, their increasingly difficult and burdensome responsibilities.

The fact that the number of Christians continued to grow during the fourth, fifth, and sixth centuries brought about changes in the organization of the churches and in the deployment of clerics. Not only were new local churches created and equipped with bishops, but existing churches found that they needed additional places for assembly and worship both in their urban centers and in the surrounding countryside. Often the buildings required for these purposes were constructed and maintained out of the common funds of the church under the direct supervision of the bishop. In that case, they were served by presbyters and deacons delegated from the central body of clergy who had always assisted the bishop, and they were regarded as places where, in principle, the bishop himself was the immediate pastor. In other cases, a building for worship might be erected and endowed by "private" wealth and supplied with clergy who lived off that endowment and who, while responsible to the bishop, did not belong to his immediate establishment. It is to such centers as these that one looks for the beginnings of the so-called "parochial" system. In some instances, rural areas were put under the immediate supervision of a "country bishop" (*chōrepiscopos*), who acted in effect as the delegate and subordinate of the bishop within whose city his territory fell. For the most part, however, it was presbyters—understood to share all the priestly powers of a bishop save that of ordination—who acted in the bishop's place as the number of centers for assembly grew. In this fashion, there gradually grew up the perception—common in medieval and later times—that the normal pastor of a congregation is a presbyter.

This same period saw the gradual appearance of customs and laws governing clerical marriage and celibacy. The high regard in which continence was held from at least the beginning of the third century—not to mention the spread of monastic ideals during the fourth century—led to the idea that clerics should be encouraged to practice celibacy. If they married, as many did, they were expected at any rate to be "the husband of one wife,"[1] which meant that remarriage was ruled out in the case of a spouse's death. After the middle of the fourth century, however, both papal admonition and synodal decree in the West demanded continence (even for married persons) after ordination as presbyter, deacon, or bishop. Though the rule was by no means universally observed, it remained the ideal. In the East, however, a different pattern developed. There a rule regarding clerical celibacy was slower to develop and more generous when it was formulated. It was only at the Quinisext or Trullan council of 692 that definitive legislation on the subject was framed. The canons of this council required all bishops to be celibate, but permitted persons already married to be ordained deacons or presbyters (though such persons might not marry after ordination). It is this legislation which accounts for the fact that in the eastern churches bishops have been chosen for the most part from the ranks of the monks.

One of the most important developments of this era, however, had to do with the structures of the church above the local level. The first Council of Nicaea, as we have seen (III:2), presupposed that the bishops of each civil province (called an "eparchy" in the East) would be associated together in synods for the regulation of matters of common interest, and it commanded that such synods should meet twice annually. Nicaea also accorded to the bishop of each provincial capital (the "metropolitan" bishop) special status and powers as the convenor and president of provincial synods. This provincial system of church administration was shortly established in the entire East save for Egypt, where all bishops seem to have answered more or less directly to the pope of Alexandria. In the West, it developed more slowly. The region of central and southern Italy under the direct jurisdiction of the Roman church had no strictly "provincial" synods, though its bishops met regularly under the

---

[1] 1 Tim. 3:2.

presidency of the bishop of Rome. In northern Italy, the churches of Milan and Aquileia also presided over areas considerably larger than a single province—partly, perhaps, because the number of cities (and hence of bishoprics) was much smaller than in the south. Only in Gaul was a strictly provincial system gradually established.

Above the provincial or regional level, two institutions came to be of special significance: the patriarchal sees, and the imperial or ecumenical councils. By the time of the Council of Chalcedon, the number of patriarchal sees had been fixed at five (Rome, Constantinople, Alexandria, Antioch, and Jerusalem). Aside from Jerusalem, whose status as a patriarchate was late (451) and largely honorary, these were not only churches which could traditionally claim apostolic foundation (Constantinople excepted) but also churches located in economic, political, and cultural centers. Of equal importance was the fact that each of them, as a matter of fact, presided over an area which represented a significant degree of linguistic and cultural cohesion. Rome was the patriarchate of the Latin West, whose only conceivable rival, Carthage, was eliminated by the successive Vandal and Arab invasions of North Africa. Antioch and Alexandria belonged to, and focused the ecclesiastical life of, those sections of the Roman Empire whose indigenous tongues were Syriac and Coptic. Constantinople, however doubtful its claims by the standard of the Roman church's Petrine theory (see III:4), established itself in the fifth and sixth centuries as the patriarchate of the Greek-speaking world of Asia Minor and Greece itself.

The system of the five patriarchates, however, provided no single central authority for the body of churches as a whole—especially since, after 381, the principal sees were continually engaged in open or concealed disputes over their relative prestige and authority. Despite the "primacy of honor" accorded the pope of Rome, and despite the claims of the Roman see to a universal authority, the only central authority for the churches in the period of the Roman Empire was the ecumenical council, and this institution rested in practice on the secular authority of the imperial office. From the days of Constantine, such assemblies were not only made possible by imperial funds and facilities but were actually summoned by the emperors; and it was they—assumed universally to have a general responsibility for the religious welfare of their peoples—who enforced (as far as possible) the decisions of general councils. It was understood, to be sure, that the doctrine and internal discipline of the churches were the responsibility of the bishops, and that this was a responsibility upon which an emperor might not encroach. This was a principle upon which all, including the emperors, normally insisted, even though it was at times violated in practice. Nevertheless, although the emperors' religious policies in the end depended upon ecclesiastical consensus, they were not above taking firm initiatives to establish such consensus, as Pulcheria and Marcian did at Chalcedon, and as Zeno did with his *Henōtikon*. In practice, then, imperial authority was both central and essential in the common life of the churches; and in the East, where

Roman rule persisted in the form of the Byzantine Empire, it continued to be so. In the West, on the other hand, imperial authority was gradually eclipsed after the reign of Justinian, and the unity and self-awareness of Latin Christianity came to depend on the leadership and the symbolic role of the Roman papacy.

Chapter 13

Worship and Piety

*T*HE FOURTH AND FIFTH CENTURIES saw a significant flowering of Christian worship and, with it, of Christian art. Set free to figure as public institutions and to own and dispose of property, the churches expanded and elaborated their use of times, spaces, and ceremonies.

This is apparent first of all in the development and articulation of the calendar of worship. The temporal rhythm of Christian life continued to revolve around the week, with its regular celebration of Sunday, and around the annual cycle, whose focus was the celebration of the Christian Passover during the fifty-day period from Easter to Pentecost. It was this latter celebration which received the earliest elaboration, as we learn from accounts given by the pilgrim Egeria of the celebration of Easter at Jerusalem toward the end of the fourth century. From her testimony, it appears that the marking of Holy Week as a commemoration of the events leading up to the resurrection of Jesus had been established there for some time. Palm Sunday, Maundy Thursday, and Good Friday as the day of the Cross were all observed with special ceremonies, and from Jerusalem these observances spread gradually, during and after the fifth century, to churches in other sectors of the Roman world. It was also during the fourth century that, following the chronology of Acts 1:3, the custom arose of marking a special feast on the fortieth day after Easter, to celebrate the Ascension of Christ. Much earlier was the growth of the season of Lent, which is mentioned in Canon 5 of the Council of Nicaea. Whatever its ultimate origins (concerning which there is still dispute among scholars), Lent in its developed form served two purposes. It was a period of fasting in preparation for Easter (eventually fixed at forty days to commemorate Jesus' fasting in the Wilderness), and it marked the time during which catechumens were instructed and made ready for baptism.

These elaborations of the yearly cycle determined by Easter and Pentecost went hand in hand with the appearance of a new annual cycle of celebration associated with the Incarnation and focused on the feasts of Christmas (December 25) and Epiphany (January 6). Each of these dates was also associated with pagan celebrations of the winter solstice. In Rome, December 25 had, since the time of the emperor Aurelian, been marked as the birthday of the Unconquered Sun; and in the East, January 6 had long had associations with the birth of the god Dionysus. Influenced by these circumstances, and by the need to lend Christian meaning to established popular feasts, the churches adapted these days to celebration of the birth and manifestation in history of the divine Logos, the Sun of Righteousness. The earlier of the two feasts to become established was that of the Epiphany, which originated in Alexandria and from an early date commemorated not only the birth of Jesus but also his baptism and the miracle at Cana, in which, as we are told by the Fourth Gospel, he "manifested his glory."[1] The Christmas celebration, on the other hand, originated in Rome early in the fourth century. By the middle of the fifth century, both feasts were known and kept in almost all sectors of the church. It was in the West that Epiphany acquired its association with the visit and adoration of the Magi.

These developments in the Christian year grew up in roughly the same era during which the initiatory rites of the churches underwent their greatest elaboration. These rites included not only the act of baptism itself and the numerous ceremonies connected with it (which differed somewhat in character and order from place to place), but also the associated actions by which persons were first admitted to the catechumenate and then enrolled as actual candidates for baptism. The development of these distinct stages in the initiatory process owed a great deal to the fact that in the fourth century—as contrasted, it seems, with the late second and the third—adult baptism had become the norm. Whether out of respect for the need of mature commitment in full members of the church, or out of a desire to postpone wholehearted dedication to the demands of the Christian way, large numbers of Christians lived a substantial part of their lives as catechumens or "hearers"—some, indeed, delaying baptism until they were near death. Such persons were understood to belong to the Christian movement, almost as a class of "fellow travelers"; but at the Sunday assemblies of the church, they were dismissed after the liturgy of the Word, having not yet been qualified through baptism for participation in the mystery of the eucharist.

With this prolongation of the initiatory process, there developed, in the fourth and fifth centuries, a strict observance of the *disciplina arcani* ("discipline of secrecy"), according to which not merely non-Christians but also catechumens were kept in ignorance of the central symbols of Christian life and faith: the

---

[1] John 2:11.

ceremonies of baptism and the eucharist and their meaning, as well as the creed and the Lord's Prayer. This practice in part reflects the assimilation of the central Christian rites and their interpretation to the awe-inspiring secret mysteries of the pagan cults. Catechumens were kept aware that they lived in the shadow of a holy reality, which they could approach only with reverence and complete commitment.

When catechumens had determined upon baptism, they presented themselves for enrollment as candidates, normally at the beginning of the season of Lent (in some places in the fourth century baptisms were performed at the Epiphany as well as at Easter). If accepted as candidates, they underwent a preliminary exorcism and spent the forty days before Easter being instructed in the meaning of the faith. During this time, they were given their church's creed to memorize and heard its meaning expounded. At the vigil conducted during the hours of darkness before Easter, the candidates came to baptism itself. They renounced Satan and his works. They were stripped of their clothes and brought naked into the waters of rebirth. There they were washed as (in the West) they confessed their faith in the triune God, or the bishop (as in Antioch) pronounced over each of them the formula "*N* is baptized in the name of the Father and of the Son and of the Holy Spirit." Often, but not invariably, there was a pre- or postbaptismal anointing by the bishop, which was specially associated with the gift of the Holy Spirit. When these ceremonies were completed, the candidate was reclothed, this time in white, and brought to the congregation to participate in the Easter eucharist. The candidate had now entered upon the fullness of Christian life.

The normal assembly of the church in each place continued, during this period, to be the Sunday-morning gathering of the faithful to hear the Scriptures read and expounded and to celebrate the eucharist. The general, though by no means invariant, practice at the liturgy of the Word originally was to read three lessons (or sets of lessons): one each from the Old Testament, the Epistles, and the Gospels. Frequently, it seems, these readings were continuous from Sunday to Sunday: i.e., a single prophecy, letter, or Gospel was read through at successive Sunday assemblies, no doubt at the choice of the local bishop. Gradually, however, special readings were assigned to individual Sundays, beginning with those in the Easter season, and by the seventh century complete lectionaries for the Sundays and the great feasts of the Christian year could be composed. Between the readings, or between two of them, a psalm was sung responsorially, and psalms were also sung at the entrance rite which preceded the liturgy of the Word, at the presentation of the bread and wine, and at the communion. A sermon, whose aim was to explain the lessons which had just been read, followed the Gospel. It was the duty of the bishop to preach, but in the East from early on, and later in the West, presbyters too bore this responsibility. It was not until the fifth and sixth centuries—the era of the great christological controversies—that the Niceno-Constantinopolitan Creed, whose original place was in the liturgy of baptism, came, in some places, to be recited in the eucharistic liturgy as well.

The eucharistic celebration proper, which invariably followed the liturgy of the Word, was simple enough in its basic outlines. It began with a presentation of the people's offerings and the preparation of the altar-table by the deacons, who laid out the bread and wine which was the focal part of the offerings. Then followed the eucharistic prayer itself, which differed from region to region but ordinarily contained certain invariant elements. It began with a dialogue between the bishop and the congregation, issuing in the "preface" and—first in the East but later in the West as well—the Cherubic Hymn of Isaiah 6:3. The prayer went on to include not only praise to God for creation and redemption in Christ, but also recitation of Christ's words of institution, a statement that this whole action was performed "in remembrance" of the Christ in his death and resurrection, a prayer of offering, and a concluding doxology, to which the people responded "Amen." In the eastern rites that took shape around the sees of Antioch and Alexandria, prominent place was given to an invocation of the Holy Spirit (the "Epiclesis"). This prayer called the Spirit down upon the offerings of bread and wine to the end that they might became the body and blood of Christ. It also asked that the Spirit descend upon the people themselves, so that in receiving the sacrament they might also receive its benefits. There are traces of such a prayer in some western liturgies, but it remains a characteristic primarily of eastern rites, and this difference eventually gave rise to controversy over the question of the liturgical "moment" when the risen Lord becomes present sacramentally for his people. Western piety tended, by contrast with that of the East, to find this moment in the recitation of the words of institution. This of course was not the only difference of form or emphasis in the eucharistic liturgies of the late patristic era. The language, order, and prominence even of the elements we have called "invariant" differed from place to place. This is the era, in fact, when regional liturgical patterns were being established around the sees of Rome, Alexandria, and Antioch (whose tradition became that of the church of Constantinople, and so of orthodox eastern Christianity).

There can be no doubt that, apart from baptism itself, the eucharist continued to be the center of Christian devotion and piety. Celebrated not only on Sundays but also on all great occasions of the church's calendar, it marked, for Christians of the fourth and later centuries, the moment when they entered most intimately into the mystery of redemption in Christ. Bringing their offerings of praise and prayer, of money, and of bread and wine, they received Christ himself, sacramentally but truly present in the consecrated elements. In this way, they were joined to the new life of the divine Victim and High Priest, whose self-offering became a present reality in their act of thanksgiving and remembrance. The sacrament was thus seen as a derivative and secondary, but entirely real, mode of the "incarnation" of God's Word.

Central though it was, however, the eucharist, associated primarily with Sundays and festivals, was by no means the sole vehicle of the church's liturgical service of God. From an early time, there is evidence that Christians in many places observed certain "hours" for private prayer. Tertullian mentions morning and evening as well as the traditional third, sixth, and ninth hours. The *Apostolic Tradition* of Hippolytus, moreover, speaks of a public morning service of teaching and prayer to which all were encouraged to come daily. In the course of the fourth century, there grew up the formal liturgical "offices"— services of praise and prayer to be carried out at particular hours of the day. One important influence on this development was the pattern of monastic prayer and devotion, which encouraged common recitation of the whole psalter in a sequence of offices over a stated interval of days or weeks. The basic pattern of offices that emerged also owed something to the practice of the bishop's church, where public services were observed in the traditional pattern at the beginning and close of the day. The interaction of these two traditions, monastic and "secular," gradually produced the system of seven offices a day,[2] supplemented by a night office,[3] which came to prevail, in slightly differing forms, in East and West alike. In its entirety, however, this system was regularly practiced only in monastic communities. The daily worship available for the participation of ordinary Christians continued to be the morning (Lauds) and the evening (Vespers) hours.

Of greater significance, however, in the popular piety of the fourth and following centuries was the cult of the martyrs. The roots of the cult lay in the second and third centuries, when a unique reverence was accorded to those who bore witness to Christ by being imprisoned for the faith (confessors) or by dying for it (martyrs). The former, after their release, were given special honor and status in the church. The latter, however, were understood to have gained already, by their witness to the point of death, the inheritance to which all believers looked forward. They were not dead Christians awaiting the resurrection, but saints living in the presence of their Lord. Even their physical remains, therefore, were holy and instinct with the powers of God's kingdom: they were buried, whenever possible, with the utmost care. This spirit of devotion was further manifested in the customs of erecting special memorials wherever a martyr was buried and of celebrating the eucharist at a martyr's tomb on the date of his or her death. After the conversion of Constantine, when the church was able to give free expression to this reverence for its heroes, great shrines were erected over the sites of their tombs. Notable examples of these were the basilica of St. Peter on the Vatican Hill near Rome and "the martyry

[2] See Psalm 119:64.   [3] Psalm 119:62.

of the holy and triumphant martyr Euphemia," where the Council of Chalcedon had assembled in 451. To such shrines, great and small, pilgrims flocked to pray and to eat and drink (not infrequently to excess) in the company of the holy one. Each sainted martyr was seen as a true patron—a living person to whom believers could belong, with whom they could be identified, and from whom they could expect a more generous justice than any ordinary human patron could or would dispense. Since the presence of the saints was associated with the presence of their physical remains, the cult of martyrs became also a cult of their relics (in which, as early as the time of Augustine, a fraudulent trade was often conducted). So deep and serious was the devotion of all classes of Christians to these saints that their feast-days became a permanent part of the churches' liturgical calendars, and in the West, at any rate, every church building became a martyr's shrine, as the custom arose of enclosing a holy relic within each altar-table.

Quite distinct from the cult of martyrs was the veneration which came to be accorded to the Mother of Jesus. From at least the time of Irenaeus—for whom Mary was the Second Eve, whose obedience to God's call reversed the effects of her counterpart's sin—Christian thinkers had assigned to the Mother of Jesus a prominent place in the history of salvation. In writers like Athanasius and Apollinaris, this estimate of Mary's role was expressed by applying to her the title Mother of God (*theotokos*). In approximately the same era, Mary's virginity—indeed, her perpetual virginity, as St. Jerome argued—made her a model for those in the West who advocated the life of monastic continence. It was not, however, until the time of the christological controversies, when the title *theotokos* became a subject of debate in the East (see III:9), that commemoration of the Virgin came to be established in the public liturgy of the church. There was a basilica dedicated to the Mother of God at Ephesus when the ecumenical council of 431 met there. A similar basilica, built at Gethsemane on a site which was believed to be that of Mary's burial, celebrated the feast of its dedication (August 15) as a commemoration of the "falling asleep" (Dormition, and later Assumption) of the Virgin. Another church, in Jerusalem proper, remembered the day of its dedication (September 8) as marking the nativity of Mary. Observance of these days—as well as of the feasts of the Annunciation (March 25) and Purification (February 2), which belong to the cycle of celebrations determined by Christmas—spread gradually from Jerusalem to the rest of the East. They came to the West only after the close of the sixth century, with a wave of refugees from the Islamic invasions. There seems little doubt that the cult of the Virgin originally attracted and replaced the devotion that had been offered to the "mother goddesses" of Egypt, Syria, and Asia Minor; at the same time, however, it was her role as the chosen vehicle of the Incarnation which set her, in Christian eyes, above martyr or apostle as the noblest and holiest of human persons.

None of these developments and elaborations of Christian worship and piety is fully comprehensible apart from the changes that occurred in the setting of the liturgy after Constantine's recognition of the church. The sense of awe and of mystery which surrounded baptism and eucharist alike, as well as the devotion accorded to saints and witnesses of the past, depended in considerable part on the character of the church's public buildings and on the systematic use of pictorial art—for the most part painting and mosaic—to adorn them. Freed by Constantine from the constraints imposed on an illegal society, the churches after 313 built their own special places of assembly. To this end, rejecting the architectural form of the pagan temple, they adopted the style of the Roman basilica, which was essentially nothing more than a rectangular public hall, capable of being adapted to many uses. In Christian use, the basilica became a longitudinal building, generally with three aisles, lit from above by clerestory windows over the central nave. Opposite the entrance was the apse, where the bishop's chair and the seats of the presbytery were arranged against the wall. The building was furnished with an altar-table placed before the apse (often set off by railings and by a canopy resting on four pillars), and with a raised ambo or *bēma* for the reading of the Scriptures. The baptistery was located in an adjacent structure. While generally very plain on the outside, the interiors of these basilicas were decorated with paintings and mosaics which, together with the vista created by their combination of height and length, invested them, as well as the rites performed in them, with solemnity and even awesomeness. It was in this sort of setting that the custom arose of venerating pictures or icons of Christ, the Virgin Mary, and the saints—a custom that caught on in the East before it did in the West, where, in any case, a more extensive use was eventually made of statues. Such veneration was encouraged by the established habit of offering reverence to portraits of the emperor, a habit which no doubt made it seem natural to accord the same respect to even greater worthies, on the principle that "the honor paid to the image passes on to the prototype."[4]

---

[4] Basil of Caesarea, *On the Holy Spirit* 47.

Chapter 14

The Latin Christian Tradition

THE CHURCHES of the Latin West played their part in the trinitarian and christological debates of the fourth century. It was not, however, either a leading or a creative part. These controversies arose in the East, and the thinkers whose ideas generated and settled them did their thinking and their writing in Greek. Until the middle of the fifth century, when Pope Leo I's *Tome,* canonized by the Council of Chalcedon, demonstrated that western theology had achieved a genuine maturity, the contribution of the Latin churches to doctrinal inquiry and argument consisted largely in the political weight which their commitments afforded to one or another party in the East. The reasons for this situation seem to have been twofold.

The first is that the issues with which western and Latin Christianity had traditionally been concerned bore little relation to the agenda of Greek Christian thought. From Tertullian and Cyprian—both natives of North Africa, which was the most fertile breeding ground of Latin theology in the Roman era— the West inherited a near obsession with questions about the church: its identity, its purity, its relation to the world around it. Tertullian, it is true, had in his treatise *Against Praxeas* (see II:7) supplied the Latin churches with a trinitarian and christological formula which, carefully interpreted, gave them useful guidance in the Arian and Nestorian controversies. Nevertheless, it was not these debates which divided the western churches in the fourth century. Their continuing concern was with the ecclesiological problems precipitated by the Donatist schism and with the questions about the nature of the Christian life which underlay the Priscillianist movement in Spain and Aquitaine. It was only through Hilary of Poitiers (d. 367), whose exile under Constantius II took him to the East at a crucial turning point in the trinitarian debate, that westerners learned not to misunderstand the theological ideas and language of their eastern contemporaries. In his treatises *On the Synods* and *On the Trinity,* written after his return from exile, Hilary made it possible for essentially ignorant Latin church leaders to acquire some appreciation of the questions and ideas which were troubling Greek-speaking Christians.

A second reason is to be found in the fact that Latin Christianity produced no theological leadership of the first rank in the century or more after the death of Cyprian. Neither in biblical exegesis nor in questions of doctrine did any teacher of distinction arise in the West until the generation of Augustine of Hippo. This does not mean, of course, that the North African, Italian, Spanish and Gallican churches were devoid of theological talent. The Donatist Tyconius (d. ca. 400) not only contributed significantly to the continuing North African debate about the church, but in his *Book of Rules* he penned a hermeneutical work which Augustine admired and drew on for his own treatment of the methods of exegesis. In the eminent philosopher and rhetorician Marius Victorinus (another African), the Roman church around the middle of the fourth century gained a convert who wrote learnedly against the Arians in the style of a Neoplatonist philosopher. But by and large Latin Christianity in this period—like Latin culture generally in an earlier period—remained largely dependent on Greek sources. Ambrose of Milan provides an illustration of this fact. A master of Greek, he exhibited in his sermons and treatises both a consuming taste for Greek learning and an admiring willingness to cull ideas—sometimes, indeed, whole passages—from eastern exegetes and thinkers. It was, therefore, only with Jerome and Rufinus of Aquileia, and Augustine of Hippo and Pelagius, that Latin theology came to intellectual and literary maturity. Their work, in fact, coincides with a general revival of Latin literature, both pagan and Christian, at the end of the fourth and the opening of the fifth century. At the same time, it marks a return of Latin Christian thought to themes and concerns that were native to the western tradition in theology.

Chapter 15

Jerome

A SUPERB LATIN STYLIST, a careful linguist, and an eloquent and unscrupulous polemicist, St. Jerome (Eusebius Hieronymus) was the greatest scholar whom the ancient western church produced. Born in 331 of a prosperous landed family whose home was at Stridon in Dalmatia (now Yugoslavia), Jerome's early life followed the course which was usual of an upper-class youth of ability. He was schooled at Rome in grammar, rhetoric, and the classics of Latin literature—three subjects of which he became not only a master but an addict. While in Rome, he acquired a circle of friends, among them Tyrannius Rufinus (d. ca. 410) of Aquileia, who later joined Jerome in making systematic translations of the works of Origen and thus in providing the only texts through which many of that thinker's writings are known. Rufinus was to share Jerome's enthusiasm for the ascetic life but ultimately to quarrel with him bitterly over the reputation and teaching of Origen. After a sojourn at the imperial capital of Trier in Germany, where he conceived his first interest in Christian literature and in the ascetic life, Jerome spent some years in Dalmatia and Aquileia in a circle of devout and literate Christians, where his taste for the life of self-discipline and retirement was further developed.

In 372, driven from this circle by attacks on his character, Jerome set out for the East. Arriving ultimately at Antioch, he there, while recovering from an illness, undertook the serious study of Greek. Not long afterward, he resolved to devote himself completely to the ascetic life. In 374, he retired (not without his library) to the wilderness north of Antioch and lived among the numerous hermits who populated its hills. As it turned out, this experiment was not a success. Jerome, a vain and irritable man at best, found it impossible to get on with his neighbors, who not only came from a completely different social and cultural milieu but had no patience with his Latin and Roman stance in the trinitarian controversy. Jerome accordingly returned to Antioch in 376 or 377. There in all probability he heard Apollinaris of Laodicea, one of the foremost exegetes of the time, lecture on the Scriptures. By 379, however, when the death of Valens and the accession of Theodosius I had turned the tide of the trinitarian controversy, Jerome was in Constantinople, where Gregory of Nazianzus instructed him in Scripture and introduced him to the works of Origen. Now for the first time, Jerome turned to translation. He rendered, edited, and amplified the *Chronicle* of Eusebius of Caesarea (an outline of world history from the birth of Abraham to 325 A.D.) and began a project of putting the homilies of Origen into Latin.

It was in Rome, however, to which he returned in 382 and where he became a kind of secretary to Pope Damasus, that he undertook, with the pope's encouragement, his greatest translation project of all—a revision of the crude Old Latin version of the Bible. Over a period of twenty-two years, he completed the Gospels of the New Testament (in Rome) and the Old Testament (in Palestine). The latter he translated from the Hebrew original, having become persuaded that the Hebrew text and canon, and not those of the Greek Septuagint, were the proper authorities for the church. It was also in Rome that he became the teacher and spiritual counselor of a group of ascetically minded, wealthy, and aristocratic women, in particular the widows Marcella and Paula, and the latter's daughter, Eustochium. Through these relationships, Jerome became notorious as an apostle of the radical eastern style of asceticism, which had many enemies and critics among Christians at Rome. Attacked for his view that the celibate state is superior to that of marriage, Jerome replied to his critics in the works *Against Helvidius* and *Against Jovinian,* defending the ideal of virginity for women as well as for men and holding up the Mother of Jesus—who, he argued, practiced virginity throughout her life—as a model for ascetics. In the process of setting forth these views, Jerome showed a tendency to attack the ordinary clergy and Christians of Rome as unworthy of their calling, thus making himself so unpopular that after the death of Damasus he was more or less driven from the city.

The remainder of Jerome's life (he died in 420) was spent at Bethlehem, where his friend Paula, with her daughter Eustochium, constructed two monasteries, one for women, which she supervised herself, and one for men, which Jerome headed. It was from this monastery that there poured his biblical commentaries and his version of the Old Testament. While there, following the lead of Bishop Epiphanius of Salamis, he took a stand against his old master, Origen. Allying himself with Theophilus of Alexandria, and standing firmly against Origen's most prominent official defender, Bishop John of Jerusalem, he succeeded in embittering permanently his relations with his old friend Rufinus. The result was a lengthy literary debate between them which ultimately made of the Origenist controversy an issue in Rome and the West. Finally, it was from Bethlehem that Jerome took the side of Augustine in the debate over the views of Pelagius. Jerome's monuments were the Vulgate Bible, which until the twentieth century remained the normative version of the Scriptures for churches in communion with the see of Rome, and his biblical commentaries (profoundly indebted to those of Origen), which were regularly consulted by medieval scholastics and evangelical reformers.

Chapter 16

Augustine of Hippo

A YOUNGER contemporary of Jerome, St. Augustine of Hippo (Aurelius Augustinus) was born in the Numidian city of Thagaste on November 13, 354. His parents belonged to the Latin-speaking middle class of a town located in an area of North Africa whose predominant language was Berber. While his father, Patricius, was a pagan, his mother, Monica, was a pious Christian in the devout and perhaps slightly superstitious North African style.

His ambitious parents sent him at the age of sixteen to the nearby city of Madaura, and after that to Carthage, to further his education and his chances of advancement. Augustine followed the course of studies which was customary in his time: grammar, the close textual study of the major Latin classics, and then, at Carthage, rhetoric. This academic training set him in the way of several possible careers: that of a lawyer, of a professional rhetorician, or of a high civil servant under the imperial government. In fact, his first job, after the death of his father, was that of a teacher in his home town, but he soon returned to Carthage to take up a post there.

During this period, Augustine, in the fashion of his age, took a concubine, with whom he was to live for fourteen years and who bore him the son, Adeodatus, whose brilliance he loved to celebrate and whose early death (at the age of seventeen or eighteen) he greatly mourned. His sojourn at Carthage also marked the beginning of his religious and philosophical quest. There Augustine read and studied Cicero's *Hortensius,* a dialogue now known only in fragments. By it, as he testifies, the young man was converted to the quest for wisdom and the fulfilled human life. It was this quest which led him, around the year 373, to join himself to the Manichaean movement (see II:18), widespread and fashionable in North Africa, which appealed to him on several grounds. One of these was that, with its systematic dualism, Manichaeanism offered an appealing solution to the problem of evil—a problem which, in one or another form, was to obsess Augustine throughout his life. Another lay in its repudiation of the Old Testament, whose literary and moral crudity had troubled the skeptical young intellectual. A third reason for its appeal was the fact that it ridiculed the Christian demand for "faith" and professed to teach only what was rationally demonstrable. Augustine's addiction to Manichaeanism was, however, of relatively short duration. In a meeting with the respected and attractive Manichaean leader Faustus, from whom he had been led to expect a resolution of his doubts and questions, he was troubled and put off by the man's superficiality and ignorance. While he continued to move in Manichaean circles (and apparently saw no positive alternative to the belief that evil "exists" in much the same sense as silver or water may be said to exist—that is, as an identifiable "substance"), his mind began to move in the direction of the Academic skepticism (see I:1) which he learned from certain writings of Cicero.

It was in this state of mind that Augustine moved, at the age of twenty-nine, from Carthage to Rome, where again he set up as a teacher. The move gives evidence of the reputation he had acquired in North Africa as an able and promising young rhetorician. Augustine was annoyed and inconvenienced, however, by the reluctance of students at Rome to pay their fees. He was not unhappy, therefore, to receive the offer of an official professorship of rhetoric at Milan, the imperial capital, tendered him by the prefect of Rome, Symmachus, and obtained through the good offices of his Manichaean friends.

To Milan accordingly he went, in the year 384, ready to embark upon what he no doubt hoped would be a distinguished public career. At Milan, however, the business of his personal life—his search for that truth which brings human fulfillment—overtook that of his professional life. For one thing, he was joined at Milan not only by two old friends, Alypius and Nebridius, who in their different fashions shared and reinforced his concern to find the true way, but also by his determined mother, Monica, who for her part sought to "settle" her son—to get his life in order and to bring him home to the Christian faith in which he had been reared. By this time, Augustine had finally separated himself from the Manichaeans, but his skepticism and disillusionment had not disappeared, and the problems which had made a Manichaean of him still haunted him. He had, to be sure, "decided to remain a catechumen in the catholic church," but only "until something clear should show me in what direction to steer my course."[1]

Another thing that happened in Milan was that Augustine began to hear the preaching of the great Ambrose, which eventually impressed him not only by its style but even more by its substance. Ambrose's typological and allegorical handling of the Old Testament dissolved one of the problems which had driven him from his parental faith. As Ambrose dealt with it, the Old Testament lost its crudity and revealed surprising depths of meaning. Again, Ambrose introduced him to the idea—revolutionary, as far as Augustine was concerned— of an immaterial reality: a nonspatial, nontangible way of being proper to God and to the soul. At the same time, through other contacts, the young rhetorician discovered circles in Milan where a new intellectual movement had taken root, one with which Ambrose himself was associated and which, in the tradition of Marius Victorinus, the Roman philosopher and rhetorician of the previous generation, wedded Christianity and Neoplatonism. Augustine came into possession of "certain books of the Platonists translated from Greek into Latin"[2] —treatises, no doubt, of Plotinus and Porphyry—and through these works, as he relates, he came to a new vision of things. Not only did they teach him that evil is not a "substance" (as the Manichaeans had alleged) but merely the negation of an existing good; they also gave him a new sense of his identity as a human being and illumined for him the meaning of the New Testament message. He was now able to see himself as a soul whose fulfillment lay in the knowledge and love of God. He learned to discern in the depths of himself the shining of "the true light that enlightens every man"[3]—and to realize, at the same time, how far away he was from that Light.

Yet even as this intellectual revolution, with all the excitement and new prospects that accompanied it, was proceeding, Augustine was still the careerist, "panting after honors, profits, and marriage."[4] His mother helped to arrange a proper, and socially and financially advantageous, match for him. Before the

---

[1] *Confessions* 5.14.   [2] Ibid., 7.9.   [3] John 1:9.   [4] *Confessions* 6.6.

betrothal (the girl was too young for actual marriage), Augustine sent away his common-law wife of many years—only to find himself compulsively taking on another sexual companion. Yet in the meantime, he and his friends were considering the advantages of a retired life devoted to reading, thought, and the common pursuit of wisdom. Under the influence of a visitor from Africa, Ponticianus, the little group was introduced to the monastic ideal of the life of renunciation and continence—an ideal which, as it was portrayed in Athanasius's *Life of Anthony,* pressed upon Augustine the inconsistency between his interior search for truth and his absorption in worldly and sexual gratification. The conflict which Augustine thus experienced was resolved when, in a garden in Milan, he overheard a child chanting a jingle: "Take and read, take and read." He took Paul's Letter to the Romans and read: ". . . not in debauchery and licentiousness, not in quarreling and jealousy. But put on the Lord Jesus Christ, and make no provision for the flesh, to gratify its desires."[5] This conversion turned him to a form of the ascetic life, and immediately afterward he retired (in the fall of 386) to an estate at Cassiciacum with his son and a group of his close friends. There for some months they read and held long discussions, the fruits of which were a series of dialogues in which Augustine dealt with some of the problems which had long troubled him. In a fashion that shows how thoroughly his mind had been imbued with a Platonist outlook, he took up questions about the possibility of assured knowledge, the problem of evil, and the nature of the fulfilled human life. When winter came, Augustine returned to Milan and enrolled himself as a candidate for baptism. After his baptism at Easter in 387, he, Monica, and Adeodatus began a journey back to Africa, where he was to spend the rest of his life. Monica died at Ostia. After an interval, Augustine continued on his way, having already begun to write the long series of works in which he turned his pen against the Manichaeanism he had earlier espoused.

Back at Thagaste, he set up a small community of ascetics and clearly envisaged spending the rest of his life in a contemplative and philosophical retirement. In 391, however, on a visit to the port city of Hippo in Numidia, he was seized by the people and, over his own tears and protests, was ordained presbyter by the bishop, Valerius, who, being a Greek, spoke Latin only haltingly and needed an associate to help him in the task of preaching. Shortly after 395, Valerius died and Augustine succeeded him. He remained the bishop of Hippo until his death in 430.

Augustine's successive ordinations marked a turning point in his life. No longer was he merely the philosopher-Christian, concerned with the dialectic of the interior search for God. Now he was also a pastor, who had to turn his attention increasingly to the Scriptures and their exposition and to the practical problems of the churches in North Africa. This crucial juncture in his life was

[5] Rom. 13:13–14.

marked by the writing of his *Confessions* (ca. 397), in which he retrospectively treats his own spiritual pilgrimage and conversion as a clue to, and an illustration of, the universal situation of human beings in relation to God. In this remarkable work, as he sums up his past and turns to the future, Augustine sounds a theme which will permeate his thinking about every major problem he would face. Though the human self is created for the knowledge and love of God and is "unquiet" until it comes to rest in God,[6] it is also turned away from God and lost in a falsely directed love. While this perversion can be described, it cannot be accounted for. Its springs in the human will lie deeper than the level of conscious choice; by the same token, its rectification depends on an impulse which human choice cannot of itself provide. Only the grace and love of God, working in ways which cannot always be discerned or understood, can redirect human loving and focus it on the ultimate source of its fulfillment—God. This theme, sounded in the very structure of the *Confessions,* appears also in Augustine's roughly contemporary studies of Paul. It marks the degree to which his attention to the Scriptures and to the teaching tradition of the church was leading him to modify and qualify his Neoplatonism, and it surfaces in his treatment of the problem which was to dominate his life and work for the fifteen years which followed his ordination as bishop—the problem of the Donatist schism.

By Augustine's time, Donatism (see III:1) had been alive in North Africa for eighty years. Under Donatus the Great (d. ca. 355) and Parmenian (d. ca. 391), Donatism, in spite of intermittent persecution by the imperial authorities (and indeed partly as a result of it), flourished in North Africa to the extent that, at the time of Augustine's ordination, it probably embraced the majority of North African Christians and was unquestionably dominant in the towns and villages of the Numidian highlands. A body puritan and exclusivist in spirit, the Donatist church stood in the tradition of Tertullian and Cyprian and, regarded itself as the one body of Christians in the Roman world which had maintained the spirit and tradition of the martyr-church of old. The catholic communion of churches it saw as "tainted"—not only by the fact that it stemmed (as was alleged) from bishops who had betrayed the faith by handing over their holy books in the persecution under Diocletian, but also (indeed above all) by the fact that it was now supported by the Roman authorities, "the world." Accordingly, as far as Donatists were concerned, the catholic body was simply not "church" at all. It was deprived of God's Spirit by the impurity and the compromises of its bishops and clergy and so was outside the realm of salvation. For this reason, Donatists refused to acknowledge baptisms performed in the catholic communion, and catholics who joined the Donatist body (and they were not few in number) were rebaptized. To the Donatists there rallied not merely persons who adhered to the traditional African conception of the church

[6] *Confessions* I.1.

as a morally and ritually "pure" outpost of God's kingdom, but also those, like the Numidian peasantry, whose opposition to "the world" stemmed partly from social and economic discontents. By Augustine's time, the opposition between Donatist and catholic was both established and embittered. Sustained by each party's cherished memories of the other's violence and reinforced by a mutual refusal of ordinary social intercourse, the schism stood as one of the given facts of North African life.

As bishop of Hippo, near whose church there rose the basilica of a Donatist congregation, Augustine refused to accept this situation. In part, his attitude stemmed from a profound antipathy to the Donatist understanding of the church. As far as he was concerned, it was simply wrong to pretend that the church could be a "pure" body. In the tradition of the third-century Roman bishops—and indeed of Cyprian of Carthage himself—Augustine saw the church as "mixed body" in which tares and wheat would grow together until the judgment. More than that, however, he believed that the holiness of the church —the presence, in and for the church, of God's Spirit—depended not (as the Donatists argued) on the sanctity or purity of the minister who baptized, celebrated the eucharist, or ordained, but simply on the gracious love of God himself. Thus, he insisted that the real and effective minister of the sacraments through which God touched and reformed human lives was not the human priest, the bishop or presbyter, but Christ himself, of whose ministry that of the human agent was merely a symbol and channel. The church lived, Augustine argued, not in virtue of its own holiness or that of its bishops, but simply in virtue of God's grace in Christ. As medieval theologians would put it much later, the sacraments were "valid" (i.e., objectively accomplished what they "said") not because of what the human minister was or did (*ex opere operantis*) but because of the church's performance of the action itself (*ex opere operato*) in dependence upon the covenanted grace of God.

This belief, however, that the church lives in and through grace led Augustine to the conviction that even the Donatist body was in a real sense "church." Its baptisms and eucharists were not meaningless ("invalid"). Rather, they were defective or inefficacious. Performed in hostile separation from the church catholic, they lacked the soil of charity in which they could bear the fruit they were intended to bear. What was needed, therefore, was the reconciliation of the Donatists to the rest of the church, and Augustine devoted himself to this end. In cooperation with his friend and colleague Aurelius, the bishop of Carthage, he sought first of all to reform, strengthen, and unify the catholic churches in Africa so that the merit of their cause might become the more apparent. At the same time, he became a propagandist, composing popular leaflets (none of them very impressive) in which he set out to controvert the Donatist version of the origins and nature of the schism. He also sought public and private occasions to conduct discussion and debate with Donatist leaders, and he replied to their theological contentions in a series of lengthy treatises.

In all this his aim was to make the catholic cause compelling and persuasive and thus to dissuade the Donatists from their separatism.

These methods did not succeed, however, nor did Donatist violence against catholics diminish. Gradually, Augustine was brought—partly by his fellow bishops and partly by his own eventual acknowledgment that a policy of conciliation was hopeless—to recognize that if the schism was to be ended, the pressure of Roman law and Roman police power must be brought to bear. Therefore, he joined in encouraging the imperial court (which was by no means reluctant) to legislate against the Donatists: to confiscate Donatist properties and to impose severe legal penalties on persons who persisted in loyalty to the schismatic body. This policy was put into final effect in 411, after a convocation in Carthage to which the Donatist bishops were summoned to make their case or suffer the consequences. Augustine justified this appeal to the power of the state in several ways. On the one hand, he quoted Luke 14:23 ("Compel people to come in"). On the other, he noted in a pragmatic vein that these legal penalties actually did induce many Donatists to return to the catholic fold and that, contrary to his original expectation, they quickly became quite normal members of their congregations. While he refused and protested any application of the death penalty to Donatists, Augustine nevertheless believed that the emperor had a right and, as a catholic Christian, an obligation to intervene in the interest of the salvation of the African schismatics. In the end, however, the policy of persecution which he came reluctantly but firmly to support did not succeed. The Donatist movement was crippled, and many of its adherents were restored to the catholic body, but it survived nonetheless, disappearing only when Islam conquered the former Roman provinces of North Africa.

After 411, the Donatist affair moved out of the center of Augustine's attention, and his mind was turned to other problems. One of these—more important to Augustine himself in his role as a religious seeker than it was to any burning public issue—was the completion of his great treatise *On the Trinity,* which he had begun more than a decade earlier but laid aside after completing a version of the first four books and of the present Book 8. Even in these sections, where there is no hint of his later so-called "psychological analogy," it is clear that the question of the Trinity had become for him not so much a problem about how the theologian is to describe God as a problem about how the human mind can rise to an apprehension of God in God's threefold being. Augustine's idea was that God is known and experienced most certainly in the act of love, of which God is the Source, the Object, and the Power. In choosing and willing love, the human self enters into the three-personed structure of God's being and acting and thus, by a kind of reflex awareness, knows and loves God. When he returned, however, after 414, to the work he had left unfinished, Augustine had read (for the first time) works of Gregory of Nazianzus and certain other Greek theologians and had ruminated on Gregory's idea that the trinitarian "persons" (hypostases) are defined and constituted by their relations to one another (see III:4). This idea that "Father," "Son," and "Spirit" are names not of different beings but of relations he then developed further. It was his conviction that the divine hypostases were not distinct actualizations of a single *ousia* (being, essence) but rather simply the substantive ways in which the one God is eternally related to himself.

It was in this connection that the "psychological analogy" came into play. Appealing to the doctrine that human beings are created "after the image of God," and insisting that this must mean creation after the image of the entire Trinity, Augustine developed a notion of the human self as subsisting in and through its own self-relatedness. Thus, he could argue that people are or become themselves as, in every act, they remember, know, and will themselves; and since these relations of remembering, knowing, and willing are ways in which one and the same self is related to itself, the threefold relationship and the unity of the person are not inconsistent but presuppose each other. Hence, there is a "clue" (*vestigium*) to God's way of being in the human way of being. More important, however, the human search for self-understanding in the end issued, as Augustine saw it, in every person's being referred "above" self to the being of God, the original of all creaturely being and so the goal of all human searching.

One central element in this idea that the "persons" of the Trinity are substantive relations in which God stands to himself was a particular understanding of the Holy Spirit. For Augustine, the Spirit is the expression of God's nature as love—is, in fact, the relation of mutual love in which the Father and the Word stand to each other. He thus spoke regularly of the Spirit as proceeding "from the Father and from the Son": the so-called doctrine of "double procession." His use of this language led eventually to the insertion in Latin versions of the Niceno-Constantinopolitan Creed of the expression *filioque* ("and from the Son")—a textual change which was in the end to become one of the principal sources of conflict between the Greek and Latin churches in medieval and modern times.

Even while he was writing his treatise *On the Trinity,* however, the fall of Rome to the Visigoths (410) and the consequent influx of refugees from Italy to North Africa compelled Augustine to turn his attention to a more burning public issue. Since the time of Constantine, Christians had tended to take the view that if the empire was faithful to Christ and his cause, God would protect and save it—a view which Constantine himself seems to have held (see III:1). Now, however, with the collapse of Rome's defenses before the Visigoths, many pagans were arguing that Rome would do better to return to her old gods, under whose sway she had been kept safe. It was in response to this problem that Augustine undertook the writing of his vast treatise *On the City of God*. His response, however, went far beyond the immediate scope of the issue which evoked it. *The City of God* is less an apology for Christianity (though it is that) than an analysis of the nature of human societies and their relation to God in history.

The work begins with a critique of pagan religion and philosophy and of their claim to bring humanity to its fulfillment. The proper goal of human striving, Augustine argues, is God himself and the society of human beings in fellowship with God ("the City of God") which will be actualized only beyond history. There is no way, therefore, in which the order established by any human government can be assigned a value which is more than provisional and passing. Rome is not, and cannot be, eternal. More than that, Augustine is convinced that earthly governments are the products of a falsely directed love: a self-centered lust for visible, ephemeral, and material goods. For just this reason, they have their root in an impulse which is intrinsically competitive and so are erected on a foundation of violence and injustice. This does not mean, however, that they cannot actualize a justice and a peace which, if relative, partial, and temporary, are nonetheless real: even a society of thieves requires and seeks some kind of order. While, then, the Roman state and all other states, as well as the institutions of slavery and of private property, exist only because of human sinfulness, they are capable of serving, in their way, the purposes of God insofar as they seek to restrain and control the effects of the very sin out of which they emerge. In the providence of God, then, the "city of man" has a role to play, and Christians have a right and an obligation to cooperate in effecting, so far as possible, the relative peace and order which a self-seeking and competitive love can contrive.

Intermingled in this society which seeks earthy goods, however, there are those who are governed by a higher love—a love for God, the good which all can share equally. Such persons compose the historical and preliminary form of the City of God, of which the church is not so much the embodiment as the ambiguous anticipation. Augustine had not forgotten the position he had taken in the Donatist controversy. The church is not a perfect society, but a body in which saints and sinners are "mixed" (*corpus permixtum*). At the same time, it is the society in which God's grace is visibly and certainly at work to turn men and women from a love falsely directed toward ephemeral and created goods to a love directed upon God himself; and for this reason the church portends and signifies the redeemed human society, the City "whose builder and maker is God." The theme of *The City of God,* then, is the theme of "the two loves," one of which is directed to ephemeral and finite, the other to eternal and infinite, good. These two loves create two kinds of human society. Moreover, each in its way attains the good at which it aims. If the "city of man"—of which Rome's empire was Augustine's symbol—does not attain a peace and an order which are indestructible and lasting, if it is vulnerable to conquest and destruction, that is because conquest and destruction are the means by which its good is achieved and because that good itself is a passing thing. The only ultimate value, because the only lasting value, is God himself, in whom all created goods are eminently contained and preserved. Thus, Augustine relativizes and, in effect, secularizes the state, denying both pagan and Christian idolizations of its order. At the same time, he affirms the significance of the relative goods it achieves. Earthly peace and justice are no mean values, even though they are not, and cannot be, the embodiments of the peace and justice of God's City.

Chapter 17

The Pelagian Controversy

THE INFLUX OF REFUGEES into North Africa after the Visigothic invasion of Italy brought Augustine, along with its cadre of Roman aristocrats, more than just one problem. Their debates over the meaning of Rome's fall diverted his attention from the domestic problems of the African churches to those of the church as a part of world history and stimulated him, as we have seen, to compose *The City of God*. At the same time, it was their arrival which compelled him to weigh, consider, and in the end attack a movement of religious reform that had been spreading from Rome through southern Italy and Sicily and which eventually came to bear the name of its leader, Pelagius.

A British ascetic (though not a cleric or a member of any monastic community), Pelagius had taken up residence in Rome around 390. There he moved and taught in the same aristocratic circles in which Jerome had once proclaimed the virtues of the ascetic life, and he acquired in the process an enthusiastic and dedicated body of followers. His message, which seems to have appealed especially to young intellectuals of noble birth, called for a strict standard of moral perfection for all Christians. Distressed by the laxity and lukewarmness of believers in Rome, critical of their excuse making, and incredulous at the notion that baptism guaranteed salvation, Pelagius asserted that it was the obligation of every Christian to achieve perfection by keeping all the commandments of God. This stern message, reminiscent of an older rigorism, turned out to be, for many of its hearers, an inspiring one as well, since Pelagius also insisted that God would not have given his commandments had he not supplied all human persons with the power to fulfill them. Perfection was truly within the reach of everyone, for everyone was endowed by God's creation—that is, as a matter of natural capacity—with freedom of choice. What is

more, God had supplied, in the Scriptures and, supremely, in the person of
Jesus, both instruction in the difference between good and evil and examples
of the virtuous life. Equipped, then, with knowledge of the good and with
freedom of choice, and drawn by the promise of eternal life for those who
should keep God's will, no one—once set right with God by the forgiveness of
sins in baptism—could lack either the necessary inducement or the necessary
capacity for perfection. Pelagius looked to a day when the virtues of the ascetic
—continence, chastity, and poverty—would belong to all Christians, and the
church would be revealed as the pure and spotless society it was called to be.

In a young lawyer named Coelestius, Pelagius won a clear-headed and
vigorous disciple and companion. Fleeing the Visigothic invasion, these two
landed at Hippo in 410, seeking to meet Augustine, another notable advocate
of the ascetic life, though one whose attitudes had already troubled and puzzled
Pelagius. The bishop was absent from the city, however, and his visitors moved
on to Carthage, whence, a year later, Pelagius departed for Palestine. The beginnings of the Pelagian controversy, therefore, were occasioned not by Pelagius
himself but by certain teachings of Coelestius. The latter had remained in
Carthage and applied to be ordained there as a presbyter. In the meantime,
moreover, he had involved himself in discussions about sin, the fall of Adam,
and baptism and had stated views on these subjects which he no doubt took
to be those of Pelagius or those which Pelagius's position presupposed. What
they were we gather from the accusations which were shortly brought against
him by one Paulinus, a Milanese deacon:

> (1) Adam was made mortal and would have died whether he had sinned or not
> sinned. (2) The sin of Adam injured himself alone, and not the human race.
> (3) New-born children are in that state in which Adam was before his fall. (4)
> Neither by the death and sin of Adam does the whole race die, nor by the resurrec-
> tion of Christ does the whole race rise. (5) The Law leads to the kingdom of heaven
> as well as the Gospel. (6) Even before the coming of the Lord there were men with-
> out sin.[1]

Coelestius did not deny that these statements represented a correct account of
his views; and there can be no doubt that they contradicted a standing tradition
of African Christian teaching, which justified the baptism of infants on the
ground that from conception they were alienated from God because of their
involvement in the original sin of Adam. Accordingly, a local synod condemned
his position (411) and refused him ordination.

Augustine was not present at this synod, and he knew of Coelestius's
teaching only by report. It was gradually and cautiously that he entered the
debate. In his treatises *On the Reward and Remission of Sins* (412) and *On
the Spirit and the Letter* (412) he made it clear what he took the underlying
issue to be. He agreed with his fellow African bishops that the baptism of

---

[1] Ayer, *Source Book,* p. 461.

infants presupposed their implication in sin—Adam's "original" sin—but he also indicated that for him the central matter in question was that of the necessity of grace. He thought that both Pelagius's moral teaching and Coelestius's six propositions called into question the truth that it is by the grace of Christ that human beings are saved—that is, by the Holy Spirit, who sheds the love of God abroad in our hearts.[2] For Augustine, salvation depended not on external obedience to prescribed modes of behavior but on the evocation of love for God in the human soul, and such human love could be evoked only as an answer to God's love. The freedom of the human person to turn wholeheartedly to God depended, then, on God's redemptive action. This the experience of his whole life, not to mention his musings on the letters of Paul and John, had taught him. Behind this conviction lay Augustine's awareness of the mystery of human sin, which for him was not simply or primarily a matter of disobedience to commands but rather of a misdirected and disoriented love. It was to explain this mystery that he appealed, with his African colleagues, to the idea of the implication of all human beings in Adam's sin and guilt—a guilt which, even in the case of infants, could be removed only by baptism.

By 415, Augustine had become perfectly clear in his mind that the assumptions underlying the views of Pelagius and Coelestius constituted a "system" which denied the very foundation of the salvation which the Christian Gospel proclaimed, though whether Pelagius explicitly maintained the doctrines which Augustine attributed to him—or saw the issues which Augustine saw—is another question. Early in that year, therefore, Augustine sent his disciple Orosius to Jerome in Palestine (where Pelagius was now residing) to encourage him in his opposition to Pelagius. Jerome did not need much encouragement, since Pelagius had become a protégé of the Origenist Bishop John of Jerusalem (see III:7). At Jerusalem, though, and later at a synod convened at Diospolis (Lydda), Pelagius disclaimed the teachings of Coelestius and assured the assembled bishops that his own views had none of the implications the Africans had seen in them. The synod accordingly received him into the full communion of the church.

To this rebuff, Augustine and his colleagues responded by assembling two councils, one at Carthage for the province of Africa and one at Mileve for the province of Numidia. These unanimously condemned the Pelagian position and appealed for confirmation of their views to Pope Innocent I (402–417). In vague and rather general terms, the Pope concurred. His successor, Zosimus (417–418), however, was of a different mind. Having received a confession of faith from Pelagius himself and an appeal in person from Coelestius, Zosimus declared that he could find no fault in them. But two developments then conspired to lead the pope to alter his position. The teaching of Coelestius in Rome

---

[2] Cf. Rom. 5:5, and *On the Spirit and the Letter*, 5.

created serious public disturbances there among the Christians, and—not without pressure from the leaders of the African church, including Augustine—the emperor Honorius issued a rescript condemning Pelagianism and ordering the exile of its adherents. Zosimus accordingly changed his mind and issued a circular letter, the so-called *Epistula tractatoria,* in which he approved the African position, which had been restated by a council at Carthage (418). From this point on, Rome stood firmly against the Pelagian party and indeed procured its condemnation, without discussion, by the ecumenical council of Ephesus (431).

These decisions did not, however, mean that the theological controversy came to a halt. For one thing, Augustine in his writings on the subject had moved to a position which troubled many who otherwise supported his stand against Pelagianism. Believing as he did that every human being is so caught up in Adam's sin and guilt that human nature itself is corrupted and incapable of turning, by its own strength, from self-love and "concupiscence" to love for God, Augustine came to stress the sole efficacy of divine grace. Accordingly, he evolved a strong doctrine of predestination, according to which it is God's choice and action, taken without regard for human merit foreseen, which at once starts people on the road to salvation and enables them to persevere in it. Furthermore, at the same time that he was trying to quiet the doubts of some of his friends about the implications of this teaching (in treatises like that of 427, *On Grace and Free Will*), Augustine was attacked by the new leader of the Pelagian cause—the brilliant and acerbic Julian, bishop of Eclanum, whose manner of combining argument, ridicule, and personal attack greatly troubled Augustine's last years and evoked from him uncharacteristically bitter replies. Julian, one of eighteen Italian bishops exiled in 419 for refusing to condemn Pelagius and Coelestius, was no ascetic in the style of his master. He conceived himself to be defending the goodness of human nature and of marriage against the dark Manichaean dualism of the provincial African position represented by Augustine. The debate between these two protagonists was cut short by Augustine's death and the Vandal conquest of Rome's North African provinces.

Chapter 18

Semi-Pelagianism

WHAT AUGUSTINE'S DEATH did not cut short was the continuing controversy over his doctrine of the sole efficacy of divine grace. Not all of those who defended his stand against Pelagius were prepared to accept his predestinarian views or his apparent contention that grace is irresistible. With the Vandal conquest of Numidia and Africa, however, the controversy over Augustine's views was transferred to the south of Gaul. There John Cassian (see III:7), the founder and guide of two monasteries near Marseilles and the principal interpreter to the West of the spirit of Egyptian monasticism, took the view—traditionally described as "semi-Pelagian"—that God's grace comes as an answer to "the beginning of a good will" in the human person.[1] In his view, "the will always remains free in man, and it can either neglect or delight in the grace of God."[2] Cassian believed not that salvation came to people apart from grace, but that "there are seeds of goodness implanted in every soul by the kindness of the Creator" and that these seeds, which enable human beings to prefer God above other goods, come to their fruition only when they are "quickened by the assistance of God."[3] There is in human nature, then, a capacity to turn to God, but this capacity is fulfilled only by God's own action.

Four years after Augustine's death, Vincent, a monk of Lérins in the south of Gaul, wrote his *Commonitorium,* in which, without attacking Augustine by name, he suggested that the latter's teachings on grace and predestination were novelties which had no support in catholic tradition. "Moreover, in the catholic church itself," he wrote, "all possible care should be taken that we hold that which has been believed everywhere, always, and by all (*quod ubique, quod semper, quod ab omnibus*)"; and clearly as far as Vincent was concerned, Augustine's position did not fulfill this criterion.[4] Some forty years later, this position was even more explicitly stated by Faustus, abbot of Lérins and later bishop of Riez. In his treatise *On the Grace of God and Free Will* (ca. 474), Faustus insisted that the beginning of faith (*initium fidei*) has its

---

[1] *Collationes* 13. [2] Ibid., 12. [3] Ibid. [4] Ayer, *Source Book*, p. 471.

root in human free will, which, in spite of the reality of original sin, has "the possibility of striving for salvation." Grace is the divine promise and warning which inclines the weakened but still free will to choose the right. It is not, as with Augustine, an inward and transforming power which works at a level deeper than that of conscious choice. In spite of his rejection of Pelagius, then, Faustus in some respects stood closer to the latter than to Augustine.

On the other side of the controversy stood Prosper of Aquitaine (ca. 390–ca. 463), who early in his career (probably as a lay monk at Marseilles) wrote Augustine to apprise him of the opposition to his views which was arising in monastic circles in Gaul. The author of works against John Cassian and Vincent of Lérins, Prosper eventually became secretary to Pope Leo I (440–461) and during his tenure of this office compiled a series of excerpts from Augustine's works. These excerpts were eventually put to good use by Caesarius (ca. 469–542), a monk of Lérins who in 502 became bishop of Arles. In 529, Caesarius held a small synod at Orange, whose canons assumed a larger significance when they were approved by Pope Boniface II (530–532). This synod affirmed a diluted form of the Augustinian position, which Caesarius himself supported. Humanity is not only implicated in the original sin of Adam, but has lost all power to turn to God of its own will. "It is brought about by the infusion of the Holy Spirit and his operation in us that we wish to be set free." It is, moreover, "by the free gift of grace, that is, by the inspiration of the Holy Spirit," that human persons have "the desire of believing" and "come to the birth of holy baptism." All human goodness, then, is the work of God. On the other hand, the synod of Orange nowhere affirmed the irresistibility of grace. On the contrary, it affirmed that human persons can "resist the same Holy Spirit." The notion of predestination to damnation was condemned. Most important of all, however, the synod bound the reception of grace to baptism and insisted that the natural fruit of this grace is good works. "We also believe this to be according to the Catholic faith, that grace having been received in baptism, all who have been baptized can and ought, by the aid and support of Christ, to perform those things which belong to the salvation of the soul, if they labor faithfully."[5] In other words, the Augustinian idea that the grace of God changes and transforms the willing of the believer was affirmed, even while the strict form of Augustine's doctrines of predestination and grace was severely qualified. These issues were not finally settled at Orange. They remained central to the agenda of Latin theology not only during the Middle Ages, but also during the Protestant Reformation and its aftermath.

[5] Ayer, *Source Book,* pp. 472–474.

Chapter 19

Gregory the Great

THE ERA of the Semi-Pelagian controversy (430–529) corresponded roughly with that of the Nestorian and Eutychian controversies in the East and their aftermath in the Acacian schism between Rome and Constantinople (see III:10). In the West, this was a time of dislocation and collapse for empire and church alike. The barbarian migrations and the decline of imperial power meant that in some outlying areas, like Britain and Pannonia, Christianity was to all intents and purposes driven out. Barbarian kingdoms were established in most of Gaul and Spain as well as in North Africa, and the constant warfare which accompanied the movements of these nations devastated cities and countryside, inhibited commerce and communication, and thus further eroded the social and economic foundations of the Roman world. The Goths, Vandals, and Burgundians, moreover, were uniformly Arian, and this meant that a religious as well as a cultural and linguistic barrier divided them from the Roman provincial society which they ruled and which, precisely because it was Roman, was devoted to the cause of catholic Christianity.

The political fate of Gaul and Spain became that of the Italian provinces as well when, with the advent (490) of the Ostrogoths under the rule of their king, Theodoric, the whole of the peninsula was occupied and subjugated by a barbarian nation, to whose members one-third of all land was assigned. Theodoric, however—who ruled formally as a governor under the emperor at Constantinople and was styled "Patrician of the Romans"—did not persecute or penalize catholic Christians. This policy was of a piece with his continuation of the system under which civil administration was exclusively in the hands of Roman citizens, while military affairs were in the hands of the Goths. Thus, Cassiodorus (see III:7) served under Theodoric as head of the civil service (*magister officiorum*), and the Christian philosopher Boethius (d. ca. 524), a member of the Anician clan and author of the famous *Consolation of Philosophy,* became an advisor of Theodoric and was elevated to the rank of consul in 514. As a king who ruled over two legally separate peoples (Goths were not Roman citizens), Theodoric seems to have aimed at a gradual romanization and civilization of his own people and to this end sought its peaceful coexistence with the Italian provincials of the empire. At the same time, to secure his political and military position, he built careful alliances with the Visigothic and Burgundian kings on his northern borders, seeking to create a stable barbarian—and Arian—entente.

Nevertheless, there were inevitable tensions and hostilities not only between the Ostrogothic invaders and the Latin-speaking population of Italy, but also between Theodoric and the imperial court at Constantinople. These showed themselves in a gradual alienation between the Ostrogothic king and the Roman senatorial aristocracy. This development was occasioned in part at least by the failure of Theodoric's system of alliances. The conversion of the Franks to catholic Christianity, their conquest of Aquitaine from the Visigoths, and, finally, the turning of the Burgundians to an alliance with Constantinople, placed Theodoric and his successors in a position of political isolation. Not unnaturally, therefore, Theodoric became uneasy about the loyalty of many of his independent-minded and catholic servants. Boethius himself died in prison under a charge of treason, and Cassiodorus ultimately retired from public service to found a school and monastery. More important still, these tensions became manifest in the determination of Emperor Justinian to reconquer Italy for the empire, an enterprise which was undertaken ten years after Theodoric's death (526). As a consequence, Italy was subjected to a series of destructive military campaigns which left poverty, famine, disease, and depopulation in their wake. Rome itself—which in the course of these wars once had its entire population deported—became a city filled with ruins, its people so reduced in numbers that much of what had been the city was returned to wilderness. The Byzantine reconquest, moreover, was followed almost immediately by the equally debilitating invasion of the pagan Lombards (568), whose leaders, by the end of the sixth century, controlled most of central and northern Italy, isolating Rome from Ravenna, the seat of the imperial exarch, as well as from the Byzantine territories in the south.

These events could not fail to affect the life of the church in Italy. The papacy, like the Latin-speaking population generally, was, during the first half of the sixth century, caught in the struggle between Constantinople and the Ostrogoths and became for a time the creature of conflicting political parties and loyalties, losing in the process much of its moral authority. The situation was changed, however, with the advent of the Lombards. With Rome cut off from the seat of the imperial exarch, who was in any case without sufficient military resources to challenge Lombard domination, the Roman bishop was constrained to become the political as well as the spiritual leader of Christians in Rome and its environs, even while he maintained, or sought to maintain, his general pastoral oversight of churches in the West.

At just this juncture in history, there came to the papal throne a man who not only rose to the challenge of his own times, but who also provided the western churches with a body of writings that did much to shape the thought, piety, and ideals of medieval Christendom: Gregory I, rightly called "the Great" and traditionally styled one of the four Latin "Doctors of the Church."

Gregory was born (ca. 540) in Rome, the offspring of a prominent senatorial family. Rising to civil eminence at an early age, he was made prefect (governor) of Rome before 573. Attracted by the monastic life, however, he disposed of his vast inheritance, devoting it to the care of the poor and to the foundation of monasteries—six in Sicily and one in Rome, which occupied his family's former palace on the Caelian Hill. This monastery Gregory entered as a simple monk. After three years, however, the reigning pope made Gregory one of Rome's seven deacons, in charge of the administration of a region of the city. Pope Pelagius II (579–590) then sent him to Constantinople as his resident ambassador (*apocrisarius*), where Gregory served with ability, though, curiously, without acquiring a knowledge of Greek. In about 586, he was once again in Rome, now acting as abbot of his monastery of St. Andrew. In 590, he was chosen pope, accepting the responsibility with great reluctance, at a time when a plague was raging in the city. He died fourteen years later on March 12, 604.

With a proper Roman magistrate's sense of duty and attentiveness to detail, Gregory set out to fulfill the obligations of his office. He fulfilled them, however, in the spirit of a Christian believer who in the events of his time saw evidence that the present age was approaching its end and knew that he was called to care for his Lord's people in view of the judgment which was soon coming to them and to him alike. Conscious of the dignity and the prerogatives of his office, he nevertheless envisaged himself as "servant of the servants of God," bound in love to admonish, protect, and assist all who were in his charge.

It was in view of this pastoral mission that he at once undertook to reform the administration of the Roman church's vast properties in Sicily, Italy, and Provence—estates whose income was as often as not appropriated by local bishops or secular rulers. As far as Gregory was concerned, these estates belonged of right to the poor, who were to be fed, clothed, and assisted by their revenues. Accordingly, he appointed personal representatives to supervise their administration and devoted much of his own time to giving precise instructions on subjects ranging from the planting of crops to the feeding of livestock. In this way, he recovered for the Roman church the revenues of the "patrimony of St. Peter" and was able to pursue his policy of support for the deprived, the underprivileged, and other victims of "the insecurity of our times."

At the same time, Gregory found himself compelled to treat with the

Lombards, who at the very time when he mounted the papal throne were threatening the city of Rome. Without reference to the imperial governor at Ravenna, Gregory in 592 contrived, by payment of tribute, a truce with the Lombard dukes of Spoleto and Beneventum and continued, throughout his pontificate, to deal in this independent fashion with the Lombard authorities, all the while pressing upon a reluctant Emperor Maurice the necessity for a general truce between Constantinople and the Lombard kingdom—a settlement which he saw to be necessitated not only by the military weakness of the empire in Italy, but also by the need of Italy and its people for peace. In the same way, his concern for the corrupt state of the church and its ministry under the exploitative policies of the Merovingian (Frankish) rulers of Gaul (see IV:2) led him both to correspond with the Merovingian kings and to advocate a permanent treaty of peace between them and the emperor: only so, he judged, could the welfare of the church and its people be maintained. Gregory thus established himself, in the pursuit of his pastoral concerns, as a virtually independent ruler in central Italy and the principal benefactor of the common folk of Italy. His policies also provided a precedent for the decision of his eighth-century successors to renounce dependence on the eastern empire and enter into alliance with a reconstituted Frankish monarchy.

Neither these political enterprises nor his concern for the administration of the Roman church's estates exhausted Gregory's activities. It was he who, when John the Faster, patriarch of Constantinople (582–595), began to use the title "ecumenical patriarch," protested in defense both of the system of the five independent patriarchates and of the prerogatives of his own see. In his view, there was no bishop who could claim such a title. Again, it was Gregory who, on learning of the marriage of the Saxon king Ethelbert of Kent to a Christian and catholic princess, promptly dispatched missionaries to England (see IV:1), thus winning England not only for Christianity but also for loyalty to the papacy and to his own project of a church reformed through the purification of its ministry.

Nothing, in fact, was closer to Gregory's heart than the regulation and reform of the ministerial office, unless it was the extension and improvement of monastic institutions. In what was perhaps his greatest—and certainly one of his most influential—works, the *Pastoral Rule,* the pope set out his own high ideal of the Christian bishop as shepherd of souls. This work, translated into Greek before Gregory's death and into Anglo-Saxon by King Alfred the Great in the ninth century, became, in the medieval West, the standard treatment of its subject. Gregory's extensive correspondence (of which some 850 letters survive) shows how he turned his ideas into practice as he directed the affairs of the Italian churches immediately under his authority. He did not confine his interest, however, to the churches of Italy alone. To the extent that the state of communications permitted, Gregory made his authority felt in correspondence with metropolitan bishops in other sectors of the West—Spain (where the Visigothic king, Recared, had renounced Arianism in 587), Gaul (where he re-established a papal vicariate at Arles), Africa, and even Illyria.

If the *Pastoral Rule* was Gregory's contribution to western understanding of the pastoral office, his *Morals on Job* (written, at least in preliminary form, while he was resident in Constantinople) was his legacy to monastic spirituality. In this work, an allegorical treatment of its text, he deals not only with the active life of morality but also with the contemplative life of the coming kingdom of God, which for him as for Augustine was the goal of human striving. Of no less importance than the *Morals,* however, were Gregory's four books of *Dialogues on the Life and Miracles of the Italian Fathers,* a work which in the centuries after its author's death circulated not only among clergy and monks but also among laity and thus did much to form popular medieval piety. This book, replete with tales of dreams, visions, and wonders which demonstrate the power of sanctity, is an admirable clue to the form in which Christian faith and life made their appeal in an age of violence, dislocation, and cultural decline. It also contains theological digressions in which, as Gregory in effect interprets and fuses his Augustinian theological heritage and the practical faith of his Roman tradition, the lineaments of later medieval thought and piety can be discerned.

There can be little doubt that Gregory's theological thought evinces the limitations imposed by his historical and cultural situation. On the one hand, his equipment and resources were slight. Of the work of his predecessors, Greek and Latin, he knew little, apart from the teachings of Augustine (whose writings he had diligently excerpted at one point in his life). On the other hand, the circumstances of his time provided little encouragement to large critical or speculative enterprises. Gregory's concern was with the practical shape of the Christian life and the path of the human self to the new age of God's kingdom, whose light was even in his day beginning to dawn. His thought therefore turned around the themes of sin, judgment, and the atonement in Christ; and on these subjects he developed Augustine's conclusions (if not the insights and perceptions in which these conclusions were rooted) in a way essentially consonant with the position of the Synod of Orange (see III:18). The human race is fettered by the sin of Adam, as is evidenced by the fact that every human person is conceived through lust. From this state the individual is rescued by the work of Christ, whose benefits are conferred in baptism through forgiveness of sins and the gift of the Holy Spirit. Nevertheless, satisfaction must be made for sins committed after baptism: no sin can go without atonement made. The essential means of satisfaction are good works undertaken in love, which are made possible by God's prevenient grace and the human will's co-operation with that grace. Such satisfaction is one of the three essential moments of *poenitentia* (repentance, penance), the others of which are confession (acknowledgment of sin) and contrition. The sinner who seeks reconciliation with God through Christ is further assisted by the eucharist, which has expiatory power because in it the benefits of Christ's self-offering to God are applied to human beings, the dead as well as the living. There is also the aid of the holy martyrs, whose prayers are heard by God. Sins for which satisfaction has not been made in this present life will be purged in the fires of purgatory after death.

This idea of the purgation of sin after death, so central to later medieval piety, was not new with Gregory. Cyprian and Augustine had considered it. To Caesarius of Arles it was a matter of certainty. Gregory, therefore, in propounding the doctrine of purgatory as an essential of the faith, was merely taking his place in a developing tradition that had its roots in early Christian discussions of the possibility and necessity of a "second repentance" (see II:15).

Gregory, then, was a theologian of little originality. His ideas, nevertheless, were crucial at every point to the shape of medieval thought and institutions. In this regard, he stands with others of his age who transmitted, though in a limited and constricted form, the wisdom of the ancient church to the churches of the medieval Latin West. Among these must be mentioned not only Cassiodorus and Boethius (whose translations of Aristotle stimulated the beginnings of medieval philosophy), but also Isidore of Seville (ca. 560–636), an almost exact contemporary of Gregory's. Isidore's *Book of Sentences*—brief statements of doctrine—became the theological textbook of the western church until the twelfth century. His *Origins or Etymologies* contained well-nigh the whole round of learning of his age, ecclesiastical and secular, and in the Middle Ages provided a principal source of knowledge of antiquity. Nevertheless, Gregory the Great stands out as one whose work shaped not merely the ideas but also the life and institutions of the church in a time of great troubles and thus did much to assure its survival as a significant force in the new barbarian world. Not without justice was Gregory described for posterity as "God's consul."

Period IV

THE MIDDLE AGES
TO THE CLOSE
OF THE
INVESTITURE
CONTROVERSY

Chapter 1

Missions in the British Isles

*T*HERE IS NO MORE striking indication of the vitality of the western churches during the centuries when Roman authority was being replaced by that of the barbarian kingdoms than the strength and persistence of the efforts made to Christianize pagan tribes which had occupied previously Roman territories or territories immediately adjoining the former borders of the empire. Nowhere did such efforts meet with a more fruitful success than in the British Isles, whose final conversion to catholic and Roman Christianity redounded to the benefit not only of the papacy but of the continental churches generally.

Christianity had existed in Britain even before the conversion of Constantine. There seems to have been a Celtic Christianity, closely related to that of Roman Gaul, in the west of England from a fairly early date. Glastonbury, in particular, which—as its location near the mouth of the Severn River attests— was an ancient port engaged in trade with Gaul and the Mediterranean, was apparently a primitive Christian holy place. Christianity also existed in the towns and villas of the Roman occupation. Three Latin-speaking British bishops were present at the Council of Arles (314).

Toward the end of the fourth century, Roman troops were gradually removed from Britain (for the most part by imperial usurpers seeking to make their fortunes in Gaul), with the result that the inhabitants of the former province were left to fend for themselves against the raids of pagan Saxons on the east coast of England and, in the north, the pressure of the Picts from Scotland. Unlike Gaul and Spain, Britain had never been thoroughly Romanized, and the departure of the imperial troops and officials meant that, in the course of the fifth century, the country gradually reverted to a tribal organization and the towns were slowly depopulated, even as the raids of the Saxons, Angles, and Jutes turned into full-scale invasion and occupation.

Christianity, however, survived. From Bede the Venerable's *Ecclesiastical History of the English People,* we learn that Bishop Germanus of Auxerre made two visits to Britain at the request of his colleagues there (429 and 444–445).

The first of these was aimed at countering the spread of Pelegianism, though, as it turned out, he was also called upon, as a former *dux* (i.e., general) in Gaul, to lead a British force against a joint Saxon and Pictish invasion in the north. By the time of his second visit, Britain's adversaries from across the North Sea had begun to occupy its eastern and southern coasts. Over the course of the next century, the British, and with them Christianity, were driven farther and farther west, until they were eventually confined to Cornwall, Wales, and, in the north, Strathclyde.

Even in the time of Germanus, however, the missionary labors which were to result in the conversion of the islands had gotten under way. In this work, the first notable name is that of Patrick (ca. 389–ca. 461), "the Apostle of Ireland." A Briton whose place of birth remains a matter for speculation, Patrick was the son of one Calpurnius, a Christian deacon and a man of curial rank in his native town. Kidnapped by Irish corsairs as a lad and put to work as a slave, the future missionary escaped after six years and ended up in Gaul (perhaps after a visit to his home in Britain). Little is known of his career in this period, though he seems to have spent some time as a member of the episcopal *familia* of Germanus of Auxerre. In 431, Pope Celestine (422–432) dispatched one Palladius to be bishop for "the Scots [i.e., Irish] who believed in Christ," but Palladius died within the year, and Patrick, now ordained a bishop, was sent to Ireland in his place. Working in the north of the island, in a society organized according to tribal territories, Patrick seems to have won significant converts among the local royalties. He apparently established territorial bishoprics (but on a tribal basis, since the "cities" of Romano-Gallic society did not exist in Ireland) and placed his own see at Armagh.

There is no reason to doubt that Patrick introduced some form of communal ascetic life into Ireland, but it was only after his death—and indeed in the next century—that monastic communities became the pastoral centers of the Irish church. This development can be dated roughly from the foundation of the monastery at Clonard in Meath by St. Finnian (ca. 540), which was swiftly followed by other foundations such as Bangor (a word which means simply "monastery"), established in Ulster by St. Comgall, and Moville, the creation of the younger St. Finnian (d. 579). The abbots who ruled such communities normally belonged to the royal families of their tribes and were frequently bishops as well. In this way, the territorial episcopate of the Roman empire was replaced by a monastically based, and essentially tribal, episcopate. The monastic communities became not merely the foci of pastoral and missionary work but also centers of learning, the arts, and education. Roughly contemporary with the flowering of Irish monasticism, and possibly even a source of it, was a parallel development of monasticism in Wales. This movement is customarily traced back to the work of St. Illtyd (d. ca. 535), the founder of the monastery later called Llanilltyd ("Illtyd's Church"), which may have been located on the Isle of Caldey. Illtyd's successor as the leader of

Welsh monasticism was St. David (fl. ca. 560), founder of the abbey at Menevia (now St. David's) and the patron saint of Wales.

Even prior to this growth of Irish and Welsh monasticism, however, and in fact during the years of Patrick's mission to Ireland, British Christianity also extended itself northward toward Scotland. The leader of this mission was St. Ninian (Nynia). Of him, Bede's *Ecclesiastical History* reports that he was a native Briton who had been instructed in the faith at Rome. Like Patrick a bishop (which suggests that there were already Christians in the area to which he was sent), Ninian established his see at Whithorn (Candida Casa) and worked in the territory north of Hadrian's Wall, where there were doubtless partly Romanized and partly Christianized Celtic tribes.

The conversion of Scotland proper, however—that is, the area north of the firths of Clyde and Forth—was the work of monastics from Ireland. From its very inception, Irish monasticism was an expanding, missionary movement. We have seen (III:7) how, toward the end of the sixth century, Columbanus, a monk of the abbey of Bangor, on a long pilgrimage set up monastic houses (which in their turn became missionary centers) in Burgundy, what is now Switzerland, and even northern Italy. Similarly, St. Kilian (d. ca. 689), of a later generation, worked in Franconia and Thuringia, establishing the see of Würzburg. The first and most notable of these Irish monastic pilgrims, however, was Columba (521–597). A product of the abbey at Clonard and a member of the royal family of the O'Neill of Connaught, Columba established a monastic community on the island of Iona, under the sponsorship and protection of the king of Dalriada (roughly the present Argyleshire), who was himself, with his people, of Irish extraction. From Iona, Columba carried out missionary work among the Pictish peoples of Caledonia, winning their chieftains to the new faith and organizing the church there on the same monastic basis that it had in Ireland.

The missionary work of the Iona community continued after the death of Columba, and at the beginning of the second third of the seventh century it was extended to the pagan Anglo-Saxon settlers of northeastern England. The occasion for this development was a request from King Oswald of Bernicia (Northumbria), who during his youth had been raised in exile among the Scots and Picts of Christian Caledonia. Regaining his throne in 633, Oswald summoned aid from Iona for the Christianization of his people. The response was the mission of St. Aidan (d. 651), who under Oswald's sponsorship established a monastery on the "Holy Isle" of Lindisfarne (634), and from it, during the reigns of Oswald (d. 641) and his brother Oswy (641–670), rooted Christianity in Northumbria. Aidan also trained a group of youths to carry on his work: among them the brothers Chad (d. 672), who ultimately became a part of the mission, begun in 654, to the kingdom of Mercia and established the see of Lichfield, and Cedd, who worked among the East Saxons, for whom he was consecrated bishop in 654.

By the time that the mission of Aidan and his successors had gotten under way, a mission dispatched by Pope Gregory the Great had already arrived in southeastern England and established itself in Kent and East Anglia. The pope's initiative was calculated to take advantage of the marriage of Ethelbert, king of Kent and Bretwalda (high king) of the Saxon territories south of the Humber, to a Christian Frankish princess, Bertha. The mission consisted originally of Augustine, the prior of Gregory's own monastery of St. Andrew at Rome, and a small group of monks. Landing in Kent in 597, Augustine—a somewhat reluctant missionary, whose zeal was maintained largely by a stream of correspondence from Pope Gregory—succeeded in converting Ethelbert, who was baptized at Easter in the year 601. According to Gregory's plan, Augustine was to establish a metropolitan see for himself at London, with twelve bishoprics under it. He was also, as the pope conceived it, to have jurisdiction over the Celtic churches of the West and, as opportunity offered, to set up a second metropolitan see at York (in the kingdom of Deira) for the north of England. These sanguine plans of the pope's, however, were not fully realized. Augustine established his own see not at London but at Canterbury, where he erected a church and, nearby, a monastery. By 604, he had founded bishoprics at Rochester (in Kent) and London (in Essex). After his death (in 604 or 605), however, and that of King Ethelbert (616), a pagan reaction revealed the shallowness of the roots which the church had put down outside of Kent. The mission dispatched (625) under Paulinus to York and the kingdom of Deira collapsed in 632 when Edwin of Deira was slain in battle. It was not until the second half of the seventh century, therefore, and then largely because of the missionary impetus which stemmed from Lindisfarne and from an independent papal mission to the West Saxons begun by one Birinus (ca. 635), that England was substantially won for Christianity.

Even at that juncture, however, a significant problem remained. There was continuing friction between the western and northern Christians of the Celtic and Irish tradition on the one hand and, on the other, the new Saxon Christians of the south, whose churches were not only organized on the continental pattern under territorial bishops but were consciously loyal to Rome and the papacy. In part, this friction had its origins in the earlier, and very long, military struggle between British Christians and pagan invaders. For the British of the West, it was not easy to envisage the Angles and Saxons, their traditional enemies, as fellow Christians. But the conflict also had ecclesiastical roots. Quite apart from obvious and definable issues like a difference over the date of Easter, the whole ethos and organization of Celtic Christianity was different from that of the Roman mission. Fortunately for the future of Christianity in the British Isles, this friction was a source of great irritation to King Oswy of Northumbria. He accordingly called for a conference or council to resolve the matter for his kingdom. The council met in 664 at Whitby on the coast of the North Sea, where a great double monastery, with houses for both men and women, had recently (659) been established under the noble abbess St. Hilda (d. 680). Wilfrid, abbot of Ripon and later bishop of York (himself a product of the Celtic community at Lindisfarne), upheld the case for loyalty to Rome, while Colman, abbot of Lindisfarne, defended the Celtic tradition. The matter was resolved when King Oswy learned that the bishop of Rome was the successor and representative of the apostle Peter, to whom the Lord himself had given the keys of the kingdom of Heaven.[1] The decision that resulted from this discovery eventually brought the whole of England under the Roman obedience, and English Christianity eventually proved a principal ally of the papacy in both the establishment and the reform of churches on the continent of Europe.

The vigor and discipline of this new Celtic-English Christianity owed much to the fortunate circumstance that, in 668, Pope Vitalian appointed one Theodore (ca. 602–690), a native of Tarsus in Asia Minor, as archbishop of Canterbury—the first occupant of that see whose authority was recognized throughout England. Theodore began his incumbency by conducting a systematic visitation of all the churches under his jurisdiction. As a result of this tour of inspection, he set about reorganizing old and establishing new dioceses. He presided over the Synod of Hertford (673), which enacted basic laws for the governance of the churches and constituted them a national body at a time when political sovereignty was still divided. It was his policy that encouraged adoption of the Celtic monastic practice of private confession and absolution, which, following Irish custom, he enjoined upon nonmonastic lay persons as an annual obligation. Theodore's organizational and pastoral abilities were revealed above all in the fact that he favored neither Saxon nor Celt, but reconciled all in a single body in which the two traditions complemented and fed each other.

The fruits of King Oswy's decision and of Theodore's skill as a ruler were soon manifested in the life of the English churches. They had a reputation for their loyalty to the see of Rome and to the standards which it set for doctrine and discipline: a fact attested by the frequency of Anglo-Saxon pilgrimages to the shrines of the apostles Peter and Paul at Rome, as well as by the introduction of the *Rule* of St. Benedict into English monastic life in the age of Theodore and his immediate successors. At the same time, the love of learning which had characterized the Irish tradition was preserved and developed in a series of monastic schools, of which perhaps the most brilliant was that of Wearmouth and Jarrow in Northumbria. There Bede the Venerable (672–735) studied and wrote in the fields of chronology, grammar, biblical exegesis, and history. Remembered above all for his *Ecclesiastical History of the English People,* he and his contemporaries brought about a minor rebirth of learning which was, in the end, to bear fruit in the ninth-century Carolingian renaissance on the continent.

---

[1] Matt. 16:18.

Chapter 2

Christianity and the Frankish Kingdom

THE CONVERSION of Clovis to catholic Christianity in 496 (see III:5) was a decisive event for both the political and the religious future of continental Europe. Under Clovis's leadership and that of his sons, the Franks conquered the former Roman territories in Gaul and in Germany and created what came to be called the *regnum Francorum* ("kingdom of the Franks"). Moving out from their original lands between the Rhine and the Somme rivers, they first overran and occupied the region previously ruled by the Roman *dux* Syagrius, roughly the area between the Somme and the Loire. Then Clovis led his followers against the Alemanni, whose kingdom straddled the Rhine to his south and east. Finally, he crossed the Loire into Aquitaine, where, at Vouillé (Vogladensis) in 507, he defeated the Visigoths and took control of the southwest of Gaul to the line of the Pyrenees. Clovis's immediate successors continued the expansion of Frankish hegemony. They incorporated Thuringia into their territories and eventually, after 532, the Burgundian kingdom, which controlled the Rhone valley and western Switzerland.

By the middle of the sixth century, then, the Frankish or "Merovingian" dynasty dominated the whole of what had been Roman territory in Gaul and Germany. This realm was frequently divided among several kings, for Frankish custom dictated that a father's property be split up among all his surviving sons. Partly in consequence of this fact, regional divisions arose within the empire which had a quasi-political, quasi-ethnic character. The first of these, Austrasia, comprised the Frankish homeland around the lower Rhine as well as Thuringia and the former territories of the Alemanni. The second, called Neustria, had its heart at Paris, which Clovis had made his capital, and extended south to the Loire and north to the Somme. Of less central importance in the political history of the Franks were the southern regions of Aquitaine and Burgundy. Despite these divisions, however, the Frankish kingdom was understood to be a single patrimony, and indeed, in the last years of Clovis's son Lothar I (d. 561), and most of the reign of Dagobert I (623–639), it enjoyed a single ruler.

The Gallo-Roman inhabitants of these areas were not unhappy with their new conquerors. Catholics themselves, they were glad to have a catholic ruler; and in any case, the Roman emperors at Constantinople gave the Frankish leaders recognition, occasional financial assistance, and, in the case of Clovis himself, the title, rank, and insignia of a consul. Nor was this gesture a mere symbol. Clovis and his successors took over what remained in Gaul of the Roman civil and financial administration. The *regnum Francorum* was, and in a certain sense remained, the formal representative of Roman authority and tradition. The Franks, moreover, unlike their predecessors the Goths, did not maintain themselves as a socially separate governing caste, but mingled and intermarried with the peoples of the territories they conquered, thus creating the foundation of a mixed culture for which vulgar Latin remained, in most of the old Roman provinces, the common tongue. In their own way, too, they fostered the spread of Christianity. Drawing initially on the strength and clerical leadership of the Gallo-Roman churches in the south and west of their territories, they supported missions to those frontier areas of the north and east where paganism persisted and where previously established Christian churches had been driven out or greatly weakened by the barbarian migrations. They further encouraged the monastic movement, which—especially perhaps after the mission of Columbanus (see III:7)—tended to become, as it had been in Britain, the principal vehicle for the spread of Christianity.

This is not to say, however, that church and society did not, in this Merovingian kingdom, continue to show signs of decline and even disintegration. The decay of the ancient cities, as well as of commerce and communication, went on apace. The real centers of life became rural manors—estates which sought to be, and in practice were, self-sufficient as far as the necessities of life were concerned. Ruled directly or indirectly by a lord who might be some magnate or the king himself, such estates afforded economic and personal security both to the owner and to his serfs or tenants. At the same time, this manorial system encouraged decentralization of authority and guaranteed that power as well as wealth would accompany land tenure, since it was the manor which produced not only food and clothing but also the men and equipment needed for the almost constant warring which marked Frankish society.

Such decentralization was further encouraged by the fact that the Franks, like all the Germanic peoples, had no idea of the state as something which, in its laws and structures, endures independently of individual persons. For them, political order was a matter of the personal loyalty of warriors to their leader: a loyalty that traditionally depended on the ability of the king to reward his followers with the spoils of successful war. This understanding of the nature of political bonds had a number of consequences in the Merovingian kingdom. For one thing, it meant that the economic resources of the "state" were identical with the personal property or wealth of the king—a situation in which the very notion of "public" property, and so of taxation, was all but inconceivable.

It also meant, therefore, that in order to retain loyalty, the Merovingian kings—once opportunities for fresh conquest had been exhausted—had to "benefice" their followers with landed estates from the royal domain. This practice had the inevitable effect of weakening the monarch, even though such benefices were technically granted only for the lifetime of the recipient.

In such a society—violent, decentralized, insecure—the traditional structures and ways of the church were bound to be affected to some degree. The most important development, perhaps, and one connected with the rise of the manorial system, was the much more frequent appearance of "proprietary" churches: i.e., church buildings erected on an estate at the private expense of the lord and provided by him with an endowment for the services of a priest. In this development, there can be seen the beginnings of the later parochial system, as well as of many later debates over lay control of clerical appointments. The bishops of the new kingdom continued their ancient habit of meeting in council to regulate common affairs, though such councils are not borne witness to frequently or regularly. They reacted to such external issues as the struggle over the Three Chapters (see III:10) and the Monothelite controversy (see III:11). Increasingly, however, the Frankish churches seem to have become isolated, even from the leadership of the papacy, though respect for the successors of Peter and the practice of pilgrimage to the tombs of the apostles at Rome by no means ceased.

In the affairs of the Frankish kingdom itself, however, the church played a central and essential role. To kings, magnates, and peasantry alike, the protection and aid of God and the saints were essential to order and justice in a disordered world. The Christian bishop, moreover, occupied a special place. Standing at once for the traditions of the ancient Roman order and for the odd tastes of the Christian God in justice and mercy, the bishop was by turns political magnate, holy man, and prophet. Literacy and learning were largely confined to the clergy, for it was only in monastic houses, and in the episcopal households where young men were educated for service as clergy, that anything like schools existed. Increasingly, therefore, churches and monastic communities were rewarded for the undoubted services they provided by being endowed with lands. This meant, however, as time went on, that bishops disposed of resources which could be of great use to the Merovingian kings. The latter, accordingly, set aside the ancient custom of the election of bishops by the people and the clergy and took to themselves the right of appointing bishops, using this right, in effect, as a way of conferring benefices upon loyal servants. Not infrequently, a ruler would go further and allow an episcopal see to remain vacant while he appropriated its revenues. Such practices—a natural if not inevitable expression of the times—were a source of dismay to successive popes; but from the time of Gregory the Great on, the bishops of Rome were unsuccessful in their efforts to bring the Merovingian house to a better mind.

Reform and renaissance in the Frankish church came about, in the end, only through the replacement of the Merovingian dynasty. This occurred gradually over a period of slightly more than a century after the death of Dagobert I (639). After his time, the degeneracy of the Merovingian line and the rise to power in Neustria, Austrasia, and Burgundy of the so-called "mayors of the palace" (i.e., the principal advisors and ministers of the king) led eventually to a new political situation. The Austrasian mayors, descendants of Bishop Arnulf of Metz (d. 641) and Pepin of Landen (d. 639), triumphed over their rivals and, in the persons of Pepin II of Heristal (d. 715) and his illegitimate son Charles (called "Martel," i.e., "the Hammer"), ruled the Frankish kingdom through a series of Merovingian shadow kings. Both Pepin and Charles, like the kings in whose names they ruled, were faithful Christians in the style of their time, endowing churches and monasteries. Their great preoccupation, however, was the reunification of their realm and the defense of its frontiers, which were threatened from the north and east by pagan German tribes and, in Charles's day, by Arab and Berber raiders from Spain, where the Visigothic kingdom had been finally overthrown by the forces of Islam. In these enterprises they were, by and large, successful. Charles in particular became famous in history and legend alike for his victory near Poitiers over the Saracens (732)— a victory which not merely preserved the Frankish kingdom but also assured the future of what would soon be called Europe, for which the Frankish realm provided the foundation. These military preoccupations, however, put the Arnulfing house in its early days in an ambiguous relation to the church. On the one hand, Pepin and, to a much greater extent, Charles regularly confiscated church properties to finance their wars. This policy was virtually forced upon them by the erosion of the Merovingian royal domain through gifts and benefices. On the other hand, as a part of their efforts at pacification of their frontiers, both leaders encouraged and supported English missionary enterprises on their northern and eastern frontiers—enterprises which brought them into close relation to the papacy, with momentous consequences for the future.

Thus, Pepin II, and Charles after him, backed the evangelistic labors of St. Willibrord (658–739), an English monk educated at Ripon and in Ireland, who in 690, with twelve associates, started his work among the Frisians in what is now Holland. Ordained bishop in 695 by Pope Sergius I, Willibrord established the see of Utrecht, though it was not until the Frankish conquest of the neighboring Saxons in the last decades of the eighth century that the Frisians were finally converted. Willibrord's work was continued by one of the most remarkable men of this era: Wynfrith, or, as he came to be called, Boniface (680–754). Born in Crediton, Devonshire, this monk came to Frisia in 716, where he worked in Willibrord's mission. Discouraged by his lack of success, he returned to England but found his way in 718 to Rome. There Pope Gregory II commissioned him as a missionary to Germany, and he took the name of the Roman martyr Boniface. His success in Thuringia and Hesse was such that in 722 he was summoned back to Rome, where he took an oath to the apostle Peter and was ordained bishop for Germany. During the next ten years, with the direct support of Charles Martel, Boniface's mission enjoyed further success in Hesse and Thuringia. Eventually, he established bishoprics for the churches not only of Hesse and Thuringia but also of Bavaria, introducing the Benedictine Rule for monks and establishing, under papal authority, his own archiepiscopal see at Mainz (ca. 747). In 744, he aided his disciple, Sturm, in the foundation of the great monastic center of Fulda, which was endowed with lands by Charles Martel's son Carloman and became a center of learning and of priestly education for west-central Germany. In all these enterprises, Boniface acted, in the spirit of the new English Christianity, as the servant of the Roman bishop and imported into the Frankish world Roman ideas of ecclesiastical order and discipline. Shortly after 747, Boniface resigned his see at Mainz to return to Frisia as a missionary, and there, after some years of work, he was martyred.

This missionary work did not spell the sum of Boniface's contributions to the Christianity of the Frankish world. In 741, Charles Martel died. His authority as mayor of the palace was inherited, in Frankish fashion, by his two sons, the elder, Carloman (741–747) of Austrasia, and the younger, Pepin III (741–768) of Neustria. From the beginning of their rule, both brothers drew closer to Boniface and, through him, to the papacy. The spirit in which they handled ecclesiastical affairs is reflected in Canon 1 of a synod called by Carloman in 742 (known as the *Concilium germanicum*):

> By the advice of my clergy and great men I [i.e., Carolman] have provided for bishops in the cities and have placed over them Boniface as archbishop—he who is sent from St. Peter. And I have ordered the yearly calling of a council in which, in my presence, canonical decrees and the laws of the church may be restored and the Christian religion emended. Further, I have restored and given back to the churches revenues wrongly taken from them; and I have removed, degraded, and forced penance upon false priests and adulterous deacons and clerics.[1]

In a series of such synods, held under Boniface's leadership, the worldliness of many clergy was rebuked, wandering bishops were censured, priestly celibacy was upheld, and, in general, stricter clerical discipline was enforced. Thus, through the co-operation of the Englishman Boniface and the sons of Charles Martel, the Frankish church was brought into moral alliance with the papacy—and, indeed, the Frankish bishops, assembled in synod in 747, explicitly recognized the jurisdiction of the Roman bishop over their affairs. In this fashion, the way was paved for an alliance of Frankish kingdom and papal authority which far transcended the level of common concern for reform of the church.

---

[1] J. M. Wallace-Hadrill, *The Barbarian West, 400–1000* (London, 1952), pp. 95–96 (slightly altered).

Chapter 3

East and West
in the Iconoclastic Controversy

THE RULE OF Charles Martel and Pepin III in the Frankish kingdom—and so also the career of St. Boniface—were roughly contemporaneous with the reigns of Emperor Leo III (717–740) and his son Constantine V (741–775) in the East. After the near collapse of the Byzantine-Roman Empire in the seventh century under the onslaughts of Islam, these founders of the Isaurian dynasty restored their realm's borders and its fortunes. Repelling the forces of Caliph Omar II (717–720) from the very gates of Constantinople, Leo and his son after him reasserted Roman control of Asia Minor. At the same time, they instituted and enforced a religious policy which demanded abolition of the veneration of icons—painted or sculpted portrayals of Christ, the Virgin Mary, the angels, and the saints. The intense and lengthy conflicts, theological and political, which this policy occasioned had abiding consequences for the life of the churches in both East and West. In the East, they resulted not only in a restoration of images, but also in a theological consensus which saw in the veneration of icons an affirmation of the Chalcedonian doctrine of the full and distinct human nature of Christ. In the West, the struggle between the iconoclastic emperors and successive bishops of Rome led to a final political split between the papacy and the empire, and thus to a new alliance of the popes with the heirs of Charles Martel and a crucial step in the growing separation between the Latin and Greek churches.

It was in the year 726 that Leo III—whose motives, though not his commitments, remain a matter of debate—made his opposition to icons known publicly and notified church leaders of his policy. He followed this action with the symbolic gesture of destroying an image of Christ which had stood above one of the entrances to the imperial palace at Constantinople. These acts not only provoked riots in the capital but also evoked the condemnation of Patriarch Germanus of Constantinople, not to mention a hostile and sometimes violent reaction among the populace of the empire and, above all, the monks. Not relenting in his policy for a moment, and strong because of the enthusiastic support of his troops, Leo proceeded in 730 to convoke a council that reiterated the prohibition of sacred images and resulted in the deposition and exile of Germanus and his replacement by a more complaisant patriarch, Anastasius.

In Italy, the opposition to Leo's actions was just as strong, but the emperor was less powerful. To be sure, significant tracts of Italian territory were still ruled by the Byzantine authorities. In the south, there were Sicily and Calabria. In the north, the empire controlled a strip of territory reaching south and west from Ravenna (the seat of the imperial exarch) on the Adriatic to the region around Rome (the so-called "Patrimony of Peter"), which was under the military command of a Roman *dux*. On north and south alike, however, this strip was beset by Lombard states. In such circumstances, the eastern emperors, whose military strength was necessarily concentrated in Asia Minor, had all they could do to maintain their Italian holdings. Moreover, it was in the Roman bishop, and not in the somewhat ineffectual governors sent to Ravenna from Constantinople, that the people of Italy saw the true representative of Roman tradition. When, therefore, St. Boniface's sponsor, Pope Gregory II (715–731), resisted and condemned the emperor's iconoclastic policy—both on the ground that it exceeded the authority of a lay ruler and on the ground that iconoclasm represented in effect a denial of the reality of the Incarnation—Leo was unable to rid himself of the pope as he had of Patriarch Germanus. Attempts to replace, and even to assassinate, Gregory were frustrated by the support not only of the common people of Rome and Ravenna but also of the Byzantine armies and even the Lombard dukes of Spoleto and Beneventum.

Another critical voice which Leo could not silence came from the very heart of the Islamic empire. This was the voice of John of Damascus (ca. 675–ca. 749), who as a youth had inherited from his Christian father a high position in the civil service of the caliphs. Compelled subsequently to relinquish this post, John spent the greater part of his adult life as a monk of the cloister of St. Sabas near Jerusalem. There he eventually wrote the great tripartite work, *The Fountain of Knowledge,* whose last division, entitled "On the Orthodox Faith," is a general and systematic presentation of Christian belief about God and the Trinity, the creation, and the Incarnation. In this work, he drew on the whole of the Greek tradition, but especially on the Cappadocian Fathers, on pseudo-Dionysius the Areopagite (see III:10), and, for his Christology, on the neo-Chalcedonianism of Leontius of Jerusalem (see III:10). Declared a "Doctor of the Church" by Pope Leo XIII in 1890, John has been appealed to regularly by orthodox eastern theologians, and he also influenced western scholastic theology through a medieval Latin translation of his major work. His contribution to the iconoclastic controversy was made in the years 726–730 in a series of discourses which answered the charge of idolatry on several grounds. In the first place, John insisted that a distinction must be made between the veneration (*proskunesis*) offered to images and the worship (*latreia*) which is properly offered to God alone. At the same time, he maintained that an icon does not pretend to be an equivalent, and therefore a substitute, for what it portrays, but is a likeness which raises the mind to its original. Both he and—at a later stage of the controversy—the monastic reformer Theodore of Studios (759–826) identified the fundamental issue in the iconoclastic controversy as christological. If Christ's humanity, which can in principle be pictured, is real, concrete, and historical; and if, at the same time, it is truly one with the hypostasis of the divine Logos, then the veneration of an image of Christ is analogous to the veneration of the Gospels, which "picture" Christ in words. Both icon and Gospel are testimonies to the ingredience of the divine in the worlds of nature and history, and both are media of access to God.

In the reign of Leo's successor, Constantine V, the iconoclastic policy took the form of a systematic attempt to destroy images and a systematic persecution of those—monks in particular, but also large sections of the general populace—who supported their veneration. In 754, Constantine convened a council which not only reasserted Leo's condemnation of the work of painters, but also made those who violated its decree subject to punishment under the laws of the state. Pursuant to this decree, icons in churches were defaced, painted over, and replaced with portrayals of nonsacred subjects. Imprisonment, torture, and exile were the lot of many image-worshipers. These measures were accompanied by severe strictures against monks, who were ridiculed and in some cases compelled to marry against their will, as well as against monasteries, which were frequently taken over and put to secular use, their estates confiscated. There was in consequence a large emigration of monastic refugees from imperially controlled territories in the East, many of whom went to southern Italy.

Not until the reign of Empress Irene—who first governed as regent for her son Constantine VI (780–797) and then, after deposing, blinding, and killing him, as sole ruler (797–802)—did the tide turn against iconoclasm. Evading the opposition of the army, which had always favored the policy of Leo III, Irene convened a council at Nicaea in 787, to which the representatives of Pope Hadrian I (772–795) were invited. This council, the seventh and last commonly called "ecumenical," restored the veneration of images and denied that icons were idols or that believers worshiped them as God. It also decreed the restitution of monastic buildings and lands which had been expropriated under the policies of Constantine V. In the early ninth century, however, under Emperor Leo V (813–820), iconoclastic policies were revived. A council held in St. Sophia in Constantinople (815) reiterated the stand of Constantine V's council of 754, and repression of image worship continued through the reigns of Michael II (820–829) and Theophilus (829–842). Empress Theodora, reigning during the minority of her son Michael III (842–867), brought the iconoclastic movement to a final close in 843, when she convoked a synod to revive the canons of the Council of Nicaea and restore the veneration of icons.

The interpretation of this "iconoclastic controversy" has been the occasion of much debate among historians, in part because many of the original sources for its history were suppressed at the time. Of the significance of its effects there can be little question; the issue, however, of the meaning and motivation of the iconoclastic movement in the life of the eastern churches is more difficult. There can be no doubt that the veneration of sacred pictures had become a vital and commonplace part of Christian piety during and after the fourth century. Neither is there any doubt that the practice had regularly met opposition from many prominent Christian thinkers and leaders, and such opposition had persisted in certain areas of the East, where many saw in this practice a reversion to paganism. Iconoclasm, therefore, had roots in the Christian tradition and can be understood, from at least one point of view, as a religiously motivated reaction to a dominant form of popular piety. Historians have pointed out, moreover, that the section of Asia Minor from which the Isaurian emperors—and the great bulk of their armies—came were areas where iconoclastic attitudes might have been stimulated by the presence of Jews and Moslems, to whom the veneration of images was simple idolatry. Unfortunately, there are almost no data to support this hypothesis, plausible though it may seem. It may be, too, that the movement was influenced by gnostic or Manichaean currents of thought; the iconoclasts seem at times to have verged on a species of dualism, opposing "worship in spirit and in truth" to the use of material representations of Christ and the saints. Monophysites, too, evidently tended to the iconoclastic point of view, since for them any portrayal of Christ was in effect an attempt, at once impossible and idolatrous, to portray the Second Person of the Trinity.

Such religious attitudes and motivations, however, have been discounted by some interpreters of the iconoclastic policies of the Isaurian emperors. Many scholars have seen in iconoclasm a disguised social or political policy; as evidence for this point of view, they point to the fact that the principal victims of iconoclasm were monastic institutions, whose number, size, and independence made them a burden on the life of the state and an obstacle to absolute imperial authority. At the same time, it is clear that the iconoclasts held a view of the emperor's role in a Christian society which made him the supreme religious authority, and one element in the polemic of the defenders of images was a protest against undue interference by the emperor in matters that ought to be reserved to ecclesiastical leaders. Certainly this was a prominent element in the attitude of Pope Gregory II, for whom iconoclasm, as we have seen, represented a double evil: a theological denial of the ingredience of God in the historical and natural order, and a false view of the authority of the head of state in religious questions.

Chapter 4

The Franks and the Papacy

GREGORY II's OPPOSITION to the iconoclastic policies of Leo III and Constantine V was continued by his successors in the Roman see, with results that could scarcely have been foreseen by anyone. It fell to the lot of Gregory III (731–741), at a council summoned in Rome just eight months after his accession, to proclaim the excommunication of any who should profane sacred images. This action, a reply to Leo III's council of 730, produced an immediate imperial response. The emperor confiscated the estates of the Roman church in southern Italy and Sicily and removed the churches in those regions, as well as in the Balkans, from papal ecclesiastical jurisdiction. Further than this, however, he did not and could not go. No attempt was made to impose iconoclastic policies on the church of Rome itself, presumably because Leo had been convinced by earlier events that he could not enforce his will against the popes in the Byzantine territories in central Italy. Thus, the regions of Ravenna, the Pentapolis, and Rome were left in practice to their own devices, though the popes continued, until 772, formally to acknowledge the sovereignty of the eastern emperors.

The independence of these territories, however, was essential to the papacy. Only by guaranteeing their integrity could the bishops of Rome avoid the prospect of trading the domination of the Lombard kings at Pavia for that of the emperor at Constantinople. Hence, in 739, after some years of playing balance-of-power games with the Lombard duchies to his south and the Lombard kingdom to his north, Gregory III turned for assistance against his enemies to Charles Martel. Furthermore, around the middle of the century, the papal secretariat produced one of the most influential forgeries in history: the so-called *Donation of Constantine*. This document, making use of the well-known legend that Pope Sylvester had cured Emperor Constantine of leprosy,[1] purported to be a grateful letter from that emperor himself. It assigned to the bishops of Rome jurisdiction over the four patriarchates of Antioch, Alexandria,

---

[1] See Gregory of Tours, *History of the Franks* 2.31, for an allusion to the story.

Constantinople, and Jerusalem and—more even than that—decreed that "the sacred see of blessed Peter shall be gloriously exalted above our empire and earthly throne."[2] Of more specific interest, Constantine was alleged to have conveyed to the popes "all provinces, palaces, and districts of the city of Rome and Italy and of the regions of the West."[3] In other words, this document (whose contents did no more than state what the papal court of the day honestly believed to be true) not only reiterated the traditional papal claim to a universal authority in the church and the traditional papal belief that the authority of the priest is superior to that of secular rulers, but it also dealt with the particular and current question of the right of the popes to govern and dispose of Rome and the other Byzantine territories in Italy.

Gregory III's appeal to Charles Martel was unsuccessful, but by the days of Pepin III the situation had changed significantly, and Pepin had as much to gain from an alliance with the popes as they had to gain from his protection against the Lombards. In 743, he and his brother Carloman, in order to legitimize their rules as mayors of the palace, had elevated the last of the Merovingians, Childeric III, to the throne of his ancestors. Four years later, however, Carloman voluntarily retired from his office to become (in 750) a monk at Monte Cassino in Italy. Pepin was thus the sole effective ruler of the Frankish kingdom and wished to enjoy the royal title as well as the substance of power. To depose the last of the Merovingian line, however, he needed the powerful sanction of the papacy. He therefore appealed to Pope Zacharias (741–752), who gave prompt consent to the deposition of Childeric and the coronation of Pepin as king of the Franks. The coronation occurred in 751 at Soissons and was carried out by St. Boniface himself, who anointed Pepin for his new calling and thus gave divine sanction to the change of rulers. Some three years later, in 754, as the Lombards, who under King Aistulf (749–756) had already occupied the Byzantine territories around Ravenna, were pressing Rome itself, Pope Stephen (752–757) journeyed to France, where he crowned and anointed Pepin and his sons afresh in the church of St. Denis at Paris. Pepin greeted the pope on foot and led his horse, while Stephen conferred on the Frankish king the title "Patrician of the Romans"—all of which suggests that Pepin had been made acquainted with, and at least in some vague sense accepted, the doctrine of the *Donation of Constantine*. Stephen also won from Pepin an agreement to protect the papacy in the possession of the Byzantine territories in central Italy, and indeed he made it clear that by anointing the new Frankish king he had constituted him and his successors the guardians of the rights of the apostle Peter. Accordingly, Pepin, in 754 or 755, brought his army to Italy and compelled Aistulf to return his conquests to the pope. Thus began the history of "The States of the Church"—that temporal sovereignty of the papacy which

[2] H. Bettenson, ed., *Documents of the Christian Church,* 2nd ed. (London, 1963), p. 138.
[3] Ibid., p. 139.

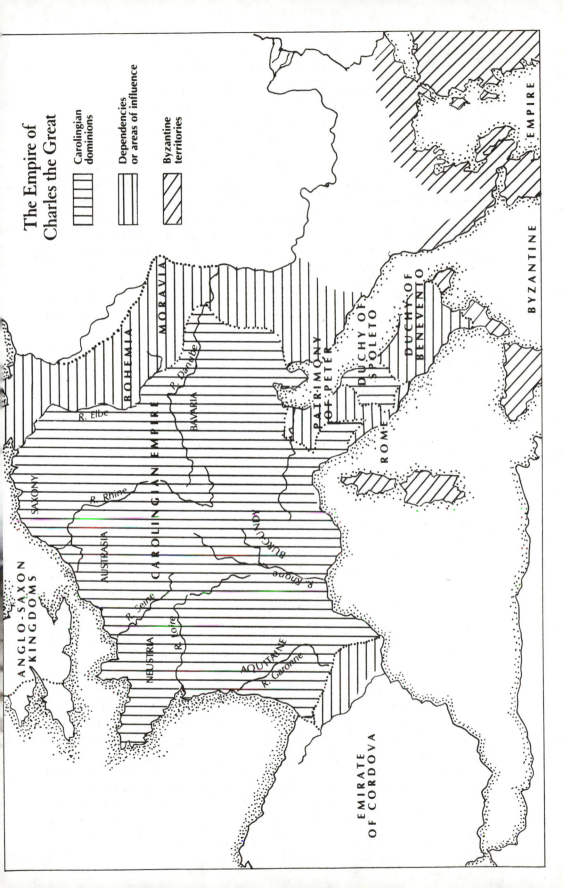

The Empire of
Charles the Great

Carolingian
dominions

Dependencies
or areas of influence

Byzantine
territories

ANGLO-SAXON
KINGDOMS

SAXONY

BOHEMIA

MORAVIA

R. Elbe

R. Rhine

AUSTRASIA

BAVARIA

R. Danube

CAROLINGIAN EMPIRE

PATRIMONY OF PETER

DUCHY OF
SPOLETO

NEUSTRIA

R. Seine

R. Loire

BURGUNDY

R. Rhone

ROME

DUCHY OF
BENEVENTO

AQUITAINE

R. Garonne

EMIRATE
OF CORDOVA

BYZANTINE
EMPIRE

was to last until 1870 and then to be renewed, if on a much smaller scale, by the creation of the State of the Vatican City.

This transaction no doubt appeared entirely ordinary and natural at the time. It recognized a state of affairs that the events of the seventh and eighth centuries had quietly but inexorably brought about. The house of Pepin II and Charles Martel, through its dealings with Boniface and the papacy, had established itself as the secular leaders of a renewed and vigorous Latin Christendom. At the same time, the popes, not without the pressures of the iconoclastic controversy and of Lombard ambitions in Italy, had recognized that their real and effective sphere of authority was the new Christian and catholic Europe which English missions and Merovingian power had created. Yet the two parties to this arrangement inevitably viewed it in different lights. For Stephen and his successors, it meant, no doubt, the visible realization of the principles of the *Donation of Constantine*. For Pepin and his, however, it meant that they had assumed, with papal blessing, the burden of the welfare of western Christendom. In this situation there was an intimation of the later struggle in the medieval West between papal and secular authorities for the headship of Latin Christendom.

Chapter 5

Charles the Great

PEPIN THE SHORT died in 768. In Frankish fashion, he divided his kingdom between his two sons, Charles and Carloman. The two brothers (who, like their father, had been anointed kings by Pope Stephen in 754) were prone to quarrel, but the conflict between them was terminated by the death of Carloman in 771. From that date until his death in 814, Charles—whose title "the Great" was eventually woven into the very name by which history has most frequently called him, "Charlemagne"—ruled, reformed, and expanded the Christian kingdom of the Franks, over which, as he understood it, a divine grace and calling had set him.

Charles was a many-sided man. A great warrior in the Frankish tradition, his annual military campaigns more than doubled his inheritance, and when he died he was the ruler of all of what is now France, Belgium, and Holland,

and of Austria, large sections of Germany and Italy, and a corner of north-eastern Spain. His military prowess, however, represented no more than a part of his gifts. Ruling as he did over a thinly populated, poor, and semibarbarous world, in which communications were slow, trade almost nonexistent, and loyalties tenuous, Charles installed an administrative system which enabled him—and even, for a time, his successors—to give religious cohesion and a measure of political unity to a society which had still not fulfilled its potential for disintegration. At the same time, he regarded himself, the anointed king of a Christian people, as the guardian of the church, whose welfare, material and spiritual, he sought to enhance. Finally, Charles was evidently a man who enjoyed learning. Though he could barely form his letters (writing was not the business of kings), he spoke Latin and even a bit of Greek, surrounded himself with learned advisors, and did all that he could to extend the benefits of education in all parts of his realm.

One of the earliest of Charles's military campaigns was undertaken to force the new Lombard king, Desiderius, to respect the independence of the papal territories in Italy. At the request of Pope Hadrian I (772–795), who was hard enough pressed by Desiderius that he was preparing Rome for a siege, Charles led two campaigns into Italy, which resulted in the extinction of Lombard independence. As of 774, therefore, Charles assumed a new title: "by the grace of God king of the Franks and of the Lombards and Patrician of the Romans." The last-mentioned title had been conferred by a grateful Pope Hadrian at Rome, when Charles had renewed the promise of Pepin to guarantee the popes in the possession of their central Italian territories. In fact, however, with the disappearance of the Lombard buffer state, the papacy found itself, in effect, a political client of the Frankish king, whose reverence for the successor of Peter was entirely real but did not outweigh his sense of being ultimately responsible, as king "by the grace of God," for the spiritual welfare of the Christian people in his charge. Charles's tendency, the natural consequence of his inherited ideal of sacred kingship, was to see the pope as the leading priest of his realm—a view which, ironically, was more consistent with the principles of the Byzantine emperors than it was with those of the *Donation of Constantine.*

Crucially important both for the integrity of his own realm and for the extension of Christianity was Charles's conquest of the Saxons, who occupied what is now northwest Germany, between the Elbe and the mouth of the Rhine. This result was achieved only after a series of bloody campaigns which lasted from 772 until 804, during which the Franks forcibly imposed Christianity on their enemies and confirmed this conversion by planting monasteries and bishoprics throughout the land. These Saxon campaigns also achieved the final Christianization of Frisia, where St. Willibrord had labored at the beginning of the century. Charles also subjugated the rebellious duke of Bavaria, Tassilo, and this enterprise led not only to the absorption of the Bavarian churches into the Frankish system, but also to successful wars against the Avars and the extension of Christianity into Austria, the "East March" of Charles's realm. In this way, the Frankish kingdom was brought into contact with the Balkan, predominantly Slavic, peoples whose territories abutted the northern border of the Byzantine Empire.

Alongside Charles the military leader and conqueror must be set the figure of Charles the reformer of church and society, who consciously employed the best and most learned minds of his day to bring order and culture to a world whose collective imagination could scarcely grasp the notion of either. Most prominent among his advisors was the English monk and deacon Alcuin, who joined Charlemagne's court in 781, after serving as master of the cathedral school in his native York. A learned and inquiring man, though by no means a deep or original thinker, Alcuin was a product of the tradition of Bede the Venerable and the monastery at Jarrow. At Charles's court, he found a company of like-minded scholars. There was Paul the Deacon (d. 799), a monk of Monte Cassino and author of *A History of the Nation of the Lombards,* whom Charles later commissioned to write a set of homilies to be read in churches throughout his realm. There was the classical scholar Peter of Pisa, and Paulinus, later archbishop of Aquileia and Charles's principal agent and representative in northern Italy. Such clerics, who were acquainted with the traditions of Roman and canon law as well as with the Scriptures and the writings of Augustine, Gregory the Great, Cassiodorus, and Isidore of Seville, served Charles in a multitude of capacities. Alcuin ran an informal school of the liberal arts in the palace, which Charles himself frequented. Created abbot of the monastery of St. Martin at Tours, he began a process of founding and expanding monastic schools, libraries, and *scriptoria* throughout Charles's kingdom. His aim was not merely to diffuse literacy and education, but also to collect and copy the documents that contained the heritage of the past; it is to the monasteries of the reigns of Charles and his successors that we owe the preservation of large numbers of classical and patristic texts, all written in the elegant hand called Carolingian minuscule. In addition, Alcuin and his associates guided Charles in his relations with the papacy and the Byzantine Empire and in his systematic efforts to reform the administration of his kingdom and the life of the church. It was they, moreover, and Alcuin in particular, who taught Charles to envisage his realm as that very "City of God," the Christian commonwealth, of which Augustine of Hippo had (as they read him) spoken almost four centuries before.

Charles's interest in, and authority over, the church extended to every area of its life. He appointed its bishops and summoned its councils, whose function in practice became that of offering him advice. At his behest, Alcuin reformed and unified the confused and diverse liturgical practices of his realm, after careful study of traditional Roman models—thus becoming responsible, among other things, for the universal employment of the so-called Apostles' Creed in the West. It was Charles's firm action which assured to bishops their right to ordain, supervise, and discipline clergy employed in village or estate churches, even in those frequent cases where it was lay patrons who had the power of appointing such priests to their pastoral charges. In this way, the growing parochial system was integrated into the governmental structures of the church. At the same time, Charles reinstituted the ancient system of metropolitan sees, whose occupants, now called archbishops, exercised jurisdiction over the other bishops within their "provinces." In addition, he interested himself in the life of those clergy—deacons and presbyters—who constituted the immediate staff or *familia* of the bishop. In their case, Charles favored and encouraged adoption of a system which had been devised by Chrodegang, bishop of Metz, in the days of Pepin the Short. Chrodegang had imposed on his clergy a semimonastic discipline, the so-called *vita canonica* ("life according to rule"), which bound them to a common life and to common recitation of the daily offices (see III:13), but which also allowed them to own property and to carry out duties inconsistent with a strict monastic vocation. It was the spread of this system which led to the custom of referring to the clergy of cathedral and collegiate churches as "canons." Above all, however, Charles was concerned with the work of clergy in local settings. It was his ideal, which he was far from achieving, to have an educated presbyter in every locale—one who could not only give instruction in Christianity to the people but could also act, in effect, as schoolmaster, bringing the benefits of literacy to all within his charge.

Needless to say, this concern for the church extended to the papacy itself, which under Hadrian I (772–795) finally terminated even formal acknowledgment of the sovereignty of the emperor at Constantinople and in effect treated Charles himself as the lay head of Christendom, a role which his conquests and his zeal for the extension and reform of the church seemed to vindicate for him. Hadrian's successor, Leo III (795–816), had reason both for gratitude and for dismay in the face of the authority which Charles thus bore. Elected pope over the objections of the rapacious Roman nobility, which aspired to control the papal office, Leo, on April 25, 799, was assaulted, kidnapped, and beaten by hired thugs. Rescued by two Frankish clerics, he fled to Charles at Paderborn, where he was received with honor. Shortly after his arrival, however, the king received letters—from the very people who had contrived the assault—accusing Leo of serious crime and immorality. Convinced that no successor of the apostle Peter could hold his sacred office with such charges outstanding against him, Charles, with a body of Frankish bishops, traveled to Rome, where, at an assembly in St. Peter's Basilica, he required Leo to exculpate himself by swearing his innocence before God. Two days later, on Christmas Day, 800, as Charles, after hearing the pope celebrate the Mass of Christ's Nativity, was praying before the shrine of St. Peter, Leo placed a diadem on his head and the assembled populace of Rome acclaimed him as "Charles Augustus, crowned by God as the great and pacific Emperor." By the pope's action, Charles was no longer merely king of the Franks and Lombards but also the successor of Constantine, the Christian emperor of the Romans.

The interpretation of this event has occasioned widespread debate among historians. Einhard, a biographer of Charles the Great, wrote that the new emperor proclaimed his displeasure at this papal action and insisted that he would never have come to St. Peter's had he known what the pope proposed to do. This statement has led many historians to see in Leo's action an attempt to reassert the principle of the *Donation of Constantine*. By creating Charles emperor, it is argued, Leo—humiliated by his need of Charles's support and by the king's requirement of an oath of innocence—was in effect reasserting his own superior authority by giving Charles what, by the testament of Constantine himself, only the pope could convey: the status and authority of emperor of the Romans. Other historians oppose this account of the matter. They see in Leo's action nothing more than a continuation of the policy of Hadrian I —who, in rejecting openly the sovereignty of the Byzantine emperors, seems to have intended a transfer of the imperial office to the West—and at the same time a confirmation of the ideology of those Frankish intellectuals who, like Alcuin, had for some years been hailing Charles as a new David and as emperor of the Latin Christendom which they now called Europe. That Leo picked this particular occasion for Charles's coronation would, on this view, be sufficiently explained by the Frankish king's intervention on behalf of the pope and by the fact that the eastern "emperor" was not only a woman, Irene, but a woman who had shocked even the Franks by the murder of her son, the legitimate monarch.

To choose between these accounts of the matter is difficult insofar as it requires a judgment of Leo's motives, for which there is little explicit evidence and which in any case may well have been mixed. What seems clear, however, is that Charles had not expected Leo's action; indeed, the emperor may well have found his new status an embarrassment, since it immediately embroiled him in diplomatic and military conflict with the Byzantine Empire. The leaders of that state, after all, could never in principle (whatever they might be pressured by circumstance to concede in practice) surrender their belief that the Christian world had, and could have, only one head, the Roman emperor throned at Constantinople. Furthermore, Charles and his advisors seem to have had a view of the imperial office different from that of either the pope or the Byzantine authorities. Charles saw himself not as emperor of the Romans but as emperor of that Latin (i.e., Frankish and Lombard) Christendom which constituted Europe. The fact is, then, that the coronation probably had different meanings for the different parties involved in it. In any case, it attests the appearance of a new Latin and Christian cultural and religious unity under the joint sponsorship of the popes as guardians of apostolic Christianity and of the Frankish monarchy—the latter now transmuted, temporarily, into a pale image of the Constantinian empire.

Chapter 6

European Christianity
in the Ninth Century

*A*NYONE WHO LOOKS AT Latin Christendom in the century following the death
of Charles the Great (814) is struck first of all by the accelerating political
disintegration of the Carolingian empire. In part, perhaps, this development can
be attributed to the ineptitude of many of Charles's successors, as well as to the
Frankish custom of dividing a patrimony among surviving male heirs. Such
factors, however, do not offer a complete explanation. More important is the
localism which was encouraged, and indeed necessitated, by the absence of
significant trade and reliable communications. This was a society whose fundamental business was subsistence farming, and its basic social unit continued to
be not the city, nor even the village, but the self-sufficient manor or estate. The
tendency toward localism was reinforced by the inability of the clumsy royal
military system to respond to the hit-and-run techniques of the Viking and
Saracen invaders who in this era tormented Europe and Britain from the sea.

Charles's successor, Louis (814–840), called "the Pious," did indeed, as his
father's only surviving legitimate son, inherit and rule the Carolingian empire
as a whole. Louis was no soldier, however, and never commanded the full respect
of his father's true source of power, the military aristocracy of the Frankish
homeland in Austrasia. Nevertheless, he held his realm together (though not
without difficulty) and shared—perhaps in too naive a way—the enthusiasm of
learned ecclesiastics for the ideology of the Latin Christian empire. Louis saw
his royal and imperial office as a calling from God to defend, expand, and rule
the Christian people, a calling given him by God in his anointing and in which
his only judges were the bishops of his realm, who were also his primary ministers and counselors. Louis accordingly continued his father's practice of acting,
in effect, as the supreme pastor of the churches, reforming and regulating every
aspect of their life.

In spite of this loyalty to the ideal of the Christian empire, however, it was
Louis who designed its partition among his sons. Furthermore, he handled this

business so clumsily that he permanently embittered their relations with himself and with one another. Their disputes continued after his death, and it was only in 843, by the treaty of Verdun, that a final settlement was reached. By this agreement, which marks the start of the separate histories of France and Germany, the empire was split into three parts. To Louis (843–875) was given the area east of the Rhine, whence he acquired the nickname "the German." To Charles (843–877), called "the Bald," came most of what is now France. Lothair I (843–855), the eldest, received, along with the imperial title, an anomalous central strip of territory which stretched from the mouth of the Rhine in the north to the Lombard kingdom of northern Italy. This initial division, however, was only the harbinger of more to come. After Lothair I's death, his territory was again divided in three, and eventually it became nothing more than a string of small principalities. In Germany and France, monarchy formally survived, but real central authority did not. When Louis the Child, last of the Carolingian kings of Germany, died in 911, the substance of power had fallen into the hands of the tribal chiefs of Bavaria, Franconia, Swabia, and Saxony, to whom the Carolingians had accorded official rank by conferring on them the ancient Roman title of *dux*—"duke." Similarly, the later Carolingian kings of France, of whom the last was Louis V (986–987), exercised less real power than many of the other magnates of their realm. The disintegration of the political unity achieved by Charles the Great was all but total.

In Italy and France, this fragmentation of power was partly a response to the external assaults which, coming from almost every quarter, threatened to overwhelm Europe in the ninth and tenth centuries. The raids of the Danish-Norwegian sea-peoples on England and France began just as the ninth century opened. While their Swedish cousins were making their way across the Baltic and down the Russian river-system to the Black Sea, the Danes and Norwegians raided up the rivers of the Anglo-Saxon and Frankish coasts, burning such towns as there were, sacking monasteries, and disappearing before the royal levies could be mustered and moved to meet them.

In England, these raids put an end to the intellectual and cultural life of the monasteries which had produced both scholars like Bede and Alcuin and the missionaries who, under Carolingian auspices, had carried out the conversion of Germany. Lindisfarne was ravaged as early as 793; by the middle of the ninth century, most of the centers of English life had been sacked, and the Danes occupied and controlled the greater part of England. The situation was saved only by the desperate valor of Alfred the Great, king of Wessex (871–899), who in 878, after a great battle at Edington, compelled the Danes under Guthrum to accept a division of territory and so created the "Danelaw," which encompassed most of central and northeastern England.

Relative peace in England, however, merely increased the pace and seriousness of Viking attacks on France and the Netherlands. While Emperor Louis II, son of Lothair I, together with a whole generation of popes, was seeking, sometimes with Byzantine co-operation, to fend off Saracen attacks in the southern half of Italy, Viking incursions in the north had struck such centers as Ghent, Cologne, and Reims. In the end, Northmen settled around the mouth of the river Seine, and the French king Charles the Simple (898–929) was compelled, after the manner of Alfred, to create his own Danelaw by treating with their leader, Rollo. The latter agreed to accept Christianity in return for the territories to be known as the Duchy of Normandy, with its center at Rouen.

In France—but not at this time, and never to the same degree, in Germany —the disintegration of Carolingian power was accompanied by the rise of what the eighteenth century called the "feudal system." This was essentially a pattern of social and political organization. Its roots lay primarily in the personal bond of reciprocal service and loyalty which had classically structured the relations of the Germanic war-leader and his crew of fighters. Its distinctive characteristics, however, were the association of this bond with land tenure and its use to define the obligations which bound subordinate rulers to the central authority of the king or other lord. In return for his loyal services, the vassal was endowed with what was (technically) only a life tenure of certain landed estates, as the means of his support. Dukes (*duces*) and counts (*comites*), who were originally, as in the Roman Empire, appointive royal officials, were normally rewarded and supported in this fashion out of royal holdings by both the Merovingians and their successors. Since, however, landed estates were the basis of both economic and military power, and since possession of a benefice or "fief" soon came in practice to pass from father to son, these officials gradually became a settled and hereditary nobility. What is more, their private wealth and power, which increasingly made them independent of the king, also made them the real source, in their regions, of public order and justice and of protection from external enemies. Thus they, too—in a world where social identity, legal rights, and safety depended on personal, quasi-familial relations with a lord—began to acquire vassals and to become little kings in their own territories, with rights of jurisdiction not only over the peasantry bound to their estates but also over the free men who were their vassals. All this, needless to say, occurred at the expense of that very royal power which had created the system as a way of rewarding and controlling its servants; and one consequence of the decline of royal authority was that monasteries and bishoprics alike fell increasingly under the control of local feudal magnates.

However, while the political unity which Charles the Great had established dissolved swiftly under the simultaneous impact of invasion and the decentralization of power, the religious unity created by the Carolingians did not suffer the same fate. Catholic and Roman Christianity remained the unifying factor in European and English culture and society. Its central institutions—the papacy, the episcopate, and the monastic communities—retained their vigor, corrupted and altered though they frequently were by the events and conditions of their time. Above all, the Carolingian ideal of an alliance of royal and ecclesiastical authority for the nurture of a Christian society continued to capture people's imaginations.

In its origins, the monastic movement had been inspired by a spirit of withdrawal from, and even of hostility to, the world for the sake of single-minded imitation of Christ. Celtic, and after it English, monasticism had by no means lost this ascetic spirit. Nevertheless, it had also engaged in pastoral and missionary activity and in the cultivation of learning, and it had become, with the support and protection of Pepin II and his successors, the primary instrument for the conversion and Christianization of pagan Europe. By the ninth century, therefore, monastic institutions, built and endowed with extensive lands by the generosity of kings and other magnates, were to be found not only scattered through the countryside but also close by every center of power, secular and ecclesiastical. The pattern of monastic life, moreover, was becoming more stable and uniform, as the Rule of St. Benedict gradually achieved universal acceptance. Louis the Pious greatly accelerated this process by bringing with him to the imperial court in 814 the Burgundian monk Benedict of Aniane (751–821), who was given a brief authorizing him to impose on all monasteries of the realm the same strict observance of the Benedictine Rule as he had enforced in his own house at Aniane. Provided with a newly founded monastic community near Louis's court, Benedict, at a council of abbots summoned by the emperor in 817 at Aix-la-Chapelle, promulgated his *Capitulare monasticum* and followed this up by composing, for the edification of monks everywhere, his *Concordia regularum* and *Codex regularum*. The response to this effort at reform was by no means universally enthusiastic, and the gradual dissolution of the Carolingian system brought disorder and corruption to many centers of monastic life. Nevertheless, Benedict succeeded in promoting a new spirit of discipline, which was eventually to bear fruit throughout Europe in a stricter and more regular monastic life.

Yet the Benedictine houses of the ninth and later centuries were not the sort of communities which their sixth-century founder had contemplated. For one thing, their members were no longer laypersons but, for the most part, clergy. For another, these clergy were not engaged in farming. Their estates, by and large, were tended, like all manors of the time, by serfs or tenants, while the monks themselves were engaged in worship and in other forms of work. Furthermore, though they were withdrawn communities, they were in many ways close to their world, and performed essential functions, symbolic and practical, in and for early medieval society. Their performance of the Divine Office, increasingly elaborate and lengthy, was understood to be not only a vicarious service of God but a perpetual struggle against the powers of evil and of disorder on behalf of the whole society that they represented. The lands with which they were endowed enabled them to provide their royal or noble patrons not only with material resources and, when necessary, soldiers, but also with a setting where highborn children whose future might otherwise be uncertain could be educated and formed for an essential and noble service. The monasteries were also the primary centers of learning and the arts. Above all, they were symbols, by their ordered, regular, and peaceful life in the service of God, of the reality and presence of the Holy in a troubled and disordered world.

This symbiosis between the monastery and its society was paralleled in the institution of the episcopate. In the society created by the early Carolingians, the bishop was above all a pastor, if an increasingly distant one. His charge was the entire population within his jurisdiction, and his ultimate support in the pastoral enterprise was the king himself, who not only appointed him and endowed his church but also summoned him to councils and saw the bishop's work as one aspect of his own call to guarantee the welfare of the Christian people. It was the bishops, then, and not merely or even primarily the pope, whose prestige and responsibility were enhanced by the alliance of church and crown in Christian Europe. Naturally enough, therefore, it was to the divinely anointed king that the bishops rallied in the first instance, putting at his service not only the resources of the estates which belonged to their churches, but their personal talents as administrators and counselors. The bishops, as we have seen, were thus treated in effect as royal ministers and vassals—and very useful ones at that, since their holdings could never become hereditary and were therefore always at the lord's disposal. In return, the bishops received, as vassals were supposed to, the protection and material support of the king for their work. Nor was this arrangement a cynical one. The Carolingian kings—and, as we shall see, their successors in Germany—accepted the guardianship of the churches as a sacred charge. In turn, they were—and increasingly so, as royal power diminished in a feudalized society—dependent on the resources of the church.

One, and not by any means the least, contribution of monastic and episcopal establishments in this era of political decentralization was the perpetuation of the tradition of learning commenced by Alcuin and his colleagues at the court of Charles the Great. After Alcuin's time, most monasteries and many episcopal "families" (the first form of the later "cathedral schools") had a teacher of greater or lesser learning who gave instruction in the seven liberal arts. Some of the more eminent monastic houses had elaborate facilities for the copying of manuscripts, not to mention schools where distinguished masters pursued inquiries not only into the theological and exegetical tradition of the ancient church but also into such matters as arithmetic, chronography, and astronomy. The spirit of this "Carolingian renaissance" was antiquarian (and sometimes playful); but it also produced the beginnings of a poetry employing accent-meter and rhyme, the beginnings of rational reflection on social problems and political theory, and the beginnings of fresh theological inquiry.

The most original theological thinker of this era was the head of the palace school of Charles the Bald. This was the Irishman John Scotus Erigena (d. ca. 877), who translated into Latin the works of pseudo-Dionysius the Areopagite (see III:10) and added to them his own ideas, conceived in a thoroughly Neoplatonist spirit, in a treatise entitled *On the Division of Nature.* John the Scot, however, had no one to continue his work, and, except through his translations, he exercised very little influence on the future. Of more interest to historians of doctrine are two debates which arose out of the monastic schools. The first of these was initiated by Paschasius Radbertus (d. ca. 860), abbot of the monastery at Corbie, whose treatise *On the Body and Blood of the Lord* seemed to some of his readers to maintain too literal and "physical" a notion of the sacramental presence of Christ in the eucharistic elements. His work caught the attention of King Charles the Bald and received replies from several thinkers. The most notable of these came from the pen of Ratramnus, a monk of Paschasius's own monastery. Ratramnus's answer, which was much admired by certain Protestant reformers of the sixteenth century, returned to the tradition of St. Augustine and emphasized that the presence of Christ in the eucharistic elements, while entirely real, was spiritual and "figurative" (i.e., not discernible by the senses but known by faith *in mysterio*). Another reply came from Rabanus Maurus (d. 856), the abbot of Fulda and (later) archbishop of Mainz. Educated by Alcuin himself, Rabanus not only replied to Paschasius but was an extensive commentator on Scripture as well as the author of a popular "encyclopedia" based on the *Etymologies* of Isidore of Seville and titled *De universo.*

Both Rabanus and Erigena had a hand in the second controversy of this era, which was occasioned by the work of the monk Gottschalk (d. ca. 868). This thinker, whose efforts to leave the monastic life and rejoin the world had been frustrated by Rabanus Maurus, had been transferred from Fulda to the abbey of Orbais in France. There he entered deeply into the study of Augustine of Hippo and eventually set out an extreme theory of double predestination (the doctrine that God decrees salvation for some and reprobation for others). This created the greatest theological storm of its time by reopening all the questions which had lay behind the Semi-Pelagian controversy of the fifth century. Replies came not only from Erigena and Rabanus Maurus but also from Hincmar (d. 882), the eminent archbishop of Reims and a former monk of the abbey of St. Denis, who was perhaps more notable as a politician, administrator, and student of canon law than as a theologian. As a result of this debate—in which Gottschalk had many defenders, including Ratramnus—he was condemned by a synod at Mainz in 848 and retired for life to the monastery of Hautvillers, where he continued to write learnedly against his opponents. Neither controversy, perhaps, was conducted with great theological sophistication, but together the two debates serve not only to demonstrate the rebirth of serious concern with theological problems in the West but also to intimate the sorts of issues which were to be central for much of later western, including Protestant, theology.

What, though, of the papacy in all this? The church of Rome and its bishop had by no means lost their pivotal character in western Christianity. As vicar and representative of the apostle Peter, the pope enjoyed an unparalleled prestige and honor, and the welfare of the Roman see was an object of at least formal concern to the later Carolingian rulers, though there was little they could do either to protect or to control it. The popes, furthermore, whose chancery records provided them with a memory longer than that of most institutions of their time, had not forgotten or deserted the principles summed up in the *Donation of Constantine*. They understood themselves to exercise a universal jurisdiction over all bishops, to be the primary source of teaching authority in the church, and to exercise a spiritual power which set them over all secular rulers in Christendom. It was one thing to claim such authority, however, and another to exercise it to the full. Nevertheless, to the extent that the circumstances and attitudes of the time allowed, this authority was exercised. There is plenty of evidence to show that the early ninth-century popes sought successfully to safeguard their rights in their own territories, to prescribe general principles for the government of the churches, and, where appropriate, to intervene in support of those principles. Yet the conditions of the ninth century forbade any direct papal administration of the ordinary affairs of the churches, just as they forbade direct royal administration of local political affairs. They also dictated that the popes of this era, given the gradual disintegration of the Carolingian empire, should become more and more absorbed in, and eventually dominated by, local Italian power struggles.

That the pope was still capable on occasion of making his authority felt, however, is demonstrated by the pontificate of Nicholas I (858–867). His predecessor but one, Leo IV (847–855), had come to the papal throne one year after Saracen raiders had penetrated into Rome and even into the basilicas of Peter and Paul. Leo's reign, therefore, was largely absorbed in problems of physical defense, and his great accomplishment was to fortify, on the right bank of the Tiber, the so-called "Leonine city"—a step which enabled him to beat off further Saracen raids. Nicholas could not and did not ignore the problem created by the Islamic onslaught, but co-operation between the papacy, Emperor Louis II (855–875), and Byzantine forces in the south of Italy temporarily stemmed the tide of the Saracen advance, and Nicholas, a tenacious leader and diplomatist, was able in two notable (and many less notable) cases to assert the authority of the pope north of the Alps, and in the process to show that neither the claims nor the prestige of the papacy had abated. The first of these cases involved him with Lothair II, king of Lorraine, who—out of dynastic concerns that made his problem a focal point of Frankish politics—divorced his childless wife, Thietberga, in favor of marriage with his concubine, Waldrada. When Thietberga appealed to the pope, Nicholas overturned the decision of a synod held in Metz (863), which had sanctioned the divorce, and at the same time deprived the archbishops of Trier and Cologne of their sees. In this fashion, he asserted papal authority over both the Frankish clergy and a reigning monarch.

More significant, perhaps, for the future was Nicholas's intervention in the affairs of the French church, when he forced Archbishop Hincmar of Reims to restore the deposed bishop of Soissons, which was in Hincmar's metropolitan jurisdiction. The broader significance of this act, which established the principle that the pope had authority to intervene in the internal affairs of an archiepiscopal province, lay in two unrelated circumstances. The first was Hincmar's conviction—which he intimated in his *Life of St. Remigius* (the bishop of Reims who had baptized Clovis) and then dramatized by his unilateral action of anointing Charles the Bald as emperor at Metz (869)—that the see of Reims had virtually supreme authority in the ecclesiastical affairs of the Franks. The second circumstance was the dissatisfaction which was just then felt by the French bishops generally at the frequent violation of canonical order and discipline in their churches—a situation occasioned above all by the growing alienation of church lands and properties by local lay magnates. This problem, a manifestation of the confusion and violence of the times, led the bishops, at Épernay in 846, to demand that the king intervene and set the state of the church to rights. Charles the Bald, however, was unwilling, probably because he was unable, to do so, and in this stand he was supported by Hincmar. In the face of this threat to traditional order and of the failure of royal authority to maintain its role as protector of the churches, the minds of at least some ecclesiastics turned to the papacy. Somewhere in the French kingdom, a group of dissident scholars composed the *Pseudo-Isidorian Decretals,* a collection of early papal and conciliar rulings, some genuine and some patently forged, which claimed to have been assembled by Isidore of Seville (see III:19). The aim of this collection (in which the *Donation of Constantine* was included) was clear. In order to protect the traditional rights of the bishops against the encroachments of the lay nobility and certain other abuses, it centered all ecclesiastical authority in the papacy, at the expense not only of royal authority, the lay nobility, and secular courts, but also of provincial archbishops. For the times, this was revolutionary doctrine. Nicholas I may have become acquainted with these decretals, and his disciplining of Hincmar of Reims can be interpreted as a sympathetic response to the plea implicit in them for an assertion of papal power. It was not until two centuries had passed, however, that the popes explicitly appealed to this collection or were able to bring about something like the state of affairs it envisaged.

These gestures toward establishing the authority of the papacy in the Frankish kingdom were paralleled by a significant intervention on Nicholas's part in the affairs of the Byzantine church. In 858, the patriarch of Constantinople, Ignatius, was deposed from his see at the instance of Emperor Michael III's uncle and chief advisor, Bardas. The occasion for this action was the systematic refusal of Ignatius, a rigid conservative, to compromise with the policies of the new government which had appeared after the forced retirement of Empress Theodora as regent (see IV:3). In Ignatius's place, Bardas appointed a layperson, Photius, one of the most learned scholars and serious theologians of the eastern church. When Ignatius refused to retire and raised questions about the legitimacy of his deposition, the emperor and Photius invited Nicholas to dispatch legates to a synod that was to deal both with certain questions about iconoclasm and with the problem of the patriarchate. Nicholas's legates, however, seem to have gone beyond their instructions. The pope's primary concern was to use this occasion to negotiate with the eastern authorities regarding the restoration of papal ecclesiastical jurisdiction in southern Italy and in the Balkans, where he was in correspondence with the Bulgarian tsar Boris over the possibility of dispatching Roman missionaries to Christianize Boris's people. His legates, however, were outmaneuvered on this issue and, contrary to the pope's desires, participated in a synod which registered papal approval of Ignatius's deposition without gaining concessions from Constantinople. Nicholas, when he heard of this, complained that his letter to Constantinople had been falsified and refused to acknowledge the acts of the synod, declaring that Ignatius was still the patriarch. In 863, he excommunicated Photius. There was no reply from Photius for four years. In 867, however—in a letter which for the first time raised the issue of the *filioque* clause, by then embedded in the Latin version of the Nicene Creed, as a bone of contention between East and West—Photius pronounced Nicholas anathema and excommunicated him. In the same year, though, a new emperor, Basil I (867–886), who had murdered both Bardas and Michael III, restored Ignatius to the patriarchal throne, and the so-called "Photian schism" came to an end. It is true that in 878, on the death of Ignatius, Photius was again elevated to the patriarchate, but it seems that Pope John VIII (872–882), contrary to an earlier view current among scholars, accepted this election as legitimate. Nicholas had succeeded in making his authority felt as the one bishop with a claim to universal authority, but in the process, relations between the eastern and western churches had taken yet another step in the direction of permanent schism.

Chapter 7

The Papacy and the Ottonian Empire

RELATIONS WITH THE EASTERN CHURCHES were scarcely the primary preoccupation of Pope John VIII when he came to power in 870. The death of Emperor Louis in 875 led to a renewal of the Saracen assault on Italy. Without even the semblance of a central authority to lead them, the minor princes of Lombardy and southern Italy, in their competitive scrambles for security and power, often preferred to deal individually with the Saracen raiders rather than to unite against them. In this situation, the invaders gained a permanent foothold near the mouth of the Garigliano River south of Rome, whence they ravaged the coast and the countryside. St. Benedict's abbey of Monte Cassino was sacked, among many others. The raiders came to the very walls of Rome. Pope John spent much of his pontificate in an attempt to rally aid for Italy from the north and to unite the Italian princes against their common enemy. In the first of these enterprises he failed; in the second, he met with reasonable success. Nevertheless, when he died—poisoned by members of his own family, it was said, who desired his wealth—Rome was under attack.

John's death in 882 marks the point after which the papacy, for almost a century, was submerged in the discord and violence of Italian politics and became the plaything of local princes and the Roman aristocracy. Historians have tended to dwell on the degradation, moral as well as institutional, of the papacy in this era: on the frequent unworthiness of those who held the office and on the use of the office itself as a pawn in family and dynastic conflicts. These strictures are no doubt accurate enough, but two other circumstances must be kept in mind in any attempt to understand this era.

For one thing, what happened to the papacy in this period was simply one instance of a situation that had come to obtain almost universally in Europe— the very sort of situation of which the French bishops had complained to Charles the Bald at Épernay in 846. With the virtual disappearance of central authority in the state, ecclesiastical institutions and properties of all sorts had come under the feudal control of local lay magnates, who used them both to expand the basis of their power and to benefice supporters and family members. The result of this situation was a sometimes scandalous moral and disciplinary laxity on the part of monks and clergy generally, which was further encouraged by the confusion and material destruction that followed in the wake of Norse and Saracen raids. In the second place, this same era of confusion and disorder almost everywhere gave birth to significant movements for restoration: movements which aimed both at the purification and reform of religious institutions, and at the revival of something like the Carolingian ideal of a society in which priest and ruler worked together for the creation of a Christian commonwealth. What is interesting about the history of the papacy in this period is not the fact that it, too, felt the effects of the disintegration of European society, but that the movement for restoration and reform (as later, in the early sixteenth century) had its roots elsewhere than in the papacy itself and only gradually took over the papal establishment.

The most scandalous period for the papacy was undoubtedly the half-century between the accession of Sergius III (904-911) and that of John XIII (965-972). During this era, traditionally known to historians as the "Pornocracy," Rome and the papacy were under the control of the family of Theophylact, "Senator of the Romans" and the highest lay official in the papal curia. It was Theophylact —together with his appointee as pope, John X (914-928)—who rallied the

Roman aristocracy to join an Italian-Byzantine force which finally drove the Saracens from their fortified camp at the mouth of the Garigliano River. The pope himself fought in the battle at the head of the Roman contingent.

The death of Theophylact (915?) left the affairs of his family and of the Roman duchy in the hands of his ambitious daughter Marozia, who was married to Alberic of Spoleto. The latter's death (after 917) led Marozia to seek to consolidate her position by a further marriage to Guy of Tuscany. John X opposed this marriage, but his opposition was eventually dealt with when Tuscan soldiers appeared in Rome, entered the Lateran, killed the pope's brother, and then imprisoned and smothered the pope himself. Marozia appointed the next three popes, the last of these, John XI (931–936), being her son (and, some said, her illegitimate son by Pope Sergius III). When her second husband also died, Marozia, looking, it appears, to the foundation of an imperial dynasty that would be truly Roman, offered her hand to Guy's half-brother, Hugh of Provence, who was called king of Italy. At the wedding festivities, however, Hugh insulted Marozia's son Alberic, who proceeded to raise the populace of Rome against his mother and her intended husband by accusing her of incest. Hugh of Provence fled Rome, Marozia was confined (and died soon afterward) and Alberic himself took over the affairs of the Roman church and duchy, with the title "Prince and Senator of all the Romans."

Alberic's rule (932–954) was no doubt arbitrary. But it was also evenhanded and obviously aimed at the restoration of order and relative prosperity to the city and its surrounding territories. Alberic devoted much attention, moreover, to the reform of monastic establishments, whose life had been disrupted and corrupted by the events of the times. In this grandson of Theophylact, who repulsed all attempts to bring Rome under the domination of external forces, the spirit of local integrity and self-sufficiency triumphed. He controlled the papacy, but the popes he appointed—and who remained loyal to him—were persons who did no indignity to their office, the functions of which in this era were in any case largely symbolic. He seems, indeed, to have sought precisely what earlier popes themselves had tried to achieve: the independence of Rome and its bishop, with the difference that in his eyes the bishop belonged to Rome and not vice versa. On the eve of his death, he attempted to unite his own office with that of the papacy by extracting an oath that his son Octavian, apparently something of a playboy, would succeed the incumbent pope, Agapetus II (946–955), on the latter's death. And so, at the age of sixteen, under the name John XII, Octavian ascended the papal throne as the successor to both Agapetus and his father. He was not to prove equal to his task.

Roughly contemporaneous with these events was the appearance in the monastic world of an institution that was to have an almost unequaled influence on the public as well as the monastic life of the early medieval world: the abbey of Cluny, which in its heyday contributed immeasurably to the moral and religious reform of church institutions. Located in Burgundy, this abbey was founded in 910 by Duke William of Aquitaine, a lay patron of more than usual piety. William took the step, exceptional for the time, of decreeing that its monks should have the right, as stipulated in Benedict's *Rule,* of electing their own abbot without interference from any secular lord. The abbey, moreover, was free not only of lay, but also of episcopal, supervision. From the beginning it was placed under the sole jurisdiction of the pope (which, in the tenth century, meant in effect no jurisdiction at all). These circumstances in themselves made Cluny a unique establishment for its time, and its distinctiveness was enhanced by a series of notable abbots: Odo (927–942), Maieul (943–994), Odilo (994–1049), and Hugh the Great (1049–1109). From the beginning, it was a reformed and reforming monastery, devoted in the tradition of Benedict of Aniane to the fullness of the Benedictine life. Its abbots, noted for their zeal and their wisdom, were consulted regularly in connection with the affairs of monastic houses all over Europe and eventually spread the spirit of their reform from England to Rome. Abbot Odo, for example, was summoned at least three times to Rome at Alberic's behest; he not only provided monks from Cluny to reform the abbey of Farfa northeast of Rome, but he also became Alberic's spiritual counselor and was put in charge of all the monasteries of Rome. By the end of the tenth century, there was a whole family of monasteries in Europe which acknowledged the authority of the abbot of Cluny, and by the opening years of the eleventh century, this family had become in effect the first formally organized religious order. What Cluny stood for was restoration of the ideals of celibacy and communal property, the abolition of lay control of the abbot's office, and the fullest dedication of the monks' time to the task of prayer and worship on behalf of the world. On the basis of this ideal, its leaders became the counselors of kings and popes, and both its example and its increasing splendor served to diffuse a high standard of morality and piety among laity and cathedral clergy as well as among monastics.

England was one place where, in the second half of the tenth century, the influence of the Cluniac ideal was felt, if only indirectly. There, under King Alfred's successors Edward the Elder (899–925) and Athelstan (925–939), the authority of the English kings over the Danelaw was reestablished and the conversion of the Danes to Christianity begun. In spite of Alfred's efforts to bring about a rebirth of learning and pastoral zeal, however, restoration of church life and property had to await the waning of the military crisis, since the kings continued to need the resources of ecclesiastical lands to create a new, mounted military force. The ecclesiastical leader of the English movement of reform, which proceeded under royal auspices, was St. Dunstan (ca. 909–988), who was made abbot of Glastonbury by King Edmund (939–946) and then, by King Edgar (960–975), archbishop of Canterbury. At Glastonbury, Dunstan—a thorough ascetic who was at the same time a learned theologian, a noted musician, an accomplished illuminator of manuscripts, and a worker in metals—recreated, apparently from almost nothing, a strict Benedictine community, which became the model for later foundations and reforms carried out by his pupil and colleague Ethelwold, bishop of Winchester. As archbishop of Canterbury, Dunstan was concerned equally with the reform and endowment of bishops' "families" and the "secular" canons of minister churches. In such places, he sought to impose the Benedictine life on the canons, who were to have no private property and to live celibate lives. These reforms brought Dunstan and his colleagues into conflict with many of the nobility, who were forced to surrender their control of monastic lands. The archbishop, however, had the support of the king. Edgar even turned royal income to the support of this major effort at a complete rebuilding of English church institutions.

In the last analysis, however, the most powerful vehicle of the movement for restoration turned out to be the Saxon dynasty of German kings, whose line began with Henry I (919–936), called "the Fowler." The situation in Germany was a distinctive one. Feudalism had not taken root there, but the Carolingian kingdom showed every sign, at the beginning of the tenth century, of being about to dissolve into its constituent tribal duchies: Bavaria, Swabia, Saxony, Franconia, and (after 929) Lorraine. That such a dissolution did not occur is attributable to two circumstances. The first of these is the phenomenon of the Hungarian (Magyar) attacks on Europe, which began toward the close of the ninth century and created, on the eastern frontier of Charles the Great's empire, a crisis just as grave as that occasioned by the Northmen and the Saracens in the west and south. A nomadic people from the steppes of Asia, the Hungarians raided on occasion as far as Italy and France, ravaging and plundering wherever they appeared. It was in the German duchies, however, that the pressure and terror of their hordes were most immediately felt. Then in the second place—and partly no doubt because of this danger—the great German ecclesiastics and the leaders of the so-called "stem" duchies decided to elect themselves another king: Henry the Fowler, duke of Saxony; and though their jealousy of his potential power compelled him to rely largely on his own resources, Henry proved a leader worthy of his commission. He drove back the Danes in the north, subdued the Slavic peoples east of the Elbe, and, in a battle at the field of the Anstrutt in 933, visited a signal defeat on the Hungarians. He was succeeded as king by his even abler son, Otto I (936–973), the architect of the German empire.

Otto's first task was the extension of his authority and the consolidation of his kingdom. His conception of his role seems to have been clear from the beginning: he had himself anointed and crowned king at Charles the Great's former seat, Aachen (Aix-la-Chapelle), by the archbishop of Mainz, the primatial see of Germany. He saw himself, then, as a sacral king, into whose hands God had committed the protection and the nurture of a Christian people. Furthermore, Otto was one of those princes, like Alfred or Edgar in England, who was himself a genuinely devout Christian (there were two canonized saints in his immediate family) and a man to whom the good estate of the churches was a matter of direct and personal concern.

At the same time, Otto was wise enough to see that the resources of the German monastic and episcopal establishments could provide him with a base of economic and military power that would enable him to dominate the restive leaders of the great duchies. From the beginning, this new king made sure that he controlled the lands of the German bishoprics and abbeys by gaining proprietary rights over their territories and by insisting upon the right of investiture—the right, that is, to invest bishops and abbots with the symbols of their office in his character as a sacral king. This meant that he could exercise control over the appointment of the higher clergy throughout his realm, since no bishop or abbot could enter upon the duties of his office without investiture. The proprietary system, and indeed the custom of investiture by lay magnates, existed elsewhere in Europe (the abbey of Cluny was a proprietary church of the pope's), and they were not generally thought inconsistent with the welfare of the church if the rights and duties of the parties were carefully defined. Otto, however, made a deliberate policy of keeping control of the German churches in his own hands, and he filled their high offices, bishoprics and abbacies, with people whom he could trust not only to be faithful to their pastoral duties but also to function as representatives of the royal authority in civil affairs.

It was not long before Otto found himself involved in the affairs of northern Italy. Partly this was the result of his own imperial ambitions, but in equal measure it was the result of the "kingdom" of Italy being inherited by a woman, Adelaide. This event precipitated interventions in Italy by the dukes of Bavaria and Swabia. It also prompted one Berengar to have himself declared king of the Lombards, seize Adelaide, and demand that she marry his son. In such circumstances, Otto had to assert the authority of the German king, and in 951 he invaded Italy, took Adelaide to wife, and—again like Charles the Great—made himself king of the Lombards. He also appeared outside Rome, requesting coronation as emperor from Pope Agapetus II; but the pope—no doubt at the behest of Alberic, who was in full possession of his own proprietary church and wanted no German intrusions upon it—refused. For the next decade, Otto was occupied by a revolt on the part of certain German nobility and by renewed pressure from the Hungarians. He sustained his cause successfully, however, and in the end rallied even the rebels to the battlefield of the Lechfield (near Augsburg), where the Hungarians were finally and completely crushed (955). Otto was acclaimed emperor by his soldiery and universally acknowledged as the savior of Christendom.

However, there was still only one way of becoming emperor, and that was by papal coronation. Accordingly, Otto had to wait for the fulfillment of his ambition. In 962, he was summoned by Alberic's son, Pope John XII, to act, in the fashion of Pepin III and Charles the Great, as the strong right arm of the

Roman church: in this instance, to defend the papal territories against the attacks of Berengar, who had not been idle while Otto was preoccupied by German affairs. In return, he was crowned by John. Otto soon made it clear what he understood his "protectorship" of the Roman church to mean. He confirmed the papacy's possession of its Italian states, but he made the people take an oath of loyalty to himself rather than to the Roman church. He also decreed that no pope could be installed henceforth without an oath of loyalty given to the emperor in person or to his delegates. At this hint that Otto saw Rome and its bishopric as a church over which the emperor had proprietary rights, John repented of his bargain with the German king and called upon his former enemies to help him against Otto. The result of this—from Otto's point of view, traitorous—action was that the emperor summoned a synod in Rome and on December 6, 963, declared John deposed. He replaced him with Leo VIII (a former layperson and a high official in the administration of the Roman church); but no sooner had Otto left Rome than its populace drove Leo out, restored John, and then, when John died in 964, elected Benedict V to succeed him, without the consent of the emperor. Otto returned to Rome, banished Benedict to Germany, and restored Leo VIII, whose successor, John XIII (965–972), was also an imperial nominee.

The dream of a Roman and Christian empire in the West was thus revived in Otto I, who even went so far as to negotiate the marriage of his eldest son to a Byzantine princess, Theophano. The dream, however, proved to be the downfall of his house, as, centuries later, it was to prove the downfall of the German kingdom which he had created. His son, Otto II (973–983), died campaigning in Italy against the Saracens. His grandson, Otto III (983–1002), who came to the throne at the age of three and effectively reigned for only eight years, was something of a prodigy of learning, piety, and idealism. Like his father, however, he deserted Germany for Italy and took up his residence in a palace on the Aventine Hill in Rome, looking forward to a true renewal of the Roman Empire, of which, for him, Charles the Great was the symbol. He again wrested the papacy from the hands of the local Roman nobility, now led by the house of the Crescentii, and in Pope Sylvester II (999–1003), his former tutor (and a man so variously learned that ordinary folk sometimes suspected him of practicing black magic), he gave Rome its most distinguished bishop in many generations—and surely the only one to recognize that the *Donation of Constantine* was a forgery. Yet the foundation of Otto's empire lay in Germany, and his neglect of German affairs meant that his successors, the Bavarian Henry II (1002–1024) and the former Franconian count Conrad II (1024–1039), had to spend their energies reconstructing the bases of royal power in Germany. They, accordingly, left Italy and the papacy largely to their own devices, and the affairs of the Roman church fell under the control of the counts of Tusculum, who in 1033 set upon the papal throne a mere youth, Benedict IX.

The Ottonian empire had restored the Carolingian ideal of a Christian society in which, under the supreme oversight of a divinely anointed ruler, ecclesiastics and ecclesiastical institutions had an organic role to play. It had also, intermittently and tantalizingly, raised the papacy again to the level of an institution of more than local influence and significance. In the end, however, the truth was to become apparent that the German Empire was in fact not Roman or (even in the West) universal and that the focus of a Latin Christian society was to lie elsewhere. Before this could become evident, however, the empire had to revivify the papacy.

Chapter 8

The Greek Church after the Iconoclastic Controversy

THE DIVISIONS BROUGHT ABOUT in the eastern empire by the iconoclastic controversy were not easily healed, and its effects, political, military, and religious, lingered. One such effect is seen in the disaffection of large sections of the army—a stronghold of iconoclasm since the time of Leo III—from rulers who favored the veneration of images. This disaffection, compounded by frequent ineptitude on the part of imperial generals and admirals, meant that under Irene (see IV:3) and her successors Nicephorus I (802–811) and Michael I (811–813), the Byzantine Empire was humbled on almost every front: by the Saracens in Sicily, Crete, and Asia Minor, and in the Balkans by the Bulgars under their war-leader Krum (d. 814). A second effect can be seen in the conflict, which persisted even after the final repudiation of iconoclasm, between a liberal and a rigorist party in the church. The latter represented the values and attitudes of the monastics who had formed the core of the opposition to iconoclasm. They saw the church and its leader, the patriarch of Constantinople, as an authority properly independent of (and in practice often hostile to) the power and policies of the emperor. The liberals, whose representatives on the patriarchal throne tended to be former laypersons and civil servants, were no less devout or orthodox in their convictions, but in practice they took the view that the emperor was the supreme authority in Christendom and that the church was a branch or arm of the Christian society which the emperor, as Christ's representative, headed.

It was in the reign of Emperor Michael III (842–867), called "the Drunkard," that the Byzantine Empire finally repudiated iconoclasm and started out on more than a century and a half of expansion and renewal, which culminated in the brilliant military successes of the emperors John Tzimiskes (969–976) and Basil II (976–1025). Michael himself was a dissolute nonentity, but under the tutelage (and domination) of his mother, Theodora, and then of his able but disreputable uncle, the Caesar Bardas, his reign saw the rebuilding of Byzantine naval and military might. Not only were the Saracen forces of the emir of Melitene signally defeated in 863, but in the same year, having heard that the Bulgar khan Boris was negotiating with the Frankish emperor Louis II for Christian missionaries of the Roman persuasion, Michael descended upon Bulgaria, compelled the conversion and baptism of Boris (who appropriately enough took the baptismal name of Michael), and thus added another nation to the jurisdiction of the patriarch of Constantinople and to the cultural sphere of the eastern empire. Needless to say, this event did not bring military or political conflict in the Balkans to an end, any more than successes on the eastern frontier brought quiet to that region. Byzantium had to struggle unceasingly on both fronts to preserve its existence. Under the Macedonian dynasty, however, which began with Michael's successor, Basil I (867–886), the forces making for recovery and expansion gradually, though with frequent setbacks, triumphed, until by 1025 the empire had recovered significant sections of Syria and Armenia, regained control of southern Italy, Crete, and the Aegean, and asserted its hegemony over the Balkans.

The era which began with the reign of Michael III also saw a significant rebirth of learning and art in the East, thanks in considerable part to the initiative of Emperor Theophilus (829–842), who restored the secular university of Constantinople, placing it under the leadership of a notable scholar, Leo the Mathematician. Among the students who gathered there were Photius, later patriarch of Constantinople, the most distinguished scholar and thinker of his day; and Constantine, who succeeded Photius as professor of philosophy and later, with his brother Methodius, devoted his life to the Christianization of the Slavic peoples of Moravia (see IV:9). This university, which Photius himself reorganized again in 863, became not only a place of training for the lay civil servants of the empire but also a center for the diffusion of Byzantine culture and faith.

Apart from the issue of iconoclasm, the chief religious problem of ninth-century Byzantium was that created by the so-called Paulicians (so named because of their special reverence for the apostle Paul). This group, which by the days of Leo III was firmly rooted in Armenia, its place of origin, and in southern Asia Minor, preached and practiced a form of Christianity reminiscent of Manichaean, gnostic, or Marcionite dualism. Holding that the visible, material cosmos is a creation of the evil power, while the soul stems from the good God, the Paulicians rejected the Old Testament, denied the physical reality of the Incarnation, therefore discounted devotion to Mary as the Mother of God, and strongly condemned the use of any material things in Christian devotion— icons above all. Persecution of the Paulicians began in 813, under Michael I. It was motivated not merely by a distaste for heresy, but also by the fact that the Paulicians, mostly frontier types and very sturdy soldiers, were as often as not allied with the Saracens in the continuous fighting along the empire's south-eastern borders. Persecution, of course, which intensified after the rejection of iconoclasm in 843, merely drove them further into the arms of the empire's enemies; a Paulician army constituted one division of the Arab force defeated by Michael III in 863.

Nevertheless, Byzantium was not destined to be rid of the Paulicians. In 757, Emperor Constantine V had moved Armenian and Syrian settlers to fortresses in Thrace, with the idea of strengthening his defenses against the Bulgarians to the north. Among these settlers were some Paulicians, who apparently spread their teaching in Thrace, whence it reached Bulgaria. Thus, in the second third of the tenth century, Tsar Peter of Bulgaria (927–969) was asking the patriarch of Constantinople how to deal with a body of heretics who derived their teaching from the priest Bogomil (Theophilus) and who clearly reproduced significant elements of the dualism which the Paulicians had espoused. Like the Gnostics before them, these Bogomils, as they were called, were convinced that the visible world was in the grip of evil, and, indeed, that matter is evil in itself. In the name of this doctrine, and preaching a message that called for personal righteousness and protested the iniquities of the social and ecclesiastical orders, the Bogomils forbade to the inner circle of their initiates not only sexual intercourse, but meat and wine as well. Their movement was not extirpated, and it spread ultimately within the Byzantine Empire as well as northward in the Balkan Peninsula. It influenced, or was a source of, the Patarene and Catharist movements in Italy and Languedoc in the twelfth century (see V:3).

In the orthodox church itself, the era of the Macedonian dynasty saw the beginnings of a theological movement which drew for its inspiration on the traditions and practice of monastic spirituality. This movement—called, in its developed form, Hesychasm (from the Greek *hēsuchos*, "quiet")—understood theology in its narrow and proper sense, as a discipline concerned with the knowledge of God. Such knowledge, however, it took to be essentially a matter of practice rather than of mere theory: the practice of a love for God which was guided by orthodox faith, sacramental worship, and exact observance of the Lord's commandments. The earliest notable leader of this movement was Simeon (949–1022), abbot of the Constantinopolitan monastery of St. Mamas, who stood in the mystical tradition of teachers like Maximus the Confessor (see III:11) and John Climacus (d. 649), abbot of the monastery of Mount Sinai and author of the influential *Ladder of Paradise*. For Simeon, theology meant above all the knowledge of God that monks attain when they are transformed and divinized through the vision of the divine light which shone in the transfigured Jesus.

Such knowledge, however, transcends anything verbal or conceptual, just as it is achieved, not by reasoning, but by moral and devotional practice. For Simeon, therefore, God is not so much known as seen, felt, and experienced through the living out of the orthodox faith. As thus apprehended, however, God is seen to be, in himself, beyond comprehension—infinite and intrinsically unknowable in his essence, as the Cappadocian fathers had taught (see III:4). What the mystic was caught up in, as Simeon understood it, was not the divine essence but the "light," the divine activity of self-communication, which immediately flowed from God's being and which was itself uncreated. The development of this teaching (which was refined further in the writings of Gregory of Palamas in the fourteenth century) won for Simeon the title of "the New Theologian," which in effect ranked him as second only to the one who was called "theologian" par excellence, Gregory of Nazianzus (see III:4). Ultimately, this "apophatic" or "negative" theology, which grew out of devotional and mystical experience and which differentiated radically between the divine being and the divine energies ("light"), was to stand as the distinguishing mark of a Greek and eastern as opposed to a Latin and western theology.

Chapter 9

Christian Expansion in the Early Middle Ages

THE NINTH, TENTH, AND ELEVENTH CENTURIES were the era during which the Christianity of Britain, of the Frankish kingdom, and of Byzantium spread to encompass not only the Northmen of Scandinavia but also the predominantly Slavic peoples of central Europe and the Balkan peninsula. In some cases, this expansion was the result of military conquest. In almost all cases, it went hand in hand with the cultural and political reconstitution of societies which had formerly been tribal in structure and, occasionally, nomadic in life style. Almost invariably, it relied on the conversion and co-operation of rulers who supported —sometimes by rather forceful means—the work of Christian missionaries among their peoples. Thus, the substantive Christianization of a people tended to follow rather than to precede its "conversion."

The diffusion of Christianity among the peoples of the Balkans and in the territories along the Danube River to the east and south of Bavaria was complicated by rivalry among German, Byzantine, and papal interests. Eastern Orthodoxy prevailed in Greece, Macedonia, and Thrace. These regions had been heavily settled by pagan Slavs as a result of the migrations and invasions of the sixth and seventh centuries (a period which also saw the appearance of a Bulgarian kingdom that straddled the Danube north of Constantinople). Their gradual Christianization occurred as a result of the reassertion of Byzantine political control, which began, apparently, under Emperor Nicephorus I (802–811). When, in the reign of the founder of the Macedonian dynasty, Basil I (867–886), Serbia also came under Byzantine domination, its ruler accepted Greek missionaries and co-operated in the Christianization of his people. The expansion of Greek Christianity from Byzantium was paralleled in the north by the spread of Latin Christianity from Bavaria under the aegis of Frankish power. This effort had its centers in the archiepiscopal sees of Salzburg and Aquileia and extended into Carinthia and Croatia, which by the beginning of the tenth century, despite strong Byzantine influence, had cast its lot with Latin Christianity.

The great missionary achievement of the ninth century, however, was the conversion to Christianity of the Bulgarian and Moravian kingdoms—the latter with its center north of the Danube along the course of the Morava River, in what is now Czechoslovakia. Both of these kingdoms originally accepted Christianity as the result of pressure from an external power. In the case of Bulgaria, as we have seen, this pressure took the form of a Byzantine invasion and the more or less forcible baptism of Tsar Boris (see IV:8). In the case of Moravia, the pressure came from the Frankish kingdom of Louis the German (see IV:6), who in 846 invaded Moravia and set over it as "duke" the prince Rastislav, who was, or shortly became, a Christian. Like Boris (who sent his son Symeon to Constantinople to be educated and ended his life as a monk), Rastislav was entirely serious in his acceptance of Christianity and co-operated with missionaries from Germany and perhaps Italy in the conversion of his people. Also like Boris, however, Rastislav wanted his Christian kingdom to be independent of foreign political and ecclesiastical domination—particularly since, during much of his reign, he was at war with his German benefactors. In order to achieve this end, both monarchs made use of the rivalry among Roman, German, and Byzantine authorities.

The upshot of this situation was that Boris began negotiations with Pope Nicholas I (see IV:6) to obtain an independent head of the Bulgarian church, a course of action that led the Byzantines to consecrate (in 870) an archbishop for Bulgaria as a way of keeping that nation within the sphere of Eastern Orthodoxy. At almost the same time, Rastislav, fearful of German domination, wrote to Emperor Michael III for missionaries from Byzantium. The patriarch Photius, quick to seize an opportunity, dispatched the two brothers Constantine (or Cyril, to use the name he took when, in 868, he became a monk in Rome) and

Methodius—both learned representatives of Greek faith and culture, and both, as natives of Thessalonika, speakers of Slavonic. It was the special contribution of these two missionaries that they began the process of translating the Christian Scriptures and liturgical books into Slavonic, for which Constantine, indeed, devised the first alphabet of that language—an enterprise that laid the foundations of a Slavonic Christian culture in the Balkans and in Russia as well. The project of developing a vernacular version of the Scriptures and the liturgy met with strong, persistent opposition from German missionaries in Moravia, who were not accustomed to any liturgical language save Latin. Constantine and Methodius therefore appealed to the pope against their German colleagues, and they received a warm welcome in Rome. There Constantine died (869), but Methodius was returned to Moravia as an archbishop with permission to continue the use of Slavonic (though not to exclude that of Latin). The liturgical use of Slavonic was eventually forbidden by the papacy, though only after Methodius's death (885?), and much of the brothers' work was brought to nothing when, after 895, the Hungarian or Magyar invasions established a new pagan kingdom in Slovakia, Pannonia, and Transylvania. Nevertheless, Moravian Christianity penetrated Bohemia to its immediate north, and the disciples of Cyril and Methodius carried their Slavonic Scriptures and liturgy to Bulgaria and other regions of the Balkans.

Completion of the work of Cyril and Methodius, which brought Hungary as well as the Moravian heartland within the sphere of Latin Christendom, thus had to wait until well after the definitive defeat of the Magyars by Otto I in 955. The work of missionaries in Hungary began in the last quarter of the tenth century, under the nation's first monarch, Geisa. It was, however, only under his son, St. Stephen (997–1038), who became the patron saint of Hungary and who himself preached among his people, that Christian faith was settled in Hungary, with the assistance of Slavic missionaries from Poland and Bohemia as well as that of Germans from the empire of Otto III.

Bohemian and Polish Christianity were established during roughly the same period as that of Hungary. Bohemia, home of the Czechs, was the area watered by the Moldau River between the Elbe and the Danube and was cut off from Germany both to the west and the north by minor mountain ranges. It had been a part of the greater Moravian kingdom in the ninth century and thus had felt the influence of the Slavonic-speaking mission of Constantine and Methodius, but paganism, no doubt increasingly associated with anti-German feeling, remained strong. King Wenceslas (ca. 924–929), an ally of the Saxon king Henry I and a leader in the cause of Christianization, was assassinated after a short reign. It was only after Otto I had brought Bohemia within the sphere of German power that Duke Boleslav II (967–999) was able effectively to establish Christianity and to found the see of Prague, whose second bishop, Adalbert (Vojtěch), was himself a Czech and eventually worked as a missionary among the Poles. Poland—roughly the area south of Pomerania between the

Oder and Vistula rivers—also became, after 965, a tributary of the Saxon empire of Otto I, and with that event began the process of its conversion. Under Boleslaus I (992–1025), who expanded Polish territories at the expense of Russia, Germany, and Hungary and took the title of king, Christianization progressed and Poland received an archiepiscopal see (Gniezno), which marked it out as an independent ecclesiastical province under Rome.

The most notable extension of Byzantine Christianity during the tenth and early eleventh centuries came about with the conversion of the Russian nation, centered in the principality of Kiev. Predominantly Slavic in make-up, the principality was nevertheless ruled by descendants of Swedish Vikings (called Varangi and Rus), who in the ninth century had taken control of the river system that ran from the Baltic to the Black Sea. Engaged in regular trade (and frequent hostilities) with Constantinople after the middle of the ninth century, the Varangi were in constant contact with Byzantium and indeed, after 911, an elite contingent of the imperial guard was drawn from their ranks. It seems likely that Greek missionaries were active in the Russian principality from the time of the patriarch Photius, so that by the middle of the tenth century there were Christians as well as non-Christians in Kiev; Olga, the wife of the ruling prince, Igor (913–945), was herself a believer. Her grandson Vladimir I (980–1015), having elected to receive baptism, took the initiative in establishing churches and monasteries and extending Orthodox Christianity from Kiev into the northern sector of his principality, whose center was at Novgorod. During his time and that of his son Yaroslav, the foundations of the Russian church and episcopate were firmly laid.

It was not until the beginning of the eleventh century that Christianity was adopted by the Norse peoples in the kingdoms of their Scandinavian homeland. To be sure, Alfred the Great in England had exacted conversion and baptism from the Danish king Guthrum as one condition of the creation of the Danelaw, and the duchy of Normandy in France was similarly Christianized as a result of Duke Rollo's treaty with Charles the Simple (911). The processes of conversion thus begun, however, had little effect in Scandinavia, though there was no want of missionary effort in that region. As early as the reign of Louis the Pious, efforts were made to bring Christianity to Denmark and Sweden—particularly to the former, where Harald, a contender for the Danish throne, sought Carolingian support for his claims and so accepted baptism in 826. In view of the prospect thus opened, Anskar (Ansgarius, d. 865), a Flemish monk originally from the monastery at Corbie, was appointed to accompany Harald to the territories at the base of the Jutland Peninsula which the latter controlled. Shortly thereafter, Anskar was also deputed to answer a call for missionaries from Sweden, and in 831 Emperor Louis established for him an archiepiscopal see at Hamburg, where he and his successors were to have a special responsibility as papal legates for the peoples of Scandinavia and the north of Germany.

Anskar's mission was not without results. At the time of his death, there were Christian believers and priests in both Denmark and Sweden. During the era of the decline of Carolingian power, however, and of the heaviest Viking assaults on Europe and the British Isles, the mission languished. By the early tenth century, it had vanished in Sweden. Under the first Saxon emperors, however—Henry the Fowler and Otto I—the new power and prestige of Frankish Christendom served to reverse the tide. King Harald Bluetooth of Denmark (d. ca. 986) was baptized, worked for the conversion of his people, and admitted Christian bishops to his realm. His son Sweyn (d. 1014), who spent much of his energy in a new attempt to conquer England, was and remained a pagan, but Sweyn's son, Canute—king of both England and Denmark from 1014 until his death in 1035—settled Christianity in his native land, using missionaries from both Germany and England.

If the conversion of Denmark owed most to the influence of the Frankish and Saxon kingdoms and to the missionary efforts of the archbishops of Hamburg, the conversion of Norway, which went on during roughly the same period, was conducted in the shadow of the English church. The second king of a united Norway, Haakon the Good (935-961), had been raised as a youth at the English court, and it was he who introduced Christianity, along with English clergy, to his realm. The missionary effort was continued, with some assistance from Harald Bluetooth, who for a time was overlord of Norway; but the pagan jarls, who no doubt associated the cause of Christianity with that of a central royal authority, consistently opposed the new religion. The final success of the church in Norway came in the reign of Olaf Tryggvesson, a proper Viking who was raised in Russia and converted by a Christian ascetic in the Scilly Islands while engaged in one of his numerous raids on England. Made king of Norway in 995, he set about the conversion of his people vigorously, firmly, and indeed violently. His death in battle in 1000 was followed by a pagan reaction, but his work was effectively completed by Olaf Haraldsson (St. Olaf of Norway, 1015-1028), again with the assistance of English clergy, and not without the use of force. Not until the twelfth century, however, did Norway become an independent province of the church under the pope, with its archiepiscopal see at Lund.

The Christianization of Sweden is customarily attributed to King Olaf Skötkonung (994-1024), a contemporary of the Norwegian Tryggvesson and his successors. Prior to his time, Christianity had reappeared in Sweden, and missionaries dispatched from both northern Germany and England (by way of Norway) had worked there. Olaf, however, while prevented from destroying the great pagan shrine at Uppsala, established the faith in the southwest of his kingdom. Nevertheless, paganism remained strong, and missionary work, punctuated by occasional presecutions of Christians, had to continue. Sweden became thoroughly Christianized only in the twelfth century, the last nation to be brought into the Frankish-Byzantine Christendom of Europe.

Chapter 10

The Reforming Papacy

THE IMPERIAL SUCCESSORS of Otto III—Henry II and the founder of the so-called Salian line, Conrad II—had by no means forgotten their role as divinely anointed rulers of the Latin Christian world and so as protectors of the church. Neither did they cease to see themselves as having the right and the responsibility of appointing and investing bishops and abbots in order to assure both the spiritual welfare of the people and the political stability of their kingdom, which continued to depend on royal proprietorship of ecclesiastical lands. Emperor Henry II styled himself "servant of the servants of Christ and emperor of the Romans in accordance with the will of God and of our Savior and Liberator"; he was not only a devout man, but also, as befitted one whose role was quasi-priestly as well as royal, a man dedicated to the reform of monastic and ecclesiastical institutions.

Reform, indeed, was in the air at the turn of the eleventh century, in spite of the fact that the obvious and shocking scandals of the late Carolingian era had been largely corrected. The ideals of Cluny continued to spread. In England, Dunstan's reforms had been initiated. In Lorraine, the work of men like the canonist Burchard, bishop of Worms (1000–1025), showed an overriding concern for the right ordering of the church and of the lives of its pastors. In Italy, this was the era of St. Romuald (950–1027), a native of Ravenna who entered the monastic life there but resigned his abbacy to take up the life of a hermit and eventually became the founder of an order—called Camaldolese, after its principal center near Arezzo—which stressed withdrawal from the world and the solitary life. Everywhere there was an awakening to the need for discipline, simplicity of life, and a spirit of single-hearted dedication in the priesthood; clerical worldliness and enslavement to secular interests were rebuked. In particular, two systematic evils were identified as roots of the corruption of the priestly order. One was simony, which, narrowly defined, meant the practice of offering or requiring payment in some form for ecclesiastical and pastoral office.[1]

[1] See Acts 5:18.

The other was the custom of clerical marriage or concubinage, which had long been forbidden by the canons of the western church, for it not only seemed inconsistent with the sacral character of the clerical calling but also appeared to bind those who practiced it to interests and needs inconsistent with a spirit of single-minded dedication.

If there was one institution that had not yet been visibly touched by the spirit of reform, it was the papacy. The fundamental reason for this was that in practice, if not in principle, the papacy in the early eleventh century was a creature of the competing local factions in Roman and Italian politics—and none of the factions seemed to share the commitment of the German emperors to nourishing and sustaining the spiritual mission of the priesthood. After the days of Otto I, to be sure, no pope entered upon his office without the consent of the emperor and no pope was in a position to oppose imperial interest or policy. On the other hand, neither Henry II nor Conrad II chose very often to make the effort required to exercise direct control over their unruly Italian domains; and in any case, their authority, perceived as German rather than Roman, was unpopular in Italy. Thus, the popes Benedict VIII (1012–1024) and John XIX (1024–1032) were both sons of Gregory, count of Tusculum, and, while pursuing policies not displeasing to the emperors, they contrived to consolidate the control of their family over Rome and in the process to weaken the faction of the Crescentii, their local opponents.

In the reign of Emperor Henry III (1039–1056)—a man distinguished by his piety, his high sense of spiritual calling, and his dedication to the program of reform in the church—a decisive crisis arose for the papacy. Benedict IX, a nephew of the two preceding popes, had been elected bishop of Rome in 1032 as a very young man. In the course of his pontificate he grew neither in grace nor in wisdom, and his lasciviousness and arbitrary cruelty eventually produced, in 1044, a rebellion at Rome which succeeded, for a brief time, in placing one Sylvester III (1045) on the papal throne. Restored by his brothers, Benedict nevertheless decided that the papacy was not for him. For the promise of a suitable pension, therefore, and with a prospect of marriage, he agreed to abdicate in favor of his godfather, Gratian, the pastor of the Church of St. John before the Lateran Gate, who succeeded him as pope with the title of Gregory VI (1045–1046). Whatever Gregory's virtues, however—and his accession was greeted with enthusiasm by clergy of a reforming bent—he lacked the imperial imprimatur.

When Henry III came to Italy in the autumn of 1046 for his imperial coronation and discovered the complexity of the situation at Rome, he ordered a synod to be convoked at Sutri so that the case might be adjudged. What Henry did was to imitate the action of Otto I in 963. He declared not only Benedict IX and Sylvester III but also Gregory VI deposed, and after this clean sweep he appointed a German, the bishop of Bamberg, as Pope Clement II (1046–1047). Clement in turn crowned Henry as emperor. Together with the emperor, he began an effort to stem the tide of simony in the church—but he died after only nine months. In Henry's absence, the Tusculan house, probably with the assistance of other Italian magnates, attempted to restore Benedict IX; imperial authority, however, imposed another German pope, Damasus II (1048), who died only twenty-three days after assuming office.

In the end, however, Henry III had his way. Upon the death of Damasus, at a synod in Worms, the emperor appointed yet a third German as pope: Bruno, bishop of Toul, an administrator and diplomat of distinction and a firm advocate of the new spirit of reform, who became Pope Leo IX (1049–1054). With Leo's pontificate, a new papacy emerges on the stage of European history. The immediate reason for this change lies in Leo's entire dedication to reforming the church by disciplining and purifying its priesthood, in which he had the cordial co-operation of Henry III. To carry this project out, however, Leo had actively to assert and enforce the authority of the papal office; and that in turn meant both that there had to be a serious reappropriation of the ideology that had traditionally undergirded papal authority and that the popes had to make themselves independent of party interests at Rome and in Italy by regaining political control of the States of the Church. It is not surprising, therefore, that a compilation of canon law made at Rome in Leo's time should show a remarkable interest in the Roman primacy and attest the currency of the sorts of ideas originally set out in the *Pseudo-Isidorian Decretals*. Neither is it odd to find Leo himself accepting from the emperor political suzerainty over Benevento (in return for the surrender of papal temporal rights over the bishopric of Bamberg) and then joining in a war against the Norman adventurers who were extending their domain in southern Italy. The central issue in each case was that of the authority and independence of the Roman see, which were necessary preconditions of the pope's ability to pursue the cause of reform.

One of the first and, in its effects, most far-reaching steps which Leo took was to import into the ranks of the "cardinal" clergy of the church of Rome certain persons who, though they belonged originally to foreign ecclesiastical jurisdictions, shared his general aims and could serve him with distinction as advisors and assistants. "Cardinals" were clergy of the Roman diocese who belonged to the immediate staff of the bishop: the priests who were pastors of the papal or "titular" churches; the seven deacons who were in charge of the administrative regions of the diocese; and (since the eighth century) the so-called "suburbicarian" bishops—the pope's episcopal assistants. Among those whom Leo introduced to their ranks were men whose work as theorists, administrators, and legates was to determine the course and character of the papal establishment for centuries to come. There was in the first place Humbert, a monk, a scholar, and a dialectician of blunt manner, from the monastery of Moyenmoutier in Lorraine. In 1050, Leo appointed him cardinal bishop of Silva Candida, and in him the new papacy found its most extreme adversary of what, for him, was the "heresy" of simony. Others were Hugh Candidus ("the White"), created cardinal priest of St. Clement, who became the most effective of the pope's representatives on legatine missions; the papal chancellor, Udo of Toul; and, not least, the former chaplain of Pope Gregory VI, a Tuscan named Hildebrand, whom Leo made administrator of the papal estates and who was later to become the revolutionary Pope Gregory VII. And in the background of Leo's pontificate—though he did not become associated with the administration of the Roman church until 1057, when he was made cardinal bishop of Ostia—was the prophetic figure of St. Peter Damian (1007–1072), prior of a monastic house at Ponte Avella, a theologian and an ascetic in the Camaldolese tradition, whose eloquent opposition to clerical marriage, to simony, and, in general, to the church's conformity to the world gave a continuing impetus to reformist zeal.

With such assistants, Leo IX set about the business of carrying his message to the churches beyond Rome. At a synod held in the Lateran in April 1049, Leo made his program clear. Under pain of papal anathema, clergy, whether bishops or others, were forbidden to accept money for ordinations, installations in office, consecrations of churches, and the like. Any ordained person who had accepted ordination from a bishop whom he knew to practice simony was required to perform extensive penance, and the simoniac bishop himself was to suffer deposition from his office. Leo did not merely formulate such rules; he applied them—frequently in person. By October 1049, he had convoked a synod at Reims, where, in the presence of the relics of St. Remigius and of crowds of common people who had come to see the successor of Peter, he demanded an accounting of the bishops present and straightforwardly deposed (or accepted the resignations of) those who had practiced simony. A similar synod was held in the same year at Mainz, in the presence of Henry III, where simony and clerical marriage alike were condemned. Similar trips in later years were taken through southern and northern Italy and through other sections of Germany. Much was accomplished by these journeys of Leo's and by those of his legates. Not only was the program of reform advanced. Not only was leadership in the cause of reform in effect snatched from the hands of the emperor. Not only did Leo show himself, in dealing with doctrinal issues (and notably with the eucharistic teaching of Berengarius of Tours, who had taken a stand in the tradition of Ratramnus), to be a teacher and judge of faith as well as of morals. Of equal importance was the fact that the pope was seen to be the effective leader and administrator of the churches, instead of a somewhat distant symbol of apostolic power and tradition.

It was this concern for the authority of the Roman see, however, which ultimately brought Leo's career to a tragic close and led to what has often been regarded as the final and irrevocable step in the separation of Greek and Latin Christianity. Relations between Rome and Constantinople had been touchy since at least the time of Nicholas I and Photius. Quite apart from the jealousy which had long existed between the two patriarchates, differences of religious custom, culture, and political allegiance tended to drive them far apart. In Leo's day, moreover, the patriarch of Constantinople was Michael Cerularius (1043–1048), a man determined not only to assert the authority of his see over the other eastern patriarchates but also to establish its equality and independence in relation to Rome. This project was threatened, however, by the unusual phenomenon of an alliance between Henry III and the pope on the one hand, and Emperor Constantine IX (1042–1055) on the other—a military alliance occasioned by the threat of the Norman invaders in southern Italy to papal and Byzantine territories alike. In the face of this reconciliation, Constantine demanded that Cerularius acknowledge the authority of Rome by writing—as he had deliberately failed to do on his accession—the traditional "synodical letter" to the pope, a letter which, by age-old custom, informed the bishop of Rome, the senior patriarch, of an election to the see of Constantinople and assured him of the new incumbent's orthodox faith.

Such a step Cerularius was not prepared to take. Instead, his first response was to close all churches of the Latin rite in Constantinople, no doubt hoping that this action would bring the new alliance to naught. Then, in 1053, he persuaded Leo of Ochrida, the Bulgarian metropolitan, to address a letter to the western churches which was little less than a denunciation of "Frankish" Christianity for a series of illicit practices which, Leo averred, prevented any union of the two churches—among them the use of unleavened bread at the eucharist and the custom of fasting on Saturdays. The original papal reply, written in some heat by Humbert of Silva Candida, set out in the most explicit terms the traditional claims of the Roman church as they had long ago been defined in the *Donation of Constantine* but its arrival seems to have been much delayed. Pope Leo IX, in the meantime, was defeated and captured at Civitate by the Normans in 1053. In the aftermath of this Norman triumph, which put the Byzantine territories in Italy in even graver danger, the authorities at Constantinople were not inclined to relinquish their alliance with the "Franks." Both Constantine and Cerularius wrote to the pope in a tone much less strident that that which had marked Leo of Ochrida's manifesto. Pope Leo accordingly sent a delegation to Constantinople—Humbert, Frederick of Lorraine, and Peter, the archbishop of Amalfi—to open conversations that would lead to union. Humbert, however, who headed the delegation, had little of the diplomat about him, and even the papal letter which he bore (and which he had written) was uncompromising in its tone. Cerularius, therefore, in spite of the emperor's desire for conciliation, chose in effect to ignore the legates and to question their credentials—a course which seemed the more plausible with the sudden announcement of the death of Leo IX. Humbert and his colleagues left Constantinople, but not before, on July 16, 1054, they had gone to the Church of the Holy Wisdom, made a public protest against the behavior of Cerularius, and then laid upon the altar a sentence of excommunication against him, which ranked him "with the devil and his angels" and ended with a triple "Amen." This action of the legates was received with satisfaction in the West, and Cerularius seems to have thought that he had got what he wanted. The schism thus formally initiated has not been healed to this day.

Chapter 11

From Reform to Revolution

T HE DEATH OF LEO IX IN 1054 created no problem for the new papal program. Emperor Henry III promptly appointed another German and another reformer to the papal throne: Gebhardt, bishop of Eichstadt, who took the title of Victor II (1055–1057). It looked as though the policies of Leo IX were to be continued without question or interruption. What did create a crisis, however, was the unexpected death of Henry III himself (1056), which placed on the German throne his six-year-old son, Henry IV, under the regency of his mother, the empress Agnes. This event, which inevitably meant a relaxation of imperial leadership in Italian and Roman affairs, was followed soon after by the death of the pope; and the question clearly was that of who, in this situation of uncertainty, was to control the appointment of the next pope.

As it turned out, the reformers in the papal curia were able to contrive the election of one of their own number, Frederick of Lorraine, as Pope Stephen IX (1057–1058). Frederick, as chance would have it, was the brother of Duke Godfrey of Lorraine, who, by his marriage to Countess Beatrice of Tuscany, had become the dominant power in northern Italy. This arrangement, which won imperial approval even though the election had been conducted without the customary consultation of the German king, satisfied both local and Italian interests as well as those of the reforming party among the cardinals. It also called attention, however, to the practical problems created by the dependence of the church on lay authorities for the provision of its leadership—a dependence which in any case was not consonant in principle with the freedom and autonomy which the priesthood required to carry out its duties.

It was under Stephen IX that Humbert of Silva Candida published a work whose teaching was to alter the whole emphasis and complexion of the reform movement: his *Three Books against the Simoniacs*. In part, this work was a reasoned development of the (by now) traditional polemic against simony, which had long been associated in the reformers' minds with their concerns for the celibacy of clergy and the Roman primacy. In his third book, however, Humbert made a systematic assault on the role of lay authorities in the affairs of the priesthood, an assault which did not stop short of the role of king or emperor. To him, there was no question of a sacred and quasi-priestly character inhering in the anointed monarch. The king was (as Ambrose, centuries before, had insisted to Theodosius the Great) simply a layperson whose authority was limited to secular affairs. When, therefore, lay magnates of any rank whatever made ecclesiastical synods the instruments of their will; or, in appointing bishops on their own authority, violated the ancient principle of the "canonical election" of bishops by clergy and people; or presumed, by investing a bishop with the symbols of ring and staff, actually to confer episcopal rank in the church—such persons were violating the rights of the priesthood, acting beyond their competence, and contravening the divinely given order of the church (which, in the early medieval world, simply meant the order of society as a whole). Humbert went so far as to argue that bishops who received their office by this means "are not to be regarded as bishops, for the manner of their appointment is upside down."[1] In this polemic against "lay investiture," Humbert was merely taking to its logical conclusion the ideal of the purification of the priesthood from involvement in, and domination by, secular interests, and to that extent his idea that lay investiture is a form of simony is understandable. Moreover, there had been earlier anticipations of his position (though he did not seem aware of them). Taken as seriously as Humbert took it, however, that position amounted to an attack on the whole social and political order of the early middle ages—in particular, on the foundations of imperial power in Germany. A program for the moral and spiritual reform of the church had become a demand for revolutionary change in the very structures of medieval society.

Not everyone agreed with Humbert's ideas. Peter Damian in particular thought that the program of reform could be carried out without a systematic attack on lay investiture. The preponderance of opinion in papal circles, however, was in Humbert's favor, and this fact soon became evident. In 1058, Stephen IX died. The Roman nobility quickly stepped in and, within a week, had contrived the election of their own candidate, Benedict X. The cardinals of the reformist party were compelled to flee Rome. Their situation was saved, however, by the leadership of Hildebrand, who rallied a part of the Roman populace and the power of Godfrey of Tuscany to the cause of Gerhard, the bishop of Florence. The consent of Empress Agnes was obtained for Gerhard's appointment, and he was accordingly elected pope at Siena. With the title Nicholas II (1058–1061), he was installed at Rome, with the support of Duke

---

[1] B. Tierney, ed., *The Crisis of Church and State, 1050–1300* (Englewood Cliffs, N.J., 1964), p. 40.

Godfrey's troops. Benedict X's election was declared uncanonical. He was confined at the church of St. Agnes in Rome, where he died some time after 1073.

Under Nicholas, the program implied in Humbert's attack on lay investiture was quickly put into law, and the papacy sought to consolidate its political independence of German, Roman, and Italian rulers alike. The first and most striking step came at the Roman synod of 1059, which passed a decree on papal elections—a decree which, though with significant modifications, governs the selection of popes to this day. In effect, what this new constitution did was to put the election of a pope into the hands of the cardinal clergy. The suburbicarian bishops were to select a candidate and then seek the advice of the cardinal priests and deacons. When a name had been agreed upon in this manner, it was submitted to the other clergy and the people, but only for their acclamation. No more than rhetorical provision was made for any imperial role, in spite of precedents reaching back to the age of Charles the Great. Having in this fashion taken a stand against lay interference in the Roman bishop's election, the same synod went on to rule out all lay investiture under any circumstances. Though no attempt was in fact made to apply or enforce this canon during Nicholas's pontificate, the papacy's stance was now clear.

How, though, were the popes to guarantee that the new process for papal elections would be carried out without external interference? Here Nicholas came up with an ingenious solution to a difficult problem. The papacy entered into an alliance with the Norman leader Robert Guiscard, who was in possession of significant tracts of southern Italy and was eager to gain papal recognition of his status. Guiscard accepted his holdings as a fief from the church of Rome and the pope, pledging, in return for his title as duke of Apulia and Calabria, to protect the pope "in holding and acquiring the temporalities and possessions of St. Peter everywhere and against all men," and, above all, to "assist in the election and consecration of a pope to the honor of St. Peter according to the advice of the leading cardinals and of the Roman clergy and people."[2] There was, in other words, to be a Norman army to guarantee that the election decree of 1059 would be carried out, and this would be the army, not of an external power, but of a vassal of the pope. This arrangement was given added strength by Nicholas's continuing alliance with the rulers of Tuscany, as well as by his close and sympathetic connection—established through the mediation of St. Peter Damian and Bishop Anselm of Lucca—with the popular party in Lombardy known as the Pataria, a movement of democratic dissent which opposed the conservative higher clergy of the region and the German establishment which they represented.

The death of Nicholas II in 1061 (the year which also saw the death of Humbert of Silva Candida) imperiled both his constitutional decree and his political arrangements. Under the leadership of Hildebrand, Bishop Anselm of

[2] Ibid., p. 44.

Lucca was elected as Pope Alexander II (1061–1073). The opponents of the new papal order, however, particularly the German and Lombard bishops, contrived a council at Basel in 1061, where Agnes, the empress-regent, was persuaded to appoint Caldalus of Parma as pope, with the title Honorius II. What saved the day for Alexander was a revolution in Germany which placed the guardianship of young King Henry in the hands of Anno, the archbishop of Cologne. Wishing to stand well with the reformist party, Anno took the side of Alexander, who was finally confirmed in his office by a synod at Mantua in 1064. A weak and divided leadership in Germany had again kept the Roman reformers in office.

No doubt with Hildebrand's counsel, Alexander II, following in the footsteps of Leo IX, made papal authority felt in Europe. Anno of Cologne himself, and Siegfried of Mainz, two of the most powerful prelates in Germany, were compelled to do penance for simony. Alexander licensed the expedition of William the Conqueror that resulted in the Norman conquest of England in 1066, and he further aided William's plans by establishing Norman bishops in the principal English sees. Papal favor toward the Normans was again manifested in Alexander's sanctioning of the efforts of the Norman leaders in southern Italy to recapture Sicily from the Saracens.

In the meanwhile, Henry IV, king of Germany, came of age (1065) and soon revealed himself to be one of the most resourceful of German rulers. That he had the opportunity to do so, however, was owed in large part to the loyalty of the German bishops, whose resources were, for the nine years of his minority, the principal force which stood against the divisive ambitions of the lay nobility. Once enthroned in his own right, Henry lost little time in establishing his power, both against the nobility and against the free peasantry of the Saxon duchy, control of which he regarded as essential to the stability of the monarchy. This power continued, as for all the German emperors since Otto I, to rest on royal control of ecclesiastical appointments and lands.

It was inevitable, then, that the papal policy regarding lay investiture should clash with essential interests and settled policies of the German king—and, for that matter, of most lay rulers in Europe. The actual occasion for conflict turned out to be a disputed succession to the archbishopric of Milan, which was not only a see of historic eminence in the church but also, by now, an extensive feudal holding which controlled access to the principal passes of the Alps. To this see Henry IV appointed Godfrey of Castiglione, a man whom Pope Alexander had already charged with simony. The pope refused to recognize Godfrey and instead acknowledged the candidate of the Milanese Pataria, Atto, as the rightful archbishop. King Henry nevertheless secured Godfrey's consecration to the post in 1073, and very shortly thereafter Alexander II died, leaving the problem to his successor, Hildebrand, who was enthroned almost in spite of himself by popular acclaim and took, in memory of his long-dead patron Gregory VI, the title Gregory VII.

Chapter 12

Hildebrand and Henry IV

ONE OF THE LAST of Leo IX's reformer-cardinals to survive, Hildebrand had, since at least the time of Pope Nicholas II, been the central figure among the papal counselors. He was not only single-minded in his devotion to the cause of reform, but as a Roman bred if not born he was equally devoted to the honor of the city and church which belonged to the apostle Peter, and therefore to the authority of the papal office. From Peter Damian, moreover, and perhaps from the letters of Gregory the Great, Hildebrand had learned that the proper constituency of the apostolic see was not the rulers and the powerful of this world (St. Augustine, after all, had traced the genealogy of royal power back to Cain the murderer), but the *pauperes Christi,* "Christ's poor ones," the downtrodden; his sympathy with the Pataria, the aspiring underprivileged, of the growing Lombard cities no doubt stemmed from this conviction. His program, therefore, was a radical and revolutionary one from the start, and like most persons of his single-minded, not to say fanatical, sort, he inspired distrust as well as admiration. Peter Damian, who had opposed Cardinal Humbert's strictures on lay investiture, is said to have described Hildebrand as a "holy Satan," while Abbot Hugh the Great of Cluny thought him an arrogant and consumingly ambitious person. But Hildebrand believed he was contending for the honor of Christ and St. Peter and for the creation of a truly Christian society.

There can be no doubt what the foundation of such a society had, in his mind, to be: it was that universal sovereignty which belonged solely to the papal office. The pope, and not the emperor, was the true vicar of Christ. In the *Dictatus Papae,* a collection of brief propositions that summarized the results of recent Roman researches into the tradition of canon law, Gregory's principles on this score were made clear: "That the Roman Church was founded by God alone." "That the Roman pontiff alone can with right be called universal." "That he alone can depose or reinstate bishops." "That he alone may use imperial insignia" (since he alone is the true successor of Constantine). "That it may be permitted him to depose Emperors." "That he himself may be judged of no one." "That he may absolve subjects from their fealty to wicked men."[1] Needless to say, these propositions were not inventions of Gregory's; the substance of the *Dictatus Papae* can be found in the *Donation of Constantine* and the *Pseudo-Isidorian Decretals*. What was new here was the pope's insistence upon these principles as a practical program which Gregory and his successors were to put into effect.

The inevitable confrontation between the new pope and Henry IV was delayed until 1075, for it was not until June of that year that Henry had consolidated the bases of his power in Germany. The pope, however, had already made his stance plain by renewing, in a Roman synod held at Easter in 1075, the absolute prohibition of lay investiture. When, therefore, the emperor once again made an appointment to the archbishopric of Milan, Gregory answered immediately with a stern letter of rebuke. Henry IV's reply to this letter was to summon a council at Worms (January 1076), where a large portion of the German bishops joined in a denunciation of Hildebrand and a rejection of his authority as pope. In this action, they were soon supported by the Lombard bishops.

Gregory VII's reply was a thunderbolt. At the Roman synod of February 22, 1076, he excommunicated Henry, forbade him to exercise royal authority in Germany and Italy, and released all Henry's subjects from their oaths of allegiance. The king answered with defiance, in a fiery letter which called Hildebrand "now no pope, but a false monk" and demanded that he relinquish his office, to make room for "another who will not cloak violence with religion" or dishonor one who had been "anointed to kingship" by God.[2]

In the end, however, Henry could not sustain his opposition, for the pope's decree had at once abashed the German bishops and given license for rebellion to the king's enemies in Germany. An assembly of lay nobility held in October 1076 declared that unless released from excommunication within a year, Henry would be deposed. It also invited the pope to an assembly at Augsburg in February 1077, where the whole German religious and political situation would be considered.

To free himself from excommunication, Henry now took a dramatic and canny step. Crossing the Alps in winter while Gregory VII was traveling north toward Germany, the king crossed the pope's path at the castle of Matilda of Tuscany at Canossa. For three successive days, he presented himself barefoot, as a penitent, before the castle gate. Gregory's companions, particularly the saintly Abbot Hugh of Cluny, pleaded for the king as, no doubt, did Gregory's priestly conscience. On January 28, 1077, therefore, Henry IV was released from excommunication. In many ways, this result represented a political triumph for the king. He had thrown his opponents into confusion. He had prevented an assembly in Augsburg under papal leadership. Nevertheless, Canossa has always

---

[1] Tierney, *Crisis of Church and State*, pp. 49f.   [2] Ibid., pp. 59f.

remained a symbol of the humiliation of the empire before the power of the church.

Yet the rest of the story of Henry IV and Gregory VII records, or seems to record, the failure of Gregory's cause. Civil war broke out in Germany when Henry's opponents there declared Rudolf of Swabia to be king. Despite a second papal decree of excommunication and deposition directed against him (1080), Henry prevailed, and at the synod of Brixen (June 1080) the king in turn deposed the pope and appointed the archbishop of Ravenna, Wibert, in his place as Clement III (d. 1100). Invading Italy in 1081, Henry gained control of Rome after three years of campaigning and combat, enthroned Wibert as pope, and had himself crowned emperor. Gregory VII, still holding the Castle of Sant' Angelo, continued to refuse compromise. In May 1084, he was rescued by a Norman army, but he spent the last year of his life in exile. "I have loved justice," he said on his deathbed, "and hated iniquity, and therefore I die in exile."[3]

Nevertheless, as the future was to show, Gregory VII had accomplished a great deal. His position on lay investiture would eventually be compromised. But the leadership of the papacy in European affairs could not now be lost, any more than could the administrative and juridical control of ecclesiastical affairs which the reforming popes had acquired. After the investiture controversy, it was the papacy, and not the German empire, which turned out to have gained the headship of Latin Christendom, though years of controversy were necessary before this fact could become apparent.

[3] Cf. Psalm 45:8.

Chapter 13

The End of the Investiture Struggle

UPON THE DEATH OF HILDEBRAND, the cardinals faithful to him (some thirteen had deserted to the cause of Wibert of Ravenna) chose the abbot of Monte Cassino, who took the name of Victor III (1086-1087), as his successor. Even in the face of Henry IV's military predominance, the reformers refused to give up their cause. Upon Victor's death, and in spite of the fact that Wibert and the imperial forces still controlled the city of Rome, they persisted in their resistance to the emperor and elected as pope Urban II (1088-1099), St. Peter Damian's successor as cardinal bishop of Ostia and a loyal pupil of Gregory VII. While devoted to Gregory's principles, Urban, a former monk of Cluny, was politically more skillful than Hildebrand, perhaps because he was more willing to be devious. A former papal legate to Germany, he rallied support for the Gregorian cause not only among the German bishops but also among cardinal clergy of Rome who had abandoned Gregory VII in his last days. Restored to the city of Rome in 1093, Urban triumphed by taking up Hildebrand's idea of a crusade to recover Jerusalem from the followers of Islam. It was at a synod in Piacenza in 1095 that Urban first announced this proposal. But it was at Clermont in France, at a similar synod in the same year, that he brought the Crusade into being—and this synod, not just incidentally, reiterated the stand of the reforming papacy against simony, lay investiture, and clerical concubinage. By the act of proclaiming the First Crusade, of which he himself, through a papal legate, was to be the leader, Urban made of the papacy, in effect, the visible and actual head of the Christian people, reinforcing the administrative and judicial authority which it had progressively acquired since the days of Leo IX.

This did not mean, however, that the controversy over investiture was settled. Urban's death in 1099 brought to the papal throne the last of the true Gregorian radicals, Paschal II (1099–1118), a former monk and papal legate in Spain. It was Paschal's fate to have to deal with Henry IV's rebellious son, Henry V (1106–1125), who had compelled his father's abdication in 1105. The new German king was no less resolved than his father to preserve royal control over the German bishoprics and abbeys; but it was a symptom of Pope Paschal's radical and reforming sentiments that he was prepared, when Henry V marched on Rome in 1110, to give the king the substance of what he wanted. If, Paschal declared, the monarchy would give up all pretense of investing bishops with the symbols of their spiritual authority, the church in turn would surrender all its rights in temporalities—the feudal lands and powers which pertained to abbots and bishops—to the king. This proposition, once announced, horrified the majority of ecclesiastics both in Rome and in Germany. Paschal had decided, in true radical fashion, that the freedom of the priesthood which the reformers had desiderated entailed its apostolic poverty—a judgment which could be expected from a man whose ideas had been formed in the new-style monastery of Vallombrosa, near Florence. The proposal pleased no one, however, and had to be repudiated.

Yet the distinction tacitly drawn in this case between temporal and spiritual investiture meant that a basis of compromise was already in sight. Two French bishops, Ivo of Chartres and Hugo of Fleury, writing between 1099 and 1106, argued that church and crown each had their distinctive rights of investiture: the former with spiritual authority and the latter with temporal. Just such a solution of the problem, moreover, had already been reached in England. There the investiture conflict—in which the protagonists were Archbishop Anselm of Canterbury (1093–1109) and King Henry I (1100–1135)—had been settled on the principle that the crown retained the right to invest a new bishop with his temporal authority, while the metropolitan archbishop invested him with ring and staff, the symbols of priestly authority. This settlement was in effect adopted in the Concordat of Worms in 1122, arranged between Henry V and Pope Calixtus II (1119–1124). By this agreement, elections of bishops and abbots in Germany were to be in free and canonical form. However, the presence of the king at the election was permitted, and in the case of a disputed outcome, he was to consult the metropolitan archbishop and the other bishops of the province. In other parts of the empire, such as Burgundy and Italy, no provision was made for the royal presence at an election. The king renounced investiture with ring and staff, but he retained the right to invest with the temporalities of the see by a touch of the royal scepter.

The effect of this agreement was, in principle, that a bishop or abbot must be acceptable to both the church and the civil ruler. The compromise would no doubt have disappointed Hildebrand, but it was the condition of a new role for the papacy in the life of European Christendom.

Period V

THE LATER
MIDDLE AGES

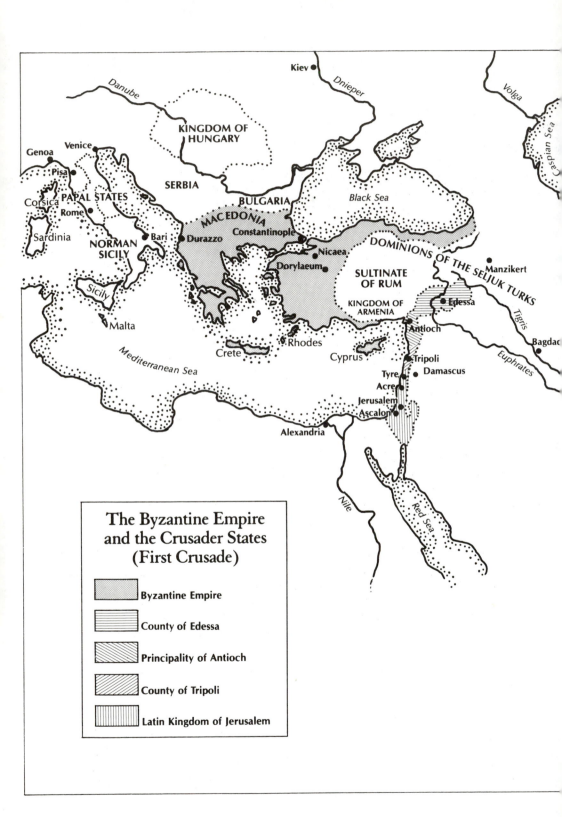

The Byzantine Empire
and the Crusader States
(First Crusade)

Byzantine Empire

County of Edessa

Principality of Antioch

County of Tripoli

Latin Kingdom of Jerusalem

Chapter 1

The Crusades

*T*HE CRUSADES ARE among the most remarkable phenomena of the Middle Ages. Their causes were many and complex. Historians who emphasize economic influences point to the rapid increase in Europe's population since the tenth century, along with a series of technical improvements in farm implements and more efficient crop cultivation, which greatly increased the productivity of the land. A surplus of people and of food made possible the growth of towns and of trade. By the end of the eleventh century, European society was pulsing with a new dynamism, and everywhere the frontiers of Christendom were gradually being pushed forward. The Crusades, extending over two centuries, may be considered a manifestation of this general European advance, evidence of the West's great expansive powers. The internal colonization of previously uninhabited regions within Europe was matched by the external colonization of lands inhabited by Muslim "infidels" or by "schismatic" Greeks.

Spiritual considerations, however, were no less influential than material ones. The whole eleventh century was a period of deepening religious feeling, which found expression in monastic and ascetic forms of piety, not least among the laity. This increasing religious zeal, animated by the Cluny movement, had been the force which reformed the church at large and nerved the papacy in its long struggle with the empire. Those regions that had come into closest relations with the reforming papacy—France, Lorraine, and southern Italy—were the recruiting grounds of the chief crusading armies. The crusader's "taking the cross," his life of self-sacrifice as Christ's liegeman, was seen as an imitation of the monastic life and as an approximation of the monk's higher spiritual perfection.

The piety of the time also placed great value on pilgrimages to holy places, above all to the land hallowed by the life, death, and resurrection of Christ. The Holy Land had been an object of pilgrimage since the days of Constantine. Pilgrimages were not only undertaken as acts of devotion; since the seventh century, they were also imposed as part of the penance of confessed sinners. Though Jerusalem had been in Muslim possession since 638, pilgrimages had

283

been, save for brief intervals, practically uninterrupted, in view of the relatively tolerant Arab rule. By the middle of the eleventh century, the number of pilgrims, as well as the frequency of pilgrimages, had reached new heights. However, the situation changed when the Seljuk Turks, beginning in 1071, conquered much of Asia Minor. By 1079, they controlled Jerusalem, and thereafter pilgrimages were virtually impossible.

It was thus to an age profoundly impressed with the spiritual advantage of pilgrimages that tidings of these events came. The time, moreover, was witnessing Christian successes in contests with Islam, at least in the West. Between 1060 and 1090, the Normans of southern Italy had wrested Sicily from Muslim control. Under Ferdinand I of Castile (1035–1065), the Christian reconquest of Spain from the Muslims had begun. The feeling was widespread that Christianity could now dispossess Islam. Love of adventure, hopes for plunder, desire for territorial acquisitions, and religious hatred undoubtedly moved the crusaders with very earthly impulses. We would wrong them, however, if we did not recognize with equal clarity that they thought they were doing something of the highest importance for their souls and for Christ.

The first impulse to the Crusades came from an appeal of the eastern emperor, Michael VII (1071–1078), to Pope Gregory VII for aid against the Seljuks. Gregory, to whom this seemed to promise the reunion of Greek and Latin Christendom and the establishment of Rome's primatial rights in Constantinople, laid plans for an expedition in 1074. The outbreak of the investiture struggle frustrated his design, but it was later to be revived by Urban II (1088–1099), the heir in so many ways of Gregory VII.

Alexius I (1081–1118), a stronger ruler than his immediate predecessors in Constantinople, saw in the divisive squabbles among the Seljuk chieftains an opportunity to take the offensive. He therefore appealed to Urban II for assistance in raising a body of western knights to help him recover his lost Asiatic provinces. Urban received the imperial messengers at the Council of Piacenza, in northern Italy, in March 1095, and promised his help. At a council held the following November at Clermont, in eastern France, Urban proclaimed the Crusade in an appeal of almost unexampled consequence. The enterprise had magnified in his conception from that of limited aid to the hardpressed Alexius to a general rescue of the holy places from Muslim hands. He called on all Christendom to take part in the work, promising a complete remission of sins to those who would make the arduous journey. Urban thus combined the old idea of pilgrimage to the Holy Land with the more recent idea of holy war against the infidel.

The crusader was at once pilgrim and soldier, bound by a solemn vow to visit the Holy Sepulcher in the ranks of an organized, armed expedition. This vow, attested by the wearing of a cross sewn to one's clothing, was a permanent obligation that could be enforced by legal sanctions. It served to keep the ranks of the crusading armies from dwindling once serious obstacles were encountered. The crusader, in turn, was the beneficiary of many special privileges, both spiritual and temporal, above all the Crusade "indulgence," which was commonly understood to wipe away all one's former sins and to restore one to a state of spiritual innocence. The crusader's vow, status, obligations, and privileges were gradually formalized by the medieval canon lawyers.

Urban's message found immediate and enthusiastic response. The chroniclers relate that his announcement of the Crusade to the people gathered outside of Clermont was greeted with a great shout of *Deus lo volt,* "God wills it!" Among the popular preachers who took up the cause, none was more famous than Peter the Hermit, a monk from Amiens or its vicinity, to whom early legend falsely attributed the origin of the Crusade. The impetus for all the Crusades lay with the papacy, just as their complex organization ultimately depended upon the unitary papal system of administration. Such was the enthusiasm engendered, especially in France, that large bands of peasants, with some knights among them, set forth in the spring of 1096, under the lead, among others, of the French knight Walter the Penniless and Peter the Hermit himself. Passing through Germany, some of these wild companies massacred many Jews in the Rhine cities, believing that the Jews of Jerusalem had helped betray that city to the Turks. (Such pogroms also disfigured later Crusades.) These plunderers often met with savage reprisals in Hungary and the Balkans when they resorted to foraging. The two relatively peaceful bands under Walter and Peter managed to reach Constantinople, and were soon transported to Asia Minor. Though warned by Alexius not to precipitate a conflict, they attempted to reach the former Seljuk capital of Nicaea and were almost entirely destroyed by the Turks in October 1096. This so-called Peoples' Crusade, remarkable for its religious fervor, proved a fiasco.

The real work of the First Crusade (1096–1099) was accomplished by the feudal nobility of Europe. Four sizable armies were raised. One was commanded by Godfrey of Bouillon, duke of Lower Lorraine, and his brothers Baldwin and Eustace of Flanders. Other armies from northern and western France were led by Robert, count of Flanders, and by the brothers of the kings of England and France—Robert, duke of Normandy, and Hugh, count of Vermandois. From southern France came a large force under Count Raymond of Toulouse, and from Norman Italy a well-equipped army led by the able, ambitious, and unprincipled Bohemond of Taranto and his nephew Tancred. No single commander led the hosts. Urban II had appointed Bishop Adhémar of Le Puy his legate; and Adhémar designated Constantinople as the gathering place. Taking three different routes, the forces arrived there in the winter and spring of 1096–1097. They caused Alexius no little difficulty by their disorder and by the initial refusal of their leaders to swear allegiance to him.

In May 1097, the crusading army began the siege of Nicaea, which surrendered in June. On July 1, a decisive victory over the Turks near Dorylaeum opened the route across Asia Minor, so that Iconium was reached, after severe losses through hunger and thirst, by the middle of August. By October, the crusading host was before the walls of Antioch. That city was captured, only after a difficult siege, on June 3, 1098. Three days later, the crusaders were besieged in the city by the Turkish ruler Kerbogha of Mosul. This time of peril and despair marked the crisis of the Crusade; but on June 28, Kerbogha was completely defeated. Yet it was not until June 1099 that Jerusalem was reached and not until July 15 that it was captured. Its inhabitants, Muslims and Jews, were put to the sword. The complete defeat of an Egyptian relieving army near Ascalon on August 12, 1099, crowned the success of the Crusade.

Upon completion of the work, Godfrey of Bouillon was named Protector of the Holy Sepulcher. He died in July 1100 and was succeeded by his abler brother Baldwin, who had earlier established a Latin county in Edessa and who now took the title of King Baldwin I (1100–1118). The conquered territory was divided and organized in western feudal fashion. Besides the kingdom of Jerusalem, it included the principality of Antioch (established by Bohemond and Tancred) and the counties of Edessa and Tripoli (the latter established by Raymond of Toulouse and his son Bertram). These fiefdoms were practically independent of the king of Jerusalem. Most of the knights were French, but the crusader states also received invaluable naval support from the fleets of Genoa, Venice, and Pisa, and important Italian commercial settlements sprang up in the towns. Under patriarchs of the Latin rite in Jerusalem and Antioch, the entire territory was divided into eight archbishoprics and sixteen bishoprics, and numerous monasteries were established.

The greatest support of the Latin kingdom soon came to be the military orders. One of these, the Knights of the Temple, or Templars, was founded by Hugo de Payens in 1119 and was granted quarters near the site of the temple —hence its name—by King Baldwin II (1118–1131). Through the hearty support of Bernard of Clairvaux, who prepared a rule for them based on that of the Cistercians (see V:2), the order received papal approval in 1128 and soon won wide popularity in the West. Its members, though technically laymen, took the usual monastic vows and also pledged themselves to fight against infidels, to defend the Holy Land, and to protect pilgrims. They were thus an order of monks in arms, symbolizing that fusion of Christian and martial ideals which the Crusades engendered. Those who supported the Crusade, but were debarred by age or sex from a personal share in the work, could secure representation in the order through gifts of money and estates. Thus richly endowed, the Templars soon became great landholders in the West. Their independence and wealth made them objects of royal jealousy, especially after their original purpose had been frustrated by the end of the Crusades, and led to their brutal suppression in France in 1307 by King Philip IV (1285–1314). But while the Crusades lasted, the Templars were a main bulwark of the kingdom of Jerusalem.

Much the same may be said of the great rivals of the Templars, the Hospitallers or Knights of St. John. In about 1070, the merchants of Amalfi, Italy, had founded in Jerusalem a hospital named for the church of St. John the Baptist, near which it stood. This foundation was made into a military order by its grand master, Raymond du Puy (1120–1160?), though without neglecting its duties to the sick. After the crusading epoch, it kept up a struggle with the Turks and Moors from its seat in Rhodes (1310–1523) and then from Malta (1530–1798). A third and later order was that of the Teutonic Knights, founded by Germans in 1190. Its chief work, however, was not to be in Palestine but, from 1226 onward, in Prussia, where it was engaged in the forcible Christianization of the pagan Slavs and in German colonization.

In spite of feudal disorganization, the kingdom of Jerusalem was fairly successful until the capture of Edessa by the Muslims in 1144 robbed it of its northeastern bulwark. In 1145, Pope Eugenius III (1145–1153) proclaimed a new Crusade. Bernard of Clairvaux, then at the height of his fame, preached the Crusade and enlisted Louis VII of France (1137–1180) and Emperor Conrad III (1138–1152) from Germany in 1146. In 1147, the Second Crusade (1147–1149) set forth; but it showed little of the fiery enthusiasm of its predecessor, its forces largely perished in Asia Minor, and those that reached Palestine were utterly unsuccessful in attempting to take Damascus in 1148. The expedition was a disastrous failure. Its collapse left a bitter feeling in the West toward the Eastern Empire, to whose princes that failure, rightly or wrongly, was charged. Bernard, for his part, attributed the debacle to the sins of Christendom.

One reason for the early success of the Latin kingdom had been the internecine quarrels among the Muslim rulers. In 1169, the famous Kurdish general Saladin (1137–1193) made himself master of Egypt; by 1174, he had secured Damascus, and by 1186, his territories surrounded the Latin kingdom on the north, east, and south. A united Muslim power now had to be met. Failing to obtain satisfactory peace terms by diplomatic means, Saladin defeated the entire Latin army at Hattin, between Tiberias and Jerusalem, in July 1187. The loss of Jerusalem and of most of the Holy Land speedily followed. The crusaders had thus held the Holy City from 1099 to 1187. Later attempts to retake it by force of arms were unsuccessful.

The news of this catastrophe roused Europe to the Third Crusade (1189–1192), proclaimed by Pope Gregory VIII (1188). None of the Crusades was more elaborately equipped. Three great armies were led by Emperor Frederick Barbarossa (1152–1190), the leading soldier of his time, by King Philip Augustus of France (1180–1223), and by King Richard "Coeur de Lion" of England (1189–1199). Frederick was accidentally drowned in Cilicia. His army, deprived of his vigorous leadership, was utterly ineffective. The constant quarrels between the kings of France and England, and Philip's return to France to promote his own political schemes, almost aborted the whole expedition. The vital port of

Acre was recovered, but Jerusalem remained in Muslim possession. Before leaving for Europe in 1192, Richard made a three-year truce with Saladin, by which the Latins were left in possession of the coast from Ascalon to Acre, with rights of access to the Holy Sepulcher. The Third Crusade had little to show for such an enormous effort.

The Fourth Crusade (1202–1204) was a small affair in terms of the numbers that were engaged, but it was of momentous political and religious consequences. Proclaimed in 1199 by a new pope, Innocent III (1198–1216), its forces came from the districts of Champagne and Blois, in northern France, and from Flanders. The crusaders, by now convinced that the key to the recovery of Jerusalem was the preliminary conquest of Egypt, bargained with the Venetians for transportation there. Unable to raise the full cost, they accepted a Venetian proposal that, in lieu of the balance due, they stop on their way and conquer for Venice, from Hungary, the Christian city of Zara on the Dalmatian coast. This they did, in 1202, to the pope's dismay.

A much greater proposal was now made to them. Alexius Angelus, son of the deposed eastern emperor Isaac II (1185–1195), promised the crusaders a large payment and help on their expedition, as well as submission of the Greek church to the papacy, provided that they stop at Constantinople and assist him in dethroning the imperial usurper, Alexius III (1195–1203). The Venetians, in particular, welcomed the proposal, which held out bright prospects of a total Venetian monopoly on eastern trade to the West. Indeed, for some time, Venice had entertained a strong interest in the destruction of the imperial authority. Western hatred of the Greeks also contributed. Though Innocent III forbad this division of purpose, most of the crusaders were persuaded. Alexius III was easily dethroned, but the other Alexius was unable to keep his promises to the crusaders, who now with the Venetians, in 1204, captured Constantinople and, in a three-day sack, plundered its treasures. Baldwin of Flanders was made Latin emperor of Constantinople, and a large portion of the Eastern Empire was divided, in feudal fashion, among western knights. Venice obtained the lion's share, as well as the desired monopoly of trade. A Latin patriarch of Constantinople was appointed, and the Greek church was made subject to the pope. The truncated Eastern Empire still continued, though it was not to regain Constantinople until 1261. This Latin conquest was disastrous for the Eastern Empire, gravely weakening it and making it vulnerable to the advances of the Ottoman Turks in the middle of the fourteenth century. It also exacerbated the hatred between Greek and Latin Christians.

A melancholy episode was the so-called Children's Crusade of 1212. In the summer of that year, thousands of children, with some adults among them, coming from the Netherlands, northeastern France, and the Rhine valley, gathered in and around Cologne. Their leader is said to have been Nicholas, a youth of Cologne, and they were apparently bound for the Holy Land, persuaded that their own boundless enthusiasm and the "hand of God" would bring them there. Their ostensible purpose was to salvage the cause which, they believed, their elders had betrayed. Their route took them up the Rhine through the Alpine passes into Italy, where many of them perished of hunger and disease. The remainder, finding no offer of transport to the Levant, were forced to straggle home in disrepute. One group, taking a different route, may have reached Marseilles, near the mouth of the Rhone, where sea passage was secured. Later accounts relate that some of the party were drowned in a storm, while the majority were sold into slavery in Egypt by unscrupulous sailors. The historicity of this "Marseilles crusade" is still debated. The summer of 1212 also witnessed marches by bands of French children to the monastery of St. Denis and to Paris, under the leadership of a visionary shepherd boy, Stephen of Cloyes. There is no firm evidence that these children were actually bound for the Holy Land, though they made their way chanting the prayer, "Lord God, restore to us the true cross." All these phenomena show the tenacious hold of the crusading idea on the popular mind, whatever one's age or social station.

Other crusading attempts were also made. An expedition against Egypt, from 1217 to 1221, had some initial success, but it ended in failure. It is usually called the Fifth Crusade. The most curious was the Sixth (1228–1229), which was more a "state visit" than a true Crusade. The free-thinking emperor Frederick II (1212–1250) had "taken the cross" in 1215, but he showed no haste to fulfill his vow. At last, in 1227, he started, but soon put back. He seems to have been seriously ill, but Pope Gregory IX (1227–1241), believing him a deserter, and having other grounds of hostility, excommunicated him. Nevertheless, Frederick went forward in 1228, and the next year he secured, by a treaty with Sultan al-Kamil of Egypt, possession of Jerusalem, Bethlehem, Nazareth, and a path to the coast. Jerusalem was once more in Christian keeping, until 1244, when it was permanently lost.

The crusading spirit was now well-nigh spent, though Louis IX of France (St. Louis, 1226–1270) led a disastrous expedition against Egypt from 1248 to 1250, in which he was taken prisoner, and an attack on Tunis in 1270, in which he lost his life. When Louis's eldest son, King Philip III (1270–1285), returned to France in 1271, he carried with him the remains of his father, his wife, his stillborn son, his brother, and his brother-in-law—all of whom had perished either in Tunisia or on the difficult homeward journey. This severe toll understandably dampened the French crusading spirit, and it well illustrates the very real perils of "taking the cross." The last considerable expedition was that of Prince Edward of England, soon to be King Edward (1272–1307), from 1271 to 1272. It accomplished nothing of military value, but it earned Edward a reputation for pious zeal. In 1291, Acre, the last of the Latin holdings in Palestine, was lost. The Crusades were over. The old crusading ideal had really died with St. Louis, though brave talk of new expeditions continued for nearly two centuries more.

Viewed by the light of their original purpose, the Crusades were failures. They made no permanent conquests of the Holy Land. They did not retard the advance of Islam. Far from aiding the Eastern Empire, they hastened its disintegration. They also revealed the continuing inability of Latin Christians to understand Greek Christians, and they hardened the schism between them. They fostered a harsh intolerance between Muslims and Christians, where before there had been a measure of mutual respect. They were marked, and marred, by a recrudescence of anti-Semitism. Though initiated in a spirit of high devotion and distinguished by innumerable acts of courage, their conduct was disgraced throughout by quarrels, divided motives, and low standards of personal conduct.

Historians were once accustomed to relieve this bleak picture by attributing important "indirect results" to the Crusades, finding in them the largest single influence in the economic advance and intellectual awakening of Europe from 1100 onward. This view can scarcely be sustained. The learning of the Muslim world, including its knowledge of Aristotle, so important for the development of Scholasticism, came to the West largely by way of Spain and Sicily, not the crusader states. Commerce between East and West, though increased by the Crusades, did not depend upon them for its existence and, indeed, antedated them. Likewise, the rise of the towns—the creation of a "third estate"—was the result of the agricultural and demographic revolutions already occurring before the First Crusade. The Crusades did not create towns and trade nor a surplus of food and of people: they presupposed these things. Still, on a more modest level, the Crusades did provide an outlet for the turbulent energy of Europe's feudal nobility and gave the populace some respite from their constant warfare. The removal of a considerable number of these unruly barons to the East also helped the growth of monarchical power in the West.

The chief beneficiary of the Crusades was the medieval papacy, whose authority and prestige were greatly enhanced by these expeditions. The popes stood forth as defenders of Christendom, proponents of a united Christendom against the infidel, inspirers of the crusading idea, protectors of the crusaders, and organizers of the military resources of the West. The Crusades also marked an important stage in the theory and practice of indulgences and in the elaboration of the church's canon law. Not least, the prosecution of holy war against infidel Muslims helped to legitimate the idea of the Crusade as an appropriate response to western schismatics, heretics, and political opponents of the papacy. The military strategy pursued in the East could also be applied to the internal problems of the western church.

Chapter 2

New Religious Movements

*T*HE CENTURY FROM 1050 to 1150, the era of the First and Second Crusades, was a great age of monasticism, but it was monasticism in a new key. Traditional Benedictine monasticism was widely felt to labor under a weight of useless customs, and it came increasingly under attack. The reformers emphasized simplicity and solitude, strict asceticism and poverty, and absolute adherence to the letter of the monastic rule.

The entire twelfth century, moreover, stimulated by the Gregorian assault on ecclesiastical corruption, witnessed a remarkable "evangelical awakening" within society at large. Many persons among the parish clergy and the laity alike were stirred by the prospect of religious renewal through a return to the primitive church and its pristine gospel—above all, to the perfection and dignity of the apostolic life. This *vita apostolica* was equated with following Christ in his self-abnegation and utter poverty and with the duty to preach repentance to a worldly church and to seal this message by personal sanctity. This way of life was open, in principle, to all believers, both men and women, not only to monks and clerics. The poverty here enjoined was not the "institutionalized" poverty of the cloister, nor the "natural" poverty of the rural and urban destitute, but the voluntary poverty of imitators of Christ and the apostles. The call to "apostolic poverty" as the basis, and proof, of the true Christian life was to resound throughout the later Middle Ages. As will be seen, it confronted the institutional church, and papal leadership, with the most serious challenges, as well as with opportunities for reform of abuses.

By 1100, Cluny had, in large measure, spent its force for church renewal. Cluny's very success, its absorption into the structures of feudal society, had led—so its critics charged—to compromise of the monastic ideal of world renunciation. New monastic communities arose in protest against this secularization. They stressed the literal observance of the original Benedictine rule, without accommodation to feudal forms and customs. These communities also answered to the quest of many monks for a more personal religion, a more intense spirituality, lived in isolation from society and even, in some cases, from one's fellow monks. Without breaking with the western tradition of cenobitic monasticism and the communal life, these new associations revived the old ideal of the eremitical life, the solitude and stern asceticism of the desert fathers (see III:7).

This new spirit is evident in the founding of the Carthusian order by Bruno of Cologne (1032?-1101). In 1080, he withdrew from his post as chancellor of the cathedral school at Reims to join a group of hermits in a desolate spot near Grenoble, in Burgundy. The bishop of Grenoble soon established him, with several companions, at a remote site in a high mountain valley. There, in 1084, he founded the monastery of La Grande Chartreuse, so named from the neighboring village of St.-Pierre-de-Chartreuse. The Carthusians were vowed to silence and lived as hermits, coming together at only a few prescribed times for worship and meals. They thus sought to combine the eremitical and the cenobitic life, holding to a modified form of the Benedictine rule. In 1127, Prior Guigo I compiled their customs in a rule that Pope Innocent II (1130-1143) approved in 1133.

"Charterhouses" were gradually founded throughout Europe, though the Carthusians had no desire to become numerous and influential. Their strict adherence to the spirit and original customs of the Chartreuse was such that the order was widely considered to be "beyond reform" precisely because it had never become "deformed" (*nunquam reformata quia nunquam deformata*). Well-known Carthusians include St. Hugh (1140?-1200), who took vows at Grande Chartreuse in 1160 and, in 1186, became bishop of Lincoln, in England; and Ludolf of Saxony (1300?-1378), whose *Life of Christ* was very popular in the late Middle Ages and also shaped the piety of Ignatius Loyola.

A hermit of a type and purpose quite different from Bruno of Cologne was Robert of Arbrissel (1060?-1117?). Formerly a priest in the household of the bishop of Rennes, Robert became an anchorite in the forests of Brittany and then a wandering preacher in the towns and villages of the Loire Valley. Going about barefoot, in poverty and in rags, with long hair and beard, he preached asceticism and the "apostolic life." Though he had been licensed to preach by Pope Urban II in 1096, his frequent attacks on clerical vices did not commend him to many of the higher clergy, who considered him an agitator. Robert's preaching attracted numerous adherents of both sexes, and he was conspicuously successful in gathering women followers, not least from among the rural nobility of Brittany, Maine, and Anjou. Abandoning their homes and possessions and calling themselves "Christ's Poor," his disciples lived the ascetic life under his direction. His innovative policy of not segregating his male and female followers evoked the opposition of the bishops of Rennes and Angers and then of a local council held at Poitiers in 1100. As a result, Robert was obliged to place the women in strict enclosure, and in about 1100 he established a cloister at Fontevrault. Thus, within the space of four years, this itinerant preacher of asceticism had become a monastic founder.

Fontevrault was in fact a "double monastery"—that is, a cloister that included men and women living in strict segregation. Double monasteries had been widespread in the early Middle Ages but had fallen into disfavor by the tenth century, only to be revived in the first half of the twelfth century. They enabled church authorities to incorporate within monastic structures the large number of women, as well as men, who responded to the popular preachers of the *vita apostolica*. Robert's double monastery was unique and innovative in that it was led by the women, specifically by an abbess who exercised jurisdiction over the entire foundation, while the men primarily cared for the liturgical and economic needs of the women. It was not as a double monastery, however, that Fontevrault endured. Within a generation, it had become the most famous nunnery of northwestern France, chiefly as a refuge for women from the great noble families of the region.

The congregation at Fontevrault, unlike that at Grande Chartreuse, did not develop into a monastic order. Of the new orders, the greatest in fame, numbers, and influence was that of the Cistercians, which dominated the twelfth century as Cluny had the eleventh. Like the Cluniacs and the Carthusians, the Cistercians were of Burgundian origin. In 1098, Robert, abbot of the monastery of Molesme, in company with a small band of monks, left Molesme to establish a monastery of great strictness at Cîteaux (Cistercium), near Dijon. From the first, the purpose of this foundation was to cultivate a strenuous, self-denying life, in which the Benedictine rule would be followed to the last letter. Its buildings and utensils, even its forms and accessories of worship, were of the plainest character. In food and clothing it exercised great austerity, adopting a habit made of cheap undyed wool (hence the designation of the Cistercians as "White Monks," in distinction to the "Black Monks" of the old Benedictine observance). The Cistercians were not hermits, but the eremitical impulse is seen both in their "puritanism" and in their withdrawal to uninhabited regions.

Under its third abbot, Stephen Harding (1109–1134), an Englishman, the influence of Cîteaux rapidly grew. By 1115, four daughter houses, including Clairvaux, had been founded elsewhere in Burgundy. Thenceforth, its progress was rapid throughout all the West. When Bernard of Clairvaux died in 1153, there were 339 houses; by the end of the thirteenth century, this number had more than doubled. This phenomenal growth occurred despite the Cistercians' break with the old practice of accepting children as oblates, to be trained in the monastery and later accepted as monks, and notwithstanding an official attempt, in 1155, to halt further expansion. While the discipline and customs of Cîteaux remained the binding model for all houses of the order, the Cistercian organization broke with the highly centralized system of Cluny. Daughter houses were subject to oversight by the abbots of their mother houses; authority thus rested with many abbots rather than with a single abbot, as in the Cluny system. All the Cistercian abbots, in turn, gathered for an annual chapter at Cîteaux, whose own abbot was only "first among equals," not an "abbot-general" of the order. The Cistercians, in short, were a federation of equally autonomous houses, with each abbot having an equal voice with all other abbots in framing legislation binding on the order as a whole. This system of organization goes back to the famous "Charter of Charity" (*Carta Caritatis*) formulated by Stephen Harding, who is justly considered the order's "second founder."

Almost from the beginning, Cistercian nunneries also sprang up, intent upon following the customs of Cîteaux. Yet early Cistercian legislation ignored the existence of their residents, and they occupied no official place in the order. A general chapter first took note of them in 1191, and from 1213 onward repeated efforts were made at the annual chapters to limit the number of nuns and to subject them to close supervision by Cistercian abbots. In 1228, the admission of any more nunneries to the order was prohibited. Such legislation was unavailing, however. By the end of the Middle Ages, there were almost as many Cistercian nunneries as there were houses for monks—a striking testimony to the wide appeal of the ascetic life and to the vigor of women's movements in the western church from 1100 onward. The Cistercian nuns, however, had no voice in the order's deliberations, and, like the Beguines at a later date (see V:4), they existed on the fringe of the official religious organization.

The Cistercian monks devoted relatively little attention to teaching or pastoral work. Their chief contribution to society, apart from their role as models of ascetic piety, was their assiduous cultivation of vast tracts of wasteland. Their houses were located, by design, in remote wilderness areas and at the expanding frontiers of Christendom. Having renounced serfs, and initially too poor to hire laborers, the Cistercians used lay brothers (the so-called *conversi*) to work the land. These lay brothers took vows and followed a simplified monastic regimen, but, being illiterate, they remained second-class monks. This system did not originate with the Cistercians, but they made the fullest use of it. It seems to have aroused little discontent during the twelfth century, the period of the order's greatest expansion. The later history of the Cistercians is a familiar one in monastic chronicles: ascetic industry created material prosperity, which then led to spiritual decline.

Not a little of the early success of the Cistercians was due to Bernard of Clairvaux (1090–1153), the greatest religious force of his age and, by common consent, one of the chief medieval saints. Born of knightly ancestry in Fontaines, near Dijon, he entered the monastery of Cîteaux in 1113 with some thirty companions, including four of his five brothers, the fruit of his powers of persuasion. In 1115, he left Cîteaux with twelve fellow monks to found the daughter house of Clairvaux, abbot of which he remained, in spite of splendid offers of ecclesiastical preferment, until his death. Ardent, uncompromising, even violent in demeanor, and given to extreme self-mortification, his prime motive was a love to Christ that found so evangelical an expression as to win the approval of Luther and Calvin. The mystic contemplation of Christ was his highest spiritual joy, and it received classic expression in his *Sermones in Cantica Canticorum* (eighty-six sermons on the Song of Solomon) and in his treatise *De diligendo Deo* (On Loving God). His mysticism was not of the "intellectualist" type of the pseudo-Dionysius, but was "practical" or "voluntarist," since for Bernard the soul's experience of divine love, rather than the mind's comprehension of God, was paramount. The return of the soul to God was always a work of the will reformed by supernatural grace. Bernard's themes reappear in the writings of two other notable Cistercian mystics of the twelfth century: William of St. Thierry (1085?–1148) and Isaac, abbot of Stella (L'Étoile) from 1147 to 1169.

Bernard was too much a man of action to be confined to the monastery. Not for nothing was he styled "the uncrowned emperor of Europe." The leading preacher of his age, and one of the greatest of all ages, he moved his hearers profoundly, whatever their social class. He conducted a vast correspondence on the problems of the time. The interests of the church, of which he was regarded as the most eminent ornament, led him into wide travels. His dominating part in organizing the unfortunate Second Crusade has already been considered (see V:1). His influence with the papacy seemed confirmed when a Cistercian abbot and former monk of Clairvaux, Bernard of Pisa, was chosen as Pope Eugenius III (1145–1153), though many of the latter's actions proved not to Bernard's liking. To Eugenius he addressed his chief literary work, *De consideratione* (On Consideration), an ecclesiological treatise castigating the secularization of the papacy due to its mixing of mundane with divine matters. Acting in defense of orthodoxy, in his role as "hammer of heretics," he secured the condemnation of Peter Abelard and Arnold of Brescia by the Council of Sens in 1141, as well as papal approval of this action; he also sought the condemnation of Gilbert de La Porrée (1076?–1154), one of the most brilliant of the early Scholastic theologians, chancellor of the cathedral school of Chartres, and later bishop of Poitiers, for his teaching on the Trinity. In 1145, Bernard preached, with some temporary success, to the heretics of southern France. In 1153, he died, the best-known and most widely mourned man of his age.

The great rivals of the Cistercians, and in many ways their antithesis, were the Augustinian canons, also known as regular canons (*canonici regulares*) and as Austin canons. They were not, strictly speaking, a monastic order, but were groups of ordained clergy who wished to live a common life of poverty, celibacy, and obedience to a superior, without withdrawal from the world. While the Cistercians aimed at reforming Benedictine monasticism through rigorous world renunciation, the regular canons claimed to be restoring the apostolic life of pastoral service to the world. They followed a rule attributed to St. Augustine, based on his letters of spiritual counsel to his clergy and to his sister's nuns; thus, they went "behind" St. Benedict and his rule—indeed, so they held, back to the Bible itself. Originally active in preaching and teaching, as well as in establishing hospitals and refuges for the sick, poor, and aged, they gradually took on all the lineaments of a monastic order. Many of their larger houses were indistinguishable from the older monastic foundations. Yet their rule was sufficiently flexible to keep them in touch with the practical needs of medieval society. Many communities of regular canons sprang up in western Europe between 1075 and 1125. By the thirteenth century, there were thousands of these communities, many of them, of course, quite small. Two twelfth-century foundations of regular canons merit special notice.

The first is that of the Premonstratensians (or Norbertines), founded by Norbert of Xanten (1080?–1134). A former cleric in the churches of Xanten and Cologne, in the German Rhineland, and subsequently in the service of Emperor Henry V (1106–1125), Norbert was early distinguished only by his loose morals and worldly ambition. In 1115, he experienced a religious conversion and resolved to enter upon an itinerant ministry of preaching to the common people. In 1118, he obtained a license to preach from Pope Gelasius II (1118–1119), and he spent the next years preaching in northern France. Like Robert of Arbrissel, he gained many adherents of both sexes, but church authority, as also in the case of Robert, did not look favorably upon a wandering band of "mixed" followers. In 1120, therefore, with the aid of the bishops of Laon and Cambrai, Norbert established a cloister in a forest near Laon. Believing the site to have been divinely indicated, he called it *Praemonstratum* (Prémontré, "the place shown beforehand"). In 1121, the house adopted the Augustinian rule, with certain additions of a Cistercian character—the product of Norbert's friendship with Bernard. The Premonstratensians, in fact, were to the regular canons as a whole what the Cistercians were to Benedictine monasticism—namely, the party of rigorists and purists. In 1126, they were approved as an order by Pope Honorius II (1124–1130). A century later, their houses numbered well over six hundred.

Norbert had originally made provision for his female adherents, in that the foundation at Prémontré, like that at Fontevrault, was a double monastery. Here, however, the women did not exercise pre-eminent authority, as they did at Fontevrault. They were subject to the governance of the abbot, performed domestic chores for the brothers, and had only a limited role in the liturgical and pastoral activity of the foundation. The establishment of double monasteries, moreover, soon evoked mounting criticism, both from within and without the order. Though twelfth-century popes endeavored to protect the rights of the women, since much of the order's property was held as gifts from or on behalf of its female members, common religious opinion continued to look upon women as temptresses and as constant threats to male chastity, especially monastic chastity. Hence, papal bulls notwithstanding, the order began to suppress its double monasteries, and before the end of the twelfth century, by decree of the general chapter at Prémontré, no more women were admitted to the order.

An equally famous house of Augustinian canons was that of the abbey of
St. Victor in Paris, founded sometime after 1108 by William of Champeaux
(1070?–1121), formerly a celebrated teacher in the cathedral school of Paris.
Though never large in numbers, the Victorines attained great prestige as
speculative theologians, mystics, and poets. Foremost among them were Hugh
of St. Victor (1096?–1142) and his disciple Richard of St. Victor (1123?–1173),
both of whom used the new dialectical method (see V:5) in the service of
mystical theology. The Victorine congregation in the later twelfth century also
included Adam of St. Victor, a hymn writer of distinction, and Walter of St.
Victor, a fierce opponent of Abelard and the "dialecticians."

A striking feature of these religious movements between 1050 and 1150 is
that the "apostolic life" was so quickly assimilated to the monastic life. The
popular preachers of the day, such as Robert of Arbrissel and Norbert of Xanten,
tended to withdraw to cloisters and even to become founders of monasteries,
and the regular canons soon developed into the equivalent of a monastic order.
Church authority clearly favored and promoted this "regularization" of the
religious life. However, it is not surprising that some individuals declined to
follow the path of assimilation. They insisted, rather, that the true *vita apostolica*
must be one of itinerant preaching to the masses, a life of Christ-like poverty
and simplicity lived "in the world," not behind the walls of cloisters, hence also
a life of unremitting opposition to wealth, luxury, and laxity among monks and
clerics alike. Beginning as reformers and revivalists, usually of orthodox belief,
some of these wandering preachers passed over from criticism of morals to
rejection of the church's approved doctrine and disciplinary authority. In a
word, they became heretics. It appears that prior to the rise and official
recognition of the mendicant friars in the early thirteenth century, the church
could harness the explosive power of the "apostolic life" movement only within
a monastic or semimonastic framework. Theological orthodoxy was thus
inseparable from traditional institutions. This limitation was of dire consequence for the medieval church.

Two popular preachers who lapsed into heresy were Peter of Bruys and
Henry the Monk. Both were active in France in the first half of the twelfth
century. Of Peter's origins and early life little is known, and most of what is
known about his teaching and his followers comes from a hostile treatise,
Contra Petrobrusianos, written by Peter the Venerable, abbot of Cluny from
1122 to 1156. Peter of Bruys was originally a priest in the small mountain
village of Bruys in the French Alps, near the mouth of the Rhone (or Bruys
may have been his birthplace). After being expelled from his parish, Peter became a heretical agitator in the region along the Rhone and then moved westward into the densely populated areas around Narbonne and Toulouse. He was
active for some twenty years, from about 1119 until his death in 1139 or 1140.
Thanks in part to his rousing oratory, he gained a large number of followers,

who were known as Petrobrusians. His root premise was that individuals bear complete responsibility for their own salvation. Hence, the clergy, infant baptism, the Mass, prayers for the dead, church ceremonial, and church buildings are superfluous. True religion does not require such "material" things. He also rejected any veneration of the cross (which should be hated, rather, as an instrument of torture). Peter practiced what he preached, and this proved his undoing: While burning crosses at the pilgrimage town of St. Gilles, near Nîmes, he was himself cast into the flames by enraged onlookers.

Henry the Monk, often called "of Lausanne" (where he preached for a time, though it is unlikely that he was born there), was a Benedictine monk who became a wandering preacher in northern and especially southern France, from 1116 until his death sometime after 1145. In 1116, he preached Lenten sermons in Le Mans and created an uproar by his attacks on the avaricious and impure clergy. After he was expelled from the city by its bishop, the learned Hildebert of Lavardin, Henry took the road southward, preaching in Poitiers and Bordeaux. Eventually, he was arrested by order of the archbishop of Arles, who brought him before Pope Innocent II at the Council of Pisa, in 1135. Here several of Henry's tenets were condemned, and he was ordered to give up his itinerant preaching and to reenter a monastery. Either he never obeyed or he soon escaped from the cloister and resumed his unauthorized preaching in the region around Toulouse, where he disappeared from the scene after 1145. In that year, Bernard of Clairvaux had conducted a preaching mission against Henry's followers in Toulouse.

At some point, Henry came into contact with Peter of Bruys in southern France—whether before or after the Council of Pisa is uncertain—and appears to have adopted from him more radical ideas. He was no mere imitator, however, and won his own considerable body of followers, known as Henricians. Like Peter, he rejected infant baptism and prayers for the dead. Unlike Peter and the Petrobrusians, he continued to honor the cross, but he went beyond them in denying the doctrine of original sin. In ancient Donatist fashion, he also denied the validity of sacraments administered by unworthy priests. The true church is a spiritual one, based on holy living and apostolic simplicity, by which standard Henry rejected the authority of the visible, hierarchical church of Rome. Henry, like Peter, insisted upon complete individual responsibility for salvation; a clergy with special sacramental functions is superfluous. The true church requires no more than poor itinerant preachers to exhort the faithful to follow the poor Christ. The teaching of both Henry the Monk and Peter of Bruys resembles that of the Cathars in several respects (see V:3), but it lacks that theological dualism which is the mark of full-blown Cathar doctrine.

Another reformist preacher of "apostolic poverty" during this period, and perhaps the best known, was Arnold of Brescia. Born at an uncertain date in or near the northern Italian city of Brescia, he began a period of study in

France in about 1115, possibly under Abelard. In 1119, he returned to his native city, where he became an Augustinian canon and abbot. Of severe austerity, he taught that the clergy, in order to be Christ's true disciples, should abandon all property and worldly power and live only on the voluntary contributions of the faithful. Arnold's teaching thus anticipated that of Valdès and the Waldenses. In Brescia, he soon roused the dissident populace against their bishop, Manfred, himself a moderate reformer. When, in 1138, the people proclaimed a commune, as a check on the clergy's political and economic power, Arnold invoked the commune's authority in support of his religious program of "apostolic" reform. Manfred, however, prevailed upon Innocent II to condemn Arnold at the Second Lateran Council in 1139 and to banish him from Italy. Arnold then sought refuge in France, where he studied with Abelard at Paris and rashly attacked Bernard of Clairvaux. Bernard, in turn, saw to it that Arnold was joined with Abelard in condemnation by the Council of Sens (1141), and he also secured Arnold's expulsion from France by King Louis VII. After finding refuge in Zurich and Bohemia, Arnold, in 1146, made his submission to the new pope, Eugenius III, who ordered him to come to Rome so that he might be kept under close watch.

Once in Rome, Arnold became even more violent in his attacks on clerical abuses and the church's temporal power. He soon became the leader of the Roman commune which, in the name of restoring the ancient republic, had driven Eugenius III from the city in January 1146. Despite his excommunication in 1148, Arnold remained influential until the vigorous Hadrian IV (1154–1159)—the only Englishman who has ever occupied the papal throne—compelled the Romans to expel him, in 1155, by placing the Holy City itself under interdict. Hadrian also bargained with the new German sovereign, Frederick Barbarossa (1152–1190), for the destruction of Arnold as the price of imperial coronation. In 1155, Arnold was executed, his body burned, and the ashes scattered on the Tiber. Never formally arraigned for heresy, Arnold's real offense was his attack upon the church's wealth and temporal power, combined with a readiness to use political force to achieve his reformist ends.

Peter of Bruys, Henry the Monk, and Arnold of Brescia have on occasion been proclaimed "Protestants before the Reformation." To do so is to treat any manifestation of opposition to the medieval church as "Protestant"—clearly an error. As has been noted, they point forward not to the sixteenth-century reformers but to the Cathars and Waldenses of the last half of the twelfth century, for whom their preaching prepared the way.

Chapter 3

Medieval Heresy—The Cathars and Waldenses; the Inquisition

THE TWELFTH CENTURY was not only a great age of religious revitalization movements among the monastic clergy, the secular clergy, and the laity. It was also a great age of heresy. The Gregorian reformation of ecclesiastical abuses and renovation of piety, with its solemn warning that the faithful should not accept the ministrations of unworthy priests, produced heretics and schismatics as well as saints. Though it called forth orthodox movements of church reform, it also created a hospitable climate in which heresy could blossom and, for a time at least, flourish.

During the last half of the twelfth century, two formidable groups of heretics appeared, the Cathars and the Waldenses, who between them threatened to carry the entire region from the Alps to the Pyrenees out of communion with the Roman Catholic church. They were "heretics" in that the church's hierarchy judged them to be obdurate opponents of the classic Christian faith as defined by Holy Scripture, the church fathers, the creeds and decrees of church councils, and the authoritative pronouncements of individual popes. Not every deviation from tradition, however, could be called heretical, and not every church teaching had received clear dogmatic definition and status. Practically speaking, therefore, the identification of what counted as heresy was a matter of papal decree. For this reason, medieval heresy was as much an issue of disobedience, of the willful rejection of church correction, as it was of false doctrine.

The heresy of the Cathars cannot be explained without postulating the outside influence of eastern heretics—specifically, the dualist Bogomils (see IV:8)—on western Catholics. Increasing contacts with the East, through pilgrimage, commerce, and the Crusades, had brought western Europeans into touch with the centers of Bogomil heresy in the Balkans, Asia Minor, and Constantinople itself. Bogomil missionaries, in turn, were active in parts of western Europe by the middle of the twelfth century. It is possible that Bogomil dualism had already penetrated the West in the first half of the eleventh century and that Peter of Bruys and the Petrobrusians were under Bogomil influence in the early decades of the twelfth century. Historians of medieval heresy find unmistakable proof of such influence, however, only in the 1140s in the Rhineland (Cologne). It is also beyond dispute that close relationships existed between the Bogomils and the Cathars after the middle of the twelfth century.

The term "Cathars" (*Catharos*) is of Greek origin and means "Pure Ones." The name has become a generic one for the sect as a whole, but, strictly speaking, it should be applied only to its leading members or adepts: those men and women who had received the *consolamentum* ("consolation")—the sect's central rite of baptism "in the Spirit" by the imposition of hands, *not* by water, through which one became a "true Christian." Their Catholic opponents called them "perfected" or "consoled" heretics, also "robed" heretics, owing to their customary black garb, but these were names which the Cathars did not use for themselves. They chose to call themselves simply "Christians" or "Good Christians," while their followers in France usually referred to them as "Good Men" (*bonshommes*). They were also called Albigenses, from the town of Albi, one of their chief seats in southern France.

In historical sources, the Cathars are often referred to as "Manichaean" or as "Manichees." There is no evidence, however, that the Manichaeanism of the later Roman Empire (see II:18), of which Augustine was once an adherent, survived in the West beyond the sixth century. It remains true, nevertheless, that the Cathars, like the ancient disciples of Mani, were theological dualists, teaching a doctrine of two opposing divine principles or even of two gods existing in open warfare from eternity. In this sense, the Cathars can be styled "medieval Manichees."

Though originating in northern Europe, in such cities as Cologne—where the first recorded outbreak took place in the early 1140s—and Liége, the dualist heresy spread southward between about 1140 and 1160. Its areas of greatest penetration and strength were northern Italy (Lombardy, Tuscany) and, above all, southern France (Languedoc), but it also continued to be widespread in Germany until the early thirteenth century. By 1167 the Cathars were sufficiently numerous to hold a well-attended council at St. Félix de Caraman, near Toulouse; and before the end of the century they had won at least the tolerance of a large section, possibly a majority, of the population of southern France, the protection of its leading nobles, and the active support of the lesser rural nobility. The sources do not permit any certain estimate of their total number. Apart from some rural areas, it is unlikely that more than a minority of the population actually adopted heretical tenets or left the Roman church. A far larger number of persons, however, while not abandoning traditional orthodoxy, probably saw no reason for hostility to men and women of exemplary life and may well have admired them as "apostolic" Christians. What is certain is that, by 1200, the Cathars of southern France and northern Italy were a serious threat to the established church.

Cathar dualism, like that of the Bogomils, was of two kinds. The original tenth-century Bogomils, in the Balkans and the Eastern Empire, were "relative" or "mitigated" dualists. They held that the good God had two sons, Satanel (the suffix "el" indicated divinity) and Christ, of whom the elder rebelled and became the leader of evil. Satan carried away with him many angels (perhaps a third of their ranks) from the heavenly realm, created the visible world, and beguiled the fallen angels to inhabit the bodies which he had created. This dualism is a "mitigated" one because it teaches that Satan is not co-eternal with the good God. At some later time—the exact date is unknown—the Bogomils adopted a "radical" or "absolute" dualism, teaching that there are two co-eternal, coequal powers, the one good, the other malign. In this version the evil power, Satan, invaded heaven, captured good angels, and forcibly imprisoned them in bodies of his evil creation. Both of these views were eventually brought to the West, where they competed with the orthodox Christian doctrine of humanity's creation and fall as ways of explaining the presence, and seeming rule, of evil in the world.

The early Cathars, like the early Bogomils, were mitigated dualists. In the late 1160s, however, the Bogomil priest (or "papa") Nicetas brought the absolute dualist position to the West from Constantinople. This most influential of medieval dualist missionaries was present at the council of Cathar leaders at St. Félix de Caraman in 1167, and he persuaded them to be rebaptized (reconsoled) in the absolute dualist tradition. While the majority of the Cathars of Languedoc were absolute dualists, both absolute and mitigated dualists maintained themselves in Italy, and their doctrinal divisions seriously weakened the Italian Cathar churches in the course of the thirteenth century.

Notwithstanding their divergent views on the ultimate origin of evil, all Cathars agreed that the visible world is the work of the evil power, in which the angelic souls—either fallen or captured from the heavenly realm of the good God—are incarcerated in bodies created by Satan. The greatest of sins, therefore—the original sin of Adam and Eve—is human reproduction, whereby the number of prison-houses is increased. Salvation comes solely by the *consolamentum,* which works forgiveness of sins, restoration of the soul to the kingdom of the good God, entrance into the state of religious perfection (which must be maintained by the most severe asceticism), and admission to the ranks of the Cathar clergy.

The *consolamentum* was ordinarily conferred only after a probationary year of fasting and instruction under the guidance of a "Perfect" (that is, one who had already received the *consolamentum*). The ceremony was divided into two parts. In the first, the "believer" (an adherent who had not yet been "consoled") received the authority to say the Lord's Prayer, for until this time one remained in Satan's realm and so had no right to call on the good God as "Father." In the second part, the believer made a formal request for baptism and heard a long sermon detailing the requirements for the new life, chiefly based on the precepts of the Sermon on the Mount.[1] The believer solemnly promised to eschew marriage (or to dissolve an existing marriage) in favor of lifelong celibacy, to avoid oaths, war, and possession of property, and never to eat meat, milk, cheese, or eggs, since all these are products of the sin of reproduction. (The eating of fish was permitted on the common medieval assumption that fish are generated not by coition, but by the water itself.) The presiding minister then held a copy of the Gospels over the believer's head and all the Cathars placed their hands on his or her body, while the minister read the first seventeen verses of the Gospel of John and recited a litany for mercy, interspersed with repetitions of the Lord's Prayer. Through this ceremony, the believer became a "good Christian," the soul having passed out of Satan's power by receiving forgiveness of sins before heaven.

Those who had thus received the *consolamentum* became members of the elect and could be certain of salvation, provided that they did not lapse from their exacting vows and so lose the "consolation." Owing to the rigors and perils of the Perfect's life, the great majority of believers deferred the *consolamentum* until death was near. If the dying person later recovered, it was expected that he or she would undergo a second baptism. There are also reports, mostly from hostile observers, that some of the Perfect committed suicide by fasting, in order to avoid the danger of sinning. This reputed practice, known as the *endura*, may have been engaged in by a few persons when the Cathar religion was in decline and under intense persecution, but it was certainly not typical practice when the sect was flourishing.

The Perfect, standing in the true apostolic succession, were the clergy of the Cathars. They were readily identifiable by their black garb (at least until persecution made this dress inadvisable), by their gaunt appearance (from regular weekly and yearly fasts, as well as their strict dietary regimen), and by their incessant repetition of the Lord's Prayer as a chain-prayer or ritual incantation. Each member of this class had the duty, and privilege, of preaching, instructing believers, and administering the consolation, above all to the dying. Each was also entitled to receive from believers a special greeting, known as the *melioramentum,* taking the form of three deep bows and a threefold request for the Perfect's mercy and blessing. Catholic writers, supposing that the Perfect were being worshiped in this act, called it "adoration."

Though every Perfect could perform clerical functions, the sect also had its hierarchy. Bishops were elected by the community of the Perfect and confirmed in their office by a special repetition of the *consolamentum*. No bishop was superior to another. The report, circulated by their thirteenth-century

[1] Matt. 5–7.

opponents, that the Cathars had a pope in the Balkans, is unfounded. Each bishop had two elected assistants, known as the "elder son" and the "younger son"—titles indicating not age, but the order of episcopal succession. The primary task of the bishops and their "sons" was to be itinerant preachers and baptizers; in times of relative security, they normally administered the consolation. Each bishop also had several deacons as subordinate assistants, whose main task was to supervise the hospices or shelters for other perfected men and women.

The *consolamentum,* as has been noted, was administered to both men and women. Women, therefore, no less than men, were admitted to the superior caste of the Perfect and could perform priestly rites. This circumstance helps to explain the great appeal of the Cathar religion to spiritually minded women, especially among the noble families of Languedoc. Women were accorded this privileged status on the supposition that physical differences between the sexes are insignificant, since sexuality was Satan's creation and has no meaningful role to play in the good God's design of things. Female Perfect were entitled to receive the *melioramentum,* took precedence over all believers, male and female, in communal gatherings, and, if no male Perfect were present, conducted prayers in such meetings. However, they were debarred from being bishops or deacons (presumably on practical rather than strictly theoretical grounds). In practice, therefore, the women adepts ordinarily led a semiretired life in houses established for them, often by noble ladies, where they instructed candidates for the *consolamentum,* preached to any willing listeners in the area, and held common meals. Here, too, hospitality was shown to the sect's officers, who used these houses as bases for their itinerant ministries. The female Perfect, in short, were normally sedentary, while the male Perfect were the sect's mobile missionaries.

Given their views on sexuality, marriage, and reproduction, it seems logical to conclude that the Cathars would have regarded casual sexual relations as preferable to marriage, since the latter institution only regularized the sinful conception of children. What was logically possible, however, has not been shown to be historically true, though the Cathars were routinely accused of all manner of sexual aberrations by their orthodox opponents. The fairest judgment appears to be that, as regards their sexual mores, the majority of Cathars were no worse than their Catholic counterparts. The Cathar Perfect, on the other hand, clearly impressed their contemporaries by their moral probity, as compared with a Catholic higher clergy in Languedoc that was notorious for its laxity. This evident contrast between the two competing priesthoods was a potent source of Cathar appeal to the masses, and it supported Cathar claims that they alone were "true Christians" leading an "apostolic life."

The Cathar leaders recognized that few persons could hope to emulate the Perfect in their total negation of the material creation. The real strength of the movement, therefore, lay with the so-called *credentes,* or "believers," who revered the Perfect and supported them with their gifts and good will. It seems that the believers were "ordinary" adherents who were allowed to marry, hold property, eat meat and other foods forbidden to the Perfect, and even outwardly to conform to the Roman church. After all, lacking the spiritual baptism that alone saves, they remained in Satan's realm and under his rule. Yet they were assured that should they receive the *consolamentum* before death, they would be saved along with the lifelong Perfect. The souls of those who died unconsoled would, in the opinion of most of the Cathars, be reincarnated in human, or even animal, bodies until at last they, too, after progressive purification from all material traces, should reascend to the celestial world whence they came. In this scheme, the orthodox doctrine of heaven and hell was meaningless, while the world itself became one vast purgatory.

The Cathars made great use of the Latin Bible, the Vulgate, portions of which they translated into the vernacular and in which they claimed to find their teachings. Some rejected the Old Testament entirely as the work of the evil power, identifying Yahweh with Satan. All believed the New Testament to come from the good God, but not all accepted every traditional New Testament saint; for example, the sainthood of John the Baptist was rejected, since he baptized merely by water and not by the Spirit. Since all things material are evil, Christ could not have had a real body or died a real death or experienced a real bodily resurrection: Cathar dualism required an uncompromising Docetism. Redemption comes not by the blood of Christ, but by submission to his teaching. The cross is but an instrument of torture, to be abhorred. The good God is dishonored by the erection of churches built and ornamented with material creations of the evil power. The sacraments, with their material elements, are evil and, in any case, could avail only for the spiritually mature.

Though profoundly heretical by orthodox Christian standards, Cathar dualism was not far removed from the language of some orthodox ascetic writers when the latter came to discuss human sexuality, marriage, the status of the female sex, and the nature of the fallen world. Certainly the majority of medieval Christians, untutored in the subtleties of orthodox dogma, were in no position to distinguish between these competing dualisms. Cathar preachers, moreover, disclosed the sect's most heretical tenets only to the inner circle of adepts. The chief appeal of the Cathar religion, in any case, was moral and ethical rather than doctrinal and intellectual. Of the effectiveness of the Cathar Perfect in gaining the allegiance of thousands, especially from the humbler ranks of medieval society, there can be no question.

Unlike the Cathars, the Waldenses originated in no conscious hostility to the church and, had they been treated with skill, would probably never have separated from it. The founder of the movement was Valdès (or Waldes), a wealthy merchant of Lyons. (The name still used by some historians, Peter

Waldo, has little historical or phonetic justification. "Peter" was added by followers in the late fourteenth century, by way of linking Valdès to the first apostle and so legitimating his mission and church.)

Sometime between 1173 and 1176, impressed by the song of a wandering minstrel recounting the sacrifices of St. Alexis, Valdès asked a master of theology "the best way to God." The theologian quoted that golden text of monasticism: "If you would be perfect, go, sell what you possess and give to the poor, and you will have treasure in heaven; and come, follow me."[2] Valdès, like Francis of Assisi a generation later, put this counsel literally into practice. Making provision for his wife, and endowing his daughters for life in the nunnery at Fontevrault, he gave the rest of his means to the poor and began preaching a life of repentance in the streets. He aimed to fulfill the directions of Christ to the apostles absolutely.[3] He would wear the clothing there prescribed. He would live only by what was given to him. To know his duty better, he procured vernacular translations of parts of the Scriptures and of the writings of the church fathers. Some people, of course, thought him mad. Others were deeply moved: here, they judged, were the true marks of the *vita apostolica,* the life of voluntary poverty and pentitential preaching. A band of followers soon formed around Valdès, arousing the suspicion and hostility of the archbishop and clergy of Lyons. Canon law, with few exceptions, restricted preaching to the clergy.

Opposed locally, Valdès and his followers appealed to the Third Lateran Council, in 1179, for papal approval of their lives of poverty and preaching. The council did not judge them to be heretics, though some of its members laughed at them as ignorant laymen. Pope Alexander III (1159–1181) applauded their devotion to poverty but denied them the right to preach without first securing permission from their bishop. Episcopal approval, as expected, was not given. For a time, the earliest Waldenses appear to have observed the papal restriction. To give up preaching, however, was unthinkable, for the Waldenses saw in the refusal of their right to preach the voice of man against that of God.[4] They soon resumed preaching, therefore, and about 1182 were excommunicated for their disobedience by the archbishop of Lyons and were expelled from the city. Some of them—now calling themselves the Poor in Spirit, and also known as the Poor of Lyons—made their way into northeast France and into German-speaking regions on the Rhine and beyond. Most of them moved southward into Languedoc and into Lombardy. In 1184, the Waldenses, together with other sects, above all the Cathars, were excommunicated at the Council of Verona by Pope Lucius III (1181–1185) in his bull *Ad abolendam,* a blanket condemnation of heresy.

These acts of the papacy and local church authorities not only forced the Waldenses out of the church against their will, but also secured them a con-

---

[2] Matt. 19:21.   [3] Matt. 10:5-23.   [4] Acts 5:29.

siderable accession. The Humiliati of northern Italy were a company of pious laborers, largely in the wool industry in Milan and other Lombard towns, who had associated themselves for a common life of penance. They, too, were forbidden to hold separate meetings, or to preach, by Alexander III, and they were also excommunicated for disobedience by Lucius III in 1184. A considerable part of these Lombard Humiliati now joined the Waldenses, as did some of the former followers of Arnold of Brescia, and came under the direction of Valdès. It is not surprising that the Waldenses, after their condemnation and excommunication, should widen their breach with the Roman church, passing from disobedience into heterodoxy, especially in Lombardy, where anticlericalism was widespread. Valdès's own role in this development is uncertain. He seems to have been more moderate than many of his followers and never to have ruled out an ultimate reconciliation with Rome.

The early characteristics of the Waldenses rapidly developed in the period between 1184 and the death of Valdès soon after 1205. Chief of all was the principle that the Bible, and especially the New Testament, is the sole rule of belief and life: whatever lacks warrant in Scripture is not justified in the church. Every prescription of the Bible, moreover, must be followed to the letter. Large portions of Scripture were learned by heart in the schools set up for training Waldensian preachers, who were the leaders of the movement (the equivalent of the Perfect among the Cathars). In keeping with Christ's instructions upon sending out the Seventy,[5] these preachers went about two by two, clad in a simple woolen robe, barefooted or wearing sandals cut in a special pattern to show their apostolic profession, enjoining repentance, hearing confessions, and rejecting oaths and all shedding of blood. Like Valdès, they renounced marriage and all earthly goods, maintaining themselves by the contributions of their adherents. They did not consider episcopal ordination necessary, and women as well as men were granted the right to preach. Lay celebration of the Lord's Supper was also permitted in regions where the sacrament was not readily available from a Catholic priest.

Besides this inner circle, the society proper, the Waldenses soon developed a body of sympathizers, "friends" (*amici*) or "believers" (*credentes*), from whom the society was recruited but who remained outwardly in communion with the Roman church. They supported the preachers by their alms, joined in the study of the vernacular Scriptures, and maintained the training schools. They rejected Masses and prayers for the dead as unbiblical, and they denied purgatory. They ordinarily used no prayer except the Lord's Prayer, and they absolutely rejected oaths, lying, and the death penalty for crime or heresy. Much of this development was due to Cathar example, yet the Waldenses strongly opposed the Cathars and justly regarded themselves as widely different.

Valdès and the French Waldenses did not reject the ministrations of suitable

[5] Luke 10:1–16.

priests among the Catholic clergy. They viewed dispensation of the sacraments as valid only if the celebrant were a priest, and they considered the Waldensian administration of the sacraments but a temporary necessity, an ad hoc arrangement. The more radical Lombard group, however, adopted the Donatist position that sacramental validity depends on "merit" or personal worthiness, not on "office." The Lombards, therefore, selected their own ministers to dispense the sacraments, appointing them for life and allowing them to support themselves by manual labor, thereby breaking with Valdès's principle that the preachers must depend solely on voluntary gifts.

These internal conflicts, and a feeling that the government of Valdès was arbitrary, even despotic, led to the secession of the Lombard branch (known as the Poor Lombards) in 1205. Attempts at reunion in 1218, at a conference held at Bergamo, failed to heal the breach. The two bodies remained estranged. The able Pope Innocent III (1198–1216), who launched the first effective counterattack against heresy, made capital of this division by countenancing in 1208 the organization of so-called Poor Catholics (*pauperes catholici*), who were allowed to carry on some of the practices of the Waldenses, chiefly itinerant preaching, under strict church oversight. Considerable numbers were thus won back to the church, including Durand of Huesca and Bernard Prim, both former leaders of the Waldenses in Languedoc. Nevertheless, the Waldensian body spread, especially among peasants and artisans. Waldenses were to be found in northern Spain, Austria, Bohemia, and eastern Germany, as well as in their original homes. They were gradually repressed and forced to lead an underground existence, until their chief seat came to be the Alpine valleys southwest of Turin. At the Reformation, many of the Waldenses accepted its principles and became fully Protestant. Their story is one of heroic endurance of persecution, and they are the only medieval sect that has survived, though with considerable modification of their original ideals and methods.

By the opening of the thirteenth century, the situation of the Roman church in southern France, northern Italy, and northern Spain was serious, even precarious. Missionary efforts to convert Cathars and Waldenses had largely failed. A crusade was ordered as early as 1181 by Pope Alexander II against the viscount of Béziers as a Cathar supporter, but it accomplished little. Under Innocent III, the storm broke. After having vainly tried preaching missions by members of the Cistercian order, and angered by the murder in 1208 of his legate, Peter of Castelnau, Innocent proclaimed a crusade against the heretics of southern France in 1209, offering the same plenary indulgence as could be earned by a crusade to the Holy Land. This strategy was agreeable to the French monarch, Philip Augustus (1180–1223), who had found the southern nobles too independent vassals, though he was reluctant to attack them—a clear breach of feudal customs—unless their heresy was definitely proved. The real work of the so-called Albigensian Crusade was undertaken by the nobles of northern France, who welcomed this unprecedented opportunity to carve out new fiefdoms in the south. They were led by Simon de Montfort, a minor noble of Île-de-France and, by marriage, titular earl of Leicester, in England. The combined interests of the pope, the king, and the northern nobles led to twenty years of destructive warfare (1209–1229), in which the power of the southern nobility was shattered and cities and provinces devastated. The defenders of the Cathars were rendered impotent or compelled to join in their extermination, though resistance did not cease until after 1243, when the Cathar bastion at Montségur was captured.

The question of the punishment of heretics had been undetermined in the earlier Middle Ages, when heresy was still sporadic. There had been a good many instances of death, generally by fire, at the hands of rulers, churchmen, or a mob, but ecclesiastics of higher standing had opposed this. The official investigation (*inquisitio*) of heresy was not as yet systematized. This task had long been left to the local bishops and ecclesiastical courts, but episcopal control was ineffective when heretics were numerous. Innocent III centralized such inquiry in the papacy by appointing special legates to hunt out heretics and present them before the church courts. It remained for Pope Gregory IX (1227–1241) to establish a regular permanent institution for the suppression of heresy—the papal Inquisition or Holy Office. In 1233, in place of special legates, he entrusted the discovery of heresy to inquisitors chosen from the mendicant orders, chiefly the Dominicans—a body formed with very different aims. These inquisitors set up their own special courts and were practically exempt from local church authority.

The papal-Dominican Inquisition quickly developed into a most formidable and fearsome organ. Its proceedings were secret, and the names of the accusers were withheld from the accused, who, by a bull of Innocent IV, in 1252, were liable to torture. Those who could not satisfactorily explain away the charges against them—a most difficult feat—and who confessed their guilt were subject to penance. Those who refused to confess, whether voluntarily or under torture, were handed over to the secular authorities for punishment, with a request for leniency but with the tacit understanding that they would be burned at the stake. The rationale for this cruel punishment was familiar and, on the whole, acceptable to medieval people: heresy, as treason against God, is far more heinous than treason against a king, itself punishable by death. Heresy, moreover, is a contagious disease within the *corpus christianum,* destroying many souls, and so requiring the most extreme countermeasures. The Inquisition, however, involved more than spiritual considerations. The confiscation of a confessed heretic's property was one of its most odious features. Since the spoils were divided between the lay and ecclesiastical authorities, this practice undoubtedly kept the fires of persecution burning where otherwise they would have died out. In any case, by means of the Inquisition, and of other less objectionable means shortly to be described, the Cathars were utterly rooted out by the middle of the fourteenth century, and the Waldenses were greatly repressed.

Historians continue to debate whether the medieval church effectively met the deep religious yearnings that welled up in the lay ascetic movements of the Middle Ages, both orthodox and heterodox. Fire and sword, Inquisition and Crusade, scarcely addressed such needs. Yet the church did not rest with coercion alone; it also pursued the way of persuasion by preaching and ex-ample—the way of the friars (*fratres,* brothers).

Chapter 4

The Dominicans, Franciscans, and Other Mendicant Orders

*T*HE CATHARS AND WALDENSES profoundly affected the medieval church. Out of an attempt to counter them with preachers of equal devotion, asceticism, and zeal, and of greater learning, grew the order of the Dominicans. In the same atmosphere of "apostolic poverty" and literal fulfillment of the commands of Christ in which the Waldenses flourished, the Franciscans had their birth. In these two orders, medieval monasticism had its noblest exemplification. In Francis of Assisi, medieval piety had its highest and most inspiring repre-sentative.

Dominic de Guzman was born at Caleruega, in Castile, between 1171 and 1173. In 1196, after years of study at Palencia, he became an Augustinian canon in the cathedral community at Osma, his native diocese located about ninety miles northeast of Madrid. Here he enjoyed the friendship of Diego of Acevedo, the bishop of Osma, with whom he traveled widely in service of the king of Castile. In 1206, returning from a trip to Rome, the two arrived in Languedoc, where the Cathars and Waldenses were then at the height of their power. There they found the Cistercian missionaries treated with contempt. At a meet-ing with the missionary leaders at Montpellier, Diego urged a complete reform of method. Only by missionaries as self-denying, as studious of "apostolic poverty," and as eager to preach as the Waldensian preachers and the Perfect of the Cathars could these heretics be won back to the fold. The Cistercian preachers endeavored to put the bishop's advice into practice and enjoyed some success, though progress was very slow. A nunnery, chiefly for converted Cathar women, was established in 1207 at Prouille, not far from Toulouse. Up to this point, Diego seems to have been the leader, but he had to return to his diocese, where he died at the end of 1207. Thenceforward, Dominic carried on the work.

The storm of the anti-Cathar war made Dominic's mission arduous and discouraging. Gradually, however, aided by the ex-Cistercian Fulk, bishop of Toulouse, and with the patronage of the crusader captain Simon de Montfort, he gathered like-minded men about him. In 1215, he was joined by Peter Seila, a wealthy citizen of Toulouse, who gave Dominic and his companions three houses for their use, while Bishop Fulk established them as preachers in the town. That same year, Dominic visited the Fourth Lateran Council in Rome, seeking papal approval for an order of preachers. It was refused, though his efforts were commended. The council had but recently forbidden the creation of new religious orders. Dominic was advised to adopt an existing rule, and he chose the one he already observed, that of St. Augustine, which was flexible enough to accommodate his purposes. Recognition amounting to the practical establishment of the order was obtained in 1216 from Pope Honorius III (1216–1227). In January 1217, Honorius officially confirmed the Order of Friars Preachers (*fratres praedicatores,* or preaching brothers, a name suggested by the pope himself).

As early as 1217, when the new association numbered but a few, Dominic, without consulting his colleagues or church authorities, decided to disperse his companions widely. Seven were sent to Paris and four to Spain, to study, preach, and found new houses; four remained in Toulouse, and Dominic himself went to Rome. This abrupt decision amounted to a revolution: an order of Augustinian canons, with special permission to preach chiefly to the heretics of southern France, became an order of preaching brothers dedicated to a world-wide mission of evangelization and the cure of souls. The great university cities of Paris and Bologna soon became the centers of the order, displacing Toulouse. Dominic wished his friars to be trained theologians; they adopted mendicancy and corporate poverty for the sake of effective preaching to a society that now included an ever-growing number of urban poor.

The first general chapters of the order were held at Bologna in 1220 and 1221, where the constitutions of the "Dominicans," as they were popularly called, were developed. At the head of the order was a master general, chosen for life by the general chapter and subject to its correction and, if need be, removal. The field was divided into provinces, each in charge of a provincial prior elected by the provincial chapter. Each convent elected its own prior. Every convent sent its prior and one brother, chosen by election, to the annual provincial chapter. The general chapter also met annually, alternating between Bologna and Paris. It was composed, for two consecutive years, of elected delegates (known as "diffinitors"), one from each province, while every third year it was composed of all the provincial priors. Most provisions in the constitutions could be changed, or new ones added, only with the concurrence of three consecutive general chapters. The system thus ingeniously combined central authority and representative government. It was the most highly developed constitutional system known in the thirteenth century.

Dominic died at Bologna in 1221 and was succeeded by Jordan of Saxony (1222–1237), a superb organizer and Dominic's first biographer. The order then numbered about twenty-five houses, divided among the eight provinces of Spain, France, Provence, Lombardy, Rome with southern Italy, Germany, Hungary, and England, to which were added, by about 1230, four more provinces—Poland, Denmark, Greece, and the Holy Land. The order grew with amazing rapidity, and by the early fourteenth century numbered about six hundred houses. Of this number, about one-fourth were houses for women. The very first "Dominican" foundation, in 1207, had been the nunnery at Prouille, and before his death Dominic had either founded or laid plans for founding three other nunneries, at Madrid, Bologna, and Rome. Yet he did not envision the proliferation of houses for women, and it appears that at life's end he was having second thoughts about such foundations. Already by 1223, there was strong opposition within the order to admitting any more nunneries, chiefly on the ground that the spiritual care of these houses by resident friars compromised the brothers' vocation as itinerant preachers and confessors. In 1228, meeting in a special general chapter at Paris, the order forbad the admission of more nunneries. (The Cistercians passed similar legislation in the same year.) This prohibition (as also in the case of the Cistercians) was unavailing. From 1245 onward, papal bulls allowed the incorporation of many additional nunneries, especially in Germany. The Dominican nuns were strictly enclosed, being forbidden to preach or to beg alms. Instead, they cultivated the inner life of "poor humility"; poverty became an interior virtue, a circumstance that helps to explain the flowering of mystical modes of piety in German Dominican nunneries in the late Middle Ages (see V:9).

Always zealous for learning, the Order of Friars Preachers sought work especially in university towns, where it found many recruits and soon became widely represented on the university faculties. Albertus Magnus and Thomas Aquinas, the theologians; Meister Eckhart and Johannes Tauler, the mystics; Girolamo Savonarola, the reformer, are but a few of the great names that adorn the catalogue of Dominicans. Their learning led to their employment as inquisitors—a role that formed no part of Dominic's ideal. The legends that represent him as an inquisitor are baseless. He would win souls, as did his example, St. Paul, by preaching. To achieve that result, he would undergo whatever sacrifice or abasement that would commend his preachers to those whom they sought. Yet it is evident that lowly and self-sacrificing as were Dominic's aims and personal demeanor, the high intellectualism of his order tended to give it a relatively aristocratic flavor. It represented, however, an emphasis on practical evangelical work, such as had appeared in the Waldenses. Its ideal was not a life of contemplation apart from the world but of service to people in their needs. In 1234, Dominic was canonized by his erstwhile friend and patron, the former Cardinal Hugolino of Ostia, now Pope Gregory IX (1227–1241).

Great as was the honor paid to Dominic and the Dominicans, it was exceeded by the popular homage given to the Franciscans and especially to their founder. The austere preacher, of blameless youth, planning in middle age how he may best reach people, and adopting poverty as a means to that end, was not so appealing a figure as that of the light-hearted young man who sacrificed all for Christ and his fellows and who adopted poverty not as a recommendation of his message but as the only means of being like his Master. In Francis of Assisi is to be seen not merely the greatest of medieval saints but one who, through his absolute sincerity of desire to imitate Christ in all things humanly possible, belongs to all ages and to the church universal.

Giovanni Bernardone was born at Assisi, in central Italy, in 1181 or 1182, the son of a wealthy cloth merchant, Pietro Bernardone, and his wife, Pica. The infant's Francophile father gave him the nickname Francesco (Francis, "Frenchman"), and it soon supplanted his baptismal name. As a young man, Francis was luxury-loving, extravagant in his dress, and generous to a fault. It little pleased his serious-minded father to see the son leading in the mischief and revelry of his companions. Francis had dreams of becoming a knight and achieving military glory. A year's experience as a prisoner of war in Perugia (1202–1203) worked a change in his spirit, as did an ensuing period of illness. He found the old entertainments insipid, and he was filled with questionings and gloom. He next (1204–1205) joined a military expedition bound for Apulia, in the heel of Italy, but he suddenly withdrew at Spoleto and returned to Assisi. His conversion to the religious life was gradual. "When I was in sin, it seemed to me very horrible to see lepers, and the Lord himself led me among them and I helped them. And when I left them that which had before seemed to me horrible was transformed into sweetness of body and soul."[1]

This note of Christ-like compassion was that to which Francis's renewed nature first responded. One day, when he was praying in the ruined church of St. Damian, just outside the walls of Assisi, he thought the painted crucifix above the altar spoke to him: "Francis, go and repair my house, which you see is falling down." Taking the words literally, he sold cloth from his father's warehouse to buy stones to rebuild the church. His irate father took him before the city magistrates and then before the bishop, seeking to force his son to restore the goods and the money from their sale; but Francis, laying

---

[1] *Testament of St. Francis,* in Rosalind Brooke, ed., *The Coming of the Friars* (London and New York, 1975), pp. 117–119. Composed in April 1226, six months before his death, this document was the point of departure for the later controversies over the true Franciscan ideal.

such money as he had as well as his clothes before the bishop's feet, declared that henceforth he had no father but the Father in heaven. This event probably occurred in 1206 or 1207. (The chronology of Francis's early life is obscure.)

For the next two years, Francis wandered in and about Assisi, aiding the unfortunate and restoring churches, of which his favorite was the Portiuncula, on the wooded plain outside the town. There, on February 24, 1208, the words of Christ to the apostles,[2] read in the service, came to him, as they had earlier to Valdès, as a trumpet call to action. He would preach repentance and the kingdom of God, without money, in the coarsest of garments, eating whatever the faithful might choose to give him. He would imitate Christ and obey his commands, in absolute poverty, in Christ-like love, and in humble deference to the priests and the pope as Christ's representatives. "The Most High himself revealed to me that I ought to live according to the pattern of the holy Gospel."[3] Like-minded associates gathered about him. For them, in 1209, he drafted a simple rule, composed of little besides selections from the Gospels, and with it, accompanied by eleven companions, he applied, in 1210, to Pope Innocent III for approval. It was practically the same request that Valdès had presented in vain to Alexander III in 1179.

Though impressed by Francis, the pope did not immediately accept his rule. Moved by a dream, however, in which he saw a poor man, whom he afterward recognized as Francis, holding up the great basilica of St. John Lateran at Rome as it was about to fall to the ground, Innocent gave his verbal approval. He licensed the brothers to preach and arranged that all twelve should receive clerical tonsure before leaving Rome. The name of the order, which Francis may have written into the original rule of 1209, was that of the Friars Minor (*fratres minores*—that is, the lesser, or humbler, brothers). Later, in 1215, Innocent formally announced to the Fourth Lateran Council that the Friars Minor were to be considered one of the existing orders of the church and thus not subject to the council's ban on new religious orders.

Francis's association was a voluntary union of imitators of Christ, bound together by love and practicing the utmost poverty, simplicity, and humility, since only thus, he believed, could the world be denied and Christ truly followed. Basing themselves at the Portiuncula, they went about, two by two, preaching repentance, singing much, aiding the peasants in their work, caring for lepers and outcasts. Soon, wide-reaching missionary plans were formed, made possible by the order's rapid growth. Francis himself wished to go to Syria to convert the Muslims and, if need be, to suffer martyrdom. In 1212, he boarded a ship at Ancona bound for the Levant, but contrary winds frustrated the journey and he returned to Italy. In 1213–1214, he was in Spain, but illness

---

[2] Matt. 10:7–14.   [3] Brooke, *The Coming of the Friars*, p. 117.

kept him from pressing on to Morocco; instead, he planted small communities of friars in a number of Spanish cities. Finally, in 1219, after the general chapter of the order held at the Portiuncula decided to send out worldwide expeditions, Francis successfully made his way by sea to Syria and thence to Egypt. Though the Fifth Crusade (1218–1221) was then in progress, he somehow managed to reach the court of Sultan al-Kamil and to hold long conversations with him, vainly imploring him to be converted and to submit to baptism.

Francis himself, unlike Dominic, was little of an organizer. But the association increased enormously, and what were adequate regulations for a handful of like-minded brethren were soon insufficient for a body numbering hundreds and then thousands. Change would have come in any event. It was hastened, however, by the organizing talents of Cardinal Hugolino, a nephew of Innocent III and himself the later Pope Gregory IX (1227–1241). Hugolino befriended Francis, as he had Dominic, and in 1217 Francis secured his appointment as "protector" of the society. Under Hugolino's influence, and that of Brother Elias of Cortona, whom Francis appointed as his vicar in 1221, the transformation of the association into a full monastic order went rapidly forward. Eleven provinces had already been established at the general chapter in 1217, each in charge of a "minister." Francis's leadership waned from the time of his absence in Syria and Egypt, and from 1221 onward he retired more and more from the scene. A new rule (the so-called *Regula Prima*) was prepared in 1221, and another in 1223 (known as the *Regula Bullata* because it was confirmed by a bull of Honorius III in that same year). The spirit of the original rule (*Regula Primitiva*) of 1209 still animated this last rule, which Francis himself drafted, but there were significant modifications. Francis was obliged to drop the requirement that a friar, on his travels, must "take nothing with him by the way," and the basic demand that postulants must renounce all possessions was subjected to the qualification that, should this prove impossible, a "good intention" would suffice.

Probably most of these changes were inevitable. They were unquestionably grievous to Francis, for he feared any form of institutional security and privilege as a threat to absolute poverty. He withdrew increasingly from the world, and was much in prayer, singing, and meditation. On September 14, 1224, at the close of a long prayerful vigil at the order's hermitage on Mount La Verna, Francis received the stigmata—wounds in his hands, feet, and side like those of the crucified Christ whose passion he yearned to share. His love of nature, always a source of peace, was never more manifest than in these last years and is displayed in his *Laudes Creaturarum*, composed in 1225. This hymn of praise, popularly known as the *Canticle of the Sun*, was a living refutation of Cathar rejection of the material creation. At last, feeble in body, totally blind, and suffering greatly from his wounds, Francis died in a little hut close by the

Portiuncula, on October 3, 1226. Two years later Pope Gregory IX—his old friend Hugolino—proclaimed him a saint of the church. Few individuals in Christian history have more richly deserved the title.

The organization of the Franciscans was similar to that of the Dominicans, though in the early years it gave more scope to autocratic tendencies than did Dominic's relatively "democratic" system. At the head stood a minister general, whom the brothers were bound to obey. He was elected by the general chapter and could be replaced by this chapter if his leadership proved "insufficient." The rule of 1223 called for a general chapter to meet every three years, or "at some other term, greater or less," at the summons of the minister general. Only after 1239 was a triennial general chapter mandated. Over each province was a provincial minister, originally appointed by the minister general but after 1239 elected by the provincial chapter. Unlike the Dominicans, the Franciscans did not at first possess regular houses or cloisters, but lived in rockhewn hermitages, wooden huts, and deserted churches. Once cloisters were established, the provinces were divided into "custodies," each in the charge of a "custos" or administrative officer. Each cloister, in turn, was under the direction of a "guardian." Originally, the custodians and guardians were appointed by the minister general; after 1239, they were appointed by the provincial minister, following consultation with the provincial chapter. Gradually, therefore, the Franciscan system more closely approximated the Dominican, though it vested greater legislative authority in the ministers and was not as fully "representational."

The Franciscans, like the Dominicans, also had almost from the first their female branch—the so-called Second Order. That of the Franciscans, known eventually as the Poor Ladies or Poor Clares, was instituted in 1212 by Francis himself, through his friend and disciple, St. Clare of Assisi (1194–1253). Francis established Clare and her associates in the church of St. Damian at Assisi, but this was the only nunnery that Francis himself can be said to have "founded," and throughout his life he was strongly opposed to admitting other nunneries to the order and to the founding and care of such houses by his friars. Soon, however, other nunneries, especially in central Italy, attached themselves to the cloister of St. Damian and an "order of St. Damian" came into being. Cardinal Hugolino gave the Poor Ladies a rule, in 1219, which was practically that of Benedictine nuns, with little in it that was specifically Franciscan, though the nuns at St. Damian continued to observe a *formula vitae,* or mode of life, that embodied the original Franciscan ideal. The later history of the Franciscan order parallels that of the Dominicans: opposition within the order to the incorporation of additional nunneries was unavailing in the face of papal directives which permitted such incorporation and, in keeping with the express wishes of the women, made provision for friars to serve as chaplains to the nuns. The women, as already at Assisi in 1212, were strictly enclosed and so could not engage in an itinerant ministry to the poor. They too, no less than their Dominican counterparts, pursued that "inward religion"—that interiorization of poverty and world-renunciation—which was a breeding ground of mysticism.

The growth of the entire Franciscan order was extremely rapid. By the early fourteenth century, it numbered about 1,400 houses (of which about one-fifth were nunneries, located mainly in the Mediterranean lands). Though Francis himself was no friend of learned theology, the Franciscans quickly established themselves in university towns and the order came to include many distinguished scholars, among them Alexander of Hales, Roger Bacon, St. Bonaventura, John Duns Scotus, and William of Ockham. More than the Dominicans, however, the Franciscans remained the order of the poor.

The Dominicans and Franciscans soon exercised an almost unbounded popular influence. Unlike the older orders, they labored primarily in towns and cities, chiefly because it was only there that mendicancy proved practicable. There can be no doubt that their work resulted in a great strengthening of religion among the laity. At the same time, they lessened the influence of the bishops and ordinary clergy, since, by virtue of papal exemptions from diocesan control, they were privileged to preach and absolve anywhere. One chief influence upon the laity was the development of the tertiaries or "Third Order," a phenomenon which first appeared in connection with the Franciscans. The Third Order, or Order of Penitence, as it was originally known, permitted men and women, still engaged in ordinary occupations, to live a semimonastic life of fasting, prayer, worship, and benevolence; they were also to abstain from oaths and from bearing arms (a constant source of friction with the civil authorities). Among the best-known Franciscan tertiaries are St. Elizabeth of Thuringia (1207–1231) and Ramón Lull (1232?–1315?); St. Catherine of Siena (1347–1380) was also a famous Dominican tertiary. Ultimately, all the mendicant orders developed tertiaries. As time went on, the system tended to become an almost complete monasticism, from which the married were excluded. It must be regarded as a successful attempt to meet the religious ideals of an age that was stirred by the quest for the *vita apostolica* and that still regarded the monastic regimen as the life of Christian perfection.

A number of other mendicant orders, besides the Dominicans and the Franciscans, were created in the thirteenth century. Most of these were short-lived, in part because the Council of Lyons (1274) sought to discourage them. Two foundations, however, proved to be of lasting importance. One was the Order of Friars of the Blessed Virgin Mary of Mount Carmel, or the Carmelites. In about 1154, a pious crusader, Berthold of Calabria (d. 1195), took up the eremitical life on Mt. Carmel in Palestine, and by 1185 he had established a community of hermits there. In 1209 or 1210, the Latin patriarch of Jerusalem gave the Carmelites a rule of strict asceticism, prescribing perpetual abstinence from meat, regular fasts, and long periods of silence. This rule was confirmed by Pope Honorius III in 1226. In 1229, a bull of Gregory IX further prescribed corporate poverty and the mendicant life. In about 1238, after the failure of the

Crusades, the Carmelites migrated from Palestine to Cyprus, Sicily, southern France, and England. Once in Europe, they ceased to be hermits, began living in cloisters in urban areas, and undertook the pastoral care of souls. These changes, which precipitated a crisis in the order, were regularized under the leadership of an English Carmelite, Simon Stock (1165?–1265), who in 1247, in extreme old age, became the general of the order. That same year, Pope Innocent IV approved the order's transformation along the lines of the Dominicans. The Carmelite friars sought to join the contemplative life with preaching, teaching, and pastoral service, and from the first they were characterized by their ardent devotion to the Virgin Mary. An order of Carmelite nuns, strictly enclosed and dedicated to the ideals of contemplation, was officially instituted by Pope Nicholas V in 1452.

The last of the four main mendicant orders—the Order of Friars Hermits of St. Augustine, known also as Austin friars—was a combination of several groups of Italian hermits dating from the twelfth and thirteenth centuries. In 1243, apparently acting at their request, Innocent IV prescribed the "rule" of St. Augustine for the hermits of Tuscany and charged Cardinal Richard Annibaldi with the task of unification, which was achieved in 1244 (the "little union"). At the direction of Alexander IV, in 1255, other eremitical communities in Italy were brought under the Augustinian rule and, in 1256, all of these groups were consolidated into one Order of Hermits of St. Augustine (the "great union"), with a constitution based on that of the Dominicans. They ceased to be hermits (in spite of their name, which points only to their historical origins) and became mendicant friars instead. Like the other mendicant orders, the Augustinian friars were granted exemption from episcopal jurisdiction, and they became a preaching order dedicated to the "apostolic" or active life of service to the world. Like the Dominicans in particular, they were devoted to theological study, above all to study of the Bible and the writings of St. Augustine, and they soon established themselves in the university towns and cities. Gregory of Rimini (d. 1358), who both studied and taught at Paris and was elected general of the order in 1357, was considered the best Augustine scholar of the Middle Ages. Gregory's works were highly valued and praised by a later member of his order, Martin Luther, who became an Augustinian hermit in 1505.

The piety of the age found many expressions other than through the mendicant orders. One important manifestation was that of the Beguines: a women's movement of sizable proportions that emerged, in about 1210, in the towns of northern France, the Netherlands, and the German Rhineland. The Beguines were pious laywomen living together in small convents or alone with their families, supporting themselves by manual labor and practicing poverty, chastity, and charitable works. They belonged to no monastic order, observed no fixed rule, and took no irrevocable vows. Because they neither had nor sought official church authorization, they were often suspected of heresy or heterodox tendencies. The name "Beguine" was probably derived from "Albigensian," the name used for a Cathar heretic of southern France. Some of the Beguines do appear to have succumbed to the teachings of the Waldenses and Cathars, but the great majority were orthodox, devoted to the church's sacramental life, and receptive to church supervision. Their houses were usually clustered around the convents of the friars, among whom they found their main support.

The movement was spontaneous and local, and it well illustrates the potent appeal of the apostolic life to medieval women as well as men. In the towns and cities, moreover, it seems that the number of women was now significantly higher than that of men. The Beguines thus provided an outlet for the spiritual and physical energies of large numbers of devout women, especially those who could not expect to find husbands and who, in any case, were too numerous to be served by the existing religious orders. There was also a parallel, but less populous, association of men, known as the "Beghards," who supported themselves largely by begging. The Council of Lyons, in 1274, included the Beguines and Beghards among the unauthorized religious associations and repeated the prohibition of the Fourth Lateran Council (1215) against new orders. The Council of Vienne, in 1312, explicitly rejected their way of life and even excluded them from the church. These harsh measures can be explained, in part, by their implication in the so-called Free Spirit heresy (see V:9). By 1400, most of the Beguines and Beghards had been absorbed into the established orders.

Dissension in the Franciscan order had already appeared during Francis's lifetime between those who held to the original ideal of simplicity, self-sacrifice, and complete personal and corporate poverty, and those who valued a relative degree of stability, security, and influence, akin to that enjoyed by the traditional orders. The stricter party, later known as "observants," looked for leadership to Brother Leo (d. 1271), who had been Francis's confessor and closest friend. The laxer party, later known as "conventuals," supported Elias of Cortona (d. 1253), Francis's vicar after 1221 and the order's minister general from 1232 to 1239. Papal policy favored the conventuals, since the church's needs would best be served by the growth and consolidation of the order along the lines of earlier monasticism. In 1230, Gregory IX declared Francis's *Testament* of 1226 to be a purely private document and so not binding on the entire order. He also allowed the friars the simple "use" (*usus rerum*) of houses, furniture, and books, as well as gifts of money, while vesting "possession" (*dominium*) or legal ownerhip of these things in such "spiritual friends" of the order as its cardinal-protector and the pope. In 1245, Pope Innocent IV (1243–1254) vested ownership of goods bequeathed to the friars in the Holy See itself, but he allowed money and property to be used not only for their "necessities" but also for their "convenience," thus opening the door to further relaxations of the rule of 1223.

The observants vigorously opposed these developments and found an able and popular leader in John of Parma (1209–1289), minister general from 1247 to 1257. The conventuals, on the other hand, who took their stand on the papal interpretations of the rule, rallied around Bonaventura, John of Parma's successor as general from 1257 to 1274. One of the greatest of the Scholastic theologians, Bonaventura supported the building of large monastic houses by appealing to the "use theory" of Gregory IX, argued that theological study—the pursuit of divine truth—is better than manual labor, and defended the friars' activity as preachers and confessors as a necessary corrective to the shortcomings of the secular clergy. He upheld Francis's ideal of absolute poverty, but he considered it only one means to Christian perfection, not an end in itself. His generalship marked a turning point in the history of the Franciscan order, and he has been justly called the order's "second founder."

Some members of the observant wing soon fell into dubious orthodoxy, or outright heresy, through their association with "Joachimism." Joachim of Fiore (1132?–1202), a former Cistercian monk and abbot in Calabria, in extreme southern Italy, was widely regarded to have been the prophet of a "new age." In a series of works known collectively as *The Everlasting Gospel,* Joachim divided the history of the world into three ages, corresponding to the Three Persons of the Trinity. That of the Father extended from Adam to the birth of Christ—the period of the Old Testament and of "patriarchal" culture. That of the Son ran from Christ down to Joachim's own lifetime—the period of the New Testament and of the Christian church, with a "priestly-clerical" culture. Joachim believed the new age of the Holy Spirit to be imminent—an egalitarian age of freedom and love which he labeled "monastic" because it would be formed by the communitarian values of the monasteries. It would be the age, indeed, when the "everlasting gospel"[4] would at last be fully revealed. Joachim was more a poet and symbolist than a theologian or exegete, and his writings have been subject to the most varied interpretations. It is unlikely that he viewed the gospel of the new age as a Third Testament, replacing the Old and New Testaments, or looked for the emergence of a new "spiritual church" to supersede the old church of pope, priests, sacraments, Bible, and theological learning. Yet his philosophy of history could be, and in fact was, read as a radical assertion of the purely contingent and temporary character of the medieval church—that is, the church of the Second Age. Therein lay the explosive ideological power of Joachimism, the source of its perennial appeal to opponents of the hierarchical church, and the ground for ecclesiastical hostility to Joachim's devotees in the later Middle Ages.

By the 1250s, many of the Franciscan rigorists, including John of Parma, were using Joachite prophecy as a framework for interpreting the world-historical significance of their order and of the original Franciscan ideal of complete personal and corporate poverty. These friars of prophetic faith were

4 Rev. 14:6.

nicknamed "Spirituals." One of them, Gerard of Borgo San Donnino, wrote a book, in 1254, entitled *Introduction to the Everlasting Gospel,* in which he identified St. Francis with the "angel of the sixth seal" in the Apocalypse[5]— that is, with the herald or forerunner of the Third Age foretold by Joachim. Gerard also hailed the strict Franciscans as the spiritual monks who truly preached the "everlasting gospel" and who thereby would bring in the new dispensation (whose advent Gerard dated in 1260). Pope Alexander IV (1254–1261) condemned Gerard's book in 1255, and Bonaventura began his generalship in 1257 by sentencing Gerard to life imprisonment (while John of Parma narrowly escaped condemnation and retired to a hermitage for the remainder of his life).

The Spirituals kept up strong resistance throughout the last half of the thirteenth century and into the early decades of the fourteenth, finding their foremost spokesman in Peter John Olivi (1248–1298), a friar of the convent at Narbonne. Olivi conceded that the Franciscans could "use" property, but he insisted that it be a genuine "poor use" (*usus pauper*)—one marked by the utmost austerity and simplicity in a friar's day-to-day living. In his *Commentary on the Apocalypse,* published around 1297, Olivi joined spiritual Franciscanism with Joachite prophecy. He envisioned an approaching cosmic struggle in which the "carnal church," opposed to the *usus pauper,* would be destroyed by God and replaced by the true "spiritual church." Though Olivi himself did not equate the carnal church with the Roman church, he showed profound hostility to the hierarchical church of his time, and his less cautious disciples among the radical Franciscans in southern France, for whom he became a cult figure, soon turned his ideas into a revolutionary doctrine.

The backbone of these opposition movements was broken during the pontificate of John XXII (1316–1334), whom the more extreme Spirituals considered the Antichrist foretold in the Apocalypse.[6] In a series of bulls issued between 1317 and 1329, John XXII declared that obedience is a greater virtue than poverty; accused the Spirituals of embracing the ancient Donatist heresy; rejected the legal validity of the distinction between "use" and "possession" that had first been recognized by Gregory IX in 1230 and had later been affirmed by Nicholas III (1277–1280) in 1279; and condemned as heretical the teaching that Christ and the apostles owned no property either in private or in common. It has been argued that the doctrine of papal infallibility in matters of faith and morals—first proclaimed a dogma of the Roman Catholic church at the First Vatican Council in 1870—actually originated with Olivi and the circle of radical Franciscans, who held, in opposition to John XXII, that the decrees of Gregory IX and Nicholas III were inerrant and indisputable and so could not be set aside by later popes. In any event, John XXII's decrees were fateful insofar as they called into question the theological foundations of the

[5] Rev. 7:2.   [6] Rev. 17:1–14.

entire "poverty movement" of the later Middle Ages and alienated the currents of "reform" within the church from papal leadership.

Opposition to John XXII quickly formed around Michael of Cesena (d. 1342), the Franciscan general from 1316 until his deposition by the pope in 1328. Cesena had been a moderate voice within the order and early opposed the Spirituals, but the pope's decrees radicalized him. In 1328, he escaped from the papal court at Avignon, where he had been detained, in company with another detainee, the great English Franciscan philosopher William of Ockham. Both men took refuge at the court of Emperor Louis of Bavaria. It was here that Ockham wrote four treatises charging the pope with heresy. Cesena and Ockham found followers in the so-called Fraticelli of Italy, but the ranks of the Spirituals were severely reduced by the Inquisition and their cause was a lost one. The older divisions between observant and conventual Franciscans continued throughout the fourteenth and fifteenth centuries. Despite many reforming attempts to keep the two parties together under the jurisdiction of a single minister general, the Order of Friars Minor was at last divided into two distinct orders, the Observants and the Conventuals, by Pope Leo X in 1517, each with its own officers and general chapters.

Chapter 5

Early Scholasticism; Anselm of Canterbury and Peter Abelard

THE SAME DYNAMIC SPIRIT in European church and society that found expression in the Crusades and in new lay, clerical, and monastic movements was also at work in the realm of ideas. Historians of medieval thought, accordingly, speak of the "renaissance" of the eleventh and twelfth centuries—a rebirth of humanistic studies and of speculative thought carried out by the medieval schools.

The educational work of cathedral and monastic schools during the early Middle Ages has already been noted in connection with Alcuin and the leading representatives of the "Carolingian renaissance" of the ninth century (see IV:5, 6). Early medieval scholarship was largely imitative of the teaching of the church fathers, especially of Augustine and Gregory the Great. Save in the remarkable case of John Scotus Erigena, it showed little that was original. Moreover, from

800 until well after 1000, education north of the Alps was primarily literary in character, based on the study of grammar and rhetoric. During these two centuries, also, Europe was besieged by invasions from the north, south, and east—by the Vikings, Muslims, and Hungarians (Magyars). Thus, in the realm of thought, there was little impetus to or occasion for philosophical activity and theological speculation. In the course of the eleventh century, however, when western Europe was at last free from external invasions, schools increased in number, especially in France. With their multiplication came a striking revival of interest in logic, or dialectic, and the application of logical method to philosophical and theological problems. The result was a fresh and fertile intellectual development, which culminated in the impressive theological syntheses (*summae*) of the thirteenth century. Since this movement originated in the schools, it has long been known as "Scholasticism."

The medieval schools differed widely in their character and influence. Throughout the eleventh century, the older monastic or cloister schools, intended for the training of oblates and young monks, were still of significance. Often, as in the case of the great Benedictine abbeys of Bec in Normandy and Monte Cassino in central Italy, they were in the vanguard of the intellectual awakening. But by 1100, at least north of the Alps, leadership had passed to the urban cathedral schools under the direction of secular masters. The most famous of these cathedral schools were located in northern France and along the borders of modern Belgium: Orléans, Chartres, Paris, Reims, Laon, Liége, and Tournai. South of the Alps, higher education flourished in the urban schools of northern Italy. These were lay schools, independent of direct church control, in which medicine and law, rather than theology, were the chief subjects of study.

Beginning in the eleventh century, a new class of professional teacher had also made its appearance: the peripatetic or wandering master (*scholasticus vagans*), who moved from place to place and attracted students by his personal magnetism and dialectical acumen. The outstanding representative of this class of scholar was Peter Abelard, but the type is already seen in Anselm of Besate (ca. 1050). The Peripatetics played a leading role in the intellectual life of the eleventh and twelfth centuries. Their very mobility—a new phenomenon, contrasting with the "stability" of the traditional monastic theologians—mirrored the intellectual restlessness and vitality of the first great age of Scholasticism.

While Scholasticism, therefore, was the kind of thought typical of the medieval schools and Schoolmen, such a definition is too broad to be of much use. It is also misleading, since not every school, nor every scholar, was "scholastic" in the strict sense. The theology taught in the monastic schools, under the tutelage of an abbot or other spiritual director, was devoted to a study of the Bible and the church fathers within the context of the daily round of monastic worship. It was predominantly contemplative or "mystical" in bent and its goal was "wisdom" (*sapientia*)—a practical experience of, and personal commitment to, the realities of the heavenly world. The monk studied a book, above all the

Bible or "sacred page" (*sacra pagina*), by reading it aloud, since one understands only what one hears, and by meditating or reflecting upon it, thereby fixing it in the mind and heart in order to put its teaching into practice. Bernard of Clairvaux was a premier type of the monastic theologian (a fact that partially explains his hostility toward Abelard).

Scholastic theology, on the other hand, was taught chiefly in the urban cathedral schools, where clerics who had already been trained in the liberal arts were prepared for an active pastoral life in the world, under the direction of a *scholasticus,* or schoolmaster. Such study was largely speculative or "theoretical" in bent and had as its purpose the attainment of "knowledge" (*scientia*), or logically defensible truth. One studied the Bible and approved authorities by the use of the dialectical or "questioning" method. Peter Abelard and Peter Lombard were eminent Scholastic theologians in the twelfth century. To be sure, there was no absolute separation between monastic and Scholastic theology. Anselm of Canterbury combined something of both modes of doing theology, carrying out a rigorous dialectical investigation of basic Christian teachings within a framework of meditation upon Holy Scripture and prayer for divine illumination. The same combination can also be seen in the writings of Hugh of St. Victor.

The distinguishing mark of Scholasticism, in the last analysis, was its adoption of a common method of inquiry: the method of discovering and defending philosophical and theological truth by means of Aristotelian logic or dialectic. The dialectical method involved three basic steps: the posing of a question (*quaestio*), followed by argument for and against answers proposed by earlier authorities (*disputatio pro et contra*), ending in a conclusion that is logically warranted (*sententia*). Until the reappearance of the total body of Aristotle's works, beginning in the middle of the twelfth century, knowledge of the dialectical method was derived from translations of portions of Aristotle's logical writings—his *Categories* and *On Interpretation* (*De Interpretatione*)—and of Porphyry's *Introduction* (*Isagoge*) to the former work. These translations, with important commentaries thereon, were all from the pen of Boethius (480?–524), one of the true founders of the Middle Ages.

In the domain of Christian theology, where the biblical revelation was understood as something given once and for all to sin-darkened minds, the dialectical method did not presume to generate new truths. Its avowed purpose, rather, was to analyze, explain, and defend the Christian faith as a body of divinely revealed truths (*corpus doctrinae*) deposited in Holy Scripture and handed on by the church's authorized teachers. Scholastic theology, therefore, moved within the framework of revelation and of the church's tradition of interpretation. In this respect, Scholasticism may be defined as the rational attempt to penetrate the revealed data of faith through a logical apparatus. Christian faith, according to the Schoolmen, is not an invitation to intellectual obscurantism; believers are obliged to understand what they already believe to be true. The Scholastic theologians, however, differed among themselves in the degree to which they held Christian revelation to be susceptible of such rational discussion and verification, as well as in their estimate of reason's capacity to penetrate revealed truths. They also differed in the degree to which they granted reason, or philosophy, relative autonomy vis-à-vis faith, or theology.

The development of Scholasticism was accompanied by a discussion about the nature of "universals"—that is, about the existence of genera and species—a debate occasioned by Porphyry's *Isagoge*. Three main positions were taken. The extreme "realists," following Platonic influences, asserted that universals exist apart from and antecedent to the individual objects—*ante rem;* i.e., the genus "man" is anterior to and determinative of the individual man. The moderate "realists," under the guidance of Aristotle, taught that universals exist only in connection with individual objects—*in re.* The "nominalists," holding that only individual things exist, maintained that universals are mere words or abstract names (*nomina*) for the resemblances of individuals and have no existence other than in thought—*post rem.* It used to be held that this quarrel between realism and nominalism dominated medieval thought and was virtually synonymous with Scholasticism. In fact, the debate was acute for only a half-century or so, from about 1080 to 1130. Later, new philosophical problems emerged as the field of speculation broadened, stimulated by the rediscovery of the "whole" Aristotle.

The first considerable Scholastic controversy was a renewal of the dispute once held between Paschasius Radbertus and Ratramnus as to the nature of Christ's presence in the Lord's Supper (see IV:6). Berengar (998?–1088), head of the cathedral school at Tours in about 1049, attacked the prevalent conception that the elements of bread and wine are changed into the actual body and blood of Christ. He argued that according to the rules of logic, a "substance" (bread, wine) must remain unchanged as long as the "accidents" (the outward appearance of the elements) remain unchanged. He was immediately opposed by Lanfranc (1010?–1089), at the time prior of the famous monastery of Bec in Normandy and later (1070) William the Conqueror's celebrated archbishop of Canterbury. The most influential theologian of his day, Lanfranc upheld a moderate use of dialectic in theology, while defending the primary authority of Scripture and tradition. Owing largely to his efforts, councils at Rome (1050) and Tours (1054) condemned Berengar's views. The debate showed that the view later (ca. 1140) to be known as "transubstantiation" had become the dominant opinion in Latin Christendom. It was to receive full approval at the Fourth Lateran Council in 1215, where it was proclaimed a dogma.

The dialectical method was also employed, with results very dissimilar to Berengar's, by Anselm of Canterbury, often called the father of Scholasticism. Born of noble family at Aosta in northern Italy in 1033, Anselm became a monk at Bec in 1060 under Lanfranc, whom he succeeded as prior in 1063, becoming abbot in 1078. Under Anselm, the school of Bec attained great distinction. In 1093, he became archbishop of Canterbury, during the reign of William II

(1087–1100), and had a stormy episcopate by reason of his Hildebrandian principles. He died in office in 1109.

One of the most original of all medieval thinkers, Anselm was convinced of the full capacity of a proper dialectic to prove the truths of theology. For him, indeed, no part of Christian faith was beyond the province of rational demonstration. Not only the existence of God, but even such "mysteries" as the Trinity, the Incarnation, and redemption, could be shown to be "necessary" truths—that is, doctrines that are congruent with the canons of logic. Unlike the later Scholastics, such as Thomas Aquinas, Anselm made no clear-cut distinction between natural truths of reason and supernatural truths known only by faith. The technical terms for such a distinction were still lacking. Faith and reason were seen as flowing together to form one harmonious body of Christian wisdom. Yet, as a leading disciple of Augustine, Anselm held that rational understanding presupposes faith. "I believe in order that I might understand" (*credo ut intelligam*) is a motto that well expresses his attitude and that of all medieval Augustinians.

Anselm's famous proof for the existence of God, set forth in his *Proslogion,* was typically Augustinian, and to that extent Neoplatonic, in that it moved entirely within the mind and its concepts, taking no account of sense experience. In keeping with the new dialectical method, Anselm began with a definition of the word "God" (*Deus*), and then logically analyzed this definition. "God" is "the being than which none greater can be conceived." He must therefore exist in reality (*in re*), as well as in thought (*in intellectu*), for if he existed in thought only, a yet greater being, existing in reality as well as in thought, could be conceived, which is impossible by definition. This proof, which already during Anselm's lifetime aroused the opposition of Gaunilo, a monk of Marmoutier, has seemed to many a logical sleight of hand, though its validity has not lacked eminent defenders, among them Descartes, Leibniz, and Hegel.

Anselm next directed his attention to Roscelin (1050–1125), a canon of Compiègne, who, under nominalist influence, had asserted that either the Father, Son, and Spirit are identical or they are three Gods. At the Council of Soissons in 1092, he was compelled to abjure this tritheism. According to Anselm, who is the main source of information about Roscelin's views, the root of his heresy was his failure to recognize universals, treating them merely as "vocal sounds" (*flatus vocis*). Hence, said Anselm, Roscelin could no more explain how several individuals are, in substance, one man than how three divine Persons are substantially one God. As an extreme realist, Anselm located all reality in timeless universals rather than in individual, transient beings. The controversy shows that the debate over universals assumed special importance because of its direct bearing on Christian dogma.

Anselm's most influential contribution to theology was his discussion of the atonement in his *Cur Deus homo* (Why God Became Man), the ablest treatment that had yet appeared. He proposed to handle this *quaestio* without recourse to any authority and to show by rational argument alone that the Incarnation and the redemption through Christ were necessary, or logically fitting. His treatment was no less revolutionary in that it totally rejected any thought, such as the early church had entertained, of a ransom paid to the devil. Man, by his sin, has dishonored God and has disturbed the divinely willed order (*rectitudo*) of the universe. His debt of justice, therefore, is owed to God alone; the devil is due nothing but contempt. Now God's justice, or rectitude, is such that he must punish sin if adequate satisfaction is not made to his injured honor (*aut poena aut satisfactio*). In order that his original purpose in creating man should not be frustrated, God, in his mercy, has chosen the way of satisfaction. Man, however, who owes obedience to God at all times, has nothing wherewith to make good past disobedience, much less to render the infinite satisfaction which will make good the injury to God's infinite honor. If satisfaction is to be made at all, therefore, it can be rendered only by one who shares human nature, who is himself man, and yet has something of infinite value to offer. Such a unique being is the sinless God-man. Hence, the Incarnation is necessary.

It will be seen that Anselm's theory rests on the "realistic" conviction that there is such an objectively existing universal as humanity which Christ could assume. Christ's voluntary self-sacrifice, moreover, not only is a satisfaction but also deserves a reward. That reward is the eternal blessedness of his disciples, for whom he perpetually intercedes and who are joined to him, in a death like his, through their own repeated acts of penance and by their faithful participation in the sacrament of his body and blood. Thus, Anselm's widely influential theory of the atonement also rested on, and supplied a theological rationale for, the developing penitential-eucharistic practice of the medieval church.

For all his radicality in "proving" Christian doctrines, Anselm remained a loyal churchman and defender of the primary authority of Scripture and church tradition. He was persuaded that dialectical explanation could but support the doctrines of the church. His bold confidence in reason was an outgrowth of his firm trust in reason's Creator and in the inherent rationality of the creation. The original title of his *Proslogion—Fides quaerens intellectum* (Faith in Search of Understanding), with its stress on the mind's active quest for the rational grounds of Christian belief—sums up the central impulses of Scholasticism and bespeaks the intellectual excitement which accompanied the revival of dialectic.

Another defender of the "churchly" use of dialectic was William of Champeaux (1070?–1121), who brought the monastic school of St. Victor, near Paris, into great repute and died as bishop of Chalons. Like Anselm, he was an extreme realist on the question of universals, until he was forced to modify his position owing to the weighty objections of his former student, Peter Abelard.

The ablest dialectician of the twelfth century, Abelard (1079–1142) was a man of charm, eloquence, vanity, and hypercritical spirit, but by no means of irreligion. Born at Pallet (Palais), in Brittany, he studied under Roscelin and William of Champeaux, both of whom he opposed and undoubtedly far surpassed in ability. On the vexed question of universals, he took a position inter-mediate between the nominalism of one teacher and the realism of the other. The universal is not a mere word (*vox*), but a word or term (*sermo*) which can be predicated of things. It is not itself a thing, but it exists in connection with things (*cum fundamento in re*). Knowledge of a universal comes through the mind's activity, whereby, working on evidence presented by the senses, it "ab-stracts" from individual things certain shared characteristics. While lacking in-dependent existence, therefore, the universal does denote something real—not a separate essence (such as "man"), but a condition or state (*status*) which a group of individuals has in common (such as "to be a man"). This view has often been called "moderate realism," but the designation is inaccurate insofar as Abelard did not treat universals metaphysically, under the category of being, but only logically, as predicates of things. Abelard thus remained, first and fore-most, a logician, and in this respect showed more affinity with nominalism than with realism.

Abelard's life, recounted in his *Historia calamitatum* (History of Calamities) was stormy. Already in 1103, he was teaching the liberal arts with great follow-ing at Melun, near Paris. Later, aspiring to theological eminence, he set up a school of his own at Laon in rivalry to that of Anselm of Laon (?–1117), the most celebrated biblical scholar of the day, whom Abelard contemptuously dis-missed as "smoke without a flame." By 1115, he was a canon of Notre Dame, with a following in Paris such as no master had yet enjoyed. Now, at the height of his fame, he fell in love with Héloïse, the niece of his fellow canon Fulbert, with whom he lodged. Héloïse gave birth to a child, named Astrolabe, and the couple entered into a secret marriage, despite the strong objections of Héloïse, who did not wish to compromise Abelard's brilliant prospects as a teacher of theology. The enraged Fulbert, believing his niece deceived and himself dis-honored, took his revenge by having Abelard emasculated. Subsequently, at Abelard's urging, Héloïse became a nun at Argentueil, and he became a monk at St. Denis. To teach was his breath of life, however, and he soon resumed lecturing, with the abbot's permission. His first published theological treatise, a reply to Roscelin's tritheism, leaned so far in the other direction that his ene-mies charged him with Sabellianism, and his views were condemned at the Council of Soissons in 1121.

Meanwhile, Abelard's denial that the founder of St. Denis was the famous Dionysius (Denis) the Areopagite brought about his expulsion from that mon-astery, and he undertook a hermit's life at a desolate spot outside Paris. Students again flocked to him and he founded a little settlement which he called the Paraclete. By his own account, however, his criticisms had aroused the hostility of that most powerful religious leader of the age, Bernard of Clairvaux, and he now sought refuge as abbot of the rough and undisciplined monastery of St. Gildas, in remote Brittany. Unable to reform the intractable monks, after several miserable years of strife, Abelard resumed his teaching career in about 1133, first at Reims and then once more at Paris on the Mont St. Geneviève. In the meantime, Héloïse had become abbess of a little nunnery at the Paraclete, and Abelard had begun his correspondence with her. The authenticity of Héloïse's letters is still debated (some scholars attribute the whole collection to Abelard himself), but the correspondence remains notable evidence for the new "humanism" of the twelfth century.

Abelard's period of intense literary activity fell in the years between 1135 and 1140, when he wrote, and constantly revised, his *Theologia christiana* (Christian Theology), portions of his *Introductio ad theologiam* (Introduction to Theology), his ethical treatise *Scito te ipsum* (Know Thyself), and his *Sic et non* (Yes and No). Versions of these works were soon brought to the attention of the formidable Bernard, who procured Abelard's second condemnation at the Council of Sens in 1141 and the rejection of his appeal by Pope Innocent II. Abelard was now a broken man. He made submission and found a magnanimous friend in Peter the Venerable, abbot of Cluny, who recounts that Abelard and Bernard were at last reconciled. In 1142, Abelard died in one of the monasteries under the jurisdiction of Cluny.

Abelard was neither a rationalist nor a skeptic. He did not reverse Anselm's motto and declare, "I understand in order that I might believe" (*intelligo ut credam*). His spirit was essentially critical and, so far as he aimed to test church doctrine by dialectic, innovative. Without rejecting Scripture, the fathers, or the creeds, he held that all tenets of faith should be subjected to logical examination and not lightly believed. But he did not think it possible fully to comprehend (*comprehendere*) divine truths; at most, one could only understand (*intelligere*) them to a degree consonant with faith. This proviso led him to define Christian belief as an "existimation" (*existimatio*) or "estimate" (*aestimatio*), by which he meant not a mere "opinion," as Bernard wrongly judged, but a mental apprehension, or "approximation," of the full truth yet to be revealed at the Last Day, when faith gives way to sight. Unlike Anselm, therefore, he did not attempt to demonstrate the cardinal Christian doctrines as "necessary" truths. Like Anselm, however, he had great confidence in the power of dialectic to explain doctrine, save that his explanations were judged to be less orthodox, and more offensive to current sensibilities, than were Anselm's.

In his *Yes and No,* for example, Abelard set forth a series of apparently contradictory texts from Scripture and the fathers on the main theological topics, without any explicit attempt at harmony or explanation. This procedure was not original to Abelard; it had already been used by the canon lawyers as a method of reconciling contradictory legal authorities. Yet it might well arouse a feeling that he was a sower of doubts, particularly when he announced in the prologue to the work, "By doubting we come to inquiry, and by inquiring we perceive the truth." His doctrine of the Trinity, condemned in 1121, was almost Sabellian. His teaching that human nature has inherited not guilt but punishment from Adam, and that grace assists rather than enables, was contrary to the

Augustinian tradition. Nor was Abelard less innovative in his conception of the atonement. Like Anselm, he rejected all thought of a ransom paid to the devil, but he repudiated Anselm's idea of a satisfaction rendered to God no less energetically. In Abelard's view, the Incarnation and death of Christ are the highest expression of God's love to undeserving people, the effect of which is to awaken their love in return—a position known as "exemplarism" or as the "moral influence theory" of the atonement. His ethical theory that good and evil inhere in the intention rather than in the act seemed to many to compromise the "objectivity" of God's law and to end in subjectivism. So also, his belief that the philosophers of antiquity were Christians before Christ, however consonant with ancient Christian opinion, was not that of his age, which saw in it a threat to the uniqueness of the biblical revelation.

Abelard, though perhaps more philosophically subtle than spiritually profound, was an immensely stimulating spirit. His direct followers were few, owing no doubt to his double condemnation and the antagonism of famous men, but his indirect influence was great. The impulse he gave to the dialectical method of theological inquiry, furthering the work of Anselm, was far-reaching. More than any other twelfth-century Parisian master, he was responsible for making that city and its later university the intellectual mistress of Europe in logic and theology. His preliminary efforts to survey the entire range of Christian doctrine, and his outlines for a "systematic" theology, stand as an important bridge between the earlier scholastic discussions of individual *quaestiones* and the great *summae,* or comprehensive surveys, of the thirteenth century.

Credit for again joining philosophical reason with traditional spirituality, as in Anselm, belongs to Hugh of St. Victor (1096?–1142). His work exhibits a moderate use of the dialectical method in the service of mystical themes drawn from the Neoplatonic tradition transmitted by Augustine and pseudo-Dionysius the Areopagite. Hugh appears to have been born of humble parents in northern France or Flanders, not of noble parents in Saxony, as formerly believed, though he was trained at a German monastery. He became an Augustinian canon at an early age and, in about 1115, entered the newly founded monastery of St. Victor, near Paris, where he attained eminence as head of its school. Known to his contemporaries as a "second Augustine," he was a quiet, modest man of profound learning and piety. His chief writings were the *Didascalion,* a very influential treatise on education, in which he extolled all human learning as an introduction to theology, and *De sacramentis christianae fidei* (The Sacraments of the Christian Faith), a much fuller survey of all the branches of theology than is to be found in Abelard's works, and thus the direct precursor of the later *summae.*

Hugh was not a mystic in the strict sense, in that he did not claim to describe the union of his own soul with God, yet he may be called a mystical theologian insofar as he traced the three stages of the soul's ascent to truth in

God. First, the "eye of the flesh" knows the world of sensible things; second, the "eye of reason," turned inward, knows itself; finally, the "eye of contemplation" comes upon God and understands all things in him. The third eye, however, has been closed by sin and must be opened by divine revelation. Faith is necessary, therefore, if the unseen God is to be believed and experienced. Such faith is more certain than mere opinion but less certain than direct knowledge—a characterization that was to become classic. For Hugh, no less than for Augustine and Bernard, the goal of theology is the personal experience and enjoyment of God, not the intellectual mastery of creedal content.

No original genius like Anselm, Abelard, and Hugh, yet a man of great intellectual service to his own age and held in honor until the Reformation and beyond, was Peter Lombard, the "Master of the Sentences" (1100?–1160?). Born near Novara, in Lombardy, he studied at Bologna, Reims, and Paris, thus combining the legal scholarship of northern Italy with the theological and dialectical learning of northern France. A friend of Bernard, who helped him on his way, Peter became, in 1140, a teacher of theology in the school of Notre Dame and, in 1159, the bishop of Paris. He certainly studied under Hugh at St. Victor, and it is likely that he was also a pupil of Abelard. Between 1150 and 1152, he wrote the work on which his fame rests, *Sententiarum libri quatuor* (Four Books of the Sentences). Under four divisions—God, Created Beings (creation and world history before Christ), Salvation (incarnation and redemption), and the Sacraments and Last Things (death, judgment, heaven, and hell)—he discussed the whole round of theology. In the fashion of Abelard's *Sic et non,* he proposed a doctrinal thesis or question for each topic; brought forward authorities for and against the thesis from Scripture, the fathers, the decrees of church councils, and papal pronouncements; and then offered a judgment (*sententia*) on the issue. To Abelard he owed his dialectical method, to Hugh his reverence for tradition and the church's teaching authority. Always displaying moderation and good sense, he produced a handbook which so fully met the needs of the age that it remained until the Reformation the main basis of theological instruction.

In the realm of canon or church law, a comparable fame and influence attended the compilation of Gratian, a monk of Bologna (d. 1159?). In about 1140, using the dialectical method perfected by Abelard and building on the work of earlier canonists such as Burchard of Worms (965?–1025) and Ivo of Chartres (1040?–1115), Gratian ordered the disparate and often conflicting mass of official church pronouncements in his *Concordia discordantium canonum* (Concordance of Discordant Canons), usually known as the *Decretum*. Like Lombard's *Sentences,* Gratian's *Decretum* soon became an authoritative text, forming the core of the church's official body of canon law, around which later collections clustered. Peter and Gratian thus demonstrated the fruitfulness of the dialectical method for systematizing the church's doctrine and law without sacrificing orthodoxy. In an age rife with dissent and heresy, they showed that one could "question" church teaching and still remain true to church tradition, that "reason" and "faith" were not inimical. Little wonder that Dante, in his *Divine Comedy,* placed Peter and Gratian side by side in Paradise.

Chapter 6

The Rediscovery of Aristotle; the Rise of the Universities

*T*HE FIRST PERIOD of Scholasticism may be said to have ended in the middle decades of the twelfth century. The schools, to be sure, continued in increasing activity, but no creative geniuses appeared during the last half of the twelfth century or the early thirteenth century, which was largely a time of further codification and compilation. This period did, however, witness two developments of profound importance for medieval intellectual and religious history: the gradual reintroduction to the West of the full corpus of Aristotle's works and the rise of the universities. Both developments, together with the rise of the mendicant orders and their dramatic impact upon the universities, resulted in a new and greater outburst of Scholastic activity in the thirteenth century.

Until about 1130, medieval thinkers had at their disposal only a fragment of Aristotle's works—the "old logic" (*logica vetus*), as it was known, comprising the *Categories* and *On Interpretation* of Aristotle himself plus the *Introduction* by Porphyry, all as translated and commented on by Boethius (see V:5). Between 1130 and 1170, the remainder of Aristotle's logical works were introduced to the West—the "new logic" (*logica nova*), comprising the *Prior Analytics* and *Posterior Analytics,* the *Topics,* and the *Sophistical Refutations.* During the course of the next hundred years, moreover, translations of Aristotle's writings on natural science (the *Physics* and *On the Heavens*), of his all-important philosophical works (*On the Soul,* the *Metaphysics,* the *Ethics*), and of his political and literary treatises (the *Politics* and *Rhetoric*) were forthcoming, so that by 1270 Latin Christendom possessed the entire Aristotelian corpus, and Aristotle's standing as "the Philosopher" was fully established. At the same time, translations of many other ancient writings also appeared, including the medical works of Hippocrates and Galen, the scientific and mathematical works of Euclid and Archimedes, and a number of the Platonic dialogues.

There were four main centers of translation activity: Antioch in Syria, Constantinople, Sicily, and, above all, Spain. The far-flung Muslim empire, stretching from India to Spain, had preserved much of the treasury of ancient thought, including Aristotle in Arabic translations (these latter often based, in turn, on earlier translations into Syriac by Nestorian Christians). Thus it came about that the Arabs of Spain served as the principal source for the infusion of the new learning into western Europe. The city of Toledo, following its reconquest by Christian forces in 1085, became a gathering place for northern scholars in search of ancient manuscripts and Greek learning. Here worked two of the most important early translators, Dominic Gundisalvi and Gerald of Cremona. Both men translated from Arabic into Latin (sometimes by way of an intermediate Spanish translation). At a later date, accurate translations, and revisions of earlier translations, were made directly from the Greek, many of them by the greatest of the medieval translators, the Flemish Dominican William of Moerbeke (1215?–1286), who for a time was a member of the papal court at Viterbo near Rome, where he came to know Thomas Aquinas.

The works of Aristotle, it must be noted, reached the West not only sporadically and piecemeal but also in an "impure" state. Apart from the inevitable textual corruptions attendant upon translations from Arabic (or Syriac) "originals," a number of works also passed as Aristotle's that were of Neoplatonic origin, namely, the so-called *Theology of Aristotle* (made up of passages from the *Enneads* of Plotinus) and the *Liber de Causis* (Book of Causes, excerpts from the *Elements of Theology* of Proclus, a disciple of Plotinus). This circumstance enabled many of the thirteenth-century Scholastics to combine Aristotelianism with the Christian Neoplatonism of Augustine and the pseudo-Dionysius and thus to soften the impact of Aristotle's "naturalism" and to render it more acceptable for traditional theological purposes.

The Aristotelian corpus also came to the West, via Spain, accompanied by a series of highly influential commentaries that had been produced from the ninth century onward by the leading Islamic and Jewish thinkers. The greatest of the medieval Jewish philosophers, whom Thomas Aquinas was to treat with the utmost respect, was Moses ben Maimon or Maimonides (born at Cordova in 1135, died in exile at Cairo in 1204), the author of the famous *Guide for the Perplexed,* a work that sought to reconcile revealed religion with the new Aristotelian philosophy. The most celebrated and influential of Aristotle's "commentators" were the two Islamic philosophers, ibn-Sina (Latinized as Avicenna, 980–1037, who lived and died in Persia) and ibn-Rushd (Averroës, born at Cordova in 1126, died at Marrakesh in 1198). Whereas Avicenna sought to establish the revealed religion of the Koran on a foundation of natural religion derived from Aristotle and certain Neoplatonic sources, Averroës considered Aristotle's teaching the supreme and final truth and sought to purge it of all Neoplatonic "contaminations." To Averroës was largely due the development in the later thirteenth century of a radical Aristotelianism, the so-called Latin Averroism, that regarded Aristotle as supreme among the teachers of truth and that was puzzled, therefore, by the problem of reconciling Christian revelation with an Aristotelian reason shorn of its Neoplatonic (theistic and mystical) accretions. The best known of these radical Aristotelians were two masters in the arts faculty at Paris in the 1260s and 1270s: Siger of Brabant and Boetius of Dacia.

It is clear, then, that medieval "Aristotelianism" was a complex admixture of Aristotle's own works and of Neoplatonic, Arabic, and Jewish components. The gradual introduction to the West of this great mass of heterogeneous material transformed the whole of late medieval thought. For the first time since the age of Augustine, Christian thinkers confronted a comprehensive vision of reality that owed nothing to specifically Christian sources of inspiration—a *Weltanschauung,* moreover, that in its strict Aristotelian form was secular and rationalistic. Throughout the thirteenth century and thereafter, theologians wrestled with the exigent issues posed by Aristotle's "naturalism"—such teachings as the eternity of the world, the soul's mortality, the dependence of virtue on "habit" (doing good), the primacy of sense-knowledge in human cognition, and the idea of the state as a purely "natural" phenomenon. The first two of these Aristotelian doctrines were in direct conflict with Christian revelation; the last three broke decisively with traditional Augustinianism. Little wonder that from the thirteenth century through the Reformation era, theologians debated the limits and contested the very legitimacy of a "Christian Aristotelianism."

The advent of "Aristotle" in the West coincided with a revolution in the medieval system of higher education: the rise of the universities. The first medieval universities came into existence during the closing years of the twelfth century. By 1500, about eighty universities had been founded throughout Europe. The historical development of the earliest universities remains too obscure to date exactly. In any event, owing to favorable geographical location and the repute of the masters who gathered there, certain towns and cities became famous educational centers: Paris and Oxford for theology, Bologna for church and civil law, Salerno and Montpellier for medicine.

The far-reaching educational changes which these institutions brought about were the standardization of teaching methods, textbooks, degrees, etc., and the association of students and teachers into collective bodies, or "universities," after the fashion of trade guilds. Such associations came about chiefly for protection, freedom from outside interference, and good order, but also for regulation of admission to the teaching profession. The original meaning of the term "university" is exhibited in the names *universitas scholarium,* the university of scholars or students, and *universitas magistrorum,* the university of masters or teachers. The beginnings of such organization may be placed about 1200.

By the end of the twelfth century, there were in Bologna two "universities" or mutual protective associations of law students. In the early thirteenth century, these two large corporations merged to form a single *universitas scholarium,* with its own elected rector. Gradually, students in the other faculties—the arts, medicine, and theology—also formed their own universities. At first, the teachers were excluded from the organization; in time, they formed their own colleges of doctors, but the nucleus of university organization in Italy, and throughout southern Europe, remained a guild of students, patterned on the Bolognese system. The system that prevailed in northern Europe, however, was that originally established at Paris—namely, a guild of masters (*universitas magistrorum*) organized for purposes of controlling admission to its ranks. The University of Paris evolved out of the cathedral school of Notre Dame and was early engaged in securing its independence from the bishop's chancellor, who alone could grant the license to teach and who sought to impose his own ordinances on the masters and scholars. Pope Innocent III (1198–1216), himself a former Paris master, intervened on behalf of the fledgling university. The corporation's earliest statutes date from about 1208 or 1209, were formalized in 1215 by the papal legate Robert de Curzon, and were subsequently confirmed by papal bulls.

By 1250, the university at Paris was composed of four distinct bodies of masters or "faculties": the masters of arts, of canon law (civil law was forbidden at Paris after 1219), of medicine, and of theology. The large arts faculty, including teachers and students, was further divided into four national groups or "nations" (another type of guild organization that seems to have originated in Bologna): the French (i.e., those from the Île-de-France and the Latin countries); the Picards (including the Low Countries); the Normans; and the English (comprising England, Germany, and northern and eastern Europe). Each nation was presided over by a proctor, and each faculty by a dean, save that of arts, which alone had a rector. By gradual stages, this rector became the head of the university.

In the arts faculty, at least in theory, the traditional seven liberal arts were taught: the *trivium* (grammar, rhetoric, and logic or dialectic) and the *quadrivium* (astronomy, arithmetic, geometry, and music). Actually, the arts course at Paris consisted almost entirely of Aristotelian logic and philosophy, plus rudimentary instruction in the natural sciences. Oxford, however, long retained more interest in the *quadrivium* than did Paris, and England in the thirteenth century could boast a succession of Oxford masters distinguished for their work in mathematics and the natural sciences. Their number included Robert Grosseteste (1168?–1253, bishop of Lincoln from 1235), who joined Aristotelian physics and metaphysics with Augustinian Neoplatonism in a creative synthesis that viewed light as the basic constituent of all reality (and thus gave a central place to astronomy and optics); and Grosseteste's leading pupil, Roger Bacon (1214?–1292?), famous for centuries as a necromancer but in modern times reputed for his insistence on the primacy of experiment in science and of experience in human life.

As regards university organization, the normal entrance age was fourteen or fifteen and presupposed only a prior education in Latin grammar and composition. Teaching in all faculties was principally by lecture or "reading" (*lectio*), in which the master "glossed" or provided a running commentary on the prescribed texts, while the students were expected to take copious notes. Difficult points in a text, as well as perennial topics of interest, had long been handled in the schools by the *quaestio,* or simple question-and-answer method, which in the universities developed into the *disputatio,* or debate, in accord with the full-blown dialectical method. The disputation could be both oral and written. The literary disputation was the characteristic form assumed by the theological masterpieces, the great *summae,* of the thirteenth century; the *Summa theologiae* of Thomas Aquinas, for example, "argues" every topic in keeping with the requirements of the Aristotelian syllogism. The oral disputation, however, was of greater practical import, since it was the second main component of university pedagogy. It was a public event, held at stated times and often lasting several days, in which a student and a master sought to arrive at a logical resolution ("determination") of two contradictory propositions, both of which were supported by seemingly valid arguments. Normally, the student presented the arguments pro and con, while the master was responsible for the final determination. The educational methods of *lectio* and *disputatio,* though prone to formalism and pedantry, enabled students to attain mastery of discrete bodies of knowledge, honed their analytical powers, and brought talent to light.

The first academic degree, that of bachelor, was similar to admission to apprenticeship in a guild. The second degree, that of master or doctor (originally synonymous terms), resembling the master workman in a guild, carried with it full authority to teach in one's own university (the *licentia docendi*) and, ultimately, the right to teach anywhere (the *ius ubique docendi*). At Paris, in 1215, the arts course lasted for six years, and one could not become a master of arts until at least age twenty. (The bachelor of arts was taken at some point along the way.) At both Paris and Oxford, the minimum age for the mastership or doctorate in theology was originally thirty-four, but this was later extended to about age forty. In order to attain this degree, one first became a master of arts and taught for a period of years in the arts faculty. The candidate then advanced through the intermediate degrees of bachelor of the Bible (*baccalaureus biblicus*) and bachelor of the *Sentences* of Peter Lombard (*baccalaureus sententiarius*), in which connection he lectured on each of these texts for several years. Relatively few students, of course, could afford the expenditure of time and money required for promotion to the doctor's degree.

The use of Latin as the sole language of the classroom made possible the assembly of students from all parts of Europe, and they flocked to the more famous universities in large numbers. The needs of these students, many of whom were of extreme poverty, early aroused the interest of benefactors. One of the most influential and oldest products of this interest was the Collège de la Sorbonne, founded for theological students at Paris around 1257 by Robert de

Sorbon (1201–1274), a chaplain to St. Louis. Many such "colleges" were established at other continental universities as well. Though they originated as endowed hospices or residence halls for indigent scholars, they became in time centers of teaching and social life and thus absorbed many of the functions of the university. They survived in France until the Revolution, but their ultimate home was England, at Oxford and Cambridge, where they became the most characteristic feature of university organization.

The medieval university was the chief beneficiary of the rediscovery of Aristotle, and it remains one of the most important and original contributions of the Middle Ages to civilization and the modern world.

Chapter 7

High Scholasticism and Its Theology; Thomas Aquinas

THE RECOVERY OF the whole of Aristotle, the rise of the universities, and the devotion of the mendicant orders to learning ushered in the period of "high Scholasticism" in the thirteenth century. An age of great intellectual ferment and remarkable creativity, it was distinguished by a series of brilliant thinkers, including several of uncontested genius, who produced comprehensive surveys (*summae*) of theology that made free and full use of philosophy and the dialectical method to establish their conclusions. Though the logic employed was invariably Aristotelian, the philosophy was usually an eclectic mix of Aristotle and Neoplatonism; and while a Christian Aristotelianism eventually prevailed within the Dominican order, it did not go unopposed either by conservative traditionalists or by the leading representatives of the Franciscan order. In any case, whatever their attitudes toward Aristotle and the new learning, virtually all the great theologians between 1250 and 1350 were members of the mendicant orders, and most were natives of either Italy or England, even though Paris continued to be the intellectual capital of Europe.

The Franciscans had come to Paris already in 1219. The founder of their school there was the most famous Parisian master of his day, the Englishman Alexander of Hales (1186?–1245), who became a friar in 1236. His university chair in theology, which he had occupied since about 1220, thus came into possession of the Franciscan order. Alexander's massive *Summa,* the literary fountainhead of the Franciscan school, was not so much a genuine "system" of theology as a stringing together of doctrines, and it owed as much to Augustine and Neoplatonism, and to the Victorines and Anselm, as it did to Aristotle. (This *Summa* is attributed to Alexander, but while he may well have planned and organized the work, it was probably written by a number of his disciples.)

The most eminent of the Franciscan doctors of the thirteenth century, a theologian who is justly considered the intellectual equal of Thomas Aquinas, was Giovanni di Fidanza (1217?–1274), generally known as Bonaventura. Born in Bagnorea, in Tuscany, he studied at Paris under Alexander of Hales and the latter's successor, John of La Rochelle, and eventually occupied the Franciscan chair in theology there from 1254 to 1257. (It was not until 1257, however, that he, along with Thomas Aquinas, was formally admitted into the ranks of the university masters.) Having entered the Franciscan order in 1243, he succeeded John of Parma as the order's minister general in 1257. In 1273, he was named cardinal bishop of Albano by Pope Gregory X; he died while attending the Council of Lyons in 1274. Famed as a teacher in Paris, especially for his brilliant *Commentary on the Sentences* (ca. 1250), he was even more distinguished for his wise leadership of the Friars Minor during difficult times (see V:4) and for his purity of life. In addition to academic works, he also wrote the "official" biography of Francis of Assisi (the *Legenda maior,* 1263) and composed an authoritative commentary on the Franciscan rule. He was canonized by Pope Sixtus IV in 1482 and declared "doctor of the church" by Sixtus V in 1587.

Spiritually a son of St. Francis, Bonaventura was intellectually a disciple of St. Augustine. Like the latter, he desired to know but two things: God, the supreme reality, and the soul's progress to union with God. Philosophy and all secular knowledge are, at best, only a means to the end of "seeing" God (the *visio Dei*). Hence, while he recognized and used Aristotle as the master dialectician, Bonaventura was far less of an Aristotelian than Thomas Aquinas and, unlike Thomas, did not articulate a system of pure philosophy to undergird his theology. Unlike Thomas, moreover, and in explicit opposition to Aristotle's theory of knowledge, he firmly held to the basic Augustinian tenet that intellectual and moral certainty requires the divine, supernatural illumination of the mind and conscience. Bonaventura was essentially a mystical theologian, deeply indebted to Dionysius the Areopagite and Richard of St. Victor as well as to Augustine and Francis. His central concerns are eloquently summarized in his brief *Itinerarium mentis in Deum* (The Journey of the Mind to God), a classic text of Franciscan spirituality and a masterpiece of mystical literature. By meditation and prayer, and aided throughout by divine grace, the mind journeys to God first by gazing upon his traces in the world at large, then by catching sight of him deep within itself, and finally by rising above itself to behold God the Holy Trinity, who is the origin and goal of all that is. At this highest stage, all intellectual operations cease; the soul (not the mind) unknowingly unites with God in the ecstasy of love and affection.

It is clear that Bonaventura's thought was largely alien to the spirit and substance of Aristotle's philosophy. In this respect, he remained a traditionalist and a less innovative theologian than Aquinas. One must remember, however, that he was called from regular academic work at a time (1257) that just antedated the great influx of Christian Aristotelianism owing to the work and writings of Albert the Great, Thomas Aquinas, and Siger of Brabant, and that his hostility to "Aristotle" was chiefly directed against the radical Aristotelians ("Latin Averroists") in the arts faculty at Paris. Furthermore, Bonaventura was in many respects a more speculative theologian than Aquinas, as is shown, for example, in his use of the orthodox (Augustinian) doctrine of the Trinity to explain the fundamental structure of the created order, and in his elaboration of a method of "introspective speculation" whereby the mind, by descending into its own inner world under the leading of grace, is enabled to ascend to the vision of God that transcends the intellect. Bonaventura was also a genuinely systematic thinker, and his works exhibit a synthetic power worthy of comparison with that of Aquinas.

The Dominicans had arrived at Paris in 1217, just two years after their founding, and they soon secured two of the university's twelve chairs in theology, beginning with Roland of Cremona (in 1229) and John of St. Giles (in 1231). The most famous of the early Dominican masters at Paris, before Aquinas, was Albert of Germany, known to his contemporaries as "the Great" (Albertus Magnus, 1200?–1280). Born of noble parentage at Lauingen, near Ulm, sometime between 1193 and 1206, Albert studied the arts at Padua, where he became a Dominican in 1223, and theology at Paris, where he later lectured as master from 1245 to 1248. In 1248, he was sent to Cologne to establish the first Dominican center of advanced studies in Germany. For a time, he also served as provincial prior of his order (1253–1256) and as bishop of Regensburg (1260–1262), but most of his career was spent in teaching and writing at Cologne.

A marvel of productivity, Albert devoted the greater part of his long career to writing a series of commentaries on the Aristotelian corpus. This vast project, begun in the early 1250s, took some twenty years to complete. Albert was an indefatigable compiler and commentator rather than an original thinker, and his Aristotelianism was modified by his acceptance of many Neoplatonic views expressed by Augustine, the pseudo-Dionysius, Avicenna, and the *Liber de Causis* (see V:6). Notwithstanding its lack of originality, his work marks an epoch in the history of Christian thought, in that Albert followed the leading Islamic and Jewish thinkers in accepting pagan philosophy, above all Aristotle's, as affording true knowledge of the natural order. Philosophy thus stands forth as an autonomous discipline worthy of credence on its own terms, inasmuch as it unfolds the divine master plan of creation. Albert's views were soon brought to a clearer and more consistent expression by his foremost pupil, Thomas Aquinas, the prince of Scholastics.

Thomas Aquinas (1224 or 1225-1274) was the son of Landulf and Theodora d'Aquino, members of the lower nobility in the Hohenstaufen kingdom of Sicily. He was born in the family castle at Roccasecca, near the ancient city of Aquino, located about halfway between Rome and Naples. At the age of five, he was brought as an oblate to the abbey of Monte Cassino, the mother house of Benedictine monasticism, with the expectation that in time he would become its abbot. (In later life, he was offered the abbacy but declined it.) Following a period of study (1239-1244) in the arts faculty at the "secular" university of Naples (founded by Emperor Frederick II in 1224), Thomas joined the Dominican order at Naples in 1244, much to the displeasure of his family, who kidnapped and detained him for over a year at Roccasecca. After his release, he rejoined the Dominicans and was sent to Paris for his novitiate and theological study under Albert the Great (1245-1248). In 1248, he accompanied Albert to Cologne for further study and for cursory lecturing on the Bible as a bachelor of theology. It was here that his fellow friars reputedly dubbed him the "dumb ox" (*bovem mutum*)—a reference to his corpulence and his personal reserve.

Thomas remained at Cologne until 1252, when he was sent back to Paris to prepare for the mastership in theology. From 1252 to 1256, he lectured on the *Sentences* of Peter Lombard. In the spring of 1256, he incepted as master of theology at Paris, occupying the second of the Dominican chairs there; but his formal reception into the consortium of university masters was delayed for sixteen months, until the fall of 1257, owing to an acrimonious dispute between the mendicant orders and the secular masters of theology (who wished to restrict the privileges of the mendicants and to limit the number of Dominican chairs in theology to one). From 1259 to 1268, Thomas was in Italy, teaching and writing at Naples, Orvieto, Rome, and Viterbo. In 1269, he returned to Paris for his second stay as master in theology; in 1272, he was called to Naples, where he established a Dominican center of studies. He died on March 7, 1274, at the Cistercian monastery of Fossanuova, on his way to the Council of Lyons. In 1323, he was canonized at Avignon by Pope John XXII. Though for centuries after his death Thomas was widely acclaimed the church's universal teacher (*doctor communis*), it was not until 1879 that Pope Leo XIII officially declared his thought the touchstone of Roman Catholic theology.

During his crowded years of teaching and preaching, Thomas was constantly consulted on important civil and ecclesiastical questions, and bitter controversies often raged about him, especially during his Paris years. Yet in spite of these distractions he remained a serene spirit and a tireless and voluminous writer. Of his writings, which number about one hundred, the most important are his two great theological syntheses: the *Summa contra gentiles,* written between 1259 and 1264 for use by Dominican missionaries preaching against Muslims, Jews, and heretical Christians in Spain; and the *Summa theologiae,* the crown of his genius, begun in 1265 as a textbook for beginners in theology and left unfinished at his death. (Thomas ceased all writing after December 6, 1273, when he had a mystical experience while celebrating Mass. The *Summa theologiae* was completed under the direction of his secretary, Friar Reginald of Piperno.) Personally, Thomas was a humble and profoundly religious man, as evidenced in the liturgy which he composed for the Feast of Corpus Christi and in his hymns, prayers, and sermons. Intellectually, his work was marked by a clarity, a logical consistency, and a breadth of presentation that places him among the greatest teachers of the church.

The aim of all theological investigation, according to Thomas, is to give true knowledge of God and of humanity's supernatural origin and destiny. Such knowledge comes in part by natural human reason, which can apprehend the rational "preambles of faith" (*praeambula fidei*)—namely, the existence of an omnipotent and omniscient God and the immortality of the soul. Thomas's insistence that these truths can be attained apart from the divine illumination of the mind, solely through inferential reasoning from the observed character of the world, was a revolutionary break with the Augustinian-Franciscan (Platonic) tradition. Thomas also defended the root Aristotelian premise that all natural knowledge—including knowledge of God—begins with sense experience. The existence of God, therefore, is not self-evident: it is known mediately through reflection on the data of experience, not immediately through the soul's probing of its own depths (Augustine-Bonaventura) or through the mind's possession of the very idea of God (Anselm).

Natural reason, to be sure, knows nothing of those "mysteries of faith" (*articuli fidei*) which are necessary to eternal beatitude, such truths, namely, as the existence of God as a Holy Trinity, the incarnation of God the Son in Jesus Christ and the world's redemption through him, the resurrection of the body and the Last Judgment, etc. Reason, therefore, must be perfected by the divine revelation (*sacra doctrina*) contained in the canonical Scriptures. The Scriptures are the only final authority (*regula fidei*), though they are always to be understood in the light of the interpretations of the church fathers, the decrees of the church councils, and the papal definitions of the faith—in short, as comprehended by the teaching authority of the church. While these revealed truths lie beyond the capacity of reason, they are not opposed to reason, and reason, illumined by faith, can show the inadequacy of objections to them. Thomas was thus far from sharing Anselm's conviction that all truths of Christianity are philosophically demonstrable; but he held that there can be no contradiction between philosophy and theology, since both are from God and truth is one.

Thomas did, however, carefully distinguish between philosophy and theology, without separating them. They are two independent "sciences," he argued, two distinct modes of knowing, but they are congruent inasmuch as the knowledge of God—natural theology—is common to both disciplines. Here, then, is the famous Thomistic synthesis of faith and reason, in which reason—specifically, Aristotelian philosophy—is granted its own integrity and authority. Yet Thomas also yoked them together as unequals, insofar as natural reason must be *completed* by divine revelation, in keeping with the fundamental Thomistic axiom that "grace does not destroy but perfects nature" (*gratia non tollit sed perficit naturam*). Thus, synthesis did not preclude subordination, and Thomas remained throughout a committed Christian theologian who viewed the function of philosophy in the light of humanity's supernatural destiny to "see" and "enjoy" God in heaven.

In treating of God, in his theology proper, Thomas made free use of biblical, Aristotelian, and Neoplatonic (Augustinian-Dionysian) conceptions. God is Pure Act, without any limitation or unrealized potentialities, and thus God alone is changeless. God is the Prime Cause, himself uncaused, and thus God alone exists in and through himself (*ens a se*). In the same way, it is true of God alone that in him essence (*quod est,* what a thing is) is identical to existence (*esse,* the fact of existing, the act of being). Hence, God is not merely "a being," or one who "has" being, but the One who simply and necessarily "is," being itself (*ipsum esse*). God, therefore, is most real and perfect being, the source and end of all that has being, the absolute plenitude of being.

The Thomist doctrine of God, though rooted in tradition, was not a mere amalgam of traditional elements. It was an original creation in that Thomas went beyond Aristotle and Greek philosophy in framing a new metaphysics of being. Whereas Aristotle (and the Greeks) had wrestled with the problem of "becoming" (what are things and how do they come to be?), Thomas made "existence" the central problem of metaphysics (why is there anything at all? why something rather than nothing?). The existence of beings which are not themselves self-caused can be explained only by the necessary existence of a First Uncaused Cause, and thus Thomas offered five proofs for the existence of God based on the argument from causality or origin. He was confident, moreover, that his philosophical language about God corresponded to, and interpreted, the biblical name for God revealed to Moses: *Qui est,* He Who Is.[1] Our knowledge of God, however, remains severely limited. Since God is infinite, and our minds finite, it is possible to know only *that* God is, but not *what* he is, other than to know what God is not (the way of negation) and to try to know the divine nature according to the analogies that hold between God the creator and his creatures (the way of analogical predication). Even the knowledge of God given to faith through revelation remains analogical, and Thomas did not hesitate to conclude that "he knows God best who acknowledges that whatever he thinks and says falls short of what God really is."[2]

---

[1] Exod. 3:14.   [2] *Expositio super librum De causis,* lectio 6.

God, being perfect, needs nothing, and therefore the creation of the world was an expression of the divine goodness which God freely bestows on the existences he thus called into being. God's providence extends to all events, and it is manifested in the predestination of some to everlasting life and in leaving others to the consequences of their self-willed sin in everlasting condemnation. Human beings have, indeed, free will, but this does not preclude the determining or permissive providence of God. The divine permission of evil results in the higher good of the whole.

In his anthropology, as in his epistemology, Thomas made a revolutionary break with the Platonic-Augustinian tradition and was soon accused of introducing a "novel" and "pernicious" doctrine. The Augustinians were intent upon upholding the soul's spirituality and unique status, its nearness to God and its categorical difference from the body. They held that the soul is a substance in its own right, and that the "form" (immanent determining principle) of the body is not the immortal soul but a distinct "form of corporeity" (*forma corporeitatis*), while the soul itself possesses a multiplicity of forms (forms of its vegetative, sensitive, and intellectual life). Thomas taught, by contrast, that the human soul, immaterial and immortal though it be, is not an independent, separate substance, which merely "uses" or "governs" a body. Each individual soul, rather, has been created by God to be the single form of the human body, so that soul and body together are one substance, and the person is a psychophysical unity. The soul thus acquires its particular natural characteristics from the body, though it does not depend on the body for its existence and survives the death of the body. Yet the soul does require the body to be a human being in the proper sense, and for Thomas this condition explains the need for the resurrection of the body at the Last Day.

As originally created, Adam had, in addition to his natural powers, a superadded gift (*donum superadditum*) which enabled him to seek the highest good and to practice the three Christian virtues—faith, hope, and love. This gift Adam lost by sin, which also corrupted his natural powers, so that his state became not merely a lack of original righteousness, but a positive turning toward lower aims. In this fallen state, it was impossible for Adam to please God, and this corruption was transmitted to all his posterity. The latter still has the power to attain the four natural virtues of prudence, justice, courage, and self-control; but these, though bringing a certain measure of temporal honor and happiness, are not sufficient to enable their possessor to attain the vision of God.

The restoration of fallen humanity is possible only through the free and unmerited grace of God, by which the superadded gift is restored to human nature, sins are forgiven, and power to practice the three Christian virtues is infused. This infused grace (*gratia infusa*) is not the indwelling of the soul by God the Holy Spirit, or "uncreated grace" (*gratia increata*), as Peter Lombard had taught. It is, rather, a love created within the soul by the sacraments of the church (*gratia creata*)—a truly human disposition or "habit" (*habitus*) of charity whereby the sinner is made acceptable before God and is enabled to live in obedience to God's will. No human act can win this grace, but salvation is impossible without the free exercise of this divinely bestowed habit of love, itself the fruit of Christ's self-sacrifice. While God could conceivably have forgiven sins and granted grace without this sacrifice—here Thomas differed from Anselm—the work of Christ was the wisest and most efficient means God could choose, and the world's entire redemption is based on it. That work involved satisfaction for sin, and Christ won a merit which deserves a reward. Christ's work also moves persons to love God and their neighbors. Thomas thus developed and combined views presented by Anselm and Abelard. Christ's satisfaction superabounds the world's sin, and the reward which Christ cannot possibly receive, since as God he needs nothing, comes to the advantage of the human race, of which Christ is the head and the exemplar of the "new humanity."

Once redeemed by Christ and empowered by sacramental grace, actively exercising the habit of charity, the believer performs works that are truly God-pleasing and fully meritorious (*merita de condigno,* merits of worthiness), themselves deserving the reward of eternal life. The faith that ultimately justifies one before God, then, is a faith that is "formed" by works of love (*fides caritate formata*); lacking these, faith remains "unformed" (*fides informis*) and so is not a living and saving faith. Yet every good work is made possible only by the prevenient and cooperating grace of God. Aquinas thus found full room for the two dominating components of medieval piety—grace and merit.

The divinely ordained vehicles of grace are the sacraments, which have been given to the church to administer and are necessary for salvation. Here, in the area of sacramental theology, Scholasticism attained far greater precision and systematic ordering than had previously existed. For the most part, however, the Scholastic theologians, and official church teaching as well, were only giving formal articulation to long-standing practices of piety and worship among the faithful. The development of sacramental theology in the Middle Ages thus exhibits the most thorough application of the ancient principle, *lex orandi lex credendi*—"the rule of prayer should prescribe the rule of faith."

The ancient feeling that all sacred actions, including monastic vows, were sacraments was still alive in the twelfth century, but Peter Lombard defined the sacraments as seven and the influence of his *Sentences* eventually prevailed. (When and where the number seven originated is uncertain; nor was this exclusive number officially recognized until the Council of Florence in 1439.) As enumerated by the Lombard, the sacraments are baptism, confirmation, the eucharist, penance, extreme unction, ordination, and matrimony. All were instituted by Christ, either directly or through the apostles, and all, according to Thomas, not only signify grace but cause (confer) grace. Without them, there is no true union between Christ the head and the members of his mystical body, the church.

Every sacrament consists of two elements defined in Aristotelian terms of "matter" and "form"—an outward action or external medium (bread, water, wine, etc.) and a formula (words of institution) conveying its purpose and effect ("I baptize you," "I absolve you," etc.). The administrant must have the intention of doing what Christ and the church appointed, and the recipient, at least in the case of those of years of discretion, must have a sincere desire to receive the benefit of the sacrament. These conditions fulfilled, the sacrament conveys grace *ex opere operato*—that is, by the act duly performed. Of this grace God is the principal cause; the sacrament itself is the instrumental cause. It is the means by which the virtue of Christ's passion is applied to his members. Hence Thomas calls the sacraments "relics of the passion of Christ."

Through baptism the recipient is regenerated, and original and previous personal sins, as well as the punishments due these sins, are pardoned, though the tendency to sin is not obliterated. Grace is given to resist sin, and the lost power to attain the Christian virtues is restored. Baptism, like confirmation and ordination, impresses on the soul an "indelible stamp" (*character indelibilis*), an indestructible spiritual disposition to honor God. (Hence, these three sacraments are not repeated for the same person.)

By 1200, the recognized language for defining Christ's real presence in the eucharistic elements was the philosophical term "transubstantiation"—a word that had appeared already in the middle of the twelfth century (though Peter Lombard in 1150 still used the old language of "conversion"). This concept was given full dogmatic authority by the Fourth Lateran Council in 1215. Thomas Aquinas but added clarity and precision of definition. At the words of consecration by the priest—through the divine power resident in the words themselves and also conferred upon the priest by ordination—the miraculous change is wrought, so that while the "accidents" of the bread and wine (shape, taste, and the like) remain unaltered, their "substance" is transformed into the very body and blood of Christ.

Thomas also accepted and elaborated the view (known as "concomitance") that the whole body and blood of Christ are present in either consecrated element. This teaching was not original to him but had developed with the increasing custom of the laity to partake of the bread only. The withdrawal of the cup from the laity did not take place at the instigation of the clergy, as is often thought, but began as a lay practice due chiefly to fear of dishonoring the sacrament by spilling the consecrated wine, i.e., the precious blood of Christ. Such anxiety had manifested itself as early as the seventh century in the widespread custom of dipping the bread in the wine—a practice (known as "intinction") that was forbidden by church synods in 675 and 1175 but was supported by lay sentiment. By the time of Aquinas, lay communion in the bread alone had become almost universal, and the doctrine of concomitance both explained and justified this practice. Lay communion under only one "species" or "kind" (*communio sub una specie*) was officially established in 1415 by decree of the Council of Constance.

Medieval piety and worship reached their highest point in the eucharist or Mass, which already in the eleventh century was beginning to displace baptism as the central sacrament. This sacrament not only causes grace, but it also contains the very author of grace, Christ himself. It was deemed altogether proper, therefore, to "adore the host," that is, to address prayers and pay vows to the consecrated bread—Christ himself—reserved in the tabernacle on the altar or carried in procession on the Feast of Corpus Christi (for which Thomas Aquinas drew up the services). The Mass is the continuation of the Incarnation, the unbloody repetition (or "re-presentation") of the passion, the source of spiritual upbuilding to the recipient, the evidence of the believer's union with Christ, and a propitiatory sacrifice well-pleasing to God, inclining him to be gracious to those in need on earth and in purgatory.

The sacrament of penance, while not reckoned of equal dignity with baptism or the eucharist, was really of great, if not prime, importance for the individual believer, given its centrality to the church's pastoral and disciplinary life. Baptism effects the forgiveness of previous sins, but for those committed after baptism penance is necessary. The sins in view here are the so-called "mortal" or "deadly" sins—those, according to Thomas, which involve a turning away from God, from immutable good—as distinct from "venial" sins, which involve only an inordinate turning toward mutable good. The "matter" of penance, for Thomas, consists of the three penitential acts: contrition, confession, and satisfaction. Contrition is sincere sorrow for the offense against God and a determination not to repeat it. Yet Thomas also holds that a penance begun in "attrition," in displeasure over sins committed and in fear of punishment, may by infused grace become a real contrition.

Private (auricular) confession to the priest had become increasingly widespread since its advocacy in the West by the Celtic and Anglo-Saxon monk-missionaries (see IV:1). Abelard and Peter Lombard were of the opinion that a true contrition was followed immediately by divine forgiveness, even without priestly confession, though they thought such confession desirable. The Fourth Lateran Council, in 1215, required lay confession to a priest at least once a year of every person who had reached the age of discretion; such annual confession thereby became church law. Thomas explained that priestly confession and absolution are necessary because only through the sacramental infusion of grace could a penance begun in uncertainty about the degree of sorrow for one's sins, or a penance begun in servile fear (attrition), become a penance of true contrition.

Though God, through priestly absolution, forgives the penitent the guilt and the eternal punishment that are the due of sin, certain temporal punishments or "satisfactions" remain as a consequence of sin. These temporal penalties satisfy the sinner's offense against God and reestablish the divine honor, so far as it is in human power to do so. They also enable the absolved person to avoid sin in the future. They are the "fruits of repentance."

On evidence of the penitent's contrition (or attrition), confession, and willingness to give satisfaction, the priest, as Christ's representative, pronounces absolution (which is the "form" of the sacrament). Without priestly pardon, no one guilty after baptism of a "deadly" sin has assurance of salvation. Following absolution, the priest imposes fitting works of satisfaction, which, if not completed in this life, will be completed in purgatory.

The century and a half before Aquinas had witnessed the rapid growth of the system of "indulgences," which was integrally bound up with the penitential satisfactions. An "indulgence" was a remission of a part or all of the temporal penalties. Bishops had long exercised the right to relax satisfactions in cases where circumstances indicated unusual contrition. Great services to the church were also held to deserve such consideration. The full indulgence system, however, seems not to have come into operation before the eleventh century. Its first conspicuous use was by Pope Urban II, who in 1095 promised a plenary indulgence to all who engaged in the First Crusade, though Pope Alexander II had given similar privileges on a smaller scale for battle against the Muslims in Spain in about 1063. Once begun, the system spread with great rapidity. Not only popes but bishops also gave indulgences, and on constantly easier terms. Pilgrimages to sacred places or at special times, and contributions to a good work, such as building a church or even a bridge or road, were deemed deserving of such reward. The financial possibilities of the system were soon perceived and exploited. Since "temporal" penalties included those of purgatory, the value of an indulgence was enormous, though undefined, and the tendency to substitute it for a real penance was one to which human nature readily responded.

Such was the practice to which Aquinas now gave the classic interpretation. Following Alexander of Hales, he taught that the superabundant merits of Christ and of the saints constitute a treasury of good works from which a portion may be transferred to the needy sinner by the authority of the church in the person of the pope (who may at will share his authority with the bishops). An indulgence can, indeed, avail only for those who are truly contrite, but for such it removes, in whole or in part, the temporal penalties here on earth and in purgatory. Indulgences were never, in church teaching, a license to commit sin. They were a remission of the penalties justly due sins already committed, repented, and forgiven. Ordinary believers, however, rarely drew the careful theological distinction between remission of temporal penalties and forgiveness of sins; official church teaching on indulgences remained inchoate; and prelates of the church routinely used the indulgence system as a partial solution to their pressing fiscal problems. Thus, the system gave rise to abuses and scandals during the later Middle Ages and thereby gave occasion to the wholesale attack on the sacrament of penance by the Protestant reformers.

At the time of death, according to Thomas, the souls of the wicked pass immediately to hell, which is endless and from which there is no release. The souls of those who have made full and faithful use of the church's sacramental graces go at once to heaven. The souls of the mass of Christians who have but imperfectly availed themselves of the means of grace must undergo a longer or shorter period of suffering and purification in purgatory.

The church is one, whether in heaven, or on earth, or in purgatory. When one member suffers, all suffer; when one does well, all share in this good work. On this unity Thomas bases prayers to the saints and for those in purgatory. The visible church, moreover, requires a visible head, namely, the Roman pontiff, subjection to whom is necessary for salvation. The pope, as vicar of Christ and St. Peter's successor, possesses a plenitude of power (*plenitudo potestatis*) over ecclesiastical affairs, has direct jurdisdiction over all souls, and can exercise his episcopal rights in every territory. To the pope also belongs the authority to determine what is correct doctrine, to summon general councils, and to issue, if need be, new definitions of faith.

Such are the leading features of Thomist theology. The history of Scholasticism after Thomas Aquinas is, in large measure, the story of critical reactions to his monumental achievement and of the development of alternative approaches to the ancient problem of "reason and revelation."

Chapter 8

Late Scholasticism; Duns Scotus and William of Ockham

THE IMPOSING Thomistic synthesis of Aristotelian philosophy and Christian theology, far from sweeping all before it, evoked strong opposition along a wide front, from conservatives among Thomas's fellow Dominicans as well as from the leading Franciscan thinkers. We have observed that Thomas, in his epistemology and psychology, appeared as a dangerous innovator vis-à-vis the older Platonic-Augustinian tradition. Some critics also associated his teaching with that of the radical Aristotelians active in the arts faculty at Paris between 1265 and 1275, the most notable of whom was Siger of Brabant (1240?–1284?). Not a few churchmen in high places were convinced that the university in Paris was a breeding ground for heresy and that pagan naturalism and rationalism were there undermining the old verities and had even contaminated the Christian Aristotelianism of Thomas Aquinas.

Thus, in 1277, exactly three years after Thomas's death, the bishop of Paris, Étienne Tempier, acting with the encouragement of Pope John XXI, issued a list of 219 condemned propositions, including a number of Thomistic theses, though Thomas was not named. A few days later, the archbishop of Canterbury, Robert Kilwardby (?–1279), himself a Dominican and a former master at Paris, "visited" Oxford and censured a number of Thomistic propositions being taught there. This latter censure was confirmed, in 1284 and again in 1286, by Kilwardby's successor in the see of Canterbury, the Franciscan John Peckham (1225?–1292). But Thomas did not lack for powerful defenders, among them his old friend and teacher, Albert the Great, and soon "Thomism" became the official doctrine of the Dominican order. Hostile attacks ceased, and the earlier condemnations were removed, when Thomas was canonized by Pope John XXII in 1323.

One result of the condemnations of 1277, and of the climate of suspicion that produced them, was the formation of distinct and often bitterly competing "schools" of thought, generally identified with the mendicant orders and their premier theologians. While the Dominicans endorsed the Christian Aristotelianism of Aquinas, the Franciscans took their bearings from the neo-Augustinianism of Alexander of Hales and Bonaventura. These schools, however, were by no means opposed at every point; all were eclectic in their use of traditional theological and philosophical resources, and even within the same school there were often sharp conflicts of opinion and teaching.

The mainstay of the Franciscan school throughout the late Middle Ages, and the most formidable of Thomas's critics, was John Duns Scotus ("the Scot," 1265?–1308), a thinker of remarkable subtlety and acuity and one of the greatest of the Scholastics. Little is known of his early life, but it is likely that he was born at Maxton, in Roxburghshire, Scotland, in 1265 or 1266. He joined the Friars Minor in 1281, was ordained priest in 1291, and studied at Oxford and Paris. He lectured on the *Sentences* at Oxford (ca. 1300) and then at Paris (1302–1303). After a brief period of enforced absence, he returned to Paris in 1304, becoming master of theology in 1305 and teaching there until 1307, when he was sent to the Franciscan house of studies at Cologne, where he died the following year. While he criticized certain doctrines of Aquinas with the utmost acumen, Scotus was no diehard conservative like John Peckham. He rejected the Augustinian doctrine of the divine illumination of the intellect, adopting in its place Aristotle's theory of knowledge, and he was much influenced by the Islamic philosopher Avicenna.

With Scotus, one observes the beginning of a dramatic change from the age of Aquinas and of "high Scholasticism." The Schoolmen of the fourteenth and fifteenth centuries no longer produced great systems of speculative divinity; instead, they wrote elaborate commentaries on the *Sentences* or critical expositions of a single topic. The logical analysis of propositions replaced the metaphysical analysis of essences. Limits were increasingly imposed on the range of natural reason; conversely, the scope of divine revelation was widened. Theologians no longer attempted, as Thomas had done, to integrate the natural and supernatural orders through the notion of God as Pure Act and First Mover Unmoved; instead, they emphasized both the unknowability of God to natural reason and the absolute freedom of God over against the world he created. Though Duns himself was the last of the great Schoolmen who sought to join the metaphysical study of being with the theological study of God, he also appears in retrospect as the harbinger of a new phase of Scholastic thought —the age of "late Scholasticism," with its conflicts between adherents of the "modern way" (*via moderna*) of Ockham and defenders of the "ancient way" (*via antiqua*) of Aquinas. As will be seen, Duns and his followers also came to be numbered among the theologians of the *via antiqua,* inasmuch as they still made room for natural (metaphysical) theology. Nonetheless, the thought of Scotus differed widely from that of Aquinas and launched a new age of Scholasticism.

Scotus argued that the Thomistic proofs for the existence of God (the "Five Ways"), all based on the principle of causality, demonstrate only the existence of a supreme mover within a hierarchy of movers, not of a unique, transcendent God: these "cosmological" proofs, in short, do not get beyond the physical world. He offered, instead, a series of "ontological" proofs, similar at points to Anselm's famous argument, but he insisted that philosophy (metaphysics) can demonstrate the existence only of a being who is infinite, not of one who is omnipotent, just, and merciful. What Christians understand by "God," as well as the truth of the soul's immortality, belongs strictly to the realm of revelation and faith. Thus, compared to Aquinas, Scotus greatly reduced the area of "overlap" between philosophy and theology and placed strict limits on the capacity of natural reason to penetrate the data of faith.

In his anthropology, Scotus also strongly opposed Aquinas. For Thomas (and the Aristotelians) the intellect is the royal faculty—a human being is a "rational animal"—and the will, being "blind," must be guided by the intellect. For Scotus (and the Augustinians), however, the will is the nobler faculty because it directs the intellect to its objects and, above all, because it is the seat of love—and love of God is greater than knowledge of him. The human will, furthermore, is essentially a free power while the intellect is not, since the mind must necessarily assent to a true proposition, once it sees its truth, whereas the will remains free to act or not to act. Thus, Scotist "voluntarism" opposes Thomist "intellectualism."

A dispute that occasioned intense controversy between Thomists (Dominicans) and Scotists (Franciscans) concerned the "immaculate conception" of the Virgin Mary. Aquinas, concerned to maintain and underline the view that Jesus Christ was the Savior of *all* persons, taught that she shared in the original sin of the human race, while conceding that she was sanctified the moment after her soul had been created. Scotus held that Mary was preserved from the stain of original sin owing to the foreseen merits of Christ—a teaching that was to be declared a dogma of the Roman church by Pope Pius IX in 1854.

The center of Scotist theology is the unconditional freedom of an omnipotent God to will whatever is not contradictory to his nature as supreme goodness. Whereas Aquinas held that God wills something because it is good, Scotus maintained that something is good solely because God wills it, and the only thing that God cannot will is hatred of himself. Since God's infinite freedom and absolute power cannot be constrained by anything creaturely and finite, even Christ's sacrifice upon the cross has only the value that God puts upon it. Any other act would have been sufficient for the world's redemption had God seen fit so to regard it. Nor can one say, with Aquinas, that Christ's death was the wisest way of salvation: that would be to limit God's will. All one can affirm is that it was the way chosen by God. The sacraments, likewise, do not intrinsically contain and convey grace, as Aquinas taught, but are the conditions appointed by God upon which, if fulfilled, grace is bestowed. Grace thus resides not in the sacraments ("signs") as instrumental causes, but solely in the divine "covenant" (*pactum*) to be present when they are duly performed.

The entire Scotist doctrine of grace and salvation diverges sharply from the Thomist doctrine. Salvation, insisted Scotus, depends solely on God's free acceptance (*acceptatio*) of persons and their meritorious works, not on any quality of their souls, even a divinely created quality. God is free to dispense with all created habits. Hence, Thomas erred in positing an intrinsic connection between salvation and the habit of charity created in the soul by the sacramental infusion of grace. Moreover, God has determined from eternity who will and will not be saved. Everything depends, therefore, on God's absolute will, which passes human understanding.

Duns acknowledged, to be sure, that according to God's "ordained" or "covenanted" will made known through revelation, those persons will be saved who avail themselves of the church's sacramental life and fully cooperate in their own salvation. In this context, Duns held, also against Thomas, that it is possible by one's natural powers (*ex suis naturalibus*) to love God above all things, and thus by a morally good act, freely willed, to "merit" the grace that makes one acceptable before God. Strictly speaking, however, this naturally good act is not a genuine "merit of worthiness" (*meritum de condigno*) that *deserves* the bestowal of sanctifying grace. It is, rather, only a "merit of fitness" (*meritum de congruo*), a "semi-merit" that God in his liberality *chooses* to reward with the gift of grace. Once equipped with sanctifying grace, the believer goes on to perform good works that are truly and fully meritorious and so deserving of eternal salvation as a just reward. Here Scotus agreed with Aquinas, though he again held that God is not bound to reward condign merits with salvation but freely accepts them to that end.

While Duns, therefore, had his distinctive doctrine of the "established" order of salvation, one that he took for granted as the normal path to blessedness, he consistently maintained that this order has no ontological necessity. God is at liberty to save persons in other ways, and, in any event, human destiny ultimately depends on God's eternal election and reprobation, as Augustine taught. Scotus believed that there was nothing "Pelagian" or anti-Augustinian about his teaching that fallen man can earn the first bestowal of grace as a congruent merit. As he saw it, his dual emphasis on God's free "acceptation" of a morally good act performed outside a state of grace, and on God's eternal predestination of the elect without any regard to their foreseen merits (*ante praevisa merita*), adequately safeguarded the Augustinian doctrine of the sovereignty of God.

It will be seen that the cardinal point of theological difference between Thomas Aquinas and Duns Scotus is the latter's insistence upon, and constant recourse to, the unconditional freedom of God. Everything outside of God, all that belongs to the created realm and to God's ordained will, is wholly contingent upon God's absolute will and in no way necessary. This contingency extends to the church and its sacraments and priesthood—in sum, to all the means of salvation. Thomas, by contrast, while no less a defender of divine sovereignty, did not thus oppose God's absolute power (*potentia absoluta*) to his ordained power (*potentia ordinata*), and so he did not make a radical distinction between God's freedom in eternity and the execution of his will in time through the agency of "secondary causes." For Thomas, rather, God's freedom shows itself precisely in creating and preserving the world that we know—a hierarchically ordered universe in which the church and its agencies of grace find their "necessary" place. In Scotist thought, however, "contingency" has replaced Thomist "necessity."

One must add that Duns was not a rebel against church authority. He did not question the legitimacy of the "ordinances" of God, including the priesthood and the sacramental system. Indeed, by his very stress on the limits of reason, he exalted the authority of the church as the bearer and interpreter of revelation. His fundamental concern, in keeping with the spirit of the condemnations of 1277, was to safeguard the unconditional freedom of God over against any form of "Greek necessitarianism," that is, over against the determinist features of Aristotelian and Arabian and even Thomist thought, which, to his mind, limited God by including him within a series of causes and thus within the created order.

The thought of Duns Scotus, and of two other notable theologians of the early fourteenth century—the Franciscan Peter Auriole (1280?–1322) and the

Dominican Durandus of St.-Pourçain (1275-1335)—became the point of departure for the work of the eminent Franciscan philosopher and theologian, William of Ockham (1285?-1349?). Ockham, like Scotus, profoundly influenced the historical course of late Scholasticism. He was the authoritative leader of the "modern way"—the thinker who was chiefly responsible for the parting of the ways between "old" and "new" Scholasticism.

William was born sometime between 1280 and 1290 in the English village of Ockham, in Surrey, near London, and entered the Franciscan order at an early age. He began his theological studies at Oxford in 1309 or 1310, and by 1319 or 1320 had completed the formal requirements for the degree of master of theology, with lectures on the *Sentences* of Peter Lombard. His teaching license was withheld, however, because he had been accused of doctrinal errors by the chancellor of the university, John Lutterell, who in 1323 went to the papal court at Avignon to prefer charges against him. In 1324, Ockham was summoned to Avignon to defend himself, and a commission of inquiry was appointed. The charges were relatively mild and no formal action appears to have been taken, but Ockham never received his doctor's license. Hence he came to be known as "the venerable inceptor" (*venerabilis inceptor*)—that is, a person who had completed the requirements for the doctorate (an "inceptor") but had never become an actual professor (a "regent master"). This title was later misconstrued to mean that he was "the founder of the nominalist school" (*inceptor scholae nominalium*).

While at Avignon, from 1324 to 1328, Ockham became deeply involved in the dispute then raging over the issue of Franciscan poverty (see V:4), and there he joined forces with the general of the Franciscan order, Michael of Cesena, who had been summoned to Avignon to answer for his opposition to Pope John XXII (1316-1334). In 1328, when it became apparent that the pope was about to condemn their position and that of the majority of Franciscans, Cesena and Ockham fled from Avignon to Munich to seek the protection of Emperor Louis of Bavaria (1314-1347). Ockham and Cesena and their companions were immediately excommunicated. There is evidence that Ockham sought reconciliation with Rome in 1349, but the outcome is uncertain, and he died, probably of the Black Death, in 1349 or 1350.

Though Ockham was an original and fiercely independent thinker, and a determined critic of Scotus no less than of Aquinas, he also shared many emphases with his great Franciscan predecessor. He took over the Scotist distinction between the absolute and the ordained power of God, making it the touchstone of his theology and giving it an even more radical application. Thus, he held that God, by his absolute power, could have made salvation dependent on hatred rather than love of him. Yet Ockham, no less than Scotus, taught that what God has ordained in time, including the priesthood and the sacramental system, is not to be despised, since it constitutes the normal path to salvation. The central concern of both Ockham and Scotus was to free

Christian theology and ethics from any trace of Greco-Islamic necessitarianism—the idea of a God who is bound to act in accordance with the dictates of "right reason."

Ockham also took over the leading features of the Scotist doctrine of God's "ordained" plan of salvation. According to this scheme, it is possible for an individual, by his own natural powers or free will, to perform a morally good act that elicits the infusion of grace as a "merit of fitness," i.e., as a semi-merit that God chooses to reward with the gift of sanctifying grace. (It will be recalled that Thomas Aquinas, in his mature works, expressly denied that one could, in a state of nature, merit the bestowal of first grace—in *any* sense of the word "merit.") Armed with sanctifying grace, the believer performs works of love that, as true "merits of worthiness," earn salvation as a due reward, inasmuch as God chooses to accept condign merits as the basis for granting eternal salvation.

The Ockhamist doctrine of salvation thus exhibits this basic pattern: God, according to his ordained will, intends to save people who do their very best (*facere quod in se est*), first by acquiring grace as a semi-merit (*de congruo*) within a state of nature, and then by earning salvation as a full merit (*de condigno*) within a state of grace. This is the meaning of the Ockhamist axiom that "God does not deny grace to those who do what is in them" (*facientibus quod in se est Deus non denegat gratiam*).

While both Ockham and Scotus, and their followers, held to the principle of "doing one's best" with one's natural abilities and in cooperation with grace, Ockham significantly modified Scotus's doctrine of salvation by rejecting his teaching that God eternally predestines the elect without any regard to their foreseen merits (*ante praevisa merita*). For Ockham, and the Ockhamist theologians, the eternal predestination of the elect is, according to God's ordained will, conditional upon God's foreknowledge of their merits (*post praevisa merita*), even as the eternal predestination of the reprobate is based upon their foreseen demerits (*post praevisa demerita*). Predestination, in short, is equivalent to the divine foreknowledge of human behavior—a doctrine that the Ockhamists considered necessary to defend human freedom and dignity. By thus linking eternal salvation with God's foreknowledge of meritorious works, the Ockhamists removed one of the main Scotist-Augustinian "safeguards" against Pelagianism. Yet they believed that their doctrine of God's free acceptance of both congruent and condign merits was itself sufficient to uphold the Augustinian doctrine that God is no one's debtor.

Later, in the sixteenth century, Luther and his fellow reformers were to argue that the entire Scholastic doctrine of salvation—chiefly Ockham's, but also that of Aquinas and Scotus—terrified rather than consoled anxious consciences, because it made salvation depend at least partly on meritorious works (a principle of uncertainty) rather than solely on God's unmerited mercy (the only ground of confidence). Yet Luther, who was trained in the

Ockhamist tradition, also appropriated features of the Scotist-Ockhamist "covenant theology," which denied any intrinsic connection between salvation and infused habits of grace and made God's "acceptation" the ultimate ground of salvation.

Ockham's true radicality over against his Scholastic predecessors, including Scotus, showed itself at two fundamental points: in his theory of knowledge and in his position on natural theology. His epistemology broke with virtually the whole medieval tradition before him. All the great Christian thinkers, from Augustine through Aquinas, held that knowledge of individuals is mediated by universals: the mind knows the particular thing (Socrates) only through the universal concept (man). These thinkers differed, of course, in their views regarding the way the mind actually comes to know universals; but whether the universal is known directly through supernatural illumination (the Augustinians) or indirectly through abstraction from sense experience (the Aristotelians), all agreed that the universal is the primary and proper object of the intellect. All agreed, likewise, that universals have an extra-mental reality, whether as self-subsisting essences apart from individual things (extreme realism) or as abstract essences inhering in things (moderate realism). Even Duns Scotus, who taught that the mind does have direct knowledge of individuals, still upheld the reality of essences, for in knowing individual things the mind actually knows the formally distinct "common natures" that constitute all being. Hence, for Scotus, the proper object of the mind is "being" in its most universal and abstract sense.

It was in this context that Ockham wielded his famous "razor" or principle of economy of explanation: "Plurality is not to be postulated without necessity," or "Whatever can be done with fewer assumptions is done in vain with more." Now the truth is, held Ockham, that only the individually existing thing is real, and direct, unmediated knowledge of individuals (what Ockham called "intuitive cognition") is possible. Hence, there is no need to explain cognition of singular things by postulating such entities as self-subsisting essences (Augustine, Anselm, Bonaventura), intelligible species (Aquinas), or common natures (Scotus). Intuitive cognition is the foundation of all knowledge, for only the immediate apprehension of an individual object enables the intellect to judge whether that object exists or not. Thus, the individual thing, not the universal, comes first both in reality (existence) and in thought (knowledge). As for universal concepts, or essences, they cannot be apprehended directly, and so they possess no reality outside the mind and its acts of judgment (what Ockham called "abstractive knowledge").

For Ockham, therefore, the universal exists only as a content of the mind —as the act whereby the intellect understands many individuals that are similar (where "similarity" does *not* mean a "common nature")—and functions within human language as a conventional sign meant to signify many things. Because Ockham and his followers thus spoke of universal concepts as mental and linguistic phenomena, they were called "termists" or "nominalists." Yet they did not consider universals to be merely subjective constructs, since these concepts arise only in connection with the mind's encounter with things that really exist outside the mind, namely, the similarities displayed by many individual beings.

Ockham's revolutionary theory of knowledge established the philosophical basis for the division between the "old way" and the "new way" in Scholasticism. The "ancients"—among whom Scotus must now be numbered, as well as Aquinas—concerned themselves with the metaphysical analysis of essences, in the conviction that universal concepts are the ultimate bearers of reality, above all of transcendent reality. The "moderns," however, led by Ockham, concerned themselves with the mind's immediate experience of individual beings and with logically valid inference from such experience, in the conviction that reality is irreducibly individual and that universal concepts are but mental constructs and linguistic signs. Since universals have no existence outside the mind and the conventions of language, and so are not "windows" on transcendent reality, natural or metaphysical theology is, for all practical purposes, impossible. There is simply no empirical evidence, provided by direct experience, of the objects of theology. The old enterprise of "natural" theology must give way, therefore, to a new "positive" theology based entirely on revelation and faith.

It has often been said that Ockham brought about the destruction of the great Scholastic endeavor, going back to the eleventh century, to put Christian faith on a rational foundation. It is true that Ockham virtually eliminated natural theology (after Scotus had reduced it to a minimum), yet he did not banish reason from the theological task; he located it, rather, *within* the bounds of revelation. Scholasticism, for Ockham and his followers, now took the form of the rational (logical) investigation of revealed first principles. And while the late medieval Schoolmen exhibited little enthusiasm for speculative metaphysics, they delighted in free philosophical speculation on theological problems, such as the question of God's knowledge of future acts and events ("future contingents"). In these respects, they continued the traditional Scholastic program of "faith in search of understanding," save that they now assigned to revelation alone much that the earlier Scholastics had considered rationally demonstrable.

Ockhamist thought, or nominalism, enjoyed widespread support throughout the late Middle Ages, among representatives of all the religious orders, but one cannot speak of a fixed "school" of Ockham's disciples, for his thought was not always taken entire. Ockhamism, moreover, did not go unopposed. The "old way" had its able defenders, among them John Capreolus (1380?–1444), a French Dominican known as the "prince of Thomists," who wrote a great commentary on and defense of the *Summa theologiae*. Thomist thought also found a home in the order of Augustinian friars, owing to the work of Giles of Rome (1247?–1316), who stoutly defended Thomism against traditional Augustinianism in the aftermath of the condemnations of 1277. Giles occupied the first Augustinian chair of theology at Paris in 1285; in 1287, his teachings were adopted as the official doctrine of the Augustinian order; and in 1292, he became the order's general. As will be seen, direct lines of connection with the thought of Albert the Great and Thomas Aquinas were also maintained by an important group of Dominican theologians and mystical writers active in Cologne and the Rhineland during the fourteenth century (see V:9).

In the middle of the fourteenth century, Ockhamist ideas and attitudes took hold at both Oxford and Paris. The "modern way" was represented at Oxford by the Franciscan Adam Woodham (?–1349) and the Dominican Robert Holcot (1285?–1349). Ockham's influence was especially strong at Paris in the 1340s, as is shown in the teachings of John of Mirecourt, a Cistercian monk, and Nicolas of Autrecourt. Both men, however, made such a radical use of Ockhamist principles that a number of their propositions were officially condemned. A much more moderate follower of Ockham was Jean Buridan (1295?–1358?), who was twice rector of the University of Paris. Buridan employed Ockham's logic and epistemology to develop a natural philosophy of an empirical type—that is, he made of physics a science of observable phenomena. Ockham's doctrine that "intuitive cognition" is the sole basis of natural knowledge helped to give late medieval science a more empirical character, as is further evidenced in the work of Buridan's two leading disciples, Albert of Saxony (1316?–1390) and Marsilius of Inghen (?–1396), both of whom originally taught at Paris and then spread Ockhamist thought to Austria and Germany.

Appraisals of late Scholasticism continue to vary widely. The *via moderna,* in particular, has often been seen as the nadir of medieval theology, chiefly by those who regard the Thomistic synthesis as the zenith of Scholastic thought. Yet it would be wrong to think that theology simply withered on the vine after Ockham. The late medieval Schoolmen exhibited much ingenuity and creativity in treating such problems as the "scientific" status of theology; God's omnipotence and the relation of the divine will to human free will in matters of sin, grace, and merit; God's knowledge of future contingents; predestination; the nature of the church and its relation to the state; Scripture and tradition; and the sacraments, especially the nature of the "change" in the eucharistic elements.

One very important result of this preoccupation with internal theological issues was the renewed search for the true interpretation of the writings of St. Augustine, particularly on the topics of predestination, prevenient grace, and the bondage of the will. This search, which generated intense debates, continued throughout the late Middle Ages and into the Reformation era. The Ockhamist scheme of salvation, with its characteristic emphasis on "doing one's best" as the basis of both congruent and condign merits, found an early and able defender in the aforementioned Dominican theologian, Robert Holcot. This doctrine was soon attacked as a species of "modern Pelagianism" by another Oxford theologian, and one of the foremost mathematicians of the day, Thomas Bradwardine (1290?–1349). His principal work, *De causa Dei contra Pelagium* (The Cause of God against the Pelagians, completed about 1344), was an uncompromising restatement and extension of Augustinian (and certain Thomistic) themes: the bondage of the fallen human will; the absolute need for prevenient grace to liberate the will; the irresistibility of such grace; the infused habit of grace as the sole basis of a meritorious act; and, undergirding all, God's eternal predestination, which elects those who will be given prevenient grace without any regard to their foreseen merit. Shortly after he had been consecrated archbishop of Canterbury, Bradwardine fell victim to the bubonic plague, or Black Death, along with Ockham, Holcot, and a whole generation of leading English thinkers.

Another stalwart opponent of the Ockhamist doctrine of salvation was Gregory of Rimini (1300?–1358), reputed to be the best Augustine scholar of the Middle Ages. Long active at Paris as both student and teacher, he became the general of the Augustinian friars in 1357, and their most influential leader since Giles of Rome. Though an adherent of Ockham and the *via moderna* in epistemology and in the doctrine of God's "two powers," his radical Augustinianism brought him into conflict with the whole Ockhamist scheme of salvation. He upheld the strict Augustinian doctrine of God's unconditional predestination of the elect and the reprobate—an absolute decree wherein God's foreknowledge of human merits or demerits plays no part.

The assaults of Bradwardine and Rimini notwithstanding, the leading Ockhamist theologians continued to hold to the essential details of their master's doctrine of salvation, always in the conviction that they, too, were "Augustinians" by virtue of their emphasis on God's free "acceptance" of meritorious works. The most prominent of these later representatives of the *via moderna* were three secular theologians: the Frenchmen Pierre d'Ailly (1350–1420) and Jean de Gerson (1363–1429), and the German Gabriel Biel (1420?–1495). D'Ailly and his pupil Gerson were leaders of the "conciliar movement," which sought to resolve the Great Schism (see V:12) by subjecting papal authority to the authority of a general council of the church. Gerson, who became chancellor of the University of Paris in 1395, sought to overcome the notorious factionalism of the Schoolmen by calling for a reunification of theology and spirituality on the model of Bernard of Clairvaux and Bonaventura. His classic work on mystical theology, *De mystica theologia* (1402), shows that the Ockhamist theologians, contrary to what is often supposed, were not in principle opposed to mysticism. Biel, known as "the last of the Scholastics," was a faithful disciple of Ockham and defended him against Rimini's attack. His balanced exposition of Ockhamist thought became an occasion, in turn, for Luther's attack on the "modern theologians" as "worse than Pelagian," while Luther's early opponents, later joined by the theologians of the Council of Trent, responded by citing Biel as a Catholic authority.

Judged on its own terms, and not merely as a "postlude" to high Scholasticism or a "prelude" to Reformation thought, the Scholastic theology of the fourteenth and fifteenth centuries is seen to possess intrinsic importance. The best minds of the age proposed new solutions to old problems concerning such matters as "nature and grace," "reason and revelation," "God and world." Their solutions perforce differed from those of their great predecessors, since they believed that earlier Scholasticism, above all the Christian Aristotelianism of Thomas Aquinas, was vulnerable to serious criticism on philosophical and theological grounds. Controversy abounded, giving way at times to sheer pedantry and logomachy, but one cannot fairly say that intellectual sterility was the order of the day or that late Scholastic thought marked the "bankruptcy" of Scholasticism. It was, rather, Scholasticism in a new key.

Chapter 9

Mysticism, the Modern Devotion, and Heresy

*T*HE LATE MIDDLE AGES were remarkable not only for important developments in Scholastic theology. The fourteenth century also witnessed a great flowering of mysticism, as well as the emergence of a new form of popular piety that sought to unite a life of inner devotion with a life of active service in and to the world. Common to these spiritual phenomena was the quest for direct personal contact with God, whether through the mystical union of the soul with God or through a cultivation of the interior life—a practice of the presence of God—that did not involve actual mystical experience. Common also was the underlying conviction that the regeneration of church and society required personal religious renewal: a religion of true inwardness rather than of mere conformity to outward rites and ceremonies.

Both the mystics and the "new devotionalists," along with groups related to them, aroused widespread suspicions of heterodoxy and in some cases met with official condemnations. These reactions were in part motivated by the fear that the "experiential way" to God would inevitably nurture indifference and hostility to the institutional church and its sacramental ministrations. This fear, as it turned out, was largely unfounded, save in the case of the "Brothers and Sisters of the Free Spirit"—a heresy based on mystical piety, but one that never amounted to an organized movement of dissent and was soon contained. To be sure, new and powerful heretical movements did arise in the late fourteenth and the early fifteenth century—not, however, among mystics and devotionalists, but among the followers of two Schoolmen—John Wyclif in England and Jan Hus in Bohemia (see V:13).

The most famous, though not the most representative, of the late medieval mystics was Johannes "Meister" Eckhart (1260?–1327 or 1328), a German Dominican who studied at Cologne and Paris, occupied a succession of high offices in the Dominican order in Germany, and from 1311 until his death served as a teacher and preacher at Paris, Strassburg, and Cologne. Toward the end of his life, he came under suspicion of heresy, and in 1329 Pope John XXII condemned twenty-eight propositions taken from his writings. Eckhart had absorbed the teaching of Albert the Great and Thomas Aquinas, more on its Neoplatonic than its Aristotelian side, and it was chiefly a series of unguarded statements of Neoplatonic provenance that brought him into condemnation.

Eckhart's central concern was the relation of the soul to God. The soul, he taught, has within it a special structure—what he variously called the "spark" (*scintilla, Fünklein*) or the "ground" (*Grund*) of the soul—which is the very likeness of God and where God dwells totally. Some of Eckhart's assertions indicate that he regarded this innermost essence of the soul as something uncreated, not only "like" God in a creaturely resemblance, but truly "one" with God because existing with God before the creation of the world and of time. Only by withdrawing from all objects of sense, thought, and will, by retreating into its "ground," can the soul experience the birth of the Word (Son) of God within itself and attain mystical union with God. This union involves far more than a perfect conformation of the human will to God's will in the ecstasy of love and affection. It is nothing less than a total transformation of the soul into God, a return of the soul to its eternal pre-existence in God— indeed, an ineffable union of the soul not with God (*Gott*) but with the abyss of pure Deity (*Gottheit*). This "essentialist" or "transformative" mysticism— so different from the "voluntarist" or "affective" mysticism of Bernard of Clairvaux—offended orthodox sensibilities as pantheistic, as merging all being into God by eliminating the ontological distance between created and uncreated being. Eckhart later admitted that he had been guilty of exaggeration, and he defended his controversial theses by offering orthodox explanations based on Augustinian and Thomist doctrine.

Eckhart's leading disciple was a fellow Dominican, Johannes Tauler (1300?–1361?), who may have studied under Eckhart at Cologne and who achieved fame as a preacher and spiritual director at Strassburg and Basel. Tauler, like Eckhart, identified within the soul a "spark" or "ground" that is the image of God and God's perpetual dwelling place, but he was careful to assert that this *Grund* is God-given, not an intrinsic property of the soul. The soul's return to its Source is an operation of grace and involves a union of the human and divine wills, not an absorption of finite being into infinite being (though some of Tauler's language does admit of the latter interpretation). Luther later hailed Tauler's sermons as a fount of "pure theology," a judgment that often led Protestant scholars to consider Tauler a forerunner of the Reformation—though what aroused Luther's admiration was not his distinctively mystical teachings, but his stress on the inward religion of suffering, self-denial, and reliance on grace.

The third of the great German Dominican mystics of the fourteenth century was Heinrich Suso (1295?–1360). A native of Constance, he entered the Dominican order at an early age and studied at Cologne, where he came into contact with Tauler and was greatly influenced by Eckhart, whom he ably defended in the aftermath of the 1329 condemnation. After a period of ascetic seclusion, he entered upon a life of preaching and pastoral ministry at Constance and Ulm. Suso, like Tauler, spoke more cautiously than Eckhart, usually describing the mystical union as one of wills rather than of substance, and insisting on the ineradicable difference between created and uncreated being. Suso's *The Little Book of Truth,* a meditation on Christ's passion, attained a popularity almost as great as that achieved later by Thomas à Kempis's *The Imitation of Christ.*

All three of the great German mystics exercised pastoral care of Dominican nuns and Beguines (see V:4) in the Rhineland and often directed their vernacular sermons and tracts to these communities of religious women. The cloistered nuns and Beguines had long since "spiritualized" the old ideal of absolute poverty by emphasizing interior self-sacrifice over outward physical renunciation. The phenomenon known as "German mysticism" may be seen as arising in this encounter between feminine piety and Dominican theology, care of souls, and vernacular preaching.

Eckhart, Tauler, and Suso were also the main sources of inspiration for a group of fourteenth-century mystics, both clerical and lay, in the Rhineland and Switzerland, who called themselves "Friends of God" (*Gottesfreunde*[1]). From this circle emerged an anonymous mystical treatise of the late fourteenth century, *Theologia Deutsch* (German Theology), which had a profound effect on the young Luther, who published it, with his own prefaces, in 1516 and 1518. It was also widely used as a basic "reform" document by the sixteenth-century Anabaptists and Spiritualists.

[1] Cf. John 15:14–15 and James 2:23.

The growth of mystical piety was furthered in the Netherlands by the greatest of the Flemish mystics, Jan van Ruysbroeck (1293–1381), who for many years was a parish priest in Brussels until, in 1343, he retired to a hermitage at Groenendael. There, in 1349, he and a group of friends and disciples established a contemplative community of Augustinian canons, of which he became the first prior. Some unguarded expressions in one of his early mystical treatises, *The Spiritual Espousals,* were to bring charges of pantheism from Jean de Gerson; however, in his later writings, such as *The Sparkling Stone,* Ruysbroeck was careful to state that the mystical union with God does not involve the loss of the contemplative's created being. He also insisted that the contemplative life of "inactive joys" must issue in the "common life" of good works.

While the German Rhineland and the Low Countries were the main centers of mystical spirituality, there was also a remarkable efflorescence of mysticism in fourteenth-century England. Unlike their continental counterparts, however, the English mystics were usually hermits and recluses, not active members of monastic communities. Both Richard Rolle (1300?–1349), author of *Fire of Love,* and Walter Hilton (?–1396), author of *The Scale of Perfection,* were hermits at the time they wrote their best-known works, though Rolle ended his life as a spiritual director of Cistercian nuns at Hampole, and Hilton later became an Augustinian canon. The anonymous author of *The Cloud of Unknowing,* who was active from about 1350 to 1380, appears to have been a solitary, and Julian of Norwich (1342?–1416), author of *Revelations of Divine Love* and one of the greatest of the women mystics of the Middle Ages, was a lifelong recluse. The English mystics varied considerably in the degree to which they were influenced by Neoplatonism—the author of *The Cloud,* for example, worked in the tradition of the pseudo-Dionysius—but all were entirely orthodox in their piety.

The foremost Italian mystic during this period was the Dominican tertiary, St. Catherine of Siena (1347–1380), who combined mystical rapture with a most active "apostolate" to church and world. Addressing herself to popes and cardinals and Christendom at large, she pressed for an end to the "captivity" of the papacy at Avignon (see V:12).

Mysticism could at times give rise to heterodox excesses. In 1312, the Council of Vienne, convoked by Pope Clement V (1305–1314), issued a decree condemning eight errors of the "abominable sect" of Beguines and Beghards (see V:4). The heretical doctrines ascribed to this "sect" were chiefly three: that it is possible in this life to achieve a state of spiritual perfection (sinlessness) by becoming fully one with God; that it is permissible for this "deified" person to dispense with all the externalities of religion, including sacramental graces and good works; and that such a one is no longer subject to church laws or even to the moral law of God. The heresy, in short, involved "autotheism" (the identification of the soul with God), "antinomianism" (the repudiation of divine law), and a radical "spiritualism" (the elimination of all outward aids to religion). In 1310, a Beguine from Hainault, Marguerite Porete, had been burned for presumably advancing such heretical notions in her book, *The Mirror of Simple Souls*. Church authorities believed that this so-called Free Spirit heresy was the work of an organized sect of international scope.

Modern research has shown that no such cohesive sect existed, though Free Spirits, of whom the majority were women, could be found in many urban areas of northern and southern Europe. Some were Beguines and Beghards, some were in clerical orders, and some were independents, having no direct links to religious communities. It appears that these Free Spirits were, on the whole, latter-day representatives of the old "apostolic life" and "voluntary poverty" movements, to which they had now added a large measure of mystical piety—the same combination that was to be found in many beguinages and nunneries since the middle of the thirteenth century. The Free Spirits were opposed by all the great mystics of northern Europe. They were certainly more radical than the orthodox mystics, Eckhart included, in their autotheism and in their often explicit denial of the liberated soul's need for the traditional means of salvation. Far from being libertines, however, they normally taught that the way to perfection requires extreme asceticism and total self-abnegation, and there is little evidence that the "perfected" engaged in licentious conduct. It is often hard to distinguish clearly between heterodox Free Spirits and orthodox mystics, as is shown in the case of Marguerite Porete. Her *Mirror of Simple Souls* was copied and translated in many late medieval monasteries, was approved in the fifteenth century by Pope Eugenius IV, and in 1927 was published in modern English under the aegis of the English Benedictines—all before it was properly identified as the work of a condemned heretic.

The most widespread and influential orthodox religious movement of the late Middle Ages was that launched in the eastern Netherlands—in Deventer and the neighboring towns of Kempen, Zwolle, and Windesheim—by Gerard Groote (1340–1384) and his disciple, Florentius Radewijns (1350–1400). The movement soon came to be known as the "Modern Devotion" (*Devotio moderna*), embracing three foundations that can be traced to the work of Groote and Radewijns in the 1370s and 1380s: the Sisters and the Brothers of the Common Life, established at Deventer, and the community of Augustinian canons established at Windesheim. The houses of the Sisters, Brothers, and Windesheimers quickly spread throughout the Low Countries, the Rhineland, and Westphalia, and thence into southern and central Germany.

Groote, a native of Deventer, was a master of arts of the University of Paris, where he had also studied law, medicine, and theology. After an early life of self-indulgence, abetted by his holding of a number of ecclesiastical benefices (though he was not in priest's orders), he experienced a conversion sometime after 1370, withdrew to the Carthusian monastery at Monnikhuizen for a period of reflection, and there studied the writings of the Rhineland mystics and especially of Ruysbroeck, whose friend he became. Inclined to neither a fully monastic nor a fully mystical life, he accepted ordination as a deacon and spent his remaining years as a missionary preacher in the diocese of Utrecht. His attacks on contemporary abuses, especially clerical and monastic immorality, led to the revocation of his preaching license in 1383. He appealed the sentence to the pope but died before any answer was made.

Before his death, Groote had established in his family house at Deventer a community of religious women that formed the nucleus of the Sisters of the Common Life. These laywomen worked for a living, took no monastic vows, adopted no habit, but sought to pursue in common a life of service to God and to society. They attracted many young women to their ranks, and Sisterhouses proliferated throughout the Low Countries and western Germany. The Sisters, however, increasingly aspired to the monastic life, and by the early fifteenth century most of them had become Franciscan tertiaries, with their houses organized into the "chapter" of Utrecht. Some of these communities also adopted the rule of St. Augustine and became strictly enclosed.

Groote's original ideal was a life of common religious observance without separation from secular society. Those who remained closest to this ideal were the lay Brothers of the Common Life, whom Radewijns had organized in his vicarage at Deventer, where he was a parish priest. The Brothers spent much of their time copying books and providing for the distribution of religious literature. Their chief work was the pastoral care of schoolboys in the city schools of the Netherlands and Germany. To this end they established hospices where some of these students could find lodging and board and where the Brothers could supply religious instruction, particularly for those whom they deemed suitable for the monastic life or the priesthood. The Brothers, with a few notable exceptions, were not university trained or theologically educated; and not until the end of the fifteenth century, when printing rendered the copying of books uneconomical, did they become teachers in the city schools or establish a few schools of their own. Both Erasmus, at Deventer, and Luther, at Magdeburg, attended schools where the Brothers were spiritual directors, but it cannot be said that the Brothers were "pioneers" of Christian humanism or of the Reformation.

In 1387, acting on the advice of Groote, Radewijns had founded a community of Augustinian canons at Windesheim, thereby making provision for at least some of the Brothers to pursue a fully monastic life. This foundation soon comprised a large number of houses over a wide territory. The Windesheim "congregation" was distinguished by its strict adherence to the Augustinian rule, and it played a leading role in the "Observantine" movement of late medieval monastic reform.

The "new devotion" practiced by the Brothers and Sisters of the Common Life, and by the Windesheimers, was based on the consciousness of a deep personal relationship to God; emphasized constant meditation on Christ's life and passion; and was nourished by the traditional spiritual practices and rites of the church. The Modern Devotionalists, though they were religious "personalists," were not anti-sacramental or anti-institutional. They aimed only to overcome formalism in religion and abuses in church life by inculcating a piety of "inward fervor." This piety, moreover, was meditative, not mystical. The devotionalists rarely embraced a full-fledged mysticism, and they largely ignored the writings of the Rhenish and Flemish mystics. The noblest fruit of this conservative piety was a book whose circulation has exceeded that of any other work of the Middle Ages: *The Imitation of Christ*, written by Thomas à Kempis (1380?–1471), who spent most of his long life in a monastery of the Windesheim congregation, Mount St. Agnes, near Zwolle.

Chapter 10

Missions and Defeats

THE PERIOD BETWEEN the Crusades and the Reformation was one of gains and losses for Christendom. In Spain, the Christian forces struggled with increasing success against the Muslims. Gradually, four Christian states dominated the peninsula. Castile conquered Toledo in 1085, defeated the Muslims at Las Navas de Tolosa in 1212, and united with Leon into a vigorous state in 1230. Little Navarre stretched on both sides of the Pyrenees. Meanwhile, Aragon to the east and Portugal to the west were winning their independence, so that by 1250 Islamic power on the peninsula was confined to the kingdom of Granada, whence it was to be driven in 1492. The Spanish Christian kingdoms were weak and were constantly warring among themselves. The real power of Spain was not to be manifest until the joint reign of Ferdinand and Isabella united Castile and Aragon in 1479.

In the East, the great Mongol empire, which began with the conquest of northern China in 1208, stretched across northern Asia, conquering most of southern Russia between 1238 and 1241 and reaching the borders of Palestine in 1258. This conquest almost annihilated the flourishing Nestorian church in central Asia (see III:9). Yet after the first rush of conquest was over, central Asia under Mongol control was accessible as it had never been before and was not to be again until the nineteenth century. In about 1260, two Venetian merchants, Niccolò and Maffeo Polo, made the long journey by land to Peking, where they were well received by the Mongol khan, Kublai. They returned to Italy in 1269 but started out again in 1271, taking Niccolò's more famous son, Marco, who entered the khan's service. Not until 1295 were the Polos back in Venice. Even before their return, an Italian Franciscan, John of Monte Corvino, had started in 1291 for Peking, where he established a church in about 1300. Christianity flourished for a time. Pope Clement V (1305–1314) appointed John an archbishop, with six bishops under him. The work came to an end, however, when the Mongols and other foreigners were expelled from China by the victorious native Ming dynasty in 1368.

Efforts were made to reach the Muslims, but with little success. Francis of Assisi himself preached to the sultan in Egypt in 1219. More famous as a missionary was the Franciscan tertiary, Ramón Lull (1232?–1315?), a native of the island of Majorca. In 1263 he was converted from a wholly worldly life, and he undertook the study of Arabic as a missionary preparation, writing also his *Ars Magna* (ca. 1274), which he intended as an irrefutable demonstration of the truth of Christianity to philosophically trained Muslims. In 1293, he began missionary work in Tunis, only to be expelled at the end of a year. He labored to induce the pope to establish schools for missionary training. He went once more to Africa in 1307 and was again driven out. His eloquence persuaded the Council of Vienne in 1311 to order teaching in Greek, Hebrew, "Chaldean," and Arabic, at Avignon, Paris, Salamanca, Bologna, and Oxford, though this remained a pious wish. Back to Tunis he went in 1314, and tradition holds that there he met a martyr's death by stoning the next year. He had little to show of missionary achievement, but much of missionary inspiration.

The prevailing characteristic of this period was the loss of once-Christian territories. The last of the crusaders' conquests in Palestine passed out of their hands in 1291. A new Islamic power was now arising in the Ottoman Turks. Sprung from central Asia, they had attained an independent position in Asia Minor by 1300. In 1354, they invaded the European portion of the Eastern Empire, capturing Adrianople in 1361 and gradually spreading their rule over the Balkans. A fragment of the empire remained until 1453, when Constantinople fell and the Byzantine Empire was at an end. The victorious advance of the Turks was to carry them, in the Reformation era, to the gates of Vienna. Christians ruled by them were deprived of political rights, though Christian worship and organization continued, under conditions of much oppression. Byzantine Christianity, however, did not suffer an abrupt decline after the fall of Constantinople. During the sixteenth and seventeenth centuries, Eastern theologians, partly in response to Protestant and Roman Catholic doctrinal definitions, set forth the distinctive teachings of Eastern Christianity in systematic formulations and comprehensive confessions of faith. The ancient Byzantine tradition also experienced a revitalization through its establishment in Russia and other Slavic lands.

Chapter 11

The Papacy at Its Height and Its Decline

THE CONTEST BETWEEN papacy and empire was by no means ended by the Concordat of Worms in 1122 (see IV:13), but the religious interest in the struggle was thereafter far less. Gregory VII's epoch-making quarrel with Henry IV had involved a great question of church purification and "defeudalization." The later disputes were plain contests for supremacy.

Frederick I "Barbarossa" (1152–1190), of the house of Hohenstaufen, was one of the ablest of the Holy Roman Emperors. His model was Charlemagne, and he aspired to a similar control of churchly affairs. In spite of the Concordat of Worms, he practically controlled the appointment of German bishops. On the other hand, his claims met with energetic resistance from the self-governing communes of northern Italy. This hostility he at first successfully overcame. In Alexander III (1159–1181), Frederick's most able enemy mounted the papal throne. The cardinals were divided in their choice, and an imperialist minority elected a rival pope, who called himself Victor IV and whom Frederick and the German bishops promptly supported. Alexander's position was long difficult. In 1176, however, Frederick was defeated at Legnano by the Lombard league of Italian cities, and he was forced to recognize Alexander. Frederick's attempt to control the papacy had been shattered, but his authority over the German bishops was scarcely diminished. In 1186, he achieved greater success by the marriage of his son Henry with the heiress of Sicily and southern Italy, thus threatening the Papal States from north and south.

Alexander also won at least an apparent victory over Henry II (1154–1189), one of the ablest of English kings, who in 1162 had secured the election of his seemingly complaisant chancellor, Thomas à Becket (1118?–1170), as archbishop of Canterbury. Once in office, Becket showed himself a determined upholder of ecclesiastical claims. In 1164, therefore, Henry secured the enactment of the Constitutions of Clarendon, limiting the right of appeal to Rome in ecclesiastical cases, restricting the power of excommunication, subjecting the clergy to civil courts, and placing the election of bishops under the control of the king, to whom they were to do homage. Becket now openly broke with

367

Henry. In 1170, a truce was brought about, but it was of short duration, and a hasty expression of anger on Henry's part led to Becket's murder at the hands of Norman knights at the close of the year. Alexander used the deed skillfully. Becket was canonized by the pope in 1173, and he continued until the Reformation to be one of the most popular of English saints. Henry was forced to abandon the Constitutions of Clarendon and to do public penance at Becket's grave. Yet in spite of this apparent papal triumph, Henry continued his control of English ecclesiastical affairs much as before.

Frederick Barbarossa died in 1190 on the Third Crusade. He was succeeded by his son, Henry VI (1190–1197), who in 1194 obtained full possession of his wife's inheritance in Sicily and southern Italy and developed ambitious plans of greatly expanding his imperial sway. The papacy, with both ends of Italy in possession of the German sovereign, was in grave political danger, but the situation was relieved by the early death of Henry VI in 1197 and the accession to the papacy in 1198 of the greatest of the medieval popes, Innocent III (1198–1216), under whom the papacy reached its highest degree of power in temporal affairs.

The death of Henry VI saw Germany divided. One party supported the claims of Henry's brother, Philip of Swabia, the other those of Otto of Brunswick, of the rival house of Welf (Guelph). Out of this confused situation, Innocent skillfully strove to bring advantage to the papacy. He secured large concessions in Italy and Germany from Otto, yet when Philip gradually gained the upper hand, Innocent won an agreement that the rival claims should be submitted to the judgment of a court controlled by the pope. The murder of Philip in 1208 frustrated this plan and put Otto once more to the fore. Innocent now obtained from Otto the desired guarantee of the extent of the Papal States and a promise to abandon control of German episcopal elections, and on the strength of these concessions he crowned Otto emperor in 1209. Otto promptly forgot all his promises. The angered pope now put forward Frederick II (1212–1250), the young son of Henry VI. Frederick was named to the German throne by elements opposed to Otto, in 1212, and he renewed all Otto's broken promises. In 1214, Otto was defeated by the French king, Philip II (1179–1223), on the field of Bouvines, and Frederick was assured of the empire. Thus, Innocent III seemed wholly to have defended papal claims and to have dictated the imperial succession. The jurisdictional supremacy of the papacy appeared realized.

Nor was Innocent III less successful in humbling the sovereigns of other lands. He compelled the powerful Philip II, by means of an interdict, to take back his queen, Ingeborg, whom Philip had unjustly divorced. He separated King Alfonso IX of Leon from a wife too closely related. King Peter of Aragon received his kingdom as a fief from the pope. Innocent's greatest apparent victory, however, occurred in England. The cruel and unpopular King John (1199–1216), following a divided election, tried to secure his candidate as archbishop of Canterbury. The dispute was appealed to Rome. The king's choice was set aside and Innocent's friend, Stephen Langton (?–1228), received the appointment in 1207. John resisted. Innocent put England under an interdict. The king drove out his clerical opponents. The pope excommunicated him, declared his throne forfeited, and proclaimed a crusade against him. The defeated king not merely made a humiliating submission to the pope, in 1213, but he also acknowledged his kingdom a fief of the papacy, agreeing to pay an annual feudal tax to the pope.

With regard to internal church affairs, Innocent's policy was strongly centralizing. He claimed for the papacy the right of decisions in all disputed episcopal elections. He asserted sole authority to sanction the transfer of bishops from one see to another. His crusade against the Cathars has already been noted (see V:3). The Fourth Lateran Council of 1215, at which transubstantiation was declared an article of faith and annual confession and communion were required, was also a papal triumph. The conquest of Constantinople by the Fourth Crusade (see V:1), though not approved by Innocent, seemed to promise the subjection of the Greek church to papal authority.

The papacy reached the summit of its worldly power in Innocent III. Succeeding popes continued the same struggle, but with decreasing success. Emperor Frederick II, ruler of Germany as well as of northern and southern Italy and Sicily, a man of much political ability and of anything but medieval piety, though put in office largely by Innocent III, soon proved the chief opponent of the political pretensions of the papacy. Under Gregory IX (1227–1241), the organizer of the Inquisition and the patron of the Franciscans, and Innocent IV (1243–1254), the papal contest was carried on against Frederick II with the utmost bitterness and with very worldly weapons. Frederick was excommunicated, and rivals were raised up against him in Germany by papal influence. The papacy seemed convinced that only the destruction of the Hohenstaufen line would assure its victory. Upon Frederick's death in 1250, it pursued his son, Conrad IV (1250–1254), with the same hostility, and gave his heritage in southern Italy and Sicily to Edmund of England, son of King Henry III.

But now a new influence, that of France, was making itself felt in papal counsels. Urban IV (1261–1264) was a Frenchman and appointed French cardinals. In 1263, he gave southern Italy and Sicily to Charles of Anjou, brother of King Louis IX of France (1226–1270). This was a turning point in papal politics, for with it the dependence of the papacy on France began. The next pope, Clement IV (1265–1268), was also a Frenchman. During his papacy, Conradin, the young son of Conrad IV, asserted his hereditary claims to southern Italy and Sicily by force of arms. He was excommunicated by Clement IV and defeated by Charles of Anjou, by whose orders he was beheaded in Naples, in 1268. With him ended the line of Hohenstaufen emperors, whom the popes had so strenuously opposed, though there is no reason to think that the pope was responsible for Conradin's execution.

These long quarrels and the consequent confusion had greatly weakened the power of the Holy Roman Empire. Thenceforward, to the Reformation, it was more a group of feeble states than an effective single sovereignty. It was able to offer little resistance to papal demands. Other forces were arising, however, that would make impossible such a sovereignty as Innocent III had exercised. One such force was a new sense of national identity, which caused people to feel that, as Frenchmen or Englishmen, they had common interests against all foreigners, even the pope himself. A second factor was the increased education, wealth, and political influence of the urban middle class. The cities were restive under ecclesiastical interference in temporal affairs. Closely associated with this development was the growth of a body of lay lawyers and the renewed study of Roman law. These laymen, who were now displacing ecclesiastics as royal advisers, gradually consolidated royal power by appealing to a body of law—the Roman—which knew nothing of medieval ecclesiastical conditions. There was also a growing conviction among thoughtful and devout people that such worldly aims as the recent papacy had followed were inconsistent with the true interests of the church. From a political point of view, the papacy was weak in that it had no adequate physical forces at its disposal. It could only balance off one competitor against another. The debacle wrought in Germany now left the door open to France to become the papacy's chief, and largely unopposed, antagonist in European politics.

Papal interference in Germany continued. Pope Gregory X (1271–1276) ordered the German electors, in 1273, to choose a king, under threat that the pope himself would make the appointment if they failed. They chose Rudolf I of Hapsburg (1273–1291), who promptly renewed the concessions to the papacy that had been once made by Otto IV and Frederick II.

The situation was quite different in France. The power of the Capetian monarchs had been rapidly growing, and in Philip IV, known as "the Fair" (1285–1314), France had a king who was unscrupulous, obstinate, and possessed of the loftiest conceptions of royal authority. The papacy was then occupied by Boniface VIII (1294–1303), a pope who was second to none in his aspirations to supreme authority in temporal affairs. In 1295, France and her ally Scotland entered into war with England, which impelled the English king, Edward I (1272–1307), to rally the support of all his subjects by inviting the representatives of the Commons to take a place in Parliament, thus giving them a permanent share in the English national councils. The war also induced the French and English kings to tax their clergy to meet expenses. The clergy complained to Pope Boniface, who in 1296 issued the bull *Clericis laicos*, inflicting excommunication on all who demanded or paid such taxes on clerical property without papal permission. Philip replied by prohibiting the export of bullion from France, thus striking at the revenues of the pope and of the Italian bankers. The latter moved Boniface to modify his position so that the clergy could make voluntary contributions. He even allowed that, in cases of urgent necessity, the king could levy a tax. It was a royal victory.

Comparative peace prevailed between Philip and Boniface for a few years, but in 1301 the struggle resumed. Philip had Bernard Saisset, bishop of Pamiers, whom the pope had recently sent to him as nuncio, arrested and charged with high treason. Boniface ordered Bernard's release and cited the French bishops, and ultimately the king himself, to Rome. In reply, Philip summoned the first French Estates-General, in which clergy, nobles, and commoners were represented. This body, in 1302, sustained the king in his attitude of resistance. The pope answered with the famous bull *Unam sanctam,* the high-water mark of papal claims to supreme jurisdictional authority over civil powers. It affirmed that temporal powers are subject to the spiritual authority, which, in the person of the pope, can be judged by God alone. It declared, following the opinion of Thomas Aquinas, "that it is altogether necessary to salvation for every human creature to be subject to the Roman pontiff"[1]—an affirmation the exact scope of which has led to much subsequent discussion. Philip answered with a new assembly, where the pope was charged with an absurd series of crimes, involving heresy and moral depravity, and an appeal was issued for a general council before which the pope might be tried. Philip was determined that this should be no idle threat. He therefore sent to Italy his able jurist vice-chancellor, Guillaume de Nogaret, who had entered into alliance with Boniface's ancient family enemy, Sciarra Colonna. Together they gathered a force and made Boniface a prisoner in Anagni, just as he was about to proclaim Philip's excommunication, in 1303. The courageous Boniface would make no concessions. His friends soon freed him, but a month later he died.

These events were a staggering blow to the temporal claims of the papacy. It was not primarily that Philip's representatives had imprisoned the pope for a short time. A new force had arisen, that of national sentiment, to which the king had appealed successfully and against which the spiritual weapons of the papacy had been of little avail. The papal hope of rulership in temporal affairs had proved impossible of permanent realization.

Worse for the papacy was soon to follow. After the death of Boniface's successor, the excellent Benedict XI (1303-1304), the cardinals chose a Frenchman, Bertrand de Got, who took the name Clement V (1305-1314). A man of weak character, little experience, and frail health, Clement was no match for the ruthless Philip. He eventually declared Philip innocent of the attack on Boniface VIII, canceled Boniface's interdicts and excommunications, and modified the bull *Unam sanctam* to please the king. Philip also compelled the hapless pope to join in the cruel destruction of the Templars (see V:1). In 1309, moreover, after four years of wandering about southern France, Clement

---

[1] H. Bettenson, ed., *Documents of the Christian Church,* 2nd ed. (London, 1963), p. 163.

V took up residence at Avignon on the river Rhone. Avignon did not belong to the French kingdom, but in popular estimate Clement's action amounted to the establishment of the papacy in France. The troubled state of Italian politics undoubtedly had something to do with this removal, though not until the pontificate of Benedict XII (1334–1342) was there any clear sign that the popes intended to stay at Avignon. Yet here the papacy was to have its seat from 1309 until 1377, a period so nearly equal to the traditional exile of the Jews as to earn the name of the "Babylonian Captivity"—a designation first employed by the Italian poet Petrarch (see V:15), who shared the contemporary judgment that the papacy was now captive to the French crown.

Clement V's stormy pontificate is also of interest as marking the conclusion of the official medieval collections of canon law. That body of ecclesiastical legislation was the product of the history of the church since the early councils, embracing their decisions as well as the decrees of synods and of individual popes. The Middle Ages had seen many collections, of which the most famous was the so-called *Decretum* of Gratian of Bologna, made about 1140 (see V:5). Pope Gregory IX caused an official collection to be formed in 1234, including new decrees up to his time. Boniface VIII published a similar addition in 1298, and Clement V enlarged it in 1314, though his work was not published till 1317, under his successor, John XXII. This great structure of ecclesiastical jurisprudence, known as the *Corpus iuris canonici,* encompassed all domains of church life. Though there was no further official collection until the twentieth century, the creation of church law continued. Finally, in 1904, Pope Pius X ordered the codification and simplification of the whole body of canon law by a special commission. In 1917, his successor, Benedict XV, promulgated the *Codex iuris canonici* (five "books" containing 2,414 canons).

Chapter 12

The Avignon Papacy; Papal Critics and Defenders; the Great Schism

WHILE THE PAPACY was at Avignon (1309–1377), the popes were all Frenchmen and the great majority of the cardinals held French episcopal sees. The ablest of the Avignon popes was unquestionably John XXII (1316–1334). The double imperial election in Germany, in 1314, had divided that land between supporters of Louis the Bavarian (1314–1347) and those of Frederick of Austria (1314–1326). John XXII, supported by King Philip V of France (1316–1322), thought the occasion ripe to diminish German influence in Italy for the benefit of the Papal States. He declined to recognize either claimant and declared, moreover, that the pope had the right to administer the empire during vacancies. When Louis interfered in Italian affairs, the pope excommunicated him, and a contest with the papacy ensued which lasted until Louis's death. In its course, the German electors issued the declaration of 1338, at Rense (confirmed by the Reichstag in Frankfurt the same year), that the chosen head of the empire needs no approval from the papacy for full entrance on or continuation in the duties of his office. In effect, the empire was divorced entirely from the papacy.

Extreme assertions of papal plenitude of power in temporal affairs had been advanced during the pontificate of Boniface VIII by two Augustinian friars, Giles of Rome (1245?–1316)—whose views informed the papal bull *Unam sanctam* (1302)—and James of Viterbo (1255?–1308). They were later joined by another Augustinian monk, Augustinus Triumphus (1243–1328), who held that all princes rule as subject to the pope, who can remove them at pleasure, whereas the pope himself can be judged by none, "since the decision and court of God and the pope are one." These papalist or "hierocratic" claims were refuted by, among others, the French Dominican John of Paris (?–1306), who argued that church and state are not related as superior to inferior, but as two autonomous powers, each sovereign in its own sphere. Another defender of this "parallelism" between the two powers was the greatest of medieval poets, Dante Alighieri (1265–1321). In his Latin treatise, *De monarchia,* written between 1308 and 1311, Dante maintained that only a universal empire, specifically that of a Roman emperor, could bring about that state of peace which is essential to civilized activity. This power of empire is as necessary to humanity's temporal happiness as papal governance is to its eternal blessedness. Each of these authorities is directly from God, and neither should interfere in the other's appropriate sphere.

Far more radical than John of Paris and Dante was the foremost "royal apologist" of the age, Marsilius of Padua (1280?–1343?), who was trained primarily in medicine, not in theology. In 1313, he became rector of the University of Paris, and there, in 1324, he completed the most remarkable of medieval political treatises, *Defensor pacis.* Its extreme views led Marsilius, in company with his assistant, John of Jandun (1275?–1328), to seek refuge at the court of Emperor Louis the Bavarian, whose protection they enjoyed for the rest of their lives. They were excommunicated by Pope John XXII in 1327, and Clement VI declared in 1343 that *Defender of Peace* was the most heretical book he had ever read.

Marsilius, who was deeply versed in Aristotle and well read in canon law, held that the basis of all power is "the people," namely, the whole body of citizens (*universitas civium*) in the state, and the whole body of believers (*universitas fidelium*) in the church. They are the legislative power; political and ecclesiastical rulers are appointed by them and remain accountable to them. The clergy possess no coercive jurisdiction whatever in temporal affairs. Their sole duty is to teach, warn, reprove, and thereby guide people to a salvation that is wholly otherworldly. The New Testament teaches that "bishop" and "priest" are equivalent designations, though it is fitting, as a purely human arrangement, to appoint some clergy superintendents over others. This appointment gives no superior spiritual power, nor has one bishop spiritual authority over another, or the pope over all, save as a traditional primacy of honor. The New Testament gives no countenance to the clergy's possession of earthly lordships and estates or to clerical exemption from civil law. No priest or prelate has authority to define normative Christian truth, to make binding church laws, or to inflict interdicts and excommunications on rulers and provinces. These acts can be done only by the whole company of believers, represented in a general council. Such a council is the supreme authority in the church, and its judgments are infallible. Since the Christian state and the Christian church are coterminous—Marsilius did not envision a fully secular state or a division between religion and politics—the executive of the state may call councils, appoint bishops, and control church property. Here were ideas that were to bear fruit in the Reformation era, but they were too radical to admit of wide acceptance in their own age.

The claims of the extreme papalists, however, were scarcely more acceptable. They were far from being shared by Germans engaged in a struggle with the papacy for the political autonomy of the empire, or by Englishmen at war with France, who considered the Avignon papacy but a tool of the French sovereign. Already in 1265, Pope Clement IV had asserted the right of the pope to appoint to any ecclesiastical office anywhere in Christendom; this novel principle was put to almost unlimited use by Clement V and the succeeding Avignon popes. Such appointees were called "provisors," and the intrusion of papal favorites in England aroused king and Parliament in 1351 to enact the Statute of Provisors, which forbad all papal provisions. This law inevitably led to disputes between papal and royal authority, and a further statute of 1353, known as that of *Praemunire,* forbad appeals outside the kingdom under penalty of outlawry. In enforcement, these statutes were largely dead letters, but they show the growth of a spirit in England which was further illustrated when Parliament, in 1366, revoked the action taken by King John in 1213, whereby he had made England a papal fief.

No feature of the Avignon papacy contributed so greatly to its criticism, or to religious and political opposition, as its oppressive taxation of church life. Such taxation had already reached scandalous proportions in the thirteenth century, but the situation was much aggravated when the papacy's removal to

Avignon largely cut off the revenues from the Papal States in central Italy without diminishing the luxury or expensiveness of the papal court. The Avignon popes developed a system of centralized administration which was the most sophisticated of the Middle Ages, and this mighty bureaucratic machine now devoted itself to increasing papal revenues. A chief means to this end was the introduction of the "annates," a tax of approximately one year's income from each new appointment. Since the "reservation" of posts to exclusive papal appointment was at the same time immensely extended, this became a large source of revenue, as did the income accruing to the papacy from vacant benefices. Taxes for bulls and other papal documents also rose rapidly in amount and productivity. These were but a portion of the papal exactions, and the total effect was the intense conviction that the papal administration was heavily and increasingly burdensome to the clergy, and through them to the people. This feeling was heightened by the ruthless manner in which churchly censures, such as excommunications, were imposed on delinquent taxpayers. The papacy seemed extravagant in expenditure and offensive in taxation. Its repute in both respects was to grow worse up to the Reformation.

Most of the Avignon popes, it should be added, were men of good character, and some tried valiantly to administer the existing arrangements without abuse; but none broke root and branch with the deleterious "benefice system" which treated church offices (*beneficia*) as pieces of property to be bought, sold, exchanged, granted as rewards, and, above all, taxed. This system was largely a revenue-raising operation and thus had little intrinsic concern for the vital pastoral activity of the church. Papal centralization, moreover, increasingly diminished the authority of bishops over their dioceses and thereby emptied the local diocese of its traditional importance as the basic unit of church life. Soon, the church at large was to suffer even greater shocks through its division into two, and then three, competing papal "obediences."

In 1367, Pope Urban V (1362–1370) returned to Rome, but in 1370 he and his court were once more at Avignon. He was succeeded by Gregory XI (1370–1378), whom St. Catherine of Siena (1347–1380) and St. Bridget of Sweden (1300?–1373) urged in the name of God to return to Rome. The distracted state of the city, in the aftermath of the popular revolution headed there in 1347 by Cola di Rienzo (1313–1354), also counseled his presence if papal interests were to be preserved. Accordingly, he transferred the papacy to Rome in January 1377. The death of Gregory XI, in March 1378, thus found most of the cardinals in Rome. The French majority among them would gladly have returned to Avignon. The Roman people, however, were determined to keep the papacy in Rome, and to that end they demanded an Italian pope. Under conditions of tumult, the cardinals chose Bartolommeo Prignano, the archbishop of Bari, who took the name Urban VI (1378–1389). A tactless man, who desired to terminate French influence over the papacy and to effect some reforms in the papal court, he soon had the hostility of the cardinals. Four months after his election, twelve of the sixteen cardinals assembled in Anagni, declared their previous choice void because dictated by mob violence, and elected Cardinal Robert of Geneva as Pope Clement VII (1378–1394). A few months later, Clement VII and his cardinals were settled at Avignon. The Great Schism had begun.

There had been many rival popes before, but they had been chosen by different elements. Here were two popes, each duly elected by a majority of one and the same body of cardinals. Latin Christendom now witnessed the spectacle of two popes fulminating against and excommunicating each other. There was apparently no power that could decide between them, and the several countries followed the one or the other as their political affinities dictated. The Roman pope was acknowledged by northern and central Italy, the greater part of Germany, Bohemia, Poland, Hungary, Scandinavia, and England. The Avignon pope had the allegiance of France, Spain, Scotland, Naples, Sicily, and some parts of Germany. It was a fairly equal division. Europe was pained and scandalized, while the papal abuses, especially of taxation, were augmented, not least because two courts (each with its own college of cardinals) now had to be maintained. Above all, the profound feeling that the church must be visibly one was offended. The papacy sank enormously in popular regard.

In Rome, Urban VI was succeeded by Boniface IX (1389–1404), and he by Innocent VII (1404–1406), who was followed by Gregory XII (1406–1415). In Avignon, Clement VII was followed by a Spaniard, Pedro de Luna, who took the name Benedict XIII (1394–1417).

The Great Schism lasted for almost forty years. It was compounded by the creation of yet a third line of popes at the ill-fated Council of Pisa in 1409; and it was not resolved until the Council of Constance (1414–1418) asserted its jurisdictional supremacy within the church and deposed, or induced to resign, the three competing popes, Gregory XII, Benedict XIII, and John XXIII (see V:14).

Chapter 13

Wyclif and Hus

BY 1400, the two great heresies which had heretofore plagued the medieval church—Catharism and Waldensianism—had been successfully contained. The Cathars, indeed, had been well-nigh destroyed. The Waldenses, though still a force to be reckoned with, had been isolated and driven underground. Likewise, the heretical dissent of the radical Franciscan groups (the Fraticelli) and of the so-called Free Spirits was no longer of pressing concern. Yet at this very time, in the half-century from 1375 to 1425, two new heretical movements, of menacing proportions, arose in two countries on the periphery of Europe, England and Bohemia—two countries, moreover, that had been notably free of heresy in the past. In each country, the new heresy was soon attributed to a single leader: John Wyclif in England and Jan Hus in Bohemia. This attribution holds good, for the most part, in Wyclif's case; Hus, however, was the heir of a native Czech tradition of religious reform.

That the teachings of Wyclif in Oxford should have found their way across the European continent to Hus in Prague was largely an "accident" of a dynastic marriage. It was not merely fortuitous, however, that the two leaders should have many points in common. Both were reacting to the profound shocks administered to Latin Christendom by the "captivity" of the papacy in Avignon and by the catastrophic Great Schism that followed. The church at large was deemed sorely in need of reform "in head and members." Thus, it is not surprising that Wyclif and Hus were at heart "moralists," or that the doctrine of the church should have become their central concern and the prime source of their heterodoxy.

John Wyclif (1325?–1384) was born in Yorkshire sometime between 1320 and 1330. His entire career, many of the details of which are matters of conjecture, was bound up with Oxford University, where he took the B.A. degree in 1356 and the M.A. in 1361. For a short time thereafter, he served as master of Balliol College. In 1361, he was also appointed rector of the parish church at Fillingham, while continuing to lecture at Oxford; in 1368, he exchanged this rectorship for that of Ludgershall, which was nearer to Oxford. It is likely that he was elected warden of Canterbury College, Oxford, in 1365, but the pope soon dismissed this election as irregular. During the 1360s, Wyclif attained great repute at Oxford, and in wider academic circles, as a brilliant lecturer and writer on logic and metaphysics; by 1369, he had completed an impressive work, *Summa de ente* (On Being). Philosophically, he was an ultrarealist, a vigorous defender of the *via antiqua* against the then prevailing nominalism. He also pursued advanced study in theology, taking the doctor's degree in 1372 and laying plans for a *Summa theologica* in twelve volumes. He was deeply influenced by the Augustinian-Platonic tradition as mediated at Oxford by Robert Grosseteste, Thomas Bradwardine, and Richard FitzRalph (1295?–1360). Disappointed in his expectation of appointment to some high church office, which apparently had been promised him by Pope Gregory XI (1370–1378), he entered the service of the crown as a theological advisor, and in 1374 he was granted the parish of Lutterworth by King Edward III. Resigning the rectorship of Ludgershall, he served the parish at Lutterworth until his death, though continuing his close association with Oxford until 1381. In 1374, Wyclif was sent to Bruges as one of the king's commissioners to meet with papal representatives in what proved to be a futile attempt to resolve the dispute over "provisors" and over England's status as a fief of the papacy.

Already in the early 1370s, Wyclif held views about "dominion" or "lordship" that would justify, under certain conditions, the state's seizure of ecclesiastical properties. These views were undoubtedly known to the crown at the time of his entry into royal service. He fully developed his position in two treatises, *On Divine Lordship* (1375) and *On Civil Lordship* (1376), based on lectures given at Oxford following his return from Bruges. God, declared Wyclif, is the supreme Lord, on whose lordship all human lordship depends. God graciously bestows all possessions and powers, civil and ecclesiastical, as stewardships, not as permanent "property" but as temporary "loans," to be held only on condition of faithful service. Since only the righteous can exercise lordship rightfully, those ecclesiastics who are living in mortal sin forfeit all claims to temporal possessions. These may justly be taken from them by the civil rulers, to whom God has given the lordship of temporal things, whereas to the church God has given the lordship only of things spiritual. This teaching, advanced in all sincerity and not a little naiveté, was certainly pleasing to the unscrupulous son of Edward III, John of Gaunt, duke of Lancaster, and to his rapacious crew of nobles, who hoped to be enriched through the "disendowment" of the "delinquent" church. It also appealed to many commoners, who had long been outspoken critics of a greedy clericalism. Nor was it displeasing to the mendicant orders, who had always, in theory at least, advocated "apostolic poverty."

In February 1377, Wyclif was summoned to appear before the bishops assembled in London for examination of his views, but the protection of John of Gaunt and the court party frustrated the proceedings. In May of that same year, Gregory XI issued a bull against Wyclif, ordering him to appear in Rome within thirty days; and in January 1378, the archbishop of London undertook further proceedings against him. All these actions, however, were rendered ineffectual by Wyclif's royal support and great popular favor.

With the beginning of the Great Schism in 1378, Wyclif became ever more radical and embittered in his views, ultimately rejecting the whole traditional structure of the medieval church. Largely abandoning the political scene, he now devoted himself to theological study and writing. In his work *On the Truth of the Holy Scriptures* (1378), he asserted that Scripture is "the highest authority for every Christian and the standard of faith and of all human perfection." Yet he did not repudiate the interpretive authority of the church fathers and the ancient doctors; thus, he was not a forerunner of the Reformation "Scripture alone." His seminal treatise *On the Church* (1378) defined the true church in Augustinian terms as "the totality of the predestined" (*universitas praedestinatorum*)—a timeless and purely spiritual, hence invisible, body of which Christ alone is the head. The pope, accordingly, is at most the head of the Roman portion of the visible church, the latter being composed of both the elect and the damned, who are known to God alone though they may be recognized, in part, by their respective "fruits."[1] Wyclif conceded in his book *On the Power of the Pope* (1379) that the visible church may well have an earthly leader, if such a one truly emulates Peter in apostolic simplicity and poverty. Such a pope would presumably be one of the elect; but a pope who grasps worldly power and is eager for riches is presumptively not of the elect and is therefore a veritable Antichrist. In any event, the papacy is of human origin—it was founded by Constantine, not Christ—and its jurisdiction is limited strictly to spiritual concerns. (Subsequently, Wyclif called for the abolition of the papacy and the total disendowment of the church.)

These treatises were followed by *On the Eucharist* (1380), wherein Wyclif rejected the dogma of transubstantiation as illogical, unscriptural, and unfaithful to the teaching of the ancient church. His own positive view, known as "remanence," holds that even after consecration the bread and wine remain material substances, since it is impossible for "accidents" to exist by themselves apart from a substance and for any really existing substance to be "annihilated." The body and blood of Christ are truly present in the elements, not materially or carnally, but symbolically or sacramentally. The bread and the wine are thus "efficacious signs" of Christ's body and blood. Though Wyclif considered preaching far more important than sacramental observation, he remained devoted to the eucharist till the end of his life. Nonetheless, his assault on one of the most cherished of church dogmas, coupled with his denunciation of the mendicant orders as "children of Cain," cost him the support of John of Gaunt and the court party, the friars, and many of his Oxford sympathizers.

---

[1] Cf. Matt. 7:16.

This tide of opposition was strengthened by political events in 1381 for which Wyclif bore no responsibility. The unrest of the lower classes, which had been growing in the wake of the severe economic dislocations caused by the Black Death of 1348–1350, culminated in 1381 in a great peasants' revolt that was suppressed with much bloodshed. Wyclif's foes charged that his heresies had licensed this violent episode. The result was a rapprochement between church and state. In 1382, William Courtenay, the new archbishop of Canterbury (1381–1396), convened a synod in London that condemned twenty-four propositions culled from Wyclif's works, though Wyclif was not cited or condemned by name. By now, the court party had abandoned Wyclif, and Courtenay was authorized to imprison any defenders of the condemned theses. Given free rein, he quickly moved against the Wyclif party at Oxford.

Wyclif himself, as noted, had withdrawn from the political arena in the closing months of 1378, and in the summer of 1381 he had retired to his parish at Lutterworth, where he remained unmolested. These last years of his life were a time of feverish literary activity. He completed the final volumes of his theological *Summa;* produced a flood of vernacular pamphlets; and worked on his *Opus evangelicum* and *Trialogus,* which summarized his main theological and philosophical themes. He also provided the inspiration and impetus for the translation of the Vulgate Bible into English. It appears that he did not contribute directly to the work of translation, which was carried out and completed, after his death, by a group of disciples at Oxford and Lutterworth, including Nicholas of Hereford and John Purvey. Wyclif also organized a large body of sermons for use by the "poor priests" who were by now spreading the gospel among the people. In their dress and demeanor, these itinerant evangelists resembled the early Waldensian or Franciscan preachers. It is unlikely that Wyclif was actively engaged in their training. His writings consumed his energies, and his health was failing. He had suffered a stroke in November 1382, which left him partly paralyzed. He suffered a second stroke on December 28, 1384, while hearing Mass, and died three days later. He was buried in the Lutterworth church graveyard, i.e., in consecrated ground, for he had not been officially excommunicated. In 1428, the bishop of Lincoln, obeying the mandate of the Council of Constance in 1415, had Wyclif's remains exhumed and burned and the ashes thrown into the River Swift.

Wyclif's followers were called "Lollards" (= "mumblers")—a derisive term, of Dutch origin, that had long been applied in the Netherlands to Beguines and Beghards. The movement was sorely disadvantaged by its lack of conspicuous intellectual leadership after Wyclif's death. The Oxford Wyclifites were assiduously rooted out by Archbishop Courtenay and his successor, Thomas Arundel (1396–1414). Even Hereford and Purvey were forced to recant. Yet in spite of the loss of Oxford and the arrest and imprisonment of Lollard preachers, the movement continued to grow throughout the reign of Richard II (1377–1399). The situation changed with the accession of the usurping house of Lancaster in the person of Henry IV (1399–1413). Anxious to placate the church, the new king was persuaded to secure the passage in 1401 of the anti-heresy statute, *De haeretico comburendo,* under which a number of Lollards were burned. Henry IV, however, spared Lollards in high station and largely treated the statute as a formality. Not so his son, Henry V (1413–1422), who enforced it ruthlessly. Under him, the most notable Lollard leader, Sir John Oldcastle, Lord Cobham, a man of the sternest religious principles, whom tradition and dramatic license transformed into the figure of Falstaff, was condemned, driven into rebellion, and executed in 1417. With his death, the political significance of Lollardy in England was at an end, though adherents survived in various rural districts and continued their underground existence until the Reformation. Wyclif's chief influence was to be in distant Bohemia rather than in the land of his birth.

Bohemia had undergone significant political, intellectual, and religious developments in the fourteenth century. The Holy Roman emperor, Charles IV (1346–1378), was also king of Bohemia and did much for that land. In 1344, he secured the establishment of Prague as an archbishopric, releasing Bohemia from ecclesiastical dependence on Mainz; in 1348, he founded at Prague the first university in central Europe. Charles was also friendly to ecclesiastical reform. During and following his reign, several preachers of power stirred Bohemia, attacking the rampant secularization of the church in the name of the "simple gospel." Most famous of these were the Austrian Augustinian canon, Conrad of Waldhausen (?–1369), and the Moravian, Milíč of Kroměříž (?–1374). They were joined by Matthew of Janov (1355?–1394) and Thomas of Štítné (1331–1409), who made notable contributions to the theological and popular religious literature of Bohemia. These preachers and writers launched the Czech religious reform, the characteristic features of which were preaching in the vernacular, moral reform of the clergy and people, the centrality of Scripture as the rule of life, and the call for frequent participation in the Lord's Supper. This native reform movement long predated the introduction of Wyclifite ideas into Bohemia. Through Matthew of Janov, a celebrated scholar, it was also linked to Czech university circles in Prague.

Politically, Bohemia was divided by strife between the immigrant German and the indigenous Czech elements of the population. The Czechs were animated by a strong desire for equality with the ruling Germans. In 1382, Bohemia, hitherto little associated with England, was brought into connection with that country by the marriage of the Bohemian princess Anne to King Richard II. Czech students were attracted to Oxford and there became acquainted with Wyclif's doctrines and writings, which they soon brought back to their native land, especially to the University of Prague. Among the professors who embraced some of Wyclif's ideas was Jan Hus, in whom Czech national aspirations found an ardent advocate and the native reform movement its outstanding leader.

Hus was born, of poor parents, in the village of Husinec in southwest

Bohemia, in 1372 or 1373. He studied at the University of Prague, where he became master of arts in 1396. In 1400, he was ordained to the priesthood, still maintaining a teaching connection with the university, where he was elected dean of the arts faculty for the winter semester of 1401–1402. By 1409, he had completed all the requirements for the doctorate in theology, with lectures on the Bible and the *Sentences* of Peter Lombard, but he never attained that degree, owing to the bitter controversies of his last years, which eventually forced him to leave the academic precincts and brought him to the stake at Constance. Sometime before his entrance into the priesthood, which he initially regarded only as a source of economic security, Hus underwent a conversion, through the study of Scripture, and became a zealous advocate of clerical reform. In 1402, he was appointed preacher at the Bethlehem Chapel in Prague, the center of the Czech reform movement, and there he soon gained an immense popular following through his fiery sermons in the Czech language.

Early in his academic career, Hus was an avid student of Wyclif's philosophical works, fully agreeing with their "realism," like most of the Czech masters at Prague. The more numerous German masters, by contrast, were largely followers of Ockham and the *via moderna*. Wyclif's theological works were not brought to Prague until shortly after 1400, initially by Hus's intimate friend and lifelong adherent, Jerome of Prague (1370?–1416), who had taken his M.A. at Oxford. Hus was not, as often thought, a "mere echo" of Wyclif, though he frequently reproduced Wyclif's language in his sermons and treatises. He owed as much to the Czech reform movement as he did to Wyclif, and his appropriation of Wyclif's theology was a critically selective one. He accepted what he considered unimpeachably orthodox in Wyclif, while usually passing over in silence those views of which he disapproved. He was also disposed to express orthodox sentiments in Wyclifite formulas—a fatal disposition, as events were to prove. Hus was entirely orthodox in his eucharistic teaching; unlike Wyclif, he did not deny transubstantiation. Like Wyclif, he did teach that the true church consists only of the predestined, of whom the head is Christ, not the pope—though if a pope lives well, he could be considered the head of the "particular" church of Rome. The life of the true church is one of Christ-like simplicity and poverty. The only law of this church is the Bible, above all the New Testament. This "Scripture principle," like Wyclif's, ruled out the extrabiblical traditions of canon law but did not deny the teaching authority of the ancient fathers and doctors.

Forty-five articles attributed to Wyclif were condemned by the majority of the Prague masters in 1403. The Czech masters, however, who were in a minority, generally defended Wyclif. Hus, of course, joined in the defense. In the meantime, his preaching at Bethlehem Chapel initially had the support of the young archbishop, Zbyněk Zajíc of Hasenburk (1401–1411); but Hus's caustic criticisms of the clergy, and his identification with the condemned Wyclifite teachings, gradually turned this favor into opposition. New grounds of controversy speedily arose. In the Great Schism, Bohemia held to the Roman pope, currently Gregory XII. As a step toward healing the breach, the king of Bohemia, Wenceslas IV (1378–1419), in 1408 declared his support for a policy of neutrality between the rival popes. Hus and the Czech element in the university stood with Wenceslas. Archbishop Zbyněk, the German clergy, and the German masters at the university clung to Gregory XII, much to the king's displeasure. In January 1409, therefore, Wenceslas abruptly changed the constitution of the university, giving the Germans but one vote to every three for the Czechs, thereby completely reversing the previous ratio. The almost immediate result was the secession of the German masters and students, numbering about 1,500, who in that same year established their own university at Leipzig. In October 1409, Hus was elected the first rector of the reorganized university. In consequence, he was long identified with perfidy and heresy in the minds of the Leipzig professors, whose enmity vented itself at Constance.

Meanwhile, the luckless Council of Pisa (1409) had run its course (see V:14). Archbishop Zbyněk now supported its pope, Alexander V (1409–1410), to whom he complained of the spread of Wyclifite teachings in Bohemia, and by whom he was commissioned to root them out. Hus protested, was excommunicated by Zbyněk in 1410, and was put under investigation by the Roman Curia. The result was great tumult in Prague, where Hus was more than ever a popular hero. King Wenceslas, whose favor was crucial, supported him. In 1411 and again in 1412, Alexander's disreputable successor, Pope John XXIII (1410–1415), promised indulgences to all participants in his planned crusade against King Ladislas of Naples (1386–1414), a supporter of the deposed Gregory XII. Hus denounced this "crusade indulgence," holding that a pope has no right to use physical force, that money payments effect no true forgiveness, and that indulgences are superfluous since forgiveness is freely given to those who are truly penitent and confess their sins. The result was an uproar. The pope's bulls were burned by the populace. Hus's principled stand, however, gravely damaged his cause. He lost many key supporters in the university, including Stanislav of Znojmo and Stephen Páleč; he was once more excommunicated; and he alienated King Wenceslas. Prague itself was placed under papal interdict. Wishing to spare the city this calamity, Hus left Prague in October 1412, taking refuge with powerful friends among the nobility in southern Bohemia.

During this time of exile, besides writing numerous vernacular tracts, Hus composed his chief work, *De ecclesia* (On the Church), a treatise greatly indebted to Wyclif's treatise of the same name, yet avoiding Wyclif's most radical conclusions. In particular, Hus stopped short of the full Donatist heresy that a sinful priest has no sacerdotal power (*potestas ordinis*), though he did hold the "semi-Donatist" position that wicked priests and prelates have no rightful jurisdictional authority (*potestas iurisdictionis*) and thus are due no obedience. For this reason, he appealed his case to "God and Christ" alone, not to a pope or to a church council—a stand that was clearly heretical in the eyes of curialists and conciliarists alike.

The great Council of Constance (1414–1418) was now approaching, and the confusion in Bohemia was certain to demand its consideration. Hus was asked to present himself before it and was given a "safe-conduct" by the Holy Roman Emperor, Sigismund (1410–1437), the brother of King Wenceslas. Though he knew himself to be in grave peril, Hus decided to go, partly believing it his duty to bear witness to what he deemed the truth, partly convinced that he could bring the council to his way of thinking. Shortly after his arrival in Constance, he was imprisoned; the council had persuaded Sigismund to disregard the promised safe-conduct. The German masters who had been expelled from Prague, as well as Hus's Czech enemies, brought bitter charges against him. The accusations of his erstwhile colleague and friend, Stephen Páleč, were given special weight by his judges, chief of whom were the renowned Pierre d'Ailly and Jean de Gerson. On May 4, 1415, confirming an action that had already been taken at a Roman synod in 1413, the council formally condemned Wyclif as a heretic and ordered his long-buried body to be removed from consecrated ground. Hus, who was now generally assumed to be the devoted disciple of the heresiarch Wyclif, could have little hope for a favorable hearing. On the basis of thirty erroneous teachings attributed to him, the council called for his complete submission. But the Czech reformer was of heroic mold. Some of the accusations he declared false, based on misrepresentation. Other positions he refused to modify unless convinced of their error by Scripture and the ancient fathers. He would not submit his conscience to the overruling judgment of the council. On July 6, 1415, he was condemned and burned, meeting his death with the most steadfast courage.

While Hus was a prisoner in Constance, his followers in Prague, in October 1414, began administering the cup to the laity in the Lord's Supper—an action which Hus approved and which soon became the badge of the Hussite movement. The news of Hus's death aroused the utmost resentment in Bohemia, to which fuel was added when the Council of Constance forbad lay use of the cup and caused Hus's more radical friend and colleague, Jerome of Prague, to be burned on May 30, 1416. Bohemia was in revolt. Two parties developed there: a moderate, aristocratic party, having its principal seat in Prague and known as the Utraquists (communion *sub utraque,* i.e., in both bread and wine) or the Calixtines (from the Latin *calix,* chalice, cup), or simply the Praguers; and a radical, democratic party, called from its fortress, Tábor, the Taborites.

The Utraquists would forbid only those practices which they deemed prohibited by the "law of God," i.e., the Bible. The Taborites repudiated all practices for which express warrant could not be found in the "law of God." The factions carried on a fierce quarrel, but in 1420 they united in adopting a common religious program, the "Four Articles of Prague," which demanded free preaching of God's Word, the cup for the laity, apostolic poverty, and strict clerical and lay life. Together they also resisted repeated crusades directed against Bohemia. Under the leadership of the one-eyed—eventually totally blind—Taborite general, Jan Žižka of Trocnov, all attempts to crush the Hussites were bloodily defeated. Nor were the Hussites' opponents more successful after Žižka's death in 1424. Under Procopius the Great, the Hussites carried the war beyond the borders of Bohemia. Some compromise seemed unavoidable. The Council of Basel, after long negotiation, met the wishes of the Hussites partway in 1433, granting the use of the cup and, to some extent, the other demands of the Four Articles. The Taborites, dissatisfied, resisted and were almost swept away by the Utraquists in 1434, at the battle of Lipany, in which Procopius was killed. The triumphant Utraquists then came to an agreement, the "Compactata," with the Council of Basel, in 1436, and on these terms they were nominally given place in the Roman communion. Yet, in 1462, Pope Pius II (1458–1464) declared this agreement void. The Utraquists nevertheless held their own, and the Bohemian Diet, in 1485 and again in 1512, declared the full equality of the Utraquists with the Catholics. At the Reformation, a considerable portion welcomed the newer ideas; a few returned to the Roman church.

The real representatives of Wyclifite principles were the Taborites rather than the Utraquists. Out of the general Hussite movement, with elements drawn from the Taborites, Utraquists, and Waldenses, there grew, from about 1458, the *Unitas Fratrum* (Unity of Bohemian Brethren), which absorbed much that was vital in Hussitism and became the spiritual ancestor of the later Moravians (see VII:6).

Wyclif and Hus have often been styled forerunners of the Reformation. The designation is appropriate if regard is given to their protest against ecclesiastical abuses, their exaltation of the Bible, and their contribution to the sum total of agitation that ultimately resulted in church reform. The fundamental doctrines of the Protestant reformers, however, owed little of their substance to the doctrines of Wyclif and Hus, and they were far more radical in their break with traditional teaching. Nevertheless, insofar as Wyclif and Hus and a great number of "orthodox" thinkers of the late Middle Ages were already confronting the same central issues that the Protestant reformers were to confront, they may be justly called "forerunners" of the Reformation. There remained a basic continuity of "questions," albeit not of "answers."

Chapter 14

The Reforming Councils

T HE PAPAL SCHISM was the scandal of Christendom, but its termination was not easy. The logic of medieval development was such that no jurisdictional power exists on earth to which the papacy was answerable. Yet good people everywhere felt that the schism must be ended, and that the church must be reformed "in head and members"—that is, in the papacy and clergy. The reforms desired were moral and administrative, not doctrinal. Foremost among those who set themselves seriously to the task of healing the schism were the teachers of the age, especially those of the University of Paris. There, in 1324, Marsilius of Padua had proclaimed the supremacy of a general council in his *Defensor pacis*. Marsilius, however, had denied all jurisdictional authority to priests and prelates and had also denied the divine foundation of the papacy. These radical ideas found no favor among the late fourteenth-century "conciliarists" at Paris and elsewhere, who drew upon entirely orthodox traditions of theology and canon law to support their basic claim that the plenitude of jurisdictional authority in the church resides in the whole body of its members, as represented in a general council. The pope, in turn, receives this fulness of power as the "principal minister" of the ecclesiastical "corporation," and he must ever exercise it for the good of the whole church. The central conciliarist principle of the superiority of a general council to the pope was first presented with scholarly rigor in treatises of 1379 and 1380 by a German doctor of canon law, Conrad of Gelnhausen (1320?–1390), then resident at Paris, and then in a treatise of 1381 by another German scholar at Paris, Heinrich of Langenstein (1330?–1397).

The thought of a general council as the best means of healing the schism— the so-called *via concilii*—quickly made converts, not only in the University of Paris, but also in the great school of canon law at Bologna and even among the cardinals. The conciliar solution, however, posed many problems, especially since canon law stipulated that the assembly had to be convened by the pope. Hence, the leaders at Paris, Pierre d'Ailly and Jean de Gerson, were slow to adopt this plan. For many years, rather, efforts were vainly made to induce the rival popes to resign—the so-called *via cessionis*. France withdrew from the Avignon pope, without recognizing the Roman, from 1398 to 1403 and again in 1408, but its example found slight following elsewhere. By 1408, d'Ailly and Gerson had come to see in a council the only hope, and they were supported by their former student and colleague at Paris, Nicholas of Clémanges (1367-1437), who had been secretary to Benedict XIII in Avignon from 1397 to 1405.

The cardinals of both popes finally became convinced of the necessity of a council. Meeting together at Leghorn in 1408, they issued a call in their own names for such an assembly to gather at Pisa on March 25, 1409. There it met with an attendance not only of cardinals, bishops, the heads of the great orders, and leading abbots, but also of doctors of theology and canon law and the representatives of lay sovereigns. Neither pope was present or acknowledged the council's legitimacy. Both were deposed by the council as schismatics and heretics. This was a practical assertion that the council was superior to the papacy. Its action, however, was too hasty, for instead of ascertaining, as d'Ailly advised, whether the person of the proposed new pope would be generally acceptable, the cardinals now elected Pietro Philarghi, archbishop of Milan, who took the name Alexander V (1409–1410). The council then dissolved, leaving the question of reform to a future council.

In many respects, the situation was now worse than before the council had met. Rome, Naples, and considerable sections of Germany clung to Gregory XII. Spain, Portugal, and Scotland supported Benedict XIII. England, France, and some portions of Germany acknowledged Alexander V. There were now three popes, three curial administrations, and three colleges of cardinals. Yet, though mismanaged, the Council of Pisa had shown that the church was one, and it increased the hope that a better council could end the schism. This assembly had been called by the cardinals—an unprecedented action. According to the eminent conciliarist Dietrich of Niem (1340?-1418), a summons by the emperor, if possible with the consent of one or more of the popes, would be consonant with the practice of the early church.

The new Holy Roman Emperor-elect, Sigismund (1410–1437), adopted Dietrich's proposal. Sigismund himself recognized as pope John XXIII (1410–1415), one of the least worthy of occupants of that office, who had been chosen successor to Alexander V in the Pisan line. Sigismund used John's difficulties with King Ladislas of Naples to secure from him joint action by which emperor-elect and pope called a council to meet in Constance on November 1, 1414. There the most brilliant and the most heavily attended gathering of the Middle Ages assembled. Sigismund attended in person, and John XXIII presided.

John hoped to secure the endorsement of the council. To this end, he had brought with him many Italian bishops. To neutralize their votes, the council (composed of patriarchs, archbishops, bishops, abbots, priors, doctors of theology and of canon law, and representatives of the sovereigns) organized itself into four "nations"—the English, German, French, and Italian. Each "nation" had but one vote, and one was assigned also to the cardinals. Despairing of the council's approval, John XXIII attempted to disrupt its session by flight, in March 1415. Under Gerson's vigorous leadership, the council, however, declared on April 6, 1415, in the famous decree *Haec sancta synodus* (or *Sacrosancta*), that "this holy Council of Constance . . . is lawfully assembled in the Holy Spirit, that it constitutes a General Council, representing the Catholic Church, and that therefore it has its authority immediately from Christ; and that all men, of every rank and condition, including the Pope himself, are bound to obey it in matters concerning the Faith, the abolition of the schism, and the reformation of the Church of God in its head and its members."[1] On May 29, the council declared John XXIII deposed on the ground of scandalous misconduct. On July 4, Gregory XII resigned, but only after formally reconvening the council on his own authority (and thereby securing, in his own mind at least, the council's tacit recognition of the legitimacy of the Roman line of popes). The council had thus rid the church of the Pisan and Roman popes by its successful assertion of its supreme authority over all in the church. It is easy to see why its leaders insisted on a full submission from Jan Hus, whose trials and martyrdom were contemporary with these events (see V:13).

The Avignon pope, Benedict XIII, proved more difficult. Sigismund himself journeyed to Spain to meet with Benedict, but that obstinate pontiff refused to resign. What Sigismund was unable to effect with Benedict he accomplished with the Spanish kingdoms. They and Scotland repudiated Benedict. The Spaniards joined the council as a fifth "nation," and, on July 26, 1417, Benedict, or Pedro de Luna, as he was once more called, was formally deposed. The careful action of the council, in contrast to the haste at Pisa, had made it certain that no considerable section of Christendom would support the former popes.

One main purpose of the Council of Constance had been moral and administrative reform. As a reformatory instrument, however, the council was a bitter disappointment, since the jealousies and rivalries of the several "nations" thwarted effective action. Its one great achievement was that it ended the schism. In November 1417, the cardinals, together with six representatives from each nation, elected a Roman cardinal, Oddo Colonna, as pope. He took the name Martin V (1417–1431). Roman Christendom once more had a single head. The council ended in April 1418, the new pope promising to call another in five years, in compliance with the council's other famous decree, *Frequens* (October 9, 1417).

The Council of Constance was a revolutionary ecclesiastical experiment. It replaced the absolute papal monarchy with the representative authority of a general council. The pope, though remaining the executive of the church, re-

---

[1] Bettenson, *Documents*, p. 192.

ceived his position and rights from the whole body of Christians acting through a general council, which was to meet at frequent intervals. The pope had become, at best, a limited constitutional monarch.

It seemed for a time that this great transformation had really been accomplished. Martin V called the next council to meet at Pavia in 1423. The plague prevented any considerable attendance and forced its transfer to Siena, where, after accomplishing little, it was peremptorily dissolved by the pope early in 1424. The pope would gladly have had no more of councils. The Hussite wars distressed Europe, however, and such pressure was brought to bear that, in January 1431, Martin V summoned a council to meet at Basel, and appointed Cardinal Giuliano Cesarini his legate to conduct it. Less than two months later, Martin V was dead and Eugenius IV (1431–1447) was pope. The council opened in July 1431, but in December Eugenius ordered it adjourned, to meet at Bologna in 1433. The council refused to adjourn and reenacted the declaration of Constance that it was superior to the pope. Thus, almost from the first, bad feelings existed between the Council of Basel and the papacy. Mindful that jealousies between "nations" had frustrated the reform plans at Constance, the council rejected such groupings and instead organized four large committees (on reform, doctrine, public peace, and general questions). It began its work with great vigor and promise of success. It made an apparent reconciliation with the moderate Hussites in 1433 (see V:13). Church unity seemed restored. The pope found little support and, before the close of 1433, formally recognized the council. Its future seemed assured.

The Council of Basel now proceeded to those administrative and moral reforms which had failed of achievement at Constance. It ordered the holding of a synod in each diocese annually, and in each archdiocese every two years, in which abuses should be examined and corrected. It provided for a general council every ten years. It reasserted the ancient rights of canonical election as against papal appointments. It limited appeals to Rome. It fixed the number of cardinals at twenty-four and ordered that no nation should be represented by more than a third of the college. It cut off the annates and the other more oppressive papal taxes entirely. However beneficial and necessary this curtailing of traditional papal privileges, the spirit in which it was done was increasingly vindictive toward Pope Eugenius. No honorable support of the papacy was provided in place of the taxes that had been abolished. This failure not only increased papal resentment but also caused division within the council. At this point a great opportunity presented itself, of which Eugenius IV made full use, and regarding which the council so put itself in the wrong as to ruin its prospects.

The Eastern Empire was now hard pressed in its final struggles with the conquering Turks. In the hope of gaining help from the West, Emperor John VIII Palaeologus (1425–1448), in company with the patriarch of Constantinople, Joseph II (1416–1439), and John Bessarion (1395–1472), the gifted archbishop of

Nicaea, was ready to enter into negotiation for the union of the Greek and Latin churches. Both pope and council were disposed to use this approach for their respective advantage. The majority of the council wished the Greeks to come to Basel or Avignon. The pope proposed an Italian city, which the Greeks preferred. The council divided on the issue in 1437, the minority seceding, including Cesarini and the heretofore staunch conciliarist, Nicholas of Cusa (1401–1464; see V:17). Eugenius IV then announced the transfer of the council to Ferrara to meet the Greeks. Thither the minority went, and there, in March 1438, the eastern emperor, with many oriental prelates, arrived. The pope had practically won. An event so full of promise as the reunion of Christendom robbed the still-continuing Council of Basel of much of its interest.

The Council of Ferrara, which was transferred to Florence in 1439, witnessed protracted discussion between Greeks and Latins, in which as a final result the primacy of the pope was accepted in rather vague terms that seemed to preserve the rights of the eastern patriarchs. The Greeks retained their distinctive liturgical practice and priestly marriage. They acknowledged the disputed *filioque* clause of the Nicene Creed, though with the understanding that they would not add it to the ancient symbol. Mark, the vigorous metropolitan of Ephesus, refused agreement, but the emperor and most of his ecclesiastical following approved, and the reunion of the two churches was joyfully proclaimed in July 1439, in the bull *Laetentur coeli*. An event so happy greatly increased the prestige of Pope Eugenius IV. The hollowness of the achievement was not at once apparent. Reunions with the Armenians, and with certain groups of Monophysites and Nestorians, were also announced in Florence or soon after the council. Yet from the first, the oriental monks were opposed. On the Greeks' return, Mark of Ephesus became the hero of the hour. Bessarion, whom Eugene had made a cardinal, had to flee to Italy, where he was to have a distinguished career of literary and ecclesiastical service. No effective military help came to the Greeks from the West, and the capture of Constantinople by the Turks in 1453 permanently frustrated those political hopes which had inspired the union efforts of 1439.

Meanwhile, the majority in Basel proceeded to more radical action, under the leadership of its only remaining cardinal, the able and excellent but dictatorial Louis d'Aleman of Arles (1380?–1450). In 1439, it deposed Eugenius IV and chose as his successor a half-monastic layman, Duke Amadeus of Savoy, who took the name Felix V. By this time, however, the Council of Basel was fast losing its remaining influence, not least because it was seen as precipitating a new papal schism. Eugenius IV, in fact, had won, and he was succeeded in Rome by Nicholas V (1447–1455). Felix V abdicated his impossible papacy in 1449. The council put the best face on its defeat by concurring in the election of Nicholas V as Felix's successor, and it then decreed its own dissolution (1449).

Though the conciliar theory still lived and was to be powerful in the Reformation age, the fiasco in Basel had really ruined the hope of transforming the papacy into a constitutional monarchy or of effecting needed reform through conciliar action. The papacy emerged in the ensuing "restoration" era as a monarchy that again was absolutist in its claims, now armed with the first conciliar definition of papal primacy, namely, that of the union decree *Laetentur coeli* of 1439.

Absolutist claims, however, once more encountered formidable opposition, not from church councils but from individual nations that had profited from the Great Schism and from the "conciliar experiment." The English kings, for example, ever since the "captivity" of the papacy at Avignon, had been notably successful in securing their share of ecclesiastical appointments and taxes, and they were determined to preserve these gains. The same was true of the French monarchs. In 1438, King Charles VII (1422–1461), with the clergy and nobles, adopted the so-called Pragmatic Sanction of Bourges, by which the greater part of the reforms attempted at Basel were enacted into law for France, which thus secured relief from the most pressing papal taxes and interferences. Germany was not so fortunate. There, in 1439, the nobles in the Reichstag at Mainz adopted an "acceptation" much resembling the French "pragmatic sanction"; but the divisions and weakness of the country gave room to papal intrigue, so that its provisions were in practical effect limited by the Concordat of Vienna in 1448. Certain privileges were granted to particular princes, but Germany as a whole remained under the weight of the papal taxation.

Throughout the period of the Great Schism and of the councils, a new force was thus manifesting itself—that of nationality. The Council of Constance had authorized the "nations" to make terms with the papacy. Bohemia had dealt with its religious situation as a nation. England and France had asserted their national rights. Germany had tried to do so. With the failure of the councils to effect thoroughgoing reform, people began asking whether what they had sought might not be secured by national action. It was a feeling that was to increase until the Reformation, and it would greatly influence the course of that struggle.

Chapter 15

The Italian Renaissance and Its Popes;
Popular Religious Leaders

THE MOST remarkable intellectual event contemporary with the papacy in Avignon and the Great Schism was the beginning of the Renaissance. That great alteration in mental outlook was long treated as without medieval antecedents. It is now recognized that the Middle Ages were not lacking in attention to the "individual" and to "humanistic" concerns, that the control of the church was never such as to make otherworldliness wholly dominant, and that the literary monuments of Latin antiquity, at least, were widely known. The revival of Roman law, beginning in about 1100, had attracted increasing attention to that normative feature of ancient thought, first in Italy and later in France and Germany. The entire twelfth century, moreover, had witnessed a revival of logic and the liberal arts in the schools, including the gradual rediscovery of the entire Aristotelian corpus, which culminated in the great theological *summae* of the thirteenth century, with their characteristic attention to "nature" no less than to "grace."

Yet when all these elements are recognized, it remains true that the Renaissance of the fourteenth, fifteenth, and early sixteenth centuries involved a subtle, and cumulatively a most significant, shift of outlook on the world, in which relatively greater emphasis was laid on the beauty, dignity, and satisfaction of the present life than on a future life of bliss or bane, and persons were accorded more value as human beings than as objects of eternal salvation or damnation. The means by which this transformation was wrought was a reappreciation of the spirit of classical antiquity, especially as manifested in its great literary monuments. In the eyes of its leading participants and patrons, the Renaissance was nothing less than a "rebirth" (Italian, *renascimento;* French, *renaissance*) of culture in general, and of classical culture in particular, after centuries of "darkness" and "barbarism."

The zeal for the recovery and study of classical literature was first exhibited in Italy, where a sophisticated urban culture had been developing since the end of the thirteenth century. The founder of Renaissance "humanism" (*studia humanitatis,* the study of the humane or liberal arts) was Francesco Petrarch (1304–1374), who was reared in Avignon, where he spent most of his life until 1353, thereafter living mainly in Milan, Venice, and Padua. He was an avid reader of the ancient Latin writers, especially Cicero and Seneca, on whom he modeled his elegant neo-Latin style. He was also a determined critic of Aristotelian-Averroistic philosophy, and hence of Scholastic theology, as inimical to the Christian religion. His rejection of Scholasticism, therefore, did not entail a rejection of Christian faith and piety; rather, it expressed a conscious preference for the classical over the medieval tradition. In Petrarch, one encounters, above all, the insistent claim that human beings and their problems, including their relationship to God, should be the center of all thought and philosophy, so that such studies are truly the "humanities" (*humaniora*). To this end, Petrarch took St. Augustine as his intellectual guide and hailed Plato as the greatest of all philosophers. In all these respects—his Ciceronian "eloquence"; his anthropocentrism; his opposition to Scholasticism; his praise of Platonic-Augustinian "wisdom"; and his conviction that classical learning and Christian faith can be reconciled—Petrarch appears as the fountainhead of the humanistic movement and the symbol of the "modern" element in Renaissance culture.

The revival of Latin literary culture, initiated by Petrarch, was soon matched by a "Greek revival," which long antedated the fall of Constantinople in 1453, though it was later given fresh impetus by refugees from that catastrophe. Already in 1360, Petrarch's friend and ally, Giovanni Boccaccio (1313–1375), the author of the famous *Decameron,* brought Leontius Pilatus from Calabria to Florence to lecture on Greek studies. In 1397, the distinguished Byzantine scholar Manuel Chrysoloras (1355?–1415) was appointed to a chair of Greek studies in the University of Florence. Among his outstanding students was Leonardo Bruni (1370?–1444), who, as a later chancellor of Florence, combined the love of learning with active participation in politics—a "civic humanism" that became a distinguishing feature of Renaissance culture. The Council of Ferrara-Florence, in 1438–1439, by bringing Greeks and Latins together, greatly fostered the desire to master the literary treasures of the East. The Greek leaders at this council included two eminent Platonists: John Bessarion (1403–1472), archbishop of Nicaea, who was a cardinal in the Roman church at the end of his life; and Georgios Gemistos Plethon (1355?–1450), who lectured on Plato in Florence and therewith inspired the Florentine populist leader, Cosimo de' Medici (1389–1464), to establish the so-called Platonic Academy, in 1462, under the direction of Marsilio Ficino (1433–1499).

Ficino, who became a priest in 1473, combined Christianity and Neoplatonism in a "Platonic theology" that identified human beings as the center of a great hierarchy of being, and Christ—the divine *Logos* made flesh—as the intermediary between the spiritual and material worlds. Ficino's "pious philosophy" exercised a profound influence beyond the Alps on such admirers as Jacques Lefèvre d'Étaples in France and John Colet in England. Colet, in turn, transmitted it to Erasmus. Almost as influential was another member of the Platonic Academy, the brilliant young philosopher Giovanni Pico della Mirandola (1463–1494), whose *Oration on the Dignity of Man* is one of the most famous of Renaissance writings. His zeal for Hebrew and the mystical lore of the Jewish Cabala was to inspire Johannes Reuchlin and, through him, to introduce Hebrew studies into northern humanism.

The humanists of the Italian Renaissance revived the literature of Christian antiquity as well as of classical culture. The Camaldolese convent of Santa Maria degli Angeli, in Florence, became a center for the study of the Greek church fathers under its humanist prior, Ambrogio Traversari (1386–1439). The study of patristic literature also engaged the energies of Bessarion, Bruni, and especially Lorenzo Valla (1406–1457). Valla, who was primarily a grammarian and philologist, developed such an acute critical and historical sense that he was able to expose the Donation of Constantine (see IV:4) as an eighth-century forgery, to show that the writings attributed to Dionysius the Areopagite (see III:10) were spurious, and to deny that the Apostles' Creed was actually composed by the apostles. He also laid the foundation of New Testament textual studies by his critical comparison of the Latin Vulgate with the Greek text.

The Renaissance was far from being a revival of paganism. To be sure, the humanists, of whom the great majority were laymen, directed much of their interest to fashioning a new "secular morality"—an ideal of virtue and the virtuous life, drawn from the ancient sages—that would be directly relevant to the commercial and political life of wealthy upper-class citizens of the Italian communes. Yet they perceived no fundamental contradiction between classical and Christian ethics, and they generally looked to classical sources for the corroboration of the truth of Christianity. Their condemnation of Scholastic theology—which must not be exaggerated, since many humanists were actually "reform-minded" Scholastics—rarely involved the rejection of basic Christian doctrine. And the leading Renaissance philosophers—Ficino, Pico, and Nicholas of Cusa (see V:17)—were "Augustinian" in their synthesis of Christianity and Platonism. Renaissance culture, in short, though primarily "secular" and "laic," was not intrinsically "irreligious" or "anticlerical."

Here it is not possible to identify, much less to survey, the remarkable, often monumental, achievements of the entire Renaissance movement in painting, sculpture, architecture, music, and vernacular literature. Mention must at least be made, however, of one epoch-making technological innovation, that of printing by movable type, which was introduced about 1450 by Johann Gutenberg of Mainz. This invention vastly enlarged the reading public, by making books available in quantity and at reasonable price, and it soon made possible the most widespread dissemination of humanist learning and, later, of Reformation teaching. By 1500, over two hundred presses had been established in European lands.

Though Florence was the "queen city" of the Renaissance, the movement was influential in many other Italian cities, not least in Rome, where it found a series of mighty patrons among the popes themselves, whose courts, and those of their cardinals, became showplaces of Renaissance opulence. The first of the Renaissance popes was Nicholas V (1447–1455), who founded the Vatican library and developed ambitious schemes for rebuilding Rome. The next pope, Alfonso Borgia, a Spaniard, who took the name Calixtus III (1455–1458), was no friend of humanism and was earnestly, though fruitlessly, intent on a crusade to drive the Turks from the recently conquered Constantinople. A most remarkable occupant of the papacy was Aeneas Silvius Piccolomini, who ruled as Pius II (1458–1464). In early life a supporter of the conciliar movement, and active at the Council of Basel, he had won renown as a humanist writer of decidedly unclerical tone. Reconciled to Eugenius IV, he became a cardinal, and ultimately pope, opposing all the conciliar views he had once supported; in the bull *Execrabilis* of 1460, he forbad all future appeals from the pope to a general council. His protracted efforts to stir Europe to a crusade against the Turks were again unavailing. In spite of his changing and often self-seeking attitude, he had the most worthy conception of the duties of the papal office of any pope of the last half of the fifteenth century. Pius II was followed by Paul II (1464–1471), a collector of antiquities and friend of learning, who nevertheless aroused the wrath of the humanists by suppressing the Roman Academy as pagan. The succeeding popes, from Sixtus IV (1471–1484) through Leo X (1513–1521), were patrons of arts and letters, and great builders who adorned Rome and made that city the focal center of Italian art.

Meanwhile, in the years after the Council of Constance, the ideals and ambitions of the papacy had undergone a dramatic change. Italy had gradually consolidated into five large states: Venice, Milan, Florence, Naples (or the Kingdom of the Two Sicilies, as it was called), and the Papal States (or States of the Church) in central Italy. Many smaller territories remained outside these larger groups and were objects of contest. The politics of Italy became a kaleidoscopic struggle to extend the possessions of the larger powers and to match one against the other, a struggle in which intrigue, murder, and duplicity were employed to an almost unparalleled extent.

Into this game of Italian politics the papacy fully plunged. Its overriding concern was to maintain political independence and to consolidate and enlarge the Papal States, the effective control of which had been rendered impossible by the stay in Avignon and the Great Schism. Beginning with the pontificate of Martin V, the pope chosen at Constance, the aims and methods of the papacy were like those of other Italian states, and, whatever its lingering aspirations to universal monarchy, the papacy now took its place as but one state among many competing states. Its occupants were reduced to the status of Italian princes, and the papal office became secularized as at no other period of its history, save possibly the tenth century. With Sixtus IV, a former general of the Franciscan order, political ambition and unabashed nepotism took almost complete control of the Holy See. Sixtus warred with Florence, sought to enrich and advance his relatives, and strove to extend the Papal States. He built extensively—the Sistine Chapel preserves his name—and spent so lavishly that only increased papal taxation could stave off bankruptcy.

The next pope, Innocent VIII (1484–1492), was notorious for the open manner in which he sought to advance the fortunes of his children (he had sired sixteen of them), his extravagant expenditures, and his sale of offices. He even received annual payment from the Turkish sultan Bayazid II for keeping the latter's brother and rival, Djem, a prisoner. Innocent's successor, Alexander VI (1492–1503), a Spaniard (Rodrigo Borgia) and a nephew of Calixtus III, obtained the papacy by bribing the cardinals. Though a man of unbridled immorality, he was a good manager of papal finances and possessed of considerable political acumen. His great concern was to advance his bastard children, especially his daughter, Lucrezia Borgia, by advantageous marriages, and his unscrupulous and murderous son, Cesare Borgia, by aiding him to carve a principality out of the Papal States. His reign saw the beginning of the collapse of Italian independence, when, in 1494, King Charles VIII of France (1483–1498) invaded Italy in an attempt to assert French dynastic claims to the kingdom of Naples. In 1499, Louis XII of France (1498–1515) conquered Milan, and in 1503 Ferdinand the Catholic, of Spain (1479–1516), secured Naples. Italy became the wretched battleground of French and Spanish rivalries.

In such circumstances, it was not easy to secure and extend the papacy's temporal power, but that task was accomplished by the most warlike of the popes, Julius II (1503–1513), the nephew of Sixtus IV. The feuding Orsini and Colonna families were reconciled, Cesare Borgia was driven from Italy, the cities of the Romagna were freed from their Venetian conquerors, and the various nations in Europe were grouped in leagues, with the result that the French were, for the time, expelled from Italy. In this contest, Louis XII secured a parody of a general council in Pisa (1511), which Julius answered by calling the Fifth Lateran Council in Rome. It met from 1512 to 1517, but though reforms were ordered, it accomplished nothing of importance. Julius II was undoubtedly a ruler of great talents, who led his soldiers personally and was animated by a desire to build up the Papal States rather than to enrich his relatives. As a patron of art and a builder he was among the most eminent of the popes. Besides launching the construction of the new basilica of St. Peter, initially under the direction of Donato Bramante (1444–1514), he commissioned Raphael (1483–1520) to execute the frescoes in the Julian apartments and Michelangelo (1475–1564) to paint those on the ceiling of the Sistine Chapel.

Julius II was succeeded by Giovanni de' Medici, who took the name Leo X (1513–1521). With all the artistic and literary tastes of the great Florentine family of which he was a member, he combined a love of display and extravagant expenditure. Far less warlike than Julius II, and free from the personal vices of some of his predecessors, he nevertheless made his prime goal the enlargement of the Papal States and the balancing of the various factions of Italy, domestic and foreign, for the political advantage of the papacy. In 1516, by means of the Concordat of Bologna with Francis I of France (1515–1547), he secured the abolition of the earlier Pragmatic Sanction of Bourges (see V:14), on terms which left to the king the nomination of all high French ecclesiastics and the right to tax the clergy, while the annates and other similar taxes went to the pope. The next year, a revolt began in Germany, the gravity of which Leo never really comprehended, but which was to tear half of Europe from the Roman obedience.

These were the popes who represented the Italian Renaissance, but they in no sense embodied the real spirit of a church which was to millions the source of comfort in this life and of hope for that to come. Nor did the papacy represent the authentic religious life of Italy. The Renaissance was an elitist movement, affecting only the educated and the upper classes. The masses responded to the appeals of penitential preachers and the example of those in whom they discerned the attributes of sainthood. During the fourteenth and fifteenth centuries, there lived in Latin Christendom some two hundred persons to whom the church, then or later, accorded beatification or sanctification. Holiness was thus both practiced and revered.

The outstanding preacher during the early Renaissance was the Spanish Dominican, St. Vincent Ferrer (1350?–1419), a native of Valencia. Between 1399 and 1419, he carried out his great missionary journeys through France, Spain, northern Italy, and parts of Switzerland, delivering thousands of sermons to immense numbers of listeners, proclaiming the imminence of the Last Day and calling the faithful to vigilance and to trust in the cross of Christ as their sole security. A supporter of the Avignon popes during the schism, Vincent sought to recall his fellow Dominicans in the Avignon obedience to a strict observance of St. Dominic's original ideal of apostolic service. He thus occupies an honored place in the late medieval "Observantine" movement of monastic reform.

Perhaps the greatest religious force in fifteenth-century Italy was the eloquent Franciscan preacher and reformer, St. Bernardino of Siena (1380–1444), known as "the Apostle of the Holy Name" (his symbol was the name of Jesus, surrounded by radiant beams of light). He was responsible for moral reforms in many Italian cities, and in 1438 he became the vicar general of the Franciscan Observants in Italy. He was aided in his reform of the Franciscan order by his disciple, St. John Capistrano (1386–1456), another preacher of eloquence, who undertook missions throughout Italy, Spain, and France, and, from 1451, was active in eastern Europe, in response to the Hussites and to the advance of the Turks.

Another highly influential religious leader, a contemporary of Vincent Ferrer, was St. Catherine of Siena (1347–1380), the best-known Italian mystic of the late Middle Ages. She was also a practical leader of affairs, a servant of the poor, sick, and imprisoned, a healer of family quarrels, a main agent in persuading the papacy to return from Avignon to Rome, a fearless denouncer of clerical evils, and an ambassador to whom popes and other leaders listened with respect.

Among her disciples were many Dominicans, including her former confessor, Raymond of Capua (1330?–1399). In 1380, Raymond became minister general of the Dominican order in the Roman obedience and, beginning in 1389, launched the reform of his order by establishing convents of Dominican Observants in Germany. Another of St. Catherine's disciples, and also Raymond's ardent follower, was John Dominici (1356?–1419), who established reformed convents in Italy. In 1393, he became vicar general of the Dominican Observants in Italy; in 1407, he was made archbishop of Ragusa and, in 1408, cardinal by Pope Gregory XII, whose legate he was at the Council of Constance. One of John's converts, St. Antonino of Florence (1389–1459), established the famous Dominican convent of San Marco in Florence, in 1436, making it a center of the Observance; in 1446, he became archbishop of Florence. That city, and the convent of San Marco (where the memory of St. Vincent Ferrer was still alive), produced one of the greatest preachers of the late Renaissance, Girolamo Savonarola (1452–1498).

A native of Ferrara, Savonarola was intended by his family for the medical profession, but a refusal of marriage turned his thoughts to the monastic life. In 1474, he became a Dominican at Bologna; in 1482, he was transferred to San Marco at Florence, of which he became the prior in 1491, restoring it to a strict observance and making it the center of a congregation of reformed houses. At first little successful as a preacher, he began in 1490 to attract huge crowds through his powerful sermons calling for repentance and conversion, and warning, in vague apocalyptic terms, of impending tribulations. The French invasion of 1494, which seemed to confirm the ascetic friar's status as a divinely inspired prophet, led to a popular revolution against the Medici, and Savonarola became the de facto ruler of Florence, which he sought to turn into a penitential city. A semimonastic life was adopted by many of its inhabitants. The carnival seasons of 1496 and 1497 witnessed the "burning of the vanities": cards, dice, jewelry, cosmetics, wigs, and lewd books and pictures were all consigned to the flames. During these years, Savonarola's message also underwent a notable shift, becoming more optimistic and heralding Florence as the "city of God" and "the heart and the center of Italy." No doubt this appeal to the Florentines' civic patriotism accounts in part for the momentary triumph of his reform program. But he also aroused formidable enemies. The adherents of the deposed Medici hated him, and Pope Alexander VI, whose evil character and misrule Savonarola denounced, was an implacable foe, owing not least to the friar's pro-French policy. Papal agents excommunicated him in 1497 and demanded his punishment. Friends sustained him for a while, but the fickle populace turned against him. In April 1498, he was arrested and cruelly tortured, and on May 23 he was hanged and his body burned by the city government.

Far less spectacular, though quietly effective, was the work in Genoa of a remarkable woman of noble birth, Caterina Fieschi Adorno, known as St. Catherine of Genoa (1447–1510). Following an ecstatic experience of conversion in 1474, she devoted herself to strict austerities and penitential vigils, and she enjoyed the rare lay privilege of daily communion. A mystical writer of note, her greatest service was the care of the poor and the hopelessly diseased at the Genoese hospital, of which she became the rector. Owing to her influence, a young lawyer, Ettore Vernazza, and three of his friends founded at Genoa, in 1497, the religious confraternity known as the Oratory of Divine Love, whose members sought to pursue a life of personal sanctification through common devotional exercises and works of charity and benevolence. Many comparable associations were founded in other Italian cities at this time.

The currents of spirituality and reform emanating from these religious leaders, and from such related movements as the Modern Devotion in northern Europe (see V:9), entered into the larger stream of religious revival that is known as the Catholic Reformation of the sixteenth century (see VI:11). Part of the tragedy of the late medieval church is that for so long the popes remained outside of these reform movements, exercising no effective leadership of them and, in the case of most of the Renaissance popes, exhibiting a life that was completely inimical to "reform in head and members."

Chapter 16

The New National Powers

THE HALF-CENTURY FROM 1450 to 1500 saw a remarkable growth in royal authority and national consciousness in the western kingdoms of Europe. France, which had seemed well-nigh ruined by the Hundred Years' War with England (1337–1453), emerged with the monarchy greatly strengthened, since these struggles had been immensely destructive to the feudal nobility. During the last stages of that war, a visionary peasant girl, St. Joan of Arc (1412–1431), "the Maid of Orleans," aroused in the French people a new sense of national identity. Subsequently, the shrewd and unscrupulous King Louis XI (1461–1483) broke the power of the feudal nobility and secured for the crown an authority it had not hitherto possessed. His son, Charles VIII (1483-1498), was able to lead the now centralized state into a career of foreign conquest in Italy that was to open a new epoch in European politics and give rise to rivalries that were to determine the political background of the whole Reformation age. What these kings had attempted in centralization at home, and in conquest abroad, was carried yet further by Louis XII (1498-1515) and by the brilliant and ambitious Francis I (1515-1547). France was now a strong, centralized monarchy, and its church was largely under royal control. The Concordat of Bologna in 1516 had increased the crown's control over clerical appointments, clerical taxation, and clerical courts, while giving the pope in turn desired taxes. The papacy, ever since the end of the Great Schism, was ready to negotiate such agreements in order to secure its political standing in Italy and regain its primacy over church councils, even at the price of tacitly surrendering its centralized control of the church at large. By the dawn of the Reformation, the church in France was, in many respects, a state church.

In England, the Wars of the Roses (1455-1485), between the houses of York and Lancaster, resulted in the destruction of the power of the high nobility to the advantage of the crown and bred in the English people a fear of civil war and a desire for strong government. Parliament survived, and with it the rule of law, but the power of Henry VII (1485-1509), the first Tudor king, was greater than that of any English sovereign for a century past, and it was exercised with remarkable skill, through a vast network of royal patronage, by his even abler son, Henry VIII (1509-1547). The English sovereigns had attained, even before the Reformation, a large degree of authority in ecclesiastical affairs, and the church in England, like that in France, was largely national at the close of the fifteenth century.

This nationalizing process was nowhere in such full development as in Spain, where it was taking the character of a religious awakening that was to make that land a pattern for a mode of reform—often, though not altogether correctly, called the Counter-Reformation—that was ultimately to hold the allegiance of half of Europe to a purified Roman church. The rise of Spain was the political wonder of the late fifteenth century. The Iberian peninsula had been almost wholly isolated from the main currents of medieval European life, and its history was that of a long, arduous crusade to throw off the Muslim yoke, which had been imposed in 711. The struggle had resulted, by the thirteenth century, in the restriction of the Moors to the kingdom of Granada and in the formation of four Christian kingdoms—Castile, Aragon, Portugal, and Navarre. These states were weak, and royal power was limited by the anarchic feudal nobility. A dramatic change came when the peninsula's two most prominent kingdoms were united, in 1469, by the marriage of Ferdinand, heir of Aragon (king, 1479-1516), with Isabella, heiress of Castile (queen, 1474-1504). Under their joint rule, Spain took a new place in European life. The turbulent nobles were repressed, the autonomy of the towns reduced, and an efficient royal bureaucracy established. In 1492, Granada was conquered and absorbed into Castile. In that same year, Columbus, sailing under Isabella's auspices, discovered the New World, which soon became a source of very considerable revenue to the royal treasury. The French invasion of Italy in 1494 led to Spanish intervention, which lodged Spain firmly in Naples by 1503 and soon rendered Spanish influence predominant throughout Italy. On Ferdinand's death in 1516, these great possessions passed to his grandson, Charles I, already heir to Austria and the Netherlands and soon to wear the imperial title as Charles V (1519–1556). Spain had suddenly become the first power in Europe.

Their Catholic Majesties, Ferdinand and Isabella, devoted themselves no less energetically to the control and reform of the church than to the extension of their temporal authority. To be sure, no nation with a history like that of Spain could desire doctrinal change or be less than devoted to the religious system of which the papacy was the spiritual head. But it believed that papal actions in administrative affairs should be limited by royal authority and that an educated, moral, and zealous clergy could, by the same power, be encouraged and maintained. These aims were especially dear to the devout Isabella, and they were so successfully carried out that the "Spanish awakening" became the model of the "Counter-Reformation."

In 1482, the joint sovereigns forced Pope Sixtus IV to agree to a concordat placing nomination to the higher ecclesiastical posts under royal control. The policy thus begun was soon extended, so that papal bulls also required royal approval for promulgation, church courts were supervised, and the clergy were taxed for the benefit of the state. Ferdinand and Isabella proceeded to fill the important stations in the Spanish church with clerics who were devoted to the royal interests and possessed of strenuous piety and disciplinary zeal. In this effort, they were aided by many able persons, chief among whom stood González (later Francisco) Jiménez de Cisneros (1436–1517).

Born of poor parents of the minor nobility, Jiménez studied law and theology at the University of Salamanca and then, in 1459, went to Rome for a period of service in the Curia. Upon his return to Spain in 1465, his talents as an administrator and preacher, combined with his force of character and intellect, commended him to the influential Pedro González de Mendoza, at the time bishop of Sigüenza and later the archbishop of Toledo. In about 1480, Mendoza appointed Jiménez vicar general of the diocese of Sigüenza. In 1484, however, Jiménez renounced all his honors and became a Franciscan friar of the strictest observance, now taking the name "Francisco" and even adopting a hermit's life. But his reputation was such that in 1492, following the fall of Granada, Queen Isabella appointed the ascetic friar her private confessor. Thereafter, his rise in the ecclesiastical hierarchy was rapid. In 1494, Jiménez became vicar general of the Franciscan Observants in Castile; in 1495, on Isabella's insistence and despite his protests, he succeeded Cardinal Mendoza as archbishop of Toledo and primate of Spain, therewith becoming also the queen's chief minister of state; in 1507, he was named cardinal and inquisitor general; twice he also served as regent for Ferdinand and Isabella. Supported by the queen, he turned all the power of his high offices to the reform of the secular and the monastic clergy, especially of the Franciscan Conventuals, whose houses he summarily gave over to the Observants. The whole of Spanish church life came under his exacting discipline.

Jiménez, though no great scholar, saw the need for an educated clergy. In 1498, he founded the University of Alcalá de Henares, to which he devoted a large part of his episcopal revenues. The university, which was opened in 1508, and which Jiménez staffed with outstanding scholars, quickly became the center of Christian humanism in Spain. The foremost Spanish humanist of the age was Antonio de Nebrija (1444–1522), whom Jiménez brought to Alcalá in 1512. Though opposed to general reading of the Bible by the laity, Jiménez believed that the Scriptures should be the principal study of the clergy. The noblest monument of this conviction was the Complutensian Polyglot Bible (Complutum was the ancient name of Alcalá), eventually published in six volumes, on which Jiménez directed the labor from 1502 to 1517. The Old Testament was presented in Hebrew, Greek, and Latin, with the Aramaic Targum on the Pentateuch; the New Testament, in Greek and Latin. The New Testament was in print already in 1514. To Jiménez and his collaborators, therefore, belongs the honor of printing the first complete edition of the New Testament in Greek. Papal permission for its publication, however, could not be obtained until 1520; hence, the *editio princeps* of the Greek New Testament was that of Erasmus, issued at Basel by the printer Johann Froben in 1516.

The intellectual impulse thus inaugurated by Jiménez led ultimately to a revival of the theology of Aquinas, begun by Francisco de Vitoria (1485?–1546) at the University of Salamanca and continued by Vitoria's disciples, the great Roman theologians of the early struggle with Protestantism, Domingo de Soto (1494–1560) and Melchior Cano (1509–1560).

The less attractive side of Jiménez's character is to be seen in his willingness to use force for the conversion of the conquered Moors of Granada. In 1492, they had been granted generous peace terms, by which they were allowed to retain their religion and ancient customs. These terms were observed until 1499, when the implacable Jiménez launched a systematic campaign of terror to enforce their conversion, until finally, in 1502, all Muslims over the age of fourteen who did not accept baptism were expelled from Castile. Already in 1492, immediately following the fall of Granada, Ferdinand and Isabella had decreed the expulsion of all professed Jews from their realms. This expulsion of the Jews and Moors undoubtedly helped to unify Spain, but only at the price of losing many skilled merchants and artisans, as well as cadres of intellectuals—losses that Spain could ill afford. (It is to be noted that the Jews had been expelled from England already in 1290, and from France in 1306.)

Characteristic of the Spanish awakening was the reorganization of the Inquisition. The Spanish temper viewed orthodoxy and patriotism as inseparable, and so it regarded professed Jews and Muslims, as well as relapsed Jewish and Muslim converts (who were ever suspected of "hypocrisy"), as perils to church and state alike. Accordingly, in 1478, Ferdinand and Isabella obtained a bull from Pope Sixtus IV establishing the Inquisition entirely under royal control, with inquisitors appointed by the crown. In Spain, therefore, the Inquisition was a uniquely "national" institution. Directed by a royal council known as the Suprema, it proved itself a fearful instrument, initially under the leadership of the Dominican inquisitor general, Tomás de Torquemada (1420–1498). The Spanish Inquisition especially concerned itself with rooting out those Jewish and Muslim converts (the Marranos and Moriscos, respectively) who had supposedly lapsed from the faith and with maintaining "purity of blood" (*limpieza de sangre*) in all offices of state and church. It was also to deal harshly with Spanish Protestants and all those suspected of "Lutheranism."

Spain therefore had, at the close of the fifteenth century, the most independent national church of any European state: one in which a moral and intellectual renewal—not destined to be permanent—was in more vigorous progress than elsewhere, and yet which was intensely medieval in doctrine and practice, and fiercely intolerant of heresy and dissent.

In Germany, the situation was very different. There was no movement toward national centralization, and the empire lacked any genuine growth of centralized government. The imperial crown, in theory elective, was worn by members of the Austrian house of Hapsburg from 1438 to 1740, but the emperors had power as possessors of their hereditary lands rather than as holders of imperial authority. Under Frederick III (1440–1493), wars between the princes and cities, and the disorder of the lower nobility, who lived too often by what was actually highway robbery, kept the land in a turmoil that the emperor was powerless to suppress. Matters were somewhat better under the popular Maximilian I (1493–1519). An attempt was made to give stronger central authority to the empire by frequent meetings of the old feudal Reichstag, the establishment of an imperial supreme court (1495) and of an imperial governing council (1500), and the division of the empire into districts for the better preservation of public peace (1512). Efforts also were made to form an imperial army and to collect imperial taxes. However, these reforms had little vitality or lasting effect. The decisions of the court could not be enforced nor could the taxes be collected. The Reichstag was, indeed, to play a great role in the Reformation years, but it was a clumsy parliament, meeting in three houses, one of the imperial electors, the second of lay and spiritual princes, and the third of delegates from the free imperial cities. The lower nobles and the common people had no share in it. One notable feature after 1461 was the increase in number and frequency of formal complaints (*gravamina*) about the "arbitrary" exercise of papal jurisdiction and fiscalism in the empire.

The imperial cities, which numbered about eighty-five in the early six-teenth century, acknowledged no superior power other than the feeble rule of the emperor. They were industrious and prosperous, and some were leading centers of humanistic activity, but by the late fifteenth century they were ex-periencing a political and economic decline. Their commercial spirit, and above all their traditional self-understanding as sovereign "sacred republics," led them to resist the exactions of clergy and princes alike. The religious message of the Protestant reformers, with their radical doctrine of the spiritual equality of laity and clergy, was to have special appeal in these cities, so jealous of their civic rights and freedoms and so intent upon recovering their old ascendancy.

In no country of Europe was the peasantry, and indeed the "common man," in a state of greater unrest, especially in southwestern Germany, where insurrections occurred in 1476 and 1493, followed by a wave of rebellions be-tween 1513 and 1517. Since the late fourteenth century, in the aftermath of the population catastrophe caused by the Black Death and the great epidemics that followed in its wake, the peasants had been subjected to increasing limitations on their freedom of movement and right of free marriage. In the process, they lost their former status as "tenants" and became "subjects" or "serfs" of their lay and ecclesiastical lords, who were bending every effort to protect their own economic and political interests by binding the peasantry to them in strict personal dependence. Such "lordship" (*Herrschaft*) brought with it higher taxes, galling restrictions on the use of communal resources (woodlands, streams, common lands), and a loss of traditional village autonomy. By the early six-teenth century, peasants throughout south and central Germany were pro-foundly disaffected, as were artisans and lesser craftsmen in many of the towns and cities, who likewise found themselves increasingly subject to oligarchic town councils and restrictive guild policies.

Yet if German national life as a whole was thus disordered and rent by disaffections, the larger territories of Germany were growing stronger and de-veloping a kind of semi-independent local national life in themselves. This was notably true of Austria, electoral and ducal Saxony, Bavaria, Brandenburg, and Hesse. Their rulers were rapidly developing centralized administrations, and they exercised a great deal of authority in church affairs, controlling the nomination of bishops and abbots, taxing the clergy, and limiting ecclesiastical jurisdiction. Yet notwithstanding the existence of a territorial or "proprietary" church in these principalities, the temporal power of the Roman church re-mained more formidable in Germany than elsewhere in Europe, since upward of one-fifth of the country was under the control of the powerful prince-bishops, and the monastic orders were also great landholders. Peasants and burghers alike found the exactions of these ecclesiastical lords especially onerous.

The years preceding the Reformation witnessed two marriages by the Hapsburg rulers of Austria that were of the utmost importance for the political background of the Reformation era. In 1477, the death of Charles the Bold,

the ambitious duke of Burgundy, left the inheritance of his Burgundian territories and the Netherlands to his daughter, Mary. Her marriage that year with
Maximilian I, to the dissatisfaction of Louis XI of France, who seized upper
Burgundy, sowed the seeds of quarrels between the kings of France and the
Hapsburg line which were largely to determine the politics of Europe until
1756. Philip, the son of Maximilian and Mary, in turn married Juana, heiress
of Ferdinand and Isabella of Spain. So it came about that Philip's and Juana's
son, Charles, became possessor of Austria, the Netherlands, and the far-flung
Spanish territories in Europe and the New World—a larger sovereignty than
had been held by a single ruler since Charlemagne—to which the imperial title
was added in 1519. Charles V became heir also to the rivalry between the
Hapsburg line and the kings of France. That rivalry and the struggle for religious reform were to interplay throughout the Reformation age, constantly
modifying each other.

Chapter 17

Humanism North of the Alps; Piety on the Eve of the Reformation

R ENAISSANCE HUMANISM came late to the countries north of the Alps, where
medieval social and cultural traditions were far more firmly entrenched
than in Italy. The "new learning" first established itself in northern Europe in
the last half of the fifteenth century, and it did not become a powerful influence
until the closing decade of the century. Its conquests were earlier in Germany
than in France, England, or Spain.

Northern scholars, to be sure, had already made some contacts with Italian
humanists in the first half of the century, most notably in the case of the
German philosopher and theologian, Nicholas of Cusa (1401-1464). Originally
a convinced conciliarist, Cusa became an ardent supporter of the papacy at the
Council of Ferrara-Florence in 1438-1439; was created a cardinal in 1448; became bishop of Brixen in 1450; and, in 1451-1452, served as papal legate in
Germany, in which capacity he sought to reform clerical and monastic life. As
a young man, he had studied canon law, mathematics, and astronomy for six

years at Padua. Here he came under humanist influence, learning Greek and classical Latin and developing a lasting admiration for the critical spirit of Lorenzo Valla. Yet he can hardly be considered a humanist, though in his writings he expressed a way of thinking which transcended that of Scholasticism. His works were first printed at Strassburg in 1490 and again in 1505 at Milan; the most important edition of them was prepared by the leading French humanist Jacques Lefèvre d'Étaples (in three volumes; Paris, 1514). Cusa stood in the tradition of Neoplatonic mysticism and developed a highly original cosmology and philosophical theology, the full importance of which was made plain only in modern times, in connection with the views of Giordano Bruno, Leibniz, and the German Idealists.

Cusa's central idea was that of the synthesis or identity of opposites (*coincidentia oppositorum*), which he expounded in his first philosophical treatise, *De docta ignorantia* (On Learned Ignorance, 1440). He saw God as the infinite unity of all finite distinctions and oppositions in the universe: because God contains all things, he is their "enfolding" (*complicatio*); because all things come forth from God, he is their "unfolding" (*explicatio*). This unity cannot be known by discursive reason (*ratio*), but only by a faculty of intuition or intelligence (*intellectus*)—a mode of understanding that amounts to a "learned ignorance" because it realizes that the coincidence of all things in God transcends our reason. This unity also transcends the power of language, and so it can be expressed only by (mathematical) symbols and analogies. Cusa's philosophical universalism further led him to search for the unity of faith in the diversity of religions. In 1453, he wrote a treatise, in the form of a Platonic dialogue, under the title *De pace seu concordantia fidei* (On the Peace or Harmony of Faith). In it he compared Christianity with Judaism and Islam and arrived at the remarkable conclusion: there is one religion in a diversity of rites, one truth resplendent in its variety. In the light of later developments, the thought of Nicholas of Cusa can be interpreted as one of the first expressions of modern universalism and individualism. In his own time, however, his genius was not recognized, and he was not then associated with humanism.

The gradual introduction of Italian humanism into the north was due, in part, to the new art of printing, which gave northern scholars ready access to the works of the Italian humanists, including their editions of the classical texts. Italian humanists also traveled to the north in various capacities—as diplomats, lecturers, church emissaries, secretaries to princely courts and city councils, and business representatives. But the real pioneers of northern humanism were the wandering scholars who acquired a love of the classics in Italy and returned home full of ardor to propagate the new learning. Some of its earlier representatives in Germany were little fitted, however, to commend it to the serious-minded. The best known of this disreputable breed was the loose-living, vagabond poet Peter Luder (1415?–1474), who in the years after

1454 passed from university to university, battling conservative professors to secure a larger place in the curriculum for classical rhetoric and poetry. A very different "apostle" was Rudolf Agricola (1444-1485), who studied in Italy for ten years (1469-1479) and had become an honored professor at the University of Heidelberg by the end of his life. Agricola was the most influential member of the older generation of German humanists, and he did much to further the teaching of Latin in the secondary schools of Germany and the Netherlands. A disciple of his, Alexander Hegius (1433-1498), directed the school of the Brothers of the Common Life at Deventer from 1483 to 1498 and made it the leading center of secondary education in the north, of which Erasmus was to be the most famous pupil.

Humanism also found footing in the German universities, as is shown by the reception accorded Agricola at Heidelberg. Another of his disciples, Conrad Celtis (1459-1508), the best lyric poet among the German humanists, was for a time professor of rhetoric at Ingolstadt; in 1497, at the invitation of Emperor Maximilian I, he went to the University of Vienna and there founded the College of Poets and Mathematicians. This initial humanist infiltration of the universities left the structure of Scholastic learning largely untouched, since the newcomers generally confined their teaching to instruction in the classical languages. By the first decade of the sixteenth century, however, humanism was pressing more aggressively into the universities of Basel, Tübingen, Ingolstadt, Heidelberg, and Erfurt. The advocates of the new learning were now beginning to infringe on the precincts of the theologians and to challenge the methods and aims of traditional theological study. Humanism also found many patrons in the wealthy commercial cities, notably Nürnberg, Strassburg, and Augsburg. So numerous were its sympathizers by the close of the fifteenth century that learned circles were being formed, like the Rhenish Literary Association organized by Celtis at Mainz in 1491, the members of which corresponded, circulated each other's works, and afforded mutual assistance. By 1500, humanism was becoming a vital factor in German intellectual life.

Northern humanism, for all its indebtedness to Italian humanism, was no mere imitation of the Italian model. Its foremost representatives distinguished themselves by their special fusion of classical learning and biblical (New Testament) piety, a combination that has gone under the name of "Christian humanism." This is not to say that the Italian humanists were pagan or anti-Christian or sub-Christian; most of them were loyal adherents of the church. Yet in their literary and scholarly writings—their works on grammar, rhetoric, history, and poetry, all based on intensive study of the Greek and Latin classics —they tended to avoid the explicit discussion of religious or theological topics. In this sense, the tone of their writing was predominantly "secular." The leading northern humanists, by contrast, expressly joined biblical scholarship to classical scholarship, intentionally returned to the sources of Christian antiquity as well as classical antiquity, and out of this union of "sacred letters" and "humane letters" fashioned a comprehensive program for the reform of church and society, including a reorientation of popular piety and of theological education. This reform program drew on medieval mysticism, Renaissance Platonism, and, in particular, on the tradition of "religious inwardness" deriving from the *Devotio moderna* (see V:9). In Germany, Christian humanism was seen at its best in its two most famous representatives, Reuchlin and Erasmus. (Erasmus, while he wished to be identified with no particular national group, was the titular leader of the German humanists.)

Johannes Reuchlin (1455–1522) was born in humble circumstances at Pforzheim. He early gained a local reputation as a Latinist and was sent as companion to the young son of the margrave of Baden to the University of Paris, in about 1472, where he began the study of Greek. In 1477, he received the master of arts degree at Basel, and he then taught Greek there. Even before his graduation, he published a Latin dictionary (1475–1476), which became very popular. He next studied law at Orléans and Poitiers, and in later life he was much employed in judicial positions; but his interests were always primarily scholarly. The service of Count Eberhard of Württemberg took him to Florence and Rome in 1482, and he visited those cities again in 1490 and 1498. At Florence, even on his first visit, his knowledge of Greek commanded admiration. There he met and was influenced by the scholars of the Platonic Academy (see V:15), and from Pico della Mirandola he acquired that interest in cabalistic doctrines that added much to his fame in Germany. Reuchlin was regarded as the ablest Greek scholar of the closing years of the fifteenth century in Germany, and his influence in promoting Greek studies was most fruitful.

Reuchlin had the humanist desire to return to the sources, and this led him, the first among non-Jewish scholars in Germany, to make a profound study of Hebrew that he might better understand the Old Testament. The fruit of twenty years of this labor was the publication in 1506 of a Hebrew grammar and lexicon, *De rudimentis Hebraicis,* which unlocked the treasures of that language to Christian students. The bitter quarrel into which the peace-loving Reuchlin was drawn by reason of his Hebrew studies, and with him all Germany, will be described in treating of the immediate antecedents of the Lutheran revolt (see VI:1). Reuchlin was no Protestant. He refused to approve the rising Reformation, which he witnessed until his death in 1522. But he rendered a service of immense importance to biblical scholarship, and his intellectual heir was to be his grandnephew, that eminent humanist scholar among the Lutheran reformers, Philip Melanchthon.

Desiderius Erasmus (1466?–1536), the illegitimate son of a priest, was born at Rotterdam or Gouda. His early schooling at Deventer, where Alexander Hegius was headmaster from 1483, awakened his love of letters and introduced him to the "modern devotion"—the inward, christocentric piety—of the Brothers of the Common Life, who also maintained a school at Hertogenbosch, which Erasmus next attended. In 1487, extreme poverty led him to enter the monastery of the Augustinian canons at Steyn, where he remained for six years, during which time he had occasion to study the classical authors and the Italian humanists. Yet he had no taste for the monastic life, nor for that of the priesthood, to which he was ordained in 1492. In 1493, he was able to leave the cloister in order to become secretary to the bishop of Cambrai. By 1495, he was studying theology in Paris, at the Collège de Montaigu (where John Calvin and Ignatius Loyola were later to enroll). His four years in Paris left him with an abiding distaste for Scholastic theology, but he also came into contact there with such French humanists as Robert Gaguin (1433–1501), a law professor and enthusiastic Ciceronian.

In 1499, a turning point in his life, Erasmus visited England and became acquainted with the realm's leading humanists, including John Colet and Thomas More, both of whom were to be his close friends. Colet, who at the time was lecturing at Oxford on Paul's epistle to the Romans, now turned Erasmus's interests to a serious study of the Bible and the church fathers. Such study required mastery of Greek (which Colet himself did not possess), and so in 1500, Erasmus returned to Paris, and during the next six years, in Paris and the Low Countries, he perfected his knowledge of Greek; laid the basis of his literary, historical, and philological scholarship; wrote a number of important works; and began a wide correspondence with the leading minds of his age. He returned to England for a brief visit early in 1506, and then, in the summer of that year, left England for a three-year sojourn in Italy. In September 1506, he took his doctor's degree in theology at the University of Turin. He passed the remainder of his stay—visiting Bologna, Florence, Venice, Padua, Siena, and Rome—pursuing his Greek and humanistic studies, basking the while in the cordial welcome he everywhere received from the Italian scholars.

In 1509, Erasmus returned to England for his third and longest visit, residing with Thomas More and, from 1511 to 1514, lecturing on Greek at Cambridge University. The years from 1514 to 1521 were spent for the most part in the Netherlands, particularly at Brussels and Louvain, with frequent trips to Basel, where the publisher Froben printed his books, including a Greek edition of the New Testament and editions of the works of the church fathers. By this time, he was universally regarded as the prince of humanistic scholars, the dominant figure in the literary world of Europe. The animosity of the theologians drove him out of Louvain in 1521, and for the next eight years he made his home in Basel. When the Reformation was introduced into that city, in 1529, he moved to Freiburg. He died during a visit to Basel in 1536.

Erasmus was, above all, a man of letters, who addressed the issues of his time with consummate wit and an unrivaled command of Latin style, put forth unsparing criticism of the clergy and civil rulers, and withal was moved by a deep sincerity of purpose. Convinced that the church of his day was over-laid with superstition, corruption, and error, that theology had been subverted by a barren, contentious dialectic, and that the monastic life was too often ignorant and unworthy, he had yet no wish to break with the church that he so freely criticized. He was too averse to strife to have sympathy with the Lutheran revolution, the "tumults" of which repelled him, and too undogmatic in his religion to approve Luther's radical assault on traditional doctrine. He was also too clear-sighted not to see, and too honest not to expose, the prevalent evils and abuses of the contemporary church and the Renaissance papacy. Hence, neither side in the great struggle that broke out in the latter part of his life fully understood him, and his memory was long condemned by polemical writers, both Protestant and Catholic.

Erasmus had his own constructive program of reform. He envisioned the renovation of church and society through education and eloquence—specifi-cally, through a return to the pristine sources of Christian truth, to the Bible and the fathers, as well as to the ethical wisdom of the ancient sages, to be instilled through the art of persuasion by pleasing discourse. Ignorance, super-stition, and immorality were also to be exposed and rooted out through irony and satire. He labored to these ends from 1500 until his death. His *Enchiridion Militis Christiani* (Handbook [Dagger] of the Christian Soldier), published in 1503, was a simple, earnest presentation of an unceremonial and undogmatic Christianity, centered on the imitation of Christ and the movement away from visible, sensible things to invisible and intelligible realities. His *Moriae En-comium* (Praise of Folly—1509), which set Europe laughing, was a biting satire on the evils of the age in church and state. His *Colloquia Familiaria* (Familiar Colloquies—1519) were witty dialogues in which the veneration of relics, pilgrimages, and similar external observances were the butts of his brilliant pen. His editorial work was of the highest importance. In 1516 came the first edition of his Greek New Testament, accompanied by a new Latin translation and critical notes. This was the pioneer publication of the Greek text, for that of Jiménez was still inaccessible (see V:16). This work was fol-lowed by a series of the Greek and Latin fathers—Jerome, Origen, Basil, Cyril, Chrysostom, Irenaeus, Ambrose, and Augustine, not all wholly from his pen, but all from his impulse, which placed scholarly knowledge of early Christianity on a new plane and thus profoundly aided the Reformation.

The *Enchiridion* is the fullest presentation of Erasmus's positive theology, which he called the "philosophy of Christ" (*philosophia Christi*). Christianity is depicted as a universal, essentially ethical religion, anticipated by the philos-ophers of antiquity and attaining its consummate expression in Christ's Sermon on the Mount. This religion is interior and spiritual, the "cult of the invisible" in the midst of worldly life, and it is animated by love for Christ and the resolve to follow in his footsteps. Erasmian thought was thus at root "optimistic," for knowledge of the truth entails the ability to do the truth, though divine grace must also assist to this end. The evident differences between Erasmus and Luther on the cardinal issues of "sin and grace" and the freedom of the human will were to lead to their famous literary exchange of 1524–1525 (see VI:2) and to a decisive parting of the ways between Erasmian humanism and Lutheran solafideism. Yet Luther and the other Protestant reformers held much in common with, and remained indebted to, Erasmus and the Christian humanists, above all in their educational preference for the Bible and the church fathers over and against the Scholastic doctors, and in their cultivation of the classical and biblical languages. The influence of Erasmus is also to be seen in the sacramental theology of such reformers as Zwingli and Oecolampadius, who came to the Reformation by way of humanism and who maintained the basic Erasmian principle that the life of the spirit is not nourished by external, corporeal things, including the physical body of Christ (see VI:3). Moreover, many of the Catholic reformers of the later sixteenth century were heirs of the Erasmian reform program, however impolitic it was to admit this. Thus, even though he had become a "heretic" to both sides by the time of his death, Erasmus's tireless labors had borne much fruit.

Though humanism exerted a greater influence in Germany at the beginning of the sixteenth century than in any other land beyond the Alps, the same impulses were stirring elsewhere. The efforts of Francisco Jiménez in Spain have already been noted (see V:16). One must add, however, that his humanistic scholarship was mainly philological in character and was used in the service of a militant Catholic orthodoxy, so much so that the Spanish church and culture proved most inhospitable to Erasmian ideas. Thus, in Spain the new learning buttressed the old theology.

In England, serious study of Greek and of the classics was introduced at Oxford in the 1490s by William Grocyn (1446?–1519) and Thomas Linacre (1460?–1524), both of whom had studied in Italy. The leader of the Christian humanists in England became John Colet (1467?–1519), who had heard the lectures of Grocyn and Linacre at Oxford. Under their influence, he went to Italy in 1493 and there developed a keen interest in Neoplatonic mysticism, as conveyed by the Florentine Platonists. Upon his return to England in 1496, he began lecturing at Oxford on the Pauline epistles, and in this connection he stirred Erasmus to biblical studies. Colet was not a distinguished classicist. His prime contribution was to introduce a literary and historical method of interpreting the Pauline texts, relating them to their historical setting and examining their rhetorical structure in order to lay bare their spiritual content. In his judgment, the Scholastic theologians had contaminated the "doctrine of Christ" with their "profane philosophy." Colet also endeavored to improve the education and morals of the clergy, and to this end he founded St. Paul's School in London in 1508.

Much more of a humanist and man of letters than Colet was his friend Thomas More (1478-1535), who was accomplished in Greek as well as classical Latin. It was while residing at More's home in London in 1509 that Erasmus wrote his *Moriae Encomium* (Praise of Folly, which can also be translated "Praise of More"). More's *Utopia* (1516) was the most famous of English humanist publications. Royal service and religious controversy were to consume his energies in later life, which ended in martyrdom (see VI:9).

The chief representative of Christian humanism in France was Jacques Lefèvre d'Étaples (Faber Stapulensis, 1460?-1536), most of whose active years were spent in or near Paris. A modest, kindly man, his religious thought was nourished not only by the Neoplatonism of Nicholas of Cusa (whose works he published) and Marsilio Ficino (with whom he became acquainted during one of his three trips to Italy), but also by his enthusiasm for the mystical theology of Dionysius the Areopagite, Richard of St. Victor, and Ramón Lull. He entered the mainstream of Christian humanism with his determination to recover the original sense of the biblical books by means of the grammatical method, in opposition to the allegorical exegesis of the medieval Schoolmen and their dialectical disputes over isolated texts. In 1509, he published the *Psalterium quincuplex,* a critical exposition of the Psalms based on a philological comparison of five different Latin versions. In 1512, there appeared his translation of the Pauline epistles, accompanied by a commentary in which he denied the justifying merits of good works and held salvation to be a free gift of God. Later, he wrote commentaries on the four Gospels (1522) and on the Catholic Epistles (1524). At the same time (1523-1525), he published French translations of the Vulgate versions of the New Testament and of the Psalter.

Though Lefèvre was attracted to the early writings of the Protestant reformers and was often suspected of being a "Lutheran," he had no intention of breaking with the Roman church. He hoped for a religious reform, chiefly on the basis of the Bible, within the framework of the established church. He gathered round himself a body of devoted pupils, destined to very diverse participation in the Reformation struggle: Guillaume Briçonnet, to be bishop of Meaux; Guillaume Budé, eminent in Greek and to be instrumental in founding the Collège de France; Louis de Berquin, to die a Protestant martyr; and Guillaume Farel, to be the intrepid reformer of French-speaking Switzerland.

Partly as a result of the humanist emphasis on the sources, but even more in consequence of the invention of printing, the latter half of the fifteenth century witnessed a wide distribution of the Bible in the Vulgate and in translation. No less than ninety-two editions of the Vulgate were issued before 1500. The first complete German Bible was printed in 1466; twenty-two editions of the complete Bible had appeared by 1522. The New Testament was printed in French in 1477, the whole bible ten years later. A Spanish Bible was printed in 1478, but it was proscribed and burned; another translation appeared in 1492. Two independent Italian versions were printed in 1471. In the Netherlands, the

Old Testament minus the Psalter was printed in 1477, to be followed in 1480 by the Psalms. Two Czech Bibles appeared in 1488 and 1489. If England had no printed Bible before the Reformation, many manuscripts of the Wyclifite Bible were in circulation.

The Middle Ages witnessed no universal and absolute prohibition of vernacular translations of the Bible and of their use by the clergy or laity. Yet efforts were often made on the local diocesan level to restrict the reading of the Vulgate and of vernacular translations by the laity and by ill-educated priests, since such "private" use of the Scriptures was considered a prime source of heresy. Thus, the central issue surrounding the increased reading of the Bible in the half-century before the Reformation was the problem of biblical interpretation, not of biblical authority as such. The medieval church never denied the normative authority of Scripture for Christian faith and life, but this authority attached to Scripture as interpreted by the fathers, the church councils, the recognized doctors, and the official pronouncements of the popes. The authority of Scripture, in short, was inseparably bound up with the church's teaching tradition and with the church's own authority as the guarantor of the "proper" interpretation and use of the Bible. Increased familiarity with the Bible inescapably raised the question of whether the church's teaching tradition was at all points faithful to the Scriptures themselves.

The Christian humanists, through their programmatic call for a literal-historical interpretation of the Bible and a return to the "old fathers," effectively undermined the interpretive authority of the Scholastic doctors and of the "allegorizing" medieval exegetes. It remained for Luther and the Protestant reformers to conclude that the church's entire teaching tradition was liable to error, and in practice had often erred, when judged by the teaching of the Scriptures alone. The radicality of the Reformation "Scripture alone" (*sola scriptura*) was thus that it broke apart the assumed coherence and congruence of Scripture and tradition, of the Bible and the age-old interpretive authority of the church. The Bible, possessed of sufficient clarity in its central message of salvation by grace through faith alone, was declared to be its own interpreter.

The growing availability of printed Bibles—above all of vernacular Bibles and of partial editions of the Psalms, Gospels, and Epistles—eventually made it possible for the reformers' radical position to commend itself to large numbers of clergy and laity, who could now read the Bible for themselves and apply its "test" to the church's teaching and practice. Even more influential was the popular preaching of the reformers, who expounded the Scriptures verse by verse for their auditors, without recourse to the traditional "glosses," and thereby equipped the people to compare the contemporary church with the New Testament church and to determine what was "true Christianity" on the basis of the "pure Word" alone. By the early 1520s, the "rediscovered" Bible had become a revolutionary force.

It would be wrong to conclude, however, that popular piety on the eve of the Reformation was already in a state of rebellion against the Roman church. To the contrary, that piety, above all in Germany, was distinguished by its "churchliness"—i.e., its loyalty to the doctrine, institutions, and sacraments of the medieval church. Popular devotion, moreover, was undergoing a remarkable intensification: the late Middle Ages were a time of religious "awakening." Much of this piety, to be sure, was marked by a frenetic preoccupation with the external forms of religion, motivated in large measure by the misery of existence, by fear of death and the devil, and by an anxious longing for the certainty of salvation.

Much in the popular life of Germany at the close of the fifteenth century tended to increase the sense of apprehension. The witchcraft delusion, though by no means new, was rapidly spreading. A bull of Pope Innocent VIII in 1484 declared Germany full of witches, and the German inquisitors, Jakob Sprenger and Heinrich Krämer, published their painfully celebrated *Malleus maleficarum* (The Hammer of Evildoers) in 1489. It was a superstition that added terror to daily life, and it was to be shared by the reformers no less than by their Roman opponents. The years from 1490 to 1503 were a period of famine in Germany. The Turkish peril was becoming threatening. The general social unrest has already been noted (see V:16). All these elements contributed to the development of a sense of the reality and nearness of the Last Day and of the urgent need to make one's peace with God and to secure one's blessedness for the life to come. This state of affairs helps to explain the heightened importance attached to the sale of indulgences, the veneration of the saints, the endowment of Masses for the dead, and the making of pilgrimages. A few of the more wealthy pilgrims journeyed to the Holy Land, more went to Rome, though the most popular foreign pilgrimage shrine was that of St. James at Compostela (Santiago de Compostela) in Spain. German shrines were also thronged, and vast collections of relics were made, notably by the Saxon elector, Frederick the Wise (1486–1525), later Luther's protector, who exhibited them in the castle church at Wittenberg.

Side by side with this external and work-trusting religious spirit, Germany displayed a very different current of piety, one marked by a quiet inwardness and tender simplicity that saw the essence of religion in the relation of the individual soul to God. This current drew on the tradition of German (Dominican) mysticism and of the *Devotio moderna,* which by the middle of the fifteenth century had attained extremely wide influence. Here, too, one finds a deep yearning for assurance of salvation in the face of death and divine judgment—save that beatitude was now to be attained not by the multiplication of pious works, or by an exaggerated religious formalism, but by cultivating the interior virtues of humility, charity, and resignation to the ineluctable will of God.

During this period, there was also an increasing sense of lay responsibility for the welfare of the church. Territorial rulers and city councils sought to improve the quality of the clergy and to reform the monasteries. In the self-governing cities of Germany and the Swiss Confederation, moreover, attempts had long been made to secure control over local church institutions, to regulate the secular and monastic clergy, and in various other ways to vindicate for the laity, as such, a central place in the religious life of the community.

It was thus no dead age to which Luther was to speak, but one stirred by an escalation of religious devotion and an immense yearning for religious consolation. The peoples of Europe were, on the whole, still loyal to the Roman church, but they were also looking to that church for satisfaction of their deepest longings and for effective leadership in a time of seething unrest, apocalyptic fears, and multitudinous unsolved problems.

Period VI

THE REFORMATION

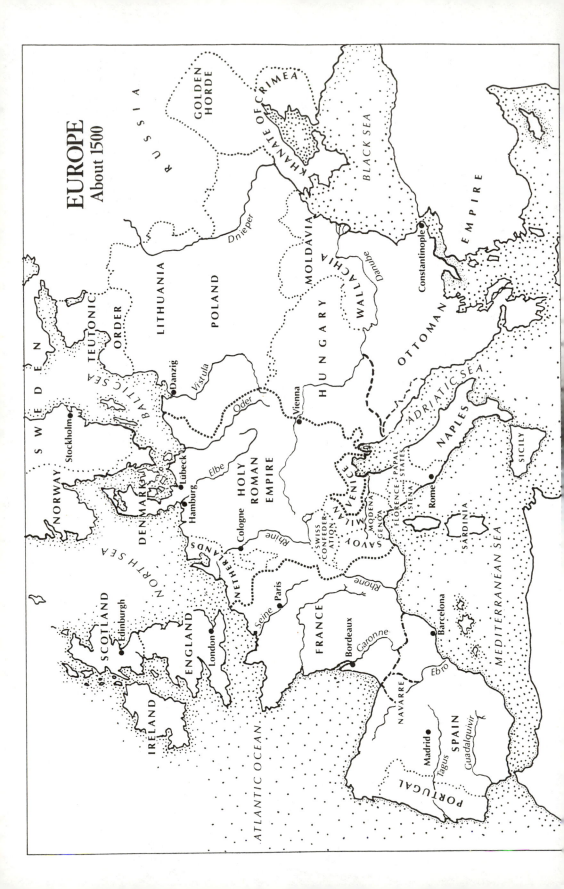

EUROPE
About 1500

RUSSIA

GOLDEN HORDE

KHANATE OF CRIMEA

BLACK SEA

EMPIRE

Dnieper

MOLDAVIA

WALLACHIA

Danube

Constantinople

TEUTONIC ORDER

LITHUANIA

POLAND

SWEDEN

BALTIC SEA

Danzig

Vistula

Oder

HUNGARY

OTTOMAN

Vienna

ADRIATIC SEA

NORWAY

Stockholm

DENMARK

Lübeck

Hamburg

Elbe

HOLY ROMAN EMPIRE

Cologne

Rhine

SWISS CONFEDERATION

MILAN

VENICE

SAVOY

MODENA

GENOA

FLORENCE

PAPAL STATES

SIENA

Rome

NAPLES

SICILY

SARDINIA

MEDITERRANEAN SEA

NORTH SEA

NETHERLANDS

Rhône

SCOTLAND

Edinburgh

ENGLAND

London

Paris

Seine

FRANCE

Bordeaux

Garonne

Barcelona

Ebro

IRELAND

ATLANTIC OCEAN

NAVARRE

Madrid

SPAIN

Tagus

Guadalquivir

PORTUGAL

Chapter 1

Luther's Development and the Beginnings of the Reformation

G ERMANY at the beginning of the sixteenth century was in many respects the most "churchly" of the European lands. The heretical outbreaks of the later Middle Ages had been successfully contained. Though the ecclesiastical hierarchy and the monastic orders continued to be objects of widespread criticism, virulent anticlericalism was little in evidence. Papal authority remained greater in Germany than in any other leading European country, apart from Italy. Lay piety and devotion, while often giving way to the wildest excesses, still ran in traditional channels. Pilgrimages and Masses for the dead were more popular than ever. Veneration of the saints, especially of the Virgin Mary and of her mother, St. Anne, had increased dramatically. Collections of relics abounded and the sale of indulgences multiplied. Many new churches, chapels, and chantries were built. Special preacherships, to ensure regular preaching, were endowed by pious laypeople in the larger towns and cities. Participation in the religious confraternities reached new heights. Devotional literature of orthodox provenance was avidly read. It cannot be said, therefore, that Germany (or any other European country, for that matter) was, in 1500, in a state of incipient revolution against the venerable rule and governance of the Roman church.

Beneath the surface, however, there were strong currents of discontent and disaffection. The bane of the church was its fiscalism. The Renaissance papacy invariably lived beyond its means and was often on the edge of bankruptcy, not least because it required immense sums to maintain its political standing in Italy. To meet expenses, the papal Curia devised new and more oppressive taxes, fees, and fines which bore heavily on the higher clergy who, in turn, passed them on to the lower clergy and, ultimately, to the laity. Rome became a byword, especially in Germany, for venality and avarice. Fiscalism brought with it, and compounded, such moral failings as clerical simony, nepotism, pluralism, absenteeism, and concubinage. The parish clergy, in particular, were in a parlous state: minimally educated, often wretchedly poor, and frequently living with concubines (for which they were fined annually by their bishops), their morale, not surprisingly, was very low. Even if these abuses and short-comings were not unprecedented and were, perhaps, no more excessive than in earlier periods, the *perception* of them as intolerable by an increasingly literate and educated laity was an ominous development.

The religious "awakening" of the late Middle Ages, like that of the twelfth century, was one of rising expectations. The institutional church was not being threatened by secularism or indifference to religion, but by demands that it truly conform itself to the "pure, apostolic church" pictured in the New Testament. Thoughtful people wanted not less religion but "better," which for them usually meant "more biblical." The old cry for "reform in head and members," going back to the conciliar movement of the early fifteenth century, was given new currency and force in the early sixteenth century by the Christian humanists, led by Erasmus. The humanists envisioned a moral and spiritual renovation of Latin Christendom through the inculcation of sacred and humane letters—Holy Scripture and the liberal arts. This drive "to the sources" (*ad fontes*) of Christian and classical culture—this program of "reformation by restoration"—was common to the humanists and the Protestant reformers alike and also shaped the outlook of the educated classes in the towns and cities. The irony is that the Roman church, in the midst of a new wave of religious devotion, failed to exercise moral and spiritual leadership at the highest echelons and was largely unable, on the parish level, to nourish and guide the burgeoning lay piety.

Popular religion on the eve of the Reformation, moreover, had a paradoxical character. It appears to have been more earnest than encouraging. The new devotion manifested a deepening sense of terror before the Last Things: the thought of death, purgatorial pains, and the universal judgment on the Last Day engendered an anxious concern for personal salvation. The church taught that one's eternal destiny would be determined by how effectively one had appropriated the church's sacramental graces in order to bring forward truly meritorious works—since only a faith active in works of love could be a saving faith. Yet this typically medieval correlation of grace and merit opened sensitive consciences to the corrosive doubt: Have I actually performed God-pleasing works? Have I done enough to be assured of divine acceptance? There is also weighty evidence that the church's entire sacramental system, above all the central sacrament of penance, was experienced by the faithful as more oppressive than liberating, not least because the spiritual benefits offered by the church were so often bound up with money matters and political purposes.

It is clear that a message of religious consolation for the anxious conscience, especially one that also held out hope for relief from ecclesiastical abuses, would have powerful appeal in wide circles and would draw in its wake a host of persons who, for reasons both spiritual and material, felt aggrieved with the

Roman church. While it is true, however, that people became adherents of the Protestant Reformation out of mixed motives, as one would expect in a society where religion and politics were virtually inseparable, it is also clear that the Reformation achieved great popular success because it satisfied, or promised to satisfy, the needs of many people who earnestly desired the consolations of the Christian religion. These people were not rapacious foes of the medieval church; they were sincere seekers after salvation who looked to the church for succor and, not finding it there, turned against the traditional religion and its representatives with all the anger of disillusioned love.

An important prelude to the Reformation in German intellectual circles was a quarrel involving one of the most peace-loving and respected of the humanists, Johannes Reuchlin (see V:17). In 1509, a recent convert from Judaism named Pfefferkorn procured a decree from Emperor Maximilian ordering the Jews to turn in their books. Pfefferkorn was supported by Jakob Hochstraten (1460–1527), the Dominican inquisitor in Cologne, while Reuchlin, in response to an inquiry from the archbishop of Mainz, defended Jewish literature as with slight exception desirable, urged a fuller knowledge of Hebrew, and advocated friendly discussion with the Jews in place of confiscating their books. A storm of controversy was the result. Reuchlin was accused of heresy and put on trial by Hochstraten. The case was appealed to Rome and dragged on until 1520, when it was decided against Reuchlin.

The advocates of the new learning looked upon the whole proceeding as an ignorant and unwarranted attack on scholarship and rallied to Reuchlin's support. From this humanist circle came one of the most successful satires ever issued—the *Letters of Obscure Men*, by Crotus Rubianus (1480?–1539?) and Ulrich von Hutten (1488–1523), published between 1515 and 1517. Purporting to be written by opponents of Reuchlin and the new learning, the *Letters* aroused widespread ridicule by their barbarous Latinity, triviality, and ignorance. They undoubtedly created the impression that the party opposed to Reuchlin was hostile to learning and progress. The effect of the Reuchlin affair was to unite German humanists and to draw a line of cleavage between them and the conservatives, of whom the Dominicans were the most prominent.

It was while this contest was at its height that a protest against an ecclesiastical abuse, made, in no unusual or spectacular fashion, by a monastic professor in a recently founded and relatively inconspicuous German university, on October 31, 1517, found immediate response and launched the greatest revolution in the history of the Christian church.

Martin Luther, from whom this protest came, is one of the few individuals of whom it may be said that the history of the world was profoundly altered by his work. Not an organizer or a politician, and by no means a self-declared revolutionary, he moved people by the power of a profound religious faith, resulting in unshakable trust in God and in direct, personal relations to God, which brought a certainty of salvation that left no room for the elaborate hierarchical and sacramental structures of the Middle Ages. For centuries an object of vitriolic attacks by Roman Catholic detractors, Luther is today widely honored in Catholic circles as a genuine *homo religiosus* and as a worthy partner in theological dialogue—a notable change that has grown out of the modern ecumenical movement and dispassionate historical scholarship. But whether honored or opposed, none can deny that Martin Luther occupies a pre-eminent place in the history of the church.

Luther was born on November 10, 1483, in Eisleben, where his father worked as a copper miner. His parents were of simple, conventional piety; there is no evidence that they treated their children with undue severity or burdened them with excessive religious demands. The father, an ambitious man of peasant origins, moved his family to Mansfeld a few months after Martin's birth, and there he won civic respect and considerable prosperity in the mining industry and determined to give Martin (the second son and one of eight children) an education fitting to a career in law. After preparatory schooling in Mansfeld, Magdeburg, and Eisenach, Martin Luther entered the University of Erfurt in 1501, where he was known as an earnest, companionable, and music-loving student. Erfurt was at that time the most humanistically advanced of the German universities, and Luther came under the influence of the new movement. Though never a humanist in the full sense, Luther did come to share the movement's enthusiasm for the study of the ancient languages, especially Greek, and its criticism of Scholastic theology on the basis of the Bible and the writings of the church fathers.

The young Luther felt strongly that deep sense of sinfulness and anxiety which was the ground note of the religious revival of the age in Germany. Following his graduation as master of arts in January 1505, he entered the law school in May. He was profoundly moved by the sudden death of a classmate and by a narrow escape from lightning while returning to Erfurt from a trip home—as a result of which he made a vow to St. Anne to become a monk. Much to his father's displeasure, he broke off his legal studies and, on July 17, 1505, entered the monastery of Augustinian hermits in Erfurt, confident that the monastic life was the surest path to his soul's salvation. The "German congregation" of Augustinian friars, recently reformed by Andreas Proles (1429-1503) and now under the supervision of Johannes von Staupitz (1460?-1524), enjoyed deserved popular respect and represented medieval monasticism at its best. The Augustinian order made much of preaching and Bible study, and it included in its number the great fourteenth-century Augustine scholar Gregory of Rimini (see V:8), whom Luther came to value most highly as the sole Scholastic theologian who was free of any taint of Pelagianism. The anti-Pelagian treatises of Augustine himself were, of course, also important for Luther's theological development. And to Staupitz, in particular, Luther was much indebted, even to the point of later giving him credit for having initiated the Reformation.

In the monastic life Luther won speedy recognition. He was ordained to the priesthood in 1507. The next year saw him in Wittenberg, at the command of his superiors, lecturing on Aristotle's ethics and preparing for a future professorship in the university which had been established there, in 1502, by the Saxon elector, Frederick III "the Wise" (1486–1525). There he graduated as a bachelor of theology in 1509, but he was sent back the same year to Erfurt to study for the degree of *sententiarius,* or licensed expounder of that great medieval textbook of theology, the *Sentences* of Peter Lombard. On business of his order, he made a memorable journey to Rome in the winter of 1510–1511. Back once more in Wittenberg, which thereafter remained his home, he became doctor of theology in 1512 and successor to Staupitz as university professor of Bible. He then entered upon a series of exegetical lectures on the Psalms (1513–1515), Romans (1515–1516), Galatians (1516–1517), and Hebrews (1517–1518). In the course of his doctoral studies, and in preparing for his early lectures, Luther familiarized himself with all the exegetical, mystical, and Scholastic traditions of medieval theology, as well as with the new humanistic scholarship of Jacques Lefèvre d'Étaples, Reuchlin, and Erasmus (see V:17). It is often overlooked, in focusing on Luther's spiritual trials (*Anfechtungen*) in the monastery, that he was a premier scholar and brilliant theologian. His practical abilities were recognized by his appointment, in 1512, as director of studies in his own cloister and, in 1515, as district vicar in charge of eleven monasteries of his order. Even earlier, he had begun the practice of regular preaching, first in his own cloister (1511) and then (1514) in the Wittenberg parish church, in which activity he displayed remarkable gifts from the outset. In his order, he thus bore the repute of a friar of singular piety, learning, dedication, and zeal.

Yet in spite of all monastic strenuousness, Luther found no peace of soul. His sense of sinfulness before a holy and righteous God overwhelmed him, and it was not relieved, but only aggravated, by the practice of penance and of ascetic works. Staupitz helped him by pointing out that true penitence begins not with fear of a punishing God, but with love to God. But if Luther could say that Staupitz first opened his eyes to the Gospel, the clarifying of his vision was a slow and gradual process. Until 1509, Luther devoted himself to the later Scholastics, the theological nominalists—Ockham, d'Ailly, and Biel. To them he owed his dialectical skills, his distrust of a speculative reason that transcends the limits of revelation, and perhaps also his emphasis on the will of God as the sole ground of salvation (for while the nominalists made room for meritorious works both before and after the sinner's justification, they ultimately traced the saving worth of such works to God's free acceptance of them). By 1510, however, Luther's study of Augustine and of the late medieval Augustinians was opening new vistas to him, leading him to a rapidly growing hostility toward the dominance of Aristotle in theology and toward nominalist theology as a "new Pelagianism."

By the time that Luther lectured on Romans, he had become convinced that salvation is a new relationship to God, based not on any human work of merit but on absolute trust in the divine promise of forgiveness for Christ's sake. The law of God, with its stern command to live in holiness before a holy God, has not been given as a means of salvation but exists to convict sinners of their sin, to humble the proud and crush the self-righteous. The Gospel, with its radical message that God "justifies the ungodly" through faith apart from works,[1] raises up self-confessed sinners and reconciles them to God. The redeemed person, therefore, while not ceasing to be a sinner, is yet freely and fully forgiven, and from this new and joyous relationship to God in Christ now flows the new life of willing conformity to God's will. Faith, understood as the firm trust of the heart (*fiducia cordis*) in God's mercy for Christ's sake, is thus active in works of love—not out of compulsion because salvation *depends* on such works, but out of gratitude because salvation has already been *assured*. Love is the spontaneous fruit of faith and is directed toward the welfare of one's neighbor; it is not a condition of one's acceptance before God. Hence faith, not love (as in Scholastic theology), is the bond that unites the soul to God.

Here was a reemphasis on a most important side of the Pauline teaching, in that Luther, like Paul, made salvation in essence a right personal relationship to God (namely, to God himself as "Uncreated Grace," rather than to the "created graces" of the church's sacraments). The ground and pledge of this right relationship is the unmerited mercy of God displayed in the sufferings of Christ on humanity's behalf. Christ has borne our sins; we, in turn, have Christ's own righteousness imputed to us and, in faith, enter into a lively union with him. Some of the German mystics, especially Tauler, with his Christ-centered religion, helped Luther to the conclusion that this transforming trust is not, as he had supposed, a work in which one has a part, but is wholly the gift of God to humble, self-accusing sinners.

Luther's development was such that in early September 1517, he prepared a *Disputation against Scholastic Theology*—ninety-seven theses presenting a truly radical attack on virtually the whole of medieval Scholasticism, including the *via antiqua* (Thomists and Scotists) as well as the *via moderna* (Ockhamists). He now declared that the nominalist emphasis on the *facere quod in se est*—the teaching that God would infallibly infuse grace into those persons who, in a state of nature, did what good was in their power—was absurd and Pelagian, indeed worse than Pelagian (see V:8). He also condemned the earlier Scholastics for teaching that justified sinners cooperate in their salvation by performing meritorious works within a state of grace (see V:7). For Luther, any talk of "merit" in the matter of justification was blasphemous and heretical

---

[1] Rom. 1:17, 4:5.

(Pelagian). He thus overthrew the basis of all that he considered work-righteousness in the church's traditional teaching.

Luther did not arrive at these views in one sudden flash of insight or illumination. His so-called "evangelical breakthrough," which scholars have often attempted to date with misplaced precision, extended over a period of years, from his first Psalms lectures of 1513–1515 to his second course of Psalms lectures beginning in late 1518. During this period, his position took on increasing clarity and certainty, not least owing to his involvement in the controversy over indulgences and his ensuing trial before church authorities. Whereas in 1515–1516 Luther could still speak of the faith that justifies as one shaped by humility, by early 1519 he was consistently teaching that the sinner is justified (accepted, acquitted, forgiven) before God by faith *alone*—that is, by absolute dependence on and trust in the Gospel of free forgiveness, the "Word of God."

By the beginning of 1517, Luther did not stand alone. In the University of Wittenberg, his opposition to Aristotelianism and Scholasticism, in favor of lectures on the Bible and the church fathers, found much sympathy. His colleagues, Andreas Bodenstein of Karlstadt (1480–1541), who, unlike Luther, had been trained in the *via antiqua,* and Nikolaus von Amsdorf (1483–1565), now became his hearty supporters. The university soon became the spearhead of the Lutheran Reformation.

In late 1517, Luther felt compelled to speak up against a crying abuse. Pope Leo X (1513–1521) had earlier issued a dispensation permitting Albrecht of Brandenburg (1490–1545) to hold at the same time the archbishopric of Mainz, the archbishopric of Magdeburg, and the administration of the bishopric of Halberstadt. This dispensation from church regulations against "pluralism" (multiple offices) cost Albrecht a great sum, which he borrowed from the Augsburg banking house of Fugger. To repay this loan, Albrecht was also permitted to share half the proceeds in his district from the sale of indulgences that the papacy had been issuing, since 1506, for building that new basilica of St. Peter which is still one of the ornaments of Rome. A commissioner for this collection was Johann Tetzel (1470–1519), a Dominican monk of eloquence, who, intent on the largest possible returns, painted the benefits of indulgences in the crassest terms. Luther himself had no knowledge of the financial transactions between Albrecht and the pope. His objections to the proceedings were pastoral and theological: indulgences create a false sense of security and are thus destructive of true Christianity, which proclaims the cross of Christ and of the Christian, not release from deserved punishment. As Tetzel approached electoral Saxony—he was not allowed to enter, though many members of the Wittenberg congregation crossed the border to buy letters of indulgence—Luther preached against the abuse of indulgences and prepared his memorable "Ninety-five Theses," copies of which he sent on

October 31, 1517, to Archbishop Albrecht of Mainz and Bishop Jerome of Brandenburg, in whose jurisdiction Wittenberg lay. Whether Luther on that day also posted his theses on the door of the castle church in Wittenberg, which served as the university bulletin board, is a matter of controversy among historians, though it seems most likely that he did.

Viewed in themselves, it may well be wondered why the Ninety-five Theses proved the spark that kindled the explosion. They were written in Latin and intended for academic debate. They are far less inflammatory in tone and content than Luther's ninety-seven theses of September 1517, albeit Luther was now attacking a lucrative source of church revenue and was also touching upon sensitive questions of papal authority. His theses, however, do not deny the right of the pope to grant indulgences. They question the extension of indulgences to purgatory, and they make evident the abuses licensed by current teaching—abuses which they imply the pope will repudiate when informed.

Yet while the theses are far from expressing the full round of Luther's thought, they display certain principles which would have revolutionary import. Repentance is not a single act of penance, but a constant change of heart and mind extending over one's lifetime. The Christian seeks rather than avoids divine discipline. The true treasure of the church is not the superabundant merits of Christ and the saints, subject to papal control, but "the most holy Gospel of the glory and grace of God," freely offered to repentant sinners by faithful preachers.[2] In the restless condition of Germany it was an event of the utmost significance that a respected, if humble, religious leader had spoken boldly against pastoral, theological, and economic abuses associated with the sacrament of penance. Within weeks, the Ninety-five Theses, translated into German, spread through the length and breadth of the empire. The primary agents in their dissemination were the humanist sodalities in the German cities, among whose ranks Luther found his earliest allies outside Wittenberg.

Luther had not anticipated the uproar. A formidable opponent soon appeared in the person of the able and disputatious Johann Maier of Eck (1486–1543), professor of theology at the University of Ingolstadt and Luther's one-time friend, who answered with a tract circulated in manuscript and entitled *Obelisci*. Luther was charged with heresy. He defended his position in a sermon entitled "Indulgence and Grace," and he replied to Eck with his own unpublished *Asterici*. By the beginning of 1518, formal charges against Luther had been lodged in Rome by Archbishop Albrecht and the Dominicans. The result was that the general of the Augustinians, Gabriel della Volta, was ordered to end the dispute, and Luther was summoned before the general chapter of the order meeting at Heidelberg in April 1518. Here, in his important "Heidelberg Theses," Luther argued against free will and the control

---

[2] J. Pelikan and H. T. Lehmann, eds., *Luther's Works,* 55 vols. (St. Louis and Philadelphia, 1955–1976), 31:31 (thesis 62). Hereafter, this work will be referred to as *"Luther's Works."*

of Aristotle in theology and outlined the leading features of his "theology of the cross." Here he also won new adherents, of whom the most important were Martin Bucer (1491–1551) and Johannes Brenz (1499–1570), later the reformers of Strassburg and Württemberg, respectively. At about this same time, Luther also sent to his publisher a more elaborate defense of his position on indulgences, the *Resolutiones* or *Explanations*.

Luther had desired no quarrel with the papacy. He seems to have believed that the pope might see the indulgence abuses as he did, but the course of events was leading to no choice save the sturdy maintenance of his views or submission. In June 1518, Pope Leo X commissioned his censor of books and master of the papal palace, the Dominican Sylvester Prierias (1456?–1523), to draft a reply to Luther, which he produced in short order. Prierias asserted that "the Roman church is representatively the college of cardinals, and moreover is virtually the supreme pontiff," and that "he who says that the Roman church cannot do what it actually does regarding indulgences is a heretic."[3] Luther was now summoned to appear in Rome within sixty days. This summons and Prierias's reply reached Luther early in August.

His case would have ended in his speedy condemnation had he not had the powerful protection of his prince, the elector Frederick. How far Frederick sympathized with Luther's religious beliefs at any time is uncertain; but, at all events, he was proud of his Wittenberg professor and averse to sending him to Rome, where he would face almost certain condemnation. Owing to Frederick's political skill, Luther was granted a hearing before the papal legate at the Reichstag in Augsburg, the learned commentator on Aquinas and theologian of European repute, Cardinal Tommaso de Vio (1469–1534), known from his birthplace (Gaeta) as Cajetan. Cajetan was already under secret instructions from the pope not to debate with Luther and, failing the latter's recantation, to obtain his arrest by any possible means. Under pressure from Frederick, Cajetan subsequently requested the Curia to adopt a more conciliatory policy, and he was permitted to grant Luther a hearing without debate. The two men held three meetings from October 12 to 14, 1518. Cajetan ordered Luther to retract, especially his criticisms of the completeness of papal power of indulgence. Luther refused, and on October 20 he fled from Augsburg, having appealed to the pope "to be better informed." Not satisfied with this, Luther appealed from Wittenberg, in November, to a future general council. How little chance of a favorable hearing he had in Rome is shown by the bull issued the same month by Leo X, defining indulgences in the sense which Luther had criticized.

The summer of 1518 had seen the installation as professor of Greek in Wittenberg of a young scholar and grandnephew of Reuchlin, Philip Melanchthon (1497–1560), who was to be singularly united with Luther in the years

---

[3] See B. J. Kidd, ed., *Documents Illustrative of the Continental Reformation* (Oxford, 1911; reprint, 1970), pp. 31–32.

to come. Never was there a greater contrast. Melanchthon was timid and retiring, but he was without a superior in scholarship, and under the strong impress of Luther's personality, he devoted his remarkable abilities, almost from his arrival in Wittenberg, to the furtherance of the Lutheran cause.

The emperor, Maximilian, was now visibly nearing the end of his life, which was to come on January 12, 1519, and the turmoil of a disputed election was impending. Pope Leo X, as an Italian prince, looked with disfavor on the candidacy of Charles of Spain or Francis of France, as increasing foreign influence in Italy, and sought the good will of Elector Frederick, whom he would gladly have seen chosen. It was no time, therefore, to proceed against Frederick's favored professor. Leo sent his chamberlain, the Saxon Karl von Miltitz, as his nuncio, with a golden rose, a present expressive of high papal favor, to the elector. Miltitz flattered himself that he could heal the ecclesiastical quarrel and went far beyond his instructions. On his own initiative he disowned Tetzel, and he then held an interview with Luther from January 4 to 6, 1519. Luther agreed to keep silent on the questions in dispute if his opponents did likewise, to submit the case, if possible, to learned German bishops, and to write a humble letter to the pope.

But any real agreement was impossible. Luther's Wittenberg colleague, Andreas Karlstadt, had argued in 1518, in opposition to Eck, that the text of the Bible is to be preferred even to the authority of the whole church. Eck demanded a public debate, to which Karlstadt agreed, and Luther soon found himself drawn into the combat, proposing to contend that the supremacy of the Roman church is unsupported by history or Scripture. In June and July 1519, the great debate was held at Leipzig. Karlstadt, who was a laborious disputant, had only moderate success in holding his own against the nimble-witted Eck. Luther's earnestness acquitted itself much better, but Eck's skill drove Luther to the damaging statements that his positions were in some respects those of Jan Hus and that in condemning Hus the revered Council of Constance had erred. To Eck, this seemed a forensic triumph, and he believed victory to be his, declaring that one who could deny the infallibility of a general council was "a heathen and a publican." It was, indeed, a momentous position into which Luther had been led. He had already rejected the inerrancy and final authority of the pope; he now proclaimed the fallibility of general councils. These steps implied a break with the entire medieval system of authority, and they seemed to allow final appeal only to the Scriptures. Eck felt that the whole controversy might now be quickly ended by a papal bull of condemnation, which he set himself to secure. This bull, *Exsurge domine,* was issued on June 15, 1520.

Luther was now in the thick of battle. His own ideas were rapidly crystallizing. Humanist supporters, like Ulrich von Hutten, were rallying to him as one who could lead in a national conflict with Rome. Luther himself, while renouncing physical force, was beginning to see his task as a spiritual liberation of Germany from a papal system of control that he was coming to regard as Antichrist. He also spelled out the direct implications of his doctrine of justification by faith alone for the Christian life of service to society. In his substantial tract *On Good Works,* of May 1520, after identifying faith in Christ as "the first, highest, and most precious of all good works," because only faith can make the sinful conscience confident before God and liberate the will for unfeigned love for one's neighbor, Luther affirmed the essential goodness of the normal trades and occupations of life and denounced those who "define good works so narrowly that they are made to consist only of praying in church, fasting, and almsgiving."[4] This vindication of ordinary life in the world as the best field for the service of God, rather than monastic-ascetic flight from the world, was to be one of Luther's most important contributions to Protestant thought, as well as one of the most significant departures from ancient and medieval conceptions of "Christian perfection."

Luther's great accomplishment of the year 1520 was the preparation of three epoch-making works. The first of these treatises was published in August and was entitled *To the Christian Nobility of the German Nation.* Written with burning conviction, by a master of the German tongue, it soon ran the breadth of the empire. It declared that the three "walls" by which the papacy had buttressed its power were now overthrown. The pretended superiority of the spiritual to the temporal estate is baseless, since all believers are priests by virtue of baptism. This truth of universal priesthood casts down the second wall as well, that of exclusive papal right to interpret the Scriptures; and the third wall also, that a reformatory council can be called by none but the pope. "A true, free council" for reform of the church should be summoned by the temporal authorities. Luther then proceeded to lay down a reform program, his suggestions being practical rather than theological. Papal misgovernment, appointments, and taxation were to be curbed, burdensome offices abolished, German ecclesiastical interests placed under a "primate of Germany," clerical marriage permitted, the far too numerous holy days reduced in the interest of industry and sobriety, beggary—including that of the mendicant orders—forbidden, brothels closed, luxury curbed, and theological education in the universities reformed. No wonder the effect of Luther's work was profound. He had voiced what earnest persons had long been thinking.

Two months later, Luther put forth in Latin his *Babylonian Captivity of the Church,* in which questions of the highest theological import, namely, the sacraments, were addressed and the teaching of the Roman church unsparingly attacked. Restricting the name of sacrament to "those promises [of forgiveness] which have signs attached to them," Luther held that Scripture recognizes only two such sacraments instituted by Christ himself: baptism and the Lord's Supper.[5] Though penance (contrition, confession, absolution) lacks

---

[4] *Luther's Works,* 44:23–24.   [5] Ibid., 36:124.

an outward sign, it has a certain sacramental value as a daily return to baptism, and Luther wished private confession retained as "a cure without equal for distressed consciences."[6] What is central to all the sacraments is not the sign (*sacramentum*) itself, but the divine word of forgiveness (the *res sacramenti*) that is to be received in faith. In this light, monastic vows, pilgrimages, and works of merit are seen to be man-made substitutes for the forgiveness of sins freely promised to faith in baptism. Luther further criticized the denial of the cup to the laity, expressed doubts about transubstantiation, and especially rejected the doctrine that the Mass is a sacrifice to God. He declared that the other Roman sacraments—confirmation, matrimony, clerical orders, and extreme unction—had no sacramental standing in Scripture.

It is one of the marvels of Luther's stormy career that he was able to compose and issue, contemporaneously with these intensely polemical treatises, and while the papal bull of condemnation was being published in Germany, his third great tractate of 1520, *The Freedom of a Christian*. In calm confidence, he presented the paradox of Christian existence: "A Christian is a perfectly free lord of all, subject to none; a Christian is a perfectly dutiful servant of all, subject to all."[7] Believers are free since they are justified by faith alone, no longer under the law of works, and in a new personal relationship with Christ. Believers are servants because they are bound by love to bring their lives into conformity to God's will and to be helpful to their neighbors. The preface to this tract, an "open letter" to Pope Leo X, is a most curious document, breathing good will to the pontiff personally but full of denunciation of the papal court and its claims for the papacy, in which the pope is represented as "sitting like a lamb in the midst of wolves." Though Luther's vision was subsequently to undergo further clarification and expansion, his theological conception of the Christian Gospel was thus practically complete in its main outlines by 1520.

Meanwhile, Eck and Girolamo Aleander (1480–1542) had come to Germany as nuncios with the papal bull. Its publication was prohibited in Wittenberg, and its reception in large parts of Germany was lukewarm or hostile, but Aleander secured its publication in the Netherlands and procured the burning of Luther's books at Louvain, Liége, Antwerp, and Cologne. On December 10, 1520, Luther answered by burning the papal bull and the canon law, in the approving presence of students and citizens of Wittenberg and without opposition from the civil authorities. It was evident that a considerable section of Germany was in ecclesiastical rebellion, and the situation demanded the cognizance of the highest authorities of the empire.

On June 18, 1519, while the Leipzig debate was in progress, Maximilian's grandson, Charles V (1500–1558), was chosen to succeed to the throne of the Holy Roman Empire. The election of Charles—already heir of Spain, the Netherlands, and the Austrian territories of the house of Hapsburg, and master

---

[6] Ibid., p. 86.   [7] Ibid., 31:344.

of a considerable portion of Italy and of newly discovered lands across the Atlantic—made him the head of a territory vaster than that of any single European ruler since Charlemagne. In Germany, however, it was an authority greatly limited by the territorial powers of the local princes. As yet Charles was young and unknown, and both sides in the religious struggles of the day had strong hope of his support. In reality, he was an earnest Catholic of the type of his grandmother, Isabella of Castile, sharing her reformatory views, desirous of improvement in clerical morals, education, and administration, but wholly unsympathetic with any departure from the doctrinal or hierarchical system of the Middle Ages.

Partly to regulate his government in Germany, partly to prepare for the war about to break out over the rival claims of France and Spain in Italy, Charles called a Reichstag to meet at Worms in January 1521. Though there was much other business, all felt the determination of Luther's case to be of high importance. The papal nuncio, Aleander, pressed for a prompt condemnation, especially after the papal bull of excommunication, *Decet pontificem romanum,* was issued on January 3, 1521. Since Luther was already condemned and excommunicated by the pope, the Reichstag had no duty, Aleander urged, but to make that judgment effective. On the other hand, Luther had wide popular support, and his ruler, the elector Frederick, a master of diplomatic intrigue, was of the opinion that Luther had never had an adequate hearing. Frederick and other nobles believed that he should be heard before the Reichstag prior to action by that body. Charles wavered between the two counsels, convinced that Luther was a damnable heretic, but politician enough not to oppose German sentiment too sharply or to throw away the possible advantage of making the heretic's fate a lever in bringing the pope to the imperial side in the struggle with France.

The result was that Luther was summoned to Worms under the protection of an imperial safe-conduct. His journey there from Wittenberg was well-nigh a popular ovation. On April 17, 1521, Luther appeared before the emperor and the Reichstag. A row of his books was pointed out to him and he was asked whether he would recant them or not. Luther requested time for reflection. A day was given him, and on the next afternoon he was once more before the assembly. Here he acknowledged that, in the heat of controversy, he had expressed himself too strongly against persons, but the substance of what he had written he could not retract, unless convinced of its wrongfulness "by the testimony of the Scriptures or by clear reason."[8] The emperor, who could hardly believe that such temerity as to deny the infallibility of a general council was possible, cut the discussion short. That Luther cried out, "I cannot do otherwise. Here I stand. God help me, Amen," is not certain, but seems not improbable. The words at least express the substance of his unshaken deter-

---

[8] Ibid., 32:112.

mination. He had borne a great historic witness to the truth of his convictions before the highest tribunal of his nation. Of his dauntless courage he had given the complete proof.

The judgment of his hearers was divided, but if he alienated the emperor and the prelates by his strong and, as it seemed to them, self-willed assertion, he made a favorable impression on many of the German nobility, including Elector Frederick. That prince, though he thought Luther too bold, was confirmed in his determination that no harm should come to the reformer. Yet the outcome seemed a defeat for Luther. A month after Luther had started on his homeward journey, he was formally put under the ban of the empire, though not until after many of the members of the Reichstag had left. He was to be seized for punishment and his books burned. This ban was never formally abrogated, and Luther remained the rest of his life under imperial condemnation as a heretic and rebel.

Had Germany been controlled by a strong central authority, Luther's career would soon have ended in martyrdom. Not even an imperial edict, however, could be executed against the will of a vigorous territorial ruler, and Frederick the Wise once more served as Luther's benefactor. Unwilling to come out openly as his defender, he had Luther seized by friendly hands, as the reformer journeyed homeward from Worms, and brought secretly to the Wartburg castle, near Eisenach. For months, Luther's hiding place was practically unknown; but that he lived, and shared in the fortunes of the struggle, his ready pen made speedily apparent. His attacks on the Roman practice grew more intense, but the most lasting fruit of this period of enforced retirement was his translation of the New Testament, begun in December 1521 and published in September of the following year.

Luther was by no means the first to translate the Scriptures into German, but the earliest versions had been made from the Vulgate and were hard and awkward in expression. Luther's work was not merely from the Greek, for which the labors of Erasmus gave the basis, but it was also idiomatic and readable. It largely determined the form of speech that should mark future German literature—that of the Saxon chancery of the time, wrought and polished by a master of popular expression. Few services greater than this translation have ever been rendered to the development of the religious life of a nation. Nor, with all his deference to Holy Scripture as the written word of God, was Luther without his own canons of criticism, namely, the relative clearness with which a biblical book testified to Christ and to justification by grace through faith alone. Judged by these standards, he felt that Hebrews, James, Jude, and Revelation were of inferior worth and did not belong to "the true and certain chief books of the New Testament."[9] Even in Scripture itself there were differences in value.

[9] Ibid., 35:394.

The month which saw the beginning of Luther's work as a translator also witnessed the publication at Wittenberg of a small volume by Melanchthon, the *Loci communes,* or *Cardinal Points of Theology*. With it the systematic presentation of Lutheran theology may be said to have begun. It was to be enlarged, developed, and modified in many later editions.

Chapter 2

Separations and Divisions

L UTHER'S SOJOURN in the Wartburg left Wittenberg without his powerful leadership, but the ecclesiastical revolution continued apace there under the guidance of his colleagues. To his earlier associates in the university— Karlstadt, Amsdorf, and Melanchthon—there were added, in the first half of 1521, Johannes Bugenhagen (1485–1558) and Justus Jonas (1493–1555). The mantle of leadership fell upon the rash and impulsive Karlstadt.

Luther's activities had as yet resulted in no changes in public worship or in monastic life, but demands for such changes were quickly forthcoming. By October 1521, Luther's fiery fellow monk, Gabriel Zwilling (1487?–1558), was denouncing the Mass and urging the abandonment of clerical vows. He soon had a large following, especially in the Augustinian monastery of Wittenberg, many of whose inmates now renounced their profession. With equal zeal, Zwilling was soon attacking images. At Christmas in 1521, Karlstadt celebrated the Lord's Supper in the castle church, without priestly garb, sacrificial offering, or elevation of the host, and with the cup offered to the laity. Auricular confession and fasts were abandoned. Karlstadt taught that all ministers should marry, and in January 1522 he himself took a wife. He was soon opposing the use of pictures, organs, and the Gregorian chant in public worship. Under his leadership, the Wittenberg city government broke up the ancient religious fraternities and confiscated their property, decreed that the services should be in German, condemned pictures in the churches, and forbad beggary, ordering that really needy cases be aided from the city treasury. The public commotion was augmented by the arrival from Zwickau, on December 27, 1521, of three radical preachers, Nicholas Storch, Marcus Thomas Stübner, and Thomas Drechsel. These "prophets" claimed immediate divine inspiration, opposed infant baptism, and announced the imminent end of the world.

This turbulence, followed by a popular attack on images, was highly displeasing to Elector Frederick the Wise, and they elicited warning protests from German princes and the imperial authorities. The city government appealed to Luther to return. The elector nominally forbad him to do so, out of political considerations, but on March 6, 1522, Luther was nevertheless once more in Wittenberg. Eight days of preaching showed his power. The Gospel, he declared, consists in the knowledge of sin, in forgiveness through Christ, and in love for one's neighbor. The alterations that had raised the turmoil had to do with externals. They should be effected only in a spirit of consideration for the weak. Luther was master of the situation. Karlstadt lost all influence and had to leave the city. Many of the changes were, for the moment, undone, and the old order of worship was largely reestablished. Luther thus showed a decidedly conservative attitude. He opposed not merely the Romanists, as heretofore, but those partisans of the revolution who would move, as he believed, too rapidly. The separations in the reform party itself had begun. Yet there can be no doubt as to Luther's wisdom. His action caused many of the German rulers to look upon him with kindliness, as one who, though condemned at Worms, was really a force for order in tumultuous times. Especially important was the continued favor of his elector, without which his cause would even now have suffered speedy defeat.

Meanwhile, the emperor was preoccupied by the war with France for the control of Italy, which was to keep him absent from Germany from 1521 to 1530. Effective interference on his part with the Reformation was impossible. Pope Leo X had died in December 1521 and had been succeeded by Charles V's old tutor as Adrian VI—a man of strict medieval orthodoxy but fully conscious of the need for moral and administrative reform in the papal court, whose brief papacy of twenty months was to be a painfully fruitless effort to check the evils for which he believed Luther's heretical movement to be a divine punishment. Sympathy with Luther was rapidly spreading, not merely throughout Saxony but in the cities of Germany as well. To the Reichstag, which met at Nürnberg in November 1522, Adrian sent a nuncio with a *Breve,* demanding the enforcement of the Edict of Worms against Luther, while admitting that much was amiss in ecclesiastical administration. The Reichstag replied by declaring the edict impossible of enforcement and by demanding a council for church reform, to meet within a year in Germany, while, pending its assembly, only the "true, pure, genuine, holy Gospel" was to be preached. The old complaints against papal misgovernment were renewed by the Reichstag. Though not in form, it was in reality a victory for Luther and his cause. It looked as if the Reformation might gain the support of the whole German nation.

Under these favorable circumstances, "evangelical" congregations (i.e., those that claimed to be "reformed in accord with the Gospel") were rapidly forming in many regions of Germany, as yet without any fixed constitution or order of service. Luther now was convinced that such associations of believers had full power to appoint and depose their pastors. He also held, however, that the temporal rulers, as leading members of the Christian community and thus as "emergency bishops," had a prime duty to further the Gospel. Luther's experiences with rebellious peasants, and the necessities of actual church organization over extensive territories, were soon to turn him from this "free churchism" to an increasing dependence on the state, though he continued to hold that the princely exercise of spiritual functions was only a temporary expedient.

To meet the demands of the new evangelical worship, Luther issued, in 1523, his *Order of Public Worship,* in which he emphasized the central place of preaching; his *Formula of the Mass,* in which, though still using Latin, he did away with the sacrificial implications, directed lay communion in both bread and wine, and urged the employment of popular hymns by the worshipers; and his *Order of Baptism,* in which he presented a brief baptismal service in German. The abandonment of private Masses and Masses for the dead, with their attendant fees, raised a serious problem of ministerial support, which Luther proposed to solve by salaries from a common chest maintained by the municipality. Luther held that great freedom was permissible in details of worship, as long as the "word of God" was kept central. The various reformed congregations, therefore, soon exhibited considerable variety, though the tendency to use German rapidly increased, Luther himself issuing a *German Mass* in 1526. Luther regarded private confession as exceedingly desirable in preparing the Christian for the Lord's Supper, but not as obligatory. Compared to the development of the Reformation elsewhere, Luther's attitude in matters of worship was strongly conservative, his principle being that "what is not contrary to Scripture is for Scripture and Scripture for it." He therefore retained much of traditional usage, such as the wearing of vestments, the altar, the sign of the cross, and the illustrative employment of images.

In the years following the Diet of Worms, the Reformation spread rapidly in almost all territories of Germany, above all in the towns and cities. During this period, everything "revolutionary" was forthwith dubbed "Lutheran," both by the revolutionaries themselves and by their Catholic opponents. The early evangelical movement, however, was far from homogeneous, and its growth was disorderly, concealing profound differences under the name of "Lutheran" preaching, liturgical reform, and political action. In 1524 and 1525, the fissures within the movement began to become apparent, the effects of which were to limit the Reformation and to make of Luther a party rather than a national leader.

The first of these separations came from the side of the humanists, among whom Luther had found his earliest cadre of supporters. Their admired leader, Erasmus, had little sympathy with Luther's doctrine of justification by faith alone. To his thinking, reform would come by education, the rejection of superstition, and a return to the "sources" of Christian truth. The stormy writings of Luther and the popular tumult were becoming increasingly odious to him. In common with humanists generally, he was alarmed by the great decline in attendance at the German universities, which set in with the rise of the religious controversy, and by the fading of interest in purely scholarly questions. Though frequently urged, he was long reluctant to attack Luther; but at last, in the autumn of 1524, he challenged Luther's denial of free will in the matter of salvation. In his carefully reasoned *Diatribe de libero arbitrio,* he argued on biblical grounds for an ethical rather than a dogmatic interpretation of religion. He concluded that the doctrine of the late medieval church asserting both human freedom of decision for God and the need of assisting grace was preferable to Luther's predestinarian extremism, because it avoided Manichaeanism as well as Pelagianism. A year later, Luther replied in his treatise *De servo arbitrio* (On the bondage of the will). He closely followed Erasmus's outline and attempted to refute it section by section. On the basis of the witness of the Bible, which he regarded as clear and unified, he argued for humanity's absolute dependence upon the all-ruling omnipotent God and his freely given gift of grace. He declared himself a predestinarian and did not hesitate to affirm doctrines that bordered on determinism. The breach between Luther and Erasmus was irreparable. While most of the older humanists deserted Luther, many of the younger humanists continued to side with him and became local leaders of the evangelical movement.

To some in Germany, Luther seemed but a halfway reformer. Such a radical was his old associate Karlstadt, who, having lost all standing in Wittenberg, went on to yet more radical views and practices and, securing a large following in Orlamünde, practically defied Luther and the Saxon government. He denied the value of education, dressed and lived like the peasantry, destroyed images, and rejected the physical presence of Christ in the Supper. Even more radical was Thomas Müntzer (1488?–1525), who upheld immediate revelation through visions and dreams and excoriated Romanists and Lutherans alike as "scribes" who suppressed the "inner word" by their slavish dependence on the letter of Scripture. A former Catholic priest, he had made a wide-ranging study of the Bible, the church fathers, and the German mystics, and had early become a follower of Luther. In 1521–1522, he worked as an ardent evangelical preacher first in Zwickau and then in Bohemia, where he hoped to build "the new apostolic church," in the conviction that the church had long since fallen from its original purity owing to the treason of the scholars and priests. In 1523, he became minister in the Thuringian town of Allstedt, where he offered an interpretation of the Gospel and a reform program that broke openly with Luther's views.

Müntzer advocated a thoroughgoing spiritualism that rendered the Bible subject to the test of religious experience: only the Spirit-possessed can rightly understand the Scriptures. The Spirit is bestowed solely upon the elect, those who have been reborn by passing through the abyss of self-despair and who have taken upon themselves the cross of the "bitter Christ." Hence, the inner baptism of the Spirit is the one true baptism; outer baptism through water is unnecessary. Müntzer was a man of great originality; the well-crafted order of worship he developed for Allstedt in 1523 was the first Protestant vernacular liturgy. A compelling preacher, he labored to establish a "covenanted" church of the elect that would bring about a new social order of justice and love. Opposing the "easygoing flesh of Wittenberg"—i.e., Luther's refusal to derive from his rediscovery of the Gospel a new law, either of morals or of social life—he advocated bloody revolution, if necessary, to put down priestly and princely injustice. It was no wonder that, in due time, he assumed a position of leadership in the peasant revolt. Luther vehemently opposed Müntzer and Karlstadt, and men like them, naming them *Schwärmer* (fanatics, enthusiasts). Their presence indicated a growing rift in the forces of reform.

Still more serious was a third separation—that caused by the great peasants' revolt, which brought Luther into open conflict with all social revolutionaries and damaged his prestige as a popular leader. The condition of the German peasantry in the late Middle Ages had been one of increasing loss of freedom and consequent unrest, especially in southwestern Germany, where the example of better conditions in neighboring Switzerland fed the discontent (see V:16). The Lutheran assault on traditional spiritual authority and the evangelical preaching of "Christian liberty" and "divine justice" were undoubtedly contributing causes of the peasant revolt. Begun in extreme southwestern Germany in May and June 1524, the insurrection had become exceedingly formidable by the spring of the following year. In February 1525, the Swabian peasants, supported by a significant number of poor burghers and guildsmen, put forth twelve articles, demanding that each community have the right to choose and depose its pastor, that the great tithes (on grain) be used for the support of the pastor and other community expenses and the small tithes (on livestock) be abolished, that serfdom be done away with, that reservations for hunting be restricted and the use of the forests allowed to the poor, and that forced labor be regulated and duly paid, just rents fixed, new laws no longer enacted, common lands restored to the communities from which they had been taken, and death taxes abolished.

Luther at first was disposed to find wrong on both sides. In his *Admonition to Peace* of April 1525, he conceded that the twelve articles contained much that was fair and just, and he blamed peasant discontent chiefly on the princes and lords, whom he denounced as "wild and dictatorial tyrants."[1] In his eyes, however, all political revolution was rebellion against God, and he looked upon the social and economic demands of the peasants, made in the name of the Bible and "divine law," as a "carnal" misinterpretation of the Gospel. As the ill-led rebellion fell into greater excesses of violence and appeared to become

[1] *Luther's Works*, 46:20.

anarchistic, Luther turned on the militant peasants with a savage pamphlet, *Against the Robbing and Murdering Hordes of Peasants,* and exhorted the rulers to crush them with force of arms. The defeat of Francis I of France by the imperial army on February 24, 1525, near Pavia, did enable the princes of Germany to put down the uprising; the peasant insurrection was stamped out in frightful bloodshed during May and June of 1525. Müntzer, whom Luther wrongly saw as the ideological leader of the entire affair, was captured, tortured, and beheaded following the battle of Frankenhausen on May 15, 1525, in which some six thousand peasants were killed.

The Peasants' War was a watershed in Reformation history, marking the end of its period of uncontrolled growth. From then on, the movement became subject to ever closer supervision by the civil authorities, who were obliged either to suppress it or to establish new evangelical church orders in their territories. The Reformation, however, though it certainly lost some of its appeal to the masses, did not cease to be a spontaneous popular movement, as is shown by its introduction in many German cities during the next decade. The initiative for reform regularly came from the commoners and craft guilds, not from the urban "patricians" or from the magistrates themselves—a fact which disproves the old belief that the Peasants' War resulted in the complete alienation of the lower classes from Luther's cause. Nevertheless, by the end of 1525 lines of division within the ranks of the reformers had been clearly drawn; opposition to the Reformation stiffened, not least because defenders of the "old faith" pointed to civil insurrection as the inevitable outcome of ecclesiastical rebellion; and the progress of the reform now became linked to authoritarian sanctions and compulsory church orders.

Meanwhile, Pope Adrian VI had died in September 1523 and had been succeeded by Giulio de' Medici as Clement VII (1523–1534)—a man of respectable character but with little sense of the importance of religious questions, and in policy primarily an Italian worldly prince. To the new Reichstag assembled at Nürnberg in the spring of 1524, Clement sent as his legate the skillful cardinal, Lorenzo Campeggio (1474–1539). With the Reichstag Campeggio could effect little. It promised to enforce the Edict of Worms against Luther "as far as possible," and it demanded a "general assembly of the German nation" to meet at Speyer the following autumn. This gathering the absent emperor succeeded in frustrating. Campeggio was much more successful outside the Reichstag. Through his efforts, a league to support the Roman cause was formed in Regensburg, on July 7, 1524, embracing the emperor's brother, Ferdinand, the dukes of Bavaria, and a number of south German bishops.

While Rome was thus strengthened in southern Germany, Luther's cause received important accessions. Chief of these was the adhesion, in 1524, of the landgrave Philip of Hesse (1518–1567), the ablest politician among the Lutheran princes. At the same time, Albert of Prussia, grand master of the Teutonic Knights, George of Brandenburg, Henry of Mecklenburg, and

Albert of Mansfeld were showing a decided interest in the evangelical cause. The important cities of Magdeburg, Nürnberg, Strassburg, Augsburg, Esslingen, and Ulm, and others of less moment, had also been won by 1524.

During the dark days of the peasant revolt, Luther's cautious protector, Frederick the Wise, died (May 5, 1525), and he was succeeded by his brother John "the Steadfast" (1525–1532). The change was favorable to Luther, for the new elector was a declared and active Lutheran. During these months also, on June 13, 1525, Luther married a former nun, Katherine von Bora (1499–1552)—a union that was to manifest some of the most winsome traits of the reformer's character.

The suppression of the peasant revolt had left the princes and the cities as the real ruling forces in Germany, and political alliances were now formed for or against the Reformation. The Catholic league of Regensburg has already been mentioned. Another league of Catholics, in central and north Germany, was instituted by Duke George of Saxony and other Catholic princes, who met at Dessau in July 1525; and as a reply, Philip of Hesse and the new elector John of Saxony organized a Lutheran league in Torgau. The imperial victory at Pavia in the previous February had resulted in the captivity of the defeated king of France, Francis I. The war had gone decisively in favor of the emperor, and its fruits seemed to be garnered by the Treaty of Madrid of January 1526, by which Francis gained his release. Both monarchs pledged themselves to combined efforts to put down heresy. The prospects of Lutheranism were indeed dark. From this peril the Lutheran cause owed its rescue primarily to the pope. Clement VII, more an Italian prince than a churchman, was thoroughly alarmed at the increase of imperial power in Italy. He formed an Italian league against the emperor, which was joined by the French king in May 1526. Francis I repudiated the Treaty of Madrid, and now the League of Cognac ranged France, the pope, Florence, and Venice against the emperor. The results of Pavia seemed lost. The war would have to be fought over again. The emperor's hands were too full to interfere in the religious struggles of Germany.

So it came about that when the new Reichstag met at Speyer in the summer of 1526, though the imperial instructions forbad alterations in religion and ordered the execution of the Edict of Worms, the Lutherans were able to urge that the situation had changed from that contemplated by the emperor when his commands were issued from Spain. The terrifying advance of the Turks, which led to the disastrous defeat of King Louis II of Hungary at Mohács on August 29, 1526, also counseled military unity. The Reichstag therefore enacted that, pending a "council or a national assembly," each of the territorial rulers of the empire is "so to live, govern, and carry himself as he hopes and trusts to answer it to God and his imperial majesty."[2]

---

[2] Kidd, *Continental Reformation*, p. 185.

This was doubtless a mere ad interim compromise, but the Lutheran princes and cities speedily interpreted it as full legal authorization to order their ecclesiastical constitutions as they saw fit. Under its shelter, the organization of Lutheran territorial churches was now rapidly accomplished. Some steps had been taken toward such territorial organization even before the Reichstag of 1526. Beyond the borders of the empire, Albert of Brandenburg (1511–1568), the grand master of the Teutonic Knights in Prussia, transformed his office into a hereditary dukedom under the overlordship of Poland, in 1525, and vigorously furthered the Lutheranization of the land. In electoral Saxony itself, Elector John was planning more active governmental control of ecclesiastical affairs, and Luther had issued his *German Mass and Order of Divine Service,* of 1526, before the Reichstag. The decree of the Reichstag greatly strengthened these tendencies.

In Saxony, which became the norm in a general way for the creation of Lutheran territorial churches, "visitors" were appointed by the elector to inquire into clerical doctrine and conduct on the basis of articles drawn up by Melanchthon in 1527 and enlarged the following year. The old jurisdiction of bishops was cast off; the land was divided into districts, each under a "superintendent" with spiritual but not administrative superiority over the parish minister and in turn responsible to the elector. Unworthy or recalcitrant clergy were driven out, similarity of worship was secured, and monastic property, altar endowment, and similar foundations were confiscated, in part for the benefit of parish churches and schools, but largely for that of the electoral treasury. In a word, a Lutheran state church, coterminous with the electoral territories and having all baptized inhabitants as its members, was substituted for the old bishop-ruled church. Other territories of evangelical Germany were similarly organized. To aid in popular religious instruction, which the confusion of a decade had reduced to a deplorable condition, Luther prepared two catechisms in 1529, of which the *Small Catechism* is one of the noblest monuments of the Reformation.

That this development of territorial churches could take place was due to favorable political conditions. The emperor had a tremendous war to wage, with domination in Italy as its prize. His brother, Ferdinand, was crowned king of Hungary on November 3, 1527, and thenceforth was engaged in struggle with the Turks. Effective intervention in Germany was impossible. But on May 6, 1527, an imperial army containing many German troops captured Rome, shut up Pope Clement VII in the castle of Sant' Angelo, and subjected the city to every barbarity. Though fortune seemed to turn toward the French in the early part of 1528, before the end of that year the imperial forces had asserted their mastery. The pope was compelled to make his peace with the emperor, at Barcelona, on June 29, 1529, and France gave up the struggle by the Peace of Cambrai, on the 5th of the following August. The war which had raged since 1521 was over, and Charles V could now turn his attention to the suppression of the Lutheran revolt. Nor had the Lutheran leaders been wholly fortunate. Deceived by Otto von Pack, an official of ducal Saxony, Landgrave Philip of Hesse and Elector John of Saxony had been convinced that the Catholics intended to attack them. Philip determined to anticipate the alleged plot and was arming for that purpose in 1528, when the letter on which Pack based his information was discovered to be a forgery. The effect of the "Pack affair" was to embitter the relations of the two great ecclesiastical parties.

In these circumstances, it was inevitable that when the next imperial diet met at Speyer, in February 1529, the Catholic majority should be strongly hostile to the Lutheran innovators. That Reichstag now ordered, by a majority decision, that no further ecclesiastical changes should be made, that Roman worship should be permitted everywhere, and that all Roman authorities and religious orders should be allowed full enjoyment of their former rights, property, and incomes. This would have meant the practical abolition of the Lutheran territorial churches. Unable to defeat this legislation, the Lutheran estates represented in the Reichstag, on April 19, 1529, entered a formal protest, the *Protestatio,* a document of historic importance, since it led to the designation of the party as "Protestant." It was supported by John of electoral Saxony, Philip of Hesse, Ernst of Lüneburg, George of Brandenburg-Ansbach, Wolfgang of Anhalt, and the cities of Strassburg, Ulm, Constance, Nürnberg, Lindau, Kempten, Memmingen, Nördlingen, Heilbronn, Isny, St. Gallen, Reutlingen, Weissenburg, and Windsheim.

Protestant prospects were dark. The situation demanded a defensive union, which Philip of Hesse undertook to organize. At this critical juncture, the Reformation cause was threatened by division between the reformers of Saxony and Switzerland and by the rapid spread of the Anabaptists.

Chapter 3

Ulrich Zwingli and the Swiss Reformation

SWITZERLAND, though nominally a part of the Holy Roman Empire, had long been practically independent. Its thirteen cantons were united in a loose confederacy, each being a self-governing republic. The land, as a whole, was deemed the freest in Europe. Its sons were in great repute as soldiers and were eagerly sought as mercenaries, particularly by the kings of France and the popes. Though the general status of education was low, humanism had penetrated the larger towns, and in the early decades of the sixteenth century had notably its home in Basel. The Swiss Reformation was to have its sources in humanism, in local self-government, in resistance to ecclesiastical dominion, and in resentment of monastic exactions, especially where the monasteries were large landowners.

Ulrich (Huldreich) Zwingli, chief of the reformers of German-speaking Switzerland, was born on January 1, 1484, in Wildhaus, where his father was the bailiff of the village and in comfortable circumstances. An uncle, the dean of Wesen, started him on the road to an education, which was continued in Basel, and then in Bern under the humanist Heinrich Wölflin (Lupulus), from 1496 to 1498. For two years (1500–1502), Zwingli was a student at the University of Vienna, where Conrad Celtis had great fame in the classics. From 1502 to 1506, he continued his studies at the University of Basel, graduating as a bachelor of arts in 1504 and receiving the master's degree two years later. At Basel, he enjoyed the instruction of the humanist Thomas Wyttenbach (1472–1526), whom he gratefully remembered as having taught him the sole authority of Scripture, the death of Christ as the only price of forgiveness, and the worthlessnes of indulgences. Under such teaching, Zwingli became naturally a humanist himself, eager to go back to the earlier sources of Christian belief and critical of what the humanists generally deemed superstition.

In 1506, Zwingli was appointed parish priest in the town of Glarus, where he remained for the next ten years. During this time, he attained proficiency in Greek, began the study of Hebrew, and absorbed the writings of Erasmus; he diligently studied the classics, the Bible (from 1516, in Erasmus's edition of the Greek New Testament), and the church fathers; he became an influential preacher and a respected member of a small group of learned northern humanists; and he opposed the employment of Swiss as mercenaries, save by the pope, from whom he received a pension in 1513. He accompanied the young men of his parish as chaplain in several Italian campaigns.

Zwingli was patriotically convinced of the moral evil of mercenary service, but the French, eager to enlist Swiss soldiers, made so much trouble in his Glarus parish that, without resigning the post, he transferred his activities in 1516 to the pilgrim shrine of Einsiedeln. The change brought him enlarged reputation as a preacher and scholar. Here also he stoutly opposed the sale of indulgences by the Franciscan monk Bernhard Sanson. By now, he had become one of the best Greek scholars north of the Alps, as well as a serious student of Hebrew. To his Einsiedeln sojourn, Zwingli, always jealous of admitting indebtedness to Luther, later ascribed his acceptance of the evangelical position. The evidence that has survived points, however, to little then beyond an Erasmian biblical humanism. In 1518, he readily accepted appointment as a papal chaplain. His private life at this time was, moreover, not free from reproach for breach of the vow of chastity.

Zwingli's opposition to foreign military service and his reputation as a preacher and scholar led to his election, in December 1518, by the chapter of the Great Minster church in Zurich as stipendiary priest, an office on which he entered on New Year's Day, 1519. He began at once the verse-by-verse exposition of entire books of the Bible, commencing with Matthew's Gospel, without any recourse to traditional (Scholastic) interpretation. In September 1519, he was brought near to death by the bubonic plague, an experience which promoted serious self-examination and awakened an intense sense of divine mission. His spiritual life was further deepened through bereavement by the death of a beloved brother in 1520, and in the same year he resigned his papal pension. By 1521, he was making careful study of Luther's writings. He continued to preach forcefully against mercenary soldiering, so that the Zurich city council ultimately (January 1523) forbad the practice.

Though Zwingli had thus long been moving in a reformist direction, it was in 1522 that his vigorous reforming work began. It is interesting to note that the question first at issue grew not out of a concern for personal assurance of salvation, as with Luther, but out of the conviction that only the Bible, evangelically interpreted, was binding on Christians. In March of that year, certain of the citizens broke the lenten fast, citing Zwingli's assertion of the sole authority of Scripture in justification. Zwingli now preached and published in their defense. The bishop of Constance, in whose diocese Zurich lay, sent a commission to repress the innovation. The cantonal civil government ruled that the New Testament imposed no fasts, but that they should be observed for the sake of good order. The importance of this compromise decision was that the civil authorities practically rejected the jurisdiction of the bishop and took full control of the Zurich churches into their own hands.

Zwingli believed that the ultimate ecclesiastical authority is the Christian community (*Gemeinde*), the local assembly of believers under the sole lordship of Christ and of the divinely inspired Scriptures that bear witness to redemption through him. This authority is exercised on the community's behalf through the duly constituted organs of civil government acting in accordance with the Scriptures. Only that which the Bible commands, or for which distinct authorization can be found in its pages, is binding or allowable. Hence, Zwingli's attitude toward the ceremonies and order of the older worship was much more radical than Luther's. The situation in Zurich was one in which the cantonal government gradually introduced the changes which Zwingli, as a trusted interpreter of Scripture and a natural popular leader, persuaded that government to sanction, not least on the grounds that its authority would be increased by allowing the proposed changes in religious policy. The city council, accordingly, ordered a public disputation, in January 1523, in which the Bible should be the exclusive touchstone. For this debate, Zwingli prepared sixty-seven brief articles, asserting that the Gospel derives no authority from the church and that salvation is by faith alone, and denying the sacrificial character of the Mass, the salvatory character of good works, the value of saintly intercessors, the binding character of monastic vows, and the existence of purgatory. He also declared Christ to be the sole head of the church, and he advocated clerical marriage. In the resulting debate, attended by over six hundred persons, the council declared Zwingli the victor over his Romanist opponents, affirming that he had not been convicted of heresy and was no innovator, judged by the scriptural standard, and directing that he should continue his preaching and that all others should preach only what could be supported by the Gospels and Holy Scripture. It was a resounding personal triumph for Zwingli, and it effectively secured the Reformation in Zurich, though not "officially" introducing it.

Growing tensions within the city, including some outbreaks of iconoclasm, now led Zwingli and his associate minister, Leo Jud (1482–1542), to propose another public debate to deal specifically with the question of the Mass and the use of images. This second disputation was held, at the order of the council, in October 1523, and was attended by some nine hundred persons. Zwingli and Jud attacked the veneration of images ("idols"), denied the sacrificial character of the Mass, asserted biblical support for lay communion in both elements, and called for a vernacular service. This disputation, like the first, was a triumph for Zwingli, but the council moved cautiously. It voted to retain the Mass in Latin and communion in one kind, and it permitted only a quiet removal of privately owned images from the churches. It also appointed a committee of fourteen, including Zwingli and Jud, to deliberate the issues. Zwingli himself favored this policy of gradualism; "by going slow," he once wrote to Jud, "we achieve our ends." Other, more radical adherents of the reform, however, wanted change to come much faster, without tarrying for the magistrates, and they thus became disillusioned with Zwingli's leadership (see VI:4).

The decisive changes, marking an open breach with Rome, came in 1524 and 1525. In June and July 1524, by order of the council, gangs of workers forcibly removed pictures, statues, and relics from the seven city churches and walled up the organ in the Great Minster. In December of that year, the monasteries were dissolved, with little opposition, and their properties put to use for educational purposes and relief of the poor. The Mass continued until Holy Week of 1525, when it too was abolished, though not without weighty opposition from the Catholic minority in the council. A simple vernacular service, with communion in both kinds as a remembrance of the Last Supper, was instituted in its place. The transformation was complete. Episcopal jurisdiction had been thrown off, the services put into German, the sermon made central, the characteristic doctrines and ceremonies of the older worship done away with. Zwingli explained and justified these changes in his chief theological work, *The Commentary on True and False Religion* (1525). Meanwhile, on April 2, 1524, Zwingli had publicly married Anna Reinhard, a widow whom he had secretly married early in 1522. All this time, the popes had made no effective intervention in the city's religious affairs, largely because they needed the military support of Zurich, the greatest of the Swiss states and heretofore the papacy's only reliable source of mercenary troops in the Swiss Confederation.

Zwingli, of course, followed with eagerness the fortunes of the ecclesiastical revolution in other parts of Switzerland and the adjacent regions of Germany, and he aided it to the utmost of his ability. Basel was won gradually for the evangelical cause, chiefly by Johannes Oecolampadius (1482–1531), who labored there continuously from 1522. There the Mass was abolished in 1529. Bern, the largest of the Swiss cantons, was won for the reform in 1528, after much preliminary evangelical labor, by a public debate in which Zwingli took a leading part. St. Gallen, under the humanist Joachim von Watt, known as Vadianus (1484–1551), was also won, as were the cantons of Schaffhausen and Glarus and the cities of Constance and Mülhausen in Alsace. Bern's decision for Zwinglian Protestantism was of the utmost importance. It saved Zurich and Zwinglianism from isolation within the Swiss Confederation, and ultimately made possible the work of John Calvin by saving Geneva from domination by the Catholic dukes of Savoy (see VI:7). Of comparable importance was the inclination of the south German city of Strassburg to the Zwinglian, rather than the Lutheran, point of view. In that city, the evangelical movement, begun in 1521 by Matthew Zell (1477–1548), had been carried forward vigorously from 1523 by Wolfgang Köpfel, or Capito (1478–1541) and by the able and peace-loving Martin Bucer (1491–1551), though not wholly completed until 1529.

Zwingli and Luther were in many matters in substantial agreement, but they were temperamentally unlike, and their intellectual and religious formation had been very different. Luther began his career as a late medieval Scholastic, Augustinian friar, and university professor of Bible, and he came to his evangelical breakthrough out of profound religious struggles in the monastery. Zwingli, parish priest and city preacher, had traveled the humanists' road, though his Erasmian humanism had been steadily deepened, and at last transformed, by his study of Paul and Augustine and by his experience of personal sinfulness and suffering. While he also learned much from Luther's early writings, his emphases were unlike Luther's. To Luther, the Christian life was one of freedom in forgiveness and reconciliation to God. To Zwingli, it was far more one of conformity to the will of God as set forth in the Bible.

In no point of Christian doctrine was his divergence from Luther more apparent than in his interpretation of the Lord's Supper, and this disagreement ultimately sundered the evangelical ranks. To Luther, Christ's words at the Last Supper, "This is my body," were literally true; hence, he taught that the body and blood of Christ are "really" or "substantially" present in the consecrated bread and wine and are truly received by all who partake of the elements—by the faithful unto salvation through forgiveness of their sins, by unbelievers to their damnation. But as early as 1521, a Dutch lawyer, Cornelius Hoen, had urged that the proper interpretation was "This *signifies* my body." Hoen's argument came to Zwingli's notice in 1523, and to him it confirmed the symbolic understanding of the words to which he was already inclined; thenceforth, he denied any bodily presence of Christ in the Supper. Christ, to be sure, is present spiritually, not in the bread and wine but in the hearts of the faithful, who alone receive the benefits of the Supper. The elements are thus outward and visible signs of an inward and spiritual grace, already present, and so "eating" is equivalent to "believing" (*edere est credere*). The Supper is a common meal of thanksgiving and remembrance and unites the assembly of believers in a common attestation of loyalty to their Lord.

By 1526, these rival interpretations had led to an embittered controversy of pamphlets, in which Luther and Bugenhagen on the one side and Zwingli and Oecolampadius on the other, and their respective associates, took part. Luther's most important work was his [*Great*] *Confession concerning Christ's Supper* (1528). Little charity was shown on either side. To Zwingli, Luther's assertion of the corporeal presence of Christ was an unreasoning remnant of Catholic superstition. A physical body can be in only one place, and the body of Christ—since the Ascension—is in heaven. Physical things, moreover, cannot contain or convey spiritual realities. To Luther, Zwingli's interpretation was a sinful exaltation of reason above the "simple words" of Scripture and a denial of the reality of Christ's Incarnation. He sought to explain the bodily presence of Christ on ten thousand altars at once by appeal to the traditional christological doctrine of the "communication of attributes" (*communicatio idiomatum*)— i.e., that the qualities of Christ's divine nature, including ubiquity, were communicated to his human nature. Luther was anxious, also, to maintain that the believer partook of the whole divine-human Christ and to avoid any dismemberment of Christ's person. Luther declared Zwingli and his supporters to be no Christians, while Zwingli affirmed that Luther was worse than the Roman champion, Eck. Zwingli's views met the approval not only of German-speaking Switzerland but of much of southwestern Germany. The Roman party rejoiced at this evident division of the evangelical forces and actively encouraged further division between German and Swiss Protestants by emphasizing the Catholic ("orthodox") elements in Lutheranism.

Zwingli was the most politically gifted of any of the reformers, and he developed plans which were far-reaching, though in the end futile. The old rural cantons of Uri, Schwyz, Unterwalden, and Zug were strongly conservative and opposed to the changes in Zurich, and with them stood Lucerne, the whole constituting a vigorous Roman party. By April 1524, they had formed a league to resist heresy. In May 1526, the Swiss Confederation convened a religious disputation at Baden. Zwingli was invited, but he declined to attend;

the evangelical position was ably represented by Oecolampadius instead. At this time, all the cantons, save Zurich, were still officially Catholic, and the result of the debate was a Catholic triumph. Zurich was, for the time being, isolated. However, after Bern became officially Protestant in February 1528, the reformed cities of Zurich, Constance, and Bern entered into a "Christian Civic Alliance" in June of that year—a formidable league to which St. Gallen was added later in 1528, and Biel, Mülhausen, Basel, and Schaffhausen in 1529. Strassburg joined early in 1530, but the league was still far less extensive than Zwingli planned. As it was, it was divisive of Swiss unity; the conservative Roman cantons formed a counter "Christian Union" and secured alliance with Austria in 1529. Hostilities were begun. But Austrian help for the Roman party was not forthcoming, and on June 25, 1529, peace was made between the two parties at Kappel, on terms very favorable to Zurich and the Zwinglians. The league with Austria was abandoned.

Zurich was now at the height of its power and was widely regarded as the political head of the evangelical cause. Yet the peace was but a truce, and when, in 1531, Zurich tried to force evangelical preaching on the Roman cantons by an embargo on shipment of food to them, war was once more certain. Zurich, in spite of Zwingli's counsels, had made no adequate preparation for the struggle. The Roman cantons moved rapidly. On October 11, 1531, they defeated the men of Zurich in battle at Kappel. Zwingli himself was discovered among the severely wounded. After refusing the ministrations of a confessor, he was killed, and his body was quartered and burned and mixed with dung, to prevent his ashes being collected as Protestant relics. In the peace that followed, Zurich was compelled to abandon its alliances, and each canton was given full right to regulate its internal religious affairs. The progress of the Reformation in German-speaking Switzerland was permanently halted. In the leadership of the Zurich church, though not in his political ambitions, Zwingli was succeeded by the able and conciliatory Heinrich Bullinger (1504–1575). The Swiss movement, as a whole, was to be modified and greatly developed by the genius of Calvin; and to the churches that trace their spiritual parentage to him, and thus in part to Zwingli, the name "Reformed," as distinguished from "Lutheran," was ultimately to be given.

Chapter 4

The Anabaptists

IT HAS BEEN SAID ABOVE, in speaking of Karlstadt, that some who once worked with Luther came to feel that he was but a halfway reformer. Such was even more largely Zwingli's experience. Among those who had been most forward in favoring innovations in Zurich were Felix Manz (1500?–1527), a scholarly priest and son of a canon of the Great Minster, and Conrad Grebel (1498–1526), scion of one of the city's most prominent families and, like Zwingli, trained as a humanist at the universities of Vienna and Basel. They and others had come, by the end of 1523, to look upon Zwingli as a false prophet, one who had failed to apply the biblical test to all religious practices in Zurich and who waited on dilatory secular authorities to enact the reforms mandated forthwith by God's word. This radical element first came into evidence during the second great disputation, in October 1523, when it looked for the immediate abolition of images and of the Mass—steps which the authorities were not yet ready to take.

An able participant in the October debate was Balthasar Hubmaier (1480?–1528), a doctor of theology of the University of Ingolstadt, where he was a pupil and then colleague of Luther's opponent, Johann Eck. In 1521, Hubmaier became preacher in Waldshut, on the northern edge of Switzerland. Led to evangelical views by Luther's writings in 1522, he successfully urged reform in his city. As early as May 1523, he had come to doubt infant baptism and had discussed it with Zwingli, who, according to Hubmaier's testimony, then sympathized with him. His criticisms were based on lack of scriptural warrant for administration to infants. By 1524, Grebel and Manz had reached the same conclusion, but it was not until early in 1525 that they or Hubmaier translated theory into practice.

Their criticisms led, on January 17, 1525, to a public debate with Zwingli, as a consequence of which the city council, on January 18, ordered all unbaptized children to be presented for baptism within eight days—there had been deliberate delay on the part of some parents—and also ordered the cessation of unauthorized preaching and illicit gatherings for worship. To the dissenters, this seemed a command by an earthly power to act counter to the word of God. On the evening of January 21, 1525, a small band gathered at a house belonging to Felix Manz's mother. After prayer, George Blaurock (1492?–1529), a married ex-priest, stood up and asked Conrad Grebel to baptize him. This Grebel did, and Blaurock then baptized fifteen others. At this very time, the council was issuing an order requiring Grebel and Manz to cease from further propaganda and banishing their associates who were not citizens of Zurich—among them Wilhelm Röubli (1484?–1559), the priest of Wytikon, and Ludwig Hätzer (1500?–1529).

The following week, these men, acting now in open defiance of the authorities, held revival meetings in the village of Zollikon near Zurich. They led prayer meetings in private homes. Those who experienced regeneration, some thirty-five in number, were baptized by affusion. Having thus instituted believers' baptism, they proceeded to celebrate their membership in the fellowship of Christ by a simple observance of the Lord's Supper. On Easter Sunday, 1525, Hubmaier was baptized in Waldshut by Röubli.

Through these fateful acts, the dissenters formed themselves into a separated community, a "gathered church" of "genuine believers." By their opponents they were nicknamed "Anabaptists," or rebaptizers. This title was both inaccurate and prejudicial, since they recognized but one baptism, that for adults only, and so denied the validity of their baptisms in infancy. They called themselves simply "brothers" and "sisters." Yet the traditional name, properly understood, is conveniently applied to this remarkable movement of the Reformation era.

Zwingli opposed these early Anabaptists (or Swiss Brethren, as they are usually called today) with much bitterness, but he had little success in winning them from their position. Grebel and his associates differed from him insofar as they saw the test of Christian faith in a discipleship of Christ that, they maintained, must be experienced in a spiritual rebirth or awakening and exhibited in a life of saintliness. The true church of God, accordingly, is made up not of all professed Christians, who have entered upon church membership through baptism in infancy, but only of all convinced believers, who have received baptism as adults in full consciousness of faith and who now display in their lives the palpable fruits of faith. Hence, the Anabaptists refused to have any part in inclusive state-churches of the kind that Zwingli established in Zurich and that were developed in other centers of the Reformation. Their beliefs impelled them, rather, to set themselves apart in free communities and conventicles of their own. Thus, they were the first to practice the complete separation of church and state. Since authentic faith is voluntary, the use of coercion in all religious matters is insupportable—a position that entailed the abandonment of the age-old requirement of religious uniformity as the guarantee of public peace and order. It was chiefly on account of this nonconformism that they were subjected to persecution. Their sectarianism was seen as an expression of hostility to ordered society, not least because they refused, on the basis of the Sermon on the Mount, to swear oaths and to undertake any form of military service—thereby undermining two fundaments of contemporary political life. In their own minds, however, they were simply carrying Zwingli's biblicism to its logical conclusion and were effecting nothing other than a restitution of primitive Christianity.

On March 7, 1526, the Zurich council ordered Anabaptists drowned, in cruel parody of their belief. This punishment was eventually inflicted on four persons by the Zurich magistracy. The first Anabaptist martyr in the canton was Felix Manz, who was drowned in the River Limmat on January 5, 1527. Grebel escaped a similar fate only because he had died of the plague shortly before.

Meanwhile, in Waldshut, Hubmaier was gathering a large Anabaptist community, and he was even more successful in propagating his opinions by pen. In his view, the Bible was the sole law of the church, and according to the scriptural test the proper order of Christian development was the proclamation of the word, repentance, faith, baptism, and works—the last indicating a life lived with the Bible as its law. Waldshut, however, was soon involved in the peasant revolt and shared the collapse of that movement. Hubmaier had to flee, and the city was once more Catholic. Imprisoned and tortured in Zurich, he fled to Augsburg and then to Moravia, where he propagated the Anabaptist movement with much success.

These persecutions had the effect of spreading the Anabaptist propaganda throughout Germany, Switzerland, and the Netherlands. The movement soon assumed sizable proportions. In the still Catholic parts of the empire, the Anabaptist propaganda practically superseded the Lutheran. The territorial rulers at first tried to check the movement by issuing mandates against it, just as the Zurich authorities had done. Ferdinand of Austria was the first to do so, and his brother, Emperor Charles V, supported him (January 4, 1528). But despite the fact that many became victims of these prohibitions, the Anabaptists became more and more troublesome. Hence, at the diets of Speyer (1529) and of Augsburg (1530), the assembled German estates, both Roman Catholic and Protestant, applied the old Roman law against heresy to them. Henceforth, membership in any Anabaptist group was punishable by death. In Roman Catholic territories, particularly Austria and Bavaria, this newly proclaimed law was executed with utmost severity. In evangelical lands, Anabaptists were treated not as heretics but as seditionists. If they were unwilling to conform to the established ecclesiastical order, they were given the chance to emigrate. If they refused to do so and continued to profess their faith publicly, they were regarded as disturbers of the peace and punished by imprisonment or death. Only in Hesse, Württemberg, and Strassburg were such "blood-judgments" avoided.

The expansion of the Anabaptist movement issued from three centers: Switzerland, south Germany, and Moravia. When Zurich began to suppress it, the earliest converts carried their faith to other parts of Switzerland. Anabaptist congregations were soon established throughout the high valleys of the Alps. That they grew rapidly is indicated by the actions which the public authorities took against them. On December 29, 1529, the city council of Basel arranged for a public discussion between evangelical preachers and spokesmen of the Anabaptists, and then it prohibited the movement. In 1530–1531, three believers were executed and many others were exiled. In the canton of Bern, a long disputation with twenty-three Anabaptists took place on July 1–9, 1532, at Zofingen. Here, too, the result was public condemnation. Between 1529 and 1571, forty public executions of Anabaptists took place. The situation was similar in the cantons of Appenzell and Aargau. The chief center of Swiss Anabaptist propaganda became Graubünden and the region around Chur. There Blaurock was the main agent, until he was burned at the stake in Tyrol on September 6, 1529. For a long time, Anabaptist groups continued to be active there, as is shown by the correspondence of Bullinger, Zwingli's successor, who was one of their most ardent literary antagonists. From Graubünden, the sectarians were in constant touch with friends and sympathizers in Moravia and upper Italy, especially Venice.

The chief German center was at first Augsburg. Here Hubmaier baptized Hans Denck (1500?–1527) in May 1526. He, in turn, shortly thereafter baptized Hans Hut, who proceeded to organize a congregation that grew rapidly, winning even members of patrician families (in March 1527, he baptized Eitelhans Langenmantel). Hut subsequently undertook missionary work in Moravia and Austria. On August 20, 1527, a large number of south German and Austrian Anabaptists held a synod (later called the "Martyrs' Synod") at Augsburg, under Denck's leadership, chiefly in order to deal with Hut's apocalyptic ideas. Hut regarded himself a divinely sent apostle or prophet, affirming that the persecution of the saints would be followed by the destruction of the empire by the Turks. Thereafter, the saints would be gathered and all priests and unworthy rulers would be destroyed by them, whereupon Christ would visibly rule on earth. The majority rejected these views and Hut promised to keep them to himself. The synod decided to send out evangelists to Austria, Bavaria, Worms, Basel, and Zurich. Almost all who went out shortly thereafter suffered the death of martyrs. Hut was imprisoned in Augsburg in September 1527. He died from burns sustained when his cell accidentally caught fire. His body was publicly burned the next day, December 7, 1527.

At the close of the synod, Denck went to Ulm and Nürnberg and then to Basel, where his career was ended by death from the plague. He was one of the most remarkable figures among the sectarians. Humanistically trained, he had become the rector of the famous school of St. Sebald in Nürnberg in 1524. He was widely respected, but he was dismissed from his post in 1525 when he expressed sympathy with the spiritualist ideas of Müntzer. Although he then joined the Anabaptists in Augsburg, probably attracted to them by their ideal of Christian discipleship and by their pacifism, his views really were those of a contemplative spiritualist. Before his death, he seems to have severed all connection with the sectarians, because he rejected all visible organization of the Christian life. His faith rested on an inner light superior to all Scripture. In Christ he saw the highest example of love, and he held that the Christian may live without sin. His writings, marked by a beautiful Christian inwardness, show that his thinking was nourished by the traditions of Christian Platonism and mysticism, especially the "German theology."

From 1526 until 1533, Strassburg was a main German center of Anabaptist activity. An indigenous Anabaptist community had existed there since 1524, founded by the gardener and lay preacher Clement Ziegler. From 1526, there was also a refugee community of Swiss Brethren led by Michael Sattler, a former monk of St. Peter's in Freiburg, who had been expelled from Zurich in late 1525. He was everywhere highly regarded because of his deep Christian piety. The Strassburg preachers, especially Capito and Matthew Zell and his wife Catherine, were friendly to him. Bucer, who saw in the Anabaptists a threat to a unified Christian community, felt that persuasion might convince them to give up their sectarianism. In the fall of 1526, Denck came to Strassburg from Augsburg and won a considerable following. On December 22, Bucer engaged him in a public discussion. As a result, Denck was ordered from the city by the council, and he then made his way to Worms and thence back to Augsburg, where in 1527 he attended the aforementioned Martyrs' Synod. Shortly after Denck's banishment from Strassburg, Sattler left voluntarily. On February 24, 1527, he presided over a synod of Swiss Brethren at Schleitheim, convened in order to combat aberrations from within the movement (the "false brethren") and to resist challenges from without. The synod adopted seven articles of faith, probably written in the main by Sattler.

This "Schleitheim Confession"—a representative statement of evangelical Anabaptist convictions—affirms believers' baptism. The church is regarded as composed only of local associations of baptized regenerated Christians, united as the body of Christ by the common observance of the Lord's Supper; its sole weapon is excommunication (the ban). Absolute rejection of all "self-indulgence of the flesh" is demanded—a disavowal of the antinomian excesses that had appeared on the fringes of the Anabaptist movement. The forms of worship of the Roman, Lutheran, and Zwinglian churches are explicitly repudiated as unchristian. The duties of the pastor—who is now regarded as a settled minister rather than an itinerant evangelist—are clearly defined: his chief responsibility is to read the Scriptures and to teach and admonish in their light; he leads in prayer; and he presides at the Supper, in which connection he disciplines and bans in the name of the church. While civil government is held to be a necessity in this imperfect world, Christians must have no share in it; they should not bear arms or use coercion, nor should they take any form of oath. These were ideas which were to be represented in varying degrees by later Baptists, Congregationalists, and Quakers, and through them to have a profound influence on the religious development of England and America. Soon after the synod, Sattler was apprehended by the Austrian authorities and burned at the stake in Rottenburg, on May 21, 1527. His wife was drowned eight days later.

The Anabaptist community in Strassburg continued to flourish, chiefly because ever new leaders sought refuge in the city. For a time, the outstanding figure was Pilgram Marpeck (1495?–1556), an engineer from the Tyrol who arrived in Strassburg in September 1528 and gained many followers. Between December 1531 and January 1532, he engaged in numerous oral and written exchanges with Bucer, and soon thereafter he was ordered to leave the city. For a time he made his headquarters in Ulm, but in 1544 he took up permanent residence in Augsburg. Marpeck was the chief formulator and organizer of south German Anabaptism from the early 1530s until his death in 1556. He defended his convictions in voluminous writings, which only recently have again come to light. In them, he sought to justify the Anabaptist doctrines on the basis of a strict biblicism. In 1542, he wrote a kind of catechism under the title *Vermahnung oder Taufbüchlein,* and during the last years of his life he completed his massive "Reply" (*Verantwortung*) to Kaspar Schwenckfeld (1489–1561), the leading spokesman of an evangelical spiritualism among the radical reformers.

From 1533 on, the Strassburg magistracy took stricter measures against the sectarians (imprisonment), chiefly because Melchior Hofmann (1495?–1543) instilled in them a fanatical apocalypticism. This strange man, born in Swabia and a tanner by profession, had been won over to Luther's cause by 1522. He then became a lay preacher, expounding his confused evangelical ideas during his travels through the Baltic countries, Sweden, Denmark, and Holstein, constantly in conflict with Roman Catholic priests and Lutheran preachers. In June of 1529, he came to Strassburg and there made contact with the Anabaptists, in time submitting to rebaptism. Their opposition to the territorial churches led him to develop an original form of apocalypticism, which he expounded in connection with the book of Revelation. He now regarded Luther, "the apostle of the beginnings," as a Judas. Proclaiming himself "apostle of the end," he predicted that the Last Judgment would come in 1533, spreading throughout the world from Strassburg. After his arrest had been ordered, he escaped from the city in April 1530 and headed for Emden, in East Friesland, where he succeeded in gaining many followers (the "Melchiorites"), filling them with the expectation that they would triumph while all others would perish by violence. When these followers experienced severe persecution at the hands of the Catholic authorities, Hofmann ordered the suspension of believers' baptism for two years (the *Stillstand*), and he returned to Strassburg, the "new Jerusalem," late in 1531. Renewed orders for his arrest forced him to withdraw from the city early in 1532. He returned yet again in the spring of 1533, and in May he was subjected to two judicial hearings and placed under mild arrest. He was then examined at length by Bucer during the course of the important Strassburg synod of June 10–13, 1533. Hofmann was sentenced to life imprisonment, and he stayed in confinement until his death in 1543, adhering to his convictions and his hope until the very end.

In Moravia, the Anabaptists found a refuge on the large estates of the lords of Liechtenstein. In July 1526, Balthasar Hubmaier came to Nikolsburg and succeeded in transforming the local German-speaking Lutheran parish into an Anabaptist congregation. Thousands of refugees, chiefly from Upper Austria and the Tyrol, now settled there and formed several communities. Hubmaier was their chief leader—the "patriarch of Nikolsburg"—until, in July 1527, he was surrendered to the Austrian authorities. He was burned at the stake in Vienna, on March 10, 1528, and a few days later his wife was drowned in the Danube.

There were many divisions among the Moravian Brethren. In May 1527, a major disputation took place in Nikolsburg between Hans Hut and Hubmaier. Hut expected the end of the world by 1528 and defended a radical pacifism. Hubmaier argued for the need of civil government and advocated submission to it, including the duty to render military service and to pay taxes. He also held that a magistrate can be expressly Christian, and he countenanced both a just war and capital punishment. (In all these respects, Hubmaier was not a typical Anabaptist.) The Brethren who sided with Hut left Nikolsburg, under the leadership of Jacob Wiedemann, and founded a community at Austerlitz, in 1528, which grew rapidly and soon comprised several thousand members. They developed a communistic social order (community of goods), one of the few groups among the Anabaptists to do so, although it was a standard charge against them, wherever they were persecuted, that they all had abolished private property.

The Austerlitz community in turn suffered many divisions and separations, until the Tyrolean apostle Jacob Hutter firmly organized them, from 1529 until 1536, when he too suffered a martyr's death by burning at Innsbruck. However, he left the "Hutterite Brethren" economically so well organized that they were able to maintain their communistic order until 1622 in Moravia, until 1685 in Hungary, and from 1770 until 1874 in the Ukraine. Between 1874 and 1877, groups of Hutterites migrated from Russia to North America and established communities in South Dakota and Montana and, later, in Manitoba and Alberta. The immediate successors of Hutter were a line of energetic bishops: Hans Amon (1536–1542); Peter Riedemann (1542–1556), who in 1540 wrote a notable book entitled *Rechenschaft* (Account of Faith), which is one of the most impressive statements of Anabaptist faith and practice; Peter Walpot (1556–1578); and Claus Braidl (1585–1611).

At the end of the Reformation period, Anabaptist congregations existed, apart from Moravia, in Switzerland, the Palatinate, the Netherlands, Friesland, Prussia, and Poland. In the thirties and forties, they had been active also in

Hesse and Saxony, the chief Lutheran territories. Philip of Hesse sought to deal leniently with them. Those among them who were apprehended and refused to recant were banished. The severest penalty imposed upon them was imprisonment. The most radical leader among the Hessian Anabaptists was Melchior Rink, a former associate of Thomas Müntzer. He spent the last ten years of his life in prison, where he died around 1540. One of the most remarkable events in Hessian Anabaptist history was a discussion which Bucer held with some of them on order of the landgrave, October 30–November 2, 1538, in Marburg. This was one of the very rare occasions when Anabaptist believers felt compelled to yield to the arguments of their opponents and to give up their faith.

In Saxony and Thuringia, the Anabaptists were vigorously suppressed. Luther, who unjustly identified them with Karlstadt and Müntzer, the *"Schwärmer,"* regarded them as perverters of the faith, because in his opinion they believed in salvation by works and by the law. The ordinarily peaceful Melanchthon was their fierce enemy. He believed them to be enemies of the social-political order. The chief Saxon literary opponent of the Anabaptists was Justus Menius. Between 1530 and 1544, he published several writings against them, the chief ones being "Doctrine and Secret of the Anabaptists, Refuted from the Bible" and "Of the Spirit of the Anabaptists."

It is a most remarkable fact that all later works of the established reformers —for example, Luther's "Commentary on the Epistle to the Galatians," first published in 1535, and Calvin's "Institutes"—expounded the evangelical faith on the one hand in opposition to Roman Catholicism and on the other by way of a contrast to the Anabaptists.

Chapter 5

German Protestantism Established

THE SUCCESSFUL CONCLUSION of the war with France and the reconciliation with Pope Clement VII had left Charles V free, in 1529, to intervene at last effectively in German affairs. The Reichstag of Speyer, in that year, alarmed at Lutheran progress and the spread of the Anabaptists, and conscious of the change in the emperor's prospects, had forbidden further Lutheran advance and practically ordered the restoration of Roman episcopal authority. The Lutheran minority had protested. In this threatening situation, Philip of Hesse had attempted to secure a defensive league of all German and Swiss evangelical forces. The chief hindrances were the doctrinal differences between the two parties, but Philip hoped that they might be adjusted by a conference. Though Luther was opposed, consent was at last secured, and on October 1, 1529, Luther and Melanchthon met face to face with Zwingli and Oecolampadius in Philip's castle at Marburg. With them were a number of the lesser leaders of both parties. Bucer and other representatives of Strassburg also attended. During the succeeding days, the "Marburg colloquy" ran its course.

Luther was somewhat suspicious of the soundness of the Swiss on the doctrines of the Trinity and original sin, but the real point of difference was Christ's bodily presence in the Supper (see VI:3). Luther held firmly to the literal interpretation of the words, "This is my body." Zwingli presented the familiar argument that a physical body could not be in two places at the same time. Agreement was impossible. Zwingli urged that both parties were, after all, Christian brethren, but Luther declared himself unwilling to accept anyone as a brother in faith unless there was unanimity in all basic articles of faith. His famous remark, "You have a different spirit than we," was addressed not to Zwingli, however, but to Bucer.

Yet Philip would not let hope of a protective league thus vanish, and he persuaded Luther to draw up fifteen articles of faith. On fourteen there was agreement. The fifteenth had to do with the Supper, and here there was unanimity on all points save the one as to the nature of Christ's presence, where the differences were stated. Both sides now signed these Marburg Articles, with the provision that "each side should show Christian love to the other side insofar as conscience will permit."[1] Luther and Zwingli each left Marburg with the conviction that he was the victor. The Lutherans now were resolved to enter any political confederation only on the basis of confessional agreement. The "Schwabach Articles," prepared by Luther and the Wittenbergers, probably in June 1529, and used by them at Marburg, were to serve such a purpose. The elector of Saxony and the margrave of Brandenburg-Ansbach now made these articles the test of political confederacy. Only Nürnberg of the great south German cities would accept them. The defensive league of evangelicals which Philip had envisioned was impossible. The Lutherans and the Swiss each went their own way, for the division was permanent.

In January 1530, the emperor sent the call from Italy, where he was about to be crowned by the pope, for a Reichstag to meet in Augsburg. With unexpected friendliness, while declaring the adjustment of religious differences to be a main object of its meeting, he promised a kindly hearing for all representations. When the Reichstag convened on June 20, the Lutherans were ready with their confession. The Wittenberg theologians had already, in the summer of 1529, drawn up a statement of their beliefs in the Schwabach Articles, and their

[1] *Luther's Works,* 38:88.

criticisms of the Roman practices were set forth in the so-called Torgau Articles of May 1530. Drawing on these two earlier sets of articles, Melanchthon drafted the Augsburg Confession, which was read in German to the emperor and the estates on June 25, 1530. It bore the approving signatures of Elector John of Saxony, his heir, John Frederick, Margrave George of Brandenburg-Ansbach, Dukes Ernst and Franz of Brunswick-Lüneburg, Landgrave Philip of Hesse, Wolfgang of Anhalt, and the representatives of Nürnberg and Reutlingen. Before the close of the Reichstag, the cities of Heilbronn, Kempten, Weissenburg, and Windsheim also signified their approval of this confession.

The Augsburg Confession was chiefly the work of the mild and conciliatory Melanchthon. Though kept closely informed of the course of events, Luther, under imperial ban, could not come to Augsburg and remained at the nearby Coburg castle. Melanchthon continued to revise the confession up until the day of its presentation; in the interest of healing the schism, he made numerous concessions to the Romanists. Yet it was not wholly conciliation that moved him. His purpose was to show that the Lutherans, far from introducing a new doctrine, had departed in no vital and essential respect from the Catholic church, or even from the Roman church, as revealed in its earlier writing. That agreement is expressly affirmed, and many ancient heresies are carefully repudiated by name. On the other hand, Zwinglian and Anabaptist positions are energetically rejected. The sole authority of Scripture is nowhere explicitly asserted. The papacy is nowhere categorically condemned. The universal priesthood of believers, transubstantiation, and purgatory are not mentioned. Yet Melanchthon gave a thoroughly evangelical tone to the confession as a whole. Justification by grace through faith alone is made the touchstone of all doctrine and life. The evangelical marks of the church are made evident. Invocation of saints, the sacrifice of the Mass, denial of the cup to the laity, monastic vows, and prescribed fasting are rejected. Luther declared himself well pleased with the confession, though noting that he could not "step so gently and softly" as Melanchthon.

Zwingli sent to the emperor a vigorous expression of his views, the *Ratio Fidei,* which received scanty attention. A more significant event was the presentation on July 9 of a joint confession by the Zwinglian-inclined south German cities (Strassburg, Constance, Memmingen, and Lindau)—the *Confessio Tetrapolitana,* largely from the pen of Bucer, in which a position intermediate between that of the Zwinglians and the Lutherans was maintained.

The papal legate, Cardinal Campeggio, advised that the Augsburg Confession be examined by the Roman theologians present in Augsburg. This the emperor approved; chief among the experts was Luther's old opponent, Eck. The Catholic theologians prepared a confutation, which was sent back to them by the emperor and Catholic princes as too polemic, and it was at last presented to the Reichstag in much milder form on August 3.

The emperor still hoped for reconciliation, and conference committees were now appointed; but their work was vain—a result to which Luther's firmness largely contributed. The Catholic majority voiced the decision of the Reichstag that the Lutherans had been duly confuted; that they be given until April 15, 1531, to conform; that combined action be taken against Zwinglians and Anabaptists; and that a general council be sought within a year to remedy abuses in the church. The reconstituted imperial law court should decide cases of secularization on terms favorable to the Catholics. The Lutherans protested, declared their confession not refuted, and called attention to Melanchthon's *Apology,* or defense of the confession, which he had hastily prepared in response to the Roman confutation. This *Apology,* rewritten and published the next year (1531), became one of the classics of Lutheranism.

Such a situation demanded defensive union. Even Luther, who had held it a sin to oppose the emperor by force, now was willing to leave the rightfulness of such resistance to the decision of the lawyers. At Christmas, the Lutheran princes assembled in Schmalkalden and laid the foundations of a league. Bucer, whose union efforts were unremitting, persuaded Strassburg to accept the Augsburg Confession—an example that had great effect on other south German cities. Finally, on February 27, 1531, the Schmalkaldic league was completed. Electoral Saxony, Hesse, Brunswick, Anhalt, and Mansfeld stood in defensive agreement with the cities of Strassburg, Constance, Ulm, Reutlingen, Memmingen, Lindau, Isny, Biberach, Magdeburg, Bremen, and Lübeck.

Strong as the position of Charles V appeared on the surface, it was not so in reality in the face of this united opposition. The Catholic princes were jealous of one another and of the emperor. The pope feared a general council. France was still to be reckoned with. The fateful April 15, 1531, therefore passed without the threatened result. In October 1531, the death of Zwingli at Kappel deprived Swiss evangelicalism of its vigorous head and inclined south German Protestantism to closer union with Wittenberg. The spring of 1532 brought a new danger to the empire as a whole, that of Turkish invasion. In 1529, the Turks had besieged Vienna, and before their advance religious differences had, in a measure, to give way. On July 23, 1532, the emperor and the Schmalkaldic league agreed to the Peace of Nürnberg, by which all existing lawsuits over secularizations would be dropped and peace was assured to the Protestants until a general council, or at least a new Reichstag, should assemble. Shortly thereafter, Charles V left Germany for Italy and Spain, not to return until 1541. Though still precarious, the Protestant position had greatly improved, and the consolidation of the churches in Protestant territories went on apace.

Lutheranism now rapidly won new territories as well. By 1534, Anhalt-Dessau, Mecklenburg, Pomerania, Hanover, Frankfurt, and Augsburg had been gained. Of even greater moment was the conquest for Lutheranism of the duchy of Württemberg, in 1534, by Philip of Hesse, from the emperor's brother, Ferdinand, and the restoration of its Duke Ulrich—a result greatly aided by Catholic jealousy of the house of Hapsburg. The death of Duke George, in 1539, was followed by the triumph of Lutheranism in ducal Saxony, and the same year a cautious adhesion to the Reformation was won from electoral Brandenburg.

This spread of Lutheranism was aided by a tragic episode of 1534–1535 that robbed Anabaptism of its influence in Germany—the Münster revolution. The Anabaptists in general were peaceable people, of great religious earnestness and patient endurance in persecution; the Münster episode was not typical of them as a whole. Yet there had arisen among them such radical leaders as Melchior Hofmann (see VI:4). The decade from 1525 to 1535, moreover, was one during which the pacifistic evangelical Anabaptists were not yet clearly distinguished from the revolutionary Anabaptists and from such revolutionary spiritualists as Thomas Müntzer.

Hofmann's apocalyptic preaching had won many disciples in the Netherlands. One of these, Jan Mathys, a baker of Haarlem, gave himself forth as the prophet Enoch, and he soon spread a fanatical propaganda widely through the Netherlands and adjacent parts of Germany. Unlike Hofmann, who would wait for the power of God to bring in the new age, Mathys would inaugurate it by force. Popular democratic discontent gave him his opportunity.

Nowhere was this new teaching more influential than in Münster in Westphalia, where Bernt Rothmann, the Lutheran preacher, had adopted Anabaptist views in January 1534. Mathys arrived soon after, and so did a tailor of Leyden, Jan (John) Bockelson. It was now assumed that God had rejected Strassburg by reason of its unbelief and had chosen Münster as the new Jerusalem in its stead. Radicals flocked there in large numbers. In February 1534, they gained mastery of the city and drove out those who would not accept the new order. The bishop of Münster laid siege to the city. Mathys was killed in a sortie in April. John of Leyden was proclaimed king. Polygamy was established, community of goods was enforced, opponents were slaughtered. The struggle, though heroically maintained, was hopeless. The bishop, aided by Catholic and Lutheran troops, captured the city on June 25, 1535, and the surviving leaders were put to death by extreme torture. For German Anabaptism, it was a catastrophe. Such fanaticism was popularly supposed to be characteristic of the Anabaptists, and the name became one of ignominy.

The Anabaptist movement was rescued, and purged of its radicalism, through the leadership of the wise, peace-loving Menno Simons (1496–1561). A native of Friesland, he had been ordained to the Catholic priesthood in 1524. In spite of growing doubts about infant baptism and transubstantiation, he remained in his priestly office until January 1536, when the debacle at Münster awakened his pastoral concern for the misguided Melchiorites, the "sheep which have no shepherd," and he now assumed the Anabaptist ministry, to which he was ordained in early 1537. Menno devoted his efforts to rehabilitating the movement and gathering its scattered remnants in the north. He and his followers, called "Mennonites," succeeded in establishing congregations in the Netherlands and northern Germany, in which the earlier form of evangelical Anabaptism was restored. His basic teachings were summarized in his influential *Foundation of Christian Doctrine* of 1540.

Charles V had never ceased to hope and to labor for a general council by which the divisions of the church could be healed and reforms effected. From Clement VII he could not secure it. Paul III (1534–1549) succeeded Clement, and, though by no means a single-hearted religious man, he had much more appreciation than Clement of the gravity of the situation caused by the Reformation. He promptly appointed as cardinals Gasparo Contarini (1483–1542), Jacopo Sadoleto (1477–1547), Reginald Pole (1500–1558), and Gian Pietro Caraffa (1476–1559), all men desirous of reform in morals, education, and administration, who laid before the pope, in 1537, extensive recommendations for ecclesiastical betterment. Paul III actually called a general council to meet at Mantua in May 1537, but a new war (1536–1538) between Charles V and Francis I made its assembly impossible. Charles had set his heart on the council, and had demanded of the Protestant leaders assembled at Schmalkalden in February 1537 that they agree to take part. The imperial order put them in a difficult position. They had long talked of a general council, and Luther had appealed to such a gathering as early as 1518. But they saw clearly that they would be outvoted, and they refused to participate in a council in an Italian city, and under the dominance of the pope.

Charles realized that a council was impossible for the time, and he now tried the experiment of reunion discussions. Such were held in Hagenau in June 1540; in Worms, later in the same year; and in Regensburg (Ratisbon) in April 1541. Melanchthon, Bucer, Calvin, and others took part in one or more of the colloquies on the Protestant side; Eck, Contarini, and others on the Catholic. For a time it appeared that agreement could be reached on the central issue of justification, but the prospect proved illusory. The differences were too profound for compromise.

It was evident to Charles V that the pathway of conciliation was blocked and that the Protestants would not share in a general council unless their military and political strength could first be reduced. The union of Protestant interests was no less a peril to imperial authority in political concerns. It was breaking what little unity was left in the empire. Charles, therefore, slowly and with many hesitations, developed his great plan. He would have a general council in being. He would so reduce the strength of Protestantism by force that the Protestants would accept the council as a final arbiter; and the council could then make such minor concessions as would be needful for the reunion of Christendom, and correct such abuses as Protestants and Catholics alike condemned. To realize this plan, he had to secure three preliminary results. He must, if possible, divide the Schmalkaldic league politically; he must ward off the danger of French attack; and the ever-threatening peril of Turkish invasion must, for a time at least, be minimized.

The emperor's purpose of dividing the Protestants was aided by one of the most curious episodes of Reformation history. Landgrave Philip of Hesse, the political genius of the Schmalkaldic league, though sacrificial in devotion to the Protestant cause, was, like most princes of that age, a man of low personal morality. Though married early to a daughter of Duke George of Saxony, who bore him seven children, he had no affection for her. His constant adulteries troubled his conscience to the extent that from 1526 to 1539 he partook of the Lord's Supper but once. He grew anxious about his soul's salvation, without improving his conduct. For some years, he entertained the thought of a second marriage as a solution to his perplexities. The Old Testament worthies had practiced polygamy and the New Testament nowhere expressly forbad it. Why should not he? This reasoning was strengthened by acquaintance with Margarete von der Saale, an attractive seventeen-year-old daughter of a lady of his sister's little court. The mother's consent was won on condition that the elector, the duke of Saxony, and some others should be informed that it was to be a real marriage. Philip's first wife also consented. Philip was fully persuaded of the rightfulness of the step, but for the sake of public opinion he desired the approval of the Wittenberg theologians. He therefore sent for Bucer of Strassburg, whom he partly persuaded, partly frightened with threats of seeking dispensation from the emperor or the pope, into full support of his plan. Bucer now became Philip's messenger to Luther and Melanchthon, and to the Saxon elector, though the matter was presented as an abstract question, without mention of the person with whom marriage was contemplated.

On December 10, 1539, Luther and Melanchthon gave their opinion. They declared polygamy to be contrary to the primal law of creation, which Christ had approved; but in cases of great distress of conscience, which they believed to be true in Philip's instance, law and precedent are transcended, though not annulled, and exceptions may be made for pastoral reasons. It would be better for Philip to marry as he proposed, therefore, than to live in adultery or to seek divorce. Luther insisted, however, that private advice given in the confessional could not be made into universally valid law; hence, the marriage must be kept absolutely secret, so that the second wife should appear to be a concubine. On March 4, 1540, Philip married Margarete in what, though private, cannot be called secret fashion. A court preacher performed the ceremony, and Melanchthon, Bucer, and a representative of the Saxon elector were among the witnesses. Though an attempt was made to keep the affair secret, that soon proved impossible. Luther advised "a good strong lie," but Philip resolutely declared, "I will not lie."

The scandal was great, both among Protestants and Catholics. Bigamy was prohibited by imperial law. A bigamous prince had to forfeit his crown. The other evangelical princes would not defend Philip's act or promise protection from its results. The emperor saw in it his opportunity. On June 13, 1541, he secured an agreement from Philip, as the price of no worse consequences, that the landgrave would neither personally, nor as representative of the Schmalkaldic league, make alliances with foreign states. The hopeful negotiations with France, England, Denmark, and Sweden, which would have greatly strengthened the power of the Schmalkaldic league against the emperor, had to be dropped. Worse than that, Philip had to promise not to aid the evangelically inclined Duke William of Cleves, whose rights over Gelders Charles disputed. Since the Saxon elector was William's brother-in-law, and determined to support him, a serious division in the Schmalkaldic league was the result, which showed its disastrous consequences when the emperor defeated William in 1543, took Gelders permanently into his own possession, and forced the duke to repudiate Lutheranism. This defeat rendered abortive a hopeful attempt to secure the archbishopric of Cologne for the Protestant cause.

Fortune favored Charles in the rest of his program as well. Paul III was persuaded to call a general council to meet at Trent, a town then belonging to the empire, but practically Italian, in 1542. War caused a postponement, but in December 1545, it at last began its sessions, which were to run a checkered and interrupted course until 1563 (see VI:11). At the Reichstag in Speyer in 1544, Charles used vague assurances to secure the passive support of the Protestants, and some active assistance, for the wars against France and the Turks. The campaign against France was brief. The emperor, in alliance with Henry VIII of England, pushed on nearly to Paris, when, to Henry's dismay and to the surprise of Europe, he made peace with the French king, apparently without gaining any of the advantages in his grasp. In fact, however, he had eliminated the possibility of French aid to German Protestantism for the immediate future. The Turks, busy with a war in Persia and beset by internal quarrels, made a truce with the emperor in October 1545. All events seemed to have worked together for his blow against German Protestantism.

It was while prospects were thus darkening for the Protestant cause that Luther died on a visit to Eisleben, the town in which he was born, on February 18, 1546. His last years had been far from happy. His health had long been wretched. The quarrels of the reformers, to which he had contributed his full share, distressed him. Above all, the failure of the pure preaching of justification by faith alone to transform the social, civic, and political life about him greatly grieved him. He was comforted by a happy home life and by full confidence in his gospel. The work which he had begun had passed far beyond the power of any one man, however gifted, to control. He was no longer needed; but his memory must always be that of one of the titanic figures in the history of the church.

Before entering on the war, Charles succeeded yet further in dividing the Protestants. Ducal Saxony had become fully Protestant under Duke Henry (1539–1541), but his short reign had been followed by the accession of his young son, Moritz (1541–1553). Of great political abilities, Moritz was a character difficult to estimate, because in an age dominated by professed religious motives, he cared nothing for the religious questions involved and everything for his own political advancement. Though son-in-law of Philip of Hesse and cousin of Elector John Frederick of Saxony (1532–1547), Moritz had quarreled with the elector and was not on very good terms with Philip. The emperor now, in June 1546, secured his support secretly, by the promise of the transfer to Moritz of his cousin's electoral dignity in case of successful war, and other important concessions. Thus at length prepared, the emperor declared John Frederick and Philip under ban for disloyalty to the empire—Charles desired the war to seem political rather than religious. The Schmalkaldic league had made no adequate preparations. Moritz's defection was a great blow. Though at first the campaign went well for the Protestants, electoral Saxony was crushed at the battle of Mühlberg on the Elbe, on April 24, 1547, in which John Frederick was captured. Philip saw the cause was hopeless and surrendered himself to the emperor. Both princes were placed under arrest. Moritz received the electoral title and half his cousin's territories. Politically, Protestantism was crushed. Only a few northern cities, of which Magdeburg was the chief, and a few minor northern princes still offered resistance.

Yet, curiously enough, the emperor who had just crushed Protestantism politically had never been on worse terms with the pope. Paul III had aided him early in the war, but had drawn back, fearing that the successful emperor might grow too powerful. Charles wished the Council of Trent to move slowly until he had the Protestants ready to recognize it. He would have it make such minor concessions as might then seem to allay Protestant prejudice. The pope wished the council to define Catholic faith quickly and go home. It had already, by April 1546, made agreement difficult by defining tradition to be a source of authority in matters of faith. To minimize imperial influence, the pope declared the council adjourned to Bologna in March 1547. This transfer the emperor refused to recognize and declined to be bound by the Tridentine decisions already framed. Some method of religious agreement was needed under which Germany could live until the healing of the schism which Charles expected from the council. The emperor therefore had an ecclesiastical commission draft an "Interim." This was essentially Roman, although granting the cup to the laity, permitting clerical marriage, and limiting slightly the powers of the pope. The Catholic princes refused to accept it as applying to them. The pope denounced it. Charles had to abandon hope of making it a temporary reunion program, but he secured its adoption on June 30, 1548, by the Reichstag in Augsburg as applying to the Protestants. This Augsburg Interim he now proceeded to enforce with a heavy hand. Moritz of Saxony had done such service to the imperial cause that a modification, known as the Leipzig Interim, was allowed in his lands. It asserted justification by faith alone but reestablished much of Roman usage and government. To it Melanchthon reluctantly consented, regarding its Roman parts as "adiaphora," or nonessential matter. For this weakness he was bitterly denounced by the defiant Lutherans of unconquered Magdeburg, notably by Matthias Flacius Illyricus (1520–1575) and Nikolaus von Amsdorf (1483–1565). Flacius, especially, did much to maintain popular Lutheranism in this dark time; but the bitter quarrels among Lutheran theologians had begun.

Superficially, it seemed that Charles was nearing his goal. Pope Paul III died in 1549 and was succeeded by Julius III (1550–1555), who proved more tractable to the emperor. The new pope summoned the council to meet once more in Trent, and several Protestant theologians actually appeared before it in 1552. In fact, Germany was profoundly disaffected, the Protestants groaning under the imperial yoke, and the Catholic princes jealous of Charles's increased power and of his apparently successful attempt to secure the imperial succession ultimately for his son, later to be famous as Philip II of Spain. Moritz of Saxony was dissatisfied that his father-in-law, Philip of Hesse, was still in chains; he felt, moreover, that he had secured all he could hope for from the emperor and, since his subjects were strongly Lutheran, that only as a Lutheran leader against the emperor could his boundless ambition be further gratified.

The reduction of defiant Magdeburg, in the name of the emperor, gave Moritz excuse for raising an army. Agreements were made with the Lutheran princes of northern Germany. The aid of King Henry II of France (1547–1559) was secured at the price of the surrender to France of the German border cities of Metz, Toul, and Verdun. Charles knew of the plot but took no adequate steps to meet it. The blow came swiftly. Henry invaded Lorraine and took the coveted cities. Moritz marched rapidly southward, almost capturing the emperor, who escaped by flight from Innsbruck. The whole structure that Charles had so laboriously built up toppled like a house of cards, not so much before the power of Lutheranism as before the territorial independence of the princes. On August 2, 1552, the Treaty of Passau brought the brief struggle to an end.

The Treaty of Passau referred the settlement of the religious question to the next Reichstag. That body was not able to meet until three years later. Princely rivalries distracted Germany. Moritz lost his life in warfare against the lawless Margrave Albrecht of Brandenburg in 1553. Charles, conscientiously unwilling to tolerate Protestantism but seeing such toleration inevitable, handed over full authority to treat to his brother Ferdinand, though the latter was not to be chosen emperor until 1558. The Reichstag met in Augsburg. The Lutherans demanded full rights, and possession of all ecclesiastical property theretofore or thereafter secularized. They asked toleration for Lutherans in all Catholic territories, but proposed to grant none to Catholics in their own. These extreme demands were naturally resisted, and the result was a compromise, the Peace of Augsburg, of September 25, 1555. By its provisions, equal rights in the empire were extended to Catholics and Lutherans—no other evangelicals were recognized. Each lay prince should determine which of the two faiths should be professed in his territory—no choice was allowed his subjects—and but one faith should be permitted in a given territory. This was the principle usually defined as *cuius regio, eius religio*. Regarding ecclesiastical territories and properties, agreement was reached that 1552, the time of the Treaty of Passau, should be the norm. All then in Lutheran possession should so remain, but a Catholic spiritual ruler turning Protestant thereafter would forfeit his position and holdings, thus insuring to the Catholics continued possession of the spiritual territories not lost by 1552. This was the "ecclesiastical reservation." Persons dissatisfied with the faith of the territory where they lived were allowed full right of unhindered emigration and a fair sale of their goods—a great advance over punishment for heresy, but the choice was only between Catholicism and Lutheranism.

So Lutheranism acquired full legal establishment. Germany was permanently divided. Luther's dream of a purification of the whole German church had vanished, but so had the Catholic conception of visible unity.

The older leaders were rapidly passing. Luther had died nine years before. Melanchthon died in 1560. Charles V resigned his possession of the Netherlands in 1555 and of Spain a year later, and he retired to San Yuste in Spain, where he died in 1558.

Chapter 6

The Scandinavian Lands

Denmark, Norway, and Sweden had been nominally united under the Danish throne since the Union of Kalmar was formed in 1397. Since 1460, Schleswig-Holstein had also been under Danish control. In none of these lands was the crown powerful. In all, the great ecclesiastics were unpopular, were oppressive, were often foreign-born, and were in rivalry with the nobility. In no part of Europe was the Reformation to be more thoroughly political. At the dawn of the Reformation, the Danish throne was occupied by Christian II (1513–1523), an enlightened despot of Renaissance sympathies. He believed the chief evil of his kingdom lay in the power wielded by the nobles and ecclesiastics. Intent upon limiting the power of the bishops by introducing the Lutheran movement, he secured in 1520 a Lutheran preacher in the person of Martin Reinhard, who proved ineffective. Karlstadt served as an adviser for a brief time in 1521. Partially at least through the latter's counsels, a law of 1521 forbad appeals to Rome, reformed the monasteries, limited the authority of the bishops, and permitted clerical marriage. Opposition prevented its enforcement, however, and the hostility of the privileged classes, which Christian II had roused in many ways, drove him from his throne in 1523. His uncle, Frederick I (1523–1533), was made king in his stead.

Though inclined to Lutheranism, Frederick was forced by the parties that had put him on the throne to promise to respect the privileges of the nobles and prevent any heretical preaching. Yet Lutheranism penetrated the land. In Hans Tausen (1494–1561), a one-time monk and former Wittenberg student, it found a preacher of popular power from 1524 onward. By 1526, King Frederick took Tausen under protection as his chaplain. The same year the king took the confirmation of the appointment of bishops into his own hands. A law of 1527 enacted this into statute, granted toleration to Lutherans, and permitted priestly marriage. These changes were aided by the support of a large section of the nobility won by the king's countenance of their attacks on ecclesiastical rights and property. In 1530, the same year as the Augsburg Confession, Tausen and his associates laid before the Danish parliament the "Forty-three Copenhagen Articles." The year before, a Danish translation of the New Testament (by Christian Petersen) had been published and was eagerly read. No decision was reached at the time, but Lutheranism made increasing progress until Frederick's demise in 1533.

The death of Frederick left all in confusion. Of his two sons, most of the nobles favored the elder, Christian III (1536–1559), a determined Lutheran, while the bishops supported the younger, Hans. A distracting period of civil conflict followed, from which Christian III emerged the victor. The bishops were imprisoned, their authority was abolished, and church property was confiscated for the crown. Christian now called on Wittenberg for aid. Johannes Bugenhagen, Luther's associate, came in 1537, and seven new Lutheran superintendents, named by the king but retaining the title "bishops," were ordained by the German reformer, who was himself superintendent of Wittenberg. The Danish church was now reorganized in fully Lutheran fashion.

Norway was a separate kingdom, but by the terms of the Union of Kalmar it was under the Danish king. The Reformation scarcely touched the land during the reign of Frederick I. In the struggles that followed, Archbishop Olaf Engelbrektssön of Trondheim, the head of the Norwegian clergy, led a temporizing party and fled the land on Christian III's success. Norway was made a Danish province, and the new Danish Lutheran religious constitution was nominally introduced. Effective preaching and superintendence in Norway was, however, largely neglected by Christian III, with the result that the Reformation, imposed from above, was long in taking effective possession of popular sympathies.

Much the same story may be told of the faraway Danish possession, Iceland. The Reformation traveled slowly thither. Bishop Gisser Einarsen of Skálholt, educated in Germany and of Lutheran sympathies, began a conservative Lutheran reformation in 1540, and the same year an Icelandic New Testament was published. In 1548, a strong Catholic reaction, led by Bishop Jon Aresen of Holum, attempted to throw off the Danish yoke. By 1554, the rebellion had been suppressed and Lutheranism forcibly established, though long with little popular approval.

The reformation of Sweden was largely bound up with a national struggle for independence. Christian II of Denmark had found bitter resistance to his efforts to secure the Swedish throne. His chief supporter was Gustaf Trolle, archbishop of Uppsala. Gustaf procured from Pope Leo X approval of the excommunication of his opponents, though that opposition was purely political. In 1520, Christian II captured Stockholm and followed his coronation as king of Sweden by a deed of the utmost cruelty. He had the unsuspecting nobles, gathered for the ceremony, executed, nominally as excommunicated heretics. The Stockholm Bath of Blood roused Sweden to a rebellion against Christian II, which soon found an energetic leader in Gustavus Vasa. The Danes were expelled and, in 1523, Gustavus was chosen king (1523–1560).

Meanwhile, Lutheran doctrine was being taught by two brothers who had returned in 1519 from studies in Wittenberg—Olaf (1493?–1552) and Lars Petersson (1499–1573), who labored in Strengnäs, and soon won the archdeacon, Lars Andersson (1482–1552). By 1524, King Gustavus was definitely favoring these leaders. Andersson (Laurentius Andreae) became his chancellor, and Lars Petersson professor of theology in Uppsala. On December 27, 1524, a discussion in Uppsala between Olaf Petersson (Olavus Petri), now preacher in Stockholm, and the Roman champion, Peter Galle, seemed a victory for the reformers. In 1526, Olavus Petri published his Swedish translation of the New Testament (with the help of his brother, he translated also the Old Testament, and the whole Swedish Bible was issued in 1541). Part of the support of the king was probably due to religious conviction, but no small portion was owing to the dire poverty of the crown, which Gustavus thought could be remedied only by extensive confiscation of church property.

In June 1527, the king struck the decisive blow. At the Diet of Västerås, Gustavus demanded and obtained from the bishops, by threat of resignation, the assignment to the crown of all episcopal or monastic property which the king should deem unnecessary for proper religious work, the surrender to the nobles of all tax-exempt lands that they had donated to the church since 1454, and the preaching of the "pure word of God." Provision was made for the reconstitution of the church under royal authority. Though master of the Swedish church, and now possessor of a large part of its property, Gustavus used his power in religion conservatively. Most of the old prelates left the land. The bishop's office was retained, though its holders were now appointed by the king. New bishops were consecrated, with the old rites, in 1528, at the hands of Bishop Peter Magni, of Västerås, who had received his office in Catholic days, and through whom apostolic succession was deemed to be transmitted to the Swedish Lutheran episcopate. Further reform measures were taken by the synod of Örebro in 1529. A Swedish service was issued in 1529, and the "Swedish Mass" in 1531. In the latter year, Lars Petersson was made archbishop of Uppsala, though without jurisdiction over his fellow bishops—that remained in the hands of the king. Most of the lower clergy accepted the Reformation and kept their places, but such changes by royal power were far from winning immediate popular approval, and it was long before Sweden became thoroughly evangelical. Its type of Lutheranism in doctrine and practice was strongly conservative. The reform of Sweden carried with it that of Finland, then part of the Swedish monarchy. The Swedish church was to pass through a period of Romanizing reaction, especially under the reign of Gustavus's son, John III (1568–1592); but this ended in 1593, when the synod of Uppsala formally adopted the Augsburg Confession as the creed of Sweden.

Chapter 7

The Reformation in French Switzerland and Geneva before Calvin

ZURICH was the strongest power in northern Switzerland, Bern in the south. The latter was in constant rivalry with the dukes of Savoy, especially for possession of French-speaking territories in the neighborhood of Lake Geneva (the Pays de Vaud). The acceptance of Protestantism by Bern on February 7, 1528, led the Bernese government to further the introduction of the Reformation into these dependent districts by encouraging the preaching of Guillaume Farel (1489–1565). Farel was a native of Gap, in the French province of Dauphiné. As a student in Paris, he came under the influence of the humanistic reformer Jacques LeFèvre d'Étaples, and by 1521 he was preaching under the auspices of the moderately reformist Guillaume Briçonnet, bishop of Meaux. An orator of fiery vehemence, intense feeling, and stentorian voice, he soon was so preaching the Reformation that he had to leave France. By 1524, he was urging the reform in Basel, but his impetuosity led to his expulsion. The next months were a period of wandering, during which he visited Strassburg and won Bucer's friendship.

In November 1526, Farel's work in French-speaking Switzerland began in Aigle, where the Bernese government defended him, though not yet itself fully committed to the Reformation. With the complete victory of the newer views in Bern, Farel's work quickened. In 1528, Aigle, Ollon, and Bex adopted the Reformation, destroying images and ending the Mass. After vainly attempting to convert Lausanne, he began a stormy attack in Neuchâtel, in November 1529, which ultimately secured the victory of the Reformation there. Morat followed in 1530; but in Grandson and Orbe, which, like Morat, were under the joint overlordship of Protestant Bern and Catholic Freiburg, he could secure only the toleration of both forms of worship. In September 1532, he was invited to attend a synod of the Waldenses in the high valleys of the Cottian Alps, which resulted in the acceptance of the Reformation by a large section of the body. The Waldenses were subsequently served by Farel's companion, Pierre Olivétan (1506?–1538), whose French translation of the Bible was published in 1535.

In October 1532, Farel made an unsuccessful attempt to preach reform in Geneva. Everywhere, he faced opposition with undaunted courage, sometimes at the risk of life and at the cost of bodily injury, but no one could be indifferent in his strenuous presence. His chief collaborator was the mild-mannered Pierre Viret (1511–1571), the future reformer of Lausanne.

Geneva, at Farel's coming in 1532, was engaged in consolidating a political revolution that had transpired during the 1520s. Situated on a main trade route across the Alps, Geneva was an energetic business community, keenly alive to its interests and liberties and of rather easygoing moral standards, in spite of its numerous monasteries and ecclesiastical foundations. Genevan liberties were being maintained with great difficulty against the encroachments of the powerful duke of Savoy. At the beginning of the sixteenth century, three powers shared the government of the city and its adjacent villages: the bishop; his *vicedominus,* or temporal administrator; and the citizens, who met annually in a General Assembly and chose four "syndics" and a treasurer. Besides the General Assembly, the citizens were ruled by a Little Council of 25, of which the syndics of the year and of the year previous were members. Questions of larger policy were discussed by a Council of Sixty appointed by the Little Council, and in 1527 a Council of Two Hundred was added, its membership including the Little Council and 175 others chosen by that inner body. The aggressive dukes of Savoy had appointed the *vicedominus* since 1290 and had controlled the bishopric since 1444. The struggle was therefore one for freedom by the citizens against Savoyard interests, represented by the bishop and the *vicedominus.*

In 1519, a revolutionary group of citizens, known as the Eidguenots (*Eidgenossen,* "confederates"), who favored a Swiss alliance against the Savoyards, entered into alliance with Catholic Freiburg; but Duke Charles III of Savoy won the upper hand, and the Genevan patriot Philibert Berthelier was beheaded. In 1525, the revolutionaries renewed the effort, under the leadership of a Genevan exile, Besançon Hugues. In 1526, Hugues negotiated an alliance with Bern and Freiburg. The General Assembly ratified the treaties and Geneva was now securely in the Swiss political camp. In August 1527, the bishop, Pierre de la Baume, fled the city, which he could not control, and fully attached himself to the Savoyard interests. The authority of the *vicedominus* was repudiated, and the traditional powers of the bishop and his deputy were assumed by the Little Council and the newly formed Council of Two Hundred. Duke Charles attacked the plucky city, but Bern and Freiburg came to its aid in October 1530, and the duke had to pledge to respect Genevan liberties.

Thus far, there was little sympathy with the Reformation in Geneva, but Bern was eager to see the evangelical faith established there. Bern, in effect, intended to control Geneva's religious destiny as well as its political revolution. Protestant agitation did not begin in the city until June 1532, when placards appeared criticizing papal claims and presenting reformed doctrine. Yet Geneva's other ally, Freiburg, was staunchly Catholic, and the Genevan government disowned any leanings toward "Lutheranism."

In October 1532, as has been noted, Farel and his associates, Pierre Olivétan and Antoine Saunier, came to Geneva, under Bernese auspices; but they could gain no foothold in the city and were obliged to flee. A month later, Farel sent his colleague Antoine Froment (1508?–1581) to Geneva, where he found a place as a schoolmaster and propagated reformed doctrine in that guise. Froment gathered a large following and on January 1, 1533, was emboldened to preach publicly, though the result was a riot and he had to flee. By the following Easter, there were enough Protestants to dare to observe the Lord's Supper. In December, Farel returned, and in January 1534 he and Pierre Viret, whom Bern had also dispatched, held a public disputation with Guy Furbity, a learned Dominican friar and the chief local defender of the Roman cause. The debate ended in a riot. In March, Farel and his followers, by now a sizable group, seized a monastic chapel for preaching purposes.

The Genevan government was in a difficult position. Its Catholic ally, Freiburg, demanded that Farel be silenced. Its Protestant ally, Bern, insisted on the arrest of Furbity, who had accused the Genevans of being Bernese pawns. The magistracy punished Furbity and broke off relations with Freiburg; Bern thus became Geneva's only Swiss ally. The exiled bishop, acting in concert with the duke of Savoy, now raised troops to attack the city and laid it under siege. His action greatly strengthened Genevan opposition, and gave Farel and Viret opportunity to advance their cause by linking Protestantism with Geneva's struggle for independence. On October 1, 1534, the Little Council declared the bishopric vacant, albeit Geneva was still far from being predominantly Protestant.

In early 1535, Farel prevailed upon the syndics to authorize a public disputation between the Protestant leaders and the Catholic clergy, but the bishop forbad the latter to participate. Farel and Viret easily prevailed over the few Roman spokesmen at the debate, which lasted most of June. Emboldened by their success, they seized the church of La Madeleine on July 23, 1535, and on August 8 took over the cathedral of St. Pierre. Iconoclastic mobs pillaged the churches. On August 10, the city government suspended the Mass. The canons of the cathedral and most of the priests, nuns, and friars left the city. On May 31, 1536, the work was completed by a vote of the General Assembly, expressing its determination "to live in this holy evangelical law and Word of God" and to abolish "all Masses and other papal ceremonies and abuses, images and idols."

Meanwhile, the bishop and the duke of Savoy had been pressing Geneva sorely. For a time, Bern refused to send assistance, but it at last, in January 1536, came powerfully to Geneva's aid. Geneva saw the peril from Savoy removed, only to be threatened with Bernese control. Yet the courage of its citizens was equal to the situation, and on August 7, 1536, Bern acknowledged Genevan independence; the city was now free. It had accepted Protestantism, albeit more for political than for religious reasons, and its religious institutions all had to be formed anew. Farel felt himself unequal to the task, and in July 1536, he constrained a young French acquaintance passing through the city to stay and aid in the work. The friend was John Calvin.

Chapter 8

John Calvin

J OHN CALVIN was born in Noyon, a city of Picardy about sixty miles northeast of Paris, on July 10, 1509. His father, Gérard Cauvin, was a self-made man who had risen to the posts of secretary of the Noyon bishopric and attorney for its cathedral chapter. He also enjoyed the friendship of the powerful noble family of Hangest, which gave two bishops to Noyon in his lifetime. John Calvin was intimately acquainted with the younger members of this family, and this friendship earned for him a familiarity with the ways of polite society such as few of the reformers enjoyed. Through the father's influence, the son received the income from certain ecclesiastical posts in and near Noyon, the earliest being assigned him before the age of twelve. He was never ordained into the Roman priesthood.

Thus provided with means, Calvin entered the University of Paris in 1523, studying first at the Collège de la Marche, where for a time he enjoyed the remarkable instruction in Latin given by Mathurin Cordier (1479-1564), to whom he owed the foundation of his brilliant literary style. He then pursued his arts course at the semimonastic Collège de Montaigu, where he was trained in Aristotelian philosophy and nominalist logic, possibly by the Scottish theologian John Major (1470–1550), and graduated as master of arts in 1528. While a student, he formed a number of warm friendships, notably with the family of Guillaume Cop, the king's physician and an eager supporter of humanism.

Calvin's father had intended him for theology and the priesthood, but by 1527 Gérard Cauvin was at odds with the Noyon cathedral chapter and determined that his son should study law. Hence, Calvin now went to the University of Orléans, where Pierre de l'Estoile (1480–1537) enjoyed great fame as a jurist, and in 1529 to the University of Bourges, to listen to Andrea Alciati (1493–1550). Humanistic interests strongly attracted him, and at both Orléans and Bourges he began the study of Greek with the aid of Melchior Wolmar (1496–1561), a German scholar who remained his lifelong friend. He took his licentiate in law; but the death of his father, in 1531, left Calvin his own master, and he now continued his Greek studies and began Hebrew at the humanist Collège de France, which King Francis I had founded at Paris in 1530. At this time, Calvin was hard at work on his first book, the *Commentary on Seneca's Treatise on Clemency,* which was published in April 1532. It was a marvel of erudition and was marked no less by a profound sense of moral values, but in it Calvin displayed no interest in the religious questions of the age. He was simply an earnest, deeply learned humanist.

Yet it was not for lack of opportunity to know the new doctrines that Calvin was still untouched by the struggle. His tutor Wolmar was committed to the Reformation, as was Calvin's kinsman and fellow student at Orléans, Pierre Robert (1506?–1538), known as Olivétan because his studiousness led him to burn the midnight oil. Humanism, moreover, had promoted in France, as elsewhere, a reformist movement. Its most conspicuous representative had long been Jacques LeFèvre d'Étaples (1460?–1536), who for some years after 1507 made his home in the monastery of St.-Germain des Prés at Paris, gathering about him a notable group of disciples. Among his pupils were Guillaume Briçonnet (1470–1534), the active leader of the French reformist party and from 1516 bishop of Meaux; Guillaume Budé (1467–1540), to whose persuasions the establishment of the Collège de France by royal authority was due; François Vatable (?–1547), Calvin's teacher of Hebrew there; Gérard Roussel (1500?–1550), Calvin's friend, later bishop of Oléron; Louis de Berquin (1490–1529), who died at the stake for his Protestantism; and Guillaume Farel, whose fiery reformist career has already been noted. With these men—none of whom, save the two last mentioned, broke with the Roman church—many humanists sympathized, such as the family of Cop, whose friendship Calvin enjoyed in Paris. They had powerful support in King Francis's gifted and popular sister, Marguerite d'Angoulême (1492–1549), from 1527 queen of Navarre, who was ultimately an unavowed Protestant. Luther's books early penetrated into France and were read in this circle. Few of its members realized, however, the gravity of the situation or were ready to pay the full price of reform, but there was no ignorance of what the main questions were in the scholarly circle in which Calvin moved. They had not as yet become important for him.

At some point between the publication of his first book in the spring of 1532 and the spring of 1534, Calvin experienced what he later called a "sudden conversion." (Some scholars date this conversion as early as 1528–1530, in which case it would be necessary to explain the absence of anything distinctly Protestant in Calvin's commentary on Seneca.) Of its circumstances nothing is known for certain, but at its center was the conviction that God, in his secret providence, had turned Calvin's course in a new direction and was subduing and making teachable his hardened heart. Religion henceforth held first place in Calvin's thoughts. Whether he even yet thought of breaking with the Roman church is doubtful. He was still a member of the humanistic circle in Paris, of which Roussel and his intimate friend Nicholas Cop were leaders.

On November 1, 1533, Cop delivered an inaugural address as newly elected rector of the University of Paris, in which he pleaded for reform, using language borrowed from Erasmus and Luther. That Calvin wrote the oration, as has often been alleged, is improbable, but he undoubtedly sympathized with its sentiments. The commotion aroused was great, and King Francis enjoined action against the "Lutherans." Cop and Calvin had to seek safety, which Calvin found in the home of a friend, Louis du Tillet, in Angoulême. Calvin's sense of the necessity of separation from the older communion was now rapidly developing, and it led him to go to Noyon to resign his benefices on May 4, 1534. But France was becoming too perilous for him, especially after Antoine Marcourt posted his injudicious theses against the Mass in October 1534, and in January 1535, Calvin was safely in Protestant Basel.

Marcourt's placards had been followed by a sharp renewal of persecution, one of the victims being Calvin's friend, the Parisian merchant, Estienne de la Forge. Francis I was coquetting for the aid of German Protestants against Charles V, and so, to explain French persecutions, he issued a public letter in February 1535, charging French Protestantism with anarchistic aims such as no government could bear. Calvin felt that he must defend his slandered fellow believers. He therefore rapidly completed a work begun in Angoulême, and published it in March 1536 as his *Institutes of the Christian Religion,* prefacing it with a letter to the French King. The letter is one of the literary masterpieces of the Reformation age. Courteous and dignified, it is a tremendously forceful presentation of the Protestant position and defense of its holders against the royal slanders. No French Protestant had yet spoken with such clearness, restraint, and power, and with it its author of twenty-six years stepped at once into the leadership of French Protestantism.

The *Institutes,* designed as a catechism of six chapters, were eventually to grow into a monumental treatise of eighty chapters in Calvin's final edition of 1559, but even in 1536 they were already the most orderly and systematic popular presentation of doctrine and of the Christian life that the Reformation produced. As a second-generation reformer, Calvin did not purport to be a "creative" thinker. He readily acknowledged that his work could not have been done without Luther's antecedent labors. He appropriated Luther's conception of justification by faith and of the sacraments as seals of God's promises. He derived much from Bucer, notably his emphasis on the glory of God as that for which all things are created, on predestination as a doctrine of Christian confidence, and on the consequences of divine election as a strenuous endeavor for a life of conformity to the will of God. But all is systematized and clarified with a skill that was Calvin's own.

The highest human knowledge, Calvin taught, is that of God and of ourselves. Enough comes by nature, through the testimony of the conscience, to leave us without excuse, but adequate saving knowledge is given only in the Scriptures, which the witness of the Spirit in the heart of the believing reader attests as the very voice of God. These divine oracles teach that God is good and is the source of all goodness everywhere. Obedience to God's will is the primal human duty. As originally created, man was good and capable of obeying God's will, but he lost goodness and power alike in Adam's fall, and is now, of himself, absolutely incapable of goodness. Hence, no human work is meritorious before God, and all persons are in a state of ruin meriting only damnation. From this helpless and hopeless condition, some are undeservedly rescued through the work of Christ. He paid the penalty due for the sins of those in whose behalf he died; yet the offer and reception of this satisfaction was a free act on God's part, so that its cause is God's love.

All that Christ has wrought is unavailing unless it becomes one's personal possession. This appropriation is effected by the Holy Spirit, who works when, how, and where he will, creating repentance and faith—a faith which, as with Luther, is a vital union between the believer and Christ. This new life of faith is salvation, but it is salvation unto righteousness. That believers now perform works pleasing to God is proof that they have entered into lively union with Christ. "We are justified not without works, yet not by works."[1] Calvin thus left room for a conception of "works" as strenuous as any advanced by the Roman church, though very different in relation to the accomplishment of salvation. The standard set before Christians is the law of God, as contained in the Scriptures, not as a basis of their salvation but as an expression of that will of God which they, as people already saved, will strive to fulfill. This emphasis on the law as the guide of Christian life was peculiarly Calvin's own. It has made Calvinism always insistent on character, though in Calvin's conception one is saved to character rather than by character. The Christian life is nourished, above all, by prayer.

[1] *Institutes*, 3.16.1 (edition of 1559). (Cf. J. T. McNeill, ed., and F. L. Battles, trans. *Calvin: Institutes of the Christian Religion*, 2 vols. [Philadelphia, 1960].)

Since all good is of God, and sinners are unable to initiate or resist their conversion, it follows that the reason some are saved and others are lost is the divine choice—election and reprobation. It is absurd to seek a reason for that choice beyond the all-determining will of God. For Calvin, however, election (predestination) was never a matter of speculation but always a doctrine of Christian comfort. That God had a plan of salvation for a person, individually, was an unshakable rock of confidence, not only for one convinced of his own unworthiness, but for one surrounded by opposing forces even if they were those of priests and kings. It made the believer a fellow laborer with God in the accomplishment of God's will.

Three institutions have been divinely established by which the Christian life is maintained: the church, the sacraments, and civil government. In the last analysis, the church consists of "all the elect of God";[2] but it also properly denotes "the whole body of mankind . . . who profess to worship one God and Christ."[3] Yet there is no true church "where lying and falsehood have gained ascendancy."[4] The New Testament recognizes as church officers only pastors, teachers, elders, and deacons, who enter on their charges with the assent of the congregation that they serve. Their "call" is twofold, the secret inclination from God and the "approbation of the people." Calvin thus gave to the congregation a voice in the choice of its officers, though circumstances at Geneva were to compel him to regard that voice there as expressed by the city government. Similarly, Calvin claimed for the church full and independent jurisdiction in discipline up to the point of excommunication. Further it could not go; but it was a retention of a freedom which all the other leaders of the Reformation had abandoned to state supervision. Civil government has, however, the divinely appointed task of fostering the church, protecting it from false doctrine, and punishing offenders for whose crimes excommunication is insufficient.

Calvin recognized only two sacraments—baptism and the Lord's Supper. Regarding the burning question of Christ's presence in the Supper, he stood, like Bucer, partway between Luther and Zwingli, nearer the Swiss reformer in form and to the German in spirit. Like Zwingli, he denied any physical presence of Christ; yet he asserted in the clearest terms a real, though spiritual, presence received by faith. "Christ, out of the substance of his flesh, breathes life into our souls, indeed, pours forth his own life into us, though the real flesh of Christ does not enter us."[5]

Upon publication of the *Institutes* in the spring of 1536, Calvin made a brief visit to the court of Ferrara, in Italy, doubtless hoping to advance the evangelical cause with his liberal-minded and hospitable countrywoman, Duchess Renée. His stay was short, and a brief visit to France followed, to settle his business affairs and to proceed to Strassburg with his brother and sister. The

[2] Ibid., 4.1.2.   [3] Ibid., 4.1.7.   [4] Ibid., 4.2.1.   [5] Ibid., 4.17.32.

perils of war forced them to make a detour to Geneva in July 1536, and there Farel's fiery exhortation, as has been seen (see VI:7), induced Calvin to remain.

Calvin's work in Geneva began very modestly, as a lecturer on the Bible. He was not appointed one of the preachers till a year later. Over Farel, however, he exercised great influence. Their first joint work was to aid the Bernese ministers and civil authorities in the effective establishment of the Reformation throughout Vaud and in Lausanne, which had just come under Bernese control. In Lausanne, Pierre Viret was appointed pastor, an office which he was to hold till 1559. With him Calvin was to enjoy close friendship. Calvin and Farel now undertook to accomplish three results in Geneva itself. In January 1537, they laid before the Little Council a series of recommendations from Calvin's pen. These proposed monthly administration of the Lord's Supper. For better preparation, the city government should appoint "certain persons of good life" for each quarter of the city, who, in connection with the ministers, might report the unworthy to the church for discipline up to excommunication. This was Calvin's first attempt to make Geneva a model community and likewise to assert the independence of the church in its own sphere. A second effort was the adoption of a catechism composed by Calvin, and a third the imposition on each citizen of a creed, probably written by Farel. These recommendations the Little Council adopted with considerable modification.

The success of Calvin's work was soon threatened. He and Farel were unjustly charged with Arianism by Pierre Caroli, then a minister at Lausanne. They vindicated their orthodoxy, but not until great publicity had been given the matter. The new discipline and the demand for individual assent to the new creed soon aroused bitter opposition in Geneva. This was strong enough to secure a vote of the Council of Two Hundred, in January 1538, that the Supper should be refused to no one, thus destroying Calvin's system of discipline. The next month, the opposition won the city election and determined to force the issue. The Bernese liturgy differed somewhat from that now established in Geneva. Bern had long wished it adopted in Geneva, and the opposition secured a vote that it be used. Calvin and Farel regarded the differences between Bernese and Genevan usage as of slight importance, but an imposition by civil authority, without consulting the ministers, they viewed as robbing the church of all freedom. Calvin and Farel refused compliance, and on April 23, 1538, they were banished. Their work in Geneva seemed to have ended in total failure.

After a vain attempt at restoration to Geneva by the intervention of Swiss Protestant authorities, Farel found a pastorate in Neuchâtel, which was thenceforth to be his home; and Calvin, at Bucer's invitation, a refuge in Strassburg. The three years Calvin spent there were in many ways the happiest of his life. He was pastor of a church of French refugees and lecturer on theology. He was honored by the city and made one of its representatives in Charles V's reunion debates between Protestants and Catholics, gaining thereby the friendship of

Melanchthon and other German reformers. In 1540, he married Idelette de Bure, who was to be his faithful companion until her death in 1549. And also while in Strassburg, he found time to write not merely an enlarged edition of the *Institutes,* but also his *Commentary on Romans,* the beginning of a series that put him in the front rank of Reformation exegetes, and his brilliant *Reply to Sadoleto,* a masterly vindication of Protestant principles.

Meanwhile, a political revolution occurred in Geneva for which Calvin was in no way responsible. The party that had secured his banishment made a disastrous treaty with Bern in 1539, which resulted in its overthrow the next year and the condemnation of the negotiators as traitors. The party friendly to Calvin was once more in power, and its leaders sought his return. He was persuaded, although with difficulty, and on September 13, 1541, he was once more in Geneva, practically on his own terms.

Calvin promptly secured the adoption of his new constitution for the Genevan church, the *Ecclesiastical Ordinances,* now far more definite than the recommendations accepted in 1537. In spite of his successful return, however, he could not have them quite all that he wished. The *Ordinances* declared that Christ has instituted in his church the four offices of pastor, teacher, elder, and deacon, and they defined the duties of each. Pastors were to meet weekly for public discussion, examination of ministerial candidates, and exegesis, in what was popularly known as the Congregation (*Congrégation*). The teachers, or doctors, were responsible for instructing believers in true doctrine and for staffing the Genevan school system, which Calvin deemed essential to the religious training of the city. To the deacons were assigned the care of the poor and the supervision of the hospital. The elders were the heart of Calvin's system. They were twelve laymen, chosen by the Little Council, two from among its own members, four from the Sixty, and six from the Two Hundred, and under the presidency of one of the syndics. They, together with the ministers (who in 1542 numbered only nine), made up the Consistory (*Consistoire*), which was to meet every Thursday and was charged with ecclesiastical discipline. They could, if need be, excommunicate the unrepentant; beyond that, if the offense demanded, they were to refer the case to the civil authorities. No right seemed to Calvin so vital to the independence of the church as this of excommunication, and for none was he compelled so to struggle, until its final establishment in 1555.

In addition to the *Ordinances,* Calvin prepared a new and much more effective catechism, and he introduced a liturgy based on that of his French congregation in Strassburg, which, in turn, was essentially a translation of the liturgy generally in use in that German city. In formulating it for Genevan use, Calvin made a good many modifications to meet Genevan customs or prejudices. It exhibited a felicitous union of fixed and free prayer. (Calvin had none of that hostility toward fixed forms which his spiritual descendants in Great Britain and America afterward manifested.) The liturgy also gave a central place to congregational singing. Calvin himself preferred a weekly celebration of the Lord's Supper, and the *Ordinances* proposed at least a monthly celebration, but the council set the number at four times a year.

Under Calvin's guidance—he held no other office than that of one of the ministers of the city, whose number had increased to nineteen by 1564—much was done for education and for improved trade, but all of Genevan life was under the constant and minute supervision of the Consistory. Calvin wished to make Geneva a model of a perfected Christian community. Its rigorous evangelicalism attracted refugees in large numbers, many of them individuals of position, learning, and wealth, principally from France, but also from Italy, the Netherlands, Scotland, and England. These soon became a very important factor in Genevan life. Calvin himself, and all his associated ministers, were foreigners. Opposition to his rule appeared practically from the first and by 1548 had grown very serious. It was made up of two elements: those to whom any discipline would have been irksome; and, much more formidable, those of old Genevan families who felt that Calvin, his fellow ministers, and the refugees were foreigners who were imposing an alien yoke on a city of heroic traditions of independence. The latter party, known as the Libertines, was under the leadership of the syndic Ami Perrin, formerly one of Calvin's staunchest supporters.

The period of sharpest struggle was from 1548 to 1555—from the time that some of the older inhabitants began to fear that they would be swamped politically by the refugees, until the refugees, almost all of whom were eager supporters of Calvin, achieved what had been dreaded: they made Calvin's position unshakable. Though constantly increasing in fame outside of Geneva, Calvin stood in imminent peril, throughout this period, of having his Genevan work overthrown.

The cases of conflict were many, but two stand out with special prominence. The first was that caused by Jerome Bolsec (?-1584), a former Carmelite friar at Paris, now a Protestant physician at Veigy, near Geneva. In a meeting of the Congregation, Bolsec charged Calvin with error in asserting predestination, namely, that his doctrine in effect made God the cause of sin. This was to attack the very foundation of Calvin's authority, for his sole hold on Geneva was as a trusted interpreter of the Scriptures. Calvin took Bolsec's charges before the city government in October 1551. The result was Bolsec's trial. The opinions of other Swiss governments were asked, and it was evident that they attached no such weight to predestination as did Calvin. It was with difficulty that Calvin procured Bolsec's banishment, and the episode led him to an even greater insistence on the vital importance of predestination as a Christian truth than heretofore. As for Bolsec, he ultimately returned to the Roman communion and avenged himself on Calvin's memory by a grossly slanderous biography.

Calvin was thus holding his power with difficulty, when in February 1553, the elections, which for some years had been fairly balanced, turned decidedly in favor of his opponents. His fall seemed inevitable, when he was rescued and put on the path to ultimate victory through his confrontation in Geneva with Michael Servetus (1511–1553), whose case forms the second of those here mentioned. Servetus was a Spaniard, almost the same age as Calvin, and undoubtedly a man of great, though erratic, genius. In 1531, he published his *De Trinitatis Erroribus* (On the Errors of the Trinity). Compelled to conceal his identity, he studied medicine at Paris under the name of Villeneuve and is reputed to have anticipated William Harvey's discovery of the circulation of the blood. He settled at Vienne in France, where he developed a large practice and became personal physician to the archbishop, but also worked secretly on his *Christianismi Restitutio* (Restitution of Christianity), which he published early in 1553. To his thinking, the Nicene doctrine of the Trinity, the Chalcedonian Christology, and infant baptism were the chief sources of the corruption of the church. As early as 1545, he had begun an exasperating correspondence with Calvin, whose *Institutes* he contemptuously criticized.

Servetus's identity and authorship were unmasked to the Roman ecclesiastical authorities in Lyons by Calvin's friend, Guillaume de Trie, who, a little later, supplied further proof obtained from Calvin himself. Servetus was condemned to be burned, though, before sentence was passed, he had escaped from prison in Vienne. For reasons hard to understand, he made his way to Geneva, and there he was arrested in August 1553. His condemnation now became a test of strength between Calvin and the opposition, which did not dare come out openly in defense of so notorious a heretic but made Calvin all the difficulties that it could. As for Servetus, he had much hope for a favorable issue; he demanded that Calvin be exiled and Calvin's goods adjudged to him. The trial ended in Servetus's conviction and death by fire on October 27, 1553. Though a few voices of protest were raised, notably that of Sebastian Castellio (1515–1563) of Basel, most people agreed with Melanchthon that it was "justly done." However odious the trial and its tragic end may seem in retrospect, for Calvin it was a great victory. It freed the Swiss churches from any imputation of unorthodoxy on the doctrine of the Trinity, while Calvin's opponents had ruined themselves by making difficult the punishment of one whom the general sentiment of that age condemned.

Calvin's improved status was soon apparent. The elections of 1554 were decidedly in his favor, those of 1555 yet more so. In January 1555, he secured permanent recognition of the right of the Consistory to proceed to excommunication without governmental interference. The now largely Calvinist government endeavored, the same year, to make its position secure by admitting a considerable number of the refugees to the franchise. A slight riot on the evening of May 16, 1555, begun by Calvin's opponents, was seized as the occasion of executing and banishing their leaders as traitors. Henceforth, the party favorable to Calvin was undisputed master of Geneva. Bern was still hostile, but in 1557 Emmanuel Philibert, duke of Savoy and victor for Spain over the French at St.-Quentin, was enabled to lay claim to his duchy, then mostly in possession of the French. This common danger to Bern and Geneva brought about a "perpetual alliance" between the two cities in January 1558, in which Geneva stood for the first time in full equality with its old ally. Thus relieved of the most pressing perils, at home and abroad, Calvin crowned his Genevan work by the foundation in 1559 of the "Genevan Academy"—in reality, as it has long since become, the University of Geneva. It became immediately the greatest center of theological instruction in the Reformed communions, as distinguished from the Lutheran, and the great seminary from which hundreds of ministers were sent forth not only to France but to the Netherlands, England, Scotland, Germany, and Italy.

Calvin's influence extended far beyond Geneva. Thanks to his *Institutes,* his pattern of church government in Geneva, his academy, his commentaries, and his constant correspondence, he molded the thought and inspired the ideals of the Protestantism of France, the Netherlands, Scotland, and the English Puritans. His influence penetrated Poland and Hungary, and before his death Calvinism was taking root in southwestern Germany. His system trained strong individuals, confident in their election to be fellow workers with God in the accomplishment of his will, courageous to do battle, insistent on character, and certain that God has given in the Scriptures the guide of all right human conduct and proper worship. The spiritual disciples of Calvin, in the most various lands, bore one common stamp. This was Calvin's work, a mastery of mind over mind, and certainly by the time of his death in Geneva, on May 27, 1564, he deserved the title of "the only international reformer."

Calvin left no successor of equal stature. The work had grown too large for any one person to direct. But in Geneva, and to a considerable extent in his labors beyond its borders, his mantle fell on the worthy shoulders of Theodore Beza (1519–1565), a man of more conciliatory spirit and gentler ways, but devoted to the same ideals.

Chapter 9

The English Reformation

THE HISTORY of the Reformation in England is the story of the gradual Protestantization of the English church and people, a process extending over the reigns of Henry VIII (1509–1547) and his three children and successors, Edward VI (1547–1553), Mary (1553–1558), and Elizabeth I (1558–1603). The immediate occasion, though not the sufficient cause, of the English Reformation was the "great question" of Henry's divorce from Catherine of Aragon, ultimately leading to the nation's severance from the Roman obedience and the drastic curtailment of the church's wealth and privileges. In this respect, the Reformation was largely an act of state, imposed from above by a willful king, his adroit ministers, and a pliable Parliament. At the same time, this political rebellion was abetted and eventually transformed by an indigenous movement of church reform and popular religious dissent that antedated the king's matrimonial problems and plans.

When Henry VIII began his reign, the church in England was beset by many evident weaknesses, both in structure and in personnel. The prelates were, on the whole, royal servants, appointed for their dedication and usefulness to the crown and because the emoluments of high church office made their appointment inexpensive for the royal treasury. By training they were primarily civil lawyers rather than theologians, a circumstance that helps to explain their virtual unanimity in following Henry when he broke with the papacy. The "careerism" of the bishops and higher clergy—their search for advancement and enrichment through royal patronage and civil service—naturally fostered the abuses of pluralism, absenteeism, and simony, and, more dangerously still, left the parishes in the hands of poorly educated and usually impecunious curates. While the parish clergy were thus ill equipped to carry out their vital pastoral functions of teaching and preaching, the monastic clergy, with some notable exceptions, had abandoned the strict observance of their rules and were no longer exemplary models for lay spirituality.

The early years of Henry's reign had witnessed a revival of Lollardy (see V:13), which sharpened and gave focus to powerful currents of anticlericalism abroad in the land. The laity deeply resented the church's heavy financial exactions and its coercive jurisdiction over their property as well as their souls. Neo-Lollardy and anticlericalism thus provided springboards for Protestantism, and so also did English humanism, with its insistent calls for ecclesiastical reform and its Bible-centered criticism of abuses. Humanism had come to England in the late fifteenth century and had found influential supporters among some of the higher clergy and in aristocratic and court circles. John Colet (1467?-1519), who in 1504 became dean of St. Paul's in London, had lectured at Oxford on the Pauline epistles in full humanistic spirit as early as 1496, and he refounded St. Paul's School in 1508. In 1512, he delivered a famous sermon to the Convocation of the Clergy, in which he censured "secular and worldly living in clerks and priests" and laid down a program of reform. The great Erasmus himself lectured at Cambridge during the years from 1511 to 1514, having first visited England in 1499 and again in 1506 and making many friends there, including John Fisher (1459?-1535), bishop of Rochester, and the famous Sir Thomas More (1478-1535).

The widespread hopes for a gradual "Erasmian" reform of the church and the commonwealth were soon to be shattered, however, by the infiltration into England of Luther's revolutionary writings, which were circulated as early as 1519-1520 and began to infect some of the younger university scholars as well as the merchants in London and other ports who carried on trade with north Germany. Beginning about 1520, a group of Cambridge scholars gathered at the White Horse Inn, dubbed "Little Germany," there to discuss the new doctrines. Among the interested disputants resident at Cambridge in the early 1520s were the leaders of the first generation of English Protestants: Robert Barnes (1495-1540), Thomas Bilney (1495?-1531), Hugh Latimer (1485?-1555), John Frith (1503?-1533), Miles Coverdale (1488-1568), Thomas Cranmer (1489-1556), Nicholas Ridley (1500?-1555), Matthew Parker (1504-1575), and perhaps also William Tyndale (1495?-1536)—five of them to become bishops and all but Coverdale and Parker to suffer martyrdom for their faith.

The most remarkable of these early Protestants was Tyndale, who died a martyr at Vilvorde, near Brussels. Having resolved about 1522 to translate the New Testament into English but finding no support for this project from Cuthbert Tunstall, bishop of London, he went to the Continent, visited Luther in 1524, and the next year published at Cologne and Worms a splendid translation based on the Greek text of Erasmus and also much indebted to Luther's German Bible. By 1526, copies of his translation were streaming into England, where the authorities made futile efforts to suppress it. It found an especially cordial reception in London, both among the merchants and among the numerous cells of Lollards who likewise advocated a strict "Bible religion." The confluence of "old Lollardy" and "new Lutheranism" virtually guaranteed the hostility of the leaders of the English church to Luther's teaching and to vernacular Bibles. Fisher and More, the realm's outstanding Erasmians, soon became the country's foremost anti-Lutherans. Yet, as will be seen, throughout the 1530s King Henry's own archbishop of Canterbury and his chief minister of state entertained strong sympathies with Lutheranism and continental Protestantism and took the lead in effecting a moderate Protestantization of the English church in spite of the king's growing conservatism and reactionary policies.

Henry VIII was a man of impressive intellectual abilities and executive force, well-read and always interested in Scholastic theology, sympathetic with humanism, popular with the mass of people, but egotistic, obstinate, and given to fitful acts of terror. In the early part of his reign, he had the aid of a superb diplomat, Thomas Wolsey (1474?–1530), who became a privy councilor in 1509, archbishop of York in 1514, and in 1515 was made lord chancellor by the king and cardinal by Pope Leo X. In 1518, the pope also made him a legate or special envoy of the Holy See. Wolsey thus exercised great power in both church and state, at the price, however, of tying his own fortunes and those of England ever more closely to the papacy. Henry, for his part, was a devoted son of the Holy See. When Luther's writings were circulated in England, their use was forbidden, and Henry published his *Assertion of the Seven Sacraments* against Luther in 1521, which won for him from Leo X the title "Defender of the Faith."

In 1509, Henry had married Catherine of Aragon, daughter of Ferdinand and Isabella of Spain, and widow, though the marriage had been one in name only, of his older brother, Arthur. A dispensation authorizing this marriage with a deceased brother's wife had been granted by Julius II in 1503. Six children were born of the union, but only one, Mary, survived infancy. By 1527, if not earlier, Henry was expressing religious scruples about the validity of his marriage, on the ground that Scripture (Lev. 20:21) expressly forbad marriage to a brother's widow. Henry's reasons, in any case, were not merely sensual. Had they been, he might well have been content with his mistresses. However, the War of the Roses had ended as recently as 1485, and the absence of a male and legitimate heir, should Henry die, would probably cause renewed civil war. Since it was not likely that Catherine would have further children, Henry wanted another wife.

Wolsey favored the king's divorce because he hoped Henry would marry a French princess and thus be drawn more firmly from the Spanish to the French side in continental politics. Henry, however, had other plans. Since 1525, he had become increasingly infatuated with Anne Boleyn, a lady of his court and sister of his mistress Mary Boleyn. A complicated negotiation followed, in which Wolsey made every effort to use his legatine powers to secure the king's divorce, while Catherine behaved with dignity and firmness, though she was treated with cruelty. An annulment of the marriage would probably have been secured from Pope Clement VII (1523–1534) had it not been for the course of European politics, which left Emperor Charles V victor in war and forced the pope into submission to the imperial policy (see VI:2). Charles was determined that Catherine, his aunt, should not be set aside. Henry, angered at Wolsey's lack of success in manipulating papal jurisdiction, dismissed him as lord chancellor in the summer of 1529. The great cardinal died on November 29, 1530, on the way to London to be tried for treason. Wolsey had been succeeded as chancellor in October 1529 by Thomas More, who immediately launched a campaign of persecution against suspected heretics, leading to the burning, among others, of Thomas Bilney and John Frith—the first Protestant martyrs in England.

Henry, still thwarted in securing his divorce, now thought well of a suggestion of Thomas Cranmer, then teaching at Cambridge and by this date strongly inclined to Protestantism, that the opinions of the European universities be sought. This was done in 1530, with only partial success; even antipapal Wittenberg upheld the legitimacy of the king's marriage to Catherine. Nevertheless, an enduring friendship was begun between the king and Cranmer that was to have momentous consequences.

Favorable action from the pope now being out of the question, Henry determined to rely on the national feeling of hostility to foreign rule, and on his own politics of menace, either to break with the papacy altogether or so to threaten papal control as to secure his wishes. In January 1531, he charged the whole body of clergy with breach of the old statute of *Praemunire* (1353) for having recognized Wolsey's authority as papal legate—an authority which Henry himself had recognized and approved. Not only did he extort a great sum as the price of pardon; he also secured the declaration by the convocations (of York and Canterbury) in which the clergy met that he was "sole protector and supreme head of the English church and clergy," to which the qualifying phrase "so far as the law of Christ allows" was added at the insistence of the clergy. Then, on May 15, 1532, following a petition to the king from the House of Commons for royal control of all ecclesiastical legislation, the convocations agreed reluctantly, in the so-called Submission of the Clergy, to make no new church laws without the king's permission and to refer all existing statutes for revision to a commission of clergy and laity approved by the king. The next day, Thomas More resigned his chancellorship. Later in 1532, Parliament passed an act forbidding the payment of all annates to Rome save with the king's consent.

In January 1533, Henry secretly married Anne Boleyn, now known to be pregnant. The following March, Parliament passed a key piece of legislation, the Act in Restraint of Appeals, which forbad all appeals to Rome in matters spiritual as well as temporal. This act virtually abolished papal authority in England. Meanwhile, Henry had used the conditional prohibition of annates to procure from Pope Clement VII confirmation of his appointment of Thomas Cranmer as archbishop of Canterbury. Cranmer was consecrated on March 30, 1533; on May 23, he held court and formally pronounced Henry's marriage to Catherine invalid, and on May 28 he declared the marriage to Anne Boleyn fully lawful. The new queen was crowned on June 1, and on September 7 she gave birth to a daughter, the princess Elizabeth.

While these events were occurring, Clement VII had prepared a bull threatening excommunication against Henry on July 11, 1533. Henry's answer was a series of statutes, enacted by Parliament in 1534, by which all payments to the pope were forbidden, all bishops were to be elected on the king's nomination, and all oaths of papal obedience, Roman licenses, and other recognition of papal authority done away with. In May 1534, the convocations formally abjured papal supremacy. On November 3, 1534, Parliament passed the famous Supremacy Act, by which Henry and his successors were declared "the only supreme head in earth of the Church of England," without qualifying clauses, and with full power to redress "heresies" and "abuses."[1] This act did not convey such spiritual rights as ordination and the administration of the sacraments, but in all else it practically put the king in place of the pope. The break with Rome was complete. Nor were these statutes in any way meaningless. In May 1535, a number of monks of one of the most respected orders in England, that of the Carthusians, or Charterhouse, were executed under circumstances of peculiar barbarity for denying the king's supremacy. In June and July, Bishop John Fisher and the ex-chancellor Sir Thomas More were beheaded for the same offense. Of the higher clergy, however, only Fisher accepted martyrdom; the rest were surprisingly compliant in following the king's lead.

The mastermind behind most of the crucial legislation enacted by the so-called Reformation Parliament of 1529–1536 was Thomas Cromwell (1485?–1540), a man of humble origin, a soldier, banker, and merchant by turns, of whom Wolsey had made much use as a business and parliamentary agent. By 1531, Cromwell was a member of the privy council; in 1534, he became the king's principal secretary; and in 1535, Henry appointed him viceregent and vicar general for ecclesiastical affairs. Cromwell's views on church and state owed much to Marsiglio of Padua's *Defensor pacis* (see V:12); he also had genuine religious leanings toward Lutheranism and showed special zeal for the translation of Scripture into the vernacular. He was in no sense an "English Machiavelli" and was far more a man of principle than traditional views of "the cynical, unscrupulous Cromwell" allow, though he was often ruthless and on occasion became a willing instrument of corrupted proceedings. He was not utterly subservient to the king, nor did he attempt to make of Henry an absolute monarch. Well-versed in common law, Cromwell was a superb parliamentary strategist and consistently worked through the House of Commons to attain his ends. To him was largely due the political transformation of England into a realm ruled by the king acting in and through Parliament. The leading Henri-

---

[1] H. Bettenson, ed., *Documents of the Christian Church*, 2nd ed. (London, 1963), p. 322.

cian reformers found in him their chief patron and the man best equipped, by ability and position, to translate theory into practice.

One of Cromwell's main plans was to secure a permanent endowment for the crown, which would necessarily involve a large-scale exploitation of ecclesiastical resources. The Reformation everywhere was marked by confiscations of church property and wealth. Cromwell, Cranmer, and their fellow reformers, moreover, were opposed to monasticism on religious grounds. In 1535, accordingly, Cromwell appointed a commission to visit the monasteries and report on their conditions. The visitation was carried out with great haste, and the report submitted to Parliament in 1536, though not without a factual basis, presented a one-sided picture of monastic decay and corruption. Parliament then adjudged to the king, "his heirs and assigns forever," all monastic establishments having an income of less than 200 pounds annually. The number of houses thus affected was about three hundred, of which some eighty secured temporary exemptions. Soon, however, the larger houses "voluntarily" dissolved themselves, the last of them in 1540. The total number of monasteries dissolved in England and Wales between 1536 and 1540 was about eight hundred. Some nine thousand monks, friars, and nuns were uprooted.

The dissolution evoked no significant opposition, neither from the religious orders nor from the people at large. Virtually all the royal officials who took the lead in dividing and selling the ex-monastic lands were themselves prominent Catholic laymen. In late 1536 and early 1537, four uprisings, known collectively as the Pilgrimage of Grace, did break out in northern England, but they were quickly suppressed. Though bound up with religious conservatism, their origins were largely economic and their aims secular; they were not "religious wars" on behalf of the monasteries or papal monarchy. There is also no solid evidence that the dissolution led to great social and economic catastrophes, such as rampant inflation, ruinous enclosure of land, or predatory rent-raising. The roots of the agrarian crises that befell England during the 1540s long antedated the dissolution of the monasteries.

The death of Catherine of Aragon in January 1536 in part relieved Henry from the threat of intervention by Charles V. By this time, Henry was tired of Anne Boleyn and unforgiving of her failure to produce a male heir, while Cromwell was suspicious of the Boleyn faction in the privy council. In May 1536, Anne was charged with adultery, and she was beheaded on May 18. On May 17, Cranmer had pronounced her marriage to Henry null and void. On May 30, Henry married Jane Seymour, who bore him the much desired son, christened Edward, on October 12, 1537. Twelve days later, Jane died.

As Henry's opposition to Rome developed, Protestant opinion spread among a considerable minority of the upper and middle classes, and even gained a strong if cautious following at the court, a conspicuous instance being the Seymour family, from which Henry had taken his third queen. By the late

1530s, the Reformation in England had become far more than a mere act of state. Cromwell and Cranmer also actively promoted the Protestant cause, so far as circumstances allowed. Henry's own religious attitude, however, remained that of Catholic orthodoxy, save on the substitution of his own authority for that of the pope. In 1535 and 1536, Cromwell had sent emissaries to Wittenberg for doctrinal discussions with the Lutheran leaders, with a view to bringing England into the orbit of the Schmalkaldic league, but Henry would have nothing to do with a distinctly Protestant formulation of faith. In 1536, chiefly in response to the pressing need of the English church for a definition of its doctrine, Henry himself drafted the so-called Ten Articles, in which he made his utmost concession to Protestantism. The authoritative standards of faith are the Bible, the three ecumenical creeds, and the first four ecumenical councils. Only three sacraments are defined: baptism, penance, and the Lord's Supper; the others are not mentioned either in approval or denial. Justification implies faith in Christ alone, but confession and absolution and works of charity are also necessary. Christ is physically present in the Supper. Images are to be honored, but with moderation. The saints are to be invoked, but not because they "will hear us sooner than Christ." Masses for the dead are desirable, but the idea that the "bishop of Rome" can deliver a soul out of purgatory is to be rejected.

A far more important act of this time, zealously promoted by Cromwell, with Cranmer's assistance, was the production of English Bibles. In 1535, Miles Coverdale, then in exile, produced the first complete English Bible and had it printed abroad, probably at Zurich, whence it was brought to England and reprinted there that same year. In 1537, a second complete vernacular Bible appeared, in a translation by John Rogers (1500?–1555); printed at London, it was known as the "Matthew Bible," because Rogers had used the pseudonym Thomas Matthew. Cranmer brought this translation to the attention of Cromwell, who in August 1537 secured the king's permission to have it put on sale in the realm; soon thereafter, he also licensed the sale of the cheaper Coverdale Bible. In 1538, Cromwell urged the bishops to promote Bible reading among the laity and ordered them to fix a date by which every parish priest was to make an English Bible available for public reading in his church. Not satisfied with the new translations, however, Cromwell entrusted a comprehensive revision to Coverdale. The result was the publication, in April 1539, of Coverdale's masterpiece, the so-called Great Bible, to which Cranmer added a famous preface for the second edition of 1540. The availability and immense appeal of the vernacular Bible proved of utmost importance for the English Reformation, chiefly by holding the contemporary church up to the mirror of original New Testament Christianity.

The publication of vernacular Bibles was attended by the printing, in 1544, of an English Litany prepared by Cranmer, which by royal command was thereafter used in the churches. The litany was the first installment of Cranmer's projects for an English prayer book, which occupied his energies from 1540 to 1547 and which were to come to fruition only during the next reign.

Since early 1536, King Henry's work had been free from foreign interference, because Charles V and Francis I were again at war from 1536 to 1538. With the arrival of peace in June 1538, the dangers to Henry greatly increased. The pope demanded a joint attack by France and Spain on the royal rebel. Henry's diplomacy and mutual jealousies warded it off, but he took several steps of importance to lessen his peril. He would show the world that he was an orthodox Catholic save in regard to the pope, and he would settle once and for all the faith of the English church. Accordingly, in June 1539, Parliament passed the Six Articles Act. It affirmed as the creed of England a strict doctrine of transubstantiation, denial of which was to be punished by fire. It repudiated priestly marriage and communion in both bread and wine. It ordered the permanent observation of vows of chastity and enjoined private Masses and auricular confession. This statute, known as "the bloody whip with six strings," remained in force until Henry's death. On the political front, Cromwell urged that Henry strengthen his position by a marriage that would please the German Protestants and unite him with those opposed to Emperor Charles V. Anne of Cleves, the elder sister of Duke William of Cleves and of the wife of John Frederick, the Saxon elector, was selected. The marriage took place on January 6, 1540.

Henry, upon first seeing her, was ill satisfied with the unattractive Anne. He found himself unable to consummate the marriage and within a short time demanded release. Cromwell procrastinated, however, because he knew that the king's choice would now fall on Catherine Howard, niece of Thomas Howard, duke of Norfolk, the powerful leader of the Catholic majority in the privy council. Norfolk's chief ally in the council was Stephen Gardiner (1490?–1555), bishop of Winchester. Cromwell was now, for the first time, seriously out of step with the king, whose own religious position, moreover, at the urging of Norfolk and Gardiner, had become increasingly reactionary. Cromwell's fall was remarkably sudden. He was arrested on June 10, 1540, and condemned without trial, by a parliamentary bill of attainder, on fabricated charges of heresy and treason. The king's greatest and most loyal servant was beheaded on July 28, 1540. Earlier, on July 10, Cranmer had pronounced Henry's marriage to Anne of Cleves invalid, and the ex-queen was handsomely compensated for her loss with crown lands. On August 9, Henry married Catherine Howard; but in November 1541, the new queen was charged with adultery. This time the charges were true; in February 1542, she was beheaded. In July 1543, Henry married Catherine Parr, who had the fortune to survive him. Henry himself died on January 28, 1547, and was succeeded by his son, who ruled as Edward VI (1547–1553).

At Henry's death, the reform party in the privy council and at court was in the ascendancy. The Howard family, the last political bulwark of Catholicism, had lost prestige through the ignominious end of Henry's fifth queen and came to further grief through the reckless adventurism of Henry Howard, earl of Surrey and son of the duke of Norfolk, who was beheaded for treason on January 19, 1547. The old duke himself would have gone to the block on January 28, had it not been for King Henry's death that same day; Norfolk remained in prison throughout the next reign. Bishop Gardiner was also imprisoned, in June 1548, and deprived of his see in 1551. The Protestant party was led by Edward Seymour, earl of Hertford, brother of Jane Seymour and uncle of the new king. This party also enjoyed the support of Catherine Parr and her circle, which favored Erasmian humanism and the type of cautious reform proposed by Archbishop Cranmer. The rise to power of the Seymour faction, combined with the evident devotion of young King Edward to Reformation religion, enabled zealous preachers and publicists to work openly for the turning of the English church away from Roman and Henrician Catholicism to a thoroughgoing Protestantism. Most of the ardent Protestants who were active during these years owed far more to the Swiss and south German reformers—to Bucer, Zwingli, Bullinger, and soon also Calvin—than to Luther and the Lutheran theologians. By the end of Edward's reign, England had become a Protestant country, at least as regards its official statements of faith and practice.

Edward VI, at his accession, was but nine years of age. Hence, the government was administered by the privy council, under the control of Hertford, who was now named protector of the realm and created duke of Somerset. An able soldier, but an irresolute politician, Somerset has traditionally been pictured as an idealist and a friend of the dispossessed, though more recent assessments have underscored his consuming ambition and ruthless acquisitiveness. In any case, he exercised an autocratic control of the state for two years, during which time a more radical Protestantism came to the fore. In 1547, Parliament abolished the existing heresy legislation as well as Henry's harsh additions to the old treason laws; repealed the Six Articles Act; removed all restrictions on the printing, reading, and teaching of the Scriptures; and ordered the administration of the cup to the laity. The same year, the last great confiscation of church lands occurred—the dissolution of the "chantries," the endowed chapels for saying Masses for the souls of their founders. The properties of free chapels, collegiate churches, hospitals (almshouses), and religious fraternities and guilds were also sequestered. Early in 1548, images were ordered removed from the churches. The marriage of priests was made legal in 1549.

The confusion soon became great, and as a means at once of advancing the reforms and securing order, Parliament, on January 21, 1549, passed an Act of Uniformity, by which the universal use of a book of common prayer in

English was required. This book, known as the First Prayer Book of Edward VI, was largely the work of Cranmer, based on the medieval liturgies of England, with some use of a revised Roman breviary published in 1535 by Cardinal Fernandez de Quiñones and of the Lutheranly inclined tentative *Consultation* of Hermann von Wied, archbishop of Cologne, issued in 1543. The 1549 Prayer Book preserved many details of older worship, such as prayers for the dead, communion at burials, anointing and exorcism in baptism, and anointing the sick, which were soon to be abandoned. The medieval vestments also survived for the time being. In the eucharist, the words used in handing the elements to the communicant implied that the body and blood of Christ were really received.

Somerset, meanwhile, was beset with political troubles. To counteract the growing power of France in Scotland he urged the union of the two British royal houses by the marriage of King Edward with the Scottish princess Mary Stuart, to be "Queen of Scots." He supported his efforts by an invasion of Scotland, in which the Scots were badly defeated, on September 10, 1547, at Pinkie; but his main purpose was thereby frustrated. The angered Scottish leaders hastened to betroth Mary to the heir of France, the later Francis II, an event of prime significance for the Reformation in Scotland. Mary was removed to France, and a powerful French army occupied England's northern border. Somerset's futile Scottish campaign also resulted in immense financial expenditures, which the nation could little afford at a time of severe price inflation and agrarian discontent. Though Parliament made some efforts to check the enclosure of common lands, a series of peasant uprisings convulsed southern England in 1549. The most serious of these occurred in Norfolk, under the capable leadership of the tradesman Robert Ket, whose forces were eventually routed by John Dudley, earl of Warwick. Somerset had badly miscalculated in failing to take the field himself, thereby thrusting Warwick to the fore as the man of the hour.

The riots and rebellions of 1549 served to discredit Somerset's rule. Having lost the support of virtually all the members of the privy council, the protector was overthrown in October 1549 by a *coup d'état*. The leader and ultimate beneficiary of this conspiracy was the earl of Warwick, who in February 1550 emerged as Somerset's successor, though he never took the title of protector. The character of Warwick, who in 1551 became duke of Northumberland, remains something of a mystery. He saved Somerset from execution at the time of the coup, yet ultimately he contrived to have him beheaded (1552), in part, it must be said, because Somerset had ever sought to undermine his rival's power. An idealized portrait of Somerset has promoted a view of Northumberland as utterly unscrupulous, avaricious, and tyrannical. Unlike Somerset, however, he sought to exercise a corporate rule through the privy council, and his regime undertook important administrative and financial reforms. His Protestantism has been taken to be purely political, yet he seems to have favored the more extreme reformers out of personal convictions as well as considerations of state. Supported by the staunchly Protestant king, his three years of rule witnessed the transformation of the English church into a Protestant body of a recognizably Reformed (Swiss) complexion.

The Prayer Book of 1549 was not popular. Conservative opposition to it had figured prominently in the 1549 rebellions in Devon and Cornwall. Protestants felt that it retained too much of Roman usage, an attitude which Cranmer himself had soon come to share. These criticisms were supported by a number of eminent Protestant refugees from the Continent who since late 1547 had found welcome in England: the Italians Pietro Martire Vermigli, or Peter Martyr (1500–1562), and Bernardino Ochino (1487–1564); the Polish reformer Jan Laski, or John Lasco (1499–1560); and most influential of all, Martin Bucer of Strassburg, who in 1551 wrote a book known as the *Censura* to show what was wrong with the 1549 Prayer Book. Cranmer and his associates, accordingly, undertook a revision of the Prayer Book, which was reissued under a new Act of Uniformity in April 1552. In this Second Prayer Book, much more of the ancient ceremonial was abolished. Prayers for the dead were omitted; a communion table was substituted for the altar; common bread, instead of a special wafer, was used in the Supper; exorcism and anointing were set aside; the medieval vestments were expressly forbidden and only the use of the surplice was required; and a new formula was introduced for delivery of the eucharistic elements that harmonized with the Zwinglian conception of the Supper.

Cranmer had long been engaged in the preparation of articles of religion, and in 1552 these were submitted by order of the council to six theologians, among whom was John Knox. The result was the Forty-two Articles, which were authorized by the young king's signature on June 12, 1553, less than a month before his death. They were decidedly more Protestant in tone than even the Second Prayer Book, though they were directed against Protestant extremism—specifically, Anabaptism—as well as against traditional Catholicism. During 1552, Cranmer also produced a comprehensive revision of the canon law—the *Reformatio Legum Ecclesiasticarum,* but this praiseworthy work failed to win authorization from either king or Parliament. Meanwhile, since 1550, vacancies in the episcopate had been filled by earnest reformers, so that the Edwardian episcopate possessed a strongly Protestant character.

Northumberland well knew that his power and personal survival depended on the king's life and on keeping Mary Tudor off the throne. By the summer of 1553, it was plain that the frail Edward was dying of tuberculosis. Northumberland now adopted a desperate plan, very possibly at the urging of Edward himself, who certainly wished to keep the English church Protestant. Henry VIII's will, in its final form, had left the crown to Edward, Mary, and Elizabeth, in that order, and had named the Grey heirs of his younger sister Mary as residuary successors after the end of the direct Tudor line. On June 11, 1553,

Edward disinherited his half sisters and settled the succession on Lady Jane Grey, the wife of Northumberland's eldest son, Guildford Dudley, and granddaughter of Henry VIII's sister Mary. Cranmer gave his reluctant consent to this wild plan. On July 6, 1553, Edward VI died.

The plot failed completely. Northumberland, in an astonishing blunder, failed to secure Mary's person, and she escaped unhindered. Even the most Protestant portions of the country, such as the city of London, rallied to her side. The people clearly preferred peace, unity, and lawful succession to civil war. Mary was soon safely on the throne and Northumberland was beheaded, abjuring his Protestantism on the scaffold. Gardiner was released from prison, was restored to his see of Winchester, and became lord chancellor. Cranmer and the leading Protestant bishops were imprisoned. In late 1553, Parliament legitimized Mary by declaring her mother's marriage to Henry VIII valid. The ecclesiastical legislation of Edward VI's reign was repealed, and public worship was restored to the forms of the last year of Henry VIII. The Supremacy Act of 1534, however, was not yet repealed. Hateful though this was to Mary, she proceeded with caution at first, guided by the advice of Simon Renard, the ambassador of her cousin, Emperor Charles V, who wished no precipitate action until Mary was safely married to his son Philip, soon to be Philip II of Spain. This marriage, on which Mary had set her heart but which for Philip was largely a dynastic duty, took place on July 25, 1554. It was exceedingly unpopular, as threatening foreign control.

Reconciliation with Rome had thus far been delayed, though bishops and other clergy of reformist sympathies had been removed. Between late 1553 and the middle of 1555, some eight hundred Protestants, both clergy and lay people, found refuge on the Continent, chiefly in the German and Swiss cities of Emden, Frankfurt, Strassburg, Basel, Zurich, and Geneva, where they were schooled in Reformed Protestantism. (The Lutheran states proved most inhospitable to these Marian exiles, viewing them as heretical in their sacramental beliefs and also fearing political repercussions.) One of the most important achievements of the exiles was the production of the so-called Geneva Bible, published in that city in April 1560. This innovative Bible, with its Calvinist flavor, became the most widely used Bible during Elizabeth's reign, without rival until the publication of the Authorized Version in 1611.

While the English Reformation thus preserved itself by flight, the Marian restoration of Catholicism proceeded slowly at home, balked in part by the widespread fear that confiscated church properties would be taken from their present holders. On assurance that this would not be the papal policy, Cardinal Reginald Pole (1500–1558), a cousin of Henry VIII, was admitted to England as legate. Parliament voted the restoration of papal authority, and on November 3, 1554, Pole absolved the nation of heresy and restored it to the Roman obedience. Parliament now reenacted the ancient laws against heresy and repealed Henry VIII's ecclesiastical legislation, thus restoring the church to the status it had occupied in 1529, save that former church property was assured by statute to its present possessors.

Severe persecution at once began. Its first victim was the Bible translator John Rogers, who was burned at London on February 4, 1555. The attitude of the people, who cheered him on the way to the stake, was ominous for this policy; nevertheless, before the end of the year, seventy-five more persons had suffered by fire in various parts of England. Of these, the most notable were the former bishops Hugh Latimer of Worcester and Nicholas Ridley of London, whose fortitude at their deaths in Oxford, on October 16, created a profound impression. Another conspicuous victim of that year was the ex-bishop of Gloucester and Worcester, John Hooper, a man whose uncompromising Zwinglian or "Swiss" principles have marked him out as a prototype of the later Puritans. Mary and Gardiner were especially determined to strike the highest of the Protestant clergy, Archbishop Cranmer. Though a man of conscience and principle, Cranmer was not of the heroic stuff of which Latimer, Ridley, Hooper, and Rogers were made. He was formally excommunicated by sentence at Rome on November 25, 1555, and Pole was shortly after made archbishop of Canterbury in his stead. Cranmer was now in an intolerable dilemma. He had sincerely maintained, since his appointment under Henry VIII, that the sovereign is the supreme authority in the English church. His Protestantism was real, but that sovereign was now a Roman Catholic. In his distress, he made submission, declaring that he recognized papal authority as established by law. Mary had no intention of sparing the man who had pronounced her mother an adulteress and herself a bastard. Cranmer must die. But it was hoped that by a public abjuration of Protestantism at his death he would discredit the Reformation. That hope was nearly realized. Cranmer signed a further recantation denying Protestantism wholly; but on the day of his execution at Oxford, March 21, 1556, his courage returned. He repudiated his retractions absolutely, declared his Protestant faith, and held the offending hand, which had signed the now renounced submissions, in the flame until it was consumed.

Philip had left England in September 1555. His absence, coupled with her own childless state, preyed on Mary's mind, inducing her to feel that she had not done enough to satisfy the judgment of God. Persecution therefore continued unabated until her death in 1558. In all, nearly three hundred persons were burned, most of them coming from southeastern England and the great majority belonging to the working classes. Their number included more than fifty women and a large proportion of young persons. Compared with the toll of sufferers in the Netherlands, the total number of Marian martyrs was scanty, though English history afforded no precedent for burnings on such a scale and English sentiment was deeply revolted. These martyrdoms—soon to be memorialized in the immensely popular *Acts and Monuments* (1563) of John Foxe (1516–1587)—probably did more for the spread of anti-Roman sentiment than all previous governmental efforts had accomplished, and they show that the Reformation had struck much deeper roots among the common people than is often supposed. Moreover, the process of theological and liturgical change begun in the 1530s under Cromwell and Cranmer, leading to the consolidation of Protestantism under Edward VI, proved irreversible. Mary could not put back the clock, and her policies increasingly took on the aspect of anachronism. The final year of her life also witnessed the surrender to the French of Calais, the last English possession on the Continent and a potent symbol of past national greatness. By the time Mary died, on November 17, 1558, to be followed a few hours later by Cardinal Pole, her reign had been discredited, and no crisis attended the accession of Elizabeth to the throne.

Elizabeth I (1558–1603) had long passed as illegitimate, though her place in the succession had been secured by act of Parliament during the lifetime of Henry VIII. Her birth and education, and the Roman denials of her mother's marriage, made her necessarily a Protestant, though under Mary, when her life had been threatened, she had conformed to the Roman ritual. While she kept her inmost religious convictions secret and was certainly no friend of Protestant extremism, she exhibited from the first a preference for a non-Catholic settlement of the religious question. Her accession had the support of Philip II of Spain, soon to be her bitterest enemy. Earnest Catholic though he was, Philip was politician enough not to wish to see France, England, and Scotland come under the rule of a single royal pair, and if Elizabeth was not queen of England, then Mary, "Queen of Scots," wife of the prince who was in 1559 to become King Francis II of France, would be entitled to the English throne. In her first measures after accession, Elizabeth enjoyed, moreover, the aid of one of the most cautious and farsighted statesmen England ever produced, William Cecil (1520–1598), better known as Lord Burghley, whom she at once made her secretary and who was to be her chief adviser until his death. For Elizabeth, it was a great advantage also that she was thoroughly English in feeling and deeply sympathetic with the political and economic ambitions of the nation. This representative quality reconciled many to her government whom mere religious considerations would have repelled. No one doubted that she put England first.

Elizabeth proceeded cautiously with her changes, too cautiously to satisfy the Protestant activists in the House of Commons, who, as matters turned out, forced the queen to move more quickly than she had intended. On April 29, 1559, Parliament passed the new Supremacy Act, over strong opposition from the Marian bishops in the House of Lords. This act rejected the pope's authority and all payments and appeals to him. A significant change of title appeared, however, by Elizabeth's own insistence. Instead of the old "Supreme Head," so obnoxious to the Catholics and scarcely more acceptable to militant Protestants, she was now styled "Supreme Governor" of the church in England—a much less objectionable phrase, though amounting to the same thing in practice. The tests of heresy were now to be the Scriptures, the first four General Councils, and the decisions of Parliament. Meanwhile, a commission had been revising the Second Prayer Book of Edward VI. While the queen herself seems to have favored the First Prayer Book of 1549, she had little choice but to accept a modified version of the Prayer Book of 1552, which had been hallowed by fire. The modifications introduced conformed to the queen's conservative tastes and also helped to render the new service more palatable to moderate Catholics. The prayer against the pope was omitted, as was the declaration that kneeling at the Supper did not imply adoration (a declaration, known as the "Black Rubric," that had been added to the 1552 Prayer Book at the insistence of John Knox). The question of Christ's physical presence in the sacrament was left intentionally undetermined by simply combining the formulas of delivery in the two Edwardian books.

The Act of Supremacy was followed immediately by the Act of Uniformity, which ordered all worship to be conducted, after June 24, 1559, in accordance with the new liturgy, and provided that the ornaments of the church and the vestments of its ministers should be those of the second year of Edward VI. This "Ornaments Rubric," which thus preserved the traditional vestments, provoked the stout opposition of the Marian exiles, who had now returned to England and from whom the leading Elizabethan bishops were recruited. This so-called Vestiarian Controversy shows that Puritanism, broadly defined as the effort to purify the church and its liturgy of "popery," was a powerful element in the origins of the Anglican church.

The oath of supremacy was refused by all but two obscure members of the Marian episcopate, though among the lower clergy generally resistance was slight, the obstinate not amounting to two hundred. New bishops had to be provided, and Elizabeth directed the election of her mother's one-time chaplain, Matthew Parker (1504–1575), as archbishop of Canterbury. Parker, like Cranmer, was scholarly and retiring; as a non-exile, he was also a Protestant of moderate views. His consecration posed difficulties, since the Marian bishops refused to participate, but there were those in England who had received consecration to the episcopal office under Henry VIII and Edward VI. On December 17, 1559, Parker was consecrated at the hands of four such—William Barlow, John Scory, Miles Coverdale, and John Hodgkin. Thus inaugurated, a new Anglican episcopate was speedily established. A definition of the creed, other than that implied in the Prayer Book, was purposely postponed; but in 1563 the Forty-two Articles of 1553 were somewhat revised, and now as the Thirty-nine Articles they became the statement of faith of the Church of England.

Thus, by 1563 the Elizabethan settlement was accomplished. It was threatened from two sides: from that of Rome, the pope having excommunicated

Elizabeth in 1570 and urged her subjects to depose her; and, with even more explosive potential, from the side of the earnest reformers who wished to go further and were soon to be nicknamed Puritans. A remarkable feature of the English Reformation is that it produced no outstanding religious leader—no Luther, Zwingli, Calvin, or Knox. Nor did it, before the beginning of Elizabeth's reign, manifest any considerable spiritual awakening among the people at all levels of society. A great revival of the religious life of England was to come, the earlier history of which was to be coincident with Elizabeth's reign, but which was to owe nothing directly to her.

Chapter 10

The Scottish Reformation

A T THE DAWN of the sixteenth century, Scotland was a poor and backward country. Its social conditions were feudal. The power of its kings was small. Its nobles were turbulent. Its church was relatively rich in land, owning about one-half that of the country, but ecclesiastical positions were largely used to supply places for younger sons of noble houses, and much clerical property was in the hands of the lay nobles. The weak monarchy had usually leaned on the church as against the lay nobility. Though universities had been founded in the fifteenth century at St. Andrews, Glasgow, and Aberdeen, they were slight compared to the continental seats of learning. The monastic foundations were generally in decline, and the parish churches were subject to scandalous neglect, staffed by ill-educated and poorly paid vicars. Reform of a disciplinary sort, of "manners and morals," was almost universally desired. When the Reformation was established in Scotland in 1560, primary attention was given to a thorough restructuring of ecclesiastical polity; theological and liturgical matters were of secondary concern.

The determining motive of most of Scottish political history in this period was fear of dominance or annexation by England, persuading it to link the fortunes of the land with those of France. Three grievous defeats by the English—Flodden (1513), Solway Moss (1542), and Pinkie (1547)—strengthened this feeling of antagonism but showed that even English superiority in force could not conquer Scotland. On the other hand, Scotland in alliance with

France was a great peril for England, the more serious when England had broken with the papacy. Therefore, England and France both sought to build up parties and strengthen factions favorable to themselves in Scotland. The powerful family of Douglas was on the whole inclined toward England, while that of Hamilton favored France. France also had strong supporters in Archbishop James Beaton (?–1539) of St. Andrews, the primate of Scotland, and his nephew, Cardinal David Beaton (1494?–1546), his successor in the same see. Though King James V (reigned 1513–1542) was a nephew of Henry VIII, and his grandson, James VI, was to become James I of England in 1603 and unite the two crowns after the death of Elizabeth, James V threw in his fortunes with France, marrying successively a daughter of Francis I and, after her death, Mary of Lorraine, of the powerful French Catholic family of Guise. This latter union, so important in the history of Scotland, was to have as its fruit Mary, "Queen of Scots" (1542–1587).

Protestant beginnings were made in Scotland not long after the Reformation got under way. Patrick Hamilton (1504?–1528), who had visited Wittenberg and studied in Marburg, preached Lutheran doctrine, and was burned on February 29, 1528. The cause grew slowly. In 1534 and 1540, there were other executions. Yet in 1543, the Scottish Parliament authorized the reading and translation of the Bible. It was but a temporary phase, due to English influence, and by 1544 Cardinal Beaton and the French party were employing strong repression. Chief of the preachers at this time was George Wishart (1513?–1546), who was burned by order of Cardinal Beaton on March 2, 1546. On May 29, Beaton himself was brutally murdered, partly in revenge for Wishart's death and partly out of hostility to his French policy. The murderers gained possession of Beaton's castle of St. Andrews and rallied their sympathizers there. In 1547, a hunted Protestant preacher, apparently a convert and certainly a friend of Wishart, of no considerable previous conspicuousness, took refuge with them and became their spiritual teacher. This was John Knox, to be the hero of the Scottish Reformation.

Born in or near Haddington between 1505 and 1515, Knox's early career was obscure. He was ordained to the priesthood, but when Wishart was arrested he was with that martyr and prepared to defend him. French forces sent to reduce the rebels in St. Andrews castle compelled its surrender, and Knox was carried to France to endure for nineteen months the cruel lot of a galley slave. Released at length, he made his way in 1549 to England, then under the Protestant government ruling in the name of Edward VI; he became one of the royal chaplains and in 1552 declined the bishopric of Rochester. The accession of Mary Tudor compelled his flight in 1554, but the English refugees whom he first joined in Frankfurt were divided by his criticisms of the Edwardian Prayer Book, and he moved on to Geneva, where he became an ardent disciple of Calvin and labored on the Genevan version of the English Bible, later so valued by the English Puritans. It was during this period of exile that Knox developed his revolutionary views on the rights of common people to take up arms against godless, idolatrous rulers—views not shared by Calvin.

Meanwhile, the English had alienated Scotland more than ever by the defeat at Pinkie, in 1547. Mary, "Queen of Scots" had been betrothed to the heir to the French throne and sent to France for safety in 1548, while her mother, the Guise, Mary of Lorraine, became regent of Scotland in 1554.

To a large portion of the Scottish nobles and people, dependence on France was as hateful as any submission to England could have been. Protestantism and national independence seemed to be bound together, and it was in this double struggle that Knox was to be the leader. Knox dared to return to Scotland, in 1555, and preached for six months; but the situation was not yet ripe for revolt, and he returned to Geneva to become the pastor of the church of English-speaking refugees there. He had, however, sowed fruitful seed. On December 3, 1557, a number of Protestant and anti-French nobles in Scotland entered into a covenant to "establish the most blessed Word of God and his congregation"—from which they were nicknamed "The Lords of the Congregation." Additional fuel was given to this dissent by the marriage of Mary Stuart to the French heir on April 24, 1558. Scotland now seemed a province of France, for should there be a son of this union he would be ruler of both lands, and the French grip was made doubly sure by an agreement signed by Mary, kept secret at the time, that France should receive Scotland should she die without heirs. Before 1558 was ended, Elizabeth was queen of England, and Mary, Queen of Scots was denouncing her as an illegitimate usurper and proclaiming herself the rightful occupant of the English throne.

In these circumstances, the advocates of Scottish independence and of Protestantism rapidly increased and became more and more fused into one party. Elizabeth, moreover, could be expected to assist, if only for her own protection. Knox saw that the time was ready. On May 2, 1559, he was back in Scotland. Nine days later, he preached in Perth. The mob destroyed the monastic establishments of the town. This action the regent naturally regarded as rank rebellion. She had French troops at her disposal, and both sides promptly armed for combat. They proved fairly equal, and the result was undecided. Churches were wrecked and monastic property sacked, to Knox's disgust, in many parts of Scotland. On July 10, 1559, Henry II of France died and Mary's husband, Francis II, became king in his stead. French reinforcements were promptly sent to the regent in Scotland. Matters went badly for the reformers. At last, in January 1560, English help came. On June 11, 1560, the regent died, and her cause perished with her. On July 6, a treaty was made between France and England by which French soldiers were withdrawn from Scotland and Frenchmen were debarred from all important posts in its government. The revolution had triumphed through English aid but without forfeiting Scottish national independence, and its inspirer had been Knox.

The victorious party pushed its triumph in the Scottish Parliament. On August 17, 1560, a Calvinistic confession of faith, largely prepared by Knox, was adopted as the creed of the realm. A week later the same body abolished papal jurisdiction and forbad the Mass under pain of death for the third offense. Though the king and queen in France refused their approval, the majority of the nation had spoken.

Knox and his associates proceeded to complete their work. In December 1560, a meeting was held which is regarded as the first Scottish "General Assembly." In January following, the *First Book of Discipline* was presented to the Parliament. It was a most remarkable document, attempting to apply the system worked out by Calvin to a whole kingdom, though the "Presbyterian" system was far from thoroughly developed as yet. In each parish, there should be a minister and elders, holding office with the consent of the congregation. Minister and elders constituted the disciplinary board—the later "session"— with power of excommunication. In the larger towns there were to be meetings for discussion, out of which the "presbyteries" would grow; over groups of ministers and congregations were synods, and over all the "General Assembly." The need of the times and the inchoate state of the church led to two further institutions: "readers," in places where there were no ministers or the work was large; and "superintendents," without spiritual authority but with administrative right to oversee the organization of parishes and recommend ministerial candidates. Besides these ecclesiastical features, the *Book* sketched out notable schemes of national education and poor relief. Knox would have had church, education, and the poor supported from the old church property; but here the *Book* met the resistance of Parliament, which did not adopt these financial proposals, though many of the body approved. The ecclesiastical constitution gradually came into force, but the nobles so possessed themselves of church lands that the church became one of the poorest in Christendom. This relative poverty stamped on it a democratic character, however, that was to make the church of Scotland the bulwark of the people against encroachments by the nobles and the crown.

All observances not having scriptural authority were swept away. Sunday was the only remaining holy day. For the conduct of public worship, Knox prepared a *Book of Common Order,* sometimes called "Knox's Liturgy," which was approved by the General Assembly in 1564. It was largely based on that of the English congregation in Geneva, which in turn was modeled on that of Calvin. It allowed, however, even more use of free prayer, the forms given being regarded as models whose strict employment was not obligatory, though the general order and content of the service were definite enough.

Knox was soon obliged to defend what he had gained. King Francis II of France died on December 5, 1560, and in the following August, Mary returned to Scotland. Her position as a youthful widow excited sympathy, which her great personal charm increased. She was no longer queen of France, and that element which had supported Protestantism not by reason of religion but from desire of national independence might well think that the pressing danger of French domination, which had induced acquiescence in the religious revolution, had passed. Mary behaved, at first, with great prudence. While she made no secret of her own faith—she had Mass said in her chapel to the furious disapproval of Knox, who was now minister of St. Giles in Edinburgh and admired by the burghers of that city—she did not interfere in the religious settlement effected in 1560. She strove to secure recognition as Elizabeth's heir to the English throne, a thing which Elizabeth had no mind to grant. Mary had the sage advice of her half brother, James Stuart (1531?–1570), later to be earl of Moray, who had been a leader of the "Lords of the Congregation." She tried by personal interviews of great skill to win Knox, but he refused any overture and remained the soul of the Protestant party. Still the prospect darkened for him. Mary won friends. The Protestant nobles were divided. The Mass was increasingly being used. Knox had good reason to fear that Mary would give a Catholic king to Scotland by marrying some great foreign prince. A marriage with the son of Philip II of Spain was seriously discussed. Even more alarming for the Protestant cause in Scotland and England was Mary's actual marriage on July 29, 1565, to her cousin, Henry Stuart, Lord Darnley (1545–1567), with whom she had fallen in love. Darnley's claim to the English throne stood next to that of Mary herself. He was popular with English Catholics, and though he had passed as a Protestant in England, he now avowed himself a Catholic. The marriage increased Elizabeth's danger at home and strengthened the Catholic party in Scotland. Moray opposed it and was driven from court and soon into exile, while Mary made much progress in subduing, one after another, the Protestant lords who sympathized with Moray. She thus lost her wisest adviser.

Thus far, Mary had acted fairly shrewdly, but Scottish Protestantism was now saved by Mary's mistakes and want of self-control. Darnley was disagreeable and vicious. Her feelings for him changed. On the other hand, his jealousy was roused by the favor which Mary showed to David Riccio, an Italian whom Mary employed as a foreign secretary and who was looked upon by the Protestant lords as their enemy. Darnley and a number of Protestant nobles entered into a plot by which Riccio was dragged from Mary's presence and murdered in the palace of Holyrood, on March 9, 1566. Mary behaved with great cunning. Dissembling her anger, she secured from Darnley the names of his fellow conspirators, outlawed those who had actually participated in the deed, and took the others back into favor, of course with the knowledge on their part that they were received on sufferance. On June 19, 1566, Mary and Darnley's son was born, the future James VI of Scotland and James I of England. Mary never seemed surer of the Scottish throne.

In reality, Mary had never forgiven her husband, and she now turned to a Protestant noble, James Hepburn, Earl of Bothwell (1536?–1578), a rough, licentious, but brave, loyal, and martial man, whose qualities contrasted with those of her weak husband. Bothwell took the lead in a conspiracy to rid Mary of Darnley, with how much share on the part of Mary herself is still a disputed question. Darnley, who was recovering from smallpox, was removed by Mary from Glasgow to a house on the edge of Edinburgh, where Mary spent part of the last evening with him. Early on the morning of February 10, 1567, the house was blown up, and Darnley's body was found near it. Public opinion charged Bothwell with the murder, and it was widely believed that Mary also was guilty of it. At all events, she heaped honors on Bothwell, who succeeded in securing acquittal by a farce of a trial. On April 24, Bothwell met Mary on one of her journeys and made her captive by a show of force—it was generally believed with her connivance. He was married, but his wife divorced him for adultery on May 3, and on May 15 he and Mary were married by Protestant rites.

These shameless transactions roused general hostility in Scotland, and they robbed Mary, for the time, of Catholic sympathy in England and on the Continent. Protestants and Catholics in Scotland joined forces against her. On July 24, 1567, she was compelled to abdicate in favor of her year-old son and appoint Moray as regent, and she was imprisoned in Lochleven Castle. On July 29, John Knox preached the sermon at James VI's coronation. With Mary's fall came the triumph of Protestantism, which was now definitely established by Parliament in December. Mary escaped from Lochleven in May 1568, but Moray promptly defeated her supporters, and she fled to England, where she was to remain, a focus of Catholic intrigue, until her execution for conspiracy against Elizabeth's life in February 1587.

Knox's fiery career was about over. He died on November 24, 1572, having influenced not merely the religion but the character of the nation more than any other person in Scottish history. Knox's work was to be taken up by Andrew Melville (1545–1623), who had taught as Beza's colleague in Geneva from 1568 until his return to Scotland in 1574. He was the educational reformer of the universities of Glasgow and St. Andrews and even more distinguished as the perfecter of the presbyterian system in Scotland and its vigorous defender against the royal and episcopal encroachments of James VI, who compelled him to spend the last sixteen years of his life in exile from his native land.

Chapter 11

The Catholic Reformation and Counter-Reformation

*B*Y THE MIDDLE OF THE sixteenth century, the steady, often spectacular, growth of Protestantism had elicited a powerful reaction from the Roman church. Beginning with Paul III (1534–1549), the popes directed churchwide efforts to repress the Protestant revolt, to correct the most glaring ecclesiastical abuses, to codify authoritative church teaching over against the Protestant schismatics and heretics, and to recover lost territories. This defensive reaction to the Protestant threat is appropriately called the Counter-Reformation; yet that designation is by no means adequate to all the facts and, taken in isolation, leads to a one-sided historical portrait. For alongside this negative response to Protestantism, one observes spontaneous movements of Catholic reform that either antedated the Protestant Reformation or originated independently of it. These movements, on the whole, stood in continuity with late medieval efforts to bring about personal religious renewal and institutional reform, as evidenced in such phenomena as the *Devotio moderna,* conciliarism, Christian humanism, penitential preaching, Observantine programs of monastic reform, and the founding of religious confraternities.

In this light, one may properly speak of an indigenous Catholic Reformation of the sixteenth century, centered on the hope of achieving a thorough reform "in head and members." In all likelihood, however, these currents of spiritual renewal would not have won the active support of popes and prelates— would not have been "institutionalized," so to speak—were it not for the profound shock administered to the church at large by the Protestant Reformation. Moreover, the exigent need to contain and counteract Protestantism largely shaped the course in which these currents flowed. Thus, the Catholic Reformation and Counter-Reformation were intimately joined.

The two main centers from which the Catholic revival radiated were Spain and Italy, though spiritual renewal in both countries owed not a little to older traditions of spirituality in the Netherlands and Germany.

It has already been noted (see V:16) that a generation before Luther's break with Rome, Spain was witnessing a vigorous reform effort led by Queen Isabella and Cardinal Franciso Jiménez de Cisneros. It combined zeal for a more moral and educated parish clergy, reform of the monasteries along Observant lines, and biblical studies based on the principles of Christian humanism, with unswerving devotion to traditional orthodoxy and repression of heresy by the Spanish Inquisition. The renewed spiritual life of Spain was also to find expression in a great flowering of quietistic mysticism, involving new techniques of meditative prayer; in a renovated Scholastic theology, involving a revival of Thomism; and not least in the founding of the most influential of the new religious orders, the Society of Jesus—developments that will be traced later in this chapter. This "Spanish awakening" was of the utmost moment for the Catholic Reformation and Counter-Reformation. Yet a rejuvenated Catholicism was no less indebted to native Italian sources of religious revival.

During the closing years of the fifteenth century and the first quarter of the sixteenth, many religious confraternities or "oratories" were established in Italy. These half-lay, half-clerical associations were devoted to the cultivation of an intense personal piety and the performance of charitable works, especially the care of orphans and of incurables (persons suffering from the new disease of syphilis). The most famous such association, predominantly lay in character, was the Oratory of Divine Love, founded at Genoa in 1497 by Ettore Vernazza, a disciple and biographer of St. Catherine of Genoa (see V:15). Sometime between 1514 and 1517, Vernazza established a branch of the oratory in Rome. Its leaders included Gaetano da Thiene (1480–1547), a devout priest and curial official, later canonized (as St. Cajetan); and Gian Pietro Caraffa (1476–1559), bishop of Chieti, papal diplomat, and later to be Pope Paul IV (1555–1559). In 1524, Gaetano and Caraffa and two other members of the Roman oratory founded the so-called Theatine Order at Rome, for which Caraffa wrote a rule in 1526. This was an order of "clerks regular," of priests, that is, who professed the monastic vows, lived in community under a superior, and sought to perfect their own priestly vocations and to raise the standard of clerical life in general. Their official name was the "Clerks Regular of the Divine Providence," but they were popularly known as the "Theatines," from Caraffa's bishopric of Chieti (= Theate, in Latin). All the first members of the order gave away their property and resigned their benefices. Their poverty, strict asceticism, and charitable work for the sick and destitute won them great popular respect. Their influence as a seedbed of Catholic reform was out of all proportion to their small number.

Many of the early leaders of the Catholic revival in Italy had close ties with the Oratorians and Theatines. This was notably true of the Venetian senator and ambassador, Gasparo Contarini (1483–1542), who from 1530 to 1535 was a member of a zealous reform group in Venice that included Caraffa (after the sack of Rome in 1527 the Theatines moved to Venice); Gregorio Cortese (d.

1548), the abbot of the Benedictine monastery of San Giorgio Maggiore; and the Englishman Reginald Pole (1500–1558), a humanistic scholar and a cousin of Henry VIII. Already in 1516, Contarini had written a treatise on the office of bishop (*De officio episcopi*), which pointed the way for the spiritual renewal of the episcopate—one of the most urgent needs of the day and subsequently a cornerstone of the Catholic Reformation. Contarini's ideal was embodied in Gian Matteo Giberti (1495–1543), the reforming bishop of Verona from 1524 until his death, who was also a devoted supporter of the Theatines. From 1527, when he took up residence in his see after fourteen years of exemplary service in the Curia, Giberti exercised the closest supervision of his clergy in order to ensure their faithful care of souls. His ordinances served as a pattern for much of the disciplinary legislation of the Council of Trent, and his example inspired the most famous pastoral bishop of the post-Tridentine church, St. Carlo Borromeo (1538–1584), the cardinal archbishop of Milan from 1560. Yet another episcopal reformer with ties to the Theatines, who may himself have been a member of the Roman oratory, was Jacopo Sadoleto (1477–1547), the scholarly bishop of Carpentras who sought to bring the Genevans back into the Roman Catholic fold and to whom Calvin addressed his famous *Reply* (see VI:8).

Two other orders of clerks regular were established in Italy at about the same time as the Theatines: the "Clerks Regular of St. Paul," founded at Milan in 1533 by St. Antonio Maria Zaccaria (d. 1539) and two associates, and popularly known as the Barnabites, from their possession of the church of St. Barnabas at Milan; and the Somaschi, founded in 1532 at Somasca in northern Italy by St. Girolamo Aemiliani (d. 1537). The Barnabites and the Somaschi, like the Theatines, were animated by motives of personal sanctification, reform of the priestly office, and active charity to the poor and afflicted, especially to the wretched victims of the wars in northern Italy.

Religious associations of women also played an important role in the Catholic revival. Chief of these was a group of unmarried women and a few widows who gathered in Brescia in 1535 under the direction of St. Angela Merici (1474?–1540). These "Ursulines," so called because of their dedication to the legendary St. Ursula, lived in their own homes and worshiped in their own parish churches, but pledged themselves to lead a self-denying life of obedience to superiors and of charitable activity, above all the religious education of young girls. The bishop of Brescia approved the foundation in 1536, and it soon spread throughout the north of Italy, especially in Milan, and later into France. Though Angela intended her foundation to be a lay association without monastic vows and enclosure, the company was gradually transformed into a full-fledged order. A habit was enjoined in 1546; simple vows and community life were introduced in 1572; and in 1612, the Ursulines of Paris were permitted strict enclosure and solemn vows according to the modified Rule of St. Augustine. Ursuline convents soon multiplied, especially in France and Canada, and achieved prominence in the education of girls. Among the most famous members of the order was Marie Guyard ("Mary of the Incarnation," 1599–1672), a noted mystic who founded the house at Quebec in 1639.

The most important of the new religious orders founded in Italy in the sixteenth century, and second only to the Jesuits in influence, was that of the Capuchins (*Capuccini,* so called because of their distinctive coarse habit with its four-pointed hood, or *capuccio*). The order was founded between 1525 and 1528 (when it received papal authorization) by Matteo da Bascio (1495?–1552) and three companions—the brothers Ludovico and Raffaele da Fossombrone and Paolo da Chioggia. All four were Franciscan Observants intent upon returning to the letter of the original Rule of St. Francis (see V:4). Hence, they committed themselves to absolute poverty, extreme physical mortification, an ordered life of prayer, itinerant preaching of a simple evangelical and moral character, and charitable work among the sick and the poor. Matteo was the first to resolve upon and assume this way of life, while Ludovico was the movement's organizer. Despite opposition from the superiors of the Observants, who understandably feared the loss of their most dedicated members, the Capuchins attained a separate organization and experienced a phenomenal growth. They counted some seven hundred members by 1535 and about twenty-five hundred by 1550. After 1572, when foundations outside Italy were permitted, the order rapidly underwent a worldwide expansion.

These forces of religious renewal emanating chiefly from Italy and Spain first achieved significant hold on the papacy during the pontificate of Paul III (1534–1549), though Adrian VI (1522–1523) had exhibited a real, though ineffective, zeal for reform during his brief and unhappy reign. By contrast, neither Leo X (1513–1521) nor Clement VII (1523–1534) was alive to the gravity of the situation, and both showed themselves incapable of putting their responsibilities as heads of the church above their political ambitions and dynastic concerns as Italian princes. Paul III, however, while not above criticism for moral lapses before taking priest's orders and for using his office to enrich his family members, was far more alert than his predecessors to the dangers confronting the church from without and within. Early in his pontificate, he appointed a number of sincere reformers to the college of cardinals. Among these were Contarini, Caraffa, Sadoleto, and Pole; subsequently, Cortese was so elevated, though Giberti declined the honor. In 1536, at Contarini's urging, Paul III appointed all of these persons, plus three others, to a commission charged with proposing reforms preparatory to a general church council. In 1537, the commission submitted its plain-spoken report, the *Consilium de emendanda ecclesia,* which identified the venality of the popes and the cardinals as the chief cause of defections from the church. Paul III adopted some of its proposals in order to eliminate the most serious abuses in the Curia.

While Caraffa was a man of unbending devotion to medieval dogma, Contarini and Pole had considerable sympathy with Luther's doctrine of justification, as did Girolamo Seripando (1492–1563), the general of the Augustinian friars. Yet these men, whose conciliatory views on justification were ultimately rejected at the Council of Trent, were far removed from authentic Protestant ideas. There were, however, a considerable number of persons in Italy—principally members of religious orders, aristocratic women, and humanists of clerical origin—whose sympathies led them much further. They were particularly numerous in Venice, where Antonio Bruccioli's Italian translation of the New Testament was printed in 1530, and of the whole Bible in 1532. Ferrara's hospitality, under Duchess Renée, has already been noted in connection with Calvin (see VI:8). The most remarkable of these groups was that gathered in Naples about Juan de Valdés (1500?–1541), a native of Castile and an Erasmian humanist who came to Rome in 1529 in the service of Charles V and settled permanently at Naples in 1534. Though he died a devout Catholic, Valdés emphasized the sole authority of Scripture and the church fathers, and he cultivated an inward, mystical piety that attached no essential importance to the church's rites and sacraments. From his disciple, Benedetto of Mantua, came about 1540 the most popular book of this circle, *The Benefits of Christ's Death*.

Among Valdés's friends were Pietro Martire Vermigli (Peter Martyr, 1500–1562), whose father had been an admirer of Savonarola, himself prior of the Augustinian monastery of St. Peter in Naples and destined to be professor of Protestant theology in Strassburg and Oxford; and Bernardino Ochino (1487–1564), the foremost preacher in Italy of his day, vicar general of the Capuchins from 1538 to 1541, later Protestant prebendary of Canterbury, pastor in Zurich, and ultimately forced to become a wanderer for his erratic opinions, dying among the Anabaptists in Moravia. (Ochino's apostasy in 1542 almost brought about the destruction of the Capuchin order.) Another friend of this group was Caraffa's nephew, Galeazzo Caraccioli, marquis of Vico, later to be Calvin's intimate associate in Geneva. These Italian evangelicals were, however, unorganized and without princely support, save very cautiously in Ferrara, nor did they gain any sizable following among the common people. In Italy they were an exotic growth, and the same may be said of the very few Protestants who were to be found in Spain.

Pope Paul III wavered for a time between the method of conciliation advocated by Contarini, who took part in the reunion discussions at Regensburg (see VI:5) as papal legate, and that of Caraffa, who urged stern repression of doctrinal divergence, while advocating administrative and moral reform. Eventually, he decided for the latter, and his decision became the policy of his successors. On Caraffa's urgent appeal, Paul III, on July 21, 1542, reorganized the Roman Inquisition, largely on the Spanish model, and extended its authority to the whole of Christendom, though its actual establishment, of course, took place only where it had the support of friendly civil authority. Before it, the feeble beginnings of Italian Protestantism rapidly disappeared. One of the main weapons of the Counter-Reformation was thus created.

Much more important was a revival of missionary zeal, which the fresh genius of Spain contributed to the kindling of Catholic enthusiasm. Viewed from any standpoint, St. Ignatius Loyola (1491–1556) is one of the master figures of the Reformation epoch. Don Iñigo de Oñez y Loyola was born of a knightly family in northern Spain. After serving as a page at the court of King Ferdinand, he became a soldier. His intrepid firmness was exhibited when Pamplona was besieged by the French in 1521, but he received there severe leg wounds that made further military service impossible. During his slow recovery he read Spanish translations of the lives of the saints and of the *Life of Christ* by Ludolph the Carthusian (see V:2). He determined that he would be a knight of Christ and of the Virgin. Recovered, in a measure, he made a pilgrimage in March 1522 to the Marian shrine at Montserrat, hung his weapons on the Virgin's altar, and exchanged his knightly garments for those of a beggar. He then re-tired to the neighboring town of Manresa, where he remained for almost a year (March 1522 to February 1523). There he pondered *The Imitation of Christ* of Thomas à Kempis, subjected himself to the harshest penances, and experi-enced a series of extraordinary raptures and visions.

Under the immediate impress of his mystical experiences at Manresa, Ignatius wrote the first draft of his *Spiritual Exercises,* a remarkable book that reached its final form at Rome in 1541. (The Latin text of the Spanish original was first published at Rome in 1548.) It is a book intended not to be read for religious edification but to be used experimentally under the guidance of a spiritual director, such use culminating in an act of will, namely, the election of a new way of life. It is thus a work designed to lead persons to the realization of their eternal destiny under God. For the sake of their soul's salvation and God's glory, they are led to make a deliberate choice for Christ, to put off their sins, and to assume an attitude of "holy disinterestedness" toward this world in order to use all its goods for the glorification of God. The Christian is led, in short, to submit wholly to God and to become an utterly disciplined member of the church, resolved to serve it in unquestioning obedience. In Ignatian spirituality, obedience to the suffering Christ and to his (hierarchical) church thus came to occupy the central place that faith in God's unmerited mercy for the crucified Christ's sake held in Luther's religion. Here may be seen a focal point of contrast between the Protestant and the Catholic Reformations.

In 1523, Ignatius went as a pilgrim to Jerusalem, resolved to serve Christ as a missionary to the Muslims, but the resident Franciscans, whom he sought to join, thought him dangerous and sent him home. Convinced that if he was to do the work he desired, he must have an education, Ignatius entered a boy's class in Barcelona (1525) and went rapidly forward to the universities of Alcalá (1526–1527) and Salamanca (1527). A born leader, he gathered like-minded companions with whom he practiced his "exercises." This aroused the suspicion of the Spanish Inquisition, and for a time he was imprisoned. In 1528, he entered the Collège de Montaigu at the University of Paris, just as

Calvin was leaving it. There he made no public demonstration but gathered round himself a handful of devoted friends and disciples—Pierre Lefèvre, Francis Xavier, Diego Lainez, Alfonso Salmerón, Nicolas Bobadilla, and Simon Rodriguez. In a small chapel in Montmartre, Paris, on August 15, 1534, these companions vowed to undertake a preaching mission to Jerusalem to work for the conversion of the Turks, or, if that proved impossible, to put themselves completely at the disposition of the pope. They were soon joined by three other recruits: Claude Le Jay, Paschase Broet, and Jean Codure.

In 1537, upon completion of their studies, the ten companions gathered in Venice to undertake fulfillment of their vow, but Jerusalem was barred by war, and so they determined to offer themselves to the pope. In the spring of 1539, Ignatius called them to Rome, and in June they formed themselves into a "Company of Jesus," intent upon serving as teachers of children and illiterates, as popular preachers, as chaplains in hospitals, and as leaders of missions or retreats. Besides their vows of chastity and poverty, already made at Montmartre, they were to take a vow of obedience to the pope, to go wherever he should send them. (It must not be thought that the company was specifically founded to combat Protestantism, though by the 1550s that had become a leading endeavor. Ignatius's vision was originally turned toward the Muslim world, and Xavier was already contemplating work in the Indies.) In spite of ecclesiastical opposition, Paul III was induced by the favorable attitude of Contarini and the skill of Ignatius to authorize the Society of Jesus on September 27, 1540, in the bull *Regimini militantis ecclesiae*. The constitution of the society was as yet indefinite, save that it was to have a head to whom full obedience was due and that it should labor wherever that head and the pope should direct. In April 1541, Ignatius was chosen the first general of the order, an office that he held until his death on July 31, 1556.

The constitution of the Jesuits was worked out gradually; indeed, it was not completed until after Ignatius's death, though its main features were his work. At the head is a general chosen for life, to whom absolute obedience is due; he, in turn, is watched by four assistants elected by the order, which can, if necessary, depose him. Over each district is a provincial, appointed by the general. Formal incorporation into the society requires a rigorous novitiate of two years, followed by the "scholasticate," a period of indefinite length devoted to studies in the humanities, philosophy, theology, etc. The scholastic takes simple vows of poverty, chastity, and obedience; if accepted into membership of the society, he is ordained and then undergoes another year of spiritual preparation, known as the "third probation" or "tertianship." After this, he is incorporated into the society either as a "formed spiritual coadjutor," to be employed in purely spiritual functions, or as a fully professed member who solemnly takes the traditional three vows. In the latter case, he could in time be allowed to take a fourth vow, that of direct personal obedience to the pope.

The governing body of the society is composed of all the "professed fathers of the fourth vow." For the sake of unimpeded pastoral service, the Jesuits are bound to no fixed hours of worship or form of dress, as are monks, and are obliged to no common recitation of the divine office—a revolutionary break with the monastic tradition. Each member is disciplined by use of Ignatius's *Spiritual Exercises*. In solitude and silence, interrupted only by the liturgy and by communications with his director, the exercitant undertakes four weeks of ordered meditation on the principal facts of the life and work of Christ and on the Christian warfare with evil. The director, for his part, adapts the technique to the particular needs and capacities of the exercitant.

The society that Ignatius constructed was, in sum, a marvelous instrument, combining the individualism of the Renaissance—each person assigned to and trained for his special work—with the sacrifice of will and complete obedience to the spirit and aims of the whole.

The Society of Jesus spread rapidly in Italy, Spain, and Portugal, numbering about one thousand members at Ignatius's death, though it was slower in gaining a foothold in France and Germany. By the latter half of the sixteenth century, it had become the single most powerful force in the Catholic revival and the advance guard of the Counter-Reformation. Its chief agencies were preaching, the confessional, its excellent schools—not for the multitude, but for the well-born and well-to-do—and its foreign missions. Under Jesuit influence, more frequent confession and communion became the rule in Catholic countries; and to aid the confessional, the Jesuit moral practice was gradually developed, largely after Ignatius's death, and especially in the early part of the seventeenth century, in a fashion that aroused the criticism not only of Protestants but of many Catholics (see VII:16). Naturally, a society thus international in character, the members of which were bound to their superiors by constant letters and reports, also speedily became a force in political life.

Together with the Society of Jesus, the Council of Trent must be classed as the primary agency of the Catholic Reformation and Counter-Reformation. That council had a checkered history. Earnestly desired by Charles V, and reluctantly called by Paul III, it finally met at Trent in December 1545. In March 1547, the Italian majority transferred it to Bologna, where it continued meeting until September 1549. In May 1551, it was back in Trent, where the Spanish majority had all along remained. On April 25, 1552, it adjourned in consequence of the successful Protestant uprising under Moritz of Saxony against the emperor (see VI:5). Not until January 1562 did it meet again, and it completed its work on December 4, 1563. In all, the council held twenty-five sessions during its three main periods. In the earliest period (1545–1547), when the most important doctrinal decisions were made, there were never more than seventy-two voters present; by the last period (1562–1563), the number had risen to over two hundred. The right to vote was confined to bishops, heads of religious orders, and influential abbots, and voting was by individuals, not (as at the Council of Constance) by nations. At all times, therefore, the majority was in Italian hands and represented the papal wish that definition of doctrine should precede reform. On the other hand, the Spanish bishops, equally orthodox in belief, stood resolutely for the emperor's desire that reform should precede doctrine. It was finally agreed that doctrine and reform should be discussed concurrently, but all decisions had to have the pope's approval, thus strengthening the papal supremacy in the church. No voices were more influential in the council than those of the pope's theological experts, the Jesuits Diego Lainez (1512–1565) and Alfonso Salmerón (1515–1585), and their influence steadily supported the anti-Protestant spirit.

The doctrinal decrees of the Council of Trent were clear and definite in their rejection of Protestant beliefs—at least of what was assumed to be the Protestant position—while they were often indecisive regarding matters of dispute in medieval controversies. Justification is not by faith alone, so the council declared, but by faith formed by works of love, and thus salvation depends on an acquired, inherent righteousness, not on an alien, imputed righteousness. Scripture and unwritten "apostolic" traditions are equally sources of divine truth and are to be received with equal reverence. The church alone has the right to determine the true sense and interpretation of Scripture. The Latin Vulgate is the sacred and canonical text. The sacraments are seven in number, not two (or three). The sacrament of penance involves works of satisfaction, as well as contrition and confession, and entails the church's power to grant indulgences. The Mass involves a transubstantiation of the consecrated elements, is a true propitiatory sacrifice that re-presents in an unbloody manner Christ's self-offering on the altar of the cross, and benefits not only the living faithful but also the souls of the faithful departed in purgatory; hence, the practice of "private Masses" is commended. The cup is to be withheld from the laity, and Latin is to remain the liturgical language.

In these and related decrees, the council had, to all appearances, shut the door completely on any compromise or modification of medieval doctrine and had rejected all the main Protestant tenets out of hand. More recent scholarship has shown, however, that the Tridentine decrees were carefully and cautiously formulated, were not as insistently hostile to Protestantism as was long believed, and are open to interpretations that make possible ecumenical dialogue and theological rapprochement. In their immediate context, however, they were seen to foreclose any possibility of reconciliation between the two great confessional camps.

Though the reforms enacted at Trent were far from realizing the wishes of many in the Roman church, they did establish a solid basis for the renewal of the church's pastoral office and, therewith, of its spiritual life. Chief among these reforms was the restoration to the bishops of effective powers of supervision in their sees, as well as the clear delineation of their pastoral duties. From now on, the bishop was to be "delegate of the Apostolic See" in his own diocese, possessed (in theory at least) of sufficient authority to prevail over those numerous exemptions from episcopal control that had been the bane of the medieval church and to curb the excessive power heretofore wielded by the Curia, legates, and nuncios. This authority was to be reinforced by the holding of regular provincial councils and of annual parochial visitations. Bishops, moreover, were bound to preach regularly, were obliged to reside in their sees, and were denied possession of more than one bishopric. The parish clergy, likewise, were to teach plainly what is needful for salvation and to be models of devout shepherds of souls. To this end, the council, in what was perhaps its most important canon, ordered the creation of seminaries— "perpetual nurseries of ministers for the worship of God." The bishop of every diocese where no university existed was to establish such a seminary for the training of worthy priests. Besides enacting reform legislation for the religious orders and issuing regulations for the prevention of clandestine marriages, the council also approved an index of prohibited books, to be prepared by the pope, following the example set by Paul IV in 1557. This latter action resulted, in 1571, in the creation by Pius V (1566–1572) of the Congregation of the Index, at Rome, to censure publications.

From a Spanish Dominican theologian influential at Trent, Melchior Cano (1509–1560), came the ablest defense of the Roman position that had yet appeared: the *De locis theologicis libri XII,* published three years after Cano's death. Theology, he taught, is based on authority. The authority of Scripture rests on the sifting and approving power of the church, which determines what is Scripture and what not; but as by no means all of Christian doctrine is contained in the Scripture, tradition, handed down and sifted by the church, is another authoritative basis. Cano had been a pupil and later the successor of Francisco de Vitoria (1485?–1546) at the University of Salamanca. He was, accordingly, a leading representative of the "new Scholasticism," initiated by Vitoria, that made the *Summa theologiae* of Thomas Aquinas the basic theological text, rather than the *Sentences* of Peter Lombard, and that endeavored to purge dogmatic and moral theology of all highly speculative elements and to base it squarely on Scripture and the church fathers.

The result of all these influences was that by 1565 an earnest and strenuous Catholicism had been revived at every level of the church's life, most importantly at its highest reaches. The popes were now prevailingly men of strict life and reformatory zeal, while Rome itself had become a more somber, and a much more ecclesiastical, city than in the Renaissance. A new spirit, intense in its opposition to Protestantism, profoundly conservative in its theology, but committed to far-reaching administrative reforms and ready to fight or suffer for its faith, was widespread. Confronted by this renewed zeal, not only did Protestantism cease to make new conquests, but its hold on the Rhineland and in southern Germany was shaken in considerable measure. Catholicism began to hope to win back all that it had lost.

The Catholic recovery of a sense of assurance was especially evident, on the scholarly level, in the writings of the great Jesuit controversialist, Roberto Bellarmino (St. Robert Bellarmine, 1542–1621), a native of Tuscany who joined the Jesuits in 1560, became a professor at their Roman college in 1576, and was made a cardinal in 1599. His *Disputations against the Heretics of Our Time* (3 vols., 1586–1593) was by far the most impressive defense of Tridentine Catholicism against the Protestant Reformation on historical and rational grounds. An equally famous defender of the historical legitimacy of Roman Catholicism was Caesar Baronius (1538–1607), a member and later superior of the Roman oratory of St. Philip Neri (see below), who was made a cardinal in 1596 and librarian of the Vatican in 1597. His *Annales Ecclesiastici* (12 vols., 1588–1607) was a work specifically directed against the *Historia Ecclesiae Christi* (13 vols., 1559–1574), prepared by the Lutheran theologian Matthias Flacius Illyricus (1520–1575) and six collaborators and known as the *Magdeburg Centuries,* because each volume covered a century of church history. Both of these monumental works were biased and poorly arranged; yet Baronius's access to the Vatican archives enabled him to present much new material and to disclose the many inaccuracies of the Magdeburg Centuriators, particularly in their handling of original texts.

The persistent theme running throughout the Catholic Reformation was the quest for a more worthy clergy. This goal inspired Gaetano da Thiene and the Theatines early in the sixteenth century, and it was no less central to the work of Filippo de' Neri (St. Philip Neri, 1515–1595) and his "Oratorians" at the end of the century. A native of Florence, educated by the Dominicans at the convent of San Marco, where the memory of Savonarola was still alive (see V:15), Neri came to Rome in 1533 and was soon devoting himself to solitary prayer vigils and works of charity on behalf of pilgrims and convalescents. In 1551, he was ordained to the priesthood, and his ensuing activity as a confessor and a leader of regular afternoon exercises in prayer, known as "oratories," quickly secured his popular reputation as the "apostle of Rome." From these activities sprang the Congregation of the Oratory (Oratorians), an order of secular priests, living in community without vows, that Pope Gregory XIII (1572–1585) formally approved in 1575. The Oratorians sought to bring people to God through prayer, preaching services, the confessional, and, not least, the attractions of good music. The "oratorio" of the next century developed out of the canticles (*laudi spirituali*) sung in their devotional exercises. The composer of many of these canticles, and the reformer of Catholic church music, Giovanni Palestrina (1525?–1594), was himself one of Neri's penitents.

In 1611, the French Congregation of the Oratorians was established at Paris by Pierre de Bérulle (1575–1629), and it soon spread throughout France and the Netherlands. Whereas the Roman oratory of Philip Neri was made up of independent houses, the French oratory of Bérulle—officially approved by Pope Paul V (1605–1621) in 1613 under the name "Oratory of Jesus Christ"—had a centralized organization governed by a superior general. It especially devoted itself to the training of priests in seminaries established in keeping with the Tridentine legislation. Bérulle himself was best known for his ardent devotion to the human nature of Jesus, to Christ as God incarnate, displayed in his most famous work, *Les Grandeurs de Jésus* (1623).

The Catholic revival was further characterized by a new flowering of mystical piety, in which, as in so much else, Spain was the leader. The chief trait of this spirituality was a self-renouncing quietism—a raising of the soul in contemplation and voiceless prayer to God—until a union in divine love, or in ecstasy of inner revelation, was believed to be attained. Prayer is possible only on the basis of self-renunciation, total forgetfulness of self, for God can fill only the soul that has emptied itself of all that is created. The outstanding representatives of this piety were Teresa de Jesús of Ávila (St. Teresa, 1515–1582) and her disciple, Juan de la Cruz of Fontiveros (St. John of the Cross, 1542–1591). Teresa provided a comprehensive, albeit rambling, description of the life of prayer in *The Way of Perfection* (1565) and *The Interior Castle* (1577), while the lyrical works of John of the Cross—*The Ascent of Mount Carmel, The Dark Night of the Soul, The Song of the Spirit, The Living Flame of Love*—afford an integrated statement of the whole of mystic doctrine and are literary masterpieces. (His works were first published, in a mutilated edition, at Alcalá in 1618; a critical edition of the authentic text was published in 1912–1914.) These two great Spanish mystics joined the contemplative life with the active. To them was due the further reform of the Carmelite order in Spain, namely, the establishment of numerous houses of Discalced (barefoot) Carmelites, friars and nuns fully committed to the ascetic rigors of their original rule (see V:4).

Teresian mysticism was spread in France chiefly by Pierre de Bérulle, but was also represented by François de Sales (St. Francis of Sales, 1567–1622), nominally bishop of Geneva from 1602, to whose efforts the winning for Catholicism of the parts of Savoy near Geneva was due; and by his disciple, Jeanne Françoise Frémiot de Chantal (St. Jane of Chantal, 1572–1641). Francis of Sales's celebrated *Introduction to the Devout Life* (1609) took contemplative piety out of the cloister and, on the basis of an optimistic view of the powers of the human will, affirmed that religious perfection is within the reach of the ordinary lay person no less than of the monk and nun. Here was a distinctively new emphasis in Catholic piety, namely, that the life of devotion is a relatively easy affair, so long as it is nourished by the church's sacraments, especially by frequent communion, and is guided by a competent spiritual director.

In 1610, Francis of Sales and Jane of Chantal established at Annency the Order of the Visitation (also known as Visitandines or Salesian Sisters). It was originally a congregation of contemplative women engaged in visiting the sick and the poor; but in 1618, it became a formally constituted religious order with solemn vows, devoted to the education of girls.

Catholic zeal also displayed itself, with momentous results, in the work of foreign missions. These were primarily the endeavor of the mendicant orders, notably the Dominicans and Franciscans, with whom from the time of its foundation the Society of Jesus eagerly shared in the labor. To the work of these religious orders, the Christianity of South, Central, and large parts of North America is due, and they also converted the Philippines. The most famous of these missionaries was Ignatius's original associate, Francisco Javier (St. Francis Xavier, 1506–1552). Appointed by Ignatius as missionary to India, at the request of King John III of Portugal, he embarked at Lisbon on April 7, 1541, reached Goa in May 1542, and began a career of vigorous activity. Making Goa his base of operations, he preached in southern India, Malaya, and the Moluccas. In 1549, he entered Japan and began a work that had reached large dimensions when its brutal repression was undertaken by the native rulers in 1614. Xavier died in 1552, just as he was about to enter China. His work was explorative rather than formative, but he opened many doors and his example was a contagious influence of far-reaching force.

The effort in China that Xavier had hoped for was begun in 1583 by the Jesuit Matteo Ricci (1552–1610). His desire to be "all things to all men," however, led him to compromise with ancestor worship, a relaxation that missionaries of other Catholic orders, especially the Dominicans, strongly opposed. In India, the early converts were almost entirely from outcastes or low-caste ranks. The Jesuit Roberto de' Nobili (1577–1656) began work for those of high caste in Madura in 1606, recognizing caste distinctions and other-wise accommodating himself to the Indian social system. His apparent success was great, but his methods aroused a storm of criticism and were ultimately prohibited by the papacy in 1744 (though in 1623 Rome refused to condemn Nobili). Probably the most famous experiment of Jesuit missions was that in Paraguay, where their work began in 1583. In 1610, they commenced gathering the natives into "reductions," or villages, each built on a similar plan, where the dwellers were kept at peace and taught the elements of religion and in-dustry but were held in strict and semi-childlike dependence on the missionaries. The system fell with the expulsion of the Jesuits in 1767 and has left few permanent results.

The rivalries of the several orders, and a desire for the more effective supervision of missionary labors, induced Pope Gregory XV (1621–1623) to found, in 1622, the *Congregatio de Propaganda Fide,* by which the whole field of missionary activity could be surveyed and superintended from Rome.

Chapter 12

Confessional Strife in France, the Netherlands, and England

*T*HE DYNASTIC RIVALRIES of France and Spain, with their political and military consequences, had made the growth of the Reformation possible and had facilitated the division of Germany between Lutherans and Catholics recorded in the Peace of Augsburg of 1555—a precarious settlement in which Calvinists (and Anabaptists) had no place. In France, Henry II (1547–1559) had succeeded Francis I, while Charles V had transferred to his son Philip II (1556–1598) the sovereignty of Spain, the Netherlands, and the Spanish territories in Italy and the New World; but the old rivalry continued. In war, Philip at first proved more successful than his father had been, and his victories at St.-Quentin in August 1557 and at Gravelines in July 1558 forced France to sign the Treaty of Cateau-Cambrésis on April 2, 1559. This treaty was a reckoning point in the history of Europe. France abandoned the long struggle for hegemony in Italy and experienced a steep decline in its fortunes through decades of civil strife and religious wars. Spain became the premier power in Europe and was largely able to induce a weakened and war-torn France to follow, or at least not to undermine, its interests.

Although the old dynastic struggles between Hapsburg and Valois diminished after 1559, Europe did not enjoy tranquillity. International relations, rather, were newly exacerbated by confessional division and dispute, above all by fierce conflict between a militant Calvinism and a revived Catholicism. The year 1559 witnessed the founding of the Genevan Academy (see VI:8), from which hundreds of dedicated ministers and evangelists were to be sent throughout Europe, above all to France and the Netherlands. Geneva under Calvin and Beza thus became the center of an international Protestant mission, intent upon winning the still "unconverted" peoples of Europe to the Reformed faith and away from "popery" and "idolatry." This militant Protestantism confronted, however, a much more united and formidable Catholicism than it had heretofore met. The

515

head of this Counter-Reformation Catholicism was Philip II of Spain. Austere, cultivated, methodical, industrious, and infinitely patient, Philip bent all his efforts to maintaining Spanish-Hapsburg ascendancy in Europe and absolute sovereignty in his dynastic lands. Joined in uneasy alliance with the post-Tridentine papacy, which chafed under its inescapable dependence on the Spanish monarchy, Philip also saw it as his God-appointed task to extirpate the detestable Protestant "heresy" in his territories, to prevent its alarming inroads in France, and to restore Christendom at large to the "true" Catholic faith. The next thirty years, the age of the "Spanish preponderance," were to be the time of chief peril in the history of nascent Protestantism.

The point of highest danger came, perhaps, in the year 1559 itself, when, after the death of Henry II in July, the French crown passed to Francis II (1559–1560), whose wife was Mary, Queen of Scots, and by her own claim queen of England also. Yet even Philip's ardent Catholicism was not willing to see a combination so dangerous to Spain as that of France, Scotland, and England under a single pair of rulers. He therefore helped Elizabeth I secure her accession to the throne.

Calvin's influence had increasingly penetrated France, and French Protestants or "Huguenots," as they were known after 1552, multiplied in spite of severe persecution. By 1559, they were strong enough to hold their first general synod in Paris, where they adopted a strongly Calvinistic creed prepared by Antoine de la Roche Chandieu and a presbyterian constitution drawn from Calvin's ecclesiastical principles. By the early 1560s, there were some two thousand Huguenot congregations and perhaps as many as a million and a half adherents (though such estimates vary widely). The great majority were from the artisan and professional classes, chiefly in the towns and cities of southern France. The party's imposing political strength resided in its accessions from the aristocracy, including some of the highest nobles of the land.

The death of Henry II and the accession of Francis II left the family of Guise, uncles of the new queen, all powerful at court. The Guises were from Lorraine, and they were looked upon by many of the French nobility as foreigners. Strenuously Catholic, its leading members were two brothers: Charles, the "cardinal of Lorraine" and head of the French clergy as archbishop of Reims, and Francis, duke of Guise and reputed to be the best soldier of France. Opposed to the Guise family was the family of Bourbon, of whom the chief in rank was Antoine of Vendôme, "first prince of the blood" and titular king of Navarre, a man of weak and vacillating spirit, and his much abler brother, Louis, prince of Condé. Also opposed to the Guises was the house of Châtillon, led by Gaspard de Coligny (1519–1572), known as Admiral Coligny, a man of sterling character and devoted to Calvinism. These high nobles were moved in large part to embrace Protestantism out of opposition to the centralization of power in the monarchy. They thus represented the hostility of the old feudal nobility to royal encroachment on their traditional "liberties." It is estimated that as many as half of the French nobles had abandoned their allegiance to Rome by the 1560s. In any case, the interests of many of the French aristocrats and those of the humbler middle-class Calvinists coincided in a desire that things should not continue on their present course, especially when persecution of the Huguenots intensified under the Guise-dominated government of Francis II. The first step toward a revolution was taken when the badly planned "Conspiracy of Amboise," in March 1560, failed in its attempt to capture the young king and to transfer the government to the Bourbons. Condé, who was implicated in the plot, would have been executed had it not been for the death of Francis II on December 5, 1560.

The accession of Charles IX (1560–1574), brother of the late king, brought a new party into the confused struggle. The Guises lost much of their power at court, but they remained the head of Catholic interests in France and entered into secret negotiations with Philip II of Spain, urging him to take the lead in an international crusade against Calvinism. That prospect, which Philip could not seriously entertain, was sufficient to bring the errant Antoine of Navarre back into the Catholic fold. The chief influence on the new sovereign, who was not yet eleven, was now that of his mother, Catherine de' Medici (1519–1589). Shrewd and unscrupulous, without any religious passion of her own, she was utterly devoted to preserving the Valois dynasty, embodied in her three surviving sons. She was determined to avoid a bloody civil war, and to maintain the rights of the crown, by pursuing a policy of religious and political reconciliation. She had the assistance of a statesman of broad and irenic views, Michel de L'Hôpital (1507–1573), who became chancellor of France in 1560. Catherine now sought a reconciliation of the two great noble factions, released Condé from prison, permitted a public discussion between Catholic and Protestant theologians at Poissy, in September 1561—in which Beza took a notable part—and followed it, in January 1562, with an edict permitting the Huguenots freedom of public worship outside walled towns, and of private worship within them. The Colloquy of Poissy and the Edict of Toleration were the high-water mark of French Protestantism.

Rather than submit to this policy of moderation, the Catholic party chose to provoke war. On March 1, 1562, the duke of Guise, on his way to Paris in arms, permitted his retainers to attack a large Huguenot congregation worshipping at Vassy (a walled town in Champagne). Well over a hundred Huguenots were killed or wounded. This "Massacre at Vassy" was followed by three savage wars between Huguenots and Catholics—1562–1563, 1567–1568, and 1568–1570—with uneasy truces between. Antoine of Navarre died of wounds (1562); Duke Francis of Guise was murdered by a Protestant assassin (1563); and Condé was captured in battle and promptly killed (1569). Coligny was left the head of the Huguenot cause. On the whole, the Huguenots held their own, and jealousy of Spanish influence helped their cause, so that, in August 1570, peace was made at St.-Germain-en-Laye, by which nobles were given complete freedom of worship and two places for worship were permitted the Huguenot common people in each governmental division of France, while four fortified cities (La Rochelle, Cognac, Montauban, and La Charité) were put in Huguenot control as a guarantee. The Huguenots had become, in effect, an armed state within the state.

The situation in France at this juncture was greatly complicated by the course of events in the Netherlands. The sources of unrest in that region were more political and economic than religious in origin, though in the struggle religion assumed a constantly increasing prominence. The Netherlands, which had come to Philip II of Spain from his father, Charles V, in 1555, were a group of seventeen provinces, tenacious of local rights, predominantly commercial and manufacturing, and disposed to resent all that interfered with existing customs or that disturbed trade. Lutheranism had entered early, but it had been largely displaced by Anabaptism among the lower stratum of the population. By 1561, when the Belgic Confession was drafted by Guy de Brès, Calvinism was steadily winning converts among the middle classes, especially in the industrial towns of the southern provinces (Artois, Hainault, Brabant, Flanders). The nobility, however, was as yet hardly touched, and in 1562 Calvinists were still a tiny minority of the population.

Charles V, though strenuously resisting the inroads of Protestantism, had largely respected the traditional rights and privileges of the provincial estates and governing class in the Low Countries. Not so Philip II. He determined to secure political and religious uniformity there similar to that in Spain. In 1559, he appointed his half sister Margaret, duchess of Parma (1522–1586), as regent, with an advisory committee of three, of which the dominant figure was his loyal minister, Antoine Perrenot, best known as Cardinal Granvelle (1517–1586). This committee practically usurped the power of the old Council of State, in which the high nobles had shared. In 1560, Philip secured from the pope a complete transformation of the ecclesiastical geography of the Netherlands, whereby eleven new dioceses and three new archdioceses were created. This scheme freed the Netherlands dioceses (originally four in number) from foreign supervision (by the archbishops of Reims and Cologne), but it aroused bitter opposition because all the new prelates were Philip's nominees, whereas the nobles had long been accustomed to placing their younger sons in these lucrative sinecures. Philip, moreover, was now using every power, including the local Inquisition, to crush heresy—a course that was deeply resented by the populace at large, especially the mercantile class, because it hurt trade and drove workers to emigration. Both nobles and merchants, therefore, were increasingly restive.

Chief among the opponents of these changes were three eminent nobles: the Catholic counts of Egmont and Horn; and the greatest of the Netherlands magnates, William of Nassau, prince of Orange (1533–1584), born a Lutheran, then at least nominally a Catholic, and to become a Calvinist in 1573 and the hero of Dutch independence. These men forced Granvelle's dismissal in 1564, and Philip came to consider them the chief hindrance to his plans. Rather than concede any measure of toleration, he demanded the enforcement of the decrees of the Council of Trent and the most rigorous punishment of heresy. By now, the lesser nobility, including William of Orange's younger brother, Louis of Nassau (1538–1574), had been moved to action. They drafted a petition of protest, calling for a change in religious policy, and presented it to the regent on April 5, 1566. The derisive nickname "Beggars" (*les Gueux*), given to its presenters on this occasion, soon became the honored name of the party of opposition. At this very time, moreover, the populace rebelled, stirred by bad economic conditions and famine. Calvinist preaching was openly heard in southern towns and villages, and in early August 1566, iconoclastic riots broke out. Within six weeks, they had spread throughout the country, and hundreds of churches were looted and wrecked. These excesses, usually carried out against the wishes of the Calvinist ministers, outraged moderate opinion and prompted most of the nobles, Protestant and Catholic alike, to withdraw their opposition to the Spanish regime. William of Orange, unable to hold together the fragile coalition of aristocrats and commoners, of Catholics, Calvinists, and Lutherans, retired to his home in Germany in April 1567. The revolt seemed over before it had barely begun.

Margaret of Parma was again in control, and severe repression seemed neither necessary nor advisable. Yet to Philip these events were an intolerable rebellion in politics and religion. He therefore dispatched his brilliant but brutal general Ferdinand Álvarez, the duke of Alba (1508–1582), with a superb Spanish army of nine thousand troops. Alba arrived in Brussels in August 1567 and immediately undertook the "reconquest" of the Netherlands. Margaret, who had counseled moderation, withdrew to Parma at the end of the year. During Alba's six years of rule (1567–1573), more than one thousand "rebels" were executed, including Egmont and Horn (on June 5, 1568). In May 1568, the exiled William of Orange launched an invasion of the Netherlands from Germany, but Alba easily beat it back. Firmly in control, Alba proceeded, in 1569, to introduce an exceedingly heavy system of taxation, including a 10 percent permanent tax on sales and exports. This tax, which was seen to threaten the Netherlands with economic ruin, thoroughly alienated the mercantile class. Alba's repressive measures thus gave new life to the nationalist cause. Yet his triumph seemed complete; the country had apparently been cowed into submission. Such opposition as there was came from the "Sea Beggars," roving Dutch, Flemish, and French privateers who had been preying on Spanish shipping to the Netherlands since 1568. They were nominally commanded by Louis of Nassau and were given semilegal status in 1570 by William of Orange, who was still in Germany attempting to gain the support of the Protestant princes. Until early 1572, the Sea Beggars were granted an uncertain refuge in English ports.

In April 1572, the Sea Beggars, having been ordered from English harbors in March, raided and captured the undefended port of Brill. Shortly thereafter, they captured Flushing, and within a few months the provinces of Holland and Zeeland had fallen almost completely under their control, aided as they were by militant Calvinists and Orangist sympathizers. Resentment of Alba's reign of terror also helped secure at least the passive support of the populace at large. In July, the leading towns of Holland, Zeeland, Friesland, and Utrecht recognized William of Orange as stadholder (viceroy). The northern provinces were largely undefended, because Alba had withdrawn his garrisons to the south, where Louis of Nassau and his allies were carrying out an invasion of Hainault with Huguenot troops from France, while William of Orange was advancing on Brabant from Germany. By early August 1572, King Charles IX of France was prepared to send an army of fifteen thousand men against the hard-pressed Alba. Spanish rule in the Netherlands was now in the greatest jeopardy.

Since the Peace of St.-Germain in 1570, the Huguenots and the opponents of Spain in France had been working for a revival of the older policy, which made France the rival instead of the ally of Spain. Immediate assistance to the Netherlands rebels, to be rewarded by accession of some territory to France, was planned, and none favored it more than Coligny, whose influence over Charles IX was extraordinary. To emphasize the reconciliation of parties in France, a marriage was arranged between Charles IX's sister, Marguerite of Valois, and Henry of Navarre, the Protestant son of the late Antoine of Navarre and of the queen of Navarre, Jeanne d'Albret, a devoted Calvinist. For the wedding, on August 18, 1572, Huguenot and Catholic nobles and their followers gathered in the fanatically Catholic city of Paris.

Catherine de' Medici had come to be increasingly displeased with the powerful influence that Coligny exercised over her son, the king. Her course of action was probably motivated by maternal jealousy and, above all, by fear that the war with Spain into which Coligny was leading Charles would be disastrous to the French crown. Apparently, what she wanted at first was Coligny's removal by murder. In this, she had the full agreement of Henry, duke of Guise, the son of the murdered Francis, who wrongly charged Coligny with responsibility for his father's assassination in 1563. On August 22, 1572, an attempt on Coligny's life was made, but he was only wounded, and the failure of the attempt caused Catherine to panic. The Huguenots had now been alienated without being deprived of their leader. She and her supporters decided on a general massacre, for which the Guise party and the fanatical Parisians furnished abundant means. On August 24, St. Bartholomew's Day, the bloody work began. Coligny was killed, and with him a great number of victims that has been most variously estimated but reaching at least three thousand in Paris and several times that number in the whole of France. Henry of Navarre saved his life by abjuring Protestantism.

The news was hailed with rejoicing in Madrid and in Rome. It had saved the Catholic cause from great peril. The policy of France was reversed. Plans for military intervention in the Netherlands were at an end. Yet Catherine and the militant Catholics gained no advantage at home, for renewed civil war was the predictable outcome of the events of August 1572. The fourth, fifth, sixth, and seventh Huguenot Wars (1572–1573, 1574–1576, 1577, and 1580) ran their course of destruction and misery, but the Huguenots were not crushed.

Charles IX died in 1574 and was succeeded by his perverse and irresolute brother, Henry III (1574–1589). A division among the French Catholics themselves was developing. There had long been a considerable element which, while Catholic in religion, felt that the protracted wars were ruining the land and permitting foreign, especially Spanish, intrigue. This group, known as the *Politiques,* believed that some basis of peace with the Huguenots should be reached, indeed was inevitable. On the other hand, those who put religion first and were willing to see France become an appanage of Spain if thereby Catholicism could triumph, had been for some time organizing associations in various parts of France to maintain the Roman church. In 1576, these were developed into a general Catholic League (or "Holy Union"), led by Henry of Guise and supported by Spain and the pope. Its existence drove the *Politiques* more and more into alliance with the Huguenots, who found their political head in Henry of Navarre, who had reasserted his Protestant faith in 1576.

The St. Bartholomew's Day massacre saved Alba and shattered the hopes of William of Orange for the speedy expulsion of Spain from the Netherlands. The two years following were those of intense struggle, in which William was the soul of the opposition. Alba's generalship seemed at first irresistible. Mons, Mechlin, Zutphen, Naarden, and Haarlem all fell before the Spanish forces, but they failed to take Alkmaar, in October 1573. Alba was recalled at his own request and was succeeded, in November, by Luis de Requeséns (1525?–1576), under whom the Spanish policy was substantially unchanged. In April 1574, Louis of Nassau was killed in a crushing defeat for the rebels at Mook, near Nijmegen; but in October, a heroic defense of Leyden succeeded, and it became evident that the northern Netherlands could not be conquered by the forces then available to Spain, not least because they were unable to win control of the sea. Requeséns died in March 1576, and on November 4 of that year the leaderless Spanish troops ran wild and sacked Antwerp. Over seven thousand citizens and soldiers died during eleven days of pillage and massacre. The revulsion against all things Spanish was sufficient to unite the northern and southern provinces in the so-called Pacification of Ghent, of November 8, 1576, which called for expulsion of the Spanish troops, suspension of Philip II's edicts against heresy, and freedom of worship for Calvinists in Holland and Zeeland, providing that they refrain from anti-Catholic activity outside their territories.

The new Spanish commander, Philip's half brother Don John of Austria (1547–1578), had little recourse but to accept the pacification. Yet the departure of the Spanish troops in March 1577 did not bring religious peace. Calvinism had enthusiastic support in the towns of Brabant and Flanders, and in 1577 and 1578 vehement Calvinist preaching, combined with popular social discontent, convulsed the southern provinces in a series of uprisings reminiscent of the iconoclastic riots of 1566. The ruling class of the French-speaking, Walloon provinces of the south now came to distrust, even despise, the leaders of the Dutch north and their zealous Calvinist preachers. In January 1579, the Walloon provinces united in the League of Arras for protection of their Catholic faith and social order. The northern provinces responded that same month with the Union of Utrecht. Protestants left the south for the north by the thousands, while many Catholics went southward. William of Orange's plans for a united Netherlands were unraveling in the face of religious factionalism and intolerance.

Meanwhile, Don John of Austria had died, a disappointed and embittered man, in October 1578. He was succeeded by his nephew and Margaret of Parma's son, Alessandro Farnese (1545–1592), prince and later duke of Parma, a general and a statesman of commanding talents. Matters soon went better for the Spanish cause. Through astute diplomacy and military success, Parma was able to consolidate royal authority in the Walloon provinces, which he made his base of operations for Spanish recovery in the Netherlands. Ultimately, he saved the ten southern provinces for Spain and Catholicism, and modern Belgium is his monument. The seven northern provinces (Holland, Zeeland, Utrecht, Gelderland, Friesland, Overijssel, and Groningen), along with Flanders and Brabant, declared their independence of Spain in 1581. Though Flanders and Brabant were reconquered by Parma within the next four years, the northern provinces successfully maintained their freedom in spite of much peril, including the murder of William of Orange on July 10, 1584, by a fanatical loyalist. (In 1580, Philip II had declared William an outlaw and put a price on his head.)

During this struggle, the Calvinistic churches of the Netherlands had been taking shape. The first national synod had been held outside of Netherlands territory, in Emden, in 1571. William of Orange had accepted Calvinism two years later. In 1575, he founded a university at Leyden, soon to be famed for its learning in theology and the sciences. The Reformed church of the Netherlands, like that of France, was presbyterian in constitution, through its degree of independence of state control was long a matter of controversy and varied with the different provinces. The severity of the struggle for national independence, the wish to secure the aid of all who were friendly to it, and the mercantile spirit led the Protestant Netherlands, by the early seventeenth century, to a larger degree of toleration than elsewhere at the time in Christendom. Catholics were not, indeed, allowed public worship or political office, but they had right of residence and employment. To the Anabaptists William of Orange granted in 1577 the first protection in rights of worship that they received anywhere. This degree of toleration, partial as it was, soon made the Netherlands a refuge for the religiously oppressed and added to the strength of the nation.

Yet the death of their leader, William of Orange, brought great peril to the Netherlands. They did not feel able to stand alone, and so they offered their sovereignty first to Henry III of France and then to Elizabeth I of England; both refused. In February 1585, Brussels surrendered to Parma, and in August Antwerp fell. Alarmed by Spanish success, Elizabeth sent an army to the Netherlands under her favorite, the earl of Leicester, in December 1585. Without her permission, Leicester accepted the title of governor general, but his rule was a failure, both diplomatically and militarily, and he returned to England in 1587. It seemed that Parma's skillful generalship might now reduce the rebellious provinces, but at this very time Philip required his services for an even greater enterprise. The Spanish king had determined on nothing less than the conquest of England.

Philip had aided Elizabeth at the beginning of her reign for political reasons, but those reasons soon ceased to apply, and Philip became her enemy, seeing in the "English Jezebel" the head of that Protestantism that he was committed to overthrow. The early part of Elizabeth's reign had been surprisingly free from trouble from her Catholic subjects. Mary, Queen of Scots was the heir to the throne, however, and she was a constant center of conspiracy after her flight to England in 1568. In 1569, a Catholic rebellion broke out in the north of England ("the Rising of the North"), encouraged by the Spanish, but it was quickly put down. On February 25, 1570, Pope Pius V issued his extraordinary bull, *Regnans in excelsis,* declaring Elizabeth excommunicate and deposed. In 1571, the so-called Ridolfi Plot—named for an Italian banker resident in England —was uncovered. It aimed to have Elizabeth assassinated and Mary joined in marriage with the duke of Norfolk, the first noble of the realm. The plot failed completely. Parliament answered by making any attacks on Elizabeth's person, orthodoxy, or title to the throne high treason. Norfolk was executed in 1572.

During Elizabeth's early years, the English Catholics had been left by Rome and their coreligionists on the Continent with surprisingly little spiritual aid or leadership. To remedy this situation, William Allen (1532–1594), an able English exile who became a cardinal in 1587, established a seminary at Douai, in Flanders, in 1568, for training missionary priests for England. His students were soon flocking to England, numbering over two hundred and fifty by 1585. Their work was almost wholly spiritual, but it was nevertheless looked upon with great hostility by the authorities. The conflict was intensified when, in 1580, the Jesuits began a small mission under the leadership of Robert Parsons (1546–1610) and Edmund Campion (1540–1581). Campion was seized and executed, though he intended no political movement. Parsons, however, escaped to the Continent, won Allen for his plans, and began a course of intrigue to bring about a Spanish invasion of England, a Catholic rising there, and the death or dethronement of Elizabeth. His work was most unfortunate for his fellow Catholics. Most of the priests laboring in England are now known to have been free of traitorous designs, but it was not so perceived at the time. The English government looked upon them all as public enemies and executed such of them as its spies could discover. Their work preserved a Roman church in England, but it was carried on at frightful cost. During Elizabeth's reign, 183 priests and lay people were executed.

In 1586, a new scheme was hatched against Elizabeth's life, the Babington Plot, in which English agents discovered that Mary, Queen of Scots was personally involved. As a consequence, she was beheaded on February 8, 1587, after a good deal of wavering on Elizabeth's part. Philip now determined on the invasion of England. Though long reluctant to go to war with Elizabeth, he greatly resented English intervention in the Netherlands under Leicester, in 1585, as well as the semipiratical raids that Sir Francis Drake carried out against Spanish settlements in the Caribbean and Gulf of Mexico that same year with Elizabeth's authorization. Before her execution, moreover, Mary had named Philip her successor to the English throne, and Philip now had reason to present himself as the avenger of the martyred queen and the defender of legitimacy. And, not least, the conquest of England would restore Catholicism there and in Scotland, would enable Parma to carry out the successful reduction of the rebellious Netherlands, and would free Philip to intervene decisively in France.

Philip's plan was this: He would collect a great fleet at Lisbon, which would proceed to ports in the Netherlands, there join forces with Parma's seasoned troops embarked in barges, and escort them across the channel for the invasion of England. The "Great Armada" was due to depart in 1587, but in April of that year Drake carried out his famous raid on Cádiz, destroying many ships and supplies and thereby delaying the venture for a year. At last, on May 28, 1588, the "invincible" armada of 130 ships and 30,000 men set sail from Lisbon. The battle in which it was about to engage was a contest between old and new naval tactics. The Spanish strategy was that of grappling and boarding. Their galleons were slow and difficult to maneuver, their guns heavy-shotted but short-ranged. The English sailing ships were longer, faster, more maneuverable, and armed with more cannon, which, though lighter, fired more accurately and at greater range. They were thus able to avoid closing and boarding and to punish the unwieldy Spanish vessels with murderous artillery fire.

On July 31, the battle was joined off Plymouth. There followed a week of running fight up the channel. Pursued relentlessly, the armada could effect no rendezvous with Parma on the Flemish coast, not least because the Netherlands had no deep-water port to accommodate the Spanish galleons (a fatal flaw in Philip's plan, which he had brushed aside in spite of Parma's well-informed objection). On August 8, after the Spanish fleet at Calais had been scattered by a terrifying attack by English ships, the remaining vessels engaged the far more numerous English ships in pitched battle off Gravelines. Hopelessly defeated, the remnant of the armada fled north, seeking to escape to Scotland and Ireland; storms completed its wreck during the retreat. Half the ships and two-thirds of the men did not return. England was the rock on which Philip's imperialist enterprise and visions of a restored Catholicism had shattered. Not only did his armada fall before English gunnery and seamanship, but the Catholic rising that he had anticipated would occur in England during the course of battle, and which men like Allen and Parsons had confidently predicted, never came.

While Philip's larger hopes were thus crushed in 1588, he held as tenaciously as ever to the plan of uprooting Protestantism in France and of keeping that country weak and divided. The death of Henry III's sole surviving brother, the duke of Anjou, in 1584, left the Huguenot Henry Bourbon of Navarre prospective heir to the throne. To prevent this succession, Philip and the Catholic league entered into a secret treaty, in January 1585, by which the crown should go to Henry of Navarre's uncle, Charles, Cardinal Bourbon, on Henry III's death. In July 1585, Henry III was forced by the league to withdraw all rights from the Huguenots, and in September a bull of Sixtus V (1585–1590) declared Henry of Navarre incapable of succeeding to the throne. The eighth and last Huguenot War (1585–1589) was the result—that known as the "War of the Three Henrys," from Henry III, Henry of Guise, the head of the league, and Henry of Navarre. Paris was entirely devoted to Henry of Guise. On May 12, 1588, its citizens compelled Henry III to leave the city. The weak king saw no way to resist the demands of the league and its imperious head and, on December 23, he had Henry of Guise treacherously murdered. Thirteen days later, Catherine de' Medici died.

Henry of Guise was succeeded in leadership of the league by his brother Charles, duke of Mayenne. Henry III now made terms with Henry of Navarre, and the two were jointly laying siege to Paris when Henry III, the last of the Valois, was stabbed by a fanatic monk and died the following day, August 2, 1589. But Henry of Navarre, or, as he now became, Henry IV of France (1589–1610), was still far from secure on his new throne. The league was defeated at Ivry, in March 1590, but Parma and his troops were again called into action from the Netherlands, this time to "save" France. They prevented Henry's capture of Paris in 1590 and of Rouen in 1592. Meanwhile, Spanish forces had invaded Brittany and Languedoc. Not until after the death of the brilliant Parma, on December 3, 1592, was Henry IV really master. For purely political reasons, Henry now declared himself a Catholic, and he was received into the Roman church on July 25, 1593, though terms were not concluded with the pope until more than two years later. However subject to moral criticism, the step pleased the vast majority of his subjects and gave peace to the distracted land. Nor did Henry forget his old associates. In April 1598, the Edict of Nantes was issued, by which the Huguenots were admitted to all public office; public worship was permitted wherever it had existed in 1597, save in Paris, Reims, Toulouse, Lyons, and Dijon; and children of Huguenots could not be forced to receive Catholic training. The Huguenots also retained their fortified towns as guarantees. In May 1598, the Franco-Spanish war, declared by Henry IV in 1595, was ended by the Treaty of Vervins, on substantially the same terms as the Treaty of Cateau-Cambrésis of 1559.

The same year (1598) Philip II died, on September 13, at the age of seventy-one. Not only had he failed to conquer England, but his military intervention in France had enabled the Dutch rebels to resume the offensive, under Maurice of Nassau (1567–1625), the young son of William of Orange. They consolidated their hold on the United Provinces and made Dutch independence assured.

Following the Edict of Nantes, the Huguenot churches entered on their most prosperous period. Their organization was completed, and their schools at Sedan, Saumur, Montauban, Nîmes, and elsewhere flourished. They were an armed political corporation within the state. As such, they were opposed by the centralizing policy of Cardinal Richelieu, the great minister of Louis XIII (1610–1643). In 1628, their fortress of La Rochelle was taken from them, after a resistance of fourteen months, and their political semi-independence ended. By the Edict of Nîmes, in 1629, their religious privileges were preserved, but they suffered increasing attack from Jesuit and other Catholic influences as the century went on. The revocation of the Edict of Nantes by Louis XIV (1643–1715), in 1685, finally reduced them to a persecuted, martyr church, to be proscribed until the eve of the French Revolution, and it also drove some three hundred thousand Huguenots into exile, to the gain of England, Holland, Prussia, and America.

Chapter 13

German Religious Controversies and the Thirty Years' War

*I*T WAS THE MISFORTUNE of Lutheranism that it had no other bond of union between its representatives in its several territories than agreement in "pure doctrine" and that differences in apprehension were regarded as incompatible with Christian fellowship. The original Lutheran conception of faith as the firm trust of the heart in God's freely promised mercy for Christ's sake tended to shade off into a more intellectualistic notion of faith as "an assent by which you accept all articles of the faith"—a definition once advanced by Melanchthon. The result was the gradual development of a new Protestant Scholasticism.

During the 1530s, Melanchthon's theological influence became even more widespread and penetrating than that of Luther himself, while Melanchthon's disciples, in turn, exercised a determinative influence on second-generation Lutheranism. Indebted to humanist thought, Melanchthon gradually moved from his original agreement with Luther to some emphases different from those of his renowned colleague. By the time of the 1535 edition of his *Loci communes,* he had come to modify Luther's doctrine of the bondage of the will and to teach that saving faith is the product of the joint operations of the preached word, the Holy Spirit, *and* the human will—a view to which the name "synergism" is usually given. He also maintained that good works are "necessary to eternal life," not as the basis of salvation but as its indispensable evidence—a position that he subsequently abandoned, though it was to be taken up by some of his pupils. Regarding the Lord's Supper, Melanchthon came to feel that Luther had too closely tied Christ's "real presence" to the sacramental elements; without quite reaching Calvin's position (see VI:8), he held that Christ is given "not in the bread, but with the bread," thereby stressing the spiritual rather than the physical reception. These newer features of Melanchthon's thinking were incorporated into his 1540 edition of the Augsburg Confession, the so-called Variata or "altered" edition. These differences never occasioned a breach with Luther, partly because of Luther's generous affection for his younger friend, and partly because of Melanchthon's caution in their expression, though they made Melanchthon uncomfortable at times in Luther's presence during that reformer's later years. They were to cause trouble enough in the Lutheran communions.

One chief cause of bad feeling was Melanchthon's reluctant consent to the Leipzig Interim, in 1548 (see VI:5). To Melanchthon, many Roman practices then reintroduced were "nonessentials" (*adiaphora*). To Matthias Flacius Illyricus and Nikolaus von Amsdorf, in the security of Magdeburg, nothing could be "nonessential" in such a time. They attacked Melanchthon bitterly and were joined in this "Adiaphoristic Controversy" by Johannes Brenz (1499–1570), who led the opposition to the Interim in south Germany. This rift was soon widened by the feeling of the princes of the old deprived Saxon electoral line that Melanchthon, by remaining in Wittenberg, which now belonged to their successful despoiler, Moritz, was guilty of deserting a family that had faithfully supported him; and they magnified the school in Jena, making it a university in 1558 and appointing Flacius to one of its professorships. The universities of Jena and Königsberg were the main centers of the "Gnesio-Lutheran" ("true Lutheran") opposition to Melanchthon and his "Philippist" supporters.

Other theological disputes arose, among them the "Osiandrian Controversy" and the "Majoristic Controversy." Andreas Osiander (1498–1552) roused the opposition of both Lutheran parties, and of John Calvin as well, by teaching that justification is a matter of the sinner's not merely "being declared righteous" but actually "being made righteous" by the substantial indwelling of the divine Christ. Georg Major (1502–1574) affirmed, in essential agreement with Melanchthon's earlier position, that it is impossible to be saved without good works, since these are necessary to conserve justification by faith. In 1552, he was bitterly assailed by Amsdorf, who went so far as to assert that good works are detrimental and injurious to salvation. The same year saw a fierce attack by Joachim Westphal (1510–1574) on Melanchthon's doctrine of the Lord's Supper as "crypto-Calvinism," or Calvinism surreptitiously introduced. It is not surprising that shortly before his death, which occurred on April 19, 1560, Melanchthon expressed his willingness to depart in order to escape "the rage of the theologians" (*rabies theologorum*).

The Protestant situation in Germany was further agitated by the victorious advance of Calvinism into the southwest. Frederick III (1559–1576), the excellent Elector Palatine, was led by studies of the discussions regarding the Lord's Supper to adopt the Calvinist position when he became elector in 1559. The young theologians Kaspar Olevianus (1536–1587) and Zacharias Ursinus (1534–1583) prepared for his territories the remarkable Heidelberg Catechism in 1562 —the most sweet-spirited and experiential of the expositions of Calvinism. It was adopted by the elector in 1563. But Calvinism had no protection under the Peace of Augsburg of 1555, and not only Catholics but Lutherans also were soon protesting against its toleration.

The disputes within Lutheranism continued with great intensity. In 1573, Elector August of Saxony (1553–1586), having assumed guardianship over the young princes of ducal Saxony, where the "Gnesio-Lutheran" foes of Melanchthon were supreme, drove out their more radical representatives. Thus far, electoral Saxony, with its universities of Wittenberg and Leipzig, had followed the Melanchthonian or "Philippist" tradition. Now, in 1574, Elector August believed he had discovered a heretofore unsuspected Calvinist propaganda regarding the Lord's Supper, in his own dominions. He had some of his principal theologians imprisoned, and one was even put to torture. "Philippism" and "crypto-Calvinism" were vigorously repressed.

Yet this acrimonious struggle gave rise, in 1577, to the last great Lutheran creed, the Formula of Concord. It was prepared by a number of irenic theologians, of whom Jakob Andreä (1528–1590) of Tübingen, Martin Chemnitz (1522–1586) of Brunswick, and Nicholas Selnecker (1532–1592) of Leipzig were chief. In June 1580, on the fiftieth anniversary of the presentation of the Augsburg Confession, it was published in the *Book of Concord,* together with the other Lutheran "symbols" or confessional statements—the three ecumenical creeds, the (Unaltered) Augsburg Confession, the *Apology* of the Augsburg Confession, the Schmalkald Articles, and the Small and Large Catechisms. The volume received the approving signatures of fifty-one princes, the representatives of thirty-five cities, and over eight thousand ministers. A number of Lutheran princes and cities refused to subscribe to the Formula of Concord, but it undoubtedly represented the majority of Lutheran Germany. It rejected the extreme positions of both the "Gnesio-Lutherans" and the "Philippists," while upholding the stricter Lutheran interpretation on all the controverted points. Though the Formula remained in substantial agreement with Luther's thinking, it was considerably more "Scholastic" in its method and mode of argument than Luther's own theological works. Thus, the Formula may be said to have inaugurated the period of Lutheran high orthodoxy, which was to receive its classic exposition in the monumental *Loci theologici* (9 vols., 1609–1622) of Johann Gerhard (1582–1637), a work distinguished by its extensive use of the dialectical method.

The repressed "Philippists" turned increasingly to Calvinism, and Calvinism made larger inroads in Germany. To the Palatinate, Nassau was added in 1577, Bremen by 1581, Anhalt in 1597, and part of Hesse in the same period. The electoral house of Brandenburg became Calvinist in 1613, though most of the inhabitants of Brandenburg remained Lutheran. This transformation was often accompanied by the retention of the Augsburg Confession. Yet though these German "Reformed" churches became Calvinist in doctrine and worship, Calvin's characteristic discipline found little foothold among them.

At the time of the Peace of Augsburg in 1555, Germany was an overwhelmingly Protestant land. The Roman Catholic church had disappeared from most of the country and was in a desperate condition. Virtually all of the secular rulers had become Protestants, but two-thirds of the ecclesiastical princes in the Reichstag, as well as the emperor, remained Catholic, and they were to provide the political base for the Catholic revival in Germany and the empire. Protestantism in Germany, moreover, reached its flood tide of territorial advance about 1566. From that time, it began to ebb. The revived Catholicism of the Counter-Reformation became increasingly aggressive, led by the Jesuits and supported by earnest Catholic princes like the dukes of Bavaria. Protestantism, divided confessionally and politically, could offer no united resistance.

In Bavaria, Duke Albert V (1550–1579) vigorously applied the principle *cuius regio, eius religio* to crush his Protestant nobility and people. The abbot of Fulda similarly attempted the repression of Protestantism in his monastic territory in 1572. Successfully opposed for a time, he accomplished the task in the years after 1602. Under Jesuit leadership, similar Catholic advances were made in many bishoprics, the inhabitants of which had embraced evangelical views. Soon Protestantism was also suppressed in the territories belonging to the three great archdioceses of Mainz, Trier, and Cologne, whose prince-bishops were numbered among the seven imperial electors. The most serious contest centered on Cologne, whose archbishop, Gebhard Truchsess, proposed to marry, in 1582, and embraced Protestantism. Little support came to him from the Protestant princes. He was forced from his strategically situated see in 1583 and the territory was fully restored to Catholicism. In Austria and Bohemia, the situation steadily became more unfavorable for Protestantism; and there as well as elsewhere in the empire, the Jesuit propaganda gained many individual converts. It was aggressive and confident of ultimate victory. Relations between Protestants and Catholics were constantly strained.

An event of the years 1606 and 1607 markedly increased this bitterness. The little imperial city of Donauwörth was almost entirely Lutheran, but a Benedictine monastery had survived there, and the monks were determined to return the city to the Catholic fold. One of their religious processions, in 1606, ended in a riot. On imperial command, Maximilian, the able Catholic duke of Bavaria (1597–1651), occupied the city and began a repression of its evangelical worship. At the Reichstag of 1608, in Regensburg, the Catholic estates demanded the restitution of all ecclesiastical property confiscated since 1555. For this claim, they had the strict letter of the law in the Peace of Augsburg; but many of these districts had become, in the two generations that had elapsed, solidly Protestant in population.

In these circumstances, a number of Protestant princes formed a defensive "union" on May 4, 1608, headed by the Calvinist Elector Frederick IV of the Palatinate (1583–1610). It was soon opposed by a "league" of Catholic princes, formed on July 10, 1609, and led by Maximilian of Bavaria. The strong Lutheran states of northern Germany were unwilling to join the union, nor was the emperor a member of the league. Had Henry IV of France lived, war would probably have broken out at this time, since the French king had allied himself with the union for a projected attack on the Spanish Netherlands; but Henry's assassination in 1610, and the uncertainty of the imperial succession in Germany, delayed it for a time.

The actual outbreak of the so-called Thirty Years' War (1618–1648) came from Bohemia. In 1609, that then-largely Protestant land had wrung from its half-demented king, Emperor Rudolf II (1576–1612), a charter—the "Letter of Majesty"—granting a high degree of religious toleration. Rudolf was succeeded, as both emperor and king, by his brother Matthias (king, 1611–1619; emperor, 1612–1619), but he was childless, and in 1617 his cousin, Ferdinand of Styria, an inflexible representative of the Counter-Reformation, succeeded in securing recognition from the Bohemian estates as Matthias's successor. Catholic violations of the "Letter of Majesty" increased, and on May 23, 1618, a party of disaffected Protestant nobles flung the two Catholic regents representing the absent Matthias from the high window of the Hradčany castle in Prague. This act— the so-called Defenestration of Prague—put Bohemia into rebellion and began the war. Its commencement was favorable for the Bohemian insurgents, and in 1619, after the death of Matthias, they elected the Calvinist elector of the Palatinate, Frederick V (1610–1632), their king. The same week, Ferdinand of Styria was chosen emperor as Ferdinand II (1619–1637).

Frederick found little support outside of Bohemia, whereas Maximilian of Bavaria and a Spanish force from the Netherlands came to Ferdinand's assistance. Under the command of a Walloon general, Jan Tserkales, count of Tilly (1559–1632), this Catholic combination overwhelmed the Bohemian forces in the Battle of White Mountain, near Prague, on November 8, 1620. Frederick fled the land. The "Letter of Majesty" was annulled, the property of Bohemian Protestants was largely confiscated, to the great financial advantage of the Jesuits, and the Counter-Reformation was enforced with a heavy hand in Bohemia and

Moravia. Among those enriched by the acquisition of confiscated property was one destined to play a great part in the further history of the war, Albrecht von Wallenstein (1583–1634). The union was dissolved. A similar repression of Protestantism now took place in Austria.

Meanwhile, Spanish troops, under Ambrosio Spinola, had invaded the Palatinate in 1620, and they were soon joined by Tilly and the army of the Catholic league. The land was conquered, Catholicism enforced, and Frederick's electoral title with a good share of the Palatinate transferred to Maximilian of Bavaria in 1623.

Northwestern Germany, where many bishoprics had become Protestant possessions since the Peace of Augsburg, was now threatened with war, and the disasters to Protestantism which had already happened aroused Protestant foreign powers. Nothing effective was done, however, except by Christian IV of Denmark (1588–1648), to whom England and the Protestant Netherlands sent some slight aid. The enmity of the Danish king seemed formidable to Emperor Ferdinand, and he therefore turned to Wallenstein to raise a new army as imperial commander-in-chief. This remarkable adventurer, born a Protestant, was nominally a Catholic, and now the richest noble of Bohemia. A natural leader, he raised an army in which he asked no questions of race or creed but simply of capacity to fight and loyalty to himself. He soon had a force of great efficiency.

On April 25, 1626, Wallenstein defeated the Protestant army under Count Ernst of Mansfeld at the Dessau bridge over the Elbe. He pursued the beaten forces through Silesia to Hungary, whither they had retreated in the vain hope of making an effective stand in conjunction with the emperor's enemy, Bethlen Gabor, the Calvinist prince of Transylvania. On August 27, 1626, Christian IV of Denmark was defeated by Tilly and the army of the Catholic league at Lutter. These successes were followed up by the Catholics in 1627 and 1628. Hanover, Brunswick, and Silesia were conquered, then Holstein, Schleswig, Pomerania, and Mecklenburg. Wallenstein, however, found it impossible to capture the Baltic seaport of Stralsund, which was aided by the Swedes, and he thought it wise to make peace before the able Swedish king, Gustavus Adolphus (1611–1632), could intervene. Accordingly, Christian IV was allowed by a treaty of May 1629 to keep his territories on condition of no further interference in German politics.

The Catholics were determined to reap the fruits of their victories. On March 6, 1629, Emperor Ferdinand issued an "Edict of Restitution" ordering the restoration to Catholic possession of all ecclesiastical property which had come into Protestant hands since 1552, the expulsion of Protestants from territories ruled by Catholics, and no recognition of any Protestants save Lutherans, thus depriving the Calvinists of any rights whatever. The events of the next few years prevented its full execution, but five bishoprics, a hundred monasteries, and hundreds of parish churches were, for a time, thus transferred. Many more would have been had Catholic success continued, and had not the Catholics themselves quarreled over the spoils. These disputes, and the jealousy of the league, headed by Maximilian of Bavaria, by reason of the great increase in imperial power which Wallenstein had effected, led to a successful demand by the league that Wallenstein be dismissed. In September 1630, the emperor was compelled to part with his able general.

Even before Wallenstein's dismissal, an event of prime importance had occurred, though its consequences were not immediately apparent. Gustavus Adolphus of Sweden had landed with a small army on the German coast in June 1630. Two motives induced his intervention in the war. He came undoubtedly as a champion of the Protestant faith; but he also desired to make the Baltic a Swedish lake, and he saw in the imperial attacks on the German Baltic seaports an immediate danger to his own kingdom. Should they be held by a hostile power, Sweden would be in great peril. Gustavus soon succeeded in driving the imperial forces out of Pomerania, but he moved slowly, since he had no adequate allies. In January 1631, however, he entered into a treaty with France, then under the masterful leadership of Louis XIII's minister, Armand du Plessis, Cardinal Richelieu (1585–1642), by which considerable financial subsidies were granted. Richelieu had resumed the historic hostility of France to the Hapsburgs of Spain and Austria, and the ancient French policy of aiding their enemies for the political advantage of the French monarchy, even if those enemies were Protestants. Gustavus's next important and difficult work was to secure the alliance of Brandenburg, which, though Protestant, had been imperialist, and of Saxony, which had been neutral. On May 20, 1631, Tilly captured Magdeburg, the inhabitants being treated with brutal ferocity and the city virtually destroyed by fire.

This loss of a Protestant stronghold was followed by an alliance in June between Gustavus and the elector of Brandenburg, and in August Saxony threw off its neutrality and joined the Swedes. On September 17, 1631, Gustavus, with little real help from the Saxons, won a victory over Tilly at Breitenfeld, close by Leipzig. The imperial power in northern Germany crumbled, and the Swedish king marched victoriously to the Rhine, establishing himself in Mainz, while the Saxons took Prague. In his extremity, the emperor called on Wallenstein once more to raise an army, and in April 1632, that general was at the head of a redoubtable force.

Gustavus now marched against Maximilian of Bavaria, defeating Tilly in a battle near Donauwörth, in which that commander was mortally wounded. Munich, the Bavarian capital, had to surrender to the Swedish king. Meanwhile, Wallenstein had driven the Saxons out of Prague and marched to meet Gustavus. For some weeks, the two armies faced each other near Nürnberg, but the fighting was indecisive, and Wallenstein marched northward to crush Saxony.

Gustavus followed him and defeated him at Lützen, near Leipzig, on November 16, 1632, in a fierce battle in which Gustavus was slain. His work was enduring. He had made the Edict of Restitution a dead letter in northern Germany, and his memory is cherished by German Protestantism.

The control of Swedish affairs passed to the able chancellor, Axel Oxenstjerna, though the most capable Protestant general was now Bernhard of Saxe-Weimar (1604–1639). In November 1633, Bernhard captured the important south German city of Regensburg and opened the line of the Danube to Protestant advance. Meanwhile, Wallenstein had remained comparatively inactive in Bohemia, partly jealous of large Spanish forces which had been sent to southern Germany, and partly intriguing with Saxony, Sweden, and France. Just what he had in mind is uncertain, but the most probable supposition is that he aimed to secure for himself the crown of Bohemia. His failure to relieve Regensburg was the last straw in rousing the suspicious hostility of the emperor, and on February 25, 1634, he was murdered by some of his own officers as a result of imperial intrigue.

On September 5 and 6, 1634, Bernhard and the Swedish troops were badly defeated at Nördlingen by combined imperial and Spanish forces. In its way, the battle was as decisive as Breitenfeld nearly three years before. That had shown that northern Germany could not be held by the Catholics, this that southern Germany could not be conquered by the Protestants. The war ought now to have ended; on June 15, 1635, peace was made at Prague between the emperor and Saxony. November 12, 1627, was taken as the normative date. All ecclesiastical properties should remain for forty years in the hands of those who then held them, and their ultimate fate should be decided by a court composed equally of Catholic and Protestant judges. No mention was made of privileges for Calvinists. To this peace most of Protestant Germany agreed in the next few weeks.

Yet no peace was to be had for the wretched land. For thirteen years more, the war continued as savagely as ever. Its original aims were practically forgotten, and it became a struggle, fought out on German soil with the aid of German parties, for the aggrandizement of Spain, France, and Sweden, in which France gained most. Ferdinand II was succeeded by his son, Ferdinand III (1637–1657), but the change brought no real alteration of the situation. Germany lacked effective leaders, the only conspicuous exception being Frederick William, the "Great Elector" (1640–1688) of Brandenburg, but though he succeeded in enlarging his territorial possessions, he was too young largely to affect the course of the war.

At last, after infinite negotiation, the Peace of Westphalia was made on October 27, 1648. Sweden was firmly settled on the German shore of the Baltic. Most of Alsace went to France. The long-existing independence of Switzerland was formally acknowledged. Brandenburg received the archbishopric of Magde-

burg and the bishoprics of Halberstadt and Minden as compensation for surrender of its claims on part of Pomerania to the Swedes. Maximilian of Bavaria
kept his title of elector and part of the Palatinate, while the rest of the Palatinate
was restored to Karl Ludwig, son of the unfortunate Frederick V, for whom a
new electoral title was created. More important was the religious settlement.
Here the ability of the "Great Elector" secured the inclusion of the Calvinists,
who, with the Lutherans, were regarded as one party as over against the
Catholics. German Calvinists at last secured full rights. The Edict of Restitution
was fully abandoned and the year 1624 taken as the norm. Whatever ecclesiastical property was then in Catholic or Protestant hands should so remain. While
the power of a lay sovereign to determine the religion of his subjects remained,
it was modified by a provision that, where divided religious worship had existed
in a territory in 1624, each party could continue it in the same proportion as
then existed. Between Lutherans and Calvinists it was agreed that the norm
should be the date of the peace and that a change of the lay ruler to one or the
other form of Protestantism thereafter should not affect his subjects. On the
other hand, by the insistence of the emperor, no privileges were accorded to
Protestants in Austria or Bohemia.

Neither side liked the peace. The pope denounced it. But all were tired of
the war, and the peace had the great merit of drawing the lines between Catholicism and Protestantism roughly, but approximately, where they really stood. As
such, it proved essentially permanent, and with it the period of the Reformation
on the Continent may be considered closed.

To Germany, the Thirty Years' War was an unmitigated and frightful evil.
The land had been ploughed from end to end for a generation by lawless and
plundering armies. Population had fallen from sixteen million to less than six.
Commerce and manufacturing were destroyed. Above all, intellectual life had
stagnated, morals had been roughened and corrupted, and religion grievously
maimed. A century after its close, the devastating consequences had not been
made good. Little evidence of spiritual life was manifested in this frightful time
of war; yet to it, in large part, and reflecting the trust of heartfelt piety in its
stress, belongs the work of perhaps the greatest of Lutheran hymn writers, Paul
Gerhardt (1607–1676). In its earlier years, also, lie the chief activities of the
influential Protestant mystic, Jakob Böhme (1575–1624), of Görlitz.

Chapter 14

Socinianism

THE REFORMATION AGE exhibited a number of departures from traditional orthodoxy regarding the person and work of Christ. Though not characteristic of Anabaptists in general, their earliest manifestation is to be found among such Anabaptists as Ludwig Hätzer and Hans Denck. Servetus's radical opinions and tragic fate have already been noted (see VI:8), but this ingenious thinker founded no school of disciples. The chief anti-Trinitarians of the age came from Italy, where elements of Anabaptism and spiritualism blended with the rationalistic spirit of Italian humanism into a radical questioning of orthodox Christian doctrine. During the 1550s, a number of the leading Italian radicals were to be found in or near Geneva, where there was a large and distinguished congregation of Italian Protestant refugees.

Among the members of this Italian diaspora who were profoundly disquieted by Servetus's execution in 1553, and who in varying degrees identified themselves with his views, were Matteo Gribaldi (1506?–1564), a celebrated professor of civil law at Padua and later at Tübingen and Grenoble, whom Calvin publicly reproved for his errors in 1555; and Giovanni Valentino Gentile (1520?–1566), who came to Geneva about 1556, was imprisoned in 1558 for heretical views, made a humiliating public recantation (mindful of Servetus's fate), and, after a wandering career that took him to Poland from 1562 to 1564, was beheaded at Bern in 1566. Of much greater importance was the Piedmontese physician Giorgio Biandrata (1515?–1588), who spent a year in Geneva as an elder of the Italian congregation, but found it wise to leave for Poland in 1558, serving as physician to the ruling families of that land and of Transylvania. In the latter region, he helped to found a Unitarian communion that, in 1571, obtained legal standing by decree of King John II Sigismund of Hungary (1540–1571)—a milestone in the history of religious toleration in Europe. Biandrata's chief ally in this remarkable work was Francis Dávid (1510?–1579), successively the superintendent of the Lutheran, the Calvinist, and the Unitarian churches in Transylvania, who in 1565 began to preach openly against the doctrine of the Trinity.

Those who were destined to give their name to the nascent anti-Trinitarian movement were the two Sozzinis, uncle and nephew. Lelio Sozzini (Socinus, 1525–1562), was of a prominent Sienese family of jurists and himself a student of law. Converted to Protestantism in the early 1540s, he passed much of his time in travels throughout Europe. He lived for a year (1550–1551) in Wittenberg, enjoying Melanchthon's friendship in spite of his "spiritualizing" view of the sacraments. He was well received in Basel and Geneva, but finally settled in Zurich, where he died. Servetus's execution had turned his attention to the problem of the Trinity, but his speculations were not made public in his lifetime. His nephew, the far more influential Fausto Sozzini (1539–1604), also a native of Siena, took up residence in Lyons from 1561 to 1563, with trips to Geneva and Zurich in 1562. In Zurich, he gathered up his deceased uncle's papers and, under their influence, composed at Lyons his *Explicatio* of the Prologue to John's Gospel. From 1563 to 1574, he again lived in Italy, outwardly conforming to the Roman church. In 1574, he settled at Basel, where he wrote his major treatise, *De Jesu Christo servatore* (1578, published in Poland in 1594). In this work, as in his earlier *Explicatio,* Fausto rejected the "natural" deity of Christ in favor of a deity and a world governance bestowed by the Father on the Son at the Ascension, in vindication of his "office" as God's righteous, suffering Servant. In 1578, he went to Transylvania, at the urging of Biandrata (who was by then bitterly at odds with Dávid owing to the latter's insistence that Christ is not to be worshiped or addressed in prayer). In 1580, Fausto went to Poland, then the most tolerant country in Europe, and he lived there until his death in 1604.

Thanks to the labors of Fausto Sozzini and others in Poland, the anti-Trinitarian Protestants—the so-called Minor Reformed Church—gained a considerable foothold and presented their beliefs effectively in the Racovian Catechism. Published in 1605 at Raków, the city from which it took its name and in which the "Polish Brethren" had their headquarters, this catechism was written by a number of Fausto's disciples. It is a remarkable combination of rationalistic reasoning and a hard supernaturalism. The basis of truth is the divinely inspired Scriptures, but confidence in the New Testament is based primarily on the miracles by which its promulgation was accompanied and especially by the crowning miracle of the Resurrection. The New Testament, thus supernaturally attested, guarantees the Old Testament. The purpose of both is to disclose to human understanding the path to eternal life. Though there may be in them matters above reason, there is nothing of value contrary to reason. Human freedom of will is asserted, and original sin and predestination are denied. The ecclesiastical dogma of the Trinity is neither biblical nor rational. The only faith that the Scriptures demand is belief that God exists and is a recompenser and a judge. Human beings are by nature mortal and cannot find the way to eternal life of themselves. Hence, God has given them the Scriptures and the life and example of Christ. Christ himself was a mortal man, yet no ordinary man.

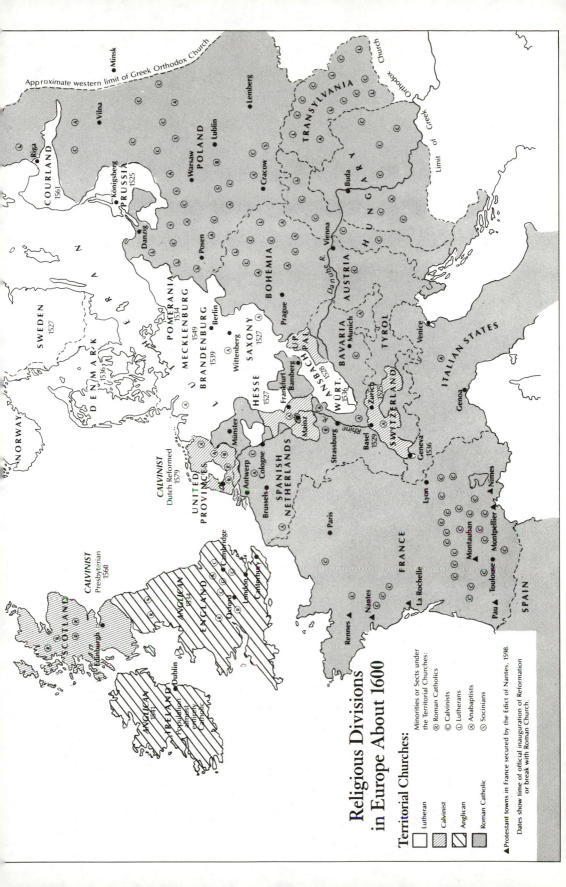

Religious Divisions
in Europe About 1600

Territorial Churches:

☐ Lutheran

▨ Calvinist

◫ Anglican

▦ Roman Catholic

Minorities or Sects under the Territorial Churches:

Ⓡ Roman Catholics

Ⓒ Calvinists

Ⓛ Lutherans

Ⓐ Anabaptists

Ⓢ Socinians

▲ Protestant towns in France secured by the Edict of Nantes, 1598.

Dates show time of official inauguration of Reformation or break with Roman Church.

Approximate western limit of Greek Orthodox Church

Limit of Greek Orthodox Church

NORWAY

SWEDEN 1527

DENMARK

COURLAND 1561

Riga

Minsk

Vilna

Königsberg 1525

PRUSSIA

Danzig

POMERANIA 1534

MECKLENBURG 1549

BRANDENBURG 1539

Berlin

Wittenberg

SAXONY 1527

Posen

Warsaw

POLAND

Lublin

Lemberg

Cracow

TRANSYLVANIA

HUNGARY

Buda

Vienna

AUSTRIA

BOHEMIA

Prague

R. Danube

BAVARIA

Munich

TYROL

Venice

ITALIAN STATES

Genoa

HESSE 1527

Frankfurt

Bamberg

ANSBACH 1528

WÜRT. 1536

Mainz

Rhine

Strassburg

Basel 1529

SWITZERLAND

Zürich

Geneva 1536

Lyon

Montauban

Montpellier

Nîmes

Toulouse

Pau

SPAIN

FRANCE

Paris

La Rochelle

Nantes

Rennes

CALVINIST
Dutch Reformed 1579

UNITED PROVINCES

Münster

Antwerp

Brussels

Cologne

SPANISH NETHERLANDS

CALVINIST
Presbyterian 1560

SCOTLAND

Edinburgh

ANGLICAN 1534

ENGLAND

London

Oxford

Cambridge

Canterbury

ANGLICAN 1541

IRELAND
Population almost entirely Catholic

Dublin

Through his miraculous birth from the Virgin Mary, he was God's only begotten Son and thus endowed with divine wisdom and might. He perfectly revealed the divine will and gave the example of the perfect moral life, sealed by his arduous death. God therefore raised him from the dead and, in the Ascension, assigned him an adoptive deity and made him coregent of the world. Hence, Christ is now worthy of adoration and invocation. The Christian life consists in joy in God, prayer and thanksgiving, renunciation of the world, humility, and patient endurance. Its consequences are forgiveness of sins and eternal life. The Lord's Supper is to be observed as an act commemorating Christ's death. Baptism has no regenerative value, is not appropriate to infants, and is at most a rite whereby converts to Christianity publicly signify their adhesion to Christ as their Master. (Fausto denied the utility of baptism for born Christians; after his death, however, believers' baptism by immersion became a distinguishing mark of Socinianism.)

Everything in Socinianism, therefore, came to focus on the moral life of the believer. Salvation is not by faith alone, but by the correct knowledge and dutiful practice of the scripturally prescribed way to eternal life—the way of active obedience to the law of God revealed and supremely exemplified by Jesus Christ. In its emphasis on faith-as-knowledge, Socinianism showed its affinity with related developments in Lutheran and Reformed orthodoxy. In its denial of justification *sola fide,* as well as in its rejection of the age-old trinitarian and christological dogmas, Socinianism broke decisively with classical Reformation Christianity.

Largely through the efforts of the Jesuits, Socinianism was banished from Poland in 1658, but it found supporters in Holland and even more in England, where it was to have considerable influence.

Chapter 15

Arminianism

IN THE LAST DECADE of the sixteenth century and the early years of the seventeenth, the Reformed church in the Netherlands (the United Provinces) was rent by a bitter controversy centering on the issues of predestination and the proper relation of church and state.

On one side stood the party of strict Calvinists, holding to the doctrine of God's unconditional predestination of the elect and the reprobate from before the foundation of the world, and asserting the right of the church to rule itself entirely, though looking to the state for protection and maintenance. These "high" Calvinists thus upheld the Genevan church polity of "noninterference" by the magistracy in spiritual affairs, and in theology they largely represented the views of Theodore Beza (1519–1605), Calvin's successor in Geneva, who took over and developed Calvin's doctrine of predestination, giving it a logical precision and systematic ordering that is not to be found in Calvin himself, and making it the center of the theological system. Most of these Geneva-oriented Calvinists were refugees from the southern Netherlands and were not inclined to tolerate any deviation from what they took to be the true "reformed" faith. On the other side was the party of "Arminians," who held that predestination has to do only with man in his fallen or sinful condition, not with man as uncreated, and that God's decree of election and reprobation is based upon his foreknowledge of the behavior of individuals. They also held that Christian magistrates are properly invested with care for the spiritual no less than the temporal welfare of the church; hence, such magistrates may enact laws regarding ecclesiastical polity and may participate in the appointment and supervision of ministers.

The embattled leader of the latter party was Jacob Harmenszoon (Jacobus Arminius, 1559/1560–1609). He has often been portrayed as a humanist or rationalist, but he is best seen as standing in a tradition of native Dutch Protestant reformers who owed little or nothing to Genevan Calvinism, who favored an inclusive church that was not insistent on sharp creedal definitions or preoccupied with "speculative" theology, and who looked to a Christian magistracy for guidance in all aspects of church life. Among these older and nondogmatic Dutch reformers, who were nourished by a biblical piety intent on a "purified" religion, were Dirck Coornhert (1522–1590) and Caspar Coolhaes (1534–1615).

Arminius, a native of Oudewater, in Holland, received his early schooling at Utrecht, possibly at the famous St. Jerome School founded in the fifteenth century by the Brothers of the Common Life. In 1575, he lost his mother, siblings, and relatives when Oudewater was ravaged by Spanish troops. Friends saw to it that he was further educated at the University of Marburg and, from 1576 to 1581, at the University of Leyden. The latter institution had been founded by William of Orange in 1575, and Arminius was among the first students to enroll there. He was next sent, at the expense of the Merchants' Guild of Amsterdam, to Geneva, and here he studied under Beza—with whom he disagreed at the outset—from 1582 until 1586, with a year's study at Basel (1583–1584). After a trip to Italy, he returned to the Netherlands in 1587, and the next year entered on a pastorate of fifteen years duration in Amsterdam, winning distinction as a preacher and pastor of irenic spirit. Though he was highly regarded by his parishioners and by the Amsterdam magistracy, his views soon aroused the ire of his fellow clergyman Petrus Plancius (1552–1622), a rigorous Calvinist who achieved fame (and wealth) as a map-maker for the Dutch East India Company. In 1603, Arminius was chosen to succeed the esteemed Franciscus Junius (1545–1602) as professor of theology at Leyden, where he remained until his death.

Within a year after his arrival at Leyden, Arminius became embroiled in an acrimonious dispute with a theological colleague, Franciscus Gomarus (1563–1641), an extreme representative of the "supralapsarian" view of predestination, as contrasted with the "sublapsarian" (or "infralapsarian") position. This issue had to do with the "order" of the divine "decree" of predestination. Did God eternally decree the election and nonelection of individuals and then permit the fall as a means by which this absolute decree could be carried out (*supra lapsum*)? Or did God permit the fall to occur and only then decree the election and nonelection of individuals (*sub* or *infra lapsum*)? Calvin himself had not elaborated on this matter, offering no explicit "order of the decrees." It remained for Beza to do this; and he, like Gomarus, taught that God eternally decreed salvation and reprobation without regard to man considered as created, much less as fallen. God's eternal, absolute decree—his all-determining sovereignty—must take priority over, and inform, all other theological and anthropological considerations.

Arminius, for his part, was neither a supralapsarian nor a sublapsarian, and herein resided one of his chief departures from "high Calvinism." The former position, in his judgment, made God the author of sin, while both positions failed to say what is decisive. He taught, rather, that God first appointed Jesus Christ as the Redeemer and Savior from sin, and that believers are predestined to salvation only in Christ. God's first and absolute decree, therefore, has Christ alone as its object, and predestination must be discussed only in this christological context. Hence, the predestination of individuals is not absolute but is conditional on their acceptance or rejection of Christ. God, that is, determines to save those whom he foresees will believe in Christ and persevere in faith, while he wills to damn those whom he foresees will not believe and will persevere in unbelief. (God's foreknowledge is thus the ground of predestination, not vice versa.) In this context, Arminius had to make room for human choice, namely, for an act of believing on the part of individuals who are saved and, conversely, for an act of rejecting God's offer of salvation on the part of the damned. The act of believing, however, is possible only by virtue of divine grace, and cannot be considered meritorious; apart from such grace, the human will is in bondage to sin and so, left to itself, resists the Holy Spirit and rejects the grace of God offered in the Gospel. Grace thus enables the individual to cooperate in the act of believing, but such cooperation is the result of renewal by the Holy Spirit, not the means to renewal. This notion of "cooperating grace," however circumscribed, had no place in strict Calvinism, but was akin to the "synergism" espoused by Philip Melanchthon in his later period (see VI:13).

After Arminius's death, in 1609, the leadership of the "Arminian" party was assumed by his intimate friend, the court preacher Johannes Uitenbogaert (1557–1644), and his former student Simon Biscop (Episcopius, 1583–1643), soon to be professor of theology at Leyden. In 1610, they and forty-two other ministers, acting in response to a prior request from the States of Holland, drew up a statement of their faith called the "Remonstrance," from which the party gained the name "Remonstrants." Over against the Calvinist doctrine of absolute predestination, the Remonstrance taught a predestination based on divine foreknowledge of the use individuals would make of the means of grace. Against the doctrine that Christ died for the elect only, it asserted that he died for all, though none receive the benefits of his death except believers. It was at one with Calvinism in denying the ability of individuals to come to repentance and faith of themselves —all depends on grace. Hence, the Arminians were not Pelagians, though that charge was repeatedly made against them. In opposition to the Calvinist doctrine of irresistible grace, they taught that grace may be rejected, and they declared uncertainty regarding the Calvinist teaching of perseverance, holding it possible that individuals may lose grace once received.

From the time of its public outbreak in late 1604, the Arminian controversy —for all its academic and abstruse character—stirred up conflict throughout the Protestant Netherlands, since theology was intimately bound up with politics. The Arminians were supported by Jan van Oldenbarneveldt (1547–1619), the civil leader of the province of Holland and the dominant figure in the States General of the United Provinces; and by the eminent jurist and historian, Hugo Grotius (1583–1645), the author of two famous works—*De jure belli ac pacis* (1625), which has earned for him the title "founder of international law," and *De veritate religionis christianae* (1622), wherein he propounded a new theory of the atonement. Oldenbarneveldt, Grotius, and the Arminians were religiously and theologically tolerant, republican in their politics, and upholders of the rights of the magistracy to exercise ecclesiastical as well as civil jurisdiction. They also favored a truce with Spain in the continuing conflict between north and south. (In 1609, the so-called Twelve Years' Truce was in fact signed.) They were opposed by the stadholder Maurice of Nassau (1587–1625), son of William of Orange and the accomplished military leader of the United Provinces, who wished to establish himself as sovereign in the north and was intent upon reconquering the southern provinces from Spain. Allied with him were the great majority of the Calvinists (the "Contra-Remonstrants"), who supported his war aims, were staunchly anti-Catholic, favored centralization in government, and insisted on a presbyterian church polity. In July 1618, Maurice used the militia to effect a *coup d'état* in the principal towns of Holland, replacing magistrates sympathetic to the Remonstrants with those favoring the Contra-Remonstrants.

Oldenbarneveldt was charged with treason and beheaded on May 13, 1619. Grotius was condemned to life imprisonment, from which he escaped with his wife's aid in 1621.

Meanwhile, a national synod had been called by the States General, now "purged" of Arminian influence, to decide the controversy. The assembly met at Dort (now Dordrecht) from November 13, 1618, to May 9, 1619. Besides representatives from the Netherlands, delegates from England, Scotland, the Palatinate, Nassau, Hesse, Bremen, and Switzerland took part in its proceedings. The Remonstrants were present only as defendants; they were not seated. The Synod of Dort, predictably, condemned Arminianism and adopted ninety-three rigorously Calvinistic "canons," which together with the Belgic Confession and the Heidelberg Catechism became the doctrinal basis of the Dutch Reformed church. Five sets of articles were adopted on April 23, 1619, which specifically affirmed the "five points" of Calvinism in rejoinder to Arminianism: (1) absolute, unconditional election; (2) an atonement whose efficacy is limited to the elect; (3) the total depravity of the "natural man"; (4) the irresistibility of grace; and (5) the final perseverance of the elect. The synod did not, however, adopt Gomarus's supralapsarian views.

In consequence of the Synod of Dort, the Arminians were forbidden to preach, and many fled the country; but on the death of Maurice, in 1625, and the accession of his brother Frederick Henry (1625–1647), who favored the Remonstrants, the measures against them became dead letters. Many of the Remonstrants returned, though their faith did not receive official recognition until 1795. In the Netherlands, the association grew slowly; it exists today as the Remonstrant Brotherhood or Remonstrant-Reformed Church. Its type of piety in the homeland was predominantly intellectual and ethical, and it was somewhat affected by Socinianism. Arminianism was to have even greater influence in England than in its homeland and was to prove, in the person of John Wesley, its possibility of association with as warm-hearted and emotional a type of piety as any interpretation of Christian belief can exhibit.

Chapter 16

Anglicanism, Puritanism, and the Free Churches in England, Episcopacy and Presbyterianism in Scotland

*A*s HER REIGN OPENED, the position of Queen Elizabeth I of England was one of exceeding difficulty. Her relations to Roman Catholics have already been considered (see VI:12). With her people far from united in religious belief, and with plots at home and enemies abroad, only by political maneuvering of extreme skillfulness was she able to steer a successful course. Her difficulties were increased by the divisions which appeared, soon after the beginning of her reign, among those who accepted her rejection of Rome. These were augmented, as that reign advanced, by the quickened popular religious life which was transforming a nation that previously had been rather spiritually apathetic during the changes under Henry VIII, Edward VI, and Mary.

Elizabeth purposely made the acceptance of her religious settlement as easy as possible. The church, in its officers and services, resembled the older worship as fully as Protestant sentiment would tolerate. All but a fragment of its parish clergy conformed, and Elizabeth was well satisfied to leave them undisturbed in their parishes, provided they remained quiet, though their hearty acceptance of Protestantism was often doubtful and their capacity to preach or their spiritual earnestness often dubious. From a political point of view, her policy was wise. England was spared such wars as those that devastated France and Germany.

From the first, however, the queen was faced by a more aggressive Protestantism, which did not find her idea of a broad, national, comprehensive church sufficiently "reformed." Many who had been exiles under Mary had come under the influence of Geneva, Zurich, or Frankfurt and returned home filled with admiration for a thoroughgoing Protestantism. They were persons prevailingly of deep religious earnestness, upon whom Elizabeth must depend in her conflict

543

with Rome. But the queen believed that, if they introduced the changes which they desired, they would disturb a situation kept at peace with difficulty at best.

From a religious point of view, the desires of such persons were quite easily understandable. For them, the Bible was the basic authority, superseding any claim of the church as interpreter or custodian of authoritative tradition. They would purge from the services what they believed to be remnants of Roman superstition and procure in every parish an earnest, spiritual-minded, preaching minister. In particular, they objected to the prescribed clerical dress as perpetuating in the popular mind the thought of the ministry as a spiritual estate of peculiar powers and hence not consistent with the priesthood of all believers, to kneeling at the reception of the Lord's Supper as implying adoration of the physical presence of Christ therein, to the use of the ring in marriage as continuing the estimate of matrimony as a sacrament, and to the use of the sign of the cross in baptism as superstitious. Because they thus desired to purify the church, they came to be called "Puritans" by the early 1560s. In 1563, they attempted to get their reform program through the convocation of the clergy of the province of Canterbury, the legislative body for most of the Church of England, but they lost by a single vote.

Many Puritans had already begun to adopt simpler practices in worship and vestment on their own. Led by Laurence Humphrey (1527–1590), president of Magdalen College, Oxford, and Thomas Sampson (1517–1589), dean of Christ Church, Oxford, both Marian exiles, a vigorous Puritan discussion concerning the use of the prescribed garments was conducted—the "Elizabethan Vestiarian Controversy." Cambridge University sympathized largely with the Puritans. But in this matter the queen's policy was strongly opposed to modification, and in 1566 Archbishop Matthew Parker issued his "Advertisements," [1] by which all preachers were required to secure fresh licenses from the bishops, controversial sermons were forbidden, kneeling at communion was required, and clerical dress was minutely prescribed. Under these regulations, a number of Puritan clergy were deprived of their positions, including Sampson, who was for a time imprisoned.

Among those who had learned in Reformed centers on the continent to feel that any worship for which biblical warrant could not be found is an insult to the divine majesty, this led to a further question—whether an ecclesiastical system which deposed ministers who refused to use vestments and ceremonies that were not delineated in Scripture was what God had intended for the church. Furthermore, as they read their New Testament through Genevan spectacles, some Puritans saw there a definite pattern of church government quite unlike that existing in England, in which effective discipline was main-

---

[1] H. Gee and W. J. Hardy, eds., *Documents Illustrative of English Church History* (London, 1896), pp. 467–475.

tained by elders, ministers were in office with the consent of the congregation, and there was essential spiritual parity among those whom, as Calvin said, Scripture, in describing them as "bishops, presbyters, and pastors," "uses the words as synonymous." [2] It was the same conviction as to the essential equality of those in spiritual office that nerved Scottish Presbyterianism to its long fight with "prelacy," or episcopal church government.

The representative and leader of this development within Puritanism was Thomas Cartwright (1535?–1603). As Lady Margaret Professor of Divinity at Cambridge University in 1569, he advocated the appointment of elders for discipline in each parish, the election of pastors by their people, the abolition of such offices as archbishops and archdeacons, and the reduction of clergy to essential parity. That was practical presbyterianism, and the more radical Puritans moved henceforth in the Presbyterian direction. Cartwright's arguments aroused the opposition of the man who was to be the chief enemy of the early Puritans, John Whitgift (1530–1604). Against Cartwright's assertion of *jure divino* presbyterianism, Whitgift was far from asserting a similar authority for episcopacy. To him it was the best form of church government, but he denied that any exact pattern is laid down in the Scriptures and affirmed that much is left to the judgment of the church. In 1572, Whitgift was able to have Cartwright, who had been removed from his professorship nearly two years before, finally deprived of his fellowship also. Cartwright thenceforth lived a wandering and persecuted life, much of the time on the Continent, laboring indefatigably to further the presbyterian Puritan cause.

The changes advocated by Cartwright were presented in an extreme but popularly effective pamphlet entitled *An Admonition to the Parliament,* written by two London ministers, John Field (?–1588) and Thomas Wilcox (1549?–1608), in 1572. To it Whitgift replied, and he was answered, in turn, by Cartwright. Some Puritans were more moderate than Cartwright and felt that relatively little alteration of the existing churchly constitution was required. The obnoxious ceremonies could be discarded, the Prayer Book revised, elders instituted in parishes, and the bishops preserved as presiding officers of the churches of each diocese organized as a synod, *primi inter pares*. But the presbyterian spirit was growing, and in the 1570s various presbyterian experiments were attempted within the framework of the establishment. Meetings of ministers and devout laymen for preaching and discussion, called "prophesyings," were undertaken. In some cases—first at Wandsworth near London in 1572—congregations voluntarily organized themselves into a kind of parochial presbytery. The presbyterian position was advanced by the publication in 1574 of *A Full and Plain Declaration of Ecclesiastical Discipline* by a former Cambridge scholar, Walter Travers (1548?–1635). All this was aided by the succes-

[2] *Institutes*, 4:3, 8.

sion to the archbishopric of Canterbury, on Parker's death in 1576, of Edmund Grindal (1519?-1583), who sympathized with the Puritans and was suspended for his conscientious objections to the queen's orders to forbid the prophesyings.

Cartwright and his fellow Puritans opposed all separation from the Church of England. Their thought was to introduce as much of Puritan discipline and practice as possible and wait for its further reformation by the government. Such a hope did not seem vain. Within a generation, the constitution and worship of the church of the land had been four times altered. Might it not soon be changed for a fifth time into what the Puritans deemed a more scriptural model? They would agitate and wait. This remained the program of the Puritans generally.

There were some, however, to whom this delay seemed unjustifiable. They would establish what they conceived to be scriptural at once. These were the "separatists," among whom proponents of congregational polity appeared. On June 19, 1567, the authorities in London seized and imprisoned some of the members of such a separatist congregation, assembled for worship ostensibly to celebrate a wedding. This company believed it could no longer freely follow the word of God within the framework of the Church of England, and it had chosen its own officers, with Richard Fitz as minister. Besides this "Plumbers' Hall" group, there were other nonconformist bodies, but in the early Puritan period separatist activities were of a fugitive and temporary character.

The first really conspicuous advocate of separatist views in England was Robert Browne (1550?-1633), a student in Cambridge in the troubled time of Cartwright's brief professorship and a graduate there in 1572. At first an advanced presbyterian Puritan, he came to adopt separatist principles by about 1580, and together with a friend, Robert Harrison, he founded an independent gathered congregation in Norwich in 1581. As a result of his preaching, he found himself several times in prison. He and the majority of his congregation sought safety in Middelburg, in the Netherlands. Here Browne had printed, in 1582, a substantial volume containing three treatises. One, directed against the Puritans who would remain in the Church of England, bears its burden in its title: *A Treatise of Reformation without Tarying for anie, and of the Wickednesse of those Preachers which will not reforme . . . till the Magistrate commaunde and compell them.* Another, *A Booke which sheweth the Life and Manners of all true Christians,* pictured the true church as composed of believers gathered together of their own volition. According to Browne, the only church is a local body of experiential believers in Christ, united to him and to one another by a voluntary covenant. Such a church has Christ as its immediate head and is ruled by officers and laws of his appointment. Each is self-governing and chooses a pastor, a teacher, elders, deacons, and widows, whom the New Testament designates; but each member has responsibility for the welfare of the whole. No church has authority over any other, but each owes brotherly helpfulness to the other.

Browne's congregational approach resembles Anabaptist views (see VI:4) at certain points. But there was no organized Anabaptist effort in England until the next century; Browne displayed no conscious indebtedness to the Anabaptists, nor did he reject infant baptism. English separatism arose out of the Puritan movement chiefly. Browne did not remain its champion very long. His stay in Holland was brief. His church was turbulent and after a period in Scotland he returned to England, where he conformed, outwardly at least, to the established church in October 1585, and spent his long remaining life, from 1591 to 1633, in its ministry.

Meanwhile, under Grindal's archbishopric, many of the main body of Puritan ministers, who remained within the established church, ceased to use the Prayer Book in whole or in part. Stress was placed on the establishment of "Holy Discipline"—Walter Travers prepared a second work on this theme as a guide for Puritan practice. Grindal was succeeded, however, from 1583 to 1604, in the see of Canterbury by Whitgift. A Calvinist in theology, Whitgift was a martinet in discipline, and in this he had the hearty support of the queen, who was implacably hostile to the Puritan movement. He promptly issued articles requiring full approval and use of the Prayer Book, prescribing clerical dress, and forbidding all private religious meetings.[3] Thenceforth, the hand of repression rested heavily on the Puritans. This hostility was embittered by the secret publication of a telling satire against the bishops, coarse and unfair but extremely witty and exasperating, plainly of Puritan origin, though disliked by the Puritans generally. Issued in 1588–1589, and known as the "Martin Marprelate Tracts," their authorship has never been fully ascertained. Probabilities point to Job Throckmorton (1545–1601), a Puritan layman, though some have suspected John Penry (1559–1593), a Welsh pamphleteer.

Puritan and separatist assertion of the divine character of their systems was now rapidly strengthening a change of attitude in the leaders of their opponents, the Anglicans. In his sermon at Paul's Cross, in London, in 1589, Richard Bancroft (1544–1610), to be Whitgift's successor as archbishop, not merely denounced Puritanism but affirmed a *jure divino* right for episcopacy. Adrian Saravia (1531–1613), a Walloon theologian domiciled in England, advocated the same view a year later, as did Thomas Bilson (1547–1616), soon to be bishop of Winchester, in his *Perpetual Government of Christ's Church,* in 1593. Less extreme was the learned Richard Hooker (1553?–1600), in his *Laws of Ecclesiastical Polity,* of 1594 and 1597. He believed that episcopacy was grounded in scripture, but his chief argument in its favor was its essential reasonableness, over against the extreme biblicism of the Puritans. The foundations of a high-church party had been laid.

The repression of Puritanism and Separatism was greatly aided by the court of the High Commission. From Henry VIII's time, it had been a favorite

---

[3] Gee and Hardy, *English Church History,* pp. 481–484.

royal expedient to control ecclesiastical affairs or persons by commissions appointed to investigate and adjudicate without being bound by the ordinary processes of law. The system was a gradual growth. Elizabeth developed it and made it more permanent, but it did not become thoroughly effective as an ecclesiastical commission until Bancroft had become one of its members in 1587. By 1592, it had fully attained its powers. The presumption of guilt was against the accused, and the nature of proof was undefined. It could examine and imprison anywhere in England and had become the right arm of episcopal authority.

Separatism had waned after Browne's return to the Church of England, but it soon reappeared. In 1587, Henry Barrow (1550?–1593), a lawyer of London, and John Greenwood (?–1593), a clergyman, were arrested for holding separatist meetings in London. From their prison, they smuggled manuscripts which appeared as printed treatises in Holland, attacking Anglicans and Puritans alike and advocating strict separatist principles more radical than those of Browne. A number of persons were won over, including Francis Johnson (1562–1618), a Puritan minister. In 1592, a separatist congregation was formally organized in London, with Johnson as pastor and Greenwood as teacher. On April 6 of the next year, Barrow and Greenwood were hanged for denying the queen's supremacy in ecclesiastical matters. The same year, Parliament passed a statute proclaiming banishment against all who challenged the queen's ecclesiastical authority, refused to go to church, or were present at some "conventicle" where other than the lawful worship was employed.[4] Under its terms, most of the London congregation were compelled to seek refuge in Amsterdam, where Johnson, after release from prison, continued as their pastor while Henry Ainsworth (1571–1623) became their teacher.

The closing years of Elizabeth's reign also saw the beginnings of a reaction from the dominant Calvinism. By 1595, a controversy broke out in Cambridge, where Peter Baro (1534–1599) had been advocating the liberal doctrines of Arminius. This discussion led to the publication, under Whitgift's auspices, of the strongly Calvinistic "Lambeth Articles";[5] but the tendency to criticize Calvinism, thus started, increased, and thorough opposition to Puritanism was to become more and more characteristic of the Anglican party.

Elizabeth's long reign ended on March 24, 1603. She was succeeded by the son of Mary, Queen of Scots, James I (1603–1625), who had already held the Scottish throne since 1567 as James VI. All religious parties in England looked with hope to his accession, the Catholics because of his parentage, the presbyterian Puritans by reason of his education, and the Anglicans on account of his high conceptions of divine right and his hostility to presbyterian rule, which had developed in his long struggles to maintain the power of the crown in

[4] Ibid., pp. 492–498.
[5] P. Schaff, ed., *Creeds of Christendom*, 6th ed., 3 vols. (New York, 1919), 3:523.

Scotland. Only the Anglicans read his character correctly. "No bishop, no king," was his favorite expression. In claim and action, he was no more arbitrary than Elizabeth, but the country would bear much from a popular and admired ruler which it resented from a disliked, undignified, and unrepresentative sovereign.

On his way to London in April 1603, James I was presented with the "Millenary Petition,"[6] so called because it professed to represent more than a thousand Englishmen, though no signatures were attached. It was a very moderate statement of the Puritan desires. As a consequence, a conference was held at Hampton Court, in January 1604, between bishops and Puritans, in the royal presence. The leading Anglican disputant, besides the king himself, was Bancroft, now bishop of London. No changes of importance desired by the Puritans were granted, except a new translation of the Bible, which resulted in the "Authorized" or "King James" version of 1611. They were ordered to conform. This Anglican victory was followed by the enactment by convocation, with royal approval, in 1604, of a series of canons elevating into church law many of the declarations and practices to which the Puritans had objected. The leading spirit here was Bancroft, who was soon to succeed Whitgift in the see of Canterbury (1604–1610). The Puritans were now thoroughly alarmed, but Bancroft was more considerate in government than his declarations and previous conduct would have prophesied, and only a relatively small number of ministers were actually deprived. Anglicanism was gaining strength also from a gradual improvement in the education and zeal of its clergy, which Whitgift and Bancroft did much to foster—a conspicuous example being the learned, saintly, and eloquent Lancelot Andrewes (1555–1626), who became bishop of Chichester in 1605.

Bancroft's successor as archbishop was George Abbot (1611–1633), a man of narrow sympathies and strong Calvinism, unpopular with the mass of the clergy and in practical disgrace in the latter part of his episcopate. The loss of such strong hands as those of Whitgift and Bancroft was felt by the Anglicans, and under these circumstances, not only Puritanism but separatism made decided progress.

A separatist movement of far-reaching ultimate consequences had its beginnings early in the origin of James I when John Smyth (1570?–1612), a former clergyman of the establishment, adopted separatist principles and became pastor of a gathered congregation at Gainsborough. Soon adherents were secured in the adjacent rural districts, and a second congregation gathered in the home of William Brewster (1560?–1644) at Scrooby. Of this Scrooby body, William Bradford (1590–1657) was a youthful member. It enjoyed the leadership of the learned and sweet-tempered John Robinson (1575?–1625), like Smyth a

---

[6] C. L. Manschreck, ed., *A History of Christianity: Readings in the History of the Church from the Reformation to the Present* (Grand Rapids, MI, 1981), pp. 197–198.

former clergyman of the Church of England and like him led to believe Separatism the only logical step. The hand of opposition being heavy upon them, the members of the Gainsborough congregation, led by Smyth, exiled themselves to Amsterdam, probably in 1608. The Scrooby congregation, under Robinson's and Brewster's leadership, followed the same road to Holland, settling finally in Leyden in 1609.

At Amsterdam, Smyth engaged in controversy with Francis Johnson, and on the basis of his own study of the New Testament became convinced that the apostolic method of admitting members to church fellowship was by baptism on profession of repentance toward God and faith in Christ. In 1608 or 1609, he therefore baptized himself by pouring, and then the others of his church, forming the first English Baptist church, though on Dutch soil. Smyth also became an Arminian, believing that Christ died not only for the elect but for all mankind. His new emphases brought him close to the Anabaptist position, and some of his congregation finally did affiliate with the Dutch Mennonites, though Smyth himself died of tuberculosis in 1612 before the transfer had been completed. A remnant of his congregation, however, clung to the English Baptist position under the leadership of Thomas Helwys (1550?–1616?) and John Murton (?–1625?). They returned to England in 1611 or 1612, becoming the first permanent Baptist congregation on English soil. Arminian in viewpoint, they were known as "General Baptists." They were ardent champions of religious toleration.

In these same years, a new Puritan position was shaped by Henry Jacob (1563–1624), who had been a member of Robinson's congregation in Leyden; William Ames (1576–1633), prominent theologian exiled to Holland; and William Bradshaw (1571–1618), leading Puritan writer. These men enunciated the Independent, or nonseparatist, Congregational position, from which modern Congregationalism has directly stemmed. Striving to avoid separation from the Church of England, they worked toward a nationwide system of established Congregational churches. Henry Jacob founded a church in Southwark in 1616, the first Congregational church to remain in continuous existence.

In the 1630s, however, a small group from Jacob's church became convinced that believers' baptism was the scriptural norm. Separating from Jacob's congregation, they started a second Baptist line in England, called the "Particular" or Calvinistic Baptists because they believed in particular or restricted atonement, confined to the elect. In about 1641, they adopted immersion as the proper mode of baptism, and it thence spread to all English Baptists.

The chief event in the history of the congregation at Leyden was the decision to send its more active minority to America. Robinson, who had been almost won to the nonseparatist Congregational position by Jacob and Ames, reluctantly stayed with the majority. In 1620, after much tiresome negotiation, the "Pilgrim Fathers" crossed the Atlantic in the *Mayflower,* under the spiritual leadership of their "elder," William Brewster. On December 21, they laid the foundations of the colony of Plymouth, of which William Bradford was soon to be the wise and self-forgetful governor. Nonseparatist and separatist streams thus flowed together in this first planting of Congregationalism in New England.

Meanwhile, under Abbot's less vigorous government, Puritanism was developing its "lectureships," the successors of the old-time "prophesyings." In parishes where the legal incumbent was hostile, or unwilling, or unable to preach, Puritan money was financing afternoon preachers of strongly Puritan cast. This was a time-tested Puritan device to allow preachers who could not conscientiously administer the sacraments in the prescribed manner to proclaim their message. Puritanism had always laid stress on a strict observance of Sunday, and its Sabbatarian tendencies were augmented by the publication, in 1595, by Nicholas Bownde (?–1613) of his *Doctrine of the Sabbath,* urging the perpetuity of the fourth commandment in Jewish rigor. Much Puritan hostility was, therefore, roused—and that of Archbishop Abbot also—when James I issued his famous *Book of Sports* in 1618, in which he commended the old popular games and dances for Sunday observance. To the Puritans, it seemed a royal command to disobey the will of God. The growth of Puritanism was further stimulated by political considerations. The king's arbitrary treatment of Parliament, his failure to support effectively the hard-pressed Protestants of Germany in the opening struggles of the Thirty Years' War, and above all his ultimately unsuccessful attempts to procure marriage with a Spanish princess for his heir, were increasingly resented and drove the Commons into a steadily growing political sympathy with Puritanism, all the more as the Anglicans were identified largely with the royal policies. By the end of his reign, in 1625, the outlook was ominous.

Nor was James's policy in his northern kingdom less fraught with future mischief. During James's childhood, the regent Morton, in 1572, had secured the nominal perpetuation of the episcopate largely as a means of getting possession of church lands. There were, therefore, bishops in name in Scotland. Their power was slight. In 1581, under the lead of Andrew Melville, the General Assembly had given full authority to presbyteries as ecclesiastical courts and had ratified the presbyterian *Second Book of Discipline.* In spite of James's opposition, the king and the Scottish Parliament had been compelled to recognize this presbyterian system as established by law in 1592.

Yet James was determined to substitute a royally controlled episcopacy for this largely self-governing Presbyterianism. He had the means at hand in the nominal bishops. By 1597, he was strong enough to insist that he alone had the right to call general assemblies, and his encroachments on Presbyterianism steadily grew. Melville and other leaders were exiled. The year 1610 saw a strong royal advance. James established two high commission courts for ecclesiastical cases in Scotland, similar to that of England, each with an arch-bishop at its head; and he procured from the English bishops episcopal conse-cration and apostolical succession for the hitherto irregular Scottish episcopate. A packed Parliament, in 1612, completed the process by giving full diocesan jurisdiction to these bishops. Thus far there had been no changes in worship, but nine years later the king forced through a cowed General Assembly, and then through Parliament, provisions for kneeling at communion, confirmation by episcopal hands, the observation of the great church festivals, and private communion and private baptism. Scotland was seething with religious discon-tent when James died.

James was succeeded, in England and Scotland, by his son Charles I (1625-1649). A man of more personal dignity than his father, of pure family life, and of sincere religion, he was quite as exalted as James in his conceptions of the divine right of kings, arbitrary in his actions, and with no capacity to understand the drift of public sentiment. He was also marked by a weakness that easily laid him open to charges of double-dealing and dishonesty. From the first he enjoyed the friendship and support of one of the most remarkable men of the time, William Laud (1573-1645).

Laud had been, under James, a leader among the younger Anglicans. A vigorous opponent of Calvinism, he had argued as early as 1604 "that there could be no true church without bishops." In 1622, in contest with the Jesuit, Fisher, he had held that the Roman church was a true church, and a branch of the Catholic church universal, of which the Church of England was the purest part. In many respects, he was a pioneer of what later was known as the Anglo-Catholic tradition, but it is not to be wondered that both the Puritans and the Roman authorities, to whom such views were then novel, believed him a Roman Catholic at heart. Twice he was offered a cardinalate. So to class him was, however, not fair to his true position. Laud was intent on uniformity in ceremony, dress, and worship. He was industrious and conscientious, but with a rough tongue and overbearing manner that made him many enemies. To the Puritans, he became a symbol of all they hated. At bottom, with all his nar-rowness of sympathy, he had a real piety of the type, though not of the win-someness, of Lancelot Andrewes. In 1628, Charles made Laud bishop of the strongly Puritan diocese of London, and in 1633 archbishop of Canterbury. To all intents, he was Charles's chief advisor also in political affairs after the mur-der of the Duke of Buckingham in 1628.

The country gentry, who formed the backbone of the House of Com-mons, were strongly Calvinist in their sympathies and disposed politically to resent the arbitrary imposition of taxes without parliamentary consent. Charles soon put himself in disfavor in both respects. Under Laud's guidance, he pro-moted Arminians to church preferments. To prevent Calvinistic discussion, in 1628 he caused a declaration to be prefixed to the Thirty-nine Articles, that no man shall "put his own sense" on any article, "but shall take it in the literal and grammatical sense."[7] Parliament resented these actions.[8] Charles had also proceeded to forced taxation, imprisoning some who refused to pay. Roger Manwaring (1590–1653), a royal chaplain, argued that as the king ruled as God's representative, those who refused taxes imposed by him were in peril of damnation. Parliament condemned Manwaring, in 1628, to fine and imprisonment, but Charles protected him by pardon and rewarded him by ecclesiastical advancement, ultimately by a bishopric. Questions of royal right to imprison without statement of cause, and of taxation, as well as of religion, embittered the relations of king and Parliament, and after dismissing the Parliament of 1629, Charles determined to rule without parliamentary aid. No Parliament was to meet until 1640. The weakness of the Anglican party was that it had identified itself with the arbitrary policy of the king.

Laud, with the support of the king, enforced conformity with a heavy hand. Lectureships were broken up. Puritan preachers were silenced. The *Book of Sports* was reissued. Under these circumstances, many Puritans began to despair of the religious and political outlook and planned to migrate to America, as the founders of Plymouth colony had already done. They did not go in search of liberty for all; rather, they sought freedom to preach and organize as they believed followed scriptural teaching. By 1628, emigration to Massachusetts had begun. In 1629, a royal charter for Massachusetts was secured, and a church was formed in Salem. The year 1630 saw the arrival of many immigrants under the leadership of John Winthrop (1588–1649). Soon there were strong churches about Massachusetts Bay, under able ministerial leaders, of whom John Cotton (1584–1652) of Boston and Richard Mather (1596–1669) of Dorchester were the most conspicuous. Connecticut colony was founded in 1636, with Thomas Hooker (1586–1647) as its chief minister at Hartford; and New Haven colony in 1638, under the spiritual guidance of John Davenport (1597–1670). These men were clergy of the English establishment. They had no fondness for Separatism. But as staunch Puritans, they looked on the Bible as the sole law of church organization, and they firmly believed it taught Congregational polity. They were able to do in New England what their fellow nonseparatist Congregationalists longed to do in old England—set up their Congregational system under the law of the state as the sole established church. Until 1640, the Puritan tide to New England ran full, at least twenty thousand crossing the Atlantic.

Charles's period of rule without Parliament was a time of considerable prosperity in England, but taxes widely believed to be illegal (such as the famous "ship-money") and enforced religious uniformity kept up the unrest. It was in Scotland, however, that the storm broke. James I had succeeded in his overthrow of Presbyterianism largely by securing the support of the nobles with grants of church lands. At the beginning of his reign, Charles, by an act

---

[7] Gee and Hardy, *English Church History*, pp. 518–520.   [8] Ibid., pp. 521–527.

of revocation that was just though impolitic, ordered the restoration of these lands, to the lasting advantage of the Scottish church, though the command was imperfectly executed. Its political effect, however, was to throw the possessors of church lands and tithes largely on the side of the discontented Presbyterians. There was now a relatively united Scotland, instead of the divisions which James had fomented to his profit.

Great as were the changes effected by James I, he had not dared alter the larger features of public worship. But in 1637, in a fatuous desire for uniformity, Charles, inspired by Laud, ordered the imposition of a liturgy which was essentially that of the Church of England. Its use in Edinburgh, on July 23, led to riot. Scotland flared in opposition. In February 1638, a National Covenant to defend the true religion was widely signed. In December, the General Assembly deposed the bishops and repudiated the whole ecclesiastical structure which James and Charles had erected. This was rebellion, and Charles raised forces to suppress it. So formidable was the Scottish attitude that an agreement patched up a truce in 1639; but in 1640, Charles determined to bring the Scots to terms. To pay the expenses of the war in prospect, Charles was at last compelled to call an English Parliament, which he did in April 1640. The old parliamentary grievances in politics and religion were at once presented, and Charles speedily dissolved this "Short Parliament." But in the brief war that followed, the Scots successfully invaded England. Charles was forced to guarantee the expenses of a Scottish army of occupation until a treaty should be completed. Of course, the English Parliament had to be summoned again, and in November 1640, the "Long Parliament" began its work. It was evident at once that Presbyterian Puritanism was in the majority. Laud was cast into prison. In July 1641, the High Commission was abolished. In January 1642, the attempt of the king to seize five members of the Commons, whom he accused of treason, led finally to the outbreak of civil war. In general, the North and West stood for the king, the South and East for Parliament.[9]

Parliament passed an act early in 1643 which abolished episcopacy before the year was out. Provision had to be made for the creed and government of the church, and therefore Parliament called an assembly of 121 clergymen and 30 laymen, whom it named, to meet in Westminster on July 1, 1643, to advise Parliament (which kept the power of enactment in its own hands). The Westminster Assembly, thus convened, contained a few Congregationalists and Episcopalians, but its overwhelming majority was Presbyterian Puritan. Meanwhile, the war had begun ill for Parliament, and to secure Scottish aid the Solemn League and Covenant, pledging the largest possible uniformity in religion in England, Scotland, and Ireland, and opposing "prelacy," was accepted by Parliament in September 1643 and was soon imposed on all Englishmen over eighteen years of age. Scottish commissioners, without vote but with much

[9] For the important documents illustrative of this period, see ibid., pp. 537–585.

influence, now sat in the Westminster Assembly. The Assembly presented to Parliament a Directory of Worship and a thoroughly Presbyterian system of church government in 1644. In January following, Parliament abolished the Prayer Book and substituted the Directory, which provided an order of worship which is substantially the one that has been used in conservative Presbyterian and Congregational churches for generations. It struck a balance between a prescribed liturgy and extemporaneous prayer. Parliament was hesitant to establish Presbyterian government but finally ordered it in part in 1646 and 1647. The work was, however, very imperfectly set in operation. In January 1645, Laud was executed under a bill of attainder—an act which must be judged one of vindictiveness. The assembly next prepared its famous confession,[10] which it laid before Parliament late in 1646. Adopted by the General Assembly of Scotland on August 27, 1647, it remains the basic standard of Scottish and American Presbyterianism. The English Parliament refused approval until June 1648, and then modified some sections. In 1647, the assembly completed two catechisms, a Larger, for pulpit exposition, and a Shorter,[11] for the training of children primarily. Both were approved by the English Parliament and the Scottish General Assembly in 1648.

The Westminster Confession and catechisms, especially the Shorter, have always ranked among the most notable expositions of Calvinism. In general, they repeat the familiar continental type. On the question of the divine decrees, they are infralapsarian (see VI:15). One of their chief features is that, in addition to the familiar derivation of original sin from the first parents as "the root of all mankind," they emphasize a "convenant of works" and a "covenant of grace." In the former, Adam is regarded as the representative head of the human race, to whom God made definite promises, which included his descendants, and which he, as their representative, forfeited by his disobedience for them as well as for himself. The "covenant of works" having failed, God offered a new "covenant of grace" through Christ. The roots of this covenant, or federal, theology can be found in the writings of Bullinger (see VI:3), though its fullest exposition was to be in the work of Johannes Cocceius (1603–1669), professor in Franeker and Leyden. It was an attempt to give a definite explanation of sin as man's own act, and to show a real human responsibility for his ruin. Another characteristic of these symbols is an emphasis on the Sabbath consonant with the Puritan development of this doctrine.

While these theological and ecclesiastical discussions were in progress, the civil war had run its early course. On July 3, 1644, the royal army had been defeated on Marston Moor near York, largely by the skill of a member of Parliament of little military experience, Oliver Cromwell (1599–1658), whose

---

[10] J. H. Leith, ed., *Creeds of the Churches: A Reader in Christian Doctrine from the Bible to the Present* (Garden City, N.Y., 1963), pp. 192–229.

[11] Schaff, *Creeds of Christendom*, 3:676–703; selections also in Manschreck, *History of Christianity*, pp. 200–203.

abilities had created a picked troop of "religious men." Not quite a year later, on June 14, 1645, Cromwell cut to pieces the last field army of the king near Naseby. The next year, Charles gave himself up to the Scots, who, in turn, surrendered him to the English Parliament. The "new model" army, as created by Cromwell, was a body of religious enthusiasts, in which little question was raised of finer distinctions of creed. So long as they opposed Rome and "prelacy," Puritans of all stripes were welcome in it. The Independents emerged as the dominant group, with Baptists and sectaries ever more in evidence. But the rigid Presbyterianism of the parliamentary majority was becoming as distasteful to the army as the older rule of bishops, and Cromwell fully shared this feeling. The army was soon demanding a large degree of toleration. Puritanism had appealed to the Bible and experience, and now men on spiritual pilgrimages—many of them in the army—were demanding the freedom to follow their convictions.

This attitude of the army prevented the full establishment of Presbyterianism which Parliament sanctioned. This displeased the Scots. Charles used this situation to intrigue with the Scots to invade England in his interest, inducing them to believe that he would support Presbyterianism. Between August 17 and 20, 1648, the invading Scottish army was scattered by Cromwell near Preston. This victory left the army supreme in England. On December 6, "Pride's Purge" expelled from Parliament the Presbyterian members, leaving the "Rump Parliament." Charles I was then tried and condemned for his alleged treasons and perfidies and was beheaded on January 30, 1649, bearing himself with great dignity. Cromwell next subjugated Ireland in 1649, reduced Scotland the next year, and overthrew Charles's son, the later Charles II (1660–1685), near Worcester in 1651. Opposition had been everywhere put down.

Cromwell, though not identified wholly with any one Puritan strand, was inclined toward the Independents. Under his protectorate, a large degree of toleration was allowed,[12] and moderate Episcopalian Puritans, Presbyterians, Independents, and some Baptists were included in a broad establishment. Since the beginning of the war, however, about two thousand Episcopal clergymen had been deprived and had suffered great hardship. But, as in earlier and later changes, it is evident, nevertheless, that the great majority of the clergy either were undisturbed or managed to adjust themselves to the new state of affairs. Able, conscientious, and statesmanlike as Cromwell was, his rule was that of military authority and was as such disliked, while the bickerings of rival religious bodies were equally distasteful to a great majority of the people of England, who could, as yet, conceive of only one established form of faith. Until his death, on September 3, 1658, Cromwell suppressed all disaffection.

Oliver Cromwell was succeeded by his son, Richard, as protector; but the new ruler was a man of no force, and practical anarchy was the result. Royalists

[12] Gee and Hardy, *English Church History,* pp. 574–585.

and Presbyterians now combined to effect a restoration of the monarchy. On April 14, 1660, Charles II issued a declaration "of liberty to tender consciences," from Breda,[13] and on May 29 he entered London. But if the Presbyterians had hopes of being included in the new religious settlement, they were doomed to bitter disappointment.

Charles II may have intended some comprehension of Presbyterians in the national church. Edward Reynolds (1599–1676), heretofore a decided Puritan, was made bishop of Norwich. The saintly Richard Baxter (1615–1691), one of the most eminent of the Presbyterian party, was offered a bishopric, but declined. A conference between bishops and Presbyterians was held by government authority at the Savoy Palace in 1661,[14] but led to little result. Charles II was unscrupulous, immoral, weak, and indifferent in religion. Little reliance could be placed on his promises. But even had he been a better or a stronger man, it is doubtful whether he could have stemmed the tide of national reaction against Puritanism. The first Parliament chosen after his restoration was fiercely royalist and Anglican. The convocations of Canterbury and York met in 1661, and some six hundred alterations were made in the Prayer Book, but none looking in the Puritan direction. In May 1662, a new Act of Uniformity received the royal assent. The use of any service other than those of the revised Prayer Book was forbidden under heavy penalties, and each clergyman was required, before August 24, to take an oath of "unfeigned assent and consent to all and everything contained and prescribed" therein; and also, "that it is not lawful, upon any pretense whatsoever, to take arms against the King."[15]

These provisions were intended to bar the Puritans from the church, and as such they were effectual. Some eighteen hundred ministers gave up their places rather than take the prescribed oaths. The Puritan party was now, what it had not been before, one outside the Church of England. Nonconformity had been forced to become Dissent. Presbyterians and Independents, the latter now organized along Congregational lines, were forced outside the establishment. Severer acts soon followed, induced in part by fear of conspiracy against the restored monarchy. By the First Conventicle Act (1664), fine, imprisonment, and banishment were the penalties for presence as a service not in accordance with the Prayer Book, attended by five or more persons not of the same household. By the "Five Mile Act" of the next year, any person "in Holy Orders or pretended Holy Orders," or who had preached to a "conventicle," and did not take the oath condemning armed resistance to the king and pledging no attempt at "any alteration of government either in church or state," was forbidden to live within five miles of any incorporated town or within the same distance of the former place of his ministry.[16] Such persons

[13] Ibid., pp. 585–588.
[14] Ibid., pp. 588–594.
[15] Ibid., pp. 600–619.
[16] Ibid., pp. 620–623; Bettenson, *Documents of the Christian Church,* pp. 404–407.

were also forbidden to teach school—about the only occupation readily open to a deprived minister. These and other acts of the so-called "Clarendon Code" were impossible of strict enforcement, but they led to a great deal of persecution of the Dissenters. The Second Conventicle Act (1670) made penalties for unlawful attendance at dissenting services less severe, but ingeniously provided that the heavy fines on preacher and hearers could be collected from any attendant, in case poverty prevented their payment by all.[17] Yet, in spite of this repression, dissenting preaching and congregations continued.

Charles II, though a man of no real religion, sympathized with the Roman faith, which he professed on his deathbed, and his brother, the later James II, was an acknowledged and earnest Catholic from 1672. Moreover, Charles was receiving secret pensions from the strongly Catholic Louis XIV of France. On March 15, 1672, with a design of aiding the Catholics and securing dissenting favor to that end, Charles issued, on his own authority, a Declaration of Indulgence, by which Protestant Dissenters were granted the right of public worship, the penal laws against the Catholics were remitted, and their worship was permitted in private houses. To Parliament, this seemed an unconstitutional favor to Rome. It forced the withdrawal of the Indulgence, in 1673, and passed the Test Act, which, though aimed at Catholics, bore hard on Protestant Dissenters. All holders of military or civil office living within thirty miles of London, with a few minor exceptions, were required to take the Lord's Supper according to the rites of the Church of England or forfeit their posts.[18] This statute was not repealed until 1828. The repression of Dissent, therefore, continued until the death of Charles II, in 1685.

For James II (1685–1688) it must be said that he saw in the establishment of Catholicism his chief aim, and his measures toward that end were vigorous but tactless. He ignored the Test Act and appointed Catholics to high office in military and civil service. He brought in Jesuits and monks. He secured from a packed Court of the King's Bench, in 1686, an acknowledgment of his right "to dispense with all penal laws in particular cases." He reestablished a High Commission Court. On April 4, 1687, he issued a Declaration of Indulgence, granting complete religious toleration.[19] In itself, it was a well-sounding and, from the modern standpoint, a praiseworthy act. Yet its motives were too obvious. Its ultimate aim was to make England once more a Roman Catholic country, and all Protestantism was alarmed, while lovers of constitutional government saw in it a nullification of the power of Parliament by arbitrary royal will. The vast majority of Dissenters, though relieved thereby from grievous disabilities, refused to support it and made common cause with the churchmen. When, in April 1688, James II ordered the Indulgence read in all churches,

---

[17] Gee and Hardy, *English Church History*, pp. 623–632.   [19] Ibid., pp. 641–644.
[18] Ibid., pp. 632–640.

seven bishops protested. They were put on trial and, to the delight of the Protestants, acquitted. James had taxed national feeling too greatly. William of Orange (1650–1702), the stadholder of the Netherlands, who had married Mary, James's daughter, was invited to head the movement against James. On November 5, 1688, he landed with an army. James fled to France. A revolution had been accomplished, and on February 13, 1689, William (III) and Mary were proclaimed joint sovereigns of England.

The clergy of the Restoration had asserted too long the doctrines of the divine right of kings and of passive obedience to royal authority to make this change palatable. Seven bishops, headed by William Sancroft (1617–1693), refused the oath of allegiance to the new sovereigns, and about four hundred clergy joined them. To them, James II was still the Lord's anointed. They were deprived, as Anglicans and Dissenters had been before, and they bore themselves with equal courage. Many of them were men of earnest piety. They formed the Nonjuror party, part of which took refuge in Scotland, there to make a genuine liturgical contribution to the Episcopal church in that country.

Under the circumstances of the Revolution of 1688, toleration could no longer be denied to Protestant Dissenters. By the Toleration Act of May 24, 1689, all who swore, or affirmed, the oaths of allegiance to William and Mary, rejected the jurisdiction of the pope, transubstantiation, the Mass, and the invocation of the Virgin and saints, and also subscribed to the doctrinal positions of the Thirty-nine Articles, were granted freedom of worship.[20] It was a personal toleration, not a territorial adjustment as in Germany at the close of the Thirty Years' War. Diverse forms of Protestant worship could now exist side by side. The Dissenters may have amounted to a tenth of the population of England, divided chiefly among the three "old denominations," Presbyterians, Congregationalists, and Baptists. They were still bound to pay tithes to the establishment, and had many other disabilities, but they had won essential religious freedom. In time, they became known as the English free churches. No such privileges as they won were granted to deniers of the Trinity or to Roman Catholics. The effective relief of the latter did not come until 1778 and 1791 and was not completed until 1829.

In Scotland, the Restoration was a time of great turmoil and suffering. The Parliament of 1661 annulled all acts favorable to the Presbyterian church since 1633. Episcopacy was therefore restored as in the time of Charles I. In September 1661, four bishops were appointed, chief of them James Sharp (1618–1679) as archbishop of St. Andrews. Consecration was obtained from England. Sharp had been a Presbyterian minister but had betrayed his party and his church. All officeholders were required by Parliament to disown the covenants of 1638 and 1643. In 1663, Parliament enacted heavy fines for absence from the

---

[20] Ibid., pp. 654–664.

now episcopally governed churches, though even it did not dare introduce a liturgy. Many Presbyterian ministers were now deprived, especially in south-western Scotland. When their parishioners absented themselves from the minis-tration of the new appointees, they were fined, and if payment was not forth-coming, soldiers were quartered on them. In 1664, a High Commission Court was added to the instruments of repression. Two years later, some of the oppressed supporters of the covenants of 1638 and 1643, or Covenanters, en-gaged in the Pentland Rising. It was ruthlessly crushed, and the Presbyterian element was thereafter treated with increasing severity. On May 3, 1679, in belated retaliation, Sharp was murdered. This crime was speedily followed by an armed rising of Covenanters, but on June 22, the revolt was crushed at Bothwell Bridge and the captured insurgents treated with great cruelty. Six months later, the king's brother, James—the later James II of England—was practically put in charge of Scottish affairs. The extremer and uncompromising Presbyterians were now a proscribed and hunted folk, known as Cameronians, from one of their leaders, Richard Cameron (1648?–1680).

The accession of James II (or VII, as he was numbered in Scotland) at first intensified the repression of the Cameronians. His first year was the "kill-ing time," and the Parliament of 1685 made death the punishment for attend-ance at a "conventicle." James, however, soon pursued the same course as in England. He filled his council with Catholics, and in 1687 he issued Letters of Indulgence granting freedom of worship. As in England, this release of Catholics from penalty aroused the hostility of all shades of Protestants. Epis-copalians and Presbyterians were alike opposed; and when William and Mary mounted the throne of England, they had many friends in the northern kingdom. Scotland was more divided than England, however. The Stuarts were Scottish, and though Episcopalians disliked the Catholicism of James, they distrusted the Calvinism of "Dutch William," whom the Presbyterians favored. The Revolution triumphed, however, and on May 11, 1689, William and Mary became rulers of Scotland. In 1690, Parliament restored all Presby-terian ministers ejected since 1661, ratified the Westminster Confession, and declared Presbyterianism the form recognized by the government. This legal establishment of the Presbyterian church was opposed by the Cameronian laity, who continued their hostility to any control of the church by civil authority and condemned the failure to renew the covenants, and by the Episcopalians, who were strong in northern Scotland. In 1707, England and Scotland were united into one kingdom of Great Britain, but the independent rights of the Church of Scotland were safeguarded. Under Queen Anne, in 1712, two im-portant acts were passed by Parliament. By one, the status of a tolerated communion was given to episcopacy, then strongly entrenched in northern Scotland. The other, destined to be the source of infinite trouble, permitted "patrons," usually the crown or the great landlords, to force appointments of Presbyterian ministers on hostile parishioners (see VII:7).

Chapter 17

The Quakers

D URING THE TURMOIL of the 1640s and 1650s in England, the number of sect movements multiplied. Some of these, like the Levelers and the Diggers, were religio-political sects. Others exhibited a strong millennial emphasis, especially the Fifth Monarchy Men. Mystical tendencies were strong in some, such as the Seekers and the Finders. By far the most significant of these movements, and one of the most remarkable products of the period of the civil wars, was the Society of Friends, popularly known as Quakers because they quaked before the Lord. George Fox (1624–1691) was one of the few religious geniuses of English history. Born in Fenny Drayton, the son of a weaver, he grew up earnest and serious-minded, having "never wronged man or woman." At nineteen, a drinking bout, to which he had been invited by some nominal Christians, so disgusted him by the contrast between practice and profession that he was set on a soul-distressing search for spiritual reality. Shams of all sorts he detested. His transforming and central experience came to Fox in 1646. Out of it came the firm conviction that every person receives from the Lord a measure of light, and that if this "inner light" is followed, it leads surely to the "light of life" and to spiritual truth. Revelation is not confined to the Scriptures, though they are a true word of God, but it enlightens all who are true disciples. The spirit of God speaks directly to them, gives them their message, and quickens them for service.

Fox began his stormy ministry in 1647. He believed that, since the inner light is given by the divine will, the true ministry is that of any man or woman God deigns to use. A professional ministry is to be rejected. The sacraments are inward and spiritual verities. The outward elements are not merely unnecessary but misleading. Oaths are a needless corroboration of the truthful word of a Christian. Servility in speech or behavior is a degradation of the true Christian respect of man to man. Artificial titles are to be rejected, though Fox did not deny legal titles like king or judge. War is unlawful for a Christian; slavery is abhorrent. All Christianity, to be true, must express itself in a transformed, consecrated life. The sincerity and spiritual earnestness of Fox's beliefs, his hatred of all that savored of formalism, and his demand for inward spiritual experience were immensely attractive forces. He drew followers from among the various Puritan parties and from the sects that had proliferated on Puritan soil. By 1652, the first Quaker community was gathered in Preston Patrick in northern England. Two years later, the Friends had spread to London, Bristol, and Norwich. Fox's most eminent early convert was Margaret Fell (1614–1702), whom he married after she became a widow, and her home, Swarthmore Hall, furnished a headquarters for his preachers.

In the circumstances of English life, such a movement met with fierce opposition. Before 1661, more than three thousand Friends, including Fox himself, had suffered imprisonment. A missionary zeal was early manifested, which sent Quakers to proclaim their faith to as far distant points as Jerusalem, the West Indies, Germany, Austria, and Holland. In 1656, they entered Massachusetts, and by 1661 four had been hanged there. There was some explanation, though no justification, for this severity in the extravagant conduct of a good many of the early Quakers, which would have aroused police interference in any age.

These extravagances were made possible by the early want of organization, as well as by belief in the immediate inspiration of the Spirit. Fox saw the necessity of order, and by 1666 the main features of the Quaker discipline had been mapped out, though in the face of considerable opposition. "Monthly Meetings" were established, by which strict watch could be kept over the life and conduct of the membership. Before Fox died, in 1691, the body had taken on the sober characteristics which have ever since distinguished it.

The laws against Dissenters at the Restoration bore with peculiar severity on the Quakers, since they, unlike the Presbyterians and Congregationalists, made no effort to conceal their meetings but defiantly maintained them in the face of hostile authority. About four hundred met their deaths in prison, and many were ruined financially by heavy fines. To this period, however, belongs their most eminent trophy and their great colonial experiment. William Penn (1644–1718), son of Admiral Sir William Penn, after inclinations toward Quakerism as early in 1661, fully embraced its beliefs in 1666 and became one of the most eminent preachers and literary defenders of the faith. He determined to find in America the freedom denied Quakers in England. After aiding in sending some eight hundred Quakers to New Jersey in 1677 and 1678, Penn obtained from Charles II the grant of Pennsylvania, in 1681, in release of a debt due from the crown to his father. In 1682, Philadelphia was founded, and a great colonial experiment had begun.

The Toleration Act of 1689 (see VI:16) relieved the Quakers, like other Dissenters, of their more pressing disabilities and granted them freedom of worship.

_____ *Period VII*

MODERN CHRISTIANITY

Chapter 1

The Beginnings of Modern Science and Philosophy

THE QUESTION has been much controverted whether the Reformation is to be reckoned to the Middle Ages or to modern history. Not a little may be urged in support of both positions. Its conceptions of a religion to be maintained by external authority, of the dominance of religion over all forms of educational and cultural life, of a single type of worship as alone allowable, at least within a given territory, of original sin, of evil spirits and witchcraft, of the immediacy and arbitrariness of the divine relations with the world, and of the otherworldliness of religious outlook—all link the Reformation to the Middle Ages. So, too, the problems primarily discussed, however different their solution from that characteristic of the Middle Ages, were essentially medieval. Sin and grace had been, since the time of Augustine if not of Tertullian, the central problems of Latin theology; they were so of the Reformation. However Luther himself might reject Aristotle, the older Protestant philosophy was thoroughly Aristotelian. Nor, though monasticism was repudiated, was the ascetic view of the world rejected, least of all by Calvinism.

On the other hand, the Reformation as a religious movement represented a new apprehension of the meaning of Christian faith. It broke the dominance of the sacramental system which had controlled Christianity for so many centuries. Baptism and the Lord's Supper were preserved and highly valued, but they were now regarded more as seals to the divine promises than as exclusive channels of grace. The Holy Spirit, whose ways are mysterious, no doubt uses them for gracious purposes, but not to the exclusion of other means. One comes to faith through the written or preached word of God. Salvation is a direct and personal relationship, wrought by God, bringing the presence of the living Christ to the believer. Faith in Christ, who is experienced as both forgiveness and power, is a gift of God. Human relationship to God is not one of debit and credit, of evil acts to be purged and merit to be acquired, but a state of reconciliation of which good works are the natural fruits. Nor was the Protestant estimate of the normal relations and occupations of life as the best fields for service to God a less radical departure from the Middle Ages. These characteristics link the Reformation with the modern world; indeed, they have contributed not a little to the shaping of the modern period. Yet if one strikes a balance, and remembers also how largely the worldly tendencies of humanism were suppressed by the Reformation, the movement in its first century and a half must be reckoned in great measure a continuance of the Middle Ages. After that, though great religious bodies still used the Reformation formulas and bore names then originating, they no longer moved in the same atmosphere.

To assign an exact line of demarcation for this change is impossible. The alteration was not due to a single leader or group of leaders. It modified Christian thought unevenly but pervasively. The transformation was aided by a great variety of causes. One of these was the steady secularization of culture since the middle of the seventeenth century. The medieval and Reformation pattern of a church-dominated state and society gave way to the drive for a religiously neutral civilization.[1] Another important factor has been the rise of the professional, mercantile, and laboring classes to constantly increasing educational and political influence. In the Reformation age, leaders of thought and sharers in government were few, but in the modern period their number and independence steadily expanded. This growth helped to bring about, and in turn was aided by, an increasing toleration on the part of the state, which made possible both the enormous subdivision of Protestantism and the rise of many groups of thinkers not directly associated with, or opposed to, organized religion.

The most potent instruments in effecting this change of atmosphere were the rise of modern science and philosophy, with the immense consequent transformations in outlook upon the universe and upon man's position in it, and the subsequent development of the historic method of examining and interpreting thought and institutions.

The early Reformation period conceived of the universe in Ptolemaic fashion. The earth was viewed as the center about which sun and stars revolved. The Renaissance had revived in Italy Greek speculations of a heliocentric system, and these were elaborately developed by Nicolaus Copernicus (1473–1543), of Thorn in Poland, and published in the year of his death. At the time, they excited slight attention, and that mostly unfavorable. But astronomical science made progress. Tycho Brahe (1546–1601), though only partially accepting the Copernican system, multiplied observations. Johannes Kepler (1571–1630), a Copernican, developed these into brilliant generalizations. Both were pursuing, though uninfluenced directly by him, the new method of Sir Francis Bacon (1561–1626), by which inductive experiment was made the basis of hypothetical

---

[1] James Hastings Nichols has remarked that the Peace of Westphalia (1648), which ended the Thirty Years' War, is as good a date as any to represent the transition to the new phase in politics, for at that time national and dynastic considerations pushed aside theological and confessional ones: *History of Christianity, 1650–1950: Secularization of the West* (NY, 1956), p. 6.

generalization. Galileo Galilei (1564-1642), of Pisa, gave to the world the thermometer, developed the pendulum, put mechanical physics on a new basis by experiment, and, above all, applied the telescope to the study of the heavens. The real triumph of the theory of Copernicus was due to him. But his explication of it, especially in his *Dialogue* of 1632, led to bitter philosophical and ecclesiastical opposition, and he was compelled to abjure it by the Inquisition the year following. The popular demonstration of the Copernican theory was, however, the work of Sir Issac Newton (1642-1727). His *Principia* of 1687 caused a European sensation, showing as it did by mathematical demonstration that the motions of the heavenly bodies were explainable by gravitation. The effect of Newton's conclusions was profound. To thinking persons, the physical universe no longer appeared as a field of arbitrary divine action, but as an interpretable realm of law—such was the conclusion of the science of that age, in strict terms of mechanical cause and effect. This earth was no longer the center of all things, but rather a mere speck in a vast realm of bodies, many of infinitely greater size and all moving in obedience to unchangeable law. Newton himself was deeply religious and much interested in theology, but his scientific findings were used by some as a means of deprecating Christianity.

While science was thus revealing a new heaven and a new earth, philosophy was no less vigorously challenging the claims of authority in the name of reason. René Descartes (1596-1650), a native of France and a devout Catholic, spent most of his active intellectual life in the Netherlands. There he wrote *Discourse on Method* (1637), *First Philosophy* (1641), and *Principia* (1644). To his thinking, only that is really knowledge which the mind fully understands. Mere erudition is not intelligence. The objects and ideas which present themselves to the mind are so involved and so dependent one on another that they must be analyzed and separated into simplicity to be really understood. Hence, the beginning of all knowledge is doubt, and no real progress can be made until a basis, or point of departure, can be found which cannot be doubted; and that Descartes found, with Augustine, in his own existence as a thinking being. Even in doubting, "I think, therefore I am." If we examine the contents of this "thinking I," we find in it ideas greater than it could of itself originate, and since nothing can be without an adequate cause, there must be a cause great enough and real enough to produce them. Hence, we are convinced of the existence of God and of God's relation to all our thinking. In God, thought and being are united. Our ideas are true and Godlike only as they are clear and distinct, with a logical clarity like the demonstrations of geometry. Matter, though equally with mind having its source in God, is in all things the opposite of mind. In the last analysis, it has only extension and the purely mechanical motion imparted to it by God. Hence, animals are merely machines, and the relations between human bodies and minds caused Descartes great perplexities.

Yet, influential as the Cartesian philosophy was, it was not its details which profoundly affected popular thought, but its assertions that all conceptions must be doubted until proved and that any adequate proof must have the certainty of mathematical demonstration. These two principles were to have momentous consequences.

The influence of the Netherlandish Hebrew, Baruch Spinoza (1632–1677), was strongly on the side of the principles of Descartes. In later centuries, both Pietists and Romanticists were to draw on Spinoza's work, with its monistic and pantheistic tendencies. He taught that all is an infinite substance, all is God or nature, known in two modes or attributes, thought and extension, of which all finite persons or attributes are the expression. In the debates of his time, however, Spinoza's contribution strengthened a developing rationalism.

But *how* do humans know? One influential answer came from the German mathematician, historian, statesman, and philosopher, Gottfried Wilhelm Leibniz (1646–1716), for the last forty years of his life librarian in Hanover, and an earnest seeker of the reunion of Catholicism and Protestantism. Unlike Spinoza, who saw in the universe one substance, Leibniz believed substances were infinite in number. Each is a "monad," an indivisible center of force. Each mirrors the universe, though the degree of consciousness in differing monads varies from practical unconsciousness to the highest activity. The greater and clearer the consciousness, the nearer the monad approaches the divine. God is the original monad, to whose perception all things are clear. All ideas are wrapped up in the monad, are innate, and need to be drawn out to clearness. Here again is the characteristic test of truth, which Descartes and Spinoza had presented. No monad influences another; all that seems to be mutual influence is the working of pre-established harmony, like perfect clocks pointing to the same hour. Nor do the aggregations of monads which constitute bodies really occupy space. Each monad is like a mathematical point, and time and space are simply the necessary aspects under which their groupings are perceived. God created the world to exhibit his perfection, and therefore, of all possible worlds, he chose the best. What seems evil is imperfection, physical pain, and limitation, or moral wrong, which is nevertheless necessary in the sense that God could not have made a better world. Leibniz's answer was, therefore, that men know by the elucidation of their innate ideas.

Very different was the answer given by the most influential English thinker of the close of the seventeenth and opening of the eighteenth centuries, John Locke (1632–1704). In his famous *Essay Concerning Human Understanding* (1690), Locke denied the existence of innate ideas. The mind is white paper, on which sensation writes its impressions, which the mind combines by reflection into ideas, and the combination of simple ideas gives rise to more complex ideas. Locke's purpose was to show that all that claims to be knowledge is justly subject to criticism as to its reasonableness judged by reason based on experience. Thus tested, he finds the existence of God demonstrated by the argument from cause and effect; morality is as demonstrable as the truths of mathematics. Religion must be essentially reasonable. It may be above reason—beyond experience—but it cannot be contradictory to reason. These views Locke developed in his *Reasonableness of Christianity* (1695); the Scriptures contain a message beyond the power of unaided reason to attain, attested by miracles; but that message cannot be contrary to reason, nor could even a miracle attest anything essentially unreasonable. Hence, though sincerely Christian, Locke had little patience with mystery in religion. For him it was enough to acknowledge Jesus as the Messiah and practice the moral virtues which he proclaimed and which are in fundamental accord with the dictates of a reason which is hardly distinguishable from enlightened common sense.

Locke was no less influential as an advocate of toleration and an opponent of all compulsion in religion. Religion's only proper weapon is essential reasonableness. Nor was Locke less formative of political theory in England and America. He had been preceded in his field, in various directions, by Grotius (1583–1645), Hobbes (1588–1679), and Pufendorf (1632–1694). In his *Treatises on Government* (1690), Locke argued that men have natural rights to life, liberty, and property. To secure these, government has been established by the consent of the governed. In such a state, the will of the majority must rule, and when that will is not carried out, or fundamental rights are violated, the people have the right of revolution. The legislative and executive functions should be carefully differentiated. The legislative is the superior. However inadequate and fanciful this may be as a historic explanation of the origin of the state, its influence in the development of English and American political theory can hardly be overestimated.

Of considerable significance in the theory of morals was the view developed by the Earl of Shaftesbury (1671–1713) in his *Characteristics of Men* (1711). Hobbes had attempted to find the basis of morality in man's constitution but had discovered there nothing but pure selfishness. To Locke, the basis which reason discovers is the law of God. Though entirely reasonable, morality is still positive to Locke, a divine command. Shaftesbury now taught that, since man is a being having personal rights and social relationships, virtue consists in the proper balancing of selfish and altruistic aims. This harmony is achieved, and the value of actions determined, by an inward "moral sense." Shaftesbury thus based right and wrong on the fundamental constitution of human nature itself, not on the will of God. This gave a reason why even one who rejected the divine existence—which was not the case with Shaftesbury—was nevertheless bound to maintain moral conduct. It removed the hope of reward or fear of punishment as prime motives for moral conduct. Atheist and rejector of morality could no longer be considered, as they had generally been, equivalent terms.

These developments in science and philosophy provided the foundations for that movement which characterized the atmosphere of the eighteenth century, the Enlightenment. The Enlightenment was the conscious effort to apply the rule of reason to the various aspects of individual and corporate life. Its fundamental principles—autonomy, reason, pre-established harmony—deeply influenced the thought and action of the modern world and conditioned the atmosphere into which Christianity moved.

Chapter 2

The Transplantation of Christianity to the Americas

CHRISTIANITY in the Americas is primarily an importation from the Old World. As the colonization of the Western Hemisphere represented many nations of Europe, so also the various types of European Christianity were reproduced in the Americas. Where, as in South and Central America, the immigration was largely of a homogeneous people, who imposed their civilization on the native inhabitants, a single type of Christianity, typically the Roman Catholic, has been dominant, however much its control has been contested by secular influences. Where, as in North America, many peoples have contributed to the population, the result has been great variety and a necessary mutual toleration (even if one form of Christianity was here and there dominant in colonial beginnings). This contributed much to the rise of full religious liberty. However, in both Americas, though the planting of Christianity may be viewed in a general way as an integral part of the developments in European Christendom, subtle changes introduced by the transition to new environments led to the evolution of distinctive forms of Christianity. In North America especially, as many Protestant denominations became independent of European mother churches, the "Americanization" and "Canadianization" of Christian traditions can be discerned.

An important aspect of the Spanish conquest of Central and South America was the establishment of Roman Catholicism. For the European settlers, secular priests working in the context of elaborate hierarchical structures were provided. The conversion of the native populations was largely the work of the monastic orders, strongly supported by the Spanish crown (the Portuguese for Brazil). Successfully protesting against the enslavement of the Indians, the monks developed the mission system. In theory an agent of the expansion of church and culture soon to be replaced by normal structures, the somewhat paternalistic system often endured for long periods. Franciscans, Dominicans, and Jesuits were especially active in the conversion of South and Central America.

In the first half of the sixteenth century, Franciscans had undertaken work in Venezuela, Mexico, Peru, and Argentina. They were the first to labor in Brazil. By the end of the century, they had founded Christian communities in what are today New Mexico and Texas. In 1770, Franciscans developed extensive mission centers in California, where their work flourished for half a century. The Franciscans found worthy competitors in the Dominicans, who were in Mexico by 1526 and soon after in Colombia, Venezuela, and Peru.

Even more extensive was the activity of the Jesuits. Beginning in 1549, they developed extensive work in Brazil. Colombia soon proved to be one of their most successful fields. They were in Peru by 1568. In 1572, they began work in Mexico. The seventeenth century witnessed their extensive activities in Ecuador, Bolivia, and Chile and saw the development of their much discussed paternally controlled Indian villages in Paraguay. These armies of monastic missionaries reproduced with fidelity the Spanish Roman Catholic Christianity to which they were so devoted.

Universities were founded in Lima and in Mexico City in 1551—the most venerable institutions of higher learning in the New World. Elementary education was kept at a minimal level, so that there was widespread illiteracy, especially among the natives, throughout the Spanish period.

The beginnings of French Canada were made in 1604. At first, there was considerable Huguenot influence, but it was soon all but displaced by Catholicism. Serious efforts were made to convert the Indians by religious orders, led by the Jesuits. The story of their heroism and sacrificial spirit is one of the classics of missionary history. In 1673, a Jesuit missionary, Jacques Marquette (1637–1675), discovered the Mississippi. A series of mission stations across the length of the Mississippi Valley, as far south as Louisiana, followed. Few permanent results accompanied this vigorous missionary thrust, however. Contrary to the pattern of South America, the tribes resisted settlement in agricultural communities, and they were ravaged by disease, drink, and intertribal war. The growth of the church in New France was the result of immigration. The molder of French Canadian Roman Catholicism was the aggressive François de Laval (1623–1708), first bishop of Quebec.

The Spanish and French colonies in the New World thus saw the importation of one dominant religious tradition, but to the English colonies a number of church bodies were drawn. The Church of England was transplanted to Virginia at its permanent founding in 1607, and it remained established by law throughout the colonial period. The lack of a resident bishop throughout the entire colonial period seriously handicapped the church, however. In the absence of adequate supervision, lay vestries often assumed control of given parishes and tended to administer them in the interests of the local aristocracy. The bishop of London exercised nominal jurisdiction over the colonial establishment; by the appointment of commissaries, some effort to fulfill these responsibilities was made. James Blair (1656–1743) served as commissary in Virginia from 1685 till his death; his most noteworthy achievement was the founding of William and Mary College in 1693. But the commissaries lacked much real authority; the church suffered from some incompetent and a few unworthy clergymen. Furthermore, some of the parishes were vast in extent, and there were usually not enough clergymen to fill them all. Hence, the establishment was not a strong one and could not effectively resist the spread of dissenting groups.

Virginia's northern neighbor, Maryland, the first English proprietary colony in what is now the United States, was chartered to Lord Baltimore, a Roman Catholic, in 1632. Anxious to secure a place of refuge and freedom under the sovereignty of England for his fellow believers, Baltimore established religious toleration. Protestants outnumbered the Catholics from the start. In 1691, Maryland was made a royal colony, and, largely through the efforts of Commissary Thomas Bray (1656–1730), the Church of England was established by law in 1702. Bray was actually in the colony only a few months, but his services, especially through the organization of the Society for Promoting Christian Knowledge (S.P.C.K.), in 1699, and the Society for the Propagation of the Gospel in Foreign Parts (S.P.G.), in 1701 (see VII:9), were invaluable. The establishment did not secure the affections of the majority of the population, however; Quakers, Presbyterians, and Baptists steadily spread. As for the Roman Catholics, they were subject to legal disabilities as in other colonies; in Catholic history, the eighteenth century, up to the Revolution, was the "penal period."

After 1689, efforts were made by the mother country to secure establishment of the Church of England where possible. The first fruit of this policy was the Maryland law; then came establishments in South and North Carolina, in 1706 and 1715 respectively. The mixed religious character of their population, including Huguenots, Scotch-Irish Presbyterians, Baptists, and Quakers, rendered these establishments largely ineffective, though they were well served by missionaries of the S.P.G., and Charleston had a distinguished succession of rectors. Church of England work began in Georgia with the founding of the colony in 1733, but establishment of the church was not effected until 1758. The policy of toleration early attracted various other Protestant groups there, and the establishment was largely nominal.

The settlement of the English Pilgrims and Puritans in New England, beginning in 1620, and the steps which led to the founding, between then and 1638, of the Congregational colonies of Plymouth, Massachusetts Bay, Connecticut, and New Haven have already been noted (see VI:16). With the able leaders of Massachusetts Bay pointing the way, serious effort to establish a holy commonwealth on earth, solidly based on the "plain law" of the Bible, was undertaken. Making the charter of their commercial company in effect the constitution of a state, for over half a century they labored to build their theocratic Bible commonwealth. Believing that their educated ministers had correctly read the Scriptures, they hastened to found Harvard College (1636), so that educated leaders might never be lacking. Nor was effort neglected for the conversion of the Indians. The work of John Eliot (1604–1690), begun in 1646, led to the formation, in 1649, of the first missionary society in England, the Society for the Propagation of the Gospel in New England (see VII:9). These early Congregationalists of New England did not differ theologically from their Puritan brethren in Great Britain—they welcomed the appearance of the Westminster Confession (see VI:16), adopted it in substance, and stressed the federal, or covenant, theology. For their first century, their controversies dealt more with the developments of polity than with questions of doctrine. By 1631 in Massachusetts, and speedily in the other Puritan colonies, Congregationalism was established by law, and the full meaning of "nonseparatist Congregationalism," which vigorously insisted on religious uniformity and sought to restrain or exclude all dissidents, became clear. The religious establishments of the Puritan colonies (Connecticut and New Haven were merged, 1662–1665; Massachusetts Bay and Plymouth were merged in 1691; New Hampshire became independent from Massachusetts in 1680) survived longer than in any other part of the country (see VII:10).

Dissent from the established order soon appeared, however. There were occasional Baptists in the Massachusetts colony almost from the beginning, and in spite of governmental repression they organized a church in Boston in 1665 and spread slowly in New England. Quakers arrived in the Bay in 1656, anxious to testify against the Puritan church-state. Within five years, four of them were hanged on Boston Common, until Charles II ordered such proceedings stopped. The Restoration government in England sought to curb the stubborn Puritans and finally had the Massachusetts Bay charter vacated (1684). With the assertion of royal control, Church of England worship finally got a permanent foothold in New England, beginning in Boston in 1687. The new charter of 1691 replaced the religious with a property qualification for the franchise, and a measure of toleration for religious minorities was granted, though various irritations, such as enforced payments for the established churches, were continued. In Massachusetts and Connecticut, exemption from taxation for the support of Congregationalism was granted to certain groups, under somewhat onerous conditions, between 1727 and 1729.

The decline of Puritan hopes for a monolithic holy commonwealth was not effected by outside forces alone, for the zeal of the founders was often not matched by their children and grandchildren. The original hope had been for a church of elect members, "proved saints" only, but soon the bars had to be lowered some by the Half-way Covenant (1657–1662). Liberal trends appeared at Harvard toward the end of the century, and the founding of the then radical Brattle Street Church in Boston in 1699 showed how far some of the descendants of the Puritan settlers had departed from the original faith. Connecticut Congregationalists, who had tended to move toward a semi-presbyterian position, were distressed by these trends in Massachusetts, and the founding of Yale College (1701) was a partial reaction to them. But dissenting groups troubled Connecticut, too; Baptists, Quakers, and an indigenous, radical, seventh-day sect called the Rogerenes began to be heard from. Episcopalians secured a foothold in Stratford in 1707 and advanced colorfully in 1722, when a small group of Congregational leaders went over to episcopacy, led by the rector, or president, of Yale, Timothy Cutler (1684–1765), and Samuel Johnson (1696–1772), who later (1754) became the first president of what is now Columbia University. The growth of the Church of England was greatly assisted by the work of the S.P.G., which sent the bulk of its missionaries to the colonies where the Episcopal church was weakest.

A highly distinctive development in New England was the settlement of Rhode Island. Providence was begun in 1636 by Roger Williams (1604?–1683), then under banishment from Massachusetts, and an opponent of coercion in matters of religion on the basis of theological principle. Rhode Island became a refuge for those seeking freedom of religious expression. In 1639, the first Baptist church in America was founded. Williams was a member of this church for a short time, spending his later life as a "Seeker" in quest of the true church. In spite of many internal troubles from an intense individualism, the broad principles of religious liberty on which Rhode Island was founded were well maintained. The Quakers, in particular, found in it a home. Williams strongly disliked and mistrusted them, but refused to violate his principles by seeking to use the arm of the state to curb them.

Thus, Anglicanism was established by law in the southern colonies and Congregationalism in New England (except Rhode Island), with dissenting groups soon in evidence both south and north. But in the middle colonies, extensive religious diversity was present early, and whatever hopes for religious establishments may have been held soon faded. New Netherland was permanently settled as a Dutch trading post in 1624. By 1628, its first Dutch Reformed church, the earliest representative of the presbyterian polity in America, was formed at New Amsterdam on Manhattan Island; Jonas Michaelius (1584–?) came from Holland as its first minister. This and other Reformed churches were established by law, but by 1644 the religious population of Manhattan included also Lutherans, Mennonites, English Puritans, and Roman Catholics. Attempts were made to prevent worship other than that of the Reformed church of Holland during the administration of Governor Peter Stuyvesant (1647–1664), though concessions were made to the presbyterially inclined Puritans. The Quakers especially were objects of repression. Dutch control ceased in 1664, when the colony passed to the English as New York. The English leaders secured the passage of a ministry act in 1693, and then attempts were made to interpret the act as establishing the Church of England in New York. But the area over which the act was effective was limited, and it did not establish the Episcopal church there in the sense of the establishments in the southern colonies. A few churches, especially Trinity beginning in 1697, did receive public funds for the support of their clergy under the act for many years, but the Dutch Reformed were protected by liberal charters, and growing toleration provided opportunities for other denominations. In 1709, a large German Reformed immigration from the Palatinate came into the colony.

The Quakers first came to America in 1656 as missionaries; persecution was their lot almost everywhere. They soon won a measure of toleration, however, and steadily they grew and developed their meetings. The visit of George Fox to the colonies in 1672 greatly aided in the stabilization of the movement. The main area of Quaker growth soon became the middle colonies. The first important Quaker experiment in government began in West Jersey, where a charter of 1677, "Laws, Concessions and Agreements," provided for religious liberty. East Jersey early had settlers representing English Puritan Presbyterianism, the Dutch Reformed, and Scotch Presbyterianism; it passed for a time into Quaker hands, though the Presbyterian element remained the strongest religious force. Before the two Jerseys were merged to form New Jersey in 1702, Quaker control had been lost.

Mention has already been made of the grant of Pennsylvania to William Penn, in 1681, and its settlement by Quakers in the following year (see VI:17). The Quaker policy of religious freedom attracted representatives of other forms of faith. Hence, no other colony presented such a variety of religious bodies as Pennsylvania. Baptists, many from England and Wales, were soon more strongly represented than elsewhere in the colonies. In 1707, the Philadelphia Baptist Association, destined to play a major role in intercolonial affairs, was organized. Mennonites from Germany and Switzerland seeking refuge flooded into Pennsylvania. Various other German bodies, such as the German Baptists (Dunkers, founded in 1708), migrated to the inviting refuge. In the eighteenth century, a great wave of German Lutherans poured in. The first Lutheran groups in America had been Swedish, in connection with the brief Swedish effort to found a colony on the Delaware River; the second period of Lutheran development had been the Dutch, focusing in the New York area. But in the eighteenth century, the German immigration centering in Pennsylvania introduced what soon became by far the most conspicuous element in colonial Lutheranism. Numbers of German Reformed came also; they enjoyed a close relationship with the Dutch Reformed leaders.

In the early eighteenth century, another wave of immigration, destined to be of great religious, economic, and political importance, brought Scotch-Irish settlers not only to the middle colonies but also to other colonies. The Scotch-Irish, from the Scottish settlements in northern Ireland, were, like most of the Scots who came at this time, devotedly Presbyterian. They found a leader and an organizer in Francis Makemie (1658–1708), to whose initiative the first American presbytery, that of Philadelphia, in 1706, was due. In this presbytery, and in many Presbyterian congregations, English Puritan Presbyterians worshiped together with Scottish and Scotch-Irish followers of Calvin. Down to the outbreak of the Revolution, the Scotch-Irish migration continued, until their presence was felt in almost every colony. Many of them pushed to the frontier, and to this energetic people is largely owed the settlement of what is now West Virginia, western North Carolina, and ultimately Kentucky and Tennessee, as well as large sections of South Carolina, and Alabama. So fast was their growth that, ten years after the formation of the first presbytery, a synod was formed, which included the presbyteries of Long Island (later New York), New Castle (Delaware), and Philadelphia.

Episcopal work had been started in the middle colonies before the beginning of the eighteenth century; its spread there in that century was largely the work of the missionaries of the S.P.G.

Thus, by the end of the first quarter of the eighteenth century, the middle colonies especially exhibited a great diversity in religion, though the multiplicity of religious bodies was felt in all the colonies. No one communion was dominant in the colonies as a whole. While particular denominations were entrenched in particular colonies, no church could become that of all the colonies. The churches that spread in America were clearly transplanted churches. But in the new environment, and especially for churches that had been established in Europe but not in the colonies, there was confusion and hesitation, because familiar practices and procedures often did not work well. Many church members who had been faithful in the Old World did not (or for reasons of distance could not) retain their religious ties in the New. The established bodies were also troubled, both by the decline in fervor of their own members and by the spread of dissidents in their midst. Furthermore, the effects of the rationalism and Deism of the Age of Reason were beginning to be felt in the churches, and many outside them were indifferent or even hostile to religion. Despite the growth of churches through immigration, a situation in which a steadily increasing segment of the population had no religious connections was developing.

Canadian life in the eighteenth century was marked by a continuing struggle between France and England for control of the northern lands, finally won by the latter. At the conclusion of Queen Anne's War (in Europe, the War of the Spanish Succession) in 1713, France surrendered Hudson's Bay, Newfoundland, and much of Nova Scotia to the English. But not until after the founding of Halifax in 1749 were permanent Protestant congregations gathered; in the next few decades, Anglican, Lutheran, Congregational, Presbyterian, Methodist, and Baptist churches were founded. Meanwhile, during the French and Indian War (the Seven Years' War) the city of Quebec fell to the English, and Montreal capitulated a year later. The Treaty of Paris in 1763 ended all French possessions on the North American continent. An effort to anglicize the province of Quebec was soon given up; by the Quebec Act of 1774, the British Parliament allowed the French Canadians to retain their own semifeudal system, admitted Roman Catholics to citizenship and to eligibility for public office, and permitted the church to retain its right to tithe the faithful. Quebec remained predominantly Catholic, but in the Maritime provinces both French- and English-speaking Catholics had to adjust to the patterns of religious pluralism that were increasingly characteristic of North American religious life.

Chapter 3

Deism and Its Opponents; Skepticism

O NE OF THE IMPORTANT consequences of the spread of the spirit of the Enlightenment (see VII:1) in the late seventeenth and early eighteenth centuries was the development of rationalism in religion. The Newtonian conception of the universe was of a realm of law, created by a "first cause" and operating in a mechanical order. The new knowledge of long-established civilizations and of other religions enlarged men's horizons and confronted them with other than Christian culture. Locke's test of truth was reasonableness, in the sense of conformity to common sense. He viewed morality as the prime content of religion. A powerful spur to the development of religious rationalism was moral reaction against the passions and brutalities of the religious wars. All these influences led to the significant departure of rationalism in English religious thought. In its milder form, it emerged as "rational supernaturalism," but in its central development it took the form of a full Christian Deism, while its radical wing turned against organized religion as anti-Christian Deism.

The pioneer Deist was Edward Herbert of Cherbury (1583–1648), who as early as 1624 had enumerated the articles of belief alleged to constitute natural religion, held by all mankind in primitive unspoiled simplicity, as being that God exists; he is to be worshiped; virtue is his true service; man must repent of wrongdoing; and there are rewards and punishments after death. But few rationalists went that far in the seventeenth century. Locke himself reserved a place for revelation in his interpretation of Christianity, though he insisted that what was revealed was basically simple and always reasonable. Not greatly dissimilar was the rational supernaturalist faith of John Tillotson (1630–1694), famous preacher, archbishop of Canterbury, and leader of the Latitudinarian party in the Church of England. For him, natural religion must be supplemented by revelation, as a divine sanction for morality is necessary. But John Toland (1670–1722), though still keeping some place for divine revelation, was moving toward a full deistic position, and his book, *Christianity Not Mysterious,* published in 1696, opened the deistic controversy in England. Those who held to a concept of revelation defended themselves by arguing that it was attested to by prophecy and miracle. But in 1713, Anthony Collins (1676–1729) published his *Discourse of Freethinking,* in which he attacked the argument from prophecy, while Thomas Woolston (1669–1733) subjected the miracles to searching criticism. In 1730 appeared a work by Matthew Tindal (1657–1733), *Christianity as Old as the Creation,* often called the Deist Bible. In the writings of these men, the main features of the deistic position were set forth. All that is acknowledged beyond or above reason is really held on belief without proof, they argued. To be rid of superstition is to be free; hence, the only rational thinker is a freethinker. The worst enemies of mankind are those who have held men in bondage to superstition, and the chief examples of these are "priests" of all sorts. All that is valuable in revelation had already been given men in natural reasonable religion; hence, "Christianity"—that is, all that is of worth in Christianity—is "as old as creation." All that is obscure or above reason in so-called "revelation" is superstitious and worthless or worse. Miracles are no real witness to revelation; they are either superfluous, for all of value in that to which they witness reason already possesses; or they are an insult to the perfect workmanship of a Creator who has set this world running by most perfect mechanical laws and does not now interfere with its ongoing. Deism thus seemed to destroy all historic Christianity and authoritative revelation. It was widely denounced as atheism, yet not justly, however destructive it may have been. In the thought of its advocates, it was a rescue of religion from bondage to the superstitious and a return to primitive rational simplicity and purity.

From a later standpoint, the weaknesses of Deism are evident. Its primitive, universal, rational religion was as much a figment of the imagination as was the primitive, unspoiled social and political state of the unspoiled child of nature so dear to the eighteenth century. Its assertion that "whatever is"—that is, whatever is natural—"is right," was shallow optimism. It had no sense of the actual facts of the historic development of religion. Its God was afar off, a being who once for all established certain religious principles, essentially rules of morality, and set a wonderfully contrived mechanical world in motion with which he has nothing now to do. Despite its profession of being grounded solidly in self-evident truth, it was itself based on a position of faith. Nevertheless, its merit was that it contributed to a generally higher level of ethical awareness and humanitarian concern.

Deism called forth many replies, and the chief proof of its power is that, relatively mediocre men as most of the Deists were, most of its opponents attempted to meet it by rational argument, often admitting a considerable share of its method, though not its results. Some few met it by a flat denial of any power of reason in the realm of religion. Such was the answer of William Law (1686–1761), in his reply to Tindal entitled *The Case of Reason* (1732). Reason, Law argued, not merely does not find truth in religion; "it is the cause of all the disorders of our passions, the corruptions of our hearts." God is above the power of man to comprehend. "His own will is wisdom and wisdom is His will. His goodness is arbitrary."

Less directly designed as an answer to Deism but believed by himself to be destructive of all "atheism" was the philosophy of George Berkeley (1685–1753), a man of most generous impulses, who attempted to found a missionary college in Bermuda for the evangelization of the American Indians, lived for a time in Rhode Island, and in 1734 became bishop of Cloyne in Ireland. To Berkeley's thinking, nothing really exists but minds and ideas. There is no other knowledge of what is called matter but an impression in our minds, and since like can only affect like, our minds must be affected only by other minds. Since ideas are universal and constant, they must be the product in our minds of a universal, eternal, and constantly working mind. Such a mind is God, to whom all our ideas are due. But ideas exist not merely subjectively in our minds. In some sense what we call nature is a range of ideas in the divine mind, impressed in a definite and constant order on our minds, though their reality to us is only in our perception of them in our own minds. By thus denying the reality of matter, Berkeley wished to destroy that whole conception of the world as a huge mechanism—a magnified watch—made once for all by an all-wise Maker, who has nothing now to do with its ongoing, which Deism had held. For it, he would substitute a universal constant divine spiritual activity. Though this conception of Berkeley has always enjoyed high philosophic respect, it is too subtle and too contrary to the evidence of the senses for the average person.

More famous in its own time, yet of far less philosophic distinction or permanent value, was a work of Joseph Butler (1692–1752), a Presbyterian by descent who had early entered the Church of England and become bishop of Bristol in 1738 and of Durham in 1750. His *Analogy of Religion* (1736) was a work of immense labor, candor, and care. In answer to the Deists, he started from the premises, held equally by the Deists and their opponents, that God exists, that nature moves in a uniform course, and that human knowledge is limited. God is admittedly the author of nature; if the same difficulties can be raised against the course of nature as against revelation, the probability is that both have the same author. Their positive resemblances also lead to the same conclusion. Immortality is at least strongly probable. As present happiness or misery depend on conduct, it is probable that future will also. In Butler's view, everyone is now in a state of "probation" as regards the use of this life; it is probable that each is also now on "probation" as to future destiny. Our limited knowledge of nature does not warrant a declaration that revelation is improbable, much less impossible, and whether there has actually been a revelation is a historic question to be tested by its attestation by miracles and fulfillment of prophecy. Believed widely in its time to be an unanswerable answer to Deism, and as such long required in English and American universities, Butler's cautious balance of probabilities utterly fails to meet modern questions and has been well criticized as raising more doubts than it answers. Its most attractive feature is its moral fervor in its exaltation of the divine regnancy of conscience over human action.

A noteworthy attack alike on Deism and on many of the defenses of Christianity against it was made by the acutest British philosopher of the eighteenth century, David Hume (1711–1776). Born in Edinburgh, he died there as well. He lived in France for some years, saw some public employment, wrote a popular but highly Tory *History of England,* and won deserved fame as a political economist. During his last years, he was regarded as the friendly, kindly head of the literary and intellectual circles of his native city. His philosophical system was ably set forth in his *Treatise of Human Nature* (1739), but this rather youthful publication attracted little notice. Very different was it when the same ideas were recast in his *Philosophical Essays* (1748) and his *Natural History of Religion* (1757). Philosophically, Hume was one of the keenest of reasoners, standing on the basis of Locke but with radical and destructive criticism of Locke's theories and with thoroughgoing religious skepticism. Experience gives us all our knowledge, but we receive it as isolated impressions and ideas. All connection between our mental impressions as related by cause and effect, or as united and borne by an underlying substance, are simply the inveterate but baseless viewpoints of our mental habit. They are the ways in which our minds are accustomed to act. What we really perceive is that, in our limited observation, certain experiences are associated. We jump to the conclusion that there is a causal relation between them. So, too, substance is "feigned." If cause and effect are therefore ruled out, the argument for a God founded thereon is baseless. The denial of substance leaves no real permanent I behind my experiences and no philosophical basis for immortality. Hume, in whom a dawning of historic criticism manifested itself, also held that history shows that polytheism preceded monotheism in human development, and thus history gives no support to the doctrine of the one originally recognized God of Deism or to the existence of the simple, primitive, rational religion of nature which Deists claimed. Most of Hume's criticisms were too subtle and too radical to be very fully understood by either the Deists or their orthodox opponents against whom they were equally directed.

Hume's greatest sensation was his criticism of miracles, then looked upon as the main defense of revelation and Christianity. His argument was twofold. Experience is the source of all our knowledge. Our experience attests to the uniformity of nature much more strongly than to the infallibility of human testimony. Hence, the probability that error, mistake, or deception has led to the report of a miracle is vastly greater than that the uniform course of nature has really been interrupted. Yet, granted that testimony may prove that unusual events have occurred, that would not prove that they established anything, unless it could be further proved that they were wrought for that special purpose by divine power, which is an even more difficult task. These positions have had lasting effect. Few who now affirm miracles view them, as the eighteenth century did, as the prime proofs of Christianity. Rather, revelation is regarded as carrying faith in the miracles far more than lending support to it. Those who accept miracles now largely regard the revelation as so supernatural and divine as to render miracles not unfitting as its accompaniment. Since Hume's criticism, the question of miracles has been increasingly felt to be one of peculiar difficulty. Hume's work was the most powerful expression of one result of the deistic controversy in England—the emergence of skepticism.

A skeptical criticism of the early history of Christianity advanced by the historian Edward Gibbon (1737–1794) in the fifteenth and sixteenth chapters of his *History of the Decline and Fall of the Roman Empire* (1776) deserves notice, not for its inherent importance, but for the controversy that it aroused and the light that it throws on the thought of the time. In accounting for the spread of Christianity, Gibbon gave as reasons its zeal inherited from the Jews, its teaching of immortality, its claim to miraculous gifts, its strict morality, and its efficient organization. Probably no modern historians would object to any of these explanations, as far as they go. What would impress them is their absolute want of comprehension of the nature of religion, whether Christian or other, and of the forces by which religion makes conquests. But that was an ignorance equally shared by Gibbon's critics in the eighteenth century. The usual orthodox explanation had been that the first disciples had been so convinced of the truth of the Gospel by miracles that they were willing to hazard their lives in its behalf. Gibbon's rather superficial explanation roused excitement because it supplied other causes, less directly supernatural, for the spread of Christianity. Its one permanent result was to aid, with other influences, toward the historical investigation of the Scriptures and Christian origins, which was to be so largely the work of the nineteenth century.

The general attitude of the period, and also the general rationalizing of even orthodox Christian presentation in England, at the close of the eighteenth century is best illustrated in the work of William Paley (1743–1805). His *View of the Evidences of Christianity* (1794) and *Natural Theology* (1802) were written with remarkable clearness of style and cogency of reasoning, and they long enjoyed great popularity. From a watch, he argued, we infer a maker; so, from the wonderful adaptation of the human body, the eye, the hand, the muscles, we infer an almighty Designer. These arguments, therefore, prove the existence of God, who has made the divine will the rule of human action and revealed it to the world. The purpose of revelation is "the proof of a future state of rewards and punishments." That revelation was given by Christ, and its convincing force to the first disciples was in the miracles by which it was accompanied. "They who acted and suffered in the cause acted and suffered for the miracles." Paley then proceeds to definition. "Virtue is the doing good to mankind, in obedience to the will of God, and for the sake of everlasting happiness." This prudential and self-regarding estimate of virtue is characteristic of Paley's age, as were his emphases on the evidential character of miracles and on a mechanical demonstration of the divine existence (which the theory of evolution has since largely robbed of force). Yet it is pleasant to note that Paley's thought of "doing good to mankind" led him to a strenuous opposition to human slavery. In many ways, Deism exerted a more profound influence through its stimulation of Christian apology on the one hand and of skeptical philosophy on the other than by its own direct efforts.

English Deism on the whole was a cautious, Christian Deism, largely restricted in influence to the upper classes. But a radical anti-Christian Deism, militant in its attack on organized Christianity, though with few supporters, accompanied it. Peter Annet (1693–?) employed a crude and iconoclastic kind of Biblical criticism in his attack. Toward the end of the century, anti-Christian Deism had a powerful popular presentation in the militant, passionate work of Thomas Paine (1737–1809), the son of an English Quaker. His *Common Sense* (1776) did great service to the American Revolution; his *Rights of Man* (1791) was no less effective in defense of the principles underlying the French Revolution. In his *Age of Reason* (1794–1796), Deism was presented in its most aggressive anti-Christian form.

English Deism influenced the development of rationalism elsewhere—in Germany, but most directly in France, where it had many advocates and became fashionable among the upper classes. Chief of the French Deists was François Marie Arouet, or, as he called himself, Voltaire (1694–1778). He had become familiar with Deism in England during a trip there from 1726 to 1729, and he was influenced by the writings of Peter Annet. In Voltaire, eighteenth-century France had its keenest wit. No philosopher, vain, self-seeking, but with genuine hatred of tyranny, especially of religious persecution, no one ever attacked organized religion with a more unsparing ridicule. Such a contest was, of necessity, more sharply drawn in France than in Great Britain. In the latter country, a certain degree of religious toleration had been achieved and great divergence of religious interpretation was allowed. In France, dogmatic Roman Catholicism was dominant; the contest was therefore between Deism or atheism, on the one hand, and a single assertive type of Christianity, on the other. Voltaire was a true Deist in his belief in the existence of God and of a primitive natural religion consisting of a simple morality and in his rejection of all that rested on the authority of Bible or church. Of the extent and significance of his work in influencing the French mind in directions that were to appear in the French Revolution, there can be no question.

Deism affected the eighteenth century widely. It was substantially the creed of Frederick the Great of Prussia (1740–1786); of Joseph II, the Holy Roman Emperor (Austria, 1765–1790); and of the marquis of Pombal (1699–1782), the greatest of Portuguese statesmen of the century. In the English colonies of North America, the deistic controversy was followed with great interest, and native exponents of the three main rationalist positions appeared. Massachusetts pastors Ebenezer Gay (1696–1787) and Jonathan Mayhew (1720–1766) were basically rational supernaturalists, while Benjamin Franklin (1706–1790) and Thomas Jefferson (1743–1826) were essentially Deistic. Anti-Christian Deism was expressed by the author of *Reason the Only Oracle of Man* (1784), Ethan Allen (1737–1789), revolutionary general, and by the blind crusader, Elihu Palmer (1764–1806).

Chapter 4

Unitarianism in England and America

IT HAS ALREADY been pointed out that, on the Continent, anti-Trinitarian views were represented by some Anabaptists (see VI:4) and by the Socinians (see VI:14). Both types penetrated into England. Under Elizabeth, "Arian Baptists" from the Netherlands were burned in 1575. Under James I, Bartholomew Legate (1575?–1612) and Edward Wightman (?–1612), of similar views, have the distinction of being the last Englishmen burned for their faith (1612). With the controversies of the civil-war period, anti-Trinitarian views became more evident. In John Biddle (1615–1662), an Oxford graduate, Socinianism had a more learned representative, who suffered much imprisonment. The great Puritan poet, John Milton (1608–1674), inclined toward Arianism in his later years. Biddle's chief convert was Thomas Firmin (1632–1697), a London layman, who furthered the publication of anti-Trinitarian tracts.

At the dawn of the eighteenth century, with its rationalizing impulses both in orthodox and Deistic circles and its inclination to see in morality the essence of religion, these anti-Trinitarian tendencies were greatly strengthened. The Presbyterian minister Thomas Emlyn (1663–1741) published his widely read *Inquiry into the Scripture Account of Jesus Christ* in 1702. In 1712, Samuel Clarke (1675–1729), rector of St. James, Westminster, and deemed the most philosophical of the Anglican clergy, published his *Scripture Doctrine of the Trinity,* in which he sought to demonstrate Arian views by a painstaking examination of the New Testament. It was, however, among the Dissenters, especially the Presbyterians and the General Baptists, that anti-Trinitarian views won the largest following. In 1717, Joseph Hallett (1691?–1744) and James Peirce (1674?–

1726), Presbyterian ministers in Exeter, sought to find a median position between orthodoxy and Arianism. The most learned of the eighteenth-century Dissenters, Nathaniel Lardner (1684–1768), held similar views, and the movement spread. On the whole, the Congregationalists and the Particular Baptists were little affected; their numbers grew as the century went on, surpassing the Presbyterians, who at the time of the Toleration Act had been the most numerous nonconformist body.

The Arian trend paved the way for the development of a separately organized Unitarianism in England. The movement was precipitated when a clergyman of the establishment, Theophilus Lindsey (1723–1808), who had adopted a Unitarian position, circulated a petition, which received some two hundred and fifty signatures, asking that clergymen be relieved from subscription to the Thirty-nine Articles, to pledge their fidelity to the Scriptures alone. Parliament in 1772 refused to receive it. In 1773, Lindsey withdrew from the establishment, and the next year he organized a Unitarian church in London. Closely associated with Lindsey was Joseph Priestley (1733–1804), a Dissenting clergyman, an eminent chemist, the discoverer of oxygen, and a sympathizer with the American and French Revolutions, who spent the last ten years of his life in Pennsylvania. Parliament in 1779 amended the Toleration Act by substituting profession of faith in the Scriptures for acceptance of the doctrinal part of the Thirty-nine Articles, and it repealed all penal acts against deniers of the Trinity in 1813. This older English Unitarianism was formal and intellectual, clear in its rejection of "creeds of human composition" and its insistence on salvation by character. It was often intellectually competent but had little influence on popular religious life.

English Unitarianism had some effect in producing a similar movement in New England, though that grew also out of the general rationalizing tendencies of the eighteenth century. The presence in the colonies of Priestley and of William Hazlitt (1737–1820) helped to precipitate its emergence as an independent movement. King's Chapel, the oldest Episcopal church in New England, became the first openly Unitarian church in 1787, under the leadership of its pastor, James Freeman (1759–1835). Many Congregationalists were in sympathy with Unitarianism, for partly in reaction to the Great Awakening (see VII:8), Arminian influences were spreading, and anti-Trinitarian views were cautiously entertained by a few. But the Congregational churches were legally established, and any outbreak of theological controversy was feared, for establishments of religion were increasingly hard to defend in a time of advancing freedoms. Not until the nineteenth century did the controversy between orthodox and liberal parties break out into the open and lead to the Unitarian schism (see VII:15).

Chapter 5

Pietism in Germany

THE DEVELOPMENT of a Scholastic Lutheranism has already been noted (see VI:13). Though based on the Scriptures, it assumed the form of a fixed dogmatic interpretation, rigid, exact, and demanding intellectual conformity. Emphasis was laid on pure doctrine and on the sacraments as constituting the sufficient elements of the Christian life. The vital relationship between the believer and God which Luther had taught had been replaced very largely by a faith which consisted in the acceptance of a dogmatic whole. The laity's role was largely passive: to accept the dogmas on the assurance that they were pure, to listen to their exposition from the pulpit, to partake of the sacraments and share in the ordinances of the church—these were the practical sum of the Christian life. Some evidences of deeper piety existed, of which the hymns of the age are ample proof, and doubtless many individual examples of real and inward religious life were to be found, but the general tendency was external and dogmatic. It was the tendency often, though only partially justly, called "dead orthodoxy." This Protestant Scholasticism was in some respects narrower than that of the medieval period, for it had unwittingly been influenced by the spirit of rationalism against which it struggled, so that it became akin to the new rationalistic currents both in temper and in method. Hence, it shared in the reactions against rationalism.

Pietism was a turning from these Scholastic tendencies, an assertion of the primacy of feeling in Christian experience, a vindication of an active share for the laity in the upbuilding of the Christian life, and a stress upon a strict ascetic attitude toward the world. Many influences contributed to the rise of the movement, and it is difficult to trace them all with certainty. The best approach to an understanding of the background and nature of the Pietist revival is through its central figure, Philipp Jacob Spener (1635–1705), one of the most notable religious figures of the seventeenth century, in whose teaching and example Pietism had its immediate source.

Born in Rappoltsweiler, in Upper Alsace, he was educated at Strassburg, where he became versed in biblical exegesis and saw a church discipline and a care in catechetical instruction far beyond what was customary in most Lutheran circles. Further studies at Basel and Geneva acquainted him with Reformed emphases without weaning him from Lutheranism. His mental and spiritual development was shaped by many factors. At Strassburg, he had studied carefully Luther's theology. He was especially stimulated by a work of the mystically inclined Johann Arndt (1555-1621), *True Christianity*, which had been published between 1605 and 1609. It is not clear how far the religious poetry of Paul Gerhardt (1607-1676) impressed him, nor is it known just how much he was indebted to the movement in Reformed churches sometimes called "Dutch Pietist" or "Dutch Precisianist." Willem Teelinck (1579-1629), Gisbert Voet (1589-1677), and Jodocus van Lodensteyn (1620-1677) were leaders in this movement, which has often been identified with English Puritanism, for the latter deeply fertilized it. But there is no doubt that Spener was strongly influenced by Puritan writings, most especially by the German translation of Lewis Bayly's (?-1631) widely read *The Practice of Pietie* and by some of the translated works of Richard Baxter (1615-1691).

In 1666, Spener became chief pastor in the prosperous commercial city of Frankfurt. He felt the need of church discipline but found himself hindered, because all authority was in the hands of the city government. Under such leadership as was permitted him, catechetical instruction speedily improved. His first considerable innovation occurred in 1670, when he gathered in his own house a little group of like-minded people for Bible reading, prayer, and the discussion of the Sunday sermons, the whole aiming at the deepening of the individual spiritual life. To these circles the name *collegia pietatis* was given, whence Pietism.

These plans for cultivating a warmer Christian life Spener put forth in his *Pia desideria* of 1675. The chief evils of the time he pictured as governmental interference, the bad example of the unworthy lives of some of the clergy, the controversial interpretations of theology, and the drunkenness, immorality, and self-seeking of the laity. By way of reform, he proposed the gathering within the various congregations of circles—*ecclesiolae in ecclesia*—for Bible reading and—since all believers are priests (a Lutheran contention which had been practically forgotten)—for mutual watch and helpfulness. Christianity is far more a life than an intellectual knowledge. Controversy is unprofitable. Better training for the clergy is desirable; an experimental knowledge of religion and a befitting life should be demanded of them. A new type of preaching should be practiced, designed to build up the Christian life of the hearers, not primarily controversial or exhibitory of the argumentative abilities of the preacher. That only is genuine Christianity which shows itself in the life. Its normal beginning is a spiritual transformation, a conscious new birth. Spener also showed certain ascetic tendencies, like the English Puritans, urging moderation in food, drink, and dress and rejecting the theater, dances, and cards, which contemporary Lutheranism regarded as "indifferent things."

Spener's efforts encountered bitter opposition and aroused enormous controversy. He was accused of heresy—falsely so, as indicating any intentional departure from Lutheran standards, but rightly so in the sense that his spirit and ideals were quite unlike those of contemporary Lutheran orthodoxy. His work involved a shift of emphasis from the creeds to the Scriptures. His feeling that, if "the heart" was right, differences of intellectual interpretation were of secondary importance, was sharply opposed by those who put the emphasis on "pure doctrine." Spener undoubtedly popularized familiarity with the Bible and weakened the authority of confessional standards as the final logical form of what the Scriptures had to teach. A result of this biblical study was to prepare the way for an investigation of the nature and history of the Scriptures. Spener greatly improved the religious instruction of youth and achieved his purpose of introducing a more strenuous, biblically nourished and warmer popular Christian life.

At Frankfurt, some of Spener's disciples, in spite of his protests, withdrew from church worship and the sacraments. Spener's meetings consequently met with police opposition, and he was glad, in 1686, to accept a call to Dresden as court preacher. Meanwhile, the Pietist movement had spread to the University of Leipzig. In 1686, one of the younger instructors, August Hermann Francke (1663-1727), and a few associates, founded there a *collegium philobiblicum* for the study of the Scriptures. Its members were at first instructors, its method scientific, and it had the approval of the university authorities. But in 1687, Francke experienced what he regarded as a divine new birth while in Lüneburg and engaged in writing a sermon on John 20:31. A couple of months' stay with Spener, in Dresden, completed his acceptance of Pietism. In 1689, Francke was back in Leipzig, lecturing to the students and to the townspeople with a great following. Leipzig was soon in a good deal of turmoil. An electoral edict soon forbad the meeting of citizens in "conventicles." Undoubtedly, Francke's lectures led some students to neglect other studies and to assume a critical attitude. Under the leadership of a Leipzig professor of theology, Johann Benedict Carpzov (1639-1699), the university authorities limited Francke's work. Carpzov became one of the most persistent of Spener's opponents. Francke's position became very uncomfortable, and in 1690 he accepted a call to Erfurt as "deacon."

Meanwhile, Spener's path in Dresden was not easy. The Saxon clergy looked upon him as a stranger; the two Saxon universities, Leipzig and Wittenberg, opposed him. His meetings for spiritual upbuilding developed criticism. The elector, John George III (1647-1691), took offense at Spener's pastoral reproof of his drunkenness. When, therefore, an invitation to Berlin came from the elector of Brandenburg, Frederick III (1688-1701), who was to become King Frederick I of Prussia (1701-1713), Spener willingly accepted it. Though Spener never won his new sovereign to Pietism, he had much support from Frederick, and his years in Berlin, where he remained until his death, were his happiest and most successful.

While in Berlin, Spener was able to do his greatest service for Pietism. Christian Thomasius (1655-1728)—a rationalist in the sense of Locke, a critic of the theological hairsplitting of the day, a creator of German jurisprudence, the first to substitute German for Latin as the language of the university instruction, a defender of religious toleration, a skeptic regarding witchcraft, and an opponent of the judicial use of torture—had been driven from Leipzig in 1690 by the hostility of the theologians. His popularity among the students was great. Thomasius was no Pietist, though he disliked the persecution of the Pietists and had done his utmost to aid Francke in the contest with the Leipzig authorities. The elector of Brandenburg, long desirous of having a university of his own, seized upon the exile of Thomasius to found a university in Halle, which was formally opened in 1694 and in which Thomasius led the faculty of law until his death. Meanwhile, Francke's energetic introduction of pietistic measures in Erfurt had roused the opposition of the clergy of the city. Carpzov's hostility pursued him, and in 1691 he was expelled by the authorities. Spener procured for him from the elector appointment to a professorship in Halle and the pastorate of the neighboring village of Glaucha, as well as the appointment of colleagues of pietistic sympathies. From the first, Francke dominated the theological methods and instruction in Halle; though he did not become formally a member of the theological faculty until 1698, he made and kept Halle a center of Pietism.

Francke was a man of unbounded energy and organizing genius. His parish of Glaucha was a model of pastoral faithfulness; his lectures in the university were largely exegetical and experiential; and his combination of the classroom and parish practice was highly helpful to his students. In 1695, he began a school for poor children, and later a preparatory school, the Paedagogium, and a Latin school. These educational establishments, all managed in the spirit of Pietism, won great renown; at Francke's death, 2,200 children were being instructed in them. He also founded an Orphan House, where 134 children were living when he died. These institutions, many of which have continued to the present, were begun almost without means; Francke sincerely believed they were maintained in answer to prayer. Gifts flowed in from all parts of Germany. Without casting doubt on Francke's faith, it is but just to note that he understood the arts of enlisting friends and winning honorable publicity. The number of nobles who were patrons of his foundations was quite remarkable. Another foundation could almost be called his: the Bible Institute, established in 1710 by his friend, Karl Hildebrand, Freiherr von Canstein (1667-1719), for the publication of the Scriptures and their circulation in inexpensive form. The institute has had a notable history.

One salient feature of these activities in Halle was the zeal for missions that was aroused there. At a time when Protestants generally still did not recognize a missionary obligation, Francke and his associates were awake to it. When Frederick IV of Denmark (1699-1730) wished to send the first Protestant missionaries to India, establishing them in 1706 in Tranquebar, then belonging to Denmark, he found them among Francke's students in Halle—Bartholomäus Ziegenbalg (1683–1719) and Heinrich Plütschau (1678–1747). During the eighteenth century, not less than sixty foreign missionaries went forth from the University of Halle and its associated institutions; the most famous of these was Christian Friedrich Schwartz (1726–1798), who served from 1750 to his death in India. Certainly Francke's name deserves high place on the roll of missionary leadership.

Pietism's influence was felt also in the German Reformed churches of the lower Rhine region, where a fusion of Reformed and Lutheran pietistic emphases was exemplified by Theodore Untereyck (1635–1693) and Joachim Neander (1650?–1680). The pietist leaven penetrated the Lutheran churches of Norway, Sweden, and Denmark, where it stimulated much religious zeal among the people; and many of the German settlers in America had been deeply affected by the movement.

In Germany, by the time of Francke's death in 1727, Pietism had passed its high-water mark. It produced no further leaders equal in ability to Spener and Francke, though it continued to spread in Germany, notably in Württemberg under the leadership of Johann Albrecht Bengel (1687–1752). A statistical estimate is difficult, as Pietists did not separate from the Lutheran churches; but Pietism undoubtedly affected Germany very widely and for good. It fostered a more vital type of piety. It greatly improved the spiritual quality of the ministry, preaching, and the Christian training of the young. It increased the share of the laity in the life of the church. It greatly augmented familiarity with the Bible and the devotional study of the Scriptures. Its shadows were its insistence on a conscious conversion through struggle as the only normal method of entrance into the kingdom of God, its ascetic attitude toward the world, illustrated in Francke's severe repression of play among the children in his foundations, its censorious judgments on those who were not Pietists as irreligious, and its neglect of the intellectual elements in religion. It produced very few intellectual leaders. But on the whole, a predominantly favorable evaluation of Pietism can be given. It did a service of great value for the religious life of Protestant Germany.

One fruit of Pietism deserves notice in a contribution of value made to the interpretation of church history by one of the most radical of the Pietists, Gottfried Arnold (1666–1714), a friend of Spener, for a short time a professor in Giessen but thereafter living in comparative retirement in Quedlinburg. Since the Reformation, church history had been polemical and had regarded all thinkers as to be rejected whom the church of their own age rejected. In his *Unparteiische Kirchen und Ketzer-Historie* of 1699 and 1700, Arnold introduced a new conception. He had read much of the ancient heretics and had concluded that no man is to be deemed a heretic because his own age so deemed him. He is to be judged on his own merits; even the views of those called heretics have their place in the history of Christian thought. As is always a danger to a man who has conceived a fruitful idea, Arnold pushed his interpretation to an extreme conclusion: that there had been more truth with the heretics than with the orthodox. Yet he gave to church history a forward step of decided importance.

Chapter 6

Zinzendorf and Moravianism

ONE OF THE MOST notable results of the pietistic awakening, though far from approved by the Pietists in general, was the reconstitution of the Unitas Fratrum, or, as they came to be known, the Moravian Brethren, under the leadership of Count Nikolaus Ludwig von Zinzendorf. Zinzendorf was born in Dresden, on May 26, 1700. His father was a high official of the Saxon electoral court and a friend of Spener. Zinzendorf's father died shortly after his son's birth, the mother married again, and the rather solitary and introspective boy was brought up by his grandmother, the Pietistic Baroness Henrietta Catherine von Gersdorf. Even as a boy, he was marked by the trait that was to dominate his religious life—passionate personal devotion to Christ. From the time he was ten until his seventeenth year, he studied in Francke's *Paedagogium* in Halle. Its rigor repelled him, but he gradually came to appreciate Francke's zeal, and his religious nature was quickened in 1715 in connection with his first communion. The insistence of his family that he should enter public employment sent him to Wittenberg from 1716 to 1719 to study law. Though a decided Pietist, his experiences in Wittenberg gave him a kindlier feeling than before toward orthodox Lutheranism. In 1719 and 1720, he took a long journey to Holland and France, forming the acquaintance of many distinguished persons and making his religious principles clearly, though tactfully, evident. On his return journey through Castell, he fell in love with his cousin, but he thought Count Heinrich XXIX von Reuss a more favored suitor for her, and so he resigned his pretensions, believing that God thereby had indicated some work for him to do. He ultimately married, in 1722, Count Heinrich's sister, Erdmuth Dorothea, who made him a most sympathetic wife.

The wishes of his relatives led him to enter the electoral service in Dresden in 1721. Yet he was primarily interested in cultivating the "heart-religion," in the pietistic sense, among his friends in Dresden, and even more on his estate of Berthelsdorf, about seventy miles east of Dresden, where as patron he appointed his like-minded friend, Johann Andreas Rothe, to the pastorate. Here, in wholly unlooked-for fashion, his lifework was to meet him.

The Unitas Fratrum (see V:13) in Bohemia and Moravia had fallen on evil days. Part of it had found refuge in Poland, where it had maintained its continued existence, but under increasing difficulties. Members persuaded Frederick III's Calvinist court preacher in Berlin, Daniel Ernst Jablonsky, by ancestry and background connected with the Unitas Fratrum, to accept episcopal ordination in 1699. The consequences of the Thirty Years' War for Czech Protestantism had been destructive, and it had persisted in Bohemia and the neighboring province of Moravia only in concealment and under persecution. As early as 1722, the German-speaking survivors of the Unitas Fratrum, residing in northern Moravia, began to seek refuge in Saxony under the leadership of a carpenter, Christian David (1690–1751). Zinzendorf allowed them to found a village on his Berthelsdorf estate, which they named Herrnhut and where they collected in considerable numbers. They were joined by many native German Pietists and other religious enthusiasts. Zinzendorf at first paid little attention to these settlers besides allowing them a refuge, but by 1727 he began to assume their spiritual leadership. The task was hard at first. The refugees were divided, and their aim was a separate church, while that of Zinzendorf and Rothe was incorporation in the Saxon Lutheran state church, though with special additional meetings as in Spener's plan of *collegia pietatis*. On the other hand, local customs permitted an organized village to give itself a secular organization and make its own rules. Under these customs, Herrnhut chose "elders" for its secular direction in 1727. Zinzendorf, as lord of the estate, had a certain indefinite right of leadership, and all this was sealed by a communion service of such spiritual power in Berthelsdorf on August 13, 1727, that that date has generally been reckoned that of the rebirth of the Unitas Fratrum, now often know as the Moravian church.

Out of these institutions for the leadership of the village of Herrnhut, originally secular, a spiritual organization soon grew. An executive committee of four developed from the eldership, and by 1730 it was regarded as exercising ministerial functions. A general eldership was formed, of which the first holder was Leonhard Dober (1706?–1766), who returned from the mission field in 1734 to assume the rôle. To Zinzendorf, the Herrnhut society came to seem a body of soldiers of Christ, to advance his cause at home and abroad—a new Protestant monasticism, without vows or celibacy but bound to their Lord by daily prayer and worship. The young men and the young women were separated from ordinary family life by 1728, and each class was placed under strict superintendence. Children were brought up away from their parents—after the manner of the Halle Orphan House. The community even attempted to regulate choices in marriage. The ideal was that of a community separate from the world yet ready to send forces to work anywhere for Christ's kingdom. Two tendencies confused this development. The Moravian element would gladly have seen the establishment of a separate denomination, a full revival of the ancient Unitas Fratrum. But Zinzendorf clung firmly to the pietistic idea of an *ecclesiola in ecclesia*. He would keep the Moravians as part of the Lutheran state church, only a special group within it, where a warmer spiritual life, a "heart-religion," should be fostered. The movement soon met much opposition, not merely from orthodox Lutherans but also from Pietists, both by reason of Herrnhut's peculiarities and because of the separatist tendency. On the whole, the separatist sentiments slowly won the upper hand, though without fully displacing the other trend.

The Moravian willingness to go anywhere in the service of Christ gave a missionary thrust to the movement which it has never lost. No Protestant body had been so awake to the duty of missions, and none was so consecrated to the service in proportion to its numbers. A journey to Copenhagen to attend the coronation of Christian VI (1730–1746) of Denmark brought Zinzendorf into contact with natives of the Danish West Indies and of Greenland. Zinzendorf returned to Herrnhut aflame with missionary enthusiasm. As a result, Leonhard Dober and David Nitschmann (1696–1772) began a mission to the West Indies in 1732, and Christian David and others to Greenland in 1733. Two years later, a considerable party, led by August Gottlieb Spangenberg (1704–1792), began labors in Georgia. For this outreaching work, Nitschmann was ordained a bishop—the first of the modern Moravian succession—by Jablonsky in 1735.

Meanwhile, Zinzendorf's relations with the Saxon government were becoming strained. The Austrian authorities complained, without ground, that he was enticing their subjects. Ecclesiastical complaints were renewed, and on March 20, 1736, he was banished from Saxony. Zinzendorf found opportunity to carry on his work in Ronneburg in western Germany and in the Baltic provinces. In 1737, he was ordained bishop by Jablonsky in Berlin. In 1738 and 1739, he journeyed to the West Indies; in 1741, he was in London, where Moravian work had been several years in progress. By December 1741, Zinzendorf was in New York, and on Christmas Eve he named the settlement which Moravians from Georgia were beginning to effect in Pennsylvania, Bethlehem—a town destined to become the American headquarters of the movement.

Zinzendorf's sojourn in America was full of activities. He made great efforts to gather the scattered German Protestant forces of Pennsylvania into a spiritual unity to be known as the "Church of God in the Spirit." He began missions to the Indians; he organized seven or eight Moravian congregations and planted schools. Itineracy was established under the superintendence of Peter Böhler (1712–1775). In January 1743, Zinzendorf sailed for Europe, and in December 1744, Spangenberg was put in charge of all the American work as bishop. Its most famous missionary to the Indians was David Zeisberger

(1721–1808), who worked among the Creeks of Georgia from 1740 and among the Iroquois from 1743 until his death.

Herrnhut thus became a hive of missionary activity. Missions were begun in Surinam, Guiana, Egypt, and South Africa. In 1771, after repeated attempts, a permanent mission was established in Labrador. The names of its early mission fields show one characteristic of Moravian effort. They were prevailingly hard places, requiring peculiar patience and devotion, and this trait characterizes Moravian missionary labors to the present.

Meanwhile, in spite of Zinzendorf's dislike of separatism, Moravianism was becoming more fully a church. In 1742, it was so recognized in Prussia by the government. By 1745, the Moravian church was thoroughly organized, with bishops, elders, and deacons, though its government was, and still is, more Presbyterian than Episcopal. The English Parliament, by a law of 1749, recognized it as "an ancient Protestant Episcopal Church." Yet Zinzendorf did not give up his theory of an *ecclesiola in ecclesia*. Negotiations with the Saxon authorities resulted in his recall from banishment in 1747, the acceptance of the Augsburg Confession by the Moravian body the next year, and recognition in 1749 as a portion of the Saxon state church, with its own special services. By this time, Moravianism was developing a liturgy of much beauty and a hymnody of rich fullness. The Moravian church remained small, but its influence spread widely through the outreach of the "diaspora" in Europe. Religious societies under Moravian auspices influenced many people whose membership in the regular state churches was not disturbed.

During the time of his banishment, Zinzendorf and some of the Moravians developed certain theological and cultural peculiarities that were the source of deserved criticism. His emphasis on the atoning death of Christ turned in a distorted direction, focusing on a morbid concentration and word-play upon the blood and wounds of the crucified Christ. This fanciful and sentimental trend was encouraged by Moravians in Wetteravia, where the movement centered at Ronneburg, Marienborn, and Herrnhaag during the banishment period, and by Zinzendorf's son, Christian Renatus (1727–1752). Zinzendorf's insistence that Christians must become as little children to enter the kingdom of God led to much puerility of expression. The peculiarities were at the height of their manifestation between 1747 and 1749, but in large measure they corrected themselves. Zinzendorf himself turned away from them. This period is called by the Moravians "the sifting time." These tendencies should be regarded at the most as but blemishes on the character of one who could say of his devotion to Christ, as few can: "I have one passion. It is He."

Zinzendorf's life from 1749 to 1755 was spent mostly in England. His property had been spent unstintedly for the Moravians, and he now found himself almost bankrupt. His debts were assumed, as was fitting, by the Moravian body and were gradually discharged. This financial need led to a growth in Moravian constitutional development. A collegiate directorate was established, which became a board of control by which Moravian affairs were superintended, and the taxes paid by the several congregations led to their representation in a general synod, meeting at regular intervals.

Zinzendorf's last few years were spent chiefly in pastoral activities. His strength had been lavishly spent, and he was bereaved of his wife and only son. On May 9, 1760, he died in Herrnhut. The Unitas Fratrum, which Zinzendorf had done so much to renew and inspire, was now firmly grounded as the Moravian church, so that his death made no serious breach. It was fortunate, however, that its practical leadership fell to Spangenberg, who was called back from America to Herrnhut in 1762 and continued his guidance until his death, thirty years later. Not a man of genius and enthusiasm like Zinzendorf, he was marked by equal devotion, great practical sense, and high organizing abilities. Under his strong, wise guidance, Moravianism strengthened and grew; its criticized peculiarities were generally discarded. His work was quiet and unpicturesque but wholly useful. The Moravian church took its accredited place among the families of Christendom, exerting wide influence through its missionary zeal and diaspora work.

Chapter 7

The Evangelical Revival in Great Britain; Wesley and Methodism

THE TRENDS in religious thought and life in England in the early part of the eighteenth century have already been described (see VII:3). The end of the struggles of the seventeenth century had been marked by a general spiritual lethargy in the established Church of England and among Dissenters alike. Rationalism had penetrated all classes of religious thinkers, so that even among the orthodox, Christianity seemed little more than a system of morality supported by divine sanctions. Joseph Butler (see VII:3) may stand as typical. His frigid probabilities may have convinced some intellects, but they can have led few to action. There were able preachers, but the characteristic sermon was the colorless essay on moral virtues. Outreaching work for the unchurched was but scanty. The condition of the lower classes was one of spiritual destitution. Popular amusements were coarse, illiteracy widespread, law savage in its enforcement, jails sinks of disease and iniquity. Drunkenness was more prevalent than at any other period in English history.

Furthermore, Great Britain stood on the eve of the industrial revolution that was to transform it in the last third of the eighteenth century from agriculture to manufacture. James Watt (1736–1819) patented the first effective steam engine in 1769. James Hargreaves (?–1778) patented the spinning jenny in 1770. Richard Arkwright (1732–1792) brought out the spinning machine in 1768. Edmund Cartwright (1743–1823) invented the power loom in 1784. Josiah Wedgwood (1730–1795) made the Staffordshire potteries operational from 1762 onward. The industrial and social changes, and the problems consequent upon the changes, were of the widest importance and involved readjustments of immense practical religious consequence.

There were not wanting people and movements, early in the eighteenth century, looking toward better things. William Law was not only a vigorous opponent of Deism but his *Serious Call to a Devout and Holy Life* (1728) profoundly influenced John Wesley and remains one of the monuments of English hortatory literature. The Congregationalist Isaac Watts (1674–1748), long since forgotten as a theologian, has well been called the founder of modern English hymnody. His *Hymns* (1707) and *The Psalms of David, Imitated in the Language of the New Testament* (1719) broke down the prejudice on both sides of the Atlantic then existing in nonprelatical English-speaking circles against the use of any but rhymed passages of Scripture. They express a deep and vital piety.

Some combined efforts of significance were being made for a warmer religious life. Such were the "religious societies," the earliest of which was formed by a group of young men in London about 1678, for prayer, reading the Scriptures, the cultivation of a religious life, frequent communion, aid to the poor and to soldiers, sailors, and prisoners, and encouragement of preaching. They spread rapidly. By 1700, there were nearly a hundred in London alone, and they were to be found in many parts of England and even in Ireland. One of these societies was formed by John Wesley's father, Samuel Wesley, in Epworth in 1702. In many ways, they resembled Spener's *collegia pietatis* (see VII:5), but they had no Spener to further them. They were composed almost exclusively of communicants of the establishment. Many of the clergy looked upon the movements as "enthusiastic," or, as would now be said, "fanatical," and after 1710 it measurably declined, though the societies were to continue and be of importance in the beginnings of Methodism.

Yet these efforts were at best local and partial in their influence. The mass of the people of England was in spiritual lethargy, yet blindly conscious of sin and convinced of the reality of future reward and retribution. Emotions of loyalty to Christ, of salvation through him, of a present transforming faith had not been aroused. It needed the appeal of vivid spiritual earnestness, directed to conviction of the heart rather than to considerations of prudence or cold logical argument. That a profound transformation was effected in England, the results of which flowed in beneficent streams to all English-speaking lands, was primarily the result of the "evangelical revival." The first signs of an awakening appeared early in the eighteenth century. In Scotland, under the leadership of Ebenezer (1680–1754) and Ralph (1685–1752) Erskine, an evangelical movement developed in the early years of the century; Ebenezer was forced to preach in a field adjacent to his church by 1714 to accommodate the crowds. Three years later, an anonymous seventeenth-century Puritan work, probably by Edward Fisher, *The Marrow of Modern Divinity,* was republished at the instigation of Thomas Boston (1677–1732) of Ettrick, a zealous popular preacher. Despite censure by the General Assembly in 1722, the "Marrow Men" with their warm evangelical spirit won much sympathy. They organized "praying societies" again suggestive of Spener's *collegia pietatis.* In Wales, Howel Harris (1714–1773) and Daniel Rowlands (1713–1790) were leaders in a revival that broke out in the mid-1730s. But only with the emergence of its three great leaders—John and Charles Wesley and George Whitefield—did the evangelical revival swell into a mighty tide. For four decades, it advanced in three identifiable but closely related strands, all related to the established Church of England: the Methodist societies under the Wesleys, the Calvinistic Methodists under Whitefield, and the Anglican Evangelicals, who operated along more traditional parish lines. Not until 1779 did the first formal separations of any of these strands from the Church of England occur.

The parents of the Wesley brothers were of nonconformist ancestry; both grandfathers had been among the ejected clergy of 1662. Their father, Samuel Wesley (1662–1735), had preferred the ministry of the establishment and was, from 1696 to his death, rector of the rough country parish of Epworth. A man of earnest religious disposition and somewhat unpractical, he was author of a *Life of Christ in Verse* and of a commentary on the book of Job. Their mother, Susanna (Annesley), was a woman of remarkable strength of character, like her husband a devoted Anglican. The sons took much from each parent, but perhaps more of force from the mother. In a household of nineteen children, even if eight died in infancy, hard work and stringent economy were perforce the rule. Of this large brood, John was the fifteenth and Charles the eighteenth.

John Wesley was born on June 17, 1703, Charles on December 18, 1707. Both were saved with difficulty from the burning rectory in 1709, an event that made an ineffaceable impression on the mind of John, who thenceforth regarded himself as literally "a brand snatched from the burning." In 1714, John entered the Charterhouse School, in London, and Charles the Westminster School two years later. Both boys distinguished themselves for scholarship. In 1720, John entered Christ Church College, Oxford, where Charles followed him six years after. Such was John's intellectual attainment that, in 1726, he was chosen a fellow of Lincoln College. To become a candidate for that honor, he had to be in holy orders, and therefore, on September 25, 1725, he was ordained a deacon. With his ordination, the spiritual struggles began which were to last until his conversion, in 1738, and perhaps in a sense beyond that time.

From 1726 to 1729, John Wesley was for the most part his father's assistant. On September 22, 1728, he was ordained a priest. During his absence from Oxford, by the spring of 1729, Charles Wesley and two fellow students, Robert Kirkham and William Morgan, formed a little club, primarily for progress in their studies, but which soon engaged in reading helpful books and frequent communion. On his return to Oxford in November 1729, John Wesley became the leader of the group, which soon attracted other students. Under his guidance, it sought to realize William Law's ideals of a consecrated life. Under Morgan's influence, it began visitation of the prisoners in the Oxford jail in August 1730. The members fasted. Their ideals were high-churchly. They were derided by the university. They were called the "Holy Club," and finally some student hit upon a nickname that stuck, the "Methodists" (a name that had been in currency in the previous century). They were very far as yet from what Methodism was to be. They were still a company painfully bent on working out the salvation of their own souls. As matters then were, they more resembled the Anglo-Catholic movement at the nineteenth century than the Methodism of history.

An important accession to the club, early in 1735, was George Whitefield. Born in Gloucester, on December 16, 1714, the son of an innkeeper, he had grown up in poverty, entering Oxford in 1733. A severe illness in the spring of 1735 brought a crisis in his religious experience, from which he emerged in joyous consciousness of peace with God. In June 1736, Whitefield sought and received episcopal ordination, and at once, young as he was, he began his marvelous career as a preacher. No Anglo-Saxon of the eighteenth century showed such pulpit power. A man largely without denominational consciousness, in an age when such feelings were usually intense, he was ready to preach anywhere and in any pulpit open to him. Sometimes censorious as to the genuineness of religious experiences unlike his own, his nature was in the highest degree simple and unself-seeking. His message was the Gospel of God's forgiving grace and of peace through acceptance of Christ by faith, and a consequent life of joyful service. His few printed sermons barely suggest his power. With a sense of the dramatic and a voice of marvelous expressiveness, he swayed vast audiences on two continents. A large part of his active ministry was spent in America. In 1738, he was in Georgia. In 1739, he was back in America, and his preaching in New England in 1740 was accompanied by the greatest spiritual upheaval ever witnessed there; nor was his success less in the middle colonies, though there and in New England there was great division of feeling as to the permanent spiritual value of his work. The years 1744 to 1748 saw him again on this side of the Atlantic, once more in 1751 and 1752, and again in 1754 and 1755. His sixth visit was from 1763 to 1765. In 1769, he came for his last preaching tour, and he died in Newburyport, Massachusetts, on

September 30, 1770. He had given himself unstintedly to the service of the American churches of every Protestant family. He was no organizer. He left no party to bear his name, but he awakened thousands.

None of the leaders of the Methodist Club was destined long to remain in Oxford, nor did their movement have much influence on the university, which was then in scholastic and religious ebb. The death of their father, on April 25, 1735, left the Wesleys less bound to home, and both now gained employment as missionaries to the new colony of Georgia, the settlement of which had been begun by General Oglethorpe, in 1733. They sailed in October 1735. On the voyage, they were unremitting in religious exercises and efforts for their fellow passengers; but in the ship was a company of twenty-six Moravians, headed by Bishop David Nitschmann. The cheerful courage of this company in a storm convinced John Wesley that the Moravians had a trust in God that was not yet his. From them he learned much. Soon after reaching Savannah, he met Spangenberg (see VII:6), who asked him the embarrassing question: "Do you know Jesus Christ?" Wesley answered: "I know He is the Saviour of the world." Spangenberg responded: "True, but do you know He has saved you?"

The Wesleys' labors in Georgia were strenuous yet unsuccessful. Charles Wesley returned home in disgust and ill health in 1736. John continued. He showed his linguistic abilities by conducting services in German, French, and Italian. In 1736, he founded a little society in Savannah for cultivating a warmer religious life. He worked indefatigably, yet with little peace of mind or comfort to others. He was a punctilious high-churchman. He lacked tact. A conspicuous case was that of Sophie Hopkey, a woman in every way suitable to be his wife. He gave her and her friends every encouragement to believe his intentions earnest, but he seesawed up and down between clerical celibacy and possible matrimony. A vein of superstition always present in Wesley, which led him to decide important questions by the first verse of Scripture to which he should open, or by drawing lots, led him now to the latter method of decision as to the marriage. The lot fell adverse, and Wesley naturally aroused the resentment of the young woman and of her relatives. In a pique, she married hastily another suitor. The husband objected to her continuance in attendance on Wesley's intimate religious discussions. Wesley now felt that she was not making proper preparation for communion, and he refused her the sacrament; her friends charged that this was the act of a disgruntled suitor. Wesley's influence in Georgia was at an end. Suits were started against him. He decided to leave the colony for home. On February 1, 1738, John Wesley was back in England. As on his outward voyage, he had feared death. In his bitterness of disappointment he could only say: "I have a fair summer religion." Yet he was a preacher of marked power, and he had labored unsparingly. He had made a good many mistakes, but they were not those which show lack of Christian consecration.

Fortunately for their distressed state of mind, within a week of John Wesley's return both brothers were in conversation with a Moravian, Peter Böhler, delayed in London until May on his way to Georgia. Böhler taught a complete self-surrendering faith, an instantaneous conversion, and a joy in believing. Before sailing, Böhler organized a "society," later to be known as the "Fetter-Lane Society," of which John Wesley was one of the original members. But neither brother was yet at peace. What Charles Wesley called his "conversion" came to him on May 21, 1738, while he was suffering from a serious illness. On May 25, the transforming experience came to John. That evening, as he recorded, he went unwillingly to a meeting of an Anglican "society" on Aldersgate Street, London, and heard Luther's preface to the *Commentary on Romans* read. "About a quarter before nine, while he [Luther] was describing the change which God works in the heart through faith in Christ, I felt my heart strangely warmed. I felt I did trust in Christ, Christ alone, for salvation; and an assurance was given me, that He had taken away my sins, even mine, and saved me from the law of sin and death." Of the far-reaching significance of this experience there can be little question. It determined thenceforth Wesley's belief about the normal mode of entrance on the Christian life. It was the light of all his theological insight. Yet it was in some measure gradually, even after it, and by preaching and observing a similar work in others and by communion with God, that he entered into full freedom from fear and complete joy in believing.

John Wesley determined to know more of the Moravians, who had helped him thus far. Less than three weeks after his conversion, he was on his way to Germany. He met Zinzendorf in Marienborn, spent two weeks in Herrnhut, and in September 1738 was back in London. It was a happy visit for Wesley. He saw much to admire. Yet he was not pleased with all. He felt that Zinzendorf was treated with too great deference and that Moravian piety was not without its subjective limitations. Much as he owed to the Moravians, Wesley was too active in religious attitude, too little mystical, too outreaching to men in their wider needs, to be fully a Moravian.

John and Charles Wesley now preached as opportunities offered, though finding many pulpits closed to their "enthusiasm" and speaking chiefly in the "societies" in and about London. Early in 1739, Whitefield was developing his work in Bristol, and there on February 17 he began preaching in the open to the coal miners of Kingswood. He entered into friendly relations with Howel Harris, who had been serving with great success since 1736 as a lay preacher in Wales. Whitefield invited John Wesley to Bristol. Wesley hesitated about "field preaching," but the opportunity to proclaim the Gospel to the needy was irresistible. On April 2, 1739, he began in Bristol what was thenceforth to be his practice for more than fifty years, as long as strength permitted. Charles Wesley soon followed his example. Though without Whitefield's dramatic power, John

Wesley was a preacher with few equals in popular effectiveness—earnest, practical, fearless. Attacked, especially in the early part of his ministry, and often in peril from mob violence, no danger could daunt him, no interruption could check him. Under his preaching, as under that of Whitefield, remarkable exhibitions of bodily excitement were frequent. Men and women cried out, fainted, were torn with convulsions. To both preachers, these seemed the working of the Spirit of God or the visible resistance of the devil. These excitements, and the disfavor with which they were often regarded, accounts for much of the opposition which these preachers encountered from the regular clergy.

John Wesley's gifts as an organizer were pre-eminent. Yet the creation of Methodism was a gradual process—an adaption of means to circumstances. In Bristol, he founded in 1739 his first really Methodist "society," and there he also began the erection of the first chapel, on May 12, 1739. Later that year, he secured in London an old "foundery," which became the first chapel in that city.

Thus far, in London, the Methodists had also joined in the Moravian Fetter-Lane Society, but Wesley's ideals were leading him away from Moravianism. This separation was increased when, in October 1739, Philipp Heinrich Molther (1714–1780), recently in touch with Zinzendorf, asserted in Fetter-Lane that if any man had doubts he had no true faith and should absent himself from the sacraments and prayer, awaiting in silence until God should renew his religious hope. Such teaching found little sympathy from Wesley's strenuous activity. The Fetter-Lane Society was divided. Wesley and his friends withdrew and founded a purely Methodist "United Society" at the Foundery, on July 23, 1740. Wesley continued on friendly terms with some of the Moravians, but thenceforth the movements were independent of each other.

Wesley had no desire or intention of breaking with the Church of England. He did not, therefore, found churches; rather, he used the device of the long-existing religious societies, which should now consist only of converted persons. These societies were from the first divided into "bands," or groups, for mutual cultivation of the Christian life. This was a Moravian device, but experience soon showed Wesley something more efficient. Soon after the Bristol society was formed, Wesley hit on the plan of giving "society tickets" to those whom he found sufficiently grounded to be full members, and receiving others on trial. These tickets were renewable quarterly and furnished a ready means of sifting the society. The debt on the Bristol chapel led to a yet more important arrangement. On February 15, 1742, the members were divided into "classes" of about twelve persons, each under a "class leader," charged to collect a penny weekly from each member. This system was introduced in London on March 25. Its advantages for spiritual oversight and mutual watch were soon even more apparent than its financial merits. It became one of the characteristic features of Methodism, though the older "bands" also long continued.

Wesley would have preferred to have all preaching done by ordained men, but few of the clergy were sympathetic with the movement. A lay preacher,

Joseph Humphreys, was helping him as early as 1738; but extensive use was not made of this arrangement until 1742, when Thomas Maxfield became regularly the earliest of what soon became a considerable company. The growth of the movement developed other lay officers: "stewards" to care for property, teachers for schools, "visitors of the sick" for the duties implied. At first, Wesley visited all the societies, which were chiefly in the regions of London and Bristol, but the task soon became too great. In 1744, he had the preachers meet him in London—the first of the "annual conferences." Two years later, the field was divided into "circuits," with traveling preachers and more stationary leaders to "assist chiefly in one place." Then an "assistant," later called a "superintendent," was placed in charge of each "circuit." Wesley endeavored by suitable publications to aid the intellectual development of his lay preachers and secured study as far as possible. He tried in vain to obtain episcopal ordination for them, but he would not allow the sacraments to be administered by unordained men.

While Wesley stood theologically on the common basis of evangelical doctrinal tradition and regarded his societies as part of the Church of England, two disputes led to considerable controversy. One was regarding perfection. Wesley believed it possible for a Christian to attain right ruling motives—love to God and to his neighbor—and that such attainment brought freedom from sin. To Wesley's cautious and sober judgment, this was an aim rather than a frequently completed achievement—however it may have appeared to some of his followers. No man was ever more positive than he that salvation evidences itself in a life of active, strenuous obedience to the will of God.

A second dispute was regarding predestination. Wesley, like the Church of England generally of his time, was Arminian, but he had derived a special parental hostility to Calvinism, which seemed to him paralyzing to moral effort. Whitefield was Calvinistic. A hot interchange of letters took place between the two evangelists in 1740 and 1741, though their good personal relations were soon restored in large measure. Whitefield found a supporter, in 1748, in Selina, Countess of Huntingdon (1707–1791), a wealthy widow, a convert to Methodism, but far too dominant a character to yield to Wesley's insistent leadership. She would be her own Wesley, and, like Wesley, founded and superintended societies and chapels—the first in Brighton in 1761, thus beginning "Lady Huntingdon's Connection." She made Whitefield her chaplain. Her "Connection" was Calvinist. In 1769, the predestinarian controversy broke out with renewed intensity. At the conference of 1770, Wesley took a strongly Arminian position, and he was defended by his devoted disciple, the Swiss John William Fletcher (1729–1785), who had settled in England and accepted a living in the established church at Madeley, where he did notable work. The effect of the controversy was to confirm the Arminian character of Wesleyan Methodism. Yet "Lady Huntingdon's Connection" of Calvinistic Methodists must be regarded as a parallel rather than as a hostile movement. Its fundamental spirit was essentially the same as that of the Wesleys.

The Wesleyan Methodist movement grew enormously. John Wesley had many friends and assistants, but few intimates who shared his responsibilities. His brother Charles long had part in his constant travels, but Charles had not the iron constitution of John. After 1756, Charles seldom itinerated. He labored in Bristol, and from 1771 to his death on March 29, 1788, he preached in London. He was always more conservative than John, and more Anglican. His great service was as a hymn writer, not merely of Methodism but of all English-speaking Christianity. John's unwise marriage to a widow, Mrs. Mary Vazeille, in 1751, was unhappy. He devoted himself all the more unreservedly to his work. Over all the multitudinous concerns of Methodism he exercised a wise but absolute authority. Naturally, as the societies grew and preachers multiplied, pressure rose for authority to administer the sacraments. This Wesley resisted long, but episcopally ordained men were few, and the force of events made the pressure irresistible in spite of Wesley's insistence that his movement was within the establishment.

Wesley won many sympathizers whose focus remained in the established Church of England. These Anglican evangelicals were generally in agreement with his religious emphases—conversion, confident faith, a religious life manifested in active work for others. On the other hand, they adopted few of his peculiar methods, and in general they were marked theologically by a moderate Calvinism rather than by Arminianism. Whitefield was the spiritual father of many of them. Not very closely organized, they developed into the Evangelical party within the Church of England. A pioneer in this position was William Grimshaw (1708–1763), vicar of Haworth, who underwent a conversion experience in 1734 which transformed him and set his feet on evangelical paths. He kept on good terms with Wesley and Whitefield. Conspicuous among the Evangelicals was John Newton (1725–1807), once a slave-dealing shipmaster. Converted, he became one of the most helpful of preachers, first in Olney and then as rector of St. Mary Woolnoth in London. His hymns express his cheerful, confident faith. Another Evangelical renowned for his hymns was Augustus Toplady (1740–1778), author of "Rock of Ages."

Thomas Scott (1747–1821), Newton's successor in Olney, was best known for his *Family Bible with Notes,* a commentary of immense popularity on both sides of the Atlantic. Richard Cecil (1748–1810) in later life was one of the most influential preachers in London. Joseph Milner (1744–1797) made Hull an Evangelical stronghold and won much influence through his *History of the Church of Christ,* continued after his death by his brother, Isaac, in which he emphasized the development of Christian biography rather than the disputes of Christianity. Isaac Milner (1750–1820) was long a professor in Cambridge and aided in making the tone of that university largely Evangelical, a work which was continued there by Charles Simeon (1759–1836).

Several not in clerical ranks were instrumental in the spread of Evangelicalism. Such was William Cowper (1731–1800), the greatest English poet of the latter half of the eighteenth century, and Newton's warm friend. In Hannah More (1745–1833), Evangelicalism had a supporter personally acquainted with the literary, artistic, and theatrical circles of London, a writer of tracts and stories of unbounded popularity, and a woman of generous and self-denying philanthropy.

The Anglican Evangelicals remained within the Church of England, but the two Methodist strands finally separated from it. In 1779, the Countess of Huntingdon and those associated with her separated from the Church of England; in time, the connection became the Welsh Methodist Church. The Wesleyan Methodists separated from the establishment by degrees, and finally only after the death (1791) of John Wesley, who had wished his followers might avoid separation. Yet in 1784, two important steps had been taken. On February 28, Wesley entered the "Deed of Declaration," which provided for the continuance of the movement after his death by naming a "Conference" of one hundred members to hold the property and assume the direction of the movement. It was a step toward the self-government of Methodism. On September 1, Wesley joined with other presbyters of the Church of England to ordain presbyters and a superintendent for America (see VII:10). This was, indeed, a breach with the Church of England, though Wesley did not then see it as such. The final separation of the Wesleyan Methodists is perhaps best marked by the "Plan of Pacification" of 1795, which stabilized the now independent church.

Wesley's strength and activities continued unabated almost to the end. On March 2, 1791, he died in London, having done a work which had largely revolutionized the religious condition of the English lower and middle classes and was even more largely to affect America.

In Scotland, actual separations from the established Presbyterian church occurred much earlier, largely because of the "patronage" system, by which the patron could force the appointment of a minister on a reluctant congregation (see VI:16). In 1733, Ebenezer Erskine of Stirling denounced such limitation of the power of the congregation to choose its minister. He was disciplined by his synod, and he and several associates were deposed by the General Assembly in 1740. Before these censures were completed, their objects had founded the first Scottish free church, ultimately known as the Secession church. It grew rapidly, but was soon in turmoil over the question of whether the burgesses of the Scottish cities could properly swear to support "the true religion . . . authorized by the laws" of Scotland. In 1747, the Secession church divided into Anti-Burgher, or Nonjuror, and Burgher sections. Further subdivisions occurred, but most of the Anti-Burghers and Burghers united, in 1820, as the United Secession church.

The question of patronage continued to be divisive. Thomas Gillespie (1708–1774), of Carnock, refused to participate in the installation of a minister over an unwilling congregation, and he was consequently deposed by the General Assembly in 1752. In 1761, he and like-minded ministers founded the organization which became the Relief church. These various secessions won large popular support, especially among the more earnest-minded. By 1765, they counted 120 congregations and one hundred thousand adherents.

These circumstances robbed the state church of a good deal of its spiritual strength. Rationalistic thought penetrated Scotland as the eighteenth century advanced, as also contemporaneously in England and Germany. Hume's speculations (see VII:3) were not without influence. The result was the growth of what was called Moderatism, which was controlling in the latter half of the eighteenth century and influential well into the nineteenth. To the Moderates generally, Christianity was largely ethical rather than strongly experiential or doctrinal. It was believed that the patronage system favored the appointment of Moderates, whereas congregations would often have chosen men of more Evangelical type. For by no means all of the awakening spirit was to be found in the separated bodies in Scotland. Within the establishment was also a "Popular" party in which there was a strong evangelical current; John Witherspoon (1723–1794), later to become president of Princeton (1768), penned his powerful satire *Ecclesiastical Characteristics* (1753) against the Moderates. But it was the latter who dominated the Church of Scotland in the closing decades of the eighteenth century; in some respects, the secessions had only strengthened their hold.

Chapter 8

The Great Awakening

THE MOST FAR-REACHING and transforming movement in the eighteenth-century religious life of America was the Great Awakening, a revival that had many phases and lasted for over half a century. Coming at a time when the familiar patterns of Christian outreach were not proving very effective, and at a time of spreading rationalism and cultural confusion, the awakening not only led to tremendous quickening of the Christian life, but also changed the conceptions of entrance upon that life in a way that profoundly affected the majority of American churches. In this respect, the Great Awakening was the analogue of Pietism in Germany and the evangelical awakening in Britain. Emphasis was placed on a transforming, regenerative change, a "conversion," as the normal method of entrance into the church. The view of the church which emphasizes its importance as a company of experiential Christians was widely extended; primary attention was not given to Christian nurture. Strict morality and earnest piety characterized the movement as a whole. Its influence spread an evangelical understanding of religion not only among churches directly affected but also among other denominations, though the movement was everywhere controversial. By providing new understandings of religious authority and new principles of action, the Great Awakening helped the Protestant communities to adjust to the realities of their time and provided a new apology for faith in the face of the challenges of rational religion. Under its influence, educational life was stimulated and new colleges were founded. An intercolonial movement, the awakening helped to bring the colonies into closer relationship and thus indirectly helped to prepare the way for the American Revolution.

Early signs of the Great Awakening appeared in the 1720s in Dutch Reformed congregations in the Raritan Valley of New Jersey. Formalism and loss of vitality were problems for a number of the Reformed congregations; many of the Dutch were content to think of their churches as symbols of their nationality and heritage. But a young pastor, Theodore J. Frelinghuysen (1691–1748), who had become acquainted with Puritan emphases in Holland, where he had been educated and ordained, challenged his people to find a deeper, more experiential knowledge of Christian faith. Though his own positive role as an awakener is not wholly clear, a revival movement arose in the churches under his care and attracted much attention. Frelinghuysen was invited to preach in many places. Others adopted the revival message and many new members were brought into the churches. But many disliked the intensity and emotionalism of the revival and opposed it; especially the New York pastors were disturbed. Despite the opposition of some, however, revival waves continued to influence the Dutch Reformed churches for many years.

Among those who were attracted to the revival was a group of Presbyterian leaders. William Tennent, Sr. (1673–1745), a man of Puritan convictions, had trained a number of young men, including three of his four sons, for the pastorate. His educational work so expanded that he finally (1736) erected a "Log College" north of Philadelphia—one of the ancestors of Princeton. His son Gilbert (1703–1764) adopted the revivalist approach, and as Presbyterian pastor at New Brunswick he became the central figure in an awakening movement in his denomination. Two strong parties were then active in Presbyterianism—one representing English Puritan concern for experiential faith, the other the Scotch-Irish insistence on correct doctrine. The Tennent group stressed the Puritan emphases, but they were in the territory where the other view was dominant, so in 1738 they organized their own, the New Brunswick, presbytery. The "Old Side" excluded this "New Side" presbytery from the synod, and from 1745 Presbyterianism was divided into two synods, the New York, representing Puritan and revivalist emphases, and the Philadelphia, adhering to the Scotch-Irish views, strict on subscription of ministers to the Westminster Confession. The trend of the times favored the growth of the New Side; the fervent preaching of George Whitefield during his American tours (see VII:7) assisted the revivalists very much. When Presbyterianism reunited in 1758, the awakening group had modified some of its more extreme positions but had won a secure place for itself in the life of the church. Thus the awakening, controversial enough to divide a denomination for a number of years, left its permanent stamp upon it.

The Great Awakening reached New England when a remarkable revival swept the town of Northampton, Massachusetts, in 1734–1735. It attracted great attention, especially when its leader, Jonathan Edwards (1703–1758), Congregational pastor at Northampton, described it in a revivalist classic, *A Faithful Narrative of the Surprising Work of God in the Conversion of Many Hundred Souls . . .* (1737). In 1739, the revival erupted again, spreading widely in New England. Congregational leaders were assisted in the work by Gilbert Tennent and George Whitefield, the latter then at the height of his youthful enthusiasm. Everywhere throngs hung on his words; faintings and outcries attended his sermons. As the awakening spread, hundreds were permanently changed. The spiritual condition of many communities was transformed. But the New England awakening was as controversial as the middle colony movement. Whitefield often denounced those who did not agree with him as unconverted, and some who were influenced by him were even more censorious and uncharitable. The revival was further troubled by the disruptive activities of the unstable James Davenport (1716–1757), who preached long, unprepared, ranting discourses in which he attacked by name many of the leading ministers as unconverted. Separate Congregational churches were formed. In protest, the "Old Lights," under the leadership of the pastor of the First Church of Boston, Charles Chauncy (1705–1787), attacked the "New Lights," who saw in the revivals a work of God. Reaction against the awakening contributed to the spread of Arminian and ultimately Unitarian thought in Congregationalism. Reaction against the revival was such that the awakening was no longer a potent force in the established Congregational churches after midcentury, though it continued strongly among the Baptists, who were now spreading rapidly in New England, profiting greatly from the awakening patterns.

The Great Awakening spread to the southern colonies, too, there contributing to the growth of the Dissenting bodies. In the 1740s and 1750s, Presbyterianism expanded rapidly in Virginia and southward, especially under the fervent preaching of Samuel Davies (1723–1761). Soon after 1750, revivals among the Baptists were touched off in Virginia by awakeners from New England, who formed many Separate Baptist churches when the Regulars resisted. High emotional enthusiasm was stirred by these revivals, and persecution at the hands of the colonial authorities served only to advance the cause. Though it is true that the Great Awakening as an intercolonial phenomenon of major proportions can be said to have terminated when the concerns of the Revolution became so absorbing, in Baptist and Methodist circles the awakening motifs strongly continued.

Methodism was late in reaching America—not until 1766 did work begin. At about the same time, Philip Embury (1728–1773) and Robert Strawbridge (?–1781) began Methodist activities in New York and Maryland respectively. A vigorous early lay preacher was Captain Thomas Webb (1724–1796) of the British army. In 1769, Wesley sent the first of eight officially appointed lay missionaries; the only one of them to remain active in American Methodism during and after the Revolution was Francis Asbury (1745–1816). During the 1770s, Methodism mushroomed chiefly in Maryland and Virginia, as a society movement loosely tied to the Church of England, as in the mother country. The first American Methodist conference was held in Philadelphia in 1773. Growth continued during the Revolution, and a number of native lay preachers were drawn into the movement.

Except for the Methodist societies, there was little interest in the awakening in the Episcopal churches. In the South, the rationalist current was strong (Latitudinarianism), in the north the high-church tendency of S.P.G. missionaries was not receptive of revival trends. The most conspicuous Episcopal evangelical was Devereux Jarratt (1733–1801), a rector in Virginia who had been converted under New Light Presbyterian preaching but had joined the Church of England because Wesley and Whitefield were within it. He did much to aid the Methodist societies before their organization into an independent church in 1784.

The Lutheran bodies were not directly much affected by the Great Awakening. Their growth in this period was largely because of the influx of German settlers. There was considerable Pietistic feeling among them, however. Their outstanding leader, Henry Melchior Muhlenberg (1711–1787), had been encouraged to come to the colonies by the leaders at Halle. He represented a balance between Pietist and orthodox emphases and was vigorous in organizing new churches among German Lutherans, who had become the largest religious group in Pennsylvania by the middle of the eighteenth century. In 1748, he organized the first Lutheran synod to enjoy permanent existence. Among some of the smaller German bodies, the Pietist spirit was much more in evidence.

Out of the discussions occasioned by the Great Awakening, there emerged in New England the most considerable contribution that eighteenth-century America made to theology—the work of Jonathan Edwards and his school. Born in a pastor's home in Connecticut in 1703, Edwards graduated from Yale in 1720. After a brief Presbyterian pastorate in New York, he became a tutor at Yale. In 1727, he became associate pastor at Northampton, then full pastor when his grandfather, Solomon Stoddard (1643–1729), died. Brilliant in intellect, Edwards read widely in the philosophic and scientific works of his time, steeping himself in the writings of Locke and Newton. Early convinced of the classic Calvinist emphases on the sovereignty of God and of predestination, Edwards shaped his theological position boldly, using as grist for his mill the most recent discoveries of the age of reason. A leader in the revivals, he defended what he felt to be true revivalism, a work of God, against those who rejected all emotionalism in religion, on the one hand, and those who exploited it, on the other. In 1746 appeared *A Treatise Concerning Religious Affections,* a theological defense of what he believed to be genuine revival, in which Edwards utilized psychological insights derived in part from Locke. A pastor and churchman, he was a champion of higher standards for church members, believing that only the saints—the true elect—should be members in full communion. When he acted on the basis of this position, no longer abiding by the laxer view, he was dismissed from his pulpit in 1750, despite a careful treatise on the subject which had appeared the year before, *Qualifications Requisite for Full Communion.*

Edwards became missionary to the Indians at Stockbridge, Massachusetts, where he found leisure to devote his theological and philosophical powers to the defense of Calvinism against Arminianism, under which term he characterized the liberal theological trends of the eighteenth century. In his *Treatise on the Will* (1754), he held that while all men have a natural ability to turn to God, they lack the moral ability—that is, the inclination—so to do. This determining inclination is the transforming gift of God's grace, though its absence is no excuse for sin. A systematic theologian, Edwards planned a massive work setting forth his entire position. Actually, he finished only a few fragments of it, though some of his earlier treatises were apparently to be fitted into it. One of the fragments was *The Nature of True Virtue,* posthumously published in 1765. To Edwards's thinking, virtue is love for intelligent Being in general. But God has infinitely the greatest share of existence, he is infinitely the greatest Being, so true virtue must essentially and radically consist in supreme love for God. Such true virtue cannot be found through reason and understanding, for it is of the affections and the disposition; it arises from the ascendancy of the supreme passion, love, over self-love. "Disinterested benevolence" is one of its tests, and it is wholly a gift of God. But Edwards's systematic work was left unfinished. Called to serve as president of Princeton, he submitted to inoculation during a smallpox epidemic, contracted the disease, and died a few weeks after assuming his new duties.

Edwards's views were championed by a group of followers: Joseph Bellamy (1719–1790), Samuel Hopkins (1721–1803), Jonathan Edwards, Jr. (1745–1801), and Nathaniel Emmons (1745–1840). These Edwardsean theologians set the pattern of theological discussion in New England for many decades; they continued to debate the issues that he had raised, engaging in arguments with the Old Calvinists, followers of the federal or covenant theology. Though the Edwardseans were competent scholars and industrious workers, they lacked the poetic insights and breadth of vision that had characterized the master.

Hopkins especially handled some of the Edwardsean positions with harsh logic, yet in stressing the theme of "disinterested benevolence" he unwittingly prepared the way for some of the theological shifts of the nineteenth century. Though the work of these Edwardseans came after the Great Awakening had passed its peak in the New England Congregational churches, they did present and defend an evangelical Calvinism that was influential in later American developments (see VII:15).

The American experience of awakening had some influence in Canada. A Great Awakening emerged in Nova Scotia in the 1770s, in historical continuity with the Separate Congregationalists of Connecticut, a number of whom had migrated to the northern province. It was led by a Rhode Islander who had gone to Nova Scotia as a boy, Henry Alline (1748–1784). Familiar with the classic accounts of conversion in evangelical Puritan writings, he responded to a call to preach immediately following his own experience of assurance in 1775. He worked out a distinctive "awakening theology," which he proclaimed on itinerant preaching tours, stimulating intense response, especially among working-class people. Alline's view of the church was decisively shaped by Separate Congregationalism; the New Light congregations which arose out of his revival efforts did not prove to be stable, however, and some, like their analogs in Connecticut, were later reconstituted as Baptist churches. Thus, in Nova Scotia as in New England, Baptists often reaped the harvest of the Great Awakening.

Chapter 9

The Impact of the Evangelical Revival; the Rise of Modern Missions

THE IMPACT of the evangelical revival in Britain was felt far beyond the range of its adherents. Its influence on the older nonconformist bodies was stimulating, though unequal. Their condition in the first half of the eighteenth century was one of decay. Their leaders looked askance at Wesley and Whitefield at first; but as the revival continued, the younger men caught its zeal. This was especially the case among the Congregationalists, who profited most of all. Their preaching was quickened, their zeal revived, their numbers rapidly increased. Many accessions came to them from those awakened by Methodism to whom the Methodist discipline was irksome. Many came to them from parishes of the establishment. By 1800, the Congregationalists occupied a very different position in England from that of 1700. The Particular Baptists also shared in this growth, as did the General Baptists, in spite of a considerable leaven of Arian thought. In 1770, an Evangelical wing separated as the General Baptist New Connection, in protest against the Unitarian tendency. The Presbyterians, on the other hand, were almost unaffected. Arianism and Socinianism were dominant among them. Their numbers dwindled. Nor were the Quakers much moved; the revival methods were too foreign to their spirit to make much impression.

The Methodist movement was forward-looking in its philanthropic sympathies, and the Evangelicals shared this trait. Methodism, under Wesley's leadership, sought to aid its poorer members financially, to provide work, to care for the sick, to furnish schools and cheap reading, and to overcome the coarseness and brutality of the lower classes.

The awakening of the new spirit of humanitarianism had one of its noblest illustrations in John Howard (1726-1790), a quiet, religious, country landlord, interested in schools and model cottages, a worshiper in Congregational and Baptist congregations. Howard was chosen high sheriff of Bedford in 1773. He was inexpressibly shocked at the moral and physical filth of the jails, their officers supported by what they could wring from the prisoners, not by salaries; no proper separation of prisoners, no release for those acquitted until their fees were discharged. Thorough in all that he did, Howard visited practically all the jails of England, and he laid the horrible results before Parliament in 1774. He then performed similar service for Scotland, Ireland, and the Continent. Much remained to be done, but he deserves the title of "father of prison reform." His last years were devoted to equally self-sacrificing efforts to ascertain methods to prevent the spread of the plague. His devotion cost him his life in southern Russia.

A group which distinguished itself for devotion to good causes gathered around Henry Venn (1725-1797), rector of Huddersfield, and his son John (1759-1813), rector of Clapham. This group, chiefly of wealthy Anglican Evangelical laymen, was dubbed "the Clapham Sect." Its members were especially influential in ridding Britain and the dominions of slavery. That evil had received John Wesley's severest condemnation. It had been vigorously opposed by the Quakers. In the early nineteenth century, the Claphamites led the successful drive to eliminate it. Zachary Macaulay (1768-1838), father of the historian, once booked passage on a slave ship to observe conditions at first hand. The most effective leader in the crusade was one of the most eminent of Evangelical laymen, William Wilberforce (1759-1833). Wealthy, popular, and a member of Parliament, he was "converted" in 1784 through the instrumentality of Isaac Milner. In 1797, he published his *Practical View of the Prevailing Religious System of Professed Christians in the Higher and Middle Classes in this Country Contrasted with Real Christianity*. It proved one of the most popular of Evangelical treatises. In 1787, he began his lifelong battle with slavery, resulting in the abolition of the slave trade in 1807 and of slavery itself throughout the British dominions in 1833.

In carrying out their religious, humane, and charitable efforts, Evangelicals of various types frequently worked together through voluntary societies. The revival movement gave a great impulse to the diffusion of Christian literature. Wesley published constantly through the Society for Promoting Christian Knowledge, which had been founded in 1699 (see VII:2). In 1799, the interdenominational Religious Tract Society was formed in London. Pietism had set the example of extensive and cheap publication of the Bible through Baron Canstein's foundation in Halle, in 1710 (see VII:5). In 1804, the British and Foreign Bible Society was founded in London through the efforts of Evangelicals. Similar societies in Ireland, Scotland, and the United States (see VII:15) were soon founded; by their work, the enormous diffusion of the Scriptures was made possible.

Some form of religious teaching of children is probably as old as organized religion, and the Reformation age made much of catechetical instruction. Though attempts were made even earlier, the first systematic and successful efforts to reach the poor and unschooled with a Christian training on a large scale were in the Sunday schools, founded in 1780 by Robert Raikes (1735–1811), an Evangelical layman of the establishment. In the absence of public education, he sought to provide training in the three Rs and in Christian fundamentals by means of paid teachers, on the only day, Sunday, when the children were free. Attendance at church was also required. Raikes was proprietor of the *Gloucester Journal,* which published accounts of these activities. The work spread with great rapidity. Wesley and the nonconformists favored them. A Society for Promoting Sunday Schools was organized in London in 1785; a similar society was formed in Philadelphia in 1791. Though the growth of the movement was as rapid as it was permanent, it was not without clerical opposition, partly on account of its novelty and partly because of its "desecration" of Sunday. The secular instruction rapidly decreased, and the paid teacher gave place to the voluntary leader. No Christian agency has become more fully part of normal modern church life.

One of the most important consequences of the evangelical revival was the rise of modern Protestant missions. The development of Roman Catholic missions in the Reformation age had been rapid and fruitful (see VI:11), but lack of geographical contact coupled with certain internal problems and theological convictions long deterred equivalent Protestant efforts. However, following the Dutch conquests in the seventeenth century, work was begun in

Ceylon, Java, and Formosa. The first English foreign missionary organization, the Society for the Propagation of the Gospel in New England, came into existence by act of Parliament in 1649, in response to John Eliot's efforts among the Massachusetts Indians (see VII:2). At its expense, his Indian Bible and other works were printed. The Society for the Propagation of the Gospel in Foreign Parts was organized in 1701 (see VII:2). German Pietism produced the Halle-Danish missions from 1705 onward (see VII:5). In 1732, the notable missionary career of the Moravians began (see VII:6). Quakers also made some missionary efforts.

Interest in non-Christian peoples was aroused in Great Britain by the voyages of discovery in the Pacific, under government auspices, conducted by Captain James Cook (1728–1779) from 1768 to his death. These discoveries awakened the missionary zeal of William Carey (1761–1834), a shoemaker and later a Baptist preacher, who was to show himself a man of remarkable talents as a linguist and a botanist, as well as of unquenchable missionary devotion. The result of his thought was his *Enquiry into the Obligation of Christians to use Means for the Conversion of the Heathens* (1792). This book and Carey's sermon on Isaiah 54:2 led to the organization of the Baptist Society for Propagating the Gospel among the Heathen. Carey was its first missionary, and his letters from India proved a powerful stimulus to other missionary endeavors. In 1795, the London Missionary Society was formed as an interdenominational enterprise, largely through the efforts of David Bogue (1750–1825), a Congregational minister of Gosport, and of Thomas Haweis (1734–1820), the Evangelical rector of Aldwinkle. Its first missionaries were sent in 1796 to Tahiti. Later it became a Congregational agency. The growing sense of missionary obligation led in 1799 to the organization of the Church Missionary Society, representative of the Evangelical wing of the establishment, through the agency of John Venn, rector of Clapham, and Thomas Scott, editor of the *Family Bible*. The Wesleyan Methodist Missionary Society of England was founded in 1817–1818. After small local beginnings in Scotland, as early as 1796, the Church of Scotland Mission boards came into being in 1825. This deepening of British missionary obligation roused wide interest in other lands. The early nineteenth century was to see the organization of extensive missionary societies, both denominational and interdenominational, in the United States and on the Continent (see VII:14, 15).

Chapter 10

The Revolutionary Epoch
in the United States

THIRTEEN OF THE ENGLISH COLONIES in North America broke free from the
mother country to become an independent nation during the last quarter
of the eighteenth century, the revolutionary epoch in America. The attention
of many was turned from the strenuous interest in religion that had marked
the Great Awakening by a long series of political and military events of absorbing concern. Increasing friction between colonies and crown led to the outbreak
of the Revolution in 1775, the Declaration of Independence in 1776, the destructive war lasting until 1783, and the protracted discussions concerning the
framework of the new nation, which did not terminate until the establishment
of government under the Constitution of the United States in 1789. The revolutionary philosophy tended to be rationalistic in its attitude to religion, minimizing the prestige of the churches. Many of the political leaders were influenced
by the Deism of England or France (see VII:3). Thus, for more than a
generation people were preoccupied with revolutionary thought and action, and
religion attracted less general attention than it had.

The event of greatest significance for religion in this period in America
was the achievement of religious freedom. This was a revolutionary step, for
it marked a radical departure from the principles of uniformity and establishment that had marked western civilization for over a thousand years. Toleration had been granted in some European countries, notably the Netherlands
and England, but the acceptance of religious freedom as a national principle
was new. It was brought about by many interwoven factors. The very multiplicity of religious organizations served to check the advance of any one church
and to prevent it from securing a majority of the population as its supporters.
The breadth of the ocean was not conducive to the maintenance of vigorous
colonial branches of European state churches, and the sheer immensity of the
continent made the maintenance of ecclesiastical establishments in it difficult.
The desire for economic prosperity in colonies where laborers were scarce

encouraged the overlooking of religious differences. The rise of toleration in England hampered efforts to maintain rigorous uniformity, as when Charles II prohibited Massachusetts Bay officials from hanging any more Quakers in 1662. Of great importance was the witness of a number of religious groups stemming from the left wing of the Reformation (Mennonites, Dunkers) and the left wing of Puritanism (Baptists, Quakers). These groups believed in religious freedom on religious principles. During the exciting days of the civil wars in England, there were forged in certain Puritan circles strong arguments for religious freedom based on broadly orthodox, classical Christian premises. In Rhode Island and Pennsylvania, representatives of these positions had opportunities to put their ideas to work and to prove that an orderly civil state could be maintained without religious uniformity or establishment. The Great Awakening further stimulated the desire for freedom in religion, and its practical effect was to contribute heavily to the growth of unestablished bodies. Finally, the representatives of rationalist views in religion were firm believers in religious liberty; they often served as leaders in drives for disestablishment.

These various factors combined in various ways in the different areas to secure religious liberty. Some of the most vigorous struggles came at the state level, in places where there had been strong establishments. In Virginia, after long years of political debate, the Virginia Statute for Religious Freedom, the original draft of which had been written by Thomas Jefferson, was passed in 1785, rationalists and Dissenters teaming up in the struggle. In New England, the rising tide of sentiment for religious liberty, coupled with the growing strength of the nonestablished bodies, led to the end of the Congregational establishments in Connecticut in 1818, New Hampshire in 1819, and Massachusetts in 1833. At the national level, the various factors combined to bring about religious freedom from the beginning. Article VI of the Constitution provided that "no religious test shall ever be required as a qualification to any office or public trust under the United States." The First Amendment (1791) to the Constitution declared that "Congress shall make no law respecting an establishment of religion, or prohibiting the free exercise thereof . . ." Thus, the patterns of establishment and uniformity were given up, and, with the disappearance of the last state establishment, all churches survived as voluntary associations, equal before the law.

The attainment of American independence thrust new problems upon all denominations. Some which had been branches of European churches now found it necessary to reorganize on an independent basis. No communion in America suffered so severely from the Revolution as the Church of England. Many of its ministers and members, especially in the north, were sympathetic with the mother country, and it emerged from the struggle in ruins. Its very name seemed unpatriotic, and that of "Protestant Episcopal" was suggested at a conference of clergy and laity of Maryland in November 1780. Two years later, William White (1748–1836), rector of Christ's Church in Philadelphia and a hearty supporter of American independence, sketched out the plan under which the American Protestant Episcopal church was essentially to be organized, in independence of the state and of English ecclesiastical control, with representative bodies composed not only of clergy but of laymen. He believed the prospect of securing an American episcopate remote. In accordance with White's suggestions, a voluntary convention, representative of eight states, met in New York City in October 1784 and called the First General Convention to gather in Philadelphia in September 1785. The Episcopal clergy of Connecticut had held aloof; it had chosen Samuel Seabury (1729–1796) as bishop, and he had gone to England for ordination in June 1783. Finding it impossible to receive consecration from the English episcopate in the absence of action by Parliament, Seabury procured it at the hands of the Nonjuror Scottish bishops in Aberdeen in November 1784.

The General Convention of 1785 adopted a constitution for the Protestant Episcopal Church in the United States, largely the work of William White. It also appealed to the English bishops for the ordination of bishops for America. Seabury's Scottish ordination might be valid, but the derivation of orders from the parent English body was desired. The local Episcopal conventions of the several states were asked to name bishops. The General Convention, reconvened in 1786, was able to report that the English bishops had procured an enabling act from Parliament and that William White had been chosen bishop of Pennsylvania and Samuel Provoost (1742–1815) of New York. On February 4, 1787, they were consecrated by the archbishop of Canterbury.

Bishop Seabury and Bishops White and Provoost, who had stood on opposite sides during the Revolution and who represented different traditions of churchmanship, looked upon each other at first with some antagonism. Connecticut had not yet been represented in the General Convention, but the decision to have both a House of Bishops and a House of Deputies in the convention, thus satisfying the demands for both clerical and lay emphases, paved the way for the adjustment of difficulties. In the General Convention of 1789, all parties united, the Prayer Book was revised and adapted to American needs, and the foundation of the Protestant Episcopal Church in the United States of America was fully laid.

American Methodism was also ripe for independent organization at the end of the Revolution. Here, too, dependence on England was no longer desirable, nor was the continued relationship with the Episcopal church very promising, in view of the latter's weakness and inability to provide the sacraments, especially in places where Methodism was rapidly moving, as on the frontier. Wesley had tried in vain, in 1780, to procure ordination for clergymen for America from the bishop of London. He had long been convinced that bishops and presbyters in the ancient church were one order. He therefore, as a presbyter, felt empowered to ordain in case of necessity. At Bristol, on September 1, 1784, he, Thomas Coke (1747–1814), and James Creighton (1739–1820), all

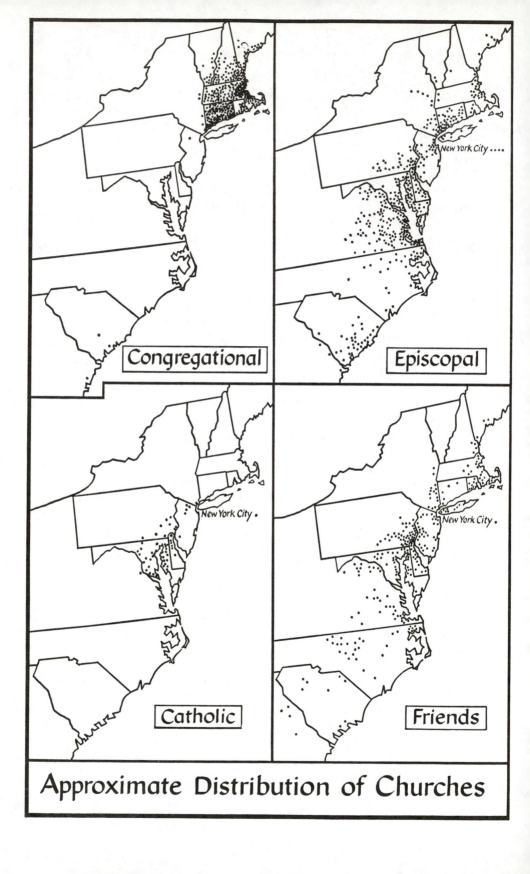

Congregational

Episcopal
New York City ....

Catholic
New York City .

Friends
New York City .

Approximate Distribution of Churches

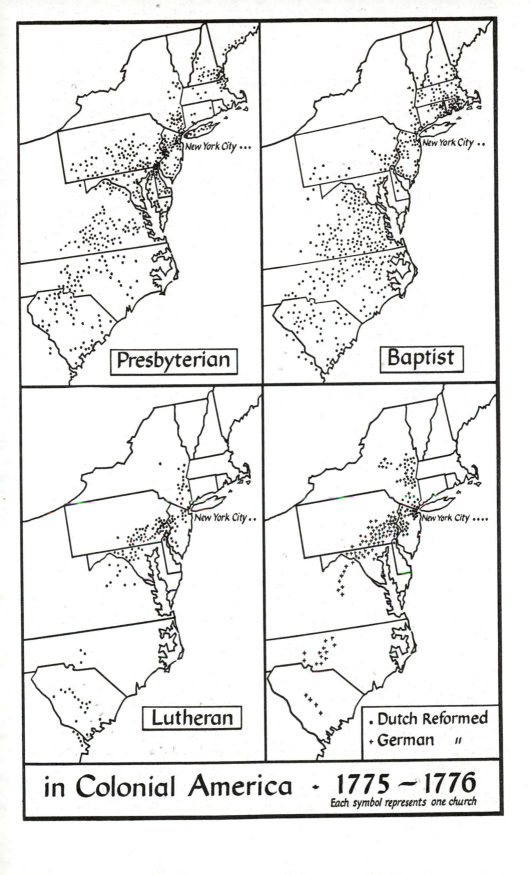

Presbyterian

Baptist

Lutheran

New York City ...

New York City ..

New York City ..

New York City ....

. Dutch Reformed
+ German   "

in Colonial America · 1775 – 1776

Each symbol represents one church

presbyters of the establishment, ordained Richard Whatcoat and Thomas Vasey deacons, and on the next day ordained them as presbyters or elders for America. On that day, too, Wesley, "assisted by other ordained ministers," "set" Coke "apart as a superintendent" for the same work.[1] Wesley sent word to the American Methodists that he had appointed Francis Asbury, who had been active among them throughout the Revolution, as well as Coke, "superintendents." But Asbury knew the American temper, and he realized that the lay preachers must meet, freely accept Wesley's plan, and elect him and Coke as superintendents. Thus, beginning December 24, 1784, the "Christmas Conference" at Baltimore did just that, forming the Methodist Episcopal Church. Asbury was ordained deacon, elder, and superintendent on successive days; a dozen other preachers were ordained as elders. A discipline was prepared. Coke and Asbury, much to Wesley's annoyance, soon began to call themselves "bishop," and in 1787 this was made official. The first General Conference met in 1792, guiding the growth of the rapidly expanding, fully independent new church.

The dependence on Holland of the Dutch and German Reformed churches had long been weakening, and the severing of the ties completely, in 1792 and 1793 respectively, was largely a formality.

The Roman Catholics, of course, did not become independent, but they did redefine their relationships and achieved a national organization. They were still a tiny minority at the time of American independence, but their position was much improved as a result of the growing tradition of religious liberty and the patriotic activities of many of them during the Revolution. They had been under the vicar apostolic of London, but with independence this was no longer feasible. In 1784, the much-respected John Carroll (1735–1815) of Maryland was appointed prefect apostolic for the United States by Pius VI (1774–1799). Internal problems soon made it highly advisable to have a bishop, but the American Catholics feared being placed under a foreign bishop, and the priests petitioned Rome for the right to elect their own. This was granted, and in 1790 Carroll was consecrated bishop of Baltimore in England. In 1791, the first Roman Catholic synod in the United States was held at the cathedral city. In 1808, Baltimore, under Carroll, was made the seat of an archbishopric, and bishoprics were established in New York, Boston, Philadelphia, and Bardstown (Kentucky). By the year of Carroll's death, the foundations of Roman Catholicism in the United States were well established, and the priesthood numbered more than one hundred, though the immigration that was so enormously to augment this communion was still in the future.

The Moravians also retained close ties with the European center at Herrnhut. In 1775, indeed, a new policy of centralization was adopted, so that the American Moravians were more than ever dependent on overseas control.

---

[1] Nehemiah Curnock, ed., *The Journal of the Rev. John Wesley, M.A.* (London, n.d.), VII, 16.

It was an unfortunate move, for overseas leaders continued to think in European state-church terms and misunderstood the opportunity offered by the freedom of the American scene. The Moravian impact soon diminished. Not until the nineteenth century did the American Moravian church become autonomous.

Some of the denominations—Congregational, Baptist, Quaker—were already independent, and the Revolution did not directly affect them organizationally. Presbyterians were also independently organized, but they seized the opportunity to reorganize. During the 1780s, they drew up a new constitution, which provided for a full presbyterian structure, headed by a General Assembly, which first met in Philadelphia in 1789. Lutherans also had been autonomous, but during the Revolutionary epoch they began to develop organizationally. Muhlenberg (see VII:8) prepared a model constitution for his Philadelphia congregation in 1762, by which all officers were chosen by the congregation itself. The two basic features of American Lutheran polity were thus sketched —congregational in respect to the local congregation, presbyterian in respect to the standing of ministers in the synod. The synodical system spread slowly. The second synod, the ministerium of New York, was organized in 1786, the third soon after in North Carolina. In 1820, a general synod was formed, but only a portion of the Lutherans supported it. Nationality and theological tensions kept the Lutherans from any overall national unity.

A religious body new in America that developed during the period of struggle for national independence was that of the Universalists. Belief in the salvation of all occasionally appeared in eighteenth-century America as elsewhere, but the father of organized Universalism was John Murray (1741–1815), who had been touched by Whitefield's preaching in his native England and by the writings of James Relly (1722?–1778), who had passed from the status of one of Whitefield's preachers to that of an advocate of universal salvation. It was as a disciple of Relly that Murray came to America in 1770 and began an itinerating ministry, chiefly in New England. A moderate Calvinist, Murray believed that Christ had made full payment for the sins not of a restricted group of the elect but of all, and immediate blessedness would be theirs at the judgment, when all unbelief in God's mercy would vanish. For those who fully believe, the divinely promised blessedness begins now.

A further impulse was given to Universalism when, in 1780, Elhanan Winchester (1751–1797), a Baptist minister of Philadelphia, independently of Murray adopted Universalist views, which he advocated with eloquence. Unlike Murray, his general opinions were Arminian. Salvation is based on the ultimate free submission of all to God, but it will not be achieved in the case of the unrepentant until their spirits have been purified by protracted, though not eternal, suffering. Even more influential was Hosea Ballou (1771–1852), long a pastor in Boston. Murray and Winchester had been Trinitarians. Ballou was an Arian, and in this Unitarian direction American Universalism has followed him. The purpose of the atonement was moral—to set forth God's love to men. Sin brings punishment, here or hereafter, until men turn from it to God.

By 1790, the Universalists were sufficiently numerous to hold a convention in Philadelphia. Three years later, a New England convention was organized, which in 1803 met in Winchester, New Hampshire, and adopted a brief creed which stated the basic tenets of the new denomination. The early converts to Universalism were prevailingly, though not always, from the humbler walks of life.

The American revolutionary epoch was momentous for religion, as currents of life and thought that had been stirred by the Great Awakening merged with other forces to mark a transition to freedom of belief. This meant a new context for the churches, in which voluntary patterns for survival and growth had to be adopted by all. The public establishment of religion that had for some fourteen centuries marked Christendom was given up at the national level, with profound consequences for religious life not only in the newly independent nation but far beyond it, as the "lively experiment" was intently watched.

Chapter 11

The German Enlightenment (Aufklärung)

ENGLAND was well advanced in its Deistic, rationalistic, and Unitarian development before the rise of Methodism. There the two streams long ran parallel. If the evangelical awakening, theologically, was in part a return to older doctrinal conceptions, it was even more an appeal to the strong, deep religious feelings of the nation. In Germany, Pietism, with its emphasis on feeling, preceded the Enlightenment (*Aufklärung*), though continuing to run parallel to the latter movement when that developed. Pietism broke the grasp of confessional orthodoxy, but it raised up no theological leaders to take the place of the older dogmatic theologians. The critical, rationalist spirit of the eighteenth century, the works of the English Deists and their opponents, the radical popular modification of Deism in France—all these invaded Germany and found the intellectual field largely barren. The result was the rapid growth of the Enlightenment, as it styled itself. Strongly rationalistic, it sheltered many shades of opinion. More than in England or in France, by its critical and constructive work it prepared the way for a significant shift in theology, which, in the nineteenth century, was to spread widely throughout Protestant lands.

Leibniz's speculations (see VII:1) were too deep to produce a powerful impression on his own age, though later they were of powerful effect. Thomasius (see VII:5) spread a rationalistic spirit, but without working out a system. His influence was marked in developing an attitude of mind, so that he has not untruly been described as the "path-breaker of the Enlightenment." Its great protagonist, however, was Christian Wolff (1679–1754). Not a creative genius, Wolff so embodied and gave expression to the unformed and inarticulate thought of his age that he became the philosophical and theological leader of two generations of his countrymen. Skilled in mathematics, like most of the philosophers of his and the preceding century, he began lecturing on mathematics in Halle in 1707. Here his philosophy rapidly developed, in close connection with that of Leibniz, whose deeper thoughts, however, he never grasped. That alone is true, Wolff held, which can be demonstrated by logical certainty akin to mathematics. Truth must thus rationally be deduced from the innate contents of the mind—the "pure reason." All that comes by experience is merely contingent and confirmatory. The world is composed of an infinite multitude of simple substances, each endowed with force, though not with all the qualities of Leibniz's monads (see VII:1). Bodies are aggregations of these substances. The world is a huge machine, ruled by mechanical laws. The soul is that in us which is conscious of itself and of other objects. It is endowed with capacities of knowledge and desire. Their completeness of fulfillment is pleasure; their incompleteness, pain.

Since the world is contingent, it must have a cause. Hence, God exists and has made the world. The laws of all rational thinking and acting give us the divine attributes. Since completeness is the highest aim of all being, all that aims at the completeness of ourselves and other men must be virtue. Hence, the principles of right action are embodied, as with the Deists, in the fundamental divinely appointed constitution of man. Wolff did not deny that there was revelation, but he declared that it could not contain anything in disagreement with reason. He felt that miracles were possible, though improbable, and that each would imply two acts of equal power, the interruption of the order of nature and its restoration after the event. Wolff's view of man was optimistic. He is going on individually, and socially, to larger completeness. All this was a breach with the older theology, both of orthodoxy and of Pietism, and one that came to its age with the conclusiveness of a logical demonstration. God, natural religion, originally implanted morality, and progress toward individual and racial perfection, not supernatural revelation or supernatural rescue from sin and ruin, are the proper objects of religious regard, even if Wolff allows a little room for revelation and miracle. Nor is man the hopeless or incapable being of the older theology.

Wolff's views aroused the hostility of his Pietistic colleagues in Halle. They procured from King Frederick William I (1713-1740) his removal in 1723. The royal sentence was even to them surprisingly strenuous: Wolff was ordered to leave the university within forty-eight hours or be hanged. He found a refuge in Marburg, and subsequently he was honorably restored to Halle in 1740 by Frederick the Great. His work had, however, became common property, and he added little to his achievements during the fourteen years in Halle before his death. His thought had become that of a large section of Germany. The sway of Pietism in Halle was over.

Less radical, but influential in aiding the new attitude of German thought, was Johann Lorenz von Mosheim (1694?-1755), professor in Helmstedt and then in Göttingen. The most admired preacher of his time, master of a style of brilliancy in Latin and in German, he was basically a rational supernaturalist. He had no sympathy with the dogmatism of the orthodox. The emphases of the Pietists awakened no response in him, nor could he support the extreme rationalism of Wolff. He touched most fields of religious thought, and his influence, on the whole, favored the spread of the Enlightenment. His chief service was in the field of history. His *Institutiones Historiae Ecclesiasticae,* issued first in 1726 and in final form in 1755, embraced the whole story of the church. In his *Commentarii de rebus Christianorum ante Constantinum* (1753), he treated the earlier centuries in ampler fashion. Mosheim well deserves the name of "father of modern church history." He desired to be free of all partisan bias, and he succeeded in remarkable measure, at the expense of some colorlessness. His is the first church history that aimed to tell events exactly as they happened, without a cause to defend. As such, and by reason of its learning and style, his work long survived his death.

More extreme rationalism also found its representatives in Germany. Hermann Samuel Reimarus (1694-1768), long a highly reputed professor of Oriental languages in Hamburg and a leader in scholarly circles there, had traveled in England in early life and had adopted Deist views, in defense of which he wrote much, though his works were not issued until after his death, when they were put forth by Lessing between 1774 and 1778 as fragments found in the library of Wolfenbüttel—hence *Wolfenbüttel Fragments,* the publication of which aroused immense discussion. As with the Deists, all that is true is that natural religion which teaches the existence of a wise Creator, a primitive morality, and immortality—all ascertainable by reason. The world itself is the only miracle and the only revelation, all others are impossible. The writers of the Bible were not even honest men; they were moved by fraud and selfishness. It is a curious commentary on the condition of thought in Germany that Reimarus's writings, though widely criticized, were no less valued by others as a defense of religion against materialism and atheism.

Gotthold Ephraim Lessing (1729-1781), to whom the publication of

Reimarus's religious writings was due (though he did not wholly agree with Reimarus), eminent as a dramatist and a literary and artistic critic and ranking as a German classic writer with Goethe and Schiller, presented in his *Education of the Human Race* (1780) a theory of much plausibility. Just as the individual passes through the successive stages of childhood, youth, and manhood, so does the race. The Scriptures have been given by God to meet these needs. Childhood is moved by immediate rewards and punishments. For men in that condition, the Old Testament is a divine book of training, with its promises of long life and temporal blessings for obedience. Youth is ready to sacrifice present ease and lesser goods for future success and happiness. For it, or for men in that state, the New Testament with its present self-surrender and eternal rewards is a fitting guide. But manhood is ruled by duty, without hope of reward or fear of punishment as its motives. Its guide is reason, though perhaps God may yet send some further revelation as its aid. Lessing's work spread wide the feeling in educated Germany that the historic Christian religion belonged to a past, or to an inferior present, stage of human development.

The effect of the Enlightenment was a wide diffusion of the views that what alone were valuable in the Scriptures were the truths of natural religion and its morality, divested of miracle or the supernatural. Jesus was a moral teacher rather than a personal center of faith. This was rationalism; it was characteristic of much of the strongest theological thinking of Germany by 1800 and was to continue powerful in the nineteenth century. Side by side with it, confessional orthodoxy and Pietism continued, though with decreasing intellectual appeal, and much which may be called semirationalism. Yet the age was characterized as well by vigorous polemic against superstitions, a large development of voluntary and popular beneficence, and provision for popular education.

The eighteenth century was also marked, and nowhere more than in Germany, by the development of textual and historical studies of the Bible, which initiated the modern period of criticism. The English scholar, John Mill (1645–1707), published a Greek Testament, based on a careful collation of manuscripts, in the year of his death. Jean le Clerc (1657–1736), brought up in Geneva, later an Arminian in Amsterdam from 1684 to his death, won fame as an exegete through his attempts to explain the teaching of the Scriptures without dogmatic prepossessions—approaching them to discover not proof texts but their actual meaning. Johann Albrecht Bengel (see VII:5), long head of the theological seminary in Denkendorf, in Württemberg, a man of pietistic leanings, was the first to recognize that New Testament manuscripts may be grouped in families, and to establish the generally accepted critical canon that a more difficult reading is to be preferred. His *Gnomon,* or Index, of the New Testament (1742), was the most remarkable commentary thus far produced. Nothing, he declared, should be read into the Scripture, and nothing there contained should be omitted which could be drawn out by the most rigid application of grammatical principles. Wesley made it the basis of his *Notes upon the New Testament* (1755). Contemporaneously, Johann Jakob Wettstein (1693–1754), of Basel and Amsterdam, spent nearly a lifetime of labor on his *Greek New Testament with Various Reading,* published in 1751–1752. Textual criticism and sound exegesis were thus given a great advance.

To Jean Astruc (1684–1766), royal professor of medicine in Paris, was due the announcement, in his *Conjectures* (1753), of the composite character of *Genesis.* The theory won essential support in 1781 from Johann Gottfried Eichhorn (1752–1827), later a rationalistic professor in Göttingen, often called the "founder of Old Testament criticism," but it was only in the later part of the nineteenth century that Astruc's discovery won extensive recognition.

In Johann August Ernesti (1707–1781), professor in Leipzig from 1742, Germany had a teacher who aided greatly that awakening of classical thought and ideals which affected German intellectual life in the closing years of the eighteenth century and who carried to New Testament interpretation the same principles that he applied to classical literature. The meaning is to be ascertained by the same grammatical and historical methods in the one field as in the other. In his seventh Fragment, published by Lessing in 1778, Reimarus for the first time subjected the life of Christ to rigid historiographical methods, like those applied to secular history. His total rejection of the supernatural, the mythical, and the legendary left his results barren enough, but he raised questions of method and conclusion which have constituted the problems of this investigation, in large measure, ever since. Johann Salomo Semler (1725–1791), professor in Halle from 1752, was of pietistic training, though in manhood a conservative rationalist. His importance was in the paths he indicated rather than in the results he achieved. He distinguished between the permanent truths in Scripture and the elements due to the times in which the several books were written. He denied the equal value of all parts of Scripture. Revelation, he taught, is in Scripture, but not all Scripture is revelation. The creeds of the church are a growth. Church history is a development. In particular, he made a distinction between Petrine, Judaizing parties, in the early church, and Pauline, anti-Judaic parties, that was to play a great rôle in later discussions.

Chapter 12

Trends in Nineteenth-Century Protestant Thought in Germany

NOTHING SEEMED more characteristic of the earlier half of the eighteenth century than the dominance of "reason," or common sense. The age was unemotional, intellectual. It did remarkable work in questioning that which had been accepted on tradition, in sweeping away ancient superstitions and abuses, and in demanding the rightfulness of that which claimed authority. But it was cold and one-sided. It was met, as the eighteenth century went on, by an immense opposition. The claims of feeling asserted themselves, voiced in a "return to nature" that was too often a nature conjured up by the imagination, but accompanied by a renewed appreciation of the classical and the medieval and the revival of a sense of the supernatural in religion, often vague and obscure but creating a totally different atmosphere in which human claims to be a feeling, rather than a purely thinking, being were asserted.

Its most effective early apostle was Jean Jacques Rousseau (1712–1778), but the movement was manifested not only in France but throughout Europe. Nowhere was it more evident than in Germany. Lessing shared it. Its most conspicuous literary representatives there were Johann Wolfgang von Goethe (1749–1832) and Johann Christoph Friedrich von Schiller (1759–1805). The older rationalism was not swept from the field, but radically different patterns of life and thought, usually referred to under the generic term Romanticism, contended on more equal terms for mastery.

Philosophy, in the eighteenth century, had seemed to lead to no thoroughfare. Leibniz had taught that all knowledge was an elucidation of that which was wrapped up innate in the monad. Wolff had affirmed the power of "pure reason" to give the only certainties. On the other hand, Locke had taught that all comes by experience, and though Hume had pushed to skepticism all conclusions based on cause and substance, he had viewed, like Locke, all knowledge as founded on experience. The British and the German tendencies were apparently mutually destructive. It was to be the work of Kant to combine and supersede both, on a new basis which should be the starting point of modern philosophy, and to give a value to feeling which none of the earlier parties had recognized. On the one hand, Kant was the climax and fulfillment of rationalistic, Enlightenment religion. But on the other hand, he was also the critic of the Enlightenment, laying bare its weaknesses and limitations, thus undermining its hold and revealing the need for fresh approaches, which came into their own in the early nineteenth century.

Immanuel Kant (1724–1804) was a native of Königsberg, where all his life was spent. His paternal ancestry, he believed, was Scottish. His earliest influences were Pietist. In 1755, Kant became a teacher in the University of Königsberg. His development was slow. He held at first to the school of Leibniz and Wolff. Study of Hume awakened doubts as to its adequacy, though he did not become Hume's disciple. Rousseau profoundly influenced him with the "discovery of the deep hidden nature of man." In 1781 came Kant's epoch-making work, the *Critique of Pure Reason*—a blow struck primarily at the then dominant philosophy of Wolff. His formative treatises rapidly followed, and his thought was soon powerful in Germany. By 1797, his mental and physical powers had begun a decline which was to end in pitiful ruin. A little man in physical stature, never married, of strict moral uprightness, he devoted himself to his task with singular simplicity and fidelity.

Kant's system was in many respects a theory of knowledge. Like Locke and Hume, he held that in our knowledge something, or some stimulus—the "percept"—comes to the mind from without. Like Leibniz and Wolff, he maintained that the mind has certain intuitional qualities that are transcendent, in the sense that they do not come by experience, and that condition and give form to that which comes from without. Time and space constitute the framework in which the perceptions are ordered. The mind classifies what comes to it from without under its own laws; these are the "categories." Knowledge is therefore the product of two elements—perception from without, to which form is given by the laws of the mind. These two elements give us experience; however, they give us knowledge not of what things are in themselves but only of what our minds make of what has come into them from without. Such a demonstration of God, natural religion, and the constitution of the universe, from "pure reason," as Wolff had attempted, is intellectually impossible. We cannot demonstrate the nature of these existences as they are in themselves. Nature may be studied as the realm of exact law, but the law is simply that of our own thinking.

While absolute knowledge of that which is beyond experience is unattainable by purely intellectual processes, one is conscious of a feeling of moral obligation when one asks what one ought to do. This problem was explored by Kant in his *Critique of Practical Reason* (1788). When one answers the question as to conduct, one feels within oneself a "categorical imperative"—an imperative because a command, and categorical because without conditions.

It is so to act that the principles of action may become those of universal law; in a phrase, "do your duty." That moral law within is the noblest of human possessions, interpreting human beings as personalities and not as machines. In this "categorical imperative," three postulates, or inseparable thoughts, are united. The most evident is that, if persons ought to do their duty, they can. Hence, they must have freedom. And freedom gives us a glimpse of a super-sensuous realm of moral purpose—a sphere of moral order. A second postulate is that of immortality, to provide fuller opportunity for the self to reach the highest good. Closely connected is the third postulate. Virtue should result in happiness, yet experience does not give that union. Hence, its accomplishment demands a power that can unite the two. The third postulate is, therefore, God, whose existence in "pure reason" is only a hypothesis; in the postulates of the practical reason, however, it become a conviction.

When Kant set forth his religious ideas, on the basis of practical rather than theoretical or pure reason, it was the familiar rationalistic Enlightenment faith that was presented. His *Religion within the Bounds of Reason Only* (1793) emphasized morality as the prime content of the practical reason and reduced religion practically to theistic ethics. Evil and the categorical impera-tive contest for human obedience. One ruled by the principle of moral good —the categorical imperative—is pleasing to God, is a child of God. Of this relationship Christ is the highest illustration. The invisible church is the ideal union of all those obedient to moral law. The visible church is a union to develop this obedience. Its complete achievement will be the kingdom of God. Kant's contribution to Christian theology was not his rationalizing inter-pretation of doctrines, but his vindication of the profoundest human feelings as bases of practical religious conviction and moral conduct. Romanticists soon developed this lead in quite a different direction than Kant's.

A decided impulse to the historical interpretation of the Bible was given by Johann Gottfried von Herder (1744-1803), in early life intimate with Goethe, later influenced by personal contact with Kant, and an eager supporter of the romantic movement. From 1776 to his death, he was court preacher in Weimar. His *Spirit of Hebrew Poetry* appeared in 1782-1783, his *Philosophy of the History of Mankind* in 1784-1791. Religion, especially Christianity, is the embodiment of that which is deepest in the feelings of humankind. The Scriptures are to be understood in the light of the views and feelings of the times in which the several books were written. They are essentially a religious literature. What is true and permanent in them must be distinguished from the temporary and local.

Out of the romantic movement came the most influential German theo-logian of the early nineteenth century, one whose work has molded religious thought far outside the borders of his native land—Friedrich Daniel Ernst Schleiermacher (1768-1834). The son of a Prussian army chaplain, he was educated by the Moravians, fell under the influence of the views of Wolff and

Semler, and was then greatly impressed by Plato, Spinoza, Kant, and Romanticism. In 1796, he became hospital chaplain in Berlin, then a center of the Enlightenment, and there published in 1799 his remarkable *Addresses on Religion,* directed to the "cultured despisers" of religion. In these, his fundamental thoughts, deeply influenced by romantic currents, were set forth. From 1804 to 1807, he was professor in Halle, and he then settled once more in Berlin, becoming a little later pastor of the Trinity Church. In 1810, on the founding of the University of Berlin, he was appointed professor of theology, a post which he occupied until his death. In 1821–1822, he set forth his mature views in his *Christian Faith according to the Principles of the Evangelical Church;* the definitive second edition appeared in 1830.

Schleiermacher's prime significance is that he took up into his own system the results of previous tendencies and gave to theology a new basis, and to the person of Christ a meaning largely ignored in his age. Both orthodoxy and rationalism had made religion essentially acceptance of an intellectual system and an externally authoritative rule of conduct. To the orthodox, religion was based on assent to the truths of revelation and obedience to the will of God. To the rationalists, it was acceptance of natural theology and of universal morality ascertained by the reason. Both parties in the eighteenth century looked upon religion and morality as primarily means for securing a happy immortality; for Kant also, religion was a type of moral action. In Schleiermacher's view, religion belongs to the realm of "feeling," not as emotion but as a sense, taste, and intuition for the infinite. In itself, religion is neither a body of doctrines, revealed or rationally certified, nor a system of conduct, though both belief and conduct flow from religion.

Schleiermacher took much from Spinoza, Leibniz, and Kant. In our experience, we perceive the antithesis of the manifold and changing over against a principle of unity and permanency. These antitheses give us the Absolute and eternal—God, without whom all would be chaos—and the world, without which all would be empty. The Absolute is throughout all. God is therefore immanent in his world. Man is, in himself, as with Leibniz, a microcosm, a reflection of the universe. As contrasted with that which is universal, absolute, and eternal, he feels himself finite, limited, temporary—in a word, dependent. This feeling of dependence is the basis of all religion. Schleiermacher taught that the piety underlying religious bodies is neither a knowing nor a doing, but a determination of feeling or of immediate self-consciousness.[1] To bridge over the gulf between the universal and the finite, to bring humanity into harmony with God, is the aim of all religions. The worth of each religion is to be measured by the degree to which this result is accomplished. Hence, religions are to be divided not into true and false, but into relative degrees

[1] Claude Welch, *Protestant Thought in the Nineteenth Century,* vol. 1, *1799–1870* (New Haven, 1972), pp. 64–68.

of adequacy. All advances in religion throughout history are in a true sense revelations, a fuller manifestation to human consciousness of the immanent God. Of all religions thus far known to men, Christianity is the best, since it most fully accomplishes what it is the aim of all religions to achieve. Its problems are those most fundamental to all religion: sin and pardon, separation and reconciliation. In the Christian religion, the person of Christ is the central element. He is himself the reconciliation of the finite with the universal, the temporal with the eternal—the union of God and man. He is, therefore, the Mediator of this reconciliation to others. Hence, Schleiermacher was strongly christocentric. The life thus uniting the temporal and the eternal—humanity and God—is now immortal. An immortality in duration is a great hope, but true immortality is a quality of life rather than a mere question of duration.

Doctrines are accounts of the religious affections set forth in speech; they are definitions and interpretations of fundamental religious experiences, but these explanations have only a relative and secondary value. They have changed and may change again. They are simply the forms in which abiding truth from time to time expresses itself.

In Schleiermacher's view, morality is the result of the proper understanding of that of which each human being is a part—the family, the community, the state, the world. Such an enlarging view of the human part in these relations will drive out selfishness and self-centering. Morality is not religion, nor religion morality; but religion is the indispensable friend and advocate of morality. It insistently asks the question: "What ought to be, in the light of the Christian consciousness?"

Schleiermacher was condemned by the orthodox of his day as too radical, by the rationalists as too visionary; but no one influenced religious thinking in Protestant circles in the nineteenth century more, or more variously.

Kant's system contained two evident points of difficulty. It denied the power of intellectual processes to give knowledge of things as they are in themselves, and it did not explain how mental processes are necessarily the same in all individuals. Philosophy was developed in the clarification of both these difficulties, under the influence of Romanticism, into idealism, by Johann Gottlieb Fichte (1762–1814), Friedrich Wilhelm Joseph von Schelling (1775–1854), and especially by Georg Wilhelm Friedrich Hegel (1770–1831). A native of Stuttgart, educated at Tübingen, Hegel taught in Jena, with a scanty following, from 1801 to 1807. From 1808 to 1816, he was the head of the *gymnasium* in Nürnberg. The year 1818 saw his appointment to a professorship in Berlin, where his fame rapidly rose to that of the first philosopher of his day in Germany. He died of cholera, at the height of his reputation and activity.

To Hegel, the universe is a constant development of the Absolute—that is, God—through struggle and effort. The Absolute is Spirit, and its development is in accordance with the laws by which Mind thinks itself out logically.

At once a dialectical thinker who continually sought the reconciliation of opposites in a higher unity, and a philosopher preoccupied with triadic patterns, which he developed in varied and complex ways, Hegel occasionally used the thesis-antithesis-synthesis terminology which was more characteristic of Fichte. A given movement, a thesis, proceeds in one direction until it encounters its opposition or its limitation, the antithesis. The contradictions are not merely apparent or accidental but necessary.[2] The dialectical tension is overcome as thesis and antithesis unite in a higher union, the synthesis. For example, over against "idea," the thesis, is "nature" as its antithesis—but the two unite in higher synthesis in "humanity," which is the union of mind and matter. Since all that exists is the Absolute developing in accordance with the laws of all thought, the laws of thought are the laws of things; and since our thinking is a fragment of that of Absolute, insofar as it is true it gives us true knowledge of the things outside our minds and is the same in all minds, since it is a part of the one Absolute. Since we are portions of the Absolute come to consciousness, a prime duty of the finite spirit is to realize its relation to the Absolute, and such realization is religion. Religion may, indeed, begin, as with Schleiermacher, in feeling; but to be true, it must become real knowledge. Every religion is an attempt thus to know God, of which Christianity is the most complete realization. God is always striving to reveal himself, but this outworking must always be through the three necessary stages of development. Thus, the Father is the divine unity—the thesis. He objectifies himself in the Son—the antithesis. The uniting love is the Holy Spirit—the synthesis. The whole process yields the Trinity. So also regarding the Incarnation: God is the thesis; he is distinguished from finite humanity, the antithesis; both unite in the higher synthesis, the God-man. Hegel's system did much to replace the older sharp distinction between the divine and the human with the sense of their fundamental unity so prevalent in nineteenth-century Protestant theology.

The breadth, power, and ingenuity of Hegel's synthesis won for him great popularity; his system became the most influential in the philosophical circles of his day and had great impact in the world of thought generally. Though Hegel was a philosopher of religion and not a theologian, his approach deeply influenced theology. His views were soon sharply challenged, but they continued to attract interpreters, especially in Great Britain and America, throughout the later half of the nineteenth century.

Hegel's theory of development received significant application to New Testament criticism in the work of Ferdinand Christian Baur (1792–1860), professor in Tübingen from 1826 to his death and founder of the Tübingen school of theology. Baur contributed extensively to church history and historiography and to the development of historical-critical theology. He rejected the choice between rationalism and supernaturalism and sought instead to over-

[2] Ibid., pp. 88–91.

come the antithesis between them. The essential features of his biblical interpretation were sketched in his account of the parties in the Corinthian church,
published in 1831, and were then developed in a series of brilliant studies,
which won many disciples. His investigations prepared him to accept much
of Hegel's work by 1835; he interpreted historical progress through the stages
of theses, antithesis, and synthesis. Semler (see VII:11) had already taught the
existence of Petrine (Judaizing) and Pauline parties in the early church. These
gave the elements of the Hegelian triad. Christianity, so Baur taught, began
as essentially a messianic Judaism. This—the thesis—was the position of all
the original apostles. The necessary antithesis arose in the form of Pauline
Christianity. Petrine and Pauline views struggled far into the second century.
The inevitable synthesis came eventually in the old Catholic church, which
honored both Peter and Paul, unconscious that they had ever stood in serious
opposition.

The most debated use made by Baur of this reconstruction of the early
history of the church was a redating of the books of the New Testament.
They must display the biases of the various aspects of this development—that
is, they must show "tendencies." Applying this test, Baur found only the
letters to the Romans, the Galatians, and the Corinthians genuinely Pauline,
since they alone showed traces of the conflict. The others did not reveal the
struggle and hence must be dated later, when it had become a forgotten
story. The book of Revelation was early and Judaizing. In 1847, Baur turned
to the investigation of the Gospels by the same methods. Matthew reveals
Judaizing tendencies and is thus the oldest. Luke is probably a reworking of
Marcion's gospel (see II:2). Mark sought to hide the conflict and is later, Baur
believed, while John not only is irenic but betrays familiarity with controversies
of the later half of the second century. The greater part of the New Testament
was therefore written in the second century.

Baur's discussion aroused advocates and opponents in great numbers. Its
ultimate effect on New Testament investigation was most fruitful. These debates immensely enlarged the knowledge of the early church and of its literature. Their results have been, however, the best answer to Baur's own theories.
He had no adequate conception of the significance of Christ in the development of the early church. There were important differences between Judaic
and Pauline Christianity, but to reduce the intellectual reactions of nascent
Christianity to these only is far too simple. There were many other shades
of unlikeness. Above all, an increasing knowledge of the second century, and
an appreciation of its atmosphere impossible in Baur's time, make it inconceivable that the books which he assigns to it could, for the most part, have
been then written. They are not of that age and outlook.

By the time that Baur began his work, and for the next generation, German theologians were divided into three main groups. On one extreme stood
the rationalists, the continuation of the type of the end of the eighteenth cen-

tury. Among them, none was of greater influence than Heinrich Eberhard Gottlob Paulus (1761–1851), professor in Jena from 1789, and then, in the latter part of his long life, professor in Heidelberg (1811–1844). An opponent of all supernaturalism, his *Life of Jesus* (1828) is typical of the woodenness of the rationalism of his period. Christ's walking on the water he explains as a misunderstanding by the disciples, who were viewing Christ through the mist as he walked on the shore. The feeding of the five thousand was accomplished by the generous freedom with which Christ bestowed the little food he had, thus awakening the generosity of those in the throng who had a larger supply. Christ's death was no real event: he revived in the tomb, aroused by an earthquake, and returned to his disciples.

Confessional orthodoxy of the most uncompromising pattern had a notable representative in Ernst Wilhelm Hengstenberg (1802–1869), professor in Berlin from 1826 to his death. He began under rationalist influence, but then for a time became leader in Pietist circles. By 1840, he emerged as a vigorous champion of strict Lutheran orthodoxy, putting emphasis on older theories of biblical inspiration and authority. Resisting both rationalist and idealist views, the confessional orthodox sought to restore the distinctive doctrine and order of the early Luthern church, to "repristinate" it. The movement was often allied with political conservatism; in Berlin, the influence of Friedrich Julius Stahl (1802–1861), professor of law, was strongly in this direction. In Mecklenburg, Theodor Kliefoth (1810–1895) and F. A. Philippi (1809–1892) asserted that purity of doctrine is the sign of the true church and that, since the Lutheran church has in its confessions of faith the full truth, it is that church.

Between the two extremes stood a "mediating" school, influenced by Schleiermacher, sharing his warmth of Christian feeling, perhaps intensified, strongly devoted, like him, to the personal Christ, but disposed to accept many of the results of criticism, especially regarding the biblical inspiration and narratives. A prominent figure among these "mediating" theologians was Johann August Wilhelm Neander (1789–1850). Of Hebrew parentage, originally David Mendel, he took the name by which he is now known at baptism in 1806, to signify his new birth. A student under Schleiermacher in Halle, it was his teacher's influence that secured for him a professorship in Berlin in 1813, which he filled with distinction until his death. Neander turned his attention to church history with a series of remarkable monographs; in 1826, he published the first volume of his *History of the Christian Religion and Church,* at which he labored for the rest of his life. Distinguished by thorough use of the sources, Neander's conception of the history of the church was that of a divine life gaining increasing control over the lives of men. That life is manifested in individuals. Hence, Neander's work was a series of striking biographical portraits. Its weaknesses were its overemphasis on the influence of individuals and its scanty appreciation of the institutional or corporate life of the church. Yet it put church history on a new plane of achievement. Quite as significant as his writings were the influence of Neander's personal interest in his students and his childlike, unaffected Christian trust. "The heart makes the theologian," frequently on his lips, expresses his character. Few men have been more personally helpful or more beloved.

A similar personal influence was exercised by Friedrich August Gottreu Tholuck (1799–1877), who became a professor in Berlin in 1823 and then held a chair in Halle from 1826 to his death. A man of pietistic sympathies, yet with acceptance of the critical views in many features, he turned Halle from the rationalism which had dominated since the time of Wolff to the evangelicalism which characterized it in the nineteenth century. As a preacher, he was distinguished. His kindness to English and American students was unwearied. Theologically, he resisted idealist philosophical influences to emphasize the specifically Christian experience of sin and regeneration and the doctrines of fall and original sin.

A third important representative of the "mediating" school, theologically the most significant, was Isaac August Dorner (1809–1884), a student in Tübingen from 1827 to 1832 and an instructor there in 1834. After service in a number of other German universities, he closed his career as professor in Berlin from 1862 to his death. Dorner's most important early publication was *Doctrine of the Person of Christ* (1839). His completed theology was formulated in fullness, late in life, in *System of the Doctrines of Faith* (1879–1881). Theology and philosophy are truly akin, but both embody themselves in a progressive historic development. Christian belief thus finds its attestation in the Christian consciousness, which in turn recognizes the validity of the spiritual experience recorded in the Scriptures and has had its growing clarification in Christian history. The central doctrine of Christianity is the Incarnation, in which Christ is the revelation of what God is and of what humanity may become. Dorner had much influence also in Great Britain and America.

A distinctive form of the mediating school was the Erlangen theology. Against the background of a religious revival in Franconia and the Neopietism of Tholuck, Adolf von Harless (1806–1879), who had been educated under Tholuck at Halle and who had experienced a profound conversion experience, was brought to the Erlangen faculty in 1833. In his teaching, three factors were interwoven: experience, Scripture, and confessionalism. The position was brought to full expression by his successor at Erlangen in 1845, Johann Christian Konrad von Hofmann (1810–1877), who sought to state old truths in a new way, blending revival theology and Schleiermacherian experimentalism with a mild biblicism and confessionalism. He endeavored to overcome previous errors in biblical interpretation by engaging in both theological and historical approaches to an understanding of "salvation history" (*Heilsgeschichte*). He developed a doctrine of the atonement which rejected the substitutionary satisfaction theory in favor of an emphasis on Christ as restorer of relationships between God and humanity.[3]

The mediating theologians, by virtue of their warm Christian faith and their partial, though cautious, acceptance of critical positions, had considerable following in the Christian world. The mediating approach, however, was not able to deal with the intellectual revolutions of the nineteenth century, and in Germany it hardly survived its principal leaders, as other positions came to dominance.

The most epoch-making book in German theological development came not from any of these schools, but from a young scholar of twenty-seven at the University of Tübingen, David Friedrich Strauss (1808–1874). Strauss had made himself at home in the Hegelian philosophy. He was familiar with the earlier positions of Baur, and he was also acquainted with the interpretation as mythical which the historian and statesman Barthold Georg Niebuhr (1776–1831) had made of the early story of Rome. These principles he now applied to the life of Christ. He was far from denying that much could be known of Jesus' earthly career; it must be viewed, however, as moving wholly in the realm of the human, like other historical events. Of the Gospel sources, he regarded that bearing the name of John as most removed in time and of the least historical worth, thus differing from much of the scholarship immediately before him, which—notably that of Schleiermacher—had preferred John to the others. Strauss gave the first place to Matthew, but none of the Gospels were by eyewitnesses. Miracles are inherently impossible, but the Gospels are full of them. The ordinary rationalistic interpretations, like those of Paulus, are ridiculous; the assertions of the ultra-rationalists, like Reimarus (see VII:11), that they were recounted with intent to deceive, are impossible. The only adequate explanation is that the simple, natural facts of Christ's life are covered over with myth. By "myth," Strauss meant the expression of an idea in the form of a historical account; the details of Old Testament prophecy provided New Testament writers the clues for interpreting Jesus' life. The people of that time were expecting a Messiah who would be a wonder-worker; they were looking for the fulfillment of Old Testament prophecy; and they had great true ideas, such as that the race is partly divine and partly human and that it rises above death by union with God. These were attributed to, or regarded as impersonated in, Christ. Jesus lived; but the Christ of the New Testament is essentially, in all his superhuman characteristics, a creation of myth.

Strauss's book aroused an enormous controversy. He had attacked the views of every party in contemporary Germany—the orthodox, the rationalists of all shades, the "mediating" theologians. He met unsparing denunciation. He was debarred from all further theological employment and lived an embittered existence. Yet his work placed the investigation of the life of Christ on a new plane,

[3] Ibid., pp. 218–225.

he answered conclusively the older rationalists, and the discussions which he inaugurated were productive for religious scholarship. Two fundamental criticisms of his approach have proven especially telling. Either the church created that which is important in the figure of Christ, albeit unconsciously, or Christ is the source of the church. If Strauss and those who shared his essential position were right, the former conclusion is true—but serious theological scholarship has found the other view prevailingly preferable. Nor has the purely human historical interpretation of the life of Christ led to the construction of a really plausible picture that could long be maintained. Albert Schweitzer (1875–1965), in his famous *The Quest of the Historical Jesus* (1910), showed how such efforts end in what is essentially failure.

The most potent influence in Germany in the latter half of the nineteenth century both in theology and in the interpretation of the history of the early church was Albrecht Ritschl (1822–1889), pioneer of liberalism, theologian of religious and moral judgments, and a forerunner of modern Luther scholarship. At a time when the approaches of Hegel were losing their appeal, Ritschl's accomplishment was to frame a new apologetic synthesis between Christian faith and the new knowledge contributed by scientific and historical scholarship. A disciple at first of the school of Baur, he broke with its main contentions when he published the second edition of his *Origin of the Old Catholic Church* in 1857. Baur's Hegelian Petrine thesis and Pauline antithesis are not adequate explanations of the growth of the early church, he asserted. There were differences, but all parties had a greater fundamental unity in owning the mastery of Jesus. Nor are the unlikenesses of early Christianity resolvable into two sharply antagonistic parties; there were many shades of opinion. Christianity came into no empty world, but one filled with religious, philosophical, and institutional ideas. By them, especially among Gentiles, the simple, primitive truths of Christianity were profoundly modified, resulting in the theology and institutions of the old Catholic church. Ritschl advocated the full use of the tools of historical criticism in order to understand the primitive Christian community and the historical Jesus. Stressing the centrality of Jesus and the given nature of the first-century church, Ritschl won a large following among Protestant scholars, in America as well as in Europe.

Ritschl began teaching in the University of Bonn in 1846. In 1864, he became professor in Göttingen, where he remained till his death. Here he published his chief theological work, *The Christian Doctrine of Justification and Reconciliation* (3 vols., 1870–1874). Ritschl had few personal disciples, but the propagating influence of his writings was great.

Ritschl was much influenced by Kant's assertion of moral feeling as the basis of practical certainty and his denial of absolute intellectual knowledge, and by Schleiermacher's affirmation of religious consciousness as the foundation of conviction. Yet Schleiermacher's assertion of the normative value of religious consciousness was, to his thinking, too individual. The real consciousness is not that of the individual, but that of the Christian community, the church. Nor is that consciousness a source of abstract speculative knowledge. It has to do with eminently practical, personal relationships—those of God and the religious community, sin and salvation. Hence, "natural" or speculative philosophic theology is valueless. Philosophy may give, as with Aristotle, a "first cause," but that is far from a loving Father. Such a practical revelation is made to us only through Christ. That revelation is mediated to us through the consciousness of the first disciples. Hence, the Old Testament, as revealing their religious background, and especially the New Testament, as recording their consciousness of Christ and his Gospel, are of supreme value. To ascertain the religious consciousness recorded in the Old and New Testaments, no theory of inspiration is necessary, only normal historical investigation.

Though Ritschl thus rejected metaphysics as an aid to Christian truth, he made much use of a theory of knowledge advocated by the philosopher Rudolf Hermann Lotze (1817–1881). While it is true, Lotze held with Kant, that things as they are in themselves cannot be known, he affirmed that they are truly known in their attributes or activities. A brick pavement is known, and truly known, to me as a sidewalk. To the ants whose mounds of sand rise between the bricks, it may be a home. What it is abstractly or in itself I have no means of knowing. If that knowledge in its attributes is one affecting my conduct, it is a "value judgment." So Ritschl held that to those who came in contact with him in the first Christian community, Christ was truly a revelation of what God is in love, the reconciler of sinful humanity to God through his sacrifice of suffering love, the pattern of spiritual lordship over the world, and the founder of the kingdom of God. As such he was truly known; but to ask whether he was pre-existent, was of two natures, or was one person of a Trinity, is to ask what the experience of the early church could not answer and what only metaphysics could assert or deny. This recognition of what Christ is and signifies arouses faith in men— that is, trust and love toward God through Christ. This new attitude is accompanied by the forgiveness and removal of sin, which constituted the barrier between humanity and God—justification—and the new relationship expresses itself in trust in God, patience amid life's trials, humility, and prayer—reconciliation. The new relationship to God also expresses itself in desires to do the will of God and to live the life of the kingdom. The Christian life is essentially social; hence, redeemer, redeemed, and the redeemed community are inseparable conceptions. The Gospel is an ellipse with two foci: justification and reconciliation, and the kingdom of God. These ideas of salvation, Ritschl believed, have never been more clearly formulated, in later church history, than by Luther.

Among the prominent Ritschlians were Wilhelm Herrmann (1846–1922) and Adolf von Harnack (1851–1930). Herrmann, professor of theology at Marburg, was a leading exponent of liberal theology. Of greatest influence in liberalism was Harnack of Berlin, prince of church historians. His outstanding work was the *History of Dogma*, which appeared in a seven-volume English edition between 1894 and 1899. His *What is Christianity?* (1901) was a classic statement of advanced liberal theology. The Ritschlian spirit, with its earnest piety and devotion to truth, had a great vogue in Germany, England, and America in the closing years of the nineteenth and opening years of the twentieth centuries.

In the 1890s, however, the Ritschlian approach was challenged by the "history of religions" school. This school sought to universalize the historical approach to religion by putting Christianity in its context with the other religions of the ancient Near East. What Ritschl had done so forcefully in tracing the historical *development* of Christian doctrine, it tried to do for the *beginnings* of Christianity itself, accusing him of provincialism in not following out his method fully. Its most distinguished exponent was Ernst Troeltsch (1865–1923). His historical work was brilliant, especially his *Social Teachings of the Christian Churches* (1912), but the relativism of the *Religionsgeschichtliche* school contributed to the crisis of liberalism.

Chapter 13

British Protestantism in the Nineteenth Century

ENGLISH RELIGIOUS LIFE in the opening years of the nineteenth century was dominated by the spiritual awakening of the evangelical revival, which was leading to much separation from the establishment (see VII:7). In the establishment, that revived zeal was represented by the Evangelical party, which in the nineteenth century became the "low-church" party, in opposition to revived "high-church" emphases. The Evangelicals, like the Methodists, were keenly alive to works of practical and missionary activity (see VII:9). The Anglican Evangelicals increased in importance in ecclesiastical affairs; they won their first bishopric in 1815 and by midcentury were the leading party of the church, with great strength among the laity. But the nineteenth century saw the shaping of a new liberal, "broad-church" movement and the revivification of the high-church tradition.

The broad-church impulse arose out of dissatisfaction with the current theological formulations. Intellectually, all parties in the Church of England at the opening of the nineteenth century stood on the basis of the rather provincial discussions of the eighteenth century. Theology was looked upon in the same rationalistic fashion—a system of intellectual demonstration, or of authoritative revelation, or of both combined. The stirrings of new intellectual forces were being felt, however. English poetry flowered into splendid blossoming in the opening years of the nineteenth century. Romanticism, as powerfully as in Germany (see VII:12), was beginning to produce an intellectual atmosphere wholly unlike that of the preceding age. The novels of Sir Walter Scott are familiar illustrations of this new outlook. A new humanitarianism, largely due to the Methodist revival, was developing and was to be manifested multitudinously in reformist movements. All the tendencies were sure to affect theological thinking and religious ideals.

Probably the most stimulating force in the religious thinking of the first quarter of the nineteenth century was that of Samuel Taylor Coleridge (1772–1834), eminent as a poet, literary critic, and philosopher. A Neoplatonist in his early sympathies, he studied in Germany in 1798 and 1799, which led to acquaintance not only with the masters of German literature but also with the thought of Kant, Fichte, and Schelling and with a philosophical outlook then largely unfamiliar in England. Coleridge never worked out a rounded system. His most significant volume was *Aids to Reflection* (1825). Over against the rationalizing of Paley (see VII:3), he held to a distinction between "reason" and "understanding." To Coleridge, "reason" was a power of intuitive perception, an "inward beholding," by which religious truths are directly perceived. This "moral reason" has, as its associate, "conscience," which is an unconditional command, and has as its postulates the moral law, a divine lawgiver, and a future life. Religious certainty is thus based not on external proofs but on religious consciousness. Hence, he has been called the "English Schleiermacher." In most respects, Coleridge was the forerunner of the broad-church way of thinking; but in his emphasis on the church as a divine institution, higher and nobler than anything "by law established," he prepared the way for the high-church party.

The work of Coleridge in its religious aspects was continued by Thomas Arnold (1795–1842), who began his famous mastership of Rugby in 1828. A man of profound and simple Christian faith, his helpfulness to his pupils was great. His views much resembled those of Herder (see VII:12). The Bible is a literature, to be understood in the light of the times in which it was written, but its divine truth finds us.

Biblical criticism was furthered, in a very moderate fashion, by Henry Hart Milman (1791–1868), dean of St. Paul's, London, from 1849, by his *History of the Jews* (1829), in which he applied critical methods to the Old Testament. His most valuable work was *History of Latin Christianity* (1855).

Not willing to be reckoned to the broad-church school, yet contributing much to its spread, was John Frederick Denison Maurice (1805–1872). The son of a Unitarian minister, he conformed to the establishment and became chaplain of Guy's Hospital in London. In 1840, he was appointed to a chair in King's College, of which he was deprived for his opinions in 1853. The year after, he founded the Working Men's College and was instrumental in inaugurating a Christian socialist movement. In 1866, he was appointed to a professorship in Cambridge. To Maurice's thinking, Christ is the Head of all humanity. None are under the curse of God. All are his children, who need no other reconciliation than a recognition by them of God's parenthood, with the filial love and service to which such recognition will naturally lead. Presumably all will ultimately be brought home to God and none forever lost.

Not very unlike Maurice in his theology, but primarily a great preacher, was Frederick William Robertson (1816–1853), educated under Evangelical influences, then passing through a period of intense questioning to a broad-church position. From 1847 until his early death, he was minister in Brighton. No English sermons of the last century were so influential on both sides of the Atlantic as those of Robertson. Spiritual truth must be spiritually discerned rather than intellectually proved. The nobility of Christ's humanity attests and leads to faith in his divinity.

Much influence in the spread of broad-church opinions was exercised by Charles Kingsley (1819–1875), rector of Eversley and a novelist, and by Alfred Lord Tennyson (1809–1892), whose *In Memoriam* (1850) was fully a broad-church poem. Similarly to be reckoned were Arthur Penrhyn Stanley (1815–1881), dean of Westminster, and Frederic William Farrar (1831–1903), dean of Canterbury. Great commotion was caused in 1860 by the *Essays and Reviews,* in which a group of Oxford scholars tried to present Christianity in the light of contemporary science and historical criticism, and by the trial of Bishop John William Colenso (1814–1883) of Natal for his Pentateuchal criticism published in 1862. Important contributions to biblical scholarship were made by three Cambridge scholars: Brooke Foss Westcott (1825–1901), Joseph Barber Lightfoot (1828–1889), and Fenton John Anthony Hort (1828–1892). Westcott and Hort's critical text of the Greek New Testament, published in 1881 after nearly thirty years of scholarly labor, became standard. The broad-church movement was never, strictly speaking, a party, and its numbers were not large, but its influence on English religious thought was widespread.

A highly significant, deeply devout, and intensely self-conscious development within the Church of England in this period was the Oxford, or Tractarian, movement, out of which came the Anglo-Catholic party. The movement gave new life and direction to the high-church tradition, which had become somewhat arid. The early years of the second quarter of the nineteenth century saw several significant breaches in the exclusive privileges of the establishment. The Test Act (see VI:16) and the Corporation Act were repealed in 1828. Roman Catholics were made eligible for the House of Commons and to most public offices in 1829. The July Revolution of 1830 in France stimulated a demand for reform in parliamentary representation, which triumphed, after heated struggles, in 1832, with the result that power was transferred from the landed gentry to the middle classes, thus increasing nonconformist influence. To many conservative church-men, it seemed that the foundations of church and state were being removed. They were disposed to raise the question of the nature of the church itself. Is it an essentially unalterable divine institution, or may it be altered, as so often since the Reformation, by government enactment? The form their answer took was to be determined largely by the romantic revival of interest in the primitive and medieval.

During these discussions, several young clergymen, mostly associated with Oriel College, Oxford, were led to take the steps that inaugurated the "Oxford movement," as it was often called. Probably the most influential of the group, while his brief life lasted, was Richard Hurrell Froude (1803-1836). To him, the church is in possession of the truth, important elements of which primitive en-dowment were repudiated by the reformers. A revival of fasting, clerical celibacy, reverence for the saints, and "Catholic usages" he deemed imperative. Closely associated with Froude was a man of great pulpit and intellectual abilities, whose early training had been evangelical but who had come to share Froude's feelings, John Henry Newman (1801-1890). A third of the Oriel group was John Keble (1792-1866), of Nonjuror ancestry and already distinguished as the author of the most popular volume of religious poetry that was issued in the nineteenth century, *The Christian Year* (1827). In hearty sympathy stood a Cambridge scholar, Hugh James Rose (1795-1838), who in 1832 founded the *British Maga-zine* to further faith in the divine authority and essential unchangeableness of the church. To all these men, the course of recent political events seemed menacing. The formal beginning of the movement is usually associated with Keble's sermon "National Apostasy," delivered in Oxford on July 14, 1833. In September of that year, Keble formulated the principles for which he and his associates stood. The way to salvation is through reception of the body and blood of Christ in the eucharist, which is validly administered only through those in apostolical succession. This is the treasure of the church—a church which must in all ways be restored to the purity of its undivided early centuries.

The same month, Newman began the publication of the famous *Tracts for the Times,* which gave to the movement they fostered the name "Tractarianism." By 1835, these associates had won the support of one who, next to Newman, and fully after Newman's defection, was to be its leader, Edward Bouverie Pusey (1800-1882). A man of great earnestness and piety, Pusey was so fully ultimately to become the head of the Anglo-Catholic movement that it was often called "Puseyism." To Pusey, it was the revival of primitive Christianity.

Ninety of the *Tracts* were issued, of which Newman wrote or edited at least twenty-eight. Keble, Pusey, Froude, and others also contributed. To Newman, the Church of England was the golden mean, the *via media,* between Prot-estantism and Rome; but as the series went on, the writers emphasized increasingly those doctrines and practices which, though undoubtedly ancient, are popularly identified with Rome. Thus, Pusey taught the regenerative nature of baptism and the sacrificial aspect of the Lord's Supper. Confession was commended. Reserve was to be practiced in the use of the Bible and the proclamation of religious truth. It was the ninetieth *Tract,* by Newman, issued in 1841, that aroused most controversy. Newman held that the Thirty-nine Articles did not intend to teach anything other than the Catholic faith and were not in conflict with genuine Roman Catholicism, even in its Tridentine form. Very few scholars or churchmen could accept this interpretation, which seemed plainly wrong, and the bishop of Oxford now forbad the continuation of the *Tracts.*

Newman was at the height of his influence when *Tract Ninety* was published. The Anglo-Catholic movement numbered hundreds of followers among the clergy. Newman was doubting, however, the catholicity of the Church of England, and on October 9, 1845, he made his submission to Rome. Several hundred clergy and laymen followed him into the Roman communion, of whom the most distinguished was Henry Edward Manning (1808–1892), who conformed to Rome in 1851 and was created a cardinal in 1875. Great excitement was caused in 1850 by the reestablishment in England by Pope Pius IX of the Roman Catholic diocesan episcopate, which had been in abeyance since the Reformation. Manning became an extreme ultramontane supporter of papal claims, unlike Newman, who was always moderate, and who, though the most eminent of English Roman Catholics, was not given a cardinalate until 1879.

These conversions to Rome ended the Oxford movement as such, but the Anglo-Catholic party which grew out of it weathered the storm, under Pusey's able leadership, and rapidly matured into an important element within the establishment. As its doctrinal modifications became accepted, it concerned itself increasingly with the "enrichment" of the liturgy, by the introduction of usages which Protestantism had discarded. These changes encountered much popular and legal opposition, but the modifications desired by the ritualists were largely secured. Any estimate of the Anglo-Catholic movement would be erroneous that failed to recognize its profound religious zeal. It not only brought a fresh Catholic emphasis into the worship and theology of the church; it also showed genuine devotion to the poor, neglected, and unchurched. It did much to regain the hold of the church on the lower classes. In 1860, the English Church Union was organized to support high-church faith and practice and to expand the influence of this significant awakening movement within the Church of England.

The parallel Protestant state church of Ireland, always an anomaly in that it was the governmentally supported church of a minority of the population, was disestablished in 1869, but the even tenor of its way was not much disturbed by the change.

The nineteenth century was marked by the steady expansion and increasing proliferation of nonconformity, in which evangelical influence was strong. Probably quite early in the century, the number of active nonconformists came to surpass the number of practicing Anglicans. Methodism, for example, increased fourfold from 1800 to 1860, even though it lost a number of factions through schisms. The other large and growing nonconformist bodies were the Congregational and the Baptist, while Quakers and Unitarians persisted as small minorities and Presbyterianism was revivified, largely by migration from Scotland. Nonconformist strength was in the middle classes. Nonconformity produced preachers of great power and had its scholars and social workers, but in its scholarship and in the work for the unchurched it was less eminent than the Church of England.

Of great importance in English life was the steady diminution of the disabilities imposed on nonconformists. In 1813, the Unitarians obtained relief by the repeal of penal acts against deniers of the Trinity. As already mentioned, the Test and Corporation acts were repealed in 1828. Marriages were permitted in dissenting places of worship in 1836. Nonconformists were freed from taxes for the benefit of the establishment in 1868. In 1871, all religious tests, save for degrees in theology, were abolished at the universities of Oxford, Cambridge, and Durham. In 1880, nonconformist services were permitted at burials in churchyards.

In the latter half of the century, nonconformity profited by what has been called the "Second Great Evangelical Awakening," a chief feature of which was the work of the American evangelist, Dwight L. Moody (1837-1899). Anglican Evangelicals also profited from these later awakenings, and their centers at Mildmay and Keswick contributed to them.

Nonconformists not only expanded in the nineteenth century; they also produced a number of new bodies. Three movements are of special interest. Edward Irving (1792-1834) was a Scottish Presbyterian minister in London, of eloquence and mystic tendencies. By 1828, he had become persuaded that the "gifts" of the apostolic age would be restored if faith was sufficient. Though no claimant to them himself, he believed by 1830 that his hopes had been fulfilled in others. In 1832, he was deposed from his Presbyterian ministry. Soon after, six apostles were believed by his followers to be designated by prophecy, which number was completed to twelve in 1835. The body thus led took the name Catholic Apostolic church. In 1842, an elaborate ritual was adopted. The apostles were regarded as organs of the Holy Spirit. The speedy coming of Christ was long expected, but the last apostle died in 1901. The church has spread to Germany and the United States.

A second movement grew out of reaction against the unspirituality of the establishment in the early years of the nineteenth century. Groups of "brethren," who claimed faith and Christian love as their only bonds, gathered in Ireland and western England. Their great increase was through the labors of John Nelson Darby (1800-1882), formerly a clergyman of the (Anglican) Church of Ireland. He was active in the vicinity of Plymouth about 1830, and his followers are therefore generally nicknamed "Plymouth Brethren." To their thinking, all believers are priests, and hence formal ministries are to be rejected. Creeds are to be refused. The Holy Spirit guides all true believers, and unites them in faith and worship after the apostolic model. The Brethren were guided by a millenarian system of biblical interpretation known as dispensationalism, in which time was divided into a series of (usually seven) dispensations. Though there were variations in detail, the last dispensation, soon to come, was generally understood to be the millennium, in which Christ would return and the Davidic monarchy would be restored to Israel. The Brethren professedly rejected all denominationalism, but they soon found themselves compelled to corporate acts of discipline, and they divided into at least six groups. Darby was an indefatigable propagandist. Through his efforts, the Brethren were planted in Switzerland, France, Germany, Canada, and the United States. Among their eminent adherents were George Müller (1805–1898), whose remarkable orphan houses in Bristol were supported, he believed, largely in direct answer to prayer; and Samuel Prideaux Tregelles (1813–1875), an eminent student of the Greek text of the New Testament.

The most important of these new organizations was the Salvation Army. Its creator, William Booth (1829–1912), was a New Connection Methodist minister, who, after successful revival work in Cardiff, began similar labors in London in 1864, out of which an organization in military form, with military obedience, developed in 1878, to which the name Salvation Army was given in 1880. Always strongly engaged in practical philanthropy as well as street evangelism, the philanthropic work was developed on a great scale beginning in 1890, when Booth published his *In Darkest England and the Way Out*. In spite of its autocratic military form, the Salvation Army is in many respects a church. Though open to the charge of occasional arbitrariness, it has done an immense and beneficent work for the defective and delinquent, and it has extended to all English-speaking lands as well as to France, Germany, Switzerland, Italy, the Scandinavian lands, and the Orient.

In the second half of the nineteenth century, English Christians of various denominations and traditions became increasingly concerned with the acute social problems of the time. Evangelicals had long engaged in charitable activities and reform movements, while churchmen like Maurice and Kingsley had pioneered in Christian Socialism at midcentury. But toward the close of the century, a wider concern for social justice and the direct facing of social issues was felt. In Anglican circles, the Christian Social Union was founded in 1889 under the leadership of Bishop Westcott, Henry Scott Holland (1847–1918), and Charles Gore (1853–1932). Strongly Anglo-Catholic in tone, it strove to apply the moral truths of Christianity to social and economic difficulties. In nonconformist circles, the social concern manifested itself especially in liberal political activity. The "nonconformist conscience" became a force to be reckoned with in

English life; its outstanding voices were Congregationalist Robert William Dale (1829–1895) of Birmingham and Methodist Hugh Price Hughes (1847–1902) of West London.

As in England, so in Scotland the story of Christianity in the nineteenth century begins with spiritual awakening. The reaction against the French Revolution, the rise of Romanticism, and the general revolt from the rationalism of the eighteenth century prepared the way for an evangelical revival north of the Tweed. Early leaders in the awakening were the Haldane brothers, Robert (1764–1842) and James Alexander (1768–1851), laymen who became active evangelists and organizers of societies to promote further revival. From 1815, when he entered on a memorable pastorate in Glasgow, the most eminent of the Evangelical party was Thomas Chalmers (1780–1847), distinguished as a preacher, a social reformer, a mathematician, a theological teacher, and an ecclesiastical statesman. Under his leadership, and in the changed spirit of the times, the Evangelical party rapidly grew in strength; a great campaign to meet the needs of the growing population of Scotland was inaugurated, which resulted by 1841 in the erection of 220 new churches by popular gifts. The old question of patronage continued a burning one. In 1834, the growing Evangelical party secured the passage by the General Assembly of a "veto" rule, by which presbyteries were forbidden to proceed to installation when a majority of the congregation was opposed to the candidate. This rule soon involved legal controversy. The courts held that the General Assembly had exceeded its powers. Parliament was asked for relief, which was refused. Under Chalmers's leadership, 474 ministers formally withdrew from the state church in the "Disruption" of 1843 and founded the Free Church of Scotland. They gave up parishes and salaries. All had to be provided anew, but the enthusiasm and sacrifice of the new body was equal to the task. In general, it was a withdrawal of the Evangelical element from the already considerably modified but less zealous and spiritual "Moderates." A third, and that the most active part, of the state church had gone out in the Disruption. Yet the example of the seceders worked ultimately for a quickening of zeal in the state church itself. In 1874, the rights of patronage, the original ground of division, were abolished by law.

The vigor of British Evangelicalism, in both established and nonconformist forms, was reflected in a missionary surge of nineteenth-century Protestantism. English-speaking Evangelicals seized the initiative in Protestant missions at the end of the eighteenth century and held it throughout the "Great Century"[1] of Protestant missionary outreach. The rapid expansion of foreign missions in the nineteenth century brought Protestantism to almost every country of the globe,

[1] The term has been popularized by a leading historian of missions, Kenneth Scott Latourette. In his seven-volume *A History of the Expansion of Christianity* (New York, 1937–45), he took three volumes to get to 1815, and then three volumes to cover the period 1815–1914, the "Great Century."

making it truly worldwide in scope. This missionary campaign centered in Great Britain, with the United States close behind. Its beginnings at the end of the eighteenth century have already been noted (see VII:9); throughout the nineteenth century, the crusade steadily expanded in extent and complexity and the organization of missionary agencies of many types continued.

The movement was led by a number of famous missionary pioneers, who followed the example of William Carey, first of the modern missionary vanguard. Those from Great Britain went especially, though by no means exclusively, into the parts of the world where the British Empire had territorial claims. In India, Anglican Evangelical Henry Martyn (1781–1812) burned himself out at an early age in his vigorous missionary efforts. The first Church of Scotland foreign missionary, Alexander Duff (1806–1878), devoted himself especially to educational work, seeking to attract the cultured classes of India. Samuel Marsden (1764–1838), another Anglican of Evangelical persuasion, labored for more than four decades to plant Christianity in Australia, New Zealand, and the Pacific islands. In Africa, Robert Moffat (1795–1883) and David Livingstone (1813–1873), both Scotsmen serving the London Missionary Society, brought the Gospel to South Africa. The same society also sent Robert Morrison (1782–1834) as the first Protestant missionary to China, in 1807. The efforts of these pioneers, heroic as they were, did not seem to yield many results at first; their task was to open doors, to found schools and stations, and above all to translate the Scriptures. But where they led, hundreds of others followed. As the century progressed, other lands were opened to Protestant effort—Japan, Korea, the Philippines. In all these lands, the missionaries brought not only the gospel but also western literature and educational methods, modern medical knowledge and hospitals, and improved techniques of agriculture and forestry. The denominational missionary societies mushroomed into vast agencies with large and complex staffs. In addition, there were nondenominational "faith missions," such as the China Inland Mission, founded in 1865 by J. Hudson Taylor (1832–1905). By the end of the century, usually small but significant Protestant minorities had developed in land after land that had had no Protestant witness before. In India and China especially, these tiny Protestant communities were an important ferment in swift-changing cultures. The missionary efforts changed the religious map of the world and enormously extended the influence of English-speaking evangelicalism. Through this missionary impulse, the foundations of the so-called "younger churches," indigenous churches in non-Christian lands, were laid. Eventually some of these churches merged with those of other backgrounds to form united churches. A forerunner was the South India United Church (see VII:18), formed in 1908 by congregations which had been associated with the United Free Church of Scotland, the London Missionary Society, the Reformed Church in America, and the American Board of Commissioners for Foreign Missions.

Chapter 14

Continental Protestantism in the Nineteenth Century

*W*HAT WAS PROBABLY the most significant development in Continental Protestantism in the nineteenth century has already been considered—the movements of Christian thought in Germany. But there were also important trends in the life of the churches, for in the nineteenth century surges of life that to a considerable extent cut across confessional and national lines swept through the Christian churches on the continent of Europe. This nineteenth-century awakening had many aspects. Of especial importance in the early part of the century was the "Réveil," the emergence of evangelical and pietistic currents reminiscent of the earlier awakenings. But in addition to this resurgence, movements of renewal stressing romantic, sacramental, and confessional elements can also be distinguished. The various aspects of the nineteenth-century awakening might be styled as low-church, broad-church, high-church, and confessionalist.

In Germany, the awakening began in the central state of Prussia during the Napoleonic occupation. The theologian Schleiermacher, preacher at Berlin's Trinity Church, led people to find depths in the Christian tradition that had long been obscured. In the 1820s and 1830s, a more pietistic movement, spearheaded by Hengstenberg's *Evangelische Kirchenzeitung,* became influential. Hengstenberg (see VII:12) stood firmly for the infallibility of the Bible and the alliance of Christianity with the conservative feudal party in German politics. Still another current in the awakening was intensely confessional. It was in part a reaction against the Prussian Union of 1817, in which the Lutheran and Reformed churches were merged at the impulse of King Frederick William III (1797–1840). Similar unions were effected in some of the other German states. But staunchly orthodox Lutherans, retaining a bitter hostility toward the Calvinists, refused to become a part of such a union. These "Old Lutherans" were subjected to considerable persecution, and not until the 1840s were they even allowed to emigrate. When they could break away, many of them went to the United States to form such conservative synods as Buffalo and Missouri. Not all the strongly confessional tendencies were to be found among the Old Lutherans, however. Hengstenberg himself broke with the pietistic movement about 1840 and became a champion of strict Lutheran orthodoxy, and there were many who were similarly disposed. Allied with this confessional trend was a high-church movement. Central figures in this development were Wilhelm Loehe (1808–1872) of Bavaria and Theodor Kliefoth (see VII:12) of Mecklenberg. These "New Lutherans" sought to stress the transmission of the saving grace of God objectively through peoples and institutions, and to revive ancient liturgical traditions.

The vitality released through these awakening currents found an outlet in the "inner mission," a multitude of evangelistic and charitable efforts reminiscent of the activities at Halle in the early days of Pietism. Johann Hinrich Wichern (1808–1881), brought up under pietistic auspices, in 1833 founded a home for underprivileged boys. Aided by his organizational skill, a vast network of hundreds of agencies to reach seamen, the unemployed, prisoners, and neglected children was spread. Above all, serious efforts to reach the masses through Sunday schools, city missions, lodging houses, and the dissemination of literature were undertaken. Many laymen were drawn into the movement, and orders of deaconesses were formed. The inner mission was supported by Protestants under the influence of various of the awakening elements, though its pietistic stamp remained strong. It also found strong response from south Germany and the lower Rhine region, where the Reformed tradition remained an important force.

Scandinavian Protestantism was also penetrated by the awakening. In Denmark, the response to the various aspects of the revival stimulated a genuinely creative period. The pietistic emphasis with its "inner mission" was welcomed into the established Lutheran church. A tendency more akin to the Romantic motifs, more "broad-church," was represented by Bishop J. P. Mynster (1775–1854), court preacher, theological professor, and primate of the Church of Denmark. The high-church aspect was represented by Nicolai Frederick Severin Grundtvig (1783–1872), who found as his rock the Apostles' Creed and who stressed the living tradition and the sacramental focus of the church. One of the products of this creative period reacted strongly against the Christianity he knew —Søren Kierkegaard (1813–1855). Stressing the paradoxical and existential aspects of Christian faith, Kierkegaard made little impression on his own time but was to be rediscovered in the twentieth century.

In Norway, the pietistic aspect of the awakening was especially felt. Hans Nielsen Hauge (1771–1824), itinerant lay evangelist, assailed the coldness of the state church and was imprisoned for almost a decade. Later, the movement he had inspired was brought into closer relation to the established Lutheran church through the efforts of Gisle Johnson (1822–1894). Both confessional and clerical emphases were evident in the work of this professor of theology at the University of Christiana. In Sweden also, the revival had a variety of aspects, but the influence of Henrik Schartau (1757–1825), pastor at Lund, was especially important. Originally under Moravian influence, he developed a high-church and sacramental bent, stressing the antiquity of the church's tradition and the real presence in the Eucharist.

The influence of the nineteenth-century Protestant awakening was also strongly felt in the Reformed churches of the Continent. In the late eighteenth century, the impact of rationalism had been very great in the Calvinist communions of Switzerland, France, and the Netherlands. The beginnings of revival can be traced in part to the evangelical movement in Scotland, for Robert Haldane was instrumental in stimulating an awakening in France and French Switzerland in 1816. A conspicuous convert to the new emphases was H. A. César Malan (1787–1864), who became a leading itinerant evangelist and writer of many hymns. In the Netherlands, an important figure in the revival was a converted Jew, Isaac de Costa (1798–1860). As in Britain, the awakening currents produced a network of voluntary societies to conduct evangelistic, missionary, and charitable undertakings. And in all these lands, exponents of the "Réveil" found themselves opposed by church leaders of rationalist leanings, and kept out of positions of power. In Holland, the tension between rationalism and awakening, represented in this case by a young pastor, Hendrik de Cock (1801–1842), who also stood for high Calvinism and strict adherence to the findings of the Synod of Dort (see VI:15), led to a schism. When de Cock was deposed in 1834, a number of congregations left the established Netherlands Reformed church to found the Christian Reformed church. Many evangelicals, however, remained within the state church. Another separation from the state church took place under Abraham Kuyper (1837–1920), a pastor who by 1870 was the leader of the strict Calvinist party. When attempts to return the established church to the status of the Synod of Dort failed, he led in the formation of what was popularly called the Free Reformed church (1886). Kuyper was not only a leading preacher and a voluminous writer, but also a politician and statesman active in the government (premier from 1901 to 1905). He was professor of systematic theology at the Free University of Amsterdam for the last forty years of his life. In Switzerland, a disruption was led by Alexander Vinet (1797–1847), the "Schleiermacher of French Protestantism." Vinet at first had been repelled by what he felt to be the crudity of the Réveil, but attracted by the emphases of the more moderate Evangelicals and by Romantic currents, and disturbed over the efforts of the rationalists to repress the Evangelicals, he himself espoused the Réveil and became an outspoken advocate of the separation of church and state. In 1846, he played a major role in gathering dissenters from the state church, which by then included a majority of the ministers and most of the theological faculty of Lausanne, to form the Free Church of Vaud.

The churches of the Continent, stimulated by the currents of awakening, contributed not a little to the missionary drive of nineteenth-century Protestantism. Many societies were organized to direct the energies stirred by revival into missionary channels. The Basel Evangelical Missionary Society dates from 1815, the Danish Missionary Society from 1821, the Berlin and Paris societies from 1824, the Rhenish Missionary Society from 1828, the Leipzig Evangelical Lutheran Mission and the North German Missionary Society from 1836—and these societies were but the more conspicuous of hundreds which sent missionaries abroad. Protestant missionaries from the Continent were especially active in the Dutch East Indies, where the greatest concentration of Protestants in the Far East developed. More than half a million baptized Protestants were there by 1914, providing solid foundations for the rise of indigenous churches. On Sumatra, for example, Ludwig I. Nommensen (1834–1918) of the (German) Rhenish Society organized and led a mission among the Bataks in the interior of Sumatra; the Batak church had grown to some 160,000 members by the eve of the First World War. Africa south of the Sahara also proved to be a fruitful field for missionaries from the continent; a growing Christian community of a million and a half had been created by 1914. Natives were recruited to serve the expanding movement, out of which arose a number of indigenous churches in the twentieth century.

In the later nineteenth century, the social interpretation of Christianity was advanced in certain quarters. The Evangelical Union church in Prussia, the largest Protestant church in the world at the time, was in many ways administered conservatively and in the interests of the state, while the inner mission had cooled to a system of organized charity. In 1874, Adolf Stöcker (1835–1909) came to Berlin as court preacher. He shared the Junker outlook, despising liberal parliamentarianism, but was greatly concerned with the alienation of the industrial masses by the forces of socialism and secularism. He advocated labor legislation and social insurance, unfortunately mingling anti-Semitic elements in his messages. But Stöcker was too politically minded for the conservative Lutheran understanding of the separation of spiritual and political spheres, and he lost his post. A more liberal middle-class social Christian message was preached by Friedrich Naumann (1860–1919), but he, too, found that the political consequences of a social ethic were difficult for Lutherans to accept, and he resigned from the ministry. Meanwhile, a "social gospel," somewhat academic in nature, was advocated by such liberal theologians as Harnack and Hermann (see VII:12).

In the Reformed churches, social Christianity found more fertile soil. Conspicuous leaders in the movement were Leonhard Ragaz (1868–1945), advocate of pacifism, cooperatives, and folk schools and settlements, and Hermann Kutter (1863–1931), author of *They Must!* (1905), a theological interpretation of socialism that also influenced developments in social Christianity in England and the United States. Though the interest of the mass of Christians in social questions never developed to the degree social Christian leaders hoped, significant changes in the way Protestants confronted social issues were effected, and thereafter narrowly individualistic ways of thinking were permanently challenged.

Chapter 15

American Protestantism in the Nineteenth Century

JUST AS THE STORY of nineteenth-century Protestantism in Great Britain and on the Continent began with the evangelical awakening, so too did the story of religion in the United States in the same period. In America, the pietistic, evangelistic, low-church current of revival became largely dominant in church life. Although there were some evidences suggestive of the other aspects of the British and Continental revival, and although some communions resisted the revivalist tide, on the whole an evangelical conception of Christian faith with characteristic attention to the winning of souls set the pace in American Protestantism. Under the influence of articulate leaders who shared in the Pietist and evangelical traditions, a conscious and often emotional conversion experience came to be widely understood as the normal way of entering the Christian life. The internal situation—church life was at a relatively low ebb during the Revolutionary period, and at the opening of the new century less than 10 per cent of the population were church members—emphasized the need for awakening. The external situation—a country which about tripled in territorial extent and increased some five times in population in half a century—played its part in focusing Christian attention on the winning of converts.

Beginning at the very end of the eighteenth century, a mighty reawakening of religious interest swept the land. In New England, what was sometimes called the "Second Great Awakening" showed its first signs as early as 1792. By 1800, revival was in full tide. Congregationalist leaders were determined that some of the excesses that had led to the decline of the earlier Great Awakening should not be repeated. Hence, in their churches the new revivals were somewhat restrained, taking place largely within the normal patterns of church life. Prominent in shaping the theology that undergirded the new revivalistic crusades was the brilliant president of Yale, Timothy Dwight (1752–1817); active in carrying on the work was the aggressive Congregational preacher, Lyman Beecher (1775–1863), and a protégé of Dwight's, Yale theologian

Nathaniel W. Taylor (1786–1858). The awakening was by no means limited to the Congregational churches, for Baptists flourished in an awakening atmosphere, and the Methodists, seeking a securer foothold in New England, freely used revivalistic practices.

The awakening also swept the Middle Atlantic states, the South, and the frontier. The easterners did their part in seeking to extend the revival westward. In 1801, the Congregational General Assembly of Connecticut and the Presbyterian General Assembly entered into a "Plan of Union," providing for the virtual merger of the denominations in frontier areas. Soon the other New England Congregational associations joined in the scheme, and many "Presbygational" churches were planted, especially in New York and Ohio. But often the westerners were impatient with the restraint of eastern revivalism and resentful of the stress on an educated clergy. It was in the frontier states of Tennessee and Kentucky that the most emotional and spectacular manifestations of the awakening occurred. There the "camp meetings" began in 1800, and there the revivals, especially at first, were marked by emotional outcries and bodily manifestations. On the whole, however, the new revival movement, which continued to ebb and flow for decades, was less marked than the eighteenth-century awakenings by these symptoms of overwrought excitement. The impact of the revival was evident in the decline of "infidelity," the lifting of the moral level of the frontier, and the steady growth of Baptist, Methodist, and Presbyterian churches.

One product of the awakening, destined to become the outstanding exponent of revivalism through a long career, was a young lawyer of upstate New York, Charles Grandison Finney (1792–1875). Converted in 1821, he set out on evangelistic tours, and despite lack of college or formal theological training, was ordained under Presbyterian auspices. Soon great revivals broke out under his fervent and intense preaching. He brought revival methods into an ordered pattern that became known as the "new measures." The measures—such as "unseasonable hours" for services, "protracted" meetings, the use of harsh and colloquial language, the specific naming of individuals in prayer and sermon, inquiry meetings, the "anxious bench"—were really not new, of course. It was the shaping of them into a system designed to produce results that was the novel feature. The effectiveness of the approach was spectacularly demonstrated in the revival of 1830–1831 in Rochester, New York. Despite the opposition of those who feared the emotionalism of frontier and "new measures" evangelism, Finney did invade the eastern cities. His tested methods soon came to be widely accepted and copied. The intensity and frequency of the revivals declined in the 1840s but burst out again in new crescendo in 1857–1858, when a nationwide revival swept thousands into the churches. Daily prayer meetings, often at unusual hours, and lay leadership were features of this great peak in revival history.

Meanwhile, from the beginning of the century, the energies produced by the revivals were being channeled into evangelical causes through a steadily expanding network of voluntary societies. Often organization began at the local level, then the small units banded together in state societies, and finally national societies completed the pattern. Whether the concern of these voluntary societies was for home or foreign missions, they often followed denominational lines. Thus, when a group of Williams College students, under the leadership of Samuel J. Mills (1783–1818), offered their services to Congregational authorities as missionaries for India, the formation of the American Board of Commissioners for Foreign Missions in 1810 was precipitated. This was basically a Congregationalist society, though Presbyterians and Reformed supported it for a time. It dispatched its first five missionaries in 1812. En route to India, two of them, Adoniram Judson (1788–1850) and Luther Rice (1783–1836), came to the conclusion that believers' baptism by immersion was the scriptural way. This, in turn, precipitated the organization of the General Missionary Convention of the Baptist Denomination in the United States for Foreign Missions. Other denominations also founded missionary societies: Presbyterians in 1817, Methodists in 1818, Episcopalians in 1820. The American Home Missionary Society was instituted in 1826 to implement the operation of the Plan of Union.

Voluntary societies were also organized for the distribution of Bibles and tracts, the promotion of educational interests and Sunday schools, and for the direction of charitable and reform efforts. The national societies were usually nondenominational, seeking the support of evangelicals of various backgrounds. Among them were the American Education Society (founded 1815), the American Bible Society (1816), the American Sunday School Union (1817–1824), and the American Tract Society (1825). The pattern of organization was consciously influenced by the British example. In the 1830s, these agencies mushroomed in size and increased in support and effectiveness. Their annual meetings, the "May anniversaries," came to be held at the same time in New York City. Their membership and their directorates were overlapping, so that they formed what has been called a "benevolent empire." Control was largely in the hands of a group of wealthy laymen, predominantly Presbyterian or Congregational, among whom the brothers Arthur Tappan (1786–1865) and Lewis Tappan (1788–1873) were central. These men recognized Finney's power, enlisted him in their causes, and when ill health necessitated the curtailment of his travels, had him called to a New York pastorate. In 1834 and 1835, Finney published his *Lectures on Revivals of Religion,* spelling out his proven ways of promoting revival. In the latter year, he went to the new Oberlin College in Ohio, where, as professor of theology and later president, he became at once the leading exponent and the major theoretician of American revivalism. His voluminous *Lectures on Systematic Theology,* first published 1846–1847, presented a theology of revival, in which a test for any doctrine was whether or not it would contribute to salvation. Finney was a leader with many followers —hosts of revivalists put his methods to work.

Vitalities stimulated by revivalism were poured directly into the benevolent empire. Never relaxing their missionary passion, its leaders attempted to utilize the voluntary society pattern to remake society by conducting great moral and humanitarian crusades. It was hoped that such evils as vice, licentiousness, juvenile delinquency, and Sabbath-breaking might be eliminated, and such causes as temperance, peace, and the abolition of slavery be promoted. Temperance, for example, had aroused the efforts of the Presbyterian General Assembly and the Congregational associations of Connecticut and Massachusetts in 1811. Lyman Beecher's sermons against drunkenness in 1813—repeated and published in 1827—attracted great attention. In 1826, the American Society for the Promotion of Temperance was added to the circle of benevolent voluntary societies. The result of all this activity was a permanent change in the drinking habits of professed Christians. Efforts then turned toward the promotion of temperance among those not actively of the church. The Washingtonian movement of 1840 sought the reformation of drunkards. Prohibition by legislation was enacted in Maine in 1846. The history of legislative prohibition, thus backed by strong Christian support, was checkered, but in the twentieth century it was to culminate in the experiment of national prohibition (1919–1933).

The American Peace Society was organized in 1828, but the greatest of the reform crusades was for abolition. Before the nineteenth century, there had been some sentiment against slaveholding, especially among Quakers. The work of John Woolman (1720–1772) had been especially important. Antipathy toward slavery was spreading in the country in the early nineteenth century. But about 1830, a great change came over the South, because of the supposed industrial necessities of the plantation system, the fear of slave uprisings, and deepening resentment against the uncompromising attacks of such northern abolitionists as William Lloyd Garrison (1805-1879). In the North, however, the abolition movement gave a cutting edge to the rather general but vague emancipation interests. In 1833, the American Anti-Slavery Society was organized as part of the benevolent empire; a Finney convert, Theodore Dwight Weld (1803-1895), became its most powerful figure in spreading abolitionist sentiment among evangelicals. As the reform concerns of northern Protestants became increasingly funneled into the abolitionist drive, the gulf between northern and southern evangelicals steadily widened.

Thus, through the revivals and through missionary organizations and voluntary societies, an evangelistic, pietistic interpretation of Christian faith became widely disseminated in America in the nineteenth century. The denominations that most fully employed the revival pattern grew to be the giants in this period of national expansion. Methodists, a scant fifteen thousand strong at the time of their independent organization in 1784 (see VII:10), were well past the million mark by 1850. The Baptists, about one hundred thousand in number at the opening of the century, had increased eightfold by midcentury. Congregationalists and Presbyterians, among whom the nineteenth-century revival had appeared so early, continued to gain from the awakening, but internal resistance in both bodies to revival emphases inhibited them, and they fell behind in comparative denominational strength, dropping from the commanding place they had held at the dawn of the century. The second awakening greatly strengthened those Massachusetts Congregationalists who considered themselves orthodox, but the "liberal" party, the rise of which has already been noted (see VII:4), was deeply opposed to it. In 1805, the liberals succeeded in placing Henry Ware (1764–1845) as Hollis Professor of Divinity at Harvard. Meanwhile, William Ellery Channing (1780–1842) had begun a greatly respected and widely influential pastorate in Boston, where he was preaching a high Arian Christology. Increasing division, caused in part by the orthodox attack upon the liberals, led in 1815 to the adoption of the Unitarian name by the liberals. But even more characteristic of them than the denial of the doctrine of the Trinity were their criticism of the doctrine of original sin and of the Calvinistic theory of predestination, and an insistence on salvation by character. A sermon by Channing in 1819 at the installation of Jared Sparks (1789–1866) as a Unitarian pastor in Baltimore was widely regarded as the authoritative statement of the liberals, and it gave to Channing henceforth an unofficial leadership in early American Unitarianism. In 1825, the American Unitarian Association was formed. The allegiance of some of the oldest Congregational churches and most eminent men of eastern Massachusetts was won to the new denomination. But the orthodox, spurred by the energetic Lyman Beecher, who became pastor of the Hanover Street Church in Boston in 1826, made renewed use of revivals and succeeded in arresting the advance of the Unitarians and in confining them largely to eastern New England.

In Connecticut, there was no such open break, but conservative Calvinists feared that the New Haven theology had gone too far in modifying Calvinism to support revivalism and meet Unitarian objections. Hence, a new "orthodox" ministerial association was formed in 1833, and a new seminary was founded at Hartford in 1834. Both the Connecticut parties continued to employ revivals, however. A brilliant pastor, Horace Bushnell (1802–1876), thoughtfully criticized the revival system in his most influential publication, *Christian Nurture,* which first appeared in 1847. He urged the quiet unfolding of the Christian nature of the child, under appropriate influences, as the normal mode of entrance into the kingdom of God, instead of the struggling conversion which Pietist and Methodist traditions had considered the only legitimate experience. An able theologian, Bushnell did much to shift the emphasis from exact dogma, demonstrable to the intellect, to religious feeling, stirring men's hearts and minds. These ideas, influenced by Romanticism and reflecting the work of

Samuel Taylor Coleridge (see VII:13) were presented in such books as *God in Christ* (1849) and *Nature and the Supernatural* (1857).

The Presbyterians were also torn by controversy. Those, often of Scotch Irish background, who held firmly to confessional standards and to traditions of an educated ministry were troubled by frontier revivalists whose doctrinal positions and ordination standards were more lax. Attempts to curb them, however, led only to schism. In 1803, Barton W. Stone (1772–1844) led a group of evangelistic Presbyterians out of the Synod of Kentucky. These "New Lights" soon dropped all "sectarian" names, seeking to be known simply as "Christians." Several years later, attempts to discipline Cumberland (Kentucky) Presbyterian revivalists led to an open break and the formation of what became the Cumberland Presbyterian Church. Some of the smaller Presbyterian bodies suffered schism, too. Thomas Campbell (1763–1854), a Seceder Presbyterian minister in the north of Ireland, came to America in 1807 and began work in western Pennsylvania. His freedom in welcoming Presbyterians of all parties to communion aroused criticism, and he was disciplined by the Seceder Presbytery of Chartiers. Campbell felt it his duty to protest against such sectarianism and to assert as the standard of all Christian discipleship the literal terms of the Bible alone, as he understood it. He broke with the Seceder Presbyterians but continued to labor in western Pennsylvania, announcing as his principle: "Where the Scriptures speak, we speak; and where the Scriptures are silent, we are silent." It was not a new denomination that he planned, but a union of all Christians on this biblical basis, without added tests of creed or ritual. In August 1809, Campbell organized the Christian Association of Washington—so called from the Pennsylvania county of its origin—and for it he prepared the "Declaration and Address" which has since been regarded as a fundamental document of what was to be known as the Disciples movement. The same year, Thomas Campbell's son, Alexander (1788–1866), emigrated to America, and he soon outstripped his father in fame as an advocate of Thomas's views.

In spite of their deprecation of sectarianism, the Campbells organized a church in Brush Run, Pennsylvania, in May 1811. The Lord's Supper was observed each Sunday from the beginning. But doubts arose as to the scriptural warrant of infant baptism. In 1812, the Campbells and a number of their associates were immersed. A year later, the Brush Run Church became a member of the Redstone Association of Baptist Churches. Points of disagreement with the Baptists soon developed, however. The Campbells disliked the Baptists' strenuous Calvinism. To the Campbells, the Old Testament was far less authoritative than the New. To the Baptists, baptism was a privilege of the already pardoned sinner; to the Campbells, it was a condition of forgiveness. Moreover, the Campbells, without being in any sense Unitarians, were influenced to some degree by the thought of the Enlightenment, and they refused to employ other than scriptural expressions regarding the Father, Son, and Holy Spirit. The result was a withdrawal from the Baptists, which may be said to have been completed by 1832, when the followers of Campbell merged with the bulk of the followers of Barton Stone to form the Disciples of Christ. Perhaps twenty-five thousand strong at that time, they passed the million mark before the turn of the century.

The loss of the more extreme revivalists from the main body of Presbyterians by no means ended the tension over revivalism within that communion. The "New School" Presbyterians, who looked with favor on the New Haven theology and worked wholeheartedly with the benevolent empire, were strengthened by the operation of the Plan of Union, which brought those of Congregational background into Presbyterian judicatories. In 1837, the "Old School" Presbyterians were strong enough to rule the suspected presbyteries out of the church, thereby dividing it almost in two. Theological tension and controversy over the voluntary societies, which were not under direct church control, were central issues in the division.

The Society of Friends was also split. An evangelical movement favoring certain revivalistic emphases and techniques was led by an English Quaker, Joseph John Gurney (1788–1846), while the liberal reaction found as its central figure Long Islander Elias Hicks (1748–1830). The "Great Separation" occurred in 1828–1829, ending in separate "Orthodox" and "Hicksite" meetings.

The resurgence of revivalism also produced controversy in Lutheran circles. The leading voice in Lutheranism in the first half of the nineteenth century was Samuel Simon Schmucker (1799–1873). He favored an "American Lutheranism," in which certain revivalistic practices would be accepted. Confessionally inclined Lutherans were troubled, and the General Synod (see VII:10), in which he was conspicuous, suffered through dissensions and withdrawals, especially as the waves of German and Scandinavian immigration brought many Lutherans who felt that the American churches had departed from the true Lutheran tradition. As the immigration strengthened confessional resurgence, Schmucker's influence declined. The General Synod came to be rivaled by the General Council in 1867, and Schmucker's seminary at Gettysburg (founded 1826) was matched by one at Mt. Airy, Pennsylvania (1864). A central figure in the latter developments was Charles Porterfield Krauth (1823–1883), author of *The Conservative Reformation and its Theology* (1871).

In some denominations, there were no overt schisms over revivalism, but considerable inner tension was created. In German Reformed churches, there was spirited resistance to the spread of the "system of the revival" by exponents of the "system of the catechism," chiefly theologian John W. Nevin (1803–1886) and church historian Philip Schaff (1819–1893) of the seminary at Mercersburg, Pennsylvania. But the Mercersburg theology made little direct contribution; its larger significance was rediscovered only in the twentieth century. In the Protestant Episcopal church, there was little revivalism as such, but there was a strong, evangelical, low-church party, in which Bishop Alexander

Viets Griswold (1766–1843) of the eastern diocese was conspicuous. The early years of the century saw the renaissance of the high-church party under the leadership of Bishop John Henry Hobart (1775–1830), a trend which the rise of Anglo-Catholicism (see VII:13) was to strengthen. The Episcopal church was small in these years, but it steadily grew, especially in the urban centers, throughout the nineteenth century.

The most extensive nineteenth-century denominational schisms occurred in connection with the struggle over slavery. Growing antipathy to slavery led to the organization, in 1843, of the Wesleyan Methodist Church of America, based on the principle that no member could own slaves. The question was thus in the foreground when the General Conference of the Methodist Episcopal church met in 1844, and an immediate struggle arose over the retention of a slaveholding bishop. Northern and southern sentiment was hopelessly divided. The conference adopted a report permitting the division of the church, with the result that the Methodist Episcopal Church, South, was constituted, in 1845.

Contemporaneously, a similar division separated the Baptists of North and South. The Alabama State Convention of Baptists demanded, in 1844, that the Foreign Mission Board make no discrimination against slaveholders in missionary appointments. The board declared that it would take no action implying approval of slavery. The result was the formation of the Southern Baptist Convention in 1845 and the cleavage of the churches.

As the Civil War (1861–1865) approached, other churches divided. The New School Presbyterian church split in 1857 and the Old School in 1861. The two southern wings merged in 1864 as the Presbyterian Church in the United States, and the two northern wings united in 1869–1870 as the Presbyterian Church in the United States of America. The Protestant Episcopal Church was divided only during the war itself; it was reunited at its close. The churches supported their respective sections through the war. Following the struggle, the great majority of black Christians became members of their own independently organized bodies, chiefly the National Baptist Convention and the smaller African Methodist Episcopal and African Methodist Episcopal Zion churches. Some of the major white denominations had significant black minorities, and there was a considerable growth in the number of black sects, especially in metropolitan areas.

The founding of many new colleges and seminaries was stimulated by the religious awakening, the controversies, and the rise of new denominations. The nineteenth century saw the beginnings of hundreds of denominational colleges, many of them short-lived. A major purpose of these schools was to help prepare men for the ministry. But the need for specialized further preparation for the ministry was increasingly felt. In 1784, the (Dutch) Reformed Church instituted ministerial training, which later developed into a theological seminary in New Brunswick, New Jersey. The Associated (later United) Presbyterians in 1794 were beginning theological instruction in a seminary which was later to find a home in Xenia, Ohio, from which it was named, and finally in Pittsburgh. The Lutherans founded such an institution in 1797, to be located in Hartwick, New York. In 1807, the Moravians established a theological school in Nazareth, Pennsylvania, later relocated to Bethlehem. The most elaborately equipped theological seminary, and in many ways the inaugurator of a new era, was that opened by the Congregationalists in Andover, Massachusetts, in 1808. Four years later, the Presbyterians founded a seminary at Princeton, New Jersey. Bangor Theological Seminary, in Maine, was founded by Congregationalists in 1814, and five years later the Divinty School of Harvard University was opened under Unitarian influence. The Baptists began a seminary at Hamilton, New York, in 1820, while the Presbyterians established a school at Auburn, New York, at about the same time. In 1822, the Congregationalists opened the Divinity School of Yale University. Then the institutions for ministerial training multiplied rapidly; by 1860, they had increased to fifty.

In the first part of the nineteenth century, in the emotional climate stimulated by the awakening, there emerged several movements that represented significant departures or distortions of the evangelical Protestant pattern. A peculiar development of prophetical interpretation was that of William Miller (1782–1849), a Baptist farmer of Low Hampton, New York. From 1831 onward, he preached widely, asserting on the basis of calculations from the book of Daniel that the second coming and the inauguration of the millennial reign

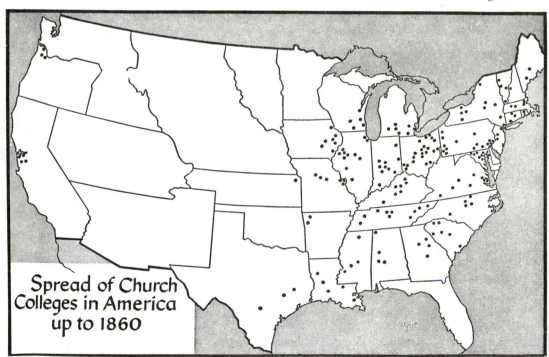

Spread of Church Colleges in America up to 1860

of Christ would occur in 1843–1844. He won thousands of followers. In spite of the failure of his prediction, his disciples held a general conference of Adventists, as they styled themselves, in 1845, and organizations of his disciples have persisted to the present, some holding to the observance of the seventh day. The most conspicuous such body has been the Seventh-day Adventists, formally organized in 1863. The Adventist faith, often coupled with pentecostal or perfectionist (holiness) emphases, played an important role in the formation of new sects in America in the latter nineteenth and early twentieth centuries. The movement that later became known as Jehovah's Witnesses, a distinctive outgrowth of Adventist teaching, began in the late 1870s under the leadership of Charles Taze Russell (1852–1916).

A movement nurtured in the revivalist atmosphere of the "burned-over" district of upstate New York but which soon went in it own highly distinctive direction was Mormonism. It was founded by Joseph Smith (1805–1844), who claimed to have dug up, near Manchester, New York, in 1827, a volume of gold plates, the Book of Mormon, supplementary to the Bible, written in mysterious characters which he was able to translate by means of a pair of magic spectacles, but the original of which was removed by angelic agency. In this book, Smith is proclaimed a prophet. The first Mormon church was organized in 1830, in Fayette, New York. It was later largely recruited in the neighborhood of Kirtland, Ohio, where Brigham Young (1801–1877) became a member. In 1838, the Mormon leaders removed to Missouri, and in 1840 they founded Nauvoo, Illinois. In spite of the monogamy enjoined by the Book of Mormon, Smith claimed to have received a revelation, in 1843, establishing polygamy. Popular hostility led to his murder by a mob the next year. The church now came under the leadership of Brigham Young, an organizer and leader of the highest ability. Under him, the Mormons marched to Salt Lake, in Utah, and a community of great material prosperity was inaugurated. Under pressure from the government, polygamy was officially abandoned in 1890. The Mormons have been indefatigable missionaries, and they have recruited many from Europe and planted their church overseas. Their system of economic and social supervision has been remarkable. Their unique theological system is based upon three sources of revelation: the Bible, the Book of Mormon, and the books recording the progressive direct revelations claimed to have been received by Joseph Smith from God, especially the "Doctrines and Covenants." Besides the main Church of Jesus Christ of Latter-Day Saints, with headquarters at Salt Lake City, Utah, there is a much smaller group with its center at Independence, Missouri.

In the period between the Civil War and the First World War, the revival emphasis of American Protestantism was strongly continued. Lay evangelist Dwight L. Moody (1837–1899) was its most conspicuous exponent. Tireless organizer and aggressive pulpiteer, Moody was a powerful force in Protestant life. His revival methods were widely copied, and his missionary enthusiasm contributed significantly to the continued growth of the foreign missionary enterprise. But the intellectual atmosphere of the late nineteenth century was swift-changing, and many new views sharply challenged ideas cherished by conservative Protestants. The impact of the revolutions in scientific and historical thought was remaking the reigning concepts of the nature of the world and its history. Those who were reared in the traditional biblical views of creation were shaken by the new ideas coming from the geologists on the one hand and the biblical critics on the other. Many Protestants reacted by holding to their views of biblical infallibility with greater rigidity. They founded a series of important Bible conferences in defense of their views—Niagara, Winona, Rocky Mountain. A popular summary of their views became known as the "five points of fundamentalism": the verbal inerrancy of Scripture, the deity of Jesus, the virgin birth, the substitutionary atonement, and the physical resurrection and bodily return of Christ. The conservative cause was strengthened by prophetic conferences, the founding of Bible schools, and the activities of many itinerant revivalists.

In the later nineteenth and early twentieth centuries, there arose several theologically conservative movements which engendered new denominational families in the United States and, through their missionary outreach, abroad. The Methodist tradition had originally claimed the possibility of perfection in Christian living (see VII:7); as this emphasis declined in the nineteenth century, a number of "Holiness" camp meetings were formed, emphasizing moral strictness and opposition to liberal tendencies. In the 1880s, a number of Holiness Methodists, along with those from other denominational backgrounds, formed separate congregations which merged in various combinations in a new range of Holiness denominations, the Church of the Nazarene becoming the most numerous. The Salvation Army (see VII:13), which reached the United States from England in 1880, was another conspicuous Holiness body, engaged especially in ministry to slum dwellers. Out of the Holiness churches in the early twentieth century came many of the leaders of another new movement, the Pentecostal. The two movements were similar in their patterns of conservative biblicism, premillennialism, strict morality, and faith healing, but the characteristic Pentecostal doctrine of the descent of the Holy Spirit as evidenced by "glossolalia," or speaking in tongues, quickly set the new movement sharply apart; in numbers, it soon surpassed the Holiness churches. An impetus for the escalation of Pentecostalism into a worldwide phenomenon came from a series of revival meetings led by a black evangelist, William J. Seymour (d. 1923), on Azusa Street in Los Angeles beginning in 1906; many received what they sincerely believed was the baptism of the Holy Spirit, a "third blessing" beyond justification and sanctification. The revival lasted for three years, and attracted hundreds and then thousands from across the country. Many who were to become leaders in the new Pentecostal movement received the third blessing there, among them both blacks and whites. As had been the case in many previous revivals, reports of what was going on varied widely and the movement became highly controversial; some believed it was the work of the Holy Spirit, while others thought it was emotional nonsense. Persons from abroad were also drawn to Azusa Street, and Pentecostalism soon became a world phenomenon as it reached Europe, Asia, Africa, and South America. In its early years as a growing movement in the United States, the movement was not sharply defined; many of those touched by the Pentecostal excitement remained at first in their old churches. Soon, however, Pentecostal churches began to form, and then divided in a range of denominations under the influence of three controversies, two theological and one primarily racial. Beginning in 1910, many Pentecostalists rejected the three-blessing doctrine and taught that that sanctification was not separated from justification but that both were part of the act of conversion based on the "finished work of Christ on Calvary," so that baptism in the Holy Spirit was the second—and final—blessing. These new views spread rapidly, and led to the formation in 1914 of the Assemblies of God, soon to become the largest American Pentecostal body. The new denomination was soon rent by a second theological issue which arose when some taught that the apostles baptized their converts in the name of Jesus only, and that there is only one personality in the Godhead, Jesus Christ, and the terms Father and Holy Spirit are only titles. This Jesus Only, or Jesus Name movement, whose followers broke with the trinitarian Assemblies of God to form the Pentecostal Assemblies of the World, eventually developed into a family of denominations. The third controversy was primarily racial as the movement which originally had been quite interracial succumbed to the color line. Among the growing number of trinitarian Pentecostal bodies, for example, the Assemblies of God remained largely white, while the Church of God in Christ, led by Charles H. Mason (1866–1961), became a black church. The first major Jesus Only group, the Pentecostal Assemblies of the World, was originally interracial, but by 1924 the whites withdrew to go into other bodies.

While many Protestants were thus oriented to conservative religious patterns, others reacted in quite another way, seeking to retain an evangelical orientation but to recast their faith so as to be in touch with the scientific and historical thought of the time. Deriving many of their ideas from the Ritschlian movement in Germany and the broad-church movement in England (see VII:12), they fought long battles for the acceptance of evolutionary thought and the critical approach to the Bible. Many seminaries championed the liberal approach; the "progressive orthodoxy" of Andover, for example, proved to be but a transition to liberalism.

A series of heresy trials marked the emergence of liberal theology. Especially conspicuous was the suspension of Professor Charles A. Briggs (1841–

1913) of Union Theological Seminary, New York, by the Presbyterian General Assembly in 1893. During the struggle, Union severed its link with the Presbyterians and emerged as a champion of the liberal way. By the dawn of the twentieth century, the liberals had won a place for themselves in many denominations. In the early decades of the new century, militant conservatives made a resolute drive to oust them in the bitter fundamentalist-modernist controversy. Largely failing by 1930, they tended to withdraw into independent churches and splinter denominations. Leadership was provided for the fundamentalists by Presbyterian professor J. Gresham Machen (1881–1937), and for the liberals by Baptist minister Harry Emerson Fosdick (1878–1969).

The 1865–1914 period witnessed an ever-enlarging recognition of the work of women in the Protestant churches. A Woman's Board of Foreign Missions was founded among the Congregationalists in 1868. The Methodist Episcopal Church, North, followed in 1869, the Northern Presbyterians in 1870, and the Protestant Episcopal Church in 1871. Similar organizations for home and foreign missions became well-nigh universal in American Protestantism. Women have long been eligible for election to the representative conventions of the Baptist and Congregational churches. They won the right of election to the Methodist general conferences in 1900. A number of denominations ordained them to the ministry, notably Baptists, Congregationalists, Disciples, Unitarians, and Universalists, and also new Holiness and Pentecostal bodies.

The same period was also marked by an increasing attention on the part of the churches to their young people. The nondenominational Christian Endeavor movement was founded by Congregationalist Francis E. Clark (1852–1927) in 1881. The denominations adopted the idea, and in 1889 the Epworth League was organized by the Methodists; the Baptist Young People's Union was formed in 1891, and the Luther League, for Lutheran young people, was set up in 1895.

An important feature of religious life after the Civil War was the steady increase in the demand for an educated ministry in those bodies which formerly had laid little stress on such training. This demand was met by constantly increasing provision, as the older theological seminaries steadily enlarged their facilities by augmented faculties and extension of the curriculum, and many new seminaries were founded. By 1900, over one hundred Protestant theological schools were functioning.

In the later nineteenth century, what have been called the "New Thought," "Mind-cure," and "Harmonial" religious movements had considerable influence within many Protestant churches, and they also led to the formation of a number of new religious bodies.[1] Distinctive among them was the Church

---

[1] See Sydney E. Ahlstrom, *A Religious History of the American People* (2 vols., Garden City, NY, 1975), vol. 2, chap. 60, pp. 528–548, "Harmonial Religion since the Later Nineteenth Century."

of Christ (Scientist), or Christian Science. Its founder, Mary Baker Eddy (1821–1910), who had long been plagued by illness, claimed that, following a fall on the ice in 1866, she had been remarkably healed and was led to the discovery of how to be in good health and how to cure others. In 1875, she published the first edition of *Science and Health with Key to the Scriptures*. In that same year, a Christian Science society was organized; in 1879, the new church was chartered in Boston. It spread to other cities and abroad, reaching an estimated size of about one hundred thousand members by the time of the founder's death. A number of other somewhat similar movements arose, some of them offshoots of Christian Science. In 1889, the Unity School of Christianity was founded in Kansas City, Missouri, by Charles and Myrtle Fillmore. Seeking to deepen the life of prayer and its healing efficacy in the churches and the larger society, Unity at first resisted becoming a new church, but it did slowly evolve into an autonomous denomination.

The late years of the nineteenth century saw the rise of deep social concern on the part of many Christians. Under the leadership of such liberal ministers as Washington Gladden (1836–1918) and Walter Rauschenbusch (1861–1918), the "social gospel" was advanced. It drew on British and Continental social Christianity (see VII:13, 14), as well as on American progressive social thought. Early nineteenth-century Protestantism had expressed its social concerns largely in individualistic terms, stressing charity and moral reform, but the social gospel focused attention on the corporate aspects of modern life and on the achievement of social justice. Great attention was devoted to the relations between capital and labor, and the movement influenced the shortening of the working day. Dedicated to the building of the kingdom of God on earth, the social gospel was especially prominent in the life and work of the Presbyterians, Baptists, and Methodists of the North, and among Congregationalists and Episcopalians. Courses on social ethics were added to seminary curricula, and denominational departments of social action were founded under social Christian influence. A number of social settlements in underprivileged areas were founded under Protestant auspices, and many institutional churches to bring social services to the urban masses were erected. The social emphasis was strongly felt in the mission field, where agricultural, medical, and educational missions were expanded.

Chapter 16

Roman Catholicism in the Modern World

*T*HE COUNTER-REFORMATION had spent its force by the middle of the seventeenth century. Its strength had been in the might of Spain and the zeal of the Jesuit order. Spain had emerged from the Thirty Years' War shorn of its power. The Jesuits, though more potent than ever in the counsels of the Roman Catholic Church, had become more worldly and had kept little of their earlier spiritual zeal. None of the popes of the seventeenth or eighteenth centuries were men of commanding force. Several, like Innocent XI (1676–1689), Innocent XII (1691–1700), and Benedict XIV (1740–1758), were of excellent character and intentions, but they were not commanding figures. The course of the Catholic Church was one of increasing feebleness in the face of the growing claims of the Catholic civil governments. A really effective attack upon Protestantism was no longer possible, save where it existed, as in France, in predominantly Roman lands. In seventeenth-century France, the Catholic position was strengthened by the attainment of a high level of Catholic piety. In 1611, Pierre de Bérulle (1575–1629) founded the French congregation of the Oratory, a great inspirer of spirituality. Bérulle's work influenced such founders of new orders and authors of spiritual writings as Saint Francis de Sales (1567–1622) and Saint Vincent de Paul (1576?–1660).

Under Louis XIV (1643–1715), the French monarchy pursued a policy dictated by the king's absolutism. As against papal claim, he asserted possession by the crown of all income of vacant bishoprics, and he favored the proclamation by the French clergy in 1682 of the "Gallican liberties"—that civil rulers have full authority in temporal affairs, that general councils are superior to the pope, that the usages of the French church limit papal interference, and that the pope is not infallible. The resulting quarrel was compromised in 1693 in such wise that the king kept the disputed income but agreed to be less insistent on the statement of the Gallican liberties, though it could still be held and taught.

Louis XIV's policy toward his own subjects was determined by his conception of national unity and Jesuit influence, especially after his marriage to Madame de Maintenon in 1684. In 1685, he revoked the Edict of Nantes (see

VI:12) and made Protestantism illegal under the severest penalties. The ultimate result was disastrous for France. Thousands of its most industrious citizens emigrated to England, Holland, Germany, and America. The former alliances with Protestant powers were ruptured, contributing much to the military failures of the latter years of Louis XIV's reign.

Jesuit influence led to equally disastrous opposition by the king and the pope to Jansenism. Cornelius Jansen (1585–1638), bishop of Ypres, an earnest Catholic, was a thoroughgoing Augustinian, convinced that the semi-Pelagian Jesuit interpretations of sin and grace must be combated. His chief work, *Augustinus,* was published in 1640, after his death. Jansen's book was condemned by Pope Urban VIII (1623–1644) in 1642, but Jansen's views found much support among the more deeply religious Catholics of France, notably in the nunnery of Port Royal, near Paris. The most influential opponent of the Jesuits was Blaise Pascal (1623–1662), especially with his *Lettres Provinciales* (1656–1657). Louis XIV supported the Jesuit hostility to Jansenism and persecuted its followers. In 1710, the buildings of Port Royal were torn down. Jansenism had found a new leader of power in Pasquier Quesnel (1634–1719), who had to seek safety in the Netherlands. His devotional commentary, *Moral Reflections on the New Testament* (1687–1692), aroused bitter hostility from the Jesuits, and through their efforts Pope Clement XI (1700–1721), by the bull *Unigenitus* of 1713, condemned one hundred and one of Quesnel's statements, some taken literally from Augustine. Louis Antoine de Noailles (1651–1729), cardinal archbishop of Paris, protested and appealed to a general council. Opposition was, however, vain. The Jesuits, supported by the French monarchy, ultimately triumphed.

Partly through this Jansenist controversy, and partly by reason of quarrels between the Jesuits and the older Roman clergy, a division occurred in Utrecht, in the Netherlands, from which in 1723 a small, independent, so-called Jansenist Catholic church originated, which still exists, with an archbishop in Utrecht and bishops in Haarlem and Deventer.

For France, the expulsion of the Huguenots and the triumph of the Jesuits were great misfortunes. While much variety of religious interpretation was possible in England, Germany, and Holland, within the bounds of Christianity, in eighteenth-century France the choice was only between Romanism of the narrow Jesuit type, which many of its own noblest sons condemned, and the rapidly rising tide of the new rationalism of a Voltaire and his associates (see VII:3). Thousands preferred the latter, and the destructive results were to be obvious in the treatment of the church during the French Revolution.

Elsewhere in Catholic circles in Europe, sentiment corresponding to the Gallican spirit in France was on the increase in the eighteenth century. In Germany, it took a conciliar form and was called "Febronianism," from the pseudonym "Justinus Febronius" taken by its most articulate exponent, Nicholas von Hontheim (1701–1790), auxiliary bishop of Trier. In Austria, it took a monarchical form and was called "Josephism," from the ecclesiastical policies of Emperor Joseph II (1765-1790).

The latter half of the eighteenth century brought to the Jesuits their greatest catastrophe. They had engaged heavily in colonial trade, in spite of its prohibition in their own constitutions; their political influence was notorious, and they had the hostility of the radical rationalism of the age. In this latter force they found their most determined foes. The powerful minister of King Joseph of Portugal (1750-1777), the marquis of Pombal (1699-1782), was a man of rationalistic sympathies. He was angered by Jesuit resistance to his policy in Paraguay, and he opposed the free-trade attitude of the Jesuits. In 1759, he enforced the deportation of all Jesuits from Portuguese territory with ruthless high hand. In France, too, sentiment against the Jesuits increased. The controlling force in the French government was that of the duke of Choiseul (1719-1785), a sympathizer with the Enlightenment. He was also aided by Madame de Pompadour, the mistress of Louis XV (1715-1774). A large part of the French clergy were also hostile to the Jesuits. In 1764, the Jesuits were suppressed in France. Spain and Naples expelled them in 1767. The rulers of these lands forced from Pope Clement XIV (1769-1774) the abolition of the order, in July 1773. These events attested the weakness of the papacy. The Jesuits continued existence in non-Roman Russia and in Protestant Prussia.

When the tremendous storm of the French Revolution broke, it swept away many of the privileges of the church, the nobility, the throne, and kindred ancient institutions. The revolutionary leaders were filled with the rationalistic spirit. They viewed the churches as religious clubs. In 1789, church lands were declared national property. In 1790, the monasteries were abolished. The same year, the Civil Constitution of the Clergy overthrew the old ecclesiastical divisions, made each "department" a bishopric, and provided for the election of all priests by the legal voters of their communities. The constitution of 1791 pledged religious liberty. Then in 1793 came a royalist and Catholic uprising in the Vendée, and in retaliation the Jacobin leaders sought to wipe out Christianity. Hundreds of ecclesiastics were beheaded. After the "terror" was over, in 1795, religious freedom was once more proclaimed, though the state, as such, was to be without religion. It was, in reality, strongly anti-Christian. This situation was extended by French conquests to the Netherlands, northern Italy, and Switzerland. In 1798, Rome was made a republic by French arms, and Pope Pius VI (1775-1799) was carried a prisoner to France, where he died.

The military events of 1800 led to the election of Pius VII (1800-1823) and the restoration of the States of the Church (see IV:4). Napoleon, on attaining power, though himself without religious feeling, recognized that a majority of the French people were Roman Catholics and that the church might be used by him. The result was the Concordat with the papacy in 1801 and the Organic Articles of 1802. By the former, the church surrendered all confiscated lands not still held by the government. Those in government possession were re-stored to it. Appointment of bishops and archbishops was to be by the pope on nomination by the state. Lower clergy were appointed by bishops, but the state had a veto power. Clergy were to be paid from the state treasury. By the Organic Articles, no papal decrees were to be published or French synods held without governmental permission. To Protestants full religious rights were accorded, at the same time, and the pay of their ministers and control of their affairs assumed by the state. Napoleon, who crowned himself emperor in 1804, soon quarreled with Pius VII, annexed the States of the Church in 1809, and held the pope a prisoner from that time until 1814. Napoleon's Concordat was to rule the relations between France and the papacy for more than a century. Intended to place the French Catholic church under the control of the government, and accomplishing that result under Napoleon, it also had the effect of making the French clergy look to the pope as their sole aid against the state. By ignoring ancient local rights, it really ruined Gallic claims to partial freedom and opened the door to that ultramontane spirit characteristic of French Catholicism throughout the nineteenth century.

The wars of the republican and Napoleonic periods resulted in far-reaching changes in Germany. The old ecclesiastical territories practically ceased to exist in 1803, and were divided between the secular states. In 1806, Francis II (1792–1835) resigned the title of Holy Roman emperor. He had already assumed that of emperor of Austria. It was the passing of a venerable institu-tion, the Holy Roman Empire, which had, indeed, been long but a shadow, but which was bound up with medieval memories of the relations of church and state.

Napoleon's downfall in 1815 was followed by universal reaction. The old seemed of value by its antiquity. It was to be years before the real progress effected by the revolutionary age was to be manifest. This reaction was aided by the rise of Romanticism, with its new appreciation of the medieval and rejection of that spirit of the eighteenth century which had been dominant in the revolution. François René de Chateaubriand (1768–1848), in his *Géne du Christianisme* (1802), showed how Catholicism could profit from Romanticist currents and contributed to the beginnings of a Catholic revival. The papacy profited by all these impulses and soon developed a strength greater than it had shown for a hundred years. A characteristic evidence of this new position of the papacy was the restoration, by Pius VII in August 1814, of the Jesuits, who speedily regained their old ascendancy in papal counsels and their widely ex-tended activities, though not their former political power. They have, in turn, been foremost in the development and support of papal authority. At the same time, the restoration of the power of the Roman Catholic Church was accom-panied and made possible by a real revival of piety that continued to char-acterize it into the twentieth century.

Roman development during the nineteenth century has been in the direction of the assertion of papal supremacy, called "ultramontanism"—i.e., "beyond the mountains," from the point of view of northern and western Europe—which is to say, Italian. The ultramontane position, with its magnification of the place of pope and king, was strengthened by the writings of the "three prophets of traditionalism"—Joseph Marie de Maistre (1754-1821), Louis Gabriel Ambroise de Bonald (1754-1840), and especially Hugues Félicité Robert de Lamennais (1782-1854). To this tendency to exalt the papacy above all national or local ecclesiaticism the Jesuits powerfully contributed. Pius VII's successor, Leo XII (1823-1829), was reactionary, condemning, like his predecessor, the work of Bible societies. Gregory XVI (1831-1846) was a patron of learning, but reactionary toward modern social and political ideals. This essentially medieval outlook and refusal to make terms with the modern world led to the formation, in the first half of the nineteenth century, of clerical and anticlerical parties in Catholic countries, whose contests largely determined the politics of those lands. An attempt on the part of the brilliant Lamennais to form an alliance of Catholicism and liberalism, especially for lands where Catholicism was in the minority, only brought about his condemnation by Gregory.

The ultramontane tendencies found conspicuous illustration in the papacy of Pius IX (1846-1878). Beginning his pontificate at a time when the States of the Church were on the edge of revolt because the leading political offices were held by the clergy, he was at first a political reformer; but the task proved too much for him and he adopted a reactionary political outlook which made it necessary to seek the support of foreign armies and rendered the people dissatisfied with his political rule. In religion, he was sincerely convinced that the papacy is a divinely appointed institution to which the modern world can appeal for the decision of its vexed religious problems. He desired to make this evident. In December 1854, after consultation with the bishops of the Catholic church, he proclaimed the immaculate conception of the Virgin—that is, that Mary shared in no taint of original sin. The question had been in discussion since the Middle Ages, though the balance of Catholic opinion in the nineteenth century was overwhelmingly in favor of the view approved by the pope. He elevated it, by his act, into a necessary dogma of faith.

In 1864, a Syllabus of Errors, prepared under papal auspices, condemned many things which most Catholics opposed, but it also repudiated much which is the foundation of modern states, like the separation of church and state, nonsectarian schools, and toleration of varieties in religion, and it concluded by condemning the claim that "the Roman Pontiff can and ought to reconcile himself to, and agree with, progress, liberalism, and civilization as lately introduced."

The crowning event of Pius IX's pontificate was the First Vatican Council. Opened on December 8, 1869, with a remarkably large attendance from all over the Roman world, its most important result was the affirmation, on July 18,

1870, of the doctrine of papal infallibility, by a vote of 533 to 2. It was far from asserting that all papal utterances are infallible. To be so, the pope must expound, in his official capacity, "the revelation or deposit of faith delivered through the Apostles." "The Roman Pontiff, when he speaks *ex cathedra,* that is, when in discharge of the office of pastor and doctor of all Christians, by virtue of his supreme apostolic authority, he defines a doctrine regarding faith or morals to be held by the universal church, by the divine assistance promised to him in blessed Peter, is possessed of that infallibility with which the divine Redeemer willed that His church should be endowed." Thus, the council sealed the triumph of ultramontanism. It was a victory for papal monarchism and a defeat for the theory of the supremacy of a general council, which had loomed so large in the fifteenth century (see V:14) and had not been without its representatives since.

Though undoubtedly the logical outcome of centuries of papal development, this doctrinal definition encountered considerable opposition, especially in Germany. The most eminent refuser of conformity was the distinguished Munich historian, Johann Joseph Ignaz von Döllinger (1799–1890); but though excommunicated, he declined to initiate a schism. What he refused, others achieved, and the result was the organization of the Old Catholics, who received episcopal ordination from the Jansenist church of Utrecht. Their chief spread has been in Germany, Switzerland, and Austria, but Old Catholics are also to be found in English-speaking lands.

Meanwhile, the tide of Italian national unity had been rising. The war carried on jointly by the kingdom of Sardinia, under Victor Emmanuel II (1849–1878), and France, under Napoleon III (1852–1870), against Austria, supplemented by Italian enthusiasm led by Giuseppe Garibaldi (1807–1882), resulted in the establishment of the kingdom of Italy under Victor Emmanuel in 1861, and the inclusion in it of the greater part of the old States of the Church. Rome and its vicinity were preserved to the pope by the ultramontane policy of Napoleon III. On the outbreak of the war between France and Germany in 1870, the French troops were withdrawn. On September 20, 1870, Victor Emmanuel captured Rome, and the inhabitants of the district voted 133,000 to 1,500 for annexation to Italy. To the pope the Italian government guaranteed the privileges of a sovereign and absolute possession of the Vatican, the Lateran, and Castel Gandolfo. Thus came to an end the States of the Church, the oldest continuous secular sovereignty then existing in Europe. Pius IX protested, declared himself the "prisoner of the Vatican," and excommunicated Victor Emmanuel. For half a century, until the Concordat with Mussolini settled the "Roman question" in 1929, the papacy refused to accept the loss of its temporal possessions. Yet it had its advantages. It aroused sympathy for the pope, and the contributions that flowed in from the Catholic world more than made up for the financial loss. It removed from the papacy a secular task which it was ill adapted to meet and the attempted accomplishment of which laid it open to well-grounded charges of maladministration. It gave to the papacy unhindered scope for the development of its spiritual functions and ultimately increased papal moral prestige.

These advantages did not immediately appear, however. For many years, it appeared that the church was retreating before the forces of the modern world, withdrawing within its own circle. In Italy, for example, Pius IX forbad Italian Catholics to participate in the political life of the kingdom of Italy. The consequence of this policy of *non expedit* was largely to strengthen the influence of radicals and socialists. In Germany in the 1870s occurred the *Kulturkampf,* which set the Catholic church against Bismarck's state; in the struggle, Catholics were often cut off from their accustomed contacts and sources of support and forced to consolidate their interests in a distinctive way.

Pius IX was succeeded by a statesman pope, Leo XIII (1878–1903). He concluded the conflicts between the papacy and the imperial government of Germany. The church had won, but at the apparent cost of becoming something of an enclave. He urged French Catholics to support the republic, but the effects of the Dreyfus case largely undid his efforts, and the struggle between church and state in France reached a climax under his successor. In Italy, Leo continued to seek the restoration of the States of the Church, and the tension between church and state continued. But he developed policies of great significance for the future. The relations of labor and capital and the interests of working men enlisted his attention. His famous encyclical of 1891, *Rerum novarum,* awoke wide Catholic concern with the issues of social justice. Leo urged the formation of a network of clerically led Catholic associations for social, benevolent, economic, and political purposes. This pattern of "Catholic Action" became an important source of strength in the twentieth century. Leo was a man of scholarly tastes, who urged the study of the Scriptures and declared that Aquinas (see V:7) was the standard of Roman Catholic instruction. He opened the treasures of the Vatican to historical scholars. He sought the reunion of the Roman and the Eastern churches, though he declared Anglican orders invalid in 1896. He was a skillful and zealous pope, who reigned in a difficult time in the life of the church.

The nineteenth century was a "great century" for Roman Catholic as well as for Protestant missions, though they were a few years later in arising and were not quite so conspicuous. The main missionary base was France, and the missionary force, chiefly monks and clergy, was strengthened by a marked increase in the number of monks serving as missionaries. Many orders and societies, some of them newly founded, participated in the movement. The restored Jesuits resumed a major missionary role, followed by the Oblates, Holy Spirit Fathers, Lazarists, Marists, Dominicans, Franciscans, Capuchins, White Fathers, and many others. New movements for the support of missions, such as the Society for the Propagation of the Faith, founded at Lyons in 1822, aroused a new interest in missions on the party of the laity. Humble lay folk were invited to pray for missions each day, and to contribute at least a penny each week. By 1914, nearly two hundred organizations to solicit lay support had been founded. An important development in nineteenth-century Catholic missions was a greatly increased role of women, primarily nuns. By the late 1870s, women from some sixty congregations provided more than half of approximately 60,000 Catholic missionaries; by the end of the century about 53,000 women were counted among the total which had increased to 70,000. The revived missionary drive, which drew much of its power from the ultramontane revival, revivified the Catholic minorities in India, which by 1870 numbered over a million, led by twenty-one bishops and nine hundred priests. In Indochina, despite persecution, the number of Catholics increased from about 300,000 in 1800 to nearly a million, about five percent of the population, by the First World War. In Africa south of the Sahara, the primitive animistic tribes were more readily drawn to Christianity than were those of Buddhist, Islamic, or Hindu background, so that by 1914 there were over a million Catholics in the central belt across Africa, with half as many in the islands, especially Madagascar and Mauritius.

Pius X (1903–1914) was, in many ways, a contrast to Leo XIII. The latter was of noble birth; Pius X was of humble origin. Leo XIII was of great diplomatic ability and far-sighted vision; Pius X was a faithful parish priest whose parish had become worldwide. He was called on to handle two questions of great difficulty. The first had to do with the relations of church and state in France. In spite of the efforts of Leo XIII, the majority of French Catholics were regarded as lukewarm toward the republic. Relations had long been growing strained. In 1901, religious orders not under state control were forbidden to engage in instruction. The refusal of conformity by some was followed in 1903 by the suppression of many monasteries and nunneries and the confiscation of their properties. In 1904, President Loubet of France paid a state visit in Rome to the king of Italy. Pius X, regarding the Italian sovereign as being in wrongful possession of Rome, protested. France withdrew its ambassador from the papal court and soon after broke off all diplomatic intercourse. In December 1905, the French government decreed the separation of church and state. All governmental aid was withdrawn from Catholics and Protestants. All churches and other church property were declared the possession of the state, to be rented for use by state-responsible local associations for worship, preference being given to those representative of the faith by which the property had last been employed. Though many French bishops were ready to form such organizations, Pius X forbade it. The result was a deadlock. Support had to be provided by voluntary gifts. Not until the 1920s was the church to have a legal basis in France.

The second problem was occasioned by the rise of the "modernists." In spite of growing ultramontanism, modern historical criticism, biblical investigation, and scientific conceptions of growth through development had found a foothold, though tenuous, in the Roman communion. To some earnest and thoughtful men, some reinterpretation of Catholicism in terms of the modern intellectual world seemed imperative. Such were Hermann Schell (1850–1906) in Germany, Alfred Loisy (1857–1940) in France, George Tyrrell (1861–1909) in England, and quite a group in Italy. Modernism was confined to no country. Against this movement Pius X set his face. By a decree, *Lamentabili,* and an encyclical, *Pascendi,* both in 1907, modernism was condemned and stringent measures were taken for its repression. Loisy and Tyrrell were excommunicated. The impression that Catholicism was retreating from the modern world was heightened.

The period of the First World War, during which Benedict XV (1914–1922) was pope, saw a marked improvement in Catholic fortunes. Catholic charitable institutions gave a good account of themselves in the struggle. The improved moral and spiritual prestige of the papacy now began to count. Rome had fought the cultural developments of the nineteenth century, but as these came into crisis during the war and after, the stand of the church appeared less anachronistic. The organizations of Catholic Action gave to Roman Catholicism an effective instrument for growth and survival in pluralistic societies.

The pontificate of able and scholarly Pius XI (1922–1939) was marked by a decided Catholic revival. Revived theological interest, a significant liturgical movement, and continued missionary interest were evident. The "Roman question" was finally settled in 1929 by the Lateran Pacts, by which the pope accepted the loss of the former States of the Church in exchange for a large sum and received the domain of the Vatican City as his own. The church sought to consolidate its new gains in Europe through a series of concordats with various governments, including agreements with Fascist Italy (1929) and Nazi Germany (1933). When those governments broke faith, Pius protested in his vigorous encyclicals, *Non abbiamo bisogno* (1931) and *Mit brennender Sorge* (1937). He was a champion of Catholic Action, later redefined as the "lay apostolate."

Roman Catholicism in the United States grew steadily throughout the nineteenth and early twentieth centuries, for the tides of immigration brought millions of that faith to American shores. In the first half of the nineteenth century, one of the chief internal problems was the desire of certain lay trustees of Catholic parishes to take on themselves the episcopal prerogative of appointing and dismissing their pastors. Schisms over "trusteeism" in some cases lasted for many years, but the bishops succeeded in securing full control. The chief external problem was the recrudescence of anti-Catholic feeling, heightened by the influx of the militantly Roman Catholic Irish in the 1840s. Meanwhile, by developing parochial schools, institutions of charity, and a Catholic press, a vigorous effort to hold the loyalty of the incoming foreigners was made.

The second half of the century was a period of naturalization and Americanization for the Catholic church. The convening of the First Plenary Council in Baltimore in 1852 was a step toward consolidating Catholic gains and toward securing a larger place in the life of the nation. By that time, Catholics were nearly two million strong—the largest single religious body in the land. The central figure in this period was James Gibbons (1834–1921), who was consecrated bishop in 1868, made archbishop in 1877, and elevated to the cardinalate in 1886. He did much to make his church at home in America and to ease the hostility against Catholics. He believed that the separation of church and state was best for America and supported it heartily. He championed the rights of working men, at a time when the shift in the main sources of immigration to southern Europe was pouring ever greater numbers of people of Catholic background into the urban centers. There were those who feared that the Roman Catholic Church in the United States was becoming *too* American in this age of Gibbons, and in 1899 a papal latter, *Testem benevolentiae,* warned against such dangers.

In the early twentieth century, Catholicism came of age in America. In 1908, the American church was removed from the jurisdiction of the Sacred Congregation for the Propagation of the Faith, its missionary status ended. The participation of Catholics in the First World War established its "Americanism" beyond any doubt and served further to diminish surviving tensions between ethnic groups. Furthermore, the National Catholic War Council (1917) proved to be such an effective instrument of consolidation and advance that it was retained as the National Catholic Welfare Conference, an instrument of the hierarchy and the dynamic center of "Catholic Action" in the United States. Increased Roman Catholic strength in America was accompanied by some increased resistance on the part of both Protestants and "other" Americans.

Chapter 17

The Eastern Churches in Modern Times[1]

THE IMPRESSION of many in the West that Eastern Christianity has had an uneventful history in modern times probably merely reflects the fact that the study of Eastern church history has been neglected in the West. Actually, the story is one of tension and conflict, much of it stemming from political

---

[1] This section is based substantially on material prepared for the second edition (1959) by the late Dr. Edward R. Hardy, then of the Berkeley Divinity School in New Haven.

pressures. The "Florentine Union" (see V:14) was quickly repudiated by the major Eastern churches. The Greek Metropolitan Isidore of Kiev was expelled when he attempted to proclaim it at Moscow, and from 1448 the Russian church was fully autonomous. At Constantinople, the Union lasted in form until the fall of the city to the Turks in 1453, but it had been definitely repudiated by a synod in 1472. The Turkish Empire continued to expand; at its height in the middle of the sixteenth century, it included most of the Balkan Peninsula, reached into Hungary, dominated the Black Sea, and embraced Asia Minor, Armenia, Georgia, the Euphrates Valley, Syria, Palestine, Egypt, and much of the north coast of Africa. For a variety of reasons, including political and military compulsion, many Christians converted to Islam. As subjects of the sultans, the Orthodox faithful were organized as a semiautonomous community, the "Rum Millet" (Roman Nation). The patriarchs exercised far more authority over their flocks than they had under the Christian emperors, sometimes abusing their civil powers. Subjected to heavy exactions and frequently deposed, they lost one ancient church after another until settled after 1603 at St. George's in the Phanar quarter of Istanbul. Other Orthodox prelates became dependent on the ecumenical patriarchate, although the Serbian and Bulgarian churches retained some autonomy until their patriarchates were suppressed in 1766–1767. From 1461, an Armenian patriarch at Istanbul had a similar position as civil representative of the Monophysites.

After 1453, the Muscovite principality replaced the Byzantine Empire as the great Orthodox state. Some ecclesiastics advanced the theory that, since Old Rome had fallen into heresy and New Rome had been conquered, Moscow with its Orthodox princes and prelates was the Third Rome, which would never fall. Monasteries such as the great Troitsky Lavra (Trinity Monastery) near Moscow, founded by St. Sergius in the fourteenth century, were the main centers of piety, learning, and church life. An interesting monastic controversy of the late fifteenth century was between the "non-possessioners," headed by Nil Sorssky, who emphasized the life of prayer and monastic poverty at the expense of limiting activities to the strictly religious, and the "possessioners," headed by Joseph of Volokolamsk, who accepted social and political responsibilities and welcomed wealth and property as a means of discharging them. The bestowal of patriarchal rank on the metropolitans (1589), like the earlier assumption of the title of tsar by the grand dukes, merely gave formal recognition to an existing situation.

In the sixteenth and seventeenth centuries, the Eastern churches had to come to terms with Western influences, both Catholic and Protestant. Luther and other Reformers appealed to the Eastern example of a non-Roman Catholicism. But when the theologians of Tübingen opened a correspondence with Patriarch Jeremias II (1574–1584), his replies stated clearly the divergence of the Greek church from the Lutheran teaching on authority, faith, grace, and the sacraments. Under obscure circumstances, the remarkable Cyril Lucar (patriarch five times between 1620 and 1638) issued a confession of a strongly Reformed character; while in the Union of Brest (1596), the metropolitan of Kiev and other prelates in what was then Polish territory accepted the Florentine terms—local autonomy and liturgical independence, subject to ultimate Roman authority in doctrine and discipline. From the Russian word *unya,* this Church of the Ukraine ("borderland") is popularly called Uniat, a term often applied (somewhat improperly) to other Eastern Rite Catholics. Under Peter Mogila, who became metropolitan in 1632, Kiev returned to the Orthodox communion. His *Confession* and *Catechism* are documents of importance in this controversy, which ended with the decrees of the Synod of Bethlehem, held under Patriarch Dositheus of Jerusalem in 1672. Though Orthodox in substance, these "confessional books" show Western influence in their form. Western methods were also used in Mogila's Theological Academy of Kiev (which was in Russian territory after 1665), where the language of instruction was neither Greek nor Slavonic, but Latin. Throughout the eighteenth century, Russian theological schools, organized on the Kiev model, followed this system.

In the sphere of influence of Catholic powers (first Portugal, later France and Austria as well as Poland), other "Uniat" churches were formed. Ethiopia was in formal union with Rome between 1624 and 1632. In India, the Syrian Christians of Malabar experienced considerable Latinization under Archbishop Menezes and Jesuit missionaries (Synod of Diamper, 1599). In 1653, a large section renounced the Roman communion and later secured the episcopal succession from the Syrian Jacobites, since the Nestorians, with whom they had once been connected, were out of reach. A section of the Nestorians were united with Rome as "Chaldeans" in the sixteenth century, and a section of Syrian Orthodox (to whom the Arabic name of the whole group, "Melkite," or royalist—i.e., Byzantine—has come to be restricted) in the eighteenth. Other small "Uniat" groups emerged in Egypt, Syria, and Armenia.

In Russia, the church was a focus of national loyalty during the wars and invasions of the "Time of Troubles," which followed the extinction of the ancient dynasty of Rurik. The defense of the Troitsky Lavra against the Poles in 1612 was one of the turning points of the period. When the new dynasty began with Michael Romanov in 1613, his father, who had been forced to take monastic vows during the wars, practically reigned with him as Patriarch Philaret. Patriarch Nikon (1652–1666), vigorous to the point of roughness, introduced practical reforms, which included a correction of the service-books from the Greek. Nikon was deposed with the assent of other patriarchs, but the reforms remained in effect. Opponents were forced into schism, as Old Believers (properly "Old Ritualists") or separatists (Raskolniki). The importance of the liturgy in Orthodox faith and life stiffened their loyalty to the details of rite and ceremonial which represented to them the strict Orthodoxy of Russia. Peter the Great's westernizing reforms intensified the difference. The Russian sects form three groups: (1) the Old Believers, of whom some (*popovtsi*) accepted priests who came over from the established church, and who in 1849 secured, irregularly from a Greek bishop, their own episcopate, while others (*bezpopovtsi*, that is, "priestless ones") held that apostasy had destroyed the orders of the church and limited themselves to such rites as laymen could administer, using consecrated wine and chrism maintained by dilution; (2) a variety of extreme or eccentric groups, some picking up survivals of paganism or ancient heresies—the pacifist Dukhobors ("spirit-wrestlers") who have migrated to Canada are the best known; and (3) since the nineteenth century, Protestant groups who have found their way into Russia in various ways.

Planning to organize church administration on the lines of a government department, Peter left the patriarchate vacant after 1700, and in 1721 he replaced it by the "Holy Governing Synod." This was composed of a few bishops and other clergy summoned by the emperor, who also appointed its lay secretary and executive, the "ober-procuror." In English he is usually called "procurator," but the barbarous title, not even good German, expresses the revolutionary character of the institution. The patriarch, who might seem to rival the tsar, was thus replaced by an administration clearly subject to him. Although the established church was not without outstanding examples of piety, learning, charity, and missionary zeal, the deepest devotion flowed in unofficial channels. The eighteenth century saw a renewal of the old monastic tradition of straightforward piety and spiritual guidance among the monks of Mount Athos, one of whom, Paisi Velichkovsky (1722–1794), later an abbot in Moldavia near the Russian border, brought this tradition back into Russian church life. Two saints canonized by the Russian church represent the same tendency, comparable in some ways to the Pietist reaction against official Protestantism—the bishop Tikhon Zadonsky (1724–1783) and the hermit of the northern woods, Seraphim of Sarov (d. 1835). One of the "elders" (*startsi*), or spiritual directors, of the Optina Monastery near Moscow is depicted in the Father Zosima of Dostoyevsky's *Brothers Karamazov*.

The rise of nationalism and modern intellectual and spiritual movements have confronted the Eastern churches with new situations, the traditional close union of people and church expressing itself in new forms. The Greek Revolution was launched at the Peloponnesian monastery of Megaspelaion (and Patriarch Gregory V, though he formally condemned the insurgents, was hanged as a Greek leader in front of his residence at the Phanar in 1821). With political independence, the church of Greece renewed its intellectual life and assumed ecclesiastical autonomy, which the patriarch of Constantinople recognized in 1851. Similar action was taken in Serbia, Romania, and Bulgaria. In 1870, the Bulgarian exarch claimed jurisdiction over Bulgars everywhere, even at Istanbul; this was condemned as "philetism ["over-nationalism," perhaps], the heresy of our age," and produced a schism between Greeks and

Bulgars from 1872 to 1945. Church life in the Balkans has continued to be unhappily involved in national conflicts.

In Syria, the Arab Christians became restive under Greek hierarchs. Since 1898, there have been Syrian patriarchs of Antioch at Damascus, but the patriarchate of Jerusalem continues to be controlled by the Brotherhood of the Holy Sepulcher (almost entirely Greek). Missionary interest helped to bring modern education to the Near East, but at the cost of further ecclesiastical divisions. The work of Eastern Catholics was extended by Latin missionaries, and small Protestant groups came into being among Greeks, Armenians, and Syrians, and a larger Evangelical church among the Copts. In India, the Anglican missionaries of the Church Missionary Society worked for a time among the Syrian Christians, an ultimate result of their influence being the separation of a more evangelical wing as the Mar Thoma Church.

The reaction against westernizing influences, whether religious or anti-religious, led to the presentation of traditional Orthodoxy in more vigorous and up-to-date forms. Westernizing and strictly Orthodox trends have competed in the theological faculties of the Balkans and among the Christian thinkers of Russia. In the later nineteenth century, the Greek church was stimulated by the vigorous if eccentric ultra-Orthodox lay theologian Apostolos Makrakis. Since that time, voluntary organizations have done much to revive preaching, organize religious education, and encourage the social activity of the church; the Zoë Brotherhood, a confraternity of celibate *theologoi* (that is, graduates in theology), lay and clerical, is the best known of these. In Russia, the Slavophils turned to the corporate and spiritual traditions of Orthodoxy, as against both the dullness of the repressed and repressing official church (at its worst perhaps under Nicholas I, 1825–1855) and the secular trends of reformers and revolutionaries. The layman Alexei Khomyakov (1804–1860) was an early leader of the school. Others were less churchly if equally religious in their interests, such as the novelist Fyodor Dostoyevsky (1821–1881) and the philosopher Vladimir Soloviev (1853–1900), whose longing for spiritual unity led him to claim the right to enter the Roman communion without abandoning his standing in the ancient Orthodox church. He believed that Russian Orthodoxy ideally expressed *sobornost* ("oneness" or "community"), which combined unity and freedom derived from the love of God. At once mystic, philosopher, theologian, prophet, and moralist, he sought to interpret Christian faith in such a way that it would become relevant to those who had discarded it and give them the hope that the truth of Christ might regenerate humanity and reform the world. The semiofficial missionary activity of the Russian church, often heroic, was at least encouraged because of its possible effect in consolidating the empire or extending its influence, as in the work of the Imperial Palestine Society and the patronage of a Russian monastery on Mount Athos. But there was also missionary work which went beyond any political connections in Alaska, a Russian outpost until 1867, and under Bishop Nicholas of Tokyo (in Japan 1860–1912), founder of Japanese Orthodoxy.

The wars and revolutions of the twentieth century have brought further changes. After the Balkan Wars, most of the dioceses of "new Greece" were in effect transferred from the jurisdiction of Constantinople to that of Athens. Somewhat later, the Albanian church became autonomous. After the First World War, Serbs and Romanians, who had been under separate jurisdictions in Austria-Hungary, were restored to their native lands and native churches; the Serbian patriarchate was restored in 1920, and the Romanian church raised to patriarchal rank in 1925. The ecumenical patriarch's direct jurisdiction was reduced to the immediate neighborhood of Istanbul by the exchange of populations between Greece and Turkey in 1923. But the Greek parishes of Europe and America remained under his jurisdiction, and his undefined primacy among Orthodox hierarchs is from time to time appealed to. Considerable feeling (and some schism) was caused in the 1920s by the adoption of the Gregorian calendar, somewhat improved, by Greeks, Syrians, and Romanians for fixed festivals—though for the sake of unity, all Orthodox still follow the Julian calendar for the calculation of Easter.

The shift of Russia from Orthodox empire to Marxist state was a blow to the church comparable to that of the Moslem conquest. In 1917, a church assembly which met at Moscow revived the patriarchate and otherwise planned for the freedom of the church. But the movement from establishment to persecution was rapid under the Bolshevik regime. Though in principle tolerating "religious profession and antireligious propaganda," the Soviet government actively promoted the latter and barely permitted the former. Many bishops and priests disappeared into prison or exile, monasteries were dissolved and most of the churches closed, church administration was impeded, and for some years the radical reforming groups commonly called the "Living Church" received relative encouragement as a further divisive factor. But the church lived on in the hearts of believers, and its leaders managed to retain some form of organization. In 1923, Patriarch Tikhon declared his political loyalty to the regime and was allowed some freedom until his death in 1925, after which Metropolitan Sergius became guardian of the patriarchal throne. Periods of antireligious pressure alternated with periods of relative calm, until the undoubted loyalty of Russian Orthodox to their country in the Second World War led to a more settled relation. A patriarchal election was allowed in 1943, and under Sergius and his successors, patriarchs Alexis (1944–1970) and Pimen (1971–   ), the Russian church has functioned more normally. Facilities are provided for its activities within the strictly religious sphere (worship, and instruction in homes when invited), and some institutions have been revived—a few monasteries and convents, seminaries, and theological academies at the Troitsky Lavra, Leningrad, and Kiev. The church and its leaders are of course expected to manifest political loyalty, and Marxist leaders still expect religion to die out in time, but they have abandoned their frontal attack. The Georgian church had been absorbed by the Russian after the country was annexed in 1801 (to this resented status may be partly due the disaffection found in its ecclesiastical schools, such as that in which the future Joseph Stalin studied), but in 1917 it again became autonomous under its own catholicos-patriarch, and it was so recognized by the Russian church in 1944. Other churches in the Soviet Union have a status similar to that of the Orthodox patriarchate—the Old Believers (at least the *popovtsi*), the Armenians (whose supreme catholicos resides at Etchmiadzin in Soviet Armenia), the Russian Baptists, and the Lutherans of the Baltic republics. In the 1920s, the Orthodox churches of areas formerly Russian but then independent received recognition of autonomous status from the ecumenical patriarch. This has been extinguished in Estonia (except for congregations in exile) and Latvia, but it survives in Poland and Finland. In the Ukraine, an autocephalous church (i.e., one that can choose its own head) was formed during the brief period of independence during the revolution, which now survives only among the Ukrainians of the United States and Canada.

The Russian Orthodox outside Russia fall into three main groups. Some remain loyal to the patriarchate in ecclesiastical matters. Others follow the lead of a group of exiled bishops headed originally by Metropolitan Anthony of Kiev, who maintain that Tikhon and his successors have been slaves of the Soviet regime and that the Russian Orthodox Church outside Russia is the true heir of its traditions. Its synod was long established at Karlovtsi in Yugoslavia, but after the Second World War it moved to Munich and then to the United States. The third group seeks to avoid political involvement by insisting on autonomy in matters of administration and church government, at least for the present, while remaining loyal to the traditions of Russian Orthodoxy. The main body of Russian Orthodox in the United States, formerly the Russian Orthodox Greek Catholic Church of North America but since 1965 the Orthodox Church in America, belongs in this group, as does an important section of the Russian church in Western Europe. In the latter, a major center of theology and church life was established in Paris in 1925, the Academy of St. Sergius, headed for many years by the distinguished theologian Sergius Bulgakov (1871–1944).

A brief survey of recent conditions and problems concludes this section. The remnant of the pre-Chalcedonian Nestorian, or Assyrian, church, which in the nineteenth century was located chiefly in the mountainous northwest region of Persia, suffered greatly in both world wars and took refuge primarily in Syria. The patriarchal family, in whom the dignity is hereditary, went into exile, and the catholicos, Mar Shimun XXIII, established his headquarters in California. The Syrian Christians of Malabar suffered another division in 1910, between the patriarch's party, willing to accept Syrian jurisdiction, and the catholicos party, desiring complete autonomy. Of other churches of the Monophysite or Jacobite communion, the Ethiopian under Emperor Haile Selassie secured its independence of the Coptic, and efforts were made to prepare it to meet the educational and other responsibilities of a national church. The Armenians recovered remarkably from the massacres and exiles of 1915–1916. Their second hierarch, the catholicos of Cilicia, once Khoren I, in Turkey, was established with his flock in Lebanon—but political movements for or against Soviet Armenia affect the life of the church.

The list of functioning Eastern Orthodox churches includes the ancient patriarchates of Constantinople, Alexandria (whose numbers have been increased in modern times by the settlement of Greeks and Syrians in Egypt), Antioch, and Jerusalem; the later patriarchates of Russia, Serbia, Romania, Bulgaria (where the title was revived), and Georgia; the autocephalous churches of Cyprus (so recognized since the Council of Ephesus and prominent in recent years through the leadership of its bishops in the national movement for union with Greece), Greece, Poland, Finland, Albania, and Czechoslovakia; and the independent monastery of Mount Sinai. Before 1917, the Russian bishopric—moved from Alaska to San Francisco in 1872, and to New York in 1905 (under Bishop Tikhon, later patriarch)—was the only organized Orthodox jurisdiction in America, and it supervised other national parishes except the Greek (the Greek were formed into an archbishopric under Constantinople in 1922). Since 1920, the Syrians, Serbians, Romanians, Bulgars, and Albanians have established American dioceses. The rise of the American-born younger generation among laity and clergy (for whom the Greeks and Russians have seminaries) marks the naturalization of Orthodoxy in America. English is increasingly used for instruction and in varying degrees for the liturgy, and in due time one may expect the majority of the national groups to join in an organizationally united Eastern Orthodox Church in America. There is also an Armenian prelacy in America and groups of Assyrian and Syrian Jacobite parishes.

A prominent ecumenical representative of Orthodoxy in the World and (American) National Councils of Churches was the theologian and historian Georges Florovsky (1893–1979). Born in Russia, he taught for more than twenty years at the Orthodox Theological Faculty of Paris before coming in 1948 to the United States, where he taught at St. Vladimir's Orthodox Seminary, Union Theological Seminary (New York), Columbia and Harvard universities and Princeton Theological Seminary. A prolific author and lecturer, he played an important ecumenical role in repesenting his tradition to others.

Until recently, the largest body of Eastern Catholics were the survivors of the Union of Brest in Galicia (after the partition of Poland, Austrian; after 1918, again Polish territory) and the related Carpatho-Russians (formerly in

Hungary, after 1918 in Czechoslovakia). The Uniat dioceses in Russian Poland were reunited to the Russian church in 1840 and 1875. A famous leader among the Galician Ukrainians was Andrew Szepticky (metropolitan of Lvov, 1900–1944), one of the Eastern Catholics who have endeavored to represent within the papal obedience the less formalized spirit of Eastern Christian piety. The Soviet occupation of these lands in 1946 was followed by the reunion of Ukrainians and Carpatho-Russians with the patriarchate of Moscow, and the Ukrainian "Unia" survives primarily in the "apostolic exarchates" established in the United States and Canada for immigrants from Galicia and Carpatho-Russia who have remained loyal to it.

Confident of the correctness of their own traditions, Eastern Christians have nevertheless been able to establish friendly contacts with others whenever the relation has not been complicated by controversy or proselytism. Friendly exchanges of various kinds have been carried on since the seventeenth century—most often, though by no means exclusively, with the Anglican communion, and since 1870 with the Old Catholics, who arrived by a different route at a position quite similar to that of the Orthodox churches. Eastern churches have participated in the ecumenical movement since the Stockholm and Lausanne conferences of 1925 and 1927—a step prepared by the synodical encyclical of 1920 (issued by the Synod of Constantinople during a vacancy in the patriarchate), which urged conference between churches on matters of practical concern. The Russian church was unhappily not able to share in such discussions in the 1920s and 1930s. But its interest was shown in the Moscow conference of 1948, following the celebrations of the 500th anniversary of its autocephaly and attended by most of the non-Greek Orthodox churches—although the immediate decisions had a rigid sound, conspicuous items being a denunciation of Vatican policy, a rejection of cooperation with the World Council of Churches, and a reservation of judgment on Anglican orders, which had been conditionally recognized by the ecumenical patriarchate and several other Orthodox churches between 1922 and 1935. In 1961, however, the Russian Orthodox Church did become a member of the World Council of Churches, so that almost every major autocephalous national Orthodox church came into full membership in that ecumenical body.

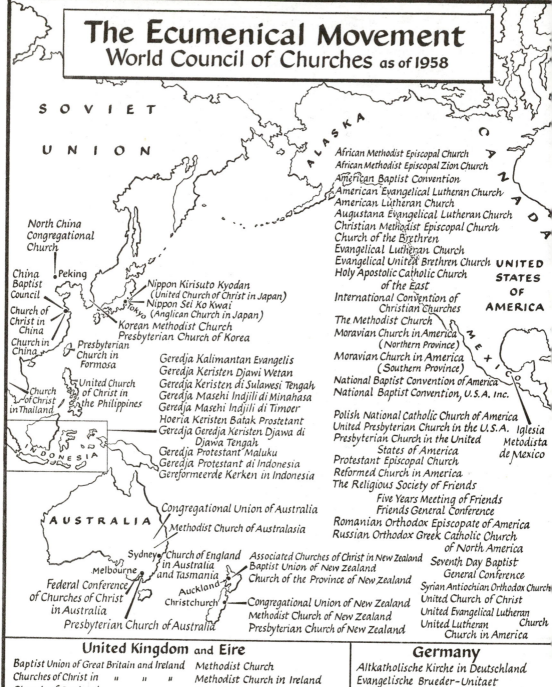

The Ecumenical Movement
World Council of Churches as of 1958

SOVIET UNION

ALASKA

CANADA

North China Congregational Church

China Baptist Council · Peking

Church of Christ in China

Church in China

Church of Christ in Thailand

Presbyterian Church in Formosa

United Church of Christ in the Philippines

Nippon Kirisuto Kyodan (United Church of Christ in Japan)
Nippon Sei Ko Kwai (Anglican Church in Japan)
Tokyo
Korean Methodist Church
Presbyterian Church of Korea

Geredja Kalimantan Evangelis
Geredja Keristen Djawi Wetan
Geredja Keristen di Sulawesi Tengah
Geredja Masehi Indjili di Minahasa
Geredja Masehi Indjili di Timoer
Hoeria Kristen Batak Prostetant
Geredja Geredja Keristen Djawa di Djawa Tengah
Geredja Protestant Maluku
Geredja Protestant di Indonesia
Gereformeerde Kerken in Indonesia

INDONESIA

AUSTRALIA

Congregational Union of Australia
Methodist Church of Australasia

Sydney · Church of England in Australia and Tasmania
Melbourne
Federal Conference of Churches of Christ in Australia
Presbyterian Church of Australia

Auckland
Christchurch
Associated Churches of Christ in New Zealand
Baptist Union of New Zealand
Church of the Province of New Zealand
Congregational Union of New Zealand
Methodist Church of New Zealand
Presbyterian Church of New Zealand

UNITED STATES OF AMERICA

African Methodist Episcopal Church
African Methodist Episcopal Zion Church
American Baptist Convention
American Evangelical Lutheran Church
American Lutheran Church
Augustana Evangelical Lutheran Church
Christian Methodist Episcopal Church
Church of the Brethren
Evangelical Lutheran Church
Evangelical United Brethren Church
Holy Apostolic Catholic Church of the East
International Convention of Christian Churches
The Methodist Church
Moravian Church in America (Northern Province)
Moravian Church in America (Southern Province)
National Baptist Convention of America
National Baptist Convention, U.S.A. Inc.
Polish National Catholic Church of America
United Presbyterian Church in the U.S.A.
Presbyterian Church in the United States of America
Protestant Episcopal Church
Reformed Church in America
The Religious Society of Friends
Five Years Meeting of Friends
Friends General Conference
Romanian Orthodox Episcopate of America
Russian Orthodox Greek Catholic Church of North America
Seventh Day Baptist General Conference
Syrian Antiochian Orthodox Church
United Church of Christ
United Evangelical Lutheran Church
United Lutheran Church in America

MEXICO

Iglesia Metodista de Mexico

United Kingdom and Eire

Baptist Union of Great Britain and Ireland
Churches of Christ in   "   "   "
Church of England
Church of Ireland
Church of Scotland
Church in Wales
Congregational Union of England and Wales
Congregational Union of Scotland
Episcopal Church in Scotland

Methodist Church
Methodist Church in Ireland
Moravian Church in Great Britain and Ireland
Presbyterian Church of England
Presbyterian Church in Ireland
Presbyterian Church of Wales
Salvation Army
United Free Church of Scotland

Germany

Altkatholische Kirche in Deutschland
Evangelische Brueder–Unitaet
Evangelische Kirche in Deutschland
Evangelische Kirche in Berlin-Brandenburg
Pommersche Evangelische Kirche
Evangelische Kirche von Schlesien
Evangelische Kirche der Kirchenprovinz Sachsen
Evangelische Kirche von Westfalen
Evangelische Kirche in Rheinland
Evangelisch-Lutherische Landeskirche Sachsens

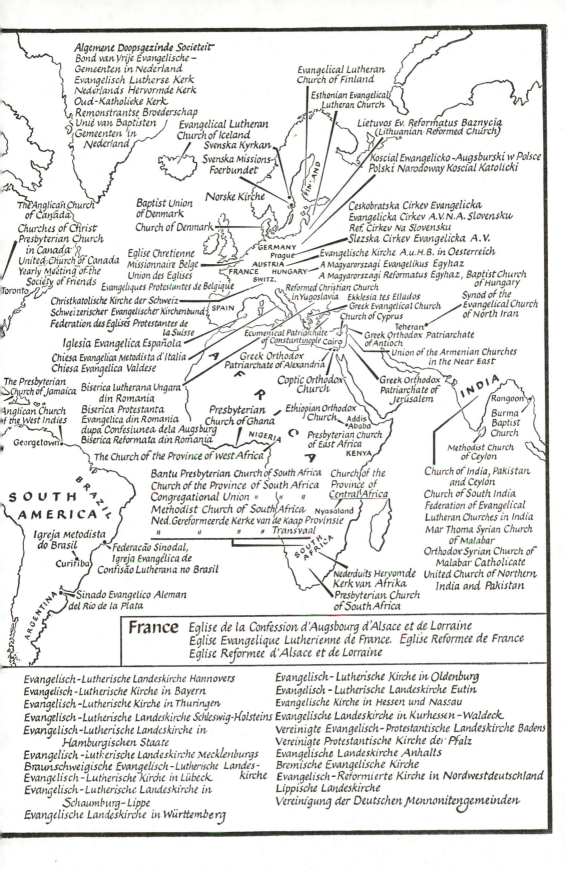

Algemene Doopsgezinde Societeit
Bond van Vrije Evangelische-
Gemeenten in Nederland
Evangelisch Lutherse Kerk
Nederlands Hervormde Kerk
Oud-Katholieke Kerk
Remonstrantse Broederschap
Unie van Baptisten
Gemeenten in
Nederland

Evangelical Lutheran
Church of Iceland
Svenska Kyrkan
Svenska Missions-
Foerbundet

Norske Kirke

Evangelical Lutheran
Church of Finland

Esthonian Evangelical
Lutheran Church

Lietuvos Ev. Reformatus Baznycia
(Lithuanian Reformed Church)

Koscial Ewangelicko-Augsburski w Polsce
Polski Narodoway Koscial Katolicki

The Anglican Church
of Canada
Churches of Christ
Presbyterian Church
in Canada
United Church of Canada
Yearly Meeting of the
Society of Friends
Toronto

Baptist Union
of Denmark
Church of Denmark

Eglise Chretienne
Missionnaire Belge
Union des Eglises
Evangeliques Protestantes de Belgique

Christkatholische Kirche der Schweiz
Schweizerischer Evangelischer Kirchenbund
Federation des Eglises Protestantes de
la Suisse
Iglesia Evangelica Española
Chiesa Evangelica Metodista d'Italia
Chiesa Evangelica Valdese

GERMANY
Prague
AUSTRIA
FRANCE HUNGARY
SWITZ.

SPAIN

Ceskobratska Cirkev Evangelicka
Evangelicka Cirkev A.V.N.A. Slovensku
Ref. Cirkev Na Slovensku
Slezska Cirkev Evangelicka A.V.
Evangelische Kirche A.u.H.B. in Oesterreich
A Magyarorszagi Evangelikus Egyhaz
A Magyarorszagi Reformatus Egyhaz, Baptist Church
of Hungary
Reformed Christian Church
in Yugoslavia
Ekklesia tes Ellados
Greek Evangelical Church
Church of Cyprus

Synod of the
Evangelical Church
of North Iran

Ecumenical Patriarchate
of Constantinople Cairo
Greek Orthodox Patriarchate
of Antioch
Teheran

Union of the Armenian Churches
in the Near East

The Presbyterian
Church of Jamaica
Anglican Church
of the West Indies
Georgetown

Biserica lutherana Ungara
din Romania
Biserica Protestanta
Evangelica din Romania
dupa Confesiunea dela Augsburg
Biserica Reformata din Romania
The Church of the Province of West Africa

Greek Orthodox
Patriarchate of Alexandria

Coptic Orthodox
Church

Presbyterian
Church of Ghana
NIGERIA

Ethiopian Orthodox
Church. Addis
Ababa
Presbyterian Church
of East Africa
KENYA

Greek Orthodox
Patriarchate of
Jerusalem

INDIA

Rangoon
Burma
Baptist
Church

Methodist Church
of Ceylon

SOUTH
AMERICA
BRAZIL

Igreja Metodista
do Brasil
Curitiba
Federação Sinodal,
Igreja Evangélica de
Confisão Lutherana no Brasil

Sinado Evangelico Aleman
del Rio de la Plata
ARGENTINA

Bantu Presbyterian Church of South Africa
Church of the Province of South Africa
Congregational Union " " "
Methodist Church of South Africa
Ned. Gereformeerde Kerke van de Kaap Provinsie
" " " Transvaal
SOUTH AFRICA

Church of the
Province of
Central Africa

Nyasaland

Nederduits Hervormde
Kerk van Afrika
Presbyterian Church
of South Africa

Church of India, Pakistan
and Ceylon
Church of South India
Federation of Evangelical
Lutheran Churches in India
Mar Thoma Syrian Church
of Malabar
Orthodox Syrian Church of
Malabar Catholicate
United Church of Northern
India and Pakistan

France Eglise de la Confession d'Augsbourg d'Alsace et de Lorraine
Eglise Evangelique Lutherienne de France. Eglise Reformee de France
Eglise Reformee d'Alsace et de Lorraine

Evangelisch-Lutherische Landeskirche Hannovers
Evangelisch-Lutherische Kirche in Bayern
Evangelisch-Lutherische Kirche in Thuringen
Evangelisch-Lutherische Landeskirche Schleswig-Holsteins
Evangelisch-Lutherische Landeskirche in
Hamburgischen Staate
Evangelisch-lutherische Landeskirche Mecklenburgs
Braunschweigische Evangelisch-Lutherische Landes-
Evangelisch-Lutherische Kirche in Lübeck kirche
Evangelisch-Lutherische Landeskirche in
Schaumburg-Lippe
Evangelische Landeskirche in Württemberg

Evangelisch-Lutherische Kirche in Oldenburg
Evangelisch-Lutherische Landeskirche Eutin
Evangelische Kirche in Hessen und Nassau
Evangelische Landeskirche in Kurhessen-Waldeck
Vereinigte Evangelisch-Protestantische Landeskirche Badens
Vereinigte Protestantische Kirche der Pfalz
Evangelische Landeskirche Anhalts
Bremische Evangelische Kirche
Evangelisch-Reformierte Kirche in Nordwestdeutschland
Lippische Landeskirche
Vereinigung der Deutschen Mennonitengemeinden

Chapter 18

The Growth of the Ecumenical Movement

THE HISTORY of the Christian church has constantly been marked by two major drives: toward expansion and toward integration. In the nineteenth century, especially in the Protestant world, the theme of expansion was dominant, but in the twentieth century the movements toward integration and consolidation have been the most conspicuous. The concern for the reintegration of Christendom has manifested itself in many ways. The term "ecumenical movement" is a generic one, which refers to a whole range of movements and tendencies toward reunion, not all of them wholly consistent with each other. Of greatest importance in Protestant affairs, the ecumenical movement has also involved most of the Eastern Orthodox churches. The Roman Catholic church for a long time took no official part in ecumenical discussion or action. The encyclical *Mortalium Animos* (1928) declared that the only way in which the unity of Christianity could be fostered would be "by furthering the return to the one true Church of Christ of those who are separated from it," which would involve their believing in "the infallibility of the Roman Pontiff in the sense of the Ecumenical Vatican Council with the same faith as they believe in the Incarnation of Our Lord." This uncompromising attitude kept the door to Catholic participation in the ecumenical movement closed until a dramatic reversal took place during the pontificate of John XXIII (see VII:19).

The ecumenical movement became prominent in the twentieth century, but its historical roots run deep, indeed as far back as the sixteenth century. It was in the nineteenth century, however, that there were launched specific movements in half a dozen areas of Protestant life and thought which were to flower into world interdenominational agencies and stimulate a number of organic church unions in the twentieth century.

The first and in many ways the most important of these areas was the missionary enterprise. On the mission fields, the evils of competitive denominationalism and the need for coordination became especially obvious. The missionary thrust of the nineteenth century had many interdenominational features from the beginning, for many of the missionary societies drew support from Christians across denominational lines. On the field, gatherings of missionaries for fellowship and discussion developed early. The first such meetings on a world scale took place in New York and in London in 1854, to be followed by others at irregular intervals. The eighth in the series of gatherings was the World Missionary Conference held at Edinburgh in 1910. This affair differed from its predecessors, however, in that most of those who attended came not only as deeply interested individuals, but also as official delegates of the various missionary societies. A feature of the assembly was its thorough advance preparation, including the preliminary circulation of carefully prepared study volumes. Representatives of the missionary or younger churches were present, giving a good account of themselves. At Edinburgh, many individuals who were to play an important role in the many areas of twentieth-century ecumenical development received inspiration and direction.

That conference marked the turning point in ecumenical history. A continuation committee, set up to preserve the gains made at Edinburgh, grew by 1921 into the International Missionary Council. Its first chairman was the American Methodist layman who had presided at Edinburgh, John R. Mott (1865–1955). Membership in the council was held chiefly by the national and regional interdenominational missionary organizations, such as the Committee of the German Evangelical Missions (founded in 1885), the Foreign Missions Conference of North America (1893), and the Conference of Missionary Societies of Great Britain and Ireland (1912). It encouraged the development of national Christian councils in the lands of the younger churches, especially in India, China, Japan, the Congo, and the Near East. This period of growing missionary cooperation was also a period of rapid devolution in the missionary enterprise, so that by the middle of the twentieth century some 90 percent of the personnel in Protestant mission fields were nationals of the country in which the mission was operating. The increasing significance of the younger churches was reflected in the meetings of the I.M.C. at Jerusalem in 1928 and Madras in 1938. At the former, the younger church leaders constituted about a quarter of the delegation; at the latter, slightly more than half.

A second area of growing ecumenical activity was that of youth work and Christian education. A pioneer, nondenominational agency of considerable ecumenical significance has been the Young Men's Christian Association, founded in London by George Williams (1821–1905) in 1844, and since spread throughout the world. The World's Alliance of the Y.M.C.A. was established in 1855. That same year, the Young Women's Christian Association was organized in London, and the World's Y.W.C.A. was founded in 1894. Another important movement among young people was the Student Volunteer Movement for Foreign Missions, which had its origins in 1886 at one of Dwight L. Moody's summer conferences at Mt. Hermon, Massachusetts. John R. Mott served as its organizer and for many years as its chairman. Under his leadership, the World's Student Christian Federation was created in Sweden in 1895.

The student Christian movements of various lands were characterized by prophetic and pioneering aspects; they served as a training ground for men and women who later became conspicuous in the various areas of ecumenical life. These world student fellowships were predominantly lay movements, and the World Christian Education movement also was strongly lay in character. World's Sunday School conventions met regularly beginning in 1889. In 1907, the World's Sunday School Association was formed. It became in 1924 a federation of national and interdenominational Christian education agencies, and then was renamed the World Council on Christian Education and Sunday School Association (1947, 1950).

A third area of ecumenical development was that of federation for Christian service and common ethical action, the area that came to be called "Life and Work." A pioneer of this general approach was Samuel S. Schmucker (see VII:15), who published his *Fraternal Appeal to the American Churches: With a Plan for Catholic Union on Apostolic Principles* in 1838. His was a federal plan, in which the existing denominations, practically intact, would become branches of the Apostolic Protestant church. Though the time was scarcely ripe for the serious discussion of such plans, they did contribute to the longing for some fuller unity. An early organizational expression in this area, though composed wholly of interested individuals, was the Evangelical Alliance, organized in London in 1846. It sponsored world conferences and served as a sounding board for evangelical opinion. It was especially active in the defense of religious liberty and accomplished much in this field. But it was not in official relationship with the communions, and as the century progressed, this was seen to be desirable. The last prominent secretary of the American branch of the Evangelical Alliance (organized in 1867) was Josiah Strong (1847–1916), but he resigned in 1898 to take an active part in the organization of the Federal Council of the Churches of Christ in America. Founded finally in 1908, it had about thirty American denominations as members, including many, but not all, of the major bodies. The professed objects of the council were: (1) to express the fellowship and catholic unity of the Christian church; (2) to bring the Christian bodies of America into united service for Christ and the world; (3) to encourage devotional fellowship and mutual counsel concerning the spiritual life and religious activities of the churches; (4) to secure a larger combined influence for the churches of Christ in all matters affecting the moral and social condition of the people, so as to promote the application of the law of Christ in every relation of human life; and (5) to assist in the organization of local branches of the council to promote its aim in their communities. In 1950, it merged with a number of other interdenominational agencies of the United States—those concerned with home and foreign missions, missionary and religious education, higher education, stewardship, and women's work—to form the National Council of the Churches of Christ in the U.S.A. In other lands, similar organizations were formed—in France in 1905, Switzerland in 1920, Britain in 1942, Canada in 1944.

On the global level, the federative approach found its most conspicuous champion in Nathan Söderblom (1866–1931), Swedish Luthern pastor and scholar, later archbishop of Uppsala. Veteran of the Student Christian Movement, he was convinced that the churches could serve together in common ethical action despite deep doctrinal differences. His driving energy led to the first Universal Christian Conference on Life and Work, held at Stockholm in 1925. The conference made a rapid survey of the social needs of the world, appealed to the conscience of the Christian world, and indicated possible lines of advance. A continuation committee grew into the Universal Christian Council for Life and Work in 1930. It called a second world gathering, the Conference on Church, Community, and State, held at Oxford in 1937. The theological foundations of ethical action, which had been "overlooked" at Stockholm, were carefully explored, and the distinctive role of the church in the world was given attention.

A fourth area of ecumenical activity was in some ways the most precarious, for it involved the frank facing of the most crucial doctrinal differences, which often did not need to be directly confronted in the other areas. The original Protestant ecumenical discussions in the sixteenth century had broken down over issues such as "faith and order," and there was hesitation in raising them again. Yet specific proposals for Christian unity in any full sense could not avoid them. For example, when the American Episcopalian William Reed Huntington (1838–1918) sought to state the minimum "essentials" of Anglicanism as a basis for reunion discussion, he named four items: (1) the Holy Scriptures as the word of God; (2) the primitive creeds as the rule of faith; (3) the two sacraments ordained by Christ himself; and (4) the historic episcopate as the keystone of the unity of church government. Approved with slight modifications by the American Episcopal House of Bishops and the Anglican Lambeth Conference in the 1880s, this "Chicago-Lambeth Quadrilateral" clearly showed how central in unity discussions matters of faith and order were. An American Episcopal missionary bishop, Charles H. Brent (1862–1929), had caught a new vision at Edinburgh in 1910—a vision of a reunited church, but it could come about only through discussion of doctrinal matters which had been omitted at Edinburgh. He called on his own communion to take the lead in the area of "faith and order." After years of preparation, the first World Conference on Faith and Order met at Lausanne in 1927. Over four hundred delegates represented over one hundred religious bodies. Some of the deepest issues between the communions were given full discussion, surprisingly large areas of agreement were found, and a spirit of friendship prevailed. A continuation committee carried on the movement, summoning the next conference for Edinburgh in 1937. That gathering prepared a remarkable statement, "The Grace of Our Lord Jesus Christ," prefaced with the judgment, "There is in connection with this subject no ground for maintaining division between Churches." But with respect to the ministry and sacraments, very deep differences were revealed, pointing to matters that needed further illumination. Yet it seemed generally accepted that, in the doctrinal realm, the agreements between the churches covered perhaps 85 percent of the ground.

Many suggestions had been advanced for the uniting of Life and Work with Faith and Order into a world council. The two 1937 conferences had been planned to meet in sequence. Both conferences voted for integration, and at Utrecht in 1938 a provisional structure for a world council was prepared. The "Basis" adopted for the council was: "The World Council of Churches is a fellowship of Churches which accept our Lord Jesus Christ as God and Saviour." Taking the lead in these developments was William Temple (1881–1944), then archbishop of York and later (1942) of Canterbury. Philosopher and theologian, Temple had played important roles in student Christian movements, the International Missionary Council, Life and Work, and Faith and Order. Now he became chairman of the provisional committee of the World Council of Churches "in process of formation." During the difficult years of the Second World War (1939–1945), the committee carried out an active role from its headquarters in Geneva in providing for orphaned missions, caring for prisoners of war, and helping with refugees. It served especially as a link between the Christian churches of Germany and those of other nations during the period of Hitler's ascendancy.

Almost immediately after the Nazis had taken power in Germany in 1933, the churches had been pressed to conform to the militaristic and anti-Semitic directions of the Third Reich. Many Christians did support the Third Reich; even after its true character became clearer, church opposition was slow in developing and was divided between those who struggled actively against it and those who engaged in passive resistance. Both types participated in the Confessing Church movement, which was supported by about a tenth of the congregations of the Protestant churches of Germany and which stated its theological opposition to Nazism in the Barmen Declaration of 1934. The state responded with restrictions on church programs and with persecution; by 1937, there were mass arrests of both lay and clerical leaders, including the famous Martin Niemöller (1892–1984), a Lutheran pastor who had been a submarine commander in the First World War. When the Second World War broke out in 1939, the restrictions and persecutions increased as Hitler sought to crush all opposition; the great majority of pastors supporting the Confessing Church were drafted into the army. The provisional committee of the World Council of Churches followed these developments closely and gave what support it could to the beleaguered churches. It maintained ties between those engaged in the church struggle in Germany and those of other lands throughout the war.[1] Seeds of later ecumenical cooperation between Protestants and Catholics were nourished as courageous underground resisters to the Nazis learned to trust each other and to work together; in the face of overwhelming common threats, the historical enmities between these traditions seemed less important.

What had been interrupted by the war was finally brought to completion at Amsterdam in 1948, when 145 churches from 44 countries participated in the completion of the organization of the World Council, approving the Basis. It was made clear that the council could have no constitutional authority over the member churches. Most of the major Protestant bodies of Europe and the British Isles, the majority of those of America and Australasia, and several of the Orthodox communions became members. Many of the younger churches of Asia and Africa also joined. The World Council continued to keep close ties with the World's Alliance of the Y.M.C.A., the World's Y.W.C.A., and the World's Student Christian Federation. World conferences of Christian youth—held at Amsterdam in 1939, Oslo in 1947, and Travancore in 1952—were initiated jointly by those world bodies.

At the second assembly of the World Council of Churches, held in Evanston, Illinois, in 1954, the delegates of 161 churches determined to "grow together," even as certain theological differences over the nature of Christian hope came into contention. The third assembly, meeting in New Delhi, India, in 1961, admitted many new churches, bringing the total membership to 198. Among the additions were the Russian Orthodox and other Slav Orthodox churches, along with a number of churches in "third world" countries, including two Pentecostal bodies. Another important step at that gathering was the merger of the International Missionary Council with the World Council.

A fifth area of ecumenical concern has been that of organic church union. Some of the specific unions have been intraconfessional or within a denominational family. Conspicuous among such achievements were the Presbyterian reunions in Scotland. The United Secession and Relief churches (see VII:7) combined as the United Presbyterian church in 1847. In 1900, the latter body combined with the majority of the Free Church of Scotland, the result of the Disruption of 1843, to form the United Free Church of Scotland. A small minority of the old Free Church (the "Wee Frees") refused to enter the union. In 1874, the rights of patronage, the original ground of the divisions, had been abolished by law. But it took many years of discussion to clear the way for the larger reunion. In 1921, Parliament passed a bill allowing the church to legislate for itself in all matters of doctrine and practice without interference by the state, but also declaring that it was the duty of the nation to render homage to God and seek to promote his kingdom. In 1929, the union was

---

[1] See Ruth Rouse and Stephen C. Neill, eds., *A History of the Ecumenical Movement, 1517–1948*, 2d ed. (Philadelphia, 1967), pp. 708–719.

consummated, and 90 percent of the Presbyterians of the country—probably more than two-thirds of the population—became members of the established Church of Scotland.

In the United States, there have been a number of denominational reunions. In 1918, the Lutheran General Synod and General Council merged with the United Synod of the South to form the United Lutheran Church. In 1930, the synods of Buffalo, Iowa, and Ohio united as the American Lutheran Church. A series of mergers in the early 1960s brought almost all Lutherans in the United States into three major bodies: the Lutheran Church in America (including the United and Augustana churches), the Lutheran Church—Missouri Synod, and The American Lutheran Church (including the American, Evangelical, and Lutheran Free churches).

The northern Presbyterian Church united with the major part of the Cumberland Presbyterian Church in 1906, and in 1958 it joined with the United Presbyterian Church to form the United Presbyterian Church in the United States of America. In 1983, this church united with the (southern) Presbyterian Church in the United States to form The Presbyterian Church (U.S.A.).

The Methodist Church was the result in 1939 of the reunion of the Methodist Episcopal Church, the Methodist Episcopal Church South, and the Methodist Protestant Church (which had broken away from the larger body of Methodists over a century earlier). Seven years later, two groups of German Methodist background united as the Evangelical United Brethren Church. This church in turn joined with the Methodists in 1968 to form the United Methodist Church. The Unitarian and Universalist churches came together in 1961 as the Unitarian Universalist Association.

Church unions across denominational lines—i.e., transconfessional—have also taken place. In Canada, diverse Protestant beginnings had led to much complexity of organization. The nineteenth century was a period of denominational consolidation. In Presbyterianism, there were nine unions, culminating in 1875, when four bodies came together to form the Presbyterian Church in Canada. Methodism saw eight unions, climaxing in 1884, when again four bodies came together to compose the Methodist Church of Canada. Many small Congregational bodies found unity as three strands came together in 1906 and 1907. But in a land of vast territory and scattered population, the need for closer Protestant accord was great, and the movement for a united church began at the turn of the century. A "Basis of Union" drew from the Presbyterian standards and the Methodist Twenty-five Articles, and the plan of government combined features from the various traditions. It was soon recognized that Anglicans and Baptists would not be included and that a large Presbyterian minority was opposed to union. Only after long years of work and many bitter exchanges was the United Church of Canada brought into being in 1925; a little more than a third of the Presbyterians remained out.

In the lands of the younger churches occurred one of the most important unions, involving Congregational, Presbyterian, and Episcopal polities. In 1908, the South India United Church (see VII:13) had brought together Presbyterian and Congregational missions. This was but the beginning; soon Methodists and Anglicans became involved in union negotiations that went on for years. The basic agreement that paved the way for larger union was that all ministers at the time of union would be accepted with equal rights and status, though congregations would be safeguarded against having thrust upon them ministries they were not prepared to accept. Then, for thirty years, all ordinations would be carried out by bishops with the assistance of presbyters. In 1947, the Church of South India was inaugurated. Five Anglican bishops were reelected, and nine new bishops were elected and consecrated. A million Indian Christians were brought together into one independent, indigenous communion.[2]

In the United States, the formation of the United Church of Christ in 1957 brought four different denominational traditions together. The Congregational and Christian churches (the latter originated in the frontier revivalist movement of the early nineteenth century) had united in 1931. Three years later, the German Reformed Church and the Evangelical Association (formed in the 1840s when groups of pietistic German-speaking immigrants of Lutheran and Reformed backgrounds began to work together) united as the Evangelical and Reformed Church. Efforts to bring these two recently merged communions together in the United Church of Christ were sharply opposed by minorities, but in 1961 the union of 1957 was ratified by an overwhelming majority of the congregations on both sides. In time, a still larger united church may develop. In 1962, a Consultation on Church Union began work. Nine denominations were participating by the end of the decade, including those of congregational, connectional, and episcopal polities, and involving three black communions of Methodist background.

A sixth area of ecumenical activity was the formation of world denominational associations or fellowships. At times, these seem to work at cross-purposes to other areas of ecumenical concern, but in general they continue on the principle that such bodies as the World Council of Churches cannot be stronger than the churches which are its members. In some respects, the Lambeth Conference of Anglican Bishops (1867) was the first such denominational world organization, though as a meeting of bishops it is quite different from the others, except perhaps the Conference of Old Catholic Bishops (1889). In 1875, what later became the World Alliance of Reformed Churches was formed, and then the World Methodist Council in 1881, the International Congregational Council in 1891, the Baptist World Alliance in 1905, the

---

[2] For a summary of the many plans for church union and reunion between 1910 and 1952, including both those completed and those then in prospect, see ibid., pp. 496–505.

Lutheran World Federation in 1923, the World Convention of the Churches of Christ in 1930, the International Association for Liberal Christianity and Religious Freedom in 1930, and the Friends' World Committee for Consultation in 1937. Most of these bodies entered into a consultative relationship with the World Council and have come to be called "Christian world fellowships."

The Protestant world was influenced in the twentieth century not only by the ecumenical movement but also by a theological revival. In the early years of the century, attention to theological issues were generally minimized. But fresh attention to biblical and systematic theology arose soon after the First World War in Europe. The most powerful spokesmen for the new "dialectical" or "crisis" theology were H. Emil Brunner (1889–1966) and especially Karl Barth (1886–1968), Reformed pastor and theologian, author of the influential *Church Dogmatics* (13 vols., 1932–1967). Criticizing the schools of Schleiermacher and Ritschl for their subjectivism and relativism, Barth put great emphasis on the otherness of God, the centrality of revelation, and the sinful nature of man. His many works have been controversial, but they have contributed to a wide and serious discussion of theological questions. The theological renaissance was further stimulated by churchly resistance to Nazi totalitarianism; the German Barmen Declaration of 1934 insisted that Jesus Christ is the only word of God that humans are to hear, trust, and obey.

In the United States, a change in theological atmosphere began in the 1930s, as "Christian realism" criticized what it saw as the idealistic assumptions and utopian illusions of much American theology, and mediated the new theological currents to the American scene. Central figures in this development were the Niebuhr brothers and Paul Tillich. The persistent search for a sound theological basis for social ethics led Reinhold Niebuhr (1892–1971) to produce works of major importance, especially *The Nature and Destiny of Man* (1941–1943). H. Richard Niebuhr (1894–1962) combined theological, sociological, and ethical analyses in his lifetime of creative work; a characteristic volume was *Christ and Culture* (1951). Tillich (1886–1965) came to America as a refugee from Hitler's Germany and became an important influence in the theological and intellectual worlds; his mature thought is presented in the three-volume *Systematic Theology* (1951–1963).

The ecumenical movement, especially as it was focused in the World Council of Churches, reflected the theological contributions of these and other biblically oriented theologians, and in turn served as a transmitter of them. A liturgical renaissance was also at work in world Protestantism, significantly changing levels of understanding and practice in worship. A number of communions revised their liturgies, while the free churches tended to incorporate certain liturgical elements into their worship. The interest of a number of Catholic and Protestant scholars in biblical study and liturgical reform helped to prepare the way for a remarkable ecumenical breakthrough in the 1960s.

Chapter 19

The Church in the World

*I*N MANY AREAS of the world immediately following the Second World War, Christian churches, especially in the West, seemed to be institutionally quite stable. The establishment of the United Nations (1945) provided an international forum for dealing with tensions between nations and maintaining peace. Though the peace was soon strained by the "cold war" between Communism and the Western powers, the churches were hopeful of continued advance.

The Roman Catholic Church, under the leadership of Eugenio Pacelli, who took the name Piux XII (1939–1958), outwardly maintained its centralized and conservative stance. Pius XII maintained in its essentials the stand that Pius IX had taken in the later nineteenth century: the church would remain in its fortress, proclaiming its truths to a world in turmoil, seeking to avoid fragmentation in the face of hostile forces. Pius XII worked for peace in time of war; he felt inhibited from speaking openly in condemnation of the Holocaust in Germany that was destroying millions of European Jews for fear of making the situation worse for them and for Catholics. His opposition to "Marxist atheism" led him to refuse any contact with Communist states, and he forbade the cooperation of Catholics with such regimes. He had no interest in the ecumenical movement, nor did he allow Catholics to participate in the World Council of Churches. Confident of the teaching authority of the Catholic church in matters of natural law and morality, he spoke and wrote on a wide variety of subjects. An austere, isolated leader, he did make effective use of the media of modern communications, and he became a familiar figure in the church and world of his time. The promulgation in 1950 of the dogma of the bodily assumption into heaven of the Virgin Mary was consistent with the spirit of the dominant nineteenth-century currents in the church, while the encyclical *Humani generis* (1950) warned against major departures in philosophical or theological thought.

The Protestant and Orthodox churches in many lands showed significant institutional resilience. In North America, there was an unexpected postwar revival of religion, while in Germany there was a notable resurgence of the laity, especially through the evangelical academies, in which laypersons planned strategies for Christian witness in their daily vocations, and through the great *Kirchentag* gatherings, which drew vast numbers into annual week-long periods of study and renewal.

The closing of mainland China to missionary work and the isolation of the remaining churches was a serious loss to world Christianity, but in other parts of the world most churches seemed to be successfully making the transition to indigenous and autonomous patterns. The World Council of Churches, under the leadership of its first general secretary, Dutch-born Willem A. Visser 't Hooft (1900–   ), enjoyed a steadily increasing membership. Though there were many theological currents flowing through the ecumenical world, the influence of revelational, christocentric biblical theology was pervasive through the 1950s.

In the next several decades, however, there was increasing concern among the churches about the trends toward secularization, especially in the West. The increase of nationalism across the world often meant that religious life was relegated more and more to the private sphere, conspicuously in communist-dominated areas, less obviously but still visibly in what had been "Christendom." References to a "post-Christian" society increased as the general cultural influence of Christianity seemed to decrease. In the United States, the postwar revival of the churches was followed by a slump in the 1960s and 1970s, in which a number of the historic major Protestant ceased growing and in some cases lost members. Other churches, especially among the more conservatively oriented traditions, continued to grow numerically. On the world scene as a whole, however, the patterns of an increasing religious pluralism combined with the eroding effects of secularism tended to weaken the public impact of the churches.

In many parts of the Christian church, therefore, there was a deep restlessness. As nation after nation of Asia and Africa became independent and threw off the bonds of colonialism, there often arose in the churches of those lands a questioning of Western ways of worshiping God, organizing churches, and formulating theologies. There surged up a conviction in the "third world" that the rich nations of Europe and North America, both capitalist and communist, especially the United States and the Soviet Union, were growing richer while the poor nations were growing relatively poorer. The institutional self-centeredness and complacency of many Western churches fell under considerable attack, both from within them and from the outside, for there was increasing conviction that churches should show much more concern than they had with the plight of the world's poorer and less powerful people, many of whom were black, or brown, or yellow.

Growing sensitivity to the world's injustices and imbalances, combined with increasing irritation over the use of military force, led to deepening criticism of the institutional barriers among Catholic, Orthodox, and Protestant Christians, for these hindered effective cooperation for human good. Collaboration between Catholics and Protestants in opposition to totalitarianism in the 1930s had provided some precedents which were not forgotten. A longing for renewal and reform at deeper levels than the postwar revival of religion had offered was frequently expressed; dissatisfactions with traditional styles of piety and organization in the church emerged. Among laypersons and youth especially, there arose considerable overt as well as covert criticism.

The impetus for renewal and reform in the Roman Catholic Church, however, came unexpectedly from the top. When Angelo Giuseppe Roncalli was elevated to the pontificate in 1958 and took the name John XXIII[1] (1958–1963), many felt that his was to be a "caretaker" administration. But as a church diplomat, he had had considerable experience with social and political movements of various kinds. His assignments in Bulgaria, Turkey, France, and Germany had brought him into contact with Orthodox and non-Catholic worlds and with many types of political groupings. As pope, he manifested a determination to guide his church toward a reconsideration of its patterns of faith and life in view of the world's needs, and also toward genuine ecumenical relations with other Christian churches. Early in 1959, he announced that he would convoke the Twenty-first Ecumenical Council (Vatican II), to which would be gathered the bishops of the Roman church from all over the world. In 1960, he established the Secretariat for Promoting Christian Unity and named Augustin Cardinal Bea (1881–1968) as its head, thus providing an effective channel for dialogue with other churches. The pope named five official observers to attend the third assembly of the World Council of Churches, and he invited Protestant and Orthodox communions to send observers to Vatican II; many accepted the invitation.

John XXIII's concern for human needs and world problems was reflected in two notable encyclicals. *Mater et magistra* (1961) was an updating of Catholic social teaching in the tradition of *Rerum novarum* and *Quadragesimo anno,* issued on the 70th and 30th anniversaries, respectively, of those documents. *Pacem in terris* (1963) was devoted to establishing conditions which could lead to universal peace in truth, justice, charity, and liberty. It declared that "all men are equal in their natural dignity" and called for the end of the arms race, stressed the growing interdependence of national economies, and instructed Catholics to work with people of other faiths for the common good.

---

[1] No pope had used the name John since 1415, when the earlier John XXIII, one of the three rival popes at the end of the great schism, had sullied the name and had been deposed at the Council of Constance (see V:14). By selecting it, Pope John restored for the papacy a name that has been much loved in Christian history and has been taken by more popes than any other.

After more than three years of preparation, Vatican II opened on October 11, 1962, in St. Peter's Basilica in Rome. It soon became apparent that the desired "updating" (*aggiornamento*) of the church would not be easy, for progressive and reactionary forces among the more than two thousand bishops present disagreed on many particulars. The spirit of reformism and ecumenism did break through during the first session, though the council adjourned on December 8 with no appreciable completed results.

John XXIII died the following June. His successor, Giovanni Battista Montini, Paul VI (1963–1978), determined to complete and implement the council, which met for three more sessions, each fall. Pope Paul did not emerge as the charismatic figure his predecessor had been, but his concern for reconciliation with others was dramatized by his journey to the Holy Land early in 1964, during which he met with the patriarch of Constantinople. An outcome was the issuance, on December 7, 1965, of identical statements from Rome and Constantinople regretting the offensive words and reprehensible gestures on both sides accompanying the sad events of the separation of 1054, and removing the sentences of excommunication.

The first completed work of Vatican II was the Constitution on the Sacred Liturgy.[2] Building on the work of the liturgical movement, it provided for the revision of the rite of the Mass and for its more communal celebration. Sixteen other texts were adopted by the council fathers, varying in length from the Declaration on the Relationship of the Church to Non-Christian Religions, which ran just over a thousand words, to the Pastoral Constitution on the Church in the Modern World, of more than twenty-three thousand words. The former referred primarily to the sensitive area of Jewish-Christian relations and has been criticized as weak in part and as somewhat abstruse. It did deplore any form of anti-Semitism and any discrimination or harassment because of race, color, condition of life, or religion, and it encouraged dialogue with members of non-Christian religions and cooperation with them for the common good. The Pastoral Constitution on the Church in the Modern World was addressed not only to the faithful but to "the whole of humanity," and it consciously directed the church to the service of the family of man. It instructed clergy and laity to collaborate in a ministry of service, so that a more human and humane world might emerge, despite the dehumanizing aspects of technological society. Many overtones of John XXIII's "social encyclicals" echoed in the text.

One of the unfinished tasks of Vatican I was the completion of a Constitution on the Church—the abrupt end of that council left only the chapters on the papacy enacted. Meanwhile, some significant statements on the church had been produced, especially Pius XII's important encyclical, *Mystici corporis*

---

[2] For the texts adopted by the council in English translation, see Austin Flannery, ed., *Vatican Council II: The Conciliar and Post-Conciliar Documents* (Wilmington, DE, 1975).

Christi (1943). Much preparation went toward Vatican II's Dogmatic Constitution on the Church; the draft was revised many times during the sessions. Widely held to be the masterpiece of the council, the text moved away from hierarchical and juridical emphases to a more biblical, historical, and dynamic position. Of central importance was the stress on collegiality, on the priestly role of all bishops who, with the pope, collectively form a "college" responsible for guiding the church. A final chapter on the Virgin was placed in this text so that Mariology would not be isolated from other theological and ecclesiological matters. Affirming the various titles that had been accorded Mary by the church, the Constitution on the Church declared that "they neither take away from nor add anything to the dignity and efficacy of Christ the one Mediator" (III, 62).[3]

Pastoral and ecumenical, this constitution opened the way for fruitful dialogue with Orthodox, Anglican, and Protestant theologians. Some of its positions were speedily implemented; early in the final session of the council, Paul VI instituted a Synod of Bishops, in which representatives of the episcopate throughout the world meet regularly at Rome.

Vatican II produced another fundamental theological document, the Dogmatic Constitution on Divine Revelation. Its text was much informed by general ecumenical scholarship on revelation and its transmission, moving away from earlier attitudes toward Scripture and tradition as "sources of revelation." It took modern methods of biblical interpretation seriously, in keeping with the tone of a forward-looking encyclical of Pius XII, *Divino afflante Spiritu* (1943). It viewed revelation as God's manifestation of himself, of his will and intentions, publicly granted to humanity. Scripture *contains* revelation in the form of a written record, along with accounts of its effects and of human reactions to it. The biblical writings are read and interpreted by the living community of the church in its ongoing tradition of understanding and explanation under the leadership of the magisterium guided by the Holy Spirit. The document closed by emphasizing the importance of easy access to Scripture by all the faithful, in suitable and correct translations. "And if, given the opportunity and the approval of Church authority, these translations are produced in cooperation with the separated brethren as well, all Christians will be able to use them" (VI, 22). One result of this judgment was the approval for Catholic use of the Revised Standard Version of the Bible, which had been prepared primarily by Protestant scholarship.

Of particular interest to the non-Catholic world was the council's Decree on Ecumenism. Down to the pontificate of John XXIII, Catholic ecumenism had meant largely work for the return of all Christians to the Roman Catholic Church, and that communion did not join officially in the many aspects of the

---

[3] Parenthetical references following a quotation from a text give the chapter and section numbers of the document from which the quotation is drawn.

ecumenical movement. The Decree on Ecumenism formally marked an about-face and put the Roman Catholic Church squarely in the ecumenical movement, calling on the faithful to take an active part in the work of ecumenism. Admitting that the divisions among Christians have been the result of sin on both sides, the text spoke of those outside the Roman church as "separated Churches and Communities" which suffer from certain defects of doctrine, discipline, or structure and yet which "have by no means been deprived of significance and importance in the mystery of salvation" (I, 3). Cooperation with them by Catholics should be encouraged especially in regions where social and technical evolution is taking place, and dialogue on matters of faith should be undertaken. Under certain special circumstances, corporate prayer is deemed desirable. Protestant comment on this decree was generally favorable, though there was some uneasiness concerning the continuing tension between its sincere ecumenical spirit and the assumption that the Roman Catholic is the only true church.

Originally a part of the draft of the Decree on Ecumenism was a section that became the Declaration on Religious Freedom. It touched off an intensive, vigorous, often emotional debate at the council, for it affirmed positions on religious freedom which had been rejected in such statements as the Syllabus of Errors. The declaration unequivocally declared that "all men are to be immune from coercion on the part of individuals or of social groups and of any human power, in such wise that in matters religious no one is to be forced to act in a manner contrary to his own beliefs" (I, 2). It affirmed that religious freedom has its foundation in the dignity of the person, which can be known both by human reason through historical experience and by revelation. The document contributed significantly to a new straightforwardness in Catholic relations with other churches and in secular affairs. But in opening up a topic for continued attention—the theological meaning of Christian freedom—the decree in time may prove to have unexpected ramifications.

Most of the other conciliar documents were decrees dealing largely with practical matters of church life, such as the episcopal office, priestly formation, the renewal of the religious life, the ministry and life of priests, missions, and education. On December 8, 1965, the council was formally closed. Prophetically, the last message of the council was to the youth of the world, who must live in it "at the period of the most gigantic transformations ever realized in its history." They were exhorted to open their hearts to the dimensions of the world, to place their energies at the service of their brothers, to build in enthusiasm a better world than their elders had.

Vatican II was accorded much attention by the press; it was a major event in world as in church history. Its impact quickly began to be felt, within the fold and in the ecumenical movement. Liturgical reform came quickly, with the very extensive use of the vernacular in the Mass. The structures of the national hierarchies were reorganized in many instances. In the United States, for example, a National Conference of Catholic Bishops was organized in 1966; it became responsible for the United States Catholic Conference, a continuation of the National Welfare Conference.

More dramatic was the rapid escalation of ecumenical contacts between Catholics and other Christians. A joint "working group" of the Secretariat for Promoting Christian Unity and the World Council of Churches was established in 1965. Official Catholic representation in the Faith and Order Commission of the World Council was initiated, and the possibility of formal Roman Catholic membership in the council was publicly discussed.

In various countries, depending on the situation, parallel manifestations developed. In the United States, a joint working group was established by the National Council of Churches and the Bishops' Committee for Ecumenical and Interreligious Affairs. The latter agency has been responsible for the initiation of a number of bilateral theological dialogues between Catholics and representatives of other traditions: Baptist, Disciples, Episcopal, Lutheran, Methodist, Reformed, Presbyterian, and Orthodox. Various Catholic parishes and dioceses joined or began to cooperate with local or regional councils of churches, which sometimes were reorganized to meet new needs. At local levels, dialogues between Catholic and other Christian laypersons developed impressively.

The epochal changes in Catholicism did raise some serious problems. A number of the faithful were bewildered by the changes and troubled by the waning of past customs. Others had their hopes for rejuvenation and freedom raised so high that the bureaucratic reformism that was offered appeared much too slow and authoritarian; some of these drifted into "free" or "underground" churches, while others abandoned the faith.

Pope Paul reaffirmed the church's traditional stand on birth control in the encyclical *Humanae vitae* (1968), in which all forms of artificial birth control were absolutely proscribed, despite the fact that the majority opinion of a special commission which had been called to give advice had advocated change. Many Catholic theologians and laymen took strong exception to the encyclical, finding that it was not in keeping with the expectations created by the Pastoral Constitution on the Church in the Modern World. A new freedom was being expressed within the church; statements even from the highest sources were being read critically. Tension over the rule of clerical celibacy was also experienced; some hoped that the longstanding rule might be relaxed. Thousands left the priesthood and the religious orders.

Despite the differences of opinion as to how far and fast the church should be renewed, Vatican II meant that a significant new step, which observers called largely irreversible, had been taken. The determination to focus on complex contemporary world problems inevitably meant that many new tensions would arise. To carry out a sweeping program of reform at a time of world turmoil, when many longed for the security of the familiar and the permanent, while others were anxious to experiment with the revolutionary, proved to be difficult. The church at the end of a decade of amazing change found itself in a time of testing as difficult as any in its history.

To summarize trends in the Protestant and Orthodox worlds for the stormy 1960s is in some ways more difficult, because there was no one center for the many communions involved—bodies with quite different traditions and styles throughout the world, most of them deployed in autonomous national structures. There was an observable trend during the decade toward deepening concern for the world, toward service to those in need and those unable to speak effectively for themselves. The move toward involvement with the secular world displayed itself in many ways, most of them controversial. In ecumenical gatherings, attention to the world and its problems absorbed increasing attention. This did not mean that questions of theology and churchmanship were neglected.

The World Council always strove to keep the interests of life and work and of faith and order in creative balance. In the first dozen years of its life, many historic misunderstandings among the member churches had to be overcome, and a considerable emphasis on theological and ecclesiastical questions was necessary. Much attention continued to be given to such matters in the 1960s, yet more was devoted to the demands of ministry and service to the world. The shift was felt early in the decade. At the third assembly in New Delhi, familiar theological questions about the nature of the church and the realization of ecclesiastical unity were much debated. One of the three main sections of the assembly considered "witness," and an important part of its report was entitled "Reshaping the Witnessing Community." The section on "unity" approved the famous paragraph that became known as the "New Delhi Statement":

> We believe that the unity which is both God's will and his gift to his Church is being made visible as all in each place who are baptized into Jesus Christ and confess him as Lord and Savior are brought by the Holy Spirit into ONE fully committed fellowship, holding the one apostolic faith, preaching the one Gospel, breaking the one bread, joining in common prayer, and having a corporate life reaching out in witness and service to all and who at the same time are united with the whole Christian fellowship in all places and all ages in such wise that ministry and members are accepted by all, and that all can act and speak together as occasion requires for the tasks to which God calls his people.

Many of the theological concerns of the World Council's early years were reflected in that paragraph; the section's commentary on it made many references to past ecclesiological discussions.

The fact that the third assembly took place in India helped to dramatize the issues of hunger and poverty in much of the world. The section on "service" insisted that many of the familiar Christian forms of philanthropy and service were so dated as to be of little use in contemporary society. New ways of expressing the obedience of the servant church in the modern world had to be found, it was declared.

Theological inspiration for much of the impulse toward "worldly Christianity" in the World Council and its members was drawn in considerable part from the unfinished work of Dietrich Bonhoeffer (1906–1945), a young German theologian who was martyred in prison in the closing months of the Second World War. Some of the advocates of "secular ecumenism," especially among the younger church leaders, were impatient with older styles of faith and order discussions. The latter were continued, but on a broader and more diversified basis. The fourth World Conference on Faith and Order was held at Montreal in 1963, with Orthodox theologians in full participation, Catholic observers present, and conservative evangelicals contributing to the debates.

The shift in ecumenical emphasis toward service to the world became more pronounced as the decade wore on. In 1966, the Church and Society department of the World Council sponsored a conference in Geneva, "Christians in the Technical and Social Revolutions of Our Time." It was a unique gathering in that a larger portion of participants came from Africa, Asia, and Latin America than any previous such conference had seen. It was also the first major ecumenical conference in which a majority of the participants were laity. The new Roman Catholic ecumenical stance was demonstrated by the presence of official observers and several main speakers. Other denominations not in World Council membership were represented. The "third world" point of view, critical of the imbalance of power by which the Soviet Union and the United States exercised such decisive sway over the entire world, was forcefully presented. The vast chasm between the rich and poor nations, between the developed and the undeveloped, was dramatized in many ways; such a situation, it was agreed, should not continue, especially in view of the fact that technological means to provide enough for all were now at hand.

There was much discussion of the relationship between the revolutionary nature of the Gospel and social revolution in the contemporary world. Some espoused Christian participation in revolutionary activity, involving violence if necessary. A section report observed that in some cases where small elites rule at the expense of the welfare of the majority, Christians should participate in political movements which work toward the achievement of a just social order as quickly as possible. In such cases, the report declared, Christians need not rule out the use of revolutionary methods a priori, for "it may very well be that the use of violent methods is the only recourse of those who wish to avoid prolongation of the vast covert violence which the existing order involves."[4]

In general, the conference agreed that the church should be on the side of social revolution against serious injustice, though it was divided about the

[4] Paul R. Albrecht and M. M. Thomas, eds., *The World Conference on Church and Society* (Geneva, 1967), p. 143.

appropriate use of violence in revolution. It was emphasized that the role of Christians and churches is to work within the secular orders to humanize them, to reform society for the sake of man. They work always from a Christian perspective, sensitive to divine judgments on human affairs. The working group on theology and social ethics explained that "the discernment by Christians of what is just and unjust, human and inhuman in the complexities of political and economic change, is a discipline exercised in continual dialogue with biblical resources, the mind of the Church through history and today, and the best insights of social scientific analysis. But it remains a discipline which aims not at a theoretical system of truth but at action in human society. Its object is not simply to understand the world but to respond to the power of God which is recreating it."[5]

The findings of a conference under World Council auspices are of quite different nature from those of a Vatican Council. The gatherings are very brief in comparison (the Geneva conference lasted two weeks), and only a few ranking officials of the churches participate. Hence, such meetings cannot speak officially for the World Council or for its member churches. But in speaking *to* them, the Geneva conference revealed a strong emerging concern in the churches for the serious social, economic, and political problems of the day.

On racial matters, the unambiguous statements of previous World Council assemblies and conferences against all forms of segregation and discrimination were restated; churches were urged to oppose, openly and actively, the perpetuation of the myth of racial superiority as it finds expression in social conditions and in human behavior as well as in laws and social structures.

A high point of the gathering was a sermon by Martin Luther King, Jr. (1929–1968), prominent nonviolent leader of the civil rights movement in the United States. Founder of the Southern Christian Leadership Conference, King played an important role in the increasing church and ecumenical support of the black community's search for justice in America. Unable to be present at Geneva because of riots in Chicago, King's sermon, rejecting senseless violence and pointing out the irony of a nation founded on the principle of freedom having to undergo a continuing struggle for human rights, was taped and flown to Geneva in time for the service. Less than two years later, King, a modern Christian martyr, was to fall by the hand of an assassin.

An important convergence of Catholic, Protestant, and Orthodox concern about the church in the world was dramatized by the Beirut Conference on World Cooperation for Development, held in 1968. Jointly planned and convened by the Roman Catholic Church and the World Council of Churches, it brought together experts on world economic and political problems to develop a "strategy for development" consistent with a theological rationale. The bases

[5] Ibid., p. 201.

for discussion were the Geneva report and an encyclical of Paul VI on development and aid to the third world, *Populorum progressio* (1967), in which it was maintained that "the new word for peace is development." The conference findings urged Christians to be politically active on an ecumenical basis in ways relevant to particular local situations, ways which might include lobbying, marches, meetings, and other forms of pressure to focus governmental responsibility for undeveloped nations. It was recommended that a joint Roman Catholic–World Council Exploratory Committee on Society, Development and Peace (SODEPAX), founded the year before, be continued.

The fourth assembly of the World Council, at Uppsala, Sweden, in 1968, continued many of these lines of thought and action. By this time, the council included in its membership most of the major and a number of the smaller Protestant and Orthodox churches and enjoyed a growing cooperation with Roman Catholicism, thus providing an arena which mirrored the various tendencies and tensions of the churches. The Uppsala assembly accepted the report of the 1966 Geneva conference and responded favorably to the recommendations of the recently adjourned Beirut conference. Characteristically seeking to keep in creative balance theological concerns and attention to action and service in the world, this assembly devoted more time and energy to the latter. Such matters as war and peace, human rights, the full participation of women in human affairs, selective conscientious objection to war, racism, refugees, economic justice, nationalism and regionalism, international structures and taxation, world hunger, and world development were discussed and recommendations drafted.

In a statement adopted by the assembly, one section declared that "to be complacent in the face of the world's need is to be guilty of practical heresy."[6] World Council members were urged to cooperate actively at every level with non-member churches, non-church groups, representatives of other religions, and persons of good will everywhere for the good of humankind, and to give sacrificially for development. The American military intervention in Vietnam was sharply criticized, by American opponents of the war as well as by others. The youth participants at Uppsala reminded the delegates pointedly that they were impatient with high-sounding reports followed by little action and tired of timidity and a "business-as-usual" attitude in the face of the unjust and inhuman treatment accorded much of the world's population.

The fourth assembly was an exciting, crowded, somewhat stormy affair. Earlier assemblies were not without their drama, but their tone was calmer than this one with its frank speeches and jarring encounters. Efforts to serve the needs of the world in relevant ways brought something of the turmoil of the world into church life.

---

[6] Norman Goodall, ed., *The Uppsala Report, 1968* (Geneva, 1968), p. 51.

Such gatherings as have been described reflected many of the pressing concerns and dominant directions of the Christian church throughout the world. In many areas, of course, Christian churches went their way little influenced if at all by what was said in world assemblies, for they were struggling with problems unique to their own situations. In many congregations of Europe and America, there was little real awareness of world needs or even of neighborhood problems, but rather an internal institutional focus, often mixed with a nostalgia for earlier and calmer days. In many lands under Communist domination, organized religion generally continued to decline, yet showed surprising persistence, often in less traditional forms.

Regional ecumenical associations to deal with church relations in particular areas were developing—the East Asia Christian Conference was founded in 1959, the continuation committee of the Pacific Church's Conference in the same year, the All-Africa Conference of Churches in 1963, and the Conference of European Churches in the following year. In Africa, the proliferation of independent prophetic movements continued, some related to the mainstream of Christian life, others moving outside of anything recognizably Christian. By the late 1960s, it was reported that in Africa south of the Sahara there were over two thousand independent churches with over a million followers. But for many of the churches of Africa, as in other areas, there was a growing relationship to the ecumenical movement, along with a clear determination to encourage the development of indigenous patterns of Christian worship and organization. In theological thought, there were many new trends in the 1960s; some of them, especially the radical "death of God" theology, briefly attracted considerable attention. More representative were efforts to frame theologies of hope and of liberation. Informed by the long history of biblical and theological reflection and shaped in the crucibles of the encounter of the church with the modern world, they were moving in the stream of life that has flowed through some of the creative periods of the church's history.

In the 1970s, a resurgence of conservative evangelical Protestantism with its traditional emphases on the Bible, mission, and evangelism became a major trend. The advance had begun in previous decades; a prominent leader was Carl F. H. Henry (1912–   ), an American theologian and founding editor of the periodical *Christianity Today* in 1956, who ten years later chaired a World Congress on Evangelism held in Berlin and attended by some 1,200 persons from more than 100 nations. Then, on July 16–25, 1974, an International Congress on World Evangelization was held at Lausanne, Switzerland, which drew twice that many participants from some 150 nations and 135 Protestant denominations, half of them from the third world. The prominent American evangelist, William F. (Billy) Graham (1918–   ) delivered an opening address on the congress's theme, "Let the Earth Hear His Voice," and at the close declared that he was satisfied with the "Lausanne Covenant" which had been completed during the meeting. It affirmed "the divine inspiration, truthfulness and authority of both Old and New Testament Scriptures in their entirety as the only written Word of God without error in all that it affirms, and the only infallible rule of faith and practice." Expressing penitence for both triumphalism and intransigency in the carrying out of the missionary task in the past and for negligence in matters of social concern, the covenant declared that "evangelism and socio-political involvement are both part of our Christian duty." It recognized that a new missionary era had dawned but reaffirmed that salvation was available only through faith in Jesus Christ.[7]

The conservative turn was further illustrated by the continued growth of the Pentecostal denominations, especially in the Americas and Africa. A standard work on these churches in North America reported that the Assemblies of God (see VII:15) had become a major denomination, with an estimated membership of 1,300,000 by the later 1970s, while the total number of Pentecostal bodies (many of them very small) had increased to 130.[8] Neopentecostal or charismatic movements also developed within many of the older churches in the United States, notably the Episcopal, Lutheran, Methodist, Presbyterian, and Roman Catholic.

The resurgence of conservative evangelicalism led to a considerable debate in ecumenical circles as to the way mission and evangelism should be understood and conducted.[9] A number of the churches represented at the meetings at Berlin and Lausanne were also members of the World Council of Churches, where a wider spectrum of theologies of mission and evangelism was evident. When the World Council assembled the year after Lausanne, there were encounters between conservative evangelicals and those who put more emphasis on dialogue with adherents of other religions and on liberation theologies and movements.

The fifth assembly of the World Council of Churches met at Nairobi, Kenya, November 23–December 10, 1975, gathering 676 voting delegates (almost half from the third world) from 271 member churches, plus a larger group of consultants, staff, press, and observers. Considerable attention was focused on the liberation theologies, with their concern for the poor, the oppressed, and the insufficiently represented (including women) in both church and world. In particular, sharp debate erupted over the World Council's Program to Combat Racism, developed as a result of decisions made at Uppsala. A number of financial grants had been made to various organizations actively involved in resisting racism, a few of the subsidies going (for humani-

[7] James D. Douglas, ed., *Let the Earth Hear His Voice* (Minneapolis, 1975), pp. 3–9.
[8] Arthur Carl Piepkorn, *Profiles in Belief: The Religious Bodies of the United States and Canada*, vol. 3 (San Francisco, 1979), p. 113.
[9] Donald McGavran, ed., *The Conciliar-Evangelical Debate: The Crucial Documents, 1964–1976* (South Pasadena, CA, 1977); C. René Padilla, ed., *The New Face of Evangelism: An International Symposium on the Lausanne Covenant* (London, 1976).

tarian purposes) to groups engaged in violent action. Though only a small percentage of the funds flowing through the World Council (those given especially for that purpose) went to the program, which was conducted by 4 of the council's 275 staff members, it became a symbolic issue of great importance. Attempts from the floor of the assembly to limit the special fund, in which those representing various points of view joined, were decisively defeated. Though a few members were lost from the council because of the way it carried out its concerns for liberation and humanization, believed by some to be too political, its membership continued to increase after the assembly, reaching a total of more than 300 by 1983, when the sixth assembly met at Vancouver, British Columbia.

At Nairobi, many other matters were considered; for example, historic ecumenical concerns for the larger unity of Christians were given vigorous expression, and there was much discussion of the concept that "the one Church is to be envisioned as a conciliar fellowship of local churches which are themselves truly united."[10] The conservative evangelical presence was especially evident in the section of the assembly that delivered a report, "Confessing Christ Today," a report that in its final form was received unanimously by the assembly. The gathering at Nairobi also approved the continuation of dialogues with representatives of other religions; in those carried on with Jews, for example, the tragic history of Jewish-Christian relations through the centuries, including attention to the Crusades, the Inquisition, and the Holocaust, have been discussed.

Though relationships between the Vatican and the World Council remained cooperative in the 1970s, the likelihood of Roman Catholic membership in the council diminished. Some reaction within the church against what was viewed as excessive ecumenical zeal and theological change was led by Pope Paul VI and by many who had been prominent leaders of the *aggiornamento*. The trend was not toward the older traditionalism, but rather in the direction of a centralist position and a centralization of authority, a trend continued after Paul VI's death in 1978. Albino Luciani, the patriarch of Venice, was elected as pope and took the name John Paul, but he died after only a few weeks in office. He was followed by the first non-Italian pope in over four centuries, a Pole, Karol Wojtyla, metropolitan archbishop of Cracow, who took the name John Paul II upon his election in October 1978.

It soon became clear that the new pope was a strong leader determined to bring new life and clear direction to Roman Catholic affairs. A colorful, outgoing, able man, at once an intellectual skilled in philosophy and languages and an administrator who had learned how to guide the faithful in a land under Communist rule, John Paul II devoted his talents to invigorating and stabilizing his church, while showing deep concern for others. A series of

[10] David M. Paton, ed., *Breaking Barriers: Nairobi, 1975* (London, 1976), p. 60.

trips to such places as Mexico, Brazil, Poland, Ireland, the United States, Canada, the United Kingdom, India, and several African and Latin American countries caused wide excitement; his charismatic personality stirred enthusiasm among Catholics and won the admiration of multitudes who were of other persuasions. Yet he sought firmly to restore order among his widely scattered flock, pressing for clear standards of doctrine and discipline, affirming clerical celibacy, and opposing the ordination of women. His visits to various shrines of the Virgin called attention again to a type of piety which had faded in popularity in the preceding decades. His ecumenical approach was sincere but cautious; without compromising Catholic doctrines, he expressed concern for the full restoration of unity, showing a particular interest in closer relations with Eastern Orthodoxy.

The long story of the Christian church is a panorama of lights and shadows, of achievements and failures, of conquests and divisions. It has exhibited the divine life marvelously transforming the lives of men and women. It has also exhibited those passions and weaknesses of which human nature is capable. Its tasks have seemed, in every age, almost insuperable. They have never been greater than at present, when confronted by a materialistic interpretation of life, and when the threat of atomic war endangers the whole fabric of civilization. Yet no Christian can survey what the church has done without confidence in its future. Its changes may be many, its struggles great. But the great hand of God which has led it hitherto will guide it to larger usefulness in the advancement of the kingdom of its Lord and toward the fulfillment of his prediction that if he be lifted up he would draw all persons unto him.

BIBLIOGRAPHICAL SUGGESTIONS

1. General Works on Church History

A. BACKGROUND AND REFERENCE

BEN-SASSON, H. H., ed. *A History of the Jewish People.* Cambridge, MA, 1976.

BETTENSON, H., ed. *Documents of the Christian Church.* 2nd ed. London, 1963.

BRAUER, J. C., ed. *The Westminster Dictionary of Church History.* Philadelphia, 1971.

CROSS, F. L., and LIVINGSTONE, E. L., eds. *The Oxford Dictionary of the Christian Church.* 2nd ed. Oxford, 1974.

DOWLEY, T., ed. *Eerdman's Handbook to the History of Christianity.* Grand Rapids, MI, 1977.

HASTINGS, J., ed. *Encyclopaedia of Religion and Ethics.* 13 vols. New York, 1908–1926.

KIDD, B. J., ed. *Documents Illustrative of the History of the Church.* 3 vols. London, 1920–1941.

LITTELL, F. H. *The Macmillan Atlas of the History of Christianity.* New York, 1976.

LOETSCHER, L. A., ed. *Twentieth-Century Encyclopedia of Religious Knowledge.* 2 vols. Grand Rapids, MI, 1955.

MACQUARRIE, J., ed. *Dictionary of Christian Ethics.* Philadelphia, 1967.

New Catholic Encyclopedia, The. 15 vols. Washington, DC, 1967.

New Schaff-Herzog Encyclopedia of Religious Knowledge, The. 3rd ed. 13 vols. New York, 1908–1912. Reprint. Grand Rapids, MI, 1951–1954.

RICHARDSON, A., ed. *A Dictionary of Christian Theology.* Philadelphia, 1969.

SMITH, W., and WACE, H., eds. *Dictionary of Christian Biography.* 4 vols. London, 1877–1878.

B. SURVEYS

ATIYA, A. S. *History of Eastern Christianity.* Notre Dame, IN, 1968.

ATTWATER, D. *The Christian Churches of the East.* 2 vols. Milwaukee, 1947, 1948.

JEDIN, H., and DOLAN, J., eds. *History of the Church.* 10 vols. New York, 1965–1981.

LATOURETTE, K. S. *A History of Christianity.* 2 vols. New York, 1975.

———. *A History of the Expansion of Christianity.* 7 vols. New York, 1937–1945.

MEYENDORFF, J. *The Orthodox Church: Its Past and Its Role in the World Today.* 3rd ed. Trans. J. Chapin. Crestwood, NY, 1981.

SCHAFF, P. *A History of the Christian Church.* 3rd rev. ed. 7 vols. in 8. New York, 1910.

C. THOUGHT AND THEOLOGY

COPLESTONE, F. *A History of Philosophy.* Rev. ed. 9 vols. London, 1951–1975.

CUNLIFFE-JONES, H., and DREWERY, B., eds. *A History of Christian Doctrine*. Philadelphia, 1980.

DENZINGER, H. J. D., ed. *The Sources of Catholic Dogma*. Trans. R. J. Deferrari. St. Louis, 1957.

GONZALEZ, J. L. *A History of Christian Thought*. 3 vols. Nashville, TN, 1970–1975.

HARNACK, A. VON. *History of Dogma*. Trans. N. Buchanan. 7 vols. Boston, 1895–1903.

LEITH, J. H., ed. *Creeds of the Churches: A Reader in Christian Doctrine from the Bible to the Present*. Garden City, NY, 1963.

LOHSE, B. *A Short History of Christian Doctrine*. Trans. F. E. Stoeffler. Philadelphia, 1966.

McGIFFERT, A. C. *A History of Christian Thought*. 2 vols. New York, 1931.

PELIKAN, J. *The Christian Tradition*. 4 vols. Chicago, 1971–1984.

REUTHER, R. R., ed. *Religion and Sexism: Images of Women in the Jewish and Christian Traditions*. New York, 1974.

SCHAFF, P., ed. *The Creeds of Christendom*. 6th ed. 3 vols. New York, 1919.

SEEBERG, R. *A Textbook of the History of Doctrines*. Trans. C. E. Hay. 2 vols. in 1. Grand Rapids, MI, 1964.

D. INSTITUTIONS: MINISTRY, POLITY, WORSHIP

ACKROYD, P. R., et al., eds. *The Cambridge History of the Bible*. 3 vols. Cambridge, 1976.

JONES, C., WAINWRIGHT, G., and YARNOLD, E., eds. *The Study of Liturgy*. New York, 1978.

MARGULL, H. J., ed. *The Councils of the Church: History and Analysis*. Trans. W. F. Bense. Philadelphia, 1966.

NEILL, S. C., and WEBER, H.-R. *The Layman in Christian History*. Philadelphia, 1963.

NIEBUHR, H. R., and WILLIAMS, D. D., eds. *The Ministry in Historical Perspective*. New York, 1956.

REUTHER, R., and McLAUGHLIN, E., eds. *Women of Spirit: Female Leadership in the Jewish and Christian Traditions*. New York, 1979.

E. SPIRITUALITY, MONASTICISM, RELIGIOUS ORDERS

BOUYER, L., et al. *A History of Christian Spirituality*. 3 vols. New York, 1963–1969.

KNOWLES, D. *Christian Monasticism*. New York and Toronto, 1969.

LOSSKY, V. *The Mystical Theology of the Eastern Church*. London, 1957.

OPSAHL, P. D. *The Holy Spirit in the Life of the Church*. Minneapolis, 1978.

POURRAT, P. *Christian Spirituality*. Trans. W. H. Mitchell and S. P. Jacques. 3 vols. London, 1922–1927.

WORKMAN, H. B. *The Evolution of Christian Monasticism*. London, 1913.

F. CHURCH AND SOCIETY

EHLER, S. Z., and MORRALL, J. B., eds. *Church and State through the Centuries*. London, 1954.

FORELL, G. W. *History of Christian Ethics*. Vol. 1. Minneapolis, 1979.

NIEBUHR, H. R. *Christ and Culture*. New York, 1951.

PARKER, T. M. *Christianity and the State in the Light of History*. London, 1955.

TROELTSCH, E. *The Social Teachings of the Christian Churches*. Trans. O. Wyon. 2 vols. New York, 1931.

2. Periods I-III: 1-600

A. BACKGROUND AND REFERENCE

Bury, J. B. *History of the Later Roman Empire*. 2nd ed. 2 vols. London, 1923. Reprint. New York, 1958.

Dill, S. *Roman Society in the Last Century of the Western Empire*. 2nd rev. ed. London, 1899. Reprint. New York, 1958.

Duckett, E. S. *Latin Writers of the Fifth Century*. New York, 1930.

Festugiere, A.-J. *Personal Religion among the Greeks*. Berkeley, 1954.

Fustel de Coulanges, N. D. *The Ancient City*. Trans. W. Small. Paris, 1864. Reprint. Garden City, NY, n.d.

Goodspeed, E. J., and Grant, R. M. *A History of Early Christian Literature*. Chicago, 1966.

Grant, M. *History of Rome*. 2nd rev. ed. London, 1979.

Jones, A. H. M. *The Later Roman Empire*. 3 vols. Oxford, 1964.

Marrou, H.-I. *A History of Education in Antiquity*. Trans. G. Lamb. New York, 1956.

Mohrmann, C., and van der Meer, F. *Atlas of the Early Christian World*. Trans. and ed. M. Hedlund and H. H. Rowley. London, 1958.

Nilsson, M. P. *Greek Piety*. Trans. H. J. Rose. Oxford, 1948.

Nock, A. D. *Conversion: The Old and the New in Religion from Alexander the Great to Augustine of Hippo*. Oxford, 1933.

Ogilvie, R. M. *The Romans and Their Gods*. London, 1969.

Peters, F. E. *The Harvest of Hellenism: A History of the Near East from Alexander the Great to the Triumph of Christianity*. New York, 1970.

Quasten, J. *Patrology*. 3 vols. Westminster, MD, 1950–1960.

Rostovtzeff, M. *Social and Economic History of the Roman Empire*. 2nd ed. 2 vols. Oxford, 1957.

Rusch, W. G. *The Later Latin Fathers*. London, 1977.

Schürer, E.; Vermes, G.; and Millar, F. *The History of the Jewish People in the Age of Jesus Christ*. 2 vols. Edinburgh, 1973–1979.

Simon, M. *Verus Israel: Étude sure les relations entre chrétiens et juifs dans l'empire romain*. 2nd ed. Paris, 1964.

Smallwood, E. M. *The Jews under Roman Rule*. Leiden, 1976.

Stewardson, J. L. *A Bibliography of Bibliographies on Patristics*. Evanston, IL, 1967.

Young, F. *From Nicaea to Chalcedon: A Guide to the Literature and Its Background*. London and Philadelphia, 1983.

B. SOURCES AND DOCUMENTS

Ayer, J. C., ed. *A Source Book for Ancient Church History*. New York, 1913.

Baillie, J.; McNeill, J. T.; and Van Dusen, H. P., eds. *The Library of Christian Classics*. 26 vols. Philadelphia, 1953–1969. (Volumes 1–8 contain works from the period of the early church.)

BETTENSON, H., ed. *The Early Christian Fathers: A Selection from the Writings of the Fathers from St. Clement of Rome to St. Athanasius.* New York, 1956.

DEFERRARI, R. J., et al., eds. *The Fathers of the Church: A New Translation.* 70 vols. New York, 1947–1984.

NORRIS, R. A., JR., trans. and ed. *The Christological Controversy.* Philadelphia, 1980.

QUASTEN, J., et al. *Ancient Christian Writers.* 42 vols. New York, 1946–1984.

ROBERTS, A., and DONALDSON, J., eds. *The Ante-Nicene Fathers.* 10 vols. Buffalo, 1884–1886.

SCHAFF, P., and WACE, H., eds. *The Nicene and Post-Nicene Fathers.* Series 1 and 2. 26 vols. New York, 1886–1895.

STEVENSON, J., ed. *Creeds, Councils and Controversies.* New York, 1966.

———, ed. *A New Eusebius.* New York, 1957.

WILES, M., and SANTER, M., eds. *Documents in Early Christian Thought.* Cambridge, 1975.

C. SURVEYS

CHADWICK, H. *The Early Church.* Baltimore, 1967.

CONZELMANN, H. *History of Primitive Christianity.* Trans. J. E. Steely. Nashville, TN, 1973.

DANIELOU, J., and MARROU, H.-I. *The First Six Hundred Years.* Vol. 1 of J. L. Rogier et al., eds., *The Christian Centuries.* Trans. V. Cronin, London, 1964.

FREND, W. H. C. *The Early Church.* Philadelphia, 1982.

LEBRETON, J., and ZEILLER, J. *The History of the Primitive Church.* Trans. E. C. Messenger. 2 vols. New York, 1949.

LIETZMANN, H. *The Beginnings of the Christian Church.* Trans. B. Woolf. New York, 1938.

———. *The Founding of the Church Universal.* Trans. B. Woolf. New York, 1938.

———. *From Constantine to Julian.* Trans. B. Woolf. New York, 1950.

———. *The Era of the Church Fathers.* Trans. B. Woolf. New York, 1951.

PALANQUE, J. R., et al. *The Church in the Christian Roman Empire.* Trans. E. C. Messenger. 2 vols. London, 1949–1952.

ZERNOV, N. *Eastern Christendom: A Study of the Origin and Development of the Eastern Orthodox Church.* New York, 1961.

D. THOUGHT AND THEOLOGY

ARMSTRONG, A. H. *An Introduction to Ancient Philosophy.* London, 1947.

———, ed. *The Cambridge History of Later Greek and Early Medieval Philosophy.* Cambridge, 1967.

CHADWICK, H. *Early Christian Thought and the Classical Tradition.* New York, 1966.

COCHRANE, C. N. *Christianity and Classical Culture.* New York, 1944.

DANIELOU, J. *A History of Early Christian Doctrine before the Council of Nicaea.* Trans. J. A. Baker. Vol. 1, *The Theology of Jewish Christianity*, Chicago, 1964. Vol. 2, *Gospel Message and Hellenistic Culture*, Philadelphia, 1973. Vol. 3, *The Origins of Latin Christianity*, Philadelphia, 1977.

EVANS, R. F. *One and Holy: The Church in Latin Patristic Thought.* London, 1972.

GRAEF, H. *Mary: A History of Doctrine and Devotion.* London, 1963.

GREENSLADE, S. L. *Schism in the Early Church.* London, 1953.

GRILLMEIER, A. *Christ in Christian Tradition.* 2nd ed. Trans. J. Bowden. London, 1975.

KELLY, J. N. D. *Early Christian Doctrines.* Rev. ed. New York, 1960.

LADNER, G. B. *The Idea of Reform: Its Impact on Christian Thought and Action in the Age of the Fathers.* Rev. ed. New York, 1967.

PELIKAN, J. *The Emergence of the Catholic Tradition.* Chicago, 1971.

PRESTIGE, G. *God in Patristic Thought.* London, 1952.

MEYENDORFF, J. *Christ in Eastern Christian Thought.* Washington, DC, and Cleveland, 1969.

STEAD, C. *Divine Substance.* Oxford, 1977.

TAVARD, G. *Women in Christian Tradition.* Notre Dame, IN, 1973.

E. SPECIAL MOVEMENTS AND PERIODS

BLACKMAN, E. C. *Marcion and His Influence.* London, 1948.

CHADWICK, H. *Priscillian of Avila: The Occult and the Charismatic in the Early Church.* Oxford, 1976.

FREND, W. H. C. *The Donatist Church.* Oxford, 1952.

——. *The Rise of the Monophysite Movement.* Cambridge, 1972.

Grant, R. M. *Gnosticism and Early Christianity.* Rev. ed. New York, 1966.

JONAS, H. *The Gnostic Religion.* 2nd rev. ed. Boston, 1963.

KOPOCEK, T. A. *A History of Neo-Arianism.* 2 vols. Cambridge, MA, 1979.

RUDOLPH, K. *Gnosis: The Nature and History of Gnosticism.* Trans. R. M. Wilson. San Francisco, 1983.

WALLACE-HADRILL, D. S. *Christian Antioch: A Study of Early Christian Thought in the East.* Cambridge, 1982.

F. INSTITUTIONS: MINISTRY, POLITY, WORSHIP

BRADSHAW, P. F. *Daily Prayer in the Early Church.* New York, 1982.

CAMPENHAUSEN, H. VON. *Ecclesiastical Authority and Spiritual Power in the Church of the First Three Centuries.* Trans. J. A. Baker. London, 1969.

——. *The Formation of the Christian Bible.* Trans. J. A. Baker. London, 1972.

GILES, E., ed. *Documents Illustrating Papal Authority, A.D. 96–454.* London, 1952.

GRABAR, A. *Christian Iconography: A Study of Its Origins.* Princeton, NJ, 1968.

Hertling, L. *Communio: Church and Papacy in Early Christianity.* Trans. J. Wicks. Chicago, 1972.

JUNGMANN, J. A. *The Early Liturgy to the Time of Gregory the Great.* Trans. F. Brunner. Notre Dame, IN, 1959.

KELLY, J. N. D. *Early Christian Creeds.* 3rd ed. New York, 1972.

KRAUTHEIMER, R. *Early Christian and Byzantine Architecture.* Baltimore, 1965.

G. SPIRITUALITY, MONASTICISM, RELIGIOUS ORDERS

AMAND, D. *L'Ascèse monastique de saint Basile.* Maredsous, 1949.

CHADWICK, H. *The Sentences of Sextus.* Cambridge, 1959.

CHITTY, D. J. *The Desert a City: An Introduction to the Study of Egyptian and Palestinian Monasticism under the Christian Empire.* Crestwood, NY, 1966.

FRY, T., et al., eds. *The Rule of St. Benedict in Latin and English, with Notes.* Collegeville, MN, 1981.

LOUTH, A. *The Origins of the Christian Mystical Tradition.* Oxford, 1981.

MORISON, E. F. *St. Basil and His Rule: A Study in Early Monasticism.* New York, 1912.

WARD, B., trans. *The Sayings of the Desert Fathers.* London, 1981.

H. CHURCH AND SOCIETY

CADOUX, C. J. *The Early Church and the World.* Edinburgh, 1925. Reprint. Edinburgh and New York, 1955.

COLEMAN-NORTON, P. R. *Roman State and Christian Church.* London, 1966.

DVORNIK, F. *Early Christian and Byzantine Political Philosophy.* 2 vols. Washington, DC, 1966.

FREND, W. H. C. *Martyrdom and Persecution in the Early Church.* Oxford, 1965.

GIET, S. *Les idées et l'action sociales de saint Basile.* Paris, 1941.

GRANT, R. M. *Early Christianity and Society.* San Francisco, 1977.

———. *The Sword and the Cross.* New York, 1955.

GREENSLADE, S. L. *Church and State from Constantine to Theodosius.* London, 1954.

MARKUS, R. A. *Saeculum: History and Society in the Theology of St. Augustine.* Cambridge, 1970.

OSBORN, E. F. *Ethical Patterns in Early Christian Thought.* Cambridge, 1976.

I. BIOGRAPHICAL STUDIES

BAUR, C. *John Chrysostom and His Time.* Trans. M. Gonzaga. 2 vols. London, 1959–1960.

BROWN, P. *Augustine of Hippo: A Biography.* Berkeley, 1969.

BROWNING, R. *The Emperor Julian.* Berkeley, 1976.

CAMPENHAUSEN, H. VON. *The Fathers of the Greek Church.* Trans. S. Godman. New York, 1959.

———. *Men Who Shaped the Western Church.* Trans. M. Hoffman. New York, 1964.

CHADWICK, O. *John Cassian.* Cambridge, 1950.

DÖRRIES, H. *Constantine the Great.* Trans. R. H. Bainton. New York, 1972.

HOMES-DUDDEN, F. *The Life and Times of St. Ambrose.* 2 vols. Oxford, 1935.

JONES, A. H. M. *Constantine and the Conversion of Europe.* Rev. ed. New York, 1962.

KELLY, J. N. D. *Jerome.* New York, 1975.

TRIGG, J. W. *Origen: The Bible and Philosophy in the Third-century Church.* Atlanta, GA, 1983.

3. Periods IV and V: The Middle Ages

A. BACKGROUND AND REFERENCE

BLOCH, M. *Feudal Society.* Trans. L. A. Manyon. London, 1961.

CARLYLE, R. W., and CARLYLE, A. J. *A History of Mediaeval Political Theory in the West.* 6 vols. Edinburgh, 1903–1936.

COULTON, G. G. *Five Centuries of Religion.* 4 vols. Cambridge, 1923–1950.

DAWSON, C. *Religion and the Rise of Western Culture.* New York, 1958.

————. *The Making of Europe.* Cleveland and New York, 1956.

FERGUSON, W. K. *Europe in Transition, 1300–1520.* Boston, 1962.

GILMORE, M. *The World of Humanism, 1453–1517.* New York, 1952.

HALE, J. R. *Renaissance Europe: Individual and Society, 1480–1520.* New York, 1973.

HAY, D., and POTTER, G. R., eds. *The New Cambridge Modern History.* Vol. 1, *The Renaissance, 1493–1520.* Cambridge, 1957.

HUIZINGA, J. *The Waning of the Middle Ages.* Trans. F. Hopman. London, 1924.

MANGO, C. *Byzantium: The Empire of New Rome.* New York, 1980.

OSTROGORSKY, G. *History of the Byzantine State.* 2nd ed. Trans. J. Hussey. Oxford, 1968.

SOUTHERN, R. W. *The Making of the Middle Ages.* New Haven, CT, 1953.

WALLACE-HADRILL, J. M. *The Barbarian West, 400–1000.* London, 1952.

B. SOURCES AND DOCUMENTS

BAILLIE, J.; McNEILL, J. T.; and VAN DUSEN, H. P., eds. *The Library of Christian Classics.* 26 vols. Philadelphia, 1953–1969. (Vols. 9–14 contain works from the early Middle Ages to the Reformation.)

BALDWIN, M. B., ed. *Christianity through the Thirteenth Century.* New York, 1970.

BROOKE, R. B., ed. *The Coming of the Friars.* London and New York, 1975.

CASSIRER, E.; KRISTELLER, P. O.; and RANDALL, J. H., eds. *The Renaissance Philosophy of Man.* Chicago, 1948.

FARRAR, C. P., and EVANS, A. P. *Bibliography of English Translations from Medieval Sources.* New York, 1946.

FERGUSON, M. A. H. *Bibliography of English Translations from Medieval Sources, 1943–1967.* New York, 1974.

OBERMAN, H. A., ed., and Nyhus, P. L., trans. *Forerunners of the Reformation: The Shape of Later Medieval Thought, Illustrated by Key Documents.* Philadelphia, 1981.

PETRY, R. C., ed. *A History of Christianity: Readings in the History of the Early and Medieval Church.* Englewood Cliffs, NJ, 1962.

WAKEFIELD, W. L., and EVANS, A. P., trans. and eds. *Heresies of the High Middle Ages: Selected Sources.* New York and London, 1969.

C. SURVEYS

BECK, H.-G., et al. *From the High Middle Ages to the Eve of the Reformation.* Trans. A. Briggs. Vol. 4 of H. Jedin and J. Dolan, *History of the Church.* New York, 1965.

KNOWLES, D., and OBOLENSKY, D. *The Middle Ages*. Vol. 2 of J. L. Rogier et al., eds., *The Christian Centuries*. London, 1968.

McNEILL, J. T. *The Celtic Churches: A History, A.D. 200 to 1200*. Chicago, 1974.

OAKLEY, F. *The Western Church in the Later Middle Ages*. Ithaca, NY, 1979.

SOUTHERN, R. W. *Western Society and the Church in the Later Middle Ages*. Baltimore, 1968.

SPINKA, M. *A History of Christianity in the Balkans*. Hamden, CT, 1968.

D. THOUGHT AND THEOLOGY

BECK, H.-G. *Kirche und theologische Literatur im byzantinischen Reich*. Munich, 1963.

CHENU, M.-D. *Nature Man and Society in the Twelfth Century*. Trans. J. Taylor and L. K. Little. Chicago, 1968.

GEANAKOPLOS, D. J. *Byzantine East and Latin West: Two Worlds of Christendom in Middle Ages and Renaissance*. New York, 1966.

GILSON, E. *A History of Christian Philosophy in the Middle Ages*. New York, 1955.

————. *Reason and Revelation in the Middle Ages*. New York, 1938.

GRABMANN, M. *Die Geschichte der scholastischen Methode*. 2 vols. Freiburg-im-Br., 1909, 1911. Reprint. Graz, 1957.

HASKINS, C. H. *The Renaissance of the Twelfth Century*. Cambridge, MA, 1927.

————. *The Rise of Universities*. Ithaca, NY, 1957.

HUSSEY, J. M. *Church and Learning in the Byzantine Empire, 867–1185*. Oxford, 1937.

KLIBANSKY, R. *The Continuity of the Platonic Tradition during the Middle Ages*. London, 1939.

KRISTELLER, P. O. *Renaissance Thought and Its Sources*. New York, 1979.

LEFF, G. *The Dissolution of the Medieval Outlook: An Essay on Intellectual and Spiritual Change in the Fourteenth Century*. New York, 1976.

————. *Medieval Thought: St. Augustine to Ockham*. Baltimore, 1958.

OBERMAN, H. A. *The Harvest of Medieval Theology: Gabriel Biel and Late Medieval Nominalism*. Cambridge, MA, 1963.

OZMENT, S. *The Age of Reform, 1250–1550: An Intellectual and Religious History of Late Medieval and Reformation Europe*. New Haven, CT, 1980.

PELIKAN, J. *Reformation of Church and Dogma (1300–1700)*. Vol. 4 of *The Christian Tradition*. Chicago, 1984.

————. *The Growth of Mediaeval Theology (600–1300)*. Vol. 3 of *The Christian Tradition*. Chicago, 1978.

————. *The Spirit of Eastern Christendom (600–1700)*. Vol. 2 of *The Christian Tradition*. Chicago, 1974.

Rashdall, H. *The Universities of Europe in the Middle Ages*. 2nd ed. rev. by F. M. Powicke and A. B. Emden. 3 vols. Oxford, 1936.

REEVES, M. *The Influence of Prophecy in the Later Middle Ages: A Study in Joachimism*. Oxford, 1969.

STEENBERGHEN, F. VAN. *Aristotle and the West*. Trans. L. Johnson. Louvain, 1955.

TAYLOR, H. O. *The Medieval Mind*. 4th ed. 2 vols. Cambridge, MA, 1949.

TRINKAUS, C. *In Our Image and Likeness: Humanity and Divinity in Italian Humanist Thought*. 2 vols. Chicago, 1970.

E. MEDIEVAL HERESY, SCHISMATIC MOVEMENTS, AND THE INQUISITION

BORST, A. *Die Katharer*. Stuttgart, 1953.

GEBHARDT, E. *Mystics and Heretics in Italy*. Trans. E. M. Hulme. London, 1922.

LAMBERT, M. D. *Medieval Heresy: Popular Movements from Bogomil to Hus*. London, 1977.

LEFF, G. *Heresy in the Late Middle Ages: The Relation of Heterodoxy to Dissent, c. 1250–c. 1450*. 2 vols. Manchester and New York, 1967.

LERNER, R. E. *The Heresy of the Free Spirit in the Later Middle Ages*. Berkeley and Los Angeles, 1972.

LOOS, M. *Dualist Heresy in the Middle Ages*. Prague, 1974.

McDONNELL, E. W. *The Beguines and Beghards in Medieval Culture*. New Brunswick, NJ, 1954.

RUSSELL, J. B. *Dissent and Reform in the Early Middle Ages*. Berkeley and Los Angeles, 1965.

———. *Witchcraft in the Middle Ages*. Ithaca, NY, 1972.

THOMSON, J. A. F. *The Later Lollards, 1414–1520*. Oxford, 1965.

TURBERVILLE, A. S. *Medieval Heresy and the Inquisition*. London, 1920.

WAKEFIELD, W. L. *Heresy, Crusade, and Inquisition in Southern France, 1100–1250*. London, 1974.

F. INSTITUTIONS: MINISTRY, POLITY, WORSHIP

BARRACLOUGH, G. *The Medieval Papacy*. London, 1968.

DVORNIK, F. *Byzantium and the Roman Primacy*. New York, 1966.

———. *The Photian Schism: History and Legend*. Cambridge, 1948.

GILL, J. *The Council of Florence*. Cambridge, 1959.

JUNGMANN, J. A. *The Mass of the Roman Rite: Its Origin and Development*. Trans. F. A. Brunner. 2 vols. New York, 1951, 1955.

KUTTNER, S. *Harmony from Dissonance: An Interpretation of Medieval Canon Law*. Latrobe, PA, 1960.

MALE, E. *The Gothic Image: Religious Art in France of the Thirteenth Century*. Trans. D. Nussey. New York, 1958.

MANN, H. K. *The Lives of the Popes in the Middle Ages*. 18 vols. London, 1906–1932.

MOLLAT, G. *The Popes at Avignon (1305–1378)*. Trans. J. Love. New York, 1963.

ROGERS, E. F. *Peter Lombard and the Sacramental System*. New York, 1917.

RUNCIMAN, S. *The Eastern Schism: A Study of the Papacy and the Eastern Churches during the XIth and XIIth Centuries*. Oxford, 1955.

SIMPSON, O. VON. *The Gothic Cathedral: Origins of Gothic Architecture and the Medieval Concept of Order*. New York, 1956.

TENTLER, T. N. *Sin and Confession on the Eve of the Reformation*. Princeton, NJ, 1977.

TIERNEY, B. *Foundations of Conciliar Theory*. Cambridge, 1955.

ULLMANN, W. *The Origins of the Great Schism*. London, 1949.

———. *A Short History of the Papacy in the Middle Ages*. London, 1974.

G. SPIRITUALITY, MONASTICISM, RELIGIOUS ORDERS

BROOKE, C., and SWAAN, W. *The Monastic World.* London and New York, 1974.

BROOKE, R., and BROOKE, C. *Popular Religion in the Middle Ages: Western Europe 1000–1300.* London and New York, 1984.

BUTLER, C. *Benedictine Monachism.* 2nd ed. Cambridge, 1961.

CONSTABLE, G. *Medieval Monasticism: A Select Bibliography.* Toronto, 1976.

DUCKETT, E. S. *The Gateway to the Middle Ages: Monasticism.* Ann Arbor, 1938.

GRUNDMANN, H. *Religiöse Bewegungen im Mittelalter.* 2nd ed. Hildesheim, 1961.

HINNEBUSCH, W. A. *A History of the Dominican Order: Origins and Growth to 1550.* Vol. 1. New York, 1965.

KNOWLES, D. *The English Mystical Tradition.* London, 1961.

————. *The Religious Orders in England.* 3 vols. Cambridge, 1948–1959.

LECLERCQ, J. *The Love of Learning and the Desire for God: A Study of Monastic Culture.* 2nd rev. ed. Trans. C. Mishrahi. New York, 1974.

LECLERCQ, J.; VANDENBROUCKE, F.; and BOUYER, L. *The Spirituality of the Middle Ages.* London, 1968.

MANSELLI, R. *La religion populaire au moyen age.* Montreal and Paris, 1975.

MOORMAN, J. R. H. *A History of the Franciscan Order.* Oxford, 1968.

NIGG, W. *The Great Religious Orders and their Founders.* Trans. M. Ilford. New York, 1972.

POST, R. R. *The Modern Devotion: Confrontation with Reformation and Humanism.* Leiden, 1968.

POWER, E. *Medieval Nunneries.* Rev. ed. Cambridge, 1940.

RYAN, J. *Irish Monasticism.* Dublin, 1931.

SMALLEY, B. *The Study of the Bible in the Middle Ages.* Notre Dame, IN, 1964.

SUMPTION, J. *Pilgrimage: An Image of Medieval Religion.* Totowa, NJ, 1975.

TRINKAUS, C., and OBERMAN, H. A., eds. *The Pursuit of Holiness in Late Medieval and Renaissance Religion.* Leiden, 1974.

H. CHURCH AND SOCIETY

HERLIHY, D. *Women in Medieval Society.* Houston, 1971.

KANTOROWICZ, E. H. *The King's Two Bodies: A Study in Medieval Political Theology.* Princeton, NJ, 1957.

NICOL, D. M. *Church and Society in the Last Centuries of Byzantium.* Cambridge, 1979.

POWER, E. *Medieval Women.* Ed. M. M. Postan. New York, 1975.

RUNCIMAN, S. *A History of the Crusades.* 3 vols. Cambridge, 1951–1954.

SCHARF, A. *Byzantine Jewry from Justinian to the Fourth Crusade.* London, 1971.

SETTON, K. M. *A History of the Crusades.* 5 vols. to date. Philadelphia, 1958–.

SOUTHERN, R. W. *Western Views of Islam in the Middle Ages.* Cambridge, MA, 1962.

SYNAN, E. A. *The Popes and the Jews in the Middle Ages.* New York, 1965.

TELLENBACH, G. *Church, State, and Christian Society at the Time of the Investiture Contest.* Trans. R. F. Bennett. New York, 1970.

TIERNEY, B., ed. *The Crisis of Church and State, 1050–1300.* Englewood Cliffs, NJ, 1964.

I. BIOGRAPHICAL STUDIES

BETTONI, E. *Duns Scotus: The Basic Principles of His Philosophy*. Trans. B. Bonansea. Washington, DC, 1961.

BOASE, T. S. R. *Boniface VIII*. London, 1933.

CHENU, M.-D. *Toward Understanding St. Thomas*. Chicago, 1964.

CLAYTON, J. *Pope Innocent III and His Times*. Milwaukee, 1940.

FATHER CUTHBERT [HESS]. *Life of St. Francis of Assisi*. London, 1912.

GILSON, E. *The Christian Philosophy of St. Thomas Aquinas*. Trans. L. K. Shook. New York, 1956.

———. *The Mystical Theology of St. Bernard*. Trans. A. H. C. Downes. New York, 1940.

———. *The Philosophy of St. Bonaventure*. Trans. I. Trethowan and F. J. Sheed. Paterson, NJ, 1965.

GRANE, L. *Peter Abelard: Philosophy and Christianity in the Middle Ages*. New York, 1970.

HOPKINS, J. *A Companion to the Study of St. Anselm*. Minneapolis, 1972.

LEFF, G. *William of Ockham: The Metamorphosis of Scholastic Discourse*. Manchester, 1975.

LONERGAN, B. *Verbum: Word and Idea in Aquinas*. Notre Dame, IN, 1967.

McFARLANE, K. B. *John Wycliffe and the Beginnings of English Nonconformity*. London, 1952.

MANDONNET, P. *Saint Dominic and His Work*. Trans. M. B. Larking. London and St. Louis, 1964.

SABATIER, P. *Life of St. Francis of Assisi*. Trans. L. S. Houghton. London, 1894.

SPINKA, M. *John Hus: A Biography*. Princeton, NJ, 1968.

VICAIRE, M. H. *Saint Dominic and His Times*. New York, 1965.

WEISHEIPL, J. A. *Friar Thomas D'Aquino: His Life, Thought, and Work*. Oxford, 1975.

WEST, D. C., ed. *Joachim of Fiore in Christian Thought: Essays on the Influence of the Calabrian Prophet*. New York, 1975.

WORKMAN, H. B. *John Wycliffe: A Study of the English Medieval Church*. 2 vols. Oxford, 1926.

4. Period VI: The Reformation

A. BACKGROUND AND REFERENCE

BAINTON, R. H., and GRITSCH, E. W. *Bibliography of the Continental Reformation: Materials Available in English*. 2nd ed. Hamden, CT, 1972.

BRAUDEL, F. *The Mediterranean and the Mediterranean World in the Age of Philip II*. 2 vols. Trans. S. Reynolds. New York, 1972, 1973.

BUCK, L. P., and ZOPHY, J. W., eds. *The Social History of the Reformation*. Columbus, OH, 1972.

DeMOLEN, R. L., ed. *The Meaning of the Renaissance and Reformation*. Boston, 1974.

ELTON, G. R., ed. *The New Cambridge Modern History.* Vol. 2, *The Reformation, 1520–1559.* Cambridge, 1958.

HURSTFIELD, J., ed. *The Reformation Crisis.* New York, 1966.

KINGDON, R. M., ed. *Transition and Revolution: Problems and Issues of European Renaissance and Reformation History.* Minneapolis, 1974.

OBERMAN, H. A., ed. *Luther and the Dawn of the Modern Era.* Leiden, 1974.

OZMENT, S., ed. *Reformation Europe: A Guide to Research.* St. Louis, 1982.

———, ed. *The Reformation in Medieval Perspective.* Chicago, 1971.

SPITZ, L. W., ed. *The Reformation: Basic Interpretations.* 2nd ed. Lexington, MA, 1972.

STRAUSS, G., ed. *Pre-Reformation Germany.* New York, 1972.

WERNHAM, R. B., ed. *The New Cambridge Modern History.* Vol. 3, *The Counter-Reformation and the Price Revolution, 1959–1610.* Cambridge, 1968.

B. SOURCES AND DOCUMENTS

BAILLIE, J.; MCNEILL, J. T.; and VAN DUSEN, H. P., eds. *The Library of Christian Classics.* Philadelphia, 1953–1969. (Vols. 15–26 contain works of the Reformation era.)

ELTON, G. R., ed. *Renaissance and Reformation, 1300–1648.* New York, 1963.

GEE, H., and HARDY, W. J., eds. *Documents Illustrative of English Church History.* London, 1896.

HILLERBRAND, H. J., ed. *The Reformation: A Narrative History Related by Contemporary Observers and Participants.* New York, 1964.

KIDD, B. J., ed. *Documents Illustrative of the Continental Reformation.* Oxford, 1911. Reprint. Oxford, 1967.

OLIN, J. C., ed. *The Catholic Reformation: Savonarola to Ignatius Loyola.* New York, 1969.

PELIKAN, J., and LEHMANN, H. T., eds. *Luther's Works.* 55 vols. St. Louis and Philadelphia, 1955–1976.

Spiritual Exercises of St. Ignatius, The. Trans. L. D. Puhl. Westminster, MD, 1951.

STRAUSS, G., ed. *Manifestations of Discontent in Germany on the Eve of the Reformation.* Bloomington, IN, 1971.

C. SURVEYS: GENERAL

BAINTON, R. H. *The Reformation of the Sixteenth Century.* Boston, 1952.

CHADWICK, O. *The Reformation.* Baltimore, 1968.

DICKENS, A. G. *Reformation and Society in Sixteenth-Century Europe.* New York, 1966.

———. *The Age of Humanism and Reformation.* Englewood Cliffs, NJ, 1972.

ELLIOTT, J. H. *Europe Divided, 1559–1598.* New York, 1959.

ELTON, G. R. *Reformation Europe, 1517–1559.* New York, 1966.

GREEN, V. H. H. *Renaissance and Reformation: A Survey of European History between 1450 and 1660.* 2nd ed. London, 1964.

GRIMM, H. J. *The Reformation Era, 1500–1650.* 2nd ed. New York, 1973.

HILLERBRAND, H. J. *The World of the Reformation.* New York, 1973.

ISERLOH, E.; GLAZIK, J.; and JEDIN, H. *Reformation and Counter-Reformation.* Vol. 5 of H. Jedin and J. Dolan, eds., *History of the Church.* New York, 1968.

KOENIGSBERGER, H. G., and MOSSE, G. L. *Europe in the Sixteenth Century*. New York, 1968.

SPITZ, L. W. *The Renaissance and Reformation Movements*. Chicago, 1971.

D. SURVEYS: REGIONAL AND TOPICAL

BERGENDORFF, C. *Olavus Petri and the Ecclesiastical Transformation of Sweden, 1520–1552*. Philadelphia, 1965.

CLASEN, C-P. *Anabaptism: A Social History, 1525–1618*. Ithaca, NY, 1972.

COLLINSON, P. *The Elizabethan Puritan Movement*. London, 1967.

DICKENS, A. G. *The Counter-Reformation*. New York, 1963.

———. *The English Reformation*. New York, 1964.

DONALDSON, G. *The Scottish Reformation*. Cambridge, 1960.

DUNCKLEY, E. H. *The Reformation in Denmark*. London, 1948.

DUNN, R. S. *The Age of Religious Wars, 1959–1689*. New York, 1970.

ELTON, G. R. *Reform and Reformation: England, 1509–1558*. Cambridge, MA, 1977.

GEYL, P. *The Revolt of the Netherlands, 1555–1609*. 2nd ed. London, 1962.

KINGDON, R. N. *Geneva and the Coming of the Wars of Religion in France, 1555–1563*. Geneva, 1956.

———. *Geneva and the Consolidation of the French Protestant Movement, 1564–1572*. Madison, WI, 1967.

LAU, F., and BIZER, E. *A History of the Reformation in Germany to 1555*. Trans. B. A. Hardy. London, 1969.

LORTZ, J. *The Reformation in Germany*. Trans. R. Walls. 2 vols. New York, 1968.

MOELLER, B. *Imperial Cities and the Reformation*. Trans. H. C. E. Midelfort and M. U. Edwards. Philadelphia, 1972.

O'CONNELL, M. R. *The Counter Reformation, 1559–1610*. New York, 1974.

OZMENT, S. *The Reformation in the Cities*. New Haven, CT, 1975.

WEDGWOOD, C. V. *The Thirty Years' War*. London, 1938.

WILBUR, E. M. *A History of Unitarianism*. 2 vols. Cambridge, MA, 1945, 1952.

WILLIAMS, G. H. *The Radical Reformation*. Philadelphia, 1962.

E. THOUGHT AND THEOLOGY

BREMOND, H. A. *A Literary History of Religious Thought in France*. Trans. K. L. Montgomery. 2 vols. New York, 1929, 1930.

DELUMEAU, J. *Catholicism between Luther and Voltaire: A New View of the Counter-Reformation*. Trans. J. Moiser. Philadelphia, 1977.

ELERT, W. *The Structure of Lutheranism*. Vol. 1. Trans. W. A. Hansen. St. Louis, 1962.

EVENNET, H. O. *The Spirit of the Counter-Reformation*. Ed. J. Bossy. Notre Dame, IN, 1970.

HARBISON, E. H. *The Christian Scholar in the Age of the Reformation*. New York, 1950.

HEPPE, H. *Reformed Dogmatics*. Ed. and rev. E. Bizer. London, 1950.

HUGHES, P. E. *The Theology of the English Reformers*. London, 1965.

JEDIN, H. *A History of the Council of Trent*. Trans. E. Graf. 2 vols. New York, 1957, 1961.

KRAHN, C. *Dutch Anabaptism: Origins, Spread, Life and Thought (1450–1600).* The Hague, 1968.

LITTELL, F. H. *The Origins of Sectarian Protestantism: A Study of the Anabaptist View of the Church.* New York, 1964.

McNEILL J. T. *The History and Character of Calvinism.* New York, 1954.

OZMENT, S. *The Age of Reform, 1250–1550: An Intellectual and Religious History of Late Medieval and Reformation Europe.* New Haven, CT, 1980.

———. *Mysticism and Dissent: Religious Ideology and Social Protest in the Sixteenth Century.* New Haven, CT, 1973.

PAUCK, W. *The Heritage of the Reformation.* 2nd ed. Glencoe, IL, 1961.

PREUS, R. D. *The Theology of Post-Reformation Lutheranism.* 2 vols. St. Louis, 1970, 1972.

REARDON, B. M. G. *Religious Thought in the Reformation.* New York, 1981.

RUPP, G. *Patterns of Reformation.* Philadelphia, 1969.

SCHWARZ, W. *Principles and Problems of Biblical Translation: Some Reformation Controversies and Their Background.* New York, 1955.

SPITZ, L. W. *The Religious Renaissance of the German Humanists.* Cambridge, MA, 1963.

F. INSTITUTIONS: MINISTRY, POLITY, WORSHIP

ARMOUR, R. *Anabaptist Baptism: A Representative Study.* Scottdale, PA, 1966.

COCHRANE, A. C., ed. *Reformed Confessions of the Sixteenth Century.* Philadelphia, 1966.

CREIGHTON, M. *A History of the Papacy during the Reformation.* 5 vols. London, 1887–1894.

DUGMORE, C. W. *The Mass and the English Reformers.* New York, 1958.

KIDD, B. J., ed. *The Thirty-Nine Articles.* 2 vols. Oxford, 1899.

McDONNELL, J. *John Calvin, the Church and the Eucharist.* Princeton, NJ, 1967.

O'DONOHOE, J. A. *Tridentine Seminary Legislation: Its Sources and Its Formation.* Louvain, 1957.

PASTOR, L. *The History of the Popes from the Close of the Middle Ages.* London, 1891–1953.

RICHARDSON, C. C. *Zwingli and Cranmer on the Eucharist.* Evanston, IL, 1949.

SASSE, H. *This Is My Body: Luther's Contention for the Real Presence in the Sacrament of the Altar.* Minneapolis, 1959.

SCHROEDER, H. J., ed. *Canons and Decrees of the Council of Trent.* St. Louis, 1941.

TAPPERT, T. G., ed. *The Book of Concord: The Confessions of the Evangelical Lutheran Church.* Philadelphia, 1959.

G. SPIRITUALITY, MONASTICISM, RELIGIOUS ORDERS

BRODRICK, J. *The Origins of the Jesuits.* London, 1940.

———. *The Progress of the Jesuits.* London, 1947.

COGNET, L. *Post-Reformation Spirituality.* London, 1959.

KNOWLES, D. *The Religious Orders in England.* 3 vols. Cambridge, 1948–1959.

MARTZ, L. L. *The Poetry of Meditation: A Study in English Religious Literature of the Seventeenth Century.* 2nd ed. New Haven, CT, 1962.

PEERS, E. A. *Studies of the Spanish Mystics.* 2nd ed. rev. 3 vols. London, 1951–1960.

H. CHURCH AND SOCIETY

BAINTON, H. *The Travail of Religious Liberty.* New York, 1958.

BLICKLE, P. *The Revolution of 1525: The German Peasants' War from a New Perspective.* Trans. T. A. Brady and H. C. E. Midelfort. Baltimore, 1981.

CRANZ, F. E. *An Essay on the Development of Luther's Thought on Justice, Law, and Society.* Cambridge, MA, 1959.

FISCHER-GALATI, S. A. *Ottoman Imperialism and German Protestantism, 1521–1555.* Cambridge, MA, 1959.

GRAHAM, W. F. *The Constructive Revolutionary: John Calvin and His Socio-Economic Impact.* Richmond, VA, 1971.

GREAVES, R. L. *Society and Religion in Elizabethan England.* Minneapolis, 1981.

GREEN, R. W., ed. *Protestantism, Capitalism, and Social Science: The Weber Thesis Controversy.* Lexington, MA, 1973.

KAMEN, H. *The Spanish Inquisition.* London, 1965.

KLASSEN, P. *The Economics of Anabaptism.* The Hague, 1964.

LECLER, J. *Toleration and the Reformation.* Trans. T. L. Weston. 2 vols., New York, 1960.

STAYER, J. M. *Anabaptists and the Sword.* Lawrence, KS, 1972.

TONKIN, J. *The Church and the Secular Order in Reformation Thought.* New York, 1971.

TREVOR-ROPER, H. R. *Religion, the Reformation and Social Change.* London, 1967.

WALTON, R. C. *Zwingli's Theocracy.* Toronto, 1967.

I. BIOGRAPHICAL STUDIES: LIFE AND THOUGHT

ALAND, K. *Four Reformers: Luther, Melanchthon, Zwingli, Calvin.* Minneapolis, 1980.

ALTHAUS, P. *The Ethics of Martin Luther.* Trans. R. C. Schultz. Philadelphia, 1972.

———. *The Theology of Martin Luther.* Trans. R. C. Schultz. Philadelphia, 1966.

BAINTON, R. H. *Erasmus of Christendom.* New York, 1969.

———. *Here I Stand: A Life of Martin Luther.* Nashville, TN, 1950.

BANGS, C. D. *Arminius: A Study in the Dutch Reformation.* Nashville, TN, 1971.

BENDER, H. *Conrad Grebel: The Founder of the Swiss Brethren.* Goshen, IN, 1950.

BRANDI, K. *The Emperor Charles V.* Trans. C. V. Wedgewood. New York, 1939.

DUDON, P. *St. Ignatius of Loyola.* Trans. W. J. Young. Milwaukee, 1949.

DYCK, C. J., ed. *A Legacy of Faith: The Heritage of Menno Simons.* Newton, KN, 1962.

EBELING, G. *Luther: An Introduction to His Thought.* Trans. R. A. Wilson. Philadelphia, 1970.

EELLS, H. *Martin Bucer.* New Haven, CT, 1931.

GERRISH, B. A., ed. *Reformers in Profile: Advocates of Reform, 1300–1600.* Philadelphia, 1969.

GRITSCH, E. *Reformer without a Church: Thomas Muentzer.* Philadelphia, 1967.

MANSCHRECK, C. *Melanchthon: The Quiet Reformer.* New York, 1958.

PARKER, T. H. L. *John Calvin: A Biography.*

POTTER, G. R. *Zwingli.* Cambridge, 1976.

RAHNER, H. *Ignatius the Theologian.* New York, 1968.

RIDLEY, J. *John Knox*. London, 1968.

———. *Thomas Cranmer*. Oxford, 1962.

SCARISBRICK, J. J. *Henry VIII*. London, 1968.

STEINMETZ, D. C. *Reformers in the Wings*. Philadelphia, 1971.

WENDEL, F. *Calvin: The Origins and Development of His Religious Thought*. Trans. P. Mairet. New York, 1963.

5. *Period VII: Modern Christianity*

A. BACKGROUND AND REFERENCE

BARRETT, D. B., ed. *World Christian Encyclopedia: A Comparative Study of Churches and Religion in the Modern World, A.D. 1900–2000*. Nairobi, 1982.

BURR, N. H. *A Critical Bibliography of Religion in America*. Princeton, NJ, 1961.

ELLIS, J. T., and TRISCO, R., eds. *A Guide to American Catholic History*. 2nd ed. Santa Barbara, CA, 1982.

GAUSTAD, E. S., ed. *Historical Atlas of Religion in America*. Rev. ed. New York, 1976.

MELTON, J. G. *The Encyclopedia of American Religions*. 2 vols. Wilmington, NC, 1978.

WILLIAMS, E. L., and BROWN, C. *The Howard University Bibliography of African and Afro-American Religious Studies*. Rev. ed. Wilmington, DE, 1977.

B. SOURCES AND DOCUMENTS

BELL, G. K. A., ed. *Documents on Christian Unity*. 4 vols. Oxford, 1929–1958.

ELLIS, J. T., ed. *Documents of American Catholic History*. Milwaukee, 1956.

FLANNERY, A., ed. *Vatican Council II: The Conciliar and Post-Conciliar Documents*. Wilmington, DE, 1975.

GAUSTAD, E. S., ed. *A Documentary History of Religion in America*. 2 vols. Grand Rapids, MI, 1982, 1983.

GEE, H., and HARDY, W. J., eds. *Documents Illustrative of English Church History*. London, 1896.

MANSCHRECK, C. L., ed. *A History of Christianity: Readings in the History of the Church from the Reformation to the Present*. Englewood Cliffs, NJ, 1964. Reprint. Grand Rapids, MI, 1981.

REARDON, B. M. G. *Religious Thought in the Nineteenth Century, Illustrated from the Writers of the Period*. Cambridge, 1966.

RUETHER, R. R., and KELLER, R. S., eds. *Women and Religion in America: A Documentary History*. 2 vols. San Francisco, 1981, 1983.

SMITH, H. S.; HANDY, R. T.; and LOETSCHER, L. A. *American Christianity: An Historical Interpretation with Representative Documents*. 2 vols. New York, 1960–1963.

VISCHER, L., ed. *A Documentary History of the Faith and Order Movement, 1927–1963*. St. Louis, 1963.

C. SURVEYS: GENERAL

FEY, H. E., ed. *The Ecumenical Advance: A History of the Ecumenical Movement.* Vol. 2, *1948–1968.* Philadelphia, 1970.

NICHOLS, J. H. *History of Christianity, 1650–1950: Secularization of the West.* New York, 1956.

NOLL, M. A., et al., eds. *Eerdmans' Handbook to Christianity in America.* Grand Rapids, MI, 1983.

NORWOOD, F. A. *The Development of Modern Christianity since 1500.* New York, 1956.

ROUSE, R., and NEILL, S. C., eds. *A History of the Ecumenical Movement, 1517–1548.* 2nd ed. Philadelphia, 1967.

VIDLER, A. R. *The Church in an Age of Revolution: 1789 to the Present Day.* Grand Rapids, MI, 1961.

D. SURVEYS: REGIONAL AND TOPICAL

AHLSTROM, S. E. *A Religious History of the American People.* 2 vols. Garden City, NY, 1975.

ALBANESE, C. L. *America: Religions and Religion.* Belmont, CA, 1981.

BILLINGTON, R. A. *The Protestant Crusade, 1800–1860.* New York, 1968.

BOLSHAKOFF, S. *Russian Nonconformity: The Story of "Unofficial" Religion in Russia.* Philadelphia, 1950.

CHADWICK, O. *The Popes and European Revolution.* Oxford, 1981.

CRAGG, G. R. *From Puritanism to the Age of Reason.* Cambridge, 1965.

DAVIES, H. *The English Free Churches.* 2nd ed. New York, 1963.

DILLENBERGER, J., and WELCH, C. *Protestant Christianity Interpreted through Its Development.* New York, 1954.

DUSSELL, E. D. *A History of the Church in Latin America: Colonialism to Liberation, 1492–1979.* Trans. A. Neely. Grand Rapids, MI, 1981.

FRAZIER, E. F., and LINCOLN, C. E. *The Negro Church in America: The Black Church since Frazier.* 2 vols. in 1. New York, 1974.

HANDY, R. T. *A History of the Churches in the United States and Canada.* New York, 1977.

HENNESEY, J. *American Catholics: A History of the Roman Catholic Community in the United States.* New York, 1981.

HOGG, W. R. *Ecumenical Foundations: A History of the International Missionary Council and Its Nineteenth-Century Background.* New York, 1952.

HOLMES, J. D. *The Papacy in the Modern World.* New York, 1981.

HUDSON, W. S. *Religion in America.* 3rd ed. New York, 1981.

JAMES, J. W., ed. *Women in American Religion.* Philadelphia, 1980.

LATOURETTE, K. S. *Christianity in a Revolutionary Age: A History of Christianity in the Nineteenth and Twentieth Centuries.* 5 vols. New York, 1958–1962.

LINDT, G. *Moravianism in Two Worlds: A Study of Changing Communities.* New York, 1967.

McNEILL, J. T. *The History and Character of Calvinism.* New York, 1954.

MARTY, M. E. *Righteous Empire: The Protestant Experience in America.* New York, 1970.

PAYNE, E. A. *The Free Church Tradition in the Life of England.* Rev. ed. London, 1951.

PHILLIPS, C. S. *The Church in France.* 2 vols. London, 1929, 1936.

RUSSELL, E. *The History of Quakerism.* New York, 1942.

E. THOUGHT AND THEOLOGY

AHLSTROM, S. E., ed. *Theology in America: The Major Voices from Puritanism to Neo-Orthodoxy.* Indianapolis, 1967.

BARTH, K. *Protestant Theology in the Nineteenth Century: Its Background and History.* London, 1972.

BAUMER, F. L. *Modern European Thought: Continuity and Change in Ideas, 1600–1950.* New York, 1977.

CAUTHEN, K. *The Impact of American Religious Liberalism,* 2nd ed. Washington, DC, 1983.

ELLIOTT-BINNS, L. E. *The Development of English Theology in the Later Nineteenth Century.* London, 1952.

GAY, P. *The Enlightenment, An Interpretation: The Rise of Modern Paganism.* New York, 1966.

GROFF, W. E., and MILLER, D. E. *The Shaping of Modern Christian Thought.* Cleveland, 1968.

HEIMERT, A. *Religion and the American Mind: From the Great Awakening to the Revolution.* Cambridge, MA, 1966.

HOOYKASS, R. *Religion and the Rise of Modern Science.* Edinburgh, 1972.

HOUGHTON, W. E. *The Victorian Frame of Mind, 1830–1870.* New Haven, CT, 1957.

HUTCHISON, W R. *The Modernist Impulse in American Protestantism.* Cambridge, MA, 1976.

LANGFORD, T. A. *In Search of Foundations: English Theology, 1900–1920.* Nashville, TN, 1969.

LOTZ, D. W. *Ritschl and Luther.* Nashville, TN, 1974.

MACQUARRIE, J. *Twentieth-Century Religious Thought.* New York, 1963.

MANUEL, F. E. *The Eighteenth Century Confronts the Gods.* Cambridge, MA, 1958.

MARSDEN, G. M. *Fundamentalism and American Culture.* New York, 1980.

MAY, H. F. *The Enlightenment in America.* New York, 1976.

MILLER, P. *The New England Mind.* 2 vols. Cambridge, MA, 1939, 1953.

MILLER, P., and JOHNSON, T. H. *The Puritans.* New York, 1938.

MOORE, J. R. *The Post-Darwinian Controversies: A Study of the Protestant Struggle to Come to Terms with Darwin in Great Britain and America, 1870–1900.* Cambridge, 1979.

NICHOLS, J. H. *Romanticism in American Theology: Nevin and Schaff at Mercersburg.* Chicago, 1961.

NIEBUHR, H. R. *The Kingdom of God in America.* New York, 1937.

PFLEIDERER, O. *The Development of Theology in Germany since Kant, and Its Progress in Great Britain since 1825.* London, 1890.

PIEPKORN, A. C. *Profiles in Belief: The Religious Bodies of the United States and Canada.* 4 vols. New York, 1977–1979.

RANDALL, J. H., JR. *The Making of the Modern Mind.* Rev. ed., Boston, 1940.

REARDON, B. M. G. *From Coleridge to Gore: A History of Nineteenth-Century Religious Thought in Britain.* London, 1971.

SANDEEN, E. R. *The Roots of Fundamentalism: British and American Millenarianism, 1800–1930.* Chicago, 1970.

SOMERVELL, D. C. *English Thought in the Nineteenth Century.* London, 1929.

TILLICH, P. *Perspectives on 19th and 20th Century Protestant Theology.* Ed. C. E. Braaten. New York, 1967.

WELCH, C. *Protestant Thought in the Nineteenth Century.* Vol. 1, *1799–1870.* New Haven, CT, 1972.

WESTFALL, R. S. *Science and Religion in Seventeenth-Century England.* New Haven, CT, 1958.

WILLEY, B. *The Seventeenth-Century Background.* London, 1942.

———. *The Eighteenth-Century Background.* London, 1941.

———. *Nineteenth-Century Studies: Coleridge to Matthew Arnold.* London, 1949.

———. *More Nineteenth-Century Studies: A Group of Honest Doubters.* New York, 1956.

WILMORE, G. S., and CONE, J. H., eds. *Black Theology: A Documentary History, 1966–1979.* Maryknoll, NY, 1979.

F. INSTITUTIONS: MINISTRY, POLITY, WORSHIP

ADAMS, D. *Meeting House to Camp Meeting: Towards a History of American Free Church Worship from 1620 to 1824.* North Aurora, IL, 1983.

DAVIES, H. *Worship and Theology in England.* 5 vols. Princeton, NJ, 1961–1975.

KOENKER, E. B. *The Liturgical Renaissance in the Roman Catholic Church.* 2nd ed. St. Louis, 1966.

SCHERER, R. P. *American Denominational Organization: A Sociological View.* Pasadena, CA, 1980.

SCOTT, D. M. *From Office to Profession: The New England Ministry, 1750–1850.* Philadelphia, 1978.

STEVICK, D. B. *Canon Law: A Handbook.* New York, 1965.

ZOLLMANN, C. F. G. *American Church Law.* St. Paul, MN, 1933.

G. SPIRITUALITY, RELIGIOUS MOVEMENTS, AND ORDERS

BANGERT, W. V. *A History of the Society of Jesus.* St. Louis, 1972.

BREMOND, H. *Histoire littéraire du sentiment religieuse en France.* 9 vols. Paris, 1916–1932.

CARWARDINE, R. *Transatlantic Revivalism: Popular Evangelicalism in Britain and America, 1790–1865.* Westport, CT, 1978.

CHADWICK, O., ed. *The Mind of the Oxford Movement.* London, 1960.

CROSS, W. R. *The Burned-over District: The Social and Intellectual History of Enthusiastic Religion in Western New York, 1800–1850.* Ithaca, NY, 1950.

ELLIOTT-BINNS, L. E. *The Early Evangelicals: A Religious and Social Study.* Greenwich, CT, 1953.

FAIRWEATHER, E. R., ed. *The Oxford Movement.* New York, 1964.

FEDOTOV, G. P., ed. *A Treasury of Russian Spirituality.* New York, 1948.

HEIMERT, A., and MILLER, P., eds. *The Great Awakening: Documents Illustrating the Crisis and Its Consequences.* Indianapolis, 1967.

KNOX, R. A. *Enthusiasm.* Oxford, 1951.

McLoughlin, W. G. *Modern Revivalism: Charles Grandison Finney to Billy Graham.* New York, 1959.

Stoeffler, F. E. *The Rise of Evangelical Pietism.* Leiden, 1965.

H. CHURCH AND SOCIETY

Blau, J. L., ed. *Cornerstones of Religious Liberty in America.* Rev. ed. New York, 1964.

Curtiss, J. S. *Church and State in Russia, 1900–1917.* New York, 1940.

————. *The Russian Church and the Soviet State.* Boston, 1953.

Helmreich, E. C. *The German Churches under Hitler: Background, Struggle, Epilogue.* Detroit, 1979.

Howe, M. D. *The Garden and the Wilderness.* Chicago, 1965.

Howse, E. M. F. *Saints in Politics: The "Clapham Sect" and the Growth of Freedom.* Toronto, 1952.

Jordan, W. K. *The Development of Religious Toleration in England.* 4 vols. London, 1932–1940.

Lincoln, C. E., ed. *The Black Experience in Religion.* New York, 1974.

McLoughlin, W. G. *New England Dissent: The Baptists and the Separation of Church and State, 1630–1833.* 2 vols. Cambridge, MA, 1971.

McManners, J. *The French Revolution and the Church.* London, 1969.

Mathews, D. G. *Religion in the Old South.* Chicago, 1977.

Mead, S. E. *The Lively Experiment: The Shaping of Christianity in America.* New York, 1963.

Pfeffer, L. *Church, State, and Freedom.* Rev. ed. Boston, 1967.

Raboteau, A. J. *Slave Religion: The "Invisible Institution" in the Antebellum South.* New York, 1978.

Sanders, T. G. *Protestant Concepts of Church and State.* New York, 1964.

Smith, E. A. *Religious Liberty in the United States.* Philadelphia, 1972.

Smith, H. S. *In His Image, But . . . : Racism in Southern Religion, 1780–1910.* Durham, 1972.

Smith, T. L. *Revivalism and Social Reform in Mid-Nineteenth Century America.* New York, 1957.

Stokes, A. P. *Church and State in the United States.* 3 vols. New York, 1950.

Stromberg, R. N. *Religious Liberty in Eighteenth-Century England.* London, 1954.

Walzer, M. *The Revolution of the Saints: A Study in the Origins of Radical Politics.* Cambridge, MA, 1965.

White, R. C., and Hopkins, C. H. *The Social Gospel: Religion and Reform in Changing America.* Philadelphia, 1976.

Wilson, J. F., ed. *Church and State in American History.* Boston, 1965.

Woodhouse, A. S. P. *Puritanism and Liberty.* 2nd ed. Chicago, 1951.

I. BIOGRAPHICAL STUDIES

Baker, F., ed. *The Works of John Wesley.* 26 vols. Oxford, 1975–1982.

Chadwick, O. *From Bossuet to Newman: The Idea of Doctrinal Development.* Cambridge, 1957.

Curnock, N., ed. *The Journal of John Wesley.* 8 vols. New York, 1909–1916.

DALLIMORE, A. A. *George Whitefield: The Life and Times of the Great Evangelist of the 18th Century Revival.* 2 vols. Westchester, IL, 1980.

ELLIS, J. T. *The Life of James Cardinal Gibbons, Archbishop of Baltimore, 1834–1921.* 2 vols. Milwaukee, 1952.

HENRY, S. C. *Unvanquished Puritan: A Portrait of Lyman Beecher.* Grand Rapids, MI, 1973.

KEGLEY, C. W., and BRETALL, R. W., eds. *Reinhold Niebuhr: His Religious, Social, and Political Thought.* Rev. ed. New York, 1982.

KURTZ, J. W. *John Frederic Oberlin.* Boulder, CO, 1976.

LEVIN, D. *Cotton Mather: The Young Life of the Lord's Remembrancer, 1663–1703.* Cambridge, MA, 1976.

LOWRIE, W. *A Short Life of Kierkegaard.* Princeton, 1942.

MARTIN, B. *John Henry Newman: His Life and Work.* London, 1982.

MILLER, P., and SMITH, J. E., eds. *The Works of Jonathan Edwards.* New Haven, CT, 1957–.

MILLER, P. *Jonathan Edwards.* New York, 1949.

MORGAN, E. S. *The Puritan Dilemma: The Story of John Winthrop.* Boston, 1958.

NELSON, R. J. *Pascal: Adversary and Advocate.* Cambridge, MA, 1981.

OUTLER, A. C., ed. *John Wesley.* New York, 1964.

PAUCK, W., and PAUCK, M. *Paul Tillich: His Life and Thought.* New York, 1976.

REDEKER, M. *Schleiermacher: Life and Thought.* Trans. J. Wallhaussen. Philadelphia, 1973.

SCHMIDT, M. *John Wesley: A Theological Biography.* Trans. N. P. Goldhawk. 2 vols. London, 1962, 1973.

Index